The Learner's
Kanji
Dictionary

Mark Spahn
Wolfgang Hadamitzky

with
Rainer Weihs
Seiko Harada
Yoko Nagai-Hintz

簡明漢英熟語字典

CHARLES E. TUTTLE COMPANY
Rutland, Vermont & Tokyo, Japan

This book has been typeset by Seiko Harada and Rainer Weihs, on a Macintosh computer, using Japanese PageMaker.

Published by Charles E. Tuttle Publishing, an imprint of Periplus Editions (HK) Ltd.

LCC Card No. 97-62030
ISBN 0-8048-2095-3

First edition, 1998

Printed in Singapore

Distributed by:
USA **Charles E. Tuttle Co., Inc.**
Airport Industrial Park
RR1 Box 231-5
North Clarendon, VT 05759
Tel: (802) 773-8930
Fax: (802) 773-6993

Japan
Tuttle Shokai Ltd.
1-21-13 Seki
Tama-ku, Kawasaki-shi
Kanagawa-ken 214, Japan
Tel: (81) (44) 833-0225
Fax: (81) (44) 822-0413

Southeast Asia
Berkeley Books Pte Ltd.
5 Little Road #08-01
Singapore 536983
Tel: (65) 280 3320
Fax: (65) 280 6290

Tokyo Editorial Office:
2-6, Suido 1-chome,
Bunkyo-ku, Tokyo 112, Japan

Boston Editorial Office:
153 Milk Street, 5th Floor
Boston, MA 02109, USA

Singapore Editorial Office:
5 Little Road #08-01
Singapore 536983

TABLES OF CONTENTS
目　次

LIST OF TABLES
図　表

APPENDICES

付録

Preface

The purpose of this *Learner's Kanji Dictionary* is to offer a handy and easy-to-use tool to look up the readings and meanings of Japanese words and names written with Chinese characters (kanji).

Each kanji entry is presented in extra-large form, with its strokes labeled in order by small numbers 1, 2, 3, ... positioned at the beginning of each stroke to show how the kanji is to be written. Handwritten pen and variant forms of the kanji are also given, along with its general structure and graphemes (graphical components) as used in recent computer programs such as *SUNRISE Kanji Dictionary* and *SUNRISE Script*.

This dictionary is a concise version of the more comprehensive *Kanji Dictionary*. For handier size, some of its less frequent characters and compounds have been dropped, but without disrupting the cross-referencing system by which each kanji is given a unique lookup identifier such as 4k7.18. In all, this *Learner's Kanji Dictionary* lists the most important 2,882 characters and 12,073 multi-character compounds, including all 1,945 *Jōyō Kanji* decreed for general use plus all 284 *Jinmei-yō Kanji* sanctioned for use in given names. In addition, the most frequently used approximately 700 surnames and 600 given names have been added.

One feature that makes this dictionary particularly useful for a beginner, or anyone else, is that every compound is listed under each of its characters. This multiple listing makes it possible to look up a compound under whichever of its characters is quickest to find, and it is a big help in deciphering sloppy handwriting or a blurred fax.

Entries are arranged according to a radical-based lookup system of the same type used in virtually all character dictionaries, but with improvements that make it particularly easy to learn and use.

And with the alphabetically arranged index of kanji readings at the back of the dictionary, the user can look up a character via any of its known readings (or look up a compound via any of the readings of any of *its* characters), without having to determine radicals or count strokes.

We welcome fan mail and criticism, especially comments about any suggested improvements, so that this dictionary can be kept always accurate and up to date.

We thank Meiji Life Insurance Company for allowing us to quote their frequency lists for given names.

Mark Spahn
Wolfgang Hadamitzky

How to Use This Dictionary

Explanation of Sample Entries

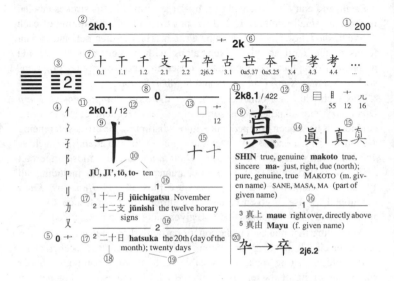

① Page number

② The range of characters on the double-page spread, identified by the descriptor of the first character on the left-hand page (2k0.1, in this case) and of the last character on the right-hand page .

③ Trailer header, indicating that this is the section of the dictionary where characters are listed whose radical consists of (in this example) 2 strokes.

④ Trailer; a string of all radicals (without variants) of a given stroke count (2, in this case).

⑤ Number indicating the residual stroke-count of the first character whose entry starts on this page (or of the last character if it is a right-hand page; 0, in this case).

⑥ The header beginning the section where all the characters having a given radical are listed. The radical is shown, along with the number-letter descriptor which identifies it (⁺ 2k, in this case).

⑦ The overview list, which presents in compact form all the characters listed under a given radical, either as main entries or as cross-references to an entry under another radical. Below each character in the overview list is printed the tail of its descriptor (or its full descriptor, if the entry is a variant or is listed under some other radical).

⑧ Number within a column-wide divider indicating that here begins the section which lists those characters under the current radical which have a given residual stroke-count (0, in this case).

⑨ The character ("head character"), with numbers showing stroke order positioned at the beginning of each stroke.

⑩ Readings and meanings of the character. *On* readings are given in all-uppercase bold letters, and *kun* readings are given in lowercase bold letters, with *okurigana* indicated within parentheses. Readings that occur as independent given names or surnames or as parts of names are indicated by a short explanation in parentheses.

⑪ The character's "descriptor", a name by which the character is identified and referred to. A descriptor (example: 2k0.1) consisting of the character's radical (2k, in this example), the number of strokes in its non-radical part (0, in this example), and, separated by a decimal point, its sequential number (1, in this example) within the group of characters having the same radical and same residual stroke-count.

The descriptor for all kanji is the same as in *The Kanji Dictionary*[1] and in *Japanese, Chinese, and Korean Surnames and How to Read Them.* [2]

⑫ The serial number of this character in the book *Kanji & Kana*[3] and in the computer program *Sunrise Script.*[4] Since *Kanji & Kana* includes only

---

[1] ***The Kanji Dictionary***
English-language edition: Tuttle (Tokyo and Rutland, Vermont)

[2] ***Japanese, Chinese, and Korean Surnames and How to Read Them.***
K. G. Saur (Munich, New Providence, London, Paris)

[3] ***Kanji & Kana***
English-language edition: Tuttle (Tokyo and Rutland, Vermont)
German editions: Langenscheidt (Berlin, Vienna, Zurich) and Enderle (Tokyo)
French edition: Maisonneuve (Paris)

[4] ***Sunrise Script***
(Seven-language edition on CD-ROM) JAPAN Media (Berlin)

the 1,945 *Jōyō Kanji* which are officially recommended for general use, plus the 284 *Jinmei-yō Kanji* sanctioned for use in given names, the presence of a *K&K* number indicates that the character is one of the *Jōyō Kanji* (numbers 1–1945) or one of the *Jinmei-yō Kanji* (numbers 2001–2284)—in general, the lower the *K&K* number, the greater the frequency of the character's occurrence.

⑬ The structure of the kanji, and up to three graphemes (graphical components) with grapheme number used as search elements in recent computer programs such as *SUNRISE Kanji Dictionary* and *SUNRISE Script*.

⑭ The character's pre-Second World War form or a variant, if any.

⑮ Two samples of the kanji in pen form.

⑯ Number giving the position of the head character within the following group of compounds; that is, whether the head character is the first, second, third, etc. kanji.

⑰ Stroke count of the second character of compounds beginning with the head character (or, if in a section of compounds where the head kanji occurs in other than first position, the stroke count of the first character). Listed under "stroke-count zero" are compounds consisting only of the head character and a word written in kana.

⑱ Compounds containing the head character. Compounds are arranged in increasing order of the stroke-count (then radical) of their second character (or, if the head character occurs in other than first position, of their first character). *Okurigana* are not indicated.

⑲ Reading(s) and meaning(s) of the compound. *Okurigana* are indicated within parentheses. Only the most important meanings of each compound are listed. Many Japanese words can, depending on context and grammatical ending, be used as either noun, verb, or adjective, but in general the English translation includes only one part of speech.

⑳ Cross-reference showing that this character is listed elsewhere. Cross-references are provided for kanji whose radical or stroke-count might be mistaken or miscounted, as well as for variant and pre-Second World War forms of kanji.

How to Look Up a Character

The characters in this dictionary are arranged according to the same general scheme adopted by virtually all character dictionaries used by Japanese: a set of character components called "radicals" is prescribed, and each character is classified according to the radical it contains, with rules for determining which radical to take when a character contains more than one.

The radicals are listed inside the front cover, arranged in groups according to the number of strokes with which they are written. Within each stroke-count group the radicals are arranged according to their usual position within a character, in the order: left side, right side, top, bottom, enclosure (on two or more sides). Each radical is identified by a number-letter name (like "3k" for radical 艹 (*kusa-kanmuri*) or "7a" for radical 言 (*gon-ben*)), where the number indicates its stroke-count. (In naming radicals, the letter "l" is skipped, lest it be confused with the digit "1".)

A character will usually contain two or more radicals, and it must be decided which radical to take. The general rule is: if the character consists of a left and right side and the left side is a radical, take the left-side radical; if the character naturally divides itself into a top and bottom and the top part is a radical, take the radical on the top. The detailed rules are given on page xi in "How to Determine the Radical of a Character", and a summary of them is given inside the back cover.

Having determined the radical of a character, then you count the number of strokes in the rest of the character (its "residual stroke-count"); the radical and residual stroke-count of the character specify where in the dictionary the character will be found. For example, the radical of the character 諸 (*SHO*) is 言 (*gon-ben*) 7a and its non-radical part 者 consists of 8 strokes. This character will therefore be found within group 7a8, the group of all characters whose radical is 7a and whose residual stroke-count is 8. The characters within this group are numbered sequentially with descriptors 7a8.1, 7a8.2, 7a8.3, etc.

Descriptors that are missing in the sequence belong to seldom-used kanji that appear in *The Kanji Dictionary* but have been dropped from this dictionary for handier size. These descriptors appearing at the top of each page indicate which characters are listed on that page. Once the search has been narrowed down this far, it is usually just a matter of flipping a few pages until the desired character is found.

When you know the radical and the residual stroke-count of the character you are looking for, you can locate it quickly with the help of the "trailer" printed in the outer margin of each page. The trailer consists of a stroke-count number followed by all the radicals having that stroke-count.

The radical of the characters which appear on the page is highlighted by a numeral indicating their residual stroke-count.

There are two other ways to locate a character. Knowing only a character's radical, the character can be found without stroke counting by scanning the "overview list" which appears at the beginning of each radical section and includes all the characters (as well as variants and cross-reference entries) which are listed under that radical.

Or, if one of the readings of a character is known, it can be located via the Readings Index at the back of the dictionary, without having to determine its radical or count strokes. Since many kanji have the same *on* reading, one should whenever possible look for the kanji under its *kun* reading. The kanji listed under a given reading are first subdivided into groups sharing the same component (generally the pronunciation-determining component), then subdivided by increasing stroke count. At the end of each group are kanji which could mistakenly be sought in this group because of the component they share with it, but which have a different reading. These kanji appear in parentheses, with their actual reading given to the right. The end of the group is denoted by a horizontal line. Following a group of kanji that share both the same component and the same reading are more kanji, arranged in order of increasing stroke count, that share the reading but are made up of different components.

This arrangement allows the user to quickly find the descriptor of the kanji of known reading that he is looking for by zeroing in on the group having the kanji's distinctive grapheme or, if not found there, the remaining kanji of the same reading. If a kanji is sought under an erroneous reading, a cross-reference directs the user to the right reading.

Other advantages of this arrangement are that it calls attention to the systematic way in which kanji are put together, it shows etymological connections, it points out the commonalities and differences between certain kanji, it provides groupings of kanji containing similar graphical components for repetition and self-testing, and it aids in expanding one's kanji vocabulary by learning new kanji in a group in which most of the kanji have already been learned.

How to Look Up a Compound

Under each character (the "head character") are listed, first, all compounds beginning with the head character. These compounds are arranged in increasing order of the stroke-count (and then the radical) of their second character. This is followed by a section of all compounds whose second character is the head character; these compounds are arranged in increasing

order of the stroke-count of their first character. Next comes a section of all compounds whose third character is the head character, likewise arranged in increasing order of the stroke-count of their first character. That is, each head character entry is followed by a list of all the compounds in which that character occurs in first, second, third, and subsequent position.

A consequence of this scheme is that each compound appears in several places in the dictionary, namely, under each of its characters. So to find the entry for a compound, just look in the proper section following whichever of its characters you can locate the most quickly and easily.

To take an example, you have a choice of about eight different ways to look up the compound 殺虫剤 (*satchūzai*). It is listed under the kanji 殺, which may be located directly by the radical system (explained below) or via its *on* reading *SATSU* or its *kun* reading *koro(su)* in the alphabetical readings index. This compound is also listed under its second kanji 虫, which may be found either directly via its radical or indirectly via its *on* reading *CHŪ* or its *kun* reading *mushi*. A third copy of this compound will be found under its third kanji 剤, whose location in the dictionary can be determined either via its radical or via its sole reading *ZAI*.

A Word about Stroke Counting

The way in which a character is actually written with pen or pencil is the criterion we adopt for counting strokes. We count as a single stroke any line which is drawn with the pen or pencil in continuous contact with the paper, no matter how the line may cusp and curve.

Taking the character 艮 as an example, the leftmost stroke is drawn by starting at the top, changing its direction at the lower left corner of the character, and continuing the stroke toward the upper right, to the center of the character. In printed versions of this character (良), however, this single stroke usually looks like two separate strokes.

When counting strokes, be aware that in this dictionary we consider the following components to consist of the following number of strokes: 丁 (1), 子 (2), 阝 (2), 辶 (2), 比 (4), 灬 (4), 臣 (7).

How to Determine the Radical of a Character

The term "radical" is used with either of two meanings: (1) any of the character components included in some specified list (in this book, in the Radical Table inside the front cover), or (2) that particular radical under which a given character is listed in a given character dictionary. Context usually makes it clear which meaning is intended (for example, "a radical"

for the first meaning and "the radical" or "its radical" for the second meaning).

To determine under which radical any given character is listed in this dictionary, go through the following checklist, stopping at the first step which applies. Look for any radicals which appear within the character.

Consider as radicals only those which consists of complete strokes not crossed by a line which is not part of the radical (for example, 寺 does not contain radical 宀 because the short vertical line at the top is only part of a stroke, and 本 does not contain the radical 木 because the 木 is crossed by the short horizontal stroke). It sometimes happens that one radical is part of another radical; in such cases, consider only the more inclusive radical.

0. All ▨ If the entire character is itself a radical (or a variant of a radical), then that is its radical.

Examples: 十 → 宀 2k, 手 → 扌 3c, 金 → 釒 8a.

(金 contains radical 2a, but remember that we always take the more inclusive radical.)

1. Left ▨ If the left side of the character is a radical, then that is the character's radical. Here we do not merely mean a radical which appears somewhere on the left side of the character (as 宀 and 田 do in 献), but rather one which forms the entire left side of the character and can be separated from the rest of the character by a straight (or nearly straight) vertical line.

Examples: 協 → 宀 2k, 休 → 亻 2a, 明 → 日 4c, 情 → 忄 4k.

About half of all characters divide themselves in a natural way into a left side and a right side, with the left side being the radical.

2. Right ▨ If the right side of the character is a radical (but the left side is not), then that is the character's radical.

Examples: 教 → 攵 4i, 別 → 刂 2f, 外 → 卜 2m, 郎 → 阝 2d.

Notice that the rule is "left before right": if both the left side and the right side of a character are radicals, as in 明, we take the left-side radical (in this example, 日 4c).

3. Up ▨ If the upper part of the character is a radical, then that is the character's radical. Here the radical must form the whole top part of the character, and it may embrace the rest of the character symmetrically like the overhanging eaves of a roof.

Examples: 芯 → ⁺⁺ 3k, 虎 → ⌐ 2m, 急 → ⁄ 2n, 企 → 𠆢 2a, 前 → ˇ 2o,
父 → 丷 2o, 翁 → ⁄⁀ 2o.

Note that some radicals (in this case "2o") may appear in different shapes as shown in the table "The 79 Radicals (with variants)" (front end paper).

4. Down ▨ If the lower part of the character is a radical (but not the upper part), then that is the character's radical.

Examples: 想 → 心 4k, 無 → 灬 4d, 攀 → 𧘇 5a, 呉 → 八 2o.

(Observe that in the last example the radical cannot be 口 because it does not "cap" the bottom part of the character and cannot be separated from the rest of the character by a horizontal line.) Notice that the rule is "top before bottom": If both the upper part and the lower part of the character are radicals, as in 共, we take the upper-part radical (⁺⁺ 3k in this example).

5. Around ▢ ▢ ▢ ▢ ▢ ▢ If the character contains a radical which encloses the rest of the character on two or more sides, then that is the character's radical.

Examples: 進 → 辶 2q, 式 → 弋 4n, 原 → 厂 2p, 区 → 匚 2t, 同 → 冂 2r, 国 → 囗 3s.

6. Everywhere ? If no radical appears in any of the positions checked so far, then look for a radical anywhere in the character.

(a) only one ① If the character contains only one radical, then there is nothing to decide; the character's sole radical is the only possible radical under which it could be classified.

Examples: 契 → ⼁ 2f, 止 → ⌐ 4m, 友 → 又 2h, 缶 → ⁺⁺ 2k, 矩 → 匚 2t.

(b) greater stroke-count > If the character contains two (or more) radicals, take the radical which consists of more strokes.

Examples: in 向 take the 3-stroke radical ⼝ 3d in preference to the 2-stroke radical 冂 2r; in 者 take the 4-stroke radical ⽇ 4c rather than the 2-stroke radical ⁺ 2k; in 鞄 take the 4-stroke radical ⾰ 4b instead of the 3-stroke radical ⁺⁺ 3k or ⁿ 3n; in 哉 the radical is the 4-stroke 戈 4n, not the 3-stroke ⼝ 3d or the 2-stroke ⁺ 2k.

(c) leftmost ⊡ If the character contains two (or more) radicals of equally greatest stroke-count, take the one whose leftmost point is farther left.

Examples: in 喪 the radicals ⼟ 3b and ⼝ 3d are of equally high

stroke-count, but since the ⼟ 3b protrudes farther left, the radical of this character is ⼟ 3b; in 鼻, 5-stroke radical ⽥ 5f extends farther left than 5-stroke radical ⽬ 5c, so we look for this character under radical ⽥ 5f; in 扳 the only possibilities are 厂 2p and 又 2h (the ⼂ 2o in the upper left is considered destroyed as a radical by the stroke which crosses it, separating its two parts), and since the 厂 2p extends farther left, 厂 2p is the radical of this character.

(d) **highest** ↑ If the character contains two (or more) radicals of equally leftmost point, then take whichever has the higher highest point.

Examples: 舖 → ⼟ 3b, 栽 → 弋 4n, 段 → 几 2s.

The steps of this whole search procedure can be neatly summarized in the mnemonic slogan "Look left, right, up, down, all around everywhere". (The "all" is out of sequence but the changed order yields the same result.)

7. **Nowhere** ⓪ If the character contains no radical at all, then it will be found in the section at the beginning of the book labeled "0a", in which such characters are listed in increasing order of stroke-count. Among these radicalless characters, characters having the same stroke-count are arranged in increasing order of number of points at which strokes intersect (then subclassified in increasing order of number of points at which strokes only touch one another; observe the progression in "0a11": 疎, 野, 爽, 肅, 彗).

(If you find it convenient, you may think of 0a as the "none of the above" radical which consists of zero strokes, thereby making it invisible and making the residual stroke-count of the character the same as its total stroke-count. For example, it is a matter of personal preference whether you think of 本 as a 5-stroke character having no radical, or as a character which "contains" the null radical 0a plus 5 strokes; in either case it will be found in group 0a5.)

Once you have understood these rules, a quick glance at the summary of them listed inside the back cover will refresh your memory should you ever be in doubt about how to apply them in a particular case.

These rules for determining the radical of a character may at first seem complex, but it takes much less time to apply them than to state them explicitly. Notice that the one-stroke radicals found in many character dictionaries are absent. This has the advantage that a meaning-bearing radical (usually the same as the traditional radical) is thereby selected, eliminating such counterintuitive results as classifying 劇 under a radical ⼃

instead of under radical 刂 2f, or 悪 under a radical 一 instead of under radical 心 4k.

How to Use other Character Dictionaries

Character Dictionaries based on the 79 radicals

In order to look up words or names not included in this dictionary, you will need to consult larger or special dictionaries. After having become familiar with this dictionary, it might be easiest for you to use a dictionary with the same search system.

Presently there are two dictionaries on the market that are based on the 79 radicals. One is *The Kanji Dictionary* (Tuttle), and the other is *Japanese, Chinese, and Korean Surnames and How to Read Them* (Saur). For more detailed bibliographic information see "OTHER TITLES BY THE SAME AUTHORS" on the last page of this volume. More dictionaries on Japanese given names, geographical names, and names of corporations will appear in the next few years.

Users of these dictionaries need not shift between different search systems. Each character in these dictionaries will even have the same descriptor. Consequently, if you have found the reading of a Japanese surname in the surname dictionary and want to know the readings and/or meanings or the stroke order of its head kanji, you can easily look it up via the descriptor in either *The Kanji Dictionary* or *The Learner's Kanji Dictionary*.

Other Character Dictionaries

The arrangement of characters in most character dictionaries is based on the classification scheme of the Kangxi zidian (康熙字典). Published in China in 1716, this 42-volume work arranged some 42,000 Chinese characters according to a system using a set of 214 radicals.

It may be argued that the compilers of the Kangxi zidian had to have so many radicals in order to classify so many characters into groups of manageable size, but a smaller set of radicals suffices for the no more than 5,000 – 6,000 characters of modern Japanese. Nevertheless, Japanese character dictionaries have usually been arranged according to the 214 traditional radicals. Indeed, to keep up with the orthographic reforms made since the Second World War, by which many characters were simplified and lost their former radical, Japanese dictionary publishers added new radicals to the traditional set, so that today many dictionaries recognize even more than 214 radicals.

To determine the radical of a character, most Japanese character dictionaries use more or less the same rule as the Kangxi zidian: the radical is usually that part of the character (or, in many cases, of its pre-1946 form) which is associated with its meaning. This presents the user with the paradoxical predicament of having to know the meaning of a character in order to locate it in a dictionary and look up its meaning. For about 85% of all characters, the traditional radical is the same as that given by the rules of the present dictionary.

Thus, the user of this dictionary who should have occasion to refer to a dictionary which is based on the historical radicals need only familiarize himself with the particular set of radicals which it uses, and be aware that the rules for determining a character's radical are somewhat different. For a comparison of the 79 radicals and the 214 historical radicals, see page 840.

Electronic Character Dictionaries

All kanji and compounds (except surnames and given names) from this dictionary plus 3,000 additional kanji and 35,000 additional compounds are contained in the CD-ROM *SUNRISE Kanji Dictionary*. With this program you can find a kanji by clicking up to six of its components (graphemes) contained in a table of 80 graphemes. You can even look up a compound by simply clicking one or two graphemes for each of its constituent kanji. With approximately 160,000 English words and 70,000 Japanese words, the program can function as a Japanese-English and English-Japanese dictionary. Since the 80 graphemes in the electronic dictionary are almost identical with the 79 radicals, users of the dictionaries based on the 79 radicals should have no problem using this electronic dictionary.

Most other electronic character dictionaries are based more or less on the traditional scheme of the 214 radicals and will be convenient if the user is familiar with that system. One problem is that displaying all 214 radicals on a small screen is impossible.

THE LEARNER'S
KANJI DICTIONARY

漢字と熟語

─ 0a1 ─

一　乙　了　丿
1.1　1.5　2c0.3　0a2.12

0a1.1 / 2

□ 一
1

ICHI, ITSU, hito(tsu), hito- one, a
HAJIME, HITOSHI, MAKOTO (m. given
name) KAZU, HI (part of given name)

─── 1 ───

1 一一 **ichi-ichi** one by one; in full
detail **hito(tsu)-hito(tsu)**
one by one

2 一丁 **itchō** one block (of tofu), one
serving (of food), one city
block

一人 **hitori, ichinin** one person

一人子 **hitorikko, hitorigo** an only
child

一人当 **hitoria(tari)** per person/
capita

一人者 **hitorimono** someone
alone; unmarried/single person

一人物 **ichijinbutsu** a person of
consequence

一人前 **ichininmae, hitorimae** one
portion/serving; full adulthood

一人娘 **hitori musume** an only
daughter

一人息子 **hitori musuko** an only
son

一人称 **ichininshō** first person (in
grammar)

一子 **isshi** a child; an only child
hitorigo an only child

3 一寸 **issun** one *sun*/inch (3.03 cm)
chotto a little; just a minute

一也 **Kazuya, Ichiya** (m. given
name)

一口 **hitokuchi** a mouthful; a unit;
a word

一山 **hitoyama** a pile (of bananas);
the whole mountain

一ヶ年 **ikkanen** one year

4 一元化 **ichigenka** unification, centralization

一夫 **Kazuo, Ichio, Itsuo** (m. given
name)

一夫多妻 **ippu-tasai** polygamy

一切 **issai** all, everything; entirely,
absolutely **hitoki(re)** a piece/
slice

一文字 **ichimonji** a straight line

一文無 **ichimonna(shi)** penniless

一片 **ippen** a piece/bit

一分 **ippun** a minute **ichibu** one
tenth; one hundredth, one percent; one quarter *ryō* (an old
coin) **ichibun** duty, honor

一分別 **hitofunbetsu** (careful) consideration

一匹 **ippiki** one animal; 20-m bolt
of cloth

一月 **ichigatsu** January **ik(ka)ge-
tsu, hitotsuki, ichigetsu** one
month

一日 **tsuitachi** the 1st (day of the
month) **ichinichi, ichijitsu**
one/a day

一日中 **ichinichi-jū** all day long

一方 **ippō** one side; on one hand, on
the other hand; one party, the
other party; nothing but, only
hitokata(narazu) greatly, immensely

一方的 **ippōteki** one-sided, unilateral

一方通行 **ippō tsūkō** one-way traffic

一心 **isshin, hito(tsu)kokoro** one
mind; the whole heart, whole-
hearted

一戸 **ikko** a house; a household

5 一本 **ippon** one (long object);
a book; one version; a blow;
a full-fledged geisha

一本立 **ipponda(chi)** independence

一本気 **ippongi** one-track mind

一本道 **ipponmichi** straight road; road with no turnoffs

一本調子 **ipponchōshi, ipponjōshi** monotony

一失 **isshitsu** a disadvantage; a defect; an error

一生涯 **isshōgai** a lifetime, one's (whole) life

一生懸命 **isshōkenmei** with all one's might

一世 **issei** a lifetime; a generation; the First; first-generation (Japanese-American) **isse** a lifetime

一世一代 **issei ichidai** once in a lifetime

一世紀 **isseiki** a century; first century

一冊 **issatsu** one copy (of a book)

一代 **ichidai** one generation; a lifetime; an age

一巡 **hitomegu(ri)** a turn/round; one full year **ichijun** a round/patrol

一打 **hitou(chi), ichida** a blow

一号 **ichigō** number one

一句 **ikku** a phrase/verse; (counter for haiku)

一字 **ichiji** a character/letter

一旦 **ittan** once

一礼 **ichirei** a bow/greeting

一石二鳥 **isseki nichō** killing two birds with one stone

一目 **hitome, ichimoku** a glance/look **hito(tsu)me** one-eyed (goblin)

一目惚 **hitomebo(re)** love at first sight

一目瞭然 **ichimoku ryōzen** clear at a glance, obvious

一皿 **hitosara** a plate/dish (of food)

6 一気 **ikki** in one breath; straight through, without a break, at a stroke

一年 **ichinen** one year **hitotose** one year, some time ago

一年中 **ichinen-jū** all year long

一年生 **ichinensei** first-year student; annual (plant)

一再 **issai** once or twice **issai(narazu)** again and again

一休 **hitoyasu(mi)** a rest

一件 **ikken** a matter, an item

一次 **ichiji** first; primary; linear (equation)

一列 **ichiretsu** a row/line

一考 **ikkō** consideration, a thought

一同 **ichidō** all concerned, all of us

一行 **ichigyō** a line (of text) **ikkō** party, group; troupe

一安心 **hitoanshin** feeling relieved for a while

一回 **ikkai** once, one time; a game; an inning **hitomawa(ri)** a turn/round

一回戦 **ikkaisen** first game/round (of tennis)

一式 **isshiki** a complete set; all, the whole

7 一身 **isshin** oneself, one's own interests

一束 **issoku, hitotaba** a bundle; a hundred

一里 **ichiri** one *ri*, 3.9 km

一位 **ichii** first place/rank

一体 **ittai** one body; (what) in the world, (how) the devil; properly speaking; generally

一対 **ittsui** a pair

一対一 **ittaiichi** one-to-one

一役 **ichiyaku** an (important) office **hitoyaku** a role

一応 **ichiō** once; tentatively; in outline

一条 **ichijō** a line/streak; a matter; a passage (from a book)

一見 **ikken** take a look at, glance at

一利 **ichiri** one advantage

一男 **Kazuo, Ichio, Ichidan** (m. given name)

一言 **hitokoto, ichigen, ichigon** a word

一言二言 **hitokoto futakoto** a word or two

一足 **issoku** a pair (of shoes) **hitoashi** a step

8 一事 **ichiji** one thing **hito(tsu)koto** the same thing

一例 **ichirei** one example, an instance

一念 **ichinen** a determined purpose

一命 **ichimei** a life; a command

一郎 **Ichirō, Kazuo** (m. given name)

一刻 **ikkoku** a minute/moment; stubborn, hotheaded

一刻千金 **ikkoku senkin** Every minute counts.

一利那 **issetsuna** an instant, a moment

一夜 **ichiya, hitoyo, hitoya** one night; all night

一斉 **issei** all at once, simultaneously

一周 **isshū** once around, a revolution/tour/lap

一泊 **ippaku** an overnight stay

一抹 **ichimatsu** a touch/tinge of

一抱 **hitokaka(e)** an armful

一味違 **hitoaji chiga(u)** with a unique flavor

一昔 **hitomukashi** about ten years ago

一定 **ittei** fixed, prescribed, regular, definite; fix, settle; standardize **ichijō** definitely settled

一歩 **ippo** a step

一国 **ikkoku** stubborn, hotheaded; the whole country

一枚 **ichimai** one sheet

一杯 **ippai** a cup of; a drink; full; to the upmost

一服 **ippuku** a dose; a smoke; a rest/break; a lull, calm market

一物 **ichimotsu** an article, a thing; ulterior motive, designs

一所 **ik(ka)sho, issho, hitotokoro** one place; the same place

一所懸命 **isshokenmei** with all one's might

一雨 **hitoame** a shower/rainfall

9 一発 **ippatsu** a shot

一巻 **ikkan** one volume **hitomaki** one roll

一重 **hitoe** one layer; single **hitokasa(ne)** a suit (of clothes); a set (of nested boxes)

一変 **ippen** a complete change

一点 **itten** a point; speck, dot, particle

一点張 **ittenba(ri)** persistence

一首 **isshu** a poem

一途 **ichizu** wholeheartedly **itto** way, course; the only way

一通 **hitotō(ri)** in general, briefly **ittsū** one copy (of a document)

一風変 **ippū kawa(tta)** eccentric, queer; unconventional, original

一段 **ichidan** one stage/step, all the more

一段落 **ichidanraku** a pause

一封 **ippū** a sealed letter/document; an enclosure

一括 **ikkatsu** one lump/bundle; summing up

一品 **ippin** an article/item; a dish/course

一律 **ichiritsu** uniform, even, equal

一荒 **hitoa(re)** a squall; a burst of anger

一度 **ichido, hitotabi** once, one time

一面 **ichimen** one side/phase; the whole surface; first page (of a newspaper)

一昨日 **issakujitsu, ototoi, ototsui** the day before yesterday

一昨年 **issakunen, ototoshi** the year before last

一神教 **isshinkyō** monotheism

一思 **hitoomo(i)** with one effort, once and for all, resolutely

一級 **ikkyū** one grade; first class

一食 **isshoku** a meal

10 一倍 **ichibai** the same number/amount; double

一部 **ichibu** a part; a copy (of a publication)

一部分 **ichibubun** a part

一部始終 **ichibu shijū** full particulars

一週間 **isshūkan** a week

一流 **ichiryū** a school (of art); first-rate, top-notch; unique

一員 **ichiin** a person; a member

一帯 **ittai** a region/zone; the whole place

一家 **ikka, ikke** a house/family/household; one's family; a style

一宮 **Ichinomiya** (city, Aichi-ken)

一挙 **ikkyo** one effort, a single action

一席 **isseki** a speech/story/feast

一桁 **hitoketa** single digit

一時 **ichiji** a time; at one time; for a time　**ittoki** twelfth part of a day　**hitotoki** a little while, a short period　**ichidoki** at a/one time

一時的 **ichijiteki** temporary

一時預場 **ichiji azukarijō** baggage safekeeping area

一致 **itchi** agree

一息 **hitoiki** a breath; a pause/break; (a little more) effort

一眠 **hitonemu(ri)** a short sleep, a nap

一般 **ippan** general

一般化 **ippanka** generalization, popularization

一軒 **ikken** a house

11 一階 **ikkai** first/ground floor

一遍 **ippen** once

一過性 **ikkasei** transient, temporary

一喝 **ikkatsu** a thundering cry, a roar

一票 **ippyō** a vote

一理 **ichiri** a principle, a reason

一族 **ichizoku** a family/household

一眼 **ichigan** one eye; single lens

一盛 **hitomo(ri)** a pile　**hitosaka(ri)** temporary prosperity

一組 **hitokumi, ichikumi** one set, one class

一粒 **hitotsubu** a grain

一転 **itten** a turn, complete change

12 一割 **ichiwari** ten percent

一着 **itchaku** first arrival; first (in a race); a suit (of clothes)

一揆 **ikki** riot, insurrection

一揃 **hitosoro(i)** a set, a suit

一握 **hitonigi(ri), ichiaku** a handful

一喜一憂 **ikki ichiyū** alternation of joy and sorrow, hope and fear

一期 **ichigo** one's lifespan　**ikki** a term, a half year, a quarter

一晩 **hitoban** a night, one evening; all night

一畳 **ichijō** one mat

一番 **ichiban** number one, the first; most, best; a game/bout

一統 **ittō** a lineage; bringing under one rule; all (of you)

一筆 **ippitsu, hitofude** a stroke of the pen, a few lines

一筋 **hitosuji** a line; earnestly, wholeheartedly

一等 **ittō** first class/rank, the most/best

一飲 **hitono(mi)** a mouthful; a swallow/sip; an easy prey

一雄 **Kazuo, Ichio, Kunio** (m. given name)

13 一際 **hitokiwa** conspicuously; still more, especially

一義的 **ichigiteki** unambiguous

一塊 **hitokatama(ri)** a lump, a group　**ikkai** a lump

一群 **hitomu(re), ichigun** a group; a flock, a crowd

一蓮托生 **ichiren-takushō** sharing fate with another

一新 **isshin** complete change, reform, renovation

一置 **hito(tsu)o(ki)** every other one

14 一髪 **ippatsu** a hair, a hair's-breadth

一層 **issō** still more, all the more

一概 **ichigai** unconditionally, sweepingly

一様 **ichiyō** uniformity, evenness; equality, impartiality

一端 **ittan** a part; a general idea

一緒 **issho** together

一箇 **ikko** one; a piece

一語 **ichigo** one word

一読 **ichidoku** a perusal/reading

一説 **issetsu** one/another view

15 一億 **ichioku** one hundred million

一審 **isshin** first instance/trial

一輝 **Kazuki** (m. given name)

16 一膳 **ichizen** a bowl (of rice); a pair (of chopsticks)

17 一覧 **ichiran** a look/glance; a summary; catalog

18 一瞬 **isshun** a moment, an instant

0a1

一癖 **hitokuse** trait, peculiarity; slyness

一難 **ichinan** one difficulty, one danger

19 一蹴 **isshū** kick; reject

20 一議 **ichigi** a word, an opinion, an objection

21 一躍 **ichiyaku** one bound; in one leap

―――― 2 ――――

1 一一 **ichi-ichi** one by one; in full detail **hito(tsu)-hito(tsu)** one by one

2 人一倍 **hito-ichibai** uncommon, more than others

十一月 **jūichigatsu** November

3 万一 **man'ichi** (if) by any chance, should happen to

4 不一致 **fuitchi** disagreement, incompatibility

5 正一 **Shōichi, Masakazu, Masaichi** (m. given name)

弘一 **Kōichi, Hirokazu, Hiroichi** (m. given name)

6 同一 **dōitsu** the same, identical, equal

7 良一 **Ryōichi, Yoshikazu** (m. given name)

伸一 **Shin'ichi, Nobukazu** (m. given name)

均一 **kin'itsu** uniform

択一 **takuitsu** choosing an alternative

8 画一 **kakuitsu** uniform, standard

刻一刻 **koku-ikkoku** moment by moment, hour by hour

幸一 **Kōichi, Yukikazu** (m. given name)

英一 **Eiichi, Hidekazu, Hideichi** (m. given name)

9 信一 **Shin'ichi, Nobukazu, Nobuichi** (m. given name)

俊一 **Shun'ichi, Toshikazu** (m. given name)

逐一 **chikuichi** one by one, in detail

通一遍 **tō(ri)-ippen** passing, casual, perfunctory

単一 **tan'itsu** single, simple, individual

祐一 **Yūichi, Sukekazu, Sukeichi** (m. given name)

10 健一 **Ken'ichi** (m. given name)

隆一 **Ryūichi, Takaichi, Takakazu** (m. given name)

浩一 **Kōichi, Hirokazu** (m. given name)

祥一 **Shōichi, Yoshikazu** (m. given name)

純一 **Jun'ichi, Yoshikazu, Jun'itsu** (m. given name)

11 唯一 **yuiitsu, tada hito(tsu)** the only, sole

第一 **dai-ichi** No. 1, first, best, main

第一人者 **dai-ichininsha** foremost/leading person

第一次 **dai-ichiji** first

12 勝一 **Katsuichi, Shōichi** (m. given name)

無一文 **muichimon** penniless

裕一 **Yūichi, Hirokazu, Hiroichi** (m. given name)

統一 **tōitsu** unity, unification, uniformity

間一髪 **kan ippatsu** a hair's breadth

順一 **Jun'ichi, Masakazu** (m. given name)

13 腹一杯 **hara ippai** full stomach; to one's heart's content

誠一 **Seiichi, Makoto** (m. given name)

14 精一杯 **sei-ippai** with all one's might

15 誰一人 **dare hitori (mo)** (with negative) no one

16 憲一 **Ken'ichi, Norikazu** (m. given name)

賢一 **Ken'ichi, Yoshikazu, Toshikazu** (m. given name)

21 鶴一声 **tsuru (no) hitokoe** the voice of authority

―――― 3 ――――

1 一世一代 **issei ichidai** once in a lifetime

一対一 **ittaiichi** one-to-one

一喜一憂 **ikki ichiyū** alternation of joy and sorrow, hope and fear

4 日本一 **Nihon-ichi, Nippon-ichi** Japan's best

⁶ 危機一髪 **kiki-ippatsu** imminent/ hairbreadth danger

百人一首 **hyakunin-isshu** 100 poems by 100 poets (a collection of 100 *tanka*; basis for the popular card game *uta karuta*)

───── 4 ─────

² 二者択一 **nisha-takuitsu** an alternative

⁶ 安全第一 **anzen dai-ichi** Safety First

0a1.5 / 983

□ 一
1

乙 乙

OTSU second (in a series), "B";

strange, queer; stylish, spicy
kinoto second calendar sign

───── 1 ─────

³ 乙女 **otome** virgin, maiden

───── 2 ─────

⁵ 甲乙 **kō-otsu** A and B; make distinctions, rank, grade

甲乙丙 **kō-otsu-hei** A, B, C; No. 1, 2, 3

了 → **2c0.3**

⼃ → ⼃ **0a2.12**

───── **0a2** ─────

二 入 丁 之 乃 〆 七 九
2.1 2.3 2.4 2.9 2.10 2.12 2.13 2.15

0a2.1 / 3

□ 二
4

二
二 フ

NI, futa(tsu), futa- two **JI** (part of given name)

───── 1 ─────

² 二人 **futari, ninin** two persons, pair, couple

二人共 **futaritomo** both (persons)

二人前 **futarimae, nininmae** enough for two, two servings

二人連 **futarizu(re)** a party of two, couple

二人称 **nininshō** second person (in grammar)

二人組 **niningumi** twosome, duo

二子 **futago** twins, a twin

二十日 **hatsuka** the 20th (day of the month); twenty days

二十代 **nijūdai** in one's twenties

二十年代 **nijūnendai** the '20s

二十歳 **hatachi** 20 years old, age 20

⁴ 二元論 **nigenron** dualism

二分 **nifun** two minutes
nibun halve, bisect

二月 **nigatsu** February
futatsuki two months

二日 **futsuka** the 2nd (day of the month); two days

二日酔 **futsukayo(i)** a hangover

二方 **futakata** both people

⁵ 二世 **nisei** (Elizabeth) II, the Second; second-generation (Japanese-American) **nise** two existences, present and future

二号 **nigō** No. 2; mistress, concubine

⁶ 二次 **niji** second(ary); quadratic, second degree (in math)
ni (no) tsugi secondary, subordinate

二次会 **nijikai** after-party party

二返事 **futa(tsu)henji** immediate reply, readily, most willingly

⁷ 二伸 **nishin** postscript, P.S.

二役 **futayaku** double role

二言 **futakoto** two words
nigon double-dealing

8 二郎 **Jirō, Nirō** (m. given name)
二枚目 **nimaime** (role of a) handsome man/beau
二枚舌 **nimaijita** forked tongue, duplicity
二者択一 **nisha-takuitsu** an alternative

9 二重 **nijū** double **futae** two-fold, two-ply, double
二重奏 **nijūsō** instrumental duet

10 二倍 **nibai** double, twice, twofold
二部 **nibu** two parts/copies; the second part
二桁 **futaketa** two digits, double-digit

11 二階建 **nikaida(te)** two-story

12 二番目 **nibanme** No. 2, second

13 二義的 **nigiteki** secondary

16 二親 **futaoya** (both) parents

———— 2 ————

2 十二支 **jūnishi** the twelve horary signs
十二月 **jūnigatsu** December

6 瓜二 **uri-futa(tsu)** alike as two halves of a split-open melon, the spitting image of each other

9 昭二 **Shōji, Akiji** (m. given name)

10 真二 **ma(p)puta(tsu)** (split) right in two
浩二 **Kōji, Hiroji** (m. given name)

12 無二 **muni** peerless, unequaled

———— 3 ————

1 一石二鳥 **isseki nichō** killing two birds with one stone
一言二言 **hitokoto futakoto** a word or two

0a2.3 / 52

NYŪ, JU, hai(ru), i(ru) go/come in, enter **i(reru)** put/let in

———— 1 ————

3 入口 **iriguchi** entrance

4 入手 **nyūshu** obtain, get
入日 **i(ri)hi** the setting sun

6 入会 **nyūkai** enrollment, admission
入江 **i(ri)e** inlet, cove
入団 **nyūdan** join, enlist

7 入来 **nyūrai** incoming, arrival, visit
入学 **nyūgaku** admission into school, matriculation
入学試験 **nyūgaku shiken** entrance exams
入社 **nyūsha** joining a company

8 入念 **nyūnen** careful, scrupulous
入国 **nyūkoku** entering a country, immigration
入物 **i(re)mono** receptacle, container
入所 **nyūsho** entrance, admission; imprisonment
入金 **nyūkin** payment, money received
入門 **nyūmon** admission, entrance; introduction, handbook, primer

9 入院 **nyūin** be admitted to hospital

10 入浴 **nyūyoku** take a bath

11 入隊 **nyūtai** enlist (in the army)
入混 **i(ri)maji(ru)** be mixed together

12 入場 **nyūjō** entrance, admission
入場料 **nyūjōryō** admission fee
入替 **i(re)ka(eru)** replace, substitute

14 入選 **nyūsen** be chosen (in a competition)
入墨 **i(re)zumi** tattooing; tattoo
入獄 **nyūgoku** imprisonment

15 入賞 **nyūshō** win a prize

20 入籍 **nyūseki** have one's name entered on the family register

———— 2 ————

4 介入 **kainyū** intervention
刈入 **ka(ri)i(re)** harvest, reaping
収入 **shūnyū** income, receipts, revenue, earnings
込入 **ko(mi)i(ru)** be complicated
手入 **tei(re)** repairs; care, tending
日入 **hi(no)i(ri)** sunset

5 出入口 **deiriguchi** entrance/exit
出入国 **shutsunyūkoku** emigration and immigration

申入 **mō(shi)i(reru)** propose, suggest

加入金 **kanyūkin** entrance/initiation fee

立入 **ta(chi)i(ru)** enter, trespass, pry into

立入禁止 **tachiiri kinshi** Keep Out

6 気入 **ki (ni) i(ru)** like, be pleased with

先入観 **sennyūkan** preconception, preoccupation, prejudice

7 没入 **botsunyū** be immersed/absorbed in

投入 **tōnyū** throw into, commit (resources); invest
na(ge)i(reru) throw into
na(ge)i(re) free-style flower arrangement

乱入 **rannyū** intrusion

8 念入 **nen'i(ri)** careful, scrupulous, conscientious

受入 **u(ke)i(re)** receiving, accepting

注入 **chūnyū** injection; pour into, infuse

押入 **o(shi)i(re)** closet, wall cupboard **o(shi)i(ru)** break into **o(shi)i(ri)** burglar

突入 **totsunyū** rush/plunge into

取入 **to(ri)i(reru)** take in, accept, adopt; harvest **to(ri)i(ru)** win (someone's) favor

金入 **kanei(re)** purse, wallet; till

9 飛入 **to(bi)i(ri)** joining in (on the spur of the moment); speckled with a different color
to(bi)i(ru) jump/dive/fly into

乗入 **no(ri)i(reru)** ride/drive into; extend (a train line) into (a city)

侵入 **shinnyū** invade, raid, break into

10 進入 **shinnyū** enter, penetrate, go/come in

挿入 **sōnyū** insert

屑入 **kuzui(re)** trash can/receptacle

書入 **ka(ki)i(reru)** write/fill in, enter

恐入 **oso(re)i(ru)** be overwhelmed (with gratitude/shame), be astonished, be sorry to trouble,

beg pardon; be defeated, yield; plead guilty

納入 **nōnyū** pay, deliver, supply

記入 **kinyū** entry (in a form/ledger)

11 混入 **konnyū** mix in, adulterate

密入国 **mitsunyūkoku** smuggle oneself into a country

袋入 **fukuroi(ri)** in bags, sacked, pouched

12 雇入 **yato(i)i(reru)** employ, hire; charter

買入 **ka(i)i(reru)** purchase, stock up on

13 嫁入 **yomei(ri)** marriage, wedding

歳入 **sainyū** annual revenue

14 導入 **dōnyū** bring in, introduce

聞入 **ki(ki)i(reru)** accede to, comply with **ki(ki)i(ru)** listen attentively

15 潜入 **sennyū** infiltrate

箱入 **hakoi(ri)** boxed, in cases

箱入娘 **hakoi(ri)musume** girl who has led a sheltered life

16 輸入 **yunyū** import

輸入税 **yunyūzei** import duties/tariff

17 購入 **kōnyū** purchase

————— 3 —————

4 不介入 **fukainyū** noninvolvement, nonintervention

8 定収入 **teishūnyū** fixed income

11 副収入 **fukushūnyū** additional/side income

————— 4 —————

5 四捨五入 **shisha-gonyū** rounding off

0a2.4 / 184

☐ 丁

14

丁 丁

CHŌ city block-size area (used in addresses); two-page leaf of paper; (counter for dishes of food, blocks of tofu, guns) **TEI** fourth (in a series), "D"; adult man; servant **hinoto** fourth calendar sign

——— 1 ———

⁵ 丁字路 **teijiro** T-junction of roads/ streets

丁目 **chōme** city block-size area (used in addresses)

⁹ 丁度 **chōdo** exactly

¹⁴ 丁寧 **teinei** polite, courteous; care- ful, meticulous

——— 2 ———

¹ 一丁 **itchō** one block (of tofu), one serving (of food), one city block

⁵ 包丁 **hōchō** kitchen knife; cooking

⁸ 庖丁 **hōchō** kitchen knife

¹² 落丁 **rakuchō** missing pages

0a2.9 / 2004

□ 一 丨
1　2

SHI, kore this **no** (the possessive particle), of **yu(ku)** go ITARU (m. given name) SHI, KORE, NO, YUKI, YOSHI, NOBU, YORI, HIDE, HISA, KUNI (part of given name)

——— 2 ———

⁷ 宏之 **Hiroyuki, Hiroshi** (m. given name)

⁸ 尚之 **Naoyuki, Hisayuki, Shōshi** (m. given name)

⁹ 俊之 **Toshiyuki, Shunshi** (m. giv- en name)

¹⁰ 浩之 **Hiroyuki** (m. given name)

¹¹ 康之 **Yasuyuki, Kōji** (m. given name)

¹² 博之 **Hiroyuki, Hiroshi, Masayuki** (m. given name)

裕之 **Hiroyuki, Yūji, Yasuyuki** (m. given name)

0a2.10 / 2003

□ カ
8

DAI, NAI your **sunawa(chi)** where- upon, accordingly **no** (the possessive

particle), of OSAMU, IMASHI (m. given name) DAI, NAI, NO, YUKI (part of given name)

0a2.12 / 1946

□ 十
12

shime closing; seal; total; ream **shime(te)** totaling

——— 1 ———

⁴ 〆切 **shimeki(ri)** deadline, closing date

0a2.13 / 9

□ 十
12

SHICHI, nana(tsu), nana, nano- seven

——— 1 ———

² 七十 **nanajū, shichijū** seventy

³ 七夕 **tanabata** Star Festival (July 7)

⁴ 七五三 **shichi-go-san** the lucky numbers 7, 5, and 3; festival for children 7, 5, and 3 years old

七月 **shichigatsu** July

七日 **nanoka, nanuka** the 7th (day of the month); seven days

——— 3 ———

⁵ 北斗七星 **Hokuto Shichisei** the Big Dipper

0a2.15 / 11

□ 十
12

KYŪ, KU, kokono(tsu), kokono- nine

——— 1 ———

⁴ 九月 **kugatsu** September **kyū(ka)getsu, ku(ka)getsu** nine months

九日 **kokonoka** the 9th (day of the month); nine days | 6 九州 **Kyūshū** (island)

— **0a3** —

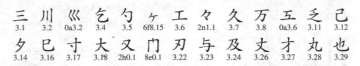

三	川	巛	乞	勹	ヶ	工	々	久	万	互	乏	己
3.1	3.2	0a3.2	3.4	3.5	6f8.15	3.6	2n1.1	3.7	3.8	0a3.6	3.11	3.12
夕	巳	寸	大	又	門	刃	与	及	丈	才	丸	也
3.14	3.16	3.17	3.18	2h0.1	8e0.1	3.22	3.23	3.24	3.26	3.27	3.28	3.29

0a3.1 / 4

日 二 一
4 1

三 三

SAN, mit(tsu), mi(tsu), mi- three ZŌ, SABU, SA, KAZU (part of given name)

— 1 —

2 三人 **sannin** three people
  三人称 **sanninshō** third person (in grammar)
  三十日 **sanjūnichi** the 30th (day of the month); 30 days **misoka** the last day of the month

3 三叉路 **sansaro** Y-junction of roads
  三千 **sanzen** 3,000; many

4 三文 **sanmon** farthing; cheap
  三分 **sanpun** three minutes
  sanbun divide into three, tri-sect
  三木 **Miki** (surname)
  三月 **sangatsu** March **san(ka)ge-tsu, mitsuki** three months
  三日 **mikka** the 3rd (day of the month); three days
  三日月 **mikazuki** crescent moon
  三日坊主 **mikka bōzu** one who can stick to nothing, "three-day monk"

5 三世 **sansei** the Third; third-genera-tion (Japanese-American) **sanze** past, present, and future existences
  三好 **Miyoshi** (surname)
  三田 **Mita** (surname)

6 三宅 **Miyake** (surname)

7 三位 **san'i, sanmi** third rank/place

三角 **sankaku** triangular
  mi(tsu)kado Y-junction of streets
三角形 **sankakkei, sankakukei** triangle
三谷 **Mitani, Mi(tsu)ya** (surname)

8 三郎 **Saburō, Mitsuo, Kazuo** (m. given name)
  三味線 **shamisen, samisen** samis-en (three-stringed instrument)

9 三重 **sanjū, mie** three-fold, three-ply, triple
  三重県 **Mie-ken** (prefecture)
  三面記事 **sanmen kiji** page-3 news, police news, human-in-terest stories
  三食 **sanshoku** three meals (a day)

10 三浦 **Miura** (surname)
  三島 **Mishima** (surname)
  三桁 **miketa** three digits

11 三菱 **Mitsubishi** (company name)

12 三揃 **mi(tsu)zoro(i)** three-piece suit

15 三権分立 **sanken bunritsu** separa-tion of powers (legislative, ex-ecutive, and judicial)

— 2 —

6 再三 **saisan** again and again, re-peatedly

8 昌三 **Shōzō, Masami, Masazō** (m. given name)

11 第三者 **dai-sansha** third person/ party

12 雄三 **Yūzō, Takemi** (m. given name)

— 3 —

2 七五三 **shichi-go-san** the lucky numbers 7, 5, and 3; festival for children 7, 5, and 3 years old

⁴ 日本三景 **Nihon sankei** Japan's three noted scenic sights (Matsushima, Miyajima, Amanohashidate)

0a3.2 / 33

SEN, kawa river

——————— 1 ———————

³ 川上 **kawakami** upstream **Kawakami, Kawaue** (surname)

川下 **kawashimo** downstream

川口 **kawaguchi** mouth of a river **Kawaguchi** (city, Saitama-ken); (surname)

⁴ 川井 **Kawai** (surname)

川辺 **kawabe** riverside

⁶ 川西 **Kawanishi** (surname)

⁷ 川村 **Kawamura** (surname)

⁸ 川沿 **kawazo(i)** along the river

川岸 **kawagishi** riverbank

⁹ 川畑 **Kawabata** (surname)

¹⁰ 川原 **Kawahara** (surname)

川島 **Kawashima** (surname)

¹¹ 川崎 **Kawasaki** (city, Kanagawa-ken); (surname)

——————— 2 ———————

³ 小川 **ogawa** brook, creek **Ogawa** (surname)

山川 **Yamakawa** (surname)

⁴ 天川 **Ama(no)kawa** the Milky Way

中川 **Nakagawa** (surname)

⁵ 市川 **Ichikawa** (city, Chiba-ken)

古川 **Furukawa** (surname)

石川 **Ishikawa** (surname)

石川県 **Ishikawa-ken** (prefecture)

立川 **Tachikawa, Tatekawa** (surname)

⁶ 西川 **Nishikawa** (surname)

江川 **Egawa** (surname)

吉川 **Yoshikawa, Kikkawa** (surname)

早川 **Hayakawa** (surname)

旭川 **Asahikawa** (city, Hokkaidō)

⁷ 佐川 **Sagawa, Sakawa** (surname)

⁸ 河川 **kasen** rivers

⁹ 前川 **Maekawa** (surname)

荒川 **Arakawa** (river in Tōkyō); (surname)

香川県 **Kagawa-ken** (prefecture)

¹¹ 淀川 **Yodogawa** (river, Ōsaka-fu)

細川 **Hosokawa** (surname)

¹³ 滝川 **Takigawa** (surname)

¹⁴ 徳川 **Tokugawa** (shogun family during Edo period); (surname)

——————— 3 ———————

⁵ 石狩川 **Ishikari-gawa** (river, Hokkaidō)

⁷ 利根川 **Tone-gawa** (river, Chiba-ken)

⁸ 長良川 **Nagara-gawa** (river, Gifu-ken)

長谷川 **Hasegawa** (surname)

⁹ 相模川 **Sagami-gawa** (river, Kanagawa-ken)

神奈川県 **Kanagawa-ken** (prefecture)

¹¹ 隅田川 **Sumida-gawa** (river, Tōkyō-to)

球磨川 **Kuma-gawa** (river, Kumamoto-ken)

¹² 最上川 **Mogami-gawa** (river, Yamagata-ken)

《《 → 川 0a3.2

0a3.4

KOTSU, KITSU, ko(u) ask for, beg

——————— 1 ———————

⁹ 乞食 **kojiki** beggar

0a3.5 / 1903   囗 ケ |
               15 2

勺

SHAKU (unit of volume, about 18 ml)

ケ → 箇   **6f8.15**

0a3.6 / 139   囗 エ
                  38

工

KŌ, KU artisan; manufacturing, construction **takumi** craftsman, workman TAKUMI (m. given name)

──────────── 1 ────────────

⁴ 工夫 **kufū** device, invention, contrivance, means   **kōfu** coolie, workman, laborer
⁶ 工合 **guai** condition, state; convenience; state of health
   工匠 **kōshō** artisan, craftsman
⁷ 工作 **kōsaku** construction, engineering; handicraft; maneuver, scheme
   工芸 **kōgei** technical arts
   工学 **kōgaku** engineering
   工学士 **kōgakushi** Bachelor of Engineering
   工学者 **kōgakusha** engineer
⁸ 工事 **kōji** construction
   工事中 **kōjichū** Under Construction
   工事場 **kōjiba** construction site
⁹ 工科 **kōka** engineering course
¹⁰ 工員 **kōin** factory worker, machine operator
¹¹ 工商 **kōshō** industry and commerce; artisans and merchants
   工務店 **kōmuten** engineering firm
¹² 工場 **kōjō, kōba** factory, workshop, mill
   工程 **kōtei** process; progress of the work
¹³ 工業 **kōgyō** industry

¹⁸ 工藤 **Kudō** (surname)

──────────── 2 ────────────

² 人工 **jinkō** artificial
³ 大工 **daiku** carpenter
⁵ 加工 **kakō** processing
⁷ 良工 **ryōkō** skilled artisan
⁸ 画工 **gakō** painter, artist
⁹ 重工業 **jūkōgyō** heavy industry
¹¹ 商工 **shōkō** commerce and industry
   商工会議所 **Shōkō Kaigisho** Chamber of Commerce and Industry
   細工 **saiku** work(manship); artifice, trick
¹² 軽工業 **keikōgyō** light industry
¹³ 鉄工場 **tekkōjō** ironworks
¹⁷ 鍛工 **tankō** metalworker, smith
¹⁸ 職工 **shokkō** (factory) worker

──────────── 3 ────────────

³ 士農工商 **shinōkōshō** samurai-farmers-artisans-merchants, the military, agricultural, industrial, and mercantile classes
⁶ 竹細工 **takezaiku** bamboo handicrafts
⁸ 金細工 **kinzaiku** goldwork, gold ware

々 →   **2n1.1**

0a3.7 / 1210   囗 ケ |
               15 2

久

KYŪ, KU, hisa(shii) long (time) HISASHI (m. given name) HISA (part of given name)

──────────── 1 ────────────

³ 久々 **hisabisa** (for the first time in) a long time
⁹ 久保 **Kubo** (surname)
   久保田 **Kubota** (surname)
   久美子 **Kumiko** (f. given name)
¹⁰ 久振 **hisa(shi)bu(ri)** (for the first time in) a long time
¹¹ 久野 **Hisano, Kuno** (surname)

0a3

— 2 —

³ 大久保 **Ōkubo** (surname)

⁵ 永久 **eikyū** permanence, perpetuity, eternity

⁹ 耐久 **taikyū** endurance, persistence, permanence, durability

持久 **jikyū** hold out, endure, persist

恒久 **kōkyū** permanence, perpetuity

0a3.8 / 16

14 1

万

萬 | 万 万

MAN ten thousand, myriad **BAN** countless, myriad; all **yorozu** ten thousand; all sorts of, everything KAZU, MA (part of given name)

— 1 —

¹ 万一 **man'ichi** (if) by any chance, should happen to

³ 万才 **banzai** hurrah

⁴ 万引 **manbi(ki)** shoplifting; shoplifter

⁶ 万年 **mannen** ten thousand years; perpetual, perennial

万年床 **mannendoko** bedding/futon left spread out on the floor during the daytime

万年筆 **mannenhitsu** fountain pen

万全 **banzen** perfect, sure, prudent

⁷ 万里 **Mari, Banri, Masato** (given name)

万里長城 **Banri (no) Chōjō** Great Wall of China

⁸ 万国 **bankoku** all nations

万物 **banbutsu, banmotsu** all things, all creation

¹⁰ 万能 **bannō** omnipotent, all-around, all-purpose

mannō all-purpose

¹¹ 万遍 **manben(naku)** equally, uniformly, without exception

¹² 万博 **banpaku** world's fair (short for 万国博覧会)

万葉集 **Man'yōshū** (Japan's oldest anthology of poems)

¹³ 万歳 **banzai** hurrah

— 2 —

³ 千万 **senman, chiyorozu** ten million; countless **senban** exceedingly, very much, indeed

⁶ 百万 **hyakuman** million

¹³ 数万 **sūman** tens of thousands

¹⁵ 億万長者 **okumanchōja** multimillionaire, billionaire

— 3 —

³ 千差万別 **sensa-banbetsu** infinite variety

 0a3.6

0a3.11 / 754

1 2

乏

乏 乏

BŌ, tobo(shii) meager, scanty, scarce

— 2 —

⁴ 欠乏 **ketsubō** lack, scarcity, shortage, deficiency

¹¹ 貧乏 **binbō** poor

貧乏人 **binbōnin** poor man, pauper

0a3.12 / 370

28

己

己 己

KO, onore oneself **KI** sixth (in a series), "F" **tsuchinoto** sixth calendar sign

— 2 —

⁶ 自己 **jiko** self-, oneself, one's own

自己紹介 **jiko shōkai** introduce oneself

⁷ 克己 **kokki** self-denial, self-control

利己 **riko** self-interest

0a3.14 / 81   □ 夕   30

タ　タ

SEKI, yū, yū(be) evening

─────── 1 ───────

4 夕月 **yūzuki** evening moon
　夕日 **yūhi** the setting sun
　夕方 **yūgata** evening
5 夕刊 **yūkan** evening paper/edition
　夕立 **yūdachi** sudden afternoon
　　　shower
9 夕食 **yūshoku** supper, evening
　　　meal
11 夕涼 **yūsuzu(mi)** enjoy the evening
　　　cool
12 夕焼 **yūya(ke)** red/glowing sunset
　夕飯 **yūhan, yūmeshi** evening
　　　meal
14 夕暮 **yūgu(re)** evening
17 夕闇 **yūyami** dusk, twilight
19 夕霧 **yūgiri** evening mist

─────── 2 ───────

2 七夕 **tanabata** Star Festival (July 7)

0a3.16 / 2060   □ 尸   40

巳 巳

SHI, mi sixth horary sign (serpent)
SHI, MI (part of given name)

0a3.17 / 1894   □ 寸   37

寸　寸

SUN small amount, just a little; (unit
of length, about 3 cm, an inch); measure

─────── 1 ───────

8 寸法 **sunpō** measurements, dimen-
　　　sions; plan, arrangement
9 寸前 **sunzen** just before

11 寸断 **sundan** cut/tear to pieces
12 寸評 **sunpyō** brief review/com-
　　　mentary

─────── 2 ───────

1 一寸 **issun** one *sun*/inch (3.03 cm)
　　　chotto a little; just a minute
10 原寸大 **gensundai** actual size

0a3.18 / 26   □ 大   34

大　大

DAI big, large, great; (university, short
for 大学); (as suffix) the size of … **TAI,
ō(kii), ō(inaru), ō-** big, large, great **ō(i
ni)** very, much, greatly **MASARU** (m.
given name) **HIRO** (part of given name)

─────── 1 ───────

0 大した **tai(shita)** much; important,
　　　serious, of great consequence
　大して **tai(shite)** very, much,
　　　greatly
　大びら/っぴら **ō(bira/ppira)**
　　　openly, publicly
　大きさ **ō(kisa)** size
2 大人 **otona** adult **otona(shii)**
　　　gentle, quiet **taijin** giant;
　　　adult; man of virtue
　大人物 **daijinbutsu** great man
3 大工 **daiku** carpenter
　大久保 **Ōkubo** (surname)
　大丈夫 **daijōbu** alright, safe, se-
　　　cure
　大凡 **ōyoso** approximately
　大小 **daishō** large and/or small size;
　　　(relative) size; long sword and
　　　short sword **dai(nari) shō-
　　　(nari)** more or less
4 大仏 **daibutsu** huge image of Bud-
　　　dha
　大切 **taisetsu** important; valuable,
　　　precious
　大文字 **ōmoji** capital letter
　　　daimonji large character; the
　　　character 大
　大分 **daibu, daibun** much, greatly,
　　　considerably **Ōita** (city,
　　　Ōita-ken)

大分県 **Ōita-ken** (prefecture)

大手 **ōte** large, major (companies); front castle gate　**ōde** both arms

大木 **Ōki** (surname)

大日本 **Dai-Nippon/-Nihon** (Great) Japan

大方 **ōkata** probably; almost, mostly; people in general

5 大半 **taihan** majority, greater part; mostly

大正 **Taishō** (era, 1912 – 1926)

大好 **daisu(ki)** very fond of, love

大字 **ōaza** major section of a village　**dai(no)ji** the character 大

大穴 **ōana** gaping hole; huge deficit; (make) a killing; (bet on) a long shot

大石 **Ōishi** (surname)

大目見 **ōme (ni) mi(ru)** overlook (faults), let go, view with tolerance

6 大多数 **daitasū** the great majority

大気 **taiki** atmosphere, the air

大気圧 **taikiatsu** atmospheric pressure

大西 **Ōnishi** (surname)

大西洋 **Taiseiyō** Atlantic Ocean

大会 **taikai** large/general meeting, conference, convention; tournament, meet

大阪 **Ōsaka** (city, Ōsaka-fu)

大汗 **ōase** profuse sweating

大地 **daichi** the ground, the (solid) earth

大地震 **ōjishin, daijishin** major earthquake

大名 **daimyō** feudal lord, daimyo　**taimei** renown

大安 **taian** lucky day

大当 **ōa(tari)** big hit, great success; (make) a killing; bumper crop

大回 **ōmawa(ri)** the long way around, circuitous route

大成 **taisei** complete, accomplish; compile; attain greatness

大自然 **daishizen** Mother Nature

大竹 **Ōtake** (surname)

7 大体 **daitai** generally, on the whole; outline, summary; in substance; originally

大作 **taisaku** masterpiece, a monumental work

大谷 **Ōtani** (surname)

大臣 **daijin** cabinet member, minister

大沢 **Ōsawa** (surname)

大役 **taiyaku** important task/role

大形 **ōgata** large size　**ōgyō** exaggeration

大学 **daigaku** university, college

大学院 **daigakuin** graduate school

大志 **taishi** ambition, aspiration

大売出 **ōu(ri)da(shi)** big sale

大声 **ōgoe** loud voice　**taisei** loud voice; sonorous voice

大男 **ōotoko** tall/large man

大系 **taikei** outline, overview, survey

8 大事 **daiji** important, precious; great thing; serious matter　**ōgoto** serious matter

大使 **taishi** ambassador

大使館 **taishikan** embassy

大卒 **daisotsu** college/university graduate (short for 大学卒業(者))

大抵 **taitei** generally, usually; probably

大昔 **ōmukashi** remote antiquity, long long ago

大空 **ōzora, taikū** the sky

大国 **taikoku** large country; major nation

大物 **ōmono** big thing; great man, big shot; big game

大和 **Yamato** ancient Japan

大和撫子 **Yamato nadeshiko** daughter/woman of Japan

大金 **taikin** large amount of money

大雨 **ōame, taiu** heavy rainfall, downpour

9 大乗仏教 **Daijō Bukkyō** Mahayana Buddhism, Great-Vehicle Buddhism

大便 **daiben** feces, excrement

大変 **taihen** serious; terrible, awful, huge, very

大負 **ōma(ke)** a crushing defeat; big price reduction

大急 **ōiso(gi)** in a big hurry/rush

大通 **ōdō(ri)** a main street, thoroughfare

大風 **ōkaze** strong wind, gale

大津 **Ōtsu** (city, Shiga-ken)

大洋 **taiyō** ocean

大洋州 **Taiyōshū** Oceania

大海 **taikai** the ocean

大型 **ōgata** large size

大要 **taiyō** summary, outline

大相撲 **ōzumō** grand sumo tournament; exciting match

大柄 **ōgara** large build; large pattern (on a kimono)

大胆 **daitan** bold, daring

大神宮 **Daijingū** the Grand Shrine (at Ise)

10 大将 **taishō** general; admiral; head, leader, boss

大陸 **tairiku** continent

大都会 **daitokai** big city

大部分 **daibubun** a large part, most; for the most part, mostly

大差 **taisa** wide difference/margin, great disparity

大酒 **ōzake, taishu** heavy drinking

大師 **daishi** great (Buddhist) teacher, saint

大家 **taika** mansion; illustrious/ wealthy family; past master, authority **taike** illustrious/ wealthy family **ōya** landlord; main building

大島 **Ōshima** (frequent name for an island); (surname)

大株主 **ōkabunushi** large shareholder

大根 **daikon** daikon, Japanese radish

大笑 **ōwara(i), taishō** a big laugh

11 大野 **Ōno** (surname)

大道 **daidō** highway, main street; great moral principle

大掃除 **ōsōji** general house-cleaning, spring/fall cleaning

大麻 **taima** marijuana; Shinto paper amulet **ōasa** hemp

大晦日 **Ōmisoka** last day of the year; New Year's Eve

大黒柱 **daikokubashira** central pillar; pillar, mainstay

大尉 **taii** captain; lieutenant

大望 **taimō, taibō** ambition, aspirations

大赦 **taisha** amnesty; plenary indulgence

大欲 **taiyoku** greed, avarice, covetousness

大規模 **daikibo** large-scale

大袈裟 **ōgesa** exaggerated

大略 **tairyaku** summary, outline; great plan; roughly, approximately

大敗 **taihai** a crushing defeat

大雪 **ōyuki, taisetsu** heavy snow

12 大違 **ōchiga(i)** big difference

大塚 **Ōtsuka** (surname)

大揺 **ōyu(re)** upheaval

大幅 **ōhaba** by a large margin, substantial

大嵐 **ōarashi** big storm

大喜 **ōyoroko(bi)** great joy

大森 **Ōmori** (surname)

大勝利 **daishōri** decisive victory

大量 **tairyō** large quantity

大量生産 **tairyō seisan** mass production

大衆 **taishū** a crowd; the masses, the general public

大衆向 **taishūmu(ki)** for the general public, popular

大統領 **daitōryō** president

大評判 **daihyōban** sensation, smash

大間違 **ōmachiga(i)** big mistake

大順 **ō(kii) jun** decreasing order, largest first

13 大業 **taigyō** a great undertaking/ achievement

大勢 **ōzei** large number of people **taisei** the general trend

大農 **dainō** large-scale farming; wealthy farmer

大損 **ōzon** heavy loss

大嫌 **daikira(i)** hate, abhor, detest

大禍 **taika** great disaster

大戦 **taisen** great/world war

大意 **taii** gist, outline, summary

大詰 **ōzu(me)** finale, final scene

14 大嘘 **ōuso** big lie

大概 **taigai** in general; mostly; probably; moderate, reasonable

大静脈 **daijōmyaku** the vena cava

大綱 **ōzuna** hawser, cable **taikō** general principles; outline, general features

大輔 **Daisuke, Taisuke** (m. given name)

大雑把 **ōzappa** rough (guess); generous

大関 **ōzeki** sumo wrestler of second-highest rank

15 大蔵省 **Ōkurashō** Ministry of Finance

大権 **taiken** supreme power/authority

大敵 **taiteki** archenemy; formidable opponent

16 大樹 **Daiki** (m. given name)

18 大儲 **ōmō(ke)** large profit

大観 **taikan** comprehensive view, general survey; philosophical outlook

大難 **tainan** great misfortune, calamity

大騒 **ōsawa(gi)** clamor, uproar

19 大願 **taigan** ambition, aspiration; earnest wish

——————— 2 ———————

4 巨大 **kyodai** huge, gigantic, enormous

5 北大西洋 **Kita Taiseiyō** the North Atlantic

広大 **kōdai** vast, extensive, huge

6 壮大 **sōdai** grand, magnificent, spectacular

7 医大 **idai** medical university (short for 医科大学)

尨大 **bōdai** enormous, extensive, bulky

宏大 **kōdai** vast, extensive, grand

私大 **shidai** private college (short for 私立大学)

8 拡大 **kakudai** magnification, expansion

拡大鏡 **kakudaikyō** magnifying glass

肥大 **hidai** fleshiness, corpulence

9 甚大 **jindai** very great, immense, serious

重大 **jūdai** important, serious

厖大 **bōdai** enormous, huge

10 莫大 **bakudai** vast, immense, enormous

党大会 **tōtaikai** (political) convention

特大 **tokudai** extra large

11 副大統領 **fukudaitōryō** vice president

商大 **shōdai** commercial college (short for 商科大学)

過大 **kadai** excessive, too much, unreasonable

盛大 **seidai** thriving, grand, magnificent

粗大 **sodai** coarse, rough, bulky

粗大ゴミ **sodai gomi** large-item trash (discarded washing machines, TV sets, etc.)

12 偉大 **idai** great, grand, mighty

短大 **tandai** junior college (short for 短期大学)

掌大 **shōdai** palm-size

最大 **saidai** maximum, greatest, largest

雄大 **yūdai** grand, magnificent **Yūdai** (m. given name)

13 寛大 **kandai** magnanimous, tolerant, lenient

誇大 **kodai** exaggeration

16 膨大 **bōdai** swelling; large, enormous

——————— 3 ———————

5 外務大臣 **gaimu daijin** Minister of Foreign Affairs

司法大臣 **shihō daijin** Minister of Justice

6 伊勢大神宮 **Ise Daijingū** the Grand Shrines of Ise

全権大使 **zenken taishi** ambassador plenipotentiary

8 奄美大島 **Amami Ōshima** (island, Kagoshima-ken)

実物大 **jitsubutsudai** actual size

10 原寸大 **gensundai** actual size

¹⁴ 総合大学 **sōgō daigaku** university
総理大臣 **sōri daijin** prime minister

又 → 又 2h0.1

門 → 門 8e0.1

0a3.22 / 1413   ... 力 ｜
                                      8   2

JIN, NIN, ha, yaiba blade

――――――――― 1 ―――――――――

⁸ 刃物 **hamono** edged tool, cutlery
¹² 刃渡 **hawata(ri)** length of a blade
¹³ 刃傷 **ninjō** bloodshed

0a3.23 / 539   ... 十 一
                                      12 1

與 ｜ 与 与

YO give; together **ata(eru)** give
kumi(suru) take part in; side with
TOMO (part of given name)

――――――――― 1 ―――――――――

¹⁰ 与党 **yotō** party in power, ruling
party
¹¹ 与野党 **yoyatō** governing and opposition parties

――――――――― 2 ―――――――――

⁵ 付与 **fuyo** give, grant, confer
¹¹ 授与 **juyo** conferring, awarding
¹² 給与 **kyūyo** allowance, grant, wages
¹⁵ 賞与金 **shōyokin** bonus
賦与 **fuyo** grant, give
¹⁸ 贈与 **zōyo** gift, donation

0a3.24 / 1257   ... 力 ｜
                                      8   2

及 及

KYŪ, oyo(bu) reach, amount to, extend to, match, equal **oyo(bosu)**
exert **oyo(bi)** and, as well as

――――――――― 1 ―――――――――

¹¹ 及第 **kyūdai** passing (an exam),
make the grade

――――――――― 2 ―――――――――

¹² 普及 **fukyū** diffusion, dissemination, wide use/ownership, popularization

0a3.26 / 1325   ... 十 ｜
                                      12 2

丈 ｜ 丈 丈

JŌ (unit of length, about 3 m); (as suffix) (title of respect, used on kabuki actor's stage name) **take** height, length

――――――――― 1 ―――――――――

⁴ 丈夫 **jōbu** strong and healthy;
strong and durable **jōfu,**
masurao manly man, hero;
gentleman

――――――――― 2 ―――――――――

² 八丈島 **Hachijōjima** (island,
Tōkyō-to)
³ 大丈夫 **daijōbu** alright, safe, secure
⁷ 身丈 **mitake, mi(no)take** one's
height
⁹ 背丈 **setake** one's height
¹⁰ 袖丈 **sodetake** sleeve length
¹³ 頑丈 **ganjō** solid, firm, robust

0a3.27 / 551   ... 十 ｜
                                      12 2

才 才

SAI ability, talent; (unit of volume or
area); (as suffix) years old

0a3

———————— 1 ————————
- ¹⁰ 才能 **sainō** talent, ability
- ¹² 才覚 **saikaku** ready wit; raise (money); a plan

———————— 2 ————————
- ² 人才 **jinzai, jinsai** man of talent
- ³ 万才 **banzai** hurrah
- ⁴ 不才 **fusai** lack of talent, incompetence
- 天才 **tensai** genius, natural gift
- ⁵ 弁才 **bensai** oratorical talent, eloquence
- ⁶ 多才 **tasai** many-talented, versatile
- ⁷ 秀才 **shūsai** talented man, bright boy/girl
- ⁸ 英才 **eisai** gifted, talented
- ⁹ 俊才 **shunsai** genius, man of exceptional talent
- ¹⁰ 鬼才 **kisai** genius, man of remarkable talent
- ¹¹ 庸才 **yōsai** mediocre talent
- 異才 **isai** genius, prodigy

0a3.28 / 644   ⊡ 十 丨
                                          12 2

丸丸

GAN, maru circle; entire, complete, full (month); (suffix for names of ships) **maru(i), maru(kkoi)** round **maru (de)** quite, utterly, completely; just like, as it were **maru(meru)** make round, form into a ball

———————— 1 ————————
- ³ 丸山 **Maruyama** (surname)
- ⁴ 丸内 **Maru(no)uchi** (area of Tōkyō)

- 丸切(り) **maru(k)ki(ri), maruki(ri)** completely, utterly
- ⁷ 丸坊主 **marubōzu** close-cropped, shaven (head)
- ¹² 丸焼 **maruya(ki)** barbecue **maruya(ke)** totally destroyed by fire
- ¹³ 丸暗記 **maruanki** learn by heart/rote
- ¹⁸ 丸儲 **marumō(ke)** clear gain/profit

———————— 2 ————————
- ⁴ 日丸 **hi(no)maru** the Japanese/red-sun flag
- ¹⁰ 真丸 **ma(n)maru, ma(n)maru(i)** perfectly round
- ¹² 弾丸 **dangan** projectile, bullet, shell

0a3.29 / 2005   ⊡ 十 丨
                                          12 2

也也

YA, nari to be, is (classical) YA, NARI, ARI, MATA, TADA, KORE (part of given name)

———————— 2 ————————
- ¹ 一也 **Kazuya, Ichiya** (m. given name)
- ⁸ 直也 **Naoya** (m. given name)
- 卓也 **Takuya, Takaya** (m. given name)
- 拓也 **Takuya** (m. given name)
- 和也 **Kazuya** (m. given name)
- ¹⁰ 哲也 **Tetsuya** (m. given name)
- ¹¹ 達也 **Tatsuya** (m. given name)
- ¹² 智也 **Tomoya** (m. given name)
- ¹³ 慎也 **Shin'ya** (m. given name)
- 雅也 **Masaya** (m. given name)

———————————————— **0a4** ————————————————

以	不	斤	云	元	幻	比	匂	勾	爪	片	勿	予
0a5.1	4.2	4.3	4.4	4.5	4.6	2m3.5	4.7	4.8	4.9	2j2.5	4.11	4.12

允	瓦	互	巴	斗	犬	太	氺	凶	天	夭	内	内
4.13	0a5.11	4.15	4.16	4.17	3g0.1	4.18	6f5.5	4.19	4.21	4.22	4.23	0a4.23

氏	卍	五	牙	夫	升	毛	丹	屯	夊	甘	丑	中
4.25	2k4.7	4.27	4.28	4.31	4.32	4.33	4.34	4.35	4.38	0a5.32	4.39	4.40

丹 弔 世 井
0a4.34 4.41 0a5.37 4.46

 → **0a5.1**

0a4.2 / 94

14 2

不

不 不

FU, BU not, un-

―――― 1 ――――

1 不一致 **fuitchi** disagreement, incompatibility

2 不人気 **funinki** unpopular

不十分 **fujūbun** insufficient, inadequate

3 不才 **fusai** lack of talent, incompetence

不干渉 **fukanshō** nonintervention

4 不毛 **fumō** barren, unproductive

不介入 **fukainyū** noninvolvement, nonintervention

不文律 **fubunritsu** unwritten law/rule

不公平 **fukōhei** unfair, unjust

5 不本意 **fuhon'i** reluctant, unwilling, to one's regret

不平 **fuhei** discontent, dissatisfaction, complaint

不平等 **fubyōdō** unequal

不正 **fusei** improper, unjust, wrong, false

不正確 **fuseikaku** inaccurate

不用 **fuyō** unused, useless, waste

不用心 **buyōjin, fuyōjin** unsafe, insecure; careless

不用意 **fuyōi** unprepared, unguarded, careless

不可 **fuka** wrong, bad, improper, disapproved

不可分 **fukabun** indivisible, inseparable

不可欠 **fukaketsu** indispensable, essential

不可抗力 **fukakōryoku** force majeure, beyond one's control, unavoidable

不可侵 **fukashin** nonaggression; inviolable

不可能 **fukanō** impossible

不可解 **fukakai** mysterious, baffling

6 不気味 **bukimi** uncanny, weird, eerie, ominous

不仲 **funaka** discord, on bad terms with

不合格 **fugōkaku** failure (in an exam), rejection, disqualification

不合理 **fugōri** unreasonable, irrational

不充分 **fujūbun** insufficient, inadequate

不孝 **fukō** disobedience to parents, lack of filial piety

不在 **fuzai** absence

不安 **fuan** uneasiness, apprehension; unsettled, precarious; suspenseful, fearful

不安定 **fuantei** unstable, shaky

不当 **futō** improper, unfair, wrongful **fua(tari)** unpopularity, failure

不朽 **fukyū** immortal, everlasting

不自由 **fujiyū** inconvenience, discomfort; privation; disability, handicap

不自然 **fushizen** unnatural

7 不良 **furyō** bad, substandard, delinquent

不承知 **fushōchi** dissent, disagreement, noncompliance

不作 **fusaku** bad harvest, crop failure

不作法 **busahō** bad manners, discourtesy

不似合 **funia(i)** unbecoming, unsuitable, ill-matched

不完全 **fukanzen** incomplete, imperfect, faulty, defective

不図 **futo** suddenly, unexpectedly, by chance

0a4

不快 **fukai** unpleasant, uncomfortable; displeased

不足 **fusoku** shortage, lack

8 不注意 **fuchūi** carelessness

不法 **fuhō** unlawful, illegal, wrongful

不況 **fukyō** recession, business slump

不治 **fuji, fuchi** incurable

不幸 **fukō** unhappiness, misfortune

不始末 **fushimatsu** mismanagement, carelessness; lavish, spendthrift

不実 **fujitsu** unfaithful, inconstant; false, untrue

不定 **futei, fujō** uncertain, indefinite, changeable

不服 **fufuku** dissatisfaction, protest

不明 **fumei** unclear, unknown; ignorance

不和 **fuwa** discord, trouble, strife

9 不信 **fushin** unfaithfulness; unbelief; distrust

不信任 **fushinnin** nonconfidence

不変 **fuhen** invariable, constant, immutable, permanent

不要 **fuyō** of no use, unneeded, waste

不思議 **fushigi** wonder, mystery, marvel

10 不倫 **furin** immoral, illicit

不健康 **fukenkō** unhealthy, unhealthful

不都合 **futsugō** inconvenience, trouble, harm; impropriety, misconduct

不真面目 **fumajime** not serious-minded, insincere

不振 **fushin** dullness, slump, stagnation

不眠症 **fuminshō** insomnia

不純 **fujun** impure

不納 **funō** nonpayment, default

11 不偏 **fuhen** impartial, fair, neutral

不動産 **fudōsan** immovable property, real estate

不運 **fuun** misfortune, bad luck

不道徳 **fudōtoku** immoral

不得意 **futokui** one's weak point

不規則 **fukisoku** irregular, unsystematic

不経済 **fukeizai** poor economy, waste

不断 **fudan** constant, ceaseless; usually

不敗 **fuhai** invincible, undefeated

12 不満 **fuman** dissatisfaction, displeasure, discontent

不覚 **fukaku** imprudence, failure, mistake

不景気 **fukeiki** business slump, recession; cheerless, gloomy

不愉快 **fuyukai** unpleasant, disagreeable

不等 **futō** inequality

13 不義 **fugi** immorality; injustice; impropriety, misconduct, adultery

不適 **futeki** unsuited, unfit, inappropriate

不滅 **fumetsu** immortal, indestructible

不意 **fui** sudden, unexpected

不詳 **fushō** unknown, unidentified

14 不精 **bushō** lazy, indolent

不精髭 **bushōhige** stubbly beard

15 不慮 **furyo** unforeseen, unexpected

不潔 **fuketsu** filthy, dirty

不器用 **bukiyō** clumsy, unskillful

不審 **fushin** dubious, suspicious; strange

不敵 **futeki** bold, daring, fearless

不調 **fuchō** failure to agree; out of sorts

不調法 **buchōhō** impoliteness; carelessness; misconduct; awkward, inexperienced

16 不衛生 **fueisei** unsanitary, unhygienic

不躾 **bushitsuke** ill-breeding, bad manners

———— 2 ————

4 手不足 **tebusoku** shorthanded, understaffed

7 良不良 **ryō-furyō** (whether) good or bad

13 寝不足 **nebusoku** lack of sleep

16 親不孝 **oyafukō** lack of filial piety

━━━━ 3 ━━━━

6 行方不明 **yukue-fumei** missing
10 消化不良 **shōka furyō** indigestion
11 運動不足 **undō-busoku** lack of exercise
欲求不満 **yokkyū fuman** frustration
14 練習不足 **renshū-busoku** out/lack of training

0a4.3 / 1897 斤
50

斤 斤

KIN (unit of weight, about 600 g); ax

0a4.4 日 二 竹
4 17

云 云

UN, i(u) say

━━━━ 1 ━━━━

3 云々 **unnun, shikajika** and so forth, and so on, and the like

0a4.5 / 137 日 二 儿
4 16

元 元

GEN origin; yuan (Chinese monetary unit); Mongol (dynasty) **GAN** origin
moto origin, basis; (as prefix) former, ex- HAJIME (m. given name)

━━━━ 1 ━━━━

3 元々 **motomoto** from the first, originally; by nature, naturally
5 元号 **gengō** era name
元旦 **gantan** New Year's Day
6 元気 **genki** vigor, energy, health, vitality, spirit, courage, pep
元年 **gannen** first year (of an era)

7 元来 **ganrai** originally, primarily, by nature, properly speaking
元利 **ganri** principal and interest
8 元金 **gankin, motokin** the principal, capital
9 元通 **motodō(ri)** as before

━━━━ 2 ━━━━

1 一元化 **ichigenka** unification, centralization
2 二元論 **nigenron** dualism
4 中元 **chūgen** 15th day of the seventh lunar month; midyear gift-giving
手元 **temoto** at hand; in one's care; ready cash
火元 **himoto** origin of a fire
6 多元論 **tagenron** pluralism
地元 **jimoto** local
7 身元 **mimoto** one's identity; one's character
9 紀元 **kigen** era (of year reckoning)
紀元前 **kigenzen** B.C.
紀元後 **kigengo** A.D.
紀元節 **kigensetsu** Empire Day
15 還元 **kangen** restore; reduce, deoxidize
窯元 **kamamoto** place where pottery is made

0a4.6 / 1227 冂 竹 一 丨
17 1 2

幻 幻

GEN, maboroshi illusion, vision, dream, apparition

━━━━ 1 ━━━━

12 幻覚 **genkaku** hallucination
13 幻滅 **genmetsu** disillusionment
幻想 **gensō** fantasy, illusion
14 幻像 **genzō** illusion, phantom

比 → **2m3.5**

0a4.7 / 1964

匂 匂匂

nio(u), nio(i) smell

――――― 1 ―――――

11 匂袋 **nioibukuro** sachet

0a4.8

勾 勾勾

KŌ be bent, slope; capture

――――― 1 ―――――

10 勾留 **kōryū** detention, custody

勾配 **kōbai** slope, incline, gradient

――――― 2 ―――――

9 急勾配 **kyūkōbai** steep slope

0a4.9

爪 爪爪

SŌ, tsume, tsuma- nail, claw, talon; plectrum

――――― 1 ―――――

4 爪切 **tsumeki(ri)** nail clippers

13 爪楊枝 **tsumayōji** toothpick

片→ **2j2.5**

0a4.11

勿 勿勿

MOCHI, BUTSU, naka(re) must not, be not

――――― 1 ―――――

7 勿体無 **mottaina(i)** more than one deserves, too good for; wasteful

15 勿論 **mochiron** of course, naturally

0a4.12 / 393

予 豫|予予

YO previously, beforehand; I, myself
arakaji(me) previously, in advance
kane(te) previously, already

――――― 1 ―――――

6 予防 **yobō** prevent, protect against

7 予告 **yokoku** advance notice; (movie) preview

予言 **yogen** prediction **kanegoto** prediction; promise

8 予定 **yotei** plan, prearrangement, expectation

予定日 **yoteibi** scheduled date, expected date (of birth)

9 予約 **yoyaku** reservations, booking, advance order, subscription, contract

11 予習 **yoshū** lesson preparation

12 予備 **yobi** preparatory, preliminary, in reserve, spare

予備校 **yobikō** preparatory school

予測 **yosoku** forecast, estimate

予報 **yohō** forecast, preannouncement

13 予想 **yosō** expect, anticipate, conjecture, imagine; estimate

予感 **yokan** premonition, hunch

14 予選 **yosen** preliminary selection/screening, elimination round

予算 **yosan** budget, estimate

――――― 2 ―――――

12 猶予 **yūyo** postponement, deferment

0a4.13 / 2022   日 竹 儿   17   16

允

允 允

IN sincere; permit IN, EN, MASA, NO-BU, YOSHI, MITSU, CHIKA, SUKE, TADA (part of given name) MAKOTO (m. given name)

―――――― 1 ――――――

11 允許 **inkyo** permission, license

瓦 → **0a5.11**

0a4.15 / 907   ⋯ 二 一 丨   4   1   2

互

互 互

GO, taga(i) mutual, reciprocal, together

―――――― 1 ――――――

12 互違 **taga(i)chiga(i)** alternating
14 互選 **gosen** co-optation, mutual election
20 互譲 **gojō** mutual concession, compromise, conciliation

―――――― 2 ――――――

9 相互 **sōgo** mutual, reciprocal

0a4.16 / 2061   ⋯ 尸 丨   40   2

巴

巴 巴

HA vortex, whirlpool, spiral **tomoe** swirling-commas design HA, TOMO (part of given name) TOMOE (f. given name)

―――――― 1 ――――――

7 巴里 **Pari** Paris

―――――― 2 ――――――

6 卍巴 **manji-tomoe** (snow falling) in swirls
11 淋巴腺 **rinpasen** lymph gland

0a4.17 / 1899   ⋯ 十 丨   12   2

斗

斗 斗

TO (unit of volume, 18 liters); ladle, dipper

―――――― 2 ――――――

5 北斗七星 **Hokuto Shichisei** the Big Dipper
14 漏斗 **rōto, jōgo** funnel

犬 → **3g0.1**

0a4.18 / 629   ⋯ 大 丨   34   2

太

太 太

TAI, TA big **futo(i)** fat **futo(ru)** get fat FUTOSHI (m. given name)

―――――― 1 ――――――

2 太子 **taishi** crown prince
5 太平洋 **Taiheiyō** the Pacific Ocean
 太字 **futoji** bold-face lettering
 太田 **Ōta** (surname)
6 太后 **taikō** empress dowager, queen mother
11 太陽 **taiyō** the sun, solar
13 太鼓 **taiko** drum
 太腹 **futo(p)para** generous; bold

―――――― 2 ――――――

5 広太郎 **Hirotarō, Kōtarō** (m. given name)
6 汎太平洋 **han-Taiheiyō** pan-Pacific
9 亮太 **Ryōta** (m. given name)
 南太平洋 **Minami Taiheiyō** the South Pacific
 祐太 **Yūta** (m. given name)
 皇太子 **kōtaishi** crown prince
 皇太后 **kōtaikō, kōtaigō** empress dowager, queen mother
10 健太 **Kenta** (m. given name)
 健太郎 **Kentarō** (m. given name)
11 涼太 **Ryōta** (m. given name)

0a4

啓太 **Keita** (m. given name)
12 翔太 **Shōta** (m. given name)
裕太 **Yūta** (m. given name)
雄太 **Yūta** (m. given name)
14 樺太 **Karafuto** Sakhalin
17 優太 **Yūta** (m. given name)

才 → 第 **6f5.5**

0a4.19 / 1280   ⊡ 冂 十
                     20 12

KYŌ evil, bad luck, misfortune; disaster; bad harvest

———————— 1 ————————

6 凶行 **kyōkō** violence, murder
7 凶作 **kyōsaku** bad harvest, crop failure
11 凶悪 **kyōaku** heinous, brutal, fiendish
13 凶漢 **kyōkan** scoundrel, outlaw, assassin
15 凶器 **kyōki** lethal weapon
凶暴 **kyōbō** ferocity, brutality, savagery

0a4.21 / 141   曰 大 一
                    34 1

TEN sky, the heavens; heaven, nature, God **ame** sky, heaven **ama-** heavenly **amatsu-** heavenly, imperial

———————— 1 ————————

3 天川 **Ama(no)kawa** the Milky Way
天才 **tensai** genius, natural gift
天下 **amakuda(ri)** descent from heaven; employment of retired officials by companies they used to regulate **tenka, tenga, ame(ga)shita** under heaven; the whole country, the public/ world; the reins of government; having one's own way
4 天井 **tenjō** ceiling
天文学 **tenmongaku** astronomy
5 天丼 **tendon** bowl of rice and tempura
6 天気 **tenki** the weather; good weather
天地 **tenchi, ametsuchi** heaven and earth, all nature; top and bottom; world, realm, sphere
天安門 **Ten'anmon** Tiananmon, Gate of Heavenly Peace (in Beijing)
7 天災 **tensai** natural disaster
8 天国 **tengoku** paradise, heaven
9 天皇 **tennō** Emperor of Japan
天皇陛下 **Tennō Heika** His Majesty the Emperor
10 天候 **tenkō** the weather
11 天野 **Amano** (surname)
12 天然 **tennen** natural
14 天罰 **tenbatsu** divine punishment
15 天敵 **tenteki** natural enemy
天麩羅 **tenpura** tempura, Japanese-style fried foods

———————— 2 ————————

3 干天 **kanten** dry weather, drought
6 仰天 **gyōten** be astounded
先天的 **sententeki** inborn, congenital, hereditary
8 青天 **seiten** the blue sky
雨天 **uten** rainy weather
11 悪天候 **akutenkō** bad weather
12 寒天 **kanten** agar-agar, gelatin; cold weather, wintry sky
13 楽天家 **rakutenka** optimist
15 摩天楼 **matenrō** skyscraper
16 曇天 **donten** cloudy/overcast sky

0a4.22   曰 大 丨
              34 2

YŌ young; death at a young age

0a4.23 / 84

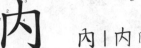

3   20

内   内丨内内

NAI, DAI inside; within; between, among **uchi** inside; house, one's home; within; between, among

――――――― 1 ―――――――

0 内ゲバ **uchigeba** internecine violence (from the German Gewalt, violence)

3 内山 **Uchiyama** (surname)

4 内心 **naishin** one's heart/mind, inward thoughts

5 内弁慶 **uchi-Benkei** tough-acting at home (but meek before outsiders)

内申 **naishin** unofficial report

内外 **naigai** inside and outside; domestic and foreign; approximately **uchi-soto** inside and out

内払 **uchibara(i)** partial payment

内田 **Uchida** (surname)

6 内向性 **naikōsei** introverted

内因 **naiin** internal cause

7 内乱 **nairan** civil war, rebellion

8 内定 **naitei** informal/tentative decision

内的 **naiteki** inner, intrinsic

内金 **uchikin** partial payment, earnest money

9 内面 **naimen** inside, interior, inner

内政 **naisei** domestic/internal affairs

内科 **naika** internal medicine

10 内部 **naibu** interior, inside, internal

内容 **naiyō** content(s), substance

11 内側 **uchigawa** inside, interior, inner

内偵 **naitei** scouting, reconnaissance; private inquiry

内密 **naimitsu** private, secret, confidential

内務省 **Naimushō** (prewar) Ministry of Home Affairs

内訳 **uchiwake** itemization, breakdown

12 内証 **naishō** secret; internal evidence; one's circumstances

13 内幕 **uchimaku** inside information

内蒙古 **Uchi Mōko** Inner Mongolia

内戦 **naisen** civil war

14 内緒 **naisho** secret

内需 **naiju** domestic demand

内閣 **naikaku** the cabinet

15 内線 **naisen** (telephone) extension; indoor wiring; inner line

内縁 **naien** common-law marriage

18 内藤 **Naitō** (surname)

内職 **naishoku** at-home work, side job, cottage industry

19 内臓 **naizō** internal organs

――――――― 2 ―――――――

3 丸内 **Maru(no)uchi** (area of Tōkyō)

山内 **Yama(no)uchi, Yamauchi** (surname)

4 木内 **Kiuchi** (surname)

5 以内 **inai** within, not more than

市内 **shinai** (within the) city

6 年内 **nennai** within the year, before the end of the year

廷内 **teinai** in the court

池内 **Ikeuchi, Ikenouchi** (surname)

寺内 **Terauchi** (surname)

竹内 **Takeuchi** (surname)

7 身内 **miuchi** relations, family, friends

体内 **tainai** inside the body, internal

社内 **shanai** in the company/shrine

車内 **shanai** inside the car

8 国内 **kokunai** domestic

武内 **Takeuchi, Takenouchi** (surname)

9 室内 **shitsunai** indoor(s), interior

屋内 **okunai** indoor(s)

10 都内 **tonai** within the capital

家内 **kanai** my wife; family, home

宮内 **Miyauchi** (surname)

宮内庁 **Kunaichō** Imperial Household Agency

案内 **annai** guidance, information

案内図 **annaizu** information map

案内所 **annaijo** information office/booth

党内 **tōnai** intra-party
11 堀内 **Horiuchi, Horinouchi** (surname)
12 港内 **kōnai** in the harbor
13 幕内 **makuuchi** senior-rank sumo wrestler **maku(no)uchi** rice-ball lunch; senior-rank sumo wrestler
14 獄内 **gokunai** in prison
構内 **kōnai** premises, grounds, precincts
16 機内 **kinai** inside the airplane

——— 3 ———
15 範囲内 **han'inai** within the limits of
19 瀬戸内海 **Setonaikai** the Inland Sea

——— 4 ———
4 水先案内 **mizusaki annai** pilot; piloting

内 → 内 **0a4.23**

0a4.25 / 566

18 12

氏 氏

SHI Mr.; family, clan; surname
uji clan; lineage, birth; surname

——— 1 ———
6 氏名 **shimei** surname and given name, (full) name
9 氏神 **ujigami** patron deity

——— 2 ———
6 両氏 **ryōshi** both men
同氏 **dōshi** the same person, said person, he, she
8 姓氏 **seishi** surname
彼氏 **kareshi** he; boyfriend, lover
9 某氏 **bōshi** a certain person
10 華氏 **kashi** Fahrenheit
13 源氏 **Genji** Genji, the Minamoto family
源氏物語 **Genji Monogatari** The Tale of Genji
摂氏 **sesshi** Celsius, centigrade

卍 → **2k4.7**

0a4.27 / 7

14 1

五 五五

GO, itsu(tsu), itsu- five I, KAZU (part of name)

——— 1 ———
2 五十音順 **gojūonjun** in "aiueo" order of the kana alphabet
五十嵐 **Igarashi** (surname)
4 五分 **gofun** five minutes **gobu** fifty percent, half; five percent
五月 **gogatsu** May **satsuki** fifth month of the lunar calendar
五月晴 **satsukiba(re)** fine weather during the rainy season
五日 **itsuka** the 5th (day of the month); five days
13 五感 **gokan** the five senses

——— 2 ———
2 七五三 **shichi-go-san** the lucky numbers 7, 5, and 3; festival for children 7, 5, and 3 years old

——— 3 ———
5 四捨五入 **shisha-gonyū** rounding off

0a4.28

14 2

牙 牙丨牙牙

GA, GE, kiba fang, canine tooth, tusk

——— 2 ———
12 象牙 **zōge** ivory
象牙塔 **zōge (no) tō** ivory tower

0a4.31 / 315

FU, FŪ husband; man otto husband
so(re) that O (part of given name)

―――――― 1 ――――――

² 夫人 **fujin** wife, married woman, Mrs.
⁸ 夫妻 **fusai** husband and wife, Mr. and Mrs.
¹¹ 夫婦 **fūfu, meoto, myōto** husband and wife, couple

―――――― 2 ――――――

¹ 一夫 **Kazuo, Ichio, Itsuo** (m. given name)
    一夫多妻 **ippu-tasai** polygamy
² 人夫 **ninpu** coolie, laborer
³ 工夫 **kufū** device, invention, contrivance, means **kōfu** coolie, workman, laborer
    丈夫 **jōbu** strong and healthy; strong and durable **jōfu, masurao** manly man, hero; gentleman
    亡夫 **bōfu** one's late husband
⁴ 文夫 **Fumio, Ayao** (m. given name)
    水夫 **suifu** sailor, seaman
⁵ 令夫人 **reifujin** Mrs., Lady, Madam; your wife
    正夫 **Masao, Tadao** (m. given name)
⁷ 辰夫 **Tatsuo, Tokio, Yoshio** (m. given name)
    坑夫 **kōfu** miner
⁸ 郁夫 **Ikuo, Kunio, Ayao** (m. given name)
⁹ 姦夫 **kanpu** adulterer
    恒夫 **Tsuneo, Hisao** (m. given name)
    紀夫 **Norio, Toshio** (m. given name)
¹¹ 道夫 **Michio, Michito** (m. given name)
    章夫 **Akio, Fumio, Yukio** (m. given name)
¹³ 農夫 **nōfu** farmer, farmhand

照夫 **Teruo, Akio, Nobuo** (m. given name)
¹⁵ 澄夫 **Sumio, Masuo** (m. given name)

―――――― 3 ――――――

³ 大丈夫 **daijōbu** alright, safe, secure

0a4.32 / 1898

SHŌ (unit of volume, 1.8 liters)
masu square measuring box
NOBORU (m. given name)

0a4.33 / 287

MŌ hair; tiny amount; 1/10,000 yen
ke hair, fur, wool

―――――― 1 ――――――

⁵ 毛皮 **kegawa** fur, skin, pelt
    毛布 **mōfu** blanket
⁶ 毛糸 **keito** wool yarn, worsted, woolen
    毛虫 **kemushi** caterpillar
⁷ 毛利 **Mōri** (surname)
¹¹ 毛深 **kebuka(i)** hairy
¹² 毛筆 **mōhitsu** writing/painting brush
¹³ 毛嫌 **kegira(i)** antipathy, aversion, prejudice
¹⁴ 毛髪 **mōhatsu** hair

―――――― 2 ――――――

⁴ 不毛 **fumō** barren, unproductive
⁶ 羽毛 **umō** feathers, plumage, down
    羊毛 **yōmō** wool
⁷ 抜毛 **nu(ke)ge** hair falling out, molting
⁹ 眉毛 **mayuge** eyebrows
¹⁰ 純毛 **junmō** all-wool
¹¹ 脱毛 **datsumō, nu(ke)ge** falling-out/removal of hair

0a4

13 睫毛 **matsuge** eyelashes
14 髪毛 **kami (no) ke** hair (on the head)
18 癖毛 **kusege** curly/kinky hair

0a4.34 / 1093   ⸤…⸥ 冂 一 ｜
                              20   1   2

丹 ｜ 丹 丹

TAN red; red lead; (suffix for medicines) **ni** red; red earth

——————— 1 ———————

8 丹念 **tannen** painstaking, elaborate
  丹波 **Tanba, Tanpa** (surname)
13 丹誠 **tansei** sincerity; diligence
14 丹精 **tansei** diligence

——————— 3 ———————

4 切支丹 **Kirishitan** (early) Japanese Christianity/Christian

0a4.35 / 1936   ⸤…⸥ 十 冂
                              12   20

屯 屯

TON ton; garrison **tamuro** garrison

——————— 2 ———————

15 駐屯地 **chūtonchi** (army) post

0a4.38 / 1902   ⸤…⸥ 宀 十
                              15   12

匁 匁

monme (unit of weight, about 3.75 g)

甘 → **0a5.32**

0a4.39 / 2001   曰 十 一
                              12   1

丑 丑

CHŪ, ushi second horary sign (cow)
CHŪ, USHI, HIRO (part of given name)

0a4.40 / 28   ⸤…⸥ 卩 ｜
                              24   2

中 中

CHŪ middle; China **-chū, -jū** throughout, during, within **naka** inside, midst **uchi** among **ATARU** (m. given name)

——————— 1 ———————

0 アル中 **aruchū** alcoholism (short for アルコール中毒)
3 中川 **Nakagawa** (surname)
  中小企業 **chūshō kigyō** small business(es)
  中山 **Nakayama** (surname)
4 中元 **chūgen** 15th day of the seventh lunar month; midyear gift-giving
  中井 **Nakai** (surname)
  中止 **chūshi** discontinue, suspend, stop, call off, cancel
  中日 **Chū-Nichi** China and Japan **chūnichi** day of the equinox **nakabi, chūnichi** the middle day (of a sumo tournament)
  中心 **chūshin** center
5 中央 **chūō** center, middle
  中世 **chūsei** the Middle Ages, medieval
  中古 **chūko** secondhand; the Middle Ages **chūburu** secondhand
  中正 **chūsei** impartial, fair
  中立 **chūritsu** neutrality
  中田 **Nakada, Nakata** (surname)
6 中年 **chūnen** middle age
  中西 **Nakanishi** (surname)

中肉中背 **chūniku-chūzei** medium height and build

中近東 **Chūkintō** the Near and Middle East

中旬 **chūjun** middle ten days of a month, mid-(May)

中米 **Chūbei** Central America

7 中身 **nakami** contents

中位 **chūi** medium, average **chūgurai, chūkurai** about medium/average

中谷 **Nakatani, Nakaya** (surname)

中沢 **Nakazawa** (surname)

中学生 **chūgakusei** junior-high-school student

中学校 **chūgakkō** junior high school

中尾 **Nakao** (surname)

中村 **Nakamura** (surname)

8 中東 **Chūtō** the Middle East, Mideast

中毒 **chūdoku** poisoning

中退 **chūtai** leaving school before graduation, dropping out

中味 **nakami** contents

中国 **Chūgoku** China; Western tip of Honshū, comprising Hiroshima, Okayama, Shimane, Tottori, and Yamaguchi prefectures

中国地方 **Chūgoku chihō** the Chūgoku region (Hiroshima, Okayama, Shimane, Tottori, and Yamaguchi prefectures)

中欧 **Chūō** central Europe

中性 **chūsei** neuter; (chemically) neutral; sterile

中和 **chūwa** neutralize

9 中南米 **Chūnanbei** Central and South America

中点 **chūten** midpoint

中途半端 **chūto-hanpa** half finished, incomplete

中指 **nakayubi, chūshi** middle finger

10 中部 **chūbu** central part **Chūbu** the central Honshū region

中原 **Nakahara** (surname)

中華人民共和国 **Chūka Jinmin Kyōwakoku** People's Republic of China

中華民国 **Chūka Minkoku** Republic of China (Taiwan)

中華料理 **chūka ryōri** Chinese cooking/food

中島 **Nakajima** (surname)

中核 **chūkaku** kernel, core, nucleus

11 中野 **Nakano** (surname)

中断 **chūdan** break off, interrupt, suspend

中頃 **nakagoro** about the middle

12 中期 **chūki** middle period

中絶 **chūzetsu** interruption, discontinuation, termination; abortion

中等 **chūtō** medium/secondary grade, average quality

中間 **chūkan** middle, midway, intermediate; midterm, interim

13 中傷 **chūshō** slander, defamation

中継 **chūkei** (remote broadcast) relay

―――――― 2 ――――――

3 上中下 **jō-chū-ge** good-fair-poor; first-second-third class; volumes/parts 1, 2, 3 (of a 3-volume/3-part series)

女中 **jochū** maid

山中 **Yamanaka** (surname)

山中湖 **Yamanaka-ko** Lake Yamanaka (near Mt. Fuji)

4 水中 **suichū** underwater, in the water

日中 **Nit-Chū** Japan and China **nitchū** during the day **hinaka** broad daylight, daytime

火中 **kachū** in the fire, midst of the flames

心中 **shinjū** lovers' double suicide; murder-suicide **shinchū** in one's heart

5 生中継 **namachūkei** live (remote) broadcast

世中 **yo(no)naka** the world, life, the times

田中 **Tanaka** (surname)

6 年中 **nenjū** all year, year-round

年中行事 **nenjū gyōji** an annual event

地中海 **Chichūkai** the Mediterranean Sea

在中 **zaichū** within

米中 **Bei-Chū** America and China

竹中 **Takenaka** (surname)

7 身中 **shinchū** one's heart, inmost thoughts

対中 **tai-Chū** toward/with China

忌中 **kichū** in mourning

車中 **shachū** in the car/vehicle

8 夜中 **yonaka** midnight, dead of night **yachū** at night **yojū** all night

卒中 **sotchū** cerebral stroke, apoplexy

空中 **kūchū** in the air/sky, aerial

的中 **tekichū** hit the mark, come true, guess right

武中 **Takenaka** (surname)

9 連中 **renchū, renjū** companions, party, company, crowd, clique

途中 **tochū** on the way, en route

途中下車 **tochū gesha** stopover, layover

背中 **senaka** one's back

10 胸中 **kyōchū** one's bosom, heart, feelings

病中 **byōchū** during an illness

11 船中 **senchū** in/aboard the ship

12 喪中 **mochū** period of mourning

御中 **onchū** To: (name of addressee organization), Dear Sirs:

掌中 **shōchū** in the hand; pocket (edition)

暑中見舞 **shochū mima(i)** inquiry after (someone's) health in the hot season

最中 **saichū, sanaka** the midst/height of **monaka** middle; bean-jam-filled wafers

集中 **shūchū** concentration

13 夢中 **muchū** rapture; absorption, intentness; frantic

話中 **hana(shi)chū** in the midst of speaking; (phone is) busy

15 熱中 **netchū** be enthusiastic/crazy about, be engrossed/absorbed in

16 懐中 **kaichū** one's pocket

懐中電灯 **kaichū dentō** flashlight

19 霧中 **muchū** in the fog

───── 3 ─────

1 一日中 **ichinichi-jū** all day long

一年中 **ichinen-jū** all year long

3 工事中 **kōjichū** Under Construction

4 中肉中背 **chūniku-chūzei** medium height and build

午前中 **gozenchū** all morning

日本中 **Nihonjū, Nipponjū** all over Japan

7 妊娠中絶 **ninshin chūzetsu** abortion

10 真夜中 **mayonaka** dead of night, midnight

真最中 **ma(s)saichū** right in the midst/middle of, at the height of

11 脳卒中 **nōsotchū** cerebral apoplexy

13 戦争中 **sensōchū** during the war

戦時中 **senjichū** during the war, wartime

───── 4 ─────

5 四六時中 **shirokujichū** 24 hours a day, constantly

12 御多忙中 **gotabōchū** while you are so busy

無我夢中 **muga-muchū** total absorption, ecstasy

丹 → 丹 0a4.34

0a4.41 / 1796   □ 弓 |

28 2

弔 弔

CHŌ, tomura(u) mourn **tomura(i)** funeral

───── 1 ─────

11 弔問 **chōmon** condolence call/visit

13 弔辞 **chōji** message of condolence, memorial address

15 弔慰 **chōi** condolences, sympathy

─────── 2 ───────
15 慶弔 **keichō** congratulations and
condolences

世 → **0a5.37**

0a4.46 / 1193   ⊡ ⧾ 一
                                  32 1

井 井

SEI, SHŌ, i (water) well

─────── 1 ───────
3 井上 **Inoue** (surname)
  井口 **Iguchi, Inoguchi** (surname)
4 井戸 **ido** (water) well
10 井原 **Ihara** (surname)

─────── 2 ───────
3 川井 **Kawai** (surname)
  土井 **Doi, Tsuchii** (surname)
4 天井 **tenjō** ceiling
  中井 **Nakai** (surname)
  今井 **Imai** (surname)
5 平井 **Hirai** (surname)
  永井 **Nagai** (surname)

白井 **Shirai** (surname)
石井 **Ishii** (surname)
6 臼井 **Usui** (surname)
向井 **Mukai** (surname)
安井 **Yasui** (surname)
吉井 **Yoshii** (surname)
7 坂井 **Sakai** (surname)
村井 **Murai** (surname)
8 長井 **Nagai** (surname)
坪井 **Tsuboi** (surname)
松井 **Matsui** (surname)
武井 **Takei** (surname)
金井 **Kanai, Kanei** (surname)
9 荒井 **Arai** (surname)
10 酒井 **Sakai** (surname)
桜井 **Sakurai** (surname)
11 細井 **Hosoi** (surname)
笠井 **Kasai** (surname)
12 筒井 **Tsutsui** (surname)
13 福井 **Fukui** (city, Fukui-ken); (sur-
      name)
福井県 **Fukui-ken** (prefecture)
新井 **Arai** (surname)
14 増井 **Masui** (surname)
15 横井 **Yokoi** (surname)
18 藤井 **Fujii** (surname)

────────────────── 0a5 ──────────────────

以   瓜   丞   北   予   巧   包   正   乍   瓦   丘   凸   凹
5.1 0a6.3 2c4.3 5.5 5.6 5.7 5.9 2m3.3 5.10 5.11 5.12 5.13 5.14

且   必   斥   矢   左   丙   出   民   半   本   末   未   失
5.15 5.16 5.18 5.19 5.20 5.21 5.22 5.23 5.24 5.25 5.26 5.27 5.28

生   弁   甘   央   甲   由   母   世   史   申   井   冊
5.29 5.30 5.32 5.33 5.34 5.35 5.36 5.37 5.38 5.39 5.40 5.42

0a5.1 / 46   ⊡ 亻 丨
                                  3 2

以 人 以

I, mot(te) with, by (means of); because
of; in view of MOCHI (part of given
name)

─────── 1 ───────
3 以上 **ijō** or more, more than, over,

above, beyond; the above;
since, so long as; that is all
以下 **ika** or less, less than; under,
below; the following
4 以内 **inai** within, not more than
5 以外 **igai** except, other than
7 以来 **irai** since
9 以降 **ikō** on and after, beginning …
以前 **izen** ago; formerly
以後 **igo** from now/then on,
(t)henceforth

0a5

—— 2 ——

9 前以 **maemot(te)** beforehand, previously

瓜→ **0a6.3**

丞→ **2c4.3**

0a5.5 / 73   口 ㅏ 一 丨
13 1 2

北北

HOKU, kita north KITA (surname)

—— 1 ——

3 北大西洋 **Kita Taiseiyō** the North Atlantic

4 北斗七星 **Hokuto Shichisei** the Big Dipper

北方 **hoppō** north, northward, northern

5 北半球 **Kita Hankyū** Northern Hemisphere

北氷洋 **Hoppyōyō, Hokuhyōyō** the Arctic Ocean

6 北西 **hokusei** northwest

北向 **kitamu(ki)** facing north

北回帰線 **Kita Kaikisen** the Tropic of Cancer

北米 **Hokubei** North America

7 北村 **Kitamura** (surname)

8 北東 **hokutō** northeast

北京 **Pekin** Peking, Beijing

北国 **hokkoku, kitaguni** northern provinces, northern countries

北欧 **Hokuō** Northern Europe

9 北風 **kitakaze, hokufū** north wind

北海道 **Hokkaidō** (prefecture)

10 北陸地方 **Hokuriku chihō** the Hokuriku region (Fukui, Ishikawa, Toyama, Niigata prefectures)

北部 **hokubu** north, northern part

北原 **Kitahara** (surname)

北島 **Kitajima** (surname)

11 北野 **Kitano** (surname)

12 北極 **hokkyoku** the North Pole

北朝鮮 **Kita Chōsen** North Korea

16 北緯 **hokui** north latitude

—— 2 ——

5 台北 **Taipei, Taihoku** Taipei (capital of Taiwan)

6 西北 **seihoku** northwest

8 東北 **tōhoku** northeast
Tōhoku (northeastern Honshū)

9 南北 **nanboku** north and south

11 敗北 **haiboku** defeat

—— 4 ——

8 東西南北 **tōzainanboku** north, south, east, and west

0a5.6 / 773   日 一 一 丨
14 1 2

矛矛

MU, hoko halberd

—— 1 ——

9 矛盾 **mujun** contradiction

0a5.7 / 1627   口 エ 一
38 14

巧巧

KŌ, taku(mi) skill

—— 1 ——

7 巧妙 **kōmyō** skillful, clever, deft

—— 2 ——

7 技巧 **gikō** art, craftsmanship, technique

0a5.9 / 804   ⋯ 弓 勹
28 15

包丨包包

HŌ, tsutsu(mu) wrap; cover, envelop; conceal **tsutsu(mi)** package
kuru(mu) wrap up, tuck in
kuru(meru) lump together
KANE (part of given name)

—————— 1 ——————

2 包丁 **hōchō** kitchen knife; cooking

4 包込 **tsutsu(mi)ko(mu)** wrap up

7 包含 **hōgan** include, comprehend; imply

包囲 **hōi** surround, encircle, besiege

9 包括 **hōkatsu** include, comprehend

10 包帯 **hōtai** bandage, dressing

包容 **hōyō** comprehend, embrace, imply; tolerate

包紙 **tsutsu(mi)gami** wrapping paper

12 包装 **hōsō** packaging, packing, wrapping

15 包蔵 **hōzō** contain, comprehend; imply; entertain (an idea)

—————— 2 ——————

3 小包 **kozutsumi** parcel, package

正→　2m3.3

0a5.10　　　□ 𠂉 ト 一
　　　　　　　　15　13　1

SA, -naga(ra) while, although; while, during

—————— 2 ——————

10 恐乍 **oso(re)naga(ra)** most humbly/respectfully

0a5.11　　　□ 厂 一 丨
　　　　　　　14　1　2

GA, kawara tile **guramu** gram

—————— 1 ——————

9 瓦屋根 **kawara yane** tiled roof

0a5.12 / 1357　　　日 斤 一
　　　　　　　　　　50　1

KYŪ, oka hill

—————— 1 ——————

10 丘陵 **kyūryō** hill

—————— 2 ——————

9 砂丘 **sakyū** dune

0a5.13 / 1892　　　□ 一 丨
　　　　　　　　　　1　2

TOTSU protrusion, bulge

—————— 1 ——————

5 凸凹 **dekoboko** uneven, bumpy, jagged

9 凸面 **totsumen** convex (surface)

—————— 2 ——————

5 凹凸 **ōtotsu** uneven, irregular, jagged; concavo-convexy

0a5.14 / 1893　　　□ 一 丨
　　　　　　　　　　1　2

Ō indentation, depression **heko(mu)** be dented, sink, collapse, give in, cave in; be daunted **heko(masu)** dent in; humiliate, put down **kubo** hollow, depression

—————— 1 ——————

5 凹凸 **ōtotsu** uneven, irregular, jagged; concavo-convexy

9 凹面 **ōmen** concave (surface)

—————— 2 ——————

5 凸凹 **dekoboko** uneven, bumpy, jagged

0a5.15 / 1926

日 月 一
42   1

且   且 且

SHO, ka(tsu) and

━━━━━━ 1 ━━━━━━

2 且又 **ka(tsu)mata** and, moreover

━━━━━━ 2 ━━━━━━

8 尚且 **naoka(tsu)** furthermore; and yet

0a5.16 / 520

�... 心 丨
51   2

必   必 必

HITSU certain, sure
kanara(zu) surely, be sure to, without fail, invariably

━━━━━━ 1 ━━━━━━

6 必死 **hisshi** certain death; desperate, frantic
9 必要 **hitsuyō** necessary
必要品 **hitsuyōhin** necessities
10 必修 **hisshū** required (subject)
12 必勝 **hisshō** sure victory
必然 **hitsuzen** inevitability, necessity
14 必読 **hitsudoku** required reading, a must read
必需品 **hitsujuhin** necessities, essentials

0a5.18 / 1401

�... 斤 丨
50   2

斤   斤 斤

SEKI repel, repulse; scout, reconnoiter **shirizo(keru)** repel, repulse; reject

━━━━━━ 1 ━━━━━━

2 斥力 **sekiryoku** repulsion, repulsive force

━━━━━━ 2 ━━━━━━

11 排斥 **haiseki** exclude, expel, ostracize, boycott

0a5.19 / 213

日 矢 ヘ
34   15

矢   矢 矢

SHI, ya arrow

━━━━━━ 1 ━━━━━━

6 矢印 **yajirushi** arrow
9 矢庭 **yaniwa (ni)** suddenly, immediately
10 矢部 **Yabe** (surname)
11 矢野 **Yano** (surname)
12 矢場 **yaba** archery ground/range

━━━━━━ 2 ━━━━━━

3 弓矢 **yumiya** bow and arrow

━━━━━━ 3 ━━━━━━

12 無理矢理 **muriyari** forcibly, under compulsion

0a5.20 / 75

日 工 十
38   12

左   左 左

SA, hidari left

━━━━━━ 1 ━━━━━━

4 左辺 **sahen** left side
左手 **hidarite** left hand
左方 **sahō** the left
5 左右 **sayū** left and right; control, dominate, govern, influence
7 左折 **sasetsu** left turn
左利 **hidariki(ki)** left-handed; left-hander; a drinker
10 左記 **saki** the following
11 左側 **hidarigawa** left side
17 左翼 **sayoku** left wing, leftist; left field (in baseball)

━━━━━━ 2 ━━━━━━

5 右左 **migi-hidari** right and left

0a5.21 / 984   … ⼀ ⼌ ⼁
14 20 2

丙   丙 丙

HEI third in a series, "C" **hinoe** third calendar sign

——————— 3 ———————

[5] 甲乙丙 **kō-otsu-hei** A, B, C; No. 1, 2, 3

0a5.22 / 53   … ⼭ ⼌
36 20

出   出 ⼭

SHUTSU, SUI, de(ru), ide(ru) go/come out, appear, emerge **de** turnout; one's turn; flow; origin **da(su), ida(su)** put/take out; send; (as verb suffix) begin to **da(shi)** broth; pretext **IZURU** (m. given name)

——————— 1 ———————

[0] お出で,お出 **(o)i(de), (o)ide** come; go; be

[2] 出入口 **deiriguchi** entrance/exit

出入国 **shutsunyūkoku** emigration and immigration

出力 **shutsuryoku** output

[3] 出口 **deguchi** exit; outlet
Deguchi (surname)

[4] 出欠 **shukketsu** attendance or absence

[5] 出生 **shusshō, shussei** birth

出世 **shusse** succeed in life, get ahead

出処 **shussho, dedokoro** source, origin

[6] 出任 **demaka(se)** saying whatever comes to mind

出合 **dea(u)** happen to meet, run into; rendezvous **da(shi)a(u)** contribute jointly, share the expenses

出廷 **shuttei** appear in court

出迎 **demuka(eru)** (go/come to) meet (someone upon his arrival)

出向 **demu(ku)** go to, leave for, repair to **shukkō** repair to; be on loan (to a subsidiary), be seconded (to another company), temporary transfer

出回 **demawa(ru)** appear on the market

出血 **shukketsu** bleeding, hemorrhage

[7] 出身 **shusshin** (as suffix) originally from …

出来 **deki(ru)** can, be able to, be possible; be done, be finished, be ready; be made of; be formed; come into being

出来上 **dekia(garu)** be finished, be ready; be cut out for

出来事 **dekigoto** incident, event, happenings

出社 **shussha** go/come to the office

[8] 出版 **shuppan** publishing

出典 **shutten** source, authority

出店 **demise** branch store
shutten open a new store

出国 **shukkoku** departure from a country

出物 **demono** rash, boil; secondhand article **da(shi)mono** performance, program

出所 **shussho** source, origin; be released from prison
dedokoro source, origin

[9] 出発 **shuppatsu** departure

出前 **demae** cooked-food home delivery **da(shi)mae** one's share (of the expenses)

出品 **shuppin** exhibit, display

[10] 出席 **shusseki** attendance

出航 **shukkō** departure, sailing

[11] 出動 **shutsudō** be sent/called out, take the field

出掛 **deka(keru)** go out, set out **de(gake)** about to go out

出張 **shutchō** business trip
deba(ri) projection, ledge

出現 **shutsugen** appear, show up

出産 **shussan** childbirth

[12] 出勤 **shukkin** go/come to work

出場 **shutsujō** appear on stage, perform; participate in, enter (a competition)

出費 **shuppi** expenses, disbursements

出雲 **Izumo** (ancient kuni, Shimane-ken)

13 出資 **shusshi** investment, financing, contribution

14 出演 **shutsuen** appear on stage, play, perform

出獄 **shutsugoku** release from prison

15 出稼 **dekase(gi)** working away from home

16 出頭 **shuttō** appear, attend, be present

19 出願 **shutsugan** application

———————— 2 ————————

2 人出 **hitode** turnout, crowd

3 口出 **kuchida(shi)** meddling, butting in

4 支出 **shishutsu** expenditure, disbursement

引出 **hi(ki)da(shi)** (desk) drawer

日出 **hi(no)de** sunrise

5 生出 **u(mi)da(su)** bring forth, produce, yield

申出 **mō(shi)de(ru)** offer, submit, report, request **mō(shi)i(de)** proposal; request, application, claim; report, notice

外出 **gaishutsu, sotode** go/step out

6 再出 **saishutsu** reappear, re-emerge

再出発 **saishuppatsu** start over, make a fresh start

吐出 **ha(ki)da(su)** vomit, disgorge, spew out

早出 **hayade** early arrival (at the office)

7 抜出 **nu(ki)da(su)** select, extract, pull out **nu(ke)da(su)** slip out, sneak away; excel; choose the best **nu(kin)de(ru), nu(ki)de(ru)** be outstanding, excel

吹出 **fu(ki)da(su)** begin to blow; breathe out; burst out laughing

芯出 **shinda(shi)** centering, aligning

見出 **miida(su)** find, discover, pick out **mida(shi)** heading, caption, headline

見出語 **mida(shi)go** headword, entry word

8 追出 **o(i)da(su)** chase/turn away, kick out, eject

抽出 **chūshutsu** extraction, sampling

呼出 **yo(bi)da(su)** call out/up/forth, summon

突出 **tsu(ki)da(su)** thrust/push/stick out **tsu(ki)de(ru)** jut/stick out, protrude **tosshutsu** projection, protrusion

届出 **todokeide, todokede** report, notification

放出 **hōshutsu** release, discharge, emit **hō(ri)da(su)** throw out; expel; abandon

取出 **to(ri)da(su)** take/pick out

9 飛出 **to(bi)da(su)** fly/jump/dart out **to(bi)de(ru)** protrude

乗出 **no(ri)da(su)** set out, embark on; lean forward

這出 **ha(i)de(ru), ha(i)da(su)** crawl out

派出 **hashutsu** dispatch, send out

派出所 **hashutsujo** police box; branch office

思出 **omo(i)de** memory, remembrance **omo(i)da(su)** remember

10 射出 **shashutsu** shoot out, emit, extrude, radiate, catapult

差出人 **sashidashinin** sender, return address

進出 **shinshutsu** advance, march, inroads, push **susu(mi)de(ru)** step forward

流出 **ryūshutsu, naga(re)de(ru), naga(re)da(su)** flow out

捜出 **saga(shi)da(su)** find out, discover, locate

振出 **fu(ri)da(su)** shake out; draw (a bill), issue (a check); infuse, decoct **fu(ri)da(shi)** start; draft, issuing

振出人 **furidashinin** remitter, issuer

家出 **iede** leave home; run away from home

笑出 **wara(i)da(su)** burst out laughing

11 運出 **hako(bi)da(su)** carry out

排出 **haishutsu** discharge, exhaust; excretion

掘出物 **ho(ri)da(shi)mono** treasure trove; lucky find, bargain

萌出 **mo(e)de(ru)** sprout, bud

脱出 **dasshutsu** escape from; prolapse **nu(ke)da(su)** slip away

現出 **genshutsu, ara(ware)de(ru)** appear, emerge

救出 **kyūshutsu** rescue **suku(i)da(su)** rescue from, help out of

産出 **sanshutsu** production, yield, output

転出 **tenshutsu** move out, be transferred

12 湧出 **wa(ki)de(ru), yūshutsu** gush forth/out, well/bubble up

提出 **teishutsu** presentation, filing

絞出 **shibo(ri)da(su)** press/ squeeze out

貸出 **ka(shi)da(su)** lend/hire out

13 歳出 **saishutsu** annual expenditures

続出 **zokushutsu** appear one after another

14 演出 **enshutsu** production, performance

漏出 **rōshutsu** leak out, escape

駆出 **ka(ke)da(su)** rush out, start running **ka(ke)da(shi)** beginner **ka(ri)da(su)** round up, muster

15 噴出 **funshutsu** eruption, gushing, spouting **fu(ki)da(su)** spew/ gush/spurt out, discharge

締出 **shi(me)da(su)** shut/lock out

輩出 **haishutsu** appear one after another

16 燃出 **mo(e)da(su)** begin to burn, ignite

輸出 **yushutsu** export

21 露出 **roshutsu** (indecent/film) exposure

───── 3 ─────

3 大売出 **ōu(ri)da(shi)** big sale

6 自費出版 **jihi shuppan** publishing at one's own expense, vanity press

14 総支出 **sōshishutsu** gross expenditures

0a5.23 / 177

40   12

民   民民

MIN, tami people, nation

───── 1 ─────

5 民本主義 **minpon shugi** democracy

民生 **minsei** the people's livelihood, welfare

民主主義 **minshu shugi** democracy

6 民有 **min'yū** privately owned

7 民芸 **mingei** folkcraft, folk art

8 民事 **minji** civil affairs; civil (law)

民法 **minpō** civil law/code

9 民俗 **minzoku** ethnic/folk customs

民政 **minsei** civil/civilian government

10 民家 **minka** private house

11 民族 **minzoku** race, a people

12 民営 **min'ei** private management, privately run

民衆 **minshū** people, populace, masses

民間 **minkan** private (not public)

13 民話 **minwa** folk tale, folklore

15 民権 **minken** civil rights

16 民謡 **min'yō** folk song

───── 2 ─────

2 人民 **jinmin** the people

4 公民館 **kōminkan** public hall, community center

5 市民 **shimin** citizen

市民権 **shiminken** citizenship, civil rights

6 自民党 **Jimintō** LDP, Liberal Democratic Party (short for 自由民主党)

7 住民 **jūmin** residents, inhabitants
村民 **sonmin** villagers
町民 **chōmin** townspeople
8 国民 **kokumin** the/a people, a national; national
国民性 **kokuminsei** national character
10 島民 **tōmin** islanders
11 貧民 **hinmin** the poor
庶民 **shomin** the (common) people
移民 **imin** immigration, emigration; immigrant, emigrant, settler
12 植民地 **shokuminchi** colony
13 農民 **nōmin** peasants, farmers
漢民族 **Kan minzoku** the Han/Chinese people
18 難民 **nanmin** refugees

――――――― 3 ―――――――

4 中華民国 **Chūka Minkoku** Republic of China (Taiwan)
6 全国民 **zenkokumin** the entire nation
先住民族 **senjū minzoku** aborigines
7 社会民主主義 **shakai minshu shugi** social democracy
10 部落民 **burakumin** (lowly class of people historically engaged in butchery and tanning)
15 避難民 **hinanmin** refugees, evacuees

――――――― 4 ―――――――

4 中華人民共和国 **Chūka Jinmin Kyōwakoku** People's Republic of China

0a5.24 / 88

```
[...]  小  二
        35   4
```

半

半 半

HAN half, semi-; odd number
naka(ba) half, semi-; middle, halfway; partly

――――――― 1 ―――――――

4 半分 **hanbun** half **hanpun** half a minute

半月 **hantsuki** half a month
hangetsu half moon, semicircle
半日 **hannichi** half day
5 半世紀 **hanseiki** half century
半田 **Handa** (surname)
6 半死半生 **hanshi-hanshō** half dead
半年 **hantoshi, hannen** half year, six months
9 半面 **hanmen** half the face; one side, half; the other side
10 半島 **hantō** peninsula
半袖 **hansode** short sleeves
12 半減期 **hangenki** halflife (in physics)
半期 **hanki** half term, half year
14 半端 **hanpa** fragment; incomplete set; fraction; remnant; incomplete
16 半濁音 **handakuon** semivoiced sound, p-sound
18 半額 **hangaku** half the amount/price

――――――― 2 ―――――――

3 大半 **taihan** majority, greater part; mostly
上半身 **jōhanshin, kamihanshin** upper half of the body
下半身 **kahanshin, shimohanshin** lower half of the body
5 北半球 **Kita Hankyū** Northern Hemisphere
6 西半球 **nishi hankyū** Western Hemisphere
9 南半球 **minami hankyū** the Southern Hemisphere
前半 **zenpan** first half
後半 **kōhan** latter half
約半分 **yaku hanbun** about half
11 過半数 **kahansū** majority, more than half
17 藁半紙 **warabanshi** (a low-grade paper)

――――――― 3 ―――――――

4 中途半端 **chūto-hanpa** half finished, incomplete
5 半死半生 **hanshi-hanshō** half dead

⁶ 伊豆半島 **Izu-hantō** Izu Peninsula (Shizuoka-ken)

¹⁰ 能登半島 **Noto-hantō** (peninsula, Ishikawa-ken)

0a5.25 / 25

41   1

HON book; this; main; origin; (counter for long objects) **moto** origin

― 1 ―

² 本人 **honnin** the person himself, the said person, the principal

³ 本土 **hondo** mainland

本山 **honzan** head temple; this temple **Motoyama** (surname)

⁴ 本文 **honbun, honmon** (main) text, body

本月 **hongetsu** this month

本日 **honjitsu** today

本心 **honshin** one's right mind, one's senses; real intention/ motive, true sentiment; conscience

⁵ 本田 **Honda, Motoda** (surname)

⁶ 本多 **Honda** (surname)

本気 **honki** serious, in earnest

本年 **honnen** this year

本州 **Honshū** (Japan's main island)

本名 **honmyō, honmei** one's real name

本当 **hontō** true, real

本旨 **honshi** the main purpose

⁷ 本来 **honrai** properly speaking; in essence, naturally; originally, primarily

本位 **hon'i** standard, basis, principle

本社 **honsha** head office; main shrine; this shrine

⁸ 本店 **honten** head office; main store; this store

本国 **hongoku** one's own country

本物 **honmono** genuine article, the real thing

本性 **honshō, honsei** true nature/ character

⁹ 本通 **hondō(ri)** main street, boulevard

本屋 **hon'ya** bookstore

本音 **honne** real intention, underlying motive

¹⁰ 本部 **honbu** headquarters

本流 **honryū** mainstream

本格的 **honkakuteki** full-scale, genuine, in earnest

本能 **honnō** instinct

¹¹ 本望 **honmō** long-cherished desire; satisfaction

¹² 本場 **honba** home, habitat, the best place for

本棚 **hondana** bookshelf

本筋 **honsuji** plot, main thread (of a story)

本間 **Honma** (surname)

¹⁵ 本質的 **honshitsuteki** in substance, essential

¹⁶ 本館 **honkan** main building; this building

¹⁸ 本職 **honshoku** one's regular occupation; an expert; I

²⁰ 本籍 **honseki** one's legal domicile

― 2 ―

¹ 一本 **ippon** one (long object); a book; one version; a blow; a full-fledged geisha

一本立 **ipponda(chi)** independence

一本気 **ippongi** one-track mind

一本道 **ipponmichi** straight road; road with no turnoffs

一本調子 **ipponchōshi, ipponjōshi** monotony

³ 山本 **Yamamoto** (surname)

⁴ 不本意 **fuhon'i** reluctant, unwilling, to one's regret

辻本 **Tsujimoto** (surname)

手本 **tehon** model, example, pattern

木本 **Kimoto** (surname)

日本 **Nihon, Nippon** Japan

日本一 **Nihon-ichi, Nippon-ichi** Japan's best

日本人 **Nihonjin, Nipponjin** a Japanese

日本刀 **nihontō** Japanese sword

日本三景 **Nihon sankei** Japan's three noted scenic sights (Matsushima, Miyajima, Amano-hashidate)

日本中 **Nihonjū, Nipponjū** all over Japan

日本史 **Nihonshi** Japanese history

日本学 **nihongaku** Japanology

日本画 **nihonga** Japanese-style painting/drawing

日本的 **nihonteki** (very) Japanese

日本風 **nihonfū** Japanese style

日本海 **Nihonkai** the Sea of Japan

日本酒 **nihonshu** saké

日本紙 **nihonshi** Japanese paper

日本晴 **nihonba(re)** clear cloudless sky, beautiful weather

日本間 **nihonma** Japanese-style room

日本製 **nihonsei** made in Japan

日本語 **nihongo** the Japanese language

5 民本主義 **minpon shugi** democracy

古本 **furuhon** used/secondhand book **kohon** secondhand book; ancient book

正本 **seihon, shōhon** an attested copy; the original (of a document) **shōhon** playbook, script; unabridged book

台本 **daihon** script, screenplay, libretto

6 西本 **Nishimoto** (surname)

阪本 **Sakamoto** (surname)

吉本 **Yoshimoto** (surname)

竹本 **Takemoto** (surname)

7 坂本 **Sakamoto** (surname)

抄本 **shōhon** excerpt, abridged transcript

杉本 **Sugimoto** (surname)

見本 **mihon** sample, specimen

8 岡本 **Okamoto** (surname)

河本 **Kōmoto, Kawamoto** (surname)

岩本 **Iwamoto** (surname)

岸本 **Kishimoto** (surname)

松本 **Matsumoto** (surname)

武本 **Takemoto** (surname)

金本 **Kanemoto, Kanamoto** (surname)

10 残本 **zanpon** unsold copies (of a book); remainders

原本 **genpon** the original (work/copy)

宮本 **Miyamoto** (surname)

根本主義 **konpon shugi** fundamentalism

根本的 **konponteki** fundamental, radical

納本 **nōhon** book delivery; presentation copy

11 基本 **kihon** basic, fundamental, standard

基本的 **kihonteki** basic, fundamental

脚本 **kyakuhon** script, play

12 塚本 **Tsukamoto** (surname)

森本 **Morimoto** (surname)

絵本 **ehon** picture book

13 滝本 **Takimoto** (surname)

資本 **shihon** capital

資本主義 **shihon shugi** capitalism

14 熊本県 **Kumamoto-ken** (prefecture)

製本 **seihon** bookbinding

読本 **tokuhon** reader, book of readings

16 橋本 **Hashimoto** (surname)

17 謄本 **tōhon** transcript, copy

18 藤本 **Fijimoto** (surname)

贈本 **zōhon** gift book, complimentary copy

———— 3 ————

3 大日本 **Dai-Nippon/-Nihon** (Great) Japan

4 文庫本 **bunkobon** small paperback book (page size 14.8 x 10.5 cm)

6 西日本 **Nishi Nihon** western Japan

全日本 **zen-Nihon, zen-Nippon** all Japan

8 表日本 **Omote Nihon** Pacific side of Japan

9 単行本 **tankōbon** separate volume, in book form

10 純日本風 **jun-Nihon-fū** classical Japanese style

12 稀覯本 **kikōbon** rare book

¹³ 裏日本 **ura-Nihon, ura-Nippon**
Sea-of-Japan side of Japan

¹⁸ 覆刻本 **fukkokubon** reissued book

0a5.26 / 305

41 1

末末

MATSU, BATSU end; powder **sue**
end; youngest child; descendant; the future; trivialities

——————— 1 ———————

² 末子 **sue(k)ko, basshi, masshi**
youngest child

⁴ 末日 **matsujitsu** last day (of a month)

⁵ 末広 **suehiro** folding fan
suehiro(gari) spreading/widening out toward the end; prospering as time goes on

⁷ 末尾 **matsubi** end, last, final

⁹ 末茶 **matcha** powdered tea

¹¹ 末梢 **masshō** tip of a twig; periphery; nonessentials, trifles

¹⁴ 末端 **mattan** end, tip, terminal

——————— 2 ———————

⁴ 月末 **getsumatsu, tsukizue** end of the month

⁶ 年末 **nenmatsu** the end of the year, year-end

⁸ 始末 **shimatsu** circumstances; manage, dispose of, take care of; economize

¹⁰ 週末 **shūmatsu** weekend
粉末 **funmatsu** powder

¹¹ 終末 **shūmatsu** end, conclusion
粗末 **somatsu** coarse, plain, crude, rough, rude

¹² 期末 **kimatsu** end of the term/period
結末 **ketsumatsu** end, conclusion, upshot

¹³ 幕末 **bakumatsu** latter days of the Tokugawa government

¹⁴ 語末 **gomatsu** word ending

——————— 3 ———————

⁴ 不始末 **fushimatsu** mismanagement, carelessness; lavish, spendthrift

⁹ 後始末 **atoshimatsu** settle, wind/finish up

¹³ 跡始末 **atoshimatsu** winding-up, settlement, straightening up (afterwards)

0a5.27 / 306

41 1

未未

MI not yet, un- **ima(da)** still, as yet, to this day, ever **mada** still, not yet
hitsuji eighth horary sign (sheep)

——————— 1 ———————

¹ 未了 **miryō** unfinished

³ 未亡人 **mibōjin** widow

⁵ 未払 **mihara(i)** unpaid

⁶ 未成年 **miseinen** minority, not of age

⁷ 未来 **mirai** future; future tense
未決 **miketsu** pending, unsettled
未完成 **mikansei** incomplete, unfinished

⁸ 未知 **michi** unknown, strange
未定 **mitei** undecided, pending
未明 **mimei** (pre-)dawn

¹¹ 未済 **misai** unpaid, unsettled, outstanding
未婚 **mikon** unmarried

¹² 未満 **miman** less than, below

¹³ 未解決 **mikaiketsu** unsolved, unsettled
未詳 **mishō** unknown, unidentified

¹⁴ 未練 **miren** lingering affection

¹⁵ 未踏 **mitō** untrodden, unexplored

——————— 3 ———————

⁶ 自殺未遂 **jisatsu misui** attempted suicide

⁹ 前代未聞 **zendai-mimon** unprecedented

0a5

0a5.28 / 311   □... 大 ケ
34 15

失   失 失

SHITSU lose; err **shis(suru)** lose, miss; forget; be excessive **ushina(u)** lose **u(seru)** disappear, vanish

───────── 1 ─────────

4 失心 **shisshin** faint, lose consciousness

5 失礼 **shitsurei** rudeness, discourtesy

6 失当 **shittō** improper, unfair, wrongful

7 失言 **shitsugen** verbal slip/impropriety

8 失効 **shikkō** lapse, lose effect, become null and void

失明 **shitsumei** lose one's eyesight, go blind

9 失陥 **shikkan** surrender, fall

失政 **shissei** misgovernment, misrule

10 失恋 **shitsuren** unrequited love

失格 **shikkaku** disqualification

11 失脚 **shikkyaku** lose one's standing, be overthrown, fall

失望 **shitsubō** disappointment, despair

失敗 **shippai** failure, blunder, mistake

12 失策 **shissaku** blunder, slip, error

失費 **shippi** expenses, expenditures

13 失業 **shitsugyō** unemployment

失業者 **shitsugyōsha** unemployed person

失意 **shitsui** despair, disappointment; adversity

14 失墜 **shittsui** lose, fall

失態 **shittai** blunder, mismanagement; disgrace

15 失権 **shikken** forfeiture of rights, disenfranchisement

失調 **shitchō** malfunction, lack of coordination

失踪 **shissō** disappear, be missing

───────── 2 ─────────

1 一失 **isshitsu** a disadvantage; a defect; an error

4 火失 **kashitsu** accidental fire

10 紛失 **funshitsu** loss, be missing

11 過失 **kashitsu** error, mistake; accident; negligence

得失 **tokushitsu** advantages and disadvantages

12 喪失 **sōshitsu** loss

焼失 **shōshitsu** be destroyed by fire

13 損失 **sonshitsu** loss

14 遺失 **ishitsu** loss

0a5.29 / 44   日 牛 一
47 1

生   生 生

SEI birth; life; (as suffix) student **SHŌ** birth; life **i(kiru)** live, be alive **i(ki)** living; fresh; stet. **i(keru)** living, alive; arrange flowers **i(kasu)** let live, revive; make best use of **nama** raw, fresh, unprocessed **u(mu)** give birth to **u(mareru)** be born **ha(eru)** grow (intr.) **ha(yasu)** grow (tr.) **o(u)** grow IKU (part of given name)

───────── 1 ─────────

0 生じる/ずる **shō(jiru/zuru)** produce, bring about; be produced, come about

生ゴミ **namagomi** biodegradable/wet garbage, kitchen scraps

生データ **namadēta** raw data

生ビール **namabīru** draft beer

3 生々 **namanama(shii)** fresh, vivid **seisei** lively

4 生中継 **namachūkei** live (remote) broadcast

生水 **namamizu** unboiled water

5 生出 **u(mi)da(su)** bring forth, produce, yield

生甲斐 **i(ki)gai** something worth living for

生母 **seibo** one's (biological) mother

生存 **seizon** existence, life, survival

生立 **u(mi)ta(te)** fresh-laid (eggs) **u(mare)ta(te)** newborn **o(i)ta(chi)** one's childhood, growing up

6 生死 **seishi** life or/and death

生気 **seiki** animation, life, vitality

生年月日 **seinengappi** date of birth

生返 **i(ki)kae(ru)** revive, be resuscitated

生返事 **namahenji** vague answer

生地 **seichi** birthplace **kiji** cloth, material; one's true colors; unadorned

生成 **seisei** creation, formation, generation

7 生身 **i(ki)mi** living body; fresh fish **namami** flesh and blood; living flesh; raw meat/fish

生体 **seitai** living body

生卵 **namatamago** raw egg

生没 **seibotsu** (year of one's) birth and death

生花 **i(ke)bana** flower arrangement **seika** flower arrangement; natural flower

8 生命 **seimei** life

生育 **seiiku** growth, development **ha(e)soda(tsu)** spring up

生茂 **o(i)shige(ru)** grow luxuriantly

生物 **seibutsu, i(ki)mono** living creature, life **namamono** uncooked food, unbaked cake

生放送 **namahōsō** live broadcast

9 生保 **seiho** life insurance (short for 生命保険)

生変 **u(mare)ka(waru)** be born again, start life afresh, be reincarnated **ha(e)ka(waru)** grow in a place of previous growth, grow in again

生前 **seizen** during one's lifetime

生活 **seikatsu** life, livelihood

生後 **seigo** after birth

生臭 **namagusa(i)** smelling of fish/blood

生計費 **seikeihi** living expenses

10 生残 **i(ki)noko(ru)** survive **seizan** survival

生残者 **seizansha** survivor

生埋 **i(ki)u(me)** burying alive

生徒 **seito** student, pupil

生家 **seika** house of one's birth

生殺 **seisatsu** life and death **namagoro(shi)** half-kill; keep in suspense

11 生涯 **shōgai** life, lifetime, career; for life, lifelong

生彩 **seisai** luster, brilliance, vividness

生理 **seiri** physiology; menstruation

生産 **seisan** production

生産物 **seisanbutsu** product, produce

生産高 **seisandaka** output, production, yield

生魚 **namazakana, seigyo** raw/fresh fish

12 生殖 **seishoku** reproduction, procreation

13 生業 **seigyō** occupation, calling

生傷 **namakizu** unhealed wound, fresh bruise

生滅 **shōmetsu** birth and death, appearance and disappearance

生暖 **namaatataka(i)** lukewarm

生意気 **namaiki** conceited, impertinent, smart-alecky

14 生態学 **seitaigaku** ecology

生憎 **ainiku** unfortunately

15 生還 **seikan** come back alive; cross home plate

16 生親 **u(mi no) oya** one's biological father; originator, creator

17 生鮮 **seisen** fresh

———— 2 ————

1 一生涯 **isshōgai** a lifetime, one's (whole) life

一生懸命 **isshōkenmei** with all one's might

2 人生 **jinsei** life, human existence

4 今生 **konjō** this life/world

双生児 **sōseiji** twins

5 出生 **shusshō, shussei** birth

民生 **minsei** the people's livelihood, welfare

史生 **Fumio, Shisei** (m. given name)

0a5

古生物学 **koseibutsugaku** paleontology

芝生 **shibafu** lawn

6 死生 **shisei** life and death

再生 **saisei** (as if) alive/born again; reclamation, regeneration, recycling; reproduction, playback

先生 **sensei** teacher, master, doctor

7 更生 **kōsei** rebirth, resuscitation; making over, rehabilitation, reorganization

余生 **yosei** the remainder of one's life

抗生物質 **kōsei busshitsu** an antibiotic

学生 **gakusei** student

私生活 **shiseikatsu** one's private life

8 長生 **nagai(ki), chōsei** long life, longevity

厚生省 **Kōseishō** Ministry of Health and Welfare

弥生 **yayoi** third lunar month; spring **Yayoi** (archaeological period, 200 B.C. – 250 A.D.); (f. given name)

往生 **ōjō** die (and be reborn in paradise); give in; be at one's wit's end

芽生 **meba(e)** bud, sprout

性生活 **sei seikatsu** sex life

9 発生 **hassei** occurrence, outbreak; genesis; generation; growth, rise, development

食生活 **shokuseikatsu** eating/dietary habits

10 残生 **zansei** one's remaining years

畜生 **chikushō** beast, brute; Dammit!

11 野生 **yasei** wild

麻生 **Asō** (surname)

13 塾生 **jukusei** cram-school student

群生 **gunsei** grow gregariously, grow in crowds

微生物 **biseibutsu** microorganism, microbe

新生活 **shinseikatsu** a new life

14 誕生 **tanjō** birth

誕生日 **tanjōbi** birthday

誕生祝 **tanjō iwa(i)** birthday celebration

16 衛生 **eisei** hygiene, sanitation

19 蘇生 **sosei** revival, resuscitation; resurrection

─────── 3 ───────

1 一年生 **ichinensei** first-year student; annual (plant)

3 大量生産 **tairyō seisan** mass production

4 不衛生 **fueisei** unsanitary, unhygienic

中学生 **chūgakusei** junior-high-school student

5 立往生 **ta(chi)ōjō** be at a standstill, be stalled/stranded; stand speechless (without a rejoinder)

6 同級生 **dōkyūsei** classmate

8 非衛生的 **hieiseiteki** unsanitary, unhygienic

10 高校生 **kōkōsei** senior-high-school student

留学生 **ryūgakusei** student studying abroad

13 適者生存 **tekisha seizon** survival of the fittest

奨学生 **shōgakusei** student on a scholarship

17 優等生 **yūtōsei** honors student

─────── 4 ───────

1 一蓮托生 **ichiren-takushō** sharing fate with another

5 半死半生 **hanshi-hanshō** half dead

0a5.30 / 711   日 艹 竹

32   17

弁

BEN speech, dialect, oratory; valve; petal; distinguish between; braid, bind
wakima(eru) discern, understand, bear in mind

─────── 1 ───────

3 弁才 **bensai** oratorical talent, eloquence

6 弁舌 **benzetsu** speech, eloquence

弁当 **bentō** (box) lunch

8 弁明 **benmei** explanation, justification

11 弁理士 **benrishi** patent attorney

13 弁解 **benkai** explanation, vindication, justification, defense, excuse, apology

15 弁論 **benron** argument, debate; oral proceedings, pleading

17 弁償 **benshō** indemnification

20 弁護士 **bengoshi** lawyer, attorney

――――――― 2 ―――――――

4 内弁慶 **uchi-Benkei** tough-acting at home (but meek before outsiders)

6 多弁 **taben** talkative

合弁会社 **gōben-gaisha** joint venture (company)

7 花弁 **hanabira, kaben** petal

10 能弁 **nōben** eloquence, oratory

11 勘弁 **kanben** pardon, forgive, tolerate

12 堪弁 **kanben** pardon, forgive

答弁 **tōben** reply, explanation, defense

13 詭弁 **kiben** sophistry, logic-chopping

詭弁家 **kibenka** sophist, quibbler

14 駄弁 **daben** foolish talk, bunk

駅弁 **ekiben** box lunch sold at a train station

0a5.32 / 1492
                                        32   4

KAN sweet; good-tasting; contented; indulgent **ama(i)** sweet; honeyed (words); lenient; easygoing, overoptimistic; sugary, sentimental **ama(eru), ama(ttareru)** act like a spoiled child, coax **ama(yakasu)** be indulgent, pamper, coddle **ama(nzuru), ama(njiru)** be content with, be resigned to **uma(i)** good tasting

――――――― 1 ―――――――

3 甘口 **amakuchi** mild, light (flavor); sweet tooth; flattery

7 甘言 **kangen** honeyed words, flattery, blarney

8 甘味料 **kanmiryō** sweetener

9 甘美 **kanbi** sweet

10 甘酒 **amazake** sweet saké

0a5.33 / 351
                                        34   20

Ō center, middle HIROSHI, HISASHI, NAKABA (m. given name) HISA (part of given name)

――――――― 2 ―――――――

4 中央 **chūō** center, middle

15 震央 **shin'ō** epicenter

0a5.34 / 982
                                        43   2

KŌ first in a series, "A"; (turtle's) shell, carapace; armor; back (of the hand), top (of the foot) **KAN** high-pitched **kinoe** first calendar sign KA, KI (part of given name)

――――――― 1 ―――――――

1 甲乙 **kō-otsu** A and B; make distinctions, rank, grade

甲乙丙 **kō-otsu-hei** A, B, C; No. 1, 2, 3

6 甲虫 **kabutomushi, kōchū** beetle

10 甲高 **kandaka(i)** high-pitched, shrill **kōdaka** having a high instep

12 甲斐 **kai** effect, result; worth, avail, use **Kai** (ancient kuni, Yamanashi-ken)

甲斐性 **kaishō** resourcefulness, competence

0a5

5 生甲斐 **i(ki)gai** something worth living for

0a5.35 / 363   ⊡ 日 ∣   43   2

由 由

YU, YŪ, YUI, yo(ru) be based on, be due to, depend on   **yoshi** purport, it is said that; reason, cause, significance; means, way

——————— 1 ———————

7 由来 **yurai** origin, derivation, how it came about; originally, by nature
8 由佳 **Yuka** (f. given name)
9 由美 **Yumi, Yoshimi** (f. given name)
   由美子 **Yumiko** (f. given name)
14 由緒 **yuisho** history, lineage
15 由縁 **yuen** relationship, reason, way

——————— 2 ———————

6 自由 **jiyū** freedom, liberty; free
   自由自在 **jiyū-jizai** free, unrestricted
   自由党 **jiyūtō** liberal party
   自由業 **jiyūgyō** freelance occupation, self-employed
8 事由 **jiyū** reason, cause
10 真由 **Mayu** (f. given name)
   真由美 **Mayumi** (f. given name)
11 理由 **riyū** reason, cause
   経由 **keiyu** via, by way of

——————— 3 ———————

4 不自由 **fujiyū** inconvenience, discomfort; privation; disability, handicap

0a5.36 / 112   ⊡ 女 ∣   25   2

母 母

BO, haha, (o)kā(san) mother

——————— 1 ———————

2 母子 **boshi, hahako** mother and child
4 母方 **hahakata** the mother's side (of the family)
7 母乳 **bonyū** mother's milk
   母系 **bokei** maternal line
8 母国 **bokoku** one's mother/native country
   母国語 **bokokugo** one's mother/native tongue
9 母胎 **botai** womb, uterus
   母音 **boin** vowel
10 母校 **bokō** one's alma mater
14 母様 **(o)kāsama** mother, mama
16 母親 **hahaoya** mother

——————— 2 ———————

3 亡母 **bōbo** one's late mother
4 父母 **fubo, chichihaha** father and mother
5 生母 **seibo** one's (biological) mother
7 伯母 **oba, hakubo** aunt
   乳母 **uba** wet nurse
   乳母車 **ubaguruma** baby carriage/buggy
8 叔母 **oba, shukubo** aunt
   実母 **jitsubo** one's biological mother
   空母 **kūbo** aircraft carrier (short for 航空母艦)
9 保母 **hobo** kindergarten teacher
   祖母 **sobo** grandmother
13 義母 **gibo** mother-in-law; foster mother; stepmother
   聖母 **Seibo** the Holy Mother
   酵母 **kōbo** yeast
15 養母 **yōbo** adoptive/foster mother

——————— 3 ———————

9 祖父母 **sofubo** grandparents
10 航空母艦 **kōkū bokan** aircraft carrier
11 曽祖母 **sōsobo, hiibaba** great-grandmother

0a5.37 / 252　　　　　... 卄 一 丨
　　　　　　　　　　　　　32　1　2

世　　　杢丨世世

SEI, SE generation; the world, society **yo** the world, society, life; age, era, generation

――――― 1 ―――――

4 世中 **yo(no)naka** the world, life, the times
5 世代 **sedai** generation
8 世事 **seji** worldly affairs
9 世相 **sesō** phase of life, the times, world conditions
　世界 **sekai** the world
　世紀 **seiki** century
10 世帯 **setai, shotai** household, home
　世帯主 **setainushi** head of a household
12 世間 **seken** the world, people, the public, society, life; rumor, gossip
13 世辞 **seji** flattery, compliment
　世話 **sewa** help, assistance; good offices, recommendation; take care of; everyday life
15 世論 **seron, yoron** public opinion

――――― 2 ―――――

1 一世 **issei** a lifetime; a generation; the First; first-generation (Japanese-American) **isse** a lifetime
　一世一代 **issei ichidai** once in a lifetime
　一世紀 **isseiki** a century; first century
2 二世 **nisei** (Elizabeth) II, the Second; second-generation (Japanese-American) **nise** two existences, present and future
3 三世 **sansei** the Third; third-generation (Japanese-American) **sanze** past, present, and future existences
4 中世 **chūsei** the Middle Ages, medieval
5 出世 **shusse** succeed in life, get ahead

半世紀 **hanseiki** half century
6 全世界 **zensekai** the whole world
　次世代 **jisedai** next-generation (product)
　近世 **kinsei** recent times, modern age; (era, 1568–1868)
　近世史 **kinseishi** modern history
7 見世物 **misemono** show, exhibition
9 浮世 **u(ki)yo** this transitory world
　浮世絵 **ukiyoe** (type of Japanese woodblock print)
　後世 **kōsei** later ages, posterity **gose** the next world
11 現世紀 **genseiki** this century
12 隔世 **kakusei** a distant age
14 厭世 **ensei** weariness with life, pessimism
　銀世界 **ginsekai** vast silvery/snowy scene

0a5.38 / 332　　　　　... 刂 十
　　　　　　　　　　　　　24　12

史　　　史丨史史

SHI history, chronicles, record; (as suffix) (title of respect) **FUMI** (f. given name) **FUMI** (part of given name)

――――― 1 ―――――

3 史上 **shijō** in history; historical
5 史生 **Fumio, Shisei** (m. given name)
8 史郎 **Shirō, Fumio** (m. given name)
　史実 **shijitsu** historical fact
　史的 **shiteki** historical
10 史家 **shika** historian
　史書 **shisho** history book, a history
15 史劇 **shigeki** historical drama
18 史観 **shikan** view of history

――――― 2 ―――――

3 女史 **joshi** Mrs., Miss, Madam
6 有史 **yūshi** historical, in recorded history
8 国史 **kokushi** national/Japanese history

0a5

10 隆史 **Takashi, Takafumi** (m. given name)
13 戦史 **senshi** military/war history
14 歴史 **rekishi** history

――――――― 3 ―――――――

4 日本史 **Nihonshi** Japanese history
6 近世史 **kinseishi** modern history
15 編年史 **hennenshi** chronicle, annals

0a5.39 / 309

申 申

SHIN, mō(su) say (humble); be named (humble) **saru** ninth horary sign (monkey) **NOBU** (part of given name)

――――――― 1 ―――――――

2 申入 **mō(shi)i(reru)** propose, suggest
3 申上 **mō(shi)a(geru)** say, tell (humble)
4 申込 **mō(shi)ko(mu)** propose, file, apply for, book
5 申出 **mō(shi)de(ru)** offer, submit, report, request **mō(shi)i(de)** proposal; request, application, claim; report, notice
申立 **mō(shi)ta(teru)** state, declare
7 申告 **shinkoku** report, declaration, notification, filing
11 申訳 **mō(shi)wake** excuse, apology
15 申請 **shinsei** application, petition

――――――― 2 ―――――――

4 内申 **naishin** unofficial report
12 答申 **tōshin** report

0a5.40

丼

丼 丼

TAN, TON, donburi bowl

――――――― 2 ―――――――

4 天丼 **tendon** bowl of rice and tempura
22 鰻丼 **unagi donburi, unadon** bowl of eel and rice

――――――― 3 ―――――――

16 親子丼 **oyako donburi** bowl of rice topped with chicken and egg

0a5.42 / 1158

冊

冊 冊 冊

SATSU, SAKU book, letter; (counter for books)

――――――― 1 ―――――――

2 冊子 **sasshi** booklet, pamphlet **sōshi** storybook

――――――― 2 ―――――――

1 一冊 **issatsu** one copy (of a book)
7 別冊 **bessatsu** separate volume, supplement

――――――――――― **0a6** ―――――――――――

州	羽	瓜	白	凸	凹	多	夛	死	弍	気	両	兇
2f4.1	2b4.5	6.3	6.4	0a5.13	0a5.14	6.5	0a6.5	6.6	4n3.3	6.8	6.11	6.12

民	朱	年	西	屯	耒	吏	曳	夷	毎	再	曲
0a5.23	6.13	6.16	6.20	3p9.1	0a7.6	6.22	6.23	6.24	6.25	6.26	6.27

州 → **2f4.1**

羽 → 羽 **2b4.5**

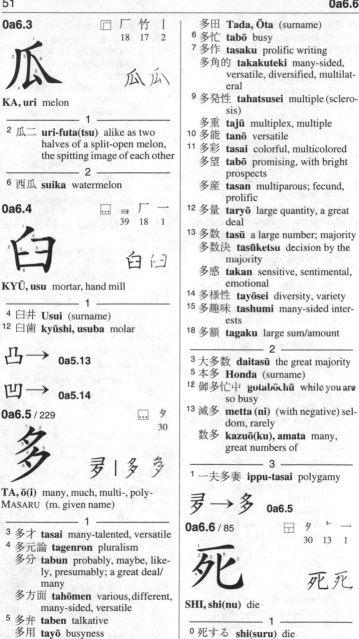

0a6.3   □ 厂 竹 |
                                                         18 17 2

瓜

KA, uri melon

——————— 1 ———————

² 瓜二 **uri-futa(tsu)** alike as two
halves of a split-open melon,
the spitting image of each other

——————— 2 ———————

⁶ 西瓜 **suika** watermelon

0a6.4   ... ⼹ 厂 一
                                                         39 18 1

臼

KYŪ, usu mortar, hand mill

——————— 1 ———————

⁴ 臼井 **Usui** (surname)
¹² 臼歯 **kyūshi, usuba** molar

凸 → **0a5.13**

凹 → **0a5.14**

0a6.5 / 229   ... 夕
                                                              30

多

TA, ō(i) many, much, multi-, poly-
MASARU (m. given name)

——————— 1 ———————

³ 多才 **tasai** many-talented, versatile
⁴ 多元論 **tagenron** pluralism
多分 **tabun** probably, maybe, like-
ly, presumably; a great deal/
many
多方面 **tahōmen** various, different,
many-sided, versatile
⁵ 多弁 **taben** talkative
多用 **tayō** busyness

多田 **Tada, Ōta** (surname)
⁶ 多忙 **tabō** busy
⁷ 多作 **tasaku** prolific writing
多角的 **takakuteki** many-sided,
versatile, diversified, multilateral
⁹ 多発性 **tahatsusei** multiple (sclerosis)
多重 **tajū** multiplex, multiple
¹⁰ 多能 **tanō** versatile
¹¹ 多彩 **tasai** colorful, multicolored
多望 **tabō** promising, with bright
prospects
多産 **tasan** multiparous; fecund,
prolific
¹² 多量 **taryō** large quantity, a great
deal
¹³ 多数 **tasū** a large number; majority
多数決 **tasūketsu** decision by the
majority
多感 **takan** sensitive, sentimental,
emotional
¹⁴ 多様性 **tayōsei** diversity, variety
¹⁵ 多趣味 **tashumi** many-sided interests
¹⁸ 多額 **tagaku** large sum/amount

——————— 2 ———————

³ 大多数 **daitasū** the great majority
⁵ 本多 **Honda** (surname)
¹² 御多忙中 **gotabōchū** while you are
so busy
¹³ 滅多 **metta (ni)** (with negative) sel-
dom, rarely
数多 **kazuō(ku), amata** many,
great numbers of

——————— 3 ———————

¹ 一夫多妻 **ippu-tasai** polygamy

夛 → 多 **0a6.5**

0a6.6 / 85   □ 夕 ⼘ 一
                                                         30 13 1

死

SHI, shi(nu) die

——————— 1 ———————

⁰ 死する **shi(suru)** die

2 死人 **shinin** dead person, the dead

3 死亡 **shibō** die

4 死火山 **shikazan** extinct volcano

5 死生 **shisei** life and death

死去 **shikyo** die

6 死刑 **shikei** capital punishment

死因 **shiin** cause of death

7 死体 **shitai** corpse, remains

死別 **shibetsu** separation by death

死角 **shikaku** dead/unseen angle

死没 **shibotsu** death

8 死命 **shimei** life or death, fate

死者 **shisha** dead person, the dead

9 死活 **shikatsu** life or death

死海 **Shikai** the Dead Sea

死後 **shigo** after death, posthumous
shi(ni)oku(reru) outlive, survive

10 死病 **shibyō** fatal disease

11 死産 **shizan** stillbirth

12 死場 **shi(ni)ba** place to die, place of death

死期 **shiki** time of death, one's last hour

死絶 **shizetsu** extinction
shi(ni)ta(eru) die out, become extinct

13 死傷者 **shishōsha** casualties, killed and wounded

死戦 **shisen** death struggle

死罪 **shizai** capital punishment

14 死語 **shigo** dead language; obsolete word

————— 2 —————

5 必死 **hisshi** certain death; desperate, frantic

半死半生 **hanshi-hanshō** half dead

生死 **seishi** life or/and death

6 仮死 **kashi** suspended animation, apparent death

老死 **rōshi** die of old age

早死 **hayaji(ni)** die young/prematurely

7 即死 **sokushi** die instantly

8 若死 **wakaji(ni)** die young

9 変死 **henshi** accidental death

急死 **kyūshi** sudden/untimely death

枯死 **koshi** wither, die

10 凍死 **tōshi, kogo(e)ji(nu), kogo(e)ji(ni)** freeze to death

致死 **chishi** fatal, lethal, deadly, mortal

病死 **byōshi** death from illness, natural death

飢死 **u(e)ji(ni)** starve to death

11 窒死 **chisshi** death from suffocation/asphyxiation

脳死 **nōshi** brain death

惨死 **zanshi** tragic/violent death

12 検死 **kenshi** coroner's inquest, autopsy

焼死 **shōshi, ya(ke)ji(ni)** be burned to death

焼死者 **shōshisha** person burned to death

悶死 **monshi, moda(e)ji(ni)** die in agony

13 溺死 **dekishi, obo(re)ji(ni)** drowning

戦死 **senshi** death in battle, killed in action

頓死 **tonshi** sudden death

15 餓死 **gashi** starve to death

19 爆死 **bakushi** death from bombing

————— 3 —————

6 安楽死 **anrakushi** euthanasia

11 過労死 **karōshi** death from overwork

弐 → **4n3.3**

0a6.8 / 134   [..] ⼃ 十 一
                     15 12 1

気   氣 ⼃ 气 気

KI, KE spirit, mind, heart; intention; mood; temperament, disposition; attention; air, atmosphere; flavor, smell

————— 1 —————

2 気入 **ki (ni) i(ru)** like, be pleased with

気力 **kiryoku** energy, vitality, mettle

4 気分 **kibun** feeling, mood

気分転換 **kibun tenkan** a (refreshing) change, diversion

5 気付 **kizu(ku)** notice, find out **kitsu(ke)** encouragement; resuscitation **-kizuke** in care of **ki (o) tsu(keru)** be careful, watch out **ki (ga) tsu(ku)** notice, realize

6 気任 **kimaka(se)** at one's pleasure/fancy

7 気体 **kitai** gas (not solid or liquid)

気折 **kio(re)** depression, dejection

気抜 **kinu(ke)** lackadaisical; dispirited

気利 **ki (ga) ki(ku)** be clever, be considerate; be stylish

8 気毒 **ki(no)doku** pitiable, regrettable, too bad

気迷 **kimayo(i)** hesitation, wavering

気味 **kimi** feeling, sensation; a touch, tinge

気苦労 **kigurō** worry, cares, anxiety

気性 **kishō** disposition, temperament, spirit

9 気重 **kiomo(i)** heavy-hearted, depressed

気変 **kiga(wari)** change one's mind, be fickle

気前 **kimae** generosity

気持 **kimo(chi)** feeling, mood

気荒 **kiara** violent-tempered

10 気候 **kikō** climate

気随 **kizui** willful, self-indulgent

気高 **kedaka(i)** noble, exalted

気兼 **kiga(ne)** feel constraint, be afraid of giving trouble

気弱 **kiyowa** timid, fainthearted

気疲 **kizuka(re)** mental fatigue, nervous strain

気紛 **kimagu(re)** whimsical, capricious

気恥 **kiha(zukashii)** embarrassed, ashamed, bashful

気配 **kehai** sign, indication **kihai** market trend **kikuba(ri)** vigilance, attentiveness

11 気掛 **kiga(kari)** anxiety

気張 **kiba(ru)** exert oneself, make an effort; be extravagant, treat oneself to

気強 **kizuyo(i)** reassuring; stouthearted, resolute

気移 **kiutsu(ri)** fickleness

12 気象 **kishō** weather; disposition, temperament

気象庁 **Kishōchō** Meteorological Agency

気遣 **kizuka(i)** anxiety, fear, worry

気違 **kichiga(i)** insanity; mania, craze; lunatic; enthusiast, fan

気落 **kio(chi)** discouragement, despondency

気晴 **kiba(rashi)** diversion, pastime, recreation

気絶 **kizetsu** faint, pass out

気軽 **kigaru** lightheartedly, readily, feel free to

13 気勢 **kisei** spirit, ardor, élan

気楽 **kiraku** feeling at ease, easygoing, comfortable

気詰 **kizu(mari)** feeling of awkwardness, ill at ease

14 気構 **kigama(e)** readiness, anticipation

気管 **kikan** windpipe, trachea

15 気質 **katagi, kishitsu** disposition, temperament, spirit

18 気難 **kimuzuka(shii)** hard to please, grouchy

29 気鬱 **kiutsu** gloom, melancholy, depression

───────── 2 ─────────

1 一気 **ikki** in one breath; straight through, without a break, at a stroke

2 人気 **ninki** popularity; popular feeling; business conditions **hitoke** signs of life (in a place)

3 大気 **taiki** atmosphere, the air

大気圧 **taikiatsu** atmospheric pressure

4 不気味 **bukimi** uncanny, weird, eerie, ominous

元気 **genki** vigor, energy, health, vitality, spirit, courage, pep

天気 **tenki** the weather; good weather

水気 **mizuke** moisture, juiciness
suiki dropsy; moisture, humidity, vapor

火気厳禁 **kaki genkin** Danger: Flammable

5 本気 **honki** serious, in earnest

生気 **seiki** animation, life, vitality

平気 **heiki** calm, cool, unconcerned, nonchalant

6 色気 **iroke** sexiness, sexuality, amorousness, romance

吐気 **ha(ki)ke** nausea

7 何気無 **nanigena(ku)** unintentionally; nonchalantly

冷気 **reiki** cold, chill, cold weather

呆気 **akke** blank amazement

呑気 **nonki** easygoing, free and easy, optimistic

狂気 **kyōki** madness, insanity

辛気臭 **shinkikusa(i)** fretful

8 毒気 **dokuke, dokki** poisonous nature, noxious air; malice, spite

侍気質 **samurai katagi** samurai spirit

味気無 **ajikena(i)** irksome, wearisome, dreary

空気 **kūki** air, atmosphere; pneumatic

怖気 **o(ji)ke, ozoke** fear, timidity, nervousness

怪気 **aya(shi)ge** suspicious, questionable, shady; faltering

9 侠気 **kyōki** chivalrous spirit

俗気 **zokke, zokuke, zokki** vulgarity, worldly ambition

勇気 **yūki** courage

負気 **ma(ken)ki** unyielding/competitive spirit

通気 **tsūki** ventilation

浮気 **uwaki** (marital) infidelity, cheating, fickle

活気 **kakki** liveliness, activity, vigor

神気 **shinki** energy, spirits; mind

怒気 **doki** (fit of) anger

臭気 **shūki** offensive odor, stink, stench

香気 **kōki** fragrance, aroma

10 陰気 **inki** gloomy, dreary

高気圧 **kōkiatsu** high atmospheric pressure

弱気 **yowaki** faintheartedness; bearishness

根気 **konki** patience, perseverance

脂気 **aburake** oily, greasy

眠気 **nemuke** sleepiness, drowsiness

病気 **byōki** sickness, illness; sick, ill

11 陽気 **yōki** cheerful, gay, convivial; season, weather

排気 **haiki** exhaust (fumes)

悪気 **warugi** evil intent, malice, ill will

12 湿気 **shikke, shikki** moisture, humidity

湯気 **yuge** steam, vapor

堅気 **katagi** honest, decent, straight

換気 **kanki** ventilation

短気 **tanki** short temper, touchiness, hastiness

蒸気 **jōki** vapor, steam; steamship

寒気 **kanki, samuke** the cold

勝気 **ka(chi)ki** determined to succeed

景気 **keiki** business conditions

無気力 **mukiryoku** spiritless, flabby, gutless

無気味 **bukimi** ominous, eerie

13 意気 **iki** spirits, morale

意気揚々 **iki-yōyō** exultant, triumphant

飾気 **kaza(ri)ke** affectation, love of display

電気 **denki** electricity; electric light

電気屋 **denkiya** electrical appliance store/dealer

14 暢気 **nonki** easygoing, happy-go-lucky

磁気 **jiki** magnetism, magnetic

19 覇気 **haki** ambition, aspirations

———— 3 ————

1 一本気 **ippongi** one-track mind

4 不人気 **funinki** unpopular

不景気 **fukeiki** business slump, recession; cheerless, gloomy

水蒸気 **suijōki** water vapor; steam

5 生意気 **namaiki** conceited, impertinent, smart-alecky

12 雾围気 **fun'iki** atmosphere, ambience

———— 4 ————

12 跛行景気 **hakō keiki** spotty boom/prosperity

0a6.11 / 200

日　㞢　冂　一
36　20　1

兩｜両両

RYŌ both; two; (obsolete Japanese coin); (counter for vehicles)

———— 1 ————

4 両氏 **ryōshi** both men
両手 **ryōte** both hands
両日 **ryōjitsu** both days; two days
両方 **ryōhō** both
5 両立 **ryōritsu** coexist, be compatible
7 両足 **ryōashi, ryōsoku** both feet/legs
8 両者 **ryōsha** both persons; both things
両性的 **ryōseiteki** bisexual, androgynous
9 両陛下 **Ryōheika** Their Majesties
両院 **ryōin** both houses (of parliament/congress)
両面刷 **ryōmenzu(ri)** printing on both sides
10 両党 **ryōtō** both (political) parties, bipartisan
11 両側 **ryōgawa** both sides
両得 **ryōtoku** double advantage
12 両極端 **ryōkyokutan** both extremes
両替 **ryōgae** money exchange
13 両義 **ryōgi** double meaning, two meanings
16 両親 **ryōshin** (both) parents
20 両議院 **ryōgiin** both houses (of parliament/congress)

———— 2 ————

7 車両 **sharyō** vehicles, cars, rolling stock

———— 3 ————

12 衆参両院 **shū-san ryōin** both Houses of the Diet

0a6.12

日　冂　十　儿
20　12　16

兇兇

KYŌ evil

———— 1 ————

6 兇行 **kyōkō** violence, murder
9 兇変 **kyōhen** disaster; assassination
13 兇漢 **kyōkan** scoundrel, assailant, assassin
15 兇器 **kyōki** lethal weapon
兇暴 **kyōbō** ferocity, brutality, savagery

民 → 0a5.23

0a6.13 / 1503

｜…｜　牛　儿
47　16

朱朱

SHU red　**AKE** (part of given name)

———— 1 ————

2 朱子学 **Shushigaku** Neo-Confucianism
6 朱肉 **shuniku** red ink pad
朱色 **shuiro** scarlet, vermilion

0a6.16 / 45

｜…｜　王　｜　亠
46　2　11

年年

NEN, toshi year

———— 1 ————

2 年子 **toshigo** children (of the same mother) born within a year of each other

0a6

³ 年上 **toshiue** older, senior

年下 **toshishita** younger, junior

年々 **nennen, toshidoshi** year by year, every year

⁴ 年内 **nennai** within the year, before the end of the year

年中 **nenjū** all year, year-round

年中行事 **nenjū gyōji** an annual event

年収 **nenshū** annual income

年月日 **nengappi** date

⁵ 年末 **nenmatsu** the end of the year, year-end

年代 **nendai** age, period, era; date

年代順 **nendaijun** chronological order

年令 **nenrei** age

年功 **nenkō** long service

年号 **nengō** era name

⁶ 年次 **nenji** annual

⁷ 年来 **nenrai** for (some) years

年忌 **nenki** anniversary of a death

年利 **nenri** annual interest

⁸ 年長者 **nenchōsha** a senior, older person

年限 **nengen** term, length of time

年金 **nenkin** annuity, pension

⁹ １９９８年型 **1998nen-gata** the 1998 model

年度 **nendo** fiscal/business year

¹⁰ 年俸 **nenpō** annual salary

¹¹ 年商 **nenshō** annual sales

年寄 **toshiyo(ri)** old person

年産 **nensan** annual production

年頃 **toshigoro** age; marriageable age

¹² 年割 **nenwa(ri)** annual installment

年報 **nenpō** annual report

年期 **nenki** term of service, apprenticeship; experience

年賀状 **nengajō** New Year's card

年間 **nenkan** period of a year; during the year

¹⁵ 年賦 **nenpu** annual installment

年輩 **nenpai** age; elderly age

¹⁶ 年頭 **nentō** beginning of the year
toshigashira the oldest person

¹⁷ 年齢 **nenrei** age

¹⁸ 年額 **nengaku** annual amount

²³ 年鑑 **nenkan** yearbook

―――― 2 ――――

¹ 一年 **ichinen** one year **hitotose** one year, some time ago

一年中 **ichinen-jū** all year long

一年生 **ichinensei** first-year student; annual (plant)

³ 万年 **mannen** ten thousand years; perpetual, perennial

万年床 **mannendoko** bedding/futon left spread out on the floor during the daytime

万年筆 **mannenhitsu** fountain pen

１ヶ年 **ikkanen** one year

⁴ 元年 **gannen** first year (of an era)

中年 **chūnen** middle age

今年 **kotoshi** this year

厄年 **yakudoshi** unlucky age, one's critical year

少年 **shōnen** boy

⁵ 半年 **hantoshi, hannen** half year, six months

本年 **honnen** this year

生年月日 **seinengappi** date of birth

幼年時代 **yōnen jidai** childhood

平年 **heinen** average/normal year; non-leap year

去年 **kyonen, kozo** last year

⁶ 毎年 **mainen, maitoshi** every year, annually

老年 **rōnen** old age

近年 **kinnen** in recent years

同年輩 **dōnenpai** persons of the same age

先年 **sennen** former years; a few years ago

光年 **kōnen** light-year

成年 **seinen** (age of) majority, adulthood

⁷ 来年 **rainen** next year

何年 **nannen** how many years; what year

享年 **kyōnen** one's age at death

忘年会 **bōnenkai** year-end party

学年 **gakunen** school year, grade in school

⁸ 長年 **naganen** many years, a long time

例年 **reinen** normal/average year; every year

周年 **shūnen** whole year, anniversary

定年 **teinen** age limit, retirement age

青年 **seinen** young man/people, a
youth

9 前年 **zennen** the preceding year,
last year

昨年 **sakunen** last year

10 高年 **kōnen** old age

11 停年 **teinen** age limit, retirement
age

翌年 **yokunen, yokutoshi** the following year

12 晩年 **bannen** latter part of one's life

幾年 **ikunen, ikutose** how many
years

閏年 **urūdoshi** leap year

13 数年 **sūnen** several years
kazo(e)doshi one's calendar-
year age (reckoned racehorse-
style)

新年 **shinnen** the New Year

14 暦年 **rekinen** calendar (not fiscal)
year; time

15 編年史 **hennenshi** chronicle, annals

─────── 3 ───────

1 一ヶ年 **ikkanen** one year

一昨年 **issakunen, ototoshi** the
year before last

2 二十年代 **nijūnendai** the '20s

5 未成年 **miseinen** minority, not of
age

8 青少年 **seishōnen** young people,
the young

─────── 4 ───────

10 恭賀新年 **kyōga shinnen** Happy
New Year

17 謹賀新年 **kinga shinnen** Happy
New Year

0a6.20 / 72

24 14 2

西西

SEI west; Spain **SAI, nishi** west
Nishi (surname)

─────── 1 ───────

3 西川 **Nishikawa** (surname)

西山 **Nishiyama** (surname)

4 西日 **nishibi** the afternoon sun

西日本 **Nishi Nihon** western Japan

西方 **seihō** west, western, westward

5 西北 **seihoku** northwest

西半球 **nishi hankyū** Western
Hemisphere

西本 **Nishimoto** (surname)

西田 **Nishida** (surname)

6 西瓜 **suika** watermelon

西向 **nishimu(ki)** facing west

7 西村 **Nishimura** (surname)

8 西岡 **Nishioka** (surname)

西岸 **seigan** west coast; west bank

西欧 **Seiō** Western Europe, the
West

9 西南 **seinan** southwest

西風 **nishikaze, seifū** west wind

西洋 **seiyō** the West, the occident

10 西部 **seibu** western part, the west

西脇 **Nishiwaki** (surname)

11 西側 **nishigawa** the western side;
the West

西崎 **Nishizaki** (surname)

14 西暦 **seireki** Christian Era, A.D.

─────── 2 ───────

3 川西 **Kawanishi** (surname)

大西 **Ōnishi** (surname)

大西洋 **Taiseiyō** Atlantic Ocean

小西 **Konishi** (surname)

4 中西 **Nakanishi** (surname)

5 北西 **hokusei** northwest

8 東西 **tōzai** east and west; Orient and
Occident; Ladies and gentle-
men!

東西南北 **tōzainanboku** north,
south, east, and west

9 南西 **nansei** southwest

14 関西 **Kansai** (region including
Ōsaka and Kyōto)

─────── 3 ───────

5 北大西洋 **Kita Taiseiyō** the North
Atlantic

─────── 4 ───────

5 古今東西 **kokon-tōzai** all ages and
places

0a6

毎回 **maikai** every time

8 毎夜 **maiyo** every evening, nightly

9 毎度 **maido** each time; frequently; always

10 毎週 **maishū** every week, weekly

12 毎朝 **maiasa** every morning

毎晩 **maiban** every evening, nightly

0a6.22 / 1007

口 十 |
24 12 2

RI an official

——— 1 ———

10 吏員 **riin** an official

0a6.23

日 十
43 12

EI, hi(ku) pull

0a6.24

大 弓
34 28

I barbarian **ebisu** barbarian, savage; Ainu

——— 2 ———

15 蝦夷 **Ezo** Ainu; Hokkaidō

0a6.25 / 116

日 女 宀 |
25 15 2

MAI, -goto every, each TSUNE (part of given name)

——— 1 ———

4 毎月 **maigetsu, maitsuki** every month, monthly

毎日 **mainichi** every day, daily

6 毎年 **mainen, maitoshi** every year, annually

0a6.26 / 782

王 冂
46 20

SAI, SA again, re-, twice, second
futata(bi) again, twice

——— 1 ———

3 再三 **saisan** again and again, repeatedly

5 再出 **saishutsu** reappear, re-emerge

再出発 **saishuppatsu** start over, make a fresh start

再生 **saisei** (as if) alive/born again; reclamation, regeneration, recycling; reproduction, playback

再犯 **saihan** second offense

6 再会 **saikai** meeting again, reunion

再考 **saikō** reconsider

7 再来週 **saraishū** the week after next

8 再使用 **saishiyō** reuse

再版 **saihan** reprint; second printing/edition

再建 **saiken** reconstruction, rebuilding

再放送 **saihōsō** rebroadcast

9 再発 **saihatsu** recurrence, relapse

再軍備 **saigunbi** rearmament

再度 **saido** twice, a second time, again

10 再帰 **saiki** recursive

再案 **saian** revised plan/draft

再挙 **saikyo** second attempt

再校 **saikō** second proof

11 再婚 **saikon** remarry

再現 **saigen** reappearance, return; revival

12 再評価 **saihyōka** reassessment, re-evaluation

妛→喜 3p9.1

耒→来 0a7.6

再開 **saikai** reopen, resume, reconvene

13 再試合 **saishiai** rematch, resumption of a game

14 再選挙 **saisenkyo** re-election

再演 **saien** repeat performance

15 再確認 **saikakunin** reaffirmation

16 再興 **saikō** revive, restore, re-establish

20 再議 **saigi** reconsideration, redeliberation

———————— 2 ————————

1 一再 **issai** once or twice
issai(narazu) again and again

0a6.27 / 366   ⊞ 日 儿
                                      43 16

曲 曲

KYOKU curve; melody **ma(garu)** bend, curve, be crooked **ma(geru)** bend, distort

———————— 1 ————————

7 曲折 **kyokusetsu** winding, twists and turns; vicissitudes, complications

曲芸 **kyokugei** acrobatics

8 曲易 **ma(ge)yasu(i)** easy to bend, supple, pliant, flexible

13 曲解 **kyokkai** strained interpretation, distortion

曲路 **ma(gari)michi** roundabout road; winding road

15 曲線 **kyokusen** a curve

———————— 2 ————————

6 名曲 **meikyoku** famous music

7 作曲家 **sakkyokuka** composer

序曲 **jokyoku** overture, prelude

8 屈曲 **kukkyoku** crookedness; refraction; curvature

9 歪曲 **waikyoku** distortion

紆曲 **ukyoku** meander

12 湾曲 **wankyoku** curve, curvature, bend

13 楽曲 **gakkyoku** musical composition/piece

15 舞曲 **bukyoku** music and dancing; dance music

戯曲 **gikyoku** drama, play

編曲 **henkyoku** (musical) arrangement

18 臍曲 **hesoma(gari)** cranky person, grouch

———————— 3 ————————

6 交響曲 **kōkyōkyoku** symphony

行進曲 **kōshinkyoku** a (musical) march

7 狂想曲 **kyōsōkyoku** rhapsody

8 協奏曲 **kyōsōkyoku** concerto

9 紆余曲折 **uyo-kyokusetsu** meandering, twists and turns, complications

14 歌謡曲 **kayōkyoku** popular song

———————————— **0a7** ————————————

巫   良   良   求   身   来   兎   承   束   肃   里   我   甫
2a5.26 0a7.3 7.3 2b5.5 7.5 7.6 0a8.5 7.7 7.8 2m6.3 7.9 7.10 7.11

曳   更   串   亜   寿   事
0a6.23 7.12 7.13 7.14 7.15 0a8.15

巫→ **2a5.26**

良→良 **0a7.3**

0a7.3 / 321   □ 食
                                      73

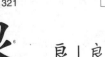

良 l 良 良

RYŌ, i(i), yo(i) good YOSHI (part of given name)

0a7

——————— 1 ———————

¹ 良一 **Ryōichi, Yoshikazu** (m. given name)

³ 良工 **ryōkō** skilled artisan

⁴ 良不良 **ryō-furyō** (whether) good or bad

良友 **ryōyū** good friend

良心 **ryōshin** conscience

良心的 **ryōshinteki** conscientious

⁵ 良平 **Ryōhei, Yoshihira** (m. given name)

良好 **ryōkō** good, favorable, satisfactory

⁷ 良医 **ryōi** good doctor, skilled physician

良否 **ryōhi** (whether) good or bad

⁸ 良法 **ryōhō** good method

良性 **ryōsei** benign (tumor)

⁹ 良品 **ryōhin** article of superior quality

¹⁰ 良案 **ryōan** good idea

¹² 良策 **ryōsaku** good plan/policy

¹⁵ 良縁 **ryōen** good (marital) match

良質 **ryōshitsu** good quality

——————— 2 ———————

⁴ 不良 **furyō** bad, substandard, delinquent

⁶ 仲良 **nakayo(ku)** on friendly terms
nakayo(shi) good friends

色良 **iroyo(i)** favorable (answer)

⁷ 奈良県 **Nara-ken** (prefecture)

改良 **kairyō** improvement, reform

⁸ 長良川 **Nagara-gawa** (river, Gifu-ken)

佳良 **karyō** excellent, good

¹¹ 野良猫 **noraneko** stray cat

¹² 最良 **sairyō** best

¹⁷ 優良 **yūryō** superior, excellent

——————— 3 ———————

⁷ 良不良 **ryō-furyō** (whether) good or bad

——————— 4 ———————

¹⁰ 消化不良 **shōka furyō** indigestion

 求 → **2b5.5**

0a7.5 / 59

日 月 丨
42 2

身

身 身

SHIN body **mi** body, one's person; one's station in life; heart, mind; flesh, meat

——————— 1 ———————

³ 身丈 **mitake, mi(no)take** one's height

身上 **shinjō** merit, strong point
shinshō one's fortune/property; household **mi(no)ue** one's fortune/future; one's circumstances; one's background

身上話 **mi(no)uebanashi** one's life story

⁴ 身元 **mimoto** one's identity; one's character

身内 **miuchi** relations, family, friends

身中 **shinchū** one's heart, inmost thoughts

身分 **mibun** social standing, status; one's circumstances

身心 **shinshin** body and mind

⁵ 身代 **shindai** fortune, property, estate **migawa(ri)** substitute, vicarious **mi(no)shiro** ransom money

身代金 **mi(no)shirokin** ransom money

⁶ 身近 **mijika** familiar, close to one

⁷ 身体 **shintai, karada** the body

身体障害者 **shintai shōgaisha** physically handicapped person

⁸ 身長 **shinchō** one's height

⁹ 身柄 **migara** one's person

¹⁰ 身振 **mibu(ri)** gesture, gesticulation

¹¹ 身動 **miugo(ki)** move about, stir

¹² 身軽 **migaru** light, agile, nimble

¹⁵ 身震 **miburu(i)** shiver, tremble, shudder

——————— 2 ———————

¹ 一身 **isshin** oneself, one's own interests

2 人身 **jinshin** the human body; one's person

4 中身 **nakami** contents

心身 **shinshin** mind and body, psychosomatic

5 出身 **shusshin** (as suffix) originally from …

生身 **i(ki)mi** living body; fresh fish **namami** flesh and blood; living flesh; raw meat/fish

白身 **shiromi** whiteness; white meat; white of an egg

6 全身 **zenshin** the whole body

7 投身 **tōshin** suicide by throwing oneself (into a river, from a building, in front of a train)

8 刺身 **sashimi** sliced raw fish, sashimi

受身 **ukemi** being acted upon; passivity; passive (in grammar)

9 保身 **hoshin** self-protection

変身 **henshin** transformation

独身 **dokushin, hito(ri)mi** unmarried

10 骨身 **honemi** flesh and bones; marrow

11 黄身 **kimi** (egg) yolk

終身刑 **shūshinkei** life sentence

12 艇身 **teishin** boat length

13 献身 **kenshin** self-sacrifice, dedication

15 膚身離 **hadami-hana(sazu)** always kept on one's person, highly treasured

16 親身 **shinmi** blood relation; kind, cordial

——————— 3 ———————

3 上半身 **jōhanshin, kamihanshin** upper half of the body

下半身 **kahanshin, shimohanshin** lower half of the body

7 私自身 **watakushi jishin** personally, as for me

——————— 4 ———————

6 自分自身 **jibun-jishin** oneself

RAI come; (as prefix) next (week); (as suffix) since **ku(ru)** come **ki(taru)** come, this coming (Sunday); be due to **ki(tasu)** cause, bring about

——————— 1 ———————

4 来月 **raigetsu** next month

来日 **rainichi** come to Japan

6 来年 **rainen** next year

9 来客 **raikyaku** visitor, caller

10 来週 **raishū** next week

11 来訪 **raihō** visit, call

15 来賓 **raihin** guest, visitor

22 来襲 **raishū** attack, raid, invasion

——————— 2 ———————

2 入来 **nyūrai** incoming, arrival, visit

4 元来 **ganrai** originally, primarily, by nature

5 以来 **irai** since

出来 **deki(ru)** can, be able to, be possible; be done, be finished, be ready; be made of; be formed; come into being

出来上 **dekia(garu)** be finished, be ready; be cut out for

出来事 **dekigoto** incident, event, happenings

本来 **honrai** properly speaking; in essence, naturally; originally, primarily

未来 **mirai** future; future tense

由来 **yurai** origin, derivation, how it came about; originally, by nature

古来 **korai** from ancient times, time-honored

外来 **gairai** foreign, imported

外来語 **gairaigo** word of foreign origin, loanword

6 年来 **nenrai** for (some) years

再来週 **saraishū** the week after next

8 到来 **tōrai** arrival, advent

0a7

往来 **ōrai** coming and going, traffic; road, street; fluctuations

10 将来 **shōrai** future

従来 **jūrai** up to now, usual, conventional

家来 **kerai** vassal, retainer, retinue

11 舶来 **hakurai** imported

舶来品 **hakuraihin** imported goods

12 渡来 **torai** introduction, influx; visit

御来光 **goraikō** sunrise viewed from a mountaintop

14 爾来 **jirai** since then

兎 → 0a8.5

0a7.7 / 942

日 氵 二 一
21 4 1

承丞

SHŌ, JŌ, uketamawa(ru) hear, listen to, be informed TSUGU (part of given name)

――― 1 ―――

8 承知 **shōchi** consent to; know, be aware of

14 承認 **shōnin** approval

15 承諾 **shōdaku** consent

――― 2 ―――

1 了承 **ryōshō** acknowledge, understand

4 不承知 **fushōchi** dissent, disagreement, noncompliance

6 伝承 **denshō** transmit, hand down (folklore)

13 継承 **keishō** succession, inheritance

継承者 **keishōsha** successor

14 領承 **ryōshō** understand, acknowledge, estimate

15 諒承 **ryōshō** acknowledge, understand, note

0a7.8 / 501

木 口
41 24

束束

SOKU bundle, sheaf, ream (of paper)
taba bundle, bunch, sheaf
taba(neru) bundle, tie in a bundle; govern, manage, control **tsuka** handbreadth; brief time; (book's) thickness
tsuka(neru) tie in bundles; fold (one's arms) TSUKANE (m. given name)

――― 1 ―――

12 束間 **tsuka(no)ma** brief time, moment

16 束縛 **sokubaku** restraint, constraint, shackles

――― 2 ―――

1 一束 **issoku, hitotaba** a bundle; a hundred

5 札束 **satsutaba** wad of money, bundle/roll of bills

7 花束 **hanataba** bouquet

8 拘束 **kōsoku** restriction, constraint

9 約束 **yakusoku** promise; appointment

12 結束 **kessoku** band together, be united

厄 → 虎 2m6.3

0a7.9 / 142

日 土
43 22

里里

RI village; (old unit of distance, about 3.9 km) **sato** village; one's parents' home

――― 1 ―――

4 里心 **satogokoro** homesickness, nostalgia

10 里帰 **satogae(ri)** bride's first visit to her old home

16 里親 **sato oya** foster parent

——————— 2 ———————

1 一里 **ichiri** one *ri*, 3.9 km

3 万里 **Mari, Banri, Masato** (given name)

万里長城 **Banri (no) Chōjō** Great Wall of China

千里眼 **senrigan** clairvoyant

4 巴里 **Pari** Paris

5 古里 **furusato** native place, home town, home

9 美里 **Misato** (f. given name)

海里 **kairi** nautical mile

10 郷里 **kyōri** one's native place, home (town)

0a7.10 / 1302   □ 戈 十 |

52 12 2

GA, wa self **wa(ga)** my, our, one's own **ware** I, oneself

——————— 1 ———————

3 我々 **wareware** we, us, our

8 我国 **wa(ga)kuni** our country

10 我流 **garyū** self-taught, one's own way

11 我張 **ga (o) ha(ru)** be self-willed, insist on having one's own way

我欲 **gayoku** selfishness

12 我等 **warera** we

14 我慢 **gaman** put up with, bear, endure, be patient

16 我儘 **wagamama** selfish, capricious, wanting to have one's own way

——————— 2 ———————

6 自我 **jiga** self, ego

8 怪我 **kega** injury, wound; accident, chance

12 無我 **muga** selflessness, self-forgetfulness

無我夢中 **muga-muchū** total absorption, ecstasy

14 瘦我慢 **ya(se)gaman** endure for sake of pride

0a7.11 / 2167   □ 月 十 |

42 12 2

HO, FU (eulogistic male name suffix); for the first time HAJIME (m. given name) HO, FU, TOSHI, SUKE, YOSHI, NAMI, MOTO, NORI, MASA (part of given name)

曳 → 曳 0a6.23

0a7.12 / 1008   □ 日 一 |

43 14 2

KŌ (two-hour) night watch; anew **sara** new thing/matter **sara (ni)** anew, again, furthermore **sara(naru)** (even) more, further **fu(kasu)** stay up till late **fu(keru)** grow late

——————— 1 ———————

5 更生 **kōsei** rebirth, resuscitation; making over, rehabilitation, reorganization

更正 **kōsei** correct, rectify

6 更衣室 **kōishitsu** clothes-changing room

7 更迭 **kōtetsu** change, reshuffle, shake-up

13 更新 **kōshin** renew, renovate, update

——————— 2 ———————

4 今更 **imasara** now, at this late date

8 尚更 **naosara** still more, all the more

9 変更 **henkō** change, alteration, amendment

10 殊更 **kotosara** especially, particularly; intentionally

0a7.13

□ 口 |
24 2

串 串

KAN pierce **kushi** spit, skewer

——— 1 ———
8 串刺 **kushiza(shi)** skewering

0a7.14 / 1616

□ 二 口 |
38 24 2

亞 | 亜 亜

A rank next, come after, sub-; -ous (in acids); Asia

——— 1 ———
10 亜流 **aryū** adherent, follower, imitator
12 亜寒帯 **akantai** subarctic zone
15 亜熱帯 **anettai** subtropics

——— 2 ———
8 東亜 **Tōa** East Asia
  欧亜 **Ō-A** Europe and Asia

0a7.15 / 1550

□ 寸 十 二
37 12 4

壽 | 寿 寿

JU, SU age; lifespan; longevity; congratulations **kotobuki** congratulations; long life **kotoho(gu)** congratulate HISASHI (m. given name) TOSHI, HISA (part of given name)

——— 1 ———
5 寿司 **sushi** sushi (raw fish and other delicacies with vinegared rice)
8 寿命 **jumyō** life, lifespan
10 寿恵 **Toshie, Hisae, Sue, Kazue** (f. given name)

——— 2 ———
8 長寿 **chōju** long life, longevity
12 喜寿 **kiju** one's 77th birthday
13 福寿 **fukuju** happiness and longevity

事 → 事 0a8.15

——————— 0a8 ———————

函	非	長	兒	亞	兩	兎	表	画	果	東	奮	垂
2b6.3	8.1	8.2	4c3.3	0a7.14	0a6.11	8.5	8.6	8.7	8.8	8.9	8.10	8.12

奉	毒	事
8.13	8.14	8.15

函 → 2b6.3

0a8.1 / 498

□ 儿 二 一
16 4 1

非 非

HI non-, un-; wrong **ara(zu)** not, not so

——— 1 ———
2 非人 **hinin** beggar; outcast

非人間的 **hiningenteki** inhuman, impersonal
3 非凡 **hibon** extraordinary, unusual
6 非合法 **higōhō** illegal
  非合理的 **higōriteki** unreasonable, irrational
  非行 **hikō** misdeed, misconduct, delinquency
7 非売品 **hibaihin** article not for sale
  非社交的 **hishakōteki** unsociable, retiring
8 非法 **hihō** illegal, unlawful, lawless
  非武装 **hibusō** demilitarized (zone), unarmed (neutrality)

⁹ 非科学的 **hikagakuteki** unscientific

¹⁰ 非能率的 **hinōritsuteki** inefficient

¹¹ 非運 **hiun** misfortune, bad luck

非常 **hijō** emergency; extraordinary; very, exceedingly, extremely

非常口 **hijōguchi** emergency exit

非現実的 **higenjitsuteki** unrealistic

¹⁵ 非課税 **hikazei** tax exemption

¹⁶ 非衛生的 **hieiseiteki** unsanitary, unhygienic

¹⁸ 非難 **hinan** criticize, denounce

──────── 2 ────────

⁷ 似非 **ni(te)hi(naru)** alike only in appearance **ese-** false, would-be, pseudo-

⁹ 是非 **zehi** right and wrong; by all means

0a8.2 / 95

日 衤 卜 二
57 13 4

CHŌ long; (especially as suffix) head, chief, director **naga(i)** long **naga(tarashii)** lengthy, long and boring **naga(raeru)** live long, live on **ta(keru)** excel in; grow older **osa** head, chief **tokoshi(e)** forever HISASHI (m. given name) TAKE, NAGA, CHŌ, OSA (part of given name) CHŌ (surname)

──────── 1 ────────

³ 長女 **chōjo** eldest daughter

⁴ 長井 **Nagai** (surname)

長引 **nagabi(ku)** be prolonged, drag on

⁵ 長生 **nagai(ki), chōsei** long life, longevity

長兄 **chōkei** eldest brother

長田 **Osada, Nagata** (surname)

⁶ 長年 **naganen** many years, a long time

長老 **chōrō** an elder

⁷ 長良川 **Nagara-gawa** (river, Gifu-ken)

長寿 **chōju** long life, longevity

長谷川 **Hasegawa** (surname)

長男 **chōnan** eldest son

⁸ 長命 **chōmei** long life, longevity

長岡 **Nagaoka** (surname)

長官 **chōkan** director, head, chief, secretary, administrator

長居 **nagai** stay too long

長所 **chōsho** one's strong point, advantages

⁹ 長途 **chōto** a long way/distance

長持 **nagamo(chi)** oblong chest; be durable, last

長音 **chōon** a long sound/vowel, long tone, dash

¹⁰ 長唄 **nagauta** song accompanied on the samisen

長島 **Nagashima** (surname)

長時間 **chōjikan** a long time

長袖 **nagasode** long sleeves

¹¹ 長野 **Nagano** (surname); (city, Nagano-ken)

長野県 **Nagano-ken** (prefecture)

長崎県 **Nagasaki-ken** (prefecture)

長蛇 **chōda** long snake; long line of people, long queue

¹² 長短 **chōtan** (relative) length; merits and demerits, advantages and disadvantages

長椅子 **nagaisu** sofa, couch

長期 **chōki** long-term, long-range

長距離 **chōkyori** long-distance, long-range

¹³ 長嘆 **chōtan** a long sigh

長靴 **nagagutsu** boots

長話 **nagabanashi** a long/tedious talk

¹⁵ 長編 **chōhen** long (article), full-length (novel), feature-length (movie)

──────── 2 ────────

⁵ 市長 **shichō** mayor

⁶ 年長者 **nenchōsha** a senior, older person

伍長 **gochō** corporal, staff sergeant

全長 **zenchō** overall length

会長 **kaichō** chairman, president

次長 **jichō** deputy director, assistant chief

成長 **seichō** growth
7 身長 **shinchō** one's height
延長 **enchō** extension, continuation, prolongation, elongation
学長 **gakuchō** dean, rector
局長 **kyokuchō** bureau chief, director, postmaster
村長 **sonchō** village mayor
社長 **shachō** company president
町長 **chōchō** town mayor
8 波長 **hachō** wavelength
店長 **tenchō** store/shop manager
所長 **shochō** director, head, manager
9 係長 **kakarichō** chief clerk
院長 **inchō** head of the hospital/school/institute
首長 **shuchō** leader, head, chief
10 部長 **buchō** department head
校長 **kōchō** principal, headmaster
班長 **hanchō** group leader
特長 **tokuchō** distinctive feature, characteristic; strong point, forte, merit
11 細長 **hosonaga(i)** long and thin
船長 **senchō** (ship's) captain
12 最長 **saichō** longest
13 園長 **enchō** head of a kindergarten/zoo
14 総長 **sōchō** (university) president
駅長 **ekichō** stationmaster
15 寮長 **ryōchō** dormitory director
横長 **yokonaga** oblong
課長 **kachō** section chief
16 機長 **kichō** (airplane) captain
館長 **kanchō** director, curator
20 議長 **gichō** chairman, president
21 艦長 **kanchō** the captain (of a warship)

——————— 3 ———————
2 八百長 **yaochō** rigged affair, fixed game
3 万里長城 **Banri (no) Chōjō** Great Wall of China
8 事務長官 **jimuchōkan** chief secretary
官房長官 **kanbō chōkan** Chief Cabinet Secretary
国務長官 **kokumu chōkan** (U.S.) Secretary of State

11 副会長 **fukukaichō** (company) vice president
理事長 **rijichō** chairman, president
13 幹事長 **kanjichō** executive secretary, secretary-general
14 総務長官 **sōmu chōkan** director-general
15 億万長者 **okumanchōja** multimillionaire, billionaire

兒 → 児   4c3.3

亞 → 亜   0a7.14

兩 → 両   0a6.11

0a8.5   日 口 儿 丨
          24   16   2

兎   兎丨兎兎

TO, usagi rabbit

0a8.6 / 272   ⊡ 衤 二
          57   4

表   表 表

HYŌ table, chart; surface; expression
arawa(su) express, manifest
arawa(reru) be expressed **omote** surface, face; front; heads (of a coin); first half (of an inning)

——————— 1 ———————
3 表口 **omoteguchi** front entrance/door
4 表日本 **Omote Nihon** Pacific side of Japan
5 表玄関 **omote genkan** front entrance/door
表札 **hyōsatsu** nameplate, doorplate
表示 **hyōji** indicate, express, display

8 表明 **hyōmei** state, express, announce

9 表面 **hyōmen** surface

表音文字 **hyōon moji** phonetic symbol/script

表看板 **omote-kanban** sign out in front; figurehead, mask

10 表紙 **hyōshi** cover, binding

表記 **hyōki** inscription, indication, declaration; orthography

11 表側 **omotegawa** the front

表現 **hyōgen** expression

表情 **hyōjō** (facial) expression

13 表意文字 **hyōi moji** ideograph

14 表彰 **hyōshō** commendation

18 表題 **hyōdai** title, heading, caption

——————— 2 ———————

3 上表紙 **uwabyōshi** outer cover, (book) jacket

4 公表 **kōhyō** official announcement

5 代表 **daihyō** representation, typical; a delegate

代表者 **daihyōsha** a representative

7 図表 **zuhyō** chart, table, graph

9 発表 **happyō** announce

10 書表 **ka(ki)ara(wasu)** express/describe in writing

12 無表情 **muhyōjō** expressionless

13 裏表 **ura-omote** both sides; reverse, inside out; two-faced

——————— 3 ———————

5 正誤表 **seigohyō** errata

6 成績表 **seisekihyō** report/score card

10 時刻表 **jikokuhyō** timetable, schedule

時間表 **jikanhyō** timetable, schedule

13 献立表 **kondatehyō** menu

0a8.7 / 343

⸬ 日 ⺾ 冂
43 14 20

GA picture, drawing, painting
KAKU stroke (of a kanji)
ega(ku) draw, paint, describe

——————— 1 ———————

1 画一 **kakuitsu** uniform, standard

3 画工 **gakō** painter, artist

5 画用紙 **gayōshi** drawing paper

画布 **gafu** a canvas

8 画法 **gahō** art of drawing/painting

9 画面 **gamen** scene, picture, (TV etc.) screen

10 画家 **gaka** painter, artist

画素 **gaso** picture element, pixel, dot

11 画廊 **garō** picture gallery

12 画期的 **kakkiteki** epoch-making, revolutionary

画然 **kakuzen (to)** distinctly, sharply

画筆 **gahitsu** artist's brush

13 画数 **kakusū** number of strokes (of a kanji)

14 画像 **gazō** portrait, picture, image

——————— 2 ———————

4 区画 **kukaku** division, section

6 企画 **kikaku** plan, planning

邦画 **hōga** Japanese movie/painting

名画 **meiga** famous picture, masterpiece

8 版画 **hanga** woodcut print

9 洋画 **yōga** Western painting/movie

映画 **eiga** movie, film

映画館 **eigakan** movie theater

計画 **keikaku** plan, project

11 描画 **byōga** drawing, painting

12 絵画 **kaiga** pictures, paintings, drawings

14 漫画 **manga** cartoon, comic book/strip

墨画 **bokuga** India-ink drawing

15 戯画 **giga** a caricature

16 壁画 **hekiga** fresco, mural

録画 **rokuga** (videotape) recording

——————— 3 ———————

3 山水画 **sansuiga** landscape painting; a landscape

4 水彩画 **suisaiga** a watercolor

水墨画 **suibokuga** India-ink painting

木炭画 **mokutanga** charcoal drawing

日本画 **nihonga** Japanese-style painting/drawing

16 諷刺画 **fūshiga** caricature, cartoon

0a8.8 / 487

43 41

KA fruit; result **ha(tasu)** carry out, accomplish **ha(tashite)** as was expected; really; ever **ha(teru)** come to an end, be exhausted; die, perish **ha(te), ha(teshi)** end, limit; result, outcome **ō(seru)** succeed in doing

—————— 1 ——————

5 果汁 **kajū** fruit juice

8 果実 **kajitsu** fruit
果物 **kudamono** fruit

12 果報 **kahō** good fortune, luck

16 果樹園 **kajuen** orchard
果糖 **katō** fruit sugar, fructose

—————— 2 ——————

6 因果 **inga** cause and effect; fate; misfortune
朽果 **ku(chi)ha(teru)** rot away
成果 **seika** result, fruit
na(ri)ha(teru) become, be reduced to **na(re)(no)ha(te)** the wreck of one's former self

7 困果 **koma(ri)ha(teru)** be greatly troubled/nonplussed

8 使果 **tsuka(i)hata(su)** use up, squander
効果 **kōka** effect, effectiveness
青果物 **seikabutsu** vegetables and fruits

9 変果 **ka(wari)ha(teru)** change completely

10 疲果 **tsuka(re)ha(teru)** get tired out, be exhausted

12 結果 **kekka** result, consequence, effect

13 戦果 **senka** war results

15 漿果 **shōka** berry

—————— 3 ——————

8 逆効果 **gyakukōka** opposite effect, counterproductive

—————— 4 ——————

11 悪因悪果 **akuin-akka** Evil breeds evil.

0a8.9 / 71

41 43

TŌ, higashi east **azuma** east; eastern Japan (east of old capital Kyōto) HIGASHI (surname) AZUMA (surname, m. given name) HARU (part of given name)

—————— 1 ——————

3 東口 **higashiguchi** east exit/entrance

4 東方 **tōhō** east, eastward, eastern

5 東北 **tōhoku** northeast **Tōhoku** (northeastern Honshū)
東芝 **Tōshiba** (company name)

6 東西 **tōzai** east and west; Orient and Occident; Ladies and gentlemen!
東西南北 **tōzainanboku** north, south, east, and west
東向 **higashimu(ki)** facing east

7 東亜 **Tōa** East Asia

8 東京 **Tōkyō** (city, capital of Japan)
東岸 **tōgan** eastern coast; east bank
東欧 **Tōō** Eastern Europe

9 東南 **tōnan** southeast
東洋 **tōyō** the Orient
東海道 **Tōkaidō** the Tōkaidō highway

11 東側 **higashigawa** east side

—————— 2 ——————

4 中東 **Chūtō** the Middle East, Mideast

5 北東 **hokutō** northeast

6 伊東 **Itō** (surname)
近東 **Kintō** the Near East

9 南東 **nantō** southeast

12 極東 **kyokutō** the Far East

14 関東 **Kantō** (region including Tōkyō)

——————— 3 ———————

⁴ 中近東 **Chūkintō** the Near and Middle East

⁵ 古今東西 **kokon-tōzai** all ages and places

¹⁰ 馬耳東風 **bajitōfū** utter indifference, turn a deaf ear

---

offer, present; revere TOMO (part of given name)

——————— 1 ———————

⁴ 奉公 **hōkō** service

⁵ 奉仕 **hōshi** service

¹⁰ 奉納 **hōnō** dedication, offering

0a8.10 ... 日 大 |
43 34 2

EN cover; sudden

——————— 1 ———————

⁹ 奄美大島 **Amami Ōshima** (island, Kagoshima-ken)

0a8.12 / 1070 ... 王 艹 一
46 32 1

SUI, **ta(reru), ta(rasu)** (intr./tr.) hang down, dangle, drip **tare** hanging, straw curtain; tassel, flap TARU (part of given name)

——————— 1 ———————

⁰ 垂とする **nanna(n to suru)** be close to

³ 垂下 **suika, ta(re)sa(garu)** hang down, dangle, droop

⁸ 垂直 **suichoku** vertical; perpendicular

——————— 2 ———————

⁸ 雨垂 **amada(re)** raindrops, eavesdrops

¹⁷ 糞垂 **kusota(re), kuso(t)ta(re)** (shit-dripping) son-of-a-bitch

0a8.13 / 1541 ... 大 二 十
34 4 12

HŌ, BU present, dedicate; obey, follow, believe in; serve **tatematsu(ru)**

0a8.14 / 522 日 土 女 一
22 25 1

DOKU poison

——————— 1 ———————

⁰ 毒ガス **doku gasu** poison gas

⁶ 毒気 **dokuke, dokki** poisonous nature, noxious air; malice, spite

毒舌 **dokuzetsu** stinging tongue, blistering remarks

毒虫 **dokumushi** poisonous insect

⁷ 毒言 **dokugen** abusive language

⁸ 毒性 **dokusei** virulence, toxicity

⁹ 毒草 **dokusō** poisonous plant

¹⁰ 毒殺 **dokusatsu** a poisoning

¹¹ 毒蛇 **dokuhebi, dokuja** poisonous snake

¹² 毒筆 **dokuhitsu** spiteful/poison pen

¹⁶ 毒薬 **dokuyaku** a poison

——————— 2 ———————

⁴ 中毒 **chūdoku** poisoning

⁶ 気毒 **ki(no)doku** pitiable, regrettable, too bad

有毒 **yūdoku** poisonous

¹⁰ 消毒 **shōdoku** disinfect, sterilize

消毒薬 **shōdokuyaku** disinfectant, antiseptic

猛毒 **mōdoku** virulent poison

¹³ 鉛毒 **endoku** lead poisoning

0a8.15 / 80 ... 口 ヨ 十
24 39 12

JI, ZU, **koto** thing, matter

0a8

—————— 1 ——————

5 事由 **jiyū** reason, cause
6 事件 **jiken** case, affair, incident
7 事局 **jikyoku** circumstances
8 事例 **jirei** example; precedent
事典 **jiten** encyclopedia, dictionary
事実 **jijitsu** fact
事実上 **jijitsujō** in fact, actually
事物 **jibutsu** things, affairs
9 事変 **jihen** accident, mishap; incident, uprising, emergency
事前 **jizen** before the fact, prior, pre-
事後 **jigo** after the fact, ex post facto, post-
事柄 **kotogara** matters, affairs, circumstances
事故 **jiko** accident; unavoidable circumstances
11 事務 **jimu** business, clerical work
事務長官 **jimuchōkan** chief secretary
事務官 **jimukan** administrative official, secretary, commissioner
事務所 **jimusho** office
事情 **jijō** circumstances, reasons
12 事項 **jikō** matters, facts, items
13 事業 **jigyō** undertakings, business, activities
14 事態 **jitai** situation, state of affairs
17 事績 **jiseki** achievements, exploits

—————— 2 ——————

1 一事 **ichiji** one thing
hito(tsu)koto the same thing
2 人事 **jinji** personal/personnel affairs **hitogoto** other people's affairs
3 工事 **kōji** construction
工事中 **kōjichū** Under Construction
工事場 **kōjiba** construction site
大事 **daiji** important, precious; great thing; serious matter **ōgoto** serious matter
4 火事 **kaji** fire, conflagration
5 民事 **minji** civil affairs; civil (law)
世事 **seji** worldly affairs
仕事 **shigoto** work

古事記 **Kojiki** (Japan's) Ancient Chronicles
用事 **yōji** business, errand, something to attend to
6 刑事 **keiji** (police) detective; criminal case
色事 **irogoto** love affair; love scene
返事 **henji** reply
行事 **gyōji** event, function, observance
7 作事 **tsuku(ri)goto** fiction, fabrication
何事 **nanigoto** what, whatever
判事 **hanji** a judge
見事 **migoto** beautiful, splendid
私事 **shiji, watakushigoto** personal affairs
8 拵事 **koshira(e)goto** fabrication, made-up story
知事 **chiji** governor
参事 **sanji** councilor
国事 **kokuji** affairs of state
炊事 **suiji** cooking
物事 **monogoto** things, matters
怪事件 **kaijiken** strange/mystery case
9 俗事 **zokuji** worldly affairs; workaday routine
軍事 **gunji** military affairs; military
変事 **henji** accident, mishap, disaster
美事 **migoto** splendid **biji** commendable act
祝事 **iwa(i)goto** auspicious/festive occasion
故事 **koji** historical event
食事 **shokuji** meal, dining
食事時 **shokujidoki** mealtime
10 従事 **jūji** engage in, carry on
家事 **kaji** housework; domestic affairs
時事 **jiji** current events
記事 **kiji** article, report
11 商事 **shōji** commercial affairs (short for 商事会社)
理事 **riji** director, trustee
理事会 **rijikai** board of directors/trustees
理事長 **rijichō** chairman, president
悪事 **akuji** evil deed

惨事 **sanji** disaster, tragic accident

12 揉事 **mo(me)goto** trouble, discord

検事 **kenji** public procurator/prosecutor

無事 **buji** safe and sound

13 隠事 **kaku(shi)goto, inji** secret

椿事 **chinji** accident; sudden occurrence

幹事長 **kanjichō** executive secretary, secretary-general

14 領事 **ryōji** consul

領事館 **ryōjikan** consulate

16 賭事 **kakegoto** betting, gambling

19 艶事 **tsuyagoto** love affair, romance

願事 **nega(i)goto** one's wish/prayer

20 議事 **giji** proceedings

議事堂 **gijidō** assembly hall, parliament/diet building

─── 3 ───

2 二返事 **futa(tsu)henji** immediate reply, readily, most willingly

4 心配事 **shinpaigoto** cares, worries, troubles

5 出来事 **dekigoto** incident, event, happenings

生返事 **namahenji** vague answer

6 百科事典 **hyakka jiten** encyclopedia

9 茶飯事 **sahanji** everyday occurrence

県知事 **kenchiji** prefectural governor

10 既成事実 **kisei jijitsu** fait accompli

針仕事 **hari shigoto** needlework, sewing

12 勝負事 **shōbugoto** game of skill/chance

14 総領事 **sōryōji** consul-general

総領事館 **sōryōjikan** consulate-general

─── 4 ───

3 三面記事 **sanmen kiji** page-3 news, police news, human-interest stories

6 年中行事 **nenjū gyōji** an annual event

─────── 0a9 ───────

歪	幽	矩	飛	発	衷	甚	巻	専	拝	毒	奏	革
2m7.4	3o6.6	2t7.1	9.4	9.5	9.9	9.10	9.11	9.16	3c5.3	0a8.14	9.17	3k6.2

重	乗
9.18	9.19

歪→ **2m7.4**

幽→ **3o6.6**

矩→ **2t7.1**

0a9.4 / 530

⌐ ⺀ 木 十一
10 12 1

飛 飛

HI, to(bu) fly; jump; skip over
to(basu) let fly; drive fast; skip over, omit

─────── 1 ───────

2 飛入 **to(bi)i(ri)** joining in (on the spur of the moment); speckled with a different color
to(bi)i(ru) jump/dive/fly into

3 飛上 **to(bi)a(garu)** fly/jump up

飛下 **tobio(ri)** jumping off

4 飛切 **tobiki(ri)** superfine, choicest, beyond compare

飛込自殺 **tobiko(mi) jisatsu** suicide by jumping in front of an oncoming train

飛火 **to(bi)hi** flying sparks, leaping flames

5 飛出 **to(bi)da(su)** fly/jump/dart out **to(bi)de(ru)** protrude

6 飛交 **to(bi)ka(u)** fly/flit about

飛行 **hikō** flight, flying, aviation

飛行士 **hikōshi** aviator

飛行機 **hikōki** airplane

飛回 **to(bi)mawa(ru)** fly/jump/rush around

9 飛降 **tobio(ri)** jumping off

11 飛掛 **to(bi)ka(karu)** pounce on, lunge for

12 飛弾 **hidan** flying bullet

飛散 **hisan, to(bi)chi(ru)** scatter, disperse

13 飛跳 **to(bi)hane(ru)** jump up and down, hop

18 飛離 **to(bi)hana(reru)** fly apart; tower above; out of the ordinary

21 飛躍 **hiyaku** leap; activity; rapid progress

飛躍的 **hiyakuteki** rapid, by leaps and bounds

────── 2 ──────

7 吹飛 **fu(ki)to(basu)** blow away

8 突飛 **toppi** wild, fantastic, reckless, eccentric **tsu(ki)to(basu)** knock down, send flying

15 撥飛 **ha(ne)to(basu)** send (something) flying; spatter, splash

19 蹴飛 **keto(basu)** kick away/out, reject

0a9.5 / 96

日	火	艹	一
	44	32	1

發 | 発 発

HATSU, HOTSU departure; shot, discharge; emit, give forth **aba(ku)** divulge, bring to light, open up

────── 1 ──────

4 発火 **hakka** ignition, combustion; discharge, firing

5 発生 **hassei** occurrence, outbreak; genesis; generation; growth, rise, development

発令 **hatsurei** announce officially, issue

発刊 **hakkan** publish, issue

発句 **hokku** first line (of a *renga*); haiku

発布 **happu** promulgation, proclamation

6 発行 **hakkō** publish, issue

7 発作 **hossa** fit, spasm, an attack of

発売 **hatsubai** sale

発見 **hakken** discover

発言 **hatsugen** utterance, speaking; proposal

発車 **hassha** start, departure (of a train)

発足 **hossoku, hassoku** start, inauguration

8 発表 **happyō** announce

発効 **hakkō** come into effect

発育 **hatsuiku** growth, development

発送 **hassō** send, ship, forward

発注 **hatchū** order (goods)

発明 **hatsumei** invention

9 発信 **hasshin** send (a message)

発音 **hatsuon** pronunciation

10 発射 **hassha** firing, launching; emanation, radiation

発案 **hatsuan** proposal

発展 **hatten** expansion, growth, development

発展途上国 **hattentojōkoku** developing country

発祥地 **hasshōchi** cradle, birthplace

発砲 **happō** firing, discharge, shooting

発病 **hatsubyō** be taken ill

発航 **hakkō** departure, sailing

11 発動 **hatsudō** put into motion, exercise, invoke

発達 **hattatsu** development, progress

発掘 **hakkutsu** excavation; disinterment

発現 **hatsugen** revelation, manifestation

発情 **hatsujō** sexual arousal, (in) heat

12 発着 **hatchaku** departures and arrivals

発揮 **hakki** exhibit, demonstrate, make manifest

発覚 **hakkaku** be detected, come to light

発散 **hassan** give forth, emit, exhale, radiate, evaporate; divergent

13 発想 **hassō** conception; expression (in music)

発意 **hatsui** initiative, suggestion, original idea

発電 **hatsuden** generation of electricity

発電所 **hatsudensho** power plant, generating station

14 発端 **hottan** origin, beginning

15 発熱 **hatsunetsu** generation of heat; have a fever

発憤 **happun** be roused to action

17 発癌 **hatsugan** cancer-causing, carcinogenic

———— 2 ————

1 一発 **ippatsu** a shot

4 反発 **hanpatsu** repel; rebound, recover; oppose

5 出発 **shuppatsu** departure

6 多発性 **tahatsusei** multiple (sclerosis)

再発 **saihatsu** recurrence, relapse

自発的 **jihatsuteki** spontaneous, voluntary

7 告発 **kokuhatsu** prosecution, indictment, accusation

8 併発 **heihatsu** break out at the same time, be complicated by

突発 **toppatsu** occur suddenly, break out

9 連発 **renpatsu** fire/shoot in rapid succession

活発 **kappatsu** active, lively

挑発的 **chōhatsuteki** provocative, suggestive

10 原発 **genpatsu** (generating electricity from) nuclear power (short for 原子力発電)

11 偶発 **gūhatsu** happen by chance

偶発的 **gūhatsuteki** accidental, incidental, occasional

12 揮発 **kihatsu** volatile, vaporize

蒸発 **jōhatsu** evaporate; disappear

開発 **kaihatsu** development

13 新発売 **shinhatsubai** new(ly marketed) product

続発 **zokuhatsu** occur one after another

14 摘発 **tekihatsu** expose, unmask, uncover

16 奮発 **funpatsu** exertion, strenuous effort; splurge

19 爆発 **bakuhatsu** explosion

爆発的 **bakuhatsuteki** explosive (popularity)

———— 3 ————

6 再出発 **saishuppatsu** start over, make a fresh start

0a9.9 / 1677　　　日 禾 口 十
　　　　　　　　　　57 24 12

 衷 ｜ 衷 衷

CHŪ heart, mind; inside TADASHI (m. given name)

———— 1 ————

4 衷心 **chūshin** one's inmost heart/feelings

11 衷情 **chūjō** one's inmost feelings

———— 2 ————

7 折衷 **setchū** compromise, cross, blending

———— 4 ————

8 和洋折衷 **wayō setchū** blending of Japanese and Western styles

0a9.10 / 1501　　　日 艹 二 儿
　　　　　　　　　　32 4 16

 甚 甚

JIN, hanaha(da), hanaha(dashii) very much, extreme, great, enormous, intense **ita(ku)** very, greatly

———— 1 ————

3 甚大 **jindai** very great, immense, serious

0a9.11 / 507 ··· 火 弓 二
44 28 4

卷

卷｜卷 卷

KAN, KEN, maki roll, reel; volume, book **ma(ku)** roll up, wind, coil

——————— 1 ———————

3 巻上 **ma(ki)a(geru)** roll/wind up, raise; take away, rob
4 巻込 **ma(ki)ko(mu)** roll up, enfold; entangle, drag into, involve in
7 巻戻 **ma(ki)modo(shi)** rewind (a tape)
8 巻物 **ma(ki)mono** scroll
10 巻起 **ma(ki)o(kosu)** stir up, create (a sensation)
11 巻添 **ma(ki)zo(e)** involvement, entanglement

——————— 2 ———————

1 一巻 **ikkan** one volume
   hitomaki one roll
3 下巻 **gekan** last volume (of two or three)
6 全１０巻 **zen-jikkan** ten volumes in all
8 虎巻 **tora(no)maki** pony, answer book; (trade) secrets
12 渦巻 **uzuma(ki)** eddy, vortex, whirlpool; spiral, coil
   葉巻 **hamaki** cigar
   絵巻物 **emakimono** picture scroll
18 襟巻 **erima(ki)** muffler, scarf

——————— 3 ———————

9 海苔巻 **norima(ki)** (vinegared) rice rolled in seaweed

0a9.16 / 600 ··· 曰 日 寸 十
43 37 12

専

專｜専 専

SEN, moppa(ra) exclusively

——————— 1 ———————

5 専用 **sen'yō** private/personal use, exclusively for
6 専任 **sennin** exclusive duty, full-time

専有権 **sen'yūken** exclusive right, monopoly
7 専売 **senbai** monopoly
専攻 **senkō** academic specialty, one's major
8 専念 **sennen** undivided/close attention
専制 **sensei** absolutism, despotism
専門 **senmon** specialty
10 専修 **senshū** specialize in
専従 **senjū** full-time (work)
11 専務 **senmu** special duty; principal business; managing/executive (director)
13 専業 **sengyō** specialty, monopoly, main occupation

拝 → 拝 **3c5.3**

毒 → 毒 **0a8.14**

0a9.17 / 1544 ··· 大 二 一
34 4 1

奏

奏 奏

SŌ play (a musical instrument); present, report (to a superior); take effect
kana(deru) play (a musical instrument)

——————— 1 ———————

13 奏楽 **sōgaku** instrumental music

——————— 2 ———————

6 合奏 **gassō** concert, ensemble
7 伴奏 **bansō** (musical) accompaniment
   吹奏楽 **suisōgaku** wind-instrument music, brass
8 協奏曲 **kyōsōkyoku** concerto
9 独奏 **dokusō** instrumental solo
14 演奏 **ensō** (musical) performance

——————— 3 ———————

2 二重奏 **nijūsō** instrumental duet
5 四重奏 **shijūsō** (instrumental) quartet

革 → **3k6.2**

0a9.18 / 227   目 車 丨 一
                69 2 1

重 重

JŪ, CHŌ heavy; serious; lie/pile on top of one another **omo(i/tai)** heavy; serious **omo(sa)** weight **omo(mi)** weight, importance **omo(njiru/nzuru)** attach importance to, honor, respect **kasa(naru/neru)** lie/pile on top of one another **-e** -fold, -ply
SHIGERU (m. given name) SHIGE (part of given name)

────────── 1 ──────────

² 重力 **jūryoku** gravity
³ 重工業 **jūkōgyō** heavy industry
   重大 **jūdai** important, serious
⁵ 重立 **omoda(tta)** principal, leading, prominent
⁶ 重任 **jūnin** heavy responsibility; re-election, reappointment
⁷ 重体 **jūtai** in serious/critical condition
   重役 **jūyaku** (company) director
   重労働 **jūrōdō** heavy/hard labor
⁸ 重味 **omomi** weight; importance; emphasis; dignity
   重苦 **omokuru(shii)** heavy, ponderous, oppressive, awkward (expression)
⁹ 重信 **Shigenobu, Jūshin** (m. given name)
   重点 **jūten** important point, priority, emphasis
   重要 **jūyō** important
¹⁰ 重病 **jūbyō** serious illness
¹¹ 重視 **jūshi** attach great importance to
   重責 **jūseki** heavy responsibility
¹² 重量 **jūryō** weight
¹³ 重傷 **jūshō, omode** serious wound, major injury
   重罪 **jūzai** serious crime, felony
¹⁴ 重態 **jūtai** in serious/critical condition
   重複 **chōfuku, jūfuku** duplication, repetition, overlapping, redundancy

¹⁶ 重篤 **jūtoku** serious (illness)

────────── 2 ──────────

¹ 一重 **hitoe** one layer; single **hitokasa(ne)** a suit (of clothes); a set (of nested boxes)
² 二重 **nijū** double **futae** two-fold, two-ply, double
   二重奏 **nijūsō** instrumental duet
³ 三重 **sanjū, mie** three-fold, three-ply, triple
   三重県 **Mie-ken** (prefecture)
⁵ 比重 **hijū** specific gravity; relative importance
   四重奏 **shijūsō** (instrumental) quartet
⁶ 多重 **tajū** multiplex, multiple
   気重 **kiomo(i)** heavy-hearted, depressed
⁷ 体重 **taijū** one's weight
⁹ 荘重 **sōchō** solemn, sublime, impressive
   珍重 **chinchō** value highly, prize
¹⁰ 荷重 **kajū** load
¹² 尊重 **sonchō** respect, esteem
   貴重 **kichō** valuable, precious
   貴重品 **kichōhin** valuables
¹³ 慎重 **shinchō** cautious
¹⁶ 積重 **tsu(mi)kasa(naru)** be piled/stacked up
¹⁷ 厳重 **genjū** strict, stringent, rigid

0a9.19 / 523   └..┘ 禾 艹 一
                56 32 1

乗 丨 乗 乗

JŌ ride; multiply, raise to a power (in math) **no(ru), no(kkaru)** ride; get on, mount; join in; be deceived, be taken in **no(seru)** give a ride, take aboard; place, put, load; let join in; deceive, take in NORI (part of given name)

────────── 1 ──────────

² 乗入 **no(ri)i(reru)** ride/drive into; extend (a train line) into (a city)
⁴ 乗切 **no(ri)ki(ru)** ride through/out, weather (a crisis)

0a10

乗心地 **no(ri)gokochi** riding comfort

5 乗出 **no(ri)da(su)** set out, embark on; lean forward

乗用車 **jōyōsha** passenger car

7 乗車 **jōsha** get on (a train)

8 乗法 **jōhō** multiplication

乗物 **no(ri)mono** vehicle

乗取 **no(t)to(ru)** hijack, commandeer, capture, occupy

9 乗除 **jōjo** multiplication and division

乗客 **jōkyaku** passenger

10 乗馬 **jōba, no(ri)uma** horseback riding; riding horse

11 乗遅 **no(ri)oku(reru)** miss (a train)

乗務員 **jōmuin** train/plane crew

乗組員 **norikumiin** crew

12 乗場 **no(ri)ba** (taxi) stand, bus stop, platform

乗換 **no(ri)ka(e)** change conveyances, transfer

13 乗損 **no(ri)soko(nau)** miss (a train)

――― 2 ―――

3 大乗仏教 **Daijō Bukkyō** Mahayana Buddhism, Great-Vehicle Buddhism

下乗 **gejō** get off (a horse), get out of (a car)

5 只乗 **tadano(ri)** free/stolen ride

6 名乗 **nano(ru)** call oneself, profess to be

自乗 **jijō** square (of a number)

8 波乗 **namino(ri)** surfing

11 添乗員 **tenjōin** tour conductor

船乗 **funano(ri)** seaman, sailor

12 搭乗 **tōjō** board, get on

搭乗券 **tōjōken** boarding pass

――― 3 ―――

5 加減乗除 **kagenjōjo** addition, subtraction, multiplication, and division

――――――――― **0a10** ―――――――――

幽	乗	套	矩	既	垂	殊	射	残	耗	耕
3o6.6	0a9.19	10.3	2t7.1	10.5	0a8.12	10.7	10.8	10.11	10.12	10.13

幽→ **3o6.6**

乗→乗 **0a9.19**

0a10.3

日 六 上 二
34 13 4

套套

TŌ cover; timeworn, trite

――― 2 ―――

5 外套 **gaitō** overcoat

11 常套 **jōtō** commonplace, conventional

矩→ **2t7.1**

0a10.5 / 1458

目 食 一 亠
73 14 11

既 旡|既旡

KI, sude (ni) already, previously

――― 1 ―――

5 既存 **kison** existing

既刊 **kikan** already published

6 既成事実 **kisei jijitsu** fait accompli

7 既決 **kiketsu** decided, settled

8 既知 **kichi** (already) known

既定 **kitei** predetermined, prearranged, fixed

11 既済 **kisai** paid-up, already settled

既婚者 **kikonsha** married person

14 既製 **kisei** ready-made

垂→垂 **0a8.12**

0a10.7 / 1505

殊殊

SHU, koto (ni) especially, in particular

------------ 1 ------------

5 殊外 **koto(no)hoka** exceedingly, exceptionally

7 殊更 **kotosara** especially, particularly; intentionally

------------ 2 ------------

10 特殊 **tokushu** special

0a10.8 / 900

射射

SHA, i(ru) shoot (an arrow) **sa(su)** shine into/upon

------------ 1 ------------

5 射出 **shashutsu** shoot out, emit, extrude, radiate, catapult

7 射利 **shari** love of money

8 射幸 **shakō** speculation

10 射殺 **shasatsu, ikoro(su)** shoot to death

12 射場 **shajō** shooting/rifle range; archery ground

射程 **shatei** range (of a gun/missile)

15 射撃 **shageki** shooting, firing

------------ 2 ------------

4 反射 **hansha** reflection, reflex

7 投射物 **tōshabutsu** projectile

8 注射 **chūsha** injection, shot

放射 **hōsha** radiation, emission, discharge

放射能 **hōshanō** radioactivity, radiation

放射線 **hōshasen** radiation

9 発射 **hassha** firing, launching; emanation, radiation

15 噴射 **funsha** jet, spray, injection

0a10.11 / 650

残丨残残

ZAN remain **noko(ru)** remain, be left over; stay, linger **noko(su)** leave behind **noko(ri)** remainder, remnant

------------ 1 ------------

5 残本 **zanpon** unsold copies (of a book); remainders

残生 **zansei** one's remaining years

残存者 **zansonsha** survivor, holdover

7 残余 **zan'yo** remainder, residual, remnant, balance

8 残念 **zannen** regrettable, too bad

残物 **zanbutsu, noko(ri)mono** remnants, scraps, leftovers

残金 **zankin** balance, surplus

9 残虐 **zangyaku** cruelty, atrocity, brutality

残品 **zanpin** remaining stock, unsold merchandise

10 残高 **zandaka** balance, remainder

残留 **zanryū** remain behind

11 残雪 **zansetsu** lingering snow

12 残期 **zanki** remaining period, unexpired term

残暑 **zansho** the lingering summer heat

13 残業 **zangyō** overtime

14 残酷 **zankoku** cruel, brutal

18 残額 **zangaku** remaining amount, balance

------------ 2 ------------

5 生残 **i(ki)noko(ru)** survive **seizan** survival

生残者 **seizansha** survivor

6 名残 **nago(ri)** farewell; remembrance, keepsake; relics, vestiges

12 勝残 **ka(chi)noko(ru)** make the finals

焼残 **ya(ke)noko(ru)** remain unburned, escape the fire

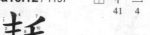

0a10.12 / 1197 ☐ 木 二 十
41 4 12

耗 | 耗 耗 耗

MŌ, KŌ decrease

― 2 ―

10 消耗 **shōmō** consumption, attrition, wear and tear

消耗品 **shōmōhin** supplies, expendables

13 損耗 **sonmō** wear and tear, loss

16 磨耗 **mamō** wear and tear, abrasion

0a10.13 / 1196 ☐ 木 艹 二
41 32 4

耕 | 耕 耕

KŌ, tagaya(su) till, plow, cultivate

― 1 ―

6 耕地 **kōchi** arable/cultivated land

7 耕作 **kōsaku** cultivation, farming

耕作物 **kōsakubutsu** farm products

― 0a11 ―

将	巣	疎	野	爽	粛	専	彗
2b8.3	3n8.1	11.4	11.5	11.7	11.8	0a9.16	11.9

將 → 将 2b8.3

巢 → 巣 3n8.1

0a11.4 / 1514 ☐ 木 口 ⼘
41 24 13

疎 | 疎 疎

SO pass through; estrangement; sparseness; shun, neglect **uto(i)** distant, estranged; be unfamiliar with, know little of **uto(mu), uto(njiru)** shun, neglect, estrange **uto(mashii)** disagreeable **oroso(ka)** negligent, remiss **maba(ra)** sparse, scattered

― 1 ―

9 疎通 **sotsū** mutual understanding

12 疎遠 **soen** estrangement; long silence

疎開 **sokai** dispersal, removal, evacuation

0a11.5 / 236 ☐ 日 土 一
43 22 14

埜 | 野 野

YA field; the opposition (parties); rustic; wild **no** field

― 1 ―

3 野口 **Noguchi** (surname)

4 野心 **yashin** ambition

5 野生 **yasei** wild

野外 **yagai** the open air, outdoor

野田 **Noda** (surname)

7 野良猫 **noraneko** stray cat

野沢 **Nozawa** (surname)

野村 **Nomura** (surname)

8 野郎 **yarō** fellow, guy, bastard

野放 **nobana(shi)** putting to pasture; leaving things to themselves

野性的 **yaseiteki** wild, rough

10 野原 **nohara** field, plain

野党 **yatō** opposition party

11 野菜 **yasai** vegetables

野崎 **Nozaki** (surname)

野球 **yakyū** baseball

野鳥 **yachō** wild birds

12 野蛮 **yaban** savage, barbarous
14 野暮 **yabo** unrefined, rustic; stupid, senseless; stale, trite
15 野趣 **yashu** rural beauty, rustic air
16 野獣 **yajū** wild animal/beast

——————— 2 ———————
3 久野 **Hisano, Kuno** (surname)
  大野 **Ōno** (surname)
  与野党 **yoyatō** governing and opposition parties
  上野 **Ueno** (section of Tōkyō) **Kōzuke** (ancient kuni, Gunma-ken)
  小野 **Ono** (surname)
4 天野 **Amano** (surname)
  中野 **Nakano** (surname)
  分野 **bun'ya** field, sphere, area, division
  水野 **Mizuno** (surname)
  日野 **Hino** (surname)
5 北野 **Kitano** (surname)
  矢野 **Yano** (surname)
  平野 **Hirano** (surname)
6 宇野 **Uno** (surname)
  吉野 **Yoshino** (surname)
7 佐野 **Sano** (surname)
8 長野 **Nagano** (city, Nagano-ken); (surname)
  長野県 **Nagano-ken** (prefecture)
  岡野 **Okano** (surname)
  河野 **Kōno, Kawano** (surname)
  牧野 **Makino** (surname)
9 浅野 **Asano** (surname)
  草野 **Kusano** (surname)
  荒野 **a(re)no, arano, kōya** wilderness, wasteland
  枯野 **ka(re)no** desolate fields
  畑野 **Hatano** (surname)
10 高野 **Takano** (surname)
  高野山 **Kōyasan** (mountain, Wakayama-ken)
  浜野 **Hamano** (surname)
  荻野 **Ogino** (surname)
11 視野 **shiya** field of vision/view
  粗野 **soya** rustic, loutish, vulgar
12 奥野 **Okuno** (surname)
13 裾野 **susono** foot of a mountain

——————— 3 ———————
4 日比野 **Hibino** (surname)

0a11.7 / 2046   □… 大 十
                            34 12

SŌ, sawa(yaka) refreshing, bracing; clear, resonant, fluent AKIRA (m. given name) SŌ, SAYA, SA, AKI, SAWA (part of given name) SAWA, SAYAKO (f. given name)

——————— 1 ———————
7 爽快 **sōkai** thrilling, exhilarating

——————— 2 ———————
14 颯爽 **sassō** dashing, smart, gallant

0a11.8 / 1695   □… 米 ヨ 儿
                            62 39 16

SHUKU rectify, admonish; reverential; solemn; quiet SUSUMU (m. given name)

——————— 1 ———————
11 粛清 **shukusei** purge, cleanup, liquidation

——————— 2 ———————
14 静粛 **seishuku** silent, still, quiet
17 厳粛 **genshuku** grave, serious, solemn

専 → 専 **0a9.16**

0a11.9 / 2066   田 ヨ 十 二
                            39 12 4

SUI comet; broom, sweep SUI, EI (part of given name)

——————— 1 ———————
9 彗星 **suisei, hōkiboshi** comet

0a13-15

鼠	業	肅	貍	爾	奬	舞	斷
13.1	13.3	0a11.8	3g7.2	14.3	3n10.4	15.1	6b5.6

13

0a13.1

日 ヨ 厂 一
39 18 1

SO, SHU, nezumi rat, mouse

— 1 —

6 鼠色 **nezumiiro** dark gray, slate
8 鼠取 **nezumito(ri)** rat poison; mousetrap, rattrap

— 2 —

10 栗鼠 **risu** squirrel

0a13.3 / 279

日 王 儿 一
46 16 1

GYŌ business, trade, industry; undertaking **GŌ** karma **waza** a work, deed, act, performance, trick **NARI** (part of given name)

— 1 —

9 業界 **gyōkai** the business world, industry, the trade
11 業務 **gyōmu** business, work, operations, duties
14 業種 **gyōshu** type of industry, category of business
17 業績 **gyōseki** (business) performance, results, achievement

— 2 —

3 工業 **kōgyō** industry
　大業 **taigyō** a great undertaking/achievement
4 分業 **bungyō** division of labor, specialization
5 失業 **shitsugyō** unemployment
　失業者 **shitsugyōsha** unemployed person
　生業 **seigyō** occupation, calling
　仕業 **shiwaza** act, deed
　巡業 **jungyō** tour (of a troupe/team)
6 休業 **kyūgyō** suspension of business, Shop Closed
　企業 **kigyō** enterprise, corporation
　企業家 **kigyōka** industrialist, entrepreneur
　早業 **hayawaza** quick work; sleight of hand
7 作業 **sagyō** work, operations
　余業 **yogyō** remaining work; avocation, sideline
8 事業 **jigyō** undertakings, business, activities
　卒業 **sotsugyō** graduation
　実業 **jitsugyō** industry, business
　林業 **ringyō** forestry
9 専業 **sengyō** specialty, monopoly, main occupation
　神業 **kamiwaza** the work of God; superhuman feat
10 残業 **zangyō** overtime
　修業 **shūgyō** pursuit of knowledge
　兼業 **kengyō** side business
　従業 **jūgyō** be employed
　従業員 **jūgyōin** employee
　家業 **kagyō** one's trade
　蚕業 **sangyō** sericulture
11 副業 **fukugyō** side business, sideline
　商業 **shōgyō** commerce, trade, business
　授業 **jugyō** teaching, instruction
　産業 **sangyō** industry
　産業界 **sangyōkai** (the) industry
　終業 **shūgyō** close of work/school
12 偉業 **igyō** great achievement, feat
　創業 **sōgyō** found, establish
　就業 **shūgyō** employment
　営業 **eigyō** (running a) business
　廃業 **haigyō** going out of business

軽業 **karuwaza** acrobatics

開業 **kaigyō** opening/starting a business

開業医 **kaigyōi** doctor in private practice

13 農業 **nōgyō** agriculture

鉱業 **kōgyō** mining

14 漁業 **gyogyō** fishery, fishing industry

15 窯業 **yōgyō** ceramics (industry)

稼業 **kagyō** one's trade/occupation

罷業 **higyō** strike, walkout

16 興業 **kōgyō** promotion of industry

操業 **sōgyō** operation, work

機業 **kigyō** the textile industry

18 職業 **shokugyō** occupation, profession

職業病 **shokugyōbyō** occupational disease

――――――――― 3 ―――――――――

3 小企業 **shōkigyō** small enterprises/business

4 水産業 **suisangyō** fisheries, marine products industry

6 自由業 **jiyūgyō** freelance occupation, self-employed

9 重工業 **jūkōgyō** heavy industry

11 接客業 **sekkyakugyō** hotel and restaurant trade

12 軽工業 **keikōgyō** light industry

13 鉄鋼業 **tekkōgyō** the steel industry

14 総罷業 **sōhigyō** general strike

18 織物業 **orimonogyō** the textile business

――――――――― 4 ―――――――――

4 中小企業 **chūshō kigyō** small business(es)

肅 → 粛 0a11.8

――――――――― 14 ―――――――――

貍 → 狸 3g7.2

0a14.3 / 2154
                          ⊡ ⻨ 儿 丨
                          75 16 2

爾   尔丨爾爾

JI, NI thou, you; so, in that way; only; since, from CHIKASHI, MITSURU, AKIRA (m. given name) JI, NI, SHIKA, MI (part of given name)

――――――――― 1 ―――――――――

7 爾来 **jirai** since then

9 爾後 **jigo** thereafter

奬 → 奨 3n10.4

――――――――― 15 ―――――――――

0a15.1 / 810   ⊞ 艹 夕 ⺅
                          32 30 15

舞   舞舞

BU, ma(u) dance; flutter about **mai** dance MAI (f. given name)

――――――――― 1 ―――――――――

3 舞上 **ma(i)a(garu)** fly up, soar

4 舞込 **ma(i)ko(mu)** drop in, visit; befall

5 舞台 **butai** stage

6 舞曲 **bukyoku** music and dancing; dance music

7 舞戻 **ma(i)modo(ru)** find one's way back, return

13 舞楽 **bugaku** old Japanese court-dance music

14 舞踊 **buyō** dancing; dance **ma(i)odo(ru)** dance

15 舞踏 **butō** dancing
舞踏会 **butōkai** ball, dance

――――――――― 2 ―――――――――

5 仕舞 **shima(u)** finish, end; put away; close, wind up

7 見舞 **mima(u)** inquire after (someone's health), visit (someone in hospital)

10 振舞 **furuma(u)** behave, conduct oneself; entertain, treat

14 歌舞伎 **kabuki** kabuki

17 檜舞台 **hinoki butai** cypress-floored stage; high-class stage, limelight

— 4 —

12 暑中見舞 **shochū mima(i)** inquiry

after (someone's) health in the hot season

— **18** —

断 → 断 **6b5.6**

— **亻 2a** —

人	个	仂	仇	仏	化	仁	分	公	介	今	久	仙
0.1	2a8.36	2a11.1	2.4	2.5	2.6	2.8	2o2.1	2o2.2	2.9	2.10	0a3.7	3.1

仕	代	他	付	以	全	令	伏	休	件	伐	伊	住
3.2	3.3	3.4	3.6	0a5.1	2r4.2	3.9	4.1	4.2	4.4	4.5	4.6	2a5.19

仲	伍	任	仰	似	伎	伝	仮	全	企	合	会	肉
4.7	4.8	4.9	4.10	2a5.11	4.13	4.14	4.15	4.16	4.17	4.18	4.19	4.20

耒	朱	位	佛	伸	伴	体	伯	佑	佐	作	似	仰
0a7.6	0a6.13	5.1	2a2.5	5.3	5.4	5.6	5.7	5.8	5.9	5.10	5.11	2a4.10

伽	但	低	佗	伶	住	何	伺	余	含	巫	依	使
5.12	5.14	5.15	2a6.14	5.17	5.19	5.21	5.23	5.25	5.26	6.1	6.2

価	侑	例	佳	侍	侃	供	侘	併	侮	侭	舍	舎
6.3	6.5	6.7	6.10	6.11	6.12	6.13	6.14	6.17	6.20	2a14.2	6.23	2a6.23

念	命	信	促	俄	侮	便	俐	係	俊	保	侵	俗
6.24	6.26	7.1	7.3	7.4	2a6.20	7.5	4k7.2	7.8	7.10	7.14	7.15	7.17

侯	臥	赴	起	乗	倒	倣	俳	併	候	修	倦	倍
7.21	7.22	3b6.14	3b7.11	0a9.19	8.5	8.7	8.8	2a6.17	8.10	8.11	8.13	8.14

俱	倭	俸	俵	借	倖	俺	倹	倫	値	健	俯	個
8.15	8.16	8.18	8.21	8.22	8.23	8.25	8.27	8.28	8.30	8.34	8.35	8.36

倉	偶	偽	假	側	倦	條	脩	偲	停	偵	偏	欧
8.37	9.1	9.2	2a4.15	9.4	2a8.13	4i4.1	9.6	9.7	9.14	9.15	9.16	5f5.5

超	越	麥	斜	敘	肅	疎	備	偉	傍	傘	禽	超
3b9.18	4n8.2	4i4.2	9.21	2h7.1	0a11.8	0a11.4	10.4	10.5	10.6	10.7	10.8	3b9.18

越	幾	疎	働	傲	傾	傳	傑	僧	傷	債	催	會
4n8.2	4n8.4	0a11.4	11.1	11.2	11.3	2a4.14	11.6	11.7	11.10	11.11	11.12	2a4.19

越	業	靴	僕	僚	僑	像	僧	趣	疑	價	儀	億
4n8.2	0a13.3	3k10.34	12.1	12.4	2a9.2	12.8	2a11.7	6e9.1	2m12.1	2a6.3	13.4	13.6

儉	趣	齒	儒	儘	儲	優	償	儲	鞭	齢
2a8.27	6e9.1	6b6.11	14.1	14.2	2a16.1	15.1	15.4	16.1	3k15.8	6b11.5

0

2a0.1 / 1   □ 亻
                                  3

人   人 人

JIN, NIN, hito man, person, human
being **TO, HITO, JIN** (part of given name)

─────────── **1** ───────────

0 アメリカ人 **Amerikajin** an American

1 人一倍 **hito-ichibai** uncommon,
   more than others

2 人力 **jinriki** human power, man-
   powered **jinryoku** human
   power/efforts

3 人工 **jinkō** artificial
   人才 **jinzai, jinsai** man of talent
   人々 **hitobito** people, everybody
   人口 **jinkō** population; common
   talk

4 人夫 **ninpu** coolie, laborer
   人文 **jinmon, jinbun** humanity,
   civilization
   人込 **hitogo(mi)** crowd of people

5 人出 **hitode** turnout, crowd
   人民 **jinmin** the people
   人生 **jinsei** life, human existence
   人付合 **hitozu(ki)a(i)** sociability
   人好 **hitozu(ki)** amiability, attractiveness

6 人気 **ninki** popularity; popular feeling; business conditions
   hitoke signs of life (in a place)
   人件費 **jinkenhi** personnel expenses
   人任 **hitomaka(se)** leaving it to
   others
   人名 **jinmei** person's name

7 人身 **jinshin** the human body; one's
   person
   人体 **jintai** the human body
   人形 **ningyō** doll, puppet
   人材 **jinzai** man of talent, personnel
   人見知 **hitomishi(ri)** be bashful
   before strangers

8 人事 **jinji** personal/personnel
   affairs **hitogoto** other people's affairs
   人命 **jinmei** (human) life
   人並 **hitona(mi)** average, ordinary
   人妻 **hitozuma** (someone else's)
   wife
   人参 **ninjin** carrot
   人物 **jinbutsu** person; one's character; character (in a story);
   man of ability
   人性 **jinsei** human nature; humanity

9 人前 **hitomae** before others, in public
   人造 **jinzō** artificial, synthetic, imitation
   人通 **hitodō(ri)** pedestrian traffic
   人相 **ninsō** facial features, physiognomy
   人柄 **hitogara** character, personality; personal appearance
   人為的 **jin'iteki** artificial

10 人真似 **hitomane** mimicry, imitations
   人差指 **hitosa(shi) yubi** index finger
   人員 **jin'in** personnel, staff, crew
   人格 **jinkaku** character, personality
   人殺 **hitogoro(shi)** murder; mur-
   derer
   人脈 **jinmyaku** (network of) personal connections

11 人達 **hitotachi** people
   人情 **ninjō** human feelings, humanity, kindness

12 人違 **hitochiga(i)** mistaken identity
   人間 **ningen** human being, man
   人間性 **ningensei** human nature,
   humanity

13 人嫌 **hitogira(i)** avoiding others'
   company; misanthrope
   人数 **ninzū, ninzu, hitokazu** number of people

14 人徳 **jintoku, nintoku** natural/per-
   sonal virtue
   人種 **jinshu** race (of people)

15 人権 **jinken** human rights
   人権蹂躙 **jinken jūrin** infringement of human rights

─────
2
─────

亻 0
⺄
孑
阝
阝
刂
力
又
亠
亠
ヒ
⺅
ク
厂
辶
冂
几
匸

人質 **hitojichi** hostage
18 人類 **jinrui** mankind, man
人類学 **jinruigaku** anthropology

1 一人 **hitori, ichinin** one person
一人子 **hitorikko, hitorigo** an only child
一人当 **hitoria(tari)** per person/capita
一人者 **hitorimono** someone alone; unmarried/single person
一人物 **ichijinbutsu** a person of consequence
一人前 **ichininmae, hitorimae** one portion/serving; full adulthood
一人娘 **hitori musume** an only daughter
一人息子 **hitori musuko** an only son
一人称 **ichininshō** first person (in grammar)

2 二人 **futari, ninin** two persons, pair, couple
二人共 **futaritomo** both (persons)
二人前 **futarimae, nininmae** enough for two, two servings
二人連 **futarizu(re)** a party of two, couple
二人称 **nininshō** second person (in grammar)
二人組 **niningumi** twosome, duo
十人十色 **jūnin-toiro** Tastes differ. To each his own.

3 三人 **sannin** three people
三人称 **sanninshō** third person (in grammar)
大人 **otona** adult **otona(shii)** gentle, quiet **taijin** giant; adult; man of virtue
大人物 **daijinbutsu** great man
凡人 **bonjin** ordinary person, man of mediocre ability
小人 **kobito** dwarf, midget **shōnin** child

4 不人気 **funinki** unpopular
夫人 **fujin** wife, married woman, Mrs.
友人 **yūjin** friend
巨人 **kyojin** giant

5 本人 **honnin** the person himself, the said person, the principal
代人 **dainin** proxy, deputy, substitute
他人 **tanin** someone else, others, outsider
玄人 **kurōto** expert, professional
外人 **gaijin** foreigner
犯人 **hannin** criminal, culprit, offender
囚人 **shūjin** prisoner, convict
四人 **yonin** four people
白人 **hakujin** a white, Caucasian
主人 **shujin** master; one's husband
主人公 **shujinkō** main character, hero (of a story)

6 死人 **shinin** dead person, the dead
仲人 **nakōdo, chūnin** go-between, matchmaker
老人 **rōjin** old man/person, the old/aged
同人 **dōjin, dōnin** the same person, said person; clique, fraternity, coterie
先人 **senjin** predecessor
名人 **meijin** master, expert, virtuoso
当人 **tōnin** the one concerned, the said person, the person himself
百人一首 **hyakunin-isshu** 100 poems by 100 poets (a collection of 100 *tanka*; basis for the popular card game *uta karuta*)
成人 **seijin** adult
成人式 **seijinshiki** Coming-of-Age-Day (Jan. 15) ceremony

7 住人 **jūnin** resident, inhabitant
何人 **nannin** how many people **nanpito(mo)** everyone, all
求人 **kyūjin** seeking workers, Help Wanted
別人 **betsujin** different person; changed man
狂人 **kyōjin** insane person, lunatic
役人 **yakunin** public official
芸人 **geinin** artiste, performer
村人 **murabito** villager
町人 **chōnin** merchant

8 非人 **hinin** beggar; outcast
非人間的 **hiningenteki** inhuman, impersonal

佳人 **kajin** beautiful woman

盲人 **mōjin** blind person

直人 **Naoto, Naondo** (m. given name)

法人 **hōjin** juridical person, legal entity, corporation

知人 **chijin** an acquaintance

若人 **wakōdo** young person, a youth

和人 **Kazuto, Kazuhito, Nagito** (m. given name)

9 俗人 **zokujin** layman; worldly-minded person

勇人 **Hayato** (m. given name)

軍人 **gunjin** soldier, military man

変人 **henjin** an eccentric

美人 **bijin** beautiful woman

狩人 **karyōdo, kariudo** hunter

茶人 **chajin, sajin** tea-ceremony expert; an eccentric

10 俳人 **haijin** haiku poet

健人 **Taketo** (m. given name)

個人 **kojin** private person, individual

個人的 **kojinteki** individual, personal, self-centered

個人差 **kojinsa** differences between individuals

恋人 **koibito** sweetheart, boyfriend, girlfriend

浪人 **rōnin** lordless samurai; unaffiliated/jobless person, high-school graduate studying to pass a university entrance exam

党人 **tōjin** party member, partisan

殺人 **satsujin** murder

恩人 **onjin** benefactor, patron

病人 **byōnin** sick person, patient, invalid

素人 **shirōto** amateur, layman

粋人 **suijin** man of refined tastes

隼人 **Hayato** (m. given name)

11 商人 **shōnin** merchant, trader, shopkeeper

達人 **tatsujin** expert, master

清人 **Kiyoto, Kiyohito, Kiyondo, Seijin** (m. given name)

婦人 **fujin** lady, woman

婦人科医 **fujinkai** gynecologist

猟人 **kariudo, karyūdo, ryōjin** hunter

黒人 **kokujin** a black, Negro

悪人 **akunin** evildoer, scoundrel, the wicked

12 善人 **zennin** virtuous man, good people

尋人 **tazu(ne)bito** person being sought, missing person

勝人 **Katsuhito, Katsuto, Katsundo** (m. given name)

無人 **mujin, munin** uninhabited; unmanned **bunin** shortage of help

雇人 **yato(i)nin** employee; servant

幾人 **ikunin** how many people

番人 **bannin** watchman, guard

証人 **shōnin** witness

13 猿人 **enjin** ape-man

聖人 **seijin** sage, saint, holy man

数人 **sūnin** several persons

新人 **shinjin** newcomer, new face

罪人 **zainin** criminal **tsumibito** sinner

痴人 **chijin** fool, idiot

詩人 **shijin** poet

雅人 **Masato, Gajin** (m. given name)

14 厭人 **enjin** misanthropy

愛人 **aijin** lover

歌人 **kajin** poet

15 隣人 **rinjin** neighbor

16 操人形 **ayatsu(ri)ningyō** puppet, marionette

賢人 **kenjin** wise man, sage, the wise

17 擬人化 **gijinka** personification

18 職人 **shokunin** craftsman, workman

雛人形 **hina ningyō** (Girls' Festival) doll

19 麗人 **reijin** beautiful woman

─────── 3 ───────

4 中華人民共和国 **Chūka Jinmin Kyōwakoku** People's Republic of China

日本人 **Nihonjin, Nipponjin** a Japanese

5 未亡人 **mibōjin** widow

仕掛人 **shika(ke)nin** intriguer, schemer, plotter

代理人 **dairinin** agent, proxy, substitute, representative

令夫人 **reifujin** Mrs., Lady, Madam; your wife

外国人 **gaikokujin** foreigner

8 知識人 **chishikijin** an intellectual

英国人 **Eikokujin** Briton, Englishman

9 保証人 **hoshōnin** guarantor

南蛮人 **nanbanjin** southern barbarians, the early Europeans

10 差出人 **sashidashinin** sender, return address

振出人 **furidashinin** remitter, issuer

料理人 **ryōrinin** a cook

11 貧乏人 **binbōnin** poor man, pauper

現代人 **gendaijin** people today

産婦人科 **sanfujinka** obstetrics and gynecology

第一人者 **dai-ichininsha** foremost/leading person

12 媒酌人 **baishakunin** matchmaker, go-between

朝鮮人 **Chōsenjin** a Korean

13 義理人情 **giri-ninjō** duty versus/ and human feelings

14 管理人 **kanrinin** manager, superintendent

15 誰一人 **dare hitori (mo)** (with negative) no one

——— 4 ———

2 八方美人 **happō bijin** one who is affable to everybody

6 同名異人 **dōmei-ijin** different person of the same name

7 社団法人 **shadan hōjin** corporate juridical person

10 財団法人 **zaidan hōjin** (incorporated) foundation

——— 1 ———

个 → 個 **2a8.36**

——— 2 ———

2a2.1 冖 亻 孑 3 6

仔 仔仔

SHI, ko (animal) offspring

——— 1 ———

4 仔犬 **koinu** puppy

11 仔細 **shisai** reasons, circumstances; significance; details

仂 → 働 **2a11.1**

2a2.4 冖 亻 十 3 12

仇 仇仇

KYŪ, ada, kataki enemy; enmity; revenge; harm, evil, ruin; invasion

——— 1 ———

10 仇討 **adau(chi)** vendetta, revenge

15 仇敵 **kyūteki** bitter enemy

2a2.5 / 583 冖 亻 竹 3 17

仏 佛｜仏仏

BUTSU Buddha, Buddhism
FUTSU France, French **hotoke** Buddha; Buddhist image; the dead

——— 1 ———

4 仏文 **Futsubun** French, French literature

仏心 **busshin, hotokegokoro** Buddha's heart

7 仏陀 **Butsuda, Budda** Buddha

8 仏典 **butten** Buddhist literature/ scriptures

仏具 **butsugu** Buddhist altar articles

10 仏徒 **butto** a Buddhist

仏教 **bukkyō** Buddhism

11 仏頂面 **butchōzura** sour face, pout, scowl

13 仏僧 **bussō** Buddhist priest

仏滅 **butsumetsu** Buddha's death; unlucky day

14 仏像 **butsuzō** image of Buddha

仏様 **hotoke-sama** a Buddha; deceased person

仏閣 **bukkaku** Buddhist temple

16 仏壇 **butsudan** household Buddhist altar

——————— 2 ———————

3 大仏 **daibutsu** huge image of Buddha

4 日仏 **Nichi-Futsu** Japan and France

石仏 **ishibotoke, sekibutsu** stone image of Buddha

9 神仏 **shinbutsu** gods and Buddha; Shinto and Buddhism

12 喉仏 **nodobotoke** Adam's apple

——————— 3 ———————

3 大乗仏教 **Daijō Bukkyō** Mahayana Buddhism, Great-Vehicle Buddhism

2a2.6 / 254

化

化化

KA make into, transform, -ization
KE, ba(kasu) bewitch, enchant, deceive **ba(keru)** take the form of, disguise oneself as

——————— 1 ———————

0 グローバル化 **gurōbaruka** globalization

6 化成 **kasei** transformation, chemical synthesis

7 化学 **kagaku** chemistry (sometimes pronounced *bakegaku* to avoid confusion with 科学, science)

8 化物 **ba(ke)mono** ghost, spook

12 化粧品 **keshōhin** cosmetics, make-up

17 化繊 **kasen** synthetic fiber

——————— 2 ———————

4 文化 **bunka** culture, civilization

文化日 **Bunka (no) Hi** Culture Day (November 3)

文化財 **bunkazai** cultural asset

6 光化学スモッグ **kōkagaku sumoggu** photochemical smog

8 厚化粧 **atsugeshō** heavy makeup

9 俗化 **zokka** vulgarization, popularization

変化 **henka** change **henge** goblin, apparition

美化 **bika** beautification; glorification

浄化 **jōka** purification

茶化 **chaka(su)** make fun of

10 帰化 **kika** become naturalized

進化 **shinka** evolution

消化 **shōka** digest

消化不良 **shōka furyō** indigestion

11 道化 **dōke** clowning

強化 **kyōka** strengthen, fortify

悪化 **akka** worsening, deterioration

軟化 **nanka** softening

12 硬化 **kōka** hardening

13 孵化 **fuka** incubation, hatching

14 酸化 **sanka** oxidation

16 激化 **gekka, gekika** intensification, aggravation

薄化粧 **usugeshō** light makeup

——————— 3 ———————

1 一元化 **ichigenka** unification, centralization

一般化 **ippanka** generalization, popularization

6 合理化 **gōrika** rationalization, streamlining

8 国際化 **kokusaika** internationalization

具体化 **gutaika** embodiment, materialization

11 現代化 **gendaika** modernization

情報化社会 **jōhōka shakai** information-oriented society

14 誤魔化 **gomaka(su)** cheat, deceive; gloss over; tamper with, doctor

16 機械化 **kikaika** mechanization, mechanized

¹⁷ 擬人化 **gijinka** personification

――――― 4 ―――――

¹² 無形文化財 **mukei-bunkazai** intangible cultural asset

2a2.8 / 1619   囗 亻 二

JIN, NI virtue, benevolence; man **NIN** kernel HITOSHI (m. given name) HITO (part of given name)

――――― 1 ―――――

¹⁰ 仁恵 **jinkei** graciousness, benevolence, mercy
¹³ 仁義 **jingi** humanity and justice; duty; moral code (of a gang)
   仁愛 **jin'ai** benevolence, charity, love

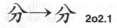 分→分 2o2.1

 公→公 2o2.2

2a2.9 / 453   日 亻 儿

KAI be in between, mediate; concern oneself with; shell, shellfish SUKE (part of male given name)

――――― 1 ―――――

² 介入 **kainyū** intervention
⁶ 介在 **kaizai** lie between
¹³ 介意 **kaii** care about, concern oneself with

――――― 2 ―――――

⁴ 不介入 **fukainyū** noninvolvement, nonintervention
   厄介 **yakkai** troublesome, burdensome; help, care
   厄介者 **yakkaimono** a dependent; nuisance

⁶ 仲介者 **chūkaisha** mediator, intermediary, middleman
¹¹ 悠介 **Yūsuke** (m. given name)
   紹介 **shōkai** introduction, presentation
   紹介状 **shōkaijō** letter of introduction
¹² 媒介 **baikai** mediation; matchmaking
   裕介 **Yūsuke** (m. given name)
¹⁷ 駿介 **Shunsuke** (m. given name)

――――― 4 ―――――

⁶ 自己紹介 **jiko shōkai** introduce oneself

2a2.10 / 51   日 亻 一

KON, KIN now, the present, this **ima, ima(ya)** now KON (surname)

――――― 1 ―――――

⁴ 今井 **Imai** (surname)
   今月 **kongetsu** this month
   今日 **kyō, konnichi** today
⁵ 今生 **konjō** this life/world
   今田 **Imada** (surname)
⁶ 今年 **kotoshi** this year
   今回 **konkai** this time, lately
⁷ 今更 **imasara** now, at this late date
   今村 **Imamura** (surname)
⁸ 今夜 **kon'ya** tonight
   今昔 **konjaku** past and present
⁹ 今後 **kongo** after this, henceforth
   今度 **kondo** this time; next time
¹⁰ 今週 **konshū** this week
   今時 **imadoki** today, nowadays; this time of day
¹¹ 今頃 **imagoro** at about this time
¹² 今期 **konki** the present/current term
   今朝 **kesa, konchō** this morning
   今晩 **konban** this evening, tonight

――――― 2 ―――――

⁵ 古今 **kokon** ancient and modern times, all ages

古今東西 **kokon-tōzai** all ages and places

古今和歌集 **Kokinwakashū** (poetry anthology, early tenth century)

古今集 **Kokinshū** (see preceding entry)

只今 **tadaima** just now

9 昨今 **sakkon** nowadays, recently

11 唯今 **tadaima** right/just now

久 → **0a3.7**

3

2a3.1 / 1891

SEN hermit; wizard

1
---

5 仙台 **Sendai** (city, Miyagi-ken)

2
---

12 雲仙岳 **Unzendake** (mountain, Nagasaki-ken)

2a3.2 / 333

SHI, JI, tsuka(eru) serve, work for

1
---

3 仕上 **shia(ge)** finish, finishing touches

4 仕切 **shiki(ri)** partition; settlement of accounts; toeing the mark (in sumo)

仕込 **shiko(mu)** train, bring up; fit into; stock up on

仕方 **shikata** way, method, means, how to

5 仕付 **shitsu(ke)** tacking, basting

仕立 **shita(te)** sewing, tailoring; outfitting

6 仕返 **shikae(shi)** get even, give tit for tat; do over again

8 仕事 **shigoto** work

仕放題 **shihōdai** have one's own way

11 仕掛 **shikaka(ri)** beginning **shika(ke)** contrivance, device; scale, size; half finished

仕掛人 **shika(ke)nin** intriguer, schemer, plotter

仕組 **shiku(mi)** construction; contrivance, mechanism; plan

13 仕業 **shiwaza** act, deed

仕損 **shisoko(nau), shison(jiru)** make a mistake, fail, blunder

14 仕様 **shiyō** specifications; way, method

15 仕舞 **shima(u)** finish, end; put away; close, wind up

2
---

8 奉仕 **hōshi** service

泥仕合 **dorojiai** mudslinging

10 針仕事 **hari shigoto** needlework, sewing

12 給仕 **kyūji** wait on; waiter, waitress, bellhop

2a3.3 / 256

DAI, TAI generation, age, era; charge, fee **ka(eru)** change, exchange, replace, substitute **ka(waru)** take the place of **yo** generation **shiro** price; substitution; materials

---
1
---

2 代人 **dainin** proxy, deputy, substitute

5 代用 **daiyō** substitute

6 代任 **dainin** acting for another; deputy

代名詞 **daimeishi** pronoun

代行者 **daikōsha** agent, proxy

7 代作 **daisaku** ghostwriting

代役 **daiyaku** substitute, stand-in, understudy

8 代表 **daihyō** representation, typical; a delegate

代表者 **daihyōsha** a representative

代金 **daikin** price, charge, the money/bill

11 代理人 **dairinin** agent, proxy, substitute, representative

代理店 **dairiten** agent, agency

12 代替 **daitai, daiga(e)** substitute, alternative

14 代演 **daien** substitute for another actor

17 代謝 **taisha** metabolism

20 代議員 **daigiin** representative, delegate

_____ 2 _____

1 一代 **ichidai** one generation; a lifetime; an age

2 十代 **jūdai** the teens, teenage

3 千代 **Chiyo** (f. given name)

千代子 **Chiyoko** (f. given name)

5 世代 **sedai** generation

古代 **kodai** ancient times, antiquity

田代 **Tashiro** (surname)

6 年代 **nendai** age, period, era; date

年代順 **nendaijun** chronological order

交代 **kōtai** take turns, alternate, relieve, work in shifts

近代 **kindai** modern

近代的 **kindaiteki** modern

7 身代 **shindai** fortune, property, estate **migawa(ri)** substitute, vicarious **mi(no)shiro** ransom money

身代金 **mi(no)shirokin** ransom money

君代 **Kimi(ga)yo** (Japan's national anthem)

初代 **shodai** the first generation; the founder

8 肩代 **kataga(wari)** change of palanquin bearers; takeover, transfer (of a business)

9 前代未聞 **zendai-mimon** unprecedented

美代子 **Miyoko** (f. given name)

10 時代 **jidai** era, period, age

時代劇 **jidaigeki** period/costume drama

11 現代 **gendai** the present age, today, modern times

現代人 **gendaijin** people today

現代化 **gendaika** modernization

現代語 **gendaigo** modern language

14 歴代 **rekidai** successive generations

嘉代 **Kayo, Yoshinori** (given name)

総代 **sōdai** representative, delegate

_____ 3 _____

2 二十代 **nijūdai** in one's twenties

6 次世代 **jisedai** next-generation (product)

13 新時代 **shinjidai** new era

_____ 4 _____

1 一世一代 **issei ichidai** once in a lifetime

2 二十年代 **nijūnendai** the '20s

5 幼年時代 **yōnen jidai** childhood

石器時代 **sekki jidai** the Stone Age

13 戦国時代 **sengoku jidai** era of civil wars

2a3.4 / 120 　　　　口 イ 十 丨
　　　　　　　　 3 12 2

他　　　　他 他

TA, hoka another, other

_____ 1 _____

2 他人 **tanin** someone else, others, outsider

他力 **tariki** outside help; salvation by faith

4 他方 **tahō** another side/direction; on the other hand

8 他国 **takoku** foreign country; another province

他所 **tasho** another place

9 他面 **tamen** the other side, on the other hand

他界 **takai** the next world; die

10 他殺 **tasatsu** murder

11 他動詞 **tadōshi** transitive verb

13 他愛 **taai** altruism

— 2 —

⁶ 自他 **jita** self and others; transitive and intransitive

¹¹ 排他的 **haitateki** exclusive

2a3.6 / 192

付 付付

FU attach, affix, set; refer, submit
tsu(keru) attach **tsu(ku)** be attached/connected; be in luck

— 1 —

³ 付与 **fuyo** give, grant, confer

⁵ 付加 **fuka** an addition **tsu(ke)kuwa(eru)** add

付加価値税 **fuka-kachi zei** value-added tax

付目 **tsu(ke)me** purpose; weak point to take advantage of

⁶ 付合 **tsu(ki)a(u)** keep company with, associate with **tsu(ke)a(wase)** vegetables added as relish

付近 **fukin** vicinity, neighborhood

⁸ 付和 **fuwa** blindly follow others

⁹ 付則 **fusoku** supplementary provisions, bylaws

¹⁰ 付値 **tsu(ke)ne** the price offered, bid

付随 **fuzui** incidental, concomitant, collateral

¹² 付着 **fuchaku** adhere, stick to

付属 **fuzoku** attached, associated, auxiliary

¹⁶ 付髭 **tsu(ke)hige** false mustache/beard

付録 **furoku** supplement, appendix

— 2 —

² 人付合 **hitozu(ki)a(i)** sociability

⁴ 片付 **katazu(keru)** put in order; put away; settle, dispose of; marry off **katazu(ku)** be put in order; be settled, be disposed of; get married off

日付 **hizuke** day, dating

火付 **hitsu(ke)** arson; instigator, firebrand **hitsu(ki)** kindling

⁵ 仕付 **shitsu(ke)** tacking, basting

目付 **metsu(ki)** a look, expression of the eyes

⁶ 気付 **kizu(ku)** notice, find out **kitsu(ke)** encouragement; resuscitation **-kizuke** in care of **ki (o) tsu(keru)** be careful, watch out **ki (ga) tsu(ku)** notice, realize

交付 **kōfu** deliver, furnish with

近付 **chikazu(ku)** come/go near, approach **chikazu(ki)** acquaintance

名付 **nazu(ke)** naming; fiancé(e) **nazu(keru)** name, call, entitle

⁷ 投付 **na(ge)tsu(keru)** throw at/against/down

吹付 **fu(ki)tsu(keru)** blow against

見付 **mitsu(keru)** find **mitsu(karu)** be found

⁸ 受付 **uketsuke** receipt, acceptance; reception desk; receptionist

追付 **o(i)tsu(ku)** catch up with

送付 **sōfu** send, forward, remit

味付 **ajitsu(ke)** seasoning

呼付 **yo(bi)tsu(keru)** call, send for, summon

⁹ 思付 **omo(i)tsu(ki)** idea, thought that comes to mind

¹⁰ 振付 **fu(ri)tsu(ke)** choreography

根付 **netsu(ke)** ornamental button for suspending a pouch from a belt

紐付 **himotsu(ki)** with strings attached

納付 **nōfu** payment, delivery

釘付 **kugizu(ke)** nailing (down); pegging (a price)

¹¹ 添付 **tenpu** attach, append

据付 **su(e)tsu(keru)** set into position, install

寄付 **kifu** contribution, donation **yo(se)tsu(keru)** let come near **yo(ri)tsu(ku)** come near; open (the day's trading)

疵付 **kizutsu(keru)** wound, injure; mar; besmirch

¹² 植付 **u(e)tsu(keru)** plant, implant

番付 **banzu(ke)** graded list, ranking

結付 **musu(bi)tsu(keru)** tie together, link

奥付 **okuzu(ke)** colophon

貼付 **chōfu, tenpu, ha(ri)tsu(keru)** stick, paste, affix

貸付 **ka(shi)tsu(keru)** lend

13 傷付 **kizutsu(keru)** injure, damage

裏付 **urazu(keru)** support, endorse, substantiate

飾付 **kaza(ri)tsu(ke)** decoration

15 瘤付 **kobutsu(ki)** wen; nuisance; with a child along

縋付 **suga(ri)tsu(ku)** cling to, depend on

糊付 **noritsu(ke)** starching; pasting

踏付 **fu(mi)tsu(keru)** trample; oppress; despise

16 燃付 **mo(e)tsu(ku)** catch fire, ignite

縛付 **shiba(ri)tsu(keru)** tie/fasten to

錆付 **sabitsu(ku)** rust (together/fast)

18 噛付 **ka(mi)tsu(ku)** bite/snap at

顔付 **kaotsu(ki)** face, look(s), expression

——————— 3 ———————

7 条件付 **jōkentsu(ki)** conditional

9 後片付 **atokatazu(ke)** straightening up afterwards, putting things in order

以→ **0a5.1**

仝→同 **2r4.2**

2a3.9 / 831   日 イ 一 丨
          3 1 2

令   令 令

REI order, command; good; (honorific prefix) **RYŌ** law YOSHI (part of given name)

——————— 1 ———————

4 令夫人 **reifujin** Mrs., Lady, Madam; your wife

7 令状 **reijō** warrant, writ

16 令嬢 **reijō** your daughter, young lady

——————— 2 ———————

5 司令 **shirei** command, control; commander

司令部 **shireibu** headquarters, the command

6 年令 **nenrei** age

7 条令 **jōrei** law, ordinance, rule, regulation

8 使令 **shirei** a directive

命令 **meirei** command, order

命令形 **meireikei** imperative form

法令 **hōrei** laws and (cabinet or ministerial) orders

9 発令 **hatsurei** announce officially, issue

勅令 **chokurei** imperial edict

指令 **shirei** order, instructions

政令 **seirei** government ordinance, cabinet order

10 訓令 **kunrei** instructions, directive

訓令式 **kunreishiki** (a system of romanization which differs from Hepburn romanization in such syllables as *shi/si, tsu/tu, cha/tya*)

——————— 3 ———————

7 戒厳令 **kaigenrei** martial law

14 総司令 **sōshirei** general headquarters, supreme command

——————— 4 ———————

2a4.1 / 1356   囗 彳 イ
          27 3

伏 伏伏

FUKU, fu(su) bend down, prostrate oneself **fu(seru)** turn downward; cover; lay (pipes); conceal **fu(shite)** bowing down; respectfully

——————— 1 ———————

6 伏在 **fukuzai** lie hidden

— 2 —

9 待伏 **ma(chi)bu(se)** ambush, lying in wait

10 俯伏 **utsubu(su)** lie face down
fufuku lie prostrate

11 捩伏 **ne(ji)fu(seru)** throw/hold (someone) down

15 潜伏 **senpuku** hide, be hidden; be dormant/latent

2a4.2 / 60 　　□ 木 イ
　　　　　　　　　41　3

休休

KYŪ, yasu(mu) rest; take the day off
yasu(meru) rest, set at ease
yasu(maru) be rested, feel at ease
yasu(mi) rest, break, vacation, absence　YASU, YOSHI (part of given name)

— 1 —

4 休止 **kyūshi** pause, suspension, dormancy

休日 **kyūjitsu** holiday, day off

休火山 **kyūkazan** dormant volcano

7 休学 **kyūgaku** absence from school

10 休校 **kyūkō** school closing

休息 **kyūsoku** rest

休航 **kyūkō** suspension of ship or airline service

12 休診 **kyūshin** see no patients, Clinic Closed

13 休業 **kyūgyō** suspension of business, Shop Closed

休暇 **kyūka** holiday, vacation, leave of absence

休戦 **kyūsen** truce, cease-fire

15 休養 **kyūyō** rest, recreation

16 休憩 **kyūkei** recess, break, intermission

18 休職 **kyūshoku** temporary retirement from office, layoff

— 2 —

1 一休 **hitoyasu(mi)** a rest

4 公休日 **kōkyūbi** legal holiday

5 冬休 **fuyuyasu(mi)** winter vacation

8 定休日 **teikyūbi** regular holiday, Closed (Tuesday)s

9 連休 **renkyū** consecutive holidays

昼休 **hiruyasu(mi)** lunch/noon-time break

10 遊休 **yūkyū** idle, unused

骨休 **honeyasu(me)** relaxation, recreation

夏休 **natsuyasu(mi)** summer vacation

息休 **kyūsoku** a rest, breather

11 運休 **unkyū** (train) cancelled, not running

12 無休 **mukyū** no holidays, always open (shop)

17 臨休 **rinkyū** special holiday (short for 臨時休校 or 臨時休業)

— 3 —

10 振替休日 **furikae kyūjitsu** substitute holiday (for one falling on a Sunday)

2a4.4 / 732 　　□ 牛 イ
　　　　　　　　　47　3

件件

KEN case, matter, item　**kudan, kudari** the aforesaid

— 2 —

1 一件 **ikken** a matter, an item

2 人件費 **jinkenhi** personnel expenses

5 用件 **yōken** business, things to be done

7 条件 **jōken** condition, stipulation

条件付 **jōkentsu(ki)** conditional

8 事件 **jiken** case, affair, incident

物件 **bukken** thing, article, physical object, a property

— 3 —

8 怪事件 **kaijiken** strange/mystery case

12 無条件 **mujōken** unconditional

2a4.5 / 1509 ⬜ 戈 亻
52 3

伐

伐 伐

BATSU, u(tsu) strike, attack; punish; cut

—————— 1 ——————

11 伐採 **bassai** felling, deforestation, cutting

—————— 2 ——————

8 征伐 **seibatsu** subjugate, conquer, punish, exterminate

2a4.6 / 2011 ⬜ ≡ 亻 丨
39 3 2

伊

伊 伊

I that one; Italy **I, KORE, YOSHI, TA-DA, ISA** (part of given name) **OSAMU** (m. given name)

—————— 1 ——————

7 伊豆半島 **Izu-hantō** Izu Peninsula (Shizuoka-ken)
8 伊東 **Itō** (surname)
11 伊達 **Date** (surname)
13 伊勢大神宮 **Ise Daijingū** the Grand Shrines of Ise
伊勢蝦 **ise-ebi** spiny lobster
18 伊藤 **Itō** (surname)

—————— 2 ——————

4 日伊 **Nichi-I** Japan and Italy

住 → 住 **2a5.19**

2a4.7 / 1347 ⬜ 口 亻 丨
24 3 2

仲

仲 仲

CHŪ, naka relationship

—————— 1 ——————

2 仲人 **nakōdo, chūnin** go-between, matchmaker
4 仲介者 **chūkaisha** mediator, intermediary, middleman
5 仲好 **nakayo(shi)** good friends
仲立 **nakada(chi)** intermediation; agent, broker; go-between
仲田 **Nakada, Nakata** (surname)
7 仲良 **nakayo(ku)** on friendly terms **nakayo(shi)** good friends
8 仲直 **nakanao(ri)** reconciliation, make up
12 仲裁 **chūsai** arbitration, mediation
仲買 **nakaga(i)** broking, brokerage
仲間 **nakama** member of a group, mate, fellow **chūgen** samurai's attendant
仲間外 **nakamahazu(re)** being left out

—————— 2 ——————

4 不仲 **funaka** discord, on bad terms with

—————— 3 ——————

4 犬猿仲 **ken'en (no) naka** hating each other

2a4.8 / 2013 ⬜ 亻 一 一
3 14 1

伍

伍 伍

GO five; five-man squad; file, line; rank/associate with **HIROSHI, ATSUMU** (m. given name) **GO, ITSU, KUMI, TOMO** (part of given name)

—————— 1 ——————

8 伍長 **gochō** corporal, staff sergeant

2a4.9 / 334 ⬜ 王 亻
46 3

任

任 任

NIN duties, responsibility; tenure **ma-ka(seru/su)** entrust to, leave it to

⁸ 任命 **ninmei** appoint, nominate

¹¹ 任務 **ninmu** duty, task, function

¹² 任期 **ninki** term of office, tenure

¹³ 任意 **nin'i** optional, voluntary, discretionary, arbitrary

— 2 —

² 人任 **hitomaka(se)** leaving it to others

³ 口任 **kuchimaka(se)** random talk

⁵ 出任 **demaka(se)** saying whatever comes to mind

代任 **dainin** acting for another; deputy

主任 **shunin** person in charge

⁶ 気任 **kimaka(se)** at one's pleasure/fancy

先任者 **senninsha** predecessor

⁷ 初任給 **shoninkyū** starting salary

⁸ 委任 **inin** trust, mandate, authorization

⁹ 専任 **sennin** exclusive duty, full-time

重任 **jūnin** heavy responsibility; re-election, reappointment

叙任 **jonin** appointment, investiture

前任者 **zenninsha** one's predecessor

赴任 **funin** proceed to one's new post

後任 **kōnin** successor

¹⁰ 兼任 **kennin** concurrent post

¹¹ 常任委員会 **jōnin iinkai** standing committee

責任 **sekinin** responsibility, liability

責任感 **sekininkan** sense of responsibility

転任 **tennin** change of assignments/personnel

¹² 就任 **shūnin** assumption of office

¹³ 解任 **kainin** dismissal, release

辞任 **jinin** resign

— 3 —

⁴ 不信任 **fushinnin** nonconfidence

¹² 無責任 **musekinin** irresponsibility

2a4.10 / 1056 　　田 亻 厂 阝
　　　　　　　　　 3　18　 7

仰

仰仰

GYŌ, KŌ, ao(gu) look up; look up to, respect; ask for, depend on; drink **os(sharu)** say (polite) **ōse** what you say (polite)

— 1 —

⁴ 仰天 **gyōten** be astounded

⁶ 仰向 **aomu(keru)** turn to face upward

— 2 —

⁹ 信仰 **shinkō** religious faith, belief in

似 → 2a5.11

2a4.13 / 2012 　　田 亻 十 又
　　　　　　　　 3　12　 9

伎

伎伎

GI deed; skill　**GI, KI, SHI** (part of given name)

— 3 —

¹⁴ 歌舞伎 **kabuki** kabuki

2a4.14 / 434 　　田 亻 二 竹
　　　　　　　　 3　 4　17

伝

傳 | 伝伝

DEN, TEN transmit; legend, tradition **tsuta(eru)** tell, convey, transmit **tsuta(waru)** be conveyed transmitted; be handed down　**tsuta(u)** go/walk along　TSUTAE (f. given name)

— 1 —

⁷ 伝承 **denshō** transmit, hand down (folklore)

⁸ 伝送 **densō** transmit, relay

⁹ 伝染病 **densenbyō** contagious/communicable disease

10 伝記 **denki** biography
11 伝達 **dentatsu** transmit, convey, propagate
伝道 **dendō** evangelism, proselytizing, missionary work
伝票 **denpyō** slip of paper
12 伝統 **dentō** tradition
伝統的 **dentōteki** traditional
14 伝説 **densetsu** legend
伝聞 **denbun** hearsay, report, rumor

───── 2 ─────

3 口伝 **kuchizute, kuchizuta(e)** word of mouth, oral tradition
6 自伝 **jiden** autobiography
7 言伝 **i(i)tsuta(eru)** hand down (a legend), spread (a rumor) **kotozu(te)** hearsay; message
9 宣伝 **senden** propaganda; advertising, publicity
宣伝部 **sendenbu** publicity department
12 超伝導 **chōdendō** superconductivity
14 遺伝 **iden** heredity

───── 3 ─────

6 自叙伝 **jijoden** autobiography

2a4.15 / 1049   囗 亻 厂 又
3 18 9

假｜仮仮

KA, KE, kari temporary, provisional; supposing; assumed (name), false

───── 1 ─────

6 仮死 **kashi** suspended animation, apparent death
仮名 **kana** kana, Japanese syllabary character **kamei, kemyō, karina** pseudonym, alias, pen name
8 仮免状 **karimenjō** temporary license; provisional diploma
仮定 **katei** supposition, assumption, hypothesis
仮性 **kasei** false (symptoms)
9 仮面 **kamen** mask, disguise

仮相 **kasō** appearance, phenomenon
10 仮眠 **kamin** nap
仮称 **kashō** tentative/provisional/working name
仮病 **kebyō** feigned illness
11 仮釈放 **karishakuhō** release on parole
12 仮装 **kasō** disguise, fancy dress; converted (cruiser)
13 仮想 **kasō** imaginary, supposed, virtual (mass), hypothetical
14 仮説 **kasetsu** hypothesis, tentative theory

───── 2 ─────

4 片仮名 **katakana** katakana, the non-cursive syllabary
5 平仮名 **hiragana** (the cursive syllabary)
8 送仮名 **oku(ri)gana** suffixed kana showing inflection
10 振仮名 **fu(ri)gana** (small kana written above or beside a kanji to show its pronunciation)

2a4.16 / 89   日 王 亻
46 3

全

全｜全全

ZEN all **matta(ku)** completely; truly, indeed **matto(u suru)** accomplish, fulfill **TAMOTSU** (m. given name) **MASA** (part of given name)

───── 1 ─────

2 全力 **zenryoku** one's every effort, full capacity
3 全土 **zendo** the whole country
4 全文 **zenbun** full text; whole sentence
全日本 **zen-Nihon, zen-Nippon** all Japan
全日空 **Zennikkū** ANA = All Nippon Airways (short for 全日本空輸)
5 全世界 **zensekai** the whole world
6 全米 **zen-Bei** all-America(n), pan-American
7 全身 **zenshin** the whole body

全体 **zentai** the whole, in all

全快 **zenkai** complete recovery, full cure

8 全長 **zenchō** overall length

全治 **zenchi, zenji** fully recover, heal completely

全知 **zenchi** onmiscience

全国 **zenkoku, zengoku** the whole country, nationwide, national

全国民 **zenkokumin** the entire nation

9 全１０巻 **zen-jikkan** ten volumes in all

全面的 **zenmenteki** all-out, full, general

10 全部 **zenbu** all, whole; entirely

全員 **zen'in** all the members, the whole staff/crew

全能 **zennō** omnipotence

全般的 **zenpanteki** general, overall, across-the-board

11 全盛期 **zenseiki** golden age, heyday

全訳 **zen'yaku** complete translation

12 全備 **zenbi** fully equipped, complete, perfect

全幅 **zenpuku** overall width; utmost

全景 **zenkei** complete view, panorama

全焼 **zenshō** be totally destroyed by fire

全然 **zenzen** entirely, utterly, (not) at all

全集 **zenshū** complete works

全開 **zenkai** open fully

13 全滅 **zenmetsu** annihilation

全損 **zenson** total loss

全数 **zensū** the whole number, all

15 全権大使 **zenken taishi** ambassador plenipotentiary

全編 **zenpen** the whole book

16 全壊 **zenkai** complete destruction

17 全優 **zen'yū** straight A's

18 全額 **zengaku** the full amount

— 2 —

3 万全 **banzen** perfect, sure, prudent

6 安全 **anzen** safety

安全第一 **anzen dai-ichi** Safety First

7 完全 **kanzen** complete, perfect

10 健全 **kenzen** healthy, sound

— 3 —

4 不完全 **fukanzen** incomplete, imperfect, faulty, defective

2a4.17 / 481

日 イ ├ 亠
3 13 11

KI, **kuwada(teru)** plan, scheme, intend; attempt, undertake **taku(ramu)** scheme, devise, contrive, plot

— 1 —

8 企画 **kikaku** plan, planning

13 企業 **kigyō** enterprise, corporation

企業家 **kigyōka** industrialist, entrepreneur

— 2 —

3 小企業 **shōkigyō** small enterprises/business

— 3 —

4 中小企業 **chūshō kigyō** small business(es)

2a4.18 / 159

目 𠘨 イ 一
24 3 1

GŌ, GA', KA' together; total; (unit of area, 0.33 square meters); (unit of volume, 180 ml); one of ten stations up a mountain; total **a(u)** fit, match, agree with, be correct **a(waseru), a(wasu)** put together, combine, compare

— 1 —

0 合カギ **aikagi** duplicate key; passkey; Keys Made

5 合弁会社 **gōben-gaisha** joint venture (company)

6 合成 **gōsei** synthetic, composite, combined

7 合作 **gassaku** joint work, collaboration

合図 **aizu** signal, sign

8 合併 **gappei** merger, consolidation

合法 **gōhō** legality, lawfulness

合金 **gōkin** alloy

9 合奏 **gassō** concert, ensemble

合点 **gaten, gatten** understand, comprehend; consent to

10 合格 **gōkaku** pass (an exam/inspection)

合致 **gatchi** agreement, concurrence, conforming to

11 合唱団 **gasshōdan** chorus, choir

合宿 **gasshuku** lodging together

合理化 **gōrika** rationalization, streamlining

合理的 **gōriteki** rational, reasonable, logical

12 合衆国 **Gasshūkoku** United States

合間 **a(i)ma** interval

13 合戦 **kassen** battle

合意 **gōi** mutual consent, agreement

16 合憲性 **gōkensei** constitutionality

20 合議制 **gōgisei** parliamentary system

———— 2 ————

3 工合 **guai** condition, state; convenience; state of health

4 不合格 **fugōkaku** failure (in an exam), rejection, disqualification

不合理 **fugōri** unreasonable, irrational

分合 **wa(ke)a(u), wa(kachi)a(u)** share

込合 **ko(mi)a(u)** be crowded

5 出合 **dea(u)** happen to meet, run into; rendezvous **da(shi)a(u)** contribute jointly, share the expenses

付合 **tsu(ki)a(u)** keep company with, associate with **tsu(ke)a(wase)** vegetables added as relish

巡合 **megu(ri)a(u)** chance to meet

打合 **u(chi)a(u)** hit each other, exchange blows **u(chi)a(waseru)** strike (one thing) against (another); prearrange **u(chi)a(wase)** previous arrangement, appointed (hour)

6 迎合 **geigō** flattery, ingratiation

向合 **mu(kai)a(u)** face each other

光合成 **kōgōsei** photosynthesis

有合 **a(ri)a(u)** happen to be on hand **a(ri)a(wase)** what is on hand

早合点 **hayagaten** hasty conclusion

百合 **yuri** lily

7 似合 **nia(u)** befit, go well with, be becoming **nia(washii)** suitable, becoming, well-matched

助合 **tasu(ke)a(u)** help one another

沖合 **okia(i)** open sea, offshore

折合 **o(ri)a(u)** come to an agreement

見合 **mia(u)** look at each other; offset **mia(i)** arranged-marriage interview **mia(waseru)** exchange glances; set off against; postpone, abandon

8 非合法 **higōhō** illegal

非合理的 **higōriteki** unreasonable, irrational

併合 **heigō** annexation, amalgamation, merger

河合 **Kawai** (surname)

押合 **o(shi)a(u)** jostle one another

抱合 **da(ki)a(u)** embrace each other **da(ki)a(waseru)** cause to embrace **hōgō** combination; embrace

知合 **shi(ri)a(i)** an acquaintance **shi(ri)a(u)** know each other

歩合 **buai** rate, percentage; commission **ayu(mi)a(u)** compromise

9 連合 **rengō** union, league, federation, alliance, combination **tsu(re)a(i)** spouse, mate

通合 **tō(ri)a(waseru)** happen to come along **tsū(ji)a(u)** plot together

待合 **ma(chi)a(waseru)** wait for (as previously arranged) **ma(chi)a(i)** waiting room; geisha entertainment place

待合室 **machiaishitsu** waiting room

相合傘 **aia(i)gasa (de)** under the same umbrella

10 都合 **tsugō** circumstances; one's convenience; opportunity; arrangements

都合上 **tsugōjō** for convenience

11 混合 **kongō** mixture, mixed, compound
ma(ze)a(waseru) mix, blend, compound

組合 **ku(mi)a(u)** form a partnership; grapple with **kumiai** association, union
ku(mi)a(waseru) combine; fit together **ku(mi)a(wase)** combination

釣合 **tsu(ri)a(u)** be in balance, match **tsu(ri)a(i)** balance, equilibrium, proportion

問合 **to(i)a(waseru), to(i)a(wasu)** inquire

頃合 **koroa(i)** suitable time; propriety; moderation

12 割合 **wariai** rate, proportion, percentage; comparatively

場合 **baai** case, occasion, circumstances

落合 **Ochiai** (surname)

結合 **ketsugō** union, combination
musu(bi)a(waseru) tie together, combine

絡合 **kara(mi)a(u)** intertwine

統合 **tōgō** unify, integrate, combine

集合 **shūgō** gathering, meeting; set (in math)

間合 **ma (ni) a(u)** be in time for; serve the purpose, suffice

13 適合 **tekigō** conform to, suit, fit

照合 **te(rashi)a(waseru)** check by comparison **shōgō** check against, verify

睨合 **nira(mi)a(u)** glare at each other **nira(mi)a(waseru)** take (something) for comparison

触合 **fu(re)a(u)** touch, come in contact with

話合 **hana(shi)a(u)** talk over, discuss

試合 **shiai** game, match

鉢合 **hachia(wase)** bump heads; run into

14 憎合 **niku(mi)a(u)** hate one another

複合 **fukugō** composite, compound, complex

複合語 **fukugōgo** compound word

綜合 **sōgō** comprehensive, composite, synthetic

総合 **sōgō** synthesis, comprehensive

総合大学 **sōgō daigaku** university

語合 **kata(ri)a(u)** talk together, chat

15 請合 **u(ke)a(u)** undertake; guarantee, vouch for **u(ke)a(i)** sure, certain, guaranteed

調合 **chōgō** compounding, mixing

16 融合 **yūgō** fusion

17 聯合 **rengō** combination, league, coalition

18 嚙合 **ka(mi)a(u)** bite each other; (gears) engage, mesh with
ka(mi)a(waseru) clench (one's teeth); engage (gears), mesh with

19 繋合 **tsuna(gi)a(waseru)** join/tie together

騙合 **dama(shi)a(i)** cheating each other

20 競合 **kyōgō** competition, rivalry
se(ri)a(u) compete with, vie for

譲合 **yuzu(ri)a(u)** defer/yield to each other, compromise

―――――― 3 ――――――

2 人付合 **hitozu(ki)a(i)** sociability

4 不似合 **funia(i)** unbecoming, unsuitable, ill-matched

不都合 **futsugō** inconvenience, trouble, harm; impropriety, misconduct

5 好都合 **kōtsugō** favorable, good

6 再試合 **saishiai** rematch, resumption of a game

7 角突合 **tsunotsu(ki)a(i)** bickering, wrangling

8 泥仕合 **dorojiai** mudslinging

12 御都合 **gotsugō** your convenience

2

4

――――― 4 ―――――
4 公定歩合 **kōtei buai** official bank rate, rediscount rate
8 国際連合 **Kokusai Rengō** United Nations

2a4.19 / 158 目 亻 二 竹
3　4　17

KAI meeting; society, association
E understanding **a(u)** meet

――――― 1 ―――――
7 会社 **kaisha** company, corporation
会社員 **kaishain** company employee
会見 **kaiken** interview
8 会長 **kaichō** chairman, president
9 会計 **kaikei** accounting; the bill
会計士 **kaikeishi** accountant
10 会員 **kaiin** member
11 会釈 **eshaku** salutation, greeting, bow
12 会場 **kaijō** meeting place; grounds
会期 **kaiki** term, session (of a legislature)
13 会話 **kaiwa** conversation
15 会談 **kaidan** conversation, conference
16 会館 **kaikan** (assembly) hall
20 会議 **kaigi** conference, meeting
会議録 **kaigiroku** minutes, proceedings

――――― 2 ―――――
2 入会 **nyūkai** enrollment, admission
子会社 **kogaisha** a subsidiary
3 大会 **taikai** large/general meeting, conference, convention; tournament, meet
4 公会 **kōkai** public meeting
5 正会員 **seikaiin** full/regular member
司会者 **shikaisha** emcee, chairman
6 再会 **saikai** meeting again, reunion
7 学会 **gakkai** academic society
社会 **shakai** society, social

社会民主主義 **shakai minshu shugi** social democracy
社会主義 **shakai shugi** socialism
社会学 **shakaigaku** sociology
社会面 **shakaimen** local-news page
社会党 **shakaitō** socialist party
社会福祉 **shakai fukushi** social welfare
8 例会 **reikai** regular meeting
協会 **kyōkai** society, association
参会 **sankai** attendance (at a meeting)
英会話 **eikaiwa** English conversation
国会 **kokkai** national assembly, parliament, diet, congress
9 茶会 **chakai** tea party/ceremony
面会 **menkai** interview, meeting
10 都会 **tokai** city **Tokai** Tōkyō Assembly
宴会 **enkai** banquet, dinner party
教会 **kyōkai** church
11 副会長 **fukukaichō** (company) vice president
商会 **shōkai** company, firm
密会 **mikkai** clandestine meeting
脱会 **dakkai** withdrawal (from an organization)
閉会 **heikai** closing, adjournment
12 集会 **shūkai** meeting, assembly
開会 **kaikai** opening a meeting
開会式 **kaikaishiki** opening ceremony
13 碁会所 **gokaisho, gokaijo** go club
14 総会 **sōkai** general meeting, plenary session
16 機会 **kikai** opportunity, occasion, chance
親会社 **oyagaisha** parent company
20 議会 **gikai** parliament, diet, congress

――――― 3 ―――――
2 二次会 **nijikai** after-party party
3 大都会 **daitokai** big city
4 公聴会 **kōchōkai** public hearing
5 主脳会談 **shunō kaidan** summit conference

主脳会議 **shunō kaigi** summit conference

6 合弁会社 **gōben-gaisha** joint venture (company)

同窓会 **dōsōkai** alumni association/meeting

有限会社 **yūgen-gaisha** limited liability company, Ltd.

7 忘年会 **bōnenkai** year-end party

8 送別会 **sōbetsukai** going-away/farewell party

委員会 **iinkai** committee

9 首脳会談 **shunō kaidan** summit conference

茶話会 **sawakai, chawakai** tea party

10 党大会 **tōtaikai** (political) convention

座談会 **zadankai** round-table discussion, symposium

展示会 **tenjikai** show, exhibition

展覧会 **tenrankai** exhibition

株式会社 **kabushiki-gaisha, kabushiki kaisha** corporation, Co., Ltd.

討論会 **tōronkai** forum, debate, discussion

記者会見 **kisha kaiken** news/press conference

11 商工会議所 **Shōkō Kaigisho** Chamber of Commerce and Industry

運送会社 **unsō-gaisha** transport/express company

運動会 **undōkai** athletic meet

理事会 **rijikai** board of directors/trustees

12 博覧会 **hakurankai** exhibition, exposition, fair

貿易会社 **bōeki-gaisha** trading firm

14 演芸会 **engeikai** an entertainment, variety show

製薬会社 **seiyaku-gaisha** pharmaceutical company

15 舞踏会 **butōkai** ball, dance

審議会 **shingikai** deliberative assembly, commission, council

歓送会 **kansōkai** farewell party, send-off

17 懇談会 **kondankai** get-together, friendly discussion

懇親会 **konshinkai** social gathering

聴聞会 **chōmonkai** public hearing

講演会 **kōenkai** lecture meeting

───── 4 ─────

8 国連総会 **Kokuren Sōkai** UN General Assembly

───── 5 ─────

11 常任委員会 **jōnin iinkai** standing committee

情報化社会 **jōhōka shakai** information-oriented society

2a4.20 / 223
             3   20

NIKU meat, flesh

───── 1 ─────

7 肉体 **nikutai** the body/flesh

肉体的 **nikutaiteki** sensual, corporal

9 肉屋 **nikuya** butcher (shop)

肉食 **nikushoku** meat eating

11 肉欲 **nikuyoku** carnal desires

肉眼 **nikugan** the naked/unaided eye

13 肉感的 **nikkanteki** suggestive, sensual, voluptuous

16 肉親 **nikushin** blood relationship/relative

───── 2 ─────

4 中肉中背 **chūniku-chūzei** medium height and build

牛肉 **gyūniku** beef

5 皮肉 **hiniku** irony, sarcasm

6 朱肉 **shuniku** red ink pad

羊肉 **yōniku** mutton

10 挽肉 **hi(ki)niku** ground meat

弱肉強食 **jakuniku-kyōshoku** survival of the fittest

桜肉 **sakuraniku** horsemeat

骨肉 **kotsuniku** one's flesh and blood, kin

2 ☰

5 イ
亻
子
阝
刂
力
又
宀
宀
艹
宀
ク
ソ
厂
辶
冂
几
匸

¹¹ 豚肉 **butaniku** pork
鳥肉 **toriniku** chicken (meat)
¹² 焼肉 **ya(ki)niku** roast/broiled meat
筋肉 **kinniku** muscle
¹⁹ 鯨肉 **geiniku** whale meat
鶏肉 **keiniku** chicken (meat)

未 → 来 0a7.6

朱 → 0a6.13

─────── 5 ───────

2a5.1 / 122   ▯ 立 イ
54 3

位位

I rank, place, grade **kurai** rank; dignity; be located; throne, crown; (decimal) place **-kurai, -gurai** to the extent of, about

─────── 1 ───────

⁸ 位取 **kuraido(ri)** positioning of the ones digit within a number
⁹ 位相 **isō** phase
¹² 位牌 **ihai** Buddhist mortuary tablet
¹³ 位置 **ichi** position, location

─────── 2 ───────

¹ 一位 **ichii** first place/rank
³ 三位 **san'i, sanmi** third rank/place
下位 **kai** low rank, subordinate
⁴ 中位 **chūi** medium, average
chūgurai, chūkurai about medium/average
水位 **suii** water level
王位 **ōi** the throne, the crown
⁵ 本位 **hon'i** standard, basis, principle
主位 **shui** leading position, first place
⁶ 地位 **chii** position, status
⁷ 学位 **gakui** academic degree
⁹ 単位 **tan'i** unit, denomination
¹² 順位 **jun'i** ranking, standing
¹⁷ 爵位 **shakui** peerage, court rank

佛 → 仏 2a2.5

2a5.3 / 1108   ▯ 日 イ |
43 3 2

伸

伸伸

SHIN stretch **no(biru)** stretch, extend (intr.); grow **no(basu)** stretch, extend (tr.) **no(su)** stretch, spread, smooth out; gain influence
no(biyaka) comfortable, carefree **NOBU, SHIN** (part of given name)

─────── 1 ───────

¹ 伸一 **Shin'ichi, Nobukazu** (m. given name)
¹⁰ 伸悩 **no(bi)naya(mu)** be sluggish, stagnate, level off, mark time
¹¹ 伸張 **shinchō** extension, expansion
¹⁷ 伸縮 **shinshuku, no(bi)chiji(mi)** expansion and contraction; elastic, flexible

─────── 2 ───────

² 二伸 **nishin** postscript, P.S.
⁴ 欠伸 **akubi** yawn
⁸ 追伸 **tsuishin** postscript, P.S.

2a5.4 / 1027   ▯ 小 イ 二
35 3 4

伴伴

BAN, HAN, tomona(u) accompany, be accompanied by **TOMO** (part of given name)

─────── 1 ───────

⁹ 伴奏 **bansō** (musical) accompaniment
伴侶 **hanryo** companion

─────── 2 ───────

⁶ 同伴 **dōhan** accompany, go with

2a5.6 / 61   囗 木 イ 一
               41 3 1

體丨体体

TAI body; object, thing; style, form
TEI appearance; condition, state
karada body

─────────── 1 ───────────

² 体力 **tairyoku** physical strength
⁴ 体内 **tainai** inside the body, internal
⁷ 体系 **taikei** system, organization
  体言 **taigen** uninflected word
⁸ 体育館 **taiikukan** gymnasium
⁹ 体重 **taijū** one's weight
  体臭 **taishū** body odor; a characteristic
¹¹ 体得 **taitoku** realization, experience; comprehension, mastery
¹² 体温計 **taionkei** (clinical) thermometer
  体裁 **teisai** decency, form, appearance, effect
¹⁴ 体罰 **taibatsu** corporal punishment
¹⁶ 体操 **taisō** calisthenics, gymnastics
  体積 **taiseki** volume
¹⁸ 体験 **taiken** experience

─────────── 2 ───────────

¹ 一体 **ittai** one body; (what) in the world, (how) the devil; properly speaking; generally
² 人体 **jintai** the human body
³ 大体 **daitai** generally, on the whole; outline, summary; in substance; originally
⁴ 勿体無 **mottaina(i)** more than one deserves, too good for; wasteful
  文体 **buntai** (literary) style
⁵ 生体 **seitai** living body
  正体 **shōtai** one's true nature/character; in one's right mind, senses
  字体 **jitai** form of a character, typeface
  主体 **shutai** the subject; main part
  立体的 **rittaiteki** three-dimensional

⁶ 死体 **shitai** corpse, remains
  気体 **kitai** gas (not solid or liquid)
  全体 **zentai** the whole, in all
  肉体 **nikutai** the body/flesh
  肉体的 **nikutaiteki** sensual, corporal
  団体 **dantai** group, organization
  自体 **jitai** itself; one's own body
⁷ 身体 **shintai, karada** the body
  身体障害者 **shintai shōgaisha** physically handicapped person
  抗体 **kōtai** antibody
  形体 **keitai** form, shape, configuration
⁸ 実体 **jittai** substance, entity; three-dimensional
  肢体 **shitai** limbs; body and limbs
  物体 **buttai** body, object, substance
  具体化 **gutaika** embodiment, materialization
  具体的 **gutaiteki** concrete, specific, definite
⁹ 重体 **jūtai** in serious/critical condition
  連体形 **rentaikei** a participial adjective
  屍体 **shitai** corpse
  政体 **seitai** form/system of government
¹⁰ 弱体 **jakutai** weak, effete
  胴体 **dōtai** the body, torso; fuselage
  書体 **shotai** style of calligraphy/type
¹¹ 液体 **ekitai** liquid
  異体 **itai** different form, variant
¹³ 解体 **kaitai** dismantle
  裸体 **ratai** naked body, nudity
¹⁴ 遺体 **itai** corpse, remains
  導体 **dōtai** conductor (of electricity/heat)
¹⁶ 機体 **kitai** fuselage

─────────── 3 ───────────

⁴ 文語体 **bungotai** literary style
⁶ 自治体 **jichitai** self-governing body, municipality
¹⁰ 流動体 **ryūdōtai** a fluid

2

イ
冫
孑
阝
卩
刂
力
又
宀
亠
十
夂
丷
厂
辶
冂
八
匸

5

¹⁶ 親団体 **oyadantai** parent organization

2a5.7 / 1176   田 日 イ ｜
                           43   3   2

伯

伯伯

HAKU count, earl; eldest brother; uncle; chief official; Brazil   NORI (part of given name)

---------- 1 ----------

⁴ 伯父 **oji, hakufu** uncle
⁵ 伯母 **oba, hakubo** aunt
¹⁷ 伯爵 **hakushaku** count, earl

---------- 2 ----------

⁷ 佐伯 **Saeki** (surname)

2a5.8 / 2015   田 口 イ 十
                           24   3   12

佑

佑佑

YŪ, U help   YŪ, U, SUKE (part of given name)   TASUKU (m. given name)

2a5.9 / 1744   田 エ イ 十
                           38   3   12

佐

佐佐

SA help   SUKE (part of given name)

---------- 1 ----------

³ 佐川 **Sagawa, Sakawa** (surname)
   佐々木 **Sasaki** (surname)
⁶ 佐竹 **Satake** (surname)
⁷ 佐伯 **Saeki** (surname)
¹¹ 佐野 **Sano** (surname)
¹² 佐渡島 **Sado(ga)shima** (island, Niigata-ken)
   佐賀県 **Saga-ken** (prefecture)
¹⁸ 佐藤 **Satō** (surname)

---------- 2 ----------

¹⁴ 輔佐 **hosa** assistance; assistant, adviser

2a5.10 / 360   口 イ ヒ
                           3   15   13

作

作作

SAKU, SA a work/production; tillage; harvest, crop   **tsuku(ru)** make

---------- 1 ----------

⁴ 作文 **sakubun** composition, writing
   作方 **tsuku(ri)kata** how to make; style of building, construction, workmanship
⁵ 作用 **sayō** action, function, effect
⁶ 作曲家 **sakkyokuka** composer
   作成 **sakusei** draw up, prepare
⁸ 作事 **tsuku(ri)goto** fiction, fabrication
   作法 **sahō** manners, etiquette
   作者 **sakusha** author
⁹ 作品 **sakuhin** a work
¹⁰ 作家 **sakka** writer, novelist
¹³ 作業 **sagyō** work, operations
   作戦 **sakusen** (military) operation, tactics
   作話 **tsuku(ri)banashi** made-up story, fabrication, fable
¹⁴ 作製 **sakusei** manufacture

---------- 2 ----------

³ 工作 **kōsaku** construction, engineering; handicraft; maneuver, scheme
   大作 **taisaku** masterpiece, a monumental work
   下作 **gesaku** poorly made, of inferior quality
⁴ 不作 **fusaku** bad harvest, crop failure
   不作法 **busahō** bad manners, discourtesy
   凶作 **kyōsaku** bad harvest, crop failure
   反作用 **hansayō** reaction

手作 **tezuku(ri)** handmade, home-made

5 代作 **daisaku** ghostwriting

6 多作 **tasaku** prolific writing

合作 **gassaku** joint work, collaboration

8 佳作 **kasaku** an excellent work

制作 **seisaku** a work, production

逆作用 **gyakusayō** adverse effect, reaction

9 発作 **hossa** fit, spasm, an attack of

造作 **zōsaku** house fixtures; facial features **zōsa** trouble, difficulty **zōsa(nai)** easy, simple

10 耕作 **kōsaku** cultivation, farming

耕作物 **kōsakubutsu** farm products

原作 **gensaku** the original work

11 偽作 **gisaku** a spurious work, a forgery

動作 **dōsa** action, movements, motion; bearing, behavior

著作 **chosaku** writing, authorship

著作権 **chosakuken** copyright

盗作 **tōsaku** plagiarism

12 創作 **sōsaku** a creation/work

無作法 **busahō** bad manners, rudeness

13 傑作 **kessaku** masterpiece

農作 **nōsaku** cultivation, tillage, farming

豊作 **hōsaku** abundant harvest

新作 **shinsaku** a new work/composition

14 製作 **seisaku** manufacturing, production

駄作 **dasaku** poor work, worthless stuff

16 操作 **sōsa** operation, handling, control

18 濫作 **ransaku** overproduction

━━━━━━━ 3 ━━━━━━━

5 礼儀作法 **reigisahō** etiquette, courtesy, propriety

処女作 **shojosaku** one's first (published) work

14 閨秀作家 **keishū sakka** woman writer

2a5.11 / 1486   ⊞ イ丨
                 3 2

似   似 似

JI, ni(ru) be similar, resemble

ni(seru) imitate; counterfeit

I (part of given name)

━━━━━━━ 1 ━━━━━━━

6 似合 **nia(u)** befit, go well with, be becoming **nia(washii)** suitable, becoming, well-matched

8 似非 **ni(te)hi(naru)** alike only in appearance **ese-** false, would-be, pseudo-

18 似顔絵 **nigaoe** portrait, likeness

━━━━━━━ 2 ━━━━━━━

4 不似合 **funia(i)** unbecoming, unsuitable, ill-matched

8 空似 **sorani** chance resemblance

10 真似 **mane** imitation, mimicry; behavior; pretense

14 疑似 **giji-** suspected, sham, pseudo-, dummy, simulated

18 類似 **ruiji** similarity, resemblance

━━━━━━━ 3 ━━━━━━━

2 人真似 **hitomane** mimicry, imitations

3 口真似 **kuchimane** mimicry

13 猿真似 **sarumane** monkey-see monkey-do

仰 → **2a4.10**

2a5.12 / 2014   ⊞ 口イ力
                24 3 8

伽   伽 伽

KYA, GA, KA, togi nursing, nurse; attend on, keep entertained; attendant

KYA, GA, KA (part of given name)

━━━━━━━ 1 ━━━━━━━

9 伽草子 **(o)togizōshi** fairy-tale book

13 伽話 **(o)togibanashi** fairy tale

2a5.14 / 1927
田 日 亻 一
43 3 1

但

tada(shi) but, however, provided
TADA (part of given name)

──────── 1 ────────

10 但書 **tada(shi)ga(ki)** proviso

2a5.15 / 561
田 亻 厂 十
3 18 12

低

TEI, hiku(i) low **hiku(meru)**
lower **hiku(maru)** become low(er)

──────── 1 ────────

3 低下 **teika** decline, go down, fall

5 低圧 **teiatsu** low pressure/voltage

7 低利 **teiri** low interest

8 低迷 **teimei** hang low, be sluggish

9 低音 **teion** bass (in music); low
voice, sotto voce

低級 **teikyū** low-grade, lowbrow,
vulgar

10 低能 **teinō** low intelligence, mentally deficient

11 低率 **teiritsu** low rate

12 低減 **teigen** decline, decrease, reduce

低落 **teiraku** fall, decline, slump

15 低調 **teichō** low-pitched; dull, inactive, sluggish (market)

──────── 2 ────────

12 最低 **saitei** lowest, minimum

佗 → 侘 **2a6.14**

2a5.17 / 2016
田 亻 一 丨
3 1 2

伶

REI entertainer, musician; clever
REI (part of given name)

2a5.19 / 156
田 王 亻 丨
46 3 2

住

JŪ dwelling, residing, living **su(mu)**,
su(mau) live, reside **su(mai)**
residence SUMI (part of given name)

──────── 1 ────────

2 住人 **jūnin** resident, inhabitant

4 住友 **Sumitomo** (company name)

住心地 **su(mi)gokochi** livability,
comfort

5 住民 **jūmin** residents, inhabitants

6 住宅 **jūtaku** dwelling, residence,
house, housing

8 住居 **jūkyo, sumai** residence,
dwelling

住所 **jūsho, su(mi)dokoro** address; residence, domicile

──────── 2 ────────

5 永住 **eijū** permanent residence

6 先住民族 **senjū minzoku** aborigines

先住者 **senjūsha** former occupant

8 佗住 **wa(bi)zu(mai)** wretched
abode; solitary life

定住者 **teijūsha** permanent resident

居住者 **kyojūsha** resident, inhabitant

11 常住 **jōjū** everlasting; always; permanently residing

移住 **ijū** migration, moving

移住者 **ijūsha** emigrant, immigrant

──────── 3 ────────

6 衣食住 **ishokujū** food, clothing,
and shelter

2a5.21 / 390
24 3 14

何

何何

KA, nani, nan what **izu(re), do(re)**
which

——————— 1

2 何人 **nannin** how many people
nanpito(mo) everyone, all
4 何分 **nanibun** anyway; please
nanpun how many minutes
nanbun what fraction
何月 **nangatsu** what month
nan(ka)getsu how many
months
何日 **nannichi** how many days;
what day of the month
5 何処 **izuko, izuku, doko** where
6 何気無 **nanigena(ku)** unintentionally; nonchalantly
何年 **nannen** how many years;
what year
何回 **nankai** how many times
8 何事 **nanigoto** what, whatever
9 何度 **nando** how many times; how
many degrees
何故 **naze, naniyue** why
10 何個 **nanko** how many (pieces)
何時 **nanji** what time, when
何時間 **nanjikan** how many hours
12 何等 **nanra** what, whatever
18 何曜日 **nan'yōbi, naniyōbi** what
day of the week

——————— 2

6 如何 **ikaga, ika (ni)** how
12 幾何学 **kikagaku** geometry

2a5.23 / 1761   口 口 亻 一
24 3 1

伺

伺伺

SHI, ukaga(u) visit; ask, inquire; hear,
be told **ukaga(i)** visit; inquiry

2a5.24 / 1063
41 3 1

余

YO remainder, the rest; other; more
than, upward of; I, myself, this writer
ama(ri) remainder, surplus; more
than, upward of; (not) very **ama(ru)**
remain left over, be more than enough;
be beyond, exceed **ama(su)** let remain, leave; save

——————— 1

4 余分 **yobun** extra, excess
5 余生 **yosei** the remainder of one's
life
6 余地 **yochi** room, place, margin,
scope
8 余命 **yomei** the remainder of one's
life
余所 **yoso** another place; other,
strange
9 余音 **yoin** lingering tone, reverberation; aftertaste, suggestiveness
余計 **yokei** more than enough, extra; unneeded, uncalled-for
10 余病 **yobyō** secondary disease,
complications
12 余程 **yohodo, yo(p)podo** very,
much, to a great degree
余裕 **yoyū** surplus, leeway, room,
margin
13 余業 **yogyō** remaining work; avocation, sideline
余暇 **yoka** spare time, leisure
15 余儀 **yogi(naku)** unavoidable, be
obliged to
余熱 **yonetsu** remaining heat
余弊 **yohei** a lingering evil
余震 **yoshin** aftershock

——————— 2

6 有余 **a(ri)ama(ru)** be superfluous,
be more than enough **yūyo**
more than
9 紆余曲折 **uyo-kyokusetsu** meandering, twists and turns, complications

10 残余 **zan'yo** remainder, residual, remnant, balance

11 剰余 **jōyo** a surplus

2a5.25 / 1249

目 口 亻 一
24 3 1

含 含

GAN, fuku(mu) contain, include; hold in the mouth; bear in mind, understand; imply, involve **fuku(meru)** include; give instructions

——————— 1 ———————

6 含有量 **gan'yūryō** quantity of a constituent substance, content

13 含意 **gan'i** implication

——————— 2 ———————

5 包含 **hōgan** include, comprehend; imply

2a5.26

⋯ 二 亻
38 3

巫 巫

FU sorcerer, sorceress

——————— 1 ———————

3 巫女 **miko, fujo** medium, sorceress; shrine maiden

——————— 6 ———————

2a6.1 / 678

目 礻 亻
57 3

依 依

I, E, yo(ru) depend on, be due to YORI (part of given name)

——————— 1 ———————

5 依存 **ison, izon** depend on, be dependent on

10 依託 **itaku** request, entrust

12 依然 **izen (to shite)** still, as ever

16 依頼 **irai** request; entrust; rely on

2a6.2 / 331

目 口 亻 十
24 3 12

使 使 使

SHI use; messenger **tsuka(u)** use **tsuka(i)** mission, errand; messenger; trainer, tamer

——————— 1 ———————

4 使分 **tsuka(i)wa(ke)** proper use

使込 **tsuka(i)ko(mu)** embezzle; accustom oneself to using

使方 **tsuka(i)kata** how to use, management

5 使令 **shirei** a directive

使用 **shiyō** use, employ, utilize

使用法 **shiyōhō** use, directions

使用者 **shiyōsha** user, consumer; employer

8 使果 **tsuka(i)hata(su)** use up, squander

使命 **shimei** mission, appointed task

使者 **shisha** messenger, envoy

13 使節 **shisetsu** envoy; mission, delegation

——————— 2 ———————

3 大使 **taishi** ambassador

大使館 **taishikan** embassy

6 再使用 **saishiyō** reuse

7 労使 **rōshi** labor and management

14 酷使 **kokushi** work (someone) hard

——————— 3 ———————

21 魔法使 **mahōtsuka(i)** magician, wizard

——————— 4 ———————

6 全権大使 **zenken taishi** ambassador plenipotentiary

2a6.3 / 421

目 口 亻
24 3 14

価 価 価

KA, atai price, cost; value, worth

—— 1 ——

10 価値 **kachi** value, merit
　　価格 **kakaku** price, cost, value

—— 2 ——

4 円価 **enka** value of the yen
5 正価 **seika** (net) price
6 地価 **chika** land value/prices
　　有価物 **yūkabutsu** valuables
　　米価 **beika** (government-set) rice price
8 定価 **teika** (fixed/set) price
　　物価 **bukka** (commodity) prices
9 単価 **tanka** unit cost/price; univalent
10 高価 **kōka** high price
　　真価 **shinka** true value
　　原価 **genka** cost price, cost
　　特価 **tokka** special/reduced price
12 評価 **hyōka** appraisal
13 廉価 **renka** low price

—— 3 ——

5 付加価値税 **fuka-kachi zei** value-added tax
6 再評価 **saihyōka** reassessment, re-evaluation

2a6.5 / 2018　　　□ 月 亻 十
　　　　　　　　　　　　42　3　12

侑侑

YŪ give, offer (food and drink)
SUSUMU, TASUKU, ATSUMU (m. given name)　YŪ, YUKI (part of given name)

2a6.7 / 612　　　□ 夕 亻 儿
　　　　　　　　　　　　30　3　16

例例

REI example; custom, practice, precedent　**tato(eru)** compare, liken
tato(eba) for example　**tameshi** instance, example; precedent; experience

—— 1 ——

4 例文 **reibun** illustrative sentence

例日 **reijitsu** weekday
5 例外 **reigai** exception
　　例示 **reiji** give an example of
6 例年 **reinen** normal/average year; every year
　　例会 **reikai** regular meeting
13 例解 **reikai** example, illustration
18 例題 **reidai** example, exercise (in a textbook)

—— 2 ——

1 一例 **ichirei** one example, an instance
3 凡例 **hanrei** explanatory notes; legend (on a map/diagram)
4 文例 **bunrei** model sentence/writing
5 比例 **hirei** proportion, ratio; proportional (representation)
　　用例 **yōrei** example, illustration
6 先例 **senrei** precedent
7 判例 **hanrei** (judicial) precedent
　　条例 **jōrei** regulation, law, ordinance, rule
8 事例 **jirei** example; precedent
　　実例 **jitsurei** example, illustration
　　定例 **teirei, jōrei** established usage, precedent; regular (meeting)
9 前例 **zenrei** precedent
　　恒例 **kōrei** established practice, custom
10 特例 **tokurei** special case, exception
11 悪例 **akurei** bad example/precedent
14 慣例 **kanrei** custom, precedent
15 範例 **hanrei** example

—— 3 ——

4 反比例 **hanpirei** in inverse proportion to

2a6.10 / 1462　　　□ 土 亻
　　　　　　　　　　　　22　3

佳佳

KA beautiful; good　**yo(i)** good　KEI (given name)　YOSHI (m. given name)
KEI, YOSHI (part of given name)

—— 1 ——

2 佳人 **kajin** beautiful woman

佳子 **Yoshiko, Keiko** (f. given name)
7 佳良 **karyō** excellent, good
佳作 **kasaku** an excellent work
佳奈 **Kana** (f. given name)
11 佳菜 **Kana** (f. given name)
19 佳麗 **karei** beautiful

——— 2 ———

5 由佳 **Yuka** (f. given name)

2a6.11 / 571   田 土 寸 亻
                    22 37 3

侍侍

JI, habe(ru) wait upon, serve
samurai warrior, samurai

——— 1 ———

6 侍気質 **samurai katagi** samurai spirit
8 侍者 **jisha** attendant, valet; altar boy

2a6.12 / 2017   田 口 亻 儿
                     24 3 16

侃侃

KAN moral strength, integrity
TSUYOSHI, TADASHI, AKIRA, SUNAO (m. given name) KAN, NAO, TADA, YASU (part of given name)

——— 1 ———

3 侃々諤々 **kankan-gakugaku** outspoken

2a6.13 / 197   田 艹 亻 儿
                    32 3 16

供供

KYŌ, KU, GU offer, submit; serve (a meal); supply **sona(eru)** make an offering, dedicate **tomo** attendant, servant, retinue

——— 1 ———

8 供物 **kumotsu, sona(e)mono** votive offering
12 供給 **kyōkyū** supply
15 供養 **kuyō, kyōyō** memorial service

——— 2 ———

2 子供 **kodomo** child
kodomo(rashii) childlike
12 提供 **teikyō** offer, present

2a6.14   田 宀 亻 艹
              33 3 12

侘|侘侘

TA lonely; other **wa(bi)** taste for the simple and quiet **wa(biru)** live a lonely life; be worried **wa(bishii)** lonely, forlorn, wretched

——— 1 ———

7 侘住 **wa(bi)zu(mai)** wretched abode; solitary life

2a6.17 / 1162   田 艹 亻 儿
                     32 3 16

併|併併

HEI, awa(seru) put together

——— 1 ———

5 併用 **heiyō** use together, use in combination
6 併合 **heigō** annexation, amalgamation, merger
9 併発 **heihatsu** break out at the same time, be complicated by
13 併置 **heichi** juxtapose, place side by side

——— 2 ———

6 合併 **gappei** merger, consolidation

2a6.20 / 1736   田 女 亻 宀
25 3 15

侮 | 侮 侮

BU, anado(ru) despise, hold in contempt

――― 1 ―――
10 侮辱 **bujoku** insult

侮 → 儘 **2a14.2**

2a6.23 / 791   日 土 口 亻
22 24 3

舍 | 舍 舍

SHA building; inn

――― 2 ―――
5 庁舎 **chōsha** government-office building
  田舎 **inaka** the country, rural areas
7 兵舎 **heisha** barracks
10 校舎 **kōsha** school building
11 宿舎 **shukusha** lodgings, quarters, billet

舎 → 舍 **2a6.23**

2a6.24 / 579   目 心 亻 一
51 3 1

念 念

NEN idea, thought, sense; desire; concern, care

――― 1 ―――
2 念入 **nen'i(ri)** careful, scrupulous, conscientious
19 念願 **nengan** one's heart's desire, earnest wish

――― 2 ―――
1 一念 **ichinen** a determined purpose
2 入念 **nyūnen** careful, scrupulous

4 丹念 **tannen** painstaking, elaborate
7 邪念 **janen** sinister intent, evil designs
8 祈念 **kinen** a prayer
9 専念 **sennen** undivided/close attention
  信念 **shinnen** faith, belief, conviction
10 残念 **zannen** regrettable, too bad
  記念 **kinen** commemoration, remembrance
  記念日 **kinenbi** memorial day, anniversary
  記念碑 **kinenhi** monument
11 執念 **shūnen** tenacity of purpose, vindictiveness
  理念 **rinen** idea, doctrine, ideology
12 無念 **munen** regret, resentment, vexation
  無念無想 **munen-musō** blank state of mind
14 疑念 **ginen** doubt, suspicion, misgivings
  概念 **gainen** general idea, concept
18 観念 **kannen** idea; sense (of duty)
20 懸念 **kenen** fear, apprehension

2a6.26 / 578   日 口 亻 阝
24 3 7

命 命

MEI, MYŌ command, order; life; fate **inochi** life **mikoto** lord, prince

――― 1 ―――
0 命じる **mei(jiru)** command; appoint
5 命令 **meirei** command, order
  命令形 **meireikei** imperative form
6 命名 **meimei** name, christen, call
14 命綱 **inochizuna** lifeline
20 命懸 **inochiga(ke)** life-or-death, risky, desperate

――― 2 ―――
1 一命 **ichimei** a life; a command
2 人命 **jinmei** (human) life
3 亡命 **bōmei** flee one's country
  亡命者 **bōmeisha** exile, emigré

7

⁵ 生命 **seimei** life

⁶ 死命 **shimei** life or death, fate

任命 **ninmei** appoint, nominate

⁷ 寿命 **jumyō** life, lifespan

余命 **yomei** the remainder of one's life

⁸ 長命 **chōmei** long life, longevity

使命 **shimei** mission, appointed task

⁹ 革命 **kakumei** revolution

¹⁰ 致命的 **chimeiteki** fatal, lethal, deadly, mortal

致命傷 **chimeishō** fatal wound/injury

¹¹ 運命 **unmei** fate, destiny

宿命 **shukumei** fate, destiny

救命 **kyūmei** lifesaving

²⁰ 懸命 **kenmei** eager, going all-out; risking one's life

---------- 3 ----------

⁴ 反革命 **hankakumei** counterrevolution

¹⁰ 祥月命日 **shōtsuki meinichi** anniversary of one's death

---------- 4 ----------

¹ 一生懸命 **isshōkenmei** with all one's might

一所懸命 **isshokenmei** with all one's might

---------- 7 ----------

2a7.1 / 157

▯ ⾔ ⺅
67 3

SHIN sincerity, trust, reliability; message, communication, signal **makoto** sincerity, fidelity AKIRA, MAKOTO (m. given name) SHIN, NOBU (part of given name)

---------- 1 ----------

⁰ 信じる/ずる **shin(jiru/zuru)** believe, believe in

¹ 信一 **Shin'ichi, Nobukazu, Nobuichi** (m. given name)

² 信子 **Nobuko** (f. given name)

⁴ 信心 **shinjin** faith, belief, piety

⁵ 信用 **shin'yō** trust, confidence; credit; reputation

信号 **shingō** signal

⁶ 信仰 **shinkō** religious faith, belief in

⁸ 信念 **shinnen** faith, belief, conviction

信者 **shinja** believer, adherent, the faithful

¹⁰ 信徒 **shinto** believer, follower, the faithful

信教 **shinkyō** religion, religious belief

信託 **shintaku** trust, entrusting

¹³ 信義 **shingi** faith, fidelity, loyalty **Nobuyoshi, Shingi** (m. given name)

¹⁶ 信憑性 **shinpyōsei** credibility, authenticity

信頼 **shinrai** reliance, trust, confidence

---------- 2 ----------

⁴ 不信 **fushin** unfaithfulness; unbelief; distrust

不信任 **fushinnin** nonconfidence

⁶ 妄信 **mōshin, bōshin** blind acceptance, credulity

返信 **henshin** reply

自信 **jishin** confidence (in oneself)

⁷ 赤信号 **akashingō** red (traffic) light

狂信 **kyōshin** fanaticism

⁸ 受信 **jushin** receipt of a message, (radio) reception

盲信 **mōshin** blind acceptance, credulity

迷信 **meishin** superstition

送信 **sōshin** transmission of a message

青信号 **aoshingō** green (traffic) light

所信 **shoshin** one's belief, conviction, opinion

⁹ 発信 **hasshin** send (a message)

重信 **Shigenobu, Jūshin** (m. given name)

通信 **teishin** communications

通信 **tsūshin** (tele)communications, correspondence, message, news, dispatch, report

¹³ 電信 **denshin** telegraph, telegram, cable

¹⁵ 確信 **kakushin** firm belief, conviction

¹⁶ 興信所 **kōshinjo** detective/investigative agency

2a7.3 / 1557   □ ⻆ 亻
                                70 3

促促

SOKU, unaga(su) urge, promote, prompt

———————— 1 ————————

⁹ 促音 **sokuon** assimilated sound (represented by a small つ or, in romanization, a doubled letter)

¹⁰ 促進 **sokushin** promote, encourage

———————— 2 ————————

¹³ 催促 **saisoku** urge, press for, demand

督促 **tokusoku** urge, press, dun

2a7.4   □ 戈 亻 ⺍
                        52 3 12

俄俄

GA, niwa(ka), niwaka sudden, unexpected

———————— 1 ————————

⁸ 俄雨 **niwakaame** (sudden) shower

侮 → 侮 **2a6.20**

2a7.5 / 330   □ 日 亻 ⼀
                                43 3 14

便|便便

BEN convenience, facilities; excrement, feces **BIN** mail; transport, flight; opportunity **tayo(ri)** news, tidings **yosuga** a means

———————— 1 ————————

⁷ 便利 **benri** convenient, handy

⁸ 便宜上 **bengijō** for convenience

便所 **benjo** toilet, lavatory

¹⁰ 便秘 **benpi** constipation

¹³ 便意 **ben'i** urge to go to the toilet, call of nature

¹⁴ 便箋 **binsen** stationery, notepaper

———————— 2 ————————

³ 大便 **daiben** feces, excrement

小便 **shōben** urine, urination

⁷ 別便 **betsubin** by separate mail

⁹ 音便 **onbin** (for sake of) euphony

¹⁰ 郵便 **yūbin** mail

郵便局 **yūbinkyoku** post office

郵便箱 **yūbinbako** mailbox

¹¹ 排便 **haiben** evacuation, defecation

船便 **funabin** sea mail; ship transportation

———————— 3 ————————

⁶ 宅配便 **takuhaibin** parcel delivery business

¹⁰ 航空便 **kōkūbin** airmail

俐 → 悧 **4k7.2**

2a7.8 / 909   □ 糸 亻 丨
                                61 3 2

係係

KEI, kakari duty, person in charge **kaka(waru), kaka(ru)** have to do with, be involved with

———————— 1 ————————

⁶ 係争 **keisō** dispute, contention

⁸ 係長 **kakarichō** chief clerk

¹⁰ 係留 **keiryū** moor, anchor

———————— 2 ————————

¹⁴ 関係 **kankei** relation(ship), connection

関係者 **kankeisha** interested party, those concerned

———————— 3 ————————

¹² 無関係 **mukankei** unrelated, irrelevant

2

7

亻
⼈
子
⻖
⼝
刂
力
又
宀
亠
艹
⺾
ノ
丷
厂
辶
冂
几
匚

——— 4 ———
7 利害関係 **rigai kankei** interests

2a7.10 / 1845   田 夂 イ 竹
                          49 3 17

俊俊

SHUN excellence, genius   SHUN,
TOSHI (part of given name)

——— 1 ———
1 俊一 **Shun'ichi, Toshikazu** (m.
   given name)
2 俊之 **Toshiyuki, Shunshi** (m. giv-
   en name)
3 俊才 **shunsai** genius, man of exceptional talent
8 俊郎 **Toshirō, Toshio, Shunrō** (m.
   given name)
10 俊逸 **shun'itsu** excellence, genius

2a7.11 / 489   田 木 口 イ
                          41 24 3

保

保保

HO, HŌ, tamo(tsu) keep, preserve,
maintain   HO, YASU (part of given
name)

——— 1 ———
5 保母 **hobo** kindergarten teacher
   保存 **hozon** preservation
6 保守的 **hoshuteki** conservative
   保有 **hoyū** possess, hold, maintain
7 保身 **hoshin** self-protection
8 保育 **hoiku** nurture, childcare, rearing
   保育所 **hoikujo** nursery school
9 保持 **hoji** maintain, preserve
10 保健 **hoken** health preservation,
   hygiene
   保険 **hoken** insurance
   保険料 **hokenryō** insurance premium
   保留 **horyū** reserve, defer
11 保菌者 **hokinsha** carrier (of a disease)

保釈 **hoshaku** bail
12 保温 **hoon** keeping warm
   保証 **hoshō** guarantee
   保証人 **hoshōnin** guarantor
13 保障 **hoshō** guarantee, security
14 保管 **hokan** custody, deposit, storage
15 保養 **hoyō** preservation of health;
   recuperation; recreation
20 保護 **hogo** protect, shelter, take care
   of

——— 2 ———
3 久保 **Kubo** (surname)
   久保田 **Kubota** (surname)
5 生保 **seiho** life insurance (short for
   生命保険)
6 安保 **anpo** (national) security (short
   for 安全保障)
8 担保 **tanpo** a security, guarantee
9 美保 **Miho, Yoshiyasu** (given
   name)
10 健保 **kenpo** health insurance (short
   for 健康保険)
15 確保 **kakuho** secure, ensure

——— 3 ———
3 大久保 **Ōkubo** (surname)

2a7.15 / 1077   田 ⇒ イ 冂
                          39 3 20

侵侵

SHIN, oka(su) invade, raid; violate, in-
fringe

——— 1 ———
2 侵入 **shinnyū** invade, raid, break
   into
5 侵犯 **shinpan** invasion, violation
9 侵食 **shinshoku** encroachment;
   erosion; pitting corrosion
10 侵害 **shingai** infringement, violation
11 侵略 **shinryaku** aggression, invasion

——— 3 ———
4 不可侵 **fukashin** nonaggression;
   inviolable

2a7.17 / 1126

□ 火 口 亻
44 24 3

俗

俗俗

ZOKU customs, manners; worldliness; laymen; vulgarity **zoku(ppoi)** lowbrow, common, vulgar

———————— 1 ————————

2 俗人 **zokujin** layman; worldly-minded person

4 俗化 **zokka** vulgarization, popularization

5 俗字 **zokuji** popular form of a kanji

6 俗気 **zokke, zokuke, zokki** vulgarity, worldly ambition

　俗名 **zokumei** common name; secular name **zokumyō** secular name

8 俗事 **zokuji** worldly affairs; workaday routine

　俗受 **zokuu(ke)** popular appeal

　俗物 **zokubutsu** worldly-minded person, person of vulgar tastes

9 俗臭 **zokushū** vulgarity, worldly-mindedness

　俗界 **zokkai** the workaday/secular world

10 俗称 **zokushō** popular/vernacular name

11 俗習 **zokushū** (popular) custom

　俗悪 **zokuaku** vulgar, coarse

14 俗語 **zokugo** colloquial language, slang

　俗説 **zokusetsu** common saying; folklore

———————— 2 ————————

5 民俗 **minzoku** ethnic/folk customs

9 通俗 **tsūzoku** popular, conventional

　風俗 **fūzoku** manners, customs, morals

　卑俗 **hizoku** vulgar, coarse

11 習俗 **shūzoku** manners and customs, usages

2a7.21 / 1924

□ 矢 亻 宀
34 3 15

侯

侯侯

KŌ marquis; lord, daimyo **KIMI** (part of given name)

———————— 1 ————————

17 侯爵 **kōshaku** marquis, marquess

2a7.22

□ 冂 亻 丨
20 3 2

臥

臥丨臥臥

GA, fu(su), fu(seru) lie down, go to bed

———————— 1 ————————

7 臥床 **gashō** be confined to bed

———————— 2 ————————

9 草臥 **kutabi(reru)** be tired/exhausted

赴 → **3b6.14**

起 → **3b7.11**

———————— 8 ————————

2a8.5 / 905

□ 土 亻 竹
22 3 17

倒

倒倒

TŌ, tao(reru), ko(keru) fall, collapse, break down **tao(su)** bring down, topple

———————— 1 ————————

11 倒産 **tōsan** bankruptcy

14 倒閣 **tōkaku** overthrowing the cabinet

16 倒壊 **tōkai** collapse, be destroyed

　倒錯 **tōsaku** perversion

亻 **8**
冫
子
阝
卩
刂
力
又
亠
十
夂
冖
厂
辶
冂
几
囗

— 2 —

5 圧倒的 **attōteki** overwhelming
打倒 **datō** overthrow
u(chi)tao(su) knock down; overthrow
6 共倒 **tomodao(re)** mutual ruin
8 押倒 **o(shi)tao(su)** push down
9 面倒 **mendō** trouble, difficulty; taking care of, tending to
面倒臭 **mendōkusa(i)** troublesome, a big bother
11 率倒 **sottō** faint, swoon
転倒 **tentō** fall down violently, turn upside down, reverse

2a8.7 / 1776 ⊞ 方 攵 亻
48 49 3

傲

傲傲

HŌ, nara(u) imitate, follow, emulate

— 2 —

14 模倣 **mohō** copy, imitation

2a8.8 / 1035 ⊞ 亻 儿 二
3 16 4

俳

俳俳

HAI actor

— 1 —

2 俳人 **haijin** haiku poet
5 俳句 **haiku** haiku
17 俳優 **haiyū** actor, actress

倂 → 併 **2a6.17**

2a8.10 / 944 ⊞ 大 亻 ー
34 3 15

候

候候

KŌ season, weather; wait for
-sōrō (classical verb ending equivalent to -masu)

— 1 —

12 候補者 **kōhosha** candidate
4 天候 **tenkō** the weather
6 気候 **kikō** climate
兆候 **chōkō** sign, indication
7 季候 **kikō** climate
8 居候 **isōrō** hanger-on, dependent, sponger
10 時候 **jikō** season, time of year; weather
時候外 **jikōhazu(re)** unseasonable
症候 **shōkō** symptom
14 徴候 **chōkō** sign, indication, symptom

— 3 —

11 悪天候 **akutenkō** bad weather

2a8.11 / 945 ⊞ 攵 彡 亻
49 31 3

修

修修

SHŪ, SHU, osa(maru) govern oneself, conduct oneself well **osa(meru)** order (one's life); study, cultivate, master OSAMU (m. given name) NOBU (part of given name)

— 1 —

1 修了 **shūryō** completion (of a course)
3 修士 **shūshi** master's degree, M.A., M.S.
5 修正 **shūsei** amendment, revision, alteration, correction
6 修行 **shūgyō, shugyō, shūkō** training, study, ascetic practices
7 修学 **shūgaku** learning
修学旅行 **shūgaku ryokō** school excursion, field trip
11 修道院 **shūdōin** monastery, convent, cloister
修理 **shūri** repair
12 修復 **shūfuku** repair
13 修業 **shūgyō** pursuit of knowledge
修辞学 **shūjigaku** rhetoric
修飾 **shūshoku** decorate, adorn; modify (in grammar)

14 修練 **shūren** training, discipline, drill
15 修養 **shūyō** cultivation of the mind, character-building
18 修繕 **shūzen** repair

───── 2 ─────

5 必修 **hisshū** required (subject)
7 学修 **gakushū** learning, study
　改修 **kaishū** repair, improvement
9 専修 **senshū** specialize in
　研修 **kenshū** study and training
13 新修 **shinshū** new compilation
15 監修 **kanshū** (editorial) supervision

2a8.13

□ 火 尸 亻
44 40 3

倦 | 倦 倦

KEN, a(kiru), agu(mu), u(mu) get tired of

───── 1 ─────

9 倦怠感 **kentaikan** fatigue

2a8.14 / 87

□ 立 口 亻
54 24 3

倍 倍

BAI double, twice; times, -fold

───── 1 ─────

11 倍率 **bairitsu** magnifying power, magnification
14 倍増 **baizō, baima(shi)** to double
18 倍額 **baigaku** double the amount

───── 2 ─────

1 一倍 **ichibai** the same number/ amount; double
2 二倍 **nibai** double, twice, twofold
7 阿倍 **Abe** (surname)
13 数倍 **sūbai** several times as (large), several-fold

───── 3 ─────

2 人一倍 **hito-ichibai** uncommon, more than others

2a8.15

□ 目 亻 儿
55 3 16

俱 俱

KU, GU, tomo together

───── 1 ─────

13 倶楽部 **kurabu** club

2a8.16 / 2019

□ 禾 女 亻
56 25 3

倭 倭

WA, Yamato ancient Japan WA, I, SHIZU, MASA, YASU, KAZU (part of given name) YAMATO (m. given name)

───── 1 ─────

11 倭寇 **wakō** Japanese pirates

2a8.18 / 1542

□ 大 亻 二
34 3 4

俸 俸

HŌ salary

───── 1 ─────

12 俸給 **hōkyū** salary

───── 2 ─────

4 月俸 **geppō** monthly salary
6 年俸 **nenpō** annual salary
12 減俸 **genpō** salary reduction
14 増俸 **zōhō** salary increase

2a8.21 / 1890

□ 耒 亻 二
57 3 4

俵 俵

HYŌ bag, bale, sack; (counter for bags) **tawara** straw bag TAWARA (surname)

───── 2 ─────

3 土俵 **dohyō** the sumo ring; sandbag

2a8.22 / 766

□ 日 艹 亻
43 32 3

借

借借

SHAKU, SHA, ka(riru), ka(ru) borrow, rent **ka(ri)** borrowing, debt, loan

———— 1 ————

4 借手 **ka(ri)te** borrower, lessee, tenant
5 借用 **shakuyō** borrowing, loan
　 借主 **ka(ri)nushi** borrower, renter
6 借地 **shakuchi, ka(ri)chi** leased land
8 借金 **shakkin** debt
10 借家 **shakuya, shakka, ka(ri)ie, ka(ri)ya** rented house, house for rent
　 借財 **shakuzai** debt
12 借款 **shakkan** loan
　 借越 **ka(ri)ko(su)** overdraw
13 借賃 **ka(ri)chin** the rent

———— 2 ————

8 拝借 **haishaku** borrow
10 家借 **kashaku** renting a house
13 賃借 **chinshaku, chinga(ri)** lease, rent, hire
　 賃借料 **chinshakuryō** rent

2a8.23 / 2020

□ 土 亻 儿
22 3 16

倖

倖倖

KŌ, shiawa(se) happiness, good fortune KŌ, GYŌ, SACHI (part of given name)

2a8.25

□ 日 大 亻
43 34 3

俺

俺俺

EN, ore I, me

2a8.27 / 878

□ 口 亻 八
24 3 14

僉

僉|僉僉

KEN thrift **tsuma(shii)** thrifty, frugal **tsuzuma(yaka)** neat and small; frugal; unpretentious; concise

———— 1 ————

9 倹約 **ken'yaku** thrift, frugality
　 倹約家 **ken'yakuka** thrifty person, economizer

2a8.28 / 1163

□ 艹 亻 冂
32 3 20

倫

倫倫

RIN road to take; sequence **tagui** kind, sort; an equal HITOSHI (m. given name) MICHI, MOTO (part of given name)

———— 1 ————

11 倫理 **rinri** ethics, morals

———— 2 ————

4 不倫 **furin** immoral, illicit

2a8.30 / 425

□ 目 亻 十
55 3 12

値

値値

CHI, ne, atai price, cost, value

———— 1 ————

3 値上 **nea(ge)** price hike
　 nea(gari) higher price
　 値下 **nesa(ge)** price reduction
　 nesa(gari) price decline, lower prices
4 値切 **negi(ru)** haggle, bargain
　 値引 **nebi(ki)** discount
5 値打 **neu(chi)** value, worth; dignity
9 値段 **nedan** price

2

⁵ 付値 **tsu(ke)ne** the price offered, bid
⁶ 安値 **yasune** low price
⁷ 売値 **u(ri)ne** selling price
⁸ 価値 **kachi** value, merit
 底値 **sokone** rock-bottom price
⁹ 卸値 **oroshine** wholesale price
¹⁰ 高値 **takane** high price
¹¹ 捨値 **su(te)ne** giveaway price
¹⁷ 闇値 **yamine** black-market price

4

⁵ 付加価値税 **fuka-kachi zei** value-added tax

2a8.34 / 893   ⊞ ⺕ 亻 辶
                    39 3 19

健健

KEN health, strength **suko(yaka)** healthy TAKESHI (m. given name) KEN, TAKE (part of given name)

1

¹ 健一 **Ken'ichi** (m. given name)
² 健人 **Taketo** (m. given name)
⁴ 健太 **Kenta** (m. given name)
 健太郎 **Kentarō** (m. given name)
⁶ 健全 **kenzen** healthy, sound
 健在 **kenzai** in good health
⁷ 健忘症 **kenbōshō** forgetfulness, amnesia
⁹ 健保 **kenpo** health insurance (short for 健康保険)
¹¹ 健康 **kenkō** health; healthy, sound
¹² 健勝 **kenshō** healthy, robust, hale and hearty
¹⁸ 健闘 **kentō** put up a good fight, make strenuous efforts

2

⁴ 不健康 **fukenkō** unhealthy, unhealthful
⁹ 保健 **hoken** health preservation, hygiene
¹⁰ 剛健 **gōken** strong and sturdy, virile
¹⁶ 穏健 **onken** moderate

2a8.35   ⊞ 寸 厂 亻
             37 18 3

俯

俯俯

FU, fu(seru) lay face down **fu(su)** prostrate oneself **utsumu(ku/keru)** look/turn downward

1

⁶ 俯伏 **utsubu(su)** lie face down **fufuku** lie prostrate
 俯向 **utsumu(keru)** turn upside down, turn downward
 utsumu(ku) look downward

2a8.36 / 973   ⊞ 口 亻 十
                    24 3 12

個

个 丨 個 個

KO individual; (counter for objects) **KA** (counter)

1

² 個人 **kojin** private person, individual
 個人的 **kojinteki** individual, personal, self-centered
 個人差 **kojinsa** differences between individuals
³ 個々 **koko** individual, separate, one by one
⁷ 個別 **kobetsu** indivudual by individual
⁸ 個性 **kosei** individuality, idiosyncrasy

2

⁷ 何個 **nanko** how many (pieces)

2a8.37 / 1307   ⊞ 食 口
                     73 24

倉

倉倉

SŌ, kura warehouse, storehouse

2

8

亻
⺡
孑
阝
卩
刂
力
又
⼇
十
夕
⼌
厂
辶
冂
八
匚

2

9

—————— 1 ——————

¹⁰ 倉庫 **sōko** warehouse

—————— 2 ——————

³ 小倉 **Ogura** (surname)

¹⁸ 鎌倉 **Kamakura** (city, Kanagawa-ken); (era, 1185 – 1333)

—————— 9 ——————

2a9.1 / 1639 | 日 亻 竹
43　3　17

偶　　偶偶

GŪ even number; couple, man and wife; same kind; doll **tama (ni)** occasionally, rarely **tamatama** by chance, unexpectedly

—————— 1 ——————

⁹ 偶発 **gūhatsu** happen by chance
偶発的 **gūhatsuteki** accidental, incidental, occasional

¹² 偶然 **gūzen** by chance, happen to …

¹³ 偶数 **gūsū** even number

¹⁴ 偶像 **gūzō** image, idol

2a9.2 / 1485 | 火 亻 十
44　3　12

偽 | 偽偽

GI, itsuwa(ru) lie, misrepresent; feign; deceive **nise** fake, counterfeit

—————— 1 ——————

⁵ 偽札 **nisesatsu** counterfeit paper money

⁶ 偽名 **gimei** assumed name, alias

⁷ 偽作 **gisaku** a spurious work, a forgery

⁸ 偽物 **gibutsu, nisemono** a counterfeit/fake

⁹ 偽造 **gizō** forgery

¹² 偽善者 **gizensha** hypocrite
偽装 **gisō** camouflage
偽証 **gishō** false testimony, perjury

—————— 2 ——————

¹⁰ 真偽 **shingi** true or false, whether genuine or spurious

假 → 仮 2a4.15

2a9.4 / 609 | 貝 亻 儿
68　3　16

側側

SOKU, kawa, -gawa side **soba** side, vicinity **hata** side, edge

—————— 1 ——————

⁶ 側近者 **sokkinsha** close associate

⁹ 側面 **sokumen** side, flank

—————— 2 ——————

⁴ 内側 **uchigawa** inside, interior, inner
片側 **katagawa, katakawa** one side

⁵ 左側 **hidarigawa** left side
外側 **sotogawa** outside, exterior
右側 **migigawa, usoku** right side

⁶ 両側 **ryōgawa** both sides
西側 **nishigawa** the western side; the West
向側 **mu(kō)gawa** the opposite side, across from

⁸ 表側 **omotegawa** the front
東側 **higashigawa** east side

⁹ 南側 **minamigawa, nansoku** south side

¹³ 裏側 **uragawa** the back side

¹⁵ 縁側 **engawa** veranda, porch, balcony

—————— 3 ——————

⁴ 反対側 **hantaigawa** the opposite side

倦 → 倦 2a8.13

條 → 条 4i4.1

2a9.6 / 2207　　　　囗　夊　月　亻
　　　　　　　　　　　49　42　3

脩脩

SHŪ dried meat; long; put in order
OSAMU (m. given name)　SHŪ, NAGA,
NOBU, OSA, HARU, SUKE, NAO, MORO,
SANE (part of given name)

2a9.7 / 2021　　　　囗　甲　心　亻
　　　　　　　　　　　58　51　3

偲偲

SHI, SAI, shino(bu) recollect,
remember　SHINOBU (given name)
SHI, SAI (part of given name)

2a9.14 / 1185　　　　囗　口　亻　宀
　　　　　　　　　　　24　3　11

停停

**TEI, todo(maru), todo(meru),
to(maru)** stop

―――――――― 1 ――――――――

⁴ 停止　**teishi** suspension, stop, halt,
cessation

⁶ 停年　**teinen** age limit, retirement
age

⁷ 停車　**teisha** stopping a vehicle

¹⁰ 停留所　**teiryūjo** stopping place,
(bus) stop

¹³ 停滞　**teitai** be stagnant, accumulate; fall into arrears

停電　**teiden** cutoff of electricity,
power outage

―――――――― 2 ――――――――

¹⁵ 調停　**chōtei** arbitration, mediation,
conciliation

―――――――― 3 ――――――――

⁶ 各駅停車　**kakuekiteisha** local
train

2a9.15 / 1928　　　　囗　貝　亻　卜
　　　　　　　　　　　68　3　13

偵偵

TEI spy

―――――――― 1 ――――――――

¹⁴ 偵察　**teisatsu** reconnaissance

⁴ 内偵　**naitei** scouting, reconnaissance; private inquiry

¹¹ 探偵　**tantei** (private) detective, investigator, spy

2a9.16 / 1159　　　　囗　尸　艹　亻
　　　　　　　　　　　40　32　3

偏|偏偏

HEN inclining; left-side part of a
kanji　**kkatayo(ru)** lean toward, be
biased　**hitoe (ni)** earnestly; humbly;
solely

―――――――― 1 ――――――――

⁶ 偏向　**henkō** leanings, deviation; deflection

⁷ 偏見　**henken** biased view, prejudice

⁸ 偏屈　**henkutsu** eccentric, bigoted,
narrow-minded

⁹ 偏食　**henshoku** unbalanced diet

¹⁶ 偏頭痛　**henzutsū, hentōtsu** migraine headache

―――――――― 2 ――――――――

⁴ 不偏　**fuhen** impartial, fair, neutral

¹² 無偏　**muhen** unbiased, impartial

歃 → 5f5.5

超 → 3b9.18

越 → 4n8.2

2

亻
冫
孑
阝
阝
刂
力
又
宀
艹
疒
冖
厂
辶
冂
几
匸

麥→麦 **4i4.2**

2a9.21 / 1069 ⊞ 木 亻 十
41 3 12

斜

斜 斜

SHA, nana(me), hasu slanting, diagonal, oblique, askew

――――― 1 ―――――
9 斜面 **shamen** slope, inclined plane
11 斜陽 **shayō** setting sun
15 斜線 **shasen** oblique line

――――― 2 ―――――
13 傾斜 **keisha** inclination, slant, slope

――――― 3 ―――――
9 急傾斜 **kyūkeisha** steep slope/incline

絞→叙 **2h7.1**

肅→ **0a11.8**

疎→ **0a11.4**

――――― 10 ―――――
2a10.4 / 768 ⊞ 月 艹 亻
42 32 3

備

備 備

BI, sona(eru) provide, furnish; provide for, make preparations; be endowed with, possess **sona(waru)** be provided/endowed with, possess

――――― 1 ―――――
6 備考 **bikō** note, remarks
9 備品 **bihin** fixtures, furnishings, equipment

――――― 2 ―――――
4 予備 **yobi** preparatory, preliminary, in reserve, spare
予備校 **yobikō** preparatory school

6 全備 **zenbi** fully equipped, complete, perfect
防備 **bōbi** defensive preparations
守備 **shubi** defense
7 完備 **kanbi** fully equipped/furnished
9 軍備 **gunbi** military preparations, preparedness
11 設備 **setsubi** equipment, facilities, accommodations
12 装備 **sōbi** equipment
13 準備 **junbi** preparations, provision, reserve
戦備 **senbi** military preparedness
16 整備 **seibi** make/keep ready for use, maintain, equip
19 警備 **keibi** security, guard, defense

――――― 3 ―――――
6 再軍備 **saigunbi** rearmament
12 無防備 **mubōbi** defenseless, unfortified

2a10.5 / 1053 ⊞ 口 亻 十
24 3 12

偉

偉 偉

I, era(i) great **era(garu)** be self-important TAKE (part of given name)

――――― 1 ―――――
3 偉大 **idai** great, grand, mighty
13 偉業 **igyō** great achievement, feat

2a10.6 / 1183 ⊞ 方 亻 亠
48 3 11

傍

傍 傍

BŌ, HŌ, katawara, soba, hata side

――――― 1 ―――――
8 傍注 **bōchū** marginal notes
17 傍聴 **bōchō** hearing, attendance, auditing
18 傍観 **bōkan** look on, remain a spectator

2a10.7 / 790　　　　⊡ 亻 ⼗
　　　　　　　　　　　　3　12

傘

傘 傘

SAN, kasa umbrella

――――― 1 ―――――
5 傘立 **kasata(te)** umbrella stand

――――― 2 ―――――
4 日傘 **higasa** parasol
8 雨傘 **amagasa** umbrella

――――― 3 ―――――
9 相々傘 **aiaigasa (de)** under the
　　　same umbrella
　相合傘 **aia(i)gasa (de)** under the
　　　same umbrella
12 落下傘 **rakkasan** parachute
15 蝙蝠傘 **kōmorigasa** umbrella

2a10.8　　　　⊟ 亻 ⼇ ⼗
　　　　　　　　3　11　12

禽

禽 禽

KIN bird; captive, capture **tori** bird

超 → **3b9.18**

越 → **4n8.2**

幾 → **4n8.4**

疎 → **0a11.4**

――――― 11 ―――――

2a11.1 / 232　　　⫼ 車 亻 力
　　　　　　　　　　69　3　8

働

仂 | 働 働

DŌ, hatara(ku) work **hatara(ki)**
work, function

――――― 1 ―――――
3 働口 **hatara(ki)guchi** job opening,
　　employment
8 働者 **hatara(ki)mono** hard worker

――――― 2 ―――――
6 共働 **tomobatara(ki)** (husband and
　　wife) both working, dual in-
　　come
7 労働 **rōdō** labor, work, toil
　労働者 **rōdōsha** worker, laborer
　労働省 **Rōdōshō** Ministry of Labor

――――― 3 ―――――
9 重労働 **jūrōdō** heavy/hard labor

2a11.2　　　⫼ 方 攵 ⼟
　　　　　　　48　49　22

傲

傲 傲

GŌ be proud

――――― 1 ―――――
14 傲慢 **gōman** proud, arrogant,
　　haughty

――――― 2 ―――――
22 驕傲 **kyōgō** arrogance, pride

2a11.3 / 1441　　⫼ 頁 亻 ⼂
　　　　　　　　　　77　3　13

傾

傾 傾

KEI, katamu(ku), kashi(gu) (intr.)
lean, incline, tilt **katamu(keru),
kashi(geru), kata(geru)** (tr.) lean

――――― 1 ―――――
6 傾向 **keikō** tendency, trend; incli-
　　nation, leanings
11 傾斜 **keisha** inclination, slant, slope
17 傾聴 **keichō** listen (attentively) to

――――― 2 ―――――
5 右傾 **ukei** leaning to the right, right-
　　ist
9 急傾斜 **kyūkeisha** steep slope/in-
　　cline

2

亻 11
冫
孑
阝
卩
刂
力
又
⼇
⼗
夂
ヽ
厂
辶
冂
八
匚

2

11

傳 → 伝 **2a4.14**

2a11.6 / 1731   ⊞ 木 夕 亻
41 30 3

傑

杰ㅣ傑傑

KETSU, sugu(reru) excel

─── 1 ───

7 傑作 **kessaku** masterpiece

─── 2 ───

14 豪傑 **gōketsu** hero, great man

2a11.7 / 1366   ⊞ 甲 日 亻
58 43 3

僧

僧ㅣ僧僧

SŌ monk, priest

─── 1 ───

9 僧侶 **sōryo** (Buddhist) priest, monk, bonze

僧院 **sōin** temple; monastery

─── 2 ───

3 小僧 **kozō** young Buddhist priest; errand boy; youngster, kid

4 仏僧 **bussō** Buddhist priest

5 尼僧 **nisō** nun

13 禅僧 **zensō** Zen priest

2a11.10 / 633   ⊞ 日 彡 亻
43 27 3

傷

傷傷

SHŌ, kizu wound, injury **ita(mu)** hurt, suffer pain/injury/damage; go bad (food) **ita(meru)** hurt, cause pain/injury/damage to

─── 1 ───

4 傷心 **shōshin** heartbreak, sorrow

5 傷付 **kizutsu(keru)** injure, damage

8 傷者 **shōsha** injured person

10 傷害 **shōgai** injury, bodily harm

─── 2 ───

3 刃傷 **ninjō** bloodshed

4 中傷 **chūshō** slander, defamation

切傷 **ki(ri)kizu** cut, gash, scar

火傷 **kashō, yakedo** a burn

5 生傷 **namakizu** unhealed wound, fresh bruise

6 死傷者 **shishōsha** casualties, killed and wounded

9 重傷 **jūshō, omode** serious wound, major injury

負傷 **fushō** sustain an injury, get hurt

10 挫傷 **zashō** sprain, fracture, bruise

11 掠傷 **kasu(ri)kizu** scratch, bruise

12 無傷 **mukizu** uninjured, undamaged, unblemished

裂傷 **resshō** laceration

軽傷 **keishō** minor injury

13 愁傷様 **(go)shūshō-sama** My heartfelt sympathy.

感傷 **kanshō** sentimentality

14 銃傷 **jūshō** gunshot wound

17 擦傷 **su(ri)kizu** abrasion, scratch

─── 3 ───

10 致命傷 **chimeishō** fatal wound/injury

17 擦過傷 **sakkashō** abrasion, scratch

2a11.11 / 1118   ⊞ 貝 土 亻
68 22 3

債

債債

SAI debt, loan

─── 1 ───

8 債券 **saiken** bond, debenture

11 債務 **saimu** debt, liabilities

15 債権 **saiken** credit, claims

─── 2 ───

4 公債 **kōsai** public debt, government bond

5 外債 **gaisai** foreign loan/bond/debt

7 社債 **shasai** (company) bonds, debentures

8 国債 **kokusai** national debt/bonds

9 負債 **fusai** debt, liabilities

2a11.12 / 1317   田 催 ⺍ 亻
                      74 36 3

催

催催

SAI, moyō(su) bring about, hold (a meeting); feel (sick)

───── 1 ─────

7 催告 **saikoku** notification, admonition
8 催物 **moyō(shi)mono** public event, show
9 催促 **saisoku** urge, press for, demand
10 催眠術 **saiminjutsu** hypnotism

───── 2 ─────

5 主催 **shusai** sponsor, promote
12 開催 **kaisai** hold (a meeting)

會 → 会 **2a4.19**

越 → **4n8.2**

業 → **0a13.3**

靴 → **3k10.34**

───── 12 ─────

2a12.1 / 1888   田 大 亻 儿
                    34 3 16

僕

僕僕

BOKU I, me; manservant **shimobe** manservant

2a12.4 / 1324   田 火 日 ⺌
                    44 43 35

僚

僚僚

RYŌ colleague; an official

───── 2 ─────

6 同僚 **dōryō** colleague, associate
8 官僚 **kanryō** bureaucracy, officialdom
  官僚的 **kanryōteki** bureaucratic
14 閣僚 **kakuryō** cabinet members

僞 → 偽 **2a9.2**

2a12.8 / 740   田 口 豸 亻
                    24 27 3

像

像像

ZŌ, SHŌ, katachi image, statue, portrait

───── 2 ─────

4 幻像 **genzō** illusion, phantom
  仏像 **butsuzō** image of Buddha
5 石像 **sekizō** stone image/statue
7 肖像 **shōzō** portrait
8 画像 **gazō** portrait, picture, image
9 映像 **eizō** image, reflection
10 胸像 **kyōzō** (sculptured) bust
11 偶像 **gūzō** image, idol
  彫像 **chōzō** carved statue, sculpture
  現像 **genzō** developing (film)
13 聖像 **seizō** sacred image, icon
  想像 **sōzō** imagine
  想像力 **sōzōryoku** (powers of) imagination
14 銅像 **dōzō** bronze statue
15 影像 **eizō** image

僧 → 僧 **2a11.7**

趣 → **6e9.1**

疑 → **2m12.1**

───── 13 ─────

價 → 価 **2a6.3**

亻 12
⺅
⼎
子
阝
阝
刂
力
又
宀
亠
十
卜
夕
⺍
厂
辶
冂
八
匚

2a13.4 / 727

田 王 戈 亻
46 52 3

儀 儀儀

GI rule; ceremony; model; affair, matter YOSHI, NORI (part of given name)

─────── 1 ───────

⁶ 儀式 **gishiki** ceremony

─────── 2 ───────

⁵ 礼儀 **reigi** courtesy, politeness, propriety

礼儀正 **reigitada(shii)** polite, courteous

礼儀作法 **reigisahō** etiquette, courtesy, propriety

⁶ 行儀 **gyōgi** manners, deportment, behavior

⁷ 余儀 **yogi(naku)** unavoidable, be obliged to

¹⁰ 流儀 **ryūgi** school (of thought), style, system, method

¹² 葬儀 **sōgi** funeral

¹³ 辞儀 **jigi** bow, greeting; decline, refuse

─────── 3 ───────

⁶ 地球儀 **chikyūgi** a globe of the world

¹² 御辞儀 **ojigi** bow, greeting

2a13.6 / 382

田 立 日 心
54 43 51

億 億丨億億

OKU hundred million, 100,000,000

─────── 1 ───────

³ 億万長者 **okumanchōja** multimillionaire, billionaire

⁷ 億劫 **okkū** bothersome, troublesome **okukō, okugō, okkō** unimaginable long time

─────── 2 ───────

¹ 一億 **ichioku** one hundred million

─────────

儉 → 倹 2a8.27

趣 → 6e9.1

歯 → 歯 6b6.11

─────── 14 ───────

2a14.1 / 1417

田 雨 亻 一
75 3 14

儒 儒儒

JU Confucianism

─────── 1 ───────

⁷ 儒学 **jugaku** Confucianism

2a14.2

田 皿 火 彐
59 44 39

儘 侭丨儘儘

JIN, mama as is, as one likes

─────── 2 ───────

⁷ 我儘 **wagamama** selfish, capricious, wanting to have one's own way

─────── 15 ───────

儲 → 儲 2a16.1

2a15.1 / 1033

田 月 心 夊
42 51 49

優 優優

YŪ superior; gentle; actor **sugu(reru), masa(ru)** excel, surpass **yasa(shii)** gentle **yasa-** gentle **yasa(shige)** gentle-looking MASARU (m. given name) YŪ, MASA (part of given name)

── 1 ──

2 優子 **Yūko, Masako** (f. given name)

4 優太 **Yūta** (m. given name)

6 優先 **yūsen** preference, priority

優劣 **yūretsu** superiority or inferiority, relative merits **masa(ru tomo) oto(ranai)** in no way inferior to, at least so good as

7 優良 **yūryō** superior, excellent

優秀 **yūshū** superior, excellent

8 優性 **yūsei** dominant (gene)

9 優香 **Yūka** (f. given name)

11 優遇 **yūgū** warm welcome, hospitality, favorable treatment

12 優勝 **yūshō** victory, championship

優越感 **yūetsukan** superiority complex

優等生 **yūtōsei** honors student

13 優勢 **yūsei** predominance, superiority, the advantage

優雅 **yūga** elegant, graceful, refined

16 優樹 **Masaki, Yūki** (m. given name)

── 2 ──

3 女優 **joyū** actress

4 心優 **kokoroyasa(shii)** kind, considerate

6 全優 **zen'yū** straight A's

7 声優 **seiyū** radio actor/actress, dubber

男優 **dan'yū** actor

10 俳優 **haiyū** actor, actress

2a15.4 / 971
貝 小 口
68 35 24

償償

SHŌ, tsuguna(u) make up for, recompense

── 1 ──

7 償却 **shōkyaku** repayment, redemption, amortization

15 償還 **shōkan** repayment, redemption, amortization

── 2 ──

5 弁償 **benshō** indemnification

12 報償 **hōshō** compensation, reward, remuneration

補償 **hoshō** compensation, indemnification

補償金 **hoshōkin** indemnity, compensation (money)

15 賠償 **baishō** reparation, indemnification

賠償金 **baishōkin** indemnities, reparations, damages

── 16 ──

2a16.1
言 日 土
67 43 22

儲 | 儲 儲

CHO, mō(karu) be profitable
mō(keru) gain, earn, make (money)
mō(ke) profits

── 1 ──

3 儲口 **mō(ke)guchi** profitable job

8 儲物 **mō(ke)mono** good bargain, windfall

── 2 ──

3 大儲 **ōmō(ke)** large profit

丸儲 **marumō(ke)** clear gain/profit

8 金儲 **kanemō(ke)** moneymaking

14 銭儲 **zenimō(ke)** money-making

鞭 → **3k15.8**

── 18 ──

齢 → 齢 **6b11.5**

2b

冰	冴	沖	次	壮	決	兆	羽	状	冴	況	冷	冶
3a1.2	2b5.2	3a4.5	4.1	4.2	3a4.6	4.4	4.5	5.1	5.2	3a5.21	5.3	5.4

求	函	飛	准	凍	将	凄	凌	涼	毬	奨	凛	凝
5.5	6.3	0a9.4	8.1	8.2	8.3	8.4	8.5	3a8.31	9.1	3n10.4	13.1	14.1

———— 4 ————

冰 → 氷 **3a1.2**

冴 → 冴 **2b5.2**

冲 → 沖 **3a4.5**

2b4.1 / 384 ☐ 欠 冫
49 5

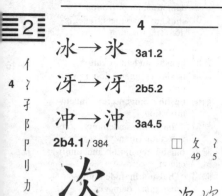

次次

JI, SHI, tsugi next **tsu(gu)** rank next to, come after

———— 1 ————

3 次々 **tsugitsugi** one by one, one after another

次女 **jijo** second daughter

5 次世代 **jisedai** next-generation (product)

6 次回 **jikai** next time

7 次男 **jinan** second son

8 次長 **jichō** deputy director, assistant chief

次官 **jikan** vice-minister, undersecretary

11 次第 **shidai** order, precedence; circumstances; as soon as; according to; gradually

———— 2 ————

1 一次 **ichiji** first; primary; linear (equation)

2 二次 **niji** second(ary); quadratic, second degree (in math) **ni(no) tsugi** secondary, subordinate

二次会 **nijikai** after-party party

5 目次 **mokuji** table of contents

6 年次 **nenji** annual

8 弥次馬 **yajiuma** bystanders, spectators, crowd of onlookers

取次 **to(ri)tsu(gu)** act as agent; transmit, convey

9 貞次 **Teiji, Sadatsugu, Sadaji** (m. given name)

逐次 **chikuji** one by one, in sequence

相次 **aitsu(gu)** follow in succession

11 副次的 **fukujiteki** secondary

12 腕次第 **ude-shidai** according to one's ability

14 漸次 **zenji** gradually

———— 3 ————

9 政務次官 **seimu jikan** parliamentary vice-minister

11 第一次 **dai-ichiji** first

2b4.2 / 1326 ☐ 士 冫 丨
22 5 2

壮

壮丨壮壮

SŌ manhood; strength; prosperity **saka(n)** prosperous

———— 1 ————

3 壮大 **sōdai** grand, magnificent, spectacular

12 壮絶 **sōzetsu** sublime, magnificent

———— 2 ————

11 強壮 **kyōsō** strong, robust, sturdy

決 → 決 **3a4.6**

2b4.4 / 1562 ☐ 冫 儿 ㇄
5 16 10

兆

兆丨兆兆

CHŌ sign, indication; trillion, 1,000,000,000,000 **kiza(shi)** signs, omen, symptoms **kiza(su)** show signs of

———— 1 ————

10 兆候 **chōkō** sign, indication

— 2 —

6 吉兆 **kitchō** good/lucky omen
9 前兆 **zenchō** portent, omen, sign

2b4.5 / 590

羽

U, ha feather **hane** feather, wing; (propeller) blade **-wa, -ba** (counter for birds)

— 1 —

4 羽毛 **umō** feathers, plumage, down
5 羽目 **hame** situation, predicament; panel, wainscoting
羽田 **Haneda** (airport in Tōkyō)
8 羽突 **hanetsu(ki)** battledore and shuttlecock (badminton-like game)
18 羽織 **haori** Japanese half-coat **hao(ru)** put on

— 5 —

2b5.1 / 626

状

JŌ condition, circumstances; form, appearance; letter

— 1 —

8 状況 **jokyō** circumstances
14 状態 **jōtai** state of affairs, situation

— 2 —

5 令状 **reijō** warrant, writ
白状 **hakujō** confess, admit
礼状 **reijō** letter of thanks
8 免状 **menjō** diploma; license
波状 **hajō** wave, undulation
実状 **jitsujō** actual state of affairs
9 悔状 **ku(yami)jō** letter of condolence
10 原状 **genjō** original state
病状 **byōjō** patient's condition
症状 **shōjō** symptoms
粉状 **funjō** powder(ed)

11 現状 **genjō** present situation, current state of affairs
情状 **jōjō** circumstances, conditions
異状 **ijō** something wrong, abnormality
12 賀状 **gajō** greeting card
13 詫状 **wa(bi)jō** written apology
15 賞状 **shōjō** certificate of merit
17 環状線 **kanjōsen** loop/belt line

— 3 —

6 年賀状 **nengajō** New Year's card
仮免状 **karimenjō** temporary license; provisional diploma
8 招待状 **shōtaijō** (written) invitation
11 推薦状 **suisenjō** letter of recommendation
紹介状 **shōkaijō** letter of introduction
12 無症状 **mushōjō** without symptoms

2b5.2 / 2023

冴

GO, sa(eru) be clear; be cold; become skilled **GO, KO, SAE** (part of given name)

— 1 —

12 冴渡 **sa(e)wata(ru)** get cold; freeze over

況 → 況 **3a5.21**

2b5.3 / 832

冷

REI, tsume(tai) cold **hi(eru)** get cold **hi(yasu)** cool, refrigerate **hi(yakasu)** banter, tease; window-shop, browse; cool in water or ice **hi(ya)** cold water/saké/rice **sa(meru)** get cold, cool down **sa(masu)** let cool; put a damper on

―――――――― 1 ――――――――

4 冷水 **reisui, hi(ya)mizu** cold water
6 冷気 **reiki** cold, chill, cold weather
冷汗 **hi(ya)ase, reikan** a cold sweat
8 冷房 **reibō** air conditioning
10 冷凍 **reitō** freezing, refrigeration
冷凍庫 **reitōko** freezer
冷笑 **reishō** derisive smile, scornful laugh, sneer
13 冷戦 **reisen** cold war
14 冷静 **reisei** calm, cool, unruffled
冷酷 **reikoku** cruel, callous
15 冷蔵庫 **reizōko** refrigerator

―――――――― 2 ――――――――

12 寒冷 **kanrei** cold, chilly
寒冷前線 **kanrei zensen** cold front

2b5.4 / 2024 ☐ 口 冫 竹
24 5 17

冶 冶冶

YA smelting; captivating **YA** (part of given name)

―――――――― 1 ――――――――

8 冶金 **yakin** metallurgy

2b5.5 / 724 灬 冫 一 丨
21 1 2

求 求 求

KYŪ, moto(meru/mu) want, seek, request, demand **MOTOMU** (m. given name) **MOTO** (part of given name)

―――――――― 1 ――――――――

2 求人 **kyūjin** seeking workers, Help Wanted
11 求婚 **kyūkon** proposal of marriage
18 求職 **kyūshoku** job hunting, Situation Wanted

―――――――― 2 ――――――――

8 追求 **tsuikyū, o(i)moto(meru)** pursue
9 要求 **yōkyū** require, demand
11 欲求 **yokkyū** wants, desires

欲求不満 **yokkyū fuman** frustration
15 請求 **seikyū** demand, request
請求書 **seikyūsho** application, claim, bill

―――――――― 6 ――――――――

2b6.3 ☐ 冫 丆 ☐
21 14 20

函 函丨函函

KAN, hako box

―――――――― 1 ――――――――

16 函館 **Hakodate** (city, Hokkaidō)

―――――――― 7 ――――――――

飛→ **0a9.4**

―――――――― 8 ――――――――

2b8.1 / 1232 ☐ 隹 冫
74 5

准 准准

JUN quasi-, semi-, associate

―――――――― 1 ――――――――

3 准士官 **junshikan** warrant officer

―――――――― 2 ――――――――

7 批准 **hijun** ratification

2b8.2 / 1205 ☐ 朿 日 冫
41 43 5

凍 凍凍

TŌ, kō(ru), kogo(eru), shi(miru), i(teru) freeze (intr.) **kō(rasu)** freeze (tr.) **kogo(eru)** be frozen, be chilled

―――――――― 1 ――――――――

6 凍死 **tōshi, kogo(e)ji(nu), kogo(e)ji(ni)** freeze to death
12 凍結 **tōketsu** freeze

─────────── 2 ───────────

⁷ 冷凍 **reitō** freezing, refrigeration
冷凍庫 **reitōko** freezer

2b8.3 / 627   田 小 寸 冫
                        35 37   5

将 | 将 将

SHŌ commander, general **masa (ni)**
just about to, on the verge of SUSUMU
(m. given name) MASA (part of given
name)

─────────── 1 ───────────

⁷ 将来 **shōrai** future
⁹ 将軍 **shōgun** general, commander,
shogun
¹² 将棋 **shōgi** shōgi, Japanese chess

─────────── 2 ───────────

³ 大将 **taishō** general; admiral; head,
leader, boss
⁵ 主将 **shushō** commander-in-chief;
captain (of a team)

2b8.4   田 ヨ 女 冫
                        39 25   5

凄 | 凄 凄

SEI, sugo(i), susa(majii) awful, tre-
mendous, terrible, enormous
sugo(mu) threaten

─────────── 1 ───────────

¹¹ 凄惨 **seisan** ghastly, gruesome, lurid

2b8.5 / 2025   田 女 土 冫
                        49 22   5

凌 凌

RYŌ, shino(gu) withstand; stave off,
keep out; tide over, pull through; surpass, outdo SHINOGU, NOBORU,
WATARU (m. given name) RYŌ
(part of given name)

─────────── 1 ───────────

¹⁰ 凌辱 **ryōjoku** insult, affront; rape
¹⁵ 凌駕 **ryōga** surpass, excel, outdo

─────────── 2 ───────────

¹² 暑凌 **atsu(sa)shino(gi)** relief from
the heat

凉 → 涼 3a8.31

─────────── 9 ───────────

2b9.1 / 2132   ⑳ 冫 艹 一
                        21 12   1

毬 毬

KYŪ, iga burr **mari** ball KYŪ,
MARI (part of given name)

─────────── 11 ───────────

奬 → 3n10.4

─────────── 13 ───────────

2b13.1 / 2026   田 ネ 口 冫
                        45 24   5

凜 | 凜 凜

RIN cold; chilling RIN (part of giv-
en name)

─────────── 1 ───────────

³ 凜々 **rinrin** severe, intense, biting;
awe-inspiring **riri(shii)** gallant, imposing

─────────── 14 ───────────

2b14.1 / 1518   田 大 冫 ト
                        34   5 13

凝 凝

GYŌ, ko(ru) get stiff; be absorbed in,
be a fanatic; to elaborate **ko(tta)** elaborate, exquisite **ko(rasu)** concentrate,
devote, apply, strain **kogo(ru)** congeal, freeze **shiko(ru)** stiffen, harden

—————— 1 ——————

8 凝固 **gyōko** solidify, congeal, coagulate **ko(ri)kata(maru)** coagulate; be fanatical

凝性 **ko(ri)shō** single-minded en-

thusiasm, fastidiousness

11 凝視 **gyōshi** stare, steady gaze, fixation

17 凝縮 **gyōshuku** condensation

—————— 子 2c ——————

子	了	孔	存	孝	丞	孟	承	孤	孫	孵	學
0.1	0.3	1.1	3.1	2k4.3	4.3	5.1	0a7.7	6.2	7.1	3n10.5	3n4.2

—————— 0 ——————

2c0.1 / 103

□ 子
6

子

子 子

SHI, SU child; (male name suffix) **ko** child, offspring; (female name suffix) **ne** first horary sign (rat) NE (part of given name)

—————— 1 ——————

6 子会社 **kogaisha** a subsidiary

子守 **komori** baby tending/sitting; nursemaid, baby sitter

8 子供 **kodomo** child **kodomo(rashii)** childlike

9 子孫 **shison** descendants

子音 **shiin** consonant

10 子宮 **shikyū** the uterus, womb

子息 **shisoku** son

—————— 2 ——————

1 一子 **isshi** a child; an only child **hitorigo** an only child

2 二子 **futago** twins, a twin

3 孔子 **Kōshi** Confucius (Chinese philosopher, 551 – 479 B.C.)

女子 **joshi** woman; women's **onna(no)ko** girl **onago** girl, woman, maid

4 太子 **taishi** crown prince

双子 **futago** twins, a twin

文子 **Fumiko, Ayako, Noriko** (f. given name)

王子 **ōji** prince

5 末子 **sue(k)ko, basshi, masshi** youngest child

母子 **boshi, hahako** mother and child

冊子 **sasshi** booklet, pamphlet **sōshi** storybook

穴子 **anago** conger eel

礼子 **Reiko, Noriko** (f. given name)

玉子 **tamago** egg

6 朱子学 **Shushigaku** Neo-Confucianism

年子 **toshigo** children (of the same mother) born within a year of each other

孝子 **Takako, Kōko** (f. given name)

老子 **Rōshi** Laozi, Lao-tzu (founder of Taoism)

竹子 **take(no)ko** bamboo shoots

7 孟子 **Mōshi** Mencius (Chinese philosopher, 372 – 289 B.C.)

卵子 **ranshi** ovum, egg cell

判子 **hanko** one's seal

弟子 **deshi, teishi** pupil, disciple, adherent, apprentice

芥子 **karashi** mustard **keshi** poppy

芥子菜 **karashina** mustard plant, rape

売子 **u(rek)ko** popular person **u(ri)ko** salesclerk

杓子 **shakushi** dipper, ladle, scoop

杏子 **Kyōko, Momoko, Yōko** (f. given name)

利子 **rishi** interest (on a loan)

男子 **danshi** man, male, boy, son **otoko(no)ko** boy

男子用 **danshiyō** for men, men's

8 佳子 **Yoshiko, Keiko** (f. given name)

郁子 **Ikuko, Fumiko** (f. given name)

京子 **Kyōko, Keiko, Takako** (f. given name)

直子 **Naoko** (f. given name)

迷子 **maigo, mayo(i)go** lost child

幸子 **Sachiko, Yukiko, Kōko, Kōshi, Toshiko** (given name)

拍子 **hyōshi** time, tempo, beat; chance, moment

妻子 **saishi** wife and child(ren)

茄子 **nasu, nasubi** eggplant

尚子 **Naoko, Hisako, Shōko, Takako, Yoshiko** (f. given name)

明子 **Akiko, Haruko, Meiko, Akeko** (f. given name)

昌子 **Masako, Shōko, Akiko** (f. given name)

金子 **Kaneko** (surname)

9 信子 **Nobuko** (f. given name)

美子 **Yoshiko, Haruko, Miko, Tomiko** (f. given name)

逗子 **Zushi** (city, Kanagawa-ken)

風子 **kaze (no) ko** (children are) outdoor creatures

洋子 **Yōko, Hiroko, Namiko** (f. given name)

独子 **hito(rik)ko, hito(ri)go** an only child

栄子 **Eiko** (f. given name)

面子 **mentsu** face, honor　**menko** cardboard game doll

柚子 **yuzu** citron

胞子 **hōshi** spore

昭子 **Akiko, Teruko** (f. given name)

祐子 **Yūko, Sachiko** (f. given name)

10 原子 **genshi** atom

原子力 **genshiryoku** atomic energy, nuclear power

浩子 **Hiroko** (f. given name)

淳子 **Atsuko, Junko** (f. given name)

恭子 **Kyōko, Yasuko, Yukiko** (f. given name)

格子 **kōshi** lattice, bars, grating, grille

祥子 **Shōko, Sachiko, Yoshiko, Yōko, Toshiko** (f. given name)

恵子 **Keiko, Shigeko** (f. given name)

息子 **musuko** son

惇子 **Junko, Atsuko** (f. given name)

扇子 **sensu** folding fan

純子 **Junko, Sumiko** (f. given name)

11 陽子 **Yōko, Haruko** (f. given name)

捻子 **neji** screw; (wind-up toy) spring

捨子 **su(te)go** abandoned child, foundling

捩子 **neji** screw; (wind-up toy) spring

啓子 **Keiko, Hiroko** (f. given name)

彩子 **Ayako, Saiko, Saeko** (f. given name)

菓子 **(o)kashi** candy, confection, pastry

菓子屋 **kashiya** candy store, confectionery shop

康子 **Yasuko, Kōko, Sadako** (f. given name)

梯子 **hashigo** ladder; barhopping, pub-crawling

粒子 **ryūshi** (atomic) particle; grain (in film)

12 揚子江 **Yōsukō** the Yangtze/Yangzi river

帽子 **bōshi** hat, cap

椰子 **yashi** palm/coconut tree

椅子 **isu** chair, seat, couch

晶子 **Akiko, Shōko** (f. given name)

敬子 **Keiko, Takako** (f. given name)

硝子 **garasu** glass

裕子 **Yūko, Hiroko** (f. given name)

順子 **Junko, Yoriko, Noriko, Nobuko** (f. given name)

13 障子 **shōji** sliding door with translucent paper panes

隠子 **kaku(shi)go** illegitimate child

嗣子 **shishi** heir

獅子 **shishi** lion

楊子江 **Yōsukō** the Yangzi/Yangtze river

2

イ
冫
子　0
阝
卩
刂
力
又
亠
十
勹
冖
厂
辶
冂
几
匚

照子 **Teruko, Shōko, Mitsuko** (f. given name)

聖子 **Seiko, Kiyoko, Satoko, Shōko** (f. given name)

碍子 **gaishi** insulator

靖子 **Yasuko, Seiko, Shizuko** (f. given name)

節子 **Setsuko, Sadako** (f. given name)

雅子 **Masako, Motoko, Utako, Tsuneko** (f. given name)

電子 **denshi** electron
denshi- electronic

電子レンジ **denshi renji** microwave oven

14 嫡子 **chakushi** legitimate child

様子 **yōsu** situation, aspect, appearance

種子島 **Tanegashima** (island, Kagoshima-ken)

踊子 **odo(ri)ko** dancer, dancing girl

15 養子 **yōshi, yashina(i)go** adopted child

慶子 **Keiko, Yoshiko** (f. given name)

調子 **chōshi** tone; mood; condition

16 親子 **oyako, shinshi** parent and child

親子丼 **oyako donburi** bowl of rice topped with chicken and egg

鍵子 **kagi(k)ko** latchkey child (who carries a key to school because no one will be home when he returns)

17 優子 **Yūko, Masako** (f. given name)

螺子 **neji** screw; stopcock; (wind-up) spring

——————— 3 ———————

1 一人子 **hitorikko, hitorigo** an only child

3 久美子 **Kumiko** (f. given name)

千代子 **Chiyoko** (f. given name)

5 由美子 **Yumiko** (f. given name)

7 伽草子 **(o)togizōshi** fairy-tale book

乳飲子 **chino(mi)go** suckling infant, babe in arms

車椅子 **kurumaisu** wheelchair

8 長椅子 **nagaisu** sofa, couch

和菓子 **wagashi** Japanese-style confections

9 美代子 **Miyoko** (f. given name)

美男子 **bidanshi, binanshi** handsome man

美智子 **Michiko** (f. given name)

茶菓子 **chagashi** teacakes

皇太子 **kōtaishi** crown prince

10 唐辛子 **tōgarashi** cayenne/red pepper

恵美子 **Emiko** (f. given name)

12 婿養子 **muko-yōshi** son-in-law adopted as an heir

富美子 **Fumiko, Tomiko** (f. given name)

——————— 4 ———————

1 一人息子 **hitori musuko** an only son

一本調子 **ipponchōshi, ipponjōshi** monotony

3 大和撫子 **Yamato nadeshiko** daughter/woman of Japan

2c0.3 / 941

RYŌ complete, finish; understand

——————— 1 ———————

7 了承 **ryōshō** acknowledge, understand

了見 **ryōken** idea; intention; decision, discretion; forgive

13 了解 **ryōkai** understand, comprehend; Roger!

——————— 2 ———————

5 未了 **miryō** unfinished

7 完了 **kanryō** complete, finish, conclude

10 修了 **shūryō** completion (of a course)

11 終了 **shūryō** end, conclusion, completion, expiration

12 満了 **manryō** expiration

15 魅了 **miryō** charm, captivate, hold spellbound

——— 1 ———

2c1.1 / 940　　　　□ 子 一
　　　　　　　　　　　　6　2

孔　　　孔孔

KŌ, KU hole; Confucius; huge **ana** hole

——— 1 ———

2 孔子 **Kōshi** Confucius (Chinese philosopher, 551 – 479 B.C.)
11 孔雀 **kujaku** peacock

——— 2 ———

10 穿孔 **senkō** perforation; punching, boring

——— 3 ———

2c3.1 / 269　　　　□ 十 子 一
　　　　　　　　　　　　12　6　2

存　　　存存

SON, ZON be, exist TAMOTSU (m. given name) ARI (part of given name)

——— 1 ———

0 存じる **zon(jiru)** know, be aware of; think, feel
4 存分 **zonbun (ni)** to one's heart's content, as much as one wants, without reserve
6 存在 **sonzai** exist
13 存続 **sonzoku** continued existence, duration

——— 2 ———

5 生存 **seizon** existence, life, survival
6 共存 **kyōson, kyōzon** coexistence
8 依存 **ison, izon** depend on, be dependent on
　並存 **heizon** coexistence
　実存 **jitsuzon** existence
9 保存 **hozon** preservation
10 既存 **kison** existing
　残存者 **zansonsha** survivor, holdover

11 現存 **genson, genzon** living, existing, extant
12 御存 **gozon(ji)** (as) you know

——— 4 ———

13 適者生存 **tekisha seizon** survival of the fittest

——— 4 ———

孝→ **2k4.3**

2c4.3 / 2002　　　　目 氵 一
　　　　　　　　　　　　21　1

丞　　　丞丞

JŌ, SHŌ help JŌ, SHŌ, SUKE, TSUGU (part of given name) SUSUMU, TASUKU, AKIRA (m. given name)

——— 5 ———

2c5.1 / 2049　　　　日 皿 子
　　　　　　　　　　　　59　6

孟　　　孟孟

MŌ beginning; leader; Mencius MŌ, TAKE, MOTO, TOMO, OSA, NAGA (part of given name) TAKESHI, TSUTOMU, HAJIME (m. given name)

——— 1 ———

2 孟子 **Mōshi** Mencius (Chinese philosopher, 372 – 289 B.C.)

承→ **0a7.7**

——— 6 ———

2c6.2 / 1480　　　　□ 子 厂 竹
　　　　　　　　　　　6　18　17

孤　　　孤孤

KO alone; orphan

——— 1 ———

5 孤立 **koritsu** be isolated
7 孤児 **koji, minashigo** orphan

⁹ 孤独 **kodoku** solitary, isolated, lonely

━━━━━━━ 7 ━━━━━━━

2c7.1 / 910　　□ 糸 子 |
　　　　　　　　　61 6 2

孫

孫 孫

SON descendants **mago** grandchild

━━━━━━━ 2 ━━━━━━━

² 子孫 **shison** descendants

━━━━━━━ 10 ━━━━━━━

孵→ **3n10.5**

━━━━━━━ 13 ━━━━━━━

學→学 **3n4.2**

━━━━━━━ 阝 2d ━━━━━━━

防 4.1	阪 4.4	那 4.6	邦 4.7	邨 4a3.11	阻 5.1	附 5.4	陀 5.5	阿 5.6	邪 5.8	邸 5.10	限 6.1	郎 6.5
郁 6.6	郊 6.8	陣 7.1	陛 7.6	降 7.7	院 7.9	除 7.10	陷 7.11	郎 2d6.5	郡 7.12	郷 2d8.14	郭 7.14	陳 8.2
陪 8.3	陸 8.4	陵 8.5	隆 8.6	陰 8.7	険 8.8	陷 2d7.11	随 8.10	陶 8.11	郵 8.12	都 8.13	郷 8.14	部 8.15
隅 9.1	陽 9.5	階 9.6	隆 2d8.6	隊 9.7	郷 2d8.14	都 2d8.13	隔 10.2	隙 10.4	郷 2d8.14	隙 2d10.4	際 11.1	障 11.2
隠 11.3	鄙 11.4	随 2d8.10	隣 13.1	鄰 2d13.1	険 2d8.8	隠 2d11.3						

━━━━━━━ 4 ━━━━━━━

2d4.1 / 513　　□ 方 阝
　　　　　　　　　48 7

防

防 防

BŌ protect against, prevent; (as prefix) anti-, -proof, -resistant **fuse(gu)** defend, protect against, prevent, resist

━━━━━━━ 1 ━━━━━━━

⁴ 防止 **bōshi** prevention
　防水 **bōsui** waterproof, watertight; flooding prevention
　防火 **bōka** fire prevention, fire fighting, fireproof
⁵ 防犯 **bōhan** crime prevention
⁸ 防空 **bōkū** air defense
⁹ 防音 **bōon** sound-deadening, soundproof(ing)
¹² 防備 **bōbi** defensive preparations

防弾 **bōdan** bulletproof; bombproof
防御 **bōgyo** defense
防寒 **bōkan** protection against the cold
¹⁴ 防腐剤 **bōfuzai** a preservative, antiseptic
¹⁶ 防衛 **bōei** defense
防衛庁 **Bōeichō** Defense Agency

━━━━━━━ 2 ━━━━━━━

⁴ 予防 **yobō** prevent, protect against
　水防 **suibō** flood prevention
⁷ 攻防 **kōbō** offense and defense
⁸ 国防 **kokubō** national defense
¹⁰ 消防 **shōbō** fire fighting, firemen
　消防署 **shōbōsho** fire station
¹² 堤防 **teibō** embankment, dike, levee
　無防備 **mubōbi** defenseless, unfortified

2d4.4 / 1947   囗 阝 厂 又
                                7 18 9

阪

阪 阪

HAN slope; embankment; Ōsaka
saka slope

——————— 1 ———————

5 阪本 **Sakamoto** (surname)
9 阪神 **Han-Shin** Ōsaka-Kōbe area

——————— 2 ———————

3 大阪 **Ōsaka** (city, Ōsaka-fu)
8 京阪神 **Kei-Han-Shin** Kyōto-Ōsaka-Kōbe

2d4.6 / 2251   囗 カ 二 阝
                                8 4 7

那

那 | 那 那

NA what, which   NA, DA, TOMO, YA-
SU, FUYU (part of given name)

——————— 1 ———————

19 那覇 **Naha** (city, Okinawa-ken)

——————— 2 ———————

4 支那 **Shina** China
5 旦那 **danna** master; husband; gen-
        tleman
8 利那 **setsuna** moment, instant

——————— 3 ———————

1 一利那 **issetsuna** an instant, a mo-
        ment

2d4.7 / 808   囗 十 二 阝
                             12 4 7

邦

邦 邦

HŌ country; our country   **kuni**
country   KUNI (part of given name)

——————— 1 ———————

5 邦字 **hōji** Japanese characters
8 邦画 **hōga** Japanese movie/painting

11 邦訳 **hōyaku** translation into Japa-
        nese
   邦貨 **hōka** Japanese currency; yen

——————— 2 ———————

9 連邦 **renpō** federation; federal

邨 → 村   **4a3.11**

——————— 5 ———————

2d5.1 / 1085   囗 月 阝 一
                               42 7 1

阻

阻 阻

SO, haba(mu) obstruct, prevent, impede, block, hamper

——————— 1 ———————

4 阻止 **soshi** obstruct, hinder, deter,
        check
10 阻害 **sogai** impede, check, hinder,
        retard

——————— 2 ———————

10 険阻 **kenso** steep

2d5.4 / 1843   囗 寸 阝 イ
                               37 7 3

附

附 附

FU attached   **tsu(ku)** be attached
tsu(keru) attach

——————— 1 ———————

12 附属 **fuzoku** attached, affiliated,
        ancillary

2d5.5   囗 宀 阝 ヒ
                             33 7 13

陀

陀 陀

DA slanting

——————— 2 ———————

4 仏陀 **Butsuda, Budda** Buddha

11 曼陀羅 **mandara** mandala, picture of Buddha

———————— 3 ————————

7 阿弥陀 **Amida** Amida Buddha; lottery; wearing a hat on the back of the head

2d5.6 / 2258

阿　阿阿

□　口　阝　一
24　7　14

A, O (used phonetically)　**omone(ru)** be obsequious　A, O, KUMA (part of given name)

———————— 1 ————————

4 阿片 **ahen** opium
5 阿古屋貝 **akoyagai** pearl oyster
7 阿呆 **ahō** fool, jackass
8 阿弥陀 **Amida** Amida Buddha; lottery; wearing a hat on the back of the head
10 阿倍 **Abe** (surname)
　 阿部 **Abe** (surname)

2d5.8 / 1457

邪　邪丨邪邪

□　一　亠　阝
14　11　7

JA evil, unjust, wicked　**yokoshima** wicked, evil, dishonest, unjust

———————— 1 ————————

8 邪念 **janen** sinister intent, evil designs
10 邪教 **jakyō** heretical religion, heathenism
11 邪推 **jasui** unjust suspicion, mistrust
21 邪魔 **jama** hinder, obstruct, get in the way, interfere, bother, disturb

———————— 2 ————————

9 風邪 **kaze, fūja** a cold

2d5.10 / 563

邸　邸邸

□　厂　十　阝
18　12　7

TEI, yashiki mansion, residence

———————— 1 ————————

6 邸宅 **teitaku** mansion, residence

———————— 2 ————————

8 官邸 **kantei** official residence

———————— 6 ————————

2d6.1 / 847

限　限限

□　食　阝
73　7

GEN, kagi(ru) limit, restrict
kagi(ri) limit(s); as far/much as possible; (as suffix) only; no later than

———————— 1 ————————

8 限定 **gentei** limit, qualify, modify; define, determine
9 限度 **gendo** limit
　 限界 **genkai** limit, boundary; marginal; critical

———————— 2 ————————

6 年限 **nengen** term, length of time
　 有限会社 **yūgen-gaisha** limited liability company, Ltd.
7 局限 **kyokugen** localize, limit
8 制限 **seigen** restriction, limitation
　 定限 **teigen** limit, restrict
　 門限 **mongen** closing time
10 時限 **jigen** time limit; time (bomb)
12 極限 **kyokugen** limit, extremity
　 期限 **kigen** term, period, due date, deadline
　 無限 **mugen** infinite
15 権限 **kengen** authority, power, jurisdiction

———————— 3 ————————

12 無期限 **mukigen** indefinite, without time limit

2d6.5 / 980 囗 食 阝 73 7

郎 郎 | 郎郎

RŌ man; husband RŌ, O (part of given name)

— 2 —

1 一郎 **Ichirō, Kazuo** (m. given name)
2 二郎 **Jirō, Nirō** (m. given name)
3 三郎 **Saburō, Mitsuo, Kazuo** (m. given name)
5 史郎 **Shirō, Fumio** (m. given name)
8 治郎 **Jirō, Haruo** (m. given name)
9 俊郎 **Toshirō, Toshio, Shunrō** (m. given name)
10 敏郎 **Toshirō, Toshio** (m. given name)
11 野郎 **yarō** fellow, guy, bastard
13 義郎 **Yoshirō, Yoshio, Girō** (m. given name)
新郎新婦 **shinrō-shinpu** the bride and groom

— 3 —

5 広太郎 **Hirotarō, Kōtarō** (m. given name)
10 健太郎 **Kentarō** (m. given name)

2d6.6 / 2252 囗 月 十 阝 42 12 7

郁 郁郁

IKU culturally advanced; fragrant IKU, KUNI, KA, AYA, FUMI (part of given name) KAORU, KAORI (f. given name) TAKASHI (m. given name)

— 1 —

2 郁子 **Ikuko, Fumiko** (f. given name)
4 郁夫 **Ikuo, Kunio, Ayao** (m. given name)
郁文堂 **Ikubundō** (publishing company)

2d6.8 / 817 日 亠 儿 十 11 16 12

郊 郊郊

KŌ suburbs; the country(side)

— 1 —

5 郊外 **kōgai** suburbs, outskirts

— 2 —

6 近郊 **kinkō** suburbs

— 7 —

2d7.1 / 1404 囗 車 阝 69 7

陣 陣陣

JIN battle array, ranks; camp; brief time, sudden

— 1 —

12 陣営 **jin'ei** camp
陣痛 **jintsū** labor (pains)

2d7.6 / 589 日 土 阝 ⺊ 22 7 13

陛 陛陛

HEI, kizahashi steps (of the throne)

— 1 —

3 陛下 **Heika** His/Her Majesty

— 2 —

6 両陛下 **Ryōheika** Their Majesties

— 3 —

4 天皇陛下 **Tennō Heika** His Majesty the Emperor
9 皇后陛下 **Kōgō Heika** Her Majesty the Empress

2d7.7 / 947

田 夂 阝 十
49 7 12

降 降降

KŌ come/go down; surrender **fu(ru)** fall, come down (rain, etc.) **o(riru)** come/go down, get off (a vehicle) **o(rosu)** take/get down (from a shelf); let (someone) alight, drop (someone) off **kuda(ru)** surrender **kuda(su)** defeat **kuda(tte)** (from then) on down; as for me

——————— 1 ———————

3 降下 **kōka** descend, fall, drop
　降口 **o(ri)guchi, o(ri)kuchi** exit (from a station)
7 降車 **kōsha** get off (a train)
8 降雨 **kōu** rain(fall)

——————— 2 ———————

3 下降 **kakō** descend, fall, sink
5 以降 **ikō** on and after, beginning ...
7 投降 **tōkō** surrender
8 昇降 **shōkō** rise and fall, ascend and descend
9 飛降 **tobio(ri)** jumping off
17 霜降 **shimofu(ri)** marbled (meat), salt-and-pepper pattern

——————— 3 ———————

3 土砂降 **doshabu(ri)** downpour

2d7.9 / 614

田 宀 阝 二
33 7 4

院 院院

IN institution, palace, temple, hospital, school, house (of a legislature); ex-emperor

——————— 1 ———————

8 院長 **inchō** head of the hospital/ school/institute

——————— 2 ———————

2 入院 **nyūin** be admitted to hospital
3 上院 **jōin** the Upper House (of a legislature), Senate

下院 **kain** the Lower House (of a legislature)
6 両院 **ryōin** both houses (of parliament/congress)
　寺院 **jiin** temple
7 学院 **gakuin** academy
8 退院 **taiin** leave the hospital
　参院 **San'in** House of Councilors (short for 参議院)
10 病院 **byōin** hospital
13 僧院 **sōin** temple; monastery
20 議院 **giin** house of a legislature, diet

——————— 3 ———————

3 大学院 **daigakuin** graduate school
6 両議院 **ryōgiin** both houses (of parliament/congress)
8 参議院 **Sangiin** House of Councilors
9 美容院 **biyōin** beauty parlor, hairdresser's
10 修道院 **shūdōin** monastery, convent, cloister
11 控訴院 **kōsoin** court of appeal
12 衆議院 **Shūgiin** the House of Representatives

——————— 4 ———————

12 衆参両院 **shū-san ryōin** both Houses of the Diet

2d7.10 / 1065

田 木 阝 亻
41 7 3

除 除除

JO, JI exclude, remove; division (in math) **nozo(ku)** exclude, except; remove, abolish, cancel **no(keru)** remove, clear out of the way, get rid of; omit **nozo(ite)** except **-yo(ke)** protection against, charm

——————— 1 ———————

5 除外 **jogai** exception
　除去 **jokyo** remove, eliminate
13 除幕式 **jomakushiki** unveiling (ceremony)

─────── 2 ───────

⁴ 切除 **setsujo** cut off/out, remove, excise

　日除 **hiyo(ke)** sunshade, awning, blind

⁶ 虫除 **mushiyo(ke)** insect repellent, charm against insects

⁸ 免除 **menjo** exemption

⁹ 乗除 **jōjo** multiplication and division

　削除 **sakujo** delete, eliminate

¹¹ 排除 **haijo** exclude, remove, eliminate

　控除 **kōjo** deduct, subtract

　掃除 **sōji** cleaning, clean-up

　掃除機 **sōjiki** vacuum cleaner

¹³ 解除 **kaijo** cancel, rescind; release from

─────── 3 ───────

³ 大掃除 **ōsōji** general house-cleaning, spring/fall cleaning

─────── 4 ───────

⁵ 加減乗除 **kagenjōjo** addition, subtraction, multiplication, and division

2d7.11 / 1218　　⊞　日　阝　宀
　　　　　　　　　　43　7　15

KAN, ochii(ru) fall/get into, sink, cave in; fall (to the enemy)
otoshii(reru) entrap, ensnare; capture (a town)

─────── 1 ───────

¹² 陥落 **kanraku** fall, surrender (of a city); sinking, a cave-in

─────── 2 ───────

⁴ 欠陥 **kekkan** defect, deficiency, shortcoming

⁵ 失陥 **shikkan** surrender, fall

郎 → 郎　**2d6.5**

2d7.12 / 193　　⊞　彐　口　阝
　　　　　　　　　　39　24　7

GUN county, district　**KUNI** (part of given name)

郷 → **2d8.14**

2d7.14 / 1673　　⊞　口　亠　子
　　　　　　　　　　24　11　6

KAKU enclosure; town wall
kuruwa area enclosed by earthwork, fortification; quarter, district; red-light district

─────── 1 ───────

⁴ 郭公 **kakkō** cuckoo

─────── 2 ───────

⁹ 城郭 **jōkaku** castle; castle walls

¹⁰ 遊郭 **yūkaku** red-light district

¹⁵ 輪郭 **rinkaku** outline, contours

─────── 8 ───────

2d8.2 / 1405　　⊞　木　日　阝
　　　　　　　　　　41　43　7

CHIN state, explain; line up; old
no(beru) state, mention, explain
NOBU (part of given name)

─────── 1 ───────

⁶ 陳列 **chinretsu** exhibit, display

⁷ 陳述書 **chinjutsusho** statement, declaration

¹¹ 陳情書 **chinjōsho** petition, representation

2d8.3 / 1943

立 口 阝
54 24 7

陪

陪陪

BAI follow, accompany, attend on

————— 1 —————

15 陪審 **baishin** jury

2d8.4 / 647

土 阝 儿
22 7 16

陸

陸陸

RIKU, ROKU, oka land RIKU (m. given name) MUTSU (part of given name)

————— 1 —————

3 陸上 **rikujō** on shore, land
9 陸軍 **rikugun** army
11 陸運 **rikuun** land transport

————— 2 —————

3 大陸 **tairiku** continent
　上陸 **jōriku** landing, going ashore
5 北陸地方 **Hokuriku chihō** the Hokuriku region (Fukui, Ishikawa, Toyama, Niigata prefectures)
12 着陸 **chakuriku** (airplane) landing
18 離陸 **ririku** (airplane) takeoff

————— 3 —————

11 軟着陸 **nanchakuriku** soft landing

2d8.5 / 1844

夂 土 阝
49 22 7

陵

陵陵

RYŌ, misasagi imperial tomb

————— 2 —————

5 丘陵 **kyūryō** hill

2d8.6 / 946

夂 牛 阝
49 47 7

隆

隆ǀ隆隆

RYŪ high; noble; flourishing
TAKASHI (m. given name) RYŪ, TAKA (part of given name)

————— 1 —————

1 隆一 **Ryūichi, Takaichi, Takakazu** (m. given name)
5 隆史 **Takashi, Takafumi** (m. given name)
　隆司 **Takashi, Ryūji, Takaji** (m. given name)
11 隆盛 **ryūsei** prosperous, flourishing, thriving

2d8.7 / 867

阝 亻 竹
7 3 17

陰

陰陰

IN, ON the yin principle; negative; shadow, hidden, back, dark, secret; sex organs; indebtedness, favor; hades
kage(ru) darken; cloud up; be obscured **kage** shade; back
(o)kage indebtedness, favor

————— 1 —————

6 陰気 **inki** gloomy, dreary
8 陰性 **insei** negative; dormant
10 陰険 **inken** tricky, wily, treacherous
　陰部 **inbu** the pubic region, the genitals
11 陰陽 **in'yō, on'yō** yin and yang, positive and negative, active and passive, male and female, sun and moon, light and shade **in (ni) yō (ni)** overtly and covertly, explicitly and implicitly
14 陰暦 **inreki** the lunar calendar
15 陰影 **in'ei** shadow; shading; gloom
16 陰謀 **inbō** conspiracy, plot, intrigue

—————— 2 ——————
⁴ 木陰 **kokage** tree shade
  日陰 **hikage** the shade
⁸ 物陰 **monokage** cover, hiding; a form, shape

2d8.8 / 533   口 ⻖ 亻
                        24 7 3

険 險┃險険

KEN steep; fearsome **kewa(shii)** steep; stern

—————— 1 ——————
⁷ 険阻 **kenso** steep
¹¹ 険悪 **ken'aku** dangerous, threatening, serious

—————— 2 ——————
⁶ 危険 **kiken** danger, risk
  危険物 **kikenbutsu** hazardous articles, explosives and combustibles
⁹ 保険 **hoken** insurance
  冒険 **bōken** adventure
¹⁰ 陰険 **inken** tricky, wily, treacherous
¹¹ 探険 **tanken** exploration, expedition

陷 → 陥 **2d7.11**

2d8.10 / 1741   口 月 ⻖ 十
                        42 7 12

随 随┃随随

ZUI, shitaga(u) follow **manimani** at the mercy of, with (the wind)

—————— 1 ——————
⁴ 随分 **zuibun** very
¹⁰ 随時 **zuiji** at any time, whenever required
¹² 随筆 **zuihitsu** essay, miscellaneous writings

¹³ 随想録 **zuisōroku** occasional thoughts, essays

—————— 2 ——————
⁵ 付随 **fuzui** incidental, concomitant, collateral
⁶ 気随 **kizui** willful, self-indulgent

—————— 3 ——————
⁸ 服装随意 **fukusō zuii** informal attire

2d8.11 / 1650   口 屮 ⻖ 勹
                        36 7 15

陶 陶陶

TŌ porcelain, pottery

—————— 1 ——————
⁷ 陶芸 **tōgei** ceramic art
¹¹ 陶酔 **tōsui** intoxication; fascination, rapture
¹⁴ 陶磁器 **tōjiki** ceramics, china and porcelain
¹⁵ 陶器 **tōki** china, ceramics, pottery

—————— 2 ——————
¹⁶ 薫陶 **kuntō** discipline, training, education
²⁹ 鬱陶 **uttō(shii)** gloomy, depressing

2d8.12 / 524   口 土 艹 ⻖
                        22 32 7

郵 郵郵

YŪ mail

—————— 1 ——————
⁸ 郵送料 **yūsōryō** postage
⁹ 郵便 **yūbin** mail
  郵便局 **yūbinkyoku** post office
  郵便箱 **yūbinbako** mailbox
  郵政省 **Yūseishō** Ministry of Posts and Telecommunications

2d8.13 / 188

口 日 土 阝
43 22 7

都

都｜都 都

TO, TSU, miyako capital, metropolis

──────── 1 ────────

4 都内 **tonai** within the capital

都心 **toshin** heart of the city, midtown

5 都市 **toshi** city

都立 **toritsu** metropolitan, municipal

6 都合 **tsugō** circumstances; one's convenience; opportunity; arrangements

都合上 **tsugōjō** for convenience

都会 **tokai** city **Tokai** Tōkyō Assembly

11 都道府県 **to-dō-fu-ken** prefectures

12 都営 **toei** city-run, metropolitan

──────── 2 ────────

3 大都会 **daitokai** big city

4 不都合 **futsugō** inconvenience, trouble, harm; impropriety, misconduct

5 好都合 **kōtsugō** favorable, good

6 宇都宮 **Utsunomiya** (city, Tochigi-ken)

8 京都 **Kyōto** (city, Kyōto-fu)

9 首都 **shuto** capital

12 御都合 **gotsugō** your convenience

2d8.14 / 855

川 食 竹 阝
73 17 7

郷

郷｜郷 郷

KYŌ, GŌ village, place, native place
Gō (surname) **SATO** (part of given name)

──────── 1 ────────

3 郷土 **kyōdo** one's native place; local

7 郷里 **kyōri** one's native place, home (town)

13 郷愁 **kyōshū** homesickness, nostalgia

──────── 2 ────────

9 故郷 **kokyō, furusato** birthplace, home town

10 帰郷 **kikyō** return home, return to one's home town

11 望郷 **bōkyō** homesickness, nostalgia

16 懐郷 **kaikyō** nostalgic reminiscence

2d8.15 / 86

口 立 口 阝
54 24 7

部

部 部

BU department; part, category; (counter for copies of a newspaper or magazine) **be** clan engaged in a certain occupation

──────── 1 ────────

3 部下 **buka** a subordinate, the people working under one

4 部分 **bubun** part **buwa(ke)** classification

部分的 **bubunteki** partial, here and there

8 部長 **buchō** department head

部門 **bumon** field, branch, line; division, section; class, category

9 部首 **bushu** radical (of a kanji)

部品 **buhin** parts

部屋 **heya** room, apartment

11 部隊 **butai** unit, corps, detachment, squad

部族 **buzoku** tribe

12 部落 **buraku** community, settlement, village

部落民 **burakumin** (lowly class of people historically engaged in butchery and tanning)

13 部数 **busū** number of copies, circulation

──────── 2 ────────

1 一部 **ichibu** a part; a copy (of a publication)

一部分 **ichibubun** a part

一部始終 **ichibu shijū** full particulars

2 二部 **nibu** two parts/copies; the second part

3 大部分 **daibubun** a large part, most; for the most part, mostly

上部 **jōbu** upper part/side, top surface

4 内部 **naibu** interior, inside, internal

中部 **chūbu** central part **Chūbu** the central Honshū region

文部省 **Monbushō** Ministry of Education

支部 **shibu** a branch (office), local chapter

5 北部 **hokubu** north, northern part

矢部 **Yabe** (surname)

本部 **honbu** headquarters

外部 **gaibu** the outside, external

主部 **shubu** main part; subject (in grammar)

6 西部 **seibu** western part, the west

全部 **zenbu** all, whole; entirely

7 阿部 **Abe** (surname)

学部 **gakubu** academic department, faculty

局部 **kyokubu** part, section; local; the affected region; one's private parts

8 服部 **Hattori** (surname)

9 軍部 **gunbu** the military

南部 **nanbu** southern part, the South

後部 **kōbu** back part, rear, stern

背部 **haibu** the back, posterior

10 陰部 **inbu** the pubic region, the genitals

胸部 **kyōbu** the chest

恥部 **chibu** the private parts

11 患部 **kanbu** diseased part, the affected area

12 渡部 **Watanabe, Watabe** (surname)

貸部屋 **ka(shi)beya** room for rent

13 腰部 **yōbu** the pelvic region, waist, hips, loins

腹部 **fukubu** abdomen, belly

幹部 **kanbu** (top) executives, management

――――― 3 ―――――

5 司令部 **shireibu** headquarters, the command

9 宣伝部 **sendenbu** publicity department

10 倶楽部 **kurabu** club

――――― 9 ―――――

2d9.1 / 1640   田 日 阝 竹
43 7 17

隅   隅隅

GŪ corner **sumi, sumi(kko)** corner, nook

――――― 1 ―――――

5 隅田川 **Sumida-gawa** (river, Tōkyō-to)

8 隈取 **kumado(ru)** tint, shade; make up (one's face) **kumado(ri)** shading; makeup

2d9.5 / 630   田 日 犭阝
43 27 7

陽   陽陽

YŌ the yang principle; positive; the sun **hi** the sun **AKIRA** (m. given name) **YŌ, HARU** (part of given name)

――――― 1 ―――――

2 陽子 **Yōko, Haruko** (f. given name)

6 陽気 **yōki** cheerful, gay, convivial; season, weather

陽当 **hia(tari)** exposure to the sun

8 陽性 **yōsei** positive

――――― 2 ―――――

4 太陽 **taiyō** the sun, solar

10 陰陽 **in'yō, on'yō** yin and yang, positive and negative, active and passive, male and female, sun and moon, light and shade **in (ni) yō (ni)** overtly and covertly, explicitly and implicitly

11 斜陽 **shayō** setting sun

2d9.6 / 588   田 日 阝 卜
            43 7 13

階

階|階

KAI stairs; step, grade; floor, story
kizahashi steps, stairway

---- 1 ----

9 階段 **kaidan** steps, stairs, stairway
   階級 **kaikyū** (social) class; (military) rank
14 階層 **kaisō** tier; social stratum, class

---- 2 ----

1 一階 **ikkai** first/ground floor
2 二階建 **nikaida(te)** two-story
9 段階 **dankai** stage, phase, step; rank, grade
   音階 **onkai** (musical) scale

隆 → 隆   **2d8.6**

2d9.7 / 795   田 犭 阝 儿
            27 7 16

隊

隊|隊隊

TAI squad, band

---- 1 ----

10 隊員 **taiin** member of a brigade/team

---- 2 ----

2 入隊 **nyūtai** enlist (in the army)
7 兵隊 **heitai** soldier; sailor
9 軍隊 **guntai** army, troops, corps
10 部隊 **butai** unit, corps, detachment, squad
11 船隊 **sentai** fleet
12 艇隊 **teitai** flotilla
13 楽隊 **gakutai** band, orchestra
21 艦隊 **kantai** fleet, squadron

---- 3 ----

6 自衛隊 **Jieitai** Self Defense Forces
13 鼓笛隊 **kotekitai** drum-and-bugle corps, fife-and-drum band
   愚連隊 **gurentai** hooligans, street gang

16 機動隊 **kidōtai** riot squad

郷 → 郷   **2d8.14**

都 → 都   **2d8.13**

---- 10 ----

2d10.2 / 1589   田 口 阝 冂
            24 7 20

隔

隔|隔隔

KAKU every other, alternate; distance between   **heda(teru)** separate, interpose, screen off; estrange, alienate **heda(taru)** be distant/separated from; become estranged

---- 1 ----

4 隔日 **kakujitsu** every other day, alternate days
5 隔世 **kakusei** a distant age
12 隔絶 **kakuzetsu** be isolated/separated
13 隔意 **kakui** reserve, estrangement
18 隔離 **kakuri** isolate, segregate

---- 2 ----

12 遠隔 **enkaku** distant, remote (control)
   間隔 **kankaku** space, spacing; interval

2d10.4   田 日 小 阝
            43 35 7

隙

隙|隙隙

GEKI crevice; spare time; discord
suki opening, crack, crevice, space; chance, opportunity; unguarded moment   **hima** (spare) time

---- 1 ----

12 隙間 **sukima** crevice, opening, gap, space

郷 → 郷   **2d8.14**

—————— 11 ——————

隙 → 隙 **2d10.4**

2d11.1 / 618   囗 ネ タ 阝
                           45 30 7

際際

SAI time, occasion, when; (as suffix)
inter- **kiwa** side, edge, verge
kiwa(doi) dangerous, critical, risky;
venturous; risqué

—————— 1 ——————

5 際立 **kiwada(tsu)** be conspicuous/
     prominent

—————— 2 ——————

1 一際 **hitokiwa** conspicuously; still
     more, especially

4 水際 **mizugiwa, migiwa** water's
     edge, shore

  手際 **tegiwa** performance, execu-
     tion; skill, deftness, workman-
     ship

6 交際 **kōsai** associate with, keep
     company with, be friends with

8 実際 **jissai** actual(ly), real(ly)

  国際 **kokusai** international

  国際化 **kokusaika** international-
     ization

  国際連合 **Kokusai Rengō** United
     Nations

12 間際 **magiwa** on the verge of, just
     before

—————— 3 ——————

19 瀬戸際 **setogiwa** crucial moment,
     crisis, brink

2d11.2 / 858   囗 立 日 阝
                           54 43 7

障障

SHŌ, sawa(ru) hinder, interfere with;
affect, hurt, harm

—————— 1 ——————

2 障子 **shōji** sliding door with trans-
     lucent paper panes

10 障害 **shōgai** obstacle, hindrance,
     impediment, handicap

  障害物 **shōgaibutsu** obstacle, ob-
     struction

—————— 2 ——————

4 支障 **shishō** hindrance, impedi-
     ment, difficulty

9 保障 **hoshō** guarantee, security

  故障 **koshō** out of order, break-
     down, trouble, accident, hin-
     drance, obstacle; objection

10 差障 **sa(shi)sawa(ri)** obstacle, hin-
     drance; offense

—————— 3 ——————

7 身体障害者 **shintai shōgaisha**
     physically handicapped person

2d11.3 / 868   囗 心 小
                           51 35 39

隠│隠隠

IN, ON, kaku(reru) (intr.) hide
kaku(su) (tr.) hide

—————— 1 ——————

2 隠子 **kaku(shi)go** illegitimate child

5 隠立 **kaku(shi)da(te)** keep secret

7 隠芸 **kaku(shi)gei** parlor trick, hid-
     den talent

  隠岐諸島 **Oki shotō** (group of is-
     lands, Shimane-ken)

8 隠事 **kaku(shi)goto, inji** secret

  隠居 **inkyo** retirement; retired per-
     son; old person

10 隠匿 **intoku** concealment

12 隠場 **kaku(re)ba** refuge, hiding
     place

  隠喩 **in'yu** metaphor

14 隠語 **ingo** secret language; argot,
     jargon

—————— 2 ——————

7 角隠 **tsunokaku(shi)** bride's wed-
     ding hood

12 雲隠 **kumogaku(re)** be hidden be-
     hind clouds; disappear

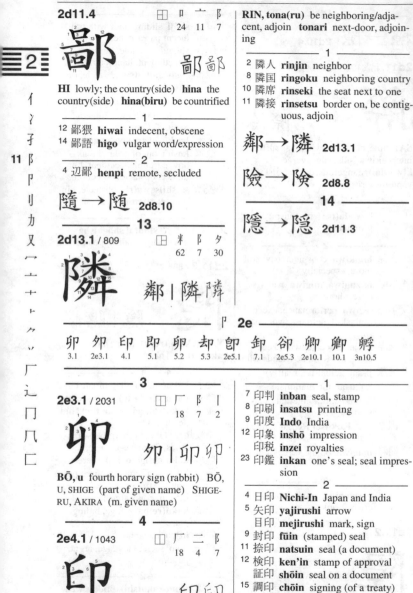

2d11.4 ⊞ 口 宀 阝
24 11 7

鄙

鄙 鄙

HI lowly; the country(side) **hina** the country(side) **hina(biru)** be countrified

――――― 1 ―――――
12 鄙猥 **hiwai** indecent, obscene
14 鄙語 **higo** vulgar word/expression

――――― 2 ―――――
4 辺鄙 **henpi** remote, secluded

隨 → 随 **2d8.10**

――――― 13 ―――――

2d13.1 / 809 ⊞ 米 阝 夕
62 7 30

隣

鄰 | 隣 隣

――――――――― 阝 **2e** ―――――――――

卯 夗 印 即 卵 却 卽 卸 卻 卿 卿 孵
3.1 2e3.1 4.1 5.1 5.2 5.3 2e5.1 7.1 2e5.3 2e10.1 10.1 3n10.5

2e3.1 / 2031 ⊞ 厂 阝 |
18 7 2

卯

夘 | 卯 卯

BŌ, u fourth horary sign (rabbit) **BŌ, U,** SHIGE (part of given name) SHIGE-RU, AKIRA (m. given name)

――――― 4 ―――――

2e4.1 / 1043 ⊞ 厂 二 阝
18 4 7

印

印 印

IN seal, stamp; India **shirushi** sign, mark, symbol

RIN, tona(ru) be neighboring/adjacent, adjoin **tonari** next-door, adjoining

――――― 1 ―――――
2 隣人 **rinjin** neighbor
8 隣国 **ringoku** neighboring country
10 隣席 **rinseki** the seat next to one
11 隣接 **rinsetsu** border on, be contiguous, adjoin

鄰 → 隣 **2d13.1**

險 → 険 **2d8.8**

――――― 14 ―――――

隱 → 隠 **2d11.3**

――――― 1 ―――――
7 印判 **inban** seal, stamp
8 印刷 **insatsu** printing
9 印度 **Indo** India
12 印象 **inshō** impression
印税 **inzei** royalties
23 印鑑 **inkan** one's seal; seal impression

――――― 2 ―――――
4 日印 **Nichi-In** Japan and India
5 矢印 **yajirushi** arrow
目印 **mejirushi** mark, sign
9 封印 **fūin** (stamped) seal
11 捺印 **natsuin** seal (a document)
12 検印 **ken'in** stamp of approval
証印 **shōin** seal on a document
15 調印 **chōin** signing (of a treaty)

――――― 4 ―――――
13 署名捺印 **shomei-natsuin** signature and seal

─────── **5** ───────

2e5.1 / 463   □ 食 阝
              73   7

即   即｜即即

SOKU immediate, as is, on the spot
sunawa(chi) namely, i.e. **tsu(ku)** ascend (a throne) CHIKASHI (m. given name)

─────── 1 ───────

0 即する **soku(suru)** conform to
4 即日 **sokujitsu** on the same day
6 即死 **sokushi** die instantly
7 即売 **sokubai** sale on the spot
   即応 **sokuō** conform/adapt to, meet
8 即刻 **sokkoku** immediately, at once
   即効 **sokkō** immediate effect
   即金 **sokkin** (payment in) cash
10 即座 **sokuza** prompt, on the spot
   即席 **sokuseki** extemporaneous, impromptu, instant (foods)
   即時 **sokuji** immediately, on the spot
12 即答 **sokutō** prompt reply
14 即製 **sokusei** manufacture on the spot
16 即興 **sokkyō** improvised, ad-lib

2e5.2 / 1058   □ 厂 阝 丨
              18   7   2

卵   卵卵

RAN, tamago egg

─────── 1 ───────

2 卵子 **ranshi** ovum, egg cell
11 卵黄 **ran'ō** yolk
   卵殻 **rankaku** eggshell

─────── 2 ───────

5 生卵 **namatamago** raw egg
9 茹卵 **yu(de)tamago, u(de)tamago** boiled egg
13 煎卵 **i(ri)tamago** scrambled eggs
   孵卵器 **furanki** incubator

19 鶏卵 **keiran** chicken egg

2e5.3 / 1783   田 土 竹 阝
              22 17   7

却   卻｜却却

KYAKU reject; contrary **kae(tte)** on the contrary, instead; rather, all the more

─────── 1 ───────

3 却下 **kyakka** reject, dismiss

─────── 2 ───────

6 返却 **henkyaku** return, repayment
8 退却 **taikyaku** retreat
10 消却 **shōkyaku** efface, erase, extinguish (a debt)
12 焼却 **shōkyaku** destroy by fire, incinerate
17 償却 **shōkyaku** repayment, redemption, amortization

─────── **7** ───────

即 → 即 **2e5.1**

2e7.1 / 707   田 工 阝 一
              38   7   1

卸   卸卸

oro(su) sell at wholesale **oroshi** wholesale

─────── 1 ───────

7 卸売 **oroshiu(ri)** wholesale
10 卸値 **oroshine** wholesale price

卻 → 却 **2e5.3**

─────── **8** ───────

卿 → 卿 **2e10.1**

亻 冫 子 阝 卩 刂 力 又 亠 十 冖 夂 丶 厂 辶 冂 八 口   **7**

— 10 —

2e10.1

川	食	厂	阝
73	18	7	

卿

卿 | 卿 卿

KEI you; state minister KYŌ (as suffix) Lord, Sir

— 11 —

孵 → 3n10.5

— 刂 2f —

刀	刈	切	分	刊	召	州	刑	列	判	免	別	制
0.1	2.1	2.2	2o2.1	3.1	3.3	4.1	4.2	4.4	5.2	2n6.1	5.3	6.1

刺	到	刻	刹	刷	券	削	剃	契	剖	剝	剥	剣
6.2	6.4	6.7	6.8	6.9	6.10	7.4	7.5	7.6	8.1	2f8.4	8.4	8.5

剤	剛	帰	剰	副	剩	割	創	剽	劍	劇	劑
8.6	8.7	8.8	9.1	9.2	2f9.1	10.1	10.3	11.1	2f8.5	13.2	2f8.6

— 0 —

2f0.1 / 37

口	力
	8

刀

釖 | 刀 刀

TŌ, katana sword

— 1 —

10 刀剣 **tōken** swords

— 2 —

6 竹刀 **shinai** bamboo sword (for kendo)
9 剃刀 **kamisori** razor
12 短刀 **tantō** short sword, dagger

— 3 —

4 日本刀 **nihontō** Japanese sword

— 2 —

2f2.1 / 1282

口	十	儿
	12	16

刈

刈 刈

KAI, GAI, ka(ru) cut, clip, shear, reap, prune

— 1 —

2 刈入 **ka(ri)i(re)** harvest, reaping

8 刈取 **ka(ri)to(ru)** mow, cut down, reap

— 2 —

5 芝刈機 **shibaka(ri)ki** lawn mower
9 草刈 **kusaka(ri)** grass cutting, mowing
14 稲刈 **ineka(ri)** rice mowing/reaping

2f2.2 / 39

口	十	力
	12	8

切

切 切

SETSU, SAI, ki(ru) cut -ki(ru) finish, do completely, be able to -ki(ri) all there is, only; since ki(ri) limit, end, place to leave off -ki(tte no) the most ... in the (whole place) ki(reru) cut well, be sharp ki(re) piece, cut, slice, scrap ki(rasu) run out of, be short of setsu (na) earnest, ardent; keen, acute setsu(nai) oppressive, suffocating; painful, distressing

— 1 —

3 切上 **ki(ri)a(ge)** end, conclusion; rounding up (to the nearest integer); revalue, up-value (a currency)

切下 **ki(ri)sa(ge)** reduction, devaluation

⁴ 切支丹 **Kirishitan** (early) Japanese Christianity/Christian

切手 **kitte** (postage) stamp

⁵ 切札 **ki(ri)fuda** trump card

⁷ 切迫 **seppaku** draw near, impend, be imminent; become acute, grow tense

⁸ 切実 **setsujitsu** acute, keen, urgent; earnest

切取 **ki(ri)to(ru)** cut off/out

⁹ 切除 **setsujo** cut off/out, remove, excise

¹¹ 切断 **setsudan** cutting, section; cut, sever, amputate

切符 **kippu** ticket

¹² 切換 **ki(ri)ka(eru)** change, exchange, convert; renew; replace; switch over

切替 **ki(ri)ka(eru)** change, exchange, convert; renew; replace; switch over

¹³ 切傷 **ki(ri)kizu** cut, gash, scar

切詰 **ki(ri)tsu(meru)** shorten; reduce, economize, curtail, retrench

¹⁸ 切離 **ki(ri)hana(su)** cut off/apart, sever, separate

—————— 2 ——————

¹ 一切 **issai** all, everything; entirely, absolutely **hitoki(re)** a piece/slice

² 〆切 **shimeki(ri)** deadline, closing date

³ 大切 **taisetsu** important; valuable, precious

丸切 **maru(k)ki(ri), maruki(ri)** completely, utterly

小切手 **kogitte** check, cheque

⁴ 爪切 **tsumeki(ri)** nail clippers

区切 **kugi(ru)** punctuate; partition

⁵ 仕切 **shiki(ri)** partition; settlement of accounts; toeing the mark (in sumo)

皮切 **kawaki(ri)** beginning, start

句切 **kugi(ru)** punctuate; mark off, partition

⁶ 缶切 **kanki(ri)** can opener

⁷ 売切 **u(ri)ki(re)** sold out

困切 **koma(ri)ki(ru)** be in a fix, be at a loss

⁹ 飛切 **tobiki(ri)** superfine, choicest, beyond compare

乗切 **no(ri)ki(ru)** ride through/out, weather (a crisis)

首切 **kubiki(ri)** decapitation, execution; dismissal, firing

品切 **shinagi(re)** out of stock, sold out

思切 **omo(i)ki(ru)** resolve, make up one's mind; resign oneself, give up **omo(i)ki(tta)** radical, drastic

食切 **ku(i)ki(ru)** bite off/through; eat (it) all up

¹⁰ 値切 **negi(ru)** haggle, bargain

息切 **ikigi(re)** shortness of breath

紙切 **kamiki(re)** scrap of paper

紋切型 **monki(ri)gata** conventional

¹¹ 張切 **ha(ri)ki(ru)** stretch tight; be tense/eager

断切 **ta(chi)ki(ru)** cut off, sever

¹² 割切 **wa(ri)ki(ru)** divide; give a clear explanation

極切 **kima(ri)ki(tta)** fixed, definite; stereotyped; self-evident

貸切 **ka(shi)ki(ri)** reservations, booking

¹³ 裏切 **uragi(ru)** betray **uragi(ri)** betrayal, treachery

適切 **tekisetsu** appropriate, pertinent

腹切 **haraki(ri)** suicide by disembowelment

数切 **kazo(e)kire(nai)** countless

¹⁵ 横切 **yokogi(ru)** cross, traverse, intersect

縁切 **enki(ri)** severing of a relationship

締切 **shi(me)ki(ru)** close **shi(me)ki(ri)** closing (date), deadline

踏切 **fu(mi)ki(ru)** cross; take the plunge, take action, make bold to **fumikiri** railroad (grade) crossing

¹⁶ 薄切 **usugi(ri)** sliced thin

親切 **shinsetsu** kind, friendly

—————— 3 ——————

⁹ 帝王切開 **teiō sekkai** Caesarean section

分 → 分　2o2.1

────────── 3 ──────────

2f3.1 / 585　　口　一　儿　一
　　　　　　　　　14　16　1

刊　　　刊刊

KAN publish; carve, engrave

────────── 1 ──────────

6 刊行 **kankō** publish

────────── 2 ──────────

3 夕刊 **yūkan** evening paper/edition

4 月刊 **gekkan** monthly publication
　日刊 **nikkan** a daily (newspaper)

7 季刊誌 **kikanshi** a quarterly (magazine)

9 発刊 **hakkan** publish, issue

10 既刊 **kikan** already published
　週刊誌 **shūkanshi** a weekly (magazine)

12 廃刊 **haikan** discontinue publication
　朝刊 **chōkan** morning paper/edition

13 新刊 **shinkan** new publication

2f3.3 / 995　　日　口　力
　　　　　　　　　24　8

召　　　召召

SHŌ summon　**me(su)** summon, call for; (honorific) eat, drink, put on, wear, take (a bath/bus), buy

────────── 1 ──────────

3 召上 **me(shi)a(garu)** (polite) eat, drink, have　**me(shi)a(geru)** confiscate

12 召集 **shōshū** call together, convene

────────── 4 ──────────

2f4.1 / 195　　皿　儿
　　　　　　　　　16

州　　　馴｜州・州

SHŪ state, province　**su** sandbank, shoals　KUNI (part of given name)

────────── 2 ──────────

2 九州 **Kyūshū** (island)

5 本州 **Honshū** (Japan's main island)

8 欧州 **Ōshū** Europe
　欧州同盟 **Ōshū Dōmei** the European Union

12 満州 **Manshū** Manchuria
　満州国 **Manshūkoku** Manchukuo

14 豪州 **Gōshū** Australia

17 濠州 **Gōshū** Australia

────────── 3 ──────────

3 大洋州 **Taiyōshū** Oceania

2f4.2 / 887　　日　艹　儿　一
　　　　　　　　　32　16　1

刑　　　刑刑

KEI penalty, punishment, criminal (law)

────────── 1 ──────────

8 刑事 **keiji** (police) detective; criminal case

11 刑務所 **keimusho** prison

12 刑期 **keiki** prison term

14 刑罰 **keibatsu** punishment, penalty

────────── 2 ──────────

5 処刑 **shokei** punish, execute

6 死刑 **shikei** capital punishment

16 磔刑 **haritsuke, takkei** crucifixion

────────── 3 ──────────

11 終身刑 **shūshinkei** life sentence

12 絞首刑 **kōshukei** (execution by) hanging

2f4.4 / 611   ⊞ 夕 儿 一
                                 30 16 1

列

列列

RETSU row, line; queue
tsura(neru) put in a row
tsura(naru) lie in a row

——————— 1 ———————
0 列する **res(suru)** attend; rank with
7 列車 **ressha** train
8 列国 **rekkoku** the powers, all nations
10 列挙 **rekkyo** enumerate, list
  列島 **rettō** archipelago
  列席 **resseki** attend, be present

——————— 2 ———————
1 一列 **ichiretsu** a row/line
6 行列 **gyōretsu** queue, procession, parade; matrix (in math)
7 系列 **keiretsu** system, series; ownership affiliation, corporate group
8 並列 **heiretsu** arrange in a row; parallel (circuit)
10 陳列 **chinretsu** exhibit, display
  配列 **hairetsu** arrangement, grouping

——————— 3 ———————
3 千島列島 **Chishima-rettō** the Kurile Islands

——————————— 5 ———————————

2f5.2 / 1026   ⊞ 小 二 儿
                                 35 4 16

判

判判

HAN, BAN one's seal; judgment
waka(ru) understand, be clear **-ban** size (of paper or books)

——————— 1 ———————
2 判子 **hanko** one's seal
7 判決 **hanketsu** judgment, (judicial) decision
8 判事 **hanji** a judge

判例 **hanrei** (judicial) precedent
判定 **hantei** judgment, decision, verdict
判明 **hanmei** become clear, be ascertained
11 判断 **handan** judgment

——————— 2 ———————
6 印判 **inban** seal, stamp
7 批判 **hihan** criticism, critique, comment
11 菊判 **kikuban** 22-by-15 cm size
12 裁判 **saiban** trial, hearing
  裁判官 **saibankan** the judge
  裁判所 **saibansho** (law) court
  評判 **hyōban** fame, popularity; rumor, gossip
15 審判 **shinpan, shinban** decision, judgment, refereeing
  審判官 **shinpankan** judge, umpire, referee

——————— 3 ———————
3 大評判 **daihyōban** sensation, smash
12 無罪判決 **muzai hanketsu** acquittal

——————— 4 ———————
12 最高裁判所 **Saikō Saibansho** Supreme Court

免 → 免 2n6.1

2f5.3 / 267   ⊞ 口 儿 宀
                                 24 16 15

別

別別

BETSU different, separate, another; special; parting, farewell; (as suffix) classified by … **waka(reru)** part, bid farewell, part company with; get divorced; diverge, branch off; disperse **wa(keru), wa(tsu)** divide, separate, distinguish **wa(kete)** above all, especially, all the more **waka(chi)** distinction, discrimination, differentiation

——————— 1 ———————
0 別に、別して **betsu (ni), bes(shite)** (not) particularly, especially

² 別人 **betsujin** different person; changed man

³ 別々 **betsubetsu** separate, individual

⁵ 別冊 **bessatsu** separate volume, supplement

⁶ 別名 **betsumei** another name, alias, pseudonym

⁸ 別居 **bekkyo** (legal) separation, living apart

⁹ 別便 **betsubin** by separate mail

別荘 **bessō** villa, country place

¹⁰ 別格 **bekkaku** special, exceptional

別書 **waka(chi)ga(ki)** write leaving a space between words

別紙 **besshi** attached sheet, enclosure

¹⁶ 別館 **bekkan** annex

¹⁸ 別離 **betsuri** parting, separation

——————— 2 ———————

⁴ 分別 **funbetsu** discretion, good judgment **bunbetsu** classification, separation, discrimination

区別 **kubetsu** distinguish between

⁶ 死別 **shibetsu** separation by death

⁸ 送別会 **sōbetsukai** going-away/farewell party

性別 **seibetsu** sex, whether male or female

¹⁰ 個別 **kobetsu** indivudual by individual

差別 **sabetsu** discrimination

格別 **kakubetsu** particularly, exceptionally

特別 **tokubetsu** special, extraordinary

¹¹ 訣別 **ketsubetsu** parting, farewell

¹⁹ 識別 **shikibetsu** discrimination, recognition

——————— 3 ———————

¹ 一分別 **hitofunbetsu** (careful) consideration

¹² 無分別 **mufunbetsu** imprudent, thoughtless, rash

無差別 **musabetsu** indiscriminate

——————— 4 ———————

³ 千差万別 **sensa-banbetsu** infinite variety

——————— 6 ———————

2f6.1 / 427

口 牛 冂 儿
47 20 16

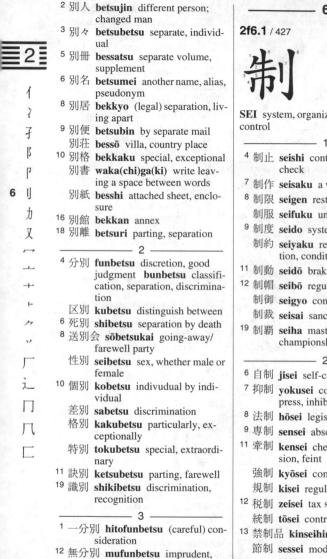

SEI system, organization; regulate, control

——————— 1 ———————

⁴ 制止 **seishi** control, restrain, keep in check

⁷ 制作 **seisaku** a work, production

⁸ 制限 **seigen** restriction, limitation

制服 **seifuku** uniform

⁹ 制度 **seido** system

制約 **seiyaku** restriction, limitation, condition

¹¹ 制動 **seidō** braking, damping

¹² 制帽 **seibō** regulation/school cap

制御 **seigyo** control

制裁 **seisai** sanctions, punishment

¹⁹ 制覇 **seiha** mastery, supremacy; championship

——————— 2 ———————

⁶ 自制 **jisei** self-control, self-restraint

⁷ 抑制 **yokusei** control, restrain, suppress, inhibit

⁸ 法制 **hōsei** legislation, laws

⁹ 専制 **sensei** absolutism, despotism

¹¹ 牽制 **kensei** check, restrain; diversion, feint

強制 **kyōsei** compulsory, forced

規制 **kisei** regulation, control

¹² 税制 **zeisei** tax system

統制 **tōsei** control, regulation

¹³ 禁制品 **kinseihin** contraband

節制 **sessei** moderation, temperance

¹⁴ 管制塔 **kanseitō** control tower

——————— 3 ———————

⁶ 合議制 **gōgisei** parliamentary system

2f6.2 / 881   囗 木 冂 儿
41 20 16

刺   刺 刺

SHI stab, pierce; name card
sa(su) stab, pierce, sting; sew, stitch
sa(saru) stick, be stuck
toge thorn, barb

———— 1 ————

7 刺身 **sashimi** sliced raw fish, sashimi

8 刺青 **shisei, irezumi** tattooing

10 刺殺 **sa(shi)koro(su)** stab to death
shisatsu stab to death; put out (a runner)

16 刺激 **shigeki** stimulus, stimulation

———— 2 ————

6 名刺 **meishi** business card

7 串刺 **kushiza(shi)** skewering

9 風刺 **fūshi** satire, sarcasm

16 諷刺 **fūshi** satire, sarcasm, lampoon

諷刺画 **fūshiga** caricature, cartoon

2f6.4 / 904   囗 土 竹 儿
22 17 16

到   到 到

TŌ, ita(ru) arrive, reach ITARU (m. given name)

———— 1 ————

7 到来 **tōrai** arrival, advent

8 到底 **tōtei** (cannot) possibly, (not) at all, utterly, absolutely

11 到達 **tōtatsu** reach, attain

12 到着 **tōchaku** arrival

———— 2 ————

10 殺到 **sattō** rush, stampede

2f6.7 / 1211   囗 宀 竹 亻
11 17 3

刻   刻 刻

KOKU time; carve, engrave
kiza(mu) cut fine, chop up; carve, engrave; notch, score, mark off
kiza(mi) notch, nick; shredded tobacco

———— 1 ————

1 刻一刻 **koku-ikkoku** moment by moment, hour by hour

———— 2 ————

1 一刻 **ikkoku** a minute/moment; stubborn, hotheaded

一刻千金 **ikkoku senkin** Every minute counts.

7 即刻 **sokkoku** immediately, at once

10 時刻表 **jikokuhyō** timetable, schedule

11 遅刻 **chikoku** be late/tardy

深刻 **shinkoku** serious, grave, acute

彫刻 **chōkoku** sculpture, carving, engraving **ho(ri)kiza(mu)** engrave, carve

18 覆刻 **fukkoku** reproduce, republish

覆刻本 **fukkokubon** reissued book

翻刻 **honkoku** reprint

———— 3 ————

8 刻一刻 **koku-ikkoku** moment by moment, hour by hour

2f6.8   囗 木 十 儿
41 12 16

刹   刹 刹

SETSU, SATSU temple

———— 1 ————

6 刹那 **setsuna** moment, instant

———— 2 ————

1 一刹那 **issetsuna** an instant, a moment

亻
冫
扌
阝
卩
刂 6
力
又
亠
亠
夂
丷
厂
辶
冂
几
匸

2f6.9 / 1044 ⬚ 尸 巾 儿
40 26 16

刷

刷 刷

SATSU, su(ru) print

———————— 1 ————————

13 刷新 **sasshin** reform, renovation

———————— 2 ————————

6 印刷 **insatsu** printing

色刷 **irozu(ri)** color printing

7 抜刷 **nu(ki)zu(ri)** offprint

17 縮刷版 **shukusatsuban** small-size edition

———————— 3 ————————

6 両面刷 **ryōmenzu(ri)** printing on both sides

2f6.10 / 506 ⬚ 火 二 力
44 4 8

券

券 券 券

KEN ticket, certificate

———————— 2 ————————

9 食券 **shokken** meal ticket

10 旅券 **ryoken** passport

12 証券 **shōken** securities

13 債券 **saiken** bond, debenture

———————— 3 ————————

6 回数券 **kaisūken** (train) coupon tickets

8 周遊券 **shūyūken** excursion ticket

9 前売券 **maeu(ri)ken** ticket sold in advance

10 航空券 **kōkūken** flight/airplane ticket

12 搭乗券 **tōjōken** boarding pass

———————— 7 ————————

2f7.4 / 1611 ⬚ 月 小 儿
42 35 16

削

削 削 削

SAKU, kezu(ru) whittle down, sharpen (a pencil); curtail; delete **so(gu), so(geru)** slice off; detract from, dampen

———————— 1 ————————

9 削除 **sakujo** delete, eliminate

12 削減 **sakugen** reduction, cutback

2f7.5 ⬚ 弓 儿 丨
28 16 2

剃

剃 剃

TEI, so(ru), su(ru) shave

———————— 1 ————————

2 剃刀 **kamisori** razor

2f7.6 / 565 ⬚ 土 大 力
22 34 8

契

契 契

KEI, chigi(ru) pledge, vow, promise

———————— 1 ————————

9 契約 **keiyaku** contract, agreement

16 契機 **keiki** opportunity, chance

———————— 8 ————————

2f8.1 / 1830 ⬚ 立 口 儿
54 24 16

剖

剖 剖 剖

BŌ divide, cut

———————— 2 ————————

13 解剖 **kaibō** dissection, autopsy; analysis

剥 → 剥 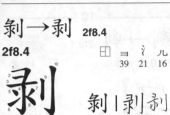 2f8.4

2f8.4 田 ヨ 冫 儿
                    39 21 16

剥 剥丨剥剥

HAKU, ha(geru) come/peel off, be worn off; fade, discolor **ha(gu), ha(gasu)** tear/peel/strip off; deprive of **mu(keru)** come/peel off **mu(ku)** peel, pare **hezu(ru)** decrease by stealing, pilfer

——— 1 ———

8 剥取 **ha(gi)to(ru)** strip/tear off; rob of

——— 2 ———

17 擦剥 **su(ri)mu(ku)** abrade, chafe

2f8.5 / 879 田 卩 亻 一
                        24 3 14

剣 剣丨剣剣

KEN, tsurugi sword

——— 1 ———

11 剣道 **kendō** Japanese fencing, kendo

——— 2 ———

2 刀剣 **tōken** swords
10 真剣 **shinken** serious

2f8.6 / 550 田 亠 十 儿
                        11 12 16

剤 剤丨剤剤

ZAI medicine, preparation

——— 2 ———

9 洗剤 **senzai** detergent
16 薬剤 **yakuzai** medicine, drugs
   薬剤師 **yakuzaishi** pharmacist
   錠剤 **jōzai** tablet, pill

——— 3 ———

6 防腐剤 **bōfuzai** a preservative, antiseptic

10 殺虫剤 **satchūzai** insecticide
11 接着剤 **setchakuzai** adhesive, glue
   脱臭剤 **dasshūzai** deodorant, deodorizer
12 覚醒剤 **kakuseizai** stimulant drugs
18 鎮痛剤 **chintsūzai** painkiller
   鎮静剤 **chinseizai** tranquilizer, sedative

2f8.7 / 1610 田 凵 冂 儿
                          36 20 16

剛 剛剛

GŌ strong, hard, rigid TAKESHI, TSUYOSHI (m. given name) TAKE (part of given name)

——— 1 ———

10 剛健 **gōken** strong and sturdy, virile
15 剛毅 **gōki** hardy, stout-hearted

2f8.8 / 317 田 ヨ 巾 儿
                        39 26 16

帰 帰丨帰帰

KI, kae(ru) return **kae(su)** let (someone) return, send (someone) back

——— 1 ———

4 帰化 **kika** become naturalized
6 帰宅 **kitaku** return/come home
8 帰国 **kikoku** return to one's country
9 帰途 **kito** homeward journey
   帰省 **kisei** returning to one's home town (for the holidays)
10 帰郷 **kikyō** return home, return to one's home town
11 帰道 **kae(ri)michi** the way back/home
12 帰着 **kichaku** return; conclusion, consequence
   帰属 **kizoku** revert to, belong to, be ascribed to

——— 2 ———

4 日帰 **higae(ri)** a one-day (trip)
6 再帰 **saiki** recursive

回帰 **kaiki** recurrent; regression (coefficient)

7 里帰 **satogae(ri)** bride's first visit to her old home

——————— 3 ———————

5 北回帰線 **Kita Kaikisen** the Tropic of Cancer

——————— 9 ———————

2f9.1 / 1068　　□　木　艹　几
　　　　　　　　　　41　32　16

剩｜剩剩

JŌ surplus **amatsusa(e)** besides

——————— 1 ———————

7 剰余 **jōyo** a surplus

10 剰員 **jōin** superfluous personnel, overstaffing

14 剰語 **jōgo** redundancy

——————— 2 ———————

11 過剰 **kajō** excess, surplus

2f9.2 / 714　　□　畐　口　几
　　　　　　　　　　58　24　16

副

副副

FUKU accompany; vice-, deputy, assistant **so(u)** accompany; marry; meet, suit, satisfy, fulfill

——————— 1 ———————

3 副大統領 **fukudaitōryō** vice president

4 副収入 **fukushūnyū** additional/ side income

6 副会長 **fukukaichō** (company) vice president

副次的 **fukujiteki** secondary

9 副食 **fukushoku** side dish; supplementary food

11 副産物 **fukusanbutsu** by-product

12 副詞 **fukushi** adverb

13 副業 **fukugyō** side business, sideline

18 副題 **fukudai** subtitle, subheading

——————— 10 ———————

剩→剩　**2f9.1**

2f10.1 / 519　　□　宀　土　口
　　　　　　　　　　33　22　24

割

割割

KATSU, wa(ru) divide, separate, split; break, crack; dilute; drop below **wa(reru)** break, crack/split apart **sa(ku)** cut up; separate; spare (time) **wari** rate; ten percent; comparatively, in comparison with

——————— 1 ———————

4 割切 **wa(ri)ki(ru)** divide; give a clear explanation

割込 **wa(ri)ko(mu)** wedge oneself in, cut/butt in **wariko(mi)** an interrupt (in computers)

割引 **waribiki** discount **wa(ri)bi(ku)** give a discount

6 割合 **wariai** rate, proportion, percentage; comparatively

割当 **wa(ri)a(teru)** allocate, allot, divide/distribute among

8 割物 **wa(re)mono** broken article; fragile article

10 割高 **waridaka** comparatively expensive

11 割勘 **wa(ri)kan** Dutch treat

14 割増 **warima(shi)** extra (charge/ payment)

割算 **wa(ri)zan** division (in math)

15 割箸 **wa(ri)bashi** half-split chopsticks

——————— 2 ———————

1 一割 **ichiwari** ten percent

4 分割 **bunkatsu** partition, division

分割払 **bunkatsubara(i)** payment in installments

水割 **mizuwa(ri)** (whiskey) diluted with water

5 四割 **yonwari, shiwari** forty percent **yo(tsu)wa(ri)** divide into four, quarter

6 年割 **nenwa(ri)** annual installment

7 役割 **yakuwa(ri)** role

2f10.3 / 1308   食 口 儿
     73 24 16

創

創創

SŌ create, originate, make; wound, injury

— 1 —

⁵ 創立 **sōritsu** establishment, founding
⁷ 創作 **sōsaku** a creation/work
⁹ 創造 **sōzō** creation
   創造力 **sōzōryoku** creative power
¹³ 創業 **sōgyō** found, establish

— 2 —

⁹ 独創 **dokusō** originality, creativity
¹¹ 絆創膏 **bansōkō** adhesive plaster

— 11 —

2f11.1   田 礻 口 一
     45 24 14

剽

剽剽

HYŌ threaten

— 1 —

⁹ 剽窃 **hyōsetsu** plagiarism, pirating

— 13 —

劍 → 剣 **2f8.5**

2f13.2 / 797   彳 厂 十
     27 18 12

劇

劇劇

GEKI drama, play; intense

— 1 —

⁶ 劇団 **gekidan** troupe, theatrical company
⁸ 劇的 **gekiteki** dramatic
¹² 劇場 **gekijō** theater
¹⁶ 劇薬 **gekiyaku** powerful medicine; deadly poison

— 2 —

⁵ 史劇 **shigeki** historical drama
¹¹ 惨劇 **sangeki** tragedy, tragic event
¹² 喜劇 **kigeki** a comedy
   悲劇 **higeki** tragedy
¹⁴ 演劇 **engeki** drama, play
   歌劇 **kageki** opera

— 3 —

¹⁰ 時代劇 **jidaigeki** period/costume drama
¹² 喜歌劇 **kikageki** comic opera

— 14 —

劑 → 剤 **2f8.6**

— 力 **2g** —

力	加	功	幼	劣	助	励	努	劼	効	券	勅	勁
0.1	3.1	3.2	3.3	3n3.4	5.1	5.4	5.6	6.1	6.2	2f6.10	7.1	7.2

勇	脅	動	勘	勤	労	勧	勢	勲	勵	勸
7.3	8.2	9.1	9.3	10.1	3n4.3	11.1	11.6	4d11.3	2g5.4	2g11.1

— 0 —

2g0.1 / 100   口 力
     8

力

力 力

RYOKU, RIKI, chikara power, force, strength **riki(mu)** exert one's strength, strain, bear down; brag, bluff, boast TSUTOMU (m. given name)

— 1 —

³ 力士 **rikishi** sumo wrestler
⁷ 力学 **rikigaku** dynamics, mechanics

2

0

イ
冫
孑
阝
卩
刂
力
又
亠
宀
冖
厂
辶
冂
八
凵

9 力持 **chikaramo(chi)** strong man
11 力動的 **rikidōteki** dynamic
力添 **chikarazo(e)** assistance
力強 **chikarazuyo(i)** forceful, vigorous, emboldened
12 力量 **rikiryō** physical strength; ability, capacity
15 力瘤 **chikarakobu** flexed biceps

─── 2 ───

2 人力 **jinriki** human power, man-powered **jinryoku** human power/efforts
4 水力 **suiryoku** water/hydro power
引力 **inryoku** gravitation, attraction
5 斥力 **sekiryoku** repulsion, repulsive force
出力 **shutsuryoku** output
他力 **tariki** outside help; salvation by faith
圧力 **atsuryoku** pressure
6 気力 **kiryoku** energy, vitality, mettle
全力 **zenryoku** one's every effort, full capacity
尽力 **jinryoku** efforts, exertions; assistance
有力 **yūryoku** influential, powerful
自力 **jiryoku** one's own strength/efforts **jiriki** one's own strength/efforts; (Buddhist) salvation by works
7 体力 **tairyoku** physical strength
助力 **joryoku** help, assistance
努力 **doryoku** effort, endeavor
迫力 **hakuryoku** (dramatic) force, intensity, appeal
学力 **gakuryoku** scholastic ability, scholarship
8 効力 **kōryoku** effectiveness, effect, validity
協力 **kyōryoku** cooperation
実力 **jitsuryoku** actual ability, competence; arms, force
底力 **sokojikara** latent energy/strength
金力 **kinryoku** the power of money
9 重力 **jūryoku** gravity
速力 **sokuryoku** speed, velocity

活力 **katsuryoku** vitality, vigor
胆力 **tanryoku** courage, mettle
威力 **iryoku** power, might, authority, influence
10 能力 **nōryoku** ability, capacity, talent
馬力 **bariki** horsepower
11 動力 **dōryoku** power, motive force
強力 **kyōryoku** strength, power **gōriki** great physical strength; mountain carrier-guide
視力 **shiryoku** visual acuity, eyesight
12 弾力性 **danryokusei** elasticity, resilience, flexibility
腕力 **wanryoku** physical strength
無力 **muryoku** powerless, ineffectual, feeble; incompetent
13 勢力 **seiryoku** influence, force
電力 **denryoku** electric power
14 精力 **seiryoku** energy, vigor, vitality
15 権力 **kenryoku** power, authority, influence
暴力 **bōryoku** violence, force
暴力団 **bōryokudan** gangster organization
魅力 **miryoku** charm, appeal, fascination
魅力的 **miryokuteki** attractive, charming, captivating
17 聴力 **chōryoku** hearing ability

─── 3 ───

9 思考力 **shikōryoku** mental faculties
10 原子力 **genshiryoku** atomic energy, nuclear power
起電力 **kidenryoku** electromotive force
11 粘着力 **nenchakuryoku** adhesion, viscosity
12 創造力 **sōzōryoku** creative power
遠心力 **enshinryoku** centrifugal force
無気力 **mukiryoku** spiritless, flabby, gutless
13 想像力 **sōzōryoku** (powers of) imagination
14 精神力 **seishinryoku** force of will

15 潜勢力 **senseiryoku** latent power, potential

――――― 4 ―――――

4 不可抗力 **fukakōryoku** force majeure, beyond one's control, unavoidable

――――― 3 ―――――

2g3.1 / 709   ☐ ⼝ ⼒
24 8

加

加口加

KA add, apply; Canada; California
kuwa(eru) add, increase; give, inflict
kuwa(waru) increase; join in

――――― 1 ―――――

2 加入金 **kanyūkin** entrance/initiation fee
3 加工 **kakō** processing
7 加奈 **Kana** (f. given name)
9 加速度 **kasokudo** acceleration
10 加害者 **kagaisha** assailant, perpetrator
加納 **Kanō** (surname)
12 加減 **kagen** addition and subtraction; degree, extent, condition; adjust, keep within bounds; state of health; seasoning, flavor; allow for
加減乗除 **kagenjōjo** addition, subtraction, multiplication, and division
13 加盟国 **kameikoku** member nation, signatory
15 加熱 **kanetsu** heating
18 加藤 **Katō** (surname)

――――― 2 ―――――

4 日加 **Nik-Ka** Japan and Canada
5 付加 **fuka** an addition
付(ke)加(eru) **tsu(ke)kuwa(eru)** add
付加価値税 **fuka-kachi zei** value-added tax
8 追加 **tsuika** addition, supplement
参加 **sanka** participate, take part
参加者 **sankasha** participant
10 冥加 **myōga** divine protection

11 添加 **tenka** annex, append, affix, add
添加物 **tenkabutsu** additives
累加 **ruika** acceleration, progressive increase
14 増加 **zōka** increase, addition, rise, growth

2g3.2 / 818   ☐ ⼯ ⼒
38 8

功

功功

KŌ merit, meritorious deed; success; credit **KU, isao** merit, meritorious deed ISAO, TSUTOMU (m. given name) NORI, YOSHI (part of given name)

――――― 1 ―――――

6 功名 **kōmyō, kōmei** great achievement
7 功労 **kōrō** meritorious service
功利 **kōri** utility; utilitarian
11 功過 **kōka** merits and demerits
17 功績 **kōseki** meritorious service

――――― 2 ―――――

6 年功 **nenkō** long service
有功 **yūkō** merit(orious)
成功 **seikō** success
15 勲功 **kunkō** distinguished service, merits

2g3.3 / 1229   ☐ ⽵ ⼒ ⼁
17 8 2

幼

幼幼

YŌ, osana(i), itokena(i), ito- very young, infant, small child

――――― 1 ―――――

4 幼友達 **osana tomodachi** childhood friend
幼心 **osanagokoro** child's mind/heart
6 幼年時代 **yōnen jidai** childhood
7 幼児 **yōji** small child, tot, baby
13 幼稚園 **yōchien** kindergarten

幼馴染 **osana najimi** childhood playmate

———————— 4 ————————

劣 → **3n3.4**

———————— 5 ————————

2g5.1 / 623   ⊞ 月 力 │
42 8 2

助 助助

JO help; (as prefix) assistant, auxiliary **tasu(keru)** help, rescue **tasu(karu)** be helped/rescued **suke** assistance; moll, broad, dame; (suffix of personification) TASUKU (m. given name) SUKE (part of given name)

———————— 1 ————————

2 助力 **joryoku** help, assistance
助力者 **joryokusha** helper, supporter
4 助手 **joshu** helper, assistant
5 助出 **tasu(ke)da(su)** help out of
6 助合 **tasu(ke)a(u)** help one another
助成金 **joseikin** subsidy, grant
7 助言 **jogen** advice
8 助長 **jochō** promote, further, encourage
10 助教授 **jokyōju** assistant professor
11 助動詞 **jodōshi** auxiliary verb
助産婦 **josanpu** midwife
助船 **tasu(ke)bune** lifeboat
12 助詞 **joshi** a particle (in grammar)
14 助演 **joen** play a supporting role, co-star

———————— 2 ————————

7 扶助 **fujo** aid, support, relief
11 救助 **kyūjo** rescue, relief, aid
12 援助 **enjo** assistance, aid
補助 **hojo** assistance, supplement, subsidy
補助金 **hojokin** subsidy, grant
15 賛助 **sanjo** support, backing

2g5.4 / 1340   ⊞ 厂 丁 力
18 14 8

励 勵 │励励

REI encouragement; diligence **hage(mu)** be diligent **hage(masu)** encourage, urge on TSUTOMU (m. given name)

———————— 1 ————————

6 励合 **hage(mi)a(u)** vie with one another
励行 **reikō** strict enforcement

———————— 2 ————————

13 奨励 **shōrei** encourage, promote, give incentive
督励 **tokurei** encourage, urge
16 激励 **gekirei** urge on, encourage

2g5.6 / 1595   ⊞ 女 又 力
25 9 8

努 努努

DO, tsuto(meru) make efforts, exert oneself, strive TSUTOMU (m. given name)

———————— 1 ————————

2 努力 **doryoku** effort, endeavor

———————— 6 ————————

2g6.1 / 1939   ⊞ 宀 竹 亻
11 17 3

劾 劾劾

GAI investigate, prosecute

———————— 2 ————————

12 弾劾 **dangai** impeachment, censure, denunciation

2g6.2 / 816   田 亠 九 十
                       11 16 12

効   效 | 効 効

KŌ, ki(ku) be effective

——————— 1 ———————

2 効力 **kōryoku** effectiveness, effect, validity
5 効用 **kōyō** use, utility, effect
   効目 **ki(ki)me** effect, efficacy
8 効果 **kōka** effect, effectiveness
10 効能 **kōnō** efficacy, effect
11 効率 **kōritsu** efficiency

——————— 2 ———————

5 失効 **shikkō** lapse, lose effect, become null and void
7 即効 **sokkō** immediate effect
8 逆効果 **gyakukōka** opposite effect, counterproductive
   実効 **jikkō** practical effect
9 発効 **hakkō** come into effect
12 無効 **mukō** null, void, invalid, ineffective
16 薬効 **yakkō** efficacy of a drug

券 → **2f6.10**

——————— 7 ———————

2g7.1 / 1886   田 木 口 力
                        41 24 8

勅   敕 | 勅 勅

CHOKU, mikotonori imperial decree

——————— 1 ———————

5 勅令 **chokurei** imperial edict
14 勅語 **chokugo** imperial rescript

——————— 2 ———————

12 詔勅 **shōchoku** imperial proclamation

2g7.2 / 2029   田 工 力 一
                       38 8 1

勁   勁 勁

KEI strong **TSUYOSHI** (m. given name) **KEI** (part of given name)

——————— 1 ———————

9 勁草 **keisō** (strong and constant as a) plant that resists the changing winds

2g7.3 / 1386   目 田 力 一
                       58 8 1

勇   勇 勇

YŪ brave, courageous **isa(mu)** be in high spirits **isa(mashii)** brave, courageous, stirring **ISAMU** (m. given name) **ISA** (part of given name)

——————— 1 ———————

2 勇人 **Hayato** (m. given name)
6 勇気 **yūki** courage
10 勇猛心 **yūmōshin** intrepid spirit
12 勇敢 **yūkan** courageous, brave, heroic

——————— 2 ———————

9 胆勇 **tan'yū** courage, pluck, dauntlessness

——————— 8 ———————

2g8.2 / 1263   目 月 力
                       42 8

脅   脅 脅

KYŌ, obiya(kasu), odo(kasu), odo(su) threaten

——————— 1 ———————

7 脅迫 **kyōhaku** threat, intimidation
9 脅威 **kyōi** threat, menace

───────── 9 ─────────

2g9.1 / 231   □□ 車 力 丨
               69 8 2

動   動 動

DŌ, ugo(ku) (intr.) move **ugo(kasu)** (tr.) move

───────── 1 ─────────

0 動じる/ずる **dō(jiru/zuru)** be perturbed
2 動力 **dōryoku** power, motive force
6 動向 **dōkō** trend, attitude
7 動作 **dōsa** action, movements, motion; bearing, behavior
   動乱 **dōran** upheaval, disturbance, riot
8 動物 **dōbutsu** animal
   動物園 **dōbutsuen** zoo
10 動員 **dōin** mobilization
12 動揺 **dōyō** shaking, pitching, rolling; excitement, commotion, unrest
   動詞 **dōshi** verb
16 動機 **dōki** motive
20 動議 **dōgi** a (parliamentary) motion

───────── 2 ─────────

2 力動的 **rikidōteki** dynamic
4 不動産 **fudōsan** immovable property, real estate
   反動 **handō** reaction; recoil
   手動 **shudō** manual, hand-operated
5 出動 **shutsudō** be sent/called out, take the field
   他動詞 **tadōshi** transitive verb
   可動 **kadō** movable, mobile
6 妄動 **mōdō, bōdō** act blindly
   行動 **kōdō** action, conduct, behavior, operations
   自動 **jidō** automatic
   自動車 **jidōsha** motor vehicle, automobile
   自動的 **jidōteki** automatic
   自動販売機 **jidōhanbaiki** vending machine
   自動詞 **jidōshi** intransitive verb
7 身動 **miugo(ki)** move about, stir

助動詞 **jodōshi** auxiliary verb
8 制動 **seidō** braking, damping
9 発動 **hatsudō** put into motion, exercise, invoke
   変動 **hendō** fluctuations
   浮動 **fudō** floating, fluctuating
   活動 **katsudō** activity
   活動的 **katsudōteki** active, dynamic
   律動 **ritsudō** rhythm, rhythmic movement
10 流動 **ryūdō** flowing, liquid (assets), current (liabilities)
   流動体 **ryūdōtai** a fluid
   振動 **shindō** vibration, oscillation
   fu(ri)ugo(ku) swing, shake, oscillate
   扇動者 **sendōsha** instigator, agitator
11 運動 **undō** motion, movement; exercise, sports; a movement, campaign
   運動不足 **undō-busoku** lack of exercise
   運動会 **undōkai** athletic meet
   運動靴 **undōgutsu** athletic shoes, sneakers
   移動 **idō** moving, migration
   異動 **idō** change, reshuffling
12 揺動 **yu(ri)ugo(kasu)** (tr.) shake
   yu(re)ugo(ku) (intr.) shake
13 鼓動 **kodō** (heart) beat
   感動 **kandō** impression, inspiration, emotion, excitement
14 鳴動 **meidō** rumbling
   総動員 **sōdōin** general mobilization
15 衝動 **shōdō** impulse, urge, drive
   震動 **shindō** tremor, vibration
16 激動 **gekidō** violent shaking; excitement, stir
   機動隊 **kidōtai** riot squad
17 聳動 **shōdō** electrify, startle, shock
18 騒動 **sōdō** disturbance, riot

───────── 3 ─────────

7 形容動詞 **keiyōdōshi** quasi-adjective used with -na (e.g., shizuka, kirei)
10 哺乳動物 **honyū dōbutsu** mammal
12 軽自動車 **keijidōsha** light car

---- 4 ----

9 単独行動 **tandoku kōdō** acting on one's own

2g9.3 / 1502   田 艹 二 儿
              32 4 16

勘   勘 勘

KAN perception, intuition, sixth sense; think over; censure

---- 1 ----

5 勘弁 **kanben** pardon, forgive, tolerate

6 勘当 **kandō** disinheritance

8 勘定 **kanjō** calculation; account; settling an account

   勘所 **kandokoro** vital point, crux

12 勘違 **kanchiga(i)** misunderstanding, mistaken idea

---- 2 ----

12 割勘 **wa(ri)kan** Dutch treat

---- 10 ----

2g10.1 / 559   田 艹 口 土
              32 24 22

勤   勤 勤 勤

KIN work **GON** Buddhist religious services **tsuto(meru)** work for, be employed by, serve **tsuto(maru)** be fit/competent for SUSUMU, TSUTOMU (m. given name)

---- 1 ----

6 勤先 **tsuto(me)saki** place of work, employer

7 勤労 **kinrō** labor, work

10 勤勉 **kinben** industrious, hardworking

11 勤務 **kinmu** service, work, duty

   勤務先 **kinmusaki** place of employment, employer

13 勤続 **kinzoku** long service

---- 2 ----

4 欠勤 **kekkin** absence (from work)

5 出勤 **shukkin** go/come to work

8 夜勤 **yakin** night duty/shift

9 通勤 **tsūkin** commute to work

   皆勤 **kaikin** perfect attendance

11 常勤 **jōkin** full-time (employment)

   転勤 **tenkin** be transferred (to another office)

14 精勤 **seikin** diligence, good attendance

勞 → 労   3n4.3

---- 11 ----

2g11.1 / 1051   田 隹 宀 力
              74 15 8

勧   勧 丨 勧 勧

KAN, susu(meru) recommend, advise, encourage; offer SUSUMU (m. given name)

---- 1 ----

7 勧告 **kankoku** recommendation, advice

14 勧誘 **kan'yū** solicitation, invitation, canvassing

2g11.6 / 646   田 土 儿 艹
              22 16 12

勢   勢 勢

SEI, SE, ikio(i) force, energy, vigor

---- 1 ----

2 勢力 **seiryoku** influence, force

12 勢揃 **seizoro(i)** array, full lineup

---- 2 ----

3 大勢 **ōzei** large number of people
           taisei the general trend

5 去勢 **kyosei** castrate

6 気勢 **kisei** spirit, ardor, élan

   伊勢大神宮 **Ise Daijingū** the Grand Shrines of Ise

   伊勢蝦 **ise-ebi** spiny lobster

7 攻勢 **kōsei** the offensive

⁸ 国勢調査 **kokusei chōsa** (national) census

⁹ 姿勢 **shisei** posture, stance

威勢 **isei** power, influence; high spirits

¹⁰ 時勢 **jisei** the times/Zeitgeist

¹¹ 運勢 **unsei** one's fate, fortune, luck

情勢 **jōsei** situation, condition, circumstances

¹⁵ 潜勢力 **senseiryoku** latent power, potential

¹⁷ 優勢 **yūsei** predominance, superiority, the advantage

²⁰ 騰勢 **tōsei** rising/upward trend

--- 3 ---

¹⁰ 高姿勢 **kōshisei** high posture/profile, aggressive attitude

--- 14 ---

勳 → 勲 4d11.3

勵 → 励 2g5.4

--- 17 ---

勸 → 勧 2g11.1

又 **2h**

又	叉	双	収	友	収	皮	叔	受	殳	版	叙	桑
0.1	1.1	2.1	2.2	2.3	2h2.2	3.1	6.1	6.2	6.3	2j6.8	7.1	8.1

叡	雙	叢
14.1	2h2.1	6e12.3

--- 0 ---

2h0.1 / 1593 □ 又 9

又

又 | 又 又

mata again; also, moreover
mata(wa) or

--- 1 ---

¹² 又貸 **mataga(shi)** lend what one has borrowed, sublet, sublease

¹⁴ 又聞 **matagi(ki)** hearsay, secondhand information

--- 2 ---

⁵ 且又 **ka(tsu)mata** and, moreover

--- 1 ---

2h1.1 ... 又 9 2

叉

叉 叉

SA, SHA, mata crotch (of a tree), fork (in a road)

--- 2 ---

³ 三叉路 **sansaro** Y-junction of roads

--- 2 ---

2h2.1 / 1594 □□ 又 9

双

雙 | 双 双

SŌ, futa pair, both

--- 1 ---

² 双子 **futago** twins, a twin

⁴ 双方 **sōhō** both parties/sides

⁵ 双生児 **sōseiji** twins

¹¹ 双眼鏡 **sōgankyō** binoculars

2h2.2 / 757 □□ 又 丨 9 2

収

収 | 収 収

SHŪ, osa(meru) obtain, collect
osa(maru) be obtained; end
OSAMU (m. given name)

—— 1 ——

2 収入 **shūnyū** income, receipts, revenue, earnings

4 収支 **shūshi** revenues and expenditures

5 収用 **shūyō** expropriation

10 収益 **shūeki** earnings, proceeds

収容 **shūyō** accommodate, admit, receive

収容所 **shūyōjo** home, asylum, camp

収納 **shūnō** receipts; harvest; put in, store

13 収賄 **shūwai** accepting bribes, graft

16 収録 **shūroku** collect, record

17 収縮 **shūshuku** contraction, constriction

18 収穫 **shūkaku** harvest

—— 2 ——

6 年収 **nenshū** annual income

吸収 **kyūshū** absorb

7 没収 **bosshū** confiscate

8 押収 **ōshū** confiscation

実収 **jisshū** actual income, take-home pay

定収入 **teishūnyū** fixed income

11 副収入 **fukushūnyū** additional/side income

接収 **sesshū** requisition, take over

12 減収 **genshū** decrease in income

税収 **zeishū** tax revenues

14 徴収 **chōshū** collect, levy, charge

領収書 **ryōshūsho** receipt

領収証 **ryōshūshō** receipt

18 贈収賄 **zōshūwai** bribery

2h2.3 / 264　　　　　　▢ 十 又
　　　　　　　　　　　　　　12　9

友

友 友

YŪ, tomo friend　YU, TOMO (part of given name)

—— 1 ——

2 友人 **yūjin** friend

5 友好 **yūkō** friendship, amity

9 友美 **Tomomi, Yumi** (f. given name)

友哉 **Tomoya** (m. given name)

11 友達 **tomodachi** friend

友情 **yūjō** friendship, fellowship

—— 2 ——

5 幼友達 **osana tomodachi** childhood friend

旧友 **kyūyū** an old friend

7 良友 **ryōyū** good friend

住友 **Sumitomo** (company name)

学友 **gakuyū** schoolmate, alumnus

8 朋友 **hōyū** friend, companion

9 級友 **kyūyū** classmate

10 校友 **kōyū** schoolmate, alumnus

16 親友 **shin'yū** close friend

—— 3 ——

収 → **2h2.2**

2h3.1 / 975　　　　　▢ 厂 又
　　　　　　　　　　　　　　18　9

皮

皮 皮

HI, kawa skin, hide, leather, pelt, bark, rind

—— 1 ——

4 皮切 **kawaki(ri)** beginning, start

6 皮肉 **hiniku** irony, sarcasm

9 皮革 **hikaku** hides, leather

15 皮膚 **hifu** skin

—— 2 ——

4 毛皮 **kegawa** fur, skin, pelt

18 鞣皮 **jūhi, name(shi)gawa** leather

20 鰐皮 **wanigawa** alligator skin

—— 6 ——

2h6.1 / 1667　　　　　田 小 上 又
　　　　　　　　　　　　　35　13　9

叔

叔 叔

SHUKU younger sibling of a parent

—— 1 ——

4 叔父 **oji, shukufu** uncle

5 叔母 **oba, shukubo** aunt

2h6.2 / 260

目 小 冂 又
35 20 9

JU, u(keru) receive, catch (a ball), undergo (an operation), take (an exam), sustain (injuries); be well received, be a hit **u(ke)** receiving; receptacle; support, prop; popularity **u(karu)** pass (an exam)

——————— 1 ———————

2 受入 **u(ke)i(re)** receiving, accepting

4 受止 **u(ke)to(meru)** stop, catch; parry, ward off

5 受付 **uketsuke** receipt, acceptance; reception desk; receptionist

7 受身 **ukemi** being acted upon; passivity; passive (in grammar)

8 受取 **u(ke)to(ru)** receive, accept, take **uketo(ri)** receipt, acknowledgment

9 受信 **jushin** receipt of a message, (radio) reception

受持 **u(ke)mo(tsu)** have/take charge of

10 受益者 **juekisha** beneficiary

受託 **jutaku** be entrusted with

11 受理 **juri** accept

12 受診 **jushin** receive a medical examination

13 受継 **u(ke)tsu(gu)** inherit, succeed to

受話器 **juwaki** (telephone) receiver

14 受領 **juryō** receive, accept

15 受賞者 **jushōsha** prizewinner

17 受講 **jukō** take lectures

18 受難 **junan** ordeal, sufferings; (Jesus's) Passion

受験 **juken** take an examination

——————— 2 ———————

4 引受 **hi(ki)u(keru)** undertake, consent to, accept responsibility for, guarantee

9 俗受 **zokuu(ke)** popular appeal

13 感受性 **kanjusei** sensibility, sensitivity

2h6.3

田 夕 宀 又
30 15 9

BOTSU, shi(nu) die

——————— 2 ———————

13 戦歿者 **senbotsusha** fallen soldier

版→ 2j6.8

——————— 7 ———————

2h7.1 / 1067

冂 木 亻 又
41 3 9

JO narrate, describe; confer (a rank)

——————— 1 ———————

6 叙任 **jonin** appointment, investiture

7 叙述 **jojutsu** description, narration

11 叙情詩 **jojōshi** lyric poem/poetry

——————— 2 ———————

6 自叙伝 **jijoden** autobiography

——————— 8 ———————

2h8.1 / 1873

目 木 又
41 9

SŌ, kuwa mulberry tree

——————— 1 ———————

5 桑田 **Kuwata, Kuwada** (surname)

10 桑原 **Kuwabara, Kuwahara** (surname)

11 皺寄 **shiwayo(se)** shifting (the burden) to

14

2h14.1 / 2032   田 日 火 宀
                          55 44 33

叡   睿 | 叡 叡

EI wise; imperial SATOSHI, AKIRA, TŌRU (m. given name) EI, TOSHI, YOSHI, MASA, TADA, SATO (part of given name)

1

12 叡智 **eichi** wisdom, intelligence; intellect

2

5 比叡山 **Hieizan** (mountain, Kyōto-fu)

16

雙 → 双 **2h2.1**

叢 → **6e12.3**

宀 **2i**

冗 写 軍 冠 冥 冨 彙 嚢
2.1 3.1 7.1 7.2 8.2 3m9.5 11.1 3d19.3

2

2i2.1 / 1614   日 几
                          20

冗   冗 | 冗 冗

JŌ uselessness

1

10 冗員 **jōin** superfluous personnel, overstaffing
12 冗費 **jōhi** unnecessary expenses
14 冗漫 **jōman** verbose, rambling
15 冗談 **jōdan** a joke

3

2i3.1 / 540   日 冂 十 一
                          20 12 1

写   寫 | 写 写

SHA, utsu(ru) be photographed, be projected (on a screen) **utsu(su)** copy, transcribe, duplicate, photograph

1

8 写実的 **shajitsuteki** realistic, true to life, graphic
10 写真 **shashin** photograph

2

8 青写真 **aojashin, aoshashin** blueprints
11 描写 **byōsha** depiction, portrayal, description
12 筆写 **hissha** copy, transcribe
14 模写 **mosha** copy, replica
   複写 **fukusha** copying, duplication; a copy, facsimile
17 謄写 **tōsha** copy, duplication
   縮写 **shukusha** reduced copy, miniature reproduction

7

2i7.1 / 438   日 車 冂
                          69 20

軍   軍 軍

GUN army, military **ikusa** war, battle

1

2 軍人 **gunjin** soldier, military man
5 軍用 **gun'yō** for military use
8 軍事 **gunji** military affairs; military
   軍国主義 **gunkoku shugi** militarism
   軍服 **gunpuku** military uniform
9 軍政 **gunsei** military government/administration
10 軍部 **gunbu** the military
11 軍隊 **guntai** army, troops, corps

亻 冫 子 阝 刂 力 又 冖 7 亠 十 ク ソ 厂 辶 冂 几 匸

12 軍備 **gunbi** military preparations, preparedness

13 軍資 **gunshi** war funds/materiel; campaign funds

14 軍需 **gunju** military demand/supplies

軍閥 **gunbatsu** military clique, militarist party

16 軍機 **gunki** military secret

17 軍縮 **gunshuku** arms reduction, disarmament

21 軍艦 **gunkan** warship, battleship

――――――― 2 ―――――――

6 再軍備 **saigunbi** rearmament

米軍 **beigun** U.S. armed forces

8 空軍 **kūgun** air force

9 海軍 **kaigun** navy

10 将軍 **shōgun** general, commander, shogun

陸軍 **rikugun** army

13 賊軍 **zokugun** rebel army, rebels

15 敵軍 **tekigun** enemy army, hostile forces

――――――― 3 ―――――――

15 駐留軍 **chūryūgun** stationed/occupying troops

2i7.2 / 1615 ⊟ 寸 冂 二　37 20 4

冠

冠 冠

KAN, kanmuri crown

――――――― 1 ―――――――

4 冠水 **kansui** be submerged/flooded

11 冠婚葬祭 **kankonsōsai** ceremonial occasions

12 冠詞 **kanshi** article (in grammar)

――――――― 2 ―――――――

10 桂冠 **keikan** crown of laurel

17 戴冠式 **taikanshiki** coronation

――――――― 8 ―――――――

2i8.2 ⊟ 日 冂 宀　43 20 11

冥

冥 冥

MEI, MYŌ dark

――――――― 1 ―――――――

5 冥加 **myōga** divine protection

7 冥利 **myōri** divine favor, providence, luck

9 冥途 **meido** hades, realm of the dead

――――――― 9 ―――――――

富 → 富 **3m9.5**

――――――― 11 ―――――――

2i11.1 ⊟ 日 木 冂　43 41 20

彙

彙 彙

I classify and compile

――――――― 1 ―――――――

12 彙報 **ihō** collection of reports, bulletin

――――――― 2 ―――――――

14 語彙 **goi** vocabulary

――――――― 16 ―――――――

囊 → 囊 **3d19.3**

――――――――――― 宀 **2j** ―――――――――――

亡	之	六	文	乏	主	市	玄	亥	亨	交	亦	衣
1.1	0a2.9	2.2	2.4	0a3.11	4f1.1	3.1	3.2	4.1	4.2	4.3	4.4	5e0.1
充	妄	享	辛	弃	忘	対	夜	卒	京	育	斉	盲
4.5	4.6	5.1	5b2.2	2j11.5	5.4	5.5	6.1	6.2	6.3	6.4	6.5	6.6
版	京	帝	変	哀	亭	亮	彦	奇	彦	衰	衷	离
6.8	2j6.3	7.1	7.3	7.4	7.5	7.6	5b4.4	3d5.17	5b4.4	8.1	0a9.9	8c10.3

恋	高	畜	率	斎	産	産	商	髙	蛮	棄	牌	斐
8.2	8.6	8.7	9.1	9.6	5b6.4	5b6.4	9.7	2j8.6	10.1	2j11.5	10.3	10.4

裏	稟	牌	棄	齊	膏	豪	毓	褒	槀	齋	囊
11.2	11.3	2j10.3	11.5	2j6.5	12.1	12.3	2j6.4	13.1	5d10.5	2j9.6	3d19.3

─────── 1 ───────

2j1.1 / 672   日 亠 丨
                      11   2

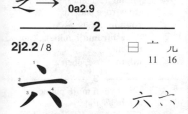

亡   亡 丨 亡 亡

BŌ, MŌ dead **na(kunaru)** die, pass away **na(ki)** the late, deceased **horo(biru)** perish, come to ruin **horo(bosu)** destroy, bring to ruin

─────── 1 ───────

4 亡夫 **bōfu** one's late husband
亡父 **bōfu** one's late father
5 亡母 **bōbo** one's late mother
8 亡命 **bōmei** flee one's country
亡命者 **bōmeisha** exile, emigré
亡妻 **bōsai** one's late wife
亡国 **bōkoku** ruined country, national ruin
15 亡霊 **bōrei** departed soul, ghost

─────── 2 ───────

5 未亡人 **mibōjin** widow
6 死亡 **shibō** die
8 逃亡 **tōbō** escape, flight, desertion
13 滅亡 **metsubō** downfall, destruction

之 → 0a2.9

─────── 2 ───────

2j2.2 / 8   日 亠 儿
                      11   16

六   六 六

ROKU, RIKU, mut(tsu), mu(tsu), mu, mui six

─────── 1 ───────

4 六月 **rokugatsu** June

六日 **muika** the sixth (day of the month); six days
8 六法 **roppō** the six directions; the six law codes

─────── 2 ───────

5 四六時中 **shirokujichū** 24 hours a day, constantly

2j2.4 / 111   日 亠 十
                      11   12

文   文 丨 文 文

BUN writing, composition, sentence, text, style; literature **MON** character, word; design; (ancient unit of money); (unit of length, about 2.4 cm) **fumi** letter, note **aya** design; figure of speech; plan, plot AYA (f. given name) FUMI, AYA (part of given name)

─────── 1 ───────

2 文子 **Fumiko, Ayako, Noriko** (f. given name)
4 文夫 **Fumio, Ayao** (m. given name)
文化 **bunka** culture, civilization
文化日 **Bunka (no) Hi** Culture Day (November 3)
文化財 **bunkazai** cultural asset
5 文句 **monku** phrase, expression; complaint, objection; excuse
文字 **moji, monji** character, letter
文字通 **mojidō(ri)** literal(ly)
7 文体 **buntai** (literary) style
文芸 **bungei** literary arts
文学 **bungaku** literature
文学士 **bungakushi** Bachelor of Arts
8 文例 **bunrei** model sentence/writing
文盲 **monmō** illiteracy
文法 **bunpō** grammar
文明 **bunmei** civilization, culture
Fumiaki, Bunmei, Fumiharu (m. given name)

─── 2 ───

亻 冫 子 阝 卩 力 又 亠 二 十 ト 夂 丷 厂 辶 冂 八 匚

9 文通 **buntsū** correspondence

10 文部省 **Monbushō** Ministry of Education

文庫 **bunko** stationery box; bookcase; library

文庫本 **bunkobon** small paperback book (page size 14.8 x 10.5 cm)

文脈 **bunmyaku** context

11 文章 **bunshō** composition, writing; article, essay

12 文集 **bunshū** anthology

13 文献 **bunken** literature (on a subject), bibliography

文楽 **bunraku** puppet theater

14 文語 **bungo** literary language

文語体 **bungotai** literary style

16 文壇 **bundan** the literary world; literary column

——————— 2 ———————

1 一文字 **ichimonji** a straight line

一文無 **ichimonna(shi)** penniless

2 人文 **jinmon, jinbun** humanity, civilization

十文字 **jūmonji** cross

3 三文 **sanmon** farthing; cheap

大文字 **ōmoji** capital letter **daimonji** large character; the character 大

小文字 **komoji** small/lowercase letters

4 不文律 **fubunritsu** unwritten law/rule

天文学 **tenmongaku** astronomy

仏文 **Futsubun** French, French literature

公文書 **kōbunsho** official document

5 本文 **honbun, honmon** (main) text, body

古文書 **komonjo, kobunsho** ancient documents

石文 **ishibumi** (inscribed) stone monument

6 全文 **zenbun** full text; whole sentence

成文 **seibun** composition, writing

7 作文 **sakubun** composition, writing

決文句 **ki(mari)monku** set phrase, conventional expression

序文 **jobun** preface, foreword, introduction

条文 **jōbun** the text, provisions

8 例文 **reibun** illustrative sentence

郁文堂 **Ikubundō** (publishing company)

注文 **chūmon** order, commission

呪文 **jumon** spell, curse, magic formula

英文 **eibun** English, English composition

英文学 **eibungaku** English literature

国文学 **kokubungaku** Japanese literature

旺文社 **Ōbunsha** (name of publishing company)

欧文 **ōbun** European language, roman script

和文 **wabun** Japanese (writing)

10 恋文 **koibumi** love letter

原文 **genbun** the text/original

純文学 **junbungaku** pure literature, belles lettres

11 脱文 **datsubun** missing passage, lacuna

12 博文 **Hirofumi, Hirobumi** (m. given name)

散文 **sanbun** prose

13 漢文 **kanbun** Chinese writing/classics

14 構文 **kōbun** sentence construction, syntax

碑文 **hibun** epitaph, inscription

15 横文字 **yokomoji** European/horizontal writing

縄文 **jōmon** (ancient Japanese) straw-rope pattern

論文 **ronbun** thesis, essay

16 頭文字 **kashiramoji** initials; capital letter

19 韻文 **inbun** verse, poetry

——————— 3 ———————

8 表音文字 **hyōon moji** phonetic symbol/script

表意文字 **hyōi moji** ideograph

12 象形文字 **shōkei moji** hieroglyphics

無一文 **muichimon** penniless

無形文化財 **mukei-bunkazai** intangible cultural asset

2j2.5 / 1045

片

片 片

HEN one (of two); fragment; just a little　**kata** one (of two), one-sided, single　**hira** leaf, sheet, petal, flake

— 1 —

3 片山 **Katayama** (surname)

4 片手 **katate** one hand, one-handed

片方 **katahō, katappō, katakata** one side/party, the other side/party

5 片付 **katazu(keru)** put in order; put away; settle, dispose of; marry off　**katazu(ku)** be put in order; be settled, be disposed of; get married off

6 片仮名 **katakana** katakana, the non-cursive syllabary

7 片言 **katakoto** baby talk, broken (English)　**hengen** few words

8 片岡 **Kataoka** (surname)

9 片思 **kataomo(i)** unrequited love

10 片桐 **Katagiri** (surname)

11 片側 **katagawa, katakawa** one side

片道 **katamichi** one way

片寄 **katayo(ru)** lean to one side; be biased

— 2 —

1 一片 **ippen** a piece/bit

7 阿片 **ahen** opium

9 後片付 **atokatazu(ke)** straightening up afterwards, putting things in order

砕片 **saihen** fragment, splinter

10 破片 **hahen** broken piece, fragment, splinter

紙片 **shihen** scrap of paper

11 断片 **danpen** fragment, snippet

乏 → **0a3.11**

3

主 → 主 **4f1.1**

2j3.1 / 181

市

市 市

SHI city, town; market　**ichi** market; fair

— 1 —

3 市川 **Ichikawa** (city, Chiba-ken)

4 市内 **shinai** (within the) city

5 市民 **shimin** citizen

市民権 **shiminken** citizenship, civil rights

市立 **shiritsu** municipal, city(-run)

7 市役所 **shiyakusho** city hall

市町村 **shichōson** cities, towns, and villages; municipalities

8 市長 **shichō** mayor

市況 **shikyō** market conditions

12 市場 **shijō** market　**ichiba** marketplace

市街 **shigai** the streets; city, town

市営 **shiei** run by the city, municipal

13 市電 **shiden** municipal railway, trolley

— 2 —

7 酉市 **tori (no) ichi** year-end fair

10 都市 **toshi** city

蚤市 **nomi (no) ichi** flea market

11 魚市場 **uoichiba** fish market

12 朝市 **asaichi** morning market/fair

13 歳市 **toshi (no) ichi** year-end market (cf. 節季市)

— 3 —

5 四日市 **Yokkaichi** (city, Mie-ken)

8 青空市場 **aozora ichiba** open-air market

10 株式市場 **kabushiki shijō** stock market

2

亻
氵
孑
阝
刂
力
又
宀
冖
冫
厂
辶
门
几
匸

3

2j3.2 / 1225 　日 亠 竹 丨
　　　　　　　11 17 2

玄

玄 玄

GEN black, mysterious, occult
HARU (part of given name)

———————— 1 ————————

2 玄人 **kurōto** expert, professional
6 玄米 **genmai** unpolished/unmilled rice
14 玄関 **genkan** entranceway, vestibule, front door

———————— 2 ————————

8 表玄関 **omote genkan** front entrance/door
9 幽玄 **yūgen** the profound, occult

———————— 4 ————————

2j4.1 / 2008 　日 亠 竹 亻
　　　　　　　11 17 3

亥

亥 亥

GAI, i twelfth horary sign (boar)　GAI, KAI, I, RI (part of given name)

2j4.2 / 2009 　目 口 亠 一
　　　　　　　24 11 1

亨

亨 亨

KŌ pass through **KYŌ** offer **HŌ** boil, cook TŌRU, AKIRA, SUSUMU (m. given name)　KŌ, KYŌ, HŌ, MICHI, YUKI, NAGA, AKI (part of given name)

2j4.3 / 114 　日 亠 儿 十
　　　　　　　11 16 12

交

交 交

KŌ intersect; coming and going; associate with **ma(jiru/zaru)** (intr.) mix **maji(eru), ma(zeru)** (tr.) mix **maji(waru)** associate with **ka(wasu)**

exchange (greetings) **-ka(u)** go past each other

———————— 1 ————————

5 交代 **kōtai** take turns, alternate, relieve, work in shifts
交付 **kōfu** deliver, furnish with
9 交通 **kōtsū** traffic, transport, communication
10 交差点 **kōsaten** crossing, intersection
交流 **kōryū** alternating current, AC; (cultural) exchange
11 交渉 **kōshō** negotiations
12 交換 **kōkan** exchange
交替 **kōtai** take turns, alternate, relieve, work in shifts
交番 **kōban** police box/stand; alternation **kawa(ri)ban(ko ni)** taking turns
13 交際 **kōsai** associate with, keep company with, be friends with
19 交響曲 **kōkyōkyoku** symphony

———————— 2 ————————

5 外交 **gaikō** diplomacy, foreign relations
外交官 **gaikōkan** diplomat
7 乱交 **rankō** orgy
社交 **shakō** society, social life
8 国交 **kokkō** diplomatic relations
性交 **seikō** sexual intercourse
9 飛交 **to(bi)ka(u)** fly/flit about
11 断交 **dankō** break off relations with
16 親交 **shinkō** friendship, intimacy

———————— 3 ————————

8 非社交的 **hishakōteki** unsociable, retiring

2j4.4 / 2007 　日 亠 儿
　　　　　　　11 16

亦

亦 亦

EKI, YAKU, mata also, again　EKI, YAKU, MATA (part of given name)

衣 → **5e0.1**

2j4.5 / 828   目 亠 竹 儿   11 17 16

充   充 充

JŪ fill **a(teru)** allocate **mi(tasu)** fulfill, satisfy **MITSURU, TAKASHI** (m. given name) **MITSU** (part of given name)

--- 1 ---

4 充分 **jūbun** enough, sufficient; thoroughly

8 充実 **jūjitsu** repletion, completion, beefing up, making substantial

12 充満 **jūman, michimichi(te iru)** be full of, be replete/teeming with

13 充電 **jūden** recharge (a battery)

--- 2 ---

4 不充分 **fujūbun** insufficient, inadequate

12 補充 **hojū** supplement, replacement

2j4.6 / 1376   目 女 亠 | 25 11 2

妄   妄 妄

BŌ, MŌ incoherent, reckless, false **mida(ri ni)** without authority; without good reason; indiscriminately, recklessly

--- 1 ---

9 妄信 **mōshin, bōshin** blind acceptance, credulity

11 妄動 **mōdō, bōdō** act blindly

13 妄想 **mōsō, bōsō** wild fantasy, delusion

--- 5 ---

2j5.1 / 1672   目 口 亠 子   24 11 6

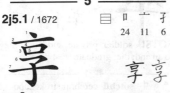

享   享 享

KYŌ enjoy; receive **u(keru)** receive **SUSUMU** (m. given name)

--- 1 ---

6 享年 **kyōnen** one's age at death

享有 **kyōyū** enjoy, possess

13 享楽 **kyōraku** enjoyment

辛 → 5b2.2

弃 → 棄 2j11.5

2j5.4 / 1374   目 心 亠 | 51 11 2

忘   忘 | 忘 忘

BŌ, wasu(reru) forget

--- 1 ---

6 忘年会 **bōnenkai** year-end party

8 忘物 **wasu(re)mono** something forgotten

--- 2 ---

8 物忘 **monowasu(re)** forgetfulness

9 度忘 **dowasu(re)** forget for the moment, slip one's mind

10 健忘症 **kenbōshō** forgetfulness, amnesia

胴忘 **dōwasu(re)** have a lapse of memory, forget for the moment

2j5.5 / 365   田 寸 亠 艹   37 11 12

対   對 | 对 対

TAI against, vis-à-vis, versus, anti-, counter- **TSUI** pair, set

--- 1 ---

0 対する **tai(suru)** be opposite to, face; toward; as opposed to; in response to

4 対中 **tai-Chū** toward/with China

対日 **tai-Nichi** toward/with Japan

5 対外 **taigai** foreign, international, overseas

対比 **taihi** contrast, comparison, opposition, analogy

2

イ 冫 孑 阝 卩 刂 力 又 宀

6 亠 亠 广 夂 宀 厂 辶 冂 几 匚

対処 **taisho** deal/cope with

対立 **tairitsu** confrontation, opposing

6 対当 **taitō** corresponding, equivalent

対米 **tai-Bei** toward/with America

7 対抗 **taikō** oppose, counter

対応 **taiō** correspond to, be equivalent to; cope with

8 対欧 **tai-Ō** toward/with Europe

9 対面 **taimen** interview, meeting; facing each other

10 対称 **taishō** symmetry; second person (in grammar)

11 対訳 **taiyaku** bilingual text (with Japanese and English side by side)

12 対象 **taishō** object, subject, target

対策 **taisaku** (counter)measures

13 対照 **taishō** contrast

15 対談 **taidan** face-to-face talk, conversation, interview

21 対露 **tai-Ro** toward/with Russia

――――― 2 ―――――

1 一対 **ittsui** a pair

一対一 **ittaiichi** one-to-one

4 反対 **hantai** opposition, against; opposite, reverse, contrary

反対側 **hantaigawa** the opposite side

反対語 **hantaigo** antonym

7 初対面 **shotaimen** first meeting

12 絶対 **zettai** absolute

15 敵対心 **tekitaishin** enmity, animosity

――――― 3 ―――――

5 正反対 **seihantai** the exact opposite

――――― 6 ―――――

2j6.1 / 471   田 夕 宀 イ
                    30 11 3

夜   夜 夜

YA, yo, yoru night

――――― 1 ―――――

4 夜中 **yonaka** midnight, dead of night **yachū** at night **yojū** all night

6 夜行 **yakō** night travel; night train

8 夜逃 **yoni(ge)** fly by night, give (creditors) the slip

夜空 **yozora** night sky

夜明 **yoa(kashi)** stay up all night **yoa(ke)** dawn, daybreak

11 夜道 **yomichi** night journey

12 夜勤 **yakin** night duty/shift

夜景 **yakei** night view

――――― 2 ―――――

1 一夜 **ichiya, hitoyo, hitoya** one night; all night

4 今夜 **kon'ya** tonight

月夜 **tsukiyo** moonlit night

日夜 **nichiya** day and night, constantly

6 毎夜 **maiyo** every evening, nightly

先夜 **sen'ya** the other night

9 前夜祭 **zen'yasai** (Christmas) Eve

昨夜 **sakuya, yūbe** last night/evening

昼夜 **chūya** day and night

10 真夜中 **mayonaka** dead of night, midnight

11 深夜 **shin'ya** late at night, the dead of night

12 幾夜 **ikuyo** how many nights; many a night

13 暗夜 **an'ya** dark night

聖夜 **seiya** Christmas Eve

15 徹夜 **tetsuya** stay up all night

17 闇夜 **yamiyo, an'ya** dark night

2j6.2 / 787   目 宀 イ 土
                    11 3 12

卒   卆 卒 卒

SOTSU soldier, private; sudden; come to an end; die; graduate

――――― 1 ―――――

4 卒中 **sotchū** cerebral stroke, apoplexy

8 卒直 **sotchoku** frank, openhearted

¹³ 卒業 **sotsugyō** graduation

—————— 2 ——————

³ 大卒 **daisotsu** college/university
graduation (short for 大学卒業
(者))

⁷ 兵卒 **heisotsu** private, enlisted man

¹⁰ 高卒 **kōsotsu** high-school graduate
(short for 高等学校卒業(者))

¹¹ 脳卒中 **nōsotchū** cerebral apo-
plexy

2j6.3 / 189

    目 日 小 亠
24 35 11

京 | 京 京

KYŌ, KEI capital, metropolis; Kyōto;
Tōkyō; ten quadrillion **miyako** capital, metropolis TAKASHI (m. given
name) MIYAKO (f. given name)
KYŌ, KEI, TAKA (part of given name)

—————— 1 ——————

² 京子 **Kyōko, Keiko, Takako** (f.
given name)

⁶ 京阪神 **Kei-Han-Shin** Kyōto-Ōsa-
ka-Kōbe

⁹ 京城 **Keijō** Seoul

¹⁰ 京都 **Kyōto** (city, Kyōto-fu)
京浜 **Kei-Hin** Tōkyō-Yokohama

—————— 2 ——————

³ 上京 **jōkyō** go/come to the capital

⁵ 北京 **Pekin** Peking, Beijing

⁸ 東京 **Tōkyō** (city, capital of Japan)

⁹ 南京 **Nankin** Nanking

2j6.4 / 246

    目 月 亠 竹
42 11 17

毓 | 育 育

IKU, soda(teru), haguku(mu) raise,
rear, bring up **soda(te)** bringing up,
raising **soda(tsu)** be raised, be
brought up, grow up **soda(chi)** upbringing; growth YASU (part of given
name)

—————— 1 ——————

⁶ 育成 **ikusei** rearing, training

⁷ 育児 **ikuji** care/raising of children

¹⁶ 育親 **soda(te no) oya** foster parent

—————— 2 ——————

⁵ 生育 **seiiku** growth, development
ha(e)soda(tsu) spring up

⁶ 成育 **seiiku** growth, development

⁷ 体育館 **taiikukan** gymnasium

⁹ 発育 **hatsuiku** growth, develop-
ment
保育 **hoiku** nurture, childcare, rearing

¹⁰ 教育 **kyōiku** education
教育費 **kyōikuhi** school/education
expenses

¹³ 飼育 **shiiku** raising, breeding

¹⁵ 養育 **yōiku** bring up, rear; support

2j6.5 / 1477

    目 亠 十 儿
11 12 16

齊 | 齊 斉

SEI in order, all together; alike
hito(shii) equal, similar HITOSHI (m.
given name) NARI (part of given
name)

—————— 1 ——————

¹⁸ 斉藤 **Saitō** (surname)

—————— 2 ——————

¹ 一斉 **issei** all at once, simultaneously

2j6.6 / 1375

    目 目 亠 丨
55 11 2

盲 | 盲 盲

MŌ, BŌ, mekura, meshii blind

—————— 1 ——————

² 盲人 **mōjin** blind person

⁷ 盲学校 **mōgakkō** school for the
blind

⁹ 盲信 **mōshin** blind acceptance, cre-
dulity

盲点 **mōten** blind spot
10 盲従 **mōjū** blind obedience
11 盲啞 **mōa** blind and mute
14 盲導犬 **mōdōken** seeing-eye dog

——————— 2 ———————

4 文盲 **monmō** illiteracy
6 色盲 **shikimō** color blindness
8 明盲 **a(ki)mekura** blind; illiterate

2j6.8 / 1046

囗 气 宀 厂
15 11 18

HAN printing block/plate; printing, edition, impression; board; roster

——————— 1 ———————

3 版下 **hanshita** art boards, mechanicals, camera-ready copy
8 版画 **hanga** woodcut print
15 版権 **hanken** copyright

——————— 2 ———————

5 出版 **shuppan** publishing
6 再版 **saihan** reprint; second printing/edition
7 初版 **shohan** first edition
13 新版 **shinpan** new publication/edition

——————— 3 ———————

7 決定版 **ketteiban** definitive edition
改訂版 **kaiteiban** revised edition
9 海賊版 **kaizokuban** pirate edition
13 新訂版 **shinteiban** newly revised edition
17 縮刷版 **shukusatsuban** small-size edition

——————— 4 ———————

6 自費出版 **jihi shuppan** publishing at one's own expense, vanity press

——————— 7 ———————

京 → 京 2j6.3

2j7.1 / 1179

目 巾 宀 儿
26 11 16

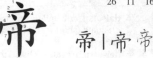

TEI emperor **mikado** emperor (of Japan)

——————— 1 ———————

4 帝王 **teiō** monarch, emperor
帝王切開 **teiō sekkai** Caesarean section
8 帝国 **teikoku** empire
帝国主義 **teikoku shugi** imperialism
9 帝室 **teishitsu** the imperial household

——————— 2 ———————

9 皇帝 **kōtei** emperor

2j7.3 / 257

目 夂 宀 儿
49 11 16

變 | 変 変

HEN change; strange; flat (in musical keys); mishap; disturbance **ka(waru)** change (intr.); be different **ka(eru)** change (tr.)

——————— 1 ———————

2 変人 **henjin** an eccentric
4 変化 **henka** change **henge** goblin, apparition
5 変目 **ka(wari)me** change, turning point, transition
6 変死 **henshi** accidental death
変色 **henshoku** change of color, discoloration
7 変身 **henshin** transformation
変更 **henkō** change, alteration, amendment
変形 **henkei** transformation, metamorphosis, modification, deformation
8 変果 **ka(wari)ha(teru)** change completely
変事 **henji** accident, mishap, disaster

9 変造 **henzō** alter, deface, falsify, forge

変革 **henkaku** change, reform, revolution

10 変容 **hen'yō** changed appearance

11 変動 **hendō** fluctuations

12 変換 **henkan** change, conversion, transformation (in math)

変装 **hensō** disguise

14 変遷 **hensen** changes, vicissitudes, transition

変貌 **henbō** transformation

変態 **hentai** metamorphosis; abnormal, perverted

15 変調 **henchō** change of tone/key; irregular, abnormal; modulation (in radio)

変質 **henshitsu** deterioration, degeneration

——————— 2 ———————

1 一変 **ippen** a complete change

3 大変 **taihen** serious; terrible, awful, huge, very

4 不変 **fuhen** invariable, constant, immutable, permanent

心変 **kokoroga(wari)** change of mind, inconstancy

5 生変 **u(mare)ka(waru)** be born again, start life afresh, be reincarnated **ha(e)ka(waru)** grow in a place of previous growth, grow in again

6 気変 **kiga(wari)** change one's mind, be fickle

兇変 **kyōhen** disaster; assassination

8 事変 **jihen** accident, mishap; incident, uprising, emergency

9 急変 **kyūhen** sudden change; emergency

風変 **fūgawa(ri)** eccentric, peculiar

相変 **aikawa(razu)** as usual

11 異変 **ihen** accident, disaster, unforeseen occurrence

——————— 3 ———————

1 一風変 **ippū kawa(tta)** eccentric, queer; unconventional, original

8 突然変異 **totsuzen hen'i** mutation

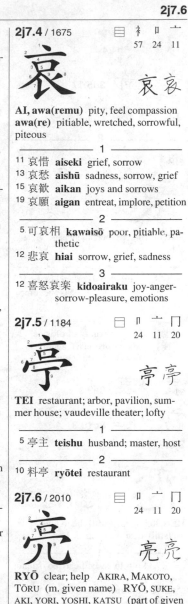

2j7.4 / 1675   目 礻 口 亠
57 24 11

哀   哀 哀

AI, awa(remu) pity, feel compassion **awa(re)** pitiable, wretched, sorrowful, piteous

——————— 1 ———————

11 哀惜 **aiseki** grief, sorrow

13 哀愁 **aishū** sadness, sorrow, grief

15 哀歓 **aikan** joys and sorrows

19 哀願 **aigan** entreat, implore, petition

——————— 2 ———————

5 可哀相 **kawaisō** poor, pitiable, pathetic

12 悲哀 **hiai** sorrow, grief, sadness

——————— 3 ———————

12 喜怒哀楽 **kidoairaku** joy-anger-sorrow-pleasure, emotions

2j7.5 / 1184   目 口 亠 冂
24 11 20

亭   亭 亭

TEI restaurant; arbor, pavilion, summer house; vaudeville theater; lofty

——————— 1 ———————

5 亭主 **teishu** husband; master, host

——————— 2 ———————

10 料亭 **ryōtei** restaurant

2j7.6 / 2010   目 口 亠 冂
24 11 20

亮   亮 亮

RYŌ clear; help AKIRA, MAKOTO, TŌRU (m. given name) RYŌ, SUKE, AKI, YORI, YOSHI, KATSU (part of given name)

——————— 1 ———————

4 亮太 **Ryōta** (m. given name)

彦 → **5b4.4**

奇 → 奇 **3d5.17**

彦 → 彦 **5b4.4**

───── 8 ─────

2j8.1 / 1676

目 禾 口 宀
57　24　11

衰　衰衰

SUI, otoro(eru) become weak, wither, ebb, go into decline

───── 1 ─────

8 衰退 **suitai** decline, degeneration
10 衰弱 **suijaku** grow weak, become feeble

───── 2 ─────

6 老衰 **rōsui** infirmity of old age
14 瘦衰 **ya(se)otoro(eru)** become emaciated, waste away

衷 → 衷 **0a9.9**

离 → 離 **8c10.3**

2j8.2 / 258

目 心 宀 儿
51　11　16

恋　戀 | 恋恋

REN, koi love　**ko(u)** be in love
koi(shii) dear, beloved

───── 1 ─────

2 恋人 **koibito** sweetheart, boyfriend, girlfriend
4 恋文 **koibumi** love letter
恋心 **koigokoro** (awakening of) love
12 恋焦 **ko(i)ko(gareru)** pine for, be desperately in love
13 恋煩 **koiwazura(i)** lovesickness

恋愛 **ren'ai** love
15 恋敵 **koigataki** one's rival in love

───── 2 ─────

5 失恋 **shitsuren** unrequited love
7 初恋 **hatsukoi** one's first love

2j8.6 / 190

目 口 宀 冂
24　11　20

高　髙 | 高高

KŌ high　taka(i) high; expensive
taka(maru) rise, increase　**taka(me-ru)** raise, heighten　**taka** amount
taka(buru) be proud/haughty; grow excited　**(o)taka(ku)** haughty, stuck up　**taka(raka)** loud　**taka(ga)** only, at most, after all　KŌ, TAKA (part of given name)

───── 1 ─────

0 ドル高 **dorudaka** strong dollar (relative to other currencies)
3 高々 **takadaka** at most; high, aloft, loudly
高山 **Takayama** (surname)
4 高木 **Takagi** (surname)
5 高石 **Takaishi** (surname)
高田 **Takada** (surname)
6 高気圧 **kōkiatsu** high atmospheric pressure
高年 **kōnen** old age
高地 **kōchi** high ground, highlands, plateau
高名 **kōmyō** fame, renown; your name　**kōmei** fame, renown
高血圧 **kōketsuatsu** high blood pressure
7 高志 **Takashi, Kōshi** (m. given name)
8 高価 **kōka** high price
高卒 **kōsotsu** high-school graduate (short for 高等学校卒業(者))
高岡 **Takaoka** (surname)
高知県 **Kōchi-ken** (prefecture)
高明 **Takaaki, Kōmei, Takaharu** (m. given name)
高所 **kōsho** elevation, height; altitude; broad view

9 高速 **kōsoku** high-speed; express-way

高姿勢 **kōshisei** high posture/profile, aggressive attitude

高度 **kōdo** high(ly developed), advanced, sophisticated; altitude

高架 **kōka** elevated, overhead

高畑 **Takabatake, Takahata** (surname)

高級 **kōkyū** high-grade, high-class; high rank

10 高値 **takane** high price

高原 **kōgen** plateau, highlands

高島 **Takashima** (surname)

高校 **kōkō** senior high school (short for 高等学校)

高校生 **kōkōsei** senior-high-school student

11 高野 **Takano** (surname)

高野山 **Kōyasan** (mountain, Wakayama-ken)

高率 **kōritsu** high rate

12 高裁 **kōsai** High Court (short for 高等裁判所)

高等 **kōtō** high-grade, high-class

14 高層 **kōsō** high-altitude, high-rise (building)

高慢 **kōman** proud, haughty, supercilious

16 高橋 **Takahashi** (surname)

17 高齢者 **kōreisha** elderly person

20 高騰 **kōtō** steep rise (in prices)

———— 2 ————

4 円高 **endaka** strong yen (exchange rate)

5 甲高 **kandaka(i)** high-pitched, shrill **kōdaka** having a high instep

6 気高 **kedaka(i)** noble, exalted

至高 **shikō** supreme, sublime, highest

名高 **nadaka(i)** famous, renowned

8 金高 **kindaka** amount of money

10 残高 **zandaka** balance, remainder

12 割高 **waridaka** comparatively expensive

最高 **saikō** maximum, best; great

最高点 **saikōten** highest point/score

最高裁判所 **Saikō Saibansho** Supreme Court

最高潮 **saikōchō** highwater mark; climax, peak

———— 3 ————

5 生産高 **seisandaka** output, production, yield

7 売上高 **uria(ge)daka** amount sold, sales

2j8.7 / 1223

目 罒 宀 竹
58　11　17

CHIKU (keep) domestic animals

———— 1 ————

5 畜生 **chikushō** beast, brute; Dammit!

11 畜産 **chikusan** livestock raising

———— 2 ————

8 牧畜 **bokuchiku** livestock/cattle raising

10 家畜 **kachiku** domestic animals, livestock

鬼畜 **kichiku** devil, brutal man

———— 9 ————

2j9.1 / 788

目 宀 冫 竹
11　5　17

RITSU rate, percentage, porportion, coefficient **SOTSU** obey; lead; all; light, easy; sudden **hiki(iru)** lead, be in command of

———— 1 ————

6 率先 **sossen** take the initiative, be the first

8 率直 **sotchoku** straightforward, frank, forthright

10 率倒 **sottō** faint, swoon

———— 2 ————

5 比率 **hiritsu** ratio, percentage

7 低率 **teiritsu** low rate

利率 **riritsu** rate of interest

8 効率 **kōritsu** efficiency

10 倍率 **bairitsu** magnifying power, magnification

高率 **kōritsu** high rate

能率 **nōritsu** efficiency

12 軽率 **keisotsu** rash, hasty

15 確率 **kakuritsu** probability

——— 3 ———

8 非能率的 **hinōritsuteki** inefficient

11 視聴率 **shichōritsu** (TV show popularity) rating

——— 1 ———

8 牽制 **kensei** check, restrain; diversion, feint

2j9.6 / 1478　　　目 小 宀 土
　　　　　　　　　　35　11　12

斎　齋｜斎斎

SAI religious purification; abstinence, fasting; Buddhist food; a room; equal **imi, monoimi** fasting, abstinence ITSUKI, HITOSHI (m. given name)

——— 1 ———

7 斎戒 **saikai** purification

18 斎藤 **Saitō** (surname)

——— 2 ———

10 書斎 **shosai** study, library, den

産 → 産 5b6.4

産 → 5b6.4

2j9.7 / 412　　　目 口 宀 儿
　　　　　　　　　　24　11　16

商　商商

SHŌ trade, merchant; quotient (in math) **akina(u)** sell, deal in, handle

——— 1 ———

2 商人 **shōnin** merchant, trader, shopkeeper

3 商工 **shōkō** commerce and industry

商工会議所 **Shōkō Kaigisho** Chamber of Commerce and Industry

商大 **shōdai** commercial college (short for 商科大学)

5 商用 **shōyō** business

商号 **shōgō** corporate name

6 商会 **shōkai** company, firm

7 商売 **shōbai** business, trade, transaction; occupation

商社 **shōsha** trading company, business firm

8 商事 **shōji** commercial affairs (short for 商事会社)

商店 **shōten** store, shop

商店街 **shōtengai** shopping area

9 商品 **shōhin** goods, merchandise

11 商務 **shōmu** commercial affairs

13 商業 **shōgyō** commerce, trade, business

15 商標 **shōhyō** trademark

商談 **shōdan** business talks/negotiations

——— 2 ———

3 工商 **kōshō** industry and commerce; artisans and merchants

4 水商売 **mizu shōbai** trades dependent on public patronage (bars, restaurants, entertainment)

6 年商 **nenshō** annual sales

——— 3 ———

12 貿易商 **bōekishō** trader

——— 4 ———

3 士農工商 **shinōkōshō** samurai-farmers-artisans-merchants, the military, agricultural, industrial, and mercantile classes

高 → 高 2j8.6

——— 10 ———

2j10.1 / 1879　　　目 虫 宀 儿
　　　　　　　　　　64　11　16

蛮　蠻｜蛮蛮

BAN barbarian

——— 2 ———

9 南蛮人 **nanbanjin** southern barbarians, the early Europeans

[11] 野蛮 **yaban** savage, barbarous

棄→ **2j11.5**

2j11.3

43 11 12

HAI label, sign; medal **pai** mahjong playing tiles

—————— 2 ——————

[7] 位牌 **ihai** Buddhhist mortuary tablet

2j10.4 / 2082

16 4 11

斐 斐

HI beautiful; bend, yield AYA (f. given name) AKIRA, AYARU (m. given name) HI, YOSHI, I, NAKA, NAGA, AYA (part of given name)

—————— 2 ——————

[5] 甲斐 **kai** effect, result; worth, avail, use **Kai** (ancient kuni, Yamanashi-ken)
甲斐性 **kaishō** resourcefulness, competence

—————— 3 ——————

[5] 生甲斐 **i(ki)gai** something worth living for

—————— 11 ——————

2j11.2 / 273

57 43 11

裡 | 裏 裏

RI, **ura** reverse side, opposite, rear; palm, sole; last half (of an inning)

—————— 1 ——————

[3] 裏口 **uraguchi** back door, rear entrance

[4] 裏切 **uragi(ru)** betray **uragi(ri)** betrayal, treachery
裏日本 **ura-Nihon, ura-Nippon** Sea-of-Japan side of Japan

[5] 裏付 **urazu(keru)** support, endorse, substantiate
裏目 **urame** the reverse (of the intended outcome)

[6] 裏返 **uragae(su)** turn the other way, turn inside out, turn over **uragae(shi)** inside out, upside down **uragae(ru)** be turned inside out; turn against (someone)

[7] 裏町 **uramachi** back street, alley

[8] 裏表 **ura-omote** both sides; reverse, inside out; two-faced

[9] 裏通 **uradō(ri)** alley, side street

[10] 裏書 **uraga(ki)** endorsement; certificate of genuineness; proof

[11] 裏側 **uragawa** the back side

[13] 裏腹 **urahara** the contrary, opposite
裏話 **urabanashi** inside story, story behind the story

2j11.3

56 24 11

稟 | 稟 稟

RIN, HIN salary paid in rice; receive; inborn

—————— 1 ——————

[20] 稟議 **ringi** decision-making by circular letter (instead of holding a meeting)

牌→ **2j10.3**

2j11.5 / 962

41 32 11

弃 | 棄 棄

KI, **su(teru)** throw away, abandon, renounce

2

亻 冫 孑 阝 卩 力 又 宀 亠 艹 夊 厂 辶 冂 几 匸

12

— 1 —
15 棄権 **kiken** abstain from voting; renounce one's rights, withdraw

— 2 —
7 投棄 **tōki** abandon, give up
8 放棄 **hōki** abandon, renounce, waive, forfeit
10 破棄 **haki** annulment, repudiation, abrogation, reversal
12 廃棄物 **haikibutsu** waste matter, wastes

— 12 —

齊 → 斉 **2j6.5**

2j12.1 目 月 口 亠 42 24 11

膏 膏 膏

KŌ ointment, grease **abura** fat, grease, tallow

— 1 —
16 膏薬 **kōyaku** salve, ointment, plaster

— 3 —
11 絆創膏 **bansōkō** adhesive plaster

2j12.3 / 1671 目 犭 口 亠 27 24 11

豪 豪 豪

GŌ strength, power; splendor, magnificence; Australia TAKESHI (m. given name) HIDE (part of given name)

— 1 —
6 豪州 **Gōshū** Australia
8 豪雨 **gōu** heavy rain, downpour
10 豪華 **gōka** luxurious, splendid, gorgeous
13 豪傑 **gōketsu** hero, great man

— 2 —
4 日豪 **Nichi-Gō** Japan and Australia

毓 → 育 **2j6.4**

— 13 —

2j13.1 / 803 目 衤 木 口 57 41 24

褒 褒 | 褒 褒

HŌ, ho(meru) praise

— 1 —
3 褒上 **ho(me)a(geru)** praise very highly
5 褒立 **ho(me)ta(teru)** praise, applaud
9 褒美 **hōbi** reward, prize
11 褒章 **hōshō** medal
15 褒賞 **hōshō** prize, reward

槁 → 稿 **5d10.5**

— 15 —

齋 → 斎 **2j9.6**

— 20 —

囊 → **3d19.3**

— 十 **2k** —

十	干	千	支	午	卆	古	芐	本	平	平	孝	考
0.1	1.1	1.2	2.1	2.2	2j6.2	3.1	0a5.37	0a5.25	2k3.4	3.4	4.3	4.4

老	岳	卍	克	求	協	幸	尭	直	阜	奔	卑	南
4.5	4.6	4.7	5.1	2b5.5	6.1	3b5.9	3b9.3	6.2	6.3	6.5	5f4.8	7.1

阜	真	索	臬	缺	皐	博	準	喪	準	献	瓶	翠
5f4.8	8.1	8.2	4c7.12	4j0.1	4c7.12	10.1	2k11.1	3b9.20	11.1	3g9.6	2o9.6	12.2

—————— 0 ——————

2k0.1 / 12

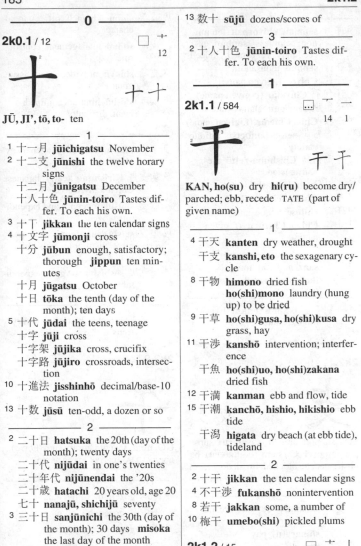

□ 十
          12

JŪ, JI', tō, to- ten

—————— 1 ——————

1 十一月 **jūichigatsu** November
2 十二支 **jūnishi** the twelve horary signs
  十二月 **jūnigatsu** December
  十人十色 **jūnin-toiro** Tastes differ. To each his own.
3 十丁 **jikkan** the ten calendar signs
4 十文字 **jūmonji** cross
  十分 **jūbun** enough, satisfactory; thorough **jippun** ten minutes
  十月 **jūgatsu** October
  十日 **tōka** the tenth (day of the month); ten days
5 十代 **jūdai** the teens, teenage
  十字 **jūji** cross
  十字架 **jūjika** cross, crucifix
  十字路 **jūjiro** crossroads, intersection
10 十進法 **jisshinhō** decimal/base-10 notation
13 十数 **jūsū** ten-odd, a dozen or so

—————— 2 ——————

2 二十日 **hatsuka** the 20th (day of the month); twenty days
  二十代 **nijūdai** in one's twenties
  二十年代 **nijūnendai** the '20s
  二十歳 **hatachi** 20 years old, age 20
  七十 **nanajū, shichijū** seventy
3 三十日 **sanjūnichi** the 30th (day of the month); 30 days **misoka** the last day of the month
4 不十分 **fujūbun** insufficient, inadequate
  五十音順 **gojūonjun** in "aiueo" order of the kana alphabet
  五十嵐 **Igarashi** (surname)
5 四十 **yonjū, shijū** forty
7 赤十字 **sekijūji** Red Cross

13 数十 **sūjū** dozens/scores of

—————— 3 ——————

2 十人十色 **jūnin-toiro** Tastes differ. To each his own.

—————— 1 ——————

2k1.1 / 584

... 一 一
          14   1

KAN, ho(su) dry hi(ru) become dry/parched; ebb, recede TATE (part of given name)

—————— 1 ——————

4 干天 **kanten** dry weather, drought
  干支 **kanshi, eto** the sexagenary cycle
8 干物 **himono** dried fish
  ho(shi)mono laundry (hung up) to be dried
9 干草 **ho(shi)gusa, ho(shi)kusa** dry grass, hay
11 干渉 **kanshō** intervention; interference
  干魚 **ho(shi)uo, ho(shi)zakana** dried fish
12 干満 **kanman** ebb and flow, tide
15 干潮 **kanchō, hishio, hikishio** ebb tide
  干潟 **higata** dry beach (at ebb tide), tideland

—————— 2 ——————

2 十干 **jikkan** the ten calendar signs
4 不干渉 **fukanshō** nonintervention
8 若干 **jakkan** some, a number of
10 梅干 **umebo(shi)** pickled plums

2k1.2 / 15

日 十 │
       12 2

SEN, chi thousand

—————————— 1 ——————————

³ 千万 **senman, chiyorozu** ten million; countless **senban** exceedingly, very much, indeed

⁴ 千分 **senbun** thousandth

⁵ 千代 **Chiyo** (f. given name)

千代子 **Chiyoko** (f. given name)

⁷ 千里眼 **senrigan** clairvoyant

⁸ 千枝 **Chie, Chieda** (f. given name)

¹⁰ 千差万別 **sensa-banbetsu** infinite variety

千島列島 **Chishima-rettō** the Kurile Islands

¹¹ 千鳥足 **chidori-ashi** tottering steps

¹² 千葉 **Chiba** (city, Chiba-ken)

¹³ 千歳 **chitose** a thousand years

²¹ 千鶴 **Chizu, Chizuru** (f. given name)

—————————— 2 ——————————

³ 三千 **sanzen** 3,000; many

¹² 幾千 **ikusen** thousands

—————————— 3 ——————————

¹ 一刻千金 **ikkoku senkin** Every minute counts.

—————————— 2 ——————————

2k2.1 / 318   日 十 又
                                  12   9

支 支

SHI support, branch **sasa(eru)** support, prop; check, stem **tsuka(eru)** be obstructed, be blocked, break down, get caught (in one's throat) **ka(u)** prop up

—————————— 1 ——————————

⁵ 支出 **shishutsu** expenditure, disbursement

支払 **shihara(u)** pay

⁶ 支那 **Shina** China

⁷ 支局 **shikyoku** a branch (office)

支社 **shisha** a branch (office)

⁸ 支店 **shiten** a branch (store/office)

⁹ 支持 **shiji** support

支度 **shitaku** preparation, arrangements

¹⁰ 支部 **shibu** a branch (office), local chapter

支配 **shihai** management, control, rule

¹² 支給 **shikyū** provide, furnish, issue, grant

¹³ 支障 **shishō** hindrance, impediment, difficulty

—————————— 2 ——————————

³ 干支 **kanshi, eto** the sexagenary cycle

⁴ 切支丹 **Kirishitan** (early) Japanese Christianity/Christian

収支 **shūshi** revenues and expenditures

¹⁰ 差支 **sa(shi)tsuka(enai)** no impediment, justifiable, allowable, may

¹⁴ 総支出 **sōshishutsu** gross expenditures

—————————— 3 ——————————

² 十二支 **jūnishi** the twelve horary signs

2k2.2 / 49   ⊡ 宀 十
                                  15   12

午 午

GO, uma seventh horary sign (horse), noon **UMA** (part of given name)

—————————— 1 ——————————

⁹ 午前 **gozen** morning, a.m.

午前中 **gozenchū** all morning

午後 **gogo** afternoon, p.m.

—————————— 2 ——————————

⁵ 正午 **shōgo** noon

¹⁴ 端午 **tango** Boys' Day (May 5)

卆 → 卒 **2j6.2**

3

2k3.1 / 172   日   口   十
            24   12

古   古 古

KO, furu(i) old **-furu(su)** wear out
furu(biru) become old
furu(bokeru) look old; wear out
furu(mekashii) old, from long ago
inishie ancient times

1

3 古川 **Furukawa** (surname)
4 古今 **kokon** ancient and modern
    times, all ages
    古今東西 **kokon-tōzai** all ages and
      places
    古今和歌集 **Kokinwakashū** (po-
      etry anthology, early tenth cen-
      tury)
    古今集 **Kokinshū** (see preceding
      entry)
    古文書 **komonjo, kobunsho** an-
      cient documents
5 古本 **furuhon** used/secondhand
    book **kohon** secondhand
    book; ancient book
    古生物学 **koseibutsugaku** paleon-
      tology
    古代 **kodai** ancient times, antiquity
    古田 **Furuta** (surname)
7 古来 **korai** from ancient times,
    time-honored
    古里 **furusato** native place, home
      town, home
8 古事記 **Kojiki** (Japan's) Ancient
    Chronicles
    古典 **koten** the classics, classic
    古典的 **kotenteki** classical
    古物 **furumono, kobutsu** old
      things, secondhand goods, cu-
      rios, antiques
9 古臭 **furukusa(i)** old, musty, out-
    dated, trite, stale
10 古流 **koryū** old style; old school (of
    art)
13 古跡 **koseki, furuato** historic spot,
    ruins

14 古語 **kogo** archaic/obsolete word;
    old saying
15 古墳 **kofun** ancient burial mound

2

4 中古 **chūko** secondhand; the Mid-
    dle Ages **chūburu** second-
    hand
6 考古学 **kōkogaku** archeology (cf.
    考現学)
    名古屋 **Nagoya** (city, Aichi-ken)
7 阿古屋貝 **akoyagai** pearl oyster
12 着古 **kifuru(su)** wear out
    最古 **saiko** oldest
13 蒙古 **Mōko** Mongolia
16 懐古 **kaiko** nostalgia
    稽古 **keiko** practice, training, drill,
      rehearsal

3

4 内蒙古 **Uchi Mōko** Inner Mongolia
5 外蒙古 **Gaimōko, Soto Mōko** Out-
    er Mongolia

苦 → 世 **0a5.37**

本 → 本 **0a5.25**

平 → 平 **2k3.4**

2k3.4 / 202   囗   小   二
            35   4

平   平 l 平 平

HEI, BYŌ flat, level; common, ordinary, average; peaceful **tai(ra)**,
hira(tai) flat, level **hira-** common, ordinary, average **TAIRA** (m. given name;
the Taira family/clan) **HEI, HIRA** (part
of given name)

1

3 平凡 **heibon** common, ordinary
    平山 **Hirayama** (surname)
4 平井 **Hirai** (surname)
    平日 **heijitsu** weekday; everyday
    平方 **heihō** square (of a number);
      square (meter)

5 平田 **Hirata** (surname)
6 平気 **heiki** calm, cool, unconcerned, nonchalant

平年 **heinen** average/normal year; non-leap year

平仮名 **hiragana** (the cursive syllabary)

平地 **heichi, hirachi** flatland, level ground, plain

平行 **heikō** parallel

平安 **heian** peace, tranquility; the Heian period (794 – 1185)

平安朝 **Heianchō** the Heian period (794 – 1185)

平成 **Heisei** (era, 1989 –)
7 平均 **heikin** average, mean; balance, equilibrium
8 平岡 **Hiraoka** (surname)

平和 **heiwa** peace
9 平屋 **hiraya** one-story house
10 平家 **hiraya** one-story house

平家 **Heike** the Taira family/clan
11 平野 **Hirano** (surname)

平常 **heijō** normal; normally, usually
12 平等 **byōdō** equality, impartiality
14 平静 **heisei** calm, serene, tranquil
16 平壌 **Heijō** Pyongyang

平衡 **heikō** equilibrium, balance

--- 2 ---

4 不平 **fuhei** discontent, dissatisfaction, complaint

不平等 **fubyōdō** unequal

太平洋 **Taiheiyō** the Pacific Ocean

公平 **kōhei** fair, just

水平 **suihei** horizontal

水平線 **suiheisen** the horizon; horizontal line
6 地平線 **chiheisen** the horizon
7 良平 **Ryōhei, Yoshihira** (m. given name)
9 扁平足 **henpeisoku** flat feet
10 真平 **mappira** (not) by any means; humbly

泰平 **taihei** peace, tranquility
13 源平 **Gen-Pei** Genji and Heike clans, the Minamoto and Taira families

--- 3 ---

4 不公平 **fukōhei** unfair, unjust
6 汎太平洋 **han-Taiheiyō** pan-Pacific
9 南太平洋 **Minami Taiheiyō** the South Pacific

--- 4 ---

2k4.3 / 542   □… 土 子 丨
22 6 2

KŌ filial piety **TAKASHI** (m. given name) **KŌ, TAKA** (part of given name)

--- 1 ---

2 孝子 **Takako, Kōko** (f. given name)
5 孝司 **Takashi, Kōji** (m. given name)
6 孝行 **kōkō** filial piety

--- 2 ---

4 不孝 **fukō** disobedience to parents, lack of filial piety
8 忠孝 **Tadataka, Tadanori, Chūkō** (m. given name)
16 親孝行 **oyakōkō** filial piety

--- 3 ---

16 親不孝 **oyafukō** lack of filial piety

2k4.4 / 541   □… 土 一
22 1

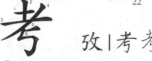

KŌ, kanga(eru) think, consider
kanga(e) thought, idea

--- 1 ---

4 考方 **kanga(e)kata** way of thinking, viewpoint
5 考古学 **kōkogaku** archeology (cf. 考現学)
8 考直 **kanga(e)nao(su)** reconsider, rethink
10 考案 **kōan** idea, conception; plan, project; design, contrivance

¹² 考違 **kanga(e)chiga(i)** mistaken idea, wrong impression

¹⁴ 考察 **kōsatsu** consideration, examination, study

¹⁵ 考慮 **kōryo** consideration, careful thought

————— 2 —————

¹ 一考 **ikkō** consideration, a thought

⁶ 再考 **saikō** reconsider

⁸ 参考 **sankō** reference, consultation
参考書 **sankōsho** reference book/work

⁹ 思考力 **shikōryoku** mental faculties

¹² 備考 **bikō** note, remarks

¹⁴ 熟考 **jukkō** mature reflection, due deliberation

¹⁵ 論考 **ronkō** a study

2k4.5 / 543   ... ⻏ ⼘ ⼁
                        22 13 2

老   老 老

RŌ old age **o(iru), fu(keru)** grow old **oi(raku)** old age **o(i)** old age; old man

————— 1 —————

² 老人 **rōjin** old man/person, the old/aged
老子 **Rōshi** Laozi, Lao-tzu (founder of Taoism)

⁴ 老込 **o(i)ko(mu)** grow old, become decrepit/senile

⁶ 老死 **rōshi** die of old age
老年 **rōnen** old age

⁸ 老若 **rōjaku, rōnyaku** young and old

¹⁰ 老衰 **rōsui** infirmity of old age
老弱 **rōjaku** infirmity/feebleness of old age

¹¹ 老婆 **rōba** old woman
老眼 **rōgan** farsightedness

¹⁴ 老熟 **rōjuku** mature skill, maturity, mellowness

¹⁵ 老舗 **rōho, shinise** long-established shop/store

¹⁷ 老齢 **rōrei** old age

————— 2 —————

⁷ 初老 **shorō** early old age (formerly 40, now about 60)

⁸ 長老 **chōrō** an elder

⁹ 海老 **ebi** shrimp, prawn; lobster

¹² 敬老 **keirō** respect for the aged

2k4.6 / 1649   ... ⼭ ⼂ 一
                        36 15 1

缶   罐 | 缶 缶

KAN, FU can **kama** steam boiler

————— 1 —————

⁴ 缶切 **kanki(ri)** can opener

¹³ 缶詰 **kanzume** canned goods

————— 2 —————

¹⁶ 薬缶 **yakan** teakettle

2k4.7   ... 一 ⼁
                   1 2

卍   卍 卍

BAN, MAN, manji fylfot, gammadion, swastika

————— 1 —————

⁴ 卍巴 **manji-tomoe** (snow falling) in swirls

————— 5 —————

2k5.1 / 1372   ⽬ ⼞ 十 ⼉
                        24 12 16

克   克 克

KOKU, ka(tsu) conquer, overcome **yo(ku)** well, skillfully MASARU (m. given name) KATSU, YOSHI (part of given name)

————— 1 —————

³ 克己 **kokki** self-denial, self-control

⁸ 克服 **kokufuku** conquest, subjugation

求→ **2b5.5**

─────── 6 ───────

2k6.1 / 234 　　田 十 力
　　　　　　　　　12 8

協 協

KYŌ cooperation **KANŌ** (m. given name)

─────── 1 ───────

2 協力 **kyōryoku** cooperation
6 協会 **kyōkai** society, association
　協同 **kyōdō** cooperation, collaboration, partnership
8 協定 **kyōtei** agreement, accord
9 協奏曲 **kyōsōkyoku** concerto
　協約 **kyōyaku** agreement, convention, pact
15 協調 **kyōchō** cooperation, conciliation
20 協議 **kyōgi** consultation, conference

─────── 2 ───────

7 妥協 **dakyō** compromise
13 農協 **nōkyō** agricultural cooperative, co-op (short for 農業共同組合)

─────── 3 ───────

11 紳士協定 **shinshi kyōtei** gentleman's agreement

幸→ **3b5.9**

尭→堯 **3b9.3**

2k6.2 / 423 　　日 日 十 ｜
　　　　　　　　55 12 2

直 直

CHOKU, JIKI straight, immediate, direct, correct **nao(su)** fix, correct; revise; convert into; (as suffix) re-, do

over **nao(ru)** return to normal, be fixed/corrected, recover **tada(chi ni)** immediately **su(gu)** immediately; readily, easily; right (near) **jika (ni)** directly, in person SUNAO, TADASHI (m. given name) TADA, NAO (part of given name)

─────── 1 ───────

2 直人 **Naoto, Naondo** (m. given name)
　直子 **Naoko** (f. given name)
3 直也 **Naoya** (m. given name)
　直々 **jikijiki** personal, direct
6 直行 **chokkō** going straight, direct, nonstop
7 直角 **chokkaku** right angle
　直売 **chokubai** direct sales
　直系 **chokkei** lineal descendant, direct line
9 直前 **chokuzen** just before
　直美 **Naomi** (f. given name)
　直通 **chokutsū** direct communication, nonstop service
　直後 **chokugo** immediately after
　直面 **chokumen** be faced with, confront
　直哉 **Naoya** (m. given name)
10 直航 **chokkō** nonstop flight, direct voyage
11 直接 **chokusetsu** direct
　直訳 **chokuyaku** literal translation
12 直結 **chokketsu** direct connection
13 直感 **chokkan** intuition
15 直線 **chokusen** straight line
16 直樹 **Naoki** (m. given name)
18 直観 **chokkan** intuition

─────── 2 ───────

5 正直 **shōjiki** honest, upright, straightforward
6 仲直 **nakanao(ri)** reconciliation, make up
　考直 **kanga(e)nao(su)** reconsider, rethink
　朴直 **bokuchoku** simple and honest, ingenuous
7 見直 **minao(su)** take another look at, reevaluate; think better of; get better
　言直 **i(i)nao(su)** rephrase, correct

⁸ 垂直 **suichoku** vertical; perpendicular

卒直 **sotchoku** frank, openhearted

居直 **inao(ru)** sit up straight; change one's attitude, come on strong; turn violent, resort to threat

¹⁰ 真直 **ma(s)su(gu)** straight; honest, upright, frank

書直 **ka(ki)nao(su)** rewrite

素直 **sunao** gentle, meek, docile; frank, honest

¹¹ 率直 **sotchoku** straightforward, frank, forthright

¹⁴ 聞直 **ki(ki)nao(su)** ask/inquire again

¹⁵ 撮直 **to(ri)nao(su)** retake (a photo)

¹⁶ 模直 **bokuchoku** simple and honest

———— 3 ————

¹⁰ 真正直 **ma(s)shōjiki** perfectly honest

2k6.3

日 尸 冂 十
40 20 12

阜 阜 阜

FU hill, mound

———— 1 ————

¹⁶ 阜頭 **futō** wharf

———— 2 ————

⁷ 岐阜県 **Gifu-ken** (prefecture)

2k6.5 / 1659

··· 大 艹 十
34 32 12

奔 奔 奔

HON, hashi(ru) run

———— 1 ————

⁷ 奔走 **honsō** running about, efforts

———— 2 ————

¹¹ 淫奔 **inpon** wanton, loose, lewd

卑 → 卑 5f4.8

———— 7 ————

2k7.1 / 74

日 月 十 儿
42 12 16

南 南 南

NAN, NA, minami south MINAMI (surname) MINA (part of given name)

———— 1 ————

³ 南口 **minamiguchi** south exit/entrance

⁴ 南太平洋 **Minami Taiheiyō** the South Pacific

南方 **nanpō** south, southern, southward

⁵ 南北 **nanboku** north and south

南半球 **minami hankyū** the Southern Hemisphere

南氷洋 **Nanpyōyō** the Antarctic Ocean

⁶ 南西 **nansei** southwest

南向 **minamimu(ki)** facing south

南米 **Nanbei** South America

⁸ 南東 **nantō** southeast

南京 **Nankin** Nanking

⁹ 南洋 **Nan'yō** the South Seas

南海 **nankai** southern sea

¹⁰ 南部 **nanbu** southern part, the South

¹¹ 南側 **minamigawa, nansoku** south side

¹² 南蛮人 **nanbanjin** southern barbarians, the early Europeans

南極 **Nankyoku** the South Pole

南極圏 **Nankyokuken** the Antarctic Circle, the Antarctic

¹⁶ 南緯 **nan'i** south latitude

———— 2 ————

⁴ 中南米 **Chūnanbei** Central and South America

⁶ 西南 **seinan** southwest

⁸ 東南 **tōnan** southeast

———— 3 ————

⁸ 東西南北 **tōzainanboku** north, south, east, and west

イ 冫 扌 阝 卩 刂 力 又 冖 亠 十 夂 冫 厂 辶 冂 几 匚

2

7

卑 → **5f4.8**

———— 8 ————

2k8.1 / 422   目 目 十 儿
                55 12 16

真   眞 | 真 真

SHIN true, genuine **makoto** true, sincere **ma-** just, right, due (north); pure, genuine, true MAKOTO (m. given name) SANE, MASA (part of given name)

———— 1 ————

2 真二 **ma(p)puta(tsu)** (split) right in two
3 真丸 **ma(n)maru, ma(n)maru(i)** perfectly round
真上 **maue** right over, directly above
真下 **mashita** right under, directly below
5 真由 **Mayu** (f. given name)
真由美 **Mayumi** (f. given name)
真平 **mappira** (not) by any means; humbly
真正直 **ma(s)shōjiki** perfectly honest
真正面 **ma(s)shōmen** directly opposite, right in front
真白 **ma(s)shiro** pure white
真冬 **mafuyu** dead of winter, midwinter
6 真向 **mamuka(i)** just opposite, right across from, face to face **ma(k)kō** forehead; front
真衣 **Mai** (f. given name)
7 真似 **mane** imitation, mimicry; behavior; pretense
8 真価 **shinka** true value
真夜中 **mayonaka** dead of night, midnight
真直 **ma(s)su(gu)** straight; honest, upright, frank
真実 **shinjitsu** truth, reality, the facts
9 真面目 **majime** serious-minded, earnest, honest

真面目 **shinmenmoku** one's true self/character; seriousness, earnestness
真相 **shinsō** the truth/facts, the real situation
真昼 **mahiru** broad daylight, midday
真彦 **Masahiko, Nobuhiko, Mahiko** (m. given name)
10 真剣 **shinken** serious
真夏 **manatsu** midsummer
11 真偽 **shingi** true or false, whether genuine or spurious
真理 **shinri** truth **Mari, Makoto, Masayoshi** (given names)
12 真最中 **ma(s)saichū** right in the midst/middle of, at the height of
13 真暗 **makkura** pitch-dark
15 真澄 **Masumi, Mazumi, Sanezumi** (given name)

———— 2 ————

2 人真似 **hitomane** mimicry, imitations
3 口真似 **kuchimane** mimicry
4 不真面目 **fumajime** not serious-minded, insincere
5 写真 **shashin** photograph
8 拓真 **Takuma** (m. given name)
13 猿真似 **sarumane** monkey-see monkey-do
17 糞真面目 **kusomajime** humorless earnestness

———— 3 ————

8 青写真 **aojashin, aoshashin** blueprints

2k8.2 / 1059   目 糸 宀 一
               61 33 1

索   索 索

SAKU rope, cord; search for

———— 1 ————

4 索引 **sakuin** index
7 索条 **sakujō** cable, rope

———— 2 ————

9 思索 **shisaku** thinking, speculation, meditation

10 捜索 **sōsaku** search

11 探索 **tansaku** search; inquiry, investigation

12 検索 **kensaku** retrieval, lookup, reference

13 摸索 **mosaku** groping

詮索 **sensaku** search, inquiry

14 模索 **mosaku** groping, trial and error

総索引 **sōsakuin** general index

皐 → 皐 4c7.12

缺 → 欠 4j0.1

─────── 9 ───────

皐 → 4c7.12

─────── 10 ───────

2k10.1 / 601 　　　田 日 寸 十
　　　　　　　　43 37 12

博 博|博博

HAKU broad, extensive; gambling; (as suffix) Ph.D.; (as suffix) exposition, fair, exhibition **BAKU** gambling HIROSHI (m. given name) HIRO (part of given name)

─────── 1 ───────

2 博之 **Hiroyuki, Hiroshi, Masayuki** (m. given name)

3 博士 **hakase, hakushi** Ph.D.

4 博文 **Hirofumi, Hirobumi** (m. given name)

5 博打 **bakuchi** gambling

7 博学 **hakugaku** broad knowledge, erudition

8 博物館 **hakubutsukan** museum

9 博美 **Hiromi, Hiroyoshi** (given name)

13 博愛 **hakuai** philanthropy

17 博覧会 **hakurankai** exhibition, exposition, fair

─────── 2 ───────

3 万博 **banpaku** world's fair (short for 万国博覧会)

13 該博 **gaihaku** profound, vast (learning)

16 賭博 **tobaku** gambling

準 → 準 2k11.1

喪 → 3b9.20

─────── 11 ───────

2k11.1 / 778 　　　田 隹 氵 十
　　　　　　　　74 21 12

準 準準

JUN quasi-, semi-; level; aim **nazora(eru)** model after, liken to, imitate HITOSHI (m. given name)

─────── 1 ───────

0 準じる/ずる **jun(jiru/zuru)** correspond to, be proportionate to, conform to

7 準決勝 **junkesshō** semifinals

8 準拠 **junkyo** conform to, be pursuant to, be based on

12 準備 **junbi** preparations, provision, reserve

─────── 2 ───────

4 水準 **suijun** water level; level, standard

11 基準 **kijun** standard, criterion, basis

15 標準 **hyōjun** standard, norm, criterion

標準語 **hyōjungo** the standard language

献 → 3g9.6

瓶 → 瓶 2o9.6

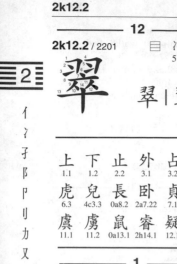

12

2k12.2 / 2201 — 目 冫 亠 亻 — 5 11 3

翠 | 翠 翆

SUI female kingfisher; green
midori green MIDORI (f. given
name) AKIRA (m. given name)
SUI (part of given name)

2m ⼕

上	下	止	外	占	正	比	乍	白	此	步	卦	卓
1.1	1.2	2.2	3.1	3.2	3.3	3.5	0a5.10	0a6.4	4.2	3n5.3	6.1	6.2

虎	兒	長	卧	貞	点	虐	歪	虚	處	套	虛	疎
6.3	4c3.3	0a8.2	2a7.22	7.1	7.2	7.3	7.4	9.1	4i2.2	0a10.3	2m9.1	0a11.4

虞	虜	鼠	睿	疑	膚	慮
11.1	11.2	0a13.1	2h14.1	12.1	13.1	13.2

1

2m1.1 / 32 — 目 卜 一 — 13 1

上 上 上

JŌ upper, top, above; first volume/part
(of a series); top-grade; emperor, sovereign; (as suffix) from the viewpoint of
SHŌ upper, above **ue** up, upper part,
top, above, over; besides, on top of; upon, after **uwa-** upper, outer **kami** upper part, top; upstream; emperor, the
authorities, a superior **a(geru)** raise,
lift up, elevate, increase; give **-a(gezu)**
every (three days) or less **a(garu)** go/
come up, rise; enter (someone's home),
call on; come to an end **a(gari)** rise, ascent; completion, finish; receipts, profit;
tea (in a restaurant); (as suffix) ex-,
former; (as suffix) (just) after (a rainfall/
bath/illness) **a(gattari)** out of business, ruined, done for **nobo(ru)** go/
come up, ascend, climb; go/come to the
capital; reach, amount to **nobo(ri)** ascent; Tōkyō-bound (train)

1

³ 上下 **jōge** top and bottom; volumes
1 and 2 (of a two-volume set);
rise and fall, go up and down;

the high and the low **shōka**
ruler and ruled **kamishimo**
the high and the low
a(gari)sa(gari) rise and fall,
fluctuations **a(ge)sa(ge)** raising and lowering; praising and
blaming; rising and falling, intonation

⁴ 上中下 **jō-chū-ge** good-fair-poor;
first-second-third class; vol-
umes/parts 1, 2, 3 (of a 3-vol-
ume/3-part series)

上辺 **uwabe** exterior, surface, outside; outward appearance

上手 **jōzu** skillful, good at **uwate**
better at, superior to; upper
part, upstream **kamite** upper
part; upstream; right side of the
stage (as seen from the audience)

⁵ 上半身 **jōhanshin, kamihanshin**
upper half of the body

上司 **jōshi** one's superior(s)

上田 **Ueda** (surname)

⁶ 上回 **uwamawa(ru)** be more than,
exceed

上旬 **jōjun** the first ten days of a
month

上衣 **uwagi** coat, jacket

⁷ 上述 **jōjutsu** the above-mentioned

上杉 **Uesugi** (surname)

上村 **Uemura, Kamimura** (surname)

8 上表紙 **uwabyōshi** outer cover, (book) jacket

上京 **jōkyō** go/come to the capital

上昇 **jōshō** rise, ascend, climb

9 上院 **jōin** the Upper House (of a legislature), Senate

上海 **Shanhai** Shanghai

上品 **jōhin** refined, elegant, genteel; first-class article

上面 **jōmen** surface, top, exterior **uwatsura, uwa(t)tsura** surface, appearances

上映 **jōei** screen, show, play (a movie)

上級 **jōkyū** upper grade, senior

10 上陸 **jōriku** landing, going ashore

上部 **jōbu** upper part/side, top surface

上流 **jōryū** upstream; upper-class

上記 **jōki** the above-mentioned/aforesaid

11 上野 **Ueno** (section of Tōkyō) **Kōzuke** (ancient kuni, Gunma-ken)

上達 **jōtatsu** make progress, become proficient

12 上着 **uwagi** coat, jacket

上等 **jōtō** first-rate, superior

14 上演 **jōen** play, stage, perform

———————— 2 ————————

3 川上 **kawakami** upstream **Kawakami, Kawaue** (surname)

4 井上 **Inoue** (surname)

切上 **ki(ri)a(ge)** end, conclusion; rounding up (to the nearest integer); revalue, up-value (a currency)

水上 **suijō** (on the) water, aquatic **minakami** headwaters, source

引上 **hi(ki)a(geru)** raise, increase; withdraw, leave

5 以上 **ijō** or more, more than, over, above, beyond; the above; since, so long as; that is all

史上 **shijō** in history; historical

申上 **mō(shi)a(geru)** say, tell (humble)

仕上 **shia(ge)** finish, finishing touches

召上 **me(shi)a(garu)** (polite) eat, drink, have **me(shi)a(geru)** confiscate

打上 **u(chi)a(geru)** shoot up, launch (a rocket), cast up on shore, wash ashore; finish, close (a performance)

右上 **migi ue** upper right

立上 **ta(chi)a(garu)** stand up; start **ta(chi)nobo(ru)** rise, ascend

目上 **meue** one's superior/senior

6 年上 **toshiue** older, senior

地上 **chijō** (on the) ground/surface; in this world

至上 **shijō** supreme, highest

向上 **kōjō** improvement, advancement

安上 **yasua(gari)** cheap, economical

机上 **kijō** desk-top, academic, theoretical, armchair

7 身上 **shinjō** merit, strong point **shinshō** one's fortune/property; household **mi(no)ue** one's fortune/future; one's circumstances; one's background

身上話 **mi(no)uebanashi** one's life story

売上 **u(ri)a(ge)** sales

売上高 **uria(ge)daka** amount sold, sales

村上 **Murakami** (surname)

車上 **shajō** aboard (the train/vehicle)

8 卓上 **takujō** table-top, desk-top

河上 **Kawakami** (surname)

炎上 **enjō** go up in flames, burst into flames

取上 **to(ri)a(geru)** take up, adopt; take away

9 飛上 **to(bi)a(garu)** fly/jump up

巻上 **ma(ki)a(geru)** roll/wind up, raise; take away, rob

這上 **ha(i)a(garu)** crawl up

造上 **tsuku(ri)a(geru)** make, build up, complete

風上 **kazakami** windward

海上 **kaijō** ocean, seagoing, marine

拾上 **hiro(i)a(geru)** pick up, pick out

屋上 **okujō** roof, rooftop

思上 **omo(i)a(garu)** be conceited

10 値上 **nea(ge)** price hike
  nea(gari) higher price

陸上 **rikujō** on shore, land

真上 **maue** right over, directly above

差上 **sa(shi)a(geru)** give; raise up

起上 **o(ki)a(garu)** get up, rise

席上 **sekijō** at the meeting, on the occasion

紙上 **shijō** on paper; by letter; in the newspapers

11 盛上 **mo(ri)a(geru)** heap/pile up

頂上 **chōjō** summit, peak, top, climax

12 湯上 **yua(gari)** just after a bath

棟上式 **munea(ge)shiki** roof-raising ceremony

晴上 **ha(re)a(garu)** clear up

最上 **saijō** best, highest

最上川 **Mogami-gawa** (river, Yamagata-ken)

焼上 **ya(ki)a(geru)** burn up; bake

煮上 **ni(e)a(garu), nia(garu)** boil up, be thoroughly cooked

買上 **ka(i)a(geru)** buy (up/out)

13 献上 **kenjō** presentation

数上 **kazo(e)a(geru)** count up, enumerate

賃上 **chin'a(ge)** raise in wages

跳上 **ha(ne)a(garu), to(bi)a(garu)** jump up

路上 **rojō** on the road

14 誌上 **shijō** in a magazine

読上 **yo(mi)a(geru)** read aloud/out; finish reading

15 舞上 **ma(i)a(garu)** fly up, soar

褒上 **ho(me)a(geru)** praise very highly

16 燃上 **mo(e)a(garu)** blaze up, burst into flames

積上 **tsu(mi)a(geru)** heap up

築上 **kizu(ki)a(geru)** build up

頭上 **zujō** overhead

  3
---

5 出来上 **dekia(garu)** be finished, be ready; be cut out for

7 形而上 **keijijō** metaphysical

8 事実上 **jijitsujō** in fact, actually

9 便宜上 **bengijō** for convenience

10 都合上 **tsugōjō** for convenience

15 論理上 **ronrijō** logically (speaking)

  4
---

9 発展途上国 **hattentojōkoku** developing country

2m1.2 / 31

14 2

KA, GE low, lower; below, under
shita lower part, below, under **shimo** lower part; downstream; the lower classes, the servants; lower part of the body **moto** under **sa(geru)** hang, suspend; lower, bring down; demote; move back; remove **sa(garu)** hang down; fall, go/come down; leave, withdraw; step back **kuda(ru)** come/go/get/step down; be given; be less than; have diarrhea **kuda(ranai)** trifling, worthless, absurd, inane **kuda(saru)** give, bestow **kuda(sai)** (indicator for polite imperative), please **kuda(su)** let down, lower; give, bestow, issue (an order), render (a judgment); have diarrhea **o(riru)** come/go/get/step down, get off (a train), get out of (a car); be discharged (from the body); be granted

---
  1
---

4 下水 **gesui** sewer, drain, drainage

下手 **heta** unskillful, poor at

下方 **kahō** lower part, downward, below

下戸 **geko** nondrinker, teetotaler

5 下半身 **kahanshin, shimohanshin** lower half of the body

下田 **Shimoda** (city; surname)

6 下向 **shitamu(ki)** downward look; downturn, decline

下回 **shitamawa(ru)** be less than, fall short of

下旬 **gejun** 21st through last day of a month

7 下位 **kai** low rank, subordinate

下作 **gesaku** poorly made, of inferior quality

下坂 **kuda(ri)zaka** downward slope, downhill

下村 **Shimomura** (surname)

下町 **shitamachi** part of the city near the sea or river, downtown

下車 **gesha** get off (a train/bus)

9 下巻 **gekan** last volume (of two or three)

下乗 **gejō** get off (a horse), get out of (a car)

下降 **kakō** descend, fall, sink

下院 **kain** the Lower House (of a legislature)

下品 **gehin** vulgar, coarse, gross

下級 **kakyū** lower grade/class, junior, subordinate

10 下流 **karyū** downstream; lower-class

下書 **shitaga(ki)** rough draft

下記 **kaki** the following

下馬評 **gebahyō** outsiders' irresponsible talk, rumor

11 下宿 **geshuku** lodging, room and board; boarding house

12 下着 **shitagi** underwear

下場 **o(ri)ba** place to get off, disembarking point

下痢 **geri** diarrhea

下等 **katō** low, lower (animals/plants), inferior, base, vulgar

14 下関 **Shimonoseki** (city, Yamaguchi-ken)

下駄 **geta** clogs

15 下敷 **shitaji(ki)** mat, desk pad; pinned under, crushed beneath; model, pattern

下請 **shitauke** subcontract

下調 **shitashira(be)** preliminary investigation; prepare (lessons)

————— 2 —————

3 川下 **kawashimo** downstream

上下 **jōge** top and bottom; volumes 1 and 2 (of a two-volume set); rise and fall, go up and down; the high and the low **shōka** ruler and ruled **kamishimo** the high and the low **a(gari)sa(gari)** rise and fall, fluctuations **a(ge)sa(ge)** raising and lowering; praising and blaming; rising and falling, intonation

口下手 **kuchibeta** awkward tongue, poor talker

山下 **Yamashita** (surname)

4 天下 **amakuda(ri)** descent from heaven; employment of retired officials by companies they used to regulate **tenka, tenga, ame(ga)shita** under heaven; the whole country, the public/world; the reins of government; having one's own way

切下 **ki(ri)sa(ge)** reduction, devaluation

引下 **hi(ki)sa(garu)** withdraw, leave **hi(ki)o(rosu)** pull down

木下 **Kinoshita** (surname)

5 以下 **ika** or less, less than; under, below; the following

右下 **migi shita** lower right

目下 **meshita** one's subordinate/junior **mokka** at present, now

6 年下 **toshishita** younger, junior

地下 **chika** underground; basement

地下室 **chikashitsu** basement, cellar

地下街 **chikagai** underground shopping mall

地下鉄 **chikatetsu** subway

吊下 **tsu(ri)sa(garu)** hang, dangle, be suspended

竹下 **Takeshita** (surname)

7 低下 **teika** decline, go down, fall

却下 **kyakka** reject, dismiss

見下 **mio(rosu)** command a view of **mikuda(su)** look down on, despise **misa(geru)** look down on, despise

足下 **ashimoto** gait, pace; at one's feet; (watch your) step
sokka at one's feet

8 垂下 **suika, ta(re)sa(garu)** hang down, dangle, droop

版下 **hanshita** art boards, mechanicals, camera-ready copy

松下 **Matsushita** (surname)

9 飛下(り) **tobio(ri)** jumping off

陛下 **Heika** His/Her Majesty

降下 **kōka** descend, fall, drop

風下 **kazashimo** leeward

城下町 **jōkamachi** castle town

10 値下 **nesa(ge)** price reduction
nesa(gari) price decline, lower prices

部下 **buka** a subordinate, the people working under one

真下 **mashita** right under, directly below

荷下 **nio(roshi)** unloading, discharge

宮下 **Miyashita** (surname)

時下 **jika** now, at present

11 廊下 **rōka** corridor, hall

12 落下傘 **rakkasan** parachute

森下 **Morishita** (surname)

最下 **saika** lowest; worst

13 靴下 **kutsushita** socks, stockings

殿下 **Denka** His/Your Highness

腹下 **harakuda(shi)** diarrhea; laxative

跳下(り) **to(bi)o(ri)** jumping off

零下 **reika** below zero, subzero

14 滴下 **tekika** drip, trickle down

───── 3 ─────

3 上中下 **jō-chū-ge** good-fair-poor; first-second-third class; volumes/parts 1, 2, 3 (of a 3-volume/3-part series)

5 氷点下 **hyōtenka** below the freezing point, below zero (Celsius)

6 両陛下 **Ryōheika** Their Majesties

妃殿下 **hidenka** Her Highness

7 形而下 **keijika** physical, material

9 途中下車 **tochū gesha** stopover, layover

12 渡廊下 **wata(ri) rōka** covered passageway

───── 4 ─────

4 天皇陛下 **Tennō Heika** His Majesty the Emperor

9 皇后陛下 **Kōgō Heika** Her Majesty the Empress

───── 2 ─────

2m2.2 / 477

13 11

止

SHI stop **to(maru)** (come to a) stop **to(meru)** (bring/put to a) stop **todo(maru)** (come to a) stop; be limited to **todo(meru)** (bring/put to a) stop; limit oneself to **todo(me)** finishing blow **ya(mu)** stop, (come to an) end, be over **ya(meru)** stop, (put to an) end, discontinue **yo(su)** stop, desist from, cut it out

───── 2 ─────

3 口止料 **kuchido(me)ryō** hush money

4 中止 **chūshi** discontinue, suspend, stop, call off, cancel

5 立止 **ta(chi)do(maru)** stop, halt, stand still

6 休止 **kyūshi** pause, suspension, dormancy

防止 **bōshi** prevention

7 阻止 **soshi** obstruct, hinder, deter, check

抑止 **yokushi** deter stave off

足止 **ashido(me)** keep indoors; induce to stay

8 制止 **seishi** control, restrain, keep in check

受止 **u(ke)to(meru)** stop, catch; parry, ward off

波止場 **hatoba** wharf, pier

10 差止 **sa(shi)to(meru)** prohibit, forbid, ban

11 停止 **teishi** suspension, stop, halt, cessation

終止 **shūshi** come to an end

12 廃止 **haishi** abolition, abrogation

痛止 **ita(mi)do(me)** painkiller

13 禁止 **kinshi** prohibition
14 静止 **seishi** still, standstill, at rest, stationary, static state
16 諫止 **kanshi** dissuade from

─────────── 3 ───────────

9 通行止 **tsūkōdo(me)** Road Closed, No Thoroughfare

─────────── 4 ───────────

5 立入禁止 **tachiiri kinshi** Keep Out
11 張紙禁止 **ha(ri)gami kinshi** Post No Bills

─────────── 3 ───────────

2m3.1 / 83

口 夕 十
30 12

外 外

GAI outside, external; foreign GE outside, external **soto** outside; outdoors **hoka** other **hazu(su)** take off, remove, disconnect; miss, fail in; avoid, leave (one's desk) **hazu(reru)** come/slip off, be/get out of place, be disconnected; miss (the target) TO (part of given name)

─────────── 1 ───────────

2 外人 **gaijin** foreigner
5 外出 **gaishutsu, sotode** go/step out
外字 **gaiji** kanji not officially recognized for everyday use; foreign letters/language
外字新聞 **gaiji shinbun** foreign-language newspaper
6 外交 **gaikō** diplomacy, foreign relations
外交官 **gaikōkan** diplomat
外向性 **gaikōsei** extroverted, outgoing
7 外来 **gairai** foreign, imported
外来語 **gairaigo** word of foreign origin, loanword
外形 **gaikei** external form, outward appearance
外車 **gaisha** foreign car
8 外国 **gaikoku** foreign country; foreign
外国人 **gaikokujin** foreigner

外国語 **gaikokugo** foreign language
9 外面 **gaimen** exterior, outward appearance, surface
外相 **gaishō** the Foreign Minister
外科 **geka** surgery
外科医 **gekai** surgeon
外食 **gaishoku** eating out
10 外套 **gaitō** overcoat
外部 **gaibu** the outside, external
11 外側 **sotogawa** outside, exterior
外務 **gaimu** foreign affairs
外務大臣 **gaimu daijin** Minister of Foreign Affairs
外務省 **Gaimushō** Ministry of Foreign Affairs
外貨 **gaika** foreign currency; imported goods
13 外債 **gaisai** foreign loan/bond/debt
外蒙古 **Gaimōko, Soto Mōko** Outer Mongolia
15 外線 **gaisen** outside (telephone) line; outside wiring
18 外観 **gaikan** external appearance

─────────── 2 ───────────

4 内外 **naigai** inside and outside; domestic and foreign; approximately **uchi-soto** inside and out
戸外 **kogai** outdoor, open-air
5 以外 **igai** except, other than
6 在外 **zaigai** overseas, abroad
当外 **a(tari)hazu(re)** hit or miss, risk **a(te)hazu(re)** a disappointment
7 対外 **taigai** foreign, international, overseas
赤外線 **sekigaisen** infrared rays
局外 **kyokugai** the outside
8 例外 **reigai** exception
郊外 **kōgai** suburbs, outskirts
並外 **namihazu(re)** out of the ordinary
的外 **matohazu(re)** wide of the mark; out of focus
取外 **to(ri)hazu(su)** remove, dismantle
門外 **mongai** outside the gate; outside one's specialty

亻
冫
子
阝
卩
刂
力
又
亠
宀
爫
ハ
厂
辶
冂
几
匸

3

門外漢 **mongaikan** outsider; layman

9 除外 **jogai** exception

海外 **kaigai** overseas, abroad

室外 **shitsugai** outdoor(s)

屋外 **okugai** outdoor(s)

思外 **omo(ino)hoka** unexpectedly, more than expected

10 殊外 **koto(no)hoka** exceedingly, exceptionally

案外 **angai** unexpectedly

桁外 **ketahazu(re)** extraordinary

時外 **tokihazu(re)** unseasonable, untimely, inopportune

11 野外 **yagai** the open air, outdoor

理外 **rigai** transcendental, supernatural

13 意外 **igai** unexpected, surprising

15 踏外 **fu(mi)hazu(su)** miss one's footing

20 欄外 **rangai** margin (of a page)

――――― 3 ―――――

6 仲間外 **nakamahazu(re)** being left out

10 時候外 **jikōhazu(re)** unseasonable

2m3.2 / 1706   日 口 ㅏ
24 13

占

占 占

SEN, shi(meru) occupy, hold
urana(u) tell fortunes

――――― 1 ―――――

6 占有 **sen'yū** exclusive possession, occupancy

9 占星術 **senseijutsu** astrology

10 占師 **uranaishi** fortuneteller

14 占領 **senryō** occupation, capture; have all to oneself

――――― 2 ―――――

9 独占 **dokusen** exclusive possession; monopoly

星占 **hoshiurana(i)** astrology, horoscope

12 買占 **ka(i)shi(meru)** buy up, corner (the market)

2m3.3 / 275   ⋯ 二 一 丨
38 1 2

正

正 正

SEI, SHŌ correct, right, just; straight; principal, original; positive (number)
tada(shii) correct, right, proper
tada(su) correct, rectify **masa (ni)** surely, indeed, truly; precisely
masa(shiku) surely, indeed, truly
TADASHI (m. given name) SHŌ, SEI, MASA, TADA (part of given name)

――――― 1 ―――――

1 正一 **Shōichi, Masakazu, Masaichi** (m. given name)

4 正夫 **Masao, Tadao** (m. given name)

正午 **shōgo** noon

正反対 **seihantai** the exact opposite

正月 **shōgatsu** the New Year; January

正方形 **seihōkei** square

5 正本 **seihon, shōhon** an attested copy; the original (of a document) **shōhon** playbook, script; unabridged book

正号 **seigō** plus sign (+)

正犯 **seihan** principal offense/offender

正字法 **seijihō** orthography

6 正会員 **seikaiin** full/regular member

正当 **seitō** proper, just, justifiable, right, fair, reasonable, legitimate

正式 **seishiki** formal, official

7 正体 **shōtai** one's true nature/character; in one's right mind, senses

正社員 **seishain** regular employee, full member of the staff

正男 **Masao** (m. given name)

8 正価 **seika** (net) price

正直 **shōjiki** honest, upright, straightforward

正治 **Masaharu, Shōji, Masaji** (m. given name)

正味 **shōmi** net (weight)

9 正美 **Masami, Masayoshi, Tada-yoshi, Matsatomi, Seibi** (given name)

正面 **shōmen** front, head-on

10 正座 **seiza** sit straight (on one's heels) **shōza** seat of honor

正教 **seikyō** orthodoxy; Greek Orthodox Church

11 正常 **seijō** normal

正規 **seiki** regular, normal, formal, legal

12 正統派 **seitōha** orthodox school, fundamentalists

正雄 **Masao** (m. given name)

13 正義 **seigi** justice, right(eousness); correct meaning **Masayoshi, Seigi** (m. given name)

14 正誤表 **seigohyō** errata

15 正確 **seikaku** exact, precise, accurate

正課 **seika** regular curriculum/course

———————— 2 ————————

3 大正 **Taishō** (era, 1912 – 1926)

4 不正 **fusei** improper, unjust, wrong, false

不正確 **fuseikaku** inaccurate

中正 **chūsei** impartial, fair

公正 **kōsei** fair, just

5 叱正 **shissei** correction

7 更正 **kōsei** correct, rectify

改正 **kaisei** revision, amendment; improvement

8 斧正 **fusei** correction, revision

9 訂正 **teisei** correction, revision

10 修正 **shūsei** amendment, revision, alteration, correction

真正直 **ma(s)shōjiki** perfectly honest

真正面 **ma(s)shōmen** directly opposite, right in front

校正 **kōsei** proofreading

純正 **junsei** pure, genuine

17 矯正 **kyōsei** correct, reform

———————— 3 ————————

5 礼儀正 **reigitada(shii)** polite, courteous

2m3.5 / 798

13

比

HI compare; ratio; the Philippines
kura(beru) compare **tagui** kind, sort, class

———————— 1 ————————

8 比例 **hirei** proportion, ratio; proportional (representation)

比物 **kura(be)mono** comparison, match

9 比重 **hijū** specific gravity; relative importance

11 比率 **hiritsu** ratio, percentage

12 比喩 **hiyu** simile, metaphor, allegory

比喩的 **hiyuteki** figurative

13 比較 **hikaku** compare; comparative (literature)

比較的 **hikakuteki** relative(ly), comparative(ly)

比較級 **hikakukyū** the comparative degree (in grammar)

16 比叡山 **Hieizan** (mountain, Kyōto-fu)

18 比類 **hirui** a parallel, an equal

———————— 2 ————————

4 反比例 **hanpirei** in inverse proportion to

日比 **Nip-Pi** Japan and the Philippines

日比野 **Hibino** (surname)

7 対比 **taihi** contrast, comparison, opposition, analogy

見比 **mikura(beru)** compare (by eying)

乍 → **0a5.10**

———————— 4 ————————

臼 → **0a6.4**

2m4.2 □ ⼑ ⼁
13 2

此

此此

SHI, ko(no), ko(re) this

――― 1 ―――

⁵ 此処 **koko** here, this place

――― 5 ―――

歩 → 歩 3n5.3

――― 6 ―――

2m6.1 田 土 ⼘
22 13

卦

卦卦

KA, KE divination sign (one of a set of eight signs, each consisting of a triplet of bars or bar-pairs; seen on the South Korean flag)

――― 2 ―――

² 八卦 **hakke** the eight divination signs; fortunetelling

2m6.2 / 1679 目 日 ⼘ ⼗
43 13 12

卓

卓卓

TAKU table, desk; excel **TAKASHI** (m. given name) TAKU, TAKA (part of given name)

――― 1 ―――

³ 卓也 **Takuya, Takaya** (m. given name)

卓上 **takujō** table-top, desk-top

¹¹ 卓球 **takkyū** table tennis, ping-pong

――― 2 ―――

⁹ 食卓 **shokutaku** dining table

¹³ 電卓 **dentaku** (desktop) calculator (short for 電子式卓上計算機)

2m6.3 / 2234 □ ⼚ ⼗ ⼉
18 12 16

虎

虎虎

KO, tora tiger; drunkard TORA (m. given name) KO, TAKE, TORA (part of given name)

――― 1 ―――

⁵ 虎穴 **koketsu** tiger's den; dangerous situation

⁹ 虎巻 **tora(no)maki** pony, answer book; (trade) secrets

兒 → 児 4c3.3

長 → 0a8.2

――― 7 ―――

臥 → 臥 2a7.22

2m7.1 / 1681 目 貝 ⼘
68 13

貞

貞貞

TEI, JŌ chastity, fidelity, virtue TEI, SADA (part of given name)

――― 1 ―――

⁶ 貞次 **Teiji, Sadatsugu, Sadaji** (m. given name)

¹¹ 貞淑 **teishuku** chastity, modesty

¹³ 貞節 **teisetsu** fidelity, chastity

2m7.2 / 169 目 火 ⼝ ⼘
44 24 13

点

點丨点点

TEN point **tomo(ru)** burn, be lighted **tomo(su)** burn, light, turn on (a lamp) **tsu(ku)** catch (fire), be lit, (lights) come on

————————— 1 —————————

⁴ 点火 **tenka** ignite

⁵ 点字 **tenji** Braille

⁶ 点灯 **tentō** light (a lamp) (cf. 消灯)

¹² 点検 **tenken** inspection

¹³ 点滅 **tenmetsu** switch/flash on and off

点数 **tensū** points, marks, score

¹⁴ 点滴 **tenteki** falling drops, raindrops; intravenous drip

¹⁵ 点線 **tensen** dotted/perforated line

————————— 2 —————————

¹ 一点 **itten** a point; speck, dot, particle

一点張 **ittenba(ri)** persistence

⁴ 中点 **chūten** midpoint

欠点 **ketten** defect, flaw, faults

⁵ 氷点下 **hyōtenka** below the freezing point, below zero (Celsius)

句点 **kuten** period (the punctuation mark)

⁶ 合点 **gaten, gatten** understand, comprehend; consent to

争点 **sōten** point of contention, issue

同点 **dōten** a tie/draw

汚点 **oten** stain, smudge, blot, disgrace

百点 **hyakuten** 100 points, perfect score

⁸ 盲点 **mōten** blind spot

沸点 **futten** boiling point

拠点 **kyoten** (military) base, position

⁹ 重点 **jūten** important point, priority, emphasis

美点 **biten** good point, virtue, merit

¹⁰ 原点 **genten** starting point

起点 **kiten** starting point

弱点 **jakuten** weak point, a weakness

班点 **hanten** spot, dot, fleck, speck

特点 **tokuten** special favor, privilege

¹¹ 採点 **saiten** marking, grading, scoring

得点 **tokuten** one's score, points made

黒点 **kokuten** black/dark spot; sunspot

視点 **shiten** center of one's field of view; viewpoint

終点 **shūten** end of the line, last stop, terminus

頂点 **chōten** zenith, peak, climax

¹² 満点 **manten** perfect score

斑点 **hanten** spot, speck

¹³ 零点 **reiten** (a score/temperature of) zero

¹⁴ 罰点 **batten** demerit marks

読点 **tōten** comma

¹⁶ 濁点 **dakuten** voiced-consonant mark

¹⁸ 観点 **kanten** viewpoint

難点 **nanten** difficult point

————————— 3 —————————

³ 小数点 **shōsūten** decimal point

⁴ 分岐点 **bunkiten** branch/ramification/turning point, fork, junction

⁵ 句読点 **kutōten** punctuation mark

⁶ 交差点 **kōsaten** crossing, intersection

早合点 **hayagaten** hasty conclusion

¹¹ 接触点 **sesshokuten** point of contact/tangency

問題点 **mondaiten** the point at issue

¹² 最高点 **saikōten** highest point/score

2m7.3 / 1574

□ 厂 十 冂
18 12 20

GYAKU, shiita(geru) oppress, tyrannize over

————————— 1 —————————

⁹ 虐待 **gyakutai** treat cruelly, mistreat

¹⁰ 虐殺 **gyakusatsu** massacre

————————— 2 —————————

¹⁰ 残虐 **zangyaku** cruelty, atrocity, brutality

2m7.4

日 工 厂 一
38 14 1

歪 歪歪

WAI, E, yuga(mu) be distorted/warped **yuga(mi)** distortion **yuga(meru)** distort, bend **hizu(mu)** be strained, warp **hizu(mi)** strain, deformation **ibitsu** oval, elliptical; distorted, warped

---1---

6 歪曲 **waikyoku** distortion

---9---

2m9.1 / 1572

厂 十 儿
18 12 16

虚 虚|虚虚

KYO, KO empty **muna(shii)** empty, vain, futile **uro** cavity, hollow, hole

---1---

8 虚実 **kyojitsu** truth or falsehood; clever fighting, trying every strategy
9 虚栄心 **kyoeishin** vanity, vainglory
10 虚弱 **kyojaku** weak, feeble, frail
12 虚無的 **kyomuteki** nihilistic
14 虚構 **kyokō** fabricated, false, unfounded

---2---

8 空虚 **kūkyo** empty, hollow; inane

處 → 処 4i2.2

套 → 0a10.3

---10---

虚 → 虚 2m9.1

疎 → 0a11.4

---11---

2m11.1 / 1941

□ 口 厂 十
24 18 12

虞 虞|虞虞

GU, osore fear, concern, risk

2m11.2 / 1385

□ 田 厂 十
58 18 12

虜 虜|虜虜

RYO captive, prisoner of war; barbarian **toriko** captive, slave

---1---

5 虜囚 **ryoshū** captive, prisoner (of war)

---2---

10 捕虜 **horyo** prisoner of war, captive

鼠 → 0a13.1

---12---

睿 → 叡 2h14.1

2m12.1 / 1516

田 大 匕 厶
34 13 15

疑 疑疑

GI, utaga(u), utaga(ru) doubt, distrust, be suspicious of **utaga(washii)** doubtful, suspicious

---1---

7 疑似 **giji-** suspected, sham, pseudo-, dummy, simulated
8 疑念 **ginen** doubt, suspicion, misgivings
11 疑深 **utaga(i)buka(i)** doubting, distrustful
　 疑問 **gimon** question, doubt
　 疑問符 **gimonfu** question mark

12 疑惑 **giwaku** suspicion, distrust, misgivings

――――― 2 ―――――

9 狐疑 **kogi** doubt, indecision
10 容疑 **yōgi** suspicion
   容疑者 **yōgisha** a suspect
13 嫌疑 **kengi** suspicion
15 質疑応答 **shitsugi-ōtō** question-and-answer (session)
16 懐疑論 **kaigiron** skepticism

――――― 13 ―――――

2m13.1 / 1269   囗 甲 月 厂
                      58 42 18

膚 膚

FU, hada skin

――――― 1 ―――――

6 膚色 **hada-iro** flesh-colored
7 膚身離 **hadami-hana(sazu)** always kept on one's person, highly treasured

13 膚触 **hadazawa(ri)** the touch, the feel

――――― 2 ―――――

5 皮膚 **hifu** skin

2m13.2 / 1384   囗 甲 心 厂
                      58 51 18

慮 慮

RYO thought, consideration
omonpaka(ri) thought, consideration, prudence; fear, apprehension

――――― 2 ―――――

4 不慮 **furyo** unforeseen, unexpected
6 考慮 **kōryo** consideration, careful thought
10 配慮 **hairyo** consideration, care
12 遠慮 **enryo** reserve, restraint, diffidence; refrain from
   enryo(naku) frankly

――――― 3 ―――――

12 無遠慮 **buenryo** unreserved, forward, impertinent

――――― ク **2n** ―――――

々	久	夕	色	争	危	角	兎	免	負	急	勉	亀
1.1	0a3.7	0a3.14	4.1	4.2	4.3	5.1	0a8.5	6.1	7.1	7.2	8.1	9.1

魚	象	解	解	豫	龜
11a0.1	10.1	4g9.1	4g9.1	0a4.12	2n9.1

――――― 1 ―――――

2n1.1   ⋯ 宀 丨
              15 2

々 々

("odoriji", "kurikaeshi kigō") (kanji repetition symbol)

――――― 2 ―――――

2 人々 **hitobito** people, everybody
3 久々 **hisabisa** (for the first time in) a long time
4 云々 **unnun, shikajika** and so forth, and so on, and the like

元々 **motomoto** from the first, originally; by nature, naturally
仄々 **honobono** dimly, faintly
少々 **shōshō** a little, a few, slightly
日々 **hibi** daily; days **nichi-nichi** daily, every day
方々 **katagata** people, ladies and gentlemen **hōbō** every direction

5 生々 **namanama(shii)** fresh, vivid **seisei** lively
白々 **shirojiro** pure white
   shirajira dawning
   shirajira(shii) feigning ignorance; barefaced (lie)
   hakuhaku very clear

6 年々 **nennen, toshidoshi** year by year, every year

次々 **tsugitsugi** one by one, one after another

色々 **iroiro** various

近々 **chikajika, kinkin** before long

先々月 **sensengetsu** the month before last

早々 **sōsō** early, immediately; Hurriedly yours, **hayabaya** early, immediately

各々 **onoono** each, every, respectively

7 我々 **wareware** we, us, our

佐々木 **Sasaki** (surname)

別々 **betsubetsu** separate, individual

延々 **en'en** repeatedly postponed, protracted, interminable

折々 **oriori** from time to time

奈々 **Nana** (f. given name)

8 侃々諤々 **kankan-gakugaku** outspoken

直々 **jikijiki** personal, direct

若々 **wakawaka(shii)** youthful

昔々 **mukashi mukashi** Once upon a time …

国々 **kuniguni** countries, nations

易々 **ii(taru), yasuyasu** easy, simple

房々 **fusafusa** tufty, bushy, profuse (hair)

9 段々 **dandan** steps, terrace; gradually, increasingly

段々畑 **dandanbatake** terraced fields

津々浦々 **tsutsu-uraura** throughout the land, the entire country

草々 **sōsō** in haste; (closing words of a letter)

荒々 **araara(shii)** rough, rude, harsh, wild, violent

茶々 **chacha** interruption

度々 **tabitabi** often, frequently

相々傘 **aiaigasa (de)** under the same umbrella

10 個々 **koko** individual, separate, one by one

高々 **takadaka** at most; high, aloft, loudly

益々 **masumasu** increasingly, more and more

弱々 **yowayowa(shii)** weak-looking, frail, delicate

徐々 **jojo** slowly, gradually

島々 **shimajima** (many) islands

朗々 **rōrō** clear, sonorous

時々 **tokidoki** sometimes

粉々 **konagona** into tiny pieces

11 渋々 **shibushibu** reluctantly, grudgingly

常々 **tsunezune** always, constantly

堂々 **dōdō(taru)** with pomp and glory, majestic, grand, magnificent

悠々 **yūyū** calm, composed, leisurely

累々 **ruirui(taru)** piled up, in heaps

細々 **komagoma** in pieces, in detail **hosoboso** slender; scanty (livelihood)

12 着々 **chakuchaku** steadily

13 遙々 **harubaru** from afar, at a great distance

微々 **bibi(taru)** slight, tiny, insignificant

楽々 **rakuraku** comfortably, with great ease

数々 **kazukazu** many

続々 **zokuzoku** successively, one after another

14 様々 **samazama** various, varied

静々 **shizushizu** quietly, calmly, gently

態々 **wazawaza** on purpose, deliberately

憎々 **nikuniku(shii)** hateful, loathsome, malicious

種々 **shuju, kusagusa** various

精々 **seizei** to the utmost; at most

賑々 **niginigi(shii)** thriving; merry, gay

15 凛々 **rinrin** severe, intense, biting; awe-inspiring **riri(shii)** gallant, imposing

蝶々 **chōchō** butterfly

諸々 **moromoro** various, all, every sort of

19 麗々 **reirei(shii)** ostentatious, pretentious

²¹ 轟々 **gōgō (to)** thunderously, with a rumble

——————— 3 ———————

⁷ 赤裸々 **sekirara** stark naked; frank, outspoken

——————— 4 ———————

⁸ 侃々諤々 **kankan-gakugaku** outspoken

⁹ 津々浦々 **tsutsu-uraura** throughout the land, the entire country

¹³ 意気揚々 **iki-yōyō** exultant, triumphant

久 → **0a3.7**

夕 → **0a3.14**

——————— 4 ———————

2n4.1 / 204

日 尸 ⺈ 丨
40 15 2

色   色 色

SHOKU, SHIKI, iro color; erotic passion

——————— 1 ———————

⁰ 色っぽい **iro(ppoi)** sexy, seductive, fascinating

³ 色々 **iroiro** various

⁶ 色気 **iroke** sexiness, sexuality, amorousness, romance

⁷ 色良 **iroyo(i)** favorable (answer)

⁸ 色事 **irogoto** love affair; love scene

色刷 **irozu(ri)** color printing

色盲 **shikimō** color blindness

⁹ 色染 **irozo(me)** dyeing

色香 **iroka** color and scent; beauty, loveliness

¹⁰ 色紙 **irogami** colored paper
shikishi (a type of calligraphy paper)

¹¹ 色彩 **shikisai** color, coloration

色情 **shikijō** sexual desire, lust

色眼鏡 **iromegane** colored glasses; prejudiced view

——————— 2 ———————

⁴ 水色 **mizu-iro** sky blue, turquoise

⁵ 好色 **kōshoku** sensuality, eroticism, lust

白色 **hakushoku** white

⁶ 朱色 **shu-iro** scarlet, vermilion

灰色 **hai-iro** gray

肌色 **hada-iro** flesh-colored

⁷ 赤色 **aka-iro, sekishoku** red

⁸ 青色 **seishoku** blue

金色 **kinshoku, kin-iro, konjiki** golden color

⁹ 変色 **henshoku** change of color, discoloration

茜色 **akane-iro** madder red, crimson

茶色 **cha-iro** (light) brown

染色 **senshoku** dyeing, staining

¹⁰ 原色 **genshoku** primary color

桃色 **momo-iro** pink

桜色 **sakura-iro** pink, cerise

特色 **tokushoku** characteristic, distinguishing feature, peculiarity

¹¹ 淡色 **tanshoku** light color

彩色 **saishiki** coloring, coloration

黄色 **ki-iro** yellow

脚色 **kyakushoku** dramatization, stage/film adaptation

脱色 **dasshoku** decoloration, bleaching

黒色 **kokushoku** black

異色 **ishoku** different color; unique, novel

紺色 **kon'iro** dark/navy blue

¹² 着色 **chakushoku** to color, tint

景色 **keshiki** scenery

無色 **mushoku** colorless, achromatic

紫色 **murasaki-iro** purple

¹³ 鼠色 **nezumi-iro** dark gray, slate

褐色 **kasshoku** brown

鉛色 **namari-iro** lead color, gray

飴色 **ame-iro** amber, light brown

¹⁴ 褪色 **taishoku** fade, lose color; faded color

緑色 **midori-iro, ryokushoku** green

銀色 **gin-iro, ginshoku** silver color

銅色 **dōshoku** copper-colored

2

イ 冫 子 阝 阝 刂 力 又 ⺈ 亠 十 匕 勹 ⼉ 厂 辶 冂 几 匚

4

15 膚色 **hada-iro** flesh-colored

18 藤色 **fuji-iro** light purple, lilac, lavender

顔色 **kaoiro, ganshoku** complexion; expression

———— 3 ————

8 青銅色 **seidōshoku** bronze-color

11 黒褐色 **kokkasshoku** blackish brown

雪景色 **yukigeshiki** snowy landscape

14 瑠璃色 **ruri-iro** sky blue, azure

16 薄茶色 **usucha-iro** light brown, buff

———— 4 ————

2 十人十色 **jūnin-toiro** Tastes differ. To each his own.

2n4.2 / 302　　　　　日 ≡ 勹 丨
　　　　　　　　　　　39 15 2

SŌ, araso(u) dispute, argue, contend for　**araso(i)** dispute, altercation

———— 1 ————

9 争点 **sōten** point of contention, issue

14 争奪 **sōdatsu** contend/scramble for

争奪戦 **sōdatsusen** contest/scramble/struggle for

15 争論 **sōron** dispute, argument, controversy

———— 2 ————

7 言争 **i(i)araso(i)** quarrel, altercation

9 係争 **keisō** dispute, contention

10 党争 **tōsō** party rivalry, factionalism

紛争 **funsō** dispute, strife

13 戦争 **sensō** war

戦争中 **sensōchū** during the war

15 論争 **ronsō** dispute, controversy

18 闘争 **tōsō** struggle, conflict; strike

19 繋争 **keisō** dispute, contention

20 競争 **kyōsō** competition

———— 3 ————

3 山猫争議 **yamaneko sōgi** wildcat strike

2n4.3 / 534　　　日 勹 厂 阝
　　　　　　　　　15 18 7

KI, abu(nai), ayau(i) dangerous
aya(bumu) fear, have misgivings about, be apprehensive about

———— 1 ————

9 危急 **kikyū** emergency, crisis

危殆 **kitai** danger, peril, jeopardy

10 危険 **kiken** danger, risk

危険物 **kikenbutsu** hazardous articles, explosives and combustibles

危害 **kigai** injury, harm

16 危機 **kiki** crisis

危機一髪 **kiki-ippatsu** imminent/hairbreadth danger

危篤 **kitoku** critically ill, near death

———— 5 ————

2n5.1 / 473　　　日 月 勹 丨
　　　　　　　　　42 15 2

KAKU angle; corner; (animal's) horn; compare, compete　**tsuno** horn, antlers　**kado** corner, angle　**sumi** corner, nook　SUMI (part of given name)

———— 1 ————

5 角立 **kadoda(tsu)** be pointed/sharp, be rough; sound harsh

角田 **Tsunoda, Kadota** (surname)

8 角突合 **tsunotsu(ki)a(i)** bickering, wrangling

9 角度 **kakudo** angle

11 角張 **kakuba(ru), kado(baru)** be angular; be stiff and formal

13 角隠 **tsunokaku(shi)** bride's wedding hood

— 2 —

3 三角 **sankaku** triangular
mi(tsu)kado Y-junction of
streets

三角形 **sankakkei, sankakukei**
triangle

5 四角 **shikaku** square;
quadrilateral **yo(tsu)kado**
four corners; intersection

四角張 **shikakuba(ru)** be formal/
stiff

6 多角的 **takakuteki** many-sided,
versatile, diversified, multilateral

死角 **shikaku** dead/unseen angle

7 折角 **sekkaku** going to (much)
trouble, on purpose, expressly;
kindly

8 直角 **chokkaku** right angle

11 視角 **shikaku** angle of vision;
viewpoint

12 街角 **machikado** street corner

— 6 —

兎 → 兎   **0a8.5**

2n6.1 / 733

目 口 卩 儿
24 15 16

MEN exemption; permission;
dismissal **manuka(reru)** escape
from; be saved; avoid, evade; be ex-
empted/spared

— 1 —

0 免じる **men(jiru)** dismiss; exempt

7 免状 **menjō** diploma; license

9 免除 **menjo** exemption

免疫 **men'eki** immunity (from a
disease)

11 免許 **menkyo** license, permission

免許証 **menkyoshō** license, certificate, permit

12 免税 **menzei** tax exemption

免税品 **menzeihin** duty-free goods

免訴 **menso** dismissal (of a case),
acquittal

18 免職 **menshoku** dismissal, discharge

— 2 —

6 仮免状 **karimenjō** temporary license; provisional diploma

11 赦免 **shamen** pardon, clemency

12 御免 **gomen** (I beg) your pardon; no
thankyou, not me; permission

無免許 **mumenkyo** without a license

15 罷免 **himen** dismissal (from one's
post)

— 7 —

2n7.1 / 510

日 貝 ⺈
68 15

FU bear, carry; be defeated; negative
(number) **ma(keru)** be defeated/beat-
en, lose; be outdone by, fall behind;
lower the price **(o)ma(ke)** a little extra
thrown in; in addition, besides
ma(kasu) defeat, beat **ma(karu)** reduce the price **o(u)** carry (on the
back), bear (responsibility/expenses),
owe, sustain (an injury) **o(waseru)**
make (someone) carry, make (someone) bear (the responsibility/expenses),
inflict (injury) **o(nbu), o(buu)** carry (a
baby) on one's back **o(busaru)** be carried piggyback; be dependent on

— 1 —

4 負犬 **ma(ke)inu** loser

5 負号 **fugō** minus sign (−)

6 負気 **ma(ken)ki** unyielding/com-
petitive spirit

8 負担 **futan** burden, load, responsibility, liability

10 負荷 **fuka** burden, load (electricity)

11 負惜 **ma(ke)o(shimi)** unwilling-
ness to admit defeat

13 負傷 **fushō** sustain an injury, get
hurt

負債 **fusai** debt, liabilities

14 負魂 **ma(keji)damashii** unyielding spirit, striving to keep
ahead of others

— 2 —

3 大負 **ōma(ke)** a crushing defeat; big price reduction

9 背負 **seo(u), sho(u)** carry on one's back, shoulder, be burdened with

12 勝負 **shōbu** victory or defeat; match, showdown

勝負事 **shōbugoto** game of skill/chance

15 請負 **u(ke)o(u)** contract for, undertake **ukeoi** contracting

2n7.2 / 303

目 心 ヨ 亠
51 39 15

KYŪ urgent, sudden, emergency; steep, sharp (turn) **iso(gu)** (be in a) hurry **se(ku)** be in a hurry, be impatient

— 1 —

4 急勾配 **kyūkōbai** steep slope

5 急用 **kyūyō** urgent business

6 急死 **kyūshi** sudden/untimely death

急行 **kyūkō** an express (train)

7 急迫 **kyūhaku** be imminent/pressing, grow acute

急足 **iso(gi)ashi** brisk pace, hurried steps

8 急性 **kyūsei** acute (not chronic)

急所 **kyūsho** vital point, vulnerable spot; crux, key (to)

9 急変 **kyūhen** sudden change; emergency

急速 **kyūsoku** prompt, swift, fast, speedy

10 急進 **kyūshin** rapid progress; radical, extreme

急病 **kyūbyō** sudden illness

11 急務 **kyūmu** urgent business, pressing need

急患 **kyūkan** emergency patient/case

急転 **kyūten** sudden change

12 急場 **kyūba** emergency, crisis

急報 **kyūhō** urgent message, alarm

13 急傾斜 **kyūkeisha** steep slope/incline

14 急増 **kyūzō** sudden increase

16 急激 **kyūgeki** sudden, abrupt, drastic

22 急襲 **kyūshū** surprise attack, raid

— 2 —

3 大急 **ōiso(gi)** in a big hurry/rush

6 危急 **kikyū** emergency, crisis

至急 **shikyū** urgent

早急 **sōkyū, sakkyū** urgently, without delay

7 応急 **ōkyū** emergency, temporary, stopgap

10 特急 **tokkyū** limited express (train)

11 救急 **kyūkyū** emergency (relief)

救急車 **kyūkyūsha** ambulance

15 緊急 **kinkyū** emergency

— 8 —

2n8.1 / 735

亠 刀 ク 儿
24 15 16

BEN diligence **tsuto(meru)** make efforts, work hard, be diligent
TSUTOMU (m. given name)

— 1 —

7 勉学 **bengaku** study

11 勉強 **benkyō** studying; diligence; sell cheap

— 2 —

12 勤勉 **kinben** industrious, hardworking

— 9 —

2n9.1 / 2284

日 刀 ク |
43 15 2

KI, kame turtle, tortoise KI, KAME, HISA, AMA, AYA (part of given name)
HISASHI, SUSUMU, NAGASHI (m. given name)

— 1 —

5 亀田 **Kameda** (surname)

12 亀裂 **kiretsu** crack, fissure

───────── 2 ─────────

9 海亀 **umigame** sea turtle

魚→ **11a0.1**

───────── 10 ─────────

2n10.1 / 739   目 口 彡 宀
            24   27   15

      象 象

SHŌ image, shape   **ZŌ** elephant
katado(ru) pattern after, imitate

───────── 1 ─────────

4 象牙 **zōge** ivory
    象牙塔 **zōge (no) tō** ivory tower
7 象形文字 **shōkei moji** hieroglyphics
14 象徴 **shōchō** symbol

───────── 2 ─────────

6 気象 **kishō** weather; disposition,
    temperament

気象庁 **Kishōchō** Meteorological
    Agency
印象 **inshō** impression
7 対象 **taishō** object, subject, target
8 抽象 **chūshō** abstraction
抽象的 **chūshōteki** abstract
具象的 **gushōteki** concrete, not ab-
    stract
11 現象 **genshō** phenomenon

───────── 11 ─────────

解→ **4g9.1**

解→解 **4g9.1**

───────── 14 ─────────

豫→予 **0a4.12**

───────── 16 ─────────

龜→亀 **2n9.1**

───────── 2o ─────────

八	分	公	父	半	羊	共	弟	谷	兵	呉	来	美
0.1	2.1	2.2	2.3	0a5.24	4.1	3k3.3	5.1	5.3	5.6	5.7	0a7.6	2o7.4

並	斧	具	典	其	券	劵	首	前	美	盆	叛	巻
6.1	6.4	5c3.1	6.5	6.6	2f6.10	2f6.10	7.2	7.3	7.4	7.6	2p7.3	0a9.11

釜	兼	差	挙	益	翁	釜	眞	瓶	恭	曾	盖	貧
2o8.7	8.1	8.4	3c6.18	8.5	8.6	8.7	2k8.1	2o9.6	3k7.16	9.3	3k10.15	9.5

黄	瓶	盾	粛	着	善	尊	尊	普	曾	巽	巽	翔
3k8.16	9.6	7b8.7	0a11.8	10.1	10.2	10.3	2o10.3	10.5	2o9.3	2o10.7	10.7	10.8

期	慈	煎	義	羨	與	業	爾	養	躾	典	輿	糞
4b8.11	11.1	11.2	11.3	11.4	0a3.23	0a13.3	0a14.3	13.1	4f12.2	14.2	15.1	6b11.3

翼	叢	蠹
15.2	6e12.3	2o10.2

───────── 0 ─────────

2o0.1 / 10   □ 儿
           16

HACHI, yat(tsu), ya(tsu), ya, yō-
eight   HACHI, HATSU   (part of given
name)

───────── 1 ─────────

3 八丈島 **Hachijōjima** (island,
    Tōkyō-to)
4 八木 **Yagi** (surname)
八月 **hachigatsu** August

八日 **yōka** eight days; the eighth (of the month)

八方 **happō** all sides/directions

八方美人 **happō bijin** one who is affable to everybody

6 八百長 **yaochō** rigged affair, fixed game

八百屋 **yaoya** vegetable store; jack-of-all-trades

8 八卦 **hakke** the eight divination signs; fortunetelling

15 八幡宮 **Hachimangū** shrine of the god of war

————————— 2 —————————

4 尺八 **shakuhachi** bamboo flute/recorder

14 嘘八百 **usohappyaku** a pack of lies

————————— 3 —————————

5 四方八方 **shihō-happō** in every direction, far and wide

四苦八苦 **shiku-hakku** agony, dire distress

——————————— 2 ———————————

2o2.1 / 38   日 儿 力
                                        16 8

分 分

BUN dividing, portion **FUN** minute (of time or arc); (unit of weight, about 375 mg) **BU** rate, percentage; one percent; thickness; (unit of length, about 3.03 cm) **wa(karu)** understand **wa(keru), wa(katsu)** divide, split up; separate, isolate; distribute; distinguish **wa(kareru)** part, leave; branch off; be divided

————————— 1 —————————

5 分立 **bunritsu** separation (of powers), independence

分目 **wa(kare)me** turning point, junction, parting of the ways

6 分合 **wa(ke)a(u), wa(kachi)a(u)** share

7 分別 **funbetsu** discretion, good judgment **bunbetsu** classification, separation, discrimination

分岐点 **bunkiten** branch/ramification/turning point, fork, junction

分局 **bunkyoku** branch office

8 分担 **buntan** apportionment, sharing

分析 **bunseki** analysis

9 分前 **wa(ke)mae** share, portion

分科 **bunka** department, section, branch, course

分界線 **bunkaisen** line of demarcation

10 分娩 **bunben** childbirth, delivery

分書 **wa(kachi)ga(ki)** writing with a space between words

分納 **bunnō** payment/delivery in installments

分配 **bunpai** division, sharing, allotment

11 分野 **bun'ya** field, sphere, area, division

12 分割 **bunkatsu** partition, division

分割払 **bunkatsubara(i)** payment in installments

分散 **bunsan** breakup, dispersion, variance

分裂 **bunretsu** dissolution, breakup, division

13 分業 **bungyō** division of labor, specialization

分解 **bunkai** analysis, breakdown, decomposition, disassembly, disintegration

18 分離 **bunri** separation, division

分類 **bunrui** classification

————————— 2 —————————

1 一分 **ippun** a minute **ichibu** one tenth; one hundredth, one percent; one quarter *ryō* (an old coin) **ichibun** duty, honor

一分別 **hitofunbetsu** (careful) consideration

2 二分 **nifun** two minutes **nibun** halve, bisect

十分 **jūbun** enough, satisfactory; thorough **jippun** ten minutes

³ 三分 **sanpun** three minutes
  sanbun divide into three, tri-
  sect

  大分 **daibu, daibun** much, greatly,
  considerably **Ōita** (city,
  Ōita-ken)

  大分県 **Ōita-ken** (prefecture)

  千分 **senbun** thousandth

⁴ 五分 **gofun** five minutes **gobu**
  fifty percent, half; five percent

  区分 **kubun, kuwa(ke)** division,
  partition; classification

  水分 **suibun** moisture, water content

  引分 **hi(ki)wa(ke)** tie, draw, stand-
  off

⁵ 半分 **hanbun** half **hanpun** half a
  minute

  存分 **zonbun (ni)** to one's heart's
  content, as much as one wants,
  without reserve

  可分 **kabun** divisible, separable

  処分 **shobun** disposal, disposition;
  punishment

⁶ 多分 **tabun** probably, maybe, like-
  ly, presumably; a great deal/
  many

  気分 **kibun** feeling, mood

  気分転換 **kibun tenkan** a (refreshing) change, diversion

  充分 **jūbun** enough, sufficient;
  thoroughly

  当分 **tōbun** for now, for a while

  早分 **hayawa(kari)** quick understanding; guide, handbook

  成分 **seibun** composition, content,
  ingredient, component

  自分 **jibun** oneself, one's own

  自分自身 **jibun-jishin** oneself

⁷ 身分 **mibun** social standing, status;
  one's circumstances

  何分 **nanibun** anyway; please
  nanpun how many minutes
  nanbun what fraction

  余分 **yobun** extra, excess

  見分 **miwa(keru)** tell apart, distinguish between, recognize;
  judge, identify

  言分 **i(i)bun** one's say; objection

⁸ 使分 **tsuka(i)wa(ke)** proper use

性分 **shōbun** nature, disposition

取分 **to(ri)wa(ke)** especially
  to(ri)wa(keru) divide, portion out **to(ri)bun** share, portion

⁹ 春分日 **shunbun (no) hi** the vernal
  equinox (a holiday, about
  March 21)

¹⁰ 随分 **zuibun** very

  部分 **bubun** part **buwa(ke)** classification

  部分的 **bubunteki** partial, here and
  there

  核分裂 **kakubunretsu** nuclear fission

  配分 **haibun** distribution, alloca-
  tion

¹¹ 過分 **kabun** excessive, undeserved

  組分 **kumiwa(ke)** sorting, grouping

¹² 無分別 **mufunbetsu** imprudent,
  thoughtless, rash

  幾分 **ikubun** some, a portion

  等分 **tōbun** (division into) equal
  parts

¹³ 塩分 **enbun** salt content, salinity

  嗅分 **ka(gi)wa(keru)** tell/differen-
  tiate by scent

¹⁵ 養分 **yōbun** nourishment

¹⁶ 親分 **oyabun** boss, chief

  糖分 **tōbun** sugar content

———————————— 3 ————————————

¹ 一部分 **ichibubun** a part

³ 三権分立 **sanken bunritsu** separation of powers (legislative, executive, and judicial)

  大部分 **daibubun** a large part,
  most; for the most part, mostly

⁴ 不十分 **fujūbun** insufficient, inadequate

  不可分 **fukabun** indivisible, inseparable

  不充分 **fujūbun** insufficient, inadequate

⁹ 約半分 **yaku hanbun** about half

¹⁴ 精神分析 **seishin bunseki** psycho-
  analysis

2o2.2 / 126 　　日 儿 竹
　　　　　　　　16　17

公 公

KŌ public; unbiased, fair; in common; prince, lord; (title of familiarity or contempt, used like -*kun*) **KU, ōyake** public **Isao, Tōru, Hiroshi** (m. given name) **Kimi, Kin** (part of given name)

──────── 1 ────────

4 公文書 **kōbunsho** official document
5 公民館 **kōminkan** public hall, community center
　公平 **kōhei** fair, just
　公正 **kōsei** fair, just
　公用 **kōyō** official business; public use; public expense
　公示 **kōji** public announcement
　公立 **kōritsu** public (institution)
6 公休日 **kōkyūbi** legal holiday
　公会 **kōkai** public meeting
　公共 **kōkyō** public society, community
　公安 **kōan** public order/safety
　公有 **kōyū** publicly owned
　公式 **kōshiki** formula, formality
7 公告 **kōkoku** public notice
　公社 **kōsha** public corporation
8 公表 **kōhyō** official announcement
　公法 **kōhō** public law
　公定歩合 **kōtei buai** official bank rate, rediscount rate
　公明 **kōmei** just, fair
　公明党 **Kōmeitō** (a political party)
10 公益 **kōeki** public benefit/interest
　公害 **kōgai** pollution
11 公務員 **kōmuin** government employee
　公設 **kōsetsu** public
12 公営 **kōei** public, government-run
　公衆 **kōshū** public (telephone, toilet, etc.)
　公開 **kōkai** open to the public
13 公債 **kōsai** public debt, government bond

公園 **kōen** park
14 公演 **kōen** public performance
　公認 **kōnin** officially authorized, certified
17 公爵 **kōshaku** prince, duke
　公聴会 **kōchōkai** public hearing

──────── 2 ────────

4 不公平 **fukōhei** unfair, unjust
8 奉公 **hōkō** service
9 郭公 **kakkō** cuckoo
13 蒲公英 **tanpopo** dandelion

──────── 3 ────────

5 主人公 **shujinkō** main character, hero (of a story)

2o2.3 / 113 　　日 儿 十
　　　　　　　　16　12

父 父

FU, chichi, (o)tō(san) father

──────── 1 ────────

4 父方 **chichikata** on the father's side, paternal
5 父母 **fubo, chichihaha** father and mother
　父兄 **fukei** parents and older brothers, guardians
9 父祖 **fuso** forefathers, ancestors
16 父親 **chichioya, teteoya** father

──────── 2 ────────

3 亡父 **bōfu** one's late father
7 伯父 **oji, hakufu** uncle
8 叔父 **oji, shukufu** uncle
　実父 **jippu** one's biological father
9 神父 **shinpu** (Catholic) priest, Father
　祖父 **sofu** grandfather
　祖父母 **sofubo** grandparents
13 義父 **gifu** father-in-law; foster father; stepfather
　継父 **keifu** stepfather
15 養父 **yōfu** adoptive/foster father
16 親父 **oyaji** one's father; the old man, the boss

11 曽祖父 **sōsofu, hiijiji** great-grandfather

------------ 3 ------------

半→ **0a5.24**

------------ 4 ------------

2o4.1 / 288　　日 王 儿
　　　　　　　　　　46 16

羊羊

YŌ, hitsuji sheep

------------ 1 ------------

4 羊毛 **yōmō** wool
6 羊肉 **yōniku** mutton
19 羊羹 **yōkan** sweet adzuki-bean jelly

------------ 2 ------------

3 山羊 **yagi** goat

共→ **3k3.3**

------------ 5 ------------

2o5.1 / 405　　日 弓 儿 丨
　　　　　　　　　28 16 2

弟弟

TEI, DAI, DE younger brother; pupil, disciple **otōto** younger brother

------------ 1 ------------

2 弟子 **deshi, teishi** pupil, disciple, adherent, apprentice
8 弟妹 **teimai** younger brothers and sisters

------------ 2 ------------

5 兄弟 **kyōdai, ani-otōto** brothers (and sisters)
10 師弟 **shitei** master and pupil
13 義弟 **gitei** younger brother-in-law

2o5.3 / 653　　日 火 口
　　　　　　　　　44 24

谷谷

KOKU, tani, -ya valley TANI (surname) YA (part of given name)

------------ 1 ------------

3 谷口 **Taniguchi** (surname)
7 谷村 **Tanimura** (surname)
8 谷底 **tanizoko, tanisoko** bottom of a valley/ravine
11 谷崎 **Tanizaki** (surname)
12 谷間 **tanima, taniai** valley, ravine

------------ 2 ------------

3 三谷 **Mitani, Mi(tsu)ya** (surname)
　 大谷 **Ōtani** (surname)
　 小谷 **Kotani, Kodani** (surname)
4 中谷 **Nakatani, Nakaya** (surname)
　 水谷 **Mizutani, Mizuya** (surname)
8 長谷川 **Hasegawa** (surname)
　 宗谷海峡 **Sōya-kaikyō** (strait between Hokkaidō and Sakhalin)
9 峡谷 **kyōkoku** gorge, ravine, canyon
　 神谷 **Kamiya** (surname)
11 渓谷 **keikoku** ravine, gorge, valley
　 細谷 **Hosoya, Hosotani** (surname)

2o5.6 / 784　　日 斤 儿 一
　　　　　　　　　50 16 1

兵兵

HEI, HYŌ soldier; warfare
tsuwamono soldier

------------ 1 ------------

3 兵士 **heishi** soldier
7 兵役 **heieki** military service
8 兵舎 **heisha** barracks
　 兵卒 **heisotsu** private, enlisted man
10 兵員 **heiin** military personnel/strength
　 兵庫県 **Hyōgo-ken** (prefecture)
11 兵隊 **heitai** soldier; sailor
15 兵器 **heiki** weapon, arms

2

イ冫孑阝卩刂カ又亠⺌厂辶冂八囗

5

— 2 —

4 水兵 **suihei** (navy) sailor

6 米兵 **beihei** U.S. soldier/sailor

9 派兵 **hahei** dispatch/send troops

10 核兵器 **kakuheiki** nuclear weapons

14 徴兵 **chōhei** conscription; draftee

— 3 —

8 狙撃兵 **sogekihei** sniper, sharp-shooter

2o5.7 / 1436 目 口 儿 一
24 16 1

呉

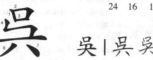

GO (region/dynasty of ancient China); China **Kure** (ancient name for China); (city, Hiroshima-ken) **ku(reru)** give; do (something) for

— 1 —

8 呉服 **gofuku** cloth/dry goods, draperies

12 呉越同舟 **Go-Etsu dōshū** enemies in the same boat

来→ **0a7.6**

— 6 —

美→ **2o7.4**

2o6.1 / 1165 目 工 儿 丨
38 16 2

並

竝 | 並 並

HEI, nara(bu) be in a row; rank with **nara(bi ni)** and, as well as **nara(beru)** arrange, put side by side, marshal **na(mi)** average, common, ordinary

— 1 —

4 並木 **namiki** row of trees; roadside tree

5 並存 **heizon** coexistence

並外 **namihazu(re)** out of the ordinary

6 並列 **heiretsu** arrange in a row; parallel (circuit)

並行 **heikō** parallel

— 2 —

2 人並 **hitona(mi)** average, ordinary

5 立並 **ta(chi)nara(bu)** stand in a row; be equal to

10 軒並 **nokina(mi), nokinara(bi)** row of houses

2o6.4 日 斤 儿 十
50 16 12

斧

FU, ono ax

— 1 —

5 斧正 **fusei** correction, revision

具→具 **5c3.1**

2o6.5 / 367 目 艹 冂 儿
32 20 16

典

TEN rule; ceremony; writing, book; pledge, pawn; model **nori** rule, law NORI (part of given name)

— 1 —

9 典型的 **tenkeiteki** typical

— 2 —

4 仏典 **butten** Buddhist literature/scriptures

5 出典 **shutten** source, authority

古典 **koten** the classics, classic

古典的 **kotenteki** classical

字典 **jiten** character dictionary

6 式典 **shikiten** ceremonies

8 事典 **jiten** encyclopedia, dictionary

11 祭典 **saiten** festival, ritual

13 聖典 **seiten** sage's writings; holy book, scriptures

辞典 **jiten** dictionary

———————— 4 ————————
6 百科事典 **hyakka jiten** encyclopedia
13 漢和辞典 **Kan-Wa jiten** kanji dictionary

2o6.6   日 艹 二 儿
                           32 4 16

其   其其

so(no) that **sore** that, it

券 → **2f6.10**

 券 → 券 **2f6.10**

———————— 7 ————————

2o7.2 / 148   日 月 儿 一
                           55 16 14

首   首首

SHU head, neck; beginning, first; (counter for poems and songs) **kubi** neck, head **kōbe** the head

———————— 1 ————————
4 首切 **kubiki(ri)** decapitation, execution; dismissal, firing
6 首吊 **kubitsu(ri)** hang oneself
8 首長 **shuchō** leader, head, chief
9 首相 **shushō** prime minister
10 首都 **shuto** capital
   首席 **shuseki** head, chief, chairman
   首班 **shuhan** head, leader
11 首脳 **shunō** leader
   首脳会談 **shunō kaidan** summit conference
13 首飾 **kubikaza(ri)** necklace

———————— 2 ————————
1 一首 **isshu** a poem
10 部首 **bushu** radical (of a kanji)
11 猪首 **ikubi** short and thick neck, bull neck

12 絞首刑 **kōshukei** (execution by) hanging
17 馘首 **kakushu** decapitate; dismissal

———————— 4 ————————
6 百人一首 **hyakunin-isshu** 100 poems by 100 poets (a collection of 100 *tanka*; basis for the popular card game *uta karuta*)

2o7.3 / 47   日 月 儿 一
                           42 16 1

前   前前

ZEN, mae before; front **SAKI** (part of given name)

———————— 1 ————————
3 前川 **Maekawa** (surname)
4 前日 **zenjitsu** the day before
   前方 **zenpō** front **maekata** before; immature
5 前以 **maemot(te)** beforehand, previously
   前半 **zenpan** first half
   前代未聞 **zendai-mimon** unprecedented
   前払 **maebara(i)** advance payment
   前田 **Maeda** (surname)
6 前年 **zennen** the preceding year, last year
   前任者 **zenninsha** one's predecessor
   前兆 **zenchō** portent, omen, sign
   前向 **maemu(ki)** forward-looking
   前回 **zenkai** last time
7 前売券 **maeu(ri)ken** ticket sold in advance
8 前例 **zenrei** precedent
   前夜祭 **zen'yasai** (Christmas) Eve
   前者 **zensha** the former
   前金 **maekin, zenkin** advance payment
9 前途 **zento** the road ahead, one's future prospects
   前後 **zengo** about, approximately; front and back, longitudinal; order, sequence
   maeushi(ro) front and back

前面 **zenmen** front, front side

前科…犯 **zenka …-han/-pan** (a criminal record of three) previous convictions

10 前進 **zenshin** advance, drive, progress

前書 **maega(ki)** preface, foreword

前記 **zenki** the above-mentioned

11 前菜 **zensai** hors d'oeuvres

前略 **zenryaku** first part omitted; (salutation in a letter)

12 前提 **zentei** premise, prerequisite

前期 **zenki** the first/preceding term

前景 **zenkei** foreground

13 前置 **maeo(ki)** preface, introduction

前触 **maebu(re)** advance notice/warning

15 前線 **zensen** front lines, the front; a (cold) front

前篇 **zenpen** the first volume/part

前輪 **zenrin, maewa** front wheel

16 前衛 **zen'ei** advance guard, vanguard

前橋 **Maebashi** (city, Gunma-ken)

——————— 2 ———————

2 人前 **hitomae** before others, in public

3 寸前 **sunzen** just before

4 午前 **gozen** morning, a.m.

午前中 **gozenchū** all morning

分前 **wa(ke)mae** share, portion

手前 **temae** you; this side of, toward oneself; out of consideration for; tea-ceremony procedures; oneself

5 以前 **izen** ago; formerly

出前 **demae** cooked-food home delivery **da(shi)mae** one's share (of the expenses)

生前 **seizen** during one's lifetime

弘前 **Hirosaki** (city, Aomori-ken)

立前 **ta(te)mae** principle, policy, official stance

目前 **me (no) mae, mokuzen** before one's eyes; immediate (gain)

6 気前 **kimae** generosity

名前 **namae** name

8 事前 **jizen** before the fact, prior, pre-

直前 **chokuzen** just before

建前 **ta(te)mae** principle, official position; erection of the framework

空前 **kūzen** unprecedented

板前 **itamae** a cook

門前払 **monzenbara(i)** turning (someone) away at the gate, refusing to see (someone)

9 神前結婚 **shinzen kekkon** Shinto wedding

食前 **shokuzen** before a meal

11 産前 **sanzen** before childbirth/delivery

12 腕前 **udemae** ability, skill

最前線 **saizensen** forefront, front lines

13 戦前 **senzen** before the war, prewar

14 駅前 **ekimae** in front of the station

16 錠前 **jōmae** a lock

——————— 3 ———————

1 一人前 **ichininmae, hitorimae** one portion/serving; full adulthood

2 二人前 **futarimae, nininmae** enough for two, two servings

9 紀元前 **kigenzen** B.C.

12 寒冷前線 **kanrei zensen** cold front

2o7.4 / 401   目 王 大 儿
                        46 34 16

美   美 美

BI beauty **utsuku(shii)** beautiful
HARU, MI, YOSHI (part of given name)

——————— 1 ———————

2 美人 **bijin** beautiful woman

美子 **Yoshiko, Haruko, Miko, Tomiko** (f. given name)

3 美女 **bijo** beautiful woman

4 美化 **bika** beautification; glorification

5 美代子 **Miyoko** (f. given name)

6 美帆 **Miho** (f. given name)

7 美里 **Misato** (f. given name)

美学 **bigaku** esthetics

美男子 **bidanshi, binanshi** handsome man

8 美事 **migoto** splendid **biji** commendable act

美味 **oi(shii)** good-tasting, delicious **bimi** good flavor; delicacies

美枝 **Mie, Yoshie** (f. given name)

美的 **biteki** esthetic

9 美保 **Miho, Yoshiyasu** (given name)

美点 **biten** good point, virtue, merit

美紀 **Miki** (f. given name)

美食家 **bishokuka** epicure, gourmet

10 美容 **biyō** beauty culture

美容院 **biyōin** beauty parlor, hairdresser's

美恵 **Mie, Yoshie** (f. given name)

11 美術 **bijutsu** art, fine arts

美術館 **bijutsukan** art gallery

12 美智子 **Michiko** (f. given name)

13 美辞麗句 **biji-reiku** flowery language

15 美穂 **Miho, Yoshiho** (given name)

16 美樹 **Miki, Yoshiki, Haruki** (given name)

18 美観 **bikan** fine view, beautiful sight

———————— 2 ————————

3 久美子 **Kumiko** (f. given name)

4 友美 **Tomomi, Yumi** (f. given name)

5 甘美 **kanbi** sweet

由美 **Yumi, Yoshimi** (f. given name)

由美子 **Yumiko** (f. given name)

正美 **Masami, Masayoshi, Tadayoshi, Masatomi, Seibi** (given name)

6 成美 **Shigemi, Shigeyoshi, Narumi, Seibi** (given name)

8 奄美大島 **Amami Ōshima** (island, Kagoshima-ken)

直美 **Naomi** (f. given name)

尚美 **Naomi, Naoyoshi, Hisayoshi, Takayoshi, Shōbi** (given name)

明美 **Akemi, Harumi** (f. given name)

和美 **Kazumi, Kazuyoshi** (given name)

10 夏美 **Natsumi** (f. given name)

恵美 **Emi** (f. given name)

恵美子 **Emiko** (f. given name)

耽美的 **tanbiteki** esthetic

11 清美 **Kiyomi, Seimi** (f. given name)

麻美 **Asami, Mami** (f. given name)

12 博美 **Hiromi, Hiroyoshi** (given name)

富美子 **Fumiko, Tomiko** (f. given name)

晴美 **Harumi, Haruyoshi** (given name)

智美 **Satomi, Tomomi** (f. given name)

裕美 **Hiromi, Yumi** (f. given name)

絵美 **Emi** (f. given name)

13 睦美 **Mutsumi, Mutsuyoshi** (given name)

雅美 **Masami, Masayoshi, Motomi, Tsuneyoshi** (given name)

15 褒美 **hōbi** reward, prize

賛美 **sanbi** praise, glorification

輝美 **Terumi, Teruyoshi** (given name)

22 讃美 **sanbi** praise, glorification

———————— 3 ————————

2 八方美人 **happō bijin** one who is affable to everybody

10 真由美 **Mayumi** (f. given name)

11 脚線美 **kyakusenbi** leg beauty/ shapeliness

2o7.6 / 1099   日 皿 儿 力   59 16 8

BON Lantern Festival, Festival of the Dead; tray

———————— 1 ————————

6 盆地 **bonchi** basin, round valley

10 盆栽 **bonsai** bonsai, potted dwarf tree

11 盆祭 **Bon-matsu(ri)** Bon Festival

— 3 —

8 盂蘭盆 **Urabon** Bon Festival

18 覆水盆返 **fukusui bon (ni) kae(razu)** No use crying over spilt milk.

叛 → **2p7.3**

巻 → **0a9.11**

— 8 —

釜 → 釜 **2o8.7**

2o8.1 / 1081   目 ヨ 儿 一
            39 16 14

兼   兼 兼

KEN and, in addition, concurrently
ka(neru) combine, double as; hold an
additional post; (as suffix) cannot
KANE (part of given name)

— 1 —

5 兼用 **ken'yō** combined use, serving two purposes

6 兼任 **kennin** concurrent post

13 兼業 **kengyō** side business

18 兼職 **kenshoku** concurrent post

— 2 —

6 気兼 **kiga(ne)** feel constraint, be afraid of giving trouble

9 待兼 **ma(chi)ka(neru)** can't stand the wait

2o8.4 / 658   目 王 エ 儿
            46 38 16

差   差 差

SA difference **sa(su)** hold (an umbrella); wear (a sword); extend (a hand);
offer; thrust; insert **sa(shi)-** (emphatic
verb prefix) **sa(shi de)** between two
persons

— 1 —

3 差上 **sa(shi)a(geru)** give; raise up

4 差支 **sa(shi)tsuka(enai)** no impediment, justifiable, allowable, may

差止 **sa(shi)to(meru)** prohibit, forbid, ban

差込 **sa(shi)ko(mu)** insert, plug in

差引 **sa(shi)hi(ku)** deduct

5 差出人 **sashidashinin** sender, return address

6 差当 **sa(shi)a(tari)** for the time being

7 差別 **sabetsu** discrimination

8 差押 **sa(shi)osa(eru)** attach, seize,
impound

11 差掛 **sa(shi)ka(karu)** hang over,
overhang; be urgent; be imminent; approach, come near
sa(shi)ka(keru) hold (an umbrella) over (someone)

差控 **sa(shi)hika(eru)** be moderate
in; withhold, refrain from

13 差障 **sa(shi)sawa(ri)** obstacle, hindrance; offense

差置 **sa(shi)o(ku)** leave, let alone;
ignore

— 2 —

2 人差指 **hitosa(shi) yubi** index finger

3 大差 **taisa** wide difference/margin,
great disparity

千差万別 **sensa-banbetsu** infinite
variety

4 水差 **mizusa(shi)** water jug, pitcher

6 交差点 **kōsaten** crossing, intersection

8 物差 **monosa(shi)** ruler, measure,
yardstick

10 格差 **kakusa** gap, differential

時差 **jisa** time difference,
staggered **jisa(boke)** jet lag

12 無差別 **musabetsu** indiscriminate

14 誤差 **gosa** error, aberration

— 3 —

10 個人差 **kojinsa** differences between individuals

12 雲泥差 **undei (no) sa** a great difference

拳 → **3c6.18**

2o8.5 / 716   目 皿 儿 一
                         59   16   1

益   益 益

EKI, YAKU gain, benefit, profit, advantage, use **ma(su)** increase
SUSUMU (m. given name) MASU
(part of given name)

———— 1 ————

3 益々 **masumasu** increasingly,
    more and more

———— 2 ————

4 収益 **shūeki** earnings, proceeds
   公益 **kōeki** public benefit/interest
6 有益 **yūeki** beneficial, profitable
7 利益 **rieki** profit, gain; benefit,
    advantage **(go)riyaku** divine
    favor
8 受益者 **juekisha** beneficiary
   実益 **jitsueki** net profit, practical
    benefit
   国益 **kokueki** national interests/
    benefit
10 純益 **jun'eki** net profit
12 無益 **mueki** useless, futile
14 総益 **sōeki** gross profit

2o8.6 / 1930   田 ヨ 儿 竹
                           39   16   17

翁   翁 翁 翁

Ō, okina old man

2o8.7   ⺌ 王 儿 十
                           46   16   12

釜   釜 釜 釜

FU, kama kettle, cooking pot

———— 1 ————

3 釜山 **Fuzan, Pusan** Pusan

眞 → 真 **2k8.1**

瓶 → **2o9.6**

恭 → **3k7.16**

———— 9 ————

2o9.3   目 田 日 儿
                       58   43   16

曽   曾 曽 曽

SO, SŌ, katsu(te) once, formerly, before; ever; former, ex-

———— 1 ————

9 曽祖父 **sōsofu, hiijiji** great-grand-
    father
   曽祖母 **sōsobo, hiibaba** great-
    grandmother

盖 → 蓋 **3k10.15**

2o9.5 / 753   日 貝 儿 力
                         68   16   8

貧   貧 貧 貧

HIN, BIN, mazu(shii) poor

———— 1 ————

3 貧乏 **binbō** poor
   貧乏人 **binbōnin** poor man, pauper
5 貧民 **hinmin** the poor
6 貧血 **hinketsu** anemia
7 貧困 **hinkon** poverty; lack
12 貧富 **hinpu** rich and poor, wealth
    and poverty

黄 → **3k8.16**

2o9.6 / 1161

田 ⺾ 儿 一
32 16 1

瓶

瓶 | 瓶 瓶

BIN, HEI bottle, jar **kame** jar, jug, vase, vat, urn

───── 1 ─────

0 ビール瓶 **bīrubin** beer bottle
13 瓶詰 **binzu(me)** bottling; bottled

───── 2 ─────

7 花瓶 **kabin, hanagame** vase
8 空瓶 **a(ki)bin** empty bottle
9 茶瓶 **chabin** teapot, tea urn

───── 3 ─────

4 火炎瓶 **kaenbin** firebomb, Molotov cocktail
21 魔法瓶 **mahōbin** thermos bottle

質 → 質   7b8.7

肅 →   0a11.8

───── 10 ─────

2o10.1 / 657

目 日 王 儿
55 46 16

着

着 著

CHAKU, JAKU arrive at; put on, wear; (counter for suits) **tsu(ku)** arrive at **ki(ru), tsu(keru)** put on, wear **ki(seru)** clothe, dress, put on

───── 1 ─────

3 着々 **chakuchaku** steadily
4 着手 **chakushu** start, commence, proceed with
着心地 **kigokochi** fit and feel (of clothes)
5 着古 **kifuru(su)** wear out
着払 **chakubara(i)** payment upon delivery, COD
6 着色 **chakushoku** to color, tint
8 着実 **chakujitsu** steady, solid, trustworthy

着服 **chakufuku** put on clothes; embezzle
着物 **kimono** clothes, kimono
10 着陸 **chakuriku** (airplane) landing
着荷 **chakuni, chakka** goods arrived
着席 **chakuseki** take a seat
11 着眼 **chakugan** notice, observe
12 着替 **kiga(e)** changing clothes; change of clothes
13 着想 **chakusō** idea, conception
着飾 **kikaza(ru)** dress up

───── 2 ─────

1 一着 **itchaku** first arrival; first (in a race); a suit (of clothes)
3 上着 **uwagi** coat, jacket
下着 **shitagi** underwear
土着 **dochaku** native, indigenous
4 水着 **mizugi** bathing suit, swimwear
5 付着 **fuchaku** adhere, stick to
辿着 **tado(ri)tsu(ku)** make it to, grope/trudge along to
6 先着順 **senchakujun** by order of arrival, in the order of receipt, (on a) first-come-first-served basis
肌着 **hadagi** underwear
7 決着 **ketchaku** conclusiveness, settlement
沈着 **chinchaku** composed, calm
8 到着 **tōchaku** arrival
厚着 **atsugi** wearing thick/heavy clothing
定着 **teichaku** fix, fasten, anchor
9 発着 **hatchaku** departures and arrivals
10 帰着 **kichaku** return; conclusion, consequence
11 執着 **shūchaku** attachment to, tenacity
接着 **setchaku** adhesion
接着剤 **setchakuzai** adhesive, glue
密着 **mitchaku** adhere to, stick fast
終着駅 **shūchakueki** terminal station
粘着 **nenchaku** adhesion
neba(ri)tsu(ku) be sticky
粘着力 **nenchakuryoku** adhesion, viscosity
軟着陸 **nanchakuriku** soft landing

12 落着 **o(chi)tsu(ku)** calm down
rakuchaku be settled

装着 **sōchaku** equip, fit, put, place

結着 **ketchaku** conclusion, settlement

悶着 **monchaku** trouble; dispute

14 漂着 **hyōchaku** drift ashore

愛着 **aichaku, aijaku** attachment, affection

15 横着 **ōchaku** dishonest; cunning; impudent; lazy; selfish

16 薄着 **usugi** lightly/thinly dressed

瞞着 **manchaku** deceive, trick, dupe

18 癒着 **yuchaku** adhere, knit together, heal up; too close a relationship (with an organization)

───── 3 ─────

12 普段着 **fudangi** everyday clothes

2o10.2 / 1139

目 王 口 儿
46 24 16

ZEN, yo(i), i(i) good YOSHI (part of given name)

───── 1 ─────

2 善人 **zennin** virtuous man, good people

6 善行 **zenkō** good conduct/deed

11 善悪 **zen'aku** good and evil
yo(shi)waru(shi), yo(shi)a(shi) good and bad, good or bad
yo(kare)a(shikare) right or wrong, for better or worse

13 善意 **zen'i** good faith; well-intentioned; favorable sense

───── 2 ─────

7 改善 **kaizen** improvement

9 独善 **hito(ri)yo(gari), dokuzen** self-righteous, complacent, smug

11 偽善者 **gizensha** hypocrite

12 最善 **saizen** (do one's) best

13 慈善 **jizen** charity

16 親善 **shinzen** friendship, amity, goodwill

2o10.3 / 704

目 酉 寸 儿
71 37 16

SON, tatto(bu), tōto(bu), tōto(mu) esteem, value, respect **tatto(i), tōto(i)** valuable, precious; noble, exalted
mikoto lord, prince TAKA (part of given name)

───── 1 ─────

9 尊重 **sonchō** respect, esteem

12 尊敬 **sonkei** respect, esteem, honor

17 尊厳 **songen** dignity

───── 2 ─────

3 女尊男卑 **joson-danpi** putting women above men

6 自尊心 **jisonshin** self-esteem; conceit

7 男尊女卑 **danson-johi** predominance of men over women

尊 → 尊 2o10.3

2o10.5 / 1166

目 日 工 儿
43 38 16

FU everywhere, general; Prussia
amane(ku) widely, generally HIRO (part of given name)

───── 1 ─────

3 普及 **fukyū** diffusion, dissemination, wide use/ownership, popularization

9 普通 **futsū** ordinary, common, usual

普段 **fudan** usual, ordinary; constant, ceaseless

普段着 **fudangi** everyday clothes

11 普遍 **fuhen** universal, general

曾 → 曽 2o9.3

巽 → 巽 2o10.7

2o10.7 / 2062 · 目 弓 艹 儿
28 32 16

巽│巽巽

SON, tatsumi southeast TATSUMI, HAJIME (m. given name) SON, YOSHI, YUKU (part of given name)

2o10.8 / 2200 · Ⅲ 彐 王 儿
39 46 16

翔翔

SHŌ, ka(keru) fly, soar, spread one's wings SHŌ (m. given name) SANE (part of given name)

─────── 1 ───────

⁴ 翔太 **Shōta** (m. given name)

期 → 期 **4b8.11**

─────── 11 ───────

2o11.1 / 1547 · 目 忄 儿 竹
51 16 17

慈│慈慈

JI, itsuku(shimu) love, be affectionate to; pity

─────── 1 ───────

¹² 慈善 **jizen** charity
慈悲 **jihi** compassion, mercy, charity

─────── 2 ───────

¹² 無慈悲 **mujihi** merciless, ruthless

2o11.2 · 目 月 火 儿
42 44 16

煎煎

SEN boil, decoct **i(ru)** roast, parch, broil, boil down

─────── 1 ───────

⁰ 煎じる **sen(jiru)** boil, decoct
⁷ 煎卵 **i(ri)tamago** scrambled eggs
⁹ 煎茶 **sencha** green tea
¹⁴ 煎餅 **senbei** (rice) cracker
¹⁶ 煎薬 **sen(ji)gusuri, sen'yaku** medical decoction, herb tea

2o11.3 / 291 · 目 王 戈 儿
46 52 16

義義

GI justice, righteousness; loyalty; non-blood family relationship; meaning, significance; substitute, artificial
TADASHI (m. given name) GI, YOSHI (part of given name)

─────── 1 ───────

⁴ 義父 **gifu** father-in-law; foster father; stepfather
⁵ 義母 **gibo** mother-in-law; foster mother; stepmother
義兄 **gikei** elder brother-in-law
⁷ 義弟 **gitei** younger brother-in-law
義足 **gisoku** artificial leg
⁸ 義郎 **Yoshirō, Yoshio, Girō** (m. given name)
義妹 **gimai** younger sister-in-law
義姉 **gishi** elder sister-in-law
義肢 **gishi** artificial limb
義明 **Yoshiaki, Noriaki, Nobuaki** (m. given name)
¹¹ 義理 **giri** sense of duty/honor, decency, courtesy, debt of gratitude
義理人情 **giri-ninjō** duty versus/ and human feelings
義務 **gimu** obligation, duty
義務的 **gimuteki** obligatory, compulsory
¹² 義歯 **gishi** artificial/false tooth, dentures
¹⁵ 義憤 **gifun** righteous indignation

─────── 2 ───────

¹ 一義的 **ichigiteki** unambiguous
² 二義的 **nigiteki** secondary

4 不義 **fugi** immorality; injustice; impropriety, misconduct, adultery

仁義 **jingi** humanity and justice; duty; moral code (of a gang)

5 正義 **seigi** justice, right(eousness); correct meaning **Masayoshi, Seigi** (m. given name)

広義 **kōgi** broad sense

主義 **shugi** -ism, principle

主義者 **shugisha** -ist, advocate (of a theory/doctrine)

6 両義 **ryōgi** double meaning, two meanings

同義語 **dōgigo** synonym

名義 **meigi** name; moral duty

8 定義 **teigi** definition

9 信義 **shingi** faith, fidelity, loyalty **Nobuyoshi, Shingi** (m. given name)

狭義 **kyōgi** narrow sense

11 道義 **dōgi** moral principles

異義 **igi** different meaning

12 奥義 **okugi, ōgi** secrets, esoteric mysteries

13 意義 **igi** meaning, significance

14 徳義 **tokugi** morality, integrity

17 講義 **kōgi** lecture

18 類義語 **ruigigo** words of similar meaning

――――――― 3 ―――――――

12 無意義 **muigi** meaningless, not significant

――――――― 4 ―――――――

5 民本主義 **minpon shugi** democracy

民主主義 **minshu shugi** democracy

6 同音異義 **dōon-igi** the same pronunciation but different meanings

共産主義 **kyōsan shugi** communism

自然主義 **shizen shugi** naturalism

7 社会主義 **shakai shugi** socialism

8 国家主義 **kokka shugi** nationalism

9 軍国主義 **gunkoku shugi** militarism

帝国主義 **teikoku shugi** imperialism

10 根本主義 **konpon shugi** fundamentalism

11 理想主義 **risō shugi** idealism

13 資本主義 **shihon shugi** capitalism

――――――― 6 ―――――――

7 社会民主主義 **shakai minshu shugi** social democracy

2o11.4   王 夂 氵
                 46 49 21

羨

SEN, **uraya(mu), uraya(mashigaru)** envy, be envious of **uraya(mashii)** enviable

――――――― 1 ―――――――

11 羨望 **senbō** envy

與 → 与 **0a3.23**

業 → **0a13.3**

――――――― 12 ―――――――

爾 → **0a14.3**

――――――― 13 ―――――――

2o13.1 / 402   目 食 王 儿
                       73 46 16

養

YŌ, **yashina(u)** nurture, bring up, rear; adopt, foster; support; promote (health); cultivate, develop YASU (part of given name)

――――――― 1 ―――――――

2 養子 **yōshi, yashina(i)go** adopted child

4 養分 **yōbun** nourishment

養父 **yōfu** adoptive/foster father

5 養母 **yōbo** adoptive/foster mother

6 養成 **yōsei** train, educate, cultivate

8 養育 **yōiku** bring up, rear; support

11 養豚 **yōton** hog raising

2
13

12 養殖 **yōshoku** raising, culture, cultivation

20 養護 **yōgo** protection, care

—————— 2 ——————

6 休養 **kyūyō** rest, recreation

7 扶養 **fuyō** support (a family)

8 供養 **kuyō, kyōyō** memorial service

9 保養 **hoyō** preservation of health; recuperation; recreation

栄養 **eiyō** nutrition, nourishment

10 修養 **shūyō** cultivation of the mind, character-building

教養 **kyōyō** culture, education, refinement

11 培養 **baiyō** cultivation, culture

12 滋養 **jiyō** nourishment

婿養子 **muko-yōshi** son-in-law adopted as an heir

14 静養 **seiyō** rest, recuperate

17 療養 **ryōyō** medical treatment/care

療養所 **ryōyōjo** sanitarium

躾 → 4f12.2

—————————— 14 ——————————

2o14.2 / 368 日 口 ヨ 厂 24 39 18

KŌ, KYŌ interest; entertainment; prosperity **oko(ru)** rise, flourish **oko(su)** revive, resuscitate, retrieve (fortunes) OKI (part of given name)

—————— 1 ——————

6 興行 **kōgyō** entertainment industry

8 興味 **kyōmi** interest

興味深 **kyōmibuka(i)** very interesting

9 興信所 **kōshinjo** detective/investigative agency

12 興廃 **kōhai** rise and fall, destiny

13 興業 **kōgyō** promotion of industry

16 興奮 **kōfun** get excited

—————— 2 ——————

6 再興 **saikō** revive, restore, re-establish

7 即興 **sokkyō** improvised, ad-lib

10 遊興 **yūkyō** pleasure seeking, merrymaking

振興 **shinkō** promotion, encouragement

13 新興 **shinkō** new, rising

—————————— 15 ——————————

2o15.1 日 車 ヨ 厂 69 39 18

YO, koshi palanquin; bier

—————— 2 ——————

12 御輿 **mikoshi** portable/palanquin shrine

糞 → 6b11.3

2o15.2 / 1062 日 田 艹 ヨ 58 32 39

YOKU wing; help **tsubasa** wing TSUBASA (m. given name)

—————— 2 ——————

5 左翼 **sayoku** left wing, leftist; left field (in baseball)

右翼 **uyoku** right wing, rightists; right flank

7 尾翼 **biyoku** tail (of an airplane)

—————————— 16 ——————————

叢 → 6e12.3

—————————— 18 ——————————

譱 → 善 2o10.2

厂 2p

厂	仄	反	厄	压	灰	辰	厚	版	厘	厖	叛	原
2p12.4	2.1	2.2	2.3	3.1	4.1	5.1	6.1	2j6.8	7.1	7.2	7.3	8.1

唇	辱	雁	農	厭	暦	歴	鴈	壓	贋
3d7.12	8.2	10.3	11.1	12.1	12.3	12.4	2p10.3	2p3.1	17.2

2

亻 冫 孑 阝 卩 刂 力 又 亠 十 亅 夂 丷 厂 辶 冂 几 匸

2

0

厂 → 歴 **2p12.4**

2

2p2.1　　　　　　　▢ 厂 亻
　　　　　　　　　　　18　3

仄仄

SOKU, honoka dim, faint, indistinct
hono(meku) be seen dimly
hono(mekasu) hint at, intimate

1

3 仄々 **honobono** dimly, faintly
13 仄暗 **honogura(i)** dim(ly lit)
14 仄聞 **sokubun** hear (by chance)

2p2.2 / 324　　　　　　▢ 厂 又
　　　　　　　　　　　18　9

反反

HAN, HON against, opposite, anti-
TAN (unit of cloth measurement, about
34 cm by 10.6 m), (unit of land area, 300
tsubo or about 992 square meters)
so(ru/rasu) (intr./tr.) warp, bend back

1

4 反日 **han-Nichi** anti-Japanese
5 反比例 **hanpirei** in inverse proportion to
6 反共 **hankyō** anticommunist
　反米 **han-Bei** anti-American
7 反作用 **hansayō** reaction
　反対 **hantai** opposition, against; opposite, reverse, contrary
　反対側 **hantaigawa** the opposite side

反対語 **hantaigo** antonym
反抗 **hankō** resistance, opposition, rebellion
反乱 **hanran** rebellion, revolt
反応 **hannō** reaction, response
反攻 **hankō** counteroffensive, counterattack
8 反逆 **hangyaku** treason, treachery, revolt
反物 **tanmono** dry/piece goods, textiles
9 反発 **hanpatsu** repel; rebound, recover; oppose
反革命 **hankakumei** counterrevolution
反面 **hanmen** the other side, on the other hand
反映 **han'ei** reflect, mirror
反省 **hansei** reflection, introspection; reconsideration
10 反射 **hansha** reflection, reflex
11 反動 **handō** reaction; recoil
反転 **hanten** turn/roll over, reverse directions, invert
12 反復 **hanpuku** repetition
13 反感 **hankan** antipathy, animosity
反戦 **hansen** antiwar
反意語 **han'igo** antonym
15 反論 **hanron** counterargument, refutation
19 反響 **hankyō** echo, reverberation; repercussions, reaction

---

2

5 正反対 **seihantai** the exact opposite
12 違反 **ihan** violation

3

9 連鎖反応 **rensa hannō** chain reaction

2p2.3 / 1341　　□ 厂 阝
18　7

厄

厄厄

YAKU misfortune, disaster

——— 1 ———

4 厄介 **yakkai** troublesome, burdensome; help, care

厄介者 **yakkaimono** a dependent; nuisance

厄日 **yakubi** unlucky/critical day

5 厄払 **yakubara(i)** exorcism

6 厄年 **yakudoshi** unlucky age, one's critical year

——— 3 ———

2p3.1 / 1342　　□ 土 厂
22　18

圧

壓 | 圧 圧

ATSU pressure　**o(su)** press, push

——— 1 ———

2 圧力 **atsuryoku** pressure

7 圧迫 **appaku** pressure, oppression, compulsion

10 圧倒的 **attōteki** overwhelming

——— 2 ———

6 血圧 **ketsuatsu** blood pressure

7 低圧 **teiatsu** low pressure/voltage

9 指圧 **shiatsu** finger pressure

13 電圧 **den'atsu** voltage

——— 3 ———

3 大気圧 **taikiatsu** atmospheric pressure

10 高気圧 **kōkiatsu** high atmospheric pressure

高血圧 **kōketsuatsu** high blood pressure

——— 4 ———

2p4.1 / 1343　　□ 火 厂
44　18

灰

灰灰

KAI, hai ash, ashes

——— 1 ———

5 灰皿 **haizara** ashtray

6 灰色 **hai-iro** gray

——— 5 ———

2p5.1 / 2246　　□ 衤 厂
57　18

辰

辰辰

SHIN, tatsu fifth horary sign (dragon)　SHIN, TATSU, TOKI, NOBU, YOSHI (part of given name)　NOBURU (m. given name)

——— 1 ———

4 辰夫 **Tatsuo, Tokio, Yoshio** (m. given name)

12 辰雄 **Tatsuo** (m. given name)

——— 6 ———

2p6.1 / 639　　□ 日 厂 子
43　18　6

厚

厚厚

KŌ, atsu(i) thick; kind, cordial　ATSUSHI (m. given name)　ATSU (part of given name)

——— 1 ———

0 厚かましい **atsu(kamashii)** shameless, brazen, impudent

4 厚化粧 **atsugeshō** heavy makeup

5 厚生省 **Kōseishō** Ministry of Health and Welfare

9 厚相 **kōshō** Welfare Minister

12 厚着 **atsugi** wearing thick/heavy clothing

13 厚意 **kōi** kindness, favor, courtesy

—— 2 ——

12 温厚 **onkō** gentle, courteous

版 → **2j6.8**

—— 7 ——

2p7.1 / 1900   厂 日 土 厂
                    43 22 18

厘

厘厘

RIN (old unit of currency, 1/1,000 yen), (unit of length, about 0.3 mm), (unit of weight, about 3.75 mg)

2p7.2   厂 犭 彡 厂
             27 31 18

厖

厖厖

BŌ large; mix

—— 1 ——

3 厖大 **bōdai** enormous, huge

2p7.3   厂 十 几 厂
             12 16 18

叛

叛叛

HAN, HON rebellion **somu(ku)** go against, disobey, rebel

—— 1 ——

7 叛乱 **hanran** rebellion, revolt
8 叛逆 **hangyaku** treason, treachery, revolt

—— 8 ——

2p8.1 / 136   厂 日 小 厂
                   43 35 18

原

原原

GEN original, fundamental; a plain **hara** field, plain; wilderness HARA (surname) MOTO (part of given name)

—— 1 ——

2 原子 **genshi** atom
  原子力 **genshiryoku** atomic energy, nuclear power
3 原寸大 **gensundai** actual size
  原口 **Haraguchi** (surname)
4 原文 **genbun** the text/original
5 原本 **genpon** the original (work/copy)
  原田 **Harada** (surname)
6 原色 **genshoku** primary color
  原因 **gen'in** cause
7 原作 **gensaku** the original work
  原状 **genjō** original state
  原告 **genkoku** plaintiff
8 原価 **genka** cost price, cost
  原油 **gen'yu** crude oil
  原始 **genshi** origin; primitive
  原始的 **genshiteki** primitive, primeval, original
9 原発 **genpatsu** (generating electricity from) nuclear power (short for 原子力発電)
  原点 **genten** starting point
  原型 **genkei** prototype, model
  原則 **gensoku** principle, general rule
10 原案 **gen'an** original proposal, draft
  原料 **genryō** raw materials
15 原稿 **genkō** manuscript
  原稿用紙 **genkō yōshi** manuscript paper
19 原爆 **genbaku** atomic bomb (short for 原子爆弾)

—— 2 ——

3 川原 **Kawahara** (surname)
4 中原 **Nakahara** (surname)
  井原 **Ihara** (surname)
  木原 **Kihara** (surname)
5 北原 **Kitahara** (surname)
  石原 **Ishihara** (surname)
  田原 **Tahara** (surname)
6 吉原 **Yoshiwara** (proper name); (a former red-light district in Tōkyō)
7 杉原 **Sugihara** (surname)
8 河原 **Kawahara** (surname)
  松原 **Matsubara** (surname)

9 草原 **sōgen** grassy plain, grasslands **kusahara** meadow, a green

柏原 **Kashiwabara** (surname)

10 桑原 **Kuwabara, Kuwahara** (surname)

高原 **kōgen** plateau, highlands

起原 **kigen** origin, beginning

11 野原 **nohara** field, plain

清原 **Kiyohara** (surname)

菅原 **Sugawara, Sugahara** (surname)

12 萩原 **Hagiwara** (surname)

14 榊原 **Sakakibara** (surname)

18 藤原 **Fujiwara** (surname)

— 3 —

3 小田原 **Odawara** (city, Kanagawa-ken)

辱→ **3d7.12**

2p8.2 / 1738   日 衤 寸 厂
57 37 18

辱辱

JOKU, hazukashi(meru) humiliate, disgrace **katajike(nai)** grateful

— 2 —

8 侮辱 **bujoku** insult

屈辱 **kutsujoku** humiliation, indignity

国辱 **kokujoku** national disgrace

10 凌辱 **ryōjoku** insult, affront; rape

恥辱 **chijoku** disgrace, humiliation

— 10 —

2p10.3   囗 隹 厂 亻
74 18 3

鴈|雁雁

GAN, kari, karigane wild goose

— 11 —

2p11.1 / 369   日 衤 日 儿
57 43 16

農農

NŌ agriculture, farming **ATSU** (part of given name)

— 1 —

4 農夫 **nōfu** farmer, farmhand

5 農民 **nōmin** peasants, farmers

7 農作 **nōsaku** cultivation, tillage, farming

農学 **nōgaku** (the science of) agriculture

農村 **nōson** farm village, rural community

8 農協 **nōkyō** agricultural cooperative, co-op (short for 農業共同組合)

農林水産省 **Nōrinsuisanshō** Ministry of Agriculture, Forestry and Fisheries

9 農相 **nōshō** Agriculture (, Forestry and Fisheries) Minister

10 農家 **nōka** farmhouse; farm household; farmer

11 農産物 **nōsanbutsu** agricultural products

12 農場 **nōjō** farm, ranch, plantation

農閑期 **nōkanki** farmers' slack season

13 農業 **nōgyō** agriculture

16 農薬 **nōyaku** agricultural chemicals

— 2 —

3 大農 **dainō** large-scale farming; wealthy farmer

士農工商 **shinōkōshō** samurai-farmers-artisans-merchants, the military, agricultural, industrial, and mercantile classes

13 酪農 **rakunō** dairy farming

12

2p12.1   日 月 犭
            43 42 27

厭 厭

EN, YŌ, a(kiru) get tired of, get fed up with **ito(u)** dislike, hate; be unwilling; grudge (effort), spare (pains); take (good) care of **i(ya)** disagreeable, detestable, hated, unwelcome

—————— 1 ——————

² 厭人 **enjin** misanthropy

⁵ 厭世 **ensei** weariness with life, pessimism

2p12.3 / 1534   木 日 厂
            41 43 18

暦 | 暦 暦

REKI, RYAKU, koyomi calendar

—————— 1 ——————

⁶ 暦年 **rekinen** calendar (not fiscal) year; time

—————— 2 ——————

⁵ 旧暦 **kyūreki** the old (lunar) calendar

⁶ 西暦 **seireki** Christian Era, A.D.

¹⁰ 陰暦 **inreki** the lunar calendar

¹⁵ 還暦 **kanreki** one's 60th birthday

2p12.4 / 480   木 厂 丄
            41 18 13

歴 | 歴 歴

REKI continuation, passage of time; successive; clear **he(ru)** pass, elapse

—————— 1 ——————

⁵ 歴史 **rekishi** history

  歴代 **rekidai** successive generations

¹² 歴然 **rekizen** clear, unmistakable

—————— 2 ——————

⁷ 学歴 **gakureki** one's academic background

¹¹ 遍歴 **henreki** travels, pilgrimage

  略歴 **ryakureki** brief personal history, résumé

  経歴 **keireki** personal history, career

¹⁵ 履歴書 **rirekisho** personal history, vita

—————— 13 ——————

鴈→雁 **2p10.3**

—————— 15 ——————

壓→圧 **2p3.1**

—————— 17 ——————

2p17.2   隹 貝 厂
            74 68 18

贋 贋

GAN counterfeit **nise** fake, counterfeit, forgery, imitation, false

—————— 1 ——————

⁵ 贋札 **nisesatsu, gansatsu** counterfeit currency

⁸ 贋物 **ganbutsu, nisemono** imitation, counterfeit, forgery

⁹ 贋造 **ganzō** counterfeiting, forgery, fabrication

———————————— 辶 **2q** ————————————

辺   辻   込   辿   迂   巡   迄   迅   廷   近   迎   返   廸

2.1   2.2   2.3   3.1   3.2   3.3   3.4   3.5   4.2   4.3   4.4   4.5   2q5.1

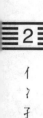

迪	迭	述	延	迫	迦	迯	迷	建	退	追	逃	逆
5.1	5.2	5.3	5.4	5.5	5.6	2q6.5	6.1	6.2	6.3	6.4	6.5	6.8

送	這	連	速	逓	逐	逝	透	造	逢	途	通	逗
6.9	7.1	7.2	7.4	7.5	7.6	7.8	7.10	7.11	7.15	7.16	7.18	7.19

進	逮	遊	達	逸	週	遇	遜	遙	達	運	遂	道
8.1	8.2	8.3	2q9.8	8.6	8.7	9.1	9.4	2q10.3	9.8	9.10	9.13	9.14

遍	遅	過	遣	遙	遠	違	遞	遭	適	遮	遷	選
9.16	9.17	9.18	10.2	10.3	10.4	10.5	2q7.5	11.2	11.3	11.4	12.1	12.3

遺	遼	遵	遲	導	避	還	邊					
12.4	12.5	12.8	2q9.17	5c9.3	13.3	13.4	2q2.1					

2

2q2.1 / 775

□ 辶 力
19 8

辺

邊 | 辺 辺

HEN side; boundary, border; vicinity
ata(ri), hoto(ri), -be vicinity

— 1 —

6 辺地 **henchi** remote/out-of-the-way place

13 辺鄙 **henpi** remote, secluded

14 辺境 **henkyō** frontier, outlying region

— 2 —

3 川辺 **kawabe** riverside

上辺 **uwabe** exterior, surface, outside; outward appearance

5 左辺 **sahen** left side

田辺 **Tanabe** (surname)

6 近辺 **kinpen** neighborhood, vicinity

8 周辺 **shūhen** periphery, environs, outskirts

9 海辺 **umibe** seashore, beach

10 浜辺 **hamabe** beach, seashore

12 渡辺 **Watanabe** (surname)

無辺 **muhen** limitless, boundless, infinite

17 磯辺 **isobe** (rocky) beach, seashore

2q2.2

□ 辶 十
19 12

辻

辻 | 辻 辻

tsuji crossroad, intersection, street corner, roadside TSUJI (surname)

— 1 —

5 辻本 **Tsujimoto** (surname)

13 辻褄 **tsujitsuma** coherence, consistency

2q2.3 / 776

□ 辶 亻
19 3

込

込 | 込 込

ko(mu) be crowded, be included; (as verb suffix) in, into **-ko(mi)** including, inclusive of **ko(meru)** include; load (a gun); concentrate, devote oneself to

— 1 —

2 込入 **ko(mi)i(ru)** be complicated

6 込合 **ko(mi)a(u)** be crowded

— 2 —

2 人込 **hitogo(mi)** crowd of people

4 引込 **hi(ki)ko(mu)** bring around, win over **hi(k)ko(mu)** draw back, retire; sink, cave in; stand back; disappear

5 包込 **tsutsu(mi)ko(mu)** wrap up

申込 **mō(shi)ko(mu)** propose, file, apply for, book

仕込 **shiko(mu)** train, bring up; fit into; stock up on

叩込 **tata(ki)ko(mu)** drive/throw into; hammer in, inculcate

立込 **ta(chi)ko(mu)** be crowded
ta(chi)ko(meru) hang over, envelop

6 老込 **o(i)ko(mu)** grow old, become decrepit/senile

吸込 **su(i)ko(mu)** inhale; suck in; swallow up

7 吹込 **fu(ki)ko(mu)** blow in; record (a song); inspire

呑込 **no(mi)ko(mu)** swallow; understand

見込 **miko(mi)** prospects, promise, hope, possibility

8 使込 **tsuka(i)ko(mu)** embezzle; accustom oneself to using

追込 **o(i)ko(mu)** corner, drive into; strike inward (a disease); make an extra effort at the end; run on (a line of print)

突込 **tsu(ki)ko(mu)**, **tsu(k)ko(mu)** thrust/poke/plunge into

9 飛込自殺 **tobiko(mi) jisatsu** suicide by jumping in front of an oncoming train

巻込 **ma(ki)ko(mu)** roll up, enfold; entangle, drag into, involve in

染込 **shi(mi)ko(mu)** soak into, permeate; be instilled with
so(me)ko(mu) dye in

思込 **omo(i)ko(mu)** have the idea that, be convinced that; set one's heart on

10 差込 **sa(shi)ko(mu)** insert, plug in

座込 **suwa(ri)ko(mu)** sit down, stage a sit-in

書込 **ka(ki)ko(mu)** write/fill in, enter

11 閉込 **to(ji)ko(meru)** shut in, confine

12 割込 **wa(ri)ko(mu)** wedge oneself in, cut/butt in **wariko(mi)** an interrupt (in computers)

落込 **o(chi)ko(mu)** fall/sink/cave in, (prices) decline

嵌込 **ha(me)ko(mu)** fit into, insert, inlay

覗込 **nozo(ki)ko(mu)** look/peek/peer into

税込 **zeiko(mi)** including tax

買込 **ka(i)ko(mu)** buy, stock up on

13 寝込 **neko(mu)** fall asleep; oversleep; be sick in bed

詰込 **tsu(me)ko(mu)** cram, stuff, pack in

14 駆込 **ka(ke)ko(mu)** rush into, seek refuge in

15 舞込 **ma(i)ko(mu)** drop in, visit; befall

黙込 **dama(ri)ko(mu)** fall silent, say no more

踏込 **fu(mi)ko(mu)** step/rush into

16 積込 **tsu(mi)ko(mu)** load, take on (board)

頼込 **tano(mi)ko(mu)** earnestly request

18 織込 **o(ri)ko(mu)** weave into

19 繰込 **ku(ri)ko(mu)** stream into; count in, round up

29 鬱込 **fusa(gi)ko(mu)** be depressed, feel low, mope

——————— 3 ———————

2q3.1

口 艹 辶
36 19

辿 | 辿 辿

TEN, tado(ru) walk along, follow (a course), trace, follow up

——————— 1 ———————

12 辿着 **tado(ri)tsu(ku)** make it to, grope/trudge along to

2q3.2

口 辶 一
19 14 1

迂 | 迂 迂

U roundabout; unrealistic

——————— 1 ———————

6 迂回 **ukai** detour

17 迂闊 **ukatsu** careless, stupid

2q3.3 / 777

□ 辶 丨
19 2

巡　巡巡

JUN, megu(ru) go around
megu(rasu) surround

――― 1 ―――

0 お巡りさん **(o)mawa(ri-san)** policeman
5 巡礼 **junrei** pilgrimage; pilgrim
6 巡合 **megu(ri)a(u)** chance to meet
巡回 **junkai** tour, patrol, one's
rounds
9 巡査 **junsa** patrolman, cop
11 巡視 **junshi** inspection tour, patrol
13 巡業 **jungyō** tour (of a troupe/team)
14 巡察 **junsatsu** patrol, one's rounds
17 巡覧 **junran** tour, sightseeing

――― 2 ―――

1 一巡 **hitomegu(ri)** a turn/round;
one full year **ichijun** a round/
patrol

2q3.4

□ 辶 ⸍ 一
19 15 1

迄 | 迄迄

KITSU, made until, up to, as far as, to
the extent of

2q3.5 / 1798

□ 辶 ⼗ 一
19 12 1

迅　迅迅

JIN fast

――― 1 ―――

9 迅速 **jinsoku** quick, prompt,
speedy

2q4.2 / 1111

□ 王 辶
46 19

廷　廷廷

TEI imperial court; law court

――― 1 ―――

4 廷内 **teinai** in the court

――― 2 ―――

5 出廷 **shuttei** appear in court
8 法廷 **hōtei** (law) court, courtroom
10 宮廷 **kyūtei** the court/place

2q4.3 / 445

□ 斤 辶
50 19

近　近近

KIN, chika(i) near CHIKA (part of
given name)

――― 1 ―――

0 近づく **chika(zuku)** come/go near,
approach
3 近々 **chikajika, kinkin** before
long
4 近辺 **kinpen** neighborhood, vicinity
近日 **kinjitsu** soon, in a few days
5 近世 **kinsei** recent times, modern
age; (era, 1568 – 1868)
近世史 **kinseishi** modern history
近代 **kindai** modern
近代的 **kindaiteki** modern
近付 **chikazu(ku)** come/go near,
approach **chikazu(ki)** acquaintance
6 近年 **kinnen** in recent years
8 近東 **Kintō** the Near East
近郊 **kinkō** suburbs
近況 **kinkyō** recent situation,
present state
近所 **kinjo** neighborhood, vicinity
9 近海 **kinkai** coastal waters, adjoining seas
11 近道 **chikamichi** short cut

近接 **kinsetsu** neighboring, contiguous, close-by

近寄 **chikayo(ru)** go/come near, approach

近視 **kinshi** nearsightedness

近眼 **kingan, chikame** nearsighted; shortsighted

近頃 **chikagoro** recently, nowadays

12 近距離 **kinkyori** short distance/range

15 近畿 **Kinki** the Ōsaka-Kyōto area

18 近藤 **Kondō** (surname)

———————— 2 ————————

4 中近東 **Chūkintō** the Near and Middle East

5 付近 **fukin** vicinity, neighborhood

7 身近 **mijika** familiar, close to one

11 側近者 **sokkinsha** close associate

接近 **sekkin** approach, draw near

12 遠近法 **enkinhō** (law of) perspective

最近 **saikin** recently; latest, newest

間近 **majika** nearby, close, affecting one personally

2q4.4 / 1055

口 辶 厂 阝
19 18 7

迎 迎

GEI, muka(eru) go to meet, receive, greet, invite, send for

———————— 1 ————————

6 迎合 **geigō** flattery, ingratiation

9 迎春 **geishun** welcoming the new year

15 迎賓館 **geihinkan** reception hall, residence for guests

———————— 2 ————————

5 出迎 **demuka(eru)** (go/come to) meet (someone upon his arrival)

15 歓迎 **kangei** welcome

2q4.5 / 442

口 辶 厂 又
19 18 9

返

返 返

HEN, kae(su) (tr.) return **kae(ru)** (intr.) return

———————— 1 ————————

5 返礼 **henrei** return gift, in return for

7 返却 **henkyaku** return, repayment

8 返事 **henji** reply

返送 **hensō** send back, return

9 返信 **henshin** reply

返咲 **kae(ri)za(ki)** second blooming; comeback

返品 **henpin** returned goods, returns

11 返済 **hensai** repayment

12 返答 **hentō** reply

15 返還 **henkan** return; repayment

———————— 2 ————————

2 二返事 **futa(tsu)henji** immediate reply, readily, most willingly

5 生返 **i(ki)kae(ru)** revive, be resuscitated

生返事 **namahenji** vague answer

仕返 **shikae(shi)** get even, give tit for tat; do over again

7 折返 **o(ri)kae(su)** fold back; double back **o(ri)kae(shi)** immediate (reply)

見返 **mikae(ru)** look back at **mikae(shi)** inside the cover

8 追返 **o(i)kae(su)** repulse, drive back, turn away

若返 **wakagae(ru)** be rejuvenated

宙返 **chūgae(ri)** somersault

取返 **to(ri)kae(su)** get back, regain, recover, recoup, catch up on **to(tte)kae(su)** hurry/double back

9 祝返 **iwa(i)gae(shi)** return gift

10 振返 **fu(ri)kae(ru)** turn one's head, look back

恩返 **ongae(shi)** repayment of a favor

12 蒸返 **mu(shi)kae(su)** reheat; repeat, rehash

13 裏返 **uragae(su)** turn the other way, turn inside out, turn over
uragae(shi) inside out, upside down **uragae(ru)** be turned inside out; turn against (someone)

跳返 **ha(ne)kae(su)** bounce back, repel

14 読返 **yo(mi)kae(su)** reread
聞返 **ki(ki)kae(su)** ask back

19 繰返 **ku(ri)kae(su)** repeat

———— 3 ————

4 引繰返 **hi(k)ku(ri)kae(ru)** be overturned, capsize, collapse; be reversed
hi(k)ku(ri)kae(su) overturn, turn upside down, turn inside out

———— 4 ————

18 覆水盆返 **fukusui bon (ni) kae(razu)** No use crying over spilt milk.

———— 5 ————

 廸 → 迪 **2q5.1**

2q5.1 / 2247   口 日 辶 丨
             43 19 2

迪 迪|廸迪

TEKI, michi path, way **michibi(ku)** guide, lead **susu(mu)** proceed, advance **ita(ru)** reach, arrive SUSUMU, TADASU, TADASHI (m. given name) TEKI, MICHI, HIRA, TADA, FUMI (part of given name)

2q5.2 / 1507   口 大 辶 ㇓
             34 19 15

 迭 迭迭

TETSU alternate

———— 2 ————

7 更迭 **kōtetsu** change, reshuffle, shake-up

2q5.3 / 968   口 木 辶 丨
             41 19 2

述 述述

JUTSU, no(beru) state, mention, refer to, explain NOBU (part of given name)

———— 1 ————

14 述語 **jutsugo** predicate

———— 2 ————

3 上述 **jōjutsu** the above-mentioned
口述 **kōjutsu** oral statement, dictation

9 叙述 **jojutsu** description, narration

10 陳述書 **chinjutsusho** statement, declaration
記述 **kijutsu** description, account

13 詳述 **shōjutsu** detailed explanation, full account

2q5.4 / 1115   口 辶 上 亠
           19 13 11

延 延延

EN stretch **no(basu)** (tr.) stretch, lengthen, extend, prolong, postpone
no(beru) (tr.) lengthen, extend
no(biru) (intr.) stretch, extend, grow, be prolonged/delayed/postponed
no(be) total, aggregate; futures transaction NOBU (part of given name)

———— 1 ————

3 延々 **en'en** repeatedly postponed, protracted, interminable

8 延長 **enchō** extension, continuation, prolongation, elongation

12 延期 **enki** postpone, defer, prolong

———— 2 ————

4 日延 **hino(be)** postponement

11 遅延 **chien** delay

19 繰延 **ku(ri)no(be)** postponement, deferment

2q5.5 / 1175

囗 日 辶 丨
43　19　2

迫　迫 迫

HAKU, sema(ru) press (someone)
for, urge; approach, draw near

――――――― 1 ―――――――

2　迫力 **hakuryoku** (dramatic) force,
intensity, appeal
10　迫害 **hakugai** persecution

――――――― 2 ―――――――

4　切迫 **seppaku** draw near, impend,
be imminent; become acute,
grow tense
5　圧迫 **appaku** pressure, oppression,
compulsion
9　急迫 **kyūhaku** be imminent/press-
ing, grow acute
10　脅迫 **kyōhaku** threat, intimidation
15　窮迫 **kyūhaku** financial distress,
poverty
　　緊迫 **kinpaku** tension

2q5.6

囗 日 辶 力
24　19　8

迦　迦丨迦 迦

KA (used phonetically)

――――――― 2 ―――――――

11　釈迦 **Shaka** Gautama, Buddha

辿 → 逃 **2q6.5**

――――――― 6 ―――――――

2q6.1 / 967

囗 米 辶
62　19

迷　迷 迷

MEI, mayo(u) go astray, get lost, be
perplexed **mayo(i)** perplexity, doubt,
delusion **mayo(wasu)** perplex; lead
astray; charm, seduce

――――――― 1 ―――――――

2　迷子 **maigo, mayo(i)go** lost child
9　迷信 **meishin** superstition
10　迷宮 **meikyū** maze, labyrinth
11　迷彩 **meisai** camouflage
12　迷惑 **meiwaku** trouble, annoyance,
inconvenience
13　迷想 **meisō** illusion, fallacy
　　迷路 **meiro** maze, labyrinth

――――――― 2 ―――――――

6　気迷 **kimayo(i)** hesitation, wavering
7　低迷 **teimei** hang low, be sluggish
8　昏迷 **konmei** be stupefied/bewil-
dered

2q6.2 / 892

囗 ヨ 辶 聿
39　19　12

建　建 建

KEN, KON, ta(teru) build **ta(tsu)**
be built **-da(te)** built in the form of
(two stories); (yen)-denominated
(loan) TAKE, TATE (part of given
name)

――――――― 1 ―――――――

5　建立 **konryū** erection, building
8　建国 **kenkoku** founding of a country
　　建物 **tatemono** a building
9　建前 **ta(te)mae** principle, official
position; erection of the framework
　　建造物 **kenzōbutsu** a building,
structure
11　建設 **kensetsu** construction
　　建設省 **Kensetsushō** Ministry of
Construction
12　建替 **ta(te)ka(e)** rebuilding, reconstruction
16　建築 **kenchiku** building, construction, architecture
　　建築家 **kenchikuka** architect,
building contractor
20　建議 **kengi** proposal

2

亻
冫
孑
阝
卩
刂
力
又
亠
宀
艹
宀
厂
辶
冂
几
匸

6

─────── 2 ───────

6 再建 **saiken** reconstruction, rebuilding

9 封建 **hōken** feudalism

─────── 3 ───────

2 二階建 **nikaida(te)** two-story

2q6.3 / 846

退 退

TAI, shirizo(ku) retreat
shirizo(keru) drive away, repel
no(ku), do(ku) get out of the way, go
away **no(keru), do(keru)** get rid of,
remove **hi(ku)** retreat; subside

─────── 1 ───────

5 退去 **taikyo** leave, withdraw, evacuate

7 退却 **taikyaku** retreat

退学 **taigaku** leave school, drop out

8 退治 **taiji** subjugation; extermination, (pest) control

退歩 **taiho** retrogress, backward
step; degeneration

退屈 **taikutsu** boring, dull

9 退院 **taiin** leave the hospital

12 退場 **taijō** leave, exit, walk out

18 退職 **taishoku** retirement

─────── 2 ───────

4 中退 **chūtai** leaving school before
graduation, dropping out

引退 **intai** retire

6 早退 **sōtai** leave early

9 後退 **kōtai** retreat, back up
atozusa(ri) move/shrink/hold
back

10 衰退 **suitai** decline, degeneration

進退 **shintai** advance or retreat,
movement; course of action, attitude; resigning or staying on

11 脱退 **dattai** secede, withdraw

2q6.4 / 1174

40 19 20

追 追

TSUI, o(u) pursue, chase after; drive
(cattle); shoo away (flies) **o(tte)** later
on, afterward

─────── 1 ───────

4 追込 **o(i)ko(mu)** corner, drive into;
strike inward (a disease); make
an extra effort at the end; run on
(a line of print)

5 追出 **o(i)da(su)** chase/turn away,
kick out, eject

追付 **o(i)tsu(ku)** catch up with

追加 **tsuika** addition, supplement

6 追返 **o(i)kae(su)** repulse, drive
back, turn away

7 追伸 **tsuishin** postscript, P.S.

追求 **tsuikyū, o(i)moto(meru)** pursue

追究 **tsuikyū** pursuit, inquiry

8 追突 **tsuitotsu** rear-end collision

追放 **tsuihō** banishment; purge

9 追風 **o(i)kaze, o(i)te** tailwind

10 追従 **tsuijū** follow, imitate; be servile to **tsuishō** flattery, bootlicking

追記 **tsuiki** postscript, P.S.

11 追掛 **o(i)ka(keru)** chase, run after

追悼 **tsuitō** mourning; memorial
(address)

12 追越 **o(i)ko(su)** overtake

13 追想 **tsuisō** recollection, reminiscences

追詰 **o(i)tsu(meru)** corner, drive to
the wall, hunt down

追跡 **tsuiseki** pursue, track, stalk

2q6.5 / 1566

19 5 16

逃 | 逃 逃

TŌ, ni(geru) flee, run away, escape
noga(reru) escape **ni(gasu),
no(gasu)** let go/escape, set free

³ 逃亡 **tōbō** escape, flight, desertion
⁷ 逃走 **tōsō** flight, escape, desertion
ni(ge)hashi(ru) run away
¹¹ 逃道 **ni(ge)michi** way of escape, way out
¹⁵ 逃避 **tōhi** escape, flight, evasion

—————— 2 ——————

⁷ 見逃 **minoga(su)** overlook
⁸ 夜逃 **yoni(ge)** fly by night, give (creditors) the slip
　　取逃 **to(ri)ni(gasu)** fail to catch, miss
²² 轢逃 **hi(ki)ni(ge)** hit-and-run

2q6.8 / 444

 辶 儿 丆
19　16　14

逆 逆逆

GYAKU, GEKI reverse, inverse, opposite; treason **saka-** reverse, inverse **saka(rau)** be contrary to

—————— 1 ——————

⁰ 逆さ/しま **saka(sa/shima)** reverse, inverted, upside down
⁵ 逆立 **sakada(chi)** handstand, standing on one's head
sakada(tsu) stand on end
sakada(teru) set on end, bristle/ruffle up
⁶ 逆行 **gyakkō** go back, move backward, run counter to
⁷ 逆作用 **gyakusayō** adverse effect, reaction
⁸ 逆効果 **gyakukōka** opposite effect, counterproductive
⁹ 逆風 **gyakufū** adverse wind, headwind
¹⁴ 逆様 **sakasama** upside-down, reverse, backwards
　　逆説 **gyakusetsu** paradox

—————— 2 ——————

⁴ 反逆 **hangyaku** treason, treachery, revolt
⁹ 叛逆 **hangyaku** treason, treachery, revolt

2q6.9 / 441

 大 辶 儿
34　19　16

送 送送

SŌ, oku(ru) send

—————— 1 ——————

⁵ 送付 **sōfu** send, forward, remit
⁶ 送仮名 **oku(ri)gana** suffixed kana showing inflection
　　送先 **oku(ri)saki** destination, consignee
⁷ 送別会 **sōbetsukai** going-away/ farewell party
⁸ 送金 **sōkin** remittance
⁹ 送信 **sōshin** transmission of a message
¹⁰ 送料 **sōryō** shipping charges, postage
¹¹ 送達 **sōtatsu** convey, deliver, dispatch

—————— 2 ——————

⁶ 伝送 **densō** transmit, relay
　　返送 **hensō** send back, return
　　回送 **kaisō** forwarding, transportation; (bus) returning to the barn, Out of Service
⁷ 見送 **mioku(ru)** see (someone) off, watch till out of sight
⁸ 油送船 **yusōsen** oil tanker
　　放送 **hōsō** broadcast
　　放送局 **hōsōkyoku** broadcasting station
⁹ 発送 **hassō** send, ship, forward
¹⁰ 郵送料 **yūsōryō** postage
¹¹ 運送 **unsō** transport, conveyance, shipping
　　運送会社 **unsō-gaisha** transport/ express company
　　転送 **tensō** transmit, forward (mail)
¹³ 電送 **densō** electrical transmission
¹⁵ 歓送会 **kansōkai** farewell party, send-off
¹⁶ 輸送 **yusō** transport
　　輸送費 **yusōhi** shipping costs

—————— 3 ——————

⁵ 生放送 **namahōsō** live broadcast
⁶ 再放送 **saihōsō** rebroadcast

─────── 7 ───────

2q7.1   口 言 辶
               67 19

這 | 這這

SHA, ha(u) crawl, creep

─────── 1 ───────

³ 這上 **ha(i)a(garu)** crawl up
⁵ 這出 **ha(i)de(ru), ha(i)da(su)** crawl out

─────── 2 ───────

¹⁵ 横這 **yokoba(i)** sidle; level off

2q7.2 / 440   口 車 辶
               69 19

連 連

REN group, accompaniment
tsu(reru) take (someone) along
tsu(re) companion **(ni) tsu(rete)** as, along with, in proportion to
tsura(naru) stand in a row
tsura(neru) link, put in a row
MURAJI (m. given name)

─────── 1 ───────

⁰ ソ連 **Soren** Soviet Union
⁴ 連中 **renchū, renjū** companions, party, company, crowd, clique
   連日 **renjitsu** day after day, every day
⁵ 連用形 **ren'yōkei** stem (of a verb)
⁶ 連休 **renkyū** consecutive holidays
   連合 **rengō** union, league, federation, alliance, combination
   tsu(re)a(i) spouse, mate
   連邦 **renpō** federation; federal
⁷ 連体形 **rentaikei** a participial adjective
⁹ 連発 **renpatsu** fire/shoot in rapid succession
¹⁰ 連帯 **rentai** solidarity; joint (liability)
¹¹ 連敗 **renpai** successive defeats, losing streak

¹² 連結 **renketsu** coupling, connection; consolidated
   連絡 **renraku** contact, liaison, communication; get/be in touch
   連絡船 **renrakusen** ferryboat
¹³ 連想 **rensō** association (of ideas)
   連盟 **renmei** league, federation, union
   連続 **renzoku** continuous, consecutive, in a row
   連載 **rensai** serialization
¹⁸ 連鎖反応 **rensa hannō** chain reaction
¹⁹ 連覇 **renpa** successive championships

─────── 2 ───────

⁸ 国連 **Kokuren** United Nations, UN (short for 国際連合)
   国連総会 **Kokuren Sōkai** UN General Assembly
¹¹ 道連 **michizu(re)** traveling companion
¹³ 愚連隊 **gurentai** hooligans, street gang
¹⁴ 関連 **kanren** connection, relation, association

─────── 3 ───────

² 二人連 **futarizu(re)** a party of two, couple
⁸ 国際連合 **Kokusai Rengō** United Nations
¹⁰ 家族連 **kazokuzu(re)** taking the family along
¹¹ 経団連 **Keidanren** Federation of Economic Organizations (Keidanren) (short for 経済団体連合)

2q7.4 / 502   口 束 口 辶
               41 24 19

速 速

SOKU, haya(i) fast **haya(meru)** quicken, accelerate **sumi(yaka)** speedy, prompt HAYA (part of given name)

─────── 1 ───────

² 速力 **sokuryoku** speed, velocity

9 速度 **sokudo** speed, velocity

速度計 **sokudokei** speedometer

10 速記 **sokki** shorthand

11 速達 **sokutatsu** special/express delivery

12 速報 **sokuhō** bulletin, news flash

――――― 2 ―――――

5 加速度 **kasokudo** acceleration

迅速 **jinsoku** quick, prompt, speedy

6 早速 **sassoku** at once, getting right to the point

7 快速 **kaisoku** high-speed; express (train)

8 拙速 **sessoku** not elaborate but fast, rough-and-ready

9 急速 **kyūsoku** prompt, swift, fast, speedy

10 高速 **kōsoku** high-speed; expressway

時速 **jisoku** speed per hour

敏速 **binsoku** promptness, alacrity

12 減速 **gensoku** speed reduction, deceleration

――――― 3 ―――――

12 超音速 **chōonsoku** supersonic speed

2q7.5 / 1937

口 巾 辶 厂
26 19 18

遞 | 逓 逓

TEI successive; relay, send

――――― 1 ―――――

9 逓信 **teishin** communications

12 逓減 **teigen** successive diminution

2q7.6 / 1134

口 豕 辶 ヒ
27 19 10

逐 逐

CHIKU drive away; one by one, one after another **o(u)** drive away, pursue, follow

――――― 1 ―――――

1 逐一 **chikuichi** one by one, in detail

6 逐次 **chikuji** one by one, in sequence

14 逐語的 **chikugoteki** word for word, literal

逐語訳 **chikugoyaku** word-for-word/literal translation

――――― 2 ―――――

14 駆逐 **kuchiku** drive away, expel, get rid of

2q7.8 / 1396

口 斤 辶
50 23 19

逝 | 逝 逝

SEI, yu(ku) die

――――― 1 ―――――

5 逝去 **seikyo** death

2q7.10 / 1685

口 禾 辶 力
56 19 8

透 透

TŌ, su(keru) shine through **su(ku)** be transparent; leave a gap **su(kasu)** look through; leave a space **su(kashi)** watermark; openwork; transparent **su(kasazu)** without delay/hesitation **tō(ru)** shine through, permeate, penetrate **tō(su)** let (light) through **TŌRU** (m. given name)

――――― 1 ―――――

8 透明 **tōmei** transparent

11 透視 **tōshi** see through; fluoroscopy; clairvoyance

12 透間 **su(ki)ma** crevice, gap, opening, space

――――― 2 ―――――

10 浸透 **shintō** permeation, infiltration, osmosis

造

造 造

ZŌ, tsuku(ru) make, produce, build

——————— 1 ———————

3 造上 **tsuku(ri)a(geru)** make, build up, complete

7 造作 **zōsaku** house fixtures; facial features **zōsa** trouble, difficulty **zōsa(nai)** easy, simple

8 造林 **zōrin** (re)forestation

11 造船 **zōsen** shipbuilding

13 造園 **zōen** landscape gardening

14 造語 **zōgo** coined word

15 造幣局 **zōheikyoku** the mint

——————— 2 ———————

2 人造 **jinzō** artificial, synthetic, imitation

8 建造物 **kenzōbutsu** a building, structure

9 変造 **henzō** alter, deface, falsify, forge

10 酒造 **shuzō** brewing, distilling

荷造 **nizuku(ri)** packing

11 偽造 **gizō** forgery

12 創造 **sōzō** creation

創造力 **sōzōryoku** creative power

13 塑造 **sozō** modeling, molding, plastic (arts)

14 構造 **kōzō** structure, construction

模造 **mozō** imitation

製造 **seizō** manufacture

15 鋳造 **chūzō** casting; minting, coinage

19 贋造 **ganzō** counterfeiting, forgery, fabrication

20 醸造 **jōzō** brewing, distilling

醸造所 **jōzōsho** brewery, distillery

逢

逢 逢

HŌ, a(u) meet

——————— 1 ———————

4 逢引 **a(i)bi(ki)** rendezvous, assignation, tryst

途

途 | 途 途

TO way, road

——————— 1 ———————

4 途中 **tochū** on the way, en route

途中下車 **tochū gesha** stopover, layover

途方暮 **tohō (ni) ku(reru)** be at a loss, not know what to do

12 途絶 **toda(eru)** come to a stop **tozetsu** suspension, interruption

14 途端 **totan** the (very) moment/minute, just when

——————— 2 ———————

1 一途 **ichizu** wholeheartedly **itto** way, course; the only way

4 中途半端 **chūto-hanpa** half finished, incomplete

5 用途 **yōto** use, purpose

8 長途 **chōto** a long way/distance

9 前途 **zento** the road ahead, one's future prospects

10 帰途 **kito** homeward journey

冥途 **meido** hades, realm of the dead

——————— 3 ———————

9 発展途上国 **hattentojōkoku** developing country

2q7.18 / 150

口　月　辶　一
42　19　1

通

通　通

TSŪ, TSU go through, pass; in common; (as suffix) thorough knowledge of, an expert; (counter for letters/copies)　**tō(ru)** go through, pass　**tō(ri)** street; way, manner　**-dō(ri)** street; as per, as, in accordance with, according to　**tō(su)** let through　**kayo(u)** go to and from, commute　MICHI (part of given name)

1

0　通じる　**tsū(jiru** pass, run, lead to; be well versed in; be understood, make oneself understood, get through

1　通一遍　**tō(ri)-ippen** passing, casual, perfunctory

5　通用　**tsūyō** be in common use, be honored/valid, pass

6　通気　**tsūki** ventilation

　通合　**tō(ri)a(waseru)** happen to come along　**tsū(ji)a(u)** plot together

　通行　**tsūkō** passing, passage, transit, traffic　**tō(ri)yu(ku)** pass by

　通行止　**tsūkōdo(me)** Road Closed, No Thoroughfare

7　通告　**tsūkoku** notification, notice

　通学　**tsūgaku** attending school

8　通知　**tsūchi** notification, notice

9　通信　**tsūshin** (tele)communications, correspondence, message, news, dispatch, report

　通俗　**tsūzoku** popular, conventional

11　通道　**tō(ri)michi** pasage, path, route, one's way to

　通帳　**tsūchō, kayo(i)chō** bankbook; chit book

　通常　**tsūjō** normal(ly), general(ly), ordinary, regular

　通産省　**Tsūsanshō** MITI, Ministry of International Trade and Industry (short for 通商産業省)

　通訳　**tsūyaku** interpreting; interpreter

　通販　**tsūhan** mail order (short for 通信販売)

　通貨　**tsūka** currency

12　通勤　**tsūkin** commute to work

　通報　**tsūhō** report, dispatch, bulletin, news

　通番号　**tō(shi)bangō** serial number

13　通話　**tsūwa** telephone call/conversation

　通路　**tsūro** aisle, passageway, path　**kayo(i)ji** path, route

---
2

1　一通　**hitotō(ri)** in general, briefly　**ittsū** one copy (of a document)

2　人通　**hitodō(ri)** pedestrian traffic

3　大通　**ōdō(ri)** a main street, thoroughfare

4　元通　**motodō(ri)** as before

　文通　**buntsū** correspondence

5　本通　**hondō(ri)** main street, boulevard

6　交通　**kōtsū** traffic, transport, communication

　共通　**kyōtsū** in common, shared

7　見通　**mitō(shi)** prospects, outlook, forecast; unobstructed view

8　直通　**chokutsū** direct communication, nonstop service

　押通　**o(shi)tō(su)** push through, accomplish

9　風通　**kazetō(shi)** ventilation

　姦通　**kantsū** adultery

　思通　**omo(i)dō(ri)** as one likes, to one's satisfaction

　食通　**shokutsū** gourmet

10　流通　**ryūtsū** distribution, circulation

11　疎通　**sotsū** mutual understanding

　望通　**nozo(mi)dō(ri)** as desired

　貫通　**kantsū** pass through, pierce　**tsuranu(ki)tō(su)** carry out (one's will)

12　普通　**futsū** ordinary, common, usual

　勝通　**ka(chi)tō(su)** win successive victories

13　裏通　**uradō(ri)** alley, side street

14　読通　**yo(mi)tō(su)** read it through

¹⁶ 融通 **yūzū** accommodation, loan; versatility

— 3 —

¹ 一方通行 **ippō tsūkō** one-way traffic

⁴ 文字通 **mojidō(ri)** literal(ly)

¹² 貯金通帳 **chokin tsūchō** bankbook

2q7.19

口 口 辶 儿
24 19 16

逗 | 逗 逗

TŌ stop

— 1 —

² 逗子 **Zushi** (city, Kanagawa-ken)

¹⁰ 逗留 **tōryū** stay, sojourn

逗留客 **tōryūkyaku** guest, visitor, sojourner

— 8 —

2q8.1 / 437

口 隹 辶
74 19

進 進

SHIN, susu(mu) advance, progress
susu(meru) advance, promote NOBU
(part of given name)

— 1 —

² 進入 **shinnyū** enter, penetrate, go/come in

⁴ 進化 **shinka** evolution

⁵ 進出 **shinshutsu** advance, march, inroads, push

進出 **susu(mi)de(ru)** step forward

⁶ 進行 **shinkō** advance, progress, proceed

⁷ 進呈 **shintei** give, present

進学 **shingaku** entrance to a higher school

⁸ 進退 **shintai** advance or retreat, movement; course of action, attitude; resigning or staying on

2 進法 **nishinhō** binary (notation)

進歩 **shinpo** progress, advance

進物 **shinmotsu** present, gift

⁹ 進級 **shinkyū** promotion (to a higher grade)

¹³ 進路 **shinro** course, way, route

— 2 —

² 十進法 **jisshinhō** decimal/base-10 notation

⁶ 先進国 **senshinkoku** advanced/developed nation

行進曲 **kōshinkyoku** a (musical) march

⁷ 改進 **kaishin** reform, progress

⁸ 昇進 **shōshin** promotion, advancement

⁹ 促進 **sokushin** promote, encourage

急進 **kyūshin** rapid progress; radical, extreme

前進 **zenshin** advance, drive, progress

後進 **kōshin** coming along behind; one's juniors/successors; back up

¹¹ 推進 **suishin** propulsion, drive

累進 **ruishin** successive promotions; progressive, graduated

累進税 **ruishinzei** progressive/graduated tax

¹⁴ 漸進 **zenshin** gradual progress, steady advance

増進 **zōshin** increase, furtherance, improvement

精進 **shōjin** diligence, devotion; purification

²¹ 躍進 **yakushin** advance by leaps and bounds

2q8.2 / 891

口 氵 ⺕ 辶
21 39 19

逮 逮

TAI catch up with

— 1 —

¹⁰ 逮捕 **taiho** arrest, capture

2q8.3 / 1003 □ 方 辶 宀
48 19 15

遊 遊

YŪ, YU play; be idle; wander
aso(bu) play, enjoy oneself; take a holiday; be idle **aso(baseru), aso(basu)**
let play; leave idle; deign to **susa(bi)**
pastime, amusement

───────── 1 ─────────

6 遊休 **yūkyū** idle, unused
8 遊歩 **yūho** walk, stroll, promenade
9 遊郭 **yūkaku** red-light district
遊相手 **aso(bi)aite** playmate
12 遊場 **aso(bl)ba** playground
13 遊園地 **yūenchi** amusement/theme
park
15 遊撃戦 **yūgekisen** guerrilla warfare
遊戯 **yūgi** games, amusement,
entertainment
aso(bi)tawamu(reru) play,
frolic
16 遊興 **yūkyō** pleasure seeking, merrymaking
17 遊覧 **yūran** excursion, sightseeing
18 遊離 **yūri** isolate, separate

───────── 2 ─────────

8 周遊券 **shūyūken** excursion ticket
9 浮遊 **fuyū** float, waft, be suspended
14 漫遊 **man'yū** trip, tour, travel

達 → 達 **2q9.8**

2q8.6 / 734 □ 口 辶 宀
24 19 15

逸 逸|逸 逸

ITSU flee, escape, be a recluse; stray
from, digress; excel; be spirited
so(reru) miss the mark; stray from,
digress **so(rasu)** avert, divert, dodge
haya(ru) be rash/impetuous/
impatient HAYA (part of given name)

───────── 1 ─────────

9 逸品 **ippin** superb article, masterpiece
13 逸楽 **itsuraku** idle pursuit of pleasure
逸話 **itsuwa** anecdote

───────── 2 ─────────

7 秀逸 **shūitsu** superb, masterly
9 俊逸 **shun'itsu** excellence, genius

2q8.7 / 92 □ 月 口 辶
42 24 19

週 週

SHŪ week

───────── 1 ─────────

4 週日 **shūjitsu** weekday
5 週末 **shūmatsu** weekend
週刊誌 **shūkanshi** a weekly (magazine)
12 週間 **shūkan** week

───────── 2 ─────────

1 一週間 **isshūkan** a week
4 今週 **konshū** this week
6 毎週 **maishū** every week, weekly
先週 **senshū** last week
7 来週 **raishū** next week

───────── 3 ─────────

6 再来週 **saraishū** the week after
next

───────── 9 ─────────

2q9.1 / 1641 □ 日 辶 竹
43 19 17

遇 遇

GŪ, GU treat, deal with; meet **a(u)**
meet, encounter

───────── 2 ─────────

5 礼遇 **reigū** cordial reception; honors, privileges

2

亻 冫 孑 阝 卩 刂 力 又 一 亠 丷 厂 辶 冂 几 匚

9

9 待遇 **taigū** treatment, reception, entertainment, (hotel) service; salary, remuneration
10 配遇者 **haigūsha** spouse
13 遭遇 **sōgū** encounter
17 優遇 **yūgū** warm welcome, hospitality, favorable treatment

2q9.4   糹 辶 子
                    61 19 6

遜 | 遜 遜

SON inferior; humble **herikuda(ru)** be humble/modest

— 2 —

17 謙遜 **kenson** modesty, humility

遥 → 遙 **2q10.3**

2q9.8 / 448   王 土 辶
                      46 22 19

達 | 達 達

TATSU reach, attain **-tachi** (plural ending) **tat(te)** earnest, urgent, pressing SUSUMU, TŌRU, ITARU (m. given name) MICHI (part of given name)

— 1 —

0 達する **tas(suru)** reach, attain; amount to; become expert in; notify
2 達人 **tatsujin** expert, master
3 達也 **Tatsuya** (m. given name)
6 達成 **tassei** achieve, attain
8 達者 **tassha** healthy, strong; proficient
12 達雄 **Tatsuo, Michio** (m. given name)
16 達磨 **Daruma** Dharma (Indian priest who brought Zen Buddhism to China circa 520 A.D.); tumbler, legless figurine

— 2 —

2 人達 **hitotachi** people

3 上達 **jōtatsu** make progress, become proficient
4 友達 **tomodachi** friend
6 伊達 **Date** (surname)
  伝達 **dentatsu** transmit, convey, propagate
  先達 **sendatsu** pioneer; leader; guide **sendat(te)** the other day, recently
7 私達 **watakushitachi** we, us, our
8 到達 **tōtatsu** reach, attain
  送達 **sōtatsu** convey, deliver, dispatch
9 発達 **hattatsu** development, progress
  速達 **sokutatsu** special/express delivery
10 配達 **haitatsu** deliver
11 雪達磨 **yuki daruma** snowman
17 闊達 **kattatsu** magnanimous, generous

— 3 —

5 幼友達 **osana tomodachi** childhood friend

2q9.10 / 439   車 辶 冂
                      69 19 20

運 運

UN fate, luck; transport; operate **hako(bu)** carry, transport KAZU (part of given name)

— 1 —

5 運出 **hako(bi)da(su)** carry out
6 運休 **unkyū** (train) cancelled, not running
  運行 **unkō** movement; operate, run (planes, trains)
8 運命 **unmei** fate, destiny
  運送 **unsō** transport, conveyance, shipping
  運送会社 **unsō-gaisha** transport/express company
  運河 **unga** canal
11 運動 **undō** motion, movement; exercise, sports; a movement, campaign

運動不足 **undō-busoku** lack of exercise

運動会 **undōkai** athletic meet

運動靴 **undōgutsu** athletic shoes, sneakers

運転 **unten** operate, run (a machine), drive (a car)

運転手 **untenshu** driver, chauffeur

12 運営 **un'ei** operation, management, administration

13 運勢 **unsei** one's fate, fortune, luck

運搬 **unpan** transport

運賃 **unchin** fare; shipping/freight charges

16 運輸 **un'yu** transport(ation)

運輸省 **Un'yushō** Ministry of Transport

――――― 2 ―――――

4 不運 **fuun** misfortune, bad luck

5 好運 **kōun** good fortune, luck

8 非運 **hiun** misfortune, bad luck

幸運 **kōun** good fortune, luck

9 海運 **kaiun** marine transport, shipping

10 陸運 **rikuun** land transport

時運 **jiun** tide of fortune

11 悪運 **aku'un** evildoer's good luck; bad luck

13 試運転 **shiunten** trial run

2q9.13 / 1133

27 19 16

SUI, to(geru) accomplish, attain, carry through **tsui(ni)** finally

――――― 1 ―――――

6 遂行 **suikō** accomplish, execute, perform

――――― 4 ―――――

6 自殺未遂 **jisatsu misui** attempted suicide

2q9.14 / 149

 55 19 16

DŌ, TŌ road; prefecture (Hokkaidō) **michi** way, path, road, street MICHI (part of given name)

――――― 1 ―――――

0 道ならぬ **michi(naranu)** improper, illicit

4 道夫 **Michio, Michito** (m. given name)

道化 **dōke** clowning

8 道具 **dōgu** tool, implement

9 道連 **michizu(re)** traveling companion

10 道教 **dōkyō** Taoism

11 道理 **dōri, kotowari** reason, right, truth

12 道場 **dōjō** (martial-arts) gymnasium; Buddhist seminary

道順 **michijun** route, itinerary

13 道義 **dōgi** moral principles

道楽 **dōraku** hobby; dissipation, debauchery

道路 **dōro** road, street, highway

14 道徳 **dōtoku** morality, morals

道端 **michibata** roadside, wayside

――――― 2 ―――――

3 大道 **daidō** highway, main street; great moral principle

弓道 **kyūdō** (Japanese) archery

4 不道徳 **fudōtoku** immoral

片道 **katamichi** one way

水道 **suidō** piped water, waterworks, aqueduct; waterway

6 伝道 **dendō** evangelism, proselytizing, missionary work

近道 **chikamichi** short cut

回道 **mawa(ri)michi** roundabout way

7 坑道 **kōdō** (mine) shaft, level, gallery, tunnel

坂道 **sakamichi** hill road

赤道 **sekidō** the equator

抜道 **nu(ke)michi** bypass; secret path; way of escape, loophole

花道 **kadō** (the art of) flower arrangement **hanamichi** runway from the stage through the audience

戻道 **modo(ri)michi** the way back

車道 **shadō** roadway

8 夜道 **yomichi** night journey

逃道 **ni(ge)michi** way of escape, way out

歩道橋 **hodōkyō** pedestrian overpass

国道 **kokudō** national highway

林道 **rindō** forest road/trail

武道 **budō** military/martial arts, bushido

9 通道 **tō(ri)michi** pasage, path, route, one's way to

茶道 **chadō, sadō** tea ceremony

県道 **kendō** prefectural highway

峠道 **tōgemichi** road through a mountain pass

柔道 **jūdō** judo

神道 **shintō** Shintoism

軌道 **kidō** (railway) track; orbit

10 修道院 **shūdōin** monastery, convent, cloister

都道府県 **to-dō-fu-ken** prefectures

剣道 **kendō** Japanese fencing, kendo

帰道 **kae(ri)michi** the way back/home

華道 **kadō** flower arranging

脇道 **wakimichi** byway, side road; digression

書道 **shodō** calligraphy

11 寄道 **yo(ri)michi** stop in on one's way

細道 **hosomichi** narrow lane, path

12 報道 **hōdō** reporting, news coverage

街道 **kaidō** highway

筋道 **sujimichi** reason, logic, coherence

13 鉄道 **tetsudō** railroad

鉄道網 **tetsudōmō** railway network

15 舗道 **hodō** paved street, pavement

横道 **yokomichi** side street, crossroad; wrong way; side issue, digression; path of evil

---

3

1 一本道 **ipponmichi** straight road; road with no turnoffs

5 北海道 **Hokkaidō** (prefecture)

8 東海道 **Tōkaidō** the Tōkaidō highway

4

15 横断歩道 **ōdan hodō** pedestrian crossing

2q9.16 / 1160

HEN widespread; (number of) times **amane(ku)** widely, generally, everywhere

---

1

14 遍歴 **henreki** travels, pilgrimage

2

1 一遍 **ippen** once

3 万遍 **manben(naku)** equally, uniformly, without exception

12 普遍 **fuhen** universal, general

3

9 通一遍 **tō(ri)-ippen** passing, casual, perfunctory

2q9.17 / 702

CHI, oso(i) late; slow **oku(reru)** be late/slow **oku(rasu)** defer, set back (a clock)

1

6 遅早 **oso(kare)haya(kare)** sooner or later

7 遅延 **chien** delay

8 遅刻 **chikoku** be late/tardy

13 遅滞 **chitai** delay; arrearage

2

4 手遅 **teoku(re)** too late, belated

9 乗遅 **no(ri)oku(reru)** miss (a train)

2q9.18 / 413

□ 口 辶 冂
24　19　20

KA excess, too much; error　**su(giru)** pass, go past; elapse; be more than, exceed; (as adjective or verb suffix) too …, over-, to excess　**su(gosu)** spend (time)　**ayama(tsu)** err　**ayama(chi)** error　**yo(giru)** pass by

——————— 1 ———————

3 過大 **kadai** excessive, too much, unreasonable

4 過分 **kabun** excessive, undeserved

5 過半数 **kahansū** majority, more than half

過失 **kashitsu** error, mistake; accident; negligence

過去 **kako** the past　**su(gi)sa(ru)** pass

7 過労 **karō** overwork

過労死 **karōshi** death from overwork

過言 **kagon, kagen** exaggeration

9 過度 **kado** excessive, too much

10 過敏 **kabin** oversensitive, nervous

11 過剰 **kajō** excess, surplus

12 過渡期 **katoki** transition period

過程 **katei** process

14 過酷 **kakoku** severe, harsh

16 過激 **kageki** radical, extreme

過激派 **kagekiha** radicals, extremists

——————— 2 ———————

1 一過性 **ikkasei** transient, temporary

5 功過 **kōka** merits and demerits

7 言過 **i(i)su(giru)** overstate, go too far

9 食過 **ta(be)su(gi), ku(i)su(gi)** overeating

11 経過 **keika** lapse, passage of time; progress, course, developments

12 超過 **chōka** exceed

焼過 **ya(ki)su(giru)** overcook

買過 **ka(i)su(giru)** buy too much/ many

飲過 **no(mi)su(giru)** drink too much

16 積過 **tsu(mi)su(giru)** overload

17 擦過傷 **sakkashō** abrasion, scratch

18 濾過 **roka** filtration

——————— 10 ———————

2q10.2 / 1173

□ 口 尸 辶
24　40　19

KEN, tsuka(wasu) send, dispatch; give　**tsuka(u)** use　**ya(ru)** give

——————— 1 ———————

4 遣方 **ya(ri)kata** way of doing, method

11 遣掛 **ya(ri)ka(keru)** begin to do, set about　**ya(ri)ka(ke)** unfinished, half done

——————— 2 ———————

3 小遣 **kozuka(i)** spending money

4 心遣 **kokorozuka(i)** solicitude, consideration　**kokoroya(ri)** diversion, recreation; thoughtfulness

6 気遣 **kizuka(i)** anxiety, fear, worry

9 派遣 **haken** dispatch, send

思遣 **omo(i)ya(ri)** consideration, sympathy, compassion

——————— 3 ———————

12 無駄遣 **mudazuka(i)** waste, squander

2q10.3 / 2248

□ 夕 屮 辶
30　36　19

YŌ, haru(ka) far off, distant; long ago; by far　HARUKA (f. given name)　YŌ, MICHI, TŌ, HARU, NOBU, SUMI, NORI (part of given name)

――――――― 1 ―――――――

³ 遙々 **harubaru** from afar, at a great distance

⁹ 遥香 **Haruka** (f. given name)

2q10.4 / 446　　　□ 礻 土 口
　　　　　　　　　　57 22 24

遠遠

EN, ON, tō(i) far, distant

――――――― 1 ―――――――

⁰ 遠ざかる **tō(zakaru)** become more distant, drift apart

遠ざける **tō(zakeru)** keep at a distance, shun, abstain from

³ 遠山 **Tōyama, Toyama** (surname)

⁴ 遠方 **enpō** great distance, long way, far-off

遠心力 **enshinryoku** centrifugal force

⁵ 遠目 **tōme** distant view; farsightedness

⁶ 遠近法 **enkinhō** (law of) perspective

遠回 **tōmawa(ri)** roundabout way, detour **tōmawa(shi)** roundabout expression

⁷ 遠足 **ensoku** excursion, outing, picnic, hike

⁸ 遠征 **ensei** (military) expedition, campaign; tour (by a team)

⁹ 遠洋 **en'yō** ocean, deep sea

¹¹ 遠視 **enshi** farsightedness

¹² 遠隔 **enkaku** distant, remote (control)

遠距離 **enkyori** long distance, long-range

¹⁴ 遠鳴 **tōna(ri)** distant sound (of thunder, the sea)

¹⁵ 遠慮 **enryo** reserve, restraint, diffidence; refrain from **enryo(naku)** frankly

¹⁸ 遠藤 **Endō** (surname)

――――――― 2 ―――――――

⁵ 永遠 **eien** eternity

¹¹ 疎遠 **soen** estrangement; long silence

望遠鏡 **bōenkyō** telescope

¹² 無遠慮 **buenryo** unreserved, forward, impertinent

敬遠 **keien** keep (someone) at a respectful distance

¹⁴ 遼遠 **ryōen** distant, remote

2q10.5 / 814　　　□ 口 艹 辶
　　　　　　　　　　24 12 19

違違

I, chiga(u) be different; be mistaken; cross/pass (someone) **chiga(eru)** alter **taga(u)** differ from; violate **taga(eru)** violate, break (a promise)

――――――― 1 ―――――――

⁰ に違いない **(ni) chiga(i nai)** for sure, no doubt

⁴ 違反 **ihan** violation

⁸ 違法 **ihō** illegal

違和感 **iwakan** feeling ill at ease, discomfort, malaise

⁹ 違約 **iyaku** breach of contract, default

¹⁶ 違憲 **iken** unconstitutionality

――――――― 2 ―――――――

² 人違 **hitochiga(i)** mistaken identity

³ 大違 **ōchiga(i)** big difference

⁴ 互違 **taga(i)chiga(i)** alternating

⁶ 気違 **kichiga(i)** insanity; mania; craze; lunatic; enthusiast, fan

考違 **kanga(e)chiga(i)** mistaken idea, wrong impression

⁷ 見違 **michiga(eru)** mistake for, not recognize **michiga(i)** misperception, mistake

⁹ 相違 **sōi** difference, discrepancy

畑違 **hatakechiga(i)** out of one's line

¹¹ 勘違 **kanchiga(i)** misunderstanding, mistaken idea

¹² 筋違 **sujichiga(e)** a cramp **sujichiga(i)** illogical; diagonal **sujika(i)** diagonal; brace

間違 **machiga(u)** be mistaken/ wrong　**machiga(eru)** mistake

13 腹違 **harachiga(i)** born of a different mother but having the same father

置違 **o(ki)chiga(eru)** put in the wrong place

14 読違 **yo(mi)chiga(i)** misreading

17 擦違 **su(re)chiga(u)** pass by each other

——— 3 ———

1 一味違 **hitoaji chiga(u)** with a unique flavor

3 大間違 **ōmachiga(i)** big mistake

4 心得違 **kokoroechiga(i)** mistaken idea; indiscretion

7 見当違 **kentōchiga(i)** wrong guess

 遰 → 逓 **2q7.5**

——— 11 ———

2q11.2 / 1643　　　□ 日 艹 辶
　　　　　　　　　　43　32　19

 遭　遭遭

SŌ, a(u) meet, encounter

——— 1 ———

11 遭遇 **sōgū** encounter

18 遭難 **sōnan** disaster, accident, mishap, distress

2q11.3 / 415　　　□ 口 辶 亠
　　　　　　　　　　24　19　11

適　適適

TEKI suitable　**kana(u)** suit, serve the purpose, be consistent with　**tama** occasional, rare

——— 1 ———

0 適する **teki(suru)** fit, suit, be qualified for

4 適切 **tekisetsu** appropriate, pertinent

5 適用 **tekiyō** apply

6 適合 **tekigō** conform to, suit, fit

適当 **tekitō** suitable, adequate

7 適応 **tekiō** adaptation, accommodation, adjustment

適材 **tekizai** the right person

8 適宜 **tekigi** suitable, proper, as one thinks best

適者生存 **tekisha seizon** survival of the fittest

適性 **tekisei** aptitude, suitability

9 適度 **tekido** proper degree/amount, moderation

10 適格 **tekikaku, tekkaku** competent, eligible

——— 2 ———

4 不適 **futeki** unsuited, unfit, inappropriate

7 快適 **kaiteki** comfortable, pleasant, agreeable

12 最適 **saiteki** optimum, best suited

2q11.4 / 1767　　　□ 火 艹 厂
　　　　　　　　　　44　32　18

 遮 | 遮遮

SHA, saegi(ru) interrupt, obstruct, block

——— 1 ———

11 遮断 **shadan** interception, isolation, cutoff

——— 12 ———

2q12.1 / 921　　　□ 口 大 弓
　　　　　　　　　　24　34　28

遷　遷遷

SEN move, change　**utsu(ru)** move, change, shift

——— 2 ———

9 変遷 **hensen** changes, vicissitudes, transition

2q12.3 / 800 　　□ 弓 艹 辶
　　　　　　　　28 32 19

選 選

SEN, era(bu), e(ru), sugu(ru), yo(ru) choose, select

―――――― 1 ――――――

4 選手 **senshu** (sports) player
7 選抜 **senbatsu, e(ri)nu(ku)** select, choose, single out
選択 **sentaku** selection, choice, option, alternative
10 選挙 **senkyo** election
選挙戦 **senkyosen** election campaign
12 選集 **senshū** selection, anthology

―――――― 2 ――――――

2 入選 **nyūsen** be chosen (in a competition)
4 予選 **yosen** preliminary selection/ screening, elimination round
互選 **gosen** co-optation, mutual election
6 再選挙 **saisenkyo** re-election
当選 **tōsen** be elected/selected, win
7 改選 **kaisen** reelection
8 抽選 **chūsen** drawing, lottery
10 特選 **tokusen** specially selected
被選挙権 **hisenkyoken** eligibility for election
12 落選 **rakusen** fail to get elected
13 詩選 **shisen** poetry anthology
14 総選挙 **sōsenkyo** general election
精選 **seisen** careful/choice selection

2q12.4 / 1172 　　□ 貝 口 辶
　　　　　　　　68 24 19

遺 遺

I, YUI, noko(su) leave behind; bequeath

―――――― 1 ――――――

5 遺失 **ishitsu** loss

6 遺伝 **iden** heredity
7 遺体 **itai** corpse, remains
遺言 **yuigon** will, last wishes
遺言書 **yuigonsho** will, testament
9 遺品 **ihin** articles left by the deceased
10 遺骨 **ikotsu** one's remains/ashes
11 遺族 **izoku** surviving family
遺産 **isan** inheritance, estate
13 遺跡 **iseki** remains, ruins, relics
14 遺漏 **irō** omission, negligence, oversight
15 遺稿 **ikō** (deceased's) unpublished works
16 遺憾 **ikan** regrettable
18 遺贈 **izō** bequest, legacy

―――――― 2 ――――――

12 補遺 **hoi** supplement, addendum, appendix

2q12.5 / 2249 　　□ 火 日 小
　　　　　　　　44 43 35

遼 | 遼 遼

RYŌ distant **HARUKA, TOSHI** (f. given name) **RYŌ, TŌ, TOSHI** (part of given name)

―――――― 1 ――――――

12 遼遠 **ryōen** distant, remote

2q12.8 / 1938 　　□ 酉 寸 辶
　　　　　　　　71 37 19

遵 遵

JUN follow, obey

―――――― 1 ――――――

6 遵守 **junshu** obey, observe
8 遵法 **junpō** law-abiding, work-to-rule (tactics)

遅 → 遅 **2q9.17**

導→ **5c9.3**

—————— 13 ——————

2q13.3 / 1491   □ 立 尸 口
54 40 24

避 避避

HI, sa(keru), yo(keru) avoid

—————— 1 ——————

7 避妊 **hinin** contraception
避妊薬 **hinin'yaku** a contraceptive, birth control pill
12 避暑地 **hishochi** summer resort
18 避難 **hinan** refuge, evacuation
避難民 **hinanmin** refugees, evacuees

—————— 2 ——————

6 回避 **kaihi** avoid
7 忌避 **kihi** evasion, shirking; (legal) challenge
8 逃避 **tōhi** escape, flight, evasion

——————————— 冂 2r ———————————

円   用   回   同   周   岡   朋   青   耐
2.1   3.1 3s3.1 4.2   6.1   6.2 4b4.1 4b4.10 7.1

—————— 2 ——————

2r2.1 / 13   □ 冂 宀
20 11

円   圓丨円円

EN circle; yen **maru(i)** round (like a disk) **maro(yaka)** round; mellow **mado(ka)** round; tranquil MADOKA (surname, f. given name)

—————— 1 ——————

7 円形 **enkei** round shape, circle
8 円価 **enka** value of the yen
10 円高 **endaka** strong yen (exchange rate)
12 円満 **enman** harmonious, smooth; well rounded

2q13.4 / 866   □ 目 衤 口
55 57 24

還 還還

KAN, GEN, kae(ru) return

—————— 1 ——————

4 還元 **kangen** restore; reduce, deoxidize
14 還暦 **kanreki** one's 60th birthday

—————— 2 ——————

5 生還 **seikan** come back alive; cross home plate
6 返還 **henkan** return; repayment
17 償還 **shōkan** repayment, redemption, amortization

—————— 15 ——————

邊→ 辺 **2q2.1**

13 円滑 **enkatsu** smooth, harmonious

—————— 2 ——————

13 楕円形 **daenkei** ellipse, oval

—————— 3 ——————

2r3.1 / 107   ⸛ 月 丨
42 2

用 用用

YŌ business, errand; (as suffix) use, for … **mochi(iru)** use

—————— 1 ——————

4 用水 **yōsui** city/irrigation water
用心 **yōjin** care, caution
用心深 **yōjinbuka(i)** careful, cautious, wary

2

イ 冫 孑 阝 卩 刂 力 又

一 亠 十 艹 夕 宀 厂 辶 **3** 冂 几 匸

---

⁶ 用件 **yōken** business, things to be done

用地 **yōchi** land for some use, lot, site

⁷ 用言 **yōgen** declinable word

⁸ 用事 **yōji** business, errand, something to attend to

用例 **yōrei** example, illustration

用法 **yōhō** how to use, directions

⁹ 用途 **yōto** use, purpose

用品 **yōhin** supplies

¹⁰ 用紙 **yōshi** form (to be filled out); stationery

¹² 用量 **yōryō** dosage, dose

¹³ 用意 **yōi** preparations, arrangements

¹⁴ 用語 **yōgo** term, terminology, vocabulary

──────── 2 ────────
---

⁴ 不用 **fuyō** unused, useless, waste

不用心 **buyōjin, fuyōjin** unsafe, insecure; careless

不用意 **fuyōi** unprepared, unguarded, careless

収用 **shūyō** expropriation

公用 **kōyō** official business; public use; public expense

引用 **in'yō** quotation, citation

引用句 **in'yōku** quotation

引用符 **in'yōfu** quotation marks

日用品 **nichiyōhin** daily necessities

⁵ 代用 **daiyō** substitute

⁶ 多用 **tayō** busyness

共用 **kyōyō** common use, shared

当用漢字 **Tōyō Kanji** (official list of 1,850 kanji recommended for general use; superseded by the 1,945 Jōyō Kanji)

有用 **yūyō** useful, serviceable, available

⁷ 作用 **sayō** action, function, effect

乱用 **ran'yō** misuse, abuse, misappropriation

応用 **ōyō** (practical) application

利用 **riyō** use, make use of

利用者 **riyōsha** user

私用 **shiyō** private use

⁸ 画用紙 **gayōshi** drawing paper

使用 **shiyō** use, employ, utilize

使用法 **shiyōhō** use, directions

使用者 **shiyōsha** user, consumer; employer

併用 **heiyō** use together, use in combination

効用 **kōyō** use, utility, effect

実用 **jitsuyō** practical use, utility

⁹ 専用 **sen'yō** private/personal use, exclusively for

乗用車 **jōyōsha** passenger car

信用 **shin'yō** trust, confidence; credit; reputation

軍用 **gun'yō** for military use

急用 **kyūyō** urgent business

連用形 **ren'yōkei** stem (of a verb)

通用 **tsūyō** be in common use, be honored/valid, pass

活用 **katsuyō** practical use; conjugate, inflect

客用 **kyakuyō** for guests

食用 **shokuyō** edible, used for food

¹⁰ 借用 **shakuyō** borrowing, loan

兼用 **ken'yō** combined use, serving two purposes

浴用 **yokuyō** for the bath

¹¹ 商用 **shōyō** business

採用 **saiyō** adopt, employ

常用 **jōyō** common/everyday/habitual use

常用漢字 **Jōyō Kanji** (official list of 1,945 kanji recommended for general use)

¹² 御用 **goyō** your order/business; official business

無用 **muyō** useless; needless; without business; prohibited

無用心 **buyōjin** unsafe; incautious

雇用 **koyō** employment

雇用者 **koyōsha** employer

費用 **hiyō** expenses, cost

飲用水 **in'yōsui** drinking water

¹³ 適用 **tekiyō** apply

¹⁴ 慣用句 **kan'yōku** idiom, common expression

慣用語 **kan'yōgo** idiom, colloquial word/phrase

誤用 **goyō** misuse

¹⁵ 器用 **kiyō** dextrous, adroit, skillful

16 薬用 **yakuyō** medicinal
18 濫用 **ran'yō** abuse, misuse, misappropriation

———————— 3 ————————

4 不器用 **bukiyō** clumsy, unskillful
反作用 **hansayō** reaction
6 再使用 **saishiyō** reuse
7 学術用語 **gakujutsu yōgo** technical term
男子用 **danshiyō** for men, men's
8 逆作用 **gyakusayō** adverse effect, reaction
10 原稿用紙 **genkō yōshi** manuscript paper
11 紳士用 **shinshiyō** men's, for men
12 無器用 **bukiyō** clumsy

———————— 4 ————————

12 廃物利用 **haibutsu riyō** recycling

囘 → 回   **3s3.1**

———————— 4 ————————

2r4.2 / 198

     □   冂   一
     24   20   1

同   全丨 同 同

DŌ, ona(ji) the same

———————— 1 ————————

1 同一 **dōitsu** the same, identical, equal
2 同人 **dōjin, dōnin** the same person, said person; clique, fraternity, coterie
3 同士 **dōshi** fellow, companion
4 同氏 **dōshi** the same person, said person, he, she
同日 **dōjitsu** the same day
6 同年輩 **dōnenpai** persons of the same age
同名異人 **dōmei-ijin** different person of the same name
同行 **dōkō** go together, accompany   **dōgyō** fellow pilgrim/esthete
7 同伴 **dōhan** accompany, go with
8 同姓 **dōsei** the same surname

同居 **dōkyo** live in the same house
同性愛 **dōseiai** homosexuality
9 同点 **dōten** a tie/draw
同封 **dōfū** enclose
同音異義 **dōon-igi** the same pronunciation but different meanings
同音語 **dōongo** homophone, homonym
同級生 **dōkyūsei** classmate
10 同時 **dōji** at the same time, simultaneous
11 同窓会 **dōsōkai** alumni association/meeting
同情 **dōjō** sympathy
12 同棲 **dōsei** live together, cohabit with
同期 **dōki** the same period; the same class; synchronous
同等 **dōtō** equal, on a par with
13 同義語 **dōgigo** synonym
同感 **dōkan** the same sentiment, sympathy, concurrence
同意 **dōi** the same meaning; the same opinion; consent, agreement
同意見 **dōiken** the same opinion, like views
同意語 **dōigo** synonym
同盟 **dōmei** alliance, league, union
14 同僚 **dōryō** colleague, associate
同様 **dōyō** the same (kind/way), similar
15 同権 **dōken** the same rights, equal rights
同調 **dōchō** alignment; tuning

———————— 2 ————————

1 一同 **ichidō** all concerned, all of us
6 共同 **kyōdō** cooperation, collaboration, joint, collective
8 協同 **kyōdō** cooperation, collaboration, partnership

———————— 3 ————————

7 呉越同舟 **Go-Etsu dōshū** enemies in the same boat
8 欧州同盟 **Ōshū Dōmei** the European Union

---------- **6** ----------

2r6.1 / 91

周　|　周　周

周 ｜ 月 口 ｜
42 24 2

SHŪ circuit, lap, circumference
MAKOTO (m. given name) **CHIKA**
(part of given name)

---------- 1 ----------

4 周辺 **shūhen** periphery, environs, outskirts
6 周年 **shūnen** whole year, anniversary
7 周囲 **shūi** circumference, perimeter; surroundings
周忌 **shūki** anniversary of a death
8 周波数 **shūhasū** frequency
周知 **shūchi** common knowledge, widely known
10 周遊券 **shūyūken** excursion ticket
11 周旋 **shūsen** good offices, recommendation, mediation
12 周期 **shūki** period, cycle

---------- 2 ----------

1 一周 **isshū** once around, a revolution/tour/lap

2r6.2 / 1948

岡

回 山 冂 儿
36 20 16

oka hill **OKA** (surname)

---------- 1 ----------

3 岡山県 **Okayama-ken** (prefecture)
5 岡本 **Okamoto** (surname)
岡田 **Okada** (surname)

7 岡村 **Okamura** (surname)
11 岡野 **Okano** (surname)
岡崎 **Okazaki** (city, Aichi-ken); (surname)

---------- 2 ----------

4 片岡 **Kataoka** (surname)
5 平岡 **Hiraoka** (surname)
6 西岡 **Nishioka** (surname)
吉岡 **Yoshioka** (surname)
8 長岡 **Nagaoka** (surname)
松岡 **Matsuoka** (surname)
10 高岡 **Takaoka** (surname)
11 盛岡 **Morioka** (city, Iwate-ken)
12 森岡 **Morioka** (surname)
14 静岡県 **Shizuoka-ken** (prefecture)
18 藤岡 **Fujioka** (surname)

朋 → 朋　**4b4.1**

青 → 青　**4b4.10**

---------- **7** ----------

2r7.1 / 1415

耐

耐 耐

田 寸 一 冂
37 14 20

TAI, ta(eru) endure, withstand

---------- 1 ----------

3 耐久 **taikyū** endurance, persistence, permanence, durability
4 耐水 **taisui** waterproof, watertight
耐火 **taika** fireproof, fire-resistant
15 耐熱 **tainetsu** heat-resistant

---------- 2 ----------

7 忍耐 **nintai** perseverance, patience, endurance
忍耐強 **nintaizuyo(i)** patient, persevering

---------- 几 **2s** ----------

凡　凧　処　凪　咒　風　段　梵　凱　鳳
1.1　3.1　4i2.2　4.3　3d5.11　7.1　7.2　4a7.27　10.1　12.1

─────── **1** ───────

2s1.1 / 1102　　　　　回 冂 丨
　　　　　　　　　　　　　　20　2

凡

凡 凡

BON, HAN common, ordinary, mediocre **oyo(so)** approximately; generally **sube(te)** all TSUNE (part of given name)

─────── 1 ───────

2 凡人 **bonjin** ordinary person, man of mediocre ability

8 凡例 **hanrei** explanatory notes; legend (on a map/diagram)

─────── 2 ───────

3 大凡 **ōyoso** approximately

5 平凡 **heibon** common, ordinary

8 非凡 **hibon** extraordinary, unusual

─────── **3** ───────

2s3.1　　　　　　　回 巾 冂
　　　　　　　　　　　　26　20

凧

凧 凧

tako kite

処 → **4i2.2**

─────── **4** ───────

2s4.3 / 2027　　　　　回 冂 丄 亠
　　　　　　　　　　　　20　13　11

凪

凪 凪

nagi lull, calm **na(gu)** become calm, die down NAGI, NAGU (part of given name)

─────── **6** ───────

咒 → 呪 **3d5.11**

─────── **7** ───────

2s7.1 / 29　　　　　回 虫 冂 丨
　　　　　　　　　　　64　20　2

風

風 風

FŪ, FU wind; appearance; style; custom **kaze, kaza-** wind; a cold **furi** deportment, behavior; form, pretense

─────── 1 ───────

2 風子 **kaze (no) ko** (children are) outdoor creatures

3 風上 **kazakami** windward
　風下 **kazashimo** leeward
　風土 **fūdo** natural features, climate
　風土記 **fudoki** description of the natural features of a region, a topography

6 風向 **fūkō** wind direction **kazemu(ki), kazamu(ki)** wind direction; situation

7 風邪 **kaze, fūja** a cold
　風呂 **furo** bath; bathtub
　風呂桶 **furooke** bathtub
　風呂場 **furoba** bathroom
　風呂敷 **furoshiki** (square of cloth used to wrap goods and presents in)
　風車 **fūsha** windmill **kazaguruma** pinwheel; windmill

8 風刺 **fūshi** satire, sarcasm
　風波 **fūha** wind and waves, storm, rough seas; discord, strife
　風雨 **fūu** wind and rain, rainstorm

9 風俗 **fūzoku** manners, customs, morals
　風変 **fūgawa(ri)** eccentric, peculiar
　風通 **kazetō(shi)** ventilation
　風紀 **fūki** discipline, public morals

10 風格 **fūkaku** character, personality, style
　風致 **fūchi** taste, elegance; scenic beauty

11 風習 **fūshū** manners, customs, ways
　風船 **fūsen** balloon

2

亻 冫 孑 阝 卩 刂 力 乂 冖 亠 十 勹 冫 厂 辶 冂 八 匚　7

¹² 風景 **fūkei** scene(ry), landscape, view

¹³ 風鈴 **fūrin** wind chime

¹⁵ 風潮 **fūchō** tide; trend of the times, the social climate

―――― 2 ――――

¹ 一風変 **ippū kawa(tta)** eccentric, queer; unconventional, original

³ 大風 **ōkaze** strong wind, gale

⁵ 北風 **kitakaze, hokufū** north wind

台風 **taifū** typhoon

⁶ 西風 **nishikaze, seifū** west wind

⁷ 狂風 **kyōfū** raging winds

⁸ 追風 **o(i)kaze, o(i)te** tailwind

逆風 **gyakufū** adverse wind, head-wind

和風 **wafū** Japanese style

⁹ 洋風 **yōfū** Western-style

屏風 **byōbu** folding screen

秋風 **akikaze, shūfū** autumn breeze

¹⁰ 扇風機 **senpūki** (electric) fan

¹¹ 涼風 **ryōfū, suzukaze** cool breeze

強風 **kyōfū** strong/high winds

¹² 蒸風呂 **mu(shi)buro** Turkish bath, sauna

寒風 **kanpū** cold wind

¹⁵ 潮風 **shiokaze** sea breeze, salt air

暴風 **bōfū** high winds, windstorm

暴風雨 **bōfūu** rainstorm

¹⁶ 薫風 **kunpū** balmy breeze

―――― 3 ――――

⁴ 日本風 **Nihon-fū** Japanese style

⁷ 季節風 **kisetsufū** seasonal wind, monsoon

―――― 4 ――――

¹⁰ 純日本風 **jun-Nihon-fū** classical Japanese style

馬耳東風 **bajitōfū** utter indifference, turn a deaf ear

2s7.2 / 362 田 厂 二 冂 18 4 20

段 段 段

DAN step; stairs; rank; column; paragraph **TAN** (unit of cloth, 10.6 m by 34 cm); (unit of land area, about 0.1 hectare)

―――― 1 ――――

³ 段々 **dandan** steps, terrace; gradually, increasingly

段々畑 **dandanbatake** terraced fields

¹¹ 段階 **dankai** stage, phase, step; rank, grade

¹² 段落 **danraku** end of a paragraph, section, period; conclusion, settlement

―――― 2 ――――

¹ 一段 **ichidan** one stage/step, all the more

一段落 **ichidanraku** a pause

⁴ 手段 **shudan** means, measures

⁵ 石段 **ishidan** stone steps

¹⁰ 値段 **nedan** price

¹¹ 階段 **kaidan** steps, stairs, stairway

¹² 普段 **fudan** usual, ordinary; constant, ceaseless

普段着 **fudangi** everyday clothes

¹⁴ 鳳凰 **hōō** mythical peacock-like bird which appears when peace and holiness prevail

梵 → **4a7.27**

―――― 10 ――――

2s10.1 / 2028 田 屮 日 儿 36 24 16

凱 凱 凱

GAI victory song; victory GAI, KAI, YOSHI, TOKI, KATSU (part of given name) TANOSHI, KATSUMI (m. given name)

―――― 1 ――――

¹¹ 凱旋門 **gaisenmon** arch of triumph

12

2s12.1 / 2274 　　　　　囗 鳥 冂 一
　　　　　　　　　　80 20 14

鳳　　　　　鳳鳳

HŌ male mythical bird HŌ, FŪ,
TAKA (part of given name) ŌTORI
(surname)

─── 1 ───

11 鳳凰 **hōō** mythical peacock-like
bird which appears when peace
and holiness prevail

─── 冂 **2t** ───

区　巨　匹　匡　匠　臣　医　殴　矩　甚　匿　區　躯
2.1　2.2　2.3　4.1　4.2　4.3　5.2　6.1　7.1　0a9.10　8.2　2t2.1　3d15.5

殴　豎　臨
2t6.1　5b9.5　15.1

─── 2 ───

2t2.1 / 183 　　　　囗 冂 十
　　　　　　　　20 12

区　　　　　區 | 区 区

KU ward, municipal administrative
district

─── 1 ───

4 区切 **kugi(ru)** punctuate; partition
区分 **kubun, kuwa(ke)** division,
partition; classification
7 区別 **kubetsu** distinguish between
区役所 **kuyakusho** ward office
8 区画 **kukaku** division, section
11 区域 **kuiki** boundary; zone, territory
12 区間 **kukan** section, interval

─── 2 ───

6 地区 **chiku** district, area, zone
14 管区 **kanku** district, precinct

2t2.2 / 1293 　　　　　囗 冂
　　　　　　　　　　20

巨　　　　　巨 巨

KYO large, gigantic HIRO, KO (part
of given name)

─── 1 ───

2 巨人 **kyojin** giant

3 巨大 **kyodai** huge, gigantic, enormous
12 巨費 **kyohi** great cost
18 巨額 **kyogaku** enormous amount,
vast sum

2t2.3 / 1500 　　　　　囗 冂 儿
　　　　　　　　　　20 16

匹　　　　　匹 匹

HITSU same kind, comparable; a
man **hiki** (counter for animals); (unit
of cloth length, about 21.8 m)

─── 1 ───

15 匹敵 **hitteki** rival, compare with, be
a match for

─── 2 ───

1 一匹 **ippiki** one animal; 20-m bolt
of cloth

─── 4 ───

2t4.1 / 2030 　　　　　囗 王 冂
　　　　　　　　　　46 20

匡　　　　　匡 匡

KYŌ correct; save; help KYŌ,
MASA, TADA (part of given name)
TADASU, TADASHI, TASUKU,
MASASHI (m. given name)

2t4.2 / 1359 ⊟ 斤 冂

50 20

匠 匠 近

SHŌ artisan, workman; idea, design
takumi artisan, mechanic, carpenter
TAKUMI (m. given name)

—— 2 ——

³ 工匠 **kōshō** artisan, craftsman

2t4.3 / 835 ⊟ 冂 丨

20 2

臣 臣 臣

SHIN, JIN, omi retainer, vassal, subject OMI, TOMI (part of given name)

—— 2 ——

³ 大臣 **daijin** cabinet member, minister

—— 4 ——

⁵ 外務大臣 **gaimu daijin** Minister of Foreign Affairs
司法大臣 **shihō daijin** Minister of Justice

¹⁴ 総理大臣 **sōri daijin** prime minister

—— 5 ——

2t5.2 / 220 ⊟ 冂 大 厶

20 34 15

医 醫 医 医

I medicine, healing art; physician

—— 1 ——

³ 医大 **idai** medical university (short for 医科大学)
⁷ 医学 **igaku** medicine, medical science
⁸ 医者 **isha** doctor, physician
¹⁰ 医師 **ishi** physician, doctor
¹⁶ 医薬品 **iyakuhin** pharmaceuticals

¹⁷ 医療 **iryō** medical treatment, health care; medical

—— 2 ——

⁵ 目医者 **meisha** ophthalmologist, optometrist
⁷ 良医 **ryōi** good doctor, skilled physician
¹⁰ 針医 **harii** acupuncturist
¹² 歯医者 **haisha** dentist
¹⁶ 獣医 **jūi** veterinarian
¹⁷ 鍼医者 **hariisha** acupuncturist
¹⁸ 藪医者 **yabuisha** a quack

—— 3 ——

⁵ 外科医 **gekai** surgeon
¹¹ 産科医 **sankai** obstetrician
¹² 歯科医 **shikai** dentist
開業医 **kaigyōi** doctor in private practice

—— 4 ——

¹¹ 婦人科医 **fujinkai** gynecologist

—— 6 ——

2t6.1 / 1940 ⊟ 冂 十 又

20 12 9

殴 毆 丨 殴 殴

Ō, nagu(ru) beat, hit, strike

—— 1 ——

⁰ ぶん殴る **(bun)nagu(ru)** beat up, give a thrashing
⁵ 殴打 **ōda** assault (and battery)
¹⁰ 殴殺 **nagu(ri)koro(su), ōsatsu** beat to death, strike dead

—— 7 ——

2t7.1 / 2175 ⊟ 大 冂 厶

34 20 15

矩 矩 矩

KU, kane, sashigane carpenter's square KU, NORI, TSUNE, KADO, KANE (part of given name) TADASHI, TADASU (m. given name)

甚 → 0a9.10

豎 → 竪 5b9.5

—————— 8 ——————

2t8.2 / 1771

田 艹 冂 口
32 20 24

匿 匿

TOKU hide **kakuma(u)** shelter, hide

———— 1 ————

⁶ 匿名 **tokumei** anonymous

———— 2 ————

¹³ 隠匿 **intoku** concealment

—————— 9 ——————

區 → 区 2t2.1

軀 → 躯 3d15.5

—————— 13 ——————

毆 → 殴 2t6.1

—————— 15 ——————

2t15.1 / 836

田 口 冂 ∕
24 20 15

臨

臨 臨

RIN look out over; go to, be present; copy; rule, subjugate **nozo(mu)** face, confront; attend, be present

———— 1 ————

⁶ 臨休 **rinkyū** special holiday (short for 臨時休校 or 臨時休業)

⁷ 臨床 **rinshō** clinical

⁹ 臨海 **rinkai** seaside, coastal, marine

臨界 **rinkai** critical (temperature)

¹⁰ 臨時 **rinji** temporary, provisional, extraordinary

¹¹ 臨終 **rinjū** one's last moments, deathbed

—————— 3a ——————

水	永	氷	汁	汀	池	汚	汗	汲	江	汐	汎	沖
0.1	1.1	1.2	2.1	2.2	3.4	3.5	3.6	3.7	3.8	3.9	3.11	4.5
決	汰	沈	沙	沒	没	汽	沢	泣	沸	油	波	泌
4.6	4.8	4.9	4.13	3a4.15	4.15	4.16	4.18	5.1	5.3	5.6	5.9	5.10
泳	泊	注	泡	法	況	注	沿	沼	治	泥	河	泉
5.14	5.15	5.16	5.18	5.20	5.21	3a5.16	5.23	5.24	5.28	5.29	5.30	5.33
泰	津	浅	洲	浮	洗	洪	洸	活	浄	洋	海	派
5.34	6.1	6.4	6.10	6.11	6.12	6.14	6.15	6.16	6.18	6.19	6.20	6.21
洵	洞	酒	浦	浪	浜	浩	流	渉	消	浸	浴	淳
6.23	6.25	7.1	7.2	7.5	7.7	7.9	7.10	3a8.20	7.16	7.17	7.18	7.19
海	涌	涙	渚	淵	淑	淋	凄	渇	混	淡	淺	溪
3a6.20	3a9.31	7.21	3a9.1	3a9.3	8.5	8.6	2b8.4	8.13	8.14	8.15	3a6.4	8.16
淫	淨	清	渋	渉	深	添	淀	液	済	涼	涙	涯
8.17	3a6.18	8.18	8.19	8.20	8.21	8.22	8.23	8.29	8.30	8.31	3a7.21	8.33
渚	淵	測	湖	港	湾	潦	温	湿	湯	渇	滞	満
9.1	9.3	9.4	9.8	9.13	9.15	3a5.33	9.21	9.22	9.23	3a8.13	3a10.14	9.25

滋	湧	渥	渡	渦	減	溺	滑	滝	溝	溜	滉	溫
9.27	9.31	9.33	9.35	9.36	9.37	10.1	10.6	10.8	10.9	10.11	10.12	3a9.21
滯	溢	溪	溶	漢	漠	滿	溢	濾	源	滅	黎	漁
10.14	3a10.19	3a8.16	10.15	10.17	10.18	3a4.16	10.19	3a15.8	10.25	10.26	10.29	11.1
漸	漱	漕	滯	漆	漫	漬	滿	漢	演	滴	漏	漿
11.2	11.4	11.7	3a10.14	11.10	11.11	11.12	3a9.25	3a10.17	11.13	11.14	11.19	11.21
潮	澂	潛	潘	潟	潔	澄	潰	澁	潤	激	澪	濃
12.1	3a12.11	12.6	3a10.11	12.9	12.10	12.11	12.14	3a8.19	12.20	13.1	13.6	13.7
澤	濁	鴻	潛	濟	濡	濯	濕	濠	澗	濫	濾	瀧
3a4.18	13.8	14.2	3a12.6	3a8.30	14.4	14.5	3a9.22	14.9	8e9.3	15.3	15.8	3a10.8
瀨	瀬	灣										
3a16.3	16.3	3a9.15										

0

3a0.1 / 21

SUI water; Wednesday **mizu** water
MI (part of given name)

1

2 水力 **suiryoku** water/hydro power
3 水上 **suijō** (on the) water, aquatic
minakami headwaters, source
4 水夫 **suifu** sailor, seaman
水中 **suichū** underwater, in the water
水分 **suibun** moisture, water content
水戸 **Mito** (city, Ibaraki-ken)
5 水平 **suihei** horizontal
水平線 **suiheisen** the horizon; horizontal line
水玉 **mizutama** drop of water/dew; polka dots
水田 **suiden** paddy
6 水気 **mizuke** moisture, juiciness
suiki dropsy; moisture, humidity, vapor
水防 **suibō** flood prevention
水色 **mizu-iro** sky blue, turquoise
水先案内 **mizusaki annai** pilot; piloting

7 水位 **suii** water level
水谷 **Mizutani, Mizuya** (surname)
水兵 **suihei** (navy) sailor
水車 **suisha** water wheel, turbine
8 水泳 **suiei** swimming
水泡 **suihō** foam, bubble
水性 **suisei** aqueous, water
mizushō flirtatious, wanton
9 水枯 **mizuga(re)** drought
水食 **suishoku** erosion
10 水差 **mizusa(shi)** water jug, pitcher
水浸 **mizubita(shi)** submerged, flooded; waterlogged
水浴 **suiyoku** bathing, cold bath
mizua(bi) bathing
水害 **suigai** flood damage, flooding
水島 **Mizushima** (surname)
11 水野 **Mizuno** (surname)
水商売 **mizu shōbai** trades dependent on public patronage (bars, restaurants, entertainment)
水道 **suidō** piped water, waterworks, city water, aqueduct; waterway, channel
水深 **suishin** (water) depth
水彩画 **suisaiga** a watercolor
水密 **suimitsu** watertight
水族館 **suizokukan** (public) aquarium
水産物 **suisanbutsu** marine products
水産業 **suisangyō** fisheries, marine products industry

12 水割 **mizuwa(ri)** (whiskey) diluted with water

水着 **mizugi** bathing suit, swimwear

水温 **suion** water temperature

水揚 **mizua(ge)** landing, unloading; earnings; watering (cut flowers so they last longer); deflowering

水蒸気 **suijōki** water vapor; steam

水晶 **suishō** quartz, crystal

水筒 **suitō** water flask, canteen

13 水際 **mizugiwa, migiwa** water's edge, shore

水準 **suijun** water level; level, standard

水溜 **mizuta(mari)** puddle, pool

水溶性 **suiyōsei** water-soluble

水源 **suigen** headwaters, source, fountainhead

水雷 **suirai** torpedo; mine

14 水滴 **suiteki** drop of water

水漏 **mizumo(ri)** leak

水増 **mizuma(shi)** water down, dilute, pad

水墨画 **suibokuga** India-ink painting

水銀 **suigin** mercury

15 水槽 **suisō** water tank/trough

18 水曜日 **suiyōbi** Wednesday

水難 **suinan** sea disaster, flood, drowning

19 水爆 **suibaku** hydrogen bomb (short for 水素爆弾)

—————— 2 ——————

3 下水 **gesui** sewer, drain, drainage

山水画 **sansuiga** landscape painting; a landscape

5 生水 **namamizu** unboiled water

用水 **yōsui** city/irrigation water

氷水 **kōrimizu** ice water; shaved ice

6 防水 **bōsui** waterproof, watertight; flooding prevention

汚水 **osui** filthy water, sewage

7 冷水 **reisui, hi(ya)mizu** cold water

8 泥水 **deisui, doromizu** muddy water

放水 **hōsui** drainage, discharge

雨水 **amamizu, usui** rainwater

9 冠水 **kansui** be submerged/flooded

耐水 **taisui** waterproof, watertight

洪水 **kōzui** flood, inundation, deluge

海水浴場 **kaisuiyokujō** bathing beach

香水 **kōsui** perfume

10 浸水 **shinsui** be inundated

配水 **haisui** water supply/distribution

11 渇水 **kassui** water shortage

淡水 **tansui** freshwater

淡水魚 **tansuigyo** freshwater fish

清水 **shimizu, seisui** pure/clear water **Shimizu** (city, Shizuoka-ken); (surname) **Kiyomizu** (temple in Kyōto)

排水 **haisui** drainage; displacement (of a ship)

断水 **dansui** water supply cutoff

12 湧水 **wa(ki)mizu** spring water

寒水 **kansui** cold water

硬水 **kōsui** hard water

給水 **kyūsui** water supply

飲水 **no(mi)mizu** drinking water

13 溝水 **dobumizu** ditch water

溜水 **tama(ri)mizu** standing/stagnant water

溢水 **issui** inundation

塩水 **shiomizu, ensui** salt water, brine

14 漏水 **rōsui** water leakage

15 潜水 **sensui** dive, submerge

潜水艦 **sensuikan** a submarine

噴水 **funsui** jet of water; fountain

18 覆水盆返 **fukusui bon (ni) kae(razu)** No use crying over spilt milk.

20 鹹水魚 **kansuigyo** saltwater fish

—————— 3 ——————

9 炭酸水 **tansansui** carbonated water

12 飲用水 **in'yōsui** drinking water

飲料水 **inryōsui** drinking water

13 農林水産省 **Nōrinsuishanshō** Ministry of Agriculture, Forestry and Fisheries

¹⁶ 樹氷 **juhyō** frost/ice on trees

― 1 ―

3a1.1 / 1207

日 氵 丨
21 2

永 永永

EI, naga(i) long (time) **HISASHI** (m. given name) **NAGA** (part of given name)

― 1 ―

³ 永久 **eikyū** permanence, perpetuity, eternity
⁴ 永井 **Nagai** (surname)
⁷ 永住 **eijū** permanent residence
¹⁰ 永島 **Nagashima** (surname)
¹² 永遠 **eien** eternity
¹³ 永続 **eizoku, nagatsuzu(ki)** perpetuity

― 2 ―

¹² 富永 **Tominaga** (surname)

3a1.2 / 1206

⋯ 氵 丨
21 2

氷 冰丨氷氷

HYŌ, kōri, hi ice **kō(ru)** freeze (up)

― 1 ―

³ 氷山 **hyōzan** iceberg
⁴ 氷水 **kōrimizu** ice water; shaved ice
⁸ 氷河 **hyōga** glacier
氷河期 **hyōgaki** glacial period, ice age
⁹ 氷点下 **hyōtenka** below the freezing point, below zero (Celsius)
氷砂糖 **kōrizatō** rock candy, crystal sugar
¹³ 氷塊 **hyōkai** lump/block of ice, ice floe
氷解 **hyōkai** thaw, melt away, be dispelled

― 2 ―

⁵ 北氷洋 **Hoppyōyō, Hokuhyōyō** the Arctic Ocean
⁹ 南氷洋 **Nanpyōyō** the Antarctic Ocean

― 2 ―

3a2.1 / 1794

⼞ 氵 十
21 12

汁 汁汁

JŪ juice **shiru, tsuyu** juice, sap; soup, broth, gravy

― 1 ―

⁸ 汁物 **shirumono** soups
¹⁰ 汁粉 **shiruko** sweet adzuki-bean soup with rice cake

― 2 ―

⁸ 果汁 **kajū** fruit juice

― 3 ―

⁸ 味噌汁 **miso shiru** miso soup

3a2.2 / 2133

⼞ 氵 一
21 14

汀 汀汀

TEI, migiwa water's edge, shore **NAGISA** (f. given name) **MIGIWA** (surname) **TEI** (part of given name)

― 3 ―

3a3.4 / 119

⼞ 氵 十 丨
21 12 2

池 池池

CHI, ike pond, reservoir

― 1 ―

⁴ 池内 **Ikeuchi, Ikenouchi** (surname)
⁵ 池田 **Ikeda** (surname)

― 2 ―

³ 小池 **Koike** (surname)
¹³ 溜池 **ta(me)ike** reservoir, cistern
電池 **denchi** battery, dry cell

― 3 ―

¹¹ 乾電池 **kandenchi** dry cell, battery

¹³ 蓄電池 **chikudenchi** storage battery

3a3.5 / 693   □ 氵 一 一
21 14 1

汚   汚汚

O, kitana(i), kega(rawashii) dirty
yogo(reru), kega(reru) become dirty
yogo(su), kega(su) make dirty

--------------- 1 ---------------

⁴ 汚水 **osui** filthy water, sewage
⁶ 汚名 **omei** blot on one's name, stigma, dishonor
⁸ 汚物 **obutsu** dirt, filth; sewage
   yogo(re)mono soiled things, the wash/laundry
⁹ 汚点 **oten** stain, smudge, blot, disgrace
   汚染 **osen** pollution, contamination
   汚臭 **oshū** foul odor
¹⁸ 汚職 **oshoku** corruption, graft

3a3.6 / 1188   □ 氵 一 一
21 14 1

汗   汗汗

KAN, ase sweat

--------------- 1 ---------------

⁰ 汗ばむ **ase(bamu)** become moist with sweat, be slightly sweaty
¹³ 汗腺 **kansen** sweat gland

--------------- 2 ---------------

³ 大汗 **ōase** profuse sweating
⁷ 冷汗 **hi(ya)ase, reikan** a cold sweat

3a3.7   □ 氵 力 |
21 8 2

汲   汲汲

KYŪ draw (water); busy **ku(mu)**
draw (water), ladle, dip, pump; consider, empathize with

---

⁸ 汲取 **ku(mi)to(ru)** draw (water), dip up (night soil); take into consideration, make allowances for

3a3.8 / 821   □ 氵 工
21 38

江   江江

KŌ river; the Yangtze/Yangzi river
e inlet, bay **E** (part of given name)

--------------- 1 ---------------

³ 江川 **Egawa** (surname)
   江口 **Eguchi** (surname)
⁴ 江戸 **Edo** (old name for Tōkyō, 1603 – 1867)
¹⁸ 江藤 **Etō** (surname)

--------------- 2 ---------------

² 入江 **i(ri)e** inlet, cove
¹⁴ 静江 **Shizue** (f. given name)

--------------- 3 ---------------

¹² 揚子江 **Yōsukō** the Yangtze/Yangzi river
¹³ 楊子江 **Yōsukō** the Yangzi/Yangtze river

3a3.9 / 2134   □ 氵 夕
21 30

汐   汐汐

SEKI, shio (evening) tide   SEKI,
SHIO, KIYO (part of given name)

3a3.11   □ 氵 冂 |
21 20 2

汎   汎汎

HAN pan-

--------------- 1 ---------------

⁴ 汎太平洋 **han-Taiheiyō** pan-Pacific

氵 ³
土
扌
口
女
巾
犭
弓
彳
彡
宀
⺌
虫
广
尸
口

— 4 —

3a4.5 / 1346　　□ 氵 口 |
21 24 2

沖

沖 | 沖 沖

CHŪ, oki open sea, offing

— 1 —

6 沖合 **okia(i)** open sea, offshore
15 沖縄県 **Okinawa-ken** (prefecture)

3a4.6 / 356　　□ 氵 大 一
21 34 1

決

決 | 決 決

KETSU, ki(meru) decide **ki(maru)**
be decided

— 1 —

0 決する **kes(suru)** determine, decide on, resolve
決して **kes(shite)** (with negative) never, by no means
4 決文句 **ki(mari)monku** set phrase, conventional expression
決心 **kesshin** determination, resolution
8 決定 **kettei** decision, determination
決定版 **ketteiban** definitive edition
11 決済 **kessai** settlement (of accounts); liquidation
決断 **ketsudan** decision, resolve
12 決着 **ketchaku** conclusiveness, settlement
決勝 **kesshō** decision (in a contest)
13 決戦 **kessen** decisive battle; play-offs
決意 **ketsui** determination, resolution
14 決算 **kessan** settlement (of accounts); liquidation
18 決闘 **kettō** duel
20 決議 **ketsugi** resolution, decision, vote

— 2 —

5 未決 **miketsu** pending, unsettled

可決 **kaketsu** approval, adoption (of a resolution)
6 先決問題 **senketsu mondai** question to be settled first
自決 **jiketsu** self-determination; resignation (from a post); suicide
7 判決 **hanketsu** judgment, (judicial) decision
否決 **hiketsu** rejection, voting down
8 取決 **toriki(me)** arrangement, agreement
10 既決 **kiketsu** decided, settled
11 採決 **saiketsu** voting
票決 **hyōketsu** vote, voting
終決 **shūketsu** settlement, conclusion
12 裁決 **saiketsu** decision, ruling
13 準決勝 **junkesshō** semifinals
解決 **kaiketsu** solution, settlement
20 議決 **giketsu** decision, resolution

— 3 —

5 未解決 **mikaiketsu** unsolved, unsettled
6 多数決 **tasūketsu** decision by the majority

— 4 —

12 無罪判決 **muzai hanketsu** acquittal

3a4.8 / 2136　　□ 氵 大 |
21 34 2

汰

汰 汰

TA wash away the bad; sort, select
TA, TAI (part of given name)

— 2 —

7 沙汰 **sata** case, matter, affair; news, notice, information; instructions; rumor

— 3 —

8 取沙汰 **to(ri)zata** rumor, gossip
12 無沙汰 **busata** silence, neglect to write/call

─────── 4 ───────

¹² 御無沙汰 **gobusata** neglect to visit/write

3a4.9 / 936

口 氵 冂 丨
21 20   2

CHIN, JIN, shizu(mu) (intr.) sink
shizu(meru) (tr.) sink

─────── 1 ───────

⁷ 沈没 **chinbotsu** sinking
¹² 沈着 **chinchaku** composed, calm
¹⁵ 沈黙 **chinmoku** silence

─────── 2 ───────

¹⁵ 撃沈 **gekichin** (attack and) sink

3a4.13 / 2135

口 氵 小 丨
21 35   2

SA, SHA, suna, isago sand SA, SHA,
SUNA, ISAGO, ISA, SU (part of given name)

─────── 1 ───────

⁷ 沙汰 **sata** case, matter, affair; news, notice, information; instructions; rumor
¹⁸ 沙織 **Saori** (f. given name)

─────── 2 ───────

⁸ 取沙汰 **to(ri)zata** rumor, gossip
¹¹ 梨沙 **Risa** (f. given name)
　理沙 **Risa** (f. given name)
¹² 無沙汰 **busata** silence, neglect to write/call

─────── 3 ───────

¹² 御無沙汰 **gobusata** neglect to visit/write

没 → 没 3a4.15

3a4.15 / 935

口 氵 冂 又
21 20   9

没｜没没

BOTSU, MOTSU sink down; die

─────── 1 ───────

⁰ 没する **bos(suru)** sink, set, go down; hide, disappear
² 没入 **botsunyū** be immersed/absorbed in
⁴ 没収 **bosshū** confiscate
¹² 没落 **botsuraku** downfall, ruin
¹⁶ 没頭 **bottō** be engrossed/absorbed in

─────── 2 ───────

⁴ 日没 **nichibotsu** sunset
⁵ 生没 **seibotsu** (year of one's) birth and death
⁶ 死没 **shibotsu** death
⁷ 沈没 **chinbotsu** sinking
¹³ 戦没者 **senbotsusha** fallen soldier

3a4.16 / 135

口 氵 ⼍ 一
21 15   1

灋｜汽汽

KI steam

─────── 1 ───────

⁷ 汽車 **kisha** train (drawn by a steam locomotive)
¹¹ 汽船 **kisen** steamship, steamer
　汽笛 **kiteki** (steam) whistle, siren

3a4.18 / 994

口 氵 尸 丨
21 40   2

澤｜沢沢

TAKU swamp; blessing **sawa** swamp, marsh

─────── 1 ───────

³ 沢山 **takusan** many, much, plenty
⁵ 沢田 **Sawada** (surname)

3

氵 4
土
扌
口
女
巾
犭
弓
彳
彡
宀
⼧
⼭
青
广
尸
口

7 沢村 **Sawamura** (surname)

11 沢庵 **takuan** pickled daikon

———— 2 ————

3 大沢 **Ōsawa** (surname)

小沢 **Ozawa** (surname)

4 中沢 **Nakazawa** (surname)

6 光沢 **kōtaku** luster, gloss, polish

吉沢 **Yoshizawa** (surname)

8 金沢 **Kanazawa** (city, Ishikawa-ken)

11 野沢 **Nozawa** (surname)

18 藤沢 **Fujisawa** (city, Kanagawa-ken)

贅沢 **zeitaku** luxury, extravagance

———— 5 ————

3a5.1 / 1236 　　□ 立 氵
　　　　　　　54 21

泣 泣

KYŪ, na(ku) cry, weep **na(kasu), na(kaseru)** let/make (someone) cry **na(keru)** be moved to tears

———— 1 ————

6 泣虫 **na(ki)mushi** crybaby

7 泣声 **na(ki)goe** crying, tearful voice, sob

12 泣落 **na(ki)o(tosu)** persuade (someone) by tears

18 泣顔 **na(ki)gao** crying/tearful face

———— 2 ————

5 号泣 **gōkyū** wailing, lamentation

9 咽泣 **muse(bi)na(ku)** sob

12 貰泣 **mora(i)na(ki)** weeping in sympathy

3a5.3 / 1792 　　□ 氵 弓 儿
　　　　　　　21 28 16

沸 沸

FUTSU, wa(ku) boil, seethe **wa(kasu)** (bring to a) boil, heat up (the bath)

———— 1 ————

5 沸立 **wa(ki)ta(tsu)** boil up, seethe

9 沸点 **futten** boiling point

20 沸騰 **futtō** boiling; excitement, agitation

———— 2 ————

12 湯沸器 **yuwa(kashi)ki** hot-water heater

煮沸 **shafutsu** boiling

11 排泄 **haisetsu** excretion, evacuation, discharge

3a5.6 / 364 　　□ 日 氵 ｜
　　　　　　　43 21 2

油 油

YU, YŪ, abura oil

———— 1 ————

0 サラダ油 **saradayu** salad/vegetable oil

5 油田 **yuden** oil field

6 油虫 **aburamushi** aphid; cockroach

8 油送船 **yusōsen** oil tanker

10 油脂 **yushi** fat, fats and oils

11 油断 **yudan** inattentiveness, lack of vigilance

12 油絵 **aburae** oil painting

———— 2 ————

5 石油 **sekiyu** petroleum, oil, kerosene

10 原油 **gen'yu** crude oil

12 給油 **kyūyu** supplying oil, fueling, oiling

給油所 **kyūyusho** filling/gas station

18 醤油 **shōyu** soy sauce

3a5.9 / 666 　　□ 氵 厂 又
　　　　　　　21 18 9

波 波

HA, nami wave

1
0 マイクロ波 **maikuroha** microwave
4 波止場 **hatoba** wharf, pier
7 波状 **hajō** wave, undulation
波乱 **haran** waves; commotion; wide fluctuations
8 波長 **hachō** wavelength
9 波乗 **namino(ri)** surfing
10 波浪 **harō** waves, billows
波紋 **hamon** ripples; repercussions

2
4 丹波 **Tanba, Tanpa** (surname)
8 周波数 **shūhasū** frequency
9 風波 **fūha** wind and waves, storm, rough seas; discord, strife
津波 **tsunami** tsunami, "tidal" wave
荒波 **aranami** rough/stormy seas
12 短波 **tanpa** shortwave
寒波 **kanpa** cold wave
筑波 **Tsukuba** (city and university, Ibaraki-ken)
13 電波 **denpa** electromagnetic waves, radio
15 穂波 **honami** waves of grain
18 難波 **Nanba** (surname)

3
12 超音波 **chōonpa** ultrasonic waves

3a5.10 / 1870   □ 心 氵 丨
51 21 2

HITSU, HI flow, secrete

1
7 泌尿科 **hinyōka** urology

3a5.14 / 1208   □ 氵 丨
21 2

EI, oyo(gu) swim

2
4 水泳 **suiei** swimming
20 競泳 **kyōei** swimming race

3a5.15 / 1177   □ 日 氵 丨
43 21 2

泊泊

HAKU overnight stay **to(maru)** stay at, put up at **to(meru)** put (someone) up (for the night)

1
9 泊客 **to(mari)kyaku** overnight guest
11 泊掛 **to(mari)ga(ke)** be staying with, visiting overnight

2
1 一泊 **ippaku** an overnight stay
11 宿泊 **shukuhaku** lodging
13 碇泊 **teihaku** lie at anchor, be berthed/moored
16 錨泊 **byōhaku** anchorage

3a5.16 / 357   □ 王 氵 丨
46 21 2

注丨注注

CHŪ note, comment; pour **tsu(gu)** pour in **soso(gu)** pour, flow **sa(su)** pour, apply (eyedrops)

1
2 注入 **chūnyū** injection; pour into, infuse
4 注文 **chūmon** order, commission
5 注目 **chūmoku** attention, notice
10 注射 **chūsha** injection, shot
13 注意 **chūi** attention, caution, warning
注意報 **chūihō** (storm) warning

2
4 不注意 **fuchūi** carelessness
9 発注 **hatchū** order (goods)
11 脚注 **kyakuchū** footnote

3 5
氵
扌
口
女
巾
犭
弓
彳
彡
艹
宀
屮
耂
广
尸
口

訳注 **yakuchū** translation and annotation

12 傍注 **bōchū** marginal notes

3a5.18 / 1765

囗 氵 弓 宀
21 28 15

泡

泡 | 泡 泡

HŌ, awa, abuku bubble, foam, froth, suds

— 1 —

5 泡立 **awada(teru)** beat into a froth, whip

— 2 —

4 水泡 **suihō** foam, bubble

3a5.20 / 123

囗 氵 土 竹
21 22 17

法

法 法

HŌ, HA', HO' law; method; religion **nori** doctrine, law; slope NORI (part of given name)

— 1 —

2 法人 **hōjin** juridical person, legal entity, corporation
4 法王 **hōō** the pope
　法王庁 **Hōōchō** the Vatican
5 法令 **hōrei** laws and (cabinet or ministerial) orders
6 法廷 **hōtei** (law) court, courtroom
7 法学 **hōgaku** law, jurisprudence
8 法制 **hōsei** legislation, laws
　法治 **hōchi** constitutional government
　法治国 **hōchikoku** constitutional state
　法定 **hōtei** legal, prescribed by law
　法的 **hōteki** legal, legalistic
9 法律 **hōritsu** law
　法相 **hōshō** Minister of Justice
　法則 **hōsoku** law, rule
10 法案 **hōan** (legislative) bill, measure

11 法曹 **hōsō** the legal profession
　法理学 **hōrigaku** jurisprudence
　法務 **hōmu** legal/judicial affairs
　法務省 **Hōmushō** Ministry of Justice
　法規 **hōki** laws and regulations

— 2 —

3 寸法 **sunpō** measurements, dimensions; plan, arrangement
4 不法 **fuhō** unlawful, illegal, wrongful
　六法 **roppō** the six directions; the six law codes
　文法 **bunpō** grammar
　公法 **kōhō** public law
　方法 **hōhō** method, way, means
5 民法 **minpō** civil law/code
　用法 **yōhō** how to use, directions
　司法 **shihō** administration of justice, judicial
　司法大臣 **shihō daijin** Minister of Justice
　礼法 **reihō** courtesy, etiquette, manners
　立法 **rippō** legislation, lawmaking
6 合法 **gōhō** legality, lawfulness
7 良法 **ryōhō** good method
　作法 **sahō** manners, etiquette
8 非法 **hihō** illegal, unlawful, lawless
　画法 **gahō** art of drawing/painting
9 乗法 **jōhō** multiplication
10 2進法 **nishinhō** binary (notation)
12 違法 **ihō** illegal
　減法 **genpō** subtraction
　無法 **muhō** unjust, unlawful, outrageous
14 遵法 **junpō** law-abiding, work-to-rule (tactics)
　語法 **gohō** phraseology, usage, diction
15 影法師 **kagebōshi** person's shadow
16 憲法 **kenpō** constitution
17 療法 **ryōhō** treatment, therapy, remedy
21 魔法使 **mahōtsuka(i)** magician, wizard
　魔法瓶 **mahōbin** thermos bottle

訳注 **yakuchū** translation and annotation
12 傍注 **bōchū** marginal notes

—————— 3 ——————

2 十進法 **jisshinhō** decimal/base-10 notation

4 不作法 **busahō** bad manners, discourtesy

不調法 **buchōhō** impoliteness; carelessness; misconduct; awkward, inexperienced

5 正字法 **seijihō** orthography

7 社団法人 **shadan hōjin** corporate juridical person

8 非合法 **higōhō** illegal

使用法 **shiyōhō** use, directions

9 独禁法 **dokkinhō** antitrust laws, the Anti-Monopoly Law (short for 独占禁止法)

10 財団法人 **zaidan hōjin** (incorporated) foundation

12 遠近法 **enkinhō** (law of) perspective

無作法 **busahō** bad manners, rudeness

無調法 **buchōhō** impolite; clumsy, unaccustomed to

—————— 4 ——————

5 礼儀作法 **reigisahō** etiquette, courtesy, propriety

3a5.21 / 850   田 氵 口 儿   21 24 16

KYŌ circumstances, situation
ma(shite) all the more so **iwa(n'ya)** all the more so, (with affirmative) still more, (with negative) much less

—————— 2 ——————

4 不況 **fukyō** recession, business slump

5 市況 **shikyō** market conditions

6 近況 **kinkyō** recent situation, present state

7 状況 **jōkyō** circumstances

8 実況 **jikkyō** actual conditions

9 政況 **seikyō** political situation

11 情況 **jōkyō** circumstances, state of affairs

12 景況 **keikyō** the situation

14 概況 **gaikyō** general situation, outlook

注 → 注   3a5.16

3a5.23 / 1607   田 氵 口 儿   21 24 16

EN follow along **so(u)** stand/lie along, run parallel to

—————— 1 ——————

8 沿岸 **engan** coast, shore

9 沿海 **enkai** coastal waters, coast

15 沿線 **ensen** along the (train) line

—————— 2 ——————

3 川沿 **kawazo(i)** along the river

3a5.24 / 996   田 氵 口 力   21 24 8

SHŌ, numa swamp, marsh

—————— 1 ——————

6 沼地 **numachi, shōchi** marshes, swampland

9 沼津 **Numazu** (city, Shizuoka-ken)

—————— 2 ——————

8 泥沼 **doronuma** bog, quagmire

3a5.28 / 493   田 氵 口 竹   21 24 17

JI, CHI peace; govern; healing
osa(meru) govern; suppress
osa(maru) be at peace, be quelled
nao(ru) (intr.) heal **nao(su)** (tr.) heal **OSAMU** (m. given name) **JI, HARU** (part of given name)

─────── 1 ───────

6 治安 **chian** public peace/order

8 治郎 **Jirō, Haruo** (m. given name)

17 治療 **chiryō** medical treatment

18 治癒 **chiyu** heal, cure, recover

─────── 2 ───────

4 不治 **fuji, fuchi** incurable

5 正治 **Masaharu, Shōji, Masaji** (m. given name)

　広治 **Hiroji, Kōji, Hiroharu** (m. given name)

6 全治 **zenchi, zenji** fully recover, heal completely

　安治 **Yasuji, Yasuharu** (m. given name)

　光治 **Kōji, Mitsuji, Mitsuharu** (m. given name)

　自治 **jichi** self-government

　自治体 **jichitai** self-governing body, municipality

　自治省 **Jichishō** Ministry of Home Affairs

8 退治 **taiji** subjugation; extermination, (pest) control

　法治 **hōchi** constitutional government

　法治国 **hōchikoku** constitutional state

　明治 **Meiji** (emperor and era, 1868 – 1912)

　明治神宮 **Meiji Jingū** Meiji Shrine

　明治維新 **Meiji Ishin** the Meiji Restoration

9 政治 **seiji** politics

　政治学 **seijigaku** political science

　政治家 **seijika** politician

10 哲治 **Tetsuji, Tetsuharu** (m. given name)

12 湯治 **tōji** hot-springs cure

　統治 **tōchi, tōji** reign, rule

　統治権 **tōchiken** sovereignty

16 憲治 **Kenji, Toshiharu** (m. given name)

17 療治 **ryōji** medical treatment, remedy

3a5.29 / 1621 　21 40 13

泥　

DEI, doro mud

─────── 1 ───────

4 泥水 **deisui, doromizu** muddy water

5 泥仕合 **dorojiai** mudslinging

8 泥沼 **doronuma** bog, quagmire

11 泥酔 **deisui** dead drunk

12 泥棒 **dorobō** thief, burglar

─────── 2 ───────

12 雲泥差 **undei (no) sa** a great difference

3a5.30 / 389 　21 24 14

河

KA river; the Yellow river　**kawa** river

─────── 1 ───────

3 河川 **kasen** rivers

　河上 **Kawakami** (surname)

　河口 **kakō** mouth of a river, estuary

5 河本 **Kōmoto, Kawamoto** (surname)

6 河合 **Kawai** (surname)

7 河村 **Kawamura** (surname)

8 河岸 **kashi** riverside; (riverside) fish market; place, scene; one's field/trade **kagan** riverside, bank/shore of a river

　河底 **kawazoko, katei** river bed/bottom

10 河原 **Kawahara** (surname)

11 河野 **Kōno, Kawano** (surname)

　河豚 **fugu** globefish, blowfish, puffer

─────── 2 ───────

5 氷河 **hyōga** glacier

　氷河期 **hyōgaki** glacial period, ice age

11 運河 **unga** canal

3a5.33 / 1192

目 日 氵 丨
43 21 2

泉 渁丨泉泉

SEN, izumi spring, fountain(head)
IZUMI (surname, f. given name)

—— 2 ——

3 小泉 **Koizumi** (surname)
12 温泉 **onsen** hot springs
13 源泉 **gensen** fountainhead, source, origin
　鉱泉 **kōsen** mineral springs

—— 3 ——

12 硫黄泉 **iōsen** sulfur springs

3a5.34 / 1545

⺍ 氵 大 二
21 34 4

泰 泰泰

TAI calm, peaceful; large, wide; proud; Thailand YASUSHI, YUTAKA (m. given name) YASU (part of given name)

—— 1 ——

5 泰平 **taihei** peace, tranquility
12 泰然 **taizen** calm, composed; firm

—— 6 ——

3a6.1 / 668

田 氵 ⺺ 十
21 39 12

津 津津

SHIN, tsu harbor, ferry; overflowing
Tsu (city, Mie-ken) ZU (part of given name)

—— 1 ——

3 津々浦々 **tsutsu-uraura** throughout the land, the entire country
7 津村 **Tsumura** (surname)
8 津波 **tsunami** tsunami, "tidal" wave

12 津軽海峡 **Tsugaru-kaikyō** (strait between Honshū and Hokkaidō)

—— 2 ——

3 大津 **Ōtsu** (city, Shiga-ken)
8 沼津 **Numazu** (city, Shizuoka-ken)
14 聞洩 **ki(ki)mo(rasu)** miss hearing, not catch

3a6.4 / 649

田 戈 氵 二
52 21 4

浅 淺丨浅浅

SEN, asa(i) shallow ASA (part of given name)

—— 1 ——

0 浅はか **asa(haka)** frivolous, shallow, rash
5 浅田 **Asada** (surname)
8 浅知恵 **asajie** shallow-witted
11 浅野 **Asano** (surname)
　浅黒 **asaguro(i)** dark-colored, swarthy
19 浅瀬 **asase** shoal, shallows, ford

3a6.10 / 2138

川 氵 九
21 16

洲 洲洲

SHŪ country, continent **su** sandbank, shoals **shima** island SHŪ, SU, SHIMA, KUNI (part of given name)

3a6.11 / 938

田 氵 小 子
21 35 6

浮 浮丨浮浮

FU, u(ku) float, rise to the surface; feel buoyant/lighthearted; (money) be left over **u(ita)** cheerful, buoyant; frivolous **u(kanu)** glum **u(ki)** a float **u(kabu)** float, rise to the surface **u(kaberu)** set afloat; show

3

氵 6

氵 土 扌 口 女 巾 犭 弓 彳 彡 艹 宀 ⺌ 山 圭 广 尸 囗

u(kareru) be in buoyant/high spirits
u(kasu) set afloat; save (money)
u(kasareru) be carried off, be captivated, be exhilarated

─────── 1 ───────

5 浮世 u(ki)yo this transitory world
浮世絵 ukiyoe (type of Japanese woodblock print)
6 浮気 uwaki (marital) infidelity, cheating, fickle
9 浮浮 u(ki)u(ki) buoyantly, jauntily
10 浮遊 fuyū float, waft, be suspended
浮浪 furō vagrant, wandering
浮浪者 furōsha street bum, tramp, hobo
11 浮動 fudō floating, fluctuating
浮彫 u(ki)bo(ri) relief, embossed carving

─────── 2 ───────

9 浮浮 u(ki)u(ki) buoyantly, jauntily

3a6.12 / 692 田 氵 土 儿
21 22 16

洗

SEN, ara(u) wash

─────── 1 ───────

5 洗礼式 senreishiki baptism (ceremony)
7 洗車 sensha car wash
9 洗面所 senmenjo washroom, lavatory
10 洗剤 senzai detergent
11 洗脳 sennō brainwashing
13 洗煉 senren refine, polish
14 洗髪 senpatsu washing the hair, shampoo ara(i)gami washed hair
洗練 senren refine, polish
17 洗濯 sentaku laundering ara(i)susu(gi) washing and rinsing
洗濯機 sentakki, sentakuki washing machine

─────── 2 ───────

4 手洗 teara(i) washing the hands; lavatory

5 皿洗 saraara(i) dishwashing; dishwasher

─────── 3 ───────

12 御手洗 oteara(i) lavatory
mitarashi holy water font at a shrine

3a6.14 / 1435 田 氵 卅 儿
21 32 16

洪

KŌ flood; vast

─────── 1 ───────

4 洪水 kōzui flood, inundation, deluge

3a6.15 / 2137 田 氵 小 丁
21 35 14

洸

KŌ sparkling (water) TAKESHI, HIROSHI, AKIRA, TAKASHI, FUKASHI (m. given name) KŌ, HIRO (part of given name)

3a6.16 / 237 田 氵 口 十
21 24 12

活

KATSU life, activity i(kiru) live, be alive i(keru) keep alive; arrange flowers i(ki) freshness; stet

─────── 1 ───────

2 活力 katsuryoku vitality, vigor
4 活火山 kakkazan active volcano
5 活用 katsuyō practical use; conjugate, inflect
6 活気 kakki liveliness, activity, vigor
9 活発 kappatsu active, lively
11 活動 katsudō activity
活動的 katsudōteki active, dynamic
21 活躍 katsuyaku be active

—————— 2 ——————

5 生活 **seikatsu** life, livelihood
6 死活 **shikatsu** life or death
7 快活 **kaikatsu** cheerful, lively, merry
10 敏活 **binkatsu** quick, alert, active, agile
12 復活 **fukkatsu** revival
復活祭 **Fukkatsusai** Easter

—————— 3 ——————

7 私生活 **shiseikatsu** one's private life
8 性生活 **sei seikatsu** sex life
9 食生活 **shokuseikatsu** eating/dietary habits
13 新生活 **shinseikatsu** a new life

3a6.18 / 664   田 氵 彐 宀
                    21 39 15

浄 | 浄 浄

JŌ pure **kiyo(meru)** purify
KIYOSHI (m. given name) **KIYO** (part of given name)

—————— 1 ——————

3 浄土 **jōdo** pure land, (Buddhist) paradise
4 浄化 **jōka** purification
14 浄瑠璃 **jōruri** (type of ballad-drama)

—————— 2 ——————

11 清浄 **seijō, shōjō** pure, clean, spotless

3a6.19 / 289   田 王 氵 儿
                    46 21 16

洋 洋

YŌ ocean; foreign, Western, occidental **HIROSHI** (m. given name)
YŌ, HIRO (part of given name)

—————— 1 ——————

2 洋子 **Yōko, Hiroko, Namiko** (f. given name)

5 洋司 **Yōji, Hiroshi, Kiyoshi** (m. given name)
6 洋式 **yōshiki** Western-style
8 洋画 **yōga** Western painting/movie
洋服 **yōfuku** (Western-type) clothes
9 洋風 **yōfū** Western-style
洋室 **yōshitsu** Western-style room
洋食 **yōshoku** Western food
12 洋裁 **yōsai** (Western) dressmaking

—————— 2 ——————

3 大洋 **taiyō** ocean
大洋州 **Taiyōshū** Oceania
6 西洋 **seiyō** the West, the occident
8 東洋 **tōyō** the Orient
和洋折衷 **wayō setchū** blending of Japanese and Western styles
9 南洋 **Nan'yo** the South Seas
海洋 **kaiyō** ocean
12 遠洋 **en'yō** ocean, deep sea

—————— 3 ——————

3 大西洋 **Taiseiyō** Atlantic Ocean
4 太平洋 **Taiheiyō** the Pacific Ocean
5 北氷洋 **Hoppyōyō, Hokuhyōyō** the Arctic Ocean
9 南氷洋 **Nanpyōyō** the Antarctic Ocean

—————— 4 ——————

5 北大西洋 **Kita Taiseiyō** the North Atlantic
6 汎太平洋 **han-Taiheiyō** pan-Pacific
9 南太平洋 **Minami Taiheiyō** the South Pacific

3a6.20 / 117   田 氵 攵 宀
                    21 25 15

海 | 海 海

KAI, umi sea, ocean **MI** (part of given name)

—————— 1 ——————

3 海上 **kaijō** ocean, seagoing, marine
4 海辺 **umibe** seashore, beach
海水浴場 **kaisuiyokujō** bathing beach

3

6

氵
士
扌
口
女
巾
犭
弓
彳
彡
艹
宀
山
吉
广
尸
口

5 海外 **kaigai** overseas, abroad
6 海老 **ebi** shrimp, prawn; lobster
7 海里 **kairi** nautical mile
　　海抜 **kaibatsu** elevation above sea level
8 海苔 **nori** laver (an edible seaweed)
　　海苔巻 **norima(ki)** (vinegared) rice rolled in seaweed
　　海岸 **kaigan** seashore, coast
　　海底 **kaitei** ocean floor, undersea
9 海軍 **kaigun** navy
　　海洋 **kaiyō** ocean
　　海草 **kaisō** seaweeds, sea plants
　　海峡 **kaikyō** strait(s), channel, sound
10 海豹 **azarashi, kaihyō** seal
11 海亀 **umigame** sea turtle
　　海運 **kaiun** marine transport, shipping
　　海深 **kaishin** ocean depth
　　海豚 **iruka** porpoise, dolphin
　　海産物 **kaisanbutsu** marine products
　　海魚 **kaigyo** ocean/saltwater fish
12 海港 **kaikō** seaport
　　海湾 **kaiwan** gulf, bay
13 海溝 **kaikō** an ocean deep, sea trench
　　海戦 **kaisen** naval battle
　　海賊 **kaizoku** pirate
　　海賊版 **kaizokuban** pirate edition
14 海鳴 **umina(ri)** roar of the ocean
　　海綿 **kaimen** sponge
18 海難 **kainan** sea disaster, shipwreck
19 海藻 **kaisō** seaweeds, marine plants

———————— 2 ————————

3 大海 **taikai** the ocean
　　上海 **Shanhai** Shanghai
5 北海道 **Hokkaidō** (prefecture)
6 死海 **Shikai** the Dead Sea
　　近海 **kinkai** coastal waters, adjoining seas
8 東海道 **Tōkaidō** the Tōkaidō highway
　　沿海 **enkai** coastal waters, coast
9 南海 **nankai** southern sea
　　荒海 **araumi** rough sea
　　紅海 **Kōkai** the Red Sea

10 航海 **kōkai** voyage, ocean navigation
11 深海 **shinkai** sea depths (200 m plus)
　　黄海 **Kōkai** the Yellow Sea
　　黒海 **Kokkai** the Black Sea
17 臨海 **rinkai** seaside, coastal, marine

———————— 3 ————————

4 日本海 **Nihonkai** the Sea of Japan
6 地中海 **Chichūkai** the Mediterranean Sea
8 宗谷海峡 **Sōya-kaikyō** (strait between Hokkaidō and Sakhalin)
9 津軽海峡 **Tsugaru-kaikyō** (strait between Honshū and Hokkaidō)
14 鳴門海峡 **Naruto-kaikyō** (strait between Shikoku and Awaji island)
　　関門海峡 **Kanmon-kaikyō** (strait between Shimonoseki and Moji)

———————— 4 ————————

19 瀬戸内海 **Setonaikai** the Inland Sea

3a6.21 / 912

口 氵 厂 乀
21　18　10

HA group, faction, sect, school (of thought/art); send, dispatch

———————— 1 ————————

4 派手 **hade** showy, flashy, gaudy
5 派出 **hashutsu** dispatch, send out
　　派出所 **hashutsujo** police box; branch office
7 派兵 **hahei** dispatch/send troops
12 派遣 **haken** dispatch, send
14 派閥 **habatsu** clique, faction

———————— 2 ————————

5 立派 **rippa** splendid, fine, magnificent
8 宗派 **shūha** sect, denomination
10 流派 **ryūha** school (of thought/art)
　　党派 **tōha** party, faction

特派員 **tokuhain** (news) corre-spondent; delegate

12 硬派 **kōha** tough elements, hardliners, hardcore

13 新派 **shinpa** new school (of thought/art)

鳩派 **hatoha** the doves, soft-liners

24 鷹派 **takaha** the hawks, hardliners

———— 3 ————

5 正統派 **seitōha** orthodox school, fundamentalists

11 過激派 **kagekiha** radicals, extremists

3a6.23 / 2139 　　囗 日 氵 宀
　　　　　　　　43 21 15

洵洵

JUN sincere　JUN, SHUN, NOBU (part of given name) MAKOTO, HITOSHI (m. given name)

3a6.25 / 1301 　　囗 氵 口 冂
　　　　　　　　21 24 20

洞

洞洞

DŌ cave; penetrate　**hora** cave, den

———— 1 ————

5 洞穴 **horaana, dōketsu** cave, den

13 洞窟 **dōkutsu** cave, cavern

14 洞察 **dōsatsu, tōsatsu** insight, discernment

———— 7 ————

3a7.1 / 517 　　囗 酉 氵
　　　　　　　71 21

酒

酒酒

SHU, sake, saka- saké, rice wine; alcoholic drink, liquor

———— 1 ————

4 酒井 **Sakai** (surname)

---

5 酒好 **sakezu(ki)** drinker

7 酒乱 **shuran** drunken frenzy/violence

8 酒店 **sakamise, saketen** liquor store

9 酒造 **shuzō** brewing, distilling

酒屋 **sakaya** wine dealer, liquor store

10 酒宴 **shuen** banquet, feast

11 酒断 **sakada(chi), sakeda(chi)** swearing off from drinking

12 酒場 **sakaba** bar, saloon, tavern

酒落 **share** play on words, pun, joke, witticism　**(o)share** dress up/stylishly　**share(ru)** pun, be witty; dress up/stylishly　**sharaku** free and easy, unconventional

酒税 **shuzei** liquor tax

酒飲 **sakeno(mi)** drinker

18 酒癖 **sakekuse, sakeguse, shuheki** drinking habits

酒類 **shurui** alcoholic beverages, liquor

———— 2 ————

3 大酒 **ōzake, taishu** heavy drinking

5 甘酒 **amazake** sweet saké

6 地酒 **jizake** locally brewed saké

11 清酒 **seishu** refined saké

13 禁酒 **kinshu** abstinence from alcohol, Prohibition

———— 3 ————

4 日本酒 **nihonshu** saké

12 葡萄酒 **budōshu** wine

3a7.2 / 1442 　　囗 月 氵 十
　　　　　　　42 21 12

浦

浦浦

HO, ura shore; inlet, bay

———— 1 ————

8 浦和 **Urawa** (city, Saitama-ken)

———— 2 ————

3 三浦 **Miura** (surname)

—— 3 ——
9 津々浦々 **tsutsu-uraura** throughout the land, the entire country

3a7.5 / 1753

口 食 氵
73 21

浪

RŌ wander; waves NAMI (part of given name)

—— 1 ——
2 浪人 **rōnin** lordless samurai; unaffiliated/jobless person, high-school graduate studying to pass a university entrance exam
12 浪費 **rōhi** waste, squander
14 浪漫的 **rōmanteki** romantic (school)

—— 2 ——
8 波浪 **harō** waves, billows
　波浪 **hōrō** wander, rove
9 浮浪 **furō** vagrant, wandering
　浮浪者 **furōsha** street bum, tramp, hobo
10 流浪 **rurō** wander about, roam

3a7.7 / 785

田 斤 氵 儿
50 21 16

浜

HIN beach, seashore; Yokohama
hama beach, seashore

—— 1 ——
3 浜口 **Hamaguchi** (surname)
4 浜辺 **hamabe** beach, seashore
5 浜田 **Hamada** (surname)
8 浜松 **Hamamatsu** (city, Shizuoka-ken)
11 浜野 **Hamano** (surname)

—— 2 ——
8 京浜 **Kei-Hin** Tōkyō-Yokohama
9 砂浜 **sunahama, sahin** sand beach
15 横浜 **Yokohama** (city, Kanagawa-ken)

3a7.9 / 2140

口 氵 土 口
21 22 24

浩

KŌ wide, vast; vigorous KŌ, HIRO, HARU, YŌ (part of given name) HIROSHI, YUTAKA, KIYOSHI, ISAMU, ŌI (m. given name)

—— 1 ——
1 浩一 **Kōichi, Hirokazu** (m. given name)
2 浩二 **Kōji, Hiroji** (m. given name)
　浩之 **Hiroyuki** (m. given name)
　浩子 **Hiroko** (f. given name)
12 浩然 **kōzen** expansive, free and easy, openly

3a7.10 / 247

田 氵 亠 竹
21 11 17

流

RYŪ, RU flow, current; (as suffix) style, school (of thought/art); (as suffix) rank, class, grade **naga(reru)** flow **naga(su)** let flow

—— 1 ——
5 流出 **ryūshutsu, naga(re)de(ru), naga(re)da(su)** flow out
　流石 **sasuga** as might be expected
6 流行 **ryūkō, haya(ru)** be popular, be in fashion; be prevalent/epidemic
　流行歌 **ryūkōka, haya(ri)uta** popular song
　流行語 **ryūkōgo** popular phrase, catchword
　流血 **ryūketsu** bloodshed
7 流図 **naga(re)zu** flowchart
9 流通 **ryūtsū** distribution, circulation
　流派 **ryūha** school (of thought/art)
　流星 **ryūsei, naga(re)boshi** meteor, shooting/falling star
10 流浪 **rurō** wander about, roam
11 流動 **ryūdō** flowing, liquid (assets), current (liabilities)
　流動体 **ryūdōtai** a fluid

流産 **ryūzan** miscarriage

13 流感 **ryūkan** flu, influenza (short for 流行性感網)

15 流儀 **ryūgi** school (of thought), style, system, method

————— 2 —————

1 一流 **ichiryū** a school (of art); first-rate, top-notch; unique

3 上流 **jōryū** upstream; upper-class

下流 **karyū** downstream; lower-class

女流 **joryū** woman (writer/singer)

5 本流 **honryū** mainstream

古流 **koryū** old style; old school (of art)

主流 **shuryū** mainstream

6 交流 **kōryū** alternating current, AC; (cultural) exchange

7 我流 **garyū** self-taught, one's own way

亜流 **aryū** adherent, follower, imitator

8 放流 **hōryū** set adrift, discharge, stock (with fish)

10 時流 **jiryū** trend of the times

12 寒流 **kanryū** cold current

13 暖流 **danryū** warm (ocean) current

電流 **denryū** electric current

14 漂流 **hyōryū** drift, be adrift; wandering

15 潮流 **chōryū** tidal current; trend of the times

涉 → 渉   **3a8.20**

3a7.16 / 845   田 月 氵 小
                       42   21   35

 消 | 消 消

SHŌ, ke(su) extinguish, turn off (a light), erase, cancel out **ki(eru)** go/die out, disappear

————— 1 —————

0 消ゴム **ke(shi)gomu** eraser

4 消化 **shōka** digest

消化不良 **shōka furyō** indigestion

消火栓 **shōkasen** fire hydrant

消火器 **shōkaki** fire extinguisher

6 消防 **shōbō** fire fighting, firemen

消防署 **shōbōsho** fire station

消灯 **shōtō** putting out the lights (cf. 点灯)

7 消却 **shōkyaku** efface, erase, extinguish (a debt)

8 消毒 **shōdoku** disinfect, sterilize

消毒薬 **shōdokuyaku** disinfectant, antiseptic

10 消耗 **shōmō** consumption, attrition, wear and tear

消耗品 **shōmōhin** supplies, expendables

消息 **shōsoku** news, hearing from (someone)

12 消極的 **shōkyokuteki** passive, negative

消費 **shōhi** consumption

消費者 **shōhisha** consumer

13 消滅 **shōmetsu** become extinct, disappear, become void, be extinguished

————— 2 —————

4 火消 **hike(shi)** firefighter; fire extinguisher

5 打消 **u(chi)ke(shi)** denial, negation, negative (in grammar)

8 抹消 **masshō** erase, cross out

取消 **to(ri)ke(su)** cancel, revoke, rescind

11 帳消 **chōke(shi)** cancellation, writing off (debts)

12 揉消 **mo(mi)ke(su)** crush out (a cigarette), hush up, suppress

13 解消 **kaishō** dissolution, liquidation; annulment; be settled/solved

19 艶消 **tsuyake(shi)** non-glossy, frosted (glass)

3a7.17 / 1078   田 氵 ョ 冂
                       21   39   20

 浸 浸

SHIN, hita(ru) be soaked/steeped in **hita(su)** soak, immerse **tsu(karu)** be soaked in; be submerged

3
7
氵
土
扌
口
女
巾
犭
弓
彳
彡
宀
艹
耂
广
尸
口

— 1 —
4 浸水 **shinsui** be inundated
9 浸透 **shintō** permeation, infiltration, osmosis
　浸食 **shinshoku** erosion, corrosion

— 2 —
4 水浸 **mizubita(shi)** submerged, flooded; waterlogged

3a7.18 / 1128 　　□ 火 氵 口
　　　　　　　　　　　　44 21 24

浴浴

YOKU bathe, bath **a(biru)** pour on oneself, bathe in, be showered with **a(biseru)** pour on, shower upon

— 1 —
5 浴用 **yokuyō** for the bath
6 浴衣 **yukata, yokui** light cotton kimono, bathrobe
7 浴室 **yokushitsu** bathroom (not toilet)
15 浴槽 **yokusō** bathtub

— 2 —
2 入浴 **nyūyoku** take a bath
4 水浴 **suiyoku** bathing, cold bath
　　　　mizua(bi) bathing

— 3 —
4 日光浴 **nikkōyoku** sunbath
9 海水浴場 **kaisuiyokujō** bathing beach

3a7.19 / 2141 　　□ 氵 口 亠
　　　　　　　　　　　　21 24 11

淳淳

JUN pure; kind, warm-hearted JUN, ATSU, KIYO (part of given name) ATSUSHI, KIYOSHI, SUNAO, MAKOTO, TADASHI (m. given name)

— 1 —
2 淳子 **Atsuko, Junko** (f. given name)
6 淳朴 **junboku** simple and honest

海→海 **3a6.20**

涌→湧 **3a9.31**

3a7.21 / 1239 　　□ 氵 尸 大
　　　　　　　　　　　　21 40 34

 涙丨涙涙

RUI, namida tear; sympathy

— 1 —
7 涙声 **namidagoe** tearful voice
18 涙顔 **namidagao** tearful face

— 2 —
8 空涙 **soranamida** crocodile tears
15 嬉涙 **ure(shi)namida** tears of joy

— 8 —
渚→渚 **3a9.1**

渕→淵 **3a9.3**

3a8.5 / 1668 　　□ 氵 小 上
　　　　　　　　　　　　21 35 13

淑淑

SHUKU good, virtuous; graceful, refined; idolize **shito(yaka)** graceful, gentle, polite TOSHI, YOSHI (part of given name)

— 2 —
9 貞淑 **teishuku** chastity, modesty

3a8.6 　　　　　　□ 木 氵
　　　　　　　　　　　　41 21

 淋淋

RIN rain, drip; lonely **sabi(shii)** lonely

— 1 —
4 淋巴腺 **rinpasen** lymph gland

¹⁰ 淋病 **rinbyō** gonorrhea

凄 → 凄   **2b8.4**

3a8.13 / 1622   田 日 氵 ⌐
             43   21   15

渇

 渇｜渇渇

KATSU, kawa(ku) dry up; be thirsty

————— 1 —————

⁴ 渇水 **kassui** water shortage

3a8.14 / 799   田 日 氵 ⊢
             43   21   13

混

 混混

KON, ma(zeru) mix; include **ma(za-ru), ma(jiru)** be mixed

————— 1 —————

² 混入 **konnyū** mix in, adulterate
⁶ 混合 **kongō** mixture, mixed, compound
     ma(ze)a(waseru) mix, blend, compound
     混血児 **konketsuji** person of mixed race, half-breed
⁷ 混乱 **konran** confusion, disorder, chaos
¹⁴ 混雑 **konzatsu** confusion, disorder, congestion

————— 2 —————

² 入混 **i(ri)maji(ru)** be mixed together
¹³ 搔混 **ka(ki)ma(zeru)** mix up, stir

3a8.15 / 1337   田 火 氵
             44   21

淡

 淡淡

TAN, awa(i) light, faint, pale; a little

————— 1 —————

⁴ 淡水 **tansui** freshwater

淡水魚 **tansuigyo** freshwater fish
⁵ 淡白 **tanpaku** light, plain, simple; candid; indifferent to
⁶ 淡色 **tanshoku** light color
¹³ 淡路島 **Awajishima** (island, Hyō-go-ken)

淺 → 浅   **3a6.4**

3a8.16 / 1884   田 氵 小 大
             21   35   34

溪

 溪｜溪溪

KEI valley

————— 1 —————

⁷ 溪谷 **keikoku** ravine, gorge, valley

3a8.17   田 王 氵 小
             46   21   35

淫

 婬｜淫淫

IN lewd, indecent; excessive
mida(ra) lewd, obscene, indecent

————— 1 —————

⁷ 淫売 **inbai** prostitution
⁸ 淫奔 **inpon** wanton, loose, lewd

————— 2 —————

⁹ 姦淫 **kan'in** illicit intercourse

淨 → 浄   **3a6.18**

3a8.18 / 660   田 月 氵 ⼟
             42   21   22

清

清｜清清

SEI, SHŌ pure, clear **SHIN** Manchu/Qing dynasty (1644 – 1911), China
kiyo(i) pure, clean, clear **kiyo(raka)** clear **kiyo(meru)** purify, cleanse
kiyo(maru) be purified/cleansed
su(masu) make clear; act nonchalant,

put on airs KIYOSHI (m. given name)
SEI, KIYO (part of given name)

————————— 1 —————————

2 清人 **Kyoto, Kiyohito, Kiyondo, Seijin** (m. given name)

4 清水 **shimizu, seisui** pure/clear water **Shimizu** (city, Shizuoka-ken); (surname) **Kiyomizu** (temple in Kyōto)

9 清美 **Kiyomi, Seimi** (f. given name)

清浄 **seijō, shōjō** pure, clean, spotless

10 清原 **Kiyohara** (surname)

清酒 **seishu** refined saké

清書 **seisho** fair/clean copy

清純 **seijun** pure (and innocent)

11 清涼 **seiryō** cool, refreshing

清涼飲料 **seiryō inryō** carbonated beverage

清掃 **seisō** cleaning

12 清朝 **Shinchō** Manchu/Qing dynasty

13 清新 **seishin** fresh, new

14 清算 **seisan** liquidation, settlement

15 清潔 **seiketsu** clean, neat, pure

————————— 2 —————————

10 祓清 **hara(i)kiyo(meru)** purify, exorcise

11 粛清 **shukusei** purge, cleanup, liquidation

渋 |渋 渋
21 13 11

JŪ, SHŪ, shibu(i) astringent, puckery; glum; quiet and tasteful **shibu(ru)** hesitate, be reluctant; have diarrhea-like bowel pains **shibu** astringent taste (of unripe persimmons)

————————— 1 —————————

3 渋々 **shibushibu** reluctantly, grudgingly

8 渋味 **shibumi** puckery taste; severe elgance

13 渋滞 **jūtai** impeded flow, congestion, delay

21 35 13

渉 |渉 渉

SHŌ go across/through; have to do with SHŌ, WATARU (m. given name)

————————— 2 —————————

3 干渉 **kanshō** intervention; interference

6 交渉 **kōshō** negotiations

————————— 3 —————————

4 不干渉 **fukanshō** nonintervention

41 21 20

深深

SHIN, fuka(i) deep **fuka(meru)** (tr.) deepen, intensify **fuka(maru)** (intr.) deepen, intensify MI (part of given name)

————————— 1 —————————

8 深刻 **shinkoku** serious, grave, acute

深夜 **shin'ya** late at night, the dead of night

9 深海 **shinkai** sea depths (200 m plus)

深度 **shindo** depth

12 深淵 **shin'en** abyss

14 深緑 **shinryoku, fukamidori** dark green

————————— 2 —————————

4 毛深 **kebuka(i)** hairy

水深 **suishin** (water) depth

9 海深 **kaishin** ocean depth

10 根深 **nebuka(i)** deep-rooted, ingrained

11 情深 **nasa(ke)buka(i)** compassionate, kindhearted

12 最深 **saishin** deepest

13 慎深 **tsutsushi(mi)buka(i)** discreet, cautious

14 疑深 **utaga(i)buka(i)** doubting, distrustful

16 憐深 **awa(remi)buka(i)** compassionate

——— 3 ———

5 用心深 **yōjinbuka(i)** careful, cautious, wary

16 興味深 **kyōmibuka(i)** very interesting

3a8.22 / 1433

□ 心 氵 大
   51   21   34

TEN, so(eru) add to, append **so(u)** accompany; marry; meet (expectations)

——— 1 ———

5 添付 **tenpu** attach, append

添加 **tenka** annex, append, affix, add

添加物 **tenkabutsu** additives

9 添乗員 **tenjōin** tour conductor

10 添書 **tensho, so(e)ga(ki)** accompanying letter; letter of introduction; additional writing, postscript

——— 2 ———

2 力添 **chikarazo(e)** assistance

3 口添 **kuchizo(e)** advice, support, recommendation

9 巻添 **ma(ki)zo(e)** involvement, entanglement

3a8.23

□ 氵 宀 丁
   21   33   14

TEN, DEN, yodo pool (in a river), backwater **yodo(mu)** stagnate, be sedimented; hesitate, stammer

——— 1 ———

3 淀川 **Yodogawa** (river, Ōsaka-fu)

3a8.29 / 472

□ 氵 夕 亠
   21   30   11

EKI liquid, fluid   **tsuyu** juice, soup, broth

——— 1 ———

7 液体 **ekitai** liquid

12 液晶 **ekishō** liquid crystal

——— 2 ———

6 血液 **ketsueki** blood

11 唾液 **daeki** saliva

粘液 **nen'eki** mucus

13 溶液 **yōeki** solution

3a8.30 / 549

□ 氵 亠 丿
   21   11   12

SAI, SEI come to an end; accomplish; save, rescue; many **su(mu)** come to an end; be paid; suffice **su(masu)** finish, settle; pay; make do, manage **su(manai)** unpardonable, (I'm) sorry **su(mimasen)** Excuse me, I'm sorry **su(mi)** settled, done **-zu(mi)** completed, done, already …ed **na(su)** pay back   WATARU (m. given name)

——— 2 ———

5 未済 **misai** unpaid, unsettled, outstanding

6 返済 **hensai** repayment

共済 **kyōsai** mutual aid

7 決済 **kessai** settlement (of accounts); liquidation

10 既済 **kisai** paid-up, already settled

11 救済 **kyūsai** relief, aid; emancipation

救済策 **kyūsaisaku** relief measure

経済 **keizai** economy, economics, economical use

経済学 **keizaigaku** economics

経済的 **keizaiteki** economic, financial; economical

経済欄 **keizairan** financial section/columns

3

4 不経済 **fukeizai** poor economy, waste

3a8.31 / 1204

田 氵 口 小
21 24 35

涼

RYŌ cool **suzu(shii)** cool, refreshing **suzu(mu)** cool off, enjoy the evening cool **SUZUSHI** (m. given name)

———— 1 ————

4 涼太 **Ryōta** (m. given name)
9 涼風 **ryōfū, suzukaze** cool breeze

———— 2 ————

3 夕涼 **yūsuzu(mi)** enjoy the evening cool
11 清涼 **seiryō** cool, refreshing
   清涼飲料 **seiryō inryō** carbonated beverage

涙 → 涙 **3a7.21**

3a8.33 / 1461

田 氵 土 厂
21 22 18

涯

GAI shore; end, limit

———— 2 ————

5 生涯 **shōgai** life, lifetime, career; for life, lifelong

———— 3 ————

1 一生涯 **isshōgai** a lifetime, one's (whole) life

———— 9 ————

3a9.1 / 2142

田 日 土 氵
43 22 21

渚

SHO, nagisa beach, shore **NAGISA** (given name) **SHO** (part of given name)

3a9.3

田 氵 儿 一
21 16 1

淵

EN edge **fuchi** deep water, abyss, depths

———— 2 ————

11 深淵 **shin'en** abyss

3a9.4 / 610

田 貝 氵 儿
68 21 16

測

SOKU, haka(ru) measure

———— 1 ————

8 測定 **sokutei** measure

———— 2 ————

4 予測 **yosoku** forecast, estimate
5 目測 **mokusoku** measure by eye
11 推測 **suisoku** conjecture, supposition
16 憶測 **okusoku** speculation, conjecture
18 観測 **kansoku** observation, survey; thinking, opinion

3a9.8 / 467

田 月 氵 口
42 21 24

湖

KO, mizuumi lake

———— 1 ————

10 湖畔 **kohan** lakeshore, lakeside

———— 3 ————

3 山中湖 **Yamanaka-ko** Lake Yamanaka (near Mt. Fuji)
12 琵琶湖 **Biwa-ko** Lake Biwa

3a9.13 / 669   囗 氵 艹 弓
                              21 32 28

港

港｜港港

KŌ, minato harbor, port

━━━━━━ 1 ━━━━━━

⁴ 港内 **kōnai** in the harbor
⁷ 港町 **minatomachi** port town/city
¹² 港湾 **kōwan** harbor

━━━━━━ 2 ━━━━━━

⁸ 空港 **kūkō** airport
⁹ 海港 **kaikō** seaport
　 香港 **Honkon** Hong Kong

3a9.15 / 670   囗 氵 弓 艹
                              21 28 11

湾

灣｜湾湾

WAN bay, gulf

━━━━━━ 1 ━━━━━━

⁶ 湾曲 **wankyoku** curve, curvature,
　 bend

━━━━━━ 2 ━━━━━━

⁵ 台湾 **Taiwan** (island country near
　 China)
⁹ 海湾 **kaiwan** gulf, bay
¹² 港湾 **kōwan** harbor

湶 → 泉　3a5.33

3a9.21 / 634   囗 皿 日 氵
                              59 43 21

温

溫｜温温

ON, atata(kai/ka) warm
atata(maru) (intr.) warm up
atata(meru) (tr.) warm up　**nuku(i)**
warm　**nuku(maru)** (intr.) warm up
(slightly)　**nuku(meru)** (tr.) warm up
(slightly)　**nukumo(ri), nuku(mi)**
(slight) warmth　ATSUSHI, YUTAKA

(m. given name)　ATSU　(part of given
name)

━━━━━━ 1 ━━━━━━

⁸ 温厚 **onkō** gentle, courteous
　 温和 **onwa** mild, gentle
⁹ 温泉 **onsen** hot springs
　 温室 **onshitsu** hothouse, green-
　　 house
　 温度 **ondo** temperature
　 温度計 **ondokei** thermometer
¹¹ 温情 **onjō** warm, cordial, kindly
¹³ 温暖 **ondan** warm, mild

━━━━━━ 2 ━━━━━━

⁴ 水温 **suion** water temperature
⁷ 体温計 **taionkei** (clinical) ther-
　　 mometer
⁹ 保温 **hoon** keeping warm
　 室温 **shitsuon** room temperature

3a9.22 / 1169   囗 日 氵 儿
                              43 21 16

湿

濕｜湿湿

SHITSU dampness, moisture
shime(ru) get damp/moist/wet
shime(su) moisten　**shime(ppoi)**
damp, humid　**shime(yaka)** quiet, gentle; gloomy

━━━━━━ 1 ━━━━━━

⁶ 湿気 **shikke, shikki** moisture, hu-
　　 midity
　 湿地 **shitchi** damp ground, bog
⁹ 湿度 **shitsudo** humidity
¹⁰ 湿疹 **shisshin** eczema, rash

3a9.23 / 632   囗 日 氵 犭
                              43 21 27

湯

湯湯

TŌ, TAN, yu hot water

━━━━━━ 1 ━━━━━━

³ 湯上 **yua(gari)** just after a bath
⁶ 湯気 **yuge** steam, vapor
⁷ 湯豆腐 **yudōfu** boiled tofu

8 湯沸器 **yuwa(kashi)ki** hot-water heater

湯治 **tōji** hot-springs cure

11 湯船 **yubune** bathtub

―――――― 2 ――――――

9 茶湯 **cha(no)yu** tea ceremony

12 煮湯 **ni(e)yu** boiling water

14 銭湯 **sentō** public bath

渇 → 渇 3a8.13

滞 → 3a10.14

3a9.25 / 201

田 氵 艹 凵
21 32 36

満 満|満満

MAN full; Manchuria **mi(chiru)** become full **mi(tasu)** fill, fulfill MITSURU (m. given name) MITSU, MA (part of given name)

―――――― 1 ――――――

1 満了 **manryō** expiration

4 満月 **mangetsu** full moon

6 満州 **Manshū** Manchuria

満州国 **Manshūkoku** Manchukuo

7 満足 **manzoku** satisfaction **mi(chi)ta(riru)** be contented

9 満点 **manten** perfect score

10 満員 **man'in** full to capacity

12 満場 **manjō** the whole assembly/ hall

満喫 **mankitsu** have one's fill of, fully enjoy

満期 **manki** expiration (date)

満開 **mankai** in full bloom

13 満腹 **manpuku** full stomach/belly

―――――― 2 ――――――

3 干満 **kanman** ebb and flow, tide

4 不満 **fuman** dissatisfaction, displeasure, discontent

円満 **enman** harmonious, smooth; well rounded

日満 **Nichi-Man** Japan and Manchuria

5 未満 **miman** less than, below

6 充満 **jūman, michimichi(te iru)** be full of, be replete/teeming with

8 肥満 **himan** corpulence, obesity

12 超満員 **chōman'in** crowded beyond capacity

13 豊満 **hōman** plump, corpulent, full-figured

飽満 **hōman** satiety, satiation

―――――― 4 ――――――

11 欲求不満 **yokkyū fuman** frustration

3a9.27 / 1549

田 氵 九 竹
21 16 17

滋

JI grow; more and more; blessing; tasty SHIGERU (m. given name) SHIGE (part of given name)

―――――― 1 ――――――

12 滋賀県 **Shiga-ken** (prefecture)

15 滋養 **jiyō** nourishment

3a9.31 / 2144

田 罒 氵 力
58 21 8

湧 涌|湧湧

YŪ, YŌ, wa(ku) boil, seethe, well up, gush forth YŪ, YŌ, WAKU, WAKI, WAKA (part of given name)

―――――― 1 ――――――

4 湧水 **wa(ki)mizu** spring water

5 湧出 **wa(ki)de(ru), yūshutsu** gush forth/out, well/bubble up

湧立 **wa(ki)ta(tsu)** well up, seethe

3a9.33 / 2143

田 氵 尸 土
21 40 22

渥

AKU kindness AKU, ATSU, HIKU (part of given name) ATSUSHI (m. given name)

3a9.35 / 378

口 氵 艹 厂
21 32 18

渡   渡渡

TO, wata(ru) cross **wata(su)** hand over

——————— 1 ———————

4 渡辺 **Watanabe** (surname)
6 渡米 **to-Bei** going to America
  渡舟 **wata(shi)bune** ferryboat
7 渡来 **torai** introduction, influx; visit
10 渡部 **Watanabe, Watabe** (surname)
  渡航 **tokō** voyage, passage, sailing, flight
11 渡廊下 **wata(ri) rōka** covered passageway
  渡船 **wata(shi)bune, tosen** ferry
  渡鳥 **wata(ri)dori** migratory bird

——————— 2 ———————

3 刃渡 **hawata(ri)** length of a blade
4 引渡 **hi(ki)wata(su)** deliver, transfer, hand over
6 先渡 **sakiwata(shi)** forward/future delivery
7 佐渡島 **Sado(ga)shima** (island, Niigata-ken)
  冴渡 **sa(e)wata(ru)** get cold; freeze over
  見渡 **miwata(su)** look out over
11 過渡期 **katoki** transition period
15 澄渡 **su(mi)wata(ru)** be crystal clear
16 橋渡 **hashiwata(shi)** bridge building; mediation
19 響渡 **hibi(ki)wata(ru)** resound, reverberate
20 譲渡 **jōto** assign, transfer, convey
  yuzu(ri)wata(su) turn over to, transfer

3a9.36 / 1810

田 氵 口 冂
21 24 20

渦   渦渦

KA, uzu swirl, vortex, whirlpool, eddy

——————— 1 ———————

9 渦巻 **uzuma(ki)** eddy, vortex, whirlpool; spiral, coil

——————— 2 ———————

13 戦渦 **senka** the turmoil of war

3a9.37 / 715

田 戈 氵 口
52 21 24

減   減減

GEN decrease **he(ru), me(ru)** decrease, diminish, dwindle **he(su), he(rasu)** reduce, decrease, curtail

0 減じる **gen(jiru)** decrease, lessen, subtract
4 減収 **genshū** decrease in income
  減少 **genshō** decrease, reduction, decline
8 減法 **genpō** subtraction
9 減速 **gensoku** speed reduction, deceleration
10 減俸 **genpō** salary reduction
  減員 **gen'in** staff reduction, personnel cutback
11 減産 **gensan** lower production
12 減税 **genzei** tax cut/reduction
  減給 **genkyū** salary reduction, pay cut

——————— 2 ———————

5 半減期 **hangenki** halflife (in physics)
  加減 **kagen** addition and subtraction; degree, extent, condition; adjust, keep within bounds; state of health; seasoning, flavor; allow for
  加減乗除 **kagenjōjo** addition, subtraction, multiplication, and division
7 低減 **teigen** decline, decrease, reduce
9 削減 **sakugen** reduction, cutback
  逓減 **teigen** successive diminution
14 漸減 **zengen** gradual decrease
  増減 **zōgen** increase and/or decrease

3

9

氵
土
扌
口
女
巾
犭
弓
彳
彡
宀
⺌
山
吉
广
尸
口

16 激減 **gekigen** sharp decrease, plummet

──────── **10** ────────

3a10.1

田 氵 弓 氵
21 28 5

溺

溺丨溺溺

DEKI, obo(reru) drown, be drowned; indulge in **obo(rasu)** drown (a cat); cause to indulge in

──────── 1 ────────

6 溺死 **dekishi, obo(re)ji(ni)** drowning

──────── 2 ────────

10 耽溺 **tandeki** addiction, dissipation

3a10.6 / 1267

田 月 氵 冂
42 21 20

滑

滑滑

KATSU, KOTSU, sube(ru) slide, glide, ski; slip; flunk an exam **sube(kkoi)** smooth, slick, slippery **name(raka)** smooth

──────── 1 ────────

5 滑台 **sube(ri)dai** (playground) slide; launching platform
7 滑走路 **kassōro** runway
滑車 **kassha** pulley
16 滑稽 **kokkei** comic, funny; joke

──────── 2 ────────

4 円滑 **enkatsu** smooth, harmonious

3a10.8 / 1759

田 立 日 氵
54 43 21

滝

瀧丨滝滝

taki waterfall TAKI (surname)

──────── 1 ────────

0 ナイアガラ滝 **Naiagara-taki** Niagara Falls
3 滝川 **Takigawa** (surname)

5 滝本 **Takimoto** (surname)

3a10.9 / 1012

田 氵 王 艹
21 46 32

溝

溝溝

KŌ, mizo ditch, gutter; groove, slot **dobu** ditch, gutter, sewer

──────── 1 ────────

4 溝水 **dobumizu** ditch water
8 溝板 **dobuita** boards covering a ditch

──────── 2 ────────

9 海溝 **kaikō** an ocean deep, sea trench

3a10.11

田 罒 氵 厂
58 21 18

溜

溜丨溜溜

RYŪ drip, condense; accumulate **tama(ru)** collect, form a mass, accumulate **ta(meru)** accumulate, save up **tama(ri)** waiting room, gathering place **ta(me)** sinkhole, cesspool

──────── 1 ────────

4 溜水 **tama(ri)mizu** standing/stagnant water
6 溜池 **ta(me)ike** reservoir, cistern
10 溜息 **ta(me)iki** sigh

──────── 2 ────────

4 水溜 **mizuta(mari)** puddle, pool
12 蒸溜 **jōryū** distill

3a10.12 / 2145

田 日 氵 小
43 21 35

滉

滉滉

KŌ deep and broad HIROSHI, AKIRA (m. given name) KŌ, HIRO (part of given name)

溫 → 温 **3a9.21**

3a10.14 / 964   ⊞ 氵 艹 巾
           21 32 26

滞   滞 | 滞 滞

TAI stay, stopping over   **todokō(ru)**
be left undone/unpaid, be overdue, fall
into arrears

———————— 1 ————————

4 滞日 **tai-Nichi** staying in Japan
6 滞在 **taizai** stay, sojourn
   滞米 **tai-Bei** staying in America
8 滞欧 **tai-Ō** staying in Europe
10 滞納 **tainō** delinquency (in pay-
      ment)

———————— 2 ————————

11 停滞 **teitai** be stagnant, accumulate;
      fall into arrears
   遅滞 **chitai** delay; arrearage
   渋滞 **jūtai** impeded flow, congestion,
      delay

溢 → 溢 **3a10.19**

溪 → 渓 **3a8.16**

3a10.15 / 1392   ⊞ 火 氵 宀
           44 21 33

溶   溶 溶

YŌ, to(keru) (intr.) melt, dissolve
to(kasu), to(ku) (tr.) melt, dissolve

———————— 1 ————————

8 溶岩 **yōgan** lava
11 溶液 **yōeki** solution
   溶接 **yōsetsu** welding
13 溶解 **yōkai** (intr.) melt, dissolve

———————— 2 ————————

4 水溶性 **suiyōsei** water-soluble

3a10.17 / 556   ⊞ 氵 艹 口
           21 32 24

漢   漢 | 漢 漢

KAN Han (dynasty); China; (as suffix)
man, fellow

———————— 1 ————————

4 漢文 **kanbun** Chinese writing/clas-
      sics
   漢方 **kanpō** Chinese herbal medi-
      cine
   漢方薬 **kanpōyaku** a herbal medi-
      cine
5 漢民族 **Kan minzoku** the Han/Chi-
      nese people
   漢字 **kanji** Chinese character, kanji
8 漢和 **Kan-Wa** China and Japan,
      Chinese and Japanese (lan-
      guages)
   漢和辞典 **Kan-Wa jiten** kanji dic-
      tionary

———————— 2 ————————

4 凶漢 **kyōkan** scoundrel, outlaw, as-
      sassin
6 兇漢 **kyōkan** scoundrel, assailant,
      assassin
8 和漢 **Wa-Kan** Japanese and Chi-
      nese
11 悪漢 **akkan** scoundrel, crook, ruffi-
      an, knave
13 痴漢 **chikan** molester of women,
      masher
15 暴漢 **bōkan** ruffian, goon, thug

———————— 3 ————————

6 当用漢字 **Tōyō Kanji** (official list
      of 1,850 kanji recommended
      for general use; superseded by
      the 1,945 Jōyō Kanji)
8 門外漢 **mongaikan** outsider; lay-
      man
11 常用漢字 **Jōyō Kanji** (official list
      of 1,945 kanji recommended
      for general use)

3a10.18 / 1427　田 日 氵 艹
43 21 32

漢　漢漢

BAKU desert; vast; vague

――――――― 1 ―――――――
12 漠然 **bakuzen** vague, obscure

――――――― 2 ―――――――
9 茫漠 **bōbaku** vague; vast
砂漠 **sabaku** desert

灖 → 汽　3a4.16

3a10.19　田 灬 氵 儿
59 21 16

溢　溢丨溢溢

ITSU, afu(reru) overflow
kobo(reru) be spilled　**kobo(su)** spill

――――――― 1 ―――――――
4 溢水 **issui** inundation

――――――― 2 ―――――――
15 横溢 **ōitsu** be filled/overflowing
with

滤 → 濾　3a15.8

3a10.25 / 580　田 日 氵 小
43 21 35

源　源源

GEN, minamoto source, origin
Minamoto the Genji family, the
Minamotos　HAJIME (m. given
name)　MOTO (part of given name)

――――――― 1 ―――――――
4 源氏 **Genji** Genji, the Minamoto
family
源氏物語 **Genji Monogatari** The
Tale of Genji

5 源平 **Gen-Pei** Genji and Heike
clans, the Minamoto and Taira
families
9 源泉 **gensen** fountainhead, source,
origin

――――――― 2 ―――――――
4 水源 **suigen** headwaters, source,
fountainhead
10 根源 **kongen** root, origin, source,
cause
財源 **zaigen** revenue source; resourcefulness
13 資源 **shigen** resources
電源 **dengen** power source
14 語源 **gogen** derivation, etymology
15 震源地 **shingenchi** epicenter

3a10.26 / 1338　田 戈 火 氵
52 44 21

滅　滅滅

METSU, horo(biru) fall into ruin, perish, die out　**horo(bosu)** ruin, destroy,
overthrow, annihilate

――――――― 1 ―――――――
3 滅亡 **metsubō** downfall, destruction
6 滅多 **metta (ni)** (with negative) sel-
dom, rarely
9 滅茶苦茶 **mechakucha** incoherent; preposterous; mess, wreck,
ruin

――――――― 2 ―――――――
4 不滅 **fumetsu** immortal, indestructible
幻滅 **genmetsu** disillusionment
仏滅 **butsumetsu** Buddha's death;
unlucky day
5 生滅 **shōmetsu** birth and death, appearance and disappearance
6 全滅 **zenmetsu** annihilation
9 点滅 **tenmetsu** switch/flash on and
off
10 消滅 **shōmetsu** become extinct,
disappear, become void, be extinguished

破滅 **hametsu** ruin, destruction, downfall

11 寂滅 **jakumetsu** Nirvana, death, annihilation

12 絶滅 **zetsumetsu** eradicate; become extinct

13 罪滅 **tsumihorobo(shi)** atonement, amends, expiation, penance, conscience money

15 撃滅 **gekimetsu** destruction, annihilation

撲滅 **bokumetsu** eradication, extermination

16 壊滅 **kaimetsu** destruction, annihilation

3a10.29 / 2282

田 禾 氵 一
56 21 15

黎黎

REI black; many; dawn   REI, RI, TAMI, ASA (part of given name)

——— 1 ———

8 黎明 **reimei** dawn, morning twilight

——— 11 ———

3a11.1 / 699

田 魚 氵
79 21

漁漁

GYO, RYŌ fishing   **isa(ru)** to fish **asa(ru)** fish; hunt for

——— 1 ———

10 漁師 **ryōshi** fisherman

11 漁船 **gyosen, ryōsen** fishing boat/vessel

12 漁場 **gyojō, ryōba** fishing ground/banks

13 漁業 **gyogyō** fishery, fishing industry

16 漁獲 **gyokaku** fishing; catch, haul

3a11.2 / 1400

田 車 斤 氵
69 50 21

漸漸

ZEN gradually   **yōya(ku)** gradually; finally; barely

——— 1 ———

6 漸次 **zenji** gradually

10 漸進 **zenshin** gradual progress, steady advance

12 漸減 **zengen** gradual decrease

3a11.4 / 2146

田 木 攵 氵
41 49 21

漱漱

SŌ, susu(gu) rinse the mouth, gargle   SUSUGU (m. given name) SŌ (part of given name)

3a11.7

田 日 氵 卅
43 21 32

漕漕

SŌ, ko(gu) row (a boat)

——— 1 ———

11 漕船 **ko(gi)bune** rowboat

3a11.9 / 924

田 木 氵 口
45 21 24

漂漂

HYŌ, tadayo(u) drift about, float

——— 1 ———

10 漂流 **hyōryū** drift, be adrift; wandering

12 漂着 **hyōchaku** drift ashore

滯 → 滞 3a10.14

3

11

田 木 氵 亻
                                  41 21 3

漆漆

SHITSU, urushi lacquer

――――― 1 ―――――

11 漆黒 **shikkoku** jet-black, pitch-black

13 漆塗 **urushinu(ri)** lacquered, japanned

15 漆器 **shikki** lacquerware

3a11.11 / 1411 田 日 目 氵
                     55 43 21

漫漫

MAN rambling, aimless; involuntarily
sozo(ro) involuntarily, in spite of oneself, somehow (or other)

――――― 1 ―――――

8 漫画 **manga** cartoon, comic book/strip

  漫歩 **manpo, sozo(ro)aru(ki)** stroll, ramble, walk

10 漫遊 **man'yū** trip, tour, travel

――――― 2 ―――――

4 冗漫 **jōman** verbose, rambling

8 放漫 **hōman** lax, loose, reckless

10 浪漫的 **rōmanteki** romantic (school)

3a11.12 / 1793 田 貝 氵 土
                     68 21 22

漬漬

SHI, tsu(keru) soak, immerse, pickle, preserve **tsu(karu)** soak, steep, be submersed; be well seasoned

――――― 1 ―――――

8 漬物 **tsukemono** pickled vegetables

満 → 満 **3a9.25**

漢 → 漢 **3a10.17**

3a11.13 / 344 田 日 氵 宀
                    43 21 33

演演

EN performance, presentation, play
NOBU (part of given name)

――――― 1 ―――――

0 演じる/ずる **en(jiru/zuru)** perform, play, act, enact

5 演出 **enshutsu** production, performance

7 演技 **engi** acting, performance

  演芸会 **engeikai** an entertainment, variety show

9 演奏 **ensō** (musical) performance

11 演習 **enshū** practice, exercises; (military) maneuvers; seminar

14 演歌 **enka** (a style of singing)

  演説 **enzetsu** speech, address

15 演劇 **engeki** drama, play

16 演壇 **endan** rostrum, platform

――――― 2 ―――――

3 上演 **jōen** play, stage, perform

4 公演 **kōen** public performance

5 出演 **shutsuen** appear on stage, play, perform

  代演 **daien** substitute for another actor

  主演 **shuen** starring

6 再演 **saien** repeat performance

  共演 **kyōen** coacting, costarring

7 助演 **joen** play a supporting role, co-star

  初演 **shoen** first performance, premiere

9 独演 **dokuen** solo performance

11 終演 **shūen** end of a performance

13 試演 **shien** rehearsal, preview

17 講演 **kōen** lecture, address

  講演会 **kōenkai** lecture meeting

3a11.14 / 1446   田 氵 口 宀
                                    21 24 11

滴

滴 滴

TEKI, shizuku a drop **shitata(ru)**
drip, trickle

─────────── 1 ───────────

3 滴下 **tekika** drip, trickle down

─────────── 2 ───────────

4 水滴 **suiteki** drop of water
8 雨滴 **uteki** raindrop
9 点滴 **tenteki** falling drops, raindrops; intravenous drip

3a11.19 / 1806   田 雨 氵 尸
                                    75 21 40

漏

漏 漏

RŌ, mo(reru), mo(ru) leak; be
disclosed **mo(rasu)** let leak; divulge

─────────── 1 ───────────

4 漏斗 **rōto, jōgo** funnel
  漏水 **rōsui** water leakage
5 漏出 **rōshutsu** leak out, escape
13 漏電 **rōden** leakage of electricity,
   short circuit

─────────── 2 ───────────

4 水漏 **mizumo(ri)** leak
14 遺漏 **irō** omission, negligence,
   oversight
   聞漏 **ki(ki)mo(rasu)** miss hearing,
   not catch
9 茶漉 **chako(shi)** tea strainer

3a11.21   田 氵 夕 寸
                        21 30 37

漿

漿 將
        氺

SHŌ juice; a drink; pasty substance

─────────── 1 ───────────

8 漿果 **shōka** berry

─────────── 12 ───────────

3a12.1 / 468   田田 月 日 氵
                                42 43 21

潮

潮 潮

CHŌ, shio tide; morning tide;
seawater **ushio** tide, seawater
USHIO (given name)

─────────── 1 ───────────

9 潮風 **shiokaze** sea breeze, salt air
10 潮流 **chōryū** tidal current; trend of
   the times
   潮時 **shiodoki** (waiting for) the
   tide, opportunity
18 潮騒 **shiosai** roar of the sea

─────────── 2 ───────────

3 干潮 **kanchō, hishio, hikishio** ebb
   tide
5 主潮 **shuchō** the main current
7 赤潮 **akashio** red tide
9 風潮 **fūchō** tide; trend of the times,
   the social climate
   紅潮 **kōchō** redden, flush, blush;
   menstruate

─────────── 3 ───────────

12 最高潮 **saikōchō** highwater mark;
   climax, peak

澂 → 澄 **3a12.11**

3a12.6 / 937   田 日 氵 大
                                43 21 34

潜

潜｜潜 潜

SEN dive; hide **mogu(ru)** dive;
crawl into **kugu(ru)** pass under
kugu(ri) wicket gate, side gate, small
doorway (built into a larger door)
hiso(mu) lurk, lie hidden
hiso(meru) conceal, hide
hiso(maru) be hushed

─────────── 1 ───────────

2 潜入 **sennyū** infiltrate

4 潜水 **sensui** dive, submerge

潜水艦 **sensuikan** a submarine

6 潜伏 **senpuku** hide, be hidden; be dormant/latent

潜在 **senzai** latent, hidden, potential (cf. 顕在)

潜在意識 **senzai ishiki** subconscious

13 潜勢力 **senseiryoku** latent power, potential

潘 → 溜 **3a10.11**

3a12.9 / 1626　　田 火 氵 ヨ
　　　　　　　　　　44 21 39

SEKI, kata beach, tideland; lagoon, inlet

————— 2 —————

3 干潟 **higata** dry beach (at ebb tide), tideland

13 新潟県 **Niigata-ken** (prefecture)

3a12.10 / 1241　　田 糸 氵 土
　　　　　　　　　　61 21 22

KETSU pure, clean **isagiyo(i)** pure-hearted, clean, righteous; manly
KIYOSHI (m. given name) KIYO (part of given name)

————— 1 —————

5 潔白 **keppaku** pure, upright, of integrity

18 潔癖 **keppeki** love of cleanliness, fastidiousness

————— 2 —————

4 不潔 **fuketsu** filthy, dirty

10 純潔 **junketsu** pure, unsullied, chaste

11 清潔 **seiketsu** clean, neat, pure

3a12.11 / 1334　　田 火 氵 口
　　　　　　　　　　44 21 24

CHŌ, su(mu) become clear
su(masu) make clear; perk up (one's ears); look nonchalant, put on airs
KIYOSHI (m. given name) SUMI (part of given name)

————— 1 —————

4 澄夫 **Sumio, Masuo** (m. given name)

12 澄渡 **su(mi)wata(ru)** be crystal clear

————— 2 —————

9 香澄 **Kasumi** (f. given name)

10 真澄 **Masumi, Mazumi, Sanezumi** (given name)

3a12.14　　田 貝 氵 口
　　　　　　　　68 21 24

KAI, tsubu(reru) be crushed/destroyed/ruined, collapse; go bankrupt; be worn down **tsubu(su)** crush, wreck; kill (time) **tsui(eru)** collapse, be utterly defeated

————— 1 —————

14 潰瘍 **kaiyō** ulcer

————— 2 —————

8 虱潰 **shiramitsubu(shi ni)** one by one, thoroughly, with a fine-tooth comb

11 酔潰 **yo(i)tsubu(reru)** be dead drunk

13 暇潰 **himatsubu(shi)** wasting/killing time

澁 → 渋 **3a8.19**

3a12.20 / 1203　　□ 門 王 氵
　　　　　　　　　　76 46 21

潤　　潤潤

JUN, uruo(u) become wet; profit by
uruo(i) moisture; gain; favor; charm
uruo(su) moisten, wet, water; profit,
enrich **uru(mu)** become wet/blurred/
clouded

―――― 1 ――――
13 潤飾 **junshoku** embellishment

―――― 2 ――――
7 利潤 **rijun** profit

―――― 13 ――――

3a13.1 / 1017　　□ 日 方 攵
　　　　　　　　　　43 48 49

激　　激激

GEKI, hage(shii) violent, fierce,
strong, intense

―――― 1 ――――
4 激化 **gekka, gekika** intensification,
aggravation
7 激励 **gekirei** urge on, encourage
8 激突 **gekitotsu** crash, collision
11 激動 **gekidō** violent shaking; excitement, stir
12 激減 **gekigen** sharp decrease, plummet
13 激戦 **gekisen** fierce fighting, hard-
fought contest
14 激増 **gekizō** sudden/sharp increase
15 激論 **gekiron** heated argument
激震 **gekishin** severe earthquake

―――― 2 ――――
8 刺激 **shigeki** stimulus, stimulation
9 急激 **kyūgeki** sudden, abrupt, drastic
11 過激 **kageki** radical, extreme
過激派 **kagekiha** radicals, extremists
13 感激 **kangeki** be deeply impressed/
grateful

3a13.6 / 2147　　□ 雨 氵 亻
　　　　　　　　　　75 21 3

澪　　澪澪

REI, mio water route, shipping
channel　**REI, RYŌ** (part of given
name)　**MIO** (f. given name)

3a13.7 / 957　　□ 衤 日 氵
　　　　　　　　　　57 43 21

濃　　濃濃

NŌ dark, thick, undiluted　**KO(I)** dark,
deep (color); dense, thick (liquid); strong
(coffee); intimate　**koma(yaka)** warm,
tender; detailed; deep, dark　**ATSUSHI**
(m. given name)

―――― 1 ――――
17 濃縮 **nōshuku** concentrate, enrich
19 濃霧 **nōmu** dense fog

―――― 2 ――――
10 脂濃 **abura(k)ko(i)** greasy, rich
(foods)

澤 → 沢　**3a4.18**

3a13.8 / 1625　　□ 虫 目 氵
　　　　　　　　　　64 55 21

濁　　濁濁

DAKU, nigo(ru) become muddy/tur-
bid; be voiced; be vague　**nigo(ri)**
muddiness, impurity; voiced sound/con-
sonant; unrefined saké　**nigo(su)** make
turbid

―――― 1 ――――
9 濁点 **dakuten** voiced-consonant
mark
濁音 **dakuon** voiced sound

―――― 2 ――――
5 半濁音 **handakuon** semivoiced
sound, p-sound

3

13

氵
土
扌
口
九
巾
犭
弓
彳
彡
艹
宀
丷
虫
亠
广
尸
囗

---------------- 14 ----------------

3a14.2 / 2275 　　▦ 鳥 氵 工
　　　　　　　　　　　80　21　38

鴻

鴻鴻

KŌ large, great; large wild goose　**HI-ROSHI, HITOSHI** (m. given name)　**KŌ, HIRO, TOKI, TAKA** (part of given name)

---------------- 1 ----------------

10 鴻恩 **kōon** great benevolence/blessings

潜 → 潜　**3a12.6**

濟 → 済　**3a8.30**

3a14.4 　　▦ 需 氵 一
　　　　　　　75　21　14

濡

濡濡

JU, nu(reru) get/be wet; make love　**nu(rasu)** wet, moisten, dip

---------------- 1 ----------------

6 濡衣 **nu(re)ginu** wet clothes; false charge

3a14.5 / 1561 　　▦ 隹 氵 ヨ
　　　　　　　74　21　39

濯

濯丨濯濯

TAKU, susu(gu), soso(gu), yusu(gu) wash, pour on, rinse

---------------- 2 ----------------

9 洗濯 **sentaku** laundering　**ara(i)susu(gi)** washing and rinsing
　洗濯機 **sentakki, sentakuki** washing machine

濕 → 湿　**3a9.22**

3a14.9 　　▦ 氵 口 犭
　　　　　　21　24　27

濠

濠濠

GŌ moat; Australia　**hori** moat

---------------- 1 ----------------

6 濠州 **Gōshū** Australia

潤 → 闊　**8e9.3**

---------------- 15 ----------------

3a15.3 / 1944 　　▦ 皿 氵 冂
　　　　　　59　21　20

濫

濫濫

RAN overflow; excessive, indiscriminate　**mida(ri ni)** without authorization; without good reason; recklessly

---------------- 1 ----------------

5 濫用 **ran'yō** abuse, misuse, misappropriation
7 濫作 **ransaku** overproduction
12 濫費 **ranpi** waste, extravagance
16 濫獲 **rankaku** overfishing, overhunting

3a15.8 　　▦ 田 心 氵
　　　　　　58　51　21

濾

濾丨濾濾

RO, ko(su) filter

---------------- 1 ----------------

10 濾紙 **roshi, ko(shi)gami** filter paper
11 濾過 **roka** filtration

---------------- 16 ----------------

瀧 → 滝　**3a10.8**

瀬 → 瀨 **3a16.3**

3a16.3 / 1513

　　　　　頁　木　氵
　　　　　77　41　21

瀨 | 瀨 瀨

se shallows, shoal, rapids

――――――― 1 ―――――――

4 瀬戸 **seto** strait(s), channel; porcelain
　瀬戸内海 **Setonaikai** the Inland Sea

瀬戸物 **setomono** porcelain, china, earthenware

瀬戸際 **setogiwa** crucial moment, crisis, brink

――――――― 2 ―――――――

5 広瀬 **Hirose** (surname)
6 早瀬 **hayase** swift current, rapids
　　Hayase (surname)
7 村瀬 **Murase** (surname)
9 浅瀬 **asase** shoal, shallows, ford

――――――― 22 ―――――――

灣 → 湾 **3a9.15**

――――――― 土 **3b** ―――――――

土	去	迄	地	圭	寺	吉	至	先	在	坊	坑	坂
0.1	2.2	3b4.9	3.1	3.2	3.5	3p3.1	3.6	3.7	3.8	4.1	4.6	4.7

均	走	赤	坐	坪	幸	城	垢	垣	型	奎	封	赳
4.8	4.9	4.10	4.11	5.4	5.9	6.1	6.3	6.5	6.11	6.12	6.13	3b7.10

赴	埋	赳	起	域	培	埼	堀	基	埜	堕	執	堪
6.14	7.2	7.10	7.11	8.3	8.6	8.8	8.11	8.12	oa11.5	8.14	8.15	9.1

堯	堙	堵	場	堤	塔	塚	塀	堅	報	超	越	喪
9.3	2r6.2	3e9.3	9.6	9.7	9.9	9.10	9.11	9.13	9.16	9.18	4n8.2	9.20

塊	塩	塚	填	塾	塑	塗	越	毀	場	境	増	塀
10.2	10.4	3b9.10	10.5	10.7	10.8	10.10	4n8.2	10.14	3b9.6	11.1	11.3	3b9.11

堕	墨	墜	臺	増	墳	墨	舗	壊	壌	壇	墾	壁
3b8.14	11.4	11.7	3d2.11	3b11.3	12.1	3b11.4	12.4	13.3	13.4	13.5	13.6	13.7

壓	壞	壤
2p3.1	3b13.3	3b13.4

――――――― 0 ―――――――

3b0.1 / 24

土 土

DO earth, soil, ground; Saturday
TO, tsuchi earth, soil, ground

――――――― 1 ―――――――

4 土井 **Doi, Tsuchii** (surname)
　土木 **doboku** civil engineering, public works

5 土台 **dodai** foundation, groundwork; utterly
6 土地 **tochi** land
7 土足厳禁 **dosoku genkin** Remove Shoes (sign)
8 土居 **Doi** (surname)
9 土砂降 **doshabu(ri)** downpour
　土砂崩 **doshakuzu(re)** landslide, washout
10 土俵 **dohyō** the sumo ring; sandbag
11 土産 **miyage** souvenir, present
12 土着 **dochaku** native, indigenous
　土焼 **tsuchiya(ki)** unglazed earthenware

3

14 土製 **dosei** earthen, terra cotta
16 土壌 **dojō** soil
土壇場 **dotanba** place of execution, eleventh hour
18 土曜日 **doyōbi** Saturday

— 2 —

5 本土 **hondo** mainland
6 全土 **zendo** the whole country
9 風土 **fūdo** natural features, climate
風土記 **fudoki** description of the natural features of a region, a topography
浄土 **jōdo** pure land, (Buddhist) paradise
10 郷土 **kyōdo** one's native place; local
14 領土 **ryōdo** territory

— 2 —

3b2.2 / 414

KYO, KO, sa(ru) leave, move away; pass, elapse

— 1 —

6 去年 **kyonen, kozo** last year
13 去勢 **kyosei** castrate

— 2 —

5 立去 **ta(chi)sa(ru)** leave, go away
6 死去 **shikyo** die
8 退去 **taikyo** leave, withdraw, evacuate
9 除去 **jokyo** remove, eliminate
逝去 **seikyo** death
11 過去 **kako** the past **su(gi)sa(ru)** pass
13 置去 **o(ki)za(ri)** desert, leave in the lurch
15 撤去 **tekkyo** withdraw, evacuate, remove

赱 → 走 **3b4.9**

— 3 —

3b3.1 / 118

CHI earth, land JI ground, land, earth; texture, fabric; field (of a flag), background; natural (voice); respectability; musical accompaniment; in actuality; narrative part

— 1 —

3 地上 **chijō** (on the) ground/surface; in this world
地下 **chika** underground; basement
地下室 **chikashitsu** basement, cellar
地下街 **chikagai** underground shopping mall
地下鉄 **chikatetsu** subway
4 地元 **jimoto** local
地中海 **Chichūkai** the Mediterranean Sea
地区 **chiku** district, area, zone
地方 **chihō** region, area **jikata** rural locality
5 地平線 **chiheisen** the horizon
地主 **jinushi** landlord
6 地名 **chimei** place name
7 地位 **chii** position, status
地図 **chizu** map
8 地価 **chika** land value/prices
地味 **jimi** plain, subdued, undemonstrative, conservative **chimi** (fertility of) the soil
9 地面 **jimen** ground, surface, land
地政学 **chiseigaku** geopolitics
10 地酒 **jizake** locally brewed saké
地帯 **chitai** zone, area, region, belt
11 地域 **chiiki** region, area, zone
地理 **chiri** geography
地球 **chikyū** earth, globe
地球儀 **chikyūgi** a globe of the world
13 地雷 **jirai** land mine
14 地獄 **jigoku** hell
地層 **chisō** stratum, layer

15 地蔵 **Jizō** (a Buddhist guardian deity of children)

地盤 **jiban** the ground; footing, base, constituency

地質 **chishitsu** geology, geological features; nature of the soil
jishitsu quality/texture (of cloth)

地震 **jishin** earthquake

────────── 2 ──────────

3 大地 **daichi** the ground, the (solid) earth

大地震 **ōjishin, daijishin** major earthquake

土地 **tochi** land

山地 **sanchi, yamachi** mountainous area

4 天地 **tenchi, ametsuchi** heaven and earth, all nature; top and bottom; world, realm, sphere

辺地 **henchi** remote/out-of-the-way place

心地 **kokochi(yoi)** pleasant, comfortable

5 生地 **seichi** birthplace **kiji** cloth, material; one's true colors; unadorned

平地 **heichi, hirachi** flatland, level ground, plain

用地 **yōchi** land for some use, lot, site

台地 **daichi** plateau, tableland, height

6 宅地 **takuchi** residential land

団地 **danchi** (public) housing development, apartment complex

各地 **kakuchi** every area; various places

7 余地 **yochi** room, place, margin, scope

8 沼地 **numachi, shōchi** marshes, swampland

実地 **jitchi** practical, on-site, in the field

服地 **fukuji** cloth, fabric, material

牧地 **bokuchi** grazing land, pasture

9 盆地 **bonchi** basin, round valley

荒地 **a(re)chi** wasteland

10 耕地 **kōchi** arable/cultivated land

借地 **shakuchi, ka(ri)chi** leased land

高地 **kōchi** high ground, highlands, plateau

11 基地 **kichi** (military) base

現地 **genchi** the actual place; on the scene, in the field, local

産地 **sanchi** producing area

転地 **tenchi** change of air/scene

12 湿地 **shitchi** damp ground, bog

番地 **banchi** lot/house number

13 墓地 **bochi** cemetery

聖地 **seichi** the Holy Land; sacred ground

戦地 **senchi** battlefield, the front

意地 **iji** temperament; will power; obstinacy

意地悪 **ijiwaru(i)** ill-tempered, crabby

路地 **roji** alley, lane, path

14 窪地 **kubochi** low ground, hollow, depression

緑地 **ryokuchi** green tract of land

19 蟻地獄 **arijigoku** antlion, doodle-bug

────────── 3 ──────────

4 中国地方 **Chūgoku chihō** the Chūgoku region (Hiroshima, Okayama, Shimane, Tottori, and Yamaguchi prefectures)

5 北陸地方 **Hokuriku chihō** the Hokuriku region (Fukui, Ishikawa, Toyama, Niigata prefectures)

6 行楽地 **kōrakuchi** pleasure resort

共有地 **kyōyūchi** public land, a common

7 住心地 **su(mi)gokochi** livability, comfort

9 発祥地 **hasshōchi** cradle, birthplace

乗心地 **no(ri)gokochi** riding comfort

10 遊園地 **yūenchi** amusement/theme park

埋立地 **u(me)ta(te)chi** reclaimed land

12 着心地 **kigokochi** fit and feel (of clothes)

棲息地 **seisokuchi** habitat

3

氵
土 3
扌
口
女
巾
犭
弓
彳
彡
艹
宀
山
言
广
尸
口

植民地 **shokuminchi** colony

¹³ 試験地獄 **shiken jigoku** the hell of (entrance) exams

¹⁵ 避暑地 **hishochi** summer resort

震源地 **shingenchi** epicenter

駐屯地 **chūtonchi** (army) post

3b3.2 / 2042 　日 土 22

KEI corner, angle; jewel　KEI, KE, TAMA, YOSHI, KIYO, KADO, KA, TAKA, AKI (part of given name)　KIYOSHI (m. given name)

─────── 1 ───────

⁹ 圭祐 **Keisuke** (m. given name)

3b3.5 / 41 　日 土 寸 22 37

寺

JI, tera temple

─────── 1 ───────

⁴ 寺内 **Terauchi** (surname)

⁵ 寺田 **Terada** (surname)

⁷ 寺社 **jisha** temples and shrines

⁹ 寺院 **jiin** temple

─────── 2 ───────

⁵ 尼寺 **amadera** convent

⁷ 社寺 **shaji** shrines and temples

¹³ 禅寺 **zendera** Zen temple

─────── 3 ───────

⁸ 金閣寺 **Kinkakuji** Temple of the Golden Pavilion

¹⁴ 銀閣寺 **Ginkakuji** (temple in Kyōto)

吉 → 吉 **3p3.1**

3b3.6 / 902 　目 土 竹 一 22 17 1

至

SHI utmost; (as prefix) to, until (place/time)　**ita(ru)** arrive, lead to, attain　**ita(ranai)** not good enough, inexperienced, careless　**ita(tte)** very　YUKI, YOSHI (part of given name)

─────── 1 ───────

³ 至上 **shijō** supreme, highest

⁸ 至所 **ita(ru) tokoro** everywhere

⁹ 至急 **shikyū** urgent

¹⁰ 至高 **shikō** supreme, sublime, highest

¹⁸ 至難 **shinan** extreme difficulty

─────── 2 ───────

⁵ 冬至 **tōji** winter solstice

⁶ 自…至… **ji…shi…** from (place/date) to (place/date)

¹⁰ 夏至 **geshi** summer solstice

3b3.7 / 50 　目 土 儿 | 22 16 2

先

SEN the future; priority, precedence　**saki** tip, point, end; (in the) lead; first priority; ahead; the future; previous, recent; objective, destination; sequel, the rest; the other party　**ma(zu)** first (of all); nearly; anyway, well

─────── 1 ───────

² 先入観 **sennyūkan** preconception, preoccupation, prejudice

先人 **senjin** predecessor

³ 先々月 **sensengetsu** the month before last

⁴ 先天的 **sententeki** inborn, congenital, hereditary

先手 **sente** the first move; the initiative　**sakite** front lines, vanguard

先月 **sengetsu** last month

先日 **senjitsu** the other day

5 先生 **sensei** teacher, master, doctor

先払 **sakibara(i)** advance payment; payment on delivery; forerunner

先立 **sakida(tsu)** go before, precede; die before; take precedence

6 先年 **sennen** former years; a few years ago

先任者 **senninsha** predecessor

先行 **senkō** precede, go first **saki-yu(ki), sakii(ki)** the future

先回 **sakimawa(ri)** anticipate, forestall; arrive ahead of

7 先住民族 **senjū minzoku** aborigines

先住者 **senjūsha** former occupant

先決問題 **senketsu mondai** question to be settled first

先見 **senken** foresight

8 先例 **senrei** precedent

先夜 **sen'ya** the other night

先妻 **sensai** one's ex-/late wife

先取 **senshu** take/score first, preoccupy **sakido(ri)** receive in advance; anticipate

9 先祖 **senzo** ancestor

先約 **sen'yaku** previous engagement; prior contract

10 先進国 **senshinkoku** advanced/developed nation

先週 **senshū** last week

先哲 **sentetsu** ancient sage

11 先達 **sendatsu** pioneer; leader; guide **sendat(te)** the other day, recently

先頃 **sakigoro** recently, the other day

12 先着順 **senchakujun** by order of arrival, in the order of receipt, (on a) first-come-first-served basis

先渡 **sakiwata(shi)** forward/future delivery

先覚者 **senkakusha** pioneer, leading spirit

先勝 **senshō** win the first game/point

先程 **sakihodo** a while ago

13 先触 **sakibu(re)** preliminary/previous announcement

14 先端 **sentan** tip, point, end; the latest, advanced (technology)

先導 **sendō** guidance, leadership

先駆 **sakiga(ke)** the lead/initiative

先駆者 **senkusha** forerunner, pioneer

15 先輩 **senpai** senior, superior, elder, older graduate

先鋭 **sen'ei** radical

16 先頭 **sentō** (in the) lead, (at the) head

———————— 2 ————————

4 水先案内 **mizusaki annai** pilot; piloting

6 行先 **yu(ki)saki** destination **yu(ku)saki** where one goes; the future

8 送先 **oku(ri)saki** destination, consignee

宛先 **atesaki** address

店先 **misesaki** storefront

届先 **todo(ke)saki** where to report, receiver's address

9 指先 **yubisaki** fingertip

春先 **harusaki** early spring

祖先 **sosen** ancestor, forefathers

10 胸先 **munasaki** the solar plexus; breast

旅先 **tabisaki** destination

軒先 **nokisaki** edge of the eaves; front of the house

11 率先 **sossen** take the initiative, be the first

12 勤先 **tsuto(me)saki** place of work, employer

筆先 **fudesaki** brush tip; writings

14 鼻先 **hanasaki** tip of the nose

15 穂先 **hosaki** tip of an ear/spear/knife/brush

17 優先 **yūsen** preference, priority

———————— 3 ————————

12 勤務先 **kinmusaki** place of employment, employer

3

氵
土
扌
口 3
女
巾
犭
弓
彳
彡
艹
宀
⺍
山
吉
广
尸
口

3b3.8 / 268 〔□ 土 龸 ｜〕
22 12 2

在在

ZAI be, exist, be located/residing in;
country(side), rural **a(ru)** be, exist, be
located in ARI (part of given name)

————— 1 —————

⁴ 在中 **zaichū** within

在日 **zai-Nichi** in Japan
a(rishi)hi bygone days; during one's lifetime

⁵ 在外 **zaigai** overseas, abroad

⁶ 在米 **zai-Bei** in America

⁷ 在学 **zaigaku** (enrolled) in school

¹⁰ 在庫 **zaiko** (in) stock, inventory

在留 **zairyū** reside, stay

¹⁸ 在職 **zaishoku** hold office, remain
in office

————— 2 —————

⁴ 不在 **fuzai** absence

介在 **kaizai** lie between

⁵ 存在 **sonzai** exist

⁶ 伏在 **fukuzai** lie hidden

⁸ 実在 **jitsuzai** real existence, reality

所在 **shozai** whereabouts, location,
site

¹⁰ 健在 **kenzai** in good health

¹¹ 現在 **genzai** now, present, current;
present tense; actually

¹³ 滞在 **taizai** stay, sojourn

¹⁵ 潜在 **senzai** latent, hidden, potential (cf. 顕在)

潜在意識 **senzai ishiki** subconscious

駐在 **chūzai** stay, residence

————— 4 —————

⁶ 自由自在 **jiyū-jizai** free, unrestricted

————————— 4 —————————

3b4.1 / 1858 〔□ 方 土〕
48 22

坊坊

BŌ, BO' priest's residence; Buddhist
priest; boy

————— 1 —————

⁰ 坊ちゃん **bot(chan)** (your) boy,
young master

⁵ 坊主 **bōzu** Buddhist priest, bonze;
shaven head; boy, rascal

坊主頭 **bōzuatama** shaven/close-
cropped head

————— 2 —————

³ 丸坊主 **marubōzu** close-cropped,
shaven (head)

⁷ 赤坊 **aka(n)bō** baby

⁹ 食坊 **ku(ishin)bō** glutton, gourmand

————— 3 —————

³ 三日坊主 **mikka bōzu** one who can
stick to nothing, "three-day
monk"

¹² 朝寝坊 **asanebō** late riser

3b4.6 / 1613 〔□ 土 亠 冂〕
22 11 20

坑坑

KŌ pit, hole, mine

————— 1 —————

⁴ 坑夫 **kōfu** miner

¹¹ 坑道 **kōdō** (mine) shaft, level, gallery, tunnel

————— 2 —————

⁹ 炭坑 **tankō** coal mine

3b4.7 / 443

□ 土 厂 又
22 18 9

坂 坂

HAN, saka slope, hill SAKA (sur-name)

——— 1 ———

3 坂口 **Sakaguchi** (surname)
4 坂井 **Sakai** (surname)
5 坂本 **Sakamoto** (surname)
  坂田 **Sakata** (surname)
11 坂道 **sakamichi** hill road

——— 2 ———

3 下坂 **kuda(ri)zaka** downward slope, downhill
  小坂 **Kosaka** (surname)
12 登坂 **nobo(ri)zaka** uphill slope, ascent

3b4.8 / 805

□ 土 ㇏ 冫
22 15 5

均 均

KIN equal, even **nara(su)** to level/average **hito(shii)** equal, equivalent HITOSHI (m. given name)

——— 1 ———

1 均一 **kin'itsu** uniform
12 均等 **kintō** equality, uniformity, parity
16 均衡 **kinkō** balance, equilibrium
  均整 **kinsei** symmetry, balance

——— 2 ———

5 平均 **heikin** average, mean; balance, equilibrium

3b4.9 / 429

□ 土 ⺊ 亻
22 13 3

走 丨走 走

SŌ, hashi(ru) run **hashi(ri)** first (produce) of the season

——— 1 ———

6 走行 **sōkō** travel, cover distance
  走回 **hashi(ri)mawa(ru)** run around
10 走書 **hashi(ri)ga(ki)** flowing/hasty handwriting
12 走程 **sōtei** distance covered

——— 2 ———

3 口走 **kuchibashi(ru)** blurt out, say
6 帆走 **hansō** sail, be under sail
8 奔走 **honsō** running about, efforts
  逃走 **tōsō** flight, escape, desertion
     ni(ge)hashi(ru) run away
11 脱走 **dassō** escape, flee
13 滑走路 **kassōro** runway
15 暴走 **bōsō** run wild, run out of control
20 競走 **kyōsō** race

——— 3 ———

12 御馳走 **gochisō** feast, banquet, treat, hospitality

3b4.10 / 207

日 土 儿
22 16

赤 赤

SEKI, SHAKU, aka(i), aka red **aka(ramu)** become red, blush **aka(rameru), aka(meru)** make red, blush

——— 1 ———

0 赤ちゃん **aka(chan)** baby
2 赤十字 **sekijūji** Red Cross
5 赤外線 **sekigaisen** infrared rays
  赤字 **akaji** deficit, in the red
6 赤色 **aka-iro, sekishoku** red
7 赤坊 **aka(n)bō** baby
9 赤信号 **akashingō** red (traffic) light
  赤面 **sekimen** a blush **akatsura** red face; villain's role
11 赤道 **sekidō** the equator
12 赤飯 **sekihan, akameshi** (festive) rice with red beans
13 赤裸々 **sekirara** stark naked; frank, outspoken

3

氵
土
扌
口
女
巾
犭
弓
彳
彡
艹
宀
⺌
⺍
聿
广
尸
口

4

¹⁴ 赤蜻蛉 **akatonbo** red dragonfly
¹⁵ 赤潮 **akashio** red tide

——— 2 ———

⁴ 日赤 **Nisseki** Japan Red Cross (short for 日本赤十字社)

3b4.11 ⟨⟩ 土 亻
22 3

ZA sit; somehow **suwa(ru)** sit (For compounds, see 座 3q7.2)

——— 5 ———

3b5.4 / 1896 □ 土 一 儿
22 14 16

HEI, tsubo (unit of area, exactly 400/121 square meters, or about 3.3 square meters)

——— 1 ———

⁴ 坪井 **Tsuboi** (surname)
¹³ 坪数 **tsubosū** number of tsubo, area

——— 2 ———

⁵ 立坪 **ta(te)tsubo** cubic *ken* (about 6 cubic meters)

3b5.9 / 684 日 立 十 一
54 12 1

KŌ, saiwa(i), shiawa(se), sachi happiness, good fortune MIYUKI (f. given name) YUKI (part of given name)

——— 1 ———

¹ 幸一 **Kōichi, Yukikazu** (m. given name)
² 幸子 **Sachiko, Yukiko, Kōko, Kōshi, Toshiko** (given name)

⁷ 幸男 **Yukio, Sachio, Yoshio** (m. given name)
¹⁰ 幸恵 **Yukie, Sachie** (f. given name)
¹¹ 幸運 **kōun** good fortune, luck
¹³ 幸福 **kōfuku** happiness

——— 2 ———

⁴ 不幸 **fukō** unhappiness, misfortune
¹⁰ 射幸 **shakō** speculation

——— 6 ———

3b6.1 / 720 □ 戈 土 亠
52 22 15

JŌ, shiro castle KI (part of given name)

——— 1 ———

³ 城下町 **jōkamachi** castle town
⁸ 城門 **jōmon** castle gate
⁹ 城郭 **jōkaku** castle; castle walls
¹⁶ 城壁 **jōheki** castle walls, ramparts

——— 2 ———

⁸ 京城 **Keijō** Seoul
⁹ 茨城県 **Ibaraki-ken** (prefecture)
¹⁰ 宮城県 **Miyagi-ken** (prefecture)

——— 4 ———

³ 万里長城 **Banri (no) Chōjō** Great Wall of China

3b6.3 □ 土 口 厂
22 24 18

KŌ, KU, aka dirt, grime, scale, (ear)wax

——— 1 ———

⁷ 垢抜 **akanu(ke)** refined, polished, urbane

3b6.5 / 1276

□ 日 土 二
43 22 4

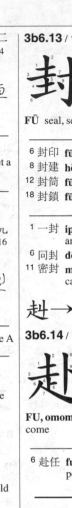

垣 垣

ＥN, kaki fence, hedge

——— 1 ———

10 垣根 **kakine** fence, hedge
12 垣間見 **kaimami(ru)** peek in, get a glimpse

——— 2 ———

5 石垣 **ishigaki** stone wall

3b6.11 / 888

田 艹 土 儿
32 22 16

型 型

KEI, kata, -gata model, form, type

——— 1 ———

0 Ａ型 **ēgata** Model A; (blood) type A

——— 2 ———

3 大型 **ōgata** large size
   小型 **kogata** small-size
6 １９９８年型 **1998nen-gata** the 1998 model
8 典型的 **tenkelteki** typical
   定型 **teikei** definite form, type
10 原型 **genkei** prototype, model
13 新型 **shingata** new model/style
14 髪型 **kamigata** hairdo
   模型 **mokei** (scale) model; a mold
15 鋳型 **igata** a mold, cast

——— 3 ———

10 紋切型 **monki(ri)gata** conventional

3b6.12 / 2045

日 大 土
34 22

奎 奎

KEI star/god ruling over literature
KEI, KE, KI, FUMI (part of given name)

3b6.13 / 1463

田 土 寸
22 37

封 封

FŪ seal, sealing HŌ fief

——— 1 ———

6 封印 **fūin** (stamped) seal
8 封建 **hōken** feudalism
12 封筒 **fūtō** envelope
18 封鎖 **fūsa** blockade; freeze (assets)

——— 2 ———

1 一封 **ippū** a sealed letter/document; an enclosure
6 同封 **dōfū** enclose
11 密封 **mippū** seal tight/up/hermetically

赴 → 3b7.10

3b6.14 / 1465

⸫ 土 ⼘ 亻
22 13 3

赴 赴

FU, omomu(ku) go, proceed to; become

——— 1 ———

6 赴任 **funin** proceed to one's new post

——— 7 ———

3b7.2 / 1826

□ 日 土
43 22

埋 埋

MAI, u(meru), uzu(meru) bury, fill up u(maru), uzu(maru) be buried (under), be filled up u(moreru), uzu(moreru) be buried; sink into obscurity i(keru) bury, bank (a fire)

3

氵 土 7
扌 扌
女 巾
犭 弓
彳 彡
艹 宀
⺌ 山
广 尸
□

3b7.10

— 1 —

5 埋立地 **u(me)ta(te)chi** reclaimed land

12 埋葬 **maisō** burial, interment

15 埋蔵 **maizō** buried stores, underground reserves

— 2 —

5 生埋 **i(ki)u(me)** burying alive

穴埋 **anau(me)** fill a gap; cover a deficit

3b7.10 / 2244

… ± ┗ ⺅
22 13 3

赳 赳

KYŪ strong and brave KYŪ, TAKE, ISA (part of given name) TAKESHI, ISAMU (m. given name)

3b7.11 / 373

… ± 弓 ┗
22 28 13

起 起

KI awakening, rise, beginning
o(kiru) get/wake/be up; occur
o(koru) occur, happen **o(kosu)** wake (someone) up; begin, start, create, cause **ta(tsu)** begin, start, rise up
OKI (part of given name)

— 1 —

3 起上 **o(ki)a(garu)** get up, rise

5 起立 **kiritsu** stand up

7 起床 **kishō** wake up, rise

9 起点 **kiten** starting point

10 起原 **kigen** origin, beginning

12 起訴 **kiso** prosecute, indict; sue, bring action against

13 起電力 **kidenryoku** electromotive force

— 2 —

6 早起 **hayao(ki)** get up early

9 巻起 **ma(ki)o(kosu)** stir up, create (a sensation)

11 捲起 **ma(ki)o(kosu)** stir up, create (a sensation)

12 揺起 **yu(ri)o(kosu)** awaken by shaking

喚起 **kanki** evoke, awaken, call forth

15 縁起 **engi** history, origin; omen, luck

— 8 —

3b8.3 / 970

⊞ 戈 ± ⼞
52 22 24

域 域

IKI region, area

— 2 —

4 区域 **kuiki** boundary; zone, territory

6 地域 **chiiki** region, area, zone

13 聖域 **seiiki** holy ground, sacred precincts

14 領域 **ryōiki** territory; domain, field

3b8.6 / 1828

⊞ 立 ± ⼞
54 22 24

培 培

BAI, tsuchika(u) cultivate, foster

— 1 —

15 培養 **baiyō** cultivation, culture

— 2 —

10 栽培 **saibai** cultivate, grow

3b8.8

⊞ ± 大 ⼞
22 34 24

埼 埼

KI, saki cape, promontory

— 1 —

5 埼玉県 **Saitama-ken** (prefecture)

3b8.11 / 1804
口 土 尸 凵
22 40 36

堀 堀堀

hori moat, ditch, canal HORI (surname)

—— 1 ——

4 堀内 **Horiuchi, Horinouchi** (surname)

5 堀田 **Hotta, Horita** (surname)

—— 2 ——

11 釣堀 **tsu(ri)bori** fishpond

3b8.12 / 450
目 艹 土 二
32 22 4

基 基基

KI basis, foundation; radical (in chemistry); (counter for heavy machines, etc.) **moto, motoi** basis, foundation, origin HAJIME (m. given name)

—— 1 ——

0 基づく **moto(zuku)** be based/founded on

5 基本 **kihon** basic, fundamental, standard

基本的 **kihonteki** basic, fundamental

6 基地 **kichi** (military) base

8 基金 **kikin** fund, endowment

13 基準 **kijun** standard, criterion, basis

15 基盤 **kiban** base, basis, foundation

18 基礎 **kiso** foundation, fundamentals

—— 2 ——

10 根基 **konki** root, origin

埜 → 野   0a11.5

3b8.14 / 1742
田 月 土 阝
42 22 7

堕 堕丨堕堕

DA fall

—— 1 ——

9 堕胎 **datai** abortion

12 堕落 **daraku** depravity, corruption

3b8.15 / 686
田 立 十 一
54 12 1

執 執執,

SHITSU, SHŪ, to(ru) take, grasp; carry out, execute

—— 1 ——

6 執行 **shikkō** performance, execution

8 執念 **shūnen** tenacity of purpose, vindictiveness

12 執着 **shūchaku** attachment to, tenacity

執筆 **shippitsu** write (for a magazine)

—— 2 ——

8 固執 **koshitsu** hold fast to, persist in, insist on

—— 9 ——

3b9.1 / 1913
田 土 艹 二
22 32 4

堪 堪堪

KAN, TAN, tae(ru) endure, withstand **kora(eru)** bear, endure; control, stifle; pardon **kota(eru)** endure **tama(ru)** bear, put up with **tama(ranai)** can't stand it

—— 1 ——

5 堪弁 **kanben** pardon, forgive

7 堪忍 **kannin** patience, forbearance; forgiveness

3

氵 土
扌 9
口
女
巾
犭
弓
彳
彡
艹
宀
屮
士
广
尸
口

8 堪性 **kora(e)shō** patience
10 堪能 **tannō** skill; be satisfied

目 土 一 丨
22 14 2

堯 | 堯 堯

GYŌ high; far GYŌ, TAKA, AKI, NORI, TOMI (part of given name)
TAKASHI, YUTAKA, AKIRA, SATORU
(m. given name)

堰 → 岡 2r6.2

壻 → 婿 3e9.3

田 日 土 彡
43 22 27

場 | 場 場

JŌ, ba place

━━━━━━ 1 ━━━━━━

6 場合 **baai** case, occasion, circumstances
　 場当 **baa(tari)** grandstanding, applause-seeking
8 場所 **basho** place, location
9 場面 **bamen** scene

━━━━━━ 2 ━━━━━━

2 入場 **nyūjō** entrance, admission
　 入場料 **nyūjōryō** admission fee
3 工場 **kōjō, kōba** factory, workshop, mill
　 下場 **o(ri)ba** place to get off, disembarking point
5 矢場 **yaba** archery ground/range
　 出場 **shutsujō** appear on stage, perform; participate in, enter (a competition)
　 本場 **honba** home, habitat, the best place for

市場 **shijō** market **ichiba** market place
穴場 **anaba** good place known to few
広場 **hiroba** plaza, public square
立場 **tachiba** standpoint, position, viewpoint
6 死場 **shi(ni)ba** place to die, place o death
会場 **kaijō** meeting place; grounds
式場 **shikijō** ceremonial hall
7 役場 **yakuba** town hall, public office
　 売場 **u(ri)ba** sales counter, place where (tickets) are sold
　 初場所 **hatsubasho** New Year's grand sumo tournament
8 退場 **taijō** leave, exit, walk out
　 牧場 **bokujō, makiba** pasture, meadow, ranch
9 乗場 **no(ri)ba** (taxi) stand, bus stop, platform
　 急場 **kyūba** emergency, crisis
　 相場 **sōba** market price; speculation; estimation
　 秋場所 **akibasho** autumn sumo tournament
10 射場 **shajō** shooting/rifle range; archery ground
　 遊場 **aso(bi)ba** playground
　 酒場 **sakaba** bar, saloon, tavern
　 夏場 **natsuba** summertime, the summer season
　 馬場 **Baba** (surname)
11 道場 **dōjō** (martial-arts) gymnasium; Buddhist seminary
　 球場 **kyūjō** baseball grounds/stadium
　 現場 **genba, genjō** the actual spot; on the scene, at the site, in the field
　 盛場 **saka(ri)ba** bustling place, popular resort, amusement center
12 満場 **manjō** the whole assembly/hall
　 登場 **tōjō** come on stage; appear on the scene
　 開場 **kaijō** opening

³ 隠場 **kaku(re)ba** refuge, hiding place

農場 **nōjō** farm, ranch, plantation

墓場 **hakaba** cemetery, graveyard

戦場 **senjō** battlefield, the front

置場 **o(ki)ba** place to put something

¹⁴ 漁場 **gyojō, ryōba** fishing ground/banks

磁場 **jiba, jijō** magnetic field

¹⁵ 劇場 **gekijō** theater

¹⁸ 職場 **shokuba** workplace, job site

²² 鱈場蟹 **tarabagani** king crab

3
---

³ 工事場 **kōjiba** construction site

土壇場 **dotanba** place of execution, eleventh hour

⁸ 波止場 **hatoba** wharf, pier

⁹ 風呂場 **furoba** bathroom

¹¹ 魚市場 **uoichiba** fish market

¹³ 鉄工場 **tekkōjō** ironworks

¹⁵ 駐車場 **chūshajō** parking lot

¹⁷ 闇相場 **yamisōba** black-market price

4
---

¹ 一時預場 **ichiji azukarijō** baggage safekeeping area

⁸ 青空市場 **aozora ichiba** open-air market

⁹ 海水浴場 **kaisuiyokujō** bathing beach

¹⁰ 株式市場 **kabushiki shijō** stock market

3b9.7 / 1592   囗 日 土 丁   43 22 14

TEI, tsutsumi bank, embankment, dike TSUTSUMI (surname)

1
---

⁶ 堤防 **teibō** embankment, dike, levee

3b9.9 / 1840   囗 土 艹 口   22 32 24

TŌ tower

2
---

⁵ 石塔 **sekitō** tombstone, stone monument

3
---

¹² 象牙塔 **zōge (no) tō** ivory tower

¹⁴ 管制塔 **kanseitō** control tower

3b9.10 / 1751   囗 土 犭 冂   22 27 20

CHŌ, tsuka mound, hillock

1
---

⁵ 塚本 **Tsukamoto** (surname)

2
---

³ 大塚 **Ōtsuka** (surname)

⁴ 手塚 **Tezuka** (surname)

¹² 飯塚 **Iizuka** (surname)

¹⁹ 蟻塚 **arizuka** anthill

3b9.11 / 1805   囗 土 尸 艹   22 40 32

HEI wall, fence

2
---

⁵ 石塀 **ishibei** stone wall

⁸ 板塀 **itabei** board fence

3b9.13 / 1289   囗 土 冂 又   22 20 9

KEN, kata(i) hard, firm, solid KATA (part of given name)

—— 1 ——

⁶ 堅気 **katagi** honest, decent, straight
⁸ 堅実 **kenjitsu** solid, sound, reliable

3b9.16 / 685

田 立 十 阝
54 12 7

報

HŌ news, report; reward, retribution
muku(iru) reward, retaliate

—— 1 ——

⁷ 報告 **hōkoku** report
　報告書 **hōkokusho** (written) report/statement
¹¹ 報道 **hōdō** reporting, news coverage
¹³ 報酬 **hōshū** remuneration
¹⁷ 報償 **hōshō** compensation, reward, remuneration

—— 2 ——

⁴ 予報 **yohō** forecast, preannouncement
⁵ 弘報 **kōhō** publicity
　広報 **kōhō** publicity
⁶ 年報 **nenpō** annual report
⁸ 果報 **kahō** good fortune, luck
　官報 **kanpō** official gazette/telegram
⁹ 急報 **kyūhō** urgent message, alarm
　速報 **sokuhō** bulletin, news flash
　通報 **tsūhō** report, dispatch, bulletin, news
¹⁰ 時報 **jihō** review; time signal
¹¹ 情報 **jōhō** information
　情報化社会 **jōhōka shakai** information-oriented society
¹² 勝報 **shōhō** news of victory
　無報酬 **muhōshū** without pay, for free
¹³ 彙報 **ihō** collection of reports, bulletin
　電報 **denpō** telegram
¹⁴ 誤報 **gohō** erroneous report/information
¹⁶ 諜報 **chōhō** intelligence, espionage
¹⁹ 警報 **keihō** warning, alarm

　警報機 **keihōki** warning device, alarm

—— 3 ——

⁸ 注意報 **chūihō** (storm) warning

3b9.18 / 1000

⋯ 土 口 ⺀
22 24 13

超

CHŌ super-, ultra-　**ko(eru)** go beyond, exceed　**ko(su)** go beyond, exceed

—— 1 ——

⁶ 超伝導 **chōdendō** superconductivity
　超自然 **chōshizen** supernatural
⁹ 超音波 **chōonpa** ultrasonic waves
　超音速 **chōonsoku** supersonic speed
¹¹ 超過 **chōka** exceed
¹² 超満員 **chōman'in** crowded beyond capacity
　超越 **chōetsu** transcend, rise above

越 → **4n8.2**

3b9.20 / 1678

田 ⺀ 口 十
57 24 12

喪

SŌ, mo mourning; loss

—— 1 ——

⁴ 喪中 **mochū** period of mourning
⁵ 喪失 **sōshitsu** loss
⁸ 喪服 **mofuku** mourning clothes

—— 10 ——

3b10.2 / 1524

田 甲 土 儿
58 22 16

塊

塊塊

KAI, katamari lump, clod, clump

— 2 —

¹ 一塊 **hitokatama(ri)** a lump, a group   **ikkai** a lump

⁵ 氷塊 **hyōkai** lump/block of ice, ice floe

石塊 **sekkai, ishikoro, ishikure** pebble, stones

3b10.4 / 1101   ⊞   ᨓ   土   口   59 22 24

鹽 | 塩塩

EN, shio salt

— 1 —

⁴ 塩分 **enbun** salt content, salinity

塩水 **shiomizu, ensui** salt water, brine

⁸ 塩味 **shioaji** salty taste

— 2 —

⁹ 食塩 **shokuen** table salt

¹⁶ 薄塩 **usujio** lightly salted

塚 → 塚 **3b9.10**

3b10.5   ⊞   ᨓ   土   十   55 22 12

塡 | 填塡

TEN fill in

— 1 —

¹² 填補 **tenpo** fill up; compensate for, make good; replenish, complete

3b10.7 / 1674   ⊞   口   土   亠   24 22 11

塾塾

JUKU private/cram school

— 1 —

⁵ 塾生 **jukusei** cram-school student

3b10.8 / 1838   ⊞   月   土   几   42 22 16

塑塑

SO (clay) molding, plastic

— 1 —

⁹ 塑造 **sozō** modeling, molding, plastic (arts)

— 2 —

⁵ 可塑 **kaso** plastic

3b10.10 / 1073   ⊞   木   氵   土   41 21 22

塗塗

TO, nu(ru) paint, apply (a coating), smear onto   **mabu(su)** smear/sprinkle/cover with   **mami(reru)** be smeared/spattered/covered with

— 1 —

⁵ 塗立 **nu(ri)ta(teru)** put on thick makeup   **nu(ri)ta(te)** freshly painted/plastered, Wet Paint

⁸ 塗物 **nu(ri)mono** lacquerware

¹⁰ 塗料 **toryō** paint, paint and varnish

¹² 塗装 **tosō** painting, coating

¹⁵ 塗箸 **nu(ri)bashi** lacquered chopsticks

— 2 —

⁶ 血塗 **chimami(re)** bloodstained   **chinu(ru)** smear with blood

¹¹ 黒塗 **kuronu(ri)** black-lacquered, painted black

¹⁴ 漆塗 **urushinu(ri)** lacquered, japanned

¹⁵ 糊塗 **koto** patch up, temporize

越 → **4n8.2**

3b10.14 田 ≡ 士 厂
39 22 18

毀

毀 毀

KI break, destroy; censure **kobo(tsu)**,
kowa(su) break, destroy **kobo(reru)**
be nicked/chipped/broken **kowa(reru)**
break, get broken, be ruined

———— 1 ————

13 毀損 **kison** damage, injure

———— 11 ————

場→場 **3b9.6**

3b11.1 / 864 ⊞ 立 日 土
54 43 22

境

境 境

KYŌ, KEI, sakai boundary

———— 1 ————

5 境目 **sakaime** borderline; crisis
9 境界 **kyōkai** boundary, border

———— 2 ————

4 辺境 **henkyō** frontier, outlying region
心境 **shinkyō** state of mind
8 苦境 **kukyō** distress, predicament,
crisis
国境 **kokkyō, kunizakai** border,
national boundary
12 越境 **ekkyō** (illegally) crossing the
border
17 環境 **kankyō** environment
環境庁 **Kankyōchō** Environment
Agency
12 廃墟 **haikyo** ruins

3b11.3 / 712 ⊞ 甲 日 土
58 43 22

増

 増丨増増

ZŌ increase **fu(eru), ma(su/saru)**
(intr.) increase, rise **fu(yasu), ma(su)**

(tr.) increase, raise **ma(shi)** increase,
extra; every (day); better, preferable

———— 1 ————

4 増井 **Masui** (surname)
5 増加 **zōka** increase, addition, rise,
growth
増田 **Masuda** (surname)
10 増俸 **zōhō** salary increase
増進 **zōshin** increase, furtherance,
improvement
11 増強 **zōkyō** reinforce, augment,
beef up
増産 **zōsan** increase in production
増設 **zōsetsu** build on, extend, establish/install more
12 増減 **zōgen** increase and/or decrease
増税 **zōzei** tax increase
16 増築 **zōchiku** build on, extend, enlarge
18 増額 **zōgaku** increase (the amount)

———— 2 ————

4 水増 **mizuma(shi)** water down, dilute, pad
日増 **hima(shi ni)** (getting ...er)
day by day
9 急増 **kyūzō** sudden increase
10 倍増 **baizō, baima(shi)** to double
12 割増 **warima(shi)** extra (charge/
payment)
16 激増 **gekizō** sudden/sharp increase

———— 3 ————

7 改訂増補 **kaitei-zōho** revised and
enlarged

塀→塀 **3b9.11**

堕→堕 **3b8.14**

3b11.4 / 1705 日 火 土
43 44 22

墨

墨丨墨墨

BOKU India ink, ink stick; Mexico;
Sumida river **sumi** India ink, ink stick

— 1 —

8 墨画 **bokuga** India-ink drawing

12 墨絵 **sumie** India-ink drawing

— 2 —

2 入墨 **i(re)zumi** tattooing; tattoo

4 水墨画 **suibokuga** India-ink painting

5 白墨 **hakuboku** chalk

3b11.7 / 1132

TSUI fall

— 1 —

12 墜落 **tsuiraku** fall, (airplane) crash

— 2 —

5 失墜 **shittsui** lose, fall

臺 → 台 **3d2.11**

— 12 —

增 → 増 **3b11.3**

3b12.1 / 1662

墳

FUN (burial) mound, tomb

— 1 —

13 墳墓 **funbo** grave, tomb

— 2 —

5 古墳 **kofun** ancient burial mound

墨 → 墨 **3b11.4**

3b12.4 / 1443

舗

HO shop, store

— 1 —

11 舗道 **hodō** paved street, pavement

12 舗装 **hosō** pavement, paving

— 2 —

6 老舗 **rōho, shinise** long-established shop/store

— 13 —

3b13.3 / 1407

壊

KAI, E break **kowa(su)** break, tear down, destroy, damage **kowa(reru)** break, get broken, be destroyed

— 1 —

13 壊滅 **kaimetsu** destruction, annihilation

— 2 —

6 全壊 **zenkai** complete destruction

8 取壊 **to(ri)kowa(su)** tear down, demolish

10 倒壊 **tōkai** collapse, be destroyed
破壊 **hakai** destroy, demolish, collapse

11 崩壊 **hōkai** collapse, disintegration

3b13.4 / 1912

JŌ soil

— 2 —

3 土壌 **dojō** soil

5 平壌 **Heijō** Pyongyang

3b13.5 / 1839

⊞ 日 土 口
43 22 24

壇 壇

DAN stage, rostrum, podium; altar; world (of art)

— 2 —

3 土壇場 **dotanba** place of execution, eleventh hour

4 仏壇 **butsudan** household Buddhist altar

文壇 **bundan** the literary world; literary column

7 花壇 **kadan** flower bed/garden

11 祭壇 **saidan** altar

14 演壇 **endan** rostrum, platform

3b13.6 / 1136

⊞ 貝 犭 土
73 27 22

墾 墾

KON open up farmland, bring under cultivation

12 開墾 **kaikon** clear (land), bring under cultivation

3b13.7 / 1489

⊞ 立 尸 口
54 40 24

壁 壁

HEKI, kabe wall

— 1 —

8 壁画 **hekiga** fresco, mural

10 壁紙 **kabegami** wallpaper

— 2 —

9 城壁 **jōheki** castle walls, ramparts

—— 14 ——

壓 → 圧 2p3.1

—— 16 ——

壞 → 壊 3b13.3

—— 17 ——

壤 → 壌 3b13.4

——— 扌 3c ———

手	払	打	扱	扱	扶	把	折	抜	抄	抑	批	抗
0.1	2.2	2.3	3.5	3c3.5	4.4	4.5	4.7	4.10	4.11	4.12	4.13	4.15
技	投	択	拒	拓	拝	押	抽	抹	拙	拂	披	拍
4.16	4.18	4.21	3c5.29	5.1	5.3	5.5	5.7	5.9	5.11	3c2.2	5.13	5.14
抱	拗	抵	担	拐	拐	招	拵	拡	拠	拘	拒	挟
5.15	5.16	5.18	5.20	5.21	3c5.21	5.22	5.24	5.25	5.26	5.28	5.29	6.1
拷	挑	持	按	括	拶	拾	指	拓	拳	挿	捕	挟
6.2	6.5	6.8	6.10	6.12	6.13	6.14	6.15	3c5.14	6.18	7.2	7.3	3c6.1
捌	捜	挨	挽	捩	振	挫	推	捷	掛	排	捲	接
7.4	7.5	7.12	7.13	3c8.31	7.14	7.15	8.1	8.4	8.6	8.8	8.9	8.10
控	捧	揭	採	授	探	捻	措	描	掃	捻	捨	捨
8.11	8.12	8.13	8.14	8.15	8.16	8.17	8.20	8.21	8.22	8.25	8.26	3c8.26
掠	挽	搔	捩	掘	据	掴	插	搜	捲	揉	揆	提
8.28	3c7.13	3c10.11	8.31	8.32	8.33	3c11.6	3c7.2	3c7.5	3c8.9	9.2	9.3	9.4
揚	揭	援	揺	搭	搔	揮	換	揃	握	搗	搬	携
9.5	3c8.13	9.7	9.8	9.10	3c10.11	9.14	9.15	9.16	9.17	10.1	10.2	10.4

摂	搾	搔	搖	損	摸	摺	摘	摑	擎	撲	撒	撤
10.6	10.9	10.11	3c9.8	10.12	10.13	11.3	11.5	11.6	11.7	12.1	12.2	12.3

撫	撰	撥	撮	擂	擇	操	擁	據	擔	擊	擧	擬
12.7	12.9	12.11	12.13	13.2	3c4.21	13.3	13.5	3c5.26	3c5.20	3c11.7	3n7.1	14.2

擦	擴	攝	攜	攣
14.5	3c5.25	3c10.6	3c10.4	19.3

3

0

手

手手

SHU, te, ta- hand

氵
土
扌
口
女
巾
犭
弓
彳
彡
宀
艹
山
亠
广
尸
囗

0

1

² 手入 **tei(re)** repairs; care, tending

⁴ 手不足 **tebusoku** shorthanded, understaffed

手元 **temoto** at hand; in one's care; ready cash

手引 **tebi(ki)** guidance; introduction, primer; good offices, introduction

⁵ 手本 **tehon** model, example, pattern

⁶ 手当 **tea(te)** (medical) treatment, care; allowance, (fringe) benefit

⁷ 手作 **tezuku(ri)** handmade, homemade

手抜 **tenu(ki)** (intentional) omission **tenu(kari)** (unintentional) omission, oversight, error

手形 **tegata** bill, (promissory) note

手芸 **shugei** handicrafts

手応 **tegota(e)** response, effect, resistance

手足 **teashi** hands and feet

⁸ 手放 **tebana(su)** let go of, part with; leave unattended **tebana(shi)** without holding on to, left unattended; unreservedly

⁹ 手前 **temae** you; this side of, toward oneself; out of consideration for; tea-ceremony procedures; oneself

手段 **shudan** means, measures

手洗 **teara(i)** washing the hands; lavatory

手拭 **tenugu(i), tefu(ki)** towel

手品 **tejina** sleight of hand, magic tricks, juggling

手品師 **tejinashi** magician, juggler

手相 **tesō** lines of the palm

手柄 **tegara** meritorious deed(s), achievement

手枷 **tekase, tegase** handcuffs, manacles

¹⁰ 手荷物 **tenimotsu** luggage, (hand) baggage

手島 **Teshima, Tejima** (surname)

手書 **shusho** write in one's own hand **tega(ki)** handwritten

手紙 **tegami** letter

手料理 **teryōri** home cooking

¹¹ 手動 **shudō** manual, hand-operated

手遅 **teoku(re)** too late, belated

手掛 **tega(kari)** handhold; clue, lead **tega(keru)** handle, deal with; have experience in; rear, look after

手帳 **techō** (pocket) notebook

手術 **shujutsu** (surgical) operation

手袋 **tebukuro** gloves, mittens

手許 **temoto** at hand; in one's care; ready cash

¹² 手塚 **Tezuka** (surname)

手落 **teo(chi)** omission, slip, oversight, neglect

手腕 **shuwan** ability, skill

手答 **tegota(e)** response, effect, resistance

手軽 **tegaru** easy, readily, simple, informal, without ado

手間 **tema** time, labor, trouble; wages

手順 **tejun** procedure, routine, process

13 手際 **tegiwa** performance, execution; skill, deftness, workmanship

手数 **tesū** trouble, pains, care **tekazu** trouble; number of moves (in a game)

手数料 **tesūryō** handling charge, fee

手続 **tetsuzu(ki)** procedure, formalities

手話 **shuwa** sign language

14 手榴弾 **shuryūdan, teryūdan** hand grenade

手慣 **tena(reru)** get used to, become practiced in

手製 **tesei** handmade, homemade

手綱 **tazuna** reins, bridle

16 手錠 **tejō** handcuffs

────── 2 ──────

2 入手 **nyūshu** obtain, get

3 大手 **ōte** large, major (companies); front castle gate **ōde** both arms

上手 **jōzu** skillful, good at **uwate** better at, superior to; upper part, upstream **kamite** upper part; upstream; right side of the stage (as seen from the audience)

下手 **heta** unskillful, poor at

山手 **yamate, yama(no)te** hilly residential section, bluff, uptown

4 切手 **kitte** (postage) stamp

片手 **katate** one hand, one-handed

5 左手 **hidarite** left hand

右手 **migite** right hand

6 両手 **ryōte** both hands

先手 **sente** the first move; the initiative **sakite** front lines, vanguard

7 助手 **joshu** helper, assistant

把手 **totte** handle, grip, knob

売手 **u(ri)te** seller

8 拍手 **hakushu** handclapping, applause **kashiwade** handclapping (at a shrine)

担手 **nina(i)te** bearer, carrier

若手 **wakate** young person/man; younger member

苦手 **nigate** one's weak point; someone hard to deal with

空手 **karate** empty-handed; karate

岩手県 **Iwate-ken** (prefecture)

9 派手 **hade** showy, flashy, gaudy

相手 **aite** the other party, partner, opponent

柏手 **kashiwade** clap one's hands (in worship at a shrine)

10 借手 **ka(ri)te** borrower, lessee, tenant

書手 **ka(ki)te** writer; calligrapher, painter

11 得手 **ete** strong point, forte, specialty

12 着手 **chakushu** start, commence, proceed with

握手 **akushu** shake hands

御手洗 **oteara(i)** lavatory **mitarashi** holy water font at a shrine

極手 **ki(me)te** winning move, decisive factor

勝手 **katte** as one pleases, arbitrary; kitchen; the situation

買手 **ka(i)te** buyer

痛手 **itade** serious wound; hard blow

13 話手 **hana(shi)te** speaker

鉤手 **kagi(no)te** right-angle bend

14 選手 **senshu** (sports) player

熊手 **kumade** rake

旗手 **kishu** standardbearer

歌手 **kashu** singer

語手 **kata(ri)te** narrator, storyteller

聞手 **ki(ki)te** listener

15 稼手 **kase(gi)te** breadwinner; hard worker

18 騎手 **kishu** rider, jockey

────── 3 ──────

3 口下手 **kuchibeta** awkward tongue, poor talker

小切手 **kogitte** check, cheque

10 遊相手 **aso(bi)aite** playmate

11 運転手 **untenshu** driver, chauffeur

13 話相手 **hanashi aite** someone to talk to; companion

—— 2 ——

3c2.2 / 582   扌   竹
              23   17

払   拂 ｜ 払 払

FUTSU, hara(u) pay; sweep/drive away

—— 1 ——

7 払戻 **hara(i)modo(su)** refund, reimburse

—— 2 ——

4 内払 **uchibara(i)** partial payment
支払 **shihara(u)** pay
厄払 **yakubara(i)** exorcism
月払 **tsukibara(i)** monthly installments
5 未払 **mihara(i)** unpaid
6 先払 **sakibara(i)** advance payment; payment on delivery; forerunner
9 前払 **maebara(i)** advance payment
咳払 **sekibara(i)** clearing one's throat
後払 **atobara(i)** deferred payment
11 酔払 **yo(p)para(i)** a drunk
12 着払 **chakubara(i)** payment upon delivery, COD

—— 3 ——

4 分割払 **bunkatsubara(i)** payment in installments
8 門前払 **monzenbara(i)** turning (someone) away at the gate, refusing to see (someone)
11 現金払 **genkinbara(i)** cash payment

3c2.3 / 1020   扌   一
              23   14

打   打 打

DA, CHŌ hit, strike **u(tsu)** hit, strike, beat, shoot **bu(tsu)** beat, strike **dāsu** dozen

—— 1 ——

3 打上 **u(chi)a(geru)** shoot up, launch (a rocket), cast up on shore, wash ashore; finish, close (a performance)
6 打合 **u(chi)a(u)** hit each other, exchange blows **u(chi)a(waseru)** strike (one thing) against (another); prearrange **u(chi)a(wase)** previous arrangement, appointed (hour)
7 打身 **u(chi)mi** bruise
8 打明 **u(chi)a(keru)** confide in, reveal
10 打倒 **datō** overthrow **u(chi)tao(su)** knock down; overthrow
打消 **u(chi)ke(shi)** denial, negation, negative (in grammar)
12 打診 **dashin** percussion, tapping (in medicine); sound/feel out
打開 **dakai** a break, development, new turn
13 打楽器 **dagakki** percussion instrument
打解 **u(chi)to(keru)** open one's heart, be frank
14 打算的 **dasanteki** calculating, mercenary
15 打撃 **dageki** blow, shock; batting, hitting

—— 2 ——

1 一打 **hitou(chi), ichida** a blow
6 舌打 **shitau(chi)** clicking one's tongue, tsk, tch
耳打 **mimiu(chi)** whisper in (someone's) ear
7 抜打的 **nu(ki)u(chi)teki** without advance warning
8 殴打 **ōda** assault (and battery)
狙打 **nera(i)u(chi)** take aim and shoot
杭打 **kuiu(chi)** pile driving
10 値打 **neu(chi)** value, worth; dignity
12 博打 **bakuchi** gambling
塁打 **ruida** base hit, single
18 鞭打症 **muchiu(chi)shō** whiplash

3

氵
扌
扌   2
口
女
巾
犭
弓
彳
彡
艹
宀
屮
圭
广
尸
口

3c3.5 / 1258 □□ 扌 力 |
23 8 2

扱   扱|扱扱

KYŪ, SŌ, atsuka(u) handle, treat, deal with **shigo(ku)** draw through the hand **shigo(ki)** squeezing through; rigorous training, hazing; woman's waistband **ko(ku)** thresh, strip off

——————— 1 ———————

3 扱下 **ko(ki)oro(su)** excoriate, criticize severely

——————— 2 ———————

8 取扱 **to(ri)atsuka(u)** treat, handle, deal with/in, carry

9 客扱 **kyakuatsuka(i)** hospitality

——————— 4 ———————

扱 → 扱 3c3.5

3c4.4 / 1721 □□ 扌 大 一
23 34 1

扶   扶扶

FU, tasu(keru) help

——————— 1 ———————

7 扶助 **fujo** aid, support, relief

15 扶養 **fuyō** support (a family)

3c4.5 / 1724 □□ 扌 尸 |
23 40 2

把   把把

HA take, grasp; (counter for bundles/sheaves)

——————— 1 ———————

4 把手 **totte** handle, grip, knob

12 把握 **haaku** grasp, comprehend

——————— 3 ———————

3 大雑把 **ōzappa** rough (guess); generous

3c4.7 / 1394 □□ 斤 扌
50 23

折   折折

SETSU, o(reru) (intr.) break, be folded, bend; turn (left/right); yield, compromise **o(ru)** (tr.) break, fold, bend **ori** occasion, opportunity

——————— 1 ———————

3 折々 **oriori** from time to time

5 折目 **o(ri)me** fold, crease

6 折合 **o(ri)a(u)** come to an agreement

折返 **o(ri)kae(su)** fold back; double back **o(ri)kae(shi)** immediate (reply)

7 折角 **sekkaku** going to (much) trouble, on purpose, expressly; kindly

9 折衷 **setchū** compromise, cross, blending

10 折紙 **o(ri)gami** the art of paper folding; colored origami paper; authentication, testimonial

12 折畳 **o(ri)tata(mu)** fold up

13 折詰 **o(ri)zu(me)** (food/lunch) packed in a cardboard/thin-wood box

15 折衝 **sesshō** negotiation

——————— 2 ———————

5 左折 **sasetsu** left turn

右折 **usetsu** turn right

6 気折 **kio(re)** depression, dejection

曲折 **kyokusetsu** winding, twists and turns; vicissitudes, complications

8 屈折 **kussetsu** bending; refraction; inflection

10 挫折 **zasetsu** setback, frustration, reverses

骨折 **kossetsu** broken bone, fracture **honeo(ru)** take pains, exert oneself

骨折損 **honeo(ri)zon** wasted effort

時折 **tokio(ri)** at times, occasionally

14 端折 **hasho(ru)** tuck up; cut short, abridge

—————— 3 ——————

8 和洋折衷 **wayō setchū** blending of Japanese and Western styles

—————— 4 ——————

9 紆余曲折 **uyo-kyokusetsu** meandering, twists and turns, complications

3c4.10 / 1713

囗 扌 十 又
23 12 9

拔 | 拔 拔

BATSU, nu(ku) pull out, remove, leave out; outdistance, surpass **-nu(ki)** without, leaving out; defeating **nu(keru)** come/fall out; be omitted; be missing; escape **nu(kasu)** omit, skip over **nu(karu)** make a blunder

—————— 1 ——————

4 抜毛 **nu(ke)ge** hair falling out, molting

5 抜出 **nu(ki)da(su)** select, extract, pull out **nu(ke)da(su)** slip out, sneak away; excel; choose the best **nu(kin)de(ru), nu(ki)de(ru)** be outstanding, excel

抜打的 **nu(ki)u(chi)teki** without advance warning

抜穴 **nu(ke)ana** secret passage/exit; loophole

8 抜刷 **nu(ki)zu(ri)** offprint

10 抜書 **nu(ki)ga(ki)** excerpt, clipping

抜粋 **bassui** excerpt, extract, selection

11 抜道 **nu(ke)michi** bypass; secret path; way of escape, loophole

13 抜群 **batsugun** pre-eminent, outstanding

—————— 2 ——————

4 手抜 **tenu(ki)** (intentional) omission **tenu(kari)** (unintentional) omission, oversight, error

引抜 **hi(ki)nu(ku)** pull out, select

6 気抜 **kinu(ke)** lackadaisical; dispirited

8 底抜 **sokonu(ke)** bottomless, unbounded

9 海抜 **kaibatsu** elevation above sea level

垢抜 **akanu(ke)** refined, polished, urbane

10 栓抜 **sennu(ki)** corkscrew; bottle opener

骨抜 **honenu(ki)** boned; emasculated, watered down

書抜 **ka(ki)nu(ku)** copy out, excerpt, abstract

12 筒抜 **tsutsunu(ke)** directly, clearly

13 腰抜 **koshinu(ke)** coward(ice), weak-kneed milksop

14 選抜 **senbatsu, e(ri)nu(ku)** select, choose, single out

3c4.11 / 1153

囗 扌 小 丨
23 35 2

抄 抄

SHŌ excerpt; make paper

—————— 1 ——————

5 抄本 **shōhon** excerpt, abridged transcript

16 抄録 **shōroku** excerpt, abstract, summary

3c4.12 / 1057

囗 扌 厂 阝
23 18 7

抑 抑

YOKU, osa(eru) hold down, hold in check, suppress, control **somosomo** in the first place; well, now

—————— 1 ——————

4 抑止 **yokushi** deter, stave off

8 抑制 **yokusei** control, restrain, suppress, inhibit

¹⁰ 抑留 **yokuryū** detention, internment

¹² 抑揚 **yokuyō** rising and falling of tones, modulation, intonation

3c4.13 / 1029

☐ 扌 卜
23 13

批

HI critique

———————— 1 ————————

⁷ 批判 **hihan** criticism, critique, comment

¹⁰ 批准 **hijun** ratification

¹² 批評 **hihyō** criticism, critique, review

²⁰ 批議 **higi** criticize, censure, blame

3c4.15 / 824

☐ 扌 亠 冂
23 11 20

抗

KŌ resist, anti-

———————— 1 ————————

⁵ 抗生物質 **kōsei busshitsu** an antibiotic

⁷ 抗体 **kōtai** antibody

抗告 **kōkoku** appeal, protest, complaint

¹³ 抗戦 **kōsen** resistance

²⁰ 抗議 **kōgi** protest, objection

———————— 2 ————————

⁴ 反抗 **hankō** resistance, opposition, rebellion

⁷ 対抗 **taikō** oppose, counter

⁸ 抵抗 **teikō** resistance

抵抗器 **teikōki** resistor, rheostat

———————— 3 ————————

⁴ 不可抗力 **fukakōryoku** force majeure, beyond one's control, unavoidable

3c4.16 / 871

☐ 扌 十 又
23 12 9

技

GI skill, art, technique **waza** technique; ability, feat

———————— 1 ————————

⁵ 技巧 **gikō** art, craftsmanship, technique

¹⁰ 技師 **gishi** engineer, technician

技能 **ginō** skill, technical ability

¹¹ 技術 **gijutsu** technology, technique, skill, art

———————— 2 ————————

⁶ 早技 **hayawaza** quick work; sleight of hand

¹¹ 球技 **kyūgi** game in which a ball is used

¹⁴ 演技 **engi** acting, performance

²⁰ 競技 **kyōgi** competition, match

3c4.18 / 1021

☐ 扌 冂 又
23 20 9

投

TŌ, na(geru) throw

———————— 1 ————————

⁰ 投じる **tō(jiru)** throw; invest in

² 投入 **tōnyū** throw into, commit (resources); invest

na(ge)i(reru) throw into

na(ge)i(re) free-style flower arrangement

⁵ 投付 **na(ge)tsu(keru)** throw at/against/down

⁷ 投身 **tōshin** suicide by throwing oneself (into a river, from a building, in front of a train)

⁹ 投降 **tōkō** surrender

投映 **tōei** project (an image), cast

¹⁰ 投射物 **tōshabutsu** projectile

投書 **tōsho** letter to the editor, contribution

¹¹ 投捨 **na(ge)su(teru)** throw away

投票 **tōhyō** vote

投票日 **tōhyōbi** voting day
13 投棄 **tōki** abandon, give up
投資 **tōshi** investment
15 投影 **tōei** projection
投影機 **tōeiki** projector
投稿 **tōkō** contribution (magazine)
16 投機 **tōki** speculation

──────── 2 ────────

12 間投詞 **kantōshi** an interjection
14 槍投 **yarina(ge)** javelin throwing

3c4.21 / 993   ⬜ ⻌ 尸 丨
                        23 40 2

択 擇｜択 択

TAKU, era(bu) choose, select

──────── 1 ────────

1 択一 **takuitsu** choosing an alternative
10 択捉島 **Etorofu-tō** (island, Russian Hokkaidō)

──────── 2 ────────

11 採択 **saitaku** adopt, select
14 選択 **sentaku** selection, choice, option, alternative

──────── 3 ────────

2 二者択一 **nisha-takuitsu** an alternative

拒→ **3c5.29**

──────── 5 ────────

3c5.1 / 1833   ⬜ 石 扌
                        53 23

拓 拓 拓

TAKU, hira(ku) open, clear, bring (land) under cultivation TAKU (part of given name)

──────── 1 ────────

3 拓也 **Takuya** (m. given name)
9 拓哉 **Takuya** (m. given name)
10 拓真 **Takuma** (m. given name)

---

12 拓殖 **takushoku** colonization, exploitation

──────── 2 ────────

12 開拓 **kaitaku** opening up land, development

3c5.3 / 1201   ⬜ 王 扌 一
                        46 23 1

拝 拜｜拝 拝

HAI worship; (prefix expressing respect) **oga(mu)** pray to, worship, venerate

──────── 1 ────────

0 拝する **hai(suru)** worship, pay respects to; receive (an imperial command); see (the emperor)
7 拝見 **haiken** see, have a look at
8 拝具 **haigu** Sincerely yours
拝金 **haikin** worship of money
10 拝借 **haishaku** borrow
11 拝啓 **haikei** Dear Sir/Madam
14 拝察 **haisatsu** infer, guess, gather
18 拝観料 **haikanryō** (museum) admission fee

──────── 2 ────────

5 礼拝 **reihai, raihai** worship, services
8 参拝 **sanpai** worship, visit (a shrine/tomb)
11 崇拝 **sūhai** worship, adoration

3c5.5 / 986   ⬜ 甲 扌 丨
                       43 23 2

押 押 押

Ō, o(su) push **o(saeru)** restrain, hold in check, suppress **o(sae)** (paper)weight; rear guard, defense; control **o(shi)** weight; authority, self-confidence; a fall (in the stock market) **o(shite)** forcibly, importunately

──────── 1 ────────

0 押ボタン **o(shi)botan** pushbutton

3

⻌ 土 扌 口 女 巾 犭 弓 彳 彡 艹 宀 ⺌ 山 ⻖ 广 尸 囗

5

2 押入 **o(shi)i(re)** closet, wall cupboard **o(shi)i(ru)** break into **o(shi)i(ri)** burglar
4 押収 **ōshū** confiscation
6 押合 **o(shi)a(u)** jostle one another
7 押売 **o(shi)u(ri)** high-pressure/importunate selling
9 押通 **o(shi)tō(su)** push through, accomplish
10 押倒 **o(shi)tao(su)** push down
11 押掛 **o(shi)ka(keru)** drop in on uninvited
押釦 **o(shi)botan** pushbutton
19 押韻 **ōin** rhyme

──────── 2 ────────

5 尻押 **shirio(shi)** push from behind, boost, back, abet; instigator, wirepuller
9 後押 **atoo(shi)** pushing from behind; backing, support
10 差押 **sa(shi)osa(eru)** attach, seize, impound

3c5.7 / 987

□ 日 扌 丨
43 23 2

CHŪ pull, extract **nu(ku)** pull out; surpass **hi(ku)** pull

──────── 1 ────────

5 抽出 **chūshutsu** extraction, sampling
12 抽象 **chūshō** abstraction
抽象的 **chūshōteki** abstract
14 抽選 **chūsen** drawing, lottery
23 抽籤 **chūsen** drawing, lottery

3c5.9 / 1914

□ 木 扌 一
41 23 1

MATSU erase, expunge; rub, paint

──────── 1 ────────

9 抹茶 **matcha** powdered tea

抹香 **makkō** incense powder; incense
10 抹消 **masshō** erase, cross out

──────── 2 ────────

1 一抹 **ichimatsu** a touch/tinge of

3c5.11 / 1801

□ 扌 ⺌ 冂
23 36 20

拙 拙

SETSU unskillful, clumsy
mazu(i) poor(ly done), clumsy, bungling, unskillful

──────── 1 ────────

9 拙速 **sessoku** not elaborate but fast, rough-and-ready
12 拙策 **sessaku** poor policy, imprudent measure

拂 → 払 3c2.2

3c5.13 / 1712

□ 扌 厂 又
23 18 9

披 披

HI open

──────── 1 ────────

21 披露 **hirō** announcement
披露宴 **hirōen** (wedding) reception

3c5.14 / 1178

□ 日 扌 丨
43 23 2

拍 拍

HAKU, HYŌ beat (in music) **u(tsu)** clap, slap

──────── 1 ────────

2 拍子 **hyōshi** time, tempo, beat; chance, moment
4 拍手 **hakushu** handclapping, applause **kashiwade** handclapping (at a shrine)

—— 2 ——

¹⁰ 脈拍 **myakuhaku** pulse (rate)

3c5.15 / 1285   扌 弓 宀
23 28 15

抱｜抱抱

HŌ, da(ku) hold in one's arms, embrace, hug **ida(ku)** embrace, harbor (feelings); hold, have **kaka(eru)** carry in one's arms; have (dependents); hire **kaka(e)** armful; employee

—— 1 ——

⁶ 抱合 **da(ki)a(u)** embrace each other **da(ki)a(waseru)** cause to embrace **hōgō** combination; embrace

⁸ 抱抱 **da(ki)kaka(eru)** hold/carry (in one's arms)

⁹ 抱括 **hōkatsu** inclusive, comprehensive

¹⁶ 抱擁 **hōyō** embrace, hug

—— 2 ——

¹ 一抱 **hitokaka(e)** an armful

⁷ 辛抱 **shinbō** perseverance, patience

⁸ 抱抱 **da(ki)kaka(eru)** hold/carry (in one's arms)

3c5.16   扌 竹 力
23 17 8

拗拗

YŌ, Ō, neji(ru) twist **neji(keru/ kureru)** be twisted/warped **koji(reru)** be twisted; go wrong, get out of order; become complicated; be peevish; get worse **koji(rasu)** make worse **su(neru)** pout, sulk

—— 1 ——

⁹ 拗音 **yōon** diphthong (written with a small や, ゅ, or ょ, as in きゅ)

3c5.18 / 560   扌 厂 十
23 18 12

抵抵

TEI touch; reach; resist

—— 1 ——

⁶ 抵当 **teitō** mortgage, hypothec
抵当物 **teitōbutsu** security, pawn, collateral

⁷ 抵抗 **teikō** resistance
抵抗器 **teikōki** resistor, rheostat

—— 2 ——

³ 大抵 **taitei** generally, usually; probably

3c5.20 / 1274   日 扌 一
43 23 1

擔｜担担

TAN carry, bear **katsu(gu)** carry on the shoulder; play a trick on **nina(u)** carry on the shoulder; bear, take on

—— 1 ——

⁴ 担手 **nina(i)te** bearer, carrier

⁶ 担当 **tantō** being in charge, overseeing
担当者 **tantōsha** the one in charge

⁹ 担保 **tanpo** a security, guarantee
担架 **tanka** stretcher

—— 2 ——

⁴ 分担 **buntan** apportionment, sharing

⁹ 負担 **futan** burden, load, responsibility, liability

¹⁰ 荷担者 **katansha** participant, supporter, accomplice

3c5.21 / 1916   扌 口 力
23 24 8

拐｜拐拐

KAI swindle; kidnap

3

氵
扌
扌   5
口
女
巾
犭
弓
彡
艹
⺌
山
青
广
尸
囗

3

5

氵
扌
口
攵
犭
引
彡
艹
宀
凵
亠
广
尸
口

— 1 —

10 拐帯 **kaitai** absconding with money

— 2 —

14 誘拐 **yūkai** kidnapping, abduction

拐 → 拐 **3c5.21**

3c5.22 / 455

□ 扌 口 力
23 24 8

招 招招

SHŌ, mane(ku) beckon to, invite, summon; cause

— 1 —

9 招待 **shōtai** invite
   招待状 **shōtaijō** (written) invitation
11 招猫 **mane(ki)neko** beckoning (porcelain) cat

3c5.24

□ 扌 十 子
23 12 6

拵 拵拵

SON, koshira(eru) make, prepare

— 1 —

8 拵事 **koshira(e)goto** fabrication, made-up story
   拵物 **koshira(e)mono** imitation, fake

3c5.25 / 1113

□ 扌 厂 竹
23 18 17

拡 擴 | 拡拡

KAKU, hiro(geru) extend, enlarge
hiro(garu) spread, expand HIROSHI
(m. given name)

— 1 —

3 拡大 **kakudai** magnification, expansion
   拡大鏡 **kakudaikyō** magnifying glass
7 拡声器 **kakuseiki** loudspeaker

---

11 拡張 **kakuchō** extension, expansion

3c5.26 / 1138

□ 攵 扌 冂
49 23 20

拠 據 | 拠拠

KYO, KO, yo(ru) be based on, be due to

— 1 —

9 拠点 **kyoten** (military) base, position

— 2 —

10 根拠 **konkyo** basis, grounds, foundation
12 証拠 **shōko** evidence, proof
13 準拠 **junkyo** conform to, be pursuant to, be based on
15 論拠 **ronkyo** grounds, basis

3c5.28 / 1800

□ 扌 口 宀
23 24 15

拘 拘拘

KŌ seize, arrest; adhere to
kakawa(ru) have to do with
kakawa(razu) in spite of, regardless of

— 1 —

4 拘引 **kōin** arrest, custody
7 拘束 **kōsoku** restriction, constraint
10 拘留 **kōryū** detention, custody
13 拘置 **kōchi** keep in detention, confine, hold

3c5.29 / 1295

□ 扌 冂
23 20

拒 拒拒

KYO, koba(mu) refuse, reject, decline

— 1 —

7 拒否 **kyohi** refusal, rejection, denial
12 拒絶 **kyozetsu** refusal, rejection, repudiation

---- 6 ----

3c6.1 / 1354   囗 扌 大 儿
                  23   34   16

挟

挟丨挟挟

KYŌ, hasa(mu), sashihasa(mu) put between, interpose **hasa(maru)** get between, be caught/hemmed/sandwiched between

3c6.2 / 1720   囗 扌 土 丨
                  23   22   2

拷

拷拷

GŌ beat, torture

---- 1 ----

11 拷問 **gōmon** torture

3c6.5 / 1564   囗 扌 冫 儿
                  23   5   16

挑

挑挑

CHŌ, ido(mu) challenge

---- 1 ----

9 挑発的 **chōhatsuteki** provocative, suggestive
13 挑戦 **chōsen** challenge

3c6.8 / 451   囗 扌 土 寸
                  23   22   37

持

持持

JI, mo(tsu) have, possess; hold, maintain; wear, last **mo(chi)** wear, durability; charge, expenses; (ladies') wear **mo(teru)** be popular with; can hold/carry; propertied, the haves **mo(taseru)** let (someone) have, give; have (someone) hold/carry/bear; pre-

serve, make last MOCHI (part of given name)

---- 1 ----

3 持久 **jikyū** hold out, endure, persist
5 持主 **mo(chi)nushi** owner, possessor
13 持続 **jizoku** continuation, maintenance

---- 2 ----

2 力持 **chikaramo(chi)** strong man
4 支持 **shiji** support
6 気持 **kimo(chi)** feeling, mood
8 長持 **nagamo(chi)** oblong chest; be durable, last
  受持 **u(ke)mo(tsu)** have/take charge of
  所持 **shoji** possess, have on one's person, carry
  金持 **kanemo(chi)** rich person
9 保持 **hoji** maintain, preserve
13 腹持 **haramo(chi)** slow digestion, feeling of fullness
14 維持 **iji** maintenance, support

---- 3 ----

8 所帯持 **shotaimo(chi)** housekeeping; married (wo)man

3c6.10   囗 扌 宀 女
                  23   33   25

按

按按

AN hold; consider; investigate

---- 1 ----

15 按摩 **anma** massage; masseur, masseuse

3c6.12 / 1260   囗 扌 口 十
                  23   24   12

括

括括

KATSU tie together **kuku(ru)** tie up/together, bundle; fasten; hang (oneself) **kuru(mu)** wrap up, tuck in **kuru(meru)** wrap up; include all **kubi(reru)** be constricted, compressed

---- 1 ----

⁹ 括弧 **kakko** parentheses, brackets

---- 2 ----

¹ 一括 **ikkatsu** one lump/bundle; summing up

⁵ 包括 **hōkatsu** include, comprehend

⁸ 抱括 **hōkatsu** inclusive, comprehensive

¹⁴ 概括 **gaikatsu** summary, generalization

総括 **sōkatsu** summarize, generalize

3c6.13

田 扌 夕 丨
23 30 2

拶　　拶 拶

SATSU be imminent

---- 2 ----

¹⁰ 挨拶 **aisatsu** greeting, salutation, courtesy call; address, message

3c6.14 / 1445

田 扌 口 亻
23 24 3

拾　　拾 拾

SHŪ, hiro(u) pick up, find **JŪ** ten (in documents)

---- 1 ----

³ 拾上 **hiro(i)a(geru)** pick up, pick out

⁸ 拾物 **hiro(i)mono** something picked up, a find; a bargain

¹¹ 拾得物 **shūtokubutsu** found article

3c6.15 / 1041

田 日 扌 卜
43 23 13

指　　指 指

SHI, yubi finger **sa(su)** point to

---- 1 ----

⁵ 指令 **shirei** order, instructions

指圧 **shiatsu** finger pressure

指示 **shiji** indication, instructions, directions **sa(shi)shime(su)** indicate, point out

⁶ 指先 **yubisaki** fingertip

指向 **shikō** directional (antenna)

指名 **shimei** nominate, designate

⁸ 指定 **shitei** appoint, designate

指定席 **shiteiseki** reserved seats

¹⁰ 指紋 **shimon** fingerprints, thumbprint

¹² 指揮 **shiki** command, lead, direct

指揮者 **shikisha** (orchestra) conductor, leader; commander, director

¹³ 指数 **shisū** index (number); exponent

指話 **shiwa** finger language, dactylology

¹⁴ 指導 **shidō** guidance, leadership

指導者 **shidōsha** leader

¹⁵ 指標 **shihyō** index, indicator

指輪 **yubiwa** (finger) ring

---- 2 ----

³ 小指 **koyubi** little finger

⁴ 中指 **nakayubi, chūshi** middle finger

⁵ 目指 **meza(su)** aim at

⁸ 物指 **monosa(shi)** ruler, measure, yardstick

¹⁶ 薬指 **kusuriyubi** third/ring finger

親指 **oyayubi** thumb

---- 3 ----

² 人差指 **hitosa(shi) yubi** index finger

拍 → 拍 3c5.14

---- 2 ----

⁴ 手拭 **tenugu(i), tefu(ki)** towel

3c6.18 / 2078

囗 火 扌 二
44 23 4

拳　　拳 | 拳 拳

KEN, GEN fist; respectful **kobushi** fist TSUTOMU, KATASHI (m. given name) KEN, GEN (part of given name)

— 1 —

¹⁴ 拳銃 **kenjū** pistol, handgun
¹⁸ 拳闘 **kentō** boxing

3c7.2 / 1651 　　　　　□｜ 日 扌 十
　　　　　　　　　　43 23 12

挿　　　插｜揷揷

SŌ, sa(su) insert **hasa(mu)** put between, insert, interpose

— 1 —

² 挿入 **sōnyū** insert
⁷ 挿図 **sōzu** figure, illustration
¹² 挿絵 **sa(shi)e** illustration (in a book)

3c7.3 / 890 　　　　　□｜ 月 扌 十
　　　　　　　　　　42 23 12

捕　　　捕捕

HO, to(raeru), to(ru), tsuka(maeru) catch, grasp **to(rawareru), tsuka(maru)** be caught; hold on to

— 1 —

¹³ 捕虜 **horyo** prisoner of war, captive
¹⁶ 捕縛 **hobaku** arrest, capture
¹⁹ 捕鯨 **hogei** whaling

— 2 —

¹⁰ 逮捕 **taiho** arrest, capture

挟 → 挾 **3c6.1**

3c7.4 　　　　　□｜｜ 扌 口 儿
　　　　　　　　　　23 24 16

捌　　　捌捌

HATSU, HACHI, BETSU, saba(ku) handle, deal with, dispose of; sell **saba(keru)** sell, be in demand; be worldly-wise; be frank/sensible/sociable **ha(ke)** drainage; sale, demand for

— 1 —

³ 捌口 **ha(ke)guchi** outlet; market

3c7.5 / 989 　　　　　□｜ 日 扌 又
　　　　　　　　　　43 23 9

捜　　　捜｜捜捜

SŌ, saga(su) look/search for

— 1 —

⁵ 捜出 **saga(shi)da(su)** find out, discover, locate
⁶ 捜回 **saga(shi)mawa(ru)** search/hunt around
⁹ 捜査 **sōsa** investigation
¹⁰ 捜索 **sōsaku** search

3c7.12 　　　　　□ 扌 六 竹
　　　　　　　　　23 34 17

挨　　　挨挨

AI push open

— 1 —

⁹ 挨拶 **aisatsu** greeting, salutation, courtesy call; address, message

3c7.13 　　　　　□ 扌 口 厂
　　　　　　　　　23 24 15

挽　　　挽｜挽挽

BAN, hi(ku) saw (wood), grind (meat, coffee beans); pull (a cart)

— 1 —

⁶ 挽肉 **hi(ki)niku** ground meat
挽回 **bankai** retrieve, recover, restore

捥 → 挽 **3c8.31**

3c7.14 / 954

57 23 18

振 振振

SHIN, fu(ru) wave, shake; jilt **fu(rareru)** be jilted/rebuffed **fu(ri)** appearance, dress; feigning, pretense; swing, wave, shake; (dance) postures; leaning, slant **-bu(ri)** after a lapse of, for the first time in (two years); for (three days); manner, style **fu(reru)** lean toward; shake, swing, wag **fu(ruu)** shake, wield; flourish, be invigorated

——————— 1 ———————

5 振出 **fu(ri)da(su)** shake out; draw (a bill), issue (a check); infuse, decoct **fu(ri)da(shi)** start; draft, issuing

振出人 **furidashinin** remitter, issuer

振付 **fu(ri)tsu(ke)** choreography

6 振仮名 **fu(ri)gana** (small kana written above or beside a kanji to show its pronunciation)

振返 **fu(ri)kae(ru)** turn one's head, look back

振向 **fu(ri)mu(ku)** turn toward, look back

振回 **fu(ri)mawa(su)** wave about, brandish

11 振動 **shindō** vibration, oscillation **fu(ri)ugo(ku)** swing, shake, oscillate

振掛 **fu(ri)ka(keru)** sprinkle on, dust, splash **fu(ri)ka(ke)** condiment mix to be sprinkled over rice

12 振替 **fu(ri)ka(eru)** change to, transfer (funds) **furika(e)** transfer

振替休日 **furikae kyūjitsu** substitute holiday (for one falling on a Sunday)

15 振舞 **furuma(u)** behave, conduct oneself; entertain, treat

16 振興 **shinkō** promotion, encouragement

——————— 2 ———————

3 久振 **hisa(shi)bu(ri)** (for the first time in) a long time

4 不振 **fushin** dullness, slump, stagnation

7 身振 **mibu(ri)** gesture, gesticulation

10 素振 **sobu(ri)** manner, bearing, behavior

——————— 3 ———————

8 武者振 **mushabu(ri)** valor, gallantry

3c7.15

23 22 3

挫 挫挫

ZA, kuji(ku) sprain, dislocate; frustrate (plans); crush, daunt **kuji(keru)** be broken/crushed/sprained, be disheartened

——————— 1 ———————

7 挫折 **zasetsu** setback, frustration, reverses

13 挫傷 **zashō** sprain, fracture, bruise

——————— 2 ———————

11 捻挫 **nenza** sprain, wrench

——————— 8 ———————

3c8.1 / 1233

74 23

推 推推

SUI inference, conjecture; push ahead **o(su)** infer, deduce; recommend, propose

——————— 1 ———————

8 推定 **suitei** presumption, estimate

10 推進 **suishin** propulsion, drive

11 推理 **suiri** reasoning, inference

推理小説 **suiri shōsetsu** detective story, whodunit

12 推測 **suisoku** conjecture, supposition

<table>
<tr><td>

14 推察 **suisatsu** guess, conjecture, surmise

推算 **suisan** calculate, reckon, estimate

16 推薦 **suisen** recommendation, nomination

推薦状 **suisenjō** letter of recommendation

</td><td>

12 掛買 **ka(ke)ga(i)** credit purchase

掛軸 **ka(ke)jiku** hanging scroll

14 掛算 **ka(ke)zan** multiplication (in math)

</td></tr>
</table>

—————— 2 ——————

7 邪推 **jasui** unjust suspicion, mistrust

3c8.4 / 2079 □ 扌 ⼘ 十
                23 39 12

捷 捷

SHŌ victory; fast SHŌ, HAYA, TOSHI, KATSU, KACHI (part of given name) SATOSHI, MASARU, SUGURU (m. given name)

—————— 1 ——————

8 捷径 **shōkei** short cut, shorter way

3c8.6 / 1464 □ 扌 土 ⼘
                23 22 13

掛 掛

ka(karu) hang (intr.); cost (money), take (time) **ka(kari), kakari** expenses, tax; relation, connection **-ga(karu)** be tinged with **-ga(kari)** taking, requiring (3 days) **ka(keru)** hang (tr.); put on top of; turn on, start; spend; multiply; (as suffix) begin to, start …ing **(ni) ka(kete wa)** in the matter of, as regards **ka(ke)** buckwheat noodles in broth; credit, account; (hat) rack, hook; (as suffix) half-(finished) **-ga(ke)** wearing, with … on; upon …ing; ten percent; times (as large)

—————— 1 ——————

5 掛布団 **ka(ke)buton** quilt, coverlet

8 掛金 **ka(ke)kin** installment (payment) **ka(ke)gane** latch, hasp

—————— 2 ——————

4 手掛 **tega(kari)** handhold; clue, lead **tega(keru)** handle, deal with; have experience in; rear, look after

引掛 **hi(k)ka(karu)** get caught/hooked/entangled **hi(k)ka(keru)** hang/hook/throw on; ensnare; cheat; have a quick drink

心掛 **kokoroga(ke)** intention; attention, care

5 出掛 **doka(keru)** go out, set out **de(gake)** about to go out

仕掛 **shikaka(ri)** beginning **shika(ke)** contrivance, device; scale, size; half finished

仕掛人 **shika(ke)nin** intriguer, schemer, plotter

6 気掛 **kiga(kari)** anxiety

7 肘掛 **hijika(ke)** arm (of a chair)

足掛 **ashiga(kari)** foothold **ashika(ke)** foothold, pedal, step; counting the first and last fractional (years of a time span) as a whole

8 追掛 **o(i)ka(keru)** chase, run after

泊掛 **to(mari)ga(ke)** be staying with, visiting overnight

押掛 **o(shi)ka(keru)** drop in on uninvited

9 飛掛 **to(bi)ka(karu)** pounce on, lunge for

思掛 **omo(i)ga(kenai)** unexpected

10 差掛 **sa(shi)ka(karu)** hang over, overhang; be urgent; be imminent; approach, come near **sa(shi)ka(keru)** hold (an umbrella) over (someone)

振掛 **fu(ri)ka(keru)** sprinkle on, dust, splash **fu(ri)ka(ke)** condiment mix to be sprinkled over rice

12 遣掛 **ya(ri)ka(keru)** begin to do, set about **ya(ri)ka(ke)** unfinished, half done

3
8

13 腰掛 **koshika(keru)** sit down
koshika(ke) seat; stepping-stone (to something else)

詰掛 **tsu(me)ka(keru)** throng to, besiege, crowd

話掛 **hana(shi)ka(keru)** speak to, accost

─────── 3 ───────

11 袈裟掛 **kesaga(ke)** hanging/slashed diagonally from the shoulder

3c8.8 / 1036   口 扌 几 二
             23 16 4

HAI exclude, reject, expel, anti-; push aside; push open; line up

─────── 1 ───────

4 排水 **haisui** drainage; displacement (of a ship)

排日 **hai-Nichi** anti-Japanese

5 排斥 **haiseki** exclude, expel, ostracize, boycott

排出 **haishutsu** discharge, exhaust; excretion

排他的 **haitateki** exclusive

6 排気 **haiki** exhaust (fumes)

排米 **hai-Bei** anti-American

7 排尿 **hainyō** urination

8 排泄 **haisetsu** excretion, evacuation, discharge

9 排便 **haiben** evacuation, defecation

排除 **haijo** exclude, remove, eliminate

3c8.9   口 火 扌 二
             44 23 4

KEN, ma(ku) roll, wind, coil
maku(ru), meku(ru) turn over (pages), roll up (one's sleeves); strip off
maku(reru) be turned/rolled up

─────── 1 ───────

10 捲起 **ma(ki)o(kosu)** stir up, create (a sensation)

3c8.10 / 486   日 立 扌 女
             54 23 25

SETSU touch, join **tsu(gu)** join to, piece together, splice **ha(gu)** patch

─────── 1 ───────

0 接する **ses(suru)** touch, come in contact with; receive (guests), attend on

4 接収 **sesshū** requisition, take over

6 接近 **sekkin** approach, draw near

7 接吻 **seppun** kiss

接尾辞 **setsubiji** suffix

接尾語 **setsubigo** suffix

9 接待 **settai** reception, welcome; serving, offering

接客業 **sekkyakugyō** hotel and restaurant trade

10 接骨 **sekkotsu** bonesetting

12 接着 **setchaku** adhesion

接着剤 **setchakuzai** adhesive, glue

13 接戦 **sessen** close combat/contest

接辞 **setsuji** an affix, prefixes and suffixes

接続詞 **setsuzokushi** a conjunction

接触 **sesshoku** touch, contact; catalytic

接触点 **sesshokuten** point of contact/tangency

14 接種 **sesshu** inoculation, vaccination

16 接頭辞 **settōji** prefix

─────── 2 ───────

6 近接 **kinsetsu** neighboring, contiguous, close-by

7 応接 **ōsetsu** reception (of visitors)

応接間 **ōsetsuma** reception room, parlor

8 直接 **chokusetsu** direct

9 面接 **mensetsu** interview

11 密接 **missetsu** close, intimate

12 間接 **kansetsu** indirect

間接税 **kansetsuzei** indirect tax
13 溶接 **yōsetsu** welding
15 隣接 **rinsetsu** border on, be contiguous, adjoin

3c8.11 / 1718

囗 扌 宀 工
23 33 38

控控

KŌ, hika(eru) hold back, refrain from; note down; wait **hika(e)** note, memo; duplicate, copy; waiting; brace, strut; a reserve

——————— 1 ———————
5 控目 **hika(e)me** moderate, reserved
9 控除 **kōjo** deduct, subtract
12 控訴院 **kōsoin** court of appeal

——————— 2 ———————
10 差控 **sa(shi)hika(eru)** be moderate in; withhold, refrain from

3c8.12

囗 扌 大 二
23 34 4

捧捧

HŌ hold in both hands; offer up
sasa(geru) lift up; give, offer, dedicate

——————— 1 ———————
7 捧呈 **hōtei** present, offer, submit

3c8.13 / 1624

囗 日 扌 匕
43 23 15

揭丨揭揭

KEI, kaka(geru) put up (a sign), hoist (a flag), display, publish, carry/run (an ad)

——————— 1 ———————
5 揭示 **keiji** notice, bulletin
揭示板 **keijiban** bulletin board

13 揭載 **keisai** publish, print, carry/run (an ad)

3c8.14 / 933

囗 木 扌 小
41 23 35

採 採丨採採

SAI, to(ru) take (on), accept, employ; collect, gather

——————— 1 ———————
5 採用 **saiyō** adopt, employ
7 採決 **saiketsu** voting
採択 **saitaku** adopt, select
8 採取 **saishu** gather, pick, harvest, extract
9 採点 **saiten** marking, grading, scoring
12 採集 **saishū** collecting (butterflies)
13 採鉱 **saikō** mining
14 採算 **saisan** profit

——————— 2 ———————
6 伐採 **bassai** felling, deforestation, cutting

3c8.15 / 602

囗 扌 小 囗
23 35 20

授授

JU, sazu(keru) give, grant; impart, teach **sazu(karu)** be granted/taught

——————— 1 ———————
3 授与 **juyo** conferring, awarding
13 授業 **jugyō** teaching, instruction
15 授賞 **jushō** awarding a prize

——————— 2 ———————
10 教授 **kyōju** professor; teaching

——————— 3 ———————
7 助教授 **jokyōju** assistant professor

——————— 4 ———————
6 名誉教授 **meiyo kyōju** professor emeritus

3

氵 土
扌 扌 8
口 女 巾
犭 弓 彳
彡 艹 宀
丷 凵 吉
广 尸 口

3c8.16 / 535 ⊞ 木 扌 冂
41 23 20

探 探探

TAN, sagu(ru) search for **saga(su)** look for

――――― 1 ―――――

7 探究 **tankyū** research, inquiry, study
10 探険 **tanken** exploration, expedition
  探索 **tansaku** search; inquiry, investigation
11 探偵 **tantei** (private) detective, investigator, spy
12 探検 **tanken** exploration, expedition

――――― 2 ―――――

10 家探 **iesaga(shi)** house hunting

3c8.17 / 2080 ⊟ 木 扌 大
45 23 34

捺 捺捺

NATSU, o(su) press down, stamp, affix a seal **NATSU, TOSHI** (part of given name)

――――― 1 ―――――

6 捺印 **natsuin** seal (a document)

――――― 3 ―――――

13 署名捺印 **shomei-natsuin** signature and seal

3c8.20 / 1200 ⊞ 日 扌 廾
43 23 32

措 措措

SO, o(ku) put aside, leave as is, desist from; except

――――― 1 ―――――

13 措置 **sochi** measure, steps

3c8.21 / 1469 ⊞ 甲 扌 艹
58 23 32

描 描描

BYŌ, ega(ku) draw, paint, sketch, depict, portray **ka(ku)** draw, paint; write, compose

――――― 1 ―――――

5 描写 **byōsha** depiction, portrayal, description
8 描画 **byōga** drawing, painting

――――― 2 ―――――

10 素描 **sobyō** rough sketch
12 絵描 **eka(ki)** painter, artist

3c8.22 / 1080 ⊞ 扌 彐 巾
23 39 26

掃 掃╷掃掃

SŌ, ha(ku) sweep

――――― 1 ―――――

9 掃除 **sōji** cleaning, clean-up
  掃除機 **sōjiki** vacuum cleaner

――――― 2 ―――――

3 大掃除 **ōsōji** general house-cleaning, spring/fall cleaning
11 清掃 **seisō** cleaning

3c8.25 ⊞ 心 扌 亻
51 23 3

捻 捻捻

NEN, hine(ru) twist; pinch **hine(ri)** a twist; a pinch **hine(kuru)** twirl, twist; tinker at **neji(ru)** twist **neji(reru)** be twisted

――――― 1 ―――――

2 捻子 **neji** screw; (wind-up toy) spring
10 捻挫 **nenza** sprain, wrench

3

氵 土 扌 口 女 巾 犭 弓 彳 彡 艹 宀 丷 屮 亠 广 尸 囗

8

3c8.26 / 1444   田 扌 土 口
                     23 22 24

捨 | 捨捨

SHA, su(teru) throw away; abandon, forsake **SUTE** (part of given name)

——————— 1 ———————

2 捨子 **su(te)go** abandoned child, foundling
10 捨値 **su(te)ne** giveaway price

——————— 2 ———————

5 四捨五入 **shisha-gonyū** rounding off
7 投捨 **na(ge)su(teru)** throw away
   見捨 **misu(teru)** desert, abandon, forsake
11 脱捨 **nu(gi)su(teru)** throw off (clothes), kick off (shoes)

捨→捨 3c8.26

3c8.28   田 扌 口 小
             23 24 35

掠掠

RYAKU, kasu(meru) rob, cheat; graze/brush/whiz/scud past **kasu(ru)** graze, glance off; squeeze, exploit **kasu(reru)** be blurred/indistinct

——————— 1 ———————

13 掠傷 **kasu(ri)kizu** scratch, bruise
14 掠奪 **ryakudatsu** plunder, loot, despoil

挽→挽 3c7.13

搔→搔 3c10.11

3c8.31   田 扌 尸 犭
             23 40 27

捩 | 捩捩

REI, RETSU, neji(ru) twist **yoji(ru)** twist **neji(reru)** be twisted **moji(ru)** twist; parody

——————— 1 ———————

2 捩子 **neji** screw; (wind-up toy) spring
6 捩伏 **ne(ji)fu(seru)** throw/hold (someone) down

3c8.32 / 1803   田 扌 尸 凵
                     23 40 36

掘

掘掘

KUTSU, ho(ru) dig

——————— 1 ———————

5 掘出物 **ho(ri)da(shi)mono** treasure trove; lucky find, bargain

——————— 2 ———————

9 発掘 **hakkutsu** excavation; disinterment

3c8.33 / 1832   田 扌 尸 口
                     23 40 24

据据

KYO, su(eru) set, place, install, put into position **su(waru)** sit, be set

——————— 1 ———————

5 据付 **su(e)tsu(keru)** set into position, install
13 据置 **su(e)o(ku)** leave as is, let stand

掴→摑 3c11.6

3

氵 土 扌 口 女 巾 犭 弓 彳 彡 艹 灬 凵 壴 广 尸 口

8

—————— 9 ——————

插→挿 3c7.2

搜→捜 3c7.5

捲→捲 3c8.9

3c9.2   田 木 扌 一
                           41 23 14

揉

揉揉

JŪ, mo(mu) rub, massage; push and shove; debate vigorously; train, coach; worry **mo(mareru)** be buffeted about **mo(meru)** get into trouble/discord; be crumpled; be worried **mo(me)** trouble, discord

---

8 揉事 **mo(me)goto** trouble, discord
10 揉消 **mo(mi)ke(su)** crush out (a cigarette), hush up, suppress

3c9.3   田 火 扌 六
                           44 23 34

揆揆

KI plan; path; uprising

—————— 2 ——————

1 一揆 **ikki** riot, insurrection

3c9.4 / 628   田 日 扌 一
                           43 23 14

提提

TEI present, submit   **CHŌ, sa(geru)** carry (in the hand)

—————— 1 ——————

5 提出 **teishutsu** presentation, filing
6 提灯 **chōchin** (paper) lantern
8 提供 **teikyō** offer, present

10 提案 **teian** proposition, proposal
13 提携 **teikei** cooperation, tie-up

—————— 2 ——————

9 前提 **zentei** premise, prerequisite
11 菩提 **bodai** Buddhahood, supreme enlightenment, salvation
菩提樹 **bodaiju** bo tree; linden tree; lime tree

3c9.5 / 631   田 日 扌 犭
                           43 23 27

揚

揚揚

YŌ raise, elevate; praise **a(garu)** rise **a(geru)** raise; fry **a(ge)** fried tofu, fried food; a tuck

—————— 1 ——————

2 揚子江 **Yōsukō** the Yangtze/Yangzi river
8 揚物 **a(ge)mono** fried food

—————— 2 ——————

4 水揚 **mizua(ge)** landing, unloading; earnings; watering (cut flowers so they last longer); deflowering
7 抑揚 **yokuyō** rising and falling of tones, modulation, intonation

—————— 3 ——————

13 意気揚々 **iki-yōyō** exultant, triumphant

揭→掲 3c8.13

3c9.7 / 1088   田 扌 小 一
                           23 35 14

援

援|援援

EN, tasu(keru) help, aid

—————— 1 ——————

7 援助 **enjo** assistance, aid
20 援護 **engo** protection, support, relief

—————— 2 ——————

7 声援 **seien** (shouts of) encouragement, cheering

応援 **ōen** aid, support

応援団 **ōendan** rooting section, cheerleaders

9 後援 **kōen** assistance, aid, support

11 救援 **kyūen** relief, rescue

3c9.8 / 1648   田 扌 小 山
                         23 35 36

YŌ, yu(reru) (lit.) shake, sway, vibrate, roll, pitch, joggle **yu(rameku)** (intr.) shake, sway, vibrate, roll, pitch, joggle **yu(rugu/ragu)** (intr.) shake, sway, vibrate, roll, pitch, joggle **yu(rasu/ru/suru)** (tr.) shake, rock, joggle **yu(rugasu/suburu/saburu)** (tr.) shake, rock, joggle

—————— 1 ——————

10 揺起 **yu(ri)o(kosu)** awaken by shaking

11 揺動 **yu(ri)ugo(kasu)** (tr.) shake **yu(re)ugo(ku)** (intr.) shake

—————— 2 ——————

3 大揺 **ōyu(re)** upheaval

11 動揺 **dōyō** shaking, pitching, rolling; excitement, commotion, unrest

3c9.10 / 1915   田 扌 艹 口
                          23 32 24

TŌ board/load (a vehicle)

—————— 1 ——————

9 搭乗 **tōjō** board, get on

搭乗券 **tōjōken** boarding pass

13 搭載 **tōsai** load; embark; mounting (of electronic components)

搔 → **3c10.11**

3c9.14 / 1652   田 車 扌 冂
                          69 23 20

KI shake, brandish; scatter; direct, command

—————— 1 ——————

9 揮発 **kihatsu** volatile, vaporize

—————— 2 ——————

9 発揮 **hakki** exhibit, demonstrate, make manifest

指揮 **shiki** command, lead, direct

指揮者 **shikisha** (orchestra) conductor, leader; commander, director

3c9.15 / 1586   田 扌 大 宀
                          23 34 15

KAN, ka(eru) substitute **ka(waru)** be replaced, change over

—————— 1 ——————

6 換気 **kanki** ventilation

7 換言 **kangen (sureba)** in other words

8 換金 **kankin** realize, convert into money

14 換算 **kansan** conversion, exchange

—————— 2 ——————

4 切換 **ki(ri)ka(eru)** change, exchange, convert; renew; replace; switch over

引換 **hi(ki)ka(eru)** exchange, change, convert

6 交換 **kōkan** exchange

9 乗換 **no(ri)ka(e)** change conveyances, transfer

変換 **henkan** change, conversion, transformation (in math)

11 転換 **tenkan** conversion, changeover; diversion

13 置換 **o(ki)kae(ru)** replace, transpose, rearrange **chikan** substitute, replace

---- 4 ----

6 気分転換 **kibun tenkan** a (refreshing) change, diversion

3c9.16 囲 月 扌 儿
42 23 16

揃 揃揃

SEN, soro(u) be complete, be all present; be uniform, be all alike **soro(i)** a set, suit, suite **soro(eru)** arrange (all together), complete; make even/uniform

---- 2 ----

1 一揃 **hitosoro(i)** a set, a suit
3 三揃 **mi(tsu)zoro(i)** three-piece suit
13 勢揃 **seizoro(i)** array, full lineup

3c9.17 / 1714 囲 扌 尸 土
23 40 22

握 握握

AKU, nigi(ru) grasp, grip, take/get hold of **nigi(ri)** grasp, grip; handful; rice/sushi ball

---- 1 ----

4 握手 **akushu** shake hands

---- 2 ----

1 一握 **hitonigi(ri), ichiaku** a handful
7 把握 **haaku** grasp, comprehend

---- 10 ----

3c10.1 囲 扌 尸 屵
23 40 36

搗 搗搗

TŌ, tsu(ku), ka(tsu) pound (rice to make mochi), hull, husk

5 搗立 **tsu(ki)ta(te)** freshly pounded (mochi)

3c10.2 / 1722 囲 舟 扌 冂
63 23 20

搬 搬搬

HAN carry, transport

---- 2 ----

11 運搬 **unpan** transport

3c10.4 / 1686 囲 隹 扌 力
74 23 8

携 攜｜携携

KEI, tazusa(eru) carry (in one's hand), have with/on one **tazusa(waru)** participate in

---- 1 ----

10 携帯 **keitai** carry with; portable

---- 2 ----

12 提携 **teikei** cooperation, tie-up

3c10.6 / 1692 囲 耳 扌 冫
65 23 5

摂 攝｜摂摂

SETSU act in place of; take **OSAMU** (m. given name)

---- 1 ----

4 摂氏 **sesshi** Celsius, centigrade
8 摂取 **sesshu** ingest, take in

3c10.9 / 1497 囲 扌 宀 儿
23 33 16

搾 搾搾

SAKU, shibo(ru) squeeze, press, extract, milk

— 1 —

⁸ 搾取 **sakushu** exploitation

3c10.11

田 虫 扌 又
64 23 9

搔 | 搔 搔

SŌ, ka(ku) scratch; rake; paddle; cut off　**ka(ki)-** (emphatic prefix)

— 1 —

⁶ 搔回 **ka(ki)mawa(su)** stir, churn; ransack, rummage around
¹¹ 搔混 **ka(ki)ma(zeru)** mix up, stir

— 2 —

⁴ 引搔回 **hi(k)ka(ki)mawa(su)** ransack, rummage through; carry on highhandedly
¹¹ 雪搔 **yukika(ki)** snow shovel(ing)/plow(ing)

搖 → 揺　**3c9.8**

3c10.12 / 350

田 貝 扌 口
68 23 24

損 損

SON loss, damage; disadvantageous
soko(nau/neru) harm, hurt, mar
-soko(nau) fail to, err in, mis-

— 1 —

⁵ 損失 **sonshitsu** loss
¹⁰ 損耗 **sonmō** wear and tear, loss
損害 **songai** damage, injury, loss
¹¹ 損得 **sontoku** advantages and disadvantages

— 2 —

³ 大損 **ōzon** heavy loss
⁴ 欠損 **kesson** deficit, loss
⁵ 仕損 **shisoko(nau), shison(jiru)** make a mistake, fail, blunder
⁶ 全損 **zenson** total loss
⁷ 言損 **i(i)soko(nau)** misspeak; fail to mention
⁹ 乗損 **no(ri)soko(nau)** miss (a train)

¹⁰ 破損 **hason** damage, breakage, breach
¹³ 毀損 **kison** damage, injure
数損 **kazo(e)soko(nau)** miscount
¹⁴ 聞損 **ki(ki)sokona(u)** mishear, not catch

— 3 —

¹⁰ 骨折損 **honeo(ri)zon** wasted effort

3c10.13

田 日 扌 艹
43 23 32

摸 摸

MO search for; copy

— 1 —

¹⁰ 摸索 **mosaku** groping

— 11 —

3c11.3

田 日 扌 彐
43 23 39

摺 | 摺 摺

SHŌ, SHŪ fold; rub; print; slide
su(ru) rub; print

— 2 —

⁴ 引摺 **hi(ki)zu(ru)** drag along
(o)hi(ki)zu(ri) slut

3c11.5 / 1447

田 扌 口 宀
23 24 11

摘 摘

TEKI, tsu(mu) pick, pluck, nip; gather　**tsuma(mu)** pick up or hold between the thumb and fingers

— 1 —

⁸ 摘取 **tsu(mi)to(ru)** pick, pluck
⁹ 摘発 **tekihatsu** expose, unmask, uncover

— 2 —

⁹ 茶摘 **chatsu(mi)** tea picking/picker

3c11.6

□ 戈 扌 口
52 23 24

掴 | 掴 掴

KAKU grab; hit **tsuka(mu)** grab, grasp, grip **tsuka(mi)** handful; grip **tsuka(maru)** hold/hang on to **tsuka(maeru)** grab, catch, nab **tsuka(maseru)** make (someone) catch hold of; bribe; palm off, foist upon

— 1 —

8 摑取 **tsuka(mi)to(ru)** snatch off, grasp

— 2 —

23 鷲摑 **washizuka(mi)** clutch, grab

3c11.7 / 1016

□ 車 扌 冂
69 23 20

撃 | 撃 撃

GEKI, u(tsu) attack; fire, shoot

— 1 —

7 撃沈 **gekichin** (attack and) sink
13 撃滅 **gekimetsu** destruction, annihilation

— 2 —

5 打撃 **dageki** blow, shock; batting, hitting
   目撃者 **mokugekisha** (eye)witness
7 攻撃 **kōgeki** attack
8 狙撃兵 **sogekihei** sniper, sharpshooter
10 射撃 **shageki** shooting, firing
   遊撃戦 **yūgekisen** guerrilla warfare
   砲撃 **hōgeki** shelling, bombardment
14 銃撃 **jūgeki** shooting
   駁撃 **bakugeki** argue against, attack, refute
15 衝撃 **shōgeki** shock
19 爆撃 **bakugeki** bombing
22 襲撃 **shūgeki** attack, assault, raid, charge

12

3c12.1 / 1889

□ 扌 六 儿
23 34 16

撲 撲

BOKU, u(tsu) hit, strike

— 1 —

10 撲殺 **bokusatsu** clubbing to death
13 撲滅 **bokumetsu** eradication, extermination

— 2 —

9 相撲 **sumō** sumo wrestling

3c12.2

□ 月 攵 扌
42 49 23

撒 撒

SAN, SATSU, ma(ku) scatter, strew; sprinkle; give (someone) the slip

— 1 —

12 撒散 **ma(ki)chi(rasu)** scatter about; squander

3c12.3 / 1423

□ 月 攵 扌
42 49 23

撤 撤

TETSU withdraw, remove

— 1 —

5 撤去 **tekkyo** withdraw, evacuate, remove
12 撤廃 **teppai** abolition, do away with, repeal

3c12.7

□ 火 扌 艹
44 23 32

撫 撫

BU, na(deru) stroke, pat, smooth down, soothe, caress

─── 2 ───

¹¹ 猫撫声 **nekona(de)goe** coaxing voice

─── 3 ───

³ 大和撫子 **Yamato nadeshiko** daughter/woman of Japan

3c12.9

田 扌 弓 艹
23 28 32

撰｜撰撰

SEN select; compose, compile
era(bu) select

─── 1 ───

¹² 撰集 **senshū** anthology

─── 2 ───

⁷ 杜撰 **zusan** slipshod, careless(ly done)

3c12.11

田 火 扌 弓
44 23 28

撥撥

HATSU, ha(neru) reject, eliminate; splash, splatter; hit, run over (a pedestrian); put an upward flip on the end of (a brush stroke in calligraphy); pronounce the kana "ん"; take a percentage/commission **ha(nekasu)** splash, splatter **bachi** plectrum, (samisen) pick; drumstick, gong stick

─── 1 ───

⁹ 撥飛 **ha(ne)to(basu)** send (something) flying; spatter, splash
撥音 **hatsuon** the sound of the kana "ん"

3c12.13 / 1520

田 耳 日 扌
65 43 23

撮撮

SATSU, tsuma(mu) grasp between thumb and fingers, pick up

tsuma(mi) knob; pinch (of salt); snack food (e.g., peanuts) to be eaten while drinking **to(ru)** take (a photo)

─── 1 ───

⁸ 撮直 **to(ri)nao(su)** retake (a photo)
¹⁵ 撮影 **satsuei** photography, filming

─── **13** ───

3c13.2

田 雷 田 扌
75 58 23

擂擂

su(ru) grind, mash

─── 1 ───

⁹ 擂砕 **su(ri)kuda(ku)** grind down/fine, pulverize

擇→択 3c4.21

3c13.3 / 1655

田 木 扌 口
41 23 24

操操

SŌ, ayatsu(ru) manipulate, operate **misao** chastity, virginity, constancy, fidelity, honor MISA (part of given name)

─── 1 ───

² 操人形 **ayatsu(ri)ningyō** puppet, marionette
⁷ 操作 **sōsa** operation, handling, control
¹² 操短 **sōtan** curtailed operations (short for 操業短縮)
¹³ 操業 **sōgyō** operation, work
¹⁶ 操縦 **sōjū** control, operate, manipulate
操縦士 **sōjūshi** pilot

─── 2 ───

⁷ 体操 **taisō** calisthenics, gymnastics
¹³ 節操 **sessō** fidelity, integrity; chastity

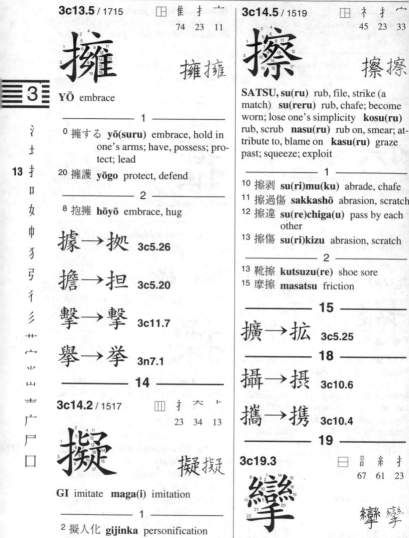

3c13.5 / 1715 　　田 隹 扌 宀
　　　　　　　　　　　　74 23 11

擁

擁擁

YŌ embrace

――――― 1 ―――――

0 擁する **yō(suru)** embrace, hold in one's arms; have, possess; protect; lead

20 擁護 **yōgo** protect, defend

――――― 2 ―――――

8 抱擁 **hōyō** embrace, hug

擄 → 拠 **3c5.26**

擔 → 担 **3c5.20**

擊 → 撃 **3c11.7**

擧 → 挙 **3n7.1**

――――― 14 ―――――

3c14.2 / 1517 　　川 扌 大 匕
　　　　　　　　　　　23 34 13

擬

擬擬

GI imitate　**maga(i)** imitation

――――― 1 ―――――

2 擬人化 **gijinka** personification

5 擬古 **giko** imitating classical style

7 擬声語 **giseigo** onomatopoetic word

――――― 2 ―――――

14 模擬 **mogi** imitation, mock, dry-run, dummy, simulated

3c14.5 / 1519 　　田 礻 扌 宀
　　　　　　　　　　45 23 33

擦

擦擦

SATSU, su(ru) rub, file, strike (a match)　**su(reru)** rub, chafe; become worn; lose one's simplicity　**kosu(ru)** rub, scrub　**nasu(ru)** rub on, smear; attribute to, blame on　**kasu(ru)** graze past; squeeze; exploit

――――― 1 ―――――

10 擦剥 **su(ri)mu(ku)** abrade, chafe

11 擦過傷 **sakkashō** abrasion, scratch

12 擦違 **su(re)chiga(u)** pass by each other

13 擦傷 **su(ri)kizu** abrasion, scratch

――――― 2 ―――――

13 靴擦 **kutsuzu(re)** shoe sore

15 摩擦 **masatsu** friction

――――― 15 ―――――

擴 → 拡 **3c5.25**

――――― 18 ―――――

攝 → 摂 **3c10.6**

攜 → 携 **3c10.4**

――――― 19 ―――――

3c19.3 　　　　日 言 糹 扌
　　　　　　　　　　67 61 23

攣

攣攣

REN crooked, bent; pine for

――――― 2 ―――――

4 引攣 **hi(ki)tsu(ru)** have a cramp/crick/tic/spasm/twitch/convulsion

12 痙攣 **keiren** cramp, spasm, convulsions

口 3d

口	叶	叱	叩	叫	只	兄	号	台	可	句	司	右
0.1	2.1	2.2	2.3	3d3.4	2.8	2.9	2.10	2.11	2.12	2.13	2.14	2.15

吐	叫	吸	吃	吊	舌	向	同	后	名	吠	吹	吟
3.1	3.4	3.5	3.7	3.8	3.9	3.10	8e3.1	3.11	3.12	4.1	4.3	4.8

呆	呈	邑	品	呉	足	呉	呂	吾	告	呑	否	谷
4.13	4.14	4.15	3d6.15	2o5.7	7d0.1	2o5.7	4.16	4.17	4.18	4.19	4.20	2o5.3

乱	呉	豆	何	伺	君	味	呼	呪	咏	知	奇	函
4.21	2o5.7	4.22	2a5.21	2a5.23	4.23	5.3	5.4	5.11	7a5.14	5.14	5.17	2b6.3

咳	咲	咽	品	哉	面	殆	唄	啞	哺	啄	唆	員
6.10	6.12	6.14	6.15	4n5.4	3s6.1	6.21	7.1	3d8.3	7.4	3d8.4	7.8	7.10

唇	哲	勉	唯	唾	啞	啄	喝	唱	啓	超	喰	啞
7.12	7.13	2n8.1	8.1	8.2	8.3	8.4	8.8	8.9	8.17	3b9.18	8.35	3d8.3

喉	喫	喝	喧	喙	喩	喚	就	單	喪	喬	登	短
9.6	9.7	3d8.8	9.12	9.14	9.15	9.19	9.21	3n6.2	3b9.20	9.25	9.26	9.27

尋	嗅	嗄	嘩	嘆	嗣	號	辞	群	羣	豊	鳴	噌
9.29	10.3	10.5	10.7	10.8	10.13	3d2.10	5b8.4	10.14	3d10.14	10.15	11.1	3d12.9

嘆	嘘	號	嘲	噛	噴	嘘	噂	嶒	噂	嘱	器	舖
3d10.8	11.7	3d2.10	12.2	3d15.2	12.8	3d11.7	3d12.10	12.9	12.10	12.11	12.13	3b12.4

毆	嘴	器	舘	竪	豫	嚇	營	矯	嚙	臨	豐	軀
2t6.1	13.7	3d12.13	8b8.3	5b9.5	0a4.12	14.1	3n9.2	14.5	15.2	2t15.1	3d10.15	15.5

艶	嚴	獻	囃	囁	囊	囑	艶	鹼
16.3	3n14.1	3g9.6	18.1	18.5	19.3	3d12.11	3d16.3	3s21.1

0

3d0.1 / 54

口 口
24

口

KŌ, KU, kuchi mouth

1
---

³ 口下手 **kuchibeta** awkward tongue, poor talker

⁴ 口止料 **kuchido(me)ryō** hush money

⁵ 口出 **kuchida(shi)** meddling, butting in

⁶ 口任 **kuchimaka(se)** random talk

口伝 **kuchizute, kuchizuta(e)** word of mouth, oral tradition

⁷ 口述 **kōjutsu** oral statement, dictation

口走 **kuchibashi(ru)** blurt out, say

⁸ 口実 **kōjitsu** excuse, pretext

¹⁰ 口真似 **kuchimane** mimicry

口座 **kōza** (bank) account

¹¹ 口添 **kuchizo(e)** advice, support, recommendation

口笛 **kuchibue** whistling

¹² 口絵 **kuchie** frontispiece

口答 **kuchigota(e)** backtalk, retort **kōtō** oral reply

口飲 **kuchino(mi)** drink from the bottle

¹⁴ 口語 **kōgo** colloquial language

口説 **kudo(ku)** persuade, entreat, woo, court **kuzetsu** quarrel; curtain lecture

¹⁸ 口癖 **kuchiguse** habit of saying, favorite saying

2
---

¹ 一口 **hitokuchi** a mouthful; a unit; a word

² 入口 **iriguchi** entrance

人口 **jinkō** population; common talk

³ 川口 **kawaguchi** mouth of a river **Kawaguchi** (city, Saitama-ken); (surname)

小口 **koguchi** in small lots, small sum; end, edge; clue; beginning

山口 **Yamaguchi** (surname)

⁴ 井口 **Iguchi, Inoguchi** (surname)

火口 **kakō** (volcano) crater **higuchi** burner; muzzle (of a gun); origin of a fire

⁵ 出口 **deguchi** exit; outlet **Deguchi** (surname)

甘口 **amakuchi** mild, light (flavor); sweet tooth; flattery

田口 **Taguchi** (surname)

⁶ 江口 **Eguchi** (surname)

早口 **hayakuchi, hayaguchi** fast talking

糸口 **itoguchi** thread end; beginning; clue

⁷ 谷口 **Taniguchi** (surname)

坂口 **Sakaguchi** (surname)

辛口 **karakuchi** salty, spicy, dry (saké); preference for sharp taste

利口 **rikō** smart, clever, bright

⁸ 表口 **omoteguchi** front entrance/door

東口 **higashiguchi** east exit/entrance

河口 **kakō** mouth of a river, estuary

⁹ 降口 **o(ri)guchi, o(ri)kuchi** exit (from a station)

南口 **minamiguchi** south exit/entrance

¹⁰ 原口 **Haraguchi** (surname)

浜口 **Hamaguchi** (surname)

捌口 **ha(ke)guchi** outlet; market

宵口 **yoi (no) kuchi** early evening

¹¹ 野口 **Noguchi** (surname)

窓口 **madoguchi** (ticket) window

悪口 **warukuchi, aku(tare)guchi, akkō** verbal abuse, speaking ill/evil of

蛇口 **jaguchi** faucet, tap

¹² 無口 **mukuchi** taciturn, reticent, laconic

¹³ 働口 **hatara(ki)guchi** job opening, employment

裏口 **uraguchi** back door, rear entrance

¹⁴ 樋口 **Higuchi** (surname)

憎口 **niku(mare)guchi** offensive/malicious remarks

関口 **Sekiguchi** (surname)

¹⁸ 儲口 **mō(ke)guchi** profitable job

───── 3 ─────

⁵ 出入口 **deiriguchi** entrance/exit

⁷ 改札口 **kaisatsuguchi** ticket gate, wicket

⁸ 非常口 **hijōguchi** emergency exit

¹² 就職口 **shūshokuguchi** job opening, employment

¹⁵ 噴火口 **funkakō** crater

───────── 2 ─────────

3d2.1 / 2033

24　12

叶

叶 叶

KYŌ, kana(eru) grant, answer, hear (a prayer) **kana(u)** be fulfilled/granted KANŌ, KANAI (surname) KYŌ (part of given name)

3d2.2 / 1963

24　12

叱

叱 叱

SHITSU, shika(ru) scold, reprimand

───────── 1 ─────────

⁵ 叱正 **shissei** correction

¹¹ 叱責 **shisseki** reproach, reprimand

3d2.3

□ 口 阝
24 7

叩

叩 叩

KŌ, tata(ku) strike, hit, knock, slap, clap, rap, pat; sound out; criticize

―――――― 1 ――――――

4 叩込 **tata(ki)ko(mu)** drive/throw into; hammer in, inculcate

16 叩頭 **kōtō** kowtow, bow deeply

―――――― 2 ――――――

19 蠅叩 **haetata(ki)** fly swatter

叫 → 叫 **3d3.4**

3d2.8 / 2034

□ 口 几
24 16

只

只 只

SHI, tada only, just; free, gratis **SHI, TADA, KORE** (part of given name)

―――――― 1 ――――――

4 只今 **tadaima** just now

9 只乗 **tadano(ri)** free/stolen ride

3d2.9 / 406

□ 口 几
24 16

兄

兄 兄

KEI, KYŌ, ani, (o)nii(san) elder brother

―――――― 1 ――――――

7 兄弟 **kyōdai, ani-otōto** brothers (and sisters)

12 兄貴 **aniki** elder brother; one's senior

―――――― 2 ――――――

4 父兄 **fukei** parents and older brothers, guardians

8 長兄 **chōkei** eldest brother

13 義兄 **gikei** elder brother-in-law

3d2.10 / 266

□ 口 一
24 14

号

號 | 号 号

GŌ number; name; signal, sign; cry out

―――――― 1 ――――――

8 号泣 **gōkyū** wailing, lamentation

―――――― 2 ――――――

1 一号 **ichigō** number one

2 二号 **nigō** No. 2; mistress, concubine

4 元号 **gengō** era name

5 正号 **seigō** plus sign (+)

6 年号 **nengō** era name

9 信号 **shingō** signal

負号 **fugō** minus sign (–)

10 称号 **shōgō** title, degree

記号 **kigō** mark, symbol

11 商号 **shōgō** corporate name

船号 **sengō** ship's name

符号 **fugō** mark, symbol, code

12 番号 **bangō** number

等号 **tōgō** equal sign (=)

13 暗号 **angō** code, cipher

15 調号 **chōgō** key signature (in music)

―――――― 3 ――――――

7 赤信号 **akashingō** red (traffic) light

8 青信号 **aoshingō** green (traffic) light

9 通番号 **tō(shi)bangō** serial number

3d2.11 / 492

□ 口 竹
24 17

台

臺 | 台 台

DAI, TAI stand, platform, base; tableland, heights; level, mark, (price/age) range; (counter for vehicles or machines) **utena** calyx, (lily) pad; stand, pedestal; tower, hall

―――――― 1 ――――――

5 台北 **Taipei, Taihoku** Taipei (capital of Taiwan)

3

氵 扌 口 女 巾 犭 弓 彳 彡 艹 宀 业 耂 广 尸 口

2

台本 **daihon** script, screenplay, libretto

6 台地 **daichi** plateau, tableland, height

8 台所 **daidokoro** kitchen

9 台風 **taifū** typhoon

12 台湾 **Taiwan** (island country near China)

台詞 **serifu** (actor's) lines, what one says

───── 2 ─────

3 土台 **dodai** foundation, groundwork; utterly

5 仙台 **Sendai** (city, Miyagi-ken)

6 灯台 **tōdai** lighthouse

13 滑台 **sube(ri)dai** (playground) slide; launching platform

寝台 **shindai** bed

15 舞台 **butai** stage

17 燭台 **shokudai** candlestick, candlestand

───── 3 ─────

17 檜舞台 **hinoki butai** cypress-floored stage; high-class stage, limelight

3d2.12 / 388

口 卩 一
24 14

可

可 可

KA possible, can, -able; good, approval

───── 1 ─────

4 可分 **kabun** divisible, separable

7 可決 **kaketsu** approval, adoption (of a resolution)

可否 **kahi** right or wrong, pro and con

9 可哀相 **kawaisō** poor, pitiable, pathetic

10 可能 **kanō** possible

可能性 **kanōsei** possibility

11 可動 **kadō** movable, mobile

13 可塑 **kaso** plastic

可愛 **kawai(i)** cute, dear, sweet

16 可燃性 **kanensei** combustible, flammable

───── 2 ─────

4 不可 **fuka** wrong, bad, improper, disapproved

不可分 **fukabun** indivisible, inseparable

不可欠 **fukaketsu** indispensable, essential

不可抗力 **fukakōryoku** force majeure, beyond one's control, unavoidable

不可侵 **fukashin** nonaggression; inviolable

不可能 **fukanō** impossible

不可解 **fukakai** mysterious, baffling

11 許可 **kyoka** permission, approval, authorization

14 認可 **ninka** approval

3d2.13 / 337

口 卩 一
24 15

句

句 句

KU phrase, sentence, verse

───── 1 ─────

4 句切 **kugi(ru)** punctuate; mark off, partition

9 句点 **kuten** period (the punctuation mark)

14 句読点 **kutōten** punctuation mark

───── 2 ─────

1 一句 **ikku** a phrase/verse; (counter for haiku)

4 文句 **monku** phrase, expression; complaint, objection; excuse

6 成句 **seiku** set phrase, idiomatic expression

9 発句 **hokku** first line (of a *renga*); haiku

10 俳句 **haiku** haiku

挙句 **ageku** in the end, ultimately

12 絶句 **zekku** stop short, forget one's lines; (Chinese poetry form)

13 禁句 **kinku** tabooed word/phrase

節句 **sekku** seasonal festival

14 語句 **goku** words and phrases

——— 3 ———

4 引用句 **in'yōku** quotation

7 決文句 **ki(mari)monku** set phrase, conventional expression

10 桃節句 **momo (no) sekku** Doll Festival (March 3)

11 菊節句 **Kiku (no) Sekku** Chrysanthemum Festival

14 慣用句 **kan'yōku** idiom, common expression

——— 4 ———

9 美辞麗句 **biji-reiku** flowery language

3d2.14 / 842
24 1

SHI an official; government office
tsukasado(ru) govern, manage, conduct **tsukasa** government office; director, official TSUKASA (m. given name)
SHI, JI, MORI (part of given name)

——— 1 ———

5 司令 **shirei** command, control; commander

司令部 **shireibu** headquarters, the command

6 司会者 **shikaisha** emcee, chairman

8 司法 **shihō** administration of justice, judicial

司法大臣 **shihō daijin** Minister of Justice

——— 2 ———

3 上司 **jōshi** one's superior(s)

6 孝司 **Takashi, Kōji** (m. given name)

7 寿司 **sushi** sushi (raw fish and other delicacies with vinegared rice)

社司 **shashi** Shinto priest

9 洋司 **Yōji, Hiroshi, Kiyoshi** (m. given name)

政司 **Masashi, Masaji** (m. given name)

10 隆司 **Takashi, Ryūji, Takaji** (m. given name)

---

11 康司 **Kōji, Yasushi, Kōshi** (m. given name)

14 総司令 **sōshirei** general headquarters, supreme command

3d2.15 / 76
24 12

U, YŪ, migi right SUKE (part of given name)

——— 1 ———

3 右上 **migi ue** upper right

右下 **migi shita** lower right

4 右手 **migite** right hand

右方 **uhō** right side, the right

5 右左 **migi-hidari** right and left

6 右回 **migimawa(ri)** clockwise

7 右折 **usetsu** turn right

右利 **migiki(ki)** righthanded; right-hander

右足 **migiashi, usoku** right foot/leg

11 右側 **migigawa, usoku** right side

12 右腕 **uwan, migiude** right arm

13 右傾 **ukei** leaning to the right, rightist

17 右翼 **uyoku** right wing, rightists; right flank

——— 2 ———

5 左右 **sayū** left and right; control, dominate, govern, influence

——— 3 ———

3d3.1 / 1253
24 22

TO, ha(ku) spew, spit out, vomit, throw up, belch, emit; express, give vent to; confess **tsu(ku)** breathe; disgorge; tell (a lie)

——— 1 ———

5 吐出 **ha(ki)da(su)** vomit, disgorge, spew out

6 吐気 **ha(ki)ke** nausea

———— 2 ————

14 嘘吐 **usotsu(ki)** liar, fibber

3d3.4 / 1252   叫 | 口 十 |
     24 12 2

叫

叫 | 叫 叫

KYŌ, sake(bu) shout, cry out

———— 1 ————

7 叫声 **sake(bi)goe** a shout, cry, scream

12 叫喚 **kyōkan** shout, shriek, scream

3d3.5 / 1256   口 力 |
     24 8 2

吸

吸 吸

KYŪ, su(u) suck; inhale; smoke (cigarettes)

———— 1 ————

4 吸収 **kyūshū** absorb

吸込 **su(i)ko(mu)** inhale; suck in; swallow up

吸引 **kyūin** absorb; attract

8 吸物 **su(i)mono** soup

11 吸殻 **su(i)gara** cigar(ette) butt

———— 2 ————

8 呼吸 **kokyū** breathing, respiration

3d3.7   田 口 宀 一
     24 15 1

吃

吃 吃

KITSU stutter; eat, drink   **domo(ru)** stutter, stammer

———— 1 ————

22 吃驚 **kikkyō, bikkuri** be surprised

3d3.8   日 口 巾
     24 26

吊

吊 吊

CHŌ, tsu(ru), tsuru(su) hang, suspend   **tsuru(shi)** ready-made/hand-me-down clothes

———— 1 ————

3 吊下 **tsu(ri)sa(garu)** hang, dangle, be suspended

9 吊革 **tsu(ri)kawa** (hanging) strap

———— 2 ————

9 首吊 **kubitsu(ri)** hang oneself

3d3.9 / 1259   日 口 十 |
     24 12 2

舌

舌 舌

ZETSU, shita tongue

———— 1 ————

5 舌打 **shitau(chi)** clicking one's tongue, tsk, tch

7 舌足 **shitata(razu)** lisping, tongue-tied

———— 2 ————

5 弁舌 **benzetsu** speech, eloquence

8 毒舌 **dokuzetsu** stinging tongue, blistering remarks

11 猫舌 **nekojita** aversion to hot foods

———— 3 ————

2 二枚舌 **nimaijita** forked tongue, duplicity

3d3.10 / 199   日 口 冂 |
     24 20 2

向

向 向

KŌ, mu(kau) face toward; proceed to   **mu(ku/keru)** (intr./tr.) turn toward   **mu(kō)** opposite side; the next (three years)

————— 1 —————

3 向上 **kōjō** improvement, advancement

4 向井 **Mukai** (surname)

6 向合 **mu(kai)a(u)** face each other

11 向側 **mu(kō)gawa** the opposite side, across from

————— 2 —————

3 下向 **shitamu(ki)** downward look; downturn, decline

4 内向性 **naikōsei** introverted

日向 **hinata(bokko)** bask in the sun **Hyūga** (ancient kuni, Miyazaki-ken)

方向 **hōkō** direction

5 北向 **kitamu(ki)** facing north

出向 **demu(ku)** go to, leave for, repair to **shukkō** repair to; be on loan (to a subsidiary), be seconded (to another company), temporary transfer

外向性 **gaikōsei** extroverted, outgoing

冬向 **fuyumu(ki)** for winter

6 西向 **nishimu(ki)** facing west

仰向 **aomu(keru)** turn to face upward

7 志向 **shikō** intention, inclination

8 東向 **higashimu(ki)** facing east

9 南向 **minamimu(ki)** facing south

前向 **maemu(ki)** forward-looking

風向 **fūkō** wind direction **kaze-mu(ki), kazamu(ki)** wind direction; situation

指向 **shikō** directional (antenna)

10 俯向 **utsumu(keru)** turn upside down, turn downward **utsumu(ku)** look downward

真向 **mamuka(i)** just opposite, right across from, face to face **ma(k)kō** forehead; front

振向 **fu(ri)mu(ku)** turn toward, look back

夏向 **natsumu(ki)** for summer

11 偏向 **henkō** leanings, deviation; deflection

動向 **dōkō** trend, attitude

13 傾向 **keikō** tendency, trend; inclination, leanings

意向 **ikō** intention, inclination

14 暮向 **ku(rashi)mu(ki)** circumstances, livelihood

15 趣向 **shukō** plan, idea

————— 3 —————

3 大衆向 **taishūmu(ki)** for the general public, popular

向 → 問 **8e3.1**

3d3.11 / 1119

口 24　厂 18　一 1

KŌ empress **GO** after **kisaki** empress, queen

————— 2 —————

4 太后 **taikō** empress dowager, queen mother

9 皇后 **kōgō** empress, queen

皇后陛下 **Kōgō Heika** Her Majesty the Empress

————— 3 —————

9 皇太后 **kōtaikō, kōtaigō** empress dowager, queen mother

3d3.12 / 82

… 30　夕 24　口

MEI, MYŌ, na name; reputation, fame

————— 1 —————

0 名づける **na(zukeru)** name, call

2 名人 **meijin** master, expert, virtuoso

5 名付 **nazu(ke)** naming; fiancé(e) **nazu(keru)** name, call, entitle

名古屋 **Nagoya** (city, Aichi-ken)

名字 **myōji** surname

名札 **nafuda** name plate/tag

名目 **meimoku** name, pretext; nominal, ostensible

6 名曲 **meikyoku** famous music

7 名声 **meisei** fame, reputation

8 名画 **meiga** famous picture, masterpiece

名刺 **meishi** business card

名物 **meibutsu** noted product (of a locality)

名所 **meisho** noted places/sights

9 名乗 **nano(ru)** call oneself, profess to be

名前 **namae** name

10 名残 **nago(ri)** farewell; remembrance, keepsake; relics, vestiges

名高 **nadaka(i)** famous, renowned

名案 **meian** splendid idea, good plan

12 名詞 **meishi** noun

13 名義 **meigi** name; moral duty

名誉 **meiyo** honor, glory, fame, prestige

名誉教授 **meiyo kyōju** professor emeritus

19 名簿 **meibo** name list, roster, roll

——————— 2 ———————

2 人名 **jinmei** person's name

3 大名 **daimyō** feudal lord, daimyo **taimei** renown

4 氏名 **shimei** surname and given name, (full) name

5 本名 **honmyō, honmei** one's real name

代名詞 **daimeishi** pronoun

功名 **kōmyō, kōmei** great achievement

6 仮名 **kana** kana, Japanese syllabary character **kamei, kemyō, karina** pseudonym, alias, pen name

同名異人 **dōmei-ijin** different person of the same name

汚名 **omei** blot on one's name, stigma, dishonor

地名 **chimei** place name

有名 **yūmei** famous

7 別名 **betsumei** another name, alias, pseudonym

芳名録 **hōmeiroku** visitor's book, name list

学名 **gakumei** scientific name

社名 **shamei** company name

改名 **kaimei** changing one's/the name

8 命名 **meimei** name, christen, call

呼名 **yo(bi)na** one's given/popular name

姓名 **seimei** name (surname and given name)

実名 **jitsumei** one's real name

宛名 **atena** address

和名 **wamyō** Japanese name (of a Chinese) **wamei** Japanese name (of a plant/animal)

9 俗名 **zokumei** common name; secular name **zokumyō** secular name

指名 **shimei** nominate, designate

10 高名 **kōmyō** fame, renown; your name **kōmei** fame, renown

匿名 **tokumei** anonymous

書名 **shomei** (book) title

記名 **kimei** register/sign one's name

11 偽名 **gimei** assumed name, alias

12 属名 **zokumei** generic name

椎名 **Shiina** (surname)

無名 **mumei** anonymous; an unknown

筆名 **hitsumei** pen name, pseudonym

13 署名 **shomei** signature

署名捺印 **shomei-natsuin** signature and seal

14 綽名 **adana** nickname

18 題名 **daimei** title

——————— 3 ———————

4 片仮名 **katakana** katakana, the non-cursive syllabary

5 平仮名 **hiragana** (the cursive syllabary)

8 送仮名 **oku(ri)gana** suffixed kana showing inflection

固有名詞 **koyū meishi** proper noun

10 振仮名 **fu(ri)gana** (small kana written above or beside a kanji to show its pronunciation)

—— 4 ——

3d4.1

口　犭
24　27

吠

吠 吠

BEI, HAI, ho(eru) bark, bay, bellow, roar, howl, cry

———— 1 ————

7 吠声 **ho(e)goe** bark, yelp, howl, roar

3d4.3 / 1255

口　攵　口
49　24

吹

吹 吹

SUI, fu(ku) blow (tr. or intr.); smelt, mint; brag

———— 1 ————

4 吹込 **fu(ki)ko(mu)** blow in; record (a song); inspire

5 吹出 **fu(ki)da(su)** begin to blow; breathe out; burst out laughing

吹付 **fu(ki)tsu(keru)** blow against

9 吹飛 **fu(ki)to(basu)** blow away

吹奏楽 **suisōgaku** wind-instrument music, brass

11 吹雪 **fubuki** snowstorm, blizzard

12 吹替 **fu(ki)ka(e)** substitute actor, stand-in; dubbing; recasting, reminting

3d4.8 / 1250

口　亻　一
24　3　1

吟

吟 吟

GIN sing, chant, recite

———— 1 ————

8 吟味 **ginmi** close inquiry, scrutiny

12 吟詠 **gin'ei** sing, recite; (compose a) poem

3d4.13

日　木　口
41　24

呆

呆 呆

HŌ stupid **BŌ, aki(reru)** be amazed/astonished/appalled/aghast/shocked

———— 1 ————

6 呆気 **akke** blank amazement

12 呆然 **bōzen (to)** in blank amazement

———— 2 ————

7 阿呆 **ahō** fool, jackass

3d4.14 / 1590

日　王　口
46　24

呈

呈 呈

TEI offer, present, exhibit

———— 1 ————

5 呈示 **teiji** present, bring up

———— 2 ————

10 進呈 **shintei** give, present

11 捧呈 **hōtei** present, offer, submit

13 献呈 **kentei** presentation (copy)

17 謹呈 **kintei** Respectfully presented, With the compliments of the author

18 贈呈 **zōtei** presentation, gift

3d4.15 / 2250

日　口　尸　|
24　40　2

邑

邑 邑

YŪ village, town; territory, dominion
YŪ, MURA, KUNI, SATO, SUMI (part of given name) SATOSHI (m. given name)

品 → 品　3d6.15

吳 → 吴　2o5.7

3

氵　　4
土
扌
口
女
巾
犭
弓
彳
彡
艹
宀
⺍
吉
广
尸
口

足→ **7d0.1**

呉→ **2o5.7**

3d4.16 / 2036 　　目 口 |
24 2

呂

呂 呂

RO, RYO backbone; tone　RO, RYO,
NAGA, TOMO, OTO, FUE　(part of given
name)

――――― 1 ―――――

9 呂律 **roretsu** articulation, pronunciation

――――― 2 ―――――

9 風呂 **furo** bath; bathtub
風呂桶 **furooke** bathtub
風呂場 **furoba** bathroom
風呂敷 **furoshiki** (square of cloth
used to wrap goods and presents in)

――――― 3 ―――――

12 蒸風呂 **mu(shi)buro** Turkish bath,
sauna

3d4.17 / 2035 　　目 口 一
24 14 1

吾

吾 吾

GO, waga my, our, one's own　**ware**
I, oneself　GO, WAGA, WARE, A, MICHI,
NORI　(part of given name)　GORŌ (m.
given name)

――――― 2 ―――――

9 省吾 **Shōgo, Seigo** (m. given name)

3d4.18 / 690 　　目 土 口 |
22 24 2

告

告 告

KOKU, tsu(geru) tell, announce, in-
form

――――― 1 ―――――

5 告白 **kokuhaku** confession
告示 **kokuji** notification
9 告発 **kokuhatsu** prosecution, indictment, accusation
12 告訴 **kokuso** accuse, charge, bring
suit

――――― 2 ―――――

4 予告 **yokoku** advance notice;
(movie) preview
公告 **kōkoku** public notice
5 申告 **shinkoku** report, declaration,
notification, filing
布告 **fukoku** proclaim, declare,
promulgate
広告 **kōkoku** advertisement
7 抗告 **kōkoku** appeal, protest, complaint
戒告 **kaikoku** warning, admonition
8 忠告 **chūkoku** advice, admonition
9 通告 **tsūkoku** notification, notice
宣告 **senkoku** sentence, verdict,
pronouncement
10 原告 **genkoku** plaintiff
被告 **hikoku** defendant
11 密告 **mikkoku** secret information
12 報告 **hōkoku** report
報告書 **hōkokusho** (written) re-
port/statement
13 催告 **saikoku** notification, admonition
勧告 **kankoku** recommendation,
advice
19 警告 **keikoku** warning, admonition

――――― 4 ―――――

9 宣戦布告 **sensen fukoku** declaration of war

3d4.19 　　⼤ 口 |
34 24 2

呑

呑 呑

DON, no(mu) drink

――――― 1 ―――――

4 呑込 **no(mi)ko(mu)** swallow; understand

⁶ 呑気 **nonki** easygoing, free and easy, optimistic

3d4.20 / 1248   ⊟ 口 一 丨
                          24 14 2

否否

HI no, negative **ina** no, nay **ina(mu)** refuse, decline; deny **ina(ya)** as soon as, no sooner than; yes or no; objection; if, whether **iya** no, nay; yes, well

——————— 1 ———————

⁷ 否決 **hiketsu** rejection, voting down
⁸ 否定 **hitei** denial, negation
¹⁴ 否認 **hinin** deny, repudiate

——————— 2 ———————

⁵ 可否 **kahi** right or wrong, pro and con
⁶ 安否 **anpi** whether safe or not, well-being
⁷ 良否 **ryōhi** (whether) good or bad
⁸ 拒否 **kyohi** refusal, rejection, denial
¹¹ 許否 **kyohi** approval or disapproval
¹⁵ 諾否 **dakuhi** acceptance or refusal, definite reply

谷→ **2o5.3**

3d4.21 / 689   ⊞ 口 十 丨
                          24 12 2

亂丨乱乱

RAN disorder; riot, rebellion **mida(su)** put in disorder **mida(reru)** be in disorder, be confused/disorganized

——————— 1 ———————

² 乱入 **rannyū** intrusion
⁵ 乱用 **ran'yō** misuse, abuse, misappropriation
⁶ 乱交 **rankō** orgy
¹² 乱筆 **ranpitsu** hasty writing, scrawl

¹³ 乱戦 **ransen** melee, free-for-all fight
¹⁴ 乱雑 **ranzatsu** disorder, confusion
¹⁵ 乱暴 **ranbō** violence; rough, reckless

——————— 2 ———————

⁴ 内乱 **nairan** civil war, rebellion
  反乱 **hanran** rebellion, revolt
⁷ 狂乱 **kyōran** frenzy, madness
⁸ 波乱 **haran** waves; commotion; wide fluctuations
⁹ 叛乱 **hanran** rebellion, revolt
  咲乱 **sa(ki)mida(reru)** bloom in profusion
¹⁰ 酒乱 **shuran** drunken frenzy/violence
¹¹ 動乱 **dōran** upheaval, disturbance, riot
  混乱 **konran** confusion, disorder, chaos
¹² 散乱 **sanran** dispersion, scattering
  chi(ri)mida(reru) be scattered about; be routed
¹³ 戦乱 **senran** the upheavals of war, war-torn (region)
¹⁶ 錯乱 **sakuran** distraction, derangement

呉→呉 **2o5.7**

3d4.22 / 958   ⋯ 口 二 儿
                          24 4 16

豆豆

TŌ, ZU bean, pea **mame** bean, pea; (as prefix) miniature

——————— 1 ———————

¹⁴ 豆腐 **tōfu** tofu, bean curd

——————— 2 ———————

³ 小豆 **azuki** adzuki beans
⁶ 伊豆半島 **Izu-hantō** Izu Peninsula (Shizuoka-ken)
⁸ 枝豆 **edamame** green soybeans
¹⁰ 納豆 **nattō** fermented soybeans
¹² 湯豆腐 **yudōfu** boiled tofu

何 → **2a5.21**

伺 → **2a5.23**

3d4.23 / 793

□... ∃ 口 丨
39 24 2

君

君 君

KUN (suffix for male names); ruler
kimi you (in masculine speech); ruler

─────── 1 ───────

5 君代 **Kimi(ga)yo** (Japan's national anthem)
君主国 **kunshukoku** a monarchy

─────── 5 ───────

3d5.3 / 307

□□ 木 口 一
41 24 1

味

味 味

MI, aji taste, flavor **aji(wau)** taste; relish, appreciate **aji(na)** clever, witty, smart

─────── 1 ───────

4 味方 **mikata** friend, ally, supporter
5 味付 **ajitsu(ke)** seasoning
6 味気無 **ajikena(i)** irksome, wearisome, dreary
12 味覚 **mikaku** sense of taste
15 味噌 **miso** miso (fermented bean paste)
味噌汁 **miso shiru** miso soup

─────── 2 ───────

1 一味違 **hitoaji chiga(u)** with a unique flavor
3 三味線 **shamisen, samisen** samisen (three-stringed instrument)
4 中味 **nakami** contents
5 甘味料 **kanmiryō** sweetener
正味 **shōmi** net (weight)
6 気味 **kimi** feeling, sensation; a touch, tinge
地味 **jimi** plain, subdued, unde-

monstrative, conservative
chimi (fertility of) the soil
旨味 **umami** tastiness, flavor
7 吟味 **ginmi** close inquiry, scrutiny
8 苦味 **nigami** bitter taste
9 重味 **omomi** weight; importance; emphasis; dignity
美味 **oi(shii)** good-tasting, delicious **bimi** good flavor; delicacies
11 渋味 **shibumi** puckery taste; severe elgance
脳味噌 **nōmiso** brains, gray matter
12 無味 **mumi** tasteless, flat, dry
13 塩味 **shioaji** salty taste
意味 **imi** meaning, significance
14 酸味 **sanmi, su(i)mi** acidity, sourness
15 賞味 **shōmi** relish, appreciate
趣味 **shumi** interest, liking, tastes; hobby
調味料 **chōmiryō** condiments, seasonings
16 興味 **kyōmi** interest
興味深 **kyōmibuka(i)** very interesting

─────── 3 ───────

4 不気味 **bukimi** uncanny, weird, eerie, ominous
6 多趣味 **tashumi** many-sided interests
有難味 **a(ri)gatami** value, worth
12 無気味 **bukimi** ominous, eerie

3d5.4 / 1254

□□ 口 十 儿
24 12 16

呼

呼 呼

KO, yo(bu) call

─────── 1 ───────

5 呼出 **yo(bi)da(su)** call out/up/forth, summon
呼付 **yo(bi)tsu(keru)** call, send for, summon
6 呼吸 **kokyū** breathing, respiration
呼名 **yo(bi)na** one's given/popular name

7 呼声 **yo(bi)goe** a call, cry, shout
8 呼物 **yo(bi)mono** attraction, feature, main event

3d5.11

田 口 儿
24 16

呪 | 呪 呪

JU spell, curse, incantation **noro(u)** curse **majina(i)** charm, spell, magical incantation

――――――― 1 ―――――――

4 呪文 **jumon** spell, curse, magic formula
11 呪術 **jujutsu** incantation, sorcery, magic

咏 → 詠 7a5.14

3d5.14 / 214

田 口 大 ㇑
24 34 15

知 知

CHI, shi(ru) (come to) know
shi(rase) information, news; omen
TOMO (part of given name)

――――――― 1 ―――――――

2 知人 **chijin** an acquaintance
6 知合 **shi(ri)a(i)** an acquaintance
     shi(ri)a(u) know each other
8 知事 **chiji** governor
     知的 **chiteki** intellectual, mental
10 知能 **chinō** intelligence
     知恵 **chie** knowledge, intelligence, wisdom
18 知顔 **shi(ran) kao, shi(ranu) kao** pretending not to know, nonchalant **shi(ri)gao** knowing look
19 知識 **chishiki** knowledge
     知識人 **chishikijin** an intellectual

――――――― 2 ―――――――

5 未知 **michi** unknown, strange
6 全知 **zenchi** omniscience
     奸知 **kanchi** cunning, guile

7 承知 **shōchi** consent to; know, be aware of
8 周知 **shūchi** common knowledge, widely known
     物知 **monoshi(ri)** knowledgeable, erudite
     物知顔 **monoshi(ri)gao** knowing look
9 通知 **tsūchi** notification, notice
     浅知恵 **asajie** shallow-witted
     県知事 **kenchiji** prefectural governor
10 既知 **kichi** (already) known
     高知県 **Kōchi-ken** (prefecture)
     恩知 **onshi(razu)** ingratitude; ingrate
     恥知 **hajishi(razu)** shameless person
11 悪知恵 **warujie** cunning, guile
12 無知 **muchi** ignorance
13 猿知恵 **sarujie** shallow cleverness
14 察知 **satchi** infer, gather, sense

――――――― 3 ―――――――

2 人見知 **hitomishi(ri)** be bashful before strangers
4 不承知 **fushōchi** dissent, disagreement, noncompliance
18 顔見知 **kaomishi(ri)** knowing someone by sight, a nodding acquaintance

3d5.17 / 1360

田 大 口 丁
34 24 14

奇 | 奇 奇

KI strange, odd; odd number
ku(shiki) strange, curious, mysterious
ku(shikumo) strange to say, mysteriously

――――――― 1 ―――――――

7 奇妙 **kimyō** strange, curious, odd
13 奇数 **kisū** odd number
     奇跡 **kiseki** miracle
19 奇麗 **kirei** pretty, beautiful; clean, neat
22 奇襲 **kishū** surprise attack

— 2 —

⁵ 好奇心 **kōkishin** curiosity, inquisitiveness

⁸ 怪奇 **kaiki** mysterious, grotesque, eerie

函 → 函 2b6.3

— 6 —

3d6.10

口　亠　竹
24　11　17

咳　　　咳 咳

GAI, seki a cough **se(ku)** cough **shiwabuki** a cough; clearing the throat

— 1 —

⁵ 咳払 **sekibara(i)** clearing one's throat

3d6.12 / 927

口　大　几
24　34　16

咲　　　咲 咲

SHŌ, sa(ku) bloom, blossom SAKI (part of given name)

— 1 —

⁷ 咲乱 **sa(ki)mida(reru)** bloom in profusion

— 2 —

⁶ 返咲 **kae(ri)za(ki)** second blooming; comeback

早咲 **hayaza(ki)** early-blooming; precocious

3d6.14

口　大
24　34

咽　　　咽 咽

IN, EN, ETSU, muse(bu) be choked up, be smothered/suffocated **nodo** throat

— 1 —

⁸ 咽泣 **muse(bi)na(ku)** sob

— 3 —

⁶ 耳鼻咽喉科 **jibiinkōka** ear, nose, and throat specialty

3d6.15 / 230

田　口
24

品　　　品 | 品 品

HIN refinement; article **shina** goods; quality

— 1 —

⁴ 品切 **shinagi(re)** out of stock, sold out

⁸ 品物 **shinamono** goods, merchandise

¹⁵ 品質 **hinshitsu** quality

— 2 —

¹ 一品 **ippin** an article/item; a dish/course

³ 上品 **jōhin** refined, elegant, genteel; first-class article

下品 **gehin** vulgar, coarse, gross

⁴ 手品 **tejina** sleight of hand, magic tricks, juggling

手品師 **tejinashi** magician, juggler

⁵ 出品 **shuppin** exhibit, display

用品 **yōhin** supplies

⁶ 返品 **henpin** returned goods, returns

⁷ 良品 **ryōhin** article of superior quality

作品 **sakuhin** a work

⁸ 物品 **buppin** goods, article, commodity

⁹ 珍品 **chinpin** rare article, curio

食品 **shokuhin** food(stuffs)

食品店 **shokuhinten** grocery store

¹⁰ 残品 **zanpin** remaining stock, unsold merchandise

部品 **buhin** parts

逸品 **ippin** superb article, masterpiece

納品 **nōhin** delivery

¹¹ 商品 **shōhin** goods, merchandise

盗品 **tōhin** stolen goods, loot

¹² 備品 **bihin** fixtures, furnishings, equipment

廃品 **haihin** scrap, waste, discards, junk

景品 **keihin** premium, present, giveaway

13 新品 **shinpin** new article, brand new

14 遺品 **ihin** articles left by the deceased

製品 **seihin** product, manufactured goods

15 賞品 **shōhin** (nonmonetary) prize

16 薬品 **yakuhin** drugs; chemicals

—— 3 ——

4 化粧品 **keshōhin** cosmetics, make-up

日用品 **nichiyōhin** daily necessities

5 必要品 **hitsuyōhin** necessities

必需品 **hitsujuhin** necessities, essentials

7 医薬品 **iyakuhin** pharmaceuticals

8 非売品 **hibaihin** article not for sale

免税品 **menzeihin** duty-free goods

9 食料品 **shokuryōhin** food(stuffs)

10 消耗品 **shōmōhin** supplies, expendables

骨董品 **kottōhin** curios, bric-a-brac

特許品 **tokkyohin** patented article

11 密輸品 **mitsuyuhin** contraband

舶来品 **hakuraihin** imported goods

12 装飾品 **sōshokuhin** ornaments, decorations, accessories

貴重品 **kichōhin** valuables

13 禁制品 **kinseihin** contraband

禁輸品 **kin'yuhin** contraband

新製品 **shinseihin** new product

哉→ 4n5.4

面→ 3s6.1

3d6.21   ⊞ 歹 24 竹 30   24   17

殆 殆

TAI, DAI, hoton(do) almost
hotohoto quite, really

—— 2 ——

6 危殆 **kitai** danger, peril, jeopardy

—— 7 ——

3d7.1 / 2039   ⊞ 貝 口   68   24

唄 唄

BAI, uta song   BAI, HAI, UTA (part of given name)

—— 2 ——

3 小唄 **kouta** ditty, ballad

8 長唄 **nagauta** song accompanied on the samisen

啞→啞 **3d8.3**

3d7.4   ⊞ 月 口 十   42   24   12

哺 哺

HO take/hold in the mouth

—— 1 ——

7 哺乳動物 **honyū dōbutsu** mammal

啄→啄 **3d8.4**

3d7.8 / 1846   ⊞ 夋 口 竹   49   24   17

唆 唆

SA, sosonoka(su) tempt, seduce, incite

—— 2 ——

5 示唆 **shisa** suggestion

10 教唆 **kyōsa** instigate, abet

3d7.10 / 163   ⊟ 貝 口   68   24

員 員

IN member; number   KAZU (part of given name)

—— 2 ——

1 一員 **ichiin** a person; a member

2 人員 **jin'in** personnel, staff, crew

3 工員 **kōin** factory worker, machine operator

4 冗員 **jōin** superfluous personnel, overstaffing

欠員 **ketsuin** vacant position, opening

6 吏員 **riin** an official

全員 **zen'in** all the members, the whole staff/crew

会員 **kaiin** member

行員 **kōin** bank clerk/employee

7 兵員 **heiin** military personnel/strength

役員 **yakuin** (company) officer, director

社員 **shain** employee, staff

8 定員 **teiin** prescribed number of personnel; (seating) capacity; quorum

店員 **ten'in** store employee, clerk

所員 **shoin** (member of the) staff, personnel

委員 **iin** committee member

委員会 **iinkai** committee

10 党員 **tōin** party member

教員 **kyōin** teacher, instructor; teaching staff

11 隊員 **taiin** member of a brigade/team

剰員 **jōin** superfluous personnel, overstaffing

動員 **dōin** mobilization

常員 **jōin** regular personnel/member

船員 **sen'in** crewman, seaman

12 満員 **man'in** full to capacity

減員 **gen'in** staff reduction, personnel cutback

艇員 **teiin** (boat's) crew

14 総員 **sōin** all hands, in full force

駅員 **ekiin** station employee/staff

18 職員 **shokuin** personnel, staff (member)

20 議員 **giin** M.P., dietman, congressman

——————— 3 ———————

4 公務員 **kōmuin** government employee

5 代議員 **daigiin** representative, delegate

正会員 **seikaiin** full/regular member

正社員 **seishain** regular employee, full member of the staff

6 会社員 **kaishain** company employee

9 乗務員 **jōmuin** train/plane crew

乗組員 **norikumiin** crew

10 従業員 **jūgyōin** employee

特派員 **tokuhain** (news) correspondent; delegate

11 添乗員 **tenjōin** tour conductor

12 超満員 **chōman'in** crowded beyond capacity

14 総動員 **sōdōin** general mobilization

——————— 4 ———————

11 常任委員会 **jōnin iinkai** standing committee

3d7.12 / 1737

日 礻 口 厂
57 24 18

SHIN, kuchibiru lip

3d7.13 / 1397

凷 斤 扌 口
50 23 24

TETSU wisdom **SATOSHI** (m. given name)

——————— 1 ———————

3 哲也 **Tetsuya** (m. given name)

7 哲学 **tetsugaku** philosophy

8 哲治 **Tetsuji, Tetsuharu** (m. given name)

——————— 2 ———————

6 先哲 **sentetsu** ancient sage

13 聖哲 **seitetsu** sage, wise man

勉→ **2n8.1**

——— 8 ———

3d8.1 / 1234

唯 唯

唯 唯

YUI, I, tada, tatta solely, only, merely TADA (part of given name)

——— 1 ———

1 唯一 **yuiitsu, tada hito(tsu)** the only, sole

4 唯今 **tadaima** right/just now

　唯心論 **yuishinron** idealism, spiritualism

8 唯物論 **yuibutsuron** materialism

3d8.2

唾

唾 唾

DA, tsuba, tsubaki saliva

——— 1 ———

11 唾液 **daeki** saliva

3d8.3

啞

啞 | 啞 啞

A, oshi mute, unable to speak

——— 1 ———

12 啞然 **azen (to)** dumbfounded, agape

——— 2 ———

8 盲啞 **mōa** blind and mute

22 聾啞 **rōa** deaf and mute

3d8.4 / 2038

啄

啄 啄

TAKU, tsuiba(mu) peck at, pick up
TAKU, TOKU (part of given name)

——— 1 ———

4 啄木鳥 **kitsutsuki** woodpecker

3d8.8 / 1919

喝

喝 | 喝 喝

KATSU scold; raise one's voice

——— 1 ———

8 喝采 **kassai** applause, cheers

——— 2 ———

1 一喝 **ikkatsu** a thundering cry, a roar

10 恐喝 **kyōkatsu** threat, intimidation, blackmail

3d8.9 / 1646

唱

唱 唱

SHŌ, tona(eru) advocate, espouse; chant; cry, yell

——— 1 ———

14 唱歌 **shōka** singing

——— 2 ———

5 主唱 **shushō** advocate, promote, suggest

6 合唱団 **gasshōdan** chorus, choir

9 独唱 **dokushō** vocal solo

14 歌唱 **kashō** singing; song

3d8.17 / 1398

田 夂 尸 口
49 40 24

啓

啓啓

KEI open; say AKIRA, HIRAKU (m. given name) HIRO, YOSHI (part of given name)

——— 1 ———

2 啓子 **Keiko, Hiroko** (f. given name)
4 啓太 **Keita** (m. given name)
5 啓示 **keiji** revelation

——— 2 ———

8 拝啓 **haikei** Dear Sir/Madam

超→ 3b9.18

——— 9 ———

3d9.1

田 食 口
73 24

喰

喰喰

ku(u), kura(u) eat, drink; receive (a blow)

啞→ 3d8.3

3d9.6

田 口 大 亻
24 34 3

喉

喉喉

KŌ, nodo throat

——— 1 ———

4 喉仏 **nodobotoke** Adam's apple

——— 4 ———

6 耳鼻咽喉科 **jibiinkōka** ear, nose, and throat specialty

3d9.7 / 1240

田 口 土 大
24 22 34

喫

喫喫

KITSU eat, drink, smoke

——— 1 ———

9 喫茶店 **kissaten** teahouse, café
13 喫煙 **kitsuen** smoking

——— 2 ———

12 満喫 **mankitsu** have one's fill of, fully enjoy

喝→喝 3d8.8

3d9.12

田 日 口 宀
43 24 33

喧

喧喧

KEN, kamabisu(shii) noisy, clamorous **yakama(shii)** noisy, boisterous; faultfinding; troublesome; much-talked-about; choosy

——— 1 ———

13 喧嘩 **kenka** quarrel

3d9.14

田 口 豸 丶
24 27 10

喙

喙喙

KAI, kuchibashi beak

3d9.15

田 月 口 亻
42 24 3

喻

喻喻

YU, tato(eru) compare, liken

——— 2 ———

5 比喻 **hiyu** simile, metaphor, allegory
比喻的 **hiyuteki** figurative
13 隠喻 **in'yu** metaphor

3d9.19 / 1587

喚喚

KAN call **wame(ku)** cry, shout, clamor

—— 1 ——
7 喚声 **kansei, wame(ki)goe** shout, yell, scream, outcry
10 喚起 **kanki** evoke, awaken, call forth

—— 2 ——
6 叫喚 **kyōkan** shout, shriek, scream

3d9.21 / 934

就就

SHŪ, JU, tsu(ku) settle in; take (a seat/position); depart; study (under a teacher) **tsu(keru)** place, appoint **(ni) tsu(ite)** concerning, about NARI (part of given name)

—— 1 ——
6 就任 **shūnin** assumption of office
13 就業 **shūgyō** employment
就寝 **shūshin** go to bed, retire
18 就職 **shūshoku** find employment
就職口 **shūshokuguchi** job opening, employment

単 → 単 **3n6.2**

喪 → **3b9.20**

3d9.25 / 2040

喬喬

KYŌ high; boast KYŌ, TAKA, NOBU, TADA, SUKE, MOTO, YASU (part of given name) TAKASHI, TADASHI (m. given name)

—— 1 ——
4 喬木 **kyōboku** tall tree

3d9.26 / 960

登登

TŌ, TO climb; attendance at one's place of duty; making an entry in an official document **nobo(ru)** climb, ascend

—— 1 ——
3 登山 **tozan** mountain climbing
7 登坂 **nobo(ri)zaka** uphill slope, ascent
10 登記 **tōki** registration, recording
12 登場 **tōjō** come on stage; appear on the scene
13 登載 **tōsai** register, record, enter
16 登録 **tōroku** registration

—— 2 ——
3 山登 **yamanobo(ri)** mountain climbing
10 能登半島 **Noto-hantō** (peninsula, Ishikawa-ken)

3d9.27 / 215

短短

TAN, mijika(i) short

—— 1 ——
2 短刀 **tantō** short sword, dagger
3 短大 **tandai** junior college (short for 短期大学)
6 短気 **tanki** short temper, touchiness, hastiness
8 短波 **tanpa** shortwave
短所 **tansho** shortcoming, defect, fault
12 短期 **tanki** short period, short-term
短絡 **tanraku** short circuit
短距離 **tankyori** short distance, short-range
14 短歌 **tanka** 31-syllable poem, tanka

3

氵
土
扌
口　9
女
巾
犭
弓
彳
彡
宀
ツ
山
青
广
厂
囗

15 短編 **tanpen** short piece/story/film

短篇小説 **tanpen shōsetsu** short story/novel

短調 **tanchō** minor key

17 短縮 **tanshuku** shorten, curtail, abridge

―――――― 2 ――――――

8 長短 **chōtan** (relative) length; merits and demerits, advantages and disadvantages

12 最短 **saitan** shortest

16 操短 **sōtan** curtailed operations (short for 操業短縮)

3d9.29 / 1082   目 ヨ 工 口
39 38 24

JIN, tazu(neru) ask (a question), inquire; seek **hiro** (unit of length, about 182 cm) HIRO (part of given name)

―――――― 1 ――――――

2 尋人 **tazu(ne)bito** person being sought, missing person

8 尋物 **tazu(ne)mono** thing being searched for, lost article

11 尋常 **jinjō** normal, ordinary

尋問 **jinmon** questioning, interrogation

―――――― **10** ――――――

3d10.3   目 目 口 犭
55 24 27

KYŪ, ka(gu) smell, sniff

―――――― 1 ――――――

4 嗅分 **ka(gi)wa(keru)** tell/differentiate by scent

12 嗅覚 **kyūkaku** sense of smell

3d10.5   目 目 夂 口
55 49 24

SA, shaga(reru), shiwaga(reru), ka(reru) become hoarse **ka(rasu)** make hoarse

―――――― 1 ――――――

7 嗄声 **shaga(re)goe** hoarse voice

3d10.7   目 王 口 艹
46 24 32

嘩 | 嘩 嘩

KA noisy

―――――― 2 ――――――

12 喧嘩 **kenka** quarrel

3d10.8 / 1246   目 口 艹 大
24 32 34

嘆 | 嘆 嘆

TAN, nage(ku) grieve, lament, bemoan; deplore, regret
nage(kawashii) deplorable

―――――― 1 ――――――

10 嘆息 **tansoku** sigh; lament

15 嘆賞 **tanshō** praise, admire

19 嘆願 **tangan** entreaty, petition

―――――― 2 ――――――

8 長嘆 **chōtan** a long sigh

12 悲嘆 **hitan** grief, sorrow

詠嘆 **eitan** exclamation; admiration

13 感嘆 **kantan** admiration, wonder, exclamation

感嘆符 **kantanfu** exclamation point (!)

慨嘆 **gaitan** regret, lament, deplore

22 驚嘆 **kyōtan** admiration, wonder

3d10.13 / 1917   ⊞ ⼝ ⼤ ⼝
                         24 32 20

嗣

嗣 嗣

SHI heir TSUGI, TSUGU (part of given name)

——— 1 ———

² 嗣子 **shishi** heir

號 → 号 **3d2.10**

辞 → **5b8.4**

3d10.14 / 794   ⊞ ⺩ ⺕ ⼝
                         46 39 24

群

羣 | 群 群

GUN, mu(re), mura group, crowd, flock, cluster, clump **mu(reru), mura(garu)** crowd, flock, swarm

——— 1 ———

⁵ 群生 **gunsei** grow gregariously, grow in crowds
¹⁰ 群島 **guntō** group of islands, archipelago
   群馬県 **Gunma-ken** (prefecture)
¹² 群衆 **gunshū** crowd, multitude
   群集 **gunshū** crowd, multitude, mob (psychology)

——— 2 ———

¹ 一群 **hitomu(re), ichigun** a group; a flock, a crowd
⁷ 抜群 **batsugun** pre-eminent, outstanding

羣 → 群 **3d10.14**

3d10.15 / 959   ⊟ ⽇ ⼝ ⼉
                         43 24 16

豊

豐 | 豊 豊

HŌ, yuta(ka) abundant, rich **toyo-** excellent, rich TOYO (part of given name)

——— 1 ———

⁵ 豊田 **Toyoda, Toyota** (surname)
⁷ 豊作 **hōsaku** abundant harvest
¹² 豊満 **hōman** plump, corpulent, full-figured
   豊富 **hōfu** abundant, affluent

——— 11 ———

3d11.1 / 925   ⊞ 鳥 ⼝
                      80 24

鳴

鳴 鳴

MEI, na(ku) (animals) cry, sing, howl **na(ru)** (intr.) sound, ring **na(rasu)** (tr.) sound, ring

——— 1 ———

⁷ 鳴声 **na(ki)goe** cry, call, chirping (of animals)
⁸ 鳴門海峡 **Naruto-kaikyō** (strait between Shikoku and Awaji island)
¹¹ 鳴動 **meidō** rumbling
¹⁹ 鳴響 **na(ri)hibi(ku)** resound, reverberate

——— 2 ———

⁶ 共鳴 **kyōmei** resonance; sympathy
   耳鳴 **mimina(ri)** ringing in the ears
⁹ 海鳴 **umina(ri)** roar of the ocean
   怒鳴 **dona(ru)** shout at
¹² 遠鳴 **tōna(ri)** distant sound (of thunder, the sea)
   悲鳴 **himei** shriek, scream
¹³ 雷鳴 **raimei** thunder
¹⁹ 鶏鳴 **keimei** cockcrow, rooster's crowing

噌 → 噌 **3d12.9**

嘆 → 嘆 **3d10.8**

3d11.7 / 1962 | □ 厂 十
24 18 12

嘘

嘘│嘘嘘

KYO, uso lie, falsehood, fib

—— 1 ——

² 嘘八百 **usohappyaku** a pack of lies
⁵ 嘘字 **usoji** miswritten kanji
⁶ 嘘吐 **usotsu(ki)** liar, fibber

—— 2 ——

³ 大嘘 **ōuso** big lie

號 → 号 **3d2.10**

—— 12 ——

3d12.2 | □ 日 月 □
43 42 24

嘲

嘲嘲

CHŌ, azake(ru) ridicule

—— 1 ——

⁷ 嘲弄 **chōrō** ridicule

嗤 → 嚙 **3d15.2**

3d12.8 / 1660 | □ 貝 □ 艹
68 24 32

噴

噴 噴

FUN, fu(ku) emit, spout, spew forth

—— 1 ——

⁴ 噴水 **funsui** jet of water; fountain
噴火 **funka** (volcanic) eruption
噴火口 **funkakō** crater
⁵ 噴出 **funshutsu** eruption, gushing, spouting **fu(ki)da(su)** spew/ gush/spurt out, discharge
¹⁰ 噴射 **funsha** jet, spray, injection

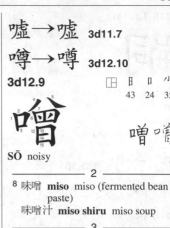

嘘 → 嘘 **3d11.7**

噂 → 噂 **3d12.10**

3d12.9 | □ 日 □ 小
43 24 35

噌

噌 噌

SŌ noisy

—— 2 ——

⁸ 味噌 **miso** miso (fermented bean paste)
味噌汁 **miso shiru** miso soup

—— 3 ——

¹¹ 脳味噌 **nōmiso** brains, gray matter

3d12.10 | □ 酉 □ 寸
71 24 37

噂

噂│噂噂

SON, uwasa rumor, gossip

—— 1 ——

¹³ 噂話 **uwasabanashi** rumor, gossip, hearsay

3d12.11 / 1638 | □ 虫 □ 尸
64 24 40

嘱

嘱│嘱嘱

SHOKU request, entrust, commission

—— 1 ——

¹⁰ 嘱託 **shokutaku** put in charge of, commission; part-time employee

3d12.13 / 527 | □ 口 大
24 34

器

器│器器

KI, utsuwa container; apparatus; capacity, ability

———— 1 ————

5 器用 **kiyō** dextrous, adroit, skillful
8 器官 **kikan** organ (of the body)
器具 **kigu** utensil, appliance, tool, apparatus
12 器量 **kiryō** looks; ability; dignity

———— 2 ————

4 不器用 **bukiyō** clumsy, unskillful
凶器 **kyōki** lethal weapon
5 石器時代 **sekki jidai** the Stone Age
6 兇器 **kyōki** lethal weapon
7 兵器 **heiki** weapon, arms
8 武器 **buki** weapon, arms
9 茶器 **chaki** tea-things
食器 **shokki** eating utensils
10 陶器 **tōki** china, ceramics, pottery
容器 **yōki** container
12 無器用 **bukiyō** clumsy
鈍器 **donki** blunt object (used as a weapon)
13 楽器 **gakki** musical instrument
14 漆器 **shikki** lacquerware
磁器 **jiki** porcelain
19 臓器 **zōki** internal organs, viscera

———— 3 ————

5 打楽器 **dagakki** percussion instrument
8 受話器 **juwaki** (telephone) receiver
抵抗器 **teikōki** resistor, rheostat
拡声器 **kakuseiki** loudspeaker
弦楽器 **gengakki** string instrument, the strings
青銅器 **seidōki** bronze ware/tools
炊飯器 **suihanki** (electric) rice cooker
10 陶磁器 **tōjiki** ceramics, china and porcelain
消火器 **shōkaki** fire extinguisher
核兵器 **kakuheiki** nuclear weapons
11 絃楽器 **gengakki** stringed instrument
12 湯沸器 **yuwa(kashi)ki** hot-water heater
13 孵卵器 **furanki** incubator

舗 → 舖   3b12.4

毆 → 殴   2t6.1

———— 13 ————

3d13.7

嘴   嘴 嘴

SHI, kuchibashi, hashi beak

器 → 器   3d12.13

舘 → 館   8b8.3

堅 → 竪   5b9.5

豫 → 予   0a4.12

———— 14 ————

3d14.1 / 1918

嚇   嚇 嚇

KAKU, odo(kasu), odo(su) threaten

———— 2 ————

9 威嚇 **ikaku** menace, threat

營 → 営   3n9.2

3d14.5 / 1925

矯   矯 矯

KYŌ, ta(meru) straighten; correct

———— 1 ————

5 矯正 **kyōsei** correct, reform

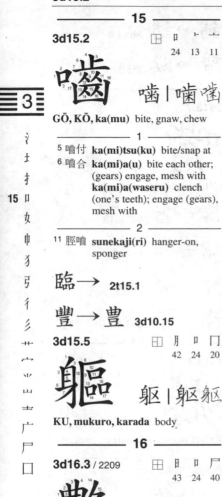

---------- 15 ----------

3d15.2

田	口	ト	一
24	13	11	

噛 ｜ 噛 噛

GŌ, KŌ, ka(mu) bite, gnaw, chew

---------- 1 ----------

5 噛付 **ka(mi)tsu(ku)** bite/snap at

6 噛合 **ka(mi)a(u)** bite each other; (gears) engage, mesh with **ka(mi)a(waseru)** clench (one's teeth); engage (gears), mesh with

---------- 2 ----------

11 脛噛 **sunekaji(ri)** hanger-on, sponger

臨→ **2t15.1**

豐→ 豊 **3d10.15**

3d15.5

田	月	口	冂
42	24	20	

躯 ｜ 躯 躯

KU, mukuro, karada body

---------- 16 ----------

3d16.3 / 2209

田	日	口	尸
43	24	40	

艶 ｜ 艶 艶

EN, tsuya gloss, luster, sheen; charm, romance, love **tsuya(meku)** be glossy; be romantic/sexy **tsuya(ppoi)** romantic, sexy, coquettish **namame(ku)** be charming/voluptuous
namame(kashii) charming, captivating, voluptuous, lucious **ade(yaka)** charming, fascinating TSUYA (f. given name) EN, YOSHI, Ō, TSUYA (part of given name)

---------- 1 ----------

8 艶事 **tsuyagoto** love affair, romance

10 艶消 **tsuyake(shi)** non-glossy, frosted (glass)

---------- 2 ----------

7 妖艶 **yōen** voluptuous charm, bewitching beauty

---------- 17 ----------

嚴→ 厳 **3n14.1**

獻→ 献 **3g9.6**

---------- 18 ----------

3d18.1

田	隹	木	口
74	41	24	

囃 ｜ 囃 囃

SŌ, haya(su) accompany (music), beat/clap time; banter **hayashi** (percussion) accompaniment

3d18.5

田	耳	口	
65	24		

囁 ｜ 囁 囁

SHŌ, sasaya(ku) whisper

---------- 19 ----------

3d19.3

田	衤	口	宀
57	24	33	

囊 ｜ 囊 囊

NŌ bag, pouch, sac

21

嚼 → 嘱 **3d12.11**

艶 → 艷 **3d16.3**

鹸 → **3s21.1**

女 3e

女	好	奴	如	妃	奸	妄	妨	姉	妊	妖	妙
0.1	2.1	2.2	3.1	3.2	3.3	2j4.6	4.1	3e5.8	4.3	4.4	4.5

妓	妥	妬	姓	妹	姉	始	妻	妾	姓	姫	姻	姦	姿
4.7	4.9	5.1	5.3	5.4	5.8	5.9	5.10	5b3.2	3e4.3	3e7.11	6.8	6.9	6.10

要	娘	娯	娠	姫	娼	婚	婬	婦	婆	媒	婿	媛
6.11	7.2	7.3	7.10	7.11	8.3	8.4	3a8.17	8.6	8.9	9.2	9.3	9.4

媚	嫌	嫁	嫌	嫉	嫡	嬌	嬉	嬢	孃
9.5	3e10.7	10 6	10.7	10.8	11.5	12.1	12.3	13.1	3e13.1

0

3e0.1 / 102

女
女女

JO, NYO, NYŌ, onna, me- woman, female

--- 1 ---

⁰ 女らしい **onna(rashii)** womanly, ladylike

² 女子 **joshi** woman; women's **onna(no)ko** girl **onago** girl, woman, maid

⁴ 女中 **jochū** maid

女王 **joō** queen

女心 **onnagokoro** a woman's heart

⁵ 女史 **joshi** Mrs., Miss, Madam

⁷ 女形 **onnagata, oyama** female role

女系 **jokei** female line(age), on the mother's side

⁸ 女性 **josei** woman; feminine gender

女房 **nyōbō** wife; court lady

⁹ 女神 **megami, joshin, nyoshin** goddess

¹⁰ 女流 **joryū** woman (writer/singer)

女殺 **onnagoro(shi)** ladykiller

女教師 **jokyōshi** female teacher

¹¹ 女盛 **onnazaka(ri)** the prime of womanhood

¹² 女尊男卑 **joson-danpi** putting women above men

¹⁵ 女権 **joken** women's rights

¹⁷ 女優 **joyū** actress

--- 2 ---

¹ 乙女 **otome** virgin, maiden

⁴ 少女 **shōjo** girl

王女 **ōjo** princess

⁵ 処女作 **shojosaku** one's first (published) work

⁶ 次女 **jijo** second daughter

⁷ 巫女 **miko, fujo** medium, sorceress; shrine maiden

男女 **danjo, nannyo** men and women

⁸ 長女 **chōjo** eldest daughter

彼女 **kanojo** she; girlfriend, lover

⁹ 美女 **bijo** beautiful woman

¹¹ 悪女 **akujo** wicked/ugly woman

²¹ 魔女 **majo** witch, sorceress

--- 3 ---

⁷ 男尊女卑 **danson-johi** predominance of men over women

───────── 2 ─────────

3e2.1 / 104　　　□ 女 子
　　　　　　　　　　　25　6

好　　　好 好

KŌ, kono(mu), su(ku), su(ki) like, be fond of **-zu(ki)** lover/fan of **yo(shi), i(i), yo(i)** good, favorable, alright YOSHI (part of given name)

───────── 1 ─────────

5 好好 **su(ki)zu(ki)** a matter of individual preferences
6 好色 **kōshoku** sensuality, eroticism, lust
8 好奇心 **kōkishin** curiosity, inquisitiveness
　 好物 **kōbutsu** a favorite food
10 好都合 **kōtsugō** favorable, good
11 好運 **kōun** good fortune, luck
12 好焼 **(o)kono(mi)ya(ki)** (unsweetened batter fried with vegetable bits into a thick griddlecake)
　 好評 **kōhyō** favorable reception, popularity
13 好嫌 **su(ki)kira(i)** likes and dislikes, preferences
　 好意 **kōi** good will, kindness, favor, friendliness
15 好調 **kōchō** good, favorable, satisfactory

───────── 2 ─────────

2 人好 **hitozu(ki)** amiability, attractiveness
3 三好 **Miyoshi** (surname)
　 大好 **daisu(ki)** very fond of, love
4 友好 **yūkō** friendship, amity
5 好好 **su(ki)zu(ki)** a matter of individual preferences
6 仲好 **nakayo(shi)** good friends
7 良好 **ryōkō** good, favorable, satisfactory
8 物好 **monozu(ki)** curious, whimsical, eccentric
9 恰好 **kakkō** shape, form, figure, appearance; reasonable; approximately
10 酒好 **sakezu(ki)** drinker
12 絶好 **zekkō** splendid, first-rate

14 愛好 **aikō** love, have a liking/taste fo

3e2.2 / 1933　　　□ 女 又
　　　　　　　　　　　25　9

奴　　　奴 奴

DO, NU, yakko manservant, slave, fellow **yatsu** guy, fellow

───────── 1 ─────────

16 奴隷 **dorei** slave

───────── 3 ─────────

6 守銭奴 **shusendo** miser, niggard

───────── 3 ─────────

3e3.1 / 1747　　　□ 女 口
　　　　　　　　　　　25　24

如　　　如 如

JO, NYO, goto(ki/ku/shi) like, such as, as if **shi(ku)** be equal to, be like **shi(kazu)** be better/best

───────── 1 ─────────

7 如何 **ikaga, ika (ni)** how

───────── 2 ─────────

8 突如 **totsujo** suddenly, unexpectedly

3e3.2 / 1756　　　□ 女 弓
　　　　　　　　　　　25　28

妃　　　妃 妃

HI (married) princess, queen

───────── 1 ─────────

13 妃殿下 **hidenka** Her Highness

3e3.3　　　　□ 女 干 一
　　　　　　　　　　25　14　1

奸　　　奸 奸

KAN wicked

——————— 1 ———————
8 奸知 **kanchi** cunning, guile

妄→ **2j4.6**

——————— 4 ———————

3e4.1 / 1182   ⊞ 方 女
                         48 25

妨 妨 妨

BŌ, samata(geru) prevent, obstruct, hamper

——————— 1 ———————
10 妨害 **bōgai** obstruction, disturbance, interference

姉→ **3e5.8**

3e4.3 / 955   ⊞ 壬 女
                         46 25

妊 妊 | 妊 妊

NIN, hara(mu) be pregnant

——————— 1 ———————
10 妊娠 **ninshin** be pregnant
    妊娠中絶 **ninshin chūzetsu** abortion
11 妊婦 **ninpu** pregnant woman
——————— 2 ———————
15 避妊 **hinin** contraception
    避妊薬 **hinin'yaku** a contraceptive, birth control pill
16 懐妊 **kainin** pregnancy

3e4.4   ⊞ 女 大 |
                         25 34 2

妖 妖 妖

YŌ bewitching, enchanting; calamity

——————— 1 ———————
19 妖艶 **yōen** voluptuous charm, bewitching beauty

3e4.5 / 1154   ⊞ 女 小 |
                         25 35 2

妙 妙 妙

MYŌ strange, odd; a mystery
tae(naru) exquisite, superb; delicate; charming; melodious TAE (part of given name)

——————— 1 ———————
10 妙案 **myōan** good idea, ingenious plan
16 妙薬 **myōyaku** wonder drug
——————— 2 ———————
5 巧妙 **kōmyō** skillful, clever, deft
8 奇妙 **kimyō** strange, curious, odd
9 神妙 **shinmyō** mysterious, marvelous; admirable; gentle
13 微妙 **bimyō** delicate, subtle

3e4.7   ⊞ 女 十 又
                         25 12 9

妓 妓 妓

GI, KI singing girl, geisha, prostitute

3e4.9 / 930   ⊟ 小 女 |
                         35 25 2

妥 妥 | 妥 妥

DA peaceful, tranquil

——————— 1 ———————
6 妥当 **datō** proper, appropriate
8 妥協 **dakyō** compromise

——————— 5 ———————

3e5.1   ⊞ 石 女
                         53 25

妬 妬 妬

TO, neta(mu) be jealous/envious of

—— 2 ——
13 嫉妬 **shitto** jealousy, envy

3e5.3 / 1746 ⊞ 女 牛 一
25 47 1

姓

姓姓

SEI, SHŌ surname **kabane** title conferred by the emperor

—— 1 ——
4 姓氏 **seishi** surname
6 姓名 **seimei** name (surname and given name)

—— 2 ——
5 旧姓 **kyūsei** former/maiden name
6 同姓 **dōsei** the same surname
百姓 **hyakushō** farmer, peasant

3e5.4 / 408 ⊞ 未 女 一
41 25 1

妹

妹妹

MAI, imōto, imo younger sister

—— 1 ——
7 妹尾 **Senoo** (surname)
12 妹御 **imōtogo** your (younger) sister

—— 2 ——
7 弟妹 **teimai** younger brothers and sisters
8 姉妹 **shimai** sister(s); sister (city), affiliated (company), companion (volume)
13 義妹 **gimai** younger sister-in-law

—— 3 ——
10 従姉妹 **itoko, jūshimai** female cousin

3e5.8 / 407 ⊞ 女 巾 宀
25 26 11

姉

姉姉

SHI, ane elder sister **(o)nē(san), nē(san)** elder sister; young lady; waitress **nē(ya)** maid

—— 1 ——
8 姉妹 **shimai** sister(s); sister (city), affiliated (company), companion (volume)
12 姉御 **anego** gang boss's wife; woman boss
14 姉様 **(o)nēsama, nēsama** elder sister

—— 2 ——
10 従姉妹 **itoko, jūshimai** female cousin
13 義姉 **gishi** elder sister-in-law

3e5.9 / 494 ⊞ 女 口 竹
25 24 17

始

始始

SHI, haji(maru), haji(meru) (intr./tr.) start, begin **HAJIME** (m. given name) **MOTO** (part of given name)

—— 1 ——
5 始末 **shimatsu** circumstances; manage, dispose of, take care of; economize
11 始終 **shijū** from first to last, all the while

—— 2 ——
4 不始末 **fushimatsu** mismanagement, carelessness; lavish, spendthrift
9 後始末 **atoshimatsu** settle, wind/finish up
10 原始 **genshi** origin; primitive
原始的 **genshiteki** primitive, primeval, original
12 開始 **kaishi** begin, commence, start
13 跡始末 **atoshimatsu** winding-up, settlement, straightening up (afterwards)

—— 3 ——
1 一部始終 **ichibu shijū** full particulars

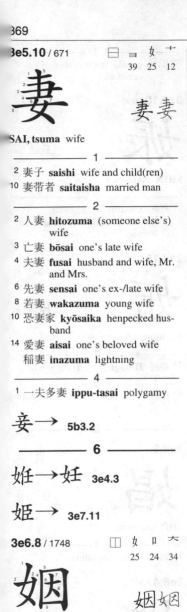

3e5.10 / 671　　日 ヨ 女 ヰ
　　　　　　　　　39 25 12

妻　妻妻

SAI, tsuma wife

——— 1 ———

2 妻子 **saishi** wife and child(ren)
10 妻帯者 **saitaisha** married man

——— 2 ———

2 人妻 **hitozuma** (someone else's) wife
3 亡妻 **bōsai** one's late wife
4 夫妻 **fusai** husband and wife, Mr. and Mrs.
6 先妻 **sensai** one's ex-/late wife
8 若妻 **wakazuma** young wife
10 恐妻家 **kyōsaika** henpecked husband
14 愛妻 **aisai** one's beloved wife
　　稲妻 **inazuma** lightning

——— 4 ———

1 一夫多妻 **ippu-tasai** polygamy

妾→ **5b3.2**

——— 6 ———

姓→妊 **3e4.3**

姫→ **3e7.11**

3e6.8 / 1748　　囗 女 口 大
　　　　　　　　　25 24 34

姻　姻姻

IN marriage

——— 2 ———

11 婚姻 **kon'in** marriage

3e6.9　　　　　　囗 女
　　　　　　　　　25

姦　姦姦

KAN wicked, immoral
kashima(shii) noisy, boisterous

——— 1 ———

4 姦夫 **kanpu** adulterer
9 姦通 **kantsū** adultery
11 姦淫 **kan'in** illicit intercourse
　　姦婦 **kanpu** adultress

——— 2 ———

11 強姦 **gōkan** rape
16 獣姦 **jūkan** bestiality

3e6.10 / 929　　囗 女 女 冫
　　　　　　　　　49 25 5

姿　姿姿

SHI, sugata form, figure, shape, appearance, posture

——— 1 ———

13 姿勢 **shisei** posture, stance

——— 2 ———

9 後姿 **ushi(ro) sugata** view (of someone) from the back
10 高姿勢 **kōshisei** high posture/profile, aggressive attitude
12 雄姿 **yūshi** gallant figure

3e6.11 / 419　　囗 口 女 一
　　　　　　　　　24 25 14

要　要|要要

YŌ main point, principal; necessary, essential **i(ru)** need, be necessary
kaname pivot; main point **KANAME** (given name)

——— 1 ———

0 要する **yō(suru)** require, need
6 要旨 **yōshi** gist, purport, substance
7 要求 **yōkyū** require, demand

3

氵
土
扌
口
女　6
巾
犭
弓
彳
彡
艹
宀
业
山
青
广
尸
口

9 要約 **yōyaku** summary
10 要素 **yōso** element, factor
11 要望 **yōbō** demand, cry for
12 要項 **yōkō** the essential point(s)
14 要領 **yōryō** gist, substance, synopsis
15 要請 **yōsei** demand, call for, require

― 2 ―

3 大要 **taiyō** summary, outline
4 不要 **fuyō** of no use, unneeded, waste
5 必要 **hitsuyō** necessary
必要品 **hitsuyōhin** necessities
主要 **shuyō** main, principal, essential, key
7 肝要 **kan'yō** important, vital
8 枢要 **sūyō** pivotal, important
9 重要 **jūyō** important
紀要 **kiyō** bulletin, record, proceedings
14 概要 **gaiyō** outline, synopsis
需要 **juyō** demand

― 7 ―

3e7.2 / 1752 □ 食 女
73 25

娘 娘娘

JŌ, musume daughter; girl, young woman

― 1 ―

12 娘婿 **musumemuko** son-in-law

― 3 ―

1 一人娘 **hitori musume** an only daughter
15 箱入娘 **hakoi(ri)musume** girl who has led a sheltered life

3e7.3 / 1437 □ 女 口 儿
25 24 16

娯 娯│娯娯

GO pleasure, enjoyment

― 1 ―

13 娯楽 **goraku** amusement, entertainment

3e7.10 / 956 □ 礻 女 厂
57 25 18

娠 娠娠

SHIN pregnancy

― 2 ―

7 妊娠 **ninshin** be pregnant
妊娠中絶 **ninshin chūzetsu** abortion

3e7.11 / 1757 □ 女 冂 丨
25 20 2

姫 姫│姫姫

KI, hime princess

― 1 ―

13 姫路 **Himeji** (city, Hyōgo-ken)

― 2 ―

13 椿姫 **Tsubakihime** (Verdi's) La Traviata

― 8 ―

3e8.3 □ 田 日 女
43 25

娼 娼娼

SHŌ prostitute

― 1 ―

11 娼婦 **shōfu** prostitute

3e8.4 / 567 □ 田 日 女 厂
43 25 18

婚 婚婚

KON marriage

—————— 1 ——————
⁹ 婚姻 **kon'in** marriage
婚約 **kon'yaku** engagement, betrothal
婚約者 **kon'yakusha** fiancé(e)

—————— 2 ——————
⁵ 未婚 **mikon** unmarried
⁶ 再婚 **saikon** remarry
早婚 **sōkon** early marriage
⁷ 求婚 **kyūkon** proposal of marriage
⁸ 金婚式 **kinkonshiki** golden wedding anniversary
⁹ 冠婚葬祭 **kankonsōsai** ceremonial occasions
¹⁰ 既婚者 **kikonsha** married person
¹² 晩婚 **bankon** late marriage
結婚 **kekkon** marriage
結婚式 **kekkonshiki** wedding
¹³ 新婚旅行 **shinkon ryokō** honeymoon
¹⁴ 銀婚式 **ginkonshiki** silver wedding anniversary
¹⁸ 離婚 **rikon** divorce

—————— 4 ——————
⁹ 神前結婚 **shinzen kekkon** Shinto wedding

婬 → 淫 **3a8.17**

3e8.6 / 316

囲 女 彐 巾
25 39 26

婦 | 婦 婦

FU woman; wife

—————— 1 ——————
² 婦人 **fujin** lady, woman
婦人科医 **fujinkai** gynecologist
¹⁹ 婦警 **fukei** policewoman

—————— 2 ——————
⁴ 夫婦 **fūfu, meoto, myōto** husband and wife, couple
⁵ 主婦 **shufu** housewife
⁷ 妊婦 **ninpu** pregnant woman
⁹ 姦婦 **kanpu** adultress
¹¹ 娼婦 **shōfu** prostitute

産婦 **sanpu** woman in/nearing childbirth
産婦人科 **sanfujinka** obstetrics and gynecology
¹³ 裸婦 **rafu** nude woman
¹⁴ 寡婦 **kafu, yamome** widow

—————— 3 ——————
⁷ 助産婦 **josanpu** midwife
売春婦 **baishunfu** prostitute
⁹ 看護婦 **kangofu** (female) nurse
¹⁰ 家政婦 **kaseifu** housekeeper
¹⁵ 慰安婦 **ianfu** comfort girl/woman, army prostitute

—————— 4 ——————
¹³ 新郎新婦 **shinrō-shinpu** the bride and groom

3e8.9 / 1931

囲 氵 女 厂
21 25 18

婆 婆

BA, babā, bā(san) old woman
bā(ya) wet nurse; elderly maid

—————— 2 ——————
⁶ 老婆 **rōba** old woman
¹¹ 産婆 **sanba** midwife

—————— 9 ——————

3e9.2 / 1496

囲 朮 女 艹
41 25 32

媒 媒

BAI, nakadachi go-between

—————— 1 ——————
⁴ 媒介 **baikai** mediation; matchmaking
⁶ 媒妁 **baishaku** matchmaking
¹⁰ 媒酌人 **baishakunin** matchmaker, go-between

(right margin, vertical)
3
9
氵
扌
口
女
巾
犭
弓
彳
彡
宀
癶
屮
广
尸
囗

3e9.3 / 1745

田 月 女 亠
42 25 14

婿　壻 | 婿 婿 婿

SEI, muko son-in-law; bridegroom

―――――― 1 ――――――

15 婿養子 **muko-yōshi** son-in-law adopted as an heir

―――――― 2 ――――――

7 花婿 **hanamuko** bridegroom
10 娘婿 **musumemuko** son-in-law

3e9.4 / 2047

田 女 小 亠
25 35 14

媛　媛 | 媛 媛

EN, hime princess EN, HIME (part of given name)

―――――― 2 ――――――

14 愛媛県 **Ehime-ken** (prefecture)

3e9.5

田 目 女 尸
55 25 40

媚　媚 媚

BI, ko(biru) flatter, humor, curry favor; flirt

―――――― 1 ――――――

14 媚態 **bitai** coquetry

―――――――――― 10 ――――――――――

嫌 → 嫌　3e10.7

3e10.6 / 1749

田 女 宀 犭
25 33 27

嫁　嫁 嫁 女家

KA marry (a man) **totsu(gu)** get married **yome** bride, young wife, daughter-in-law

―――――― 1 ――――――

2 嫁入 **yomei(ri)** marriage, wedding

―――――― 2 ――――――

7 花嫁 **hanayome** bride

3e10.7 / 1688

田 女 彐 儿
25 39 16

嫌　嫌 | 嫌 嫌

KEN, GEN, kira(u), kira(i) dislike, hate **iya** disagreeable **iya(garu)** dislike, hate; be unwilling (to do something)

―――――― 1 ――――――

0 嫌らしい **iya(rashii)** unpleasant, offensive
11 嫌悪 **ken'o** hatred, dislike, loathing
14 嫌疑 **kengi** suspicion

―――――― 2 ――――――

2 人嫌 **hitogira(i)** avoiding others' company; misanthrope
3 大嫌 **daikira(i)** hate, abhor, detest
4 毛嫌 **kegira(i)** antipathy, aversion, prejudice
5 好嫌 **su(ki)kira(i)** likes and dislikes, preferences
7 男嫌 **otokogira(i)** man-hater
16 機嫌 **kigen** mood, humor, temper

3e10.8

田 疒 女 大
60 25 34

嫉　嫉 嫉

SHITSU, sone(mu) be jealous of, envy

―――――― 1 ――――――

8 嫉妬 **shitto** jealousy, envy

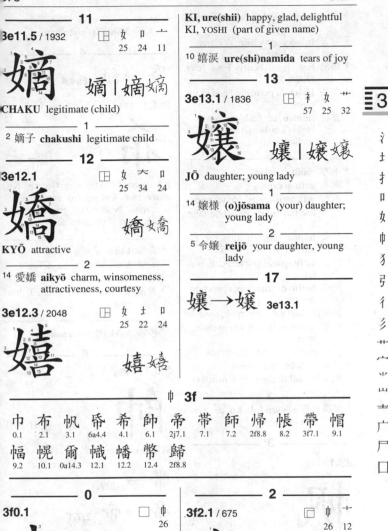

— 11 —

3e11.5 / 1932 　　　田 女 口 亠
　　　　　　　　　　25 24 11

嫡 ｜ 嫡 嫡

CHAKU legitimate (child)

— 1 —

² 嫡子 **chakushi** legitimate child

— 12 —

3e12.1 　　　田 女 大 口
　　　　　　　25 34 24

嬌 嬌

KYŌ attractive

— 2 —

¹⁴ 愛嬌 **aikyō** charm, winsomeness,
attractiveness, courtesy

3e12.3 / 2048 　　　田 女 土 口
　　　　　　　　　25 22 24

嬉 嬉

KI, **ure(shii)** happy, glad, delightful
KI, YOSHI (part of given name)

— 1 —

¹⁰ 嬉涙 **ure(shi)namida** tears of joy

— 13 —

3e13.1 / 1836 　　　田 耂 女 艹
　　　　　　　　　57 25 32

孃 ｜ 嬢 嬢

JŌ daughter; young lady

— 1 —

¹⁴ 嬢様 **(o)jōsama** (your) daughter;
young lady

— 2 —

⁵ 令嬢 **reijō** your daughter, young
lady

— 17 —

孃 → 嬢 **3e13.1**

巾 3f

巾	布	帆	咼	希	帥	帝	帯	師	帰	帳	帶	帽
0.1	2.1	3.1	6a4.4	4.1	6.1	2j7.1	7.1	7.2	2f8.8	8.2	3f7.1	9.1

幅	幌	爾	幟	幡	幣	歸
9.2	10.1	0a14.3	12.1	12.2	12.4	2f8.8

— 0 —

3f0.1 　　　　　　　□ 巾
　　　　　　　　　　26

巾 巾

KIN a cloth, rag, towel **haba** width,
breadth

— 2 —

⁵ 布巾 **fukin** dishcloth

— 2 —

3f2.1 / 675 　　　　田 巾 十
　　　　　　　　　26 12

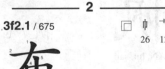

布 布

FU, HO cloth; spread **nuno** cloth

— 1 —

³ 布巾 **fukin** dishcloth

6 布団 **futon** bedding, sleeping mat, futon

7 布告 **fukoku** proclaim, declare, promulgate

9 布施 **fuse** alms, charity **Fuse** (city, Ōsaka-fu)

11 布袋 **Hotei** (a potbellied god of fortune)

布設 **fusetsu** lay (cable/mines), build (a railway/road) (also spelled 敷設)

――――― 2 ―――――

4 毛布 **mōfu** blanket

8 画布 **gafu** a canvas

若布 **wakame** (an edible seaweed)

昆布 **konbu, kobu** sea tangle, tang, kelp

9 発布 **happu** promulgation, proclamation

10 財布 **saifu** purse, pocketbook, wallet

配布 **haifu** distribution, apportionment

11 掛布団 **ka(ke)buton** quilt, coverlet

麻布 **asanuno, mafu** hemp cloth, linen

13 頒布 **hanpu** distribute, circulate

15 敷布 **shikifu** (bed) sheet

敷布団 **shikibuton** floor mattress

――――― 3 ―――――

9 宣戦布告 **sensen fukoku** declaration of war

――――― 3 ―――――

3f3.1 / 1103 　　□ 巾 冂 丨
　　　　　　　　26 20 2

帆帆

HAN, ho sail

――――― 1 ―――――

5 帆立貝 **hotategai** scallop (shell)

7 帆走 **hansō** sail, be under sail

9 帆柱 **hobashira** mast

11 帆船 **hansen, hobune** sailing ship, sailboat

――――― 2 ―――――

9 美帆 **Miho** (f. given name)

――――― 4 ―――――

昻 → 紙 6a4.4

3f4.1 / 676 　　日 巾 十
　　　　　　　　26 12

希 希

KI desire, hope for; rare; Greece **KE, mare** rare **koinega(u)** entreat; desire, wish **NOZOMI** (f. given name) **MARE** (part of given name)

――――― 1 ―――――

4 希少 **kishō** scarce

11 希望 **kibō** wish, hope, desire

希釈 **kishaku** dilute

16 希薄 **kihaku** dilute, rarefied, thin, sparse

――――― 2 ―――――

10 紗希 **Saki** (f. given name)

――――― 6 ―――――

3f6.1 / 1935 　　囗 尸 巾 冂
　　　　　　　40 26 20

帥 帥

SUI leading troops

帯 → **3f7.1**

帝 → 帝 2j7.1

――――― 7 ―――――

3f7.1 / 963 　　日 艹 巾 宀
　　　　　　　32 26 11

帯 丨 帯 帯

TAI belt; zone **obi** obi **o(biru)** wear/carry (a sword); have (the character of), be tinged with

—————— 2 ——————

1 一帯 **ittai** a region/zone; the whole place
5 包帯 **hōtai** bandage, dressing
世帯 **setai, shotai** household, home
世帯主 **setainushi** head of a household
6 地帯 **chitai** zone, area, region, belt
8 拐帯 **kaitai** absconding with money
妻帯者 **saitaisha** married man
所帯 **shotai** household, home
所帯持 **shotaimo(chi)** housekeeping; married (wo)man
9 連帯 **rentai** solidarity; joint (liability)
12 寒帯 **kantai** frigid zone
13 携帯 **keitai** carry with; portable
15 熱帯 **nettai** torrid zone, the tropics

—————— 3 ——————

7 亜寒帯 **akantai** subarctic zone
亜熱帯 **anettai** subtropics

3f7.2 / 409   🔲 尸 巾 冂
                    40 26 20

師師

SHI teacher, master; army

—————— 1 ——————

6 師団 **shidan** (army) division
7 師弟 **shitei** master and pupil
15 師範 **shihan** teacher, instructor

—————— 2 ——————

3 大師 **daishi** great (Buddhist) teacher, saint
5 占師 **uranaishi** fortuneteller
7 医師 **ishi** physician, doctor
技師 **gishi** engineer, technician
8 牧師 **bokushi** pastor, minister
10 教師 **kyōshi** instructor, teacher
恩師 **onshi** one's honored teacher
11 猟師 **ryōshi** hunter
14 漁師 **ryōshi** fisherman
17 講師 **kōshi** lecturer, instructor

—————— 3 ——————

3 女教師 **jokyōshi** female teacher
4 手品師 **tejinashi** magician, juggler
9 宣教師 **senkyōshi** missionary
11 理髪師 **rihatsushi** barber, hairdresser
12 詐欺師 **sagishi** swindler, con man
15 影法師 **kagebōshi** person's shadow
16 薬剤師 **yakuzaishi** pharmacist

—————— 4 ——————

10 家庭教師 **katei kyōshi** (private) tutor

帰 → **2f8.8**

—————— 8 ——————

3f8.2 / 1107   🔲 耒 巾 ⼘
                     57 26 13

帳帳

CHŌ notebook, register, (telephone) directory, (bank)book **tobari** curtain

—————— 1 ——————

10 帳消 **chōke(shi)** cancellation, writing off (debts)
19 帳簿 **chōbo** (account) books, book (value)

—————— 2 ——————

2 几帳面 **kichōmen** methodical, precise, punctilious
4 手帳 **techō** (pocket) notebook
9 通帳 **tsūchō, kayo(i)chō** bankbook; chit book
10 蚊帳 **kaya, kachō** mosquito net

—————— 3 ——————

13 電話帳 **denwachō** telephone directory

—————— 4 ——————

12 貯金通帳 **chokin tsūchō** bankbook

带 → 帯 **3f7.1**

9

3f9.1 / 1105 　田　目　日　巾
　　　　　　　55　43　26

帽　　　帽帽

BŌ cap, hat, headgear

1

2 帽子 **bōshi** hat, cap

2

8 制帽 **seibō** regulation/school cap
11 脱帽 **datsubō** take off one's hat/cap

3f9.2 / 1380 　田　甲　巾　口
　　　　　　　58　26　24

幅　　　幅幅

FUKU width; (counter for) hanging scrolls **haba** width, breadth, range; influence

1

5 幅広 **habahiro(i)** broad, extensive
　　　habahiro wide
13 幅跳 **habato(bi)** long jump

2

3 大幅 **ōhaba** by a large margin, substantial
6 全幅 **zenpuku** overall width; utmost
15 横幅 **yokohaba** width, breadth

10

3f10.1 / 1976 　田　日　巾　小
　　　　　　　43　26　35

幌　　　幌幌

KŌ, horo awning, hood, (folding) top

2

5 札幌 **Sapporo** (city, Hokkaidō)

11

爾 → **0a14.3**

12

3f12.1 　田　戈　日　巾
　　　　　　52　43　26

幟　　　幟幟

SHI, nobori banner, streamer

2

18 鯉幟 **koinobori** carp streamer
　　　(Boys' Festival decoration)

3f12.2 　田　米　甲　巾
　　　　　　62　58　26

幡　　　幡幡

HAN, hata flag

2

2 八幡宮 **Hachimangū** shrine of the god of war

3f12.4 / 1781 　田　攵　小　巾
　　　　　　49　35　26

幣　　　幣｜幣幣

HEI Shinto zigzag paper offerings; money **nusa** Shinto offerings of cloth, rope, or cut paper

2

9 造幣局 **zōheikyoku** the mint
10 紙幣 **shihei** paper money
11 貨幣 **kahei** money, currency, coin

15

歸 → 帰 **2f8.8**

犭 3g

犬	犯	状	尨	狂	犹	狀	狙	狗	狐	独	狭	狐
0.1	2.1	2b5.1	3j4.2	4.2	3g9.5	2b5.1	5.3	5.5	3g6.4	6.1	6.2	6.4

狩	狸	狭	狼	猛	猪	猫	猟	就	猪	猥	猶	献
6.5	7.2	3g6.2	7.3	7.4	8.1	8.5	8.6	3d9.21	3g8.1	9.2	9.5	9.6

獅	猿	獄	獎	獣	獣	獨	獲	獵	獸	獻
10.1	10.3	11.1	3n10.4	4d11.5	12.3	3g6.1	13.1	3g8.6	3g12.3	3g9.6

3g0.1 / 280

犬

KEN, Inu dog

— 1 —
3 犬小屋 **inugoya** doghouse, kennel
13 犬猿仲 **ken'en (no) naka** hating each other

— 2 —
3 小犬 **koinu** puppy
4 仔犬 **koinu** puppy
6 牝犬 **mesu inu, meinu** female dog, bitch
7 狂犬病 **kyōkenbyō** rabies
9 負犬 **ma(ke)inu** loser
10 猛犬 **mōken** vicious dog
柴犬 **Shiba-inu** (a breed of small dog)
11 猟犬 **ryōken** hunting dog
12 番犬 **banken** watchdog
雄犬 **osuinu** male dog
13 飼犬 **ka(i)inu** pet dog
14 愛犬 **aiken** pet dog
雌犬 **mesuinu** female dog, bitch
16 橇犬 **soriinu** sled dog
18 闘犬 **tōken** dogfight(ing); fighting dog

— 3 —
8 盲導犬 **mōdōken** seeing-eye dog

3g2.1 / 882

犯

HAN crime; (counter for criminal offenses) **oka(su)** commit (a crime), violate

— 1 —
2 犯人 **hannin** criminal, culprit, offender
6 犯行 **hankō** crime
13 犯罪 **hanzai** crime

— 2 —
5 正犯 **seihan** principal offense/offender
6 再犯 **saihan** second offense
防犯 **bōhan** crime prevention
共犯者 **kyōhansha** accomplice
8 性犯罪 **sei hanzai** sex crime
9 侵犯 **shinpan** invasion, violation
11 累犯 **ruihan** repeated offense
13 戦犯 **senpan** war crime/criminal

— 3 —
9 前科…犯 **zenka …-han/-pan** (a criminal record of three) previous convictions
窃盗犯 **settōhan** thief
11 現行犯 **genkōhan** crime/criminal witnessed in the act, flagrante delicto

— 3 —
状 → 2b5.1

彪 → 3j4.2

4

3g4.2 / 883 　　　　田 王 犭
　　　　　　　　　46　27

狂　　　　狂狂

KYŌ go mad/crazy; (as suffix) craze, mania; enthusiast **kuru(u)** go crazy; run amuck; get out of order **kuru(waseru/wasu)** drive mad; upset (plans) **kuru(i)** madness; out of order; going wide of the mark **kuru(oshii)** mad (with grief) **kuru(washii)** appearing to be crazy **fu(reru)** go mad/crazy

──────── 1 ────────

² 狂人 **kyōjin** insane person, lunatic
⁴ 狂犬病 **kyōkenbyō** rabies
⁶ 狂気 **kyōki** madness, insanity
⁷ 狂乱 **kyōran** frenzy, madness
　 狂言 **kyōgen** play, drama; program; Noh farce; trick, sham
⁹ 狂信 **kyōshin** fanaticism
　 狂風 **kyōfū** raging winds
¹³ 狂想曲 **kyōsōkyoku** rhapsody

──────── 2 ────────

⁹ 荒狂 **a(re)kuru(u)** rage, run amuck
¹⁰ 能狂言 **nōkyōgen** Noh farce; Noh drama and *kyōgen* farce
¹⁵ 暴狂 **aba(re)kuru(u)** run amuck
　 熱狂 **nekkyō** wild enthusiasm, frenzy, mania

犹 → 猶 3g9.5

狀 → 状 2b5.1

──────── 5 ────────

3g5.3 　　　　田 月 犭 一
　　　　　　　　42　27　1

狙　　　　狙狙

SO, nera(u) aim at

──────── 1 ────────

⁵ 狙打 **nera(i)u(chi)** take aim and shoot
⁸ 狙所 **nera(i)dokoro** aim, objective
¹⁵ 狙撃兵 **sogekihei** sniper, sharpshooter

──────── 3 ────────

⁸ 空巣狙 **a(ki)sunera(i)** sneak thief, prowler

3g5.5 　　　　田 犭 口 ハ
　　　　　　　27　24　15

狗　　　　狗狗

KU dog, puppy

狐 → 3g6.4

──────── 6 ────────

3g6.1 / 219 　　　　田 虫 犭
　　　　　　　64　27

独　　　　獨 | 独独

DOKU alone, on one's own; Germany **hito(ri)** alone **hito(rideni)** by itself, of its own accord

──────── 1 ────────

⁰ 独りぼっち/りぼっち **hito(ribotchi/ripotchi)** all alone
² 独子 **hito(rik)ko, hito(ri)go** an only child
⁵ 独占 **dokusen** exclusive possession; monopoly
　 独立 **dokuritsu** independence
⁶ 独自 **dokuji** original, characteristic, individual, personal
⁷ 独身 **dokushin, hito(ri)mi** unmarried
　 独学 **dokugaku** self-study
　 独言 **hito(ri)goto** talking to oneself; soliloquy; monolog
⁸ 独者 **hito(ri)mono** single/unmarried person

独和 **Doku-Wa** German-Japanese (dictionary)

9 独奏 **dokusō** instrumental solo

0 独特 **dokutoku** unique, peculiar to

1 独唱 **dokushō** vocal solo

12 独創 **dokusō** originality, creativity

独善 **hito(ri)yo(gari), dokuzen** self-righteous, complacent, smug

独裁 **dokusai** autocracy, dictatorship

13 独禁法 **dokkinhō** antitrust laws, the Anti-Monopoly Law (short for 独占禁止法)

14 独演 **dokuen** solo performance

独暮 **hito(ri)gu(rashi)** living alone

——————— 2 ———————

4 日独 **Nichi-Doku** Japan and Germany

8 孤独 **kodoku** solitary, isolated, lonely

和独 **Wa-Doku** Japanese-German (dictionary), Japan and Germany

9 単独 **tandoku** independent, single-handed

単独行動 **tandoku kōdō** acting on one's own

3g6.2 / 1353

□ 犭 六 儿
27 34 16

狭 | 狭 狭

KYŌ, sema(i) narrow, small (in area) **seba(maru), seba(meru)** (intr./tr.) become/make narrow, contract **sa-** (prefix used for euphony) SA (part of given name)

——————— 1 ———————

4 狭心症 **kyōshinshō** stricture of the heart, angina pectoris

8 狭苦 **semakuru(shii)** cramped

13 狭義 **kyōgi** narrow sense

3g6.4

□ 犭 厂 竹
27 18 17

狐 狐

KO, kitsune fox

——————— 1 ———————

14 狐疑 **kogi** doubt, indecision

3g6.5 / 1581

□ 犭 宀 寸
27 33 37

狩 狩

SHU, ka(ru) hunt **ka(ri), -ga(ri)** hunting

——————— 1 ———————

2 狩人 **karyūdo, kariudo** hunter

11 狩猟 **shuryō** hunting

——————— 2 ———————

5 石狩川 **Ishikari-gawa** (river, Hokkaidō)

24 鷹狩 **takaga(ri)** falconry

3g7.2

□ 日 犭 土
43 27 22

狸 | 狸 狸

RI, tanuki raccoon dog; cunning person

狭 → 狭   3g6.2

3g7.3

□ 飠 犭
73 27

狼 狼

RŌ wolf; confusion **ōkami** wolf

——————— 1 ———————

10 狼狽 **rōbai** consternation, confusion, panic

3g7.4 / 1579

田 皿 犭 子
59 27 6

猛　猛猛

MŌ fierce, strong, intense **ta(keru)**
rush forth, rage, rave TAKESHI (m.
given name) TAKE (part of given
name)

――― 1 ―――

4 猛犬 **mōken** vicious dog
8 猛毒 **mōdoku** virulent poison
猛者 **mosa** man of courage, stalwart, veteran
10 猛烈 **mōretsu** fierce, violent, intense
12 猛暑 **mōsho** intense heat
16 猛獣 **mōjū** ferocious animal

――― 2 ―――

9 勇猛心 **yūmōshin** intrepid spirit

――― 8 ―――

3g8.1 / 2155

田 日 犭 土
43 27 22

猪　猪│猪猪

CHO, inoshishi wild boar CHO, I,
SHISHI (part of given name)

――― 1 ―――

9 猪首 **ikubi** short and thick neck,
bull neck

3g8.5 / 1470

田 甲 犭 艹
58 27 32

猫　猫猫

BYŌ, neko cat

――― 1 ―――

6 猫舌 **nekojita** aversion to hot foods
15 猫撫声 **nekona(de)goe** coaxing
voice

――― 2 ―――

3 小猫 **koneko** kitten
山猫争議 **yamaneko sōgi** wildcat
strike
8 招猫 **mane(ki)neko** beckoning
(porcelain) cat

――― 3 ―――

11 野良猫 **noraneko** stray cat

3g8.6 / 1580

田 犭 小 冂
27 35 20

猟　獵│猟猟

RYŌ, ka(ri) hunting

――― 1 ―――

2 猟人 **kariudo, karyūdo, ryōjin**
hunter
4 猟犬 **ryōken** hunting dog
10 猟師 **ryōshi** hunter
14 猟銃 **ryōjū** hunting gun, shotgun

――― 2 ―――

9 狩猟 **shuryō** hunting
11 密猟 **mitsuryō** poaching

就 → 3d9.21

――― 9 ―――

猪 → 猪 3g8.1

3g9.2

田 甲 耂 犭
58 57 27

猥　猥猥

WAI obscene mida(ra) indecent,
lewd mida(rigamashii) indecent, immoral

――― 1 ―――

15 猥談 **waidan** indecent talk, dirty
story
17 猥褻 **waisetsu** obscene, lewd

――― 2 ―――

13 鄙猥 **hiwai** indecent, obscene

3g9.5 / 1583

酉 犭 儿
71   27   16

猶 猶

YŪ delay; still, still more   **nao** also, moreover; still; still more   NAO (part of given name)

― 1 ―

4 猶予 **yūyo** postponement, deferment

3g9.6 / 1355

犭 十 冂
27   12   20

獻 | 献 献

KEN, sasa(geru) offer, present, dedicate   **KON** (counter for drinks)

― 1 ―

3 献上 **kenjō** presentation
5 献立 **kondate** menu; arrangements, plan, program
   献立表 **kondatehyō** menu
6 献血 **kenketsu** blood donation
7 献身 **kenshin** self-sacrifice, dedication
   献呈 **kentei** presentation (copy)
8 献金 **kenkin** gift of money, contribution

― 2 ―

4 文献 **bunken** literature (on a subject), bibliography
10 貢献 **kōken** contribution, services

― 10 ―

3g10.1

犭 尸 巾
27   40   26

獅 獅

SHI, shishi lion

― 1 ―

2 獅子 **shishi** lion

3g10.3 / 1584

礻 犭 土
57   27   22

猿 猿

EN, saru, mashira monkey

― 1 ―

2 猿人 **enjin** ape-man
8 猿知恵 **sarujie** shallow cleverness
10 猿真似 **sarumane** monkey-see monkey-do

― 2 ―

4 犬猿仲 **ken'en (no) naka** hating each other

― 11 ―

3g11.1 / 884

言 犭
67   27

獄 獄

GOKU prison

― 1 ―

4 獄内 **gokunai** in prison
5 獄囚 **gokushū** prisoner

― 2 ―

2 入獄 **nyūgoku** imprisonment
5 出獄 **shutsugoku** release from prison
6 地獄 **jigoku** hell
7 牢獄 **rōgoku** prison, jail
11 脱獄 **datsugoku** escape from prison, jailbreak

― 3 ―

19 蟻地獄 **arijigoku** antlion, doodlebug

― 4 ―

13 試験地獄 **shiken jigoku** the hell of (entrance) exams

獎 → 奨   3n10.4

12

默 → 黙　4d11.5

3g12.3 / 1582

田　小　口
58　35　24

獣

獣｜獣獣

JŪ, kemono, kedamono animal, beast

— 1 —

7 獣医 **jūi** veterinarian
9 獣姦 **jūkan** bestiality
18 獣類 **jūrui** beasts, animals, brutes

— 2 —

10 猛獣 **mōjū** ferocious animal
11 野獣 **yajū** wild animal/beast
　　鳥獣 **chōjū** birds and animals, wildlife

— 13 —

獨 → 独　3g6.1

3g13.1 / 1313

隹　犭　艹
74　27　32

獲

獲獲

KAKU, e(ru) obtain, acquire, gain

— 1 —

8 獲物 **emono** game, a catch, spoils
11 獲得 **kakutoku** acquire, gain, win

— 2 —

14 漁獲 **gyokaku** fishing; catch, haul
18 濫獲 **rankaku** overfishing, overhunting

— 15 —

獵 → 猟　3g8.6

獸 → 獣　3g12.3

— 16 —

獻 → 献　3g9.6

── 弓 3h ──

弓	引	弘	弦	弥	弧	弱	張	強	弾	發	彈	彌
0.1	1.1	2.1	5.1	5.2	6.2	7.2	8.1	8.3	9.3	0a9.5	3h9.3	3h5.2

0

3h0.1 / 212

弓
28

弓

弓弓

KYŪ, yumi bow (for archery/violin)
YU (part of given name)

— 1 —

5 弓矢 **yumiya** bow and arrow
7 弓形 **kyūkei** bow-shaped; circle segment **yuminari, yumigata** arch, arc, curve
11 弓道 **kyūdō** (Japanese) archery
　　弓術 **kyūjutsu** (Japanese) archery

1

3h1.1 / 216

弓｜
28　2

引

引引

IN, hi(ku) pull; attract; retreat, recede, withdraw; reduce, discount **-biki** (30%) discount **hi(keru)** close, be over

— 1 —

2 引力 **inryoku** gravitation, attraction
3 引上 **hi(ki)a(geru)** raise, increase; withdraw, leave

引下 **hi(ki)sa(garu)** withdraw, leave **hi(ki)o(rosu)** pull down

⁴ 引分 **hi(ki)wa(ke)** tie, draw, stand-off

引込 **hi(ki)ko(mu)** bring around, win over **hi(k)ko(mu)** draw back, retire; sink, cave in; stand back; disappear

⁵ 引出 **hi(ki)da(shi)** (desk) drawer

引用 **in'yō** quotation, citation

引用句 **in'yōku** quotation

引用符 **in'yōfu** quotation marks

⁷ 引抜 **hi(ki)nu(ku)** pull out, select

⁸ 引受 **hi(ki)u(keru)** undertake, consent to, accept responsibility for, guarantee

引退 **intai** retire

¹¹ 引掛 **hi(k)ka(karu)** get caught/hooked/entangled **hi(k)ka(keru)** hang/hook/throw on; ensnare; cheat; have a quick drink

引張 **hi(p)pa(ru)** pull, drag, tug at; take (someone) to

引寄 **hi(ki)yo(seru)** draw near/toward; attract

¹² 引渡 **hi(ki)wata(su)** deliver, transfer, hand over

引換 **hi(ki)ka(eru)** exchange, change, convert

引替 **hikika(e)** exchange, conversion

引越 **hi(k)ko(su)** move (to a new residence)

¹³ 引掻回 **hi(k)ka(ki)mawa(su)** ransack, rummage through; carry on highhandedly

引続 **hi(ki)tsuzu(ki)** continuing

¹⁴ 引摺 **hi(ki)zu(ru)** drag along **(o)hi(ki)zu(ri)** slut

引算 **hi(ki)zan** subtraction (in math)

¹⁵ 引締 **hi(ki)shi(meru)** tighten, stiffen, brace

¹⁸ 引離 **hi(ki)hana(su)** pull apart; outdistance

¹⁹ 引繰返 **hi(k)ku(ri)kae(ru)** be overturned, capsize, collapse; be reversed **hi(k)ku(ri)kae(su)** overturn, turn upside down, turn inside out

²³ 引攣 **hi(ki)tsu(ru)** have a cramp/crick/tic/spasm/twitch/convulsion

───── 2 ─────

³ 万引 **manbi(ki)** shoplifting; shoplifter

⁴ 手引 **tebi(ki)** guidance; introduction, primer; good offices, introduction

⁵ 字引 **jibiki** dictionary

⁶ 吸引 **kyūin** absorb; attract

早引 **hayabi(ki)** leave early

⁸ 長引 **nagabi(ku)** be prolonged, drag on

拘引 **kōin** arrest, custody

取引 **torihiki** transaction, deal, business

⁹ 逢引 **a(i)bi(ki)** rendezvous, assignation, tryst

¹⁰ 値引 **nebi(ki)** discount

索引 **sakuin** index

差引 **sa(shi)hi(ku)** deduct

¹¹ 強引 **gōin** by force, forcibly

¹² 割引 **waribiki** discount **wa(ri)bi(ku)** give a discount

棚引 **tanabi(ku)** trail, hang over (fog/smoke)

¹⁴ 駆引 **ka(ke)hi(ki)** bargaining, haggling, maneuvering

²³ 籤引 **kujibi(ki)** drawing lots

───── 3 ─────

¹⁴ 総索引 **sōsakuin** general index

¹⁷ 闇取引 **yamitorihiki** black-market dealings, illegal transaction

───── 2 ─────

3h2.1 / 2064   □ 弓 竹
                                    28   17

KŌ, KŪ, hiro(i) broad, wide KŌ, HI-RO, MITSU, O (part of given name) HIROSHI, HIROMU (m. given name)

3

氵土扌口女巾犭弓彳彡艹宀艸吉广尸囗

5

1

¹ 弘一 **Kōichi, Hirokazu, Hiroichi** (m. given name)
⁹ 弘前 **Hirosaki** (city, Aomori-ken)
¹² 弘報 **kōhō** publicity
¹⁶ 弘樹 **Hiroki** (m. given name)

5

3h5.1 / 1226 　　口 弓 宀 竹
　　　　　　　　　　　28 11 17

弦　　　　弦 弦

GEN bowstring; (violin) string; chord (in geometry); hypotenuse; quarter (phase of the moon) **tsuru** bowstring **YUZURU** (m. given name)

1

¹³ 弦楽器 **gengakki** string instrument, the strings
¹⁴ 弦管 **genkan** wind and string instruments
¹⁵ 弦線 **gensen** (violin) string, catgut

2

¹⁴ 管弦楽団 **kangen gakudan** orchestra

3h5.2 / 2065　　口 弓 小 宀
　　　　　　　　　　　28 35 15

弥　　　　彌 弥 弥

BI, MI, ya, iya all the more, increasingly BI, MI, IYA, YA, MITSU, HISA, MI, HIRO, YOSHI (part of given name) HISASHI, WATARU (m. given name)

1

⁵ 弥生 **yayoi** third lunar month; spring **Yayoi** (archaeological period, 200 B.C. – 250 A.D.**);** (f. given name)
⁶ 弥次馬 **yajiuma** bystanders, spectators, crowd of onlookers

2

⁷ 阿弥陀 **Amida** Amida Buddha; lottery; wearing a hat on the back of the head

---

6

3h6.2 / 1481　　口 弓 厂 竹
　　　　　　　　　　　28 18 17

弧　　　　弧 弧

KO arc

2

⁹ 括弧 **kakko** parentheses, brackets

7

3h7.2 / 218　　口 弓 冫
　　　　　　　　　　28 5

弱　　　弱 | 弱 弱

JAKU weak; (as suffix) a little less than **yowa(i)** weak **yowa(maru)** grow weak **yowa(meru)** make weak, weaken **yowa(ru)** grow weak; be nonplussed/floored

---

1

³ 弱々 **yowayowa(shii)** weak-looking, frail, delicate
⁶ 弱気 **yowaki** faintheartedness; bearishness
　弱肉強食 **jakuniku-kyōshoku** survival of the fittest
　弱虫 **yowamushi** weakling, coward, sissy
⁷ 弱体 **jakutai** weak, effete
⁹ 弱点 **jakuten** weak point, a weakness

2

⁶ 気弱 **kiyowa** timid, fainthearted
　老弱 **rōjaku** infirmity/feebleness of old age
⁹ 柔弱 **nyūjaku** weakness, enervation
¹⁰ 衰弱 **suijaku** grow weak, become feeble
　脆弱 **zeijaku** fragile, frail, flimsy, brittle
　病弱 **byōjaku** delicate constitution
¹¹ 虚弱 **kyojaku** weak, feeble, frail
　軟弱 **nanjaku** weak(-kneed)
¹⁶ 薄弱 **hakujaku** feeble, flimsy

17 懦弱 **dajaku** effete, soft

繊弱 **senjaku** frail, delicate

— 8 —

3h8.1 / 1106   田 衤 弓 卜
                    57 28 13

張

張 張

CHŌ stretch, spread; assert, boast;
(counter for bows, string instruments,
curtains) **ha(ru)** stretch, spread

— 1 —

4 張切 **ha(ri)ki(ru)** stretch tight; be
tense/eager

10 張紙禁止 **ha(ri)gami kinshi** Post
No Bills

— 2 —

4 引張 **hi(p)pa(ru)** pull, drag, tug at;
take (someone) to

5 出張 **shutchō** business trip
deba(ri) projection, ledge

主張 **shuchō** assertion, claim, contention

6 気張 **kiba(ru)** exert oneself, make
an effort; be extravagant, treat
oneself to

7 我張 **ga (o) ha(ru)** be self-willed,
insist on having one's own way

伸張 **shinchō** extension, expansion

角張 **kakuba(ru), kado(baru)** be
angular; be stiff and formal

見張 **miha(ru)** watch, be on the
lookout for, stake out; open
(one's eyes) wide

言張 **i(i)ha(ru)** insist on, maintain

8 拡張 **kakuchō** extension, expansion

9 威張 **iba(ru)** be proud, swagger

11 強張 **kowaba(ru)** become stiff

欲張 **yokuba(ri)** greed, covetousness

13 嵩張 **kasaba(ru)** be bulky/un-
wieldly

誇張 **kochō** exaggeration

頑張 **ganba(ru)** persist in, stick to
it, hang in there

15 縄張 **nawaba(ri)** rope off; one's
domain, bailiwick

緊張 **kinchō** tension

踏張 **fu(n)ba(ru)** brace one's legs,
stand firm, hold out, persist in

16 膨張 **bōchō** swelling, expansion

— 3 —

1 一点張 **ittenba(ri)** persistence

5 四角張 **shikakuba(ru)** be formal/
stiff

3h8.3 / 217   田 虫 弓 竹
                   64 28 17

強

強 強

KYŌ, GŌ, tsuyo(i) strong
tsuyo(maru) become strong(er)
tsuyo(meru) make strong(er),
strengthen **shi(iru)** force, compel
anaga(chi) (not) necessarily
kowa(i) tough, hard, stiff TSUTOMU,
TSUYOSHI (m. given name)

— 1 —

2 強力 **kyōryoku** strength, power
gōriki great physical strength;
mountain carrier-guide

4 強化 **kyōka** strengthen, fortify

強引 **gōin** by force, forcibly

6 強壮 **kyōsō** strong, robust, sturdy

強行 **kyōkō** (en)force, ram through

8 強制 **kyōsei** compulsory, forced

強国 **kyōkoku** strong country,
great power

9 強風 **kyōfū** strong/high winds

強姦 **gōkan** rape

10 強烈 **kyōretsu** strong, intense,
powerful

11 強張 **kowaba(ru)** become stiff

強欲 **gōyoku** greedy, avaricious

強情 **gōjō** stubbornness, obstinacy

強盗 **gōtō** burglar(y), robber(y)

12 強硬 **kyōkō** firm, resolute, vigorous

14 強奪 **gōdatsu** rob, plunder, hijack,
hold up

15 強調 **kyōchō** emphasis, stress

強震 **kyōshin** violent earthquake

— 2 —

2 力強 **chikarazuyo(i)** forceful, vigorous, emboldened

4 心強 **kokorozuyo(i)** reassuring,
heartening

3

氵 土 扌 口 女 巾 犭 弓 彳 彡 艹 宀 山 青 广 尸 口

8

6 気強 **kizuyo(i)** reassuring; stout-hearted, resolute

10 勉強 **benkyō** studying; diligence; sell cheap

根強 **nezuyo(i)** firmly rooted/established

11 粘強 **neba(ri)zuyo(i)** tenacious, persistent

12 最強 **saikyō** strongest

14 増強 **zōkyō** reinforce, augment, beef up

—————— 3 ——————

7 忍耐強 **nintaizuyo(i)** patient, persevering

10 弱肉強食 **jakuniku-kyōshoku** survival of the fittest

—————— 9 ——————

3h9.3 / 1539　　　田　日　弓　小
　　　　　　　　　　　43　28　35

弾　　　弾｜弾弾

DAN bullet, shell; bounce, rebound; pluck, play (a string instrument); censure, denounce **tama** bullet **hi(ku)** play (guitar/piano) **hazu(mu)** bounce, become lively; fork out, splurge on **haji(keru)** split open; spring off

haji(ku) snap, pluck; repel (water); work (a soroban) **haji(ki)** (metal) spring; marbles; (slang) pistol

—————— 1 ——————

2 弾力性 **danryokusei** elasticity, resilience, flexibility

3 弾丸 **dangan** projectile, bullet, shell

8 弾劾 **dangai** impeachment, censure, denunciation

16 弾薬 **dan'yaku** ammunition

—————— 2 ——————

6 防弾 **bōdan** bulletproof; bombproof

8 実弾 **jitsudan** live ammunition; money

9 飛弾 **hidan** flying bullet

10 砲弾 **hōdan** shell, cannonball

14 銃弾 **jūdan** bullet

19 爆弾 **bakudan** bomb

—————— 3 ——————

4 手榴弾 **shuryūdan, teryūdan** hand grenade

發 → 発　**0a9.5**

—————— 12 ——————

彈 → 弾　**3h9.3**

—————— 14 ——————

彌 → 弥　**3h5.2**

———————————————— 彳 **3i** ————————————————

行	役	牲	彼	低	径	往	律	待	後	徑	徒	徐
3.1	4.2	3i5.6	5.2	2a5.15	5.5	5.6	6.1	6.4	6.5	3i5.5	7.1	7.2

従	御	術	得	從	御	街	復	循	微	徴	微	徳
7.3	3i9.1	8.2	8.4	3i7.3	9.1	9.4	9.6	10.1	11.2	3i10.1	11.3	

衝	徹	徴	德	衡	衛	衞	徽
12.1	12.2	3i11.2	3i11.3	13.1	13.3	3i13.3	20.1

—————— 3 ——————

3i3.1 / 68　　　田　彳　二　｜
　　　　　　　　　　29　4　2

行　　　　　　　行 行

KŌ go, proceed; do, carry out; bank

GYŌ line (of text), row; walk along; do, carry out **AN** go, travel; carry with **i(ku), yu(ku)** go **i(keru)** can go; be good **okona(u)** do, carry out, conduct **kudari** (vertical) line (of text) YUKI, IKU (part of given name)

—————— 1 ——————

0 行きずり **yu(kizuri)** passing, casual

4 行方不明 **yukue-fumei** missing
6 行列 **gyōretsu** queue, procession, parade; matrix (in math)
　行先 **yu(ki)saki** destination **yu(ku)saki** where one goes; the future
7 行男 **Yukio, Ikuo** (m. given name)
8 行事 **gyōji** event, function, observance
9 行為 **kōi** act, deed, conduct
　行政 **gyōsei** administration
10 行進曲 **kōshinkyoku** a (musical) march
　行員 **kōin** bank clerk/employee
11 行動 **kōdō** action, conduct, behavior, operations
12 行程 **kōtei** distance; journey; march; itinerary; stroke (of a piston)
13 行楽地 **kōrakuchi** pleasure resort
　行詰 **yu(ki)zu(mari), i(ki)zu(mari)** dead end, deadlock, standstill
15 行儀 **gyōgi** manners, deportment, behavior

――――――― 2 ―――――――

1 一行 **ichigyō** a line (of text) **ikkō** party, group; troupe
4 凶行 **kyōkō** violence, murder
5 代行者 **daikōsha** agent, proxy
　刊行 **kankō** publish
　平行 **heikō** parallel
　犯行 **hankō** crime
6 兇行 **kyōkō** violence, murder
　孝行 **kōkō** filial piety
　同行 **dōkō** go together, accompany **dōgyō** fellow pilgrim/esthete
　先行 **senkō** precede, go first **sak-iyu(ki), sakii(ki)** the future
　成行 **na(ri)yu(ki)** course (of events), developments
7 励行 **reikō** strict enforcement
　走行 **sōkō** travel, cover distance
　尾行 **bikō** shadow, tail (someone)
8 非行 **hikō** misdeed, misconduct, delinquency
　夜行 **yakō** night travel; night train
　直行 **chokkō** going straight, direct, nonstop
　並行 **heikō** parallel
　逆行 **gyakkō** go back, move backward, run counter to

実行 **jikkō** put into practice, carry out, realize
歩行 **hokō** walking, ambulatory
歩行者 **hokōsha** pedestrian
9 飛行 **hikō** flight, flying, aviation
　飛行士 **hikōshi** aviator
　飛行機 **hikōki** airplane
　発行 **hakkō** publish, issue
　急行 **kyūkō** an express (train)
　通行 **tsūkō** passing, passage, transit, traffic **tō(ri)yu(ku)** pass by
　通行止 **tsūkōdo(me)** Road Closed, No Thoroughfare
　単行本 **tankōbon** separate volume, in book form
　施行 **shikō** enforce; put into operation
　紀行 **kikō** account of a journey
10 修行 **shūgyō, shugyō, shūkō** training, study, ascetic practices
　進行 **shinkō** advance, progress, proceed
　流行 **ryūkō, haya(ru)** be popular, be in fashion; be prevalent/epidemic
　流行歌 **ryūkōka, haya(ri)uta** popular song
　流行語 **ryūkōgo** popular phrase, catchword
　徐行 **jokō** go/drive slowly
　旅行 **ryokō** trip, travel
　旅行者 **ryokōsha** traveler, tourist
　航行 **kōkō** navigation, sailing
11 運行 **unkō** movement; operate, run (planes, trains)
　遂行 **suikō** accomplish, execute, perform
　執行 **shikkō** performance, execution
　強行 **kyōkō** (en)force, ram through
　現行犯 **genkōhan** crime/criminal witnessed in the act, flagrante delicto
　悪行 **akugyō, akkō** evildoing, wickedness
　移行 **ikō** move, shift to
　蛇行 **dakō** meander, zigzag
12 善行 **zenkō** good conduct/deed
　奥行 **okuyu(ki)** depth (vs. height and width)

跛行景気 **hakō keiki** spotty boom/prosperity

13 試行錯誤 **shikō-sakugo** trial and error

14 銀行 **ginkō** bank

15 履行 **rikō** perform, fulfill, implement

暴行 **bōkō** act of violence, assault, outrage

16 興行 **kōgyō** entertainment industry

————— 3 —————

6 年中行事 **nenjū gyōji** an annual event

9 単独行動 **tandoku kōdō** acting on one's own

16 親孝行 **oyakōkō** filial piety

————— 4 —————

1 一方通行 **ippō tsūkō** one-way traffic

10 修学旅行 **shūgaku ryokō** school excursion, field trip

13 新婚旅行 **shinkon ryokō** honeymoon

————————— 4 —————————

3i4.2 / 375

□ 彳 冂 又
29 20 9

役

役役

YAKU service, use; office, post
EKI service; battle

————— 1 —————

2 役人 **yakunin** public official

5 役立 **yakuda(tsu), yaku (ni) ta(tsu)** be useful, serve the purpose

役目 **yakume** one's duty, role

8 役者 **yakusha** player, actor

役所 **yakusho** government office

10 役員 **yakuin** (company) officer, director

12 役割 **yakuwa(ri)** role

役場 **yakuba** town hall, public office

————— 2 —————

1 一役 **ichiyaku** an (important) office **hitoyaku** a role

2 二役 **futayaku** double role

3 大役 **taiyaku** important task/role

4 区役所 **kuyakusho** ward office

5 代役 **daiyaku** substitute, stand-in, understudy

市役所 **shiyakusho** city hall

主役 **shuyaku** major role; star

7 兵役 **heieki** military service

9 重役 **jūyaku** (company) director

10 荷役 **niyaku** loading and unloading, cargo handling

11 悪役 **akuyaku** the villain('s role)

18 懲役 **chōeki** penal servitude, imprisonment

22 纏役 **mato(me)yaku** mediator

————— 3 —————

8 取締役 **torishimariyaku** (company) director

————————— 5 —————————

徃 → 往 **3i5.6**

3i5.2 / 977

□ 彳 厂 又
29 18 9

彼

彼彼

HI he; that **kare** he **ka(no), a(no)** that, the **are** that

————— 1 —————

3 彼女 **kanojo** she; girlfriend, lover

4 彼氏 **kareshi** he; boyfriend, lover

8 彼岸 **higan** equinoctal week; Buddhist services during equinoctal week; the other shore; goal

3i5.3 / 1114

□ 彳 エ 一
29 38 1

征

征征

SEI go afar; conquer, vanquish
MASA, YUKI (part of given name)

————— 1 —————

6 征伐 **seibatsu** subjugate, conquer, punish, exterminate

7 征男 **Masao, Yukio, Ikuo** (m. given name)

8 征服 **seifuku** conquer, subjugate; master

─────── 2 ───────

12 遠征 **ensei** (military) expedition, campaign; tour (by a team)

低 → 低 **2a5.15**

3i5.5 / 1475

田 彳 土 又
29 22 9

径　徑 | 径 径

KEI path; diameter

─────── 1 ───────

13 径路 **keiro** course, route, process

─────── 2 ───────

11 捷径 **shōkei** short cut, shorter way

3i5.6 / 918

田 王 彳 丨
46 29 2

往　徃 | 往 往

Ō go; the first　**yu(ku)** go　**i(nasu)** let go; parry (an attack in sumo)

─────── 1 ───────

5 往生 **ōjō** die (and be reborn in paradise); give in; be at one's wit's end

7 往来 **ōrai** coming and going, traffic; road, street; fluctuations

12 往復 **ōfuku** going and returning, round trip; correspondence; association

─────── 2 ───────

5 立往生 **ta(chi)ōjō** be at a standstill, be stalled/stranded; stand speechless (without a rejoinder)

─────── 6 ───────

3i6.1 / 667

田 彳 ヨ 十
29 39 12

律　律 律

RITSU, RICHI law, regulation; rhythm　NORI (part of given name)

─────── 1 ───────

11 律動 **ritsudō** rhythm, rhythmic movement

─────── 2 ───────

1 一律 **ichiritsu** uniform, even, equal
6 自律 **jiritsu** autonomy, self-control
7 呂律 **roretsu** articulation, pronunciation
8 法律 **hōritsu** law
11 旋律 **senritsu** melody

─────── 3 ───────

4 不文律 **fubunritsu** unwritten law/rule

3i6.4 / 452

田 彳 土 寸
29 22 37

待　待 待

TAI, ma(tsu) wait, wait for

─────── 1 ───────

0 待ちぼうけ **ma(chibōke)** getting stood up

6 待伏 **ma(chi)bu(se)** ambush, lying in wait

待合 **ma(chi)a(waseru)** wait for (as previously arranged) **ma(chi)a(i)** waiting room; geisha entertainment place

待合室 **machiaishitsu** waiting room

10 待兼 **ma(chi)ka(neru)** can't stand the wait

11 待遇 **taigū** treatment, reception, entertainment, (hotel) service; salary, remuneration

待望 **taibō** wait for expectantly, hope for, look forward to

3

16 待機 **taiki** wait for an opportunity, watch and wait, stand by

───── 2 ─────

7 応待 **ōtai** receive (visitors), wait on (customers)

8 招待 **shōtai** invite
招待状 **shōtaijō** (written) invitation

9 虐待 **gyakutai** treat cruelly, mistreat

11 接待 **settai** reception, welcome; serving, offering

12 期待 **kitai** expect, anticipate, place one's hopes on
款待 **kantai** warm welcome, hospitality

15 歓待 **kantai** hospitality

3i6.5 / 48

日 夂 彳 竹
49 29 17

後 後

GO, nochi after, later   **KŌ, ushi(ro)** behind   **ato** afterward, subsequent; back, retro-   **oku(reru)** be late, lag behind

───── 1 ─────

0 その後 **(sono)go** thereafter, later

4 後片付 **atokatazu(ke)** straightening up afterwards, putting things in order
後日 **gojitsu, gonichi** the future, another day

5 後半 **kōhan** latter half
後世 **kōsei** later ages, posterity
gose the next world
後払 **atobara(i)** deferred payment

6 後任 **kōnin** successor

7 後足 **atoashi** hind leg/foot

8 後退 **kōtai** retreat, back up
atozusa(ri) move/shrink/hold back
後押 **atoo(shi)** pushing from behind; backing, support
後始末 **atoshimatsu** settle, wind/finish up
後者 **kōsha** the latter

9 後姿 **ushi(ro) sugata** view (of someone) from the back
後悔 **kōkai** regret

10 後部 **kōbu** back part, rear, stern
後進 **kōshin** coming along behind; one's juniors/successors; back up
後書 **atoga(ki)** postscript
後記 **kōki** postscript

11 後祭 **ato (no) matsu(ri)** too late (for the fair)

12 後援 **kōen** assistance, aid, support
後期 **kōki** latter period/term, late (Nara); latter half (of the year)
後程 **nochihodo** later on

13 後楯 **ushi(ro)date** backing, support
後裔 **kōei** descendant
後継者 **kōkeisha** successor

15 後編 **kōhen** concluding part/volume
後輩 **kōhai** one's junior, younger generation

16 後衛 **kōei** rear guard

18 後藤 **Gotō** (surname)

───── 2 ─────

4 今後 **kongo** after this, henceforth
午後 **gogo** afternoon, p.m.

5 以後 **igo** from now/then on, (t)henceforth
生後 **seigo** after birth

6 死後 **shigo** after death, posthumous
shi(ni)oku(reru) outlive, survive

8 事後 **jigo** after the fact, ex post facto, post-
直後 **chokugo** immediately after
国後島 **Kunashiri-tō** (island, Russian Hokkaidō)
明後日 **myōgonichi** the day after tomorrow

9 前後 **zengo** about, approximately; front and back, longitudinal; order, sequence
maeushi(ro) front and back
背後 **haigo** back, rear, behind
食後 **shokugo** after a meal

10 病後 **byōgo** after an illness, convalescence

11 産後 **sango** after childbirth

12 最後 **saigo** the last; the end

13 戦後 **sengo** after the war, postwar

¹⁴ 爾後 **jigo** thereafter

― 3 ―

⁹ 紀元後 **kigengo** A.D.

― 7 ―

徑 → 径 3i5.5

3i7.1 / 430 田 彳 土 卜
29 22 13

徒徒

TO on foot; companions; vain, useless **ada** empty, vain **itazu(ra)** in vain, to no purpose **tada** in vain, only, merely **muda** in vain, wasted, futile **kachi** walking

― 1 ―

⁷ 徒労 **torō** wasted effort
⁸ 徒歩 **toho** walking

― 2 ―

⁴ 仏徒 **butto** a Buddhist
⁵ 生徒 **seito** student, pupil
⁸ 宗徒 **shūto** adherent, believer
　　muneto principal vassals
⁹ 信徒 **shinto** believer, follower, the faithful
¹⁰ 教徒 **kyōto** believer, adherent
¹³ 賊徒 **zokuto** rebels, traitors

― 3 ―

⁶ 回教徒 **kaikyōto** a Moslem

3i7.2 / 1066 田 木 彳 亻
41 29 3

徐徐

JO, omomu(ro) slowly, gradually

― 1 ―

³ 徐々 **jojo** slowly, gradually
⁶ 徐行 **jokō** go/drive slowly

3i7.3 / 1482 田 彳 几 丆
29 16 14

從 | 従従

JŪ, JU, SHŌ follow, obey; junior, subordinate **shitaga(u)** obey, comply with, follow **shitaga(tte)** consequently, therefore; in accordance with, in proportion to, as **shitaga(eru)** be attended by; conquer

― 1 ―

⁷ 従来 **jūrai** up to now, usual, conventional
⁸ 従事 **jūji** engage in, carry on
　　従姉妹 **itoko, jūshimai** female cousin
¹⁰ 従容 **shōyō** calm, composed, serene
¹² 従属的 **jūzokuteki** subordinate, dependent
¹³ 従業 **jūgyō** be employed
　　従業員 **jūgyōin** employee

― 2 ―

⁸ 盲従 **mōjū** blind obedience
　　追従 **tsuijū** follow, imitate; be servile to **tsuishō** flattery, bootlicking
　　服従 **fukujū** obey, submit to
⁹ 専従 **senjū** full-time (work)
¹⁶ 隷従 **reijū** slavery

― 8 ―

御 → 3i9.1

3i8.2 / 187 田 木 彳 二
41 29 4

術 | 術術

JUTSU art, technique, means; conjury **sube** way, means, what to do

― 1 ―

¹² 術策 **jussaku** stratagem, artifice, tricks

― 2 ―

³ 弓術 **kyūjutsu** (Japanese) archery

3

氵
扌
口
女
巾
犭
弓
彳 8
彡
艹
宀
山
土
广
尸
口

4 手術 **shujutsu** (surgical) operation

7 技術 **gijutsu** technology, technique, skill, art

芸術 **geijutsu** art

芸術家 **geijutsuka** artist

学術 **gakujutsu** science, learning

学術用語 **gakujutsu yōgo** technical term

8 呪術 **jujutsu** incantation, sorcery, magic

武術 **bujutsu** military/martial arts

9 美術 **bijutsu** art, fine arts

美術館 **bijutsukan** art gallery

10 馬術 **bajutsu** horseback riding, dressage

13 戦術 **senjutsu** tactics

17 鍼術 **shinjutsu** acupuncture

21 魔術 **majutsu** magic, sorcery, witchcraft

—————— 3 ——————

5 占星術 **senseijutsu** astrology

13 催眠術 **saiminjutsu** hypnotism

3i8.4 / 374

43   29   37

TOKU profit, advantage **e(ru), u(ru)** gain, acquire, earn, win; (as suffix) can, be able to **e(tari)** fine, excellent **e(te)** apt to NARI (part of given name)

—————— 1 ——————

0 得する **toku(suru)** gain, come out ahead

4 得手 **ete** strong point, forte, specialty

5 得失 **tokushitsu** advantages and disadvantages

9 得点 **tokuten** one's score, points made

13 得意 **tokui** pride, triumph; one's strong point; customer; prosperity

—————— 2 ——————

4 不得意 **futokui** one's weak point

心得 **kokoroe** knowledge, understanding **kokoroe(ru)** know, understand

心得違 **kokoroechiga(i)** mistaken idea; indiscretion

6 両得 **ryōtoku** double advantage

有得 **a(ri)u(ru)** could be, possible

7 体得 **taitoku** realization, experience; comprehension, mastery

8 所得 **shotoku** income, earnings

所得税 **shotokuzei** income tax

9 拾得物 **shūtokubutsu** found article

10 納得 **nattoku** assent to, be convinced of

11 習得 **shūtoku** learn, master

12 勝得 **ka(chi)e(ru)** win, achieve, earn, gain

13 損得 **sontoku** advantages and disadvantages

14 説得 **settoku** persuasion

16 獲得 **kakutoku** acquire, gain, win

従 → 従 **3i7.3**

—————— 9 ——————

3i9.1 / 708

29   38   7

御御

GYO control; (imperial honorific prefix) **GO-, o-, on-, mi-** (honorific prefix) MI (part of given name)

—————— 1 ——————

0 御する **gyo(suru)** control, manage

4 御中 **onchū** To: (name of addressee organization), Dear Sirs:

御手洗 **oteara(i)** lavatory **mitarashi** holy water font at a shrine

5 御存 **gozon(ji)** (as) you know

御用 **goyō** your order/business; official business

6 御多忙中 **gotabōchū** while you are so busy

7 御来光 **goraikō** sunrise viewed from a mountaintop

8 御免 **gomen** (I beg) your pardon; no thankyou, not me; permission

御苑 **gyoen** imperial garden

御所 **gosho** imperial palace

10 御都合 **gotsugō** your convenience

12 御無沙汰 **gobusata** neglect to visit/ write

御飯 **gohan** boiled rice; a meal

御飯時 **gohandoki** mealtime

13 御蔭 **okage** indebtedness, favor, thanks to

御辞儀 **ojigi** bow, greeting

御馳走 **gochisō** feast, banquet, treat, hospitality

17 御輿 **mikoshi** portable/palanquin shrine

御覧 **goran** see, look at; give it a try

─────────── 2 ───────────

6 防御 **bōgyo** defense

8 制御 **seigyo** control

妹御 **imōtogo** your (younger) sister

姉御 **anego** gang boss's wife; woman boss

3i9.2 / 186

街 街街

GAI, KAI street **machi** town; streets, neighborhood

─────────── 1 ───────────

6 街灯 **gaitō** street lamp

7 街角 **machikado** street corner

11 街道 **kaidō** highway

13 街路 **gairo** street

16 街頭 **gaitō** street

─────────── 2 ───────────

5 市街 **shigai** the streets; city, town

─────────── 3 ───────────

6 地下街 **chikagai** underground shopping mall

11 商店街 **shōtengai** shopping area

15 歓楽街 **kanrakugai** amusement center

16 繁華街 **hankagai** busy (shopping/ entertainment) area

18 観楽街 **kanrakugai** amusement district

3i9.4 / 917

復 復復

FUKU return to, be restored **mata** again MATA (part of given name)

─────────── 1 ───────────

5 復旧 **fukkyū, fukukyū** restoration, recovery

9 復活 **fukkatsu** revival

復活祭 **Fukkatsusai** Easter

11 復習 **fukushū** review

23 復讐 **fukushū** revenge

─────────── 2 ───────────

4 反復 **hanpuku** repetition

6 回復 **kaifuku** recovery

8 往復 **ōfuku** going and returning, round trip; correspondence; association

10 修復 **shūfuku** repair

3i9.6 / 1479

循 循循

JUN follow; circulate

─────────── 1 ───────────

17 循環 **junkan** circulation, cycle

─────────── 2 ───────────

11 悪循環 **akujunkan** vicious cycle/ spiral

─────────── 10 ───────────

3i10.1 / 1419

微 微|微微

BI, MI minute, slight **kasu(ka)** faint, dim

3

---- 1 ----

3 微々 **bibi(taru)** slight, tiny, insignificant

5 微生物 **biseibutsu** microorganism, microbe

7 微妙 **bimyō** delicate, subtle

10 微笑 **bishō, hohoe(mi)** smile

11 微細 **bisai** minute, fine, detailed

15 微熱 **binetsu** a slight fever

微震 **bishin** slight earthquake/tremor

---- 11 ----

3i11.2 / 1420 ⊞ 王 攵 彳 46 49 29

徴 | 徴 徴

CHŌ collect, demand; sign, indication
shirushi sign, indication AKIRA (m. given name)

---- 1 ----

0 徴する **chō(suru)** collect, charge (a fee), solicit, seek, demand

4 徴収 **chōshū** collect, levy, charge

7 徴兵 **chōhei** conscription; draftee

10 徴候 **chōkō** sign, indication, symptom

12 徴税 **chōzei** tax collection, taxation

---- 2 ----

10 特徴 **tokuchō** distinctive feature

12 象徴 **shōchō** symbol

微 → 微 **3i10.1**

3i11.3 / 1038 ⊞ 日 心 彳 55 51 29

徳 | 德 德

TOKU virtue NORI, TOKU, NARU (part of given name)

---- 1 ----

3 徳川 **Tokugawa** (shogun family during Edo period); (surname)

7 徳利 **tokuri, tokkuri** (pinchnecked) saké bottle

8 徳明 **Noriaki, Tokuaki, Naruaki, Tokumei, Akira** (m. given name)

10 徳島県 **Tokushima-ken** (prefecture)

13 徳義 **tokugi** morality, integrity

---- 2 ----

2 人徳 **jintoku, nintoku** natural/personal virtue

6 有徳 **yūtoku** virtuous

11 道徳 **dōtoku** morality, morals

13 頌徳 **shōtoku** eulogizing someone's virtures

---- 3 ----

4 不道徳 **fudōtoku** immoral

---- 12 ----

3i12.1 / 1772 ⊞ 車 彳 二 69 29 4

衝 衝

SHŌ collide; highway; important point; (planets in) opposition

---- 1 ----

8 衝突 **shōtotsu** collision; clash

11 衝動 **shōdō** impulse, urge, drive

15 衝撃 **shōgeki** shock

---- 2 ----

7 折衝 **sesshō** negotiation

3i12.2 / 1422 ⊞ 月 攵 彳 42 49 29

徹 徹

TETSU go through TŌRU (m. given name)

---- 1 ----

0 徹する **tes(suru)** pierce, penetrate; go all-out; stay up (all night)

8 徹夜 **tetsuya** stay up all night

徹底的 **tetteiteki** thorough, exhaustive

---2---

11 貫徹 **kantetsu** carry through, attain, realize

徴 → 徴 3i11.2

德 → 德 3i11.3

---13---

3i13.1 / 1585 　田 彳 大
　　　　　58　29　34

衡 衡

KŌ scales, weigh　HIRA (part of given name)

---2---

5 平衡 **heikō** equilibrium, balance
7 均衡 **kinkō** balance, equilibrium

3i13.3 / 815 　彳 口 十
　　　　　29　24　12

衛 | 衛 衛

EI defend, protect　MAMORU (m. given name)　MORI (part of given name)

---1---

5 衛生 **eisei** hygiene, sanitation
9 衛星 **eisei** satellite

---2---

4 不衛生 **fueisei** unsanitary, unhygienic
6 防衛 **bōei** defense
　防衛庁 **Bōeichō** Defense Agency
　守衛 **shuei** (security) guard
　自衛隊 **Jieitai** Self Defense Forces
8 非衛生的 **hieiseiteki** unsanitary, unhygienic
9 前衛 **zen'ei** advance guard, vanguard
　後衛 **kōei** rear guard
20 護衛 **goei** guard, escort

儒 → 衛 3i13.3

---20---

3i20.1 　田 火 攵 彳
　　　　　44　49　29

黴 黴

BAI, kabi mold, mildew, fungus
ka(biru), kabi(ru) get moldy/musty

---1---

9 黴臭 **kabikusa(i)** moldy, musty

---彡 3j---

川	巛	形	尨	參	彩	彫	参	彪	須	髪	影	髮
0a3.2	0a3.2	4.1	4.2	5.1	8.1	8.2	3j5.1	8.3	9.1	11.3	12.1	3j11.3

髭		
13.2		

---0---

川 → 0a3.2

巛 → 川 0a3.2

---4---

3j4.1 / 395 　田 艹 彡 一
　　　　　32　31　1

形 形

KEI, GYŌ, katachi, kata, -gata form, shape　**nari** form, figure, appearance

———— 1 ————

0 ハート形 **hātogata** heart-shaped

6 形而上 **keijijō** metaphysical

形而下 **keijika** physical, material

形成 **keisei** formation, makeup

形式 **keishiki** form; formality

7 形体 **keitai** form, shape, configuration

形見 **katami** keepsake, memento

10 形容 **keiyō** form, appearance; describe, qualify, modify; figure of speech

形容動詞 **keiyōdōshi** quasi-adjective used with *-na* (e.g., *shizuka, kirei*)

形容詞 **keiyōshi** adjective

13 形跡 **keiseki** traces, signs, evidence

14 形態 **keitai** form, shape, configuration

———— 2 ————

2 人形 **ningyō** doll, puppet

3 大形 **ōgata** large size **ōgyō** exaggeration

女形 **onnagata, oyama** female role

弓形 **kyūkei** bow-shaped; circle segment **yuminari, yumigata** arch, arc, curve

小形 **kogata** small-size

4 円形 **enkei** round shape, circle

手形 **tegata** bill, (promissory) note

5 外形 **gaikei** external form, outward appearance

9 変形 **henkei** transformation, metamorphosis, modification, deformation

10 扇形 **ōgigata, senkei** fan shape, sector, segment

11 菱形 **hishigata** diamond shape, rhombus

球形 **kyūkei** spherical, globular

12 象形文字 **shōkei moji** hieroglyphics

無形文化財 **mukei-bunkazai** intangible cultural asset

13 畸形 **kikei** deformity, abnormality

畸形児 **kikeiji** deformed child

16 整形 **seikei** orthopedics

———— 3 ————

3 三角形 **sankakkei, sankakukei** triangle

5 正方形 **seihōkei** square

8 命令形 **meireikei** imperative form

9 連用形 **ren'yōkei** stem (of a verb)

連体形 **rentaikei** a participial adjective

13 楕円形 **daenkei** ellipse, oval

16 操人形 **ayatsu(ri)ningyō** puppet, marionette

18 雛人形 **hina ningyō** (Girls' Festival) doll

3j4.2

⊡ 犭 彡
27 31

龙 龙

BŌ, muku shaggy dog

———— 1 ————

3 龙大 **bōdai** enormous, extensive, bulky

———— 5 ————

3j5.1 / 710

日 大 彡 竹
34 31 17

参 | 参 参

SAN go, come, visit; three (in documents); participate **mai(ru)** go, come, visit; visit a temple/shrine; be nonplussed **(o)mai(ri)** visit to a temple/shrine

5 参加 **sanka** participate, take part

参加者 **sankasha** participant

6 参会 **sankai** attendance (at a meeting)

参考 **sankō** reference, consultation

参考書 **sankōsho** reference book/work

8 参事 **sanji** councilor

参拝 **sanpai** worship, visit (a shrine/tomb)

9 参院 **San'in** House of Councilors (short for 参議院)

13 参照 **sanshō** refer to, see, compare

16 参謀 **sanbō** staff officer; adviser

18 参観 **sankan** visit, inspect

²⁰ 参議院 **Sangiin** House of Councilors

——— 2 ———

² 人参 **ninjin** carrot

¹⁰ 宮参 **miyamai(ri)** visit to a shrine

¹² 衆参両院 **shū-san ryōin** both Houses of the Diet

¹³ 墓参 **hakamai(ri), bosan** visit to a grave

——— 8 ———

3j8.1 / 932   田 木 小 彡
41 35 31

彩

彩彩

SAI, irodo(ru) color ΛYA (f. given name) AYA (part of given name)

——— 1 ———

² 彩子 **Ayako, Saiko, Saeko** (f. given name)

⁶ 彩色 **saishiki** coloring, coloration

⁹ 彩香 **Ayaka** (f. given name)

¹⁰ 彩華 **Ayaka** (f. given name)

——— 2 ———

⁴ 水彩画 **suisaiga** a watercolor

⁵ 生彩 **seisai** luster, brilliance, vividness

⁶ 多彩 **tasai** colorful, multicolored

色彩 **shikisai** color, coloration

⁸ 迷彩 **meisai** camouflage

3j8.2 / 1149   田 月 日 彡
42 24 31

彫

彫彡 彫彡

CHŌ, ho(ru) carve, engrave, chisel, sculpt

——— 1 ———

⁸ 彫刻 **chōkoku** sculpture, carving, engraving **ho(ri)kiza(mu)** engrave, carve

¹⁴ 彫像 **chōzō** carved statue, sculpture

——— 2 ———

⁴ 木彫 **kibo(ri), mokuchō** wood carving

⁹ 浮彫 **u(ki)bo(ri)** relief, embossed carving

參 → 参 **3j5.1**

3j8.3 / 2068   ⋯ 彡 厂 十
31 18 12

彪

彪彪

HYŌ spotted, mottled, patterned; small tiger HYŌ, HYŪ, TAKE, AYA, TORA (part of given name) AKIRA, TAKESHI, TSUYOSHI, KAORU (m. given name)

——— 9 ———

3j9.1 / 2263   田 頁 彡
77 31

須

須 須

SU, SHU, subeka(raku) should, ought, necessary MOTOMU (m. given name) SU, SHU, MOCHI, MATSU (part of given name)

——— 11 ———

3j11.1 / 1827   田 立 日 彡
54 43 31

彰

彰 彰

SHŌ clear AKIRA (m. given name) AKI, TERU (part of given name)

——— 1 ———

⁷ 彰男 **Akio, Teruo** (m. given name)

——— 2 ———

⁸ 表彰 **hyōshō** commendation

3j11.3 / 1148   田 彡 𠂤 二
31 13 4

髪

髪 ┃ 髪 髪

HATSU, kami hair (on the head)

— 1 —

4 髪毛 **kami (no) ke** hair (on the head)
9 髪型 **kamigata** hairdo

— 2 —

1 一髪 **ippatsu** a hair, a hair's-breadth
4 毛髪 **mōhatsu** hair
5 白髪 **hakuhatsu, shiraga** white/gray hair
8 金髪 **kinpatsu** blond hair
9 洗髪 **senpatsu** washing the hair, shampoo **ara(i)gami** washed hair
11 黒髪 **kurokami, kokuhatsu** black hair
理髪店 **rihatsuten** barbershop
理髪師 **rihatsushi** barber, hairdresser
12 散髪 **sanpatsu** get/give a haircut; disheveled hair
16 頭髪 **tōhatsu** hair (on the head)

— 3 —

12 間一髪 **kan ippatsu** a hair's breadth

— 4 —

6 危機一髪 **kiki-ippatsu** imminent/hairbreadth danger

12

3j12.1 / 854

日 口 小
43 24 35

影

影 影

EI, kage light; shadow, silhouette, image, reflection, figure, trace

— 1 —

3 影山 **Kageyama** (surname)
8 影法師 **kagebōshi** person's shadow
12 影絵 **kagee** shadow picture, silhouette
14 影像 **eizō** image
19 影響 **eikyō** effect, influence

— 2 —

4 日影 **hika(ge)** sunlight; shadow
6 灯影 **tōei** flicker of light
7 投影 **tōei** projection
投影機 **tōeiki** projector
8 物影 **monokage** a form, shape
9 面影 **omokage** face, looks; trace, vestiges
10 陰影 **in'ei** shadow; shading; gloom
15 撮影 **satsuei** photography, filming

髮 → 髪 3j11.3

13

3j13.2

彡 ⺊ 二
31 13 4

髭

髭 髭

SHI, hige mustache

— 2 —

5 付髭 **tsu(ke)hige** false mustache/beard
14 鼻髭 **hanahige** mustache

— 3 —

4 不精髭 **bushōhige** stubbly beard

艹 3k

芝 2.1	甘 0a5.32	芋 3.1	共 3.3	芳 4.1	芦 4.3	芙 4.4	芹 4.5	芭 4.6	芽 3k5.9	花 4.7	芥 4.10	芸 4.12
苗 5.2	苺 5.4	英 5.5	茉 5.6	茂 5.7	芽 5.9	若 5.12	苑 5.17	茄 5.19	茎 5.23	苦 5.24	茅 5.26	苔 5.27
昔 5.28	苛 5.30	尭 3b9.3	茸 6.1	革 6.2	茜 6.3	茫 6.6	茹 6.7	茨 6.11	荘 6.12	草 6.13	荒 6.18	茶 6.19
華 7.1	莉 7.5	莊 3k6.12	荿 3k13.11	荻 7.8	荷 7.10	莫 7.13	莖 3k5.23	莞 7.14	恭 7.16	莓 3k5.4	菫 8.1	菓 8.2

著	萠	萌	黄	菱	菱	菩	菖	葛	菜	菅	菴	菊
8.4	3k8.11	8.11	8.16	8.18	8.20	8.21	8.22	3k9.22	8.25	8.27	3q8.6	8.30

萄	菌	董	萬	著	萩	葫	落	葬	葵	蒸	葱	葉
8.31	8.32	9.1	0a3.8	3k8.4	9.5	9.7	9.13	9.15	9.17	9.19	9.20	9.21

葛	募	葺	萱	蓮	葡	黄	蒜	蒔	蒲	蔭	曹	蒐
9.22	9.23	9.25	9.26	3k10.31	9.30	3k8.16	10.5	10.7	10.8	10.10	4c7.10	10.12

夢	蓋	蓄	墓	幕	蓉	葦	蒼	蒙	蓮	靴	蔦	蔑
10.14	10.15	10.16	10.18	10.19	10.20	10.21	10.22	10.23	10.31	10.34	11.1	11.11

慕	暮	鞄	蔽	蕩	蕉	蕪	蕎	蔵	薮	薪	蕗	薄
11.12	11.14	11.25	12.1	12.4	12.6	12.7	12.8	12.17	3k15.1	13.3	13.4	13.11

薇	薩	薬	燕	薫	薔	薗	薦	藉	薰	舊	橐	藪
13.13	13.14	13.15	13.16	13.17	13.20	3s10.1	13.25	14.2	3k13.17	4c1.1	14.6	15.1

藤	藩	藥	藝	藍	繭	藏	鞭	蘇	蘓	藻	蘆
15.3	15.4	3k13.15	3k4.12	15.5	15.7	3k12.17	15.8	16.1	3k16.1	16.8	3k4.3	16.9

蘭
3k16.9

3 ⌇ 氵 土 扌 口 女 巾 犭 弓 彳 彡 艹 3 宀 屮 卉 广 尸 口

2

3k2.1 / 250   〓 艹 一 丨
    32   1   2

芝

芝 芝

SHI, shiba lawn, turf

--- 1 ---

4 芝刈機 **shibaka(ri)ki** lawn mower
5 芝生 **shibafu** lawn
8 芝居 **shibai** stage play, theater

--- 2 ---

8 東芝 **Tōshiba** (company name)

甘 → **0a5.32**

--- 3 ---

3k3.1 / 1909   〓 艹 干 一
    32   14   1

芋

芋 芋

U, imo potato

1

0 じゃが芋 **jagaimo** (white/Irish) potato

--- 3 ---

16 薩摩芋 **satsumaimo** sweet potato

3k3.3 / 196   〓 艹 儿 一
    32   16   1

共

共 共

KYŌ, tomo both, all, as well as, including, together with

--- 1 ---

5 共存 **kyōson, kyōzon** coexistence
   共用 **kyōyō** common use, shared
   共犯者 **kyōhansha** accomplice
6 共同 **kyōdō** cooperation, collaboration, joint, collective
   共有 **kyōyū** joint ownership
   共有地 **kyōyūchi** public land, a common
7 共学 **kyōgaku** coeducation
8 共和国 **kyōwakoku** republic
   共和党 **kyōwatō** republican party
9 共通 **kyōtsū** in common, shared
10 共倒 **tomodao(re)** mutual ruin

3 ≡

氵
扌
扌
口
女
巾
犭
弓
彳
彡

4 艹
宀
丷
屮
耂
广
尸
口

11 共済 **kyōsai** mutual aid
共産 **kyōsan** communist
共産主義 **kyōsan shugi** communism
共産党 **kyōsantō** communist party
13 共働 **tomobatara(ki)** (husband and wife) both working, dual income
14 共演 **kyōen** coacting, costarring
共鳴 **kyōmei** resonance; sympathy
15 共稼 **tomokase(gi)** (husband and wife) both working, dual income
共編 **kyōhen** joint editorship
16 共謀 **kyōbō** conspiracy

──────── 2 ────────

4 公共 **kōkyō** public society, community
反共 **hankyō** anticommunist

──────── 3 ────────

2 二人共 **futaritomo** both (persons)

──────── 5 ────────

4 中華人民共和国 **Chūka Jinmin Kyōwakoku** People's Republic of China

──────── 4 ────────

3k4.1 / 1775

日 方 艹
48 32

芳

芳芳

HŌ fragrance; (honorific prefix) **kan-ba(shii)**, **kō(bashii)** fragrant; favorable **KAORU** (f. given name) **YOSHI** (part of given name)

──────── 1 ────────

6 芳名録 **hōmeiroku** visitor's book, name list
9 芳香 **hōkō** fragrance, perfume, aroma(tic)
5 芯出 **shinda(shi)** centering, aligning

3k4.3

日 艹 尸
32 40

芦

蘆 | 芦 芦

RO, ashi, yoshi reed, rush

3k4.4 / 2211

日 艹 大 一
32 34 1

芙

芙芙

FU lotus; Mt. Fuji **FU, HASU** (part of given name)

3k4.5 / 2210

日 斤 艹
50 32

芹

芹芹

KIN, seri parsley **KIN, KI, SERI** (part of given name)

3k4.6

日 艹 尸 |
32 40 2

芭

芭芭

BA plantain, banana plant

──────── 1 ────────

15 芭蕉 **bashō** plantain, banana plant **Bashō** (haiku poet, 1644 – 1694)

芽 → 芽 **3k5.9**

3k4.7 / 255

日 艹 亻
32 3 13

花

花 | 花 花

KA, KE, hana flower **hana(yaka)** showy, gaudy, gay **hana(yagu)** become showy/brilliant

──────── 1 ────────

4 花火 **hanabi** fireworks
5 花弁 **hanabira, kaben** petal
花札 **hanafuda** floral playing cards
7 花束 **hanataba** bouquet
花見 **hanami** viewing cherry blossoms

9 花屋 **hanaya** flower shop, florist
花柳 **karyū** blossoms and willows; demimonde; red-light district
花畑 **hanabatake** flower bed/garden

11 花瓶 **kabin, hanagame** vase
花道 **kadō** (the art of) flower arrangement **hanamichi** runway from the stage through the audience
花盛 **hanazaka(ri)** in full bloom

12 花婿 **hanamuko** bridegroom

13 花嫁 **hanayome** bride
花園 **hanazono** flower garden

14 花模様 **hanamoyō** floral pattern/design

16 花壇 **kadan** flower bed/garden

— 2 —

5 生花 **i(ke)bana** flower arrangement **seika** flower arrangement; natural flower

10 桃花 **Momoka** (f. given name)

11 雪花 **sekka** snowflakes

12 開花 **kaika** bloom, flower, blossom

3k4.10

芥

芥芥

日 艹 亻 儿
32 3 16

KAI mustard; tiny; trash **karashi** mustard **akuta, gomi** trash, rubbish

— 1 —

2 芥子 **karashi** mustard **keshi** poppy
芥子菜 **karashina** mustard plant, rape

15 芥箱 **gomibako** garbage box/bin, waste basket

3k4.12 / 435

芸

藝 | 芸芸

目 艹 二 竹
32 4 17

GEI art, craft; accomplishment, (dog's) trick

— 1 —

2 芸人 **geinin** artiste, performer

8 芸者 **geisha** geisha

10 芸能 **geinō** (public) entertainment; accomplishments, attainments

11 芸術 **geijutsu** art
芸術家 **geijutsuka** artist

— 2 —

3 工芸 **kōgei** technical arts

4 文芸 **bungei** literary arts
手芸 **shugei** handicrafts

5 民芸 **mingei** folkcraft, folk art

6 曲芸 **kyokugei** acrobatics

10 陶芸 **tōgei** ceramic art

13 隠芸 **kaku(shi)gei** parlor trick, hidden talent
園芸 **engei** gardening

14 演芸会 **engeikai** an entertainment, variety show

— 5 —

3k5.2 / 1468

苗

苗苗

日 甲 艹
58 32

BYŌ, MYŌ, nae, nawa seedling, sapling, shoot

— 1 —

5 苗字 **myōji** surname

— 2 —

12 痘苗 **tōbyō** vaccine

3k5.4

苺

苺 | 苺苺

日 艹 母 丨
32 25 2

BAI, MAI, ichigo strawberry

— 2 —

4 木苺 **kiichigo** raspberry

3
冫
扌
口
女
巾
犭
弓
彳
彡
艹
宀
山
圭
广
尸
口

5

3k5.5 / 353

日 艹 大 冂
32 34 20

英英

EI Britain, England, English; brilliant, talented, gifted HANABUSA (surname) SUGURU (m. given name) HIDE (part of given name)

————— 1 —————

1 英一 **Eiichi, Hidekazu, Hideichi** (m. given name)
3 英才 **eisai** gifted, talented
4 英文 **eibun** English, English composition
英文学 **eibungaku** English literature
5 英字新聞 **eiji shinbun** English-language newspaper
6 英会話 **eikaiwa** English conversation
英米 **Ei-Bei** Britain and the U.S.
8 英国 **Eikoku** Britain, the U.K.
英国人 **Eikokujin** Briton, Englishman
英和 **Ei-Wa** English-Japanese (dictionary)
11 英訳 **eiyaku** English translation
12 英雄 **eiyū** hero
英雄 **Hideo, Fusao** (m. given name)
14 英語 **eigo** the English language

————— 2 —————

4 日英 **Nichi-Ei** Japan and Britain/England
8 和英 **Wa-Ei** Japanese-English (dictionary), Japan and England

————— 3 —————

13 蒲公英 **tanpopo** dandelion

3k5.6 / 2215

日 耒 艹 一
41 32 1

茉茉

MATSU jasmine MATSU, MA (part of given name)

3k5.7 / 1467

日 戈 艹 丨
52 32 2

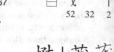
楙丨茂茂

MO, shige(ru) grow thick/rank/luxuriantly SHIGE (part of given name)

————— 2 —————

5 生茂 **o(i)shige(ru)** grow luxuriantly
16 繁茂 **hanmo** luxuriant/dense growth

3k5.9 / 1455

日 艹 乛 十
32 14 11

芽丨芽芽

GA, me a sprout, bud, germ
me(gumu) bud, sprout

————— 1 —————

0 芽キャベツ **mekyabetsu** Brussels sprouts
5 芽生 **meba(e)** bud, sprout

————— 2 —————

11 萌芽 **hōga** germination; germ, sprout

3k5.12 / 544

日 艹 口 十
32 24 12

若若

JAKU, NYAKU, waka(i) young
mo(shi) if, supposing **mo(shikuwa)**
or **shi(ku)** be equal to, compare with
WAKA (part of given name)

————— 1 —————

2 若人 **wakōdo** young person, a youth
3 若干 **jakkan** some, a number of
若々 **wakawaka(shii)** youthful
4 若手 **wakate** young person/man; younger member
5 若布 **wakame** (an edible seaweed)
6 若死 **wakaji(ni)** die young

若返 **wakagae(ru)** be rejuvenated
7 若杉 **Wakasugi** (surname)
8 若妻 **wakazuma** young wife
若松 **Wakamatsu** (surname)
若者 **wakamono** young person/people
12 若葉 **wakaba** new leaves, fresh verdure
19 若鶏 **wakadori** (spring) chicken, pullet

——— 2 ———

6 老若 **rōjaku, rōnyaku** young and old

3k5.17 / 2212 🔲 艹 夕 阝
32 30 7

EN garden, farm   **EN, ON,** SONO (part of given name)   SHIGERU (m. given name)

——— 2 ———

12 御苑 **gyoen** imperial garden

——— 3 ———

5 広辞苑 **Kōjien** (name of a dictionary)

3k5.19 / 2213 🔲 艹 口 力
32 24 8

KA eggplant   **KA** (part of given name)

——— 1 ———

2 茄子 **nasu, nasubi** eggplant

3k5.23 / 1474 🔲 艹 土 又
32 22 9

茎 莖|茎 莖

KEI, kuki stem, stalk

3k5.24 / 545   🔲 艹 口 十
32 24 12

苦 苦

KU, kuru(shimu/shigaru) suffer **kuru(shimeru)** torment **kuru(shii)** painful **niga(i)** bitter **niga(ru)** scowl

——— 1 ———

4 苦手 **nigate** one's weak point; someone hard to deal with
苦心 **kushin** pains, efforts
7 苦労 **kurō** trouble, hardships, adversity
8 苦味 **nigami** bitter taste
10 苦悩 **kunō** suffering, agony, distress
苦笑 **kushō, nigawara(i)** bitter/wry smile
11 苦情 **kujō** complaint, grievance
12 苦痛 **kutsū** pain
14 苦境 **kukyō** distress, predicament, crisis

——— 2 ———

5 四苦八苦 **shiku-hakku** agony, dire distress
6 気苦労 **kigurō** worry, cares, anxiety
7 辛苦 **shinku** hardship, privation, trouble
8 固苦 **katakuru(shii)** stiff, formal, strict
9 重苦 **omokuru(shii)** heavy, ponderous, oppressive, awkward (expression)
狭苦 **semakuru(shii)** cramped
10 胸苦 **munaguru(shii)** feeling oppressed in the chest
病苦 **byōku** suffering from illness
12 暑苦 **atsukuru(shii), atsuguru(shii)** oppressively hot, sultry, sweltering
15 熱苦 **atsukuru(shii)** sultry, sweltering, stifling

——— 3 ———

13 滅茶苦茶 **mechakucha** incoherent; preposterous; mess, wreck, ruin

3

氵 土 扌 口 女 巾 犭 弓 彳 彡 艹 宀 ⺍ 丰 广 尸 口 5

— 4 —

5 四苦八苦 **shiku-hakku** agony, dire distress

3k5.26 / 2214　　日 艹 亠 一
　　　　　　　　　　32 14 1

茅　　茅 茅

BŌ, kaya any of various grasses or rushes suitable for thatching　BŌ, KAYA, CHI (part of given name)

— 1 —

12 茅葺 **kayabu(ki)** thatched

3k5.27　　　目 艹 口 竹
　　　　　　　　32 24 17

苔　　苔 苔

TAI, koke moss, lichen

— 2 —

9 海苔 **nori** laver (an edible seaweed)
　　海苔巻 **norima(ki)** (vinegared) rice rolled in seaweed

3k5.28 / 764　　日 日 艹 一
　　　　　　　　43 32 1

昔　　昔 昔

SEKI, SHAKU, mukashi antiquity, long ago

— 1 —

3 昔々 **mukashi mukashi** Once upon a time …
13 昔話 **mukashibanashi** old tale, legend

— 2 —

1 一昔 **hitomukashi** about ten years ago
3 大昔 **ōmukashi** remote antiquity, long long ago
4 今昔 **konjaku** past and present

3k5.30　　　日 艹 口 一
　　　　　　　　32 24 14

苛　　苛 苛

KA harsh **iji(meru)** torment, bully, pick on **saina(mu)** torment, harass; chastise

— 1 —

5 苛立 **irada(tsu)** get irritated/ exasperated **irada(teru)** irritate, exasperate
14 苛酷 **kakoku** harsh, rigorous, cruel

尭 → 堯　3b9.3

— 6 —

3k6.1　　　日 耳 艹
　　　　　　　65 32

茸　　茸 茸

JŌ grow thick **take, kinoko** mushroom

— 2 —

8 松茸 **matsutake, matsudake** (a kind of edible mushroom)
12 椎茸 **shiitake** (a variety of edible mushroom)

3k6.2 / 1075　　… 艹 口 一
　　　　　　　　　32 24 14

革　　革 革

KAKU reform; leather **kawa** leather

— 1 —

8 革命 **kakumei** revolution
13 革靴 **kawagutsu** leather shoes/ boots
　　革新 **kakushin** reform, innovation

— 2 —

4 反革命 **hankakumei** counterrevolution

5 皮革 **hikaku** hides, leather

6 吊革 **tsu(ri)kawa** (hanging) strap

7 改革 **kaikaku** reform, reorganization

9 変革 **henkaku** change, reform, revolution

3k6.3 / 2216

囗 艹 口 一
      32 24 14

茜

SEN, akane madder; madder red
AKANE (f. given name)　SEN (part of given name)

——— 1 ———

6 茜色 **akane-iro** madder red, crimson

3k6.6

囗 艹 氵 亠
      32 21 11

茫

BŌ far and wide; vague

——— 1 ———

12 茫然 **bōzen** vacantly, in a daze

13 茫漠 **bōbaku** vague; vast

3k6.7

囗 艹 女 口
      32 25 24

茹

JO, yu(deru), u(deru) (tr.) boil
yu(daru), u(daru) (intr.) boil

——— 1 ———

7 茹卵 **yu(de)tamago, u(de)tamago** boiled egg

3k6.11

囗 夂 艹 冫
      49 32 5

茨

SHI thatch; brier　**ibara** brier

——— 1 ———

9 茨城県 **Ibaraki-ken** (prefecture)

3k6.12 / 1327

囗 艹 土 冫
      32 22 5

荘

SŌ solemn; villa, inn; village　**SHŌ** manor　SHŌ (part of given name)

——— 1 ———

9 荘重 **sōchō** solemn, sublime, impressive

17 荘厳 **sōgon** sublime, grand, majestic

——— 2 ———

7 別荘 **bessō** villa, country place

3k6.13 / 249

囗 日 艹 十
      43 32 12

草

SŌ grass, small plants; original; first draft; cursive handwriting　**kusa** grass, small plants

——— 1 ———

3 草々 **sōsō** in haste; (closing words of a letter)

4 草刈 **kusaka(ri)** grass cutting, mowing

9 草臥 **kutabi(reru)** be tired/exhausted

10 草原 **sōgen** grassy plain, grasslands
　　　kusahara meadow, a green

　草案 **sōan** (rough) draft

　草書 **sōsho** cursive form of kanji, "grass hand"

11 草野 **Kusano** (surname)

12 草葺 **kusabu(ki)** thatch

15 草履 **zōri** sandals, zori

草稿 **sōkō** (rough) draft, notes, manuscript

─────── 2 ───────

3 干草 **ho(shi)gusa, ho(shi)kusa** dry grass, hay

7 伽草子 **(o)togizōshi** fairy-tale book

8 毒草 **dokusō** poisonous plant

牧草 **bokusō** grass, pasturage, meadow

9 勁草 **keisō** (strong and constant as a) plant that resists the changing winds

海草 **kaisō** seaweeds, sea plants

10 笑草 **wara(i)gusa** topic of amusement

12 絵草紙 **ezōshi** picture book

19 藻草 **mogusa** water plant

3k6.18 / 1377

KŌ, ara(i), ara(ppoi) rough, wild, violent **a(reru)** become rough/stormy, run wild; go to ruin **a(re)** stormy weather; roughness, chapping **a(rasu)** devastate, lay waste **ara(rageru)** raise (one's voice) **susa(bu), susa(mu)** grow wild; become rough

─────── 1 ───────

3 荒川 **Arakawa** (river in Tōkyō); (surname)

荒々 **araara(shii)** rough, rude, harsh, wild, violent

4 荒井 **Arai** (surname)

荒木 **Araki** (surname)

5 荒立 **arada(tsu)** be agitated/aggravated **arada(teru)** exacerbate, exasperate

6 荒地 **a(re)chi** wasteland

7 荒狂 **a(re)kuru(u)** rage, run amuck

8 荒波 **aranami** rough/stormy seas

9 荒海 **araumi** rough sea

11 荒野 **a(re)no, arano, kōya** wilderness, wasteland

─────── 2 ───────

1 一荒 **hitoa(re)** a squall; a burst of anger

6 気荒 **kiara** violent-tempered

3k6.19 / 251

CHA, SA tea; light brown

─────── 1 ───────

2 茶人 **chajin, sajin** tea-ceremony expert; an eccentric

3 茶々 **chacha** interruption

4 茶化 **chaka(su)** make fun of

6 茶会 **chakai** tea party/ceremony

茶色 **cha-iro** (light) brown

茶托 **chataku** teacup holder, saucer

9 茶室 **chashitsu** tea-ceremony room

茶屋 **chaya** teahouse; tea dealer

茶畑 **chabatake** tea plantation

11 茶瓶 **chabin** teapot, tea urn

茶道 **chadō, sadō** tea ceremony

茶菓子 **chagashi** teacakes

12 茶湯 **cha(no)yu** tea ceremony

茶飯事 **sahanji** everyday occurrence

茶間 **cha(no)ma** living room

13 茶園 **chaen, saen** tea plantation

茶碗 **chawan** teacup; (rice) bowl

茶碗蒸 **chawanmu(shi)** steamed non-sweet custard of vegetables, egg, and meat

茶話会 **sawakai, chawakai** tea party

14 茶漉 **chako(shi)** tea strainer

茶摘 **chatsu(mi)** tea picking/picker

15 茶器 **chaki** tea-things

─────── 2 ───────

5 末茶 **matcha** powdered tea

8 抹茶 **matcha** powdered tea

9 紅茶 **kōcha** black tea

12 喫茶店 **kissaten** teahouse, café

焙茶 **hō(ji)cha** toasted/roasted tea

無茶 **mucha** absurd; rash; excessive

番茶 **bancha** coarse tea

³ 煎茶 **sencha** green tea
滅茶苦茶 **mechakucha** incoherent; preposterous; mess, wreck, ruin
⁴ 銘茶 **meicha** quality-brand tea
⁶ 薄茶色 **usucha-iro** light brown, buff

———— 4 ————

³ 滅茶苦茶 **mechakucha** incoherent; preposterous; mess, wreck, ruin

———— 7 ————

3k7.1 / 1074

日　王　艹
46　32

華

華　華

KA flowery, brilliant; China **KE**, **hana** flower, florid, showy, brilliant
hana(yaka) showy, gaudy, gay
hana(yagu) become showy/brilliant

———— 1 ————

⁴ 華氏 **kashi** Fahrenheit
¹¹ 華道 **kadō** flower arranging
¹⁴ 華僑 **Kakyō** overseas Chinese
¹⁹ 華麗 **karei** splendid, magnificent

———— 2 ————

⁴ 中華人民共和国 **Chūka Jinmin Kyōwakoku** People's Republic of China
中華民国 **Chūka Minkoku** Republic of China (Taiwan)
中華料理 **chūka ryōri** Chinese cooking/food
¹¹ 彩華 **Ayaka** (f. given name)
¹³ 蓮華 **renge** lotus, lotus flower
¹⁴ 豪華 **gōka** luxurious, splendid, gorgeous
精華 **seika** (quint)essence
¹⁶ 繁華街 **hankagai** busy (shopping/entertainment) area

3k7.5 / 2218

日　禾　艹　儿
56　32　16

莉

莉　莉

RI jasmine RI, REI (part of given name)

莊 → 莊 **3k6.12**

莕 → 薄 **3k13.11**

3k7.8

日　火　艹　犭
44　32　27

荻

荻　荻

TEKI, ogi reed, rush

———— 1 ————

¹¹ 荻野 **Ogino** (surname)

3k7.10 / 391

日　艹　口　亻
32　24　3

荷

荷　荷

KA, ni load, cargo, baggage

———— 1 ————

³ 荷下 **nio(roshi)** unloading, discharge
⁷ 荷役 **niyaku** loading and unloading, cargo handling
⁸ 荷担者 **katansha** participant, supporter, accomplice
荷物 **nimotsu** baggage; load
⁹ 荷重 **kajū** load
荷造 **nizuku(ri)** packing

———— 2 ————

⁴ 手荷物 **tenimotsu** luggage, (hand) baggage
⁹ 負荷 **fuka** burden, load (electricity)
¹¹ 船荷 **funani** (ship's) cargo
¹² 着荷 **chakuni, chakka** goods arrived
¹⁴ 稲荷 **Inari** god of harvests, fox deity
¹⁶ 積荷 **tsu(mi)ni** load, freight, cargo, shipment

3 〔 7 〕
氵 扌 口 巾 犭 弓 彳 彡 艹 宀 ⺌ 吉 广 尸 口

3k7.13

目 日 艹 大
43 32 34

莫

莫莫

BAKU empty; vast **BO, naka(re)** must not, do not, be not

―――― 1 ――――
³ 莫大 **bakudai** vast, immense, enormous

莖 → 茎 3k5.23

3k7.14 / 2217

目 艹 宀 二
32 33 4

莞

莞莞

KAN reed, rush **KAN** (part of given name)

3k7.16 / 1434

目 心 艹 儿
51 32 16

恭

恭恭

KYŌ, uyauya(shii) respectful, reverent, deferential **YASUSHI** (m. given name) **YASU** (part of given name)

―――― 1 ――――
² 恭子 **Kyōko, Yasuko, Yukiko** (f. given name)
¹² 恭賀新年 **kyōga shinnen** Happy New Year

苺 → 苺 3k5.4

―――― 8 ――――

3k8.1 / 2219

目 王 艹 口
46 32 24

 菫

菫菫

KIN, sumire a violet SUMIRE (f. given name) KIN, TADA (part of given name)

3k8.2 / 1535

目 日 木 艹
43 41 32

菓

菓菓

KA cake; fruit

―――― 1 ――――
² 菓子 **(o)kashi** candy, confection, pastry
菓子屋 **kashiya** candy store, confectionery shop

―――― 2 ――――
⁸ 和菓子 **wagashi** Japanese-style confections
⁹ 茶菓子 **chagashi** teacakes
¹⁶ 糖菓 **tōka** candy, sweets

3k8.4 / 859

目 日 艹 土
43 32 22

著

 著 | 著著

CHO literary work; clearly apparent **CHAKU** arrival; (counter for suits) **arawa(su)** write, publish **ichijiru(shii)** marked, striking, remarkable, conspicuous **ki(ru)** put on, wear, don **AKI** (part of given name)

―――― 1 ――――
⁷ 著作 **chosaku** writing, authorship
著作権 **chosakuken** copyright
⁸ 著者 **chosha** author

―――― 2 ――――
¹⁸ 顕著 **kencho** notable, striking, marked

萠 → 萌 3k8.11

3k8.11 / 2221

43 42 32

萌

崩 | 萌 萌

HŌ, BŌ, mo(eru) sprout, bud, put forth
shoots **mo(yashi)** bean sprouts; malt
kiza(su) show signs of **kiza(shi)**
sprouting, germination; signs HŌ, BŌ,
MOE, ME, MEMI, MOYU (part of given
name) KIZASHI, MEGUMI (m. given
name) MOE (f. given name)

---- 1 ----

5 萌出 **mo(e)de(ru)** sprout, bud
8 萌芽 **hōga** germination; germ,
   sprout

3k8.16 / 780

43 32 14

黄

黄 | 黄 黄

KŌ, Ō, ki, ko yellow **ki(bamu)** turn
yellowish

---- 1 ----

6 黄色 **ki-iro** yellow
7 黄身 **kimi** (egg) yolk
8 黄金 **ōgon, kogane** gold
9 黄海 **Kōkai** the Yellow Sea
13 黄禍 **kōka** the Yellow Peril
15 黄熱 **ōnetsu, kōnetsu** yellow fever

---- 2 ----

7 卵黄 **ran'ō** yolk
12 硫黄 **iō** sulfur
   硫黄泉 **iōsen** sulfur springs

3k8.18

56 32 25

萎

I, na(eru) wither, droop, weaken;
go numb, be paralyzed **shibo(mu),**
shio(reru), shina(biru) wither, droop,
shrivel

17 萎縮 **ishuku** wither, atrophy; be
    dispirited

3k8.20 / 1970

49 32 22

菱

RYŌ, hishi water chestnut; diamond
shape, rhombus

---- 1 ----

7 菱形 **hishigata** diamond shape,
   rhombus

---- 2 ----

3 三菱 **Mitsubishi** (company name)

3k8.21

54 32 24

菩

BO (used phonetically)

---- 1 ----

12 菩提 **bodai** Buddhahood, supreme
   enlightenment, salvation
   菩提樹 **bodaiju** bo tree; linden tree;
   lime tree
16 菩薩 **bosatsu** bodhisattva, Buddhist saint

3k8.22 / 2220

43 32

菖

SHŌ iris, flag (the flower) AYAME (f.
given name) SHŌ (part of given
name)

---- 1 ----

13 菖蒲 **ayame, shōbu** iris, flag

葛 → 葛 3k9.22

3k8.25 / 931 　　目 朩 艹 小
　　　　　　　　　41 32 35

菜

菜 | 菜 菜

SAI vegetables **na** vegetables; rape, mustard plant

——————— 1 ———————

0 サラダ菜 **saradana** romaine lettuce
4 菜月 **Natsuki** (f. given name)
9 菜食 **saishoku** vegetarian/herbivorous diet
13 菜園 **saien** vegetable garden

——————— 2 ———————

8 佳菜 **Kana** (f. given name)
9 前菜 **zensai** hors d'oeuvres
　 春菜 **Haruna** (f. given name)
11 野菜 **yasai** vegetables

——————— 3 ———————

7 芥子菜 **karashina** mustard plant, rape

3k8.27 　　　　目 艹 宀 尸
　　　　　　　　　32 33 40

菅

菅 菅

KAN, suge sedge **KAN, SUGA** (surname)

——————— 1 ———————

10 菅原 **Sugawara, Sugahara** (surname)

菴 → 庵 3q8.6

3k8.30 / 475 　　目 米 艹 勹
　　　　　　　　　62 32 15

菊

菊 菊

KIKU chrysanthemum

——————— 1 ———————

5 菊田 **Kikuta** (surname)

7 菊判 **kikuban** 22-by-15 cm size
13 菊節句 **Kiku (no) Sekku** Chrysanthemum Festival

3k8.31 　　　　目 艹 出 勹
　　　　　　　　　32 36 15

萄

萄 萄

TŌ, DŌ grape

——————— 2 ———————

12 葡萄 **budō** grape
　 葡萄酒 **budōshu** wine

3k8.32 / 1222 　　目 禾 艹 口
　　　　　　　　　56 32 24

菌

菌 菌

KIN bacteria, germ, fungus

——————— 2 ———————

9 保菌者 **hokinsha** carrier (of a disease)
10 殺菌 **sakkin** sterilize, disinfect, pasteurize

——————— 9 ———————

3k9.1 　　　　目 車 艹 一
　　　　　　　　　69 32 1

董

董 董

TŌ correct, set right

——————— 2 ———————

10 骨董品 **kottōhin** curios, bric-a-brac

萬 → 万 0a3.8

著 → 著 3k8.4

3k9.5 / 2223
田 禾 火
56 44 32

萩   萩萩

SHŪ, hagi bush clover SHŪ, HAGI
(part of given name)

———————— 1 ————————

¹⁰ 萩原 **Hagiwara** (surname)

3k9.7
田 月 艹 口
42 32 24

葫   葫葫

KO, ninniku garlic

3k9.13 / 839
田 夂 艹 氵
49 32 21

落   落落

RAKU, o(chiru) fall **o(chi)** omission, error; point (of a joke); outcome
o(tosu) drop, let fall; lose **o(toshi)**
trap; false bottom; sluice

———————— 1 ————————

⁰ 落ちこぼれる **o(chikoboreru)**
(cart-loaded grain) fallen off
and left behind, fallen/left behind (academically)
² 落丁 **rakuchō** missing pages
³ 落下傘 **rakkasan** parachute
⁴ 落込 **o(chi)ko(mu)** fall/sink/cave
in, (prices) decline
⁵ 落穴 **o(toshi)ana** pitfall, trap
落主 **o(toshi)nushi** owner of a lost/
found article
落目 **o(chi)me** declining fortunes,
on the wane
⁶ 落合 **Ochiai** (surname)
⁸ 落物 **o(toshi)mono** lost article
⁹ 落胆 **rakutan** be discouraged/dis-
heartened
¹⁰ 落書 **rakuga(ki)** graffiti, scribblings

¹¹ 落第 **rakudai** failure in an exam
¹² 落着 **o(chi)tsu(ku)** calm down
rakuchaku be settled
落葉 **o(chi)ba** fallen leaves
rakuyō shed leaves
落葉樹 **rakuyōju** deciduous tree
¹³ 落雷 **rakurai** be struck by lightning
¹⁴ 落選 **rakusen** fail to get elected
落語 **rakugo** comic storytelling
落語家 **rakugoka** comic storyteller
¹⁵ 落魄 **rakuhaku** straitened circumstances

———————— 2 ————————

⁴ 手落 **teo(chi)** omission, slip, oversight, neglect
⁶ 気落 **kio(chi)** discouragement, despondency
⁷ 低落 **teiraku** fall, decline, slump
没落 **botsuraku** downfall, ruin
奈落 **naraku** hell, hades; theater
basement
⁸ 泣落 **na(ki)o(tosu)** persuade
(someone) by tears
⁹ 陥落 **kanraku** fall, surrender (of a
city); sinking, a cave-in
段落 **danraku** end of a paragraph,
section, period; conclusion,
settlement
¹⁰ 部落 **buraku** community, settlement, village
部落民 **burakumin** (lowly class of
people historically engaged in
butchery and tanning)
洒落 **share** play on words, pun,
joke, witticism **(o)share**
dress up/stylishly **share(ru)**
pun, be witty; dress up/
stylishly **sharaku** free and
easy, unconventional
¹¹ 堕落 **daraku** depravity, corruption
脱落 **datsuraku** fall off, molt; be
omitted; defect, desert, drop
out
転落 **tenraku, koro(ge)o(chiru)**
fall, slip down
¹² 腑落 **fu (ni) o(chinai)** cannot fath-
om/understand
¹⁴ 墜落 **tsuiraku** fall, (airplane) crash
読落 **yo(mi)o(tosu)** overlook in
reading

3

氵
土
扌
口
女
巾
犭
弓
彳
彡
艹   9
宀
⺌
⺕
广
尸
口

説落 **to(ki)o(tosu)** win over, talk into

─────── 3 ───────

[1] 一段落 **ichidanraku** a pause

3k9.15 / 812 　 目 艹 夕 卜
　　　　　　　　　　32 30 13

葬 葬葬

SŌ, hōmu(ru) bury, inter

─────── 1 ───────

[6] 葬式 **sōshiki** funeral
[15] 葬儀 **sōgi** funeral

─────── 2 ───────

[4] 火葬 **kasō** cremation
[8] 国葬 **kokusō** state funeral
[10] 埋葬 **maisō** burial, interment

─────── 3 ───────

[9] 冠婚葬祭 **kankonsōsai** ceremonial occasions

3k9.17 / 2222 　 目 火 艹 大
　　　　　　　　　　44 32 34

葵 葵葵

KI, aoi mallow, hollyhock **KI, GI** (part of given name) **MAMORU** (m. given name) **AOI** (f. given name)

─────── 2 ───────

[3] 山葵 **wasabi** Japanese horseradish

3k9.19 / 943 　 目 火 氵 艹
　　　　　　　　　　44 21 32

蒸 蒸蒸

JŌ, mu(su) steam; be sultry
mu(reru) be steamed; get hot and stuffy **mu(rasu)** steam **fu(kasu)** steam **fu(keru)** be steamed/boiled

─────── 1 ───────

[6] 蒸気 **jōki** vapor, steam; steamship

蒸返 **mu(shi)kae(su)** reheat; repeat, rehash

[9] 蒸発 **jōhatsu** evaporate; disappear
蒸風呂 **mu(shi)buro** Turkish bath, sauna

[12] 蒸暑 **mu(shi)atsu(i)** hot and humid, sultry

[13] 蒸溜 **jōryū** distill

─────── 2 ───────

[4] 水蒸気 **suijōki** water vapor; steam

─────── 3 ───────

[9] 茶碗蒸 **chawanmu(shi)** steamed non-sweet custard of vegetables, egg, and meat

3k9.20 　 目 心 艹 犭
　　　　　　　　 51 32 27

葱 葱葱

SŌ, negi stone leek, Welsh/long onion

3k9.21 / 253 　 目 木 艹 一
　　　　　　　　　　41 32 1

葉 葉葉

YŌ leaf; (counter for thin flat objects)
ha, ha(ppa) leaf

─────── 1 ───────

[9] 葉巻 **hamaki** cigar
[10] 葉書 **hagaki** postcard

─────── 2 ───────

[3] 万葉集 **Man'yōshū** (Japan's oldest anthology of poems)
千葉 **Chiba** (city, Chiba-ken)

[4] 木葉 **ki(no)ha, ko(no)ha** tree leaves, foliage

[7] 言葉 **kotoba** words, expression, language **koto(no)ha** words; *tanka* poem

[8] 若葉 **wakaba** new leaves, fresh verdure
松葉 **matsuba** pine needle
松葉杖 **matsubazue** crutches

枝葉 **shiyō, edaha** branches and leaves; ramifications; unimportant details

青葉 **aoba** green leaves/foliage, greenery

9 枯葉 **ka(re)ha** dead leaf

紅葉 **kōyō** red (autumn) leaves
momiji maple tree; red (autumn) leaves

10 針葉樹 **shin'yōju** needle-leaf tree, conifer

12 落葉 **o(chi)ba** fallen leaves
rakuyō shed leaves

落葉樹 **rakuyōju** deciduous tree

絵葉書 **ehagaki** picture postcard

――――――― 3 ―――――――

7 忌言葉 **i(mi)kotoba** tabooed word

10 書言葉 **ka(ki)kotoba** written language

13 話言葉 **hana(shi)kotoba** spoken language

3k9.22

目 日 艹 冖
43 32 15

葛 | 葛 葛

KATSU kudzu, arrowroot; vines **kuzu, tsuzura** kudzu, arrowroot

――――――― 1 ―――――――

18 葛藤 **kattō** entanglements, discord, trouble

3k9.23 / 1430

目 日 艹 大
43 32 34

募 募

BO, tsuno(ru) appeal for, invite, raise; grow intense

――――――― 1 ―――――――

8 募金 **bokin** fund raising

12 募集 **boshū** recruiting; solicitation

――――――― 2 ―――――――

7 応募 **ōbo** answer (an ad), apply for, enroll, enlist, subscribe for (shares)

3k9.25

目 耳 艹 口
65 32 24

葺 葺

SHŪ reed, rush **fu(ku)** to thatch, shingle, tile, install roofing

――――――― 2 ―――――――

8 茅葺 **kayabu(ki)** thatched

9 草葺 **kusabu(ki)** thatch

12 萱葺 **kayabu(ki)** thatched

17 藁葺 **warabu(ki)** straw thatching

3k9.26

目 日 艹 宀
43 32 33

萱 萱

KEN, kaya day lily; reed, rush

――――――― 1 ―――――――

12 萱葺 **kayabu(ki)** thatched

蓮→蓮 3k10.31

3k9.30

目 月 艹 冖
42 32 15

葡 葡

BU, HO grape

――――――― 1 ―――――――

11 葡萄 **budō** grape

葡萄酒 **budōshu** wine

黄→黄 3k8.16

――――――― 10 ―――――――

3k10.5

田 木 艹
45 32

蒜 蒜

SAN garlic

3

氵 土 扌 口 女 巾 犭 弓 彳 彡 艹 10 宀 ⺌ 业 耂 广 尸 口

3k10.7 / 2224

田 日 艹 土
43 32 22

蒔

蒔 蒔

JI, SHI, ma(ku) sow (seeds) JI, SHI, MAKI (part of given name)

───── 1 ─────

12 蒔絵 **makie** (gold) lacquerwork

3k10.8

田 月 艹 氵
42 32 21

蒲

蒲 蒲

HO, FU, BU, gama cattail, bulrush, purple willow

───── 1 ─────

4 蒲公英 **tanpopo** dandelion
6 蒲団 **futon** futon, mattress, bedding
14 蒲鉾 **kamaboko** boiled fish paste

───── 2 ─────

10 座蒲団 **zabuton** cushion
11 菖蒲 **ayame, shōbu** iris, flag

3k10.10

田 艹 阝 亻
32 7 3

蔭

蔭 蔭

IN, kage shade; assistance

───── 2 ─────

12 御蔭 **okage** indebtedness, favor, thanks to

曹 → **4c7.10**

3k10.12

目 田 艹 儿
58 32 16

蒐

蒐 蒐

SHŪ gather

───── 1 ─────

12 蒐集 **shūshū** collect, gather, accumulate

3k10.14 / 811

目 目 艹 夕
55 32 30

夢

梦丨夢 夢

MU, yume dream

───── 1 ─────

4 夢中 **muchū** rapture; absorption, intentness; frantic
7 夢見 **yumemi** dreaming, dream
11 夢現 **yumeutsutsu** dream and reality; half-dreaming
13 夢想 **musō** dream, vision, fancy
   夢想家 **musōka** dreamer, visionary

───── 2 ─────

11 悪夢 **akumu** nightmare, disturbing dream

───── 3 ─────

12 無我夢中 **muga-muchū** total absorption, ecstasy

3k10.15

目 皿 艹 土
59 32 22

蓋

盖丨蓋 蓋

GAI, futa cover, lid **keda(shi)** probably

───── 1 ─────

12 蓋然性 **gaizensei** probability

3k10.16 / 1224

目 田 艹 宀
58 32 11

蓄

蓄 蓄

CHIKU, takuwa(eru) store, save, put aside

───── 1 ─────

13 蓄電池 **chikudenchi** storage battery

¹⁶ 蓄積 **chikuseki** accumulation, amassing

——————— 2 ———————

¹² 貯蓄 **chochiku** savings

3k10.18 / 1429   目 日 艹 大
43 32 34

墓

墓墓

BO, haka a grave

——————— 1 ———————

⁵ 墓穴 **boketsu** grave (pit)
墓石 **hakaishi, boseki** gravestone
⁶ 墓地 **bochi** cemetery
⁸ 墓参 **hakamai(ri), bosan** visit to a grave
¹² 墓場 **hakaba** cemetery, graveyard
¹⁴ 墓碑 **bohi** tombstone
墓銘 **bomei** epitaph

——————— 2 ———————

¹⁵ 墳墓 **funbo** grave, tomb

3k10.19 / 1432   目 日 艹 大
43 32 34

幕

幕幕

MAKU (stage) curtain; act (of a play)
BAKU shogunate

——————— 1 ———————

⁴ 幕内 **makuuchi** senior-rank sumo wrestler **maku(no)uchi** rice-ball lunch; senior-rank sumo wrestler
⁵ 幕末 **bakumatsu** latter days of the Tokugawa government
¹² 幕開 **makua(ki), makua(ke)** opening of a play; beginning

——————— 2 ———————

⁴ 内幕 **uchimaku** inside information
⁵ 字幕 **jimaku** captions, superimposed dialog
⁹ 除幕式 **jomakushiki** unveiling (ceremony)
¹¹ 黒幕 **kuromaku** black curtain; be

hind-the-scenes mastermind, wirepuller
終幕 **shūmaku** curtainfall, end, close
¹² 開幕 **kaimaku** opening/raising the curtain

3k10.20 / 2226   目 火 艹 宀
44 32 33

3

蓉

蓉蓉

YŌ lotus **YŌ, HASU** (part of given name)

3k10.21   目 艹 口 卜
32 24 12

葦

葦葦

I, ashi, yoshi reed, bulrush

3k10.22 / 2225   目 艹 食 口
32 73 24

蒼

蒼蒼

SŌ, ao blue; pale **SHIGERU** (m. given name) **SŌ, TAMI** (part of given name)

——————— 1 ———————

⁵ 蒼白 **sōhaku** pale, pallid, wan

3k10.23   目 艹 犭 冂
32 27 20

蒙

蒙蒙

MŌ Spanish moss; ignorance, darkness **kōmu(ru)** receive, be subjected to

——————— 1 ———————

⁵ 蒙古 **Mōko** Mongolia

——————— 2 ———————

⁴ 内蒙古 **Uchi Mōko** Inner Mongolia

⁵ 外蒙古 **Gaimōko, Soto Mōko** Outer Mongolia

CHŌ, tsuta ivy　CHŌ, TSUTA (part of given name)

3k10.31 / 2227　　　　日　車　艹　辶
　　　　　　　　　　　　　69　32　19

蓮　　　蓮｜蓮蓮

REN, hasu lotus　REN, HASU (part of given name)

—————— 1 ——————

¹⁰ 蓮華 **renge** lotus, lotus flower

—————— 2 ——————

¹ 一蓮托生 **ichiren-takushō** sharing fate with another
⁴ 日蓮 **Nichiren** Buddhist priest (1222 – 1282) who founded the Nichiren sect

3k10.34 / 1076　　　　川　艹　⺆　一
　　　　　　　　　　　　　32　24　14

靴　　　靴靴

KA, kutsu shoe, boot

—————— 1 ——————

³ 靴下 **kutsushita** socks, stockings
⁹ 靴屋 **kutsuya** shoe store, shoemaker
¹⁰ 靴紐 **kutsuhimo** shoelaces
¹⁷ 靴擦 **kutsuzu(re)** shoe sore

—————— 2 ——————

⁸ 長靴 **nagagutsu** boots
　　雨靴 **amagutsu** rubbers, overshoes
⁹ 革靴 **kawagutsu** leather shoes/boots

—————— 3 ——————

¹¹ 運動靴 **undōgutsu** athletic shoes, sneakers

—————— 11 ——————

3k11.1 / 2228　　　　日　鳥　艹
　　　　　　　　　　　　　80　32

蔦　　　蔦蔦

BETSU, sagesu(mu) despise, scorn

3k11.11　　　　　日　目　戈　艹
　　　　　　　　　　　55　52　32

蔑　　　蔑蔑

BETSU, sagesu(mu) despise, scorn

—————— 1 ——————

⁰ 蔑ろにする **naigashi(ro ni suru)** despise, look down on, set at naught
¹¹ 蔑視 **besshi** look down on, regard with contempt

—————— 2 ——————

¹² 軽蔑 **keibetsu** contempt, scorn, disdain

3k11.12 / 1431　　　　日　日　心　艹
　　　　　　　　　　　43　51　32

慕　　　慕慕

BO, shita(u) yearn for, dearly love; idolize　**shita(washii)** dear, beloved

—————— 1 ——————

¹¹ 慕情 **bojō** longing, love, affection

—————— 2 ——————

⁹ 思慕 **shibo** yearning, deep affection
¹⁴ 愛慕 **aibo** love, attachment, yearning

3k11.14 / 1428　　　　日　日　艹　大
　　　　　　　　　　　43　32　34

暮　　　暮暮

BO, ku(reru) (the day/year) come to an end　**ku(re)** nightfall; year-end; end　**ku(rasu)** live　**ku(rashi)** (daily) living, life

—————— 1 ——————

⁴ 暮方 **ku(re)gata** dusk, evening
　　ku(rashi)kata manner of living

6 暮向 **ku(rashi)mu(ki)** circumstances, livelihood

———— 2 ————

3 夕暮 **yūgu(re)** evening

9 独暮 **hito(ri)gu(rashi)** living alone

11 野暮 **yabo** unrefined, rustic; stupid, senseless; stale, trite

13 歳暮 **seibo** year's end; year-end present

———— 3 ————

9 途方暮 **tohō (ni) ku(reru)** be at a loss, not know what to do

3k11.25

田 艹 日 弓
32 24 28

鞄   鞄 | 鞄 鞄

HŌ, kaban suitcase, briefcase, bag

———— 12 ————

3k12.1

田 夂 艹 小
49 32 35

蔽   蔽 | 蔽 蔽

HEI, ō(u) cover, conceal

3k12.4

田 日 艹 氵
43 32 21

蕩   蕩 蕩

TŌ move; loose, licentious; enchant
toro(kasu) charm, captivate
toro(keru) be enraptured

3k12.6 / 2229

目 隹 火 艹
74 44 32

蕉   蕉 蕉

SHŌ banana   **SHŌ** (part of given name)

———— 2 ————

7 芭蕉 **bashō** plantain, banana plant
Bashō (haiku poet, 1644 – 1694)

3k12.7

目 火 艹 宀
44 32 15

蕪   蕪 蕪

BU grow wild/rank; turnip   **kabu, kabura** turnip

3k12.8

目 艹 大 口
32 34 24

蕎   蕎 蕎

KYŌ buckwheat

———— 1 ————

7 蕎麦 **soba** buckwheat; buckwheat noodles

3k12.17 / 1286

目 戈 艹 冂
52 32 20

蔵   藏 | 蔵 蔵

ZŌ, kura storehouse, warehouse, repository   **OSAMU** (m. given name)

———— 1 ————

9 蔵相 **zōshō** Finance Minister

10 蔵書 **zōsho** book collection, one's library

———— 2 ————

3 大蔵省 **Ōkurashō** Ministry of Finance

5 包蔵 **hōzō** contain, comprehend; imply; entertain (an idea)

6 地蔵 **Jizō** (a Buddhist guardian deity of children)

7 冷蔵庫 **reizōko** refrigerator

8 所蔵 **shozō** in one's possession
武蔵 **Musashi** (ancient kuni, Saitama-ken and Tōkyō-to)

3

氵 扌 土 艹
口 女 巾
犭 弓 彳
彡 艹 12
宀 ⺌ 山 耂 广 尸 囗

10 埋蔵 **maizō** buried stores, underground reserves

秘蔵 **hizō** treasure, prize, cherish

12 貯蔵 **chozō** storage, preservation

13 腹蔵 **fukuzō** being reserved, holding back

---------- 13 ----------

薮 → 藪 3k15.1

3k13.3 / 1910 　田 立 木 斤 54 41 50

薪 新

SHIN, takigi, maki firewood

3k13.4 / 2230 　田 昆 夂 艹 70 49 32

蕗 蕗

RO, fuki butterbur, bog rhubarb　RO, FUKI (part of given name)

3k13.11 / 1449 　田 日 艹 氵 43 32 21

茇 薄 薄

HAKU, usu(i) thin (paper), weak (tea), light (color)　**usu(meru)** dilute
usu(maru/(ragu/reru) thin out, fade
usu(ppera) thin; shallow, superficial, frivolous　**susuki** eulalia (a grass associated with autumn)

---------- 1 ----------

4 薄化粧 **usugeshō** light makeup

薄切 **usugi(ri)** sliced thin

9 薄茶色 **usucha-iro** light brown, buff

10 薄弱 **hakujaku** feeble, flimsy

11 薄黒 **usuguro(i)** dark, dusky, umber

薄情 **hakujō** unfeeling, heartless, coldhearted

12 薄着 **usugi** lightly/thinly dressed

13 薄塩 **usujio** lightly salted

薄暗 **usugura(i), usukura(gari)** dimly lit, semi-dark, twilight

---------- 2 ----------

7 希薄 **kihaku** dilute, rarefied, thin, sparse

12 軽薄 **keihaku** insincere, frivolous, fickle

3k13.13 　田 夂 艹 彳 49 32 29

薇 薇 薇

BI, zenmai osmund (a coiling edible fern)

---------- 2 ----------

16 薔薇 **bara, shōbi** rose, rosebush

3k13.14 　田 立 艹 土 54 32 22

薩 薩 薩

SATSU salvation; Buddha

---------- 1 ----------

15 薩摩 **Satsuma** (ancient kuni, Kagoshima-ken)

薩摩芋 **satsumaimo** sweet potato

---------- 2 ----------

11 菩薩 **bosatsu** bodhisattva, Buddhist saint

3k13.15 / 359 　田 日 木 艹 43 41 32

藥 薬 薬

YAKU, kusuri medicine; chemical

---------- 1 ----------

4 薬方 **yakuhō** prescription

5 薬用 **yakuyō** medicinal

6 薬缶 **yakan** teakettle

7 薬学 **yakugaku** pharmacology
薬局 **yakkyoku** pharmacy
8 薬効 **yakkō** efficacy of a drug
薬物 **yakubutsu** medicines, drugs
9 薬指 **kusuriyubi** third/ring finger
薬品 **yakuhin** drugs; chemicals
薬屋 **kusuriya** drugstore
10 薬剤 **yakuzai** medicine, drugs
薬剤師 **yakuzaishi** pharmacist
23 薬罐 **yakan** teakettle

―――――― 2 ――――――

7 医薬品 **iyakuhin** pharmaceuticals
妙薬 **myōyaku** wonder drug
8 毒薬 **dokuyaku** a poison
10 眠薬 **nemu(ri)gusuri** sleeping
drug/pills
11 麻薬 **mayaku** narcotics, drugs
12 弾薬 **dan'yaku** ammunition
13 煎薬 **sen(ji)gusuri, sen'yaku** medical decoction, herb tea
農薬 **nōyaku** agricultural chemicals
痺薬 **shibi(re)gusuri** anesthetic
14 膏薬 **kōyaku** salve, ointment, plaster
製薬会社 **seiyaku-gaisha** pharmaceutical company
15 劇薬 **gekiyaku** powerful medicine;
deadly poison
19 爆薬 **bakuyaku** explosives

―――――― 3 ――――――

9 胃腸薬 **ichōyaku** stomach and
bowel medicine
10 消毒薬 **shōdokuyaku** disinfectant,
antiseptic
13 漢方薬 **kanpōyaku** a herbal medicine
睡眠薬 **suimin'yaku** sleeping
drug/pills
15 避妊薬 **hinin'yaku** a contraceptive, birth control pill

3k13.16   目 火 艹 口
                                44 32 24

EN, tsubame swallow (the bird) (cf.
嚥 3d16.2)

―――――― 1 ――――――

7 燕尾服 **enbifuku** swallow-tailed
coat

3k13.17 / 1774   目 車 火 艹
                          69 44 32

薫 | 薫薫

KUN, kao(ru) be fragrant, smell
good **SHIGE** (part of given name)

―――――― 1 ――――――

9 薫風 **kunpū** balmy breeze
10 薫陶 **kuntō** discipline, training, education

3k13.20   目 艹 土 口
                          32 22 24

薔 薔

SHŌ water pepper (a kind of grass)

―――――― 1 ――――――

16 薔薇 **bara, shōbi** rose, rosebush

 園 **3s10.1**

3k13.25 / 1631   目 火 艹 厂
                          44 32 18

薦 薦

SEN, susu(meru) recommend; encourage, offer **komo** straw mat

―――――― 2 ――――――

11 推薦 **suisen** recommendation,
nomination
推薦状 **suisenjō** letter of recommendation

────── 14 ──────

3k14.2

田 木 日 艹
41 43 32

藉 藉

SHA, SEKI rug; borrow, lend; make excuses; spread out; step on

薫 → 薫 **3k13.17**

舊 → 旧 **4c1.1**

3k14.6

日 木 艹 口
41 32 24

藁 藁

KŌ, wara straw

────── 1 ──────

5 藁半紙 **warabanshi** (a low-grade paper)

12 藁葺 **warabu(ki)** straw thatching

────── 15 ──────

3k15.1

田 夂 艹 口
49 32 24

藪 | 藪 藪

SŌ, yabu thicket, grove

────── 1 ──────

7 藪医者 **yabuisha** a quack

────── 2 ──────

6 竹藪 **takeyabu** bamboo grove/thicket

11 笹藪 **sasayabu** bamboo-grass thicket

3k15.3 / 2231

田 月 火 艹
42 44 32

藤 | 藤 藤

TŌ, fuji wisteria TŌ, DŌ, TSU, HISA, FUJI (part of given name) FUJI, KATSURA (surname)

────── 1 ──────

3 藤山 **Fujiyama** (surname)

4 藤井 **Fujii** (surname)

5 藤本 **Fijimoto** (surname)

  藤田 **Fujita** (surname)

6 藤色 **fuji-iro** light purple, lilac, lavender

7 藤沢 **Fujisawa** (city, Kanagawa-ken)

  藤村 **Fujimura** (surname)

8 藤岡 **Fujioka** (surname)

10 藤原 **Fujiwara** (surname)

  藤島 **Fujishima** (surname)

────── 2 ──────

3 工藤 **Kudō** (surname)

4 内藤 **Naitō** (surname)

5 加藤 **Katō** (surname)

6 伊藤 **Itō** (surname)

  近藤 **Kondō** (surname)

  江藤 **Etō** (surname)

  安藤 **Andō** (surname)

7 佐藤 **Satō** (surname)

8 斉藤 **Saitō** (surname)

  武藤 **Mutō** (surname)

9 後藤 **Gotō** (surname)

11 斎藤 **Saitō** (surname)

12 遠藤 **Endō** (surname)

  葛藤 **kattō** entanglements, discord, trouble

3k15.4 / 1382

田 米 田 艹
62 58 32

藩 藩

HAN feudal clan/lord; enclosure

────── 1 ──────

5 藩主 **hanshu** lord of a feudal clan

14 藩閥 **hanbatsu** clanship, clannishness

藥 → 薬 **3k13.15**

藝 → 芸 3k4.12

3k15.5 / 2232 目 皿 艹 口
59 32 20

藍藍

RAN, ai indigo plant; indigo (the color) **RAN, AI** (part of given name)

3k15.7 / 1911 目 糸 虫 艹
61 64 32

繭繭

KEN, mayu cocoon

藏 → 蔵 3k12.17

3k15.8 田 日 艹 日
43 32 24

鞭鞭

BEN, muchi whip, rod

——————— 1 ———————

5 鞭打症 **muchiu(chi)shō** whiplash
15 鞭撻 **bentatsu** whip, lash; urge/
spur on, goad

——————— 16 ———————

3k16.1 田 魚 禾 艹
79 56 32

蘓 | 蘇蘇

SO, SU, yomigae(ru) come back to life, be revived/resuscitated

5 蘇生 **sosei** revival, resuscitation;
resurrection

蘓 → 蘇 3k16.1

3k16.8 / 1657 田 木 艹 氵
41 32 21

藻藻

SŌ, mo water plant

——————— 1 ———————

9 藻草 **mogusa** water plant
18 藻類 **sōrui** water plants, seaweeds

——————— 2 ———————

9 海藻 **kaisō** seaweeds, marine plants

蘆 → 芦 3k4.3

3k16.9 / 2233 目 門 木 日
76 41 43

蘭 | 蘭蘭

RAN orchid; Dutch **RAN, KA** (part of given name)

——————— 1 ———————

7 蘭学 **Rangaku** study of the Dutch
language and Western learning

——————— 2 ———————

8 盂蘭盆 **Urabon** o-Bon festival
9 室蘭 **Muroran** (city, Hokkaidō)
13 鈴蘭 **suzuran** lily-of-the-valley

——————— 17 ———————

蘭 → 蘭 3k16.9

——————— 宀 3m ———————

字	穴	安	守	宇	宅	宋	牢	宏	究	完	宗	宝
2.1	2.2	3.1	3.2	3.3	3.4	4.1	4.2	4.3	4.5	4.6	5.1	5.2

3

氵 土 扌 口 女 巾 犭 弓 彡 艹 16 宀 丷 耂 广 尸 口

実	宙	官	宜	定	宛	突	空	宥	宣	客	室	窃
5.4	5.5	5.6	5.7	5.8	5.9	5.11	5.12	6.1	6.2	6.3	6.4	6.5
突	窄	家	宰	宴	害	宮	案	宵	容	穿	窄	寂
3m5.11	6.6	7.1	7.2	7.3	7.4	7.5	7.6	7.7	7.8	7.10	7.11	8.2
宿	寅	密	窓	寄	室	寓	寒	富	窗	寝	塞	寛
8.3	8.4	8.5	8.7	8.8	8.9	9.1	9.3	9.5	3m8.7	10.1	10.2	10.3
窟	寡	察	蜜	寧	賓	實	寢	窪	寬	審	寮	賓
10.6	11.2	11.6	11.7	11.8	3m12.3	3m5.4	3m10.1	11.9	3m10.3	12.1	12.2	12.3
窮	寫	窯	窰	憲	寠	實	竊					
12.4	2i3.1	12.5	3m12.5	13.2	13.5	3m5.2	3m6.5					

3
氵
扌
扌
口
女
巾
犭
弓
彳
彡
艹
2
宀
山
土
广
尸
口

---

2 ---

3m2.1 / 110

日 宀 子
33 6

字 字

JI character, letter **aza** section of a village **azana** nickname, one's popular name

--- 1 ---

4 字引 **jibiki** dictionary
7 字体 **jitai** form of a character, typeface
8 字典 **jiten** character dictionary
13 字幕 **jimaku** captions, superimposed dialog

--- 2 ---

1 一字 **ichiji** a character/letter
2 丁字路 **teijiro** T-junction of roads/ streets
十字 **jūji** cross
十字架 **jūjika** cross, crucifix
十字路 **jūjiro** crossroads, intersection
3 大字 **ōaza** major section of a village **dai(no)ji** the character 大
4 太字 **futoji** bold-face lettering
文字 **moji, monji** character, letter
文字通 **mojidō(ri)** literal(ly)
5 外字 **gaiji** kanji not officially recognized for everyday use; foreign letters/language

外字新聞 **gaiji shinbun** foreign-language newspaper
正字法 **seijihō** orthography
6 邦字 **hōji** Japanese characters
名字 **myōji** surname
当字 **a(te)ji** kanji used phonetically; kanji used purely ideographically, disregarding usual readings
7 赤字 **akaji** deficit, in the red
8 苗字 **myōji** surname
英字新聞 **eiji shinbun** English-language newspaper
国字 **kokuji** native script; made-in-Japan kanji not found in Chinese
9 俗字 **zokuji** popular form of a kanji
点字 **tenji** Braille
11 脱字 **datsuji** omitted character/word
習字 **shūji** penmanship, calligraphy
黒字 **kuroji** in the black
略字 **ryakuji** simplified character; abbreviation
12 植字 **shokuji** typesetting
13 漢字 **kanji** Chinese character, kanji
数字 **sūji** digit, numeral, figures
14 嘘字 **usoji** miswritten kanji
誤字 **goji** incorrect character, misprint
15 篆字 **tenji** seal characters
16 親字 **oyaji** first character (of a dictionary entry)

--- 3 ---

1 一文字 **ichimonji** a straight line
2 十文字 **jūmonji** cross

³ 大文字 **ōmoji** capital letter
daimonji large character; the character 大

小文字 **komoji** small/lowercase letters

⁷ 赤十字 **sekijūji** Red Cross

¹⁵ 横文字 **yokomoji** European/horizontal writing

¹⁶ 頭文字 **kashiramoji** initials; capital letter

───── 4 ─────

⁶ 当用漢字 **Tōyō Kanji** (official list of 1,850 kanji recommended for general use; superseded by the 1,945 Jōyō Kanji)

⁸ 表音文字 **hyōon moji** phonetic symbol/script

表意文字 **hyōi moji** ideograph

¹¹ 常用漢字 **Jōyō Kanji** (official list of 1,945 kanji recommended for general use)

¹² 象形文字 **shōkei moji** hieroglyphics

3m2.2 / 899   日 宀 儿
               33   16

穴 | 穴 穴

KETSU, ana hole; cave, den

───── 1 ─────

² 穴子 **anago** conger eel

¹⁰ 穴埋 **anau(me)** fill a gap; cover a deficit

¹² 穴場 **anaba** good place known to few

───── 2 ─────

³ 大穴 **ōana** gaping hole; huge deficit; (make) a killing; (bet on) a long shot

⁷ 抜穴 **nu(ke)ana** secret passage/exit; loophole

⁸ 虎穴 **koketsu** tiger's den; dangerous situation

⁹ 洞穴 **horaana, dōketsu** cave, den

¹² 落穴 **o(toshi)ana** pitfall, trap

覗穴 **nozo(ki)ana** peephole

¹³ 墓穴 **boketsu** grave (pit)

¹⁶ 鍵穴 **kagiana** keyhole

───── 3 ─────

3m3.1 / 105   日 宀 女
               33   25

安 安

AN peacefulness **yasu(i)** cheap, inexpensive **yasu(raka)** peaceful, tranquil YASUSHI (m. given name) YASU (part of given name)

───── 1 ─────

⁰ ドル安 **doruyasu** weak dollar (relative to other currencies)

³ 安上 **yasua(gari)** cheap, economical

⁴ 安井 **Yasui** (surname)

安月給 **yasugekkyū** meager salary

安心 **anshin** feel relieved/reassured

⁵ 安田 **Yasuda** (surname)

⁶ 安全 **anzen** safety

安全第一 **anzen dai-ichi** Safety First

⁷ 安否 **anpi** whether safe or not, well-being

安売 **yasuu(ri)** sell cheap

⁸ 安治 **Yasuji, Yasuharu** (m. given name)

安定 **antei** stability

安易 **an'i** easy, easygoing

安物 **yasumono** cheap goods

⁹ 安保 **anpo** (national) security (short for 安全保障)

¹⁰ 安値 **yasune** low price

安息 **ansoku** rest, repose

安息日 **ansokubi** sabbath **ansokunichi** the (Jewish) sabbath **ansokujitsu** the (Christian) sabbath

¹¹ 安産 **anzan** easy delivery/childbirth

¹³ 安楽 **anraku** ease, comfort

安楽死 **anrakushi** euthanasia

¹⁴ 安寧秩序 **annei-chitsujo** peace and order

¹⁸ 安藤 **Andō** (surname)

───── 2 ─────

¹ 一安心 **hitoanshin** feeling relieved for a while

³ 大安 **taian** lucky day

⁴ 不安 **fuan** uneasiness, apprehension; unsettled, precarious; suspenseful, fearful

不安定 **fuantei** unstable, shaky

天安門 **Ten'anmon** Tiananmon, Gate of Heavenly Peace (in Beijing)

公安 **kōan** public order/safety

⁵ 平安 **heian** peace, tranquility; the Heian period (794 – 1185)

平安朝 **Heianchō** the Heian period (794 – 1185)

目安 **meyasu** standard, yardstick

⁸ 治安 **chian** public peace/order

¹⁰ 格安 **kakuyasu** inexpensive

¹⁵ 慰安 **ian** comfort, recreation, amusement

慰安婦 **ianfu** comfort girl/woman, army prostitute

¹⁸ 職安 **shokuan** (public) employment security office (short for 公共職業安定所)

3m3.2 / 490

日 宀 寸
33 37

守

守 守

SHU, SU, mamo(ru) protect; obey, abide by   **mori** babysitter; (lighthouse) keeper   **kami** feudal lord
MORI (part of given name)

——————— 1 ———————

⁰ お守り **(o)mamo(ri)** charm, amulet

⁵ 守田 **Morita** (surname)

⁹ 守神 **mamo(ri)gami** guardian deity

¹² 守備 **shubi** defense

¹⁴ 守銭奴 **shusendo** miser, niggard

¹⁶ 守衛 **shuei** (security) guard

——————— 2 ———————

² 子守 **komori** baby tending/sitting; nursemaid, baby sitter

⁷ 見守 **mimamo(ru)** watch over

⁹ 保守的 **hoshuteki** conservative

¹⁰ 留守 **rusu** absence, being away from home; looking after the house (while someone is away); neglecting

留守番 **rusuban** looking after the house (while someone is away); caretaker

留守番電話 **rusuban denwa** answering machine

¹⁴ 遵守 **junshu** obey, observe

¹⁵ 監守 **kanshu** keeping watch over, custody

¹⁷ 厳守 **genshu** strict observance/adherence

——————— 3 ———————

⁸ 居留守 **irusu** pretend not to be in (to avoid callers)

3m3.3 / 990

日 宀 丁 一
33 14 1

宇

宇 宇

U sky, heavens; eaves, roof, house; country's border

——————— 1 ———————

⁸ 宇宙 **uchū** space, the universe

宇宙船 **uchūsen** spaceship

¹⁰ 宇都宮 **Utsunomiya** (city, Tochigi-ken)

¹¹ 宇野 **Uno** (surname)

3m3.4 / 178

日 宀 丶 亅
33 12 2

宅

宅 宅

TAKU house, home, residence

——————— 1 ———————

⁰ お宅 **(o)taku** your house/company; you

⁶ 宅地 **takuchi** residential land

¹⁰ 宅配便 **takuhaibin** parcel delivery business

——————— 2 ———————

³ 三宅 **Miyake** (surname)

⁶ 自宅 **jitaku** at one's home

⁷ 住宅 **jūtaku** dwelling, residence, house, housing

邸宅 **teitaku** mansion, residence

¹⁰ 帰宅 **kitaku** return/come home

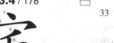

家宅 **kataku** house, premises

─────── **4** ───────

3m4.1
日 木 宀
41　33

宋　　宋宋

SŌ Song/Sung (dynasty); dwell

─────── 1 ───────

12 宋朝 **Sōchō** Song dynasty

3m4.2
日 牛 宀
47　33

牢　　牢牢

RŌ prison, jail; hardness

─────── 1 ───────

8 牢固 **rōko** firm, solid, inflexible
9 牢屋 **rōya** prison, jail
10 牢破 **rōyabu(ri)** jailbreak
14 牢獄 **rōgoku** prison, jail

3m4.3 / 2050
日 宀 十 竹
33　12　17

宏　　宏宏

KŌ vast, large　KŌ, HIRO, ATSU (part of given name)　HIROSHI, FUKASHI (m. given name)

─────── 1 ───────

2 宏之 **Hiroyuki, Hiroshi** (m. given name)
3 宏大 **kōdai** vast, extensive, grand

3m4.5 / 895
日 宀 儿 十
33　16　12

究　　究究

KYŪ, kiwa(meru) investigate thoroughly/exhaustively　KIWAMU (m. given name)

─────── 1 ───────

8 究明 **kyūmei** study, investigation, inquiry
12 究極 **kyūkyoku** final, ultimate

─────── 2 ───────

8 追究 **tsuikyū** pursuit, inquiry
9 研究 **kenkyū** research
研究所 **kenkyūjo** (research) institute, laboratory
研究室 **kenkyūshitsu** laboratory, study room
11 探究 **tankyū** research, inquiry, study

3m4.6 / 613
日 宀 二 儿
33　4　16

完　　完完

KAN completion

─────── 1 ───────

1 完了 **kanryō** complete, finish, conclude
6 完全 **kanzen** complete, perfect
完成 **kansei** completion, accomplishment
11 完敗 **kanpai** complete defeat
12 完備 **kanbi** fully equipped/furnished
17 完璧 **kanpeki** perfect, flawless

─────── 2 ───────

4 不完全 **fukanzen** incomplete, imperfect, faulty, defective
5 未完成 **mikansei** incomplete, unfinished

─────── **5** ───────

3m5.1 / 616
日 礻 宀
45　33

宗　　宗宗

SHŪ religion, sect, denomination
SŌ head, leader　**mune** main/important point　MUNE (part of given name)

氵
土
扌
口
女
巾
犭
弓
彳
彡
艹　5
宀
⺍
耂
广
尸
口

———————— 1 ————————

7 宗谷海峡 **Sōya-kaikyō** (strait between Hokkaidō and Sakhalin)

9 宗派 **shūha** sect, denomination

宗祖 **shūso** founder of a sect

10 宗徒 **shūto** adherent, believer
muneto principal vassals

宗教 **shūkyō** religion

———————— 2 ————————

7 改宗 **kaishū** conversion (to another religion)

13 禅宗 **zenshū** the Zen sect

3m5.2 / 296

日 王 宀 |
46 33 2

HŌ, takara treasure TOMI (part of given name)

———————— 1 ————————

5 宝石 **hōseki** precious stone, gem, jewel

8 宝物 **takaramono, hōmotsu** treasure

23 宝籤 **takarakuji** lottery, raffle

———————— 2 ————————

8 国宝 **kokuhō** national treasure

3m5.4 / 203

日 宀 大 二
33 34 4

JITSU actual, real, true; sincerity **mi** fruit, nut **mino(ru)** bear fruit **makoto** sincerity **sane** seed inside a (peach) stone; clitoris MAKOTO, MINORU (m. given name) SANE (part of given name)

———————— 1 ————————

2 実力 **jitsuryoku** actual ability, competence; arms, force

4 実収 **jisshū** actual income, take-home pay

実父 **jippu** one's biological father

5 実母 **jitsubo** one's biological mother

実存 **jitsuzon** existence

実用 **jitsuyō** practical use, utility

6 実地 **jitchi** practical, on-site, in the field

実在 **jitsuzai** real existence, reality

実名 **jitsumei** one's real name

実行 **jikkō** put into practice, carry out, realize

7 実体 **jittai** substance, entity; three-dimensional

実状 **jitsujō** actual state of affairs

8 実例 **jitsurei** example, illustration

実効 **jikkō** practical effect

実況 **jikkyō** actual conditions

実物 **jitsubutsu** the real thing, the original

実物大 **jitsubutsudai** actual size

10 実益 **jitsueki** net profit, practical benefit

実家 **jikka** one's parent's home

11 実習 **jisshū** practice, drill

実現 **jitsugen** come true, realize, materialize

実情 **jitsujō** actual state of affairs

12 実弾 **jitsudan** live ammunition; money

実証 **jisshō** actual proof

実費 **jippi** actual expense; cost price

13 実業 **jitsugyō** industry, business

実際 **jissai** actual(ly), real(ly)

実感 **jikkan** actual sensation, realization

実践 **jissen** in practice

14 実態 **jittai** actual conditions

15 実権 **jikken** real power

実質的 **jisshitsuteki** substantial, essential, material, real

17 実績 **jisseki** actual results, record of performance

18 実験 **jikken** experiment

実験室 **jikkenshitsu** laboratory

———————— 2 ————————

3 口実 **kōjitsu** excuse, pretext

4 不実 **fujitsu** unfaithful, inconstant; false, untrue

切実 **setsujitsu** acute, keen, urgent; earnest

木実 **ki(no)mi, ko(no)mi** fruit, nut, berry

5 史実 **shijitsu** historical fact

写実的 **shajitsuteki** realistic, true to life, graphic

6 充実 **jūjitsu** repletion, completion, beefing up, making substantial

8 果実 **kajitsu** fruit

事実 **jijitsu** fact

事実上 **jijitsujō** in fact, actually

忠実 **chūjitsu** faithful, devoted, loyal

10 真実 **shinjitsu** truth, reality, the facts

核実験 **kakujikken** nuclear testing

11 虚実 **kyojitsu** truth or falsehood, clever fighting, trying every strategy

現実 **genjitsu** actuality, reality

12 着実 **chakujitsu** steady, solid, trustworthy

堅実 **kenjitsu** solid, sound, reliable

13 誠実 **seijitsu** sincere, faithful, truthful

15 確実 **kakujitsu** certain, reliable

———————— 3 ————————

8 非現実的 **higenjitsuteki** unrealistic

———————— 4 ————————

10 既成事実 **kisei jijitsu** fait accompli

3m5.5 / 991

口 日 宀 |
43 33 2

宙 宙

CHŪ midair, space, heaven　HIROSHI (m. given name)

———————— 1 ————————

6 宙返 **chūgae(ri)** somersault

———————— 2 ————————

6 宇宙 **uchū** space, the universe

宇宙船 **uchūsen** spaceship

3m5.6 / 326

曰 宀 尸 冂
33 40 20

官 官 官

KAN government, the authorities; the (imperial) court; (as suffix) an official, officer

———————— 1 ————————

5 官庁 **kanchō** government office/authorities

6 官有 **kan'yū** government-owned

7 官邸 **kantei** official residence

8 官房長官 **kanbō chōkan** Chief Cabinet Secretary

官金 **kankin** government funds

10 官能 **kannō** bodily functions; sensual, carnal

12 官報 **kanpō** official gazette/telegram

官営 **kan'ei** government-run

官費 **kanpi** government expense

14 官僚 **kanryō** bureaucracy, officialdom

官僚的 **kanryōteki** bureaucratic

———————— 2 ————————

6 次官 **jikan** vice-minister, undersecretary

8 長官 **chōkan** director, head, chief, secretary, administrator

9 神官 **shinkan** Shinto priest

11 尉官 **ikan** officer below the rank of major

15 器官 **kikan** organ (of the body)

19 警官 **keikan** policeman

———————— 3 ————————

5 外交官 **gaikōkan** diplomat

8 事務官 **jimukan** administrative official, secretary, commissioner

9 政務官 **seimukan** parliamentary official

10 准士官 **junshikan** warrant officer

12 検査官 **kensakan** inspector, examiner

裁判官 **saibankan** the judge

15 審判官 **shinpankan** judge, umpire, referee

19 警察官 **keisatsukan** police officer

────── 4 ──────

8 事務長官 **jimuchōkan** chief secretary

官房長官 **kanbō chōkan** Chief Cabinet Secretary

国務長官 **kokumu chōkan** (U.S.) Secretary of State

9 政務次官 **seimu jikan** parliamentary vice-minister

14 総務長官 **sōmu chōkan** director-general

3m5.7 / 1086

目 月 宀 一
42 33 1

GI, yoro(shii) good, alright **yoro(shiku)** regards, greetings; well, suitably **mube** true, well said YOSHI (part of given name)

────── 2 ──────

9 便宜上 **bengijō** for convenience

13 適宜 **tekigi** suitable, proper, as one thinks best

3m5.8 / 355

日 宀 丁 亻
33 14 3

TEI, JŌ definite, fixed, constant, regular **sada(meru)** determine, decide **sada(me)** rule, provision; decision; arrangements; karma **sada(maru)** be determined/decided **sada(ka)** definite, certain SADA (part of given name)

────── 1 ──────

4 定収入 **teishūnyū** fixed income

定日 **teijitsu** fixed/appointed date

6 定年 **teinen** age limit, retirement age

定休日 **teikyūbi** regular holiday, Closed (Tuesday)s

定吉 **Sadakichi, Sadayoshi, Teikichi** (m. given name)

定式 **jōshiki, teishiki** prescribed/established form, formula, formality

7 定住者 **teijūsha** permanent resident

8 定価 **teika** (fixed/set) price

定例 **teirei, jōrei** established usage, precedent; regular (meeting)

定限 **teigen** limit, restrict

9 定型 **teikei** definite form, type

定食 **teishoku** regular meal, table d'hôte

10 定員 **teiin** prescribed number of personnel; (seating) capacity; quorum

定時 **teiji** regular time/intervals, fixed period

11 定常 **teijō** steady, stationary, regular, routine

定規 **teiki** prescribed **jōgi** ruler, (T-)square; standard

12 定着 **teichaku** fix, fasten, anchor

定期 **teiki** fixed period/term/intervals, regular (meeting); (train) pass, commuting ticket (short for 定期券)

定量 **teiryō** fixed quantity; to measure; dose

定款 **teikan** articles of incorporation, charter

13 定義 **teigi** definition

14 定説 **teisetsu** established/accepted opinion

18 定礎式 **teisoshiki** cornerstone-laying ceremony

定職 **teishoku** regular occupation, steady job

定額 **teigaku** fixed amount, flat sum

────── 2 ──────

1 一定 **ittei** fixed, prescribed, regular, definite; fix, settle; standardize **ichijō** definitely settled

4 不定 **futei, fujō** uncertain, indefinite, changeable

予定 **yotei** plan, prearrangement, expectation

予定日 **yoteibi** scheduled date, expected date (of birth)

内定 **naitei** informal/tentative decision

公定歩合 **kōtei buai** official bank rate, rediscount rate

5 未定 **mitei** undecided, pending

6 仮定 **katei** supposition, assumption, hypothesis

安定 **antei** stability

7 判定 **hantei** judgment, decision, verdict

決定 **kettei** decision, determination

決定版 **ketteiban** definitive edition

否定 **hitei** denial, negation

8 限定 **gentei** limit, qualify, modify; define, determine

協定 **kyōtei** agreement, accord

法定 **hōtei** legal, prescribed by law

国定 **kokutei** quasi-national, state-prescribed

固定 **kotei** fixed

肯定 **kōtei** affirm

肯定的 **kōteiteki** affirmative

所定 **shotei** fixed, prescribed, stated

9 指定 **shitei** appoint, designate

指定席 **shiteiseki** reserved seats

査定 **satei** assessment

10 既定 **kitei** predetermined, prearranged, fixed

特定 **tokutei** specify

11 勘定 **kanjō** calculation; account; settling an account

推定 **suitei** presumption, estimate

規定 **kitei** stipulations, provisions, regulations

設定 **settei** establishment, creation

12 測定 **sokutei** measure

検定 **kentei** official approval, inspection

裁定 **saitei** decision, ruling, arbitration

13 禅定 **zenjō** meditative concentration

14 算定 **santei** calculate, estimate

認定 **nintei** approval, acknowledgment

15 暫定 **zantei** tentative, provisional

確定 **kakutei** decision, definite

20 議定書 **giteisho, gijōsho** a protocol

23 鑑定 **kantei** appraisal, expert opinion

———— 3 ————

4 不安定 **fuantei** unstable, shaky

———— 4 ————

11 紳士協定 **shinshi kyōtei** gentleman's agreement

3m5.9 / 1984

　　33　30　7

宛　宛宛

EN just like, as if　**a(teru)** address (a letter)　**-ate** addressed to　**sanaga(ra)** just like　**-zutsu** apiece, each

———— 1 ————

6 宛先 **atesaki** address

宛名 **atena** address

3m5.11 / 898

日　宀　大　儿　33　34　16

突　突|突突

TOTSU, tsu(ku) thrust, poke, strike
tsutsu(ku) poke, peck, pick at

———— 1 ————

2 突入 **totsunyū** rush/plunge into

4 突込 **tsu(ki)ko(mu), tsu(k)ko(mu)** thrust/poke/plunge into

5 突出 **tsu(ki)da(su)** thrust/push/stick out　**tsu(ki)de(ru)** jut/stick out, protrude　**tosshutsu** projection, protrusion

6 突如 **totsujo** suddenly, unexpectedly

突当 **tsu(ki)a(taru)** run/bump into; reach the end　**tsu(ki)a(tari)** collision; end (of a street/corridor)

9 突飛 **toppi** wild, fantastic, reckless, eccentric　**tsu(ki)to(basu)** knock down, send flying

突発 **toppatsu** occur suddenly, break out

10 突破 **toppa** break through, overcome　**tsu(ki)yabu(ru)** break/crash through

12 突然 **totsuzen** suddenly, unexpectedly

突然変異 **totsuzen hen'i** mutation

—————— 2 ——————

6 羽突 **hanetsu(ki)** battledore and
   shuttlecock (badminton-like
   game)

7 角突合 **tsunotsu(ki)a(i)** bickering,
   wrangling

8 追突 **tsuitotsu** rear-end collision

13 楯突 **tatetsu(ku)** oppose, defy
   煙突 **entotsu** chimney

15 衝突 **shōtotsu** collision; clash

16 激突 **gekitotsu** crash, collision

3m5.12 / 140

目 宀 工 儿
33 38 16

空 空

KŪ sky; empty **sora** sky **su(ku),
a(ku)** be empty/unoccupied **a(keru)**
empty, leave blank **kara, kara(ppo)**
empty **muna(shii)** empty, vain,
futile **utsu(ro)** hollow, blank
utsuke empty(-headed)

—————— 1 ——————

0 空オケ **karaoke** prerecorded or-
   chestral accompaniment (tape
   and amplification system for
   amateur singers)

4 空中 **kūchū** in the air/sky, aerial
   空手 **karate** empty-handed; karate

5 空母 **kūbo** aircraft carrier (short for
   航空母艦)

   空白 **kūhaku** blank, empty space,
   vacuum

6 空気 **kūki** air, atmosphere; pneumatic

7 空似 **sorani** chance resemblance
   空車 **kūsha, karaguruma** empty
   car, (taxi) For Hire

9 空軍 **kūgun** air force
   空前 **kūzen** unprecedented

10 空涙 **soranamida** crocodile tears
   空家 **a(ki)ya** vacant house
   空席 **kūseki** vacant seat, vacancy

11 空虚 **kūkyo** empty, hollow; inane
   空瓶 **a(ki)bin** empty bottle
   空巣狙 **a(ki)sunera(i)** sneak thief,
   prowler

12 空港 **kūkō** airport

空間 **kūkan** space **a(ki)ma** vacant room

13 空腹 **kūfuku, su(ki)hara** empty
   stomach, hunger

   空想 **kūsō** idle fancy, fiction, daydream

   空路 **kūro** air route; by air/plane

14 空模様 **soramoyō** looks of the sky,
   weather

16 空輸 **kūyu** air transport

20 空欄 **kūran** blank column

22 空襲 **kūshū** air raid/strike

—————— 2 ——————

3 大空 **ōzora, taikū** the sky

5 冬空 **fuyuzora** winter sky

6 防空 **bōkū** air defense

8 夜空 **yozora** night sky
   青空 **aozora** the blue sky
   青空市場 **aozora ichiba** open-air
   market

9 架空 **kakū** overhead, aerial; fanci-
   ful, fictitious
   星空 **hoshizora** starry sky
   秋空 **akizora** autumn sky

10 航空 **kōkū** aviation, flight, aero-
   航空母艦 **kōkū bokan** aircraft carrier

   航空券 **kōkūken** flight/airplane
   ticket

   航空便 **kōkūbin** airmail
   航空路 **kōkūro** air route

11 雪空 **yukizora** snowy sky

12 寒空 **samuzora** wintry sky, cold
   weather

—————— 3 ——————

6 全日空 **Zennikkū** ANA = All Nippon Airways (short for 全日本
   空輸)

—————— 6 ——————

3m6.1 / 2051

日 月 宀 十
42 33 12

宥 宥

YŪ, nada(meru) soothe, placate HI-
ROSHI, YUTAKA (m. given name) **YŪ,
HIRO, SUKE** (part of given name)

⁸ 宥和 **yūwa** appease, placate

3m6.2 / 625

目 日 宀 一
43 33 1

宣   宣宣

SEN announce **no(beru)** state, declare NOBU, NORI (part of given name)

— 1 —

⁶ 宣伝 **senden** propaganda; advertising, publicity

宣伝部 **sendenbu** publicity department

⁷ 宣告 **senkoku** sentence, verdict, pronouncement

宣言 **sengen** declaration, statement

¹⁰ 宣教師 **senkyōshi** missionary

¹³ 宣戦布告 **sensen fukoku** declaration of war

¹⁴ 宣誓 **sensei** oath, vow, pledge

3m6.3 / 641

目 夂 宀 口
49 33 24

客   客客

KYAKU guest, customer, passenger
KAKU guest, customer, passenger; (as prefix) last (year)

— 1 —

⁵ 客用 **kyakuyō** for guests

⁶ 客扱 **kyakuatsuka(i)** hospitality

⁹ 客室 **kyakushitsu** guest room, stateroom

¹⁰ 客席 **kyakuseki** seats for guests

¹¹ 客船 **kyakusen** passenger ship/boat

¹² 客間 **kyakuma** guest room, parlor

¹⁸ 客観的 **kyakkanteki, kakkanteki** objective

— 2 —

⁷ 来客 **raikyaku** visitor, caller

⁸ 泊客 **to(mari)kyaku** overnight guest

⁹ 乗客 **jōkyaku** passenger

¹⁰ 旅客機 **ryokakki** passenger plane

¹¹ 接客業 **sekkyakugyō** hotel and restaurant trade

常客 **jōkyaku** regular customer/visitor

船客 **senkyaku** (ship) passenger

訪客 **hōkyaku, hōkaku** visitor, guest

¹² 棋客 **kikyaku, kikaku** go/shogi player

¹⁵ 賓客 **hinkaku, hinkyaku** honored guest, visitor

¹⁸ 観客 **kankyaku** audience, spectators

— 3 —

⁹ 逗留客 **tōryūkyaku** guest, visitor, sojourner

¹⁰ 観光客 **kankōkyaku** tourist, sightseer

3m6.4 / 166

目 宀 士 竹
33 22 17

室   室室

SHITSU room, chamber **muro** greenhouse; cellar

— 1 —

⁴ 室内 **shitsunai** indoor(s), interior

⁵ 室外 **shitsugai** outdoor(s)

⁷ 室町 **Muromachi** (era, 1338–1573)

¹² 室温 **shitsuon** room temperature

¹⁹ 室蘭 **Muroran** (city, Hokkaidō)

— 2 —

⁸ 和室 **washitsu** Japanese-style room

⁹ 帝室 **teishitsu** the imperial household

洋室 **yōshitsu** Western-style room

茶室 **chashitsu** tea-ceremony room

客室 **kyakushitsu** guest room, stateroom

皇室 **Kōshitsu** the Imperial Household, the reigning line

¹⁰ 浴室 **yokushitsu** bathroom (not toilet)

教室 **kyōshitsu** classroom

病室 **byōshitsu** sickroom, ward, infirmary

11 船室 **senshitsu** cabin, stateroom
12 温室 **onshitsu** hothouse, greenhouse
13 寝室 **shinshitsu** bedroom
   暗室 **anshitsu** darkroom

——————— 3 ———————

6 地下室 **chikashitsu** basement, cellar
7 更衣室 **kōishitsu** clothes-changing room
8 実験室 **jikkenshitsu** laboratory
9 待合室 **machiaishitsu** waiting room
   研究室 **kenkyūshitsu** laboratory, study room
15 閲覧室 **etsuranshitsu** reading room

3m6.5 / 1717   田 宀 儿 十
                     33 16 12

窃   竊｜窃窃

SETSU, nusu(mu) steal **hiso(ka)** secret, stealthy

——————— 1 ———————

8 窃取 **sesshu** steal
11 窃盗 **settō** theft, larceny; thief
   窃盗犯 **settōhan** thief
   窃盗罪 **settōzai** theft, larceny

——————— 2 ———————

13 剽窃 **hyōsetsu** plagiarism, pirating

突 → 突 **3m5.11**

3m6.6   田 宀 艹 儿
              33 32 16

穽   穽穽

SEI pitfall

——————— 7 ———————

3m7.1 / 165   田 宀 犭 匕
                    33 27 10

家   家家

KA house, family; (as suffix) -er, person, profession **KE** house, family; (as suffix) the … family, the house of …
ie house **-ya, ya-** house; shop

——————— 1 ———————

4 家内 **kanai** my wife; family, home
5 家出 **iede** leave home; run away from home
   家主 **yanushi, ienushi** houseowner, landlord
6 家宅 **kataku** house, premises
7 家来 **kerai** vassal, retainer, retinue
   家系図 **kakeizu** family tree
8 家事 **kaji** housework; domestic affairs
   家具 **kagu** furniture, furnishings
9 家庭 **katei** home; family
   家庭教師 **katei kyōshi** (private) tutor
   家屋 **kaoku** house; building
   家柄 **iegara** lineage, parentage; (of) good family
   家政婦 **kaseifu** housekeeper
   家計 **kakei** family finances; livelihood
10 家借 **kashaku** renting a house
   家畜 **kachiku** domestic animals, livestock
   家紋 **kamon** family crest
11 家探 **iesaga(shi)** house hunting
   家族 **kazoku** family
   家族連 **kazokuzu(re)** taking the family along
13 家業 **kagyō** one's trade
   家賃 **yachin** (house) rent
   家電 **kaden** household electrical products/appliances, consumer electronics (short for 家庭用電気製品)
19 家譜 **kafu** a genealogy, family tree

——————— 2 ———————

1 一家 **ikka, ikke** a house/family/household; one's family; a style
3 大家 **taika** mansion; illustrious/wealthy family; past master, authority **taike** illustrious/wealthy family **ōya** landlord; main building
5 民家 **minka** private house

生家 **seika** house of one's birth
史家 **shika** historian
平家 **hiraya** one-story house
Heike the Taira family/clan
6 自家製 **jikasei** homemade, home-brewed
7 作家 **sakka** writer, novelist
売家 **u(ri)ya, u(ri)ie** house for sale
8 画家 **gaka** painter, artist
実家 **jikka** one's parent's home
空家 **a(ki)ya** vacant house
国家 **kokka** state, nation, country
国家主義 **kokka shugi** nationalism
武家 **buke** samurai
10 借家 **shakuya, shakka, ka(ri)ie, ka(ri)ya** rented house, house for rent
書家 **shoka** good penman, calligrapher
12 貸家 **ka(shi)ie, kashiya** house for rent
13 農家 **nōka** farmhouse; farm household; farmer
17 檀家 **danka** family supporting a temple

————— 3 —————
3 小説家 **shōsetsuka** novelist, (fiction) writer
6 企業家 **kigyōka** industrialist, entrepreneur
7 作曲家 **sakkyokuka** composer
芸術家 **geijutsuka** artist
8 建築家 **kenchikuka** architect, building contractor
9 美食家 **bishokuka** epicure, gourmet
政治家 **seijika** politician
音楽家 **ongakka, ongakuka** musician
思想家 **shisōka** thinker
10 倹約家 **ken'yakuka** thrifty person, economizer
恐妻家 **kyōsaika** henpecked husband
11 理想家 **risōka** idealist
12 落語家 **rakugoka** comic storyteller
評論家 **hyōronka** critic, commentator
13 夢想家 **musōka** dreamer, visionary
楽天家 **rakutenka** optimist

詭弁家 **kibenka** sophist, quibbler
16 親日家 **shin-Nichika** Nippophile
篤志家 **tokushika** benefactor, volunteer

————— 4 —————
14 閨秀作家 **keishū sakka** woman writer

3m7.2 / 1488   54 33 12

SAI manage, rule OSAMU, TSUKASA (m. given name)

————— 1 —————
9 宰相 **saishō** prime minister, premier

————— 2 —————
5 主宰者 **shusaisha** president, chairman

3m7.3 / 640   43 33 25

EN feast, banquet **utage** party, banquet

————— 1 —————
6 宴会 **enkai** banquet, dinner party

————— 2 —————
9 祝宴 **shukuen** congratulatory banquet, feast
10 酒宴 **shuen** banquet, feast

————— 3 —————
8 披露宴 **hirōen** (wedding) reception

3m7.4 / 518   33 22 24

GAI damage, harm, injury

1

⁶ 害虫 **gaichū** harmful insect, pest

¹¹ 害悪 **gaiaku** an evil (influence), harm

2

⁴ 公害 **kōgai** pollution

水害 **suigai** flood damage, flooding

⁵ 加害者 **kagaisha** assailant, perpetrator

⁶ 危害 **kigai** injury, harm

有害 **yūgai** harmful, noxious, injurious

虫害 **chūgai** damage from insects

⁷ 阻害 **sogai** impede, check, hinder, retard

迫害 **hakugai** persecution

妨害 **bōgai** obstruction, disturbance, interference

旱害 **kangai** drought damage

災害 **saigai** disaster, accident

利害 **rigai** advantages and disadvantages, interests

利害関係 **rigai kankei** interests

⁹ 侵害 **shingai** infringement, violation

¹⁰ 殺害 **satsugai** murder

被害 **higai** damage, harm, injury

被害者 **higaisha** victim

¹² 寒害 **kangai** damage from cold/frost

無害 **mugai** harmless

¹³ 傷害 **shōgai** injury, bodily harm

障害 **shōgai** obstacle, hindrance, impediment, handicap

障害物 **shōgaibutsu** obstacle, obstruction

損害 **songai** damage, injury, loss

雹害 **hyōgai** hail damage

¹⁵ 弊害 **heigai** an evil, ill effects

震害 **shingai** earthquake damage

¹⁷ 霜害 **sōgai** frost damage

4

⁷ 身体障害者 **shintai shōgaisha** physically handicapped person

---

33 24 2

KYŪ, GŪ, KU, miya palace; prince, princess

1

³ 宮下 **Miyashita** (surname)

⁴ 宮内 **Miyauchi** (surname)

宮内庁 **Kunaichō** Imperial Household Agency

⁵ 宮本 **Miyamoto** (surname)

宮田 **Miyata** (surname)

⁶ 宮廷 **kyūtei** the court/place

⁸ 宮参 **miyamai(ri)** visit to a shrine

⁹ 宮城県 **Miyagi-ken** (prefecture)

¹¹ 宮崎 **Miyazaki** (city, Miyazaki-ken); (surname)

宮崎県 **Miyazaki-ken** (prefecture)

¹³ 宮殿 **kyūden** palace

¹⁴ 宮様 **miyasama** prince, princess

2

¹ 一宮 **Ichinomiya** (city, Aichi-ken)

² 子宮 **shikyū** the uterus, womb

³ 小宮 **Komiya** (surname)

⁸ 迷宮 **meikyū** maze, labyrinth

⁹ 神宮 **jingū** Shinto shrine; the Ise Shrines

¹⁸ 離宮 **rikyū** detached palace

3

² 八幡宮 **Hachimangū** shrine of the god of war

³ 大神宮 **Daijingū** the Grand Shrine (at Ise)

⁶ 宇都宮 **Utsunomiya** (city, Tochigi-ken)

4

⁸ 明治神宮 **Meiji Jingū** Meiji Shrine

5

⁶ 伊勢大神宮 **Ise Daijingū** the Grand Shrines of Ise

3m7.6 / 106

日 木 宀 女
41 33 25

案

AN plan, proposal

――――――― 1 ―――――――

0 案じる/ずる **an(jiru/zuru)** worry,
    be anxious; ponder
4 案内 **annai** guidance, information
    案内図 **annaizu** information map
    案内所 **annaijo** information office/
    booth
5 案外 **angai** unexpectedly

――――――― 2 ―――――――

4 方案 **hōan** plan
6 再案 **saian** revised plan/draft
    考案 **kōan** idea, conception; plan,
    project; design, contrivance
    名案 **meian** splendid idea, good
    plan
7 良案 **ryōan** good idea
    妙案 **myōan** good idea, ingenious
    plan
    図案 **zuan** (ornamental) design, de-
    vice
    私案 **shian** one's own plan
8 法案 **hōan** (legislative) bill, measure
9 発案 **hatsuan** proposal
    草案 **sōan** (rough) draft
    思案 **shian** thought, consideration,
    mulling over; plan
10 原案 **gen'an** original proposal, draft
    教案 **kyōan** teaching/lesson plan
12 提案 **teian** proposition, proposal
13 試案 **shian** draft, tentative plan

――――――― 3 ―――――――

4 水先案内 **mizusaki annai** pilot;
    piloting

3m7.7 / 1854

目 月 宀 小
42 33 35

宵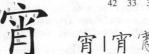

SHŌ, yoi evening, early night hours

――――――― 1 ―――――――

3 宵口 **yoi (no) kuchi** early evening
11 宵祭(り) **yoimatsu(ri)** eve (of a festi-
    val), vigil

3m7.8 / 654

日 火 宀 口
44 33 24

容

YŌ form, appearance; content; put/let
in **i(reru)** put/let in, admit, accept;
permit **YASU** (part of given name)

――――――― 1 ―――――――

8 容易 **yōi** easy, simple
11 容赦 **yōsha** mercy, pardon, forgive-
    ness
12 容量 **yōryō** capacity, volume; ca-
    pacitance
14 容疑 **yōgi** suspicion
    容疑者 **yōgisha** a suspect
    容貌 **yōbō** looks, personal appear-
    ance
    容態 **yōdai** (patient's) condition
15 容器 **yōki** container

――――――― 2 ―――――――

4 内容 **naiyō** content(s), substance
    収容 **shūyō** accommodate, admit,
    receive
    収容所 **shūyōjo** home, asylum,
    camp
5 包容 **hōyō** comprehend, embrace,
    imply; tolerate
7 形容 **keiyō** form, appearance; de-
    scribe, qualify, modify; figure
    of speech
    形容動詞 **keiyōdōshi** quasi-adjec-
    tive used with -na (e.g., shi-
    zuka, kirei)
    形容詞 **keiyōshi** adjective
9 変容 **hen'yō** changed appearance
    美容 **biyō** beauty culture
    美容院 **biyōin** beauty parlor, hair-
    dresser's
10 従容 **shōyō** calm, composed, serene
11 許容 **kyoyō** permission, tolerance
13 寛容 **kan'yō** magnanimity, gener-
    osity, forbearance

¹⁴ 認容 **nin'yō** admit, accept

3m7.10

日 宀 儿 干
33 16 14

穿 穿

SEN, uga(tsu) dig, drill, bore, pierce, penetrate; be incisive/apt/astute **hojiku(ru), hoji(ru)** dig up; pick (one's nose); examine closely **ha(ku)** wear, put on (shoes/pants)

───── 1 ─────

³ 穿孔 **senkō** perforation; punching, boring

3m7.11

日 宀 儿 宀
33 16 15

窄 窄

SAKU narrow **subo(mu/maru), tsubo(maru)** become narrow(er) **subo(meru), tsubo(meru)** make narrow(er), shrug (one's shoulders), purse (one's lips)

───── 8 ─────

3m8.2 / 1669

日 宀 小 上
33 35 13

寂 寂

JAKU, SEKI, sabi(shii) lonely **sabi(reru)** decline in prosperity **sabi** elegant simplicity

───── 1 ─────

¹² 寂然 **sekizen, jakunen** lonesome, desolate
¹³ 寂滅 **jakumetsu** Nirvana, death, annihilation

───── 2 ─────

⁴ 心寂 **kokorosabi(shii)** lonely, lonesome
¹⁴ 静寂 **seijaku** silent, still, quiet

3m8.3 / 179

曰 日 宀 亻
43 33 3

宿 宿

SHUKU, yado lodging, inn **yado(ru)** take shelter; be pregnant **yado(ri)** (taking) shelter **yado(su)** give shelter; conceive (a child)

───── 1 ─────

⁸ 宿舎 **shukusha** lodgings, quarters, billet
宿命 **shukumei** fate, destiny
宿泊 **shukuhaku** lodging
⁹ 宿屋 **yadoya** inn
¹¹ 宿望 **shukubō** long-cherished desire
¹³ 宿賃 **yadochin** hotel charges
¹⁸ 宿題 **shukudai** homework

───── 2 ─────

³ 下宿 **geshuku** lodging, room and board; boarding house
⁶ 合宿 **gasshuku** lodging together
¹¹ 寄宿 **kishuku** lodging, board

3m8.4 / 2052

曰 日 宀 干
43 33 14

寅 寅

IN, tora third horary sign (tiger) IN, I, TORA, NOBU, TAKA, TOMO, TSURA, FUSA (part of given name)

3m8.5 / 806

曰 心 宀 山
51 33 36

密 密

MITSU close, dense, crowded; minute, fine; secret; (as suffix) (water)-tight **hiso(ka)** secret, private, stealthy

───── 1 ─────

² 密入国 **mitsunyūkoku** smuggle oneself into a country

6 密会 **mikkai** clandestine meeting

7 密告 **mikkoku** secret information

密売 **mitsubai** illicit sale, smuggling, bootlegging

8 密林 **mitsurin** jungle, dense forest

9 密封 **mippū** seal tight/up/hermetically

密度 **mitsudo** density

10 密教 **mikkyō** esoteric Buddhism; religious mysteries

密航者 **mikkōsha** stowaway

11 密接 **missetsu** close, intimate

密猟 **mitsuryō** poaching

12 密着 **mitchaku** adhere to, stick fast

16 密輸 **mitsuyu** smuggling; contraband

密輸品 **mitsuyuhin** contraband

———————— 2 ————————

4 内密 **naimitsu** private, secret, confidential

水密 **suimitsu** watertight

10 秘密 **himitsu** a secret, confidential

11 細密 **saimitsu** minute, close, miniature

14 綿密 **menmitsu** minute, close, meticulous

精密 **seimitsu** precision

15 緊密 **kinmitsu** close, tight

16 機密 **kimitsu** secret, secrecy

緻密 **chimitsu** fine, close, minute, exact

17 厳密 **genmitsu** strict, precise

3m8.7 / 698

目 心 宀 儿
51 33 16

SŌ, mado window

———————— 1 ————————

3 窓口 **madoguchi** (ticket) window

———————— 2 ————————

6 同窓会 **dōsōkai** alumni association/meeting

7 車窓 **shasō** car/train window

3m8.8 / 1361

目 宀 大 口
33 34 24

寄寄

KI depend on; give; call at **yo(ru)** approach, draw near; meet; drop in **yo(seru)** bring near; push aside; gather together; send YORI (part of given name)

———————— 1 ————————

5 寄付 **kifu** contribution, donation
yo(se)tsu(keru) let come near **yo(ri)tsu(ku)** come near; open (the day's trading)

10 寄席 **yose** variety-show hall

11 寄道 **yo(ri)michi** stop in on one's way

寄宿 **kishuku** lodging, board

18 寄贈 **kizō** donate, present

———————— 2 ————————

4 片寄 **katayo(ru)** lean to one side; be biased

引寄 **hi(ki)yo(seru)** draw near/toward; attract

5 立寄 **ta(chi)yo(ru)** drop in on, stop at

6 年寄 **toshiyo(ri)** old person

近寄 **chikayo(ru)** go/come near, approach

14 駆寄 **ka(ke)yo(ru)** rush up to

15 皺寄 **shiwayo(se)** shifting the burden) to

23 躙寄 **niji(ri)yo(ru)** edge/crawl/sidle up to

3m8.9 / 1716

目 宀 土 儿
33 22 16

CHITSU plug up, obstruct; nitrogen

———————— 1 ————————

6 窒死 **chisshi** death from suffocation/asphyxiation

10 窒息 **chissoku** suffocation, asphyxiation

——— 9 ———

3m9.1

日 日 宀 竹
43 33 17

寓寓

GŪ temporary abode; imply

——— 1 ———

13 寓意 **gūi** allegory, moral

寓話 **gūwa** fable, parable, allegory

3m9.3 / 457

目 宀 艹 二
33 32 4

寒│寒寒

KAN cold; midwinter **samu(i)** cold, chilly

——— 1 ———

4 寒天 **kanten** agar-agar, gelatin; cold weather, wintry sky

寒水 **kansui** cold water

6 寒気 **kanki, samuke** the cold

7 寒冷 **kanrei** cold, chilly

寒冷前線 **kanrei zensen** cold front

8 寒波 **kanpa** cold wave

寒空 **samuzora** wintry sky, cold weather

9 寒風 **kanpū** cold wind

10 寒流 **kanryū** cold current

寒帯 **kantai** frigid zone

寒害 **kangai** damage from cold/ frost

——— 2 ———

6 防寒 **bōkan** protection against the cold

肌寒 **hadazamu(i), hadasamu(i)** chilly

7 亜寒帯 **akantai** subarctic zone

3m9.5 / 713

目 田 宀 口
58 33 24

富│富富

FU, FŪ, to(mu) be/become rich, abound in **tomi** wealth **TO** (part of given name)

——— 1 ———

3 富山 **Tomiyama, Toyama** (surname)

富山県 **Toyama-ken** (prefecture)

富士山 **Fuji-san** Mt. Fuji

5 富永 **Tominaga** (surname)

富田 **Tomita** (surname)

9 富美子 **Fumiko, Tomiko** (f. given name)

12 富裕 **fuyū** wealthy, affluent

——— 2 ———

8 国富 **kokufu** national wealth

11 貧富 **hinpu** rich and poor, wealth and poverty

13 豊富 **hōfu** abundant, affluent

 窗 → 窓 3m8.7

——— 10 ———

3m10.1 / 1079

田 宀 ヨ 冫
33 39 5

寝│寝寝

SHIN, ne(ru) go to bed, sleep **ne** sleep **ne(kasu)** put to bed

——— 1 ———

4 寝不足 **nebusoku** lack of sleep

寝込 **neko(mu)** fall asleep; oversleep; be sick in bed

5 寝台 **shindai** bed

7 寝床 **nedoko** bed

8 寝具 **shingu** bedding

9 寝室 **shinshitsu** bedroom

11 寝惚 **nebo(keru)** be half asleep

寝袋 **nebukuro** sleeping bag

—— 2 ——

6 早寝 **hayane** retiring early

9 昼寝 **hirune** nap, siesta

2 就寝 **shūshin** go to bed, retire

朝寝坊 **asanebō** late riser

3m10.2

目 宀 艹 土
33 32 22

SOKU, SAI, fusa(gu) stop/plug up, close off, block, obstruct, fill **fusa(garu)** be closed/blocked/clogged/filled **se(ku)** dam up; check, stop, stem

—— 1 ——

10 塞栓 **sokusen** an embolism

—— 2 ——

11 梗塞 **kōsoku** stoppage; (monetary) stringency; infarction

閉塞 **heisoku** blockade; obstruction

3m10.3 / 1050

目 貝 宀 艹
68 33 32

KAN magnanimity, leniency, generosity **kutsuro(gu)** relax, feel at home **kutsuro(geru)** loosen, relax
HIROSHI, YUTAKA (m. given name)
HIRO (part of given name)

—— 1 ——

3 寛大 **kandai** magnanimous, tolerant, lenient

10 寛容 **kan'yō** magnanimity, generosity, forbearance

3m10.6

目 宀 尸 山
33 40 36

KUTSU, iwaya cave, den

—— 2 ——

9 洞窟 **dōkutsu** cave, cavern

—————— 11 ——————

3m11.2 / 1851

目 月 宀 一
42 33 14

KA few, small; alone, widowed

—— 1 ——

11 寡婦 **kafu, yamome** widow

15 寡黙 **kamoku** taciturn, reticent

3m11.6 / 619

目 礻 宀 夕
45 33 30

SATSU infer, see

—— 1 ——

0 察する **sas(suru)** surmise, judge; understand; sympathize with

8 察知 **satchi** infer, gather, sense

—— 2 ——

5 巡察 **junsatsu** patrol, one's rounds

6 考察 **kōsatsu** consideration, examination, study

8 拝察 **haisatsu** infer, guess, gather

明察 **meisatsu** discernment, insight

9 洞察 **dōsatsu, tōsatsu** insight, discernment

11 偵察 **teisatsu** reconnaissance

推察 **suisatsu** guess, conjecture, surmise

視察 **shisatsu** inspection, observance

12 検察 **kensatsu** investigation and prosecution

診察 **shinsatsu** medical examination

15 監察 **kansatsu** inspection; inspector, supervisor

18 観察 **kansatsu** observe, view

19 警察 **keisatsu** police

氵 土
扌 口
女 巾
犭 弓
彳 纟
艹
宀 11
丷
吉
广 尸
口

警察庁 **Keisatsuchō** National Police Agency

警察官 **keisatsukan** police officer

3m11.7

目 虫 心 宀
64 51 33

MITSU honey; nectar, molasses

――――― 1 ―――――

9 蜜柑 **mikan** mandarin orange, tangerine

13 蜜蜂 **mitsubachi** honeybee

――――― 2 ―――――

13 蜂蜜 **hachimitsu** honey

3m11.8 / 1412

目 目 心 宀
55 51 33

NEI peaceful, quiet **mushi(ro)** rather, preferably YASUSHI (m. given name)

――――― 2 ―――――

2 丁寧 **teinei** polite, courteous; careful, meticulous

6 安寧秩序 **annei-chitsujo** peace and order

賓 → 賓 3m12.3

實 → 実 3m5.4

寢 → 寝 3m10.1

3m11.9

田 宀 氵 土
33 21 22

WA, A, kubo(mu) cave in, sink, become hollow **kubo(mi)** hollow, dent **kubo** depression, hollow

――――― 1 ―――――

5 窪田 **Kubota** (surname)

6 窪地 **kubochi** low ground, hollow, depression

寬 → 寛 3m10.3

――――― 12 ―――――

3m12.1 / 1383

目 米 田 宀
62 58 33

SHIN hearing, investigation, trial **tsumabi(raka)** fully known, in detail

――――― 1 ―――――

7 審判 **shinpan, shinban** decision, judgment, refereeing

審判官 **shinpankan** judge, umpire, referee

9 審査 **shinsa** examination, investigation

11 審問 **shinmon** trial, hearing, inquiry

20 審議会 **shingikai** deliberative assembly, commission, council

――――― 2 ―――――

1 一審 **isshin** first instance/trial

4 不審 **fushin** dubious, suspicious; strange

10 陪審 **baishin** jury

11 終審 **shūshin** final trial, last instance

14 誤審 **goshin** error in refereeing

3m12.2 / 1323

目 火 日 宀
44 43 33

RYŌ dormitory, hostel

――――― 1 ―――――

8 寮長 **ryōchō** dormitory director

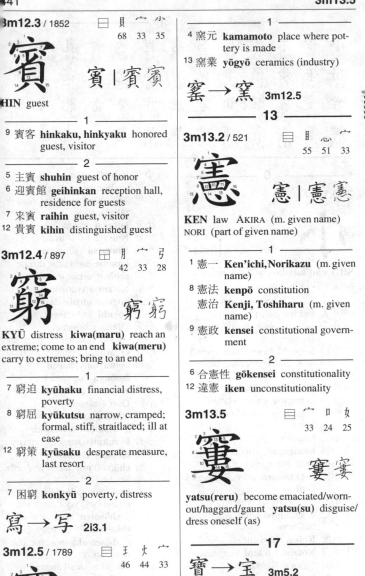

3m12.3 / 1852   日 貝 宀 小   68 33 35

賓 | 賓 賓

HIN guest

— 1 —

9 賓客 **hinkaku, hinkyaku** honored guest, visitor

— 2 —

5 主賓 **shuhin** guest of honor
6 迎賓館 **geihinkan** reception hall, residence for guests
7 来賓 **raihin** guest, visitor
12 貴賓 **kihin** distinguished guest

3m12.4 / 897   田 月 宀 弓   42 33 28

窮 窮

KYŪ distress **kiwa(maru)** reach an extreme; come to an end **kiwa(meru)** carry to extremes; bring to an end

— 1 —

7 窮迫 **kyūhaku** financial distress, poverty
8 窮屈 **kyūkutsu** narrow, cramped; formal, stiff, straitlaced; ill at ease
12 窮策 **kyūsaku** desperate measure, last resort

— 2 —

7 困窮 **konkyū** poverty, distress

寫 → 写 **2i3.1**

3m12.5 / 1789   田 王 火 宀   46 44 33

窯 | 窯 窯

YŌ, kama kiln

4 窯元 **kamamoto** place where pottery is made
13 窯業 **yōgyō** ceramics (industry)

窰 → 窯 **3m12.5**

— 13 —

3m13.2 / 521   目 目 心 宀   55 51 33

憲 | 憲 憲

KEN law **AKIRA** (m. given name) **NORI** (part of given name)

— 1 —

1 憲一 **Ken'ichi, Norikazu** (m. given name)
8 憲法 **kenpō** constitution
憲治 **Kenji, Toshiharu** (m. given name)
9 憲政 **kensei** constitutional government

— 2 —

6 合憲性 **gōkensei** constitutionality
12 違憲 **iken** unconstitutionality

3m13.5   目 宀 口 女   33 24 25

嫠 嫠

yatsu(reru) become emaciated/worn-out/haggard/gaunt **yatsu(su)** disguise/dress oneself (as)

— 17 —

寶 → 宝 **3m5.2**

— 19 —

竊 → 窃 **3m6.5**

3n

小	少	尔	尖	光	当	劣	肖	学	労	乳	币	尚
0.1	1.1	0a14.3	3.1	3.2	3.3	3.4	4.1	4.2	4.3	4.4	0a13.1	5.2

峃	争	歩	栄	単	県	省	拳	党	将	雀	巣	蛍
5f5.4	2n4.2	5.3	6.1	6.2	6.3	5c4.7	7.1	7.2	2b8.3	8c3.2	8.1	8.2

常	堂	雀	営	覚	掌	就	嘗	誉	當	亂	舜	奨
8.3	8.4	8c3.2	9.2	9.3	9.4	3d9.21	3n11.1	10.1	3n3.3	3d4.21	10.2	10.4

孵	嘗	裳	賞	輝	鴬	静	厳	黨
10.5	11.1	11.2	12.1	7c8.8	11b10.9	4b10.9	14.1	3n7.2

0

3n0.1 / 27

□ 小
35

小

小 小

SHŌ, chii(sai), ko-, o- little, small
SA (part of given name)

1

² 小人 **kobito** dwarf, midget
³ 小川 **ogawa** brook, creek **Ogawa** (surname)
　小口 **koguchi** in small lots, small sum; end, edge; clue; beginning
　小山 **Koyama** (surname)
⁴ 小切手 **kogitte** check, cheque
　小文字 **komoji** small/lowercase letters
　小犬 **koinu** puppy
⁵ 小包 **kozutsumi** parcel, package
　小田 **Oda** (surname)
　小田原 **Odawara** (city, Kanagawa-ken)
⁶ 小西 **Konishi** (surname)
　小企業 **shōkigyō** small enterprises/business
　小池 **Koike** (surname)
⁷ 小谷 **Kotani, Kodani** (surname)
　小沢 **Ozawa** (surname)
　小坂 **Kosaka** (surname)
　小豆 **azuki** adzuki beans
　小形 **kogata** small-size
　小学校 **shōgakkō** elementary school

　小売 **kou(ri)** retail
　小児科 **shōnika** pediatrics
　小児麻痺 **shōni mahi** infantile paralysis, polio
　小麦 **komugi** wheat
⁸ 小林 **Kobayashi** (surname)
　小松 **Komatsu** (surname)
　小雨 **kosame** light rain, drizzle
⁹ 小便 **shōben** urine, urination
　小泉 **Koizumi** (surname)
　小型 **kogata** small-size
　小指 **koyubi** little finger
　小畑 **Obata** (surname)
　小計 **shōkei** subtotal
¹⁰ 小倉 **Ogura** (surname)
　小唄 **kouta** ditty, ballad
　小宮 **Komiya** (surname)
　小島 **Kojima** (surname)
¹¹ 小野 **Ono** (surname)
　小猫 **koneko** kitten
　小規模 **shōkibo** small-scale
¹² 小遣 **kozuka(i)** spending money
　小森 **Komori** (surname)
　小順 **chii(sai) jun** increasing order, smallest first
¹³ 小僧 **kozō** young Buddhist priest; errand boy; youngster, kid
　小数点 **shōsūten** decimal point
¹⁴ 小説 **shōsetsu** novel, story, fiction
　小説家 **shōsetsuka** novelist, (fiction) writer
¹⁸ 小額 **shōgaku** small amount

2

³ 大小 **daishō** large and/or small size; (relative) size; long sword and short sword **dai(nari) shō(nari)** more or less

⁴ 中小企業 **chūshō kigyō** small business(es)

犬小屋 **inugoya** doghouse, kennel

⁷ 私小説 **watakushi shōsetsu** novel narrated in the first person; autobiographical novel
shishōsetsu autobiographical novel

¹ 袋小路 **fukurokōji** blind alley, cul-de-sac

² 最小 **saishō** smallest, minimum

⁷ 縮小 **shukushō** reduction, cut

——————— 3 ———————

¹ 推理小説 **suiri shōsetsu** detective story, whodunit

¹² 短篇小説 **tanpen shōsetsu** short story/novel

——————— 1 ———————

3n1.1 / 144   ⊡ 小 丨
                 35   2

少   少 少

SHŌ, suko(shi) a little, a few
suku(nai) little, few

——————— 1 ———————

³ 少々 **shōshō** a little, a few, slightly

少女 **shōjo** girl

⁶ 少年 **shōnen** boy

¹² 少量 **shōryō** small quantity/dose

¹³ 少数 **shōsū** few; minority

——————— 2 ———————

⁷ 希少 **kishō** scarce

⁸ 青少年 **seishōnen** young people, the young

¹² 減少 **genshō** decrease, reduction, decline

最少 **saishō** fewest; youngest

——————— 2 ———————

尓 → 爾   **0a14.3**

——————— 3 ———————

3n3.1   ⊡ 小 大
                    35   34

尖   尖 尖

SEN, toga(ru), tonga(ru) be pointed/sharp; be displeased **toga(rasu)** make pointed, sharpen

——————— 1 ———————

¹⁴ 尖端 **sentan** pointed tip; spearhead, leading edge, latest (technology)

¹⁵ 尖鋭 **sen'ei** acute; radical

3n3.2 / 138   ⊡ 小 一 丨
                  35   14   2

光   光 光

KŌ, hikari light **hika(ru)** shine
HIKARU, AKIRA (m. given name)
TERU, MITSU (part of given name)

——————— 1 ———————

⁰ 光ファイバー **hikari faibā** optical fiber

⁴ 光化学スモッグ **kōkagaku sumoggu** photochemical smog

⁶ 光年 **kōnen** light-year

光合成 **kōgōsei** photosynthesis

⁷ 光沢 **kōtaku** luster, gloss, polish

⁸ 光治 **Kōji, Mitsuji, Mitsuharu** (m. given name)

⁹ 光栄 **kōei** honor, glory, privilege

¹⁵ 光熱費 **kōnetsuhi** heating and electricity expenses

——————— 2 ———————

⁴ 月光 **gekkō** moonlight

日光 **nikkō** sunshine, sunlight
Nikkō (town in Tochigi-ken)

日光浴 **nikkōyoku** sunbath

⁵ 白光 **hakkō** white light; corona

⁶ 灯光 **tōkō** light, lamplight, flashlight

⁹ 栄光 **eikō** glory

¹⁰ 閃光 **senkō** flash

¹¹ 蛍光灯 **keikōtō** fluorescent lamp

¹⁴ 稲光 **inabikari** lightning

¹⁸ 観光 **kankō** sightseeing

観光客 **kankōkyaku** tourist, sight-seer

—————— 3 ——————

¹² 御来光 **goraikō** sunrise viewed from a mountaintop

3n3.3 / 77

日 小 ヨ
35 39

當 | 当 当

TŌ (as prefix) this, the said, that
a(taru) hit, be on target; correspond to
a(tari) a hit/success; (as suffix) per
a(teru) hit the mark; guess at; apply, put, place; allocate **a(te)** aim, goal; expectations; reliance, trustworthiness
masa (ni) properly, just; indeed, truly; just about to, on the verge of

—————— 1 ——————

² 当人 **tōnin** the one concerned, the said person, the person himself

⁴ 当分 **tōbun** for now, for a while

当方 **tōhō** I, we, on our part/side

⁵ 当外 **a(tari)hazu(re)** hit or miss, risk **a(te)hazu(re)** a disappointment

当用漢字 **Tōyō Kanji** (official list of 1,850 kanji recommended for general use; superseded by the 1,945 Jōyō Kanji)

当字 **a(te)ji** kanji used phonetically; kanji used purely ideographically, disregarding usual readings

⁷ 当局 **tōkyoku** the authorities

当社 **tōsha** this/our company; this shrine

¹² 当然 **tōzen** of course, naturally

当惑 **tōwaku** be perplexed/nonplussed, be at a loss

当番 **tōban** being on duty

¹⁴ 当選 **tōsen** be elected/selected, win

²³ 当籤 **tōsen** win (a lottery)

—————— 2 ——————

³ 大当 **ōa(tari)** big hit, great success; (make) a killing; bumper crop

⁴ 不当 **futō** improper, unfair, wrongful **fua(tari)** unpopularity, failure

手当 **tea(te)** (medical) treatment, care; allowance, (fringe) benefit

日当 **hia(tari)** exposure to the sun; sunny place **nittō** per-diem allowance, daily wages

⁵ 本当 **hontō** true, real

失当 **shittō** improper, unfair, wrongful

弁当 **bentō** (box) lunch

正当 **seitō** proper, just, justifiable, right, fair, reasonable, legitimate

⁷ 対当 **taitō** corresponding, equivalent

妥当 **datō** proper, appropriate

見当 **miata(ru)** be found, turn up **kentō** aim, mark, guess, estimate, hunch; direction; approximately

見当違 **kentōchiga(i)** wrong guess

⁸ 抵当 **teitō** mortgage, hypothec

抵当物 **teitōbutsu** security, pawn, collateral

担当 **tantō** being in charge, overseeing

担当者 **tantōsha** the one in charge

突当 **tsu(ki)a(taru)** run/bump into; reach the end **tsu(ki)a(tari)** collision; end (of a street/corridor)

⁹ 相当 **sōtō** suitable, appropriate; considerable; be equivalent to, correspond to

¹⁰ 差当 **sa(shi)a(tari)** for the time being

配当 **haitō** allotment, share, dividend

¹¹ 陽当 **hia(tari)** exposure to the sun

勘当 **kandō** disinheritance

¹² 割当 **wa(ri)a(teru)** allocate, allot, divide/distribute among

場当 **baa(tari)** grandstanding, applause-seeking

¹³ 適当 **tekitō** suitable, adequate

該当 **gaitō** pertain to, come/fall under

該当者 **gaitōsha** the said person

14 罰当 **bachia(tari)** damned, cursed

16 穏当 **ontō** proper, reasonable, moderate

――― 3 ―――

1 一人当 **hitoria(tari)** per person/capita

13 蛸配当 **takohaitō** bogus dividends

3n3.4 / 1150

　　　　　　　　35　8　2

劣劣

RETSU, oto(ru) be inferior to

――― 1 ―――

12 劣等 **rettō** inferiority

劣等感 **rettōkan** inferiority complex

――― 2 ―――

8 陋劣 **rōretsu** mean, base, low, nasty, sneaky

9 卑劣 **hiretsu** mean, contemptible, sneaking

13 愚劣 **guretsu** stupid, foolish

17 優劣 **yūretsu** superiority or inferiority, relative merits **masa(ru tomo) oto(ranai)** in no way inferior to, at least so good as

――― 4 ―――

3n4.1 / 844

　　　　　　　　42　35

肖肖

SHŌ resemble **ayaka(ru)** be similarly lucky

――― 1 ―――

14 肖像 **shōzō** portrait

3n4.2 / 109

　目　小　冂　子

　　　　　　　　35　20　6

學｜学学

GAKU learning, study, science; (as suffix) -ology **mana(bu)** learn, study
SATORU (m. given name)

――― 1 ―――

2 学力 **gakuryoku** scholastic ability, scholarship

3 学士 **gakushi** Bachelor of Arts, university graduate

4 学友 **gakuyū** schoolmate, alumnus

5 学生 **gakusei** student

6 学年 **gakunen** school year, grade in school

学会 **gakkai** academic society

学名 **gakumei** scientific name

7 学位 **gakui** academic degree

8 学長 **gakuchō** dean, rector

学者 **gakusha** scholar

9 学院 **gakuin** academy

学界 **gakkai** academic/scientific world

学級 **gakkyū** school class, grade

10 学修 **gakushū** learning, study

学部 **gakubu** academic department, faculty

学校 **gakkō** school

11 学術 **gakujutsu** science, learning

学術用語 **gakujutsu yōgo** technical term

学問 **gakumon** learning, scholarship, education, science

12 学期 **gakki** school term, semester

13 学園 **gakuen** academy; campus

14 学歴 **gakureki** one's academic background

学閥 **gakubatsu** clique of graduates from the same school, old boy network

15 学課 **gakka** lessons, schoolwork

17 学績 **gakuseki** student's record

――― 2 ―――

2 入学 **nyūgaku** admission into school, matriculation

3

氵土扌口女巾犭弓彳彡艹宀屮吉广尸口

4

入学試験 **nyūgaku shiken** entrance exams

力学 **rikigaku** dynamics, mechanics

3 工学 **kōgaku** engineering

工学士 **kōgakushi** Bachelor of Engineering

工学者 **kōgakusha** engineer

大学 **daigaku** university, college

大学院 **daigakuin** graduate school

小学校 **shōgakkō** elementary school

4 中学生 **chūgakusei** junior-high-school student

中学校 **chūgakkō** junior high school

化学 **kagaku** chemistry (sometimes pronounced *bakegaku* to avoid confusion with 科学, science)

文学 **bungaku** literature

文学士 **bungakushi** Bachelor of Arts

6 休学 **kyūgaku** absence from school

在学 **zaigaku** (enrolled) in school

共学 **kyōgaku** coeducation

7 医学 **igaku** medicine, medical science

見学 **kengaku** study by observation, tour (a factory)

私学 **shigaku** private school

8 盲学校 **mōgakkō** school for the blind

退学 **taigaku** leave school, drop out

法学 **hōgaku** law, jurisprudence

国学者 **kokugakusha** Japanese-classics scholar

9 美学 **bigaku** esthetics

通学 **tsūgaku** attending school

独学 **dokugaku** self-study

神学 **shingaku** theology

研学 **kengaku** study

科学 **kagaku** science

科学的 **kagakuteki** scientific

科学者 **kagakusha** scientist

10 修学 **shūgaku** learning

修学旅行 **shūgaku ryokō** school excursion, field trip

勉学 **bengaku** study

進学 **shingaku** entrance to a higher school

哲学 **tetsugaku** philosophy

留学 **ryūgaku** studying abroad

留学生 **ryūgakusei** student studying abroad

11 理学 **rigaku** physical sciences, science

12 博学 **hakugaku** broad knowledge, erudition

無学 **mugaku** unlettered, ignorant

13 農学 **nōgaku** (the science of) agriculture

奨学生 **shōgakusei** student on a scholarship

奨学金 **shōgakukin** a scholarship

数学 **sūgaku** mathematics

14 碩学 **sekigaku** erudition; great scholar

語学 **gogaku** language learning; linguistics

雑学 **zatsugaku** knowledge of various subjects

16 儒学 **jugaku** Confucianism

薬学 **yakugaku** pharmacology

篤学 **tokugaku** love of learning

19 蘭学 **Rangaku** study of the Dutch language and Western learning

———— 3 ————

2 人類学 **jinruigaku** anthropology

3 山林学 **sanringaku** forestry

4 天文学 **tenmongaku** astronomy

日本学 **nihongaku** Japanology

心理学 **shinrigaku** psychology

5 生態学 **seitaigaku** ecology

6 朱子学 **Shushigaku** Neo-Confucianism

考古学 **kōkogaku** archeology (cf. 考現学)

地政学 **chiseigaku** geopolitics

光化学スモッグ **kōkagaku sumoggu** photochemical smog

7 社会学 **shakaigaku** sociology

言語学 **gengogaku** linguistics, philology

8 非科学的 **hikagakuteki** unscientific

法理学 **hōrigaku** jurisprudence

英文学 **eibungaku** English literature

国文学 **kokubungaku** Japanese literature

物理学 **butsurigaku** physics

9 政治学 **seijigaku** political science

政経学 **seikeigaku** politics and economics

10 修辞学 **shūjigaku** rhetoric

病理学 **byōrigaku** pathology

純文学 **junbungaku** pure literature, belles lettres

11 経済学 **keizaigaku** economics

12 幾何学 **kikagaku** geometry

—————— 4 ——————

5 古生物学 **koseibutsugaku** palcontology

6 自然科学 **shizen kagaku** the natural sciences

14 総合大学 **sōgō daigaku** university

3n4.3 / 233 　　　目 小 冖 力
　　　　　　　　　　35 20 8

労 労 | 労 劳

RŌ labor, toil **itawa(ru)** sympathize with, be kind to, take good care of **negira(u)** thank for, show appreciation, reward

—————— 1 ——————

8 労使 **rōshi** labor and management

11 労組 **rōso, rōkumi** labor union (short for 労働組合)

13 労働 **rōdō** labor, work, toil

労働者 **rōdōsha** worker, laborer

労働省 **Rōdōshō** Ministry of Labor

労資 **rōshi** labor(ers) and capital(ists)

—————— 2 ——————

5 功労 **kōrō** meritorious service

8 苦労 **kurō** trouble, hardships, adversity

9 重労働 **jūrōdō** heavy/hard labor

10 徒労 **torō** wasted effort

疲労 **hirō** fatigue

11 過労 **karō** overwork

過労死 **karōshi** death from overwork

12 勤労 **kinrō** labor, work

—————— 3 ——————

6 気苦労 **kigurō** worry, cares, anxiety

3n4.4 / 939 　　田 小 子 丨
　　　　　　　　35 6 2

乳 乳 乳

NYŪ, chi, chichi mother's milk; the breasts

—————— 1 ——————

5 乳母 **uba** wet nurse

乳母車 **ubaguruma** baby carriage/buggy

7 乳児 **nyūji** suckling baby, infant

8 乳房 **chibusa** breast

12 乳飲子 **chino(mi)go** suckling infant, babe in arms

17 乳癌 **nyūgan** breast cancer

—————— 2 ——————

4 牛乳 **gyūnyū** (cow's) milk

5 母乳 **bonyū** mother's milk

10 哺乳動物 **honyū dōbutsu** mammal

—————— 5 ——————

甶 → 鼠 **0a13.1**

3n5.2 / 1853 　　目 小 口 冂
　　　　　　　　35 24 20

尚 尚 | 尚 尚

SHŌ value, respect; further, still **nao** further(more), still (more) HISASHI (m. given name) NAO, HISA, TAKA (part of given name)

—————— 1 ——————

2 尚之 **Naoyuki, Hisayuki, Shōshi** (m. given name)

尚子 **Naoko, Hisako, Shōko, Takako, Yoshiko** (f. given name)

3

氵
扌
口
女
巾
犭
弓
彳
彡
艹
宀
⺌
音
寺
广
尸
口

5

⁵ 尚且 **naoka(tsu)** furthermore; and yet

⁷ 尚更 **naosara** still more, all the more

⁹ 尚美 **Naomi, Naoyoshi, Hisayoshi, Takayoshi, Shōbi** (given name)

畄 → 留 5f5.4

爭 → 争 2n4.2

3n5.3 / 431 ☰ 小 ⌐ ⊥
                  35 13 11

歩   歩 | 歩 歩

HO step, pace **BU** rate; 1 percent; (unit of area, same as *tsubo*) **FU** pawn (in Japanese chess) **aru(ku), ayu(mu)** walk AYUMI (f. given name) AYUMU (m. given name)

─────── 1 ───────

⁶ 歩合 **buai** rate, percentage; commission **ayu(mi)a(u)** compromise

歩行 **hokō** walking, ambulatory

歩行者 **hokōsha** pedestrian

⁹ 歩度 **hodo** pace, cadence

¹¹ 歩道橋 **hodōkyō** pedestrian overpass

¹⁵ 歩調 **hochō** pace, step

─────── 2 ───────

¹ 一歩 **ippo** a step

⁷ 初歩 **shoho** rudiments, ABCs

⁸ 退歩 **taiho** retrogress, backward step; degeneration

¹⁰ 進歩 **shinpo** progress, advance

遊歩 **yūho** walk, stroll, promenade

徒歩 **toho** walking

¹² 散歩 **sanpo** walk, stroll

¹⁴ 漫歩 **manpo, sozo(ro)aru(ki)** stroll, ramble, walk

─────── 3 ───────

⁴ 公定歩合 **kōtei buai** official bank rate, rediscount rate

¹⁵ 横断歩道 **ōdan hodō** pedestrian crossing

─────────── 6 ───────────

3n6.1 / 723 ☰ 木 小 ⌐

                  41 35 20

栄   榮 | 栄 栄

EI prosperity, glory **saka(eru)** thrive, flourish, prosper **ha(eru)** shine, be brilliant **ha(e)** glory, honor, splendor SAKAE (f. given name) SHIGE, HIDE, YOSHI (part of given name)

─────── 1 ───────

² 栄子 **Eiko** (f. given name)

⁶ 栄光 **eikō** glory

¹⁵ 栄養 **eiyō** nutrition, nourishment

─────── 2 ───────

⁶ 光栄 **kōei** honor, glory, privilege

⁷ 見栄 **mie** (for sake of) appearance, show

¹¹ 虚栄心 **kyoeishin** vanity, vainglory

¹⁶ 繁栄 **han'ei** prosperity

3n6.2 / 300 ☰ 日 小 ⊥
                  43 35 12

単   單 | 単 単

TAN single, simple, mere; (as prefix) mono-, uni-

─────── 1 ───────

¹ 単一 **tan'itsu** single, simple, individual

⁶ 単行本 **tankōbon** separate volume, in book form

⁷ 単位 **tan'i** unit, denomination

⁸ 単価 **tanka** unit cost/price; univalent

⁹ 単独 **tandoku** independent, single-handed

単独行動 **tandoku kōdō** acting on one's own

¹⁰ 単純 **tanjun** simple

¹³ 単数 **tansū** singular (not plural)

14 単語 **tango** word
15 単調 **tanchō** monotonous

――――― 2 ―――――

18 簡単 **kantan** simple, brief

3n6.3 / 194

    55 35 2

    縣｜県 県

KEN prefecture **agata** (ancient administrative district) AGATA (m. given name)

――――― 1 ―――――

5 県立 **kenritsu** prefectural
8 県知事 **kenchiji** prefectural governor
11 県道 **kendō** prefectural highway
12 県営 **ken'ei** run by the prefecture

――――― 2 ―――――

8 府県 **fuken** prefectures

――――― 3 ―――――

3 三重県 **Mie-ken** (prefecture)
　大分県 **Ōita-ken** (prefecture)
　山梨県 **Yamanashi-ken** (prefecture)
5 広島県 **Hiroshima-ken** (prefecture)
　石川県 **Ishikawa-ken** (prefecture)
7 佐賀県 **Saga-ken** (prefecture)
　兵庫県 **Hyōgo-ken** (prefecture)
　沖縄県 **Okinawa-ken** (prefecture)
　岐阜県 **Gifu-ken** (prefecture)
　奈良県 **Nara-ken** (prefecture)
8 長野県 **Nagano-ken** (prefecture)
　長崎県 **Nagasaki-ken** (prefecture)
　岡山県 **Okayama-ken** (prefecture)
　岩手県 **Iwate-ken** (prefecture)
　青森県 **Aomori-ken** (prefecture)
9 茨城県 **Ibaraki-ken** (prefecture)
　栃木県 **Tochigi-ken** (prefecture)
　秋田県 **Akita-ken** (prefecture)
　香川県 **Kagawa-ken** (prefecture)
10 高知県 **Kōchi-ken** (prefecture)
　宮城県 **Miyagi-ken** (prefecture)
　宮崎県 **Miyazaki-ken** (prefecture)
　島根県 **Shimane-ken** (prefecture)

11 埼玉県 **Saitama-ken** (prefecture)
　鳥取県 **Tottori-ken** (prefecture)
12 滋賀県 **Shiga-ken** (prefecture)
　富山県 **Toyama-ken** (prefecture)
13 群馬県 **Gunma-ken** (prefecture)
　福井県 **Fukui-ken** (prefecture)
　新潟県 **Niigata-ken** (prefecture)
14 徳島県 **Tokushima-ken** (prefecture)
　静岡県 **Shizuoka-ken** (prefecture)
　熊本県 **Kumamoto-ken** (prefecture)
　愛媛県 **Ehime-ken** (prefecture)

――――― 4 ―――――

8 和歌山県 **Wakayama-ken** (prefecture)
9 神奈川県 **Kanagawa-ken** (prefecture)
10 都道府県 **to-dō-fu-ken** prefectures
11 鹿児島県 **Kagoshima-ken** (prefecture)

省 → 5c4.7

――――― 7 ―――――

3n7.1 / 801

    35 23 16

擧｜挙 挙

KYO arrest, capture; name, give, cite **a(geru)** name, give, enumerate; arrest, apprehend **a(gete)** all, whole, in a body **a(garu)** be apprehended, be found/recovered **kozo(tte)** all, all together TAKA (part of given name)

――――― 1 ―――――

5 挙句 **ageku** in the end, ultimately
6 挙式 **kyoshiki** (wedding) ceremony

――――― 2 ―――――

1 一挙 **ikkyo** one effort, a single action
6 再挙 **saikyo** second attempt
　列挙 **rekkyo** enumerate, list
12 検挙 **kenkyo** arrest, apprehend
14 選挙 **senkyo** election

選挙戦 **senkyosen** election campaign

———— 3 ————

6 再選挙 **saisenkyo** re-election
10 被選挙権 **hisenkyoken** eligibility for election
14 総選挙 **sōsenkyo** general election

3n7.2 / 495

目 小 口 冂
35 24 20

党 黨 | 党 党

TŌ party, faction

———— 1 ————

2 党人 **tōjin** party member, partisan
3 党大会 **tōtaikai** (political) convention
4 党内 **tōnai** intra-party
6 党争 **tōsō** party rivalry, factionalism
9 党派 **tōha** party, faction
10 党員 **tōin** party member
14 党閥 **tōbatsu** faction, clique
15 党輩 **tōhai** companions, associates

———— 2 ————

3 与党 **yotō** party in power, ruling party
6 両党 **ryōtō** both (political) parties, bipartisan
9 政党 **seitō** political party
11 野党 **yatō** opposition party
　脱党 **dattō** leave/bolt the party

———— 3 ————

3 与野党 **yoyatō** governing and opposition parties
4 公明党 **Kōmeitō** (a political party)
6 共和党 **kyōwatō** republican party
　共産党 **kyōsantō** communist party
　自民党 **Jimintō** LDP, Liberal Democratic Party (short for 自由民主党)
　自由党 **jiyūtō** liberal party
7 社会党 **shakaitō** socialist party

将→ **2b8.3**

———— 8 ————

雀→ **8c3.2**

3n8.1 / 1538

目 日 木 小
43 41 35

巢 巢 | 巢 巣

SŌ, su nest, (spider) web, (bee)hive
su(kuu) build a nest

———— 1 ————

5 巣立 **suda(chi)** leave the nest, become independent

———— 2 ————

8 空巣狙 **a(ki)sunera(i)** sneak thief, prowler
13 蜂巣 **hachi (no) su** beehive, honeycomb

———— 3 ————

14 蜘蛛巣 **kumo(no)su** spiderweb

3n8.2 / 1878

目 虫 小 冂
64 35 20

蛍 螢 | 蛍 蛍

KEI, hotaru firefly

———— 1 ————

6 蛍光灯 **keikōtō** fluorescent lamp

3n8.3 / 497

目 小 口 巾
35 24 26

常 常 常

JŌ, tsune normal, usual, continual; always, continually **toko-** ever-, everlasting

———— 1 ————

3 常々 **tsunezune** always, constantly
5 常用 **jōyō** common/everyday/habitual use

常用漢字 **Jōyō Kanji** (official list of 1,945 kanji recommended for general use)

6 常任委員会 **jōnin iinkai** standing committee

7 常住 **jōjū** everlasting; always; permanently residing

9 常客 **jōkyaku** regular customer/visitor

10 常套 **jōtō** commonplace, conventional

常員 **jōin** regular personnel/member

常時 **jōji** usually, habitually, ordinarily

11 常習 **jōshū** custom, common practice, habit

常習者 **jōshūsha** habitual offender

常務 **jōmu** regular business, routine duties, executive (director)

12 常勤 **jōkin** full-time (employment)

15 常駐 **jōchū** permanently stationed

19 常識 **jōshiki** common sense/knowledge

常識的 **jōshikiteki** matter-of-fact, practical

――――― 2 ―――――

4 日常 **nichijō** everyday, routine

5 平常 **heijō** normal; normally, usually

正常 **seijō** normal

8 非常 **hijō** emergency; extraordinary; very, exceedingly, extremely

非常口 **hijōguchi** emergency exit

定常 **teijō** steady, stationary, regular, routine

9 通常 **tsūjō** normal(ly), general(ly), ordinary, regular

恒常的 **kōjōteki** constant

12 尋常 **jinjō** normal, ordinary

3n8.4 / 496

目 小 口 土
35 24 22

堂 堂

DŌ temple; hall

――――― 1 ―――――

3 堂々 **dōdō(taru)** with pomp and glory, majestic, grand, magnificent

――――― 2 ―――――

9 食堂 **shokudō** dining hall, cafeteria

13 聖堂 **seidō** Confucian temple; sanctuary, church

――――― 3 ―――――

8 郁文堂 **Ikubundō** (publishing company)

20 議事堂 **gijidō** assembly hall, parliament/diet building

 雀 → **8c3.2**

――――― 9 ―――――

3n9.2 / 722

目 小 口 冂
35 24 20

営 営

EI run (a business); build; camp, barracks **itona(mu)** conduct (business), operate, perform; build

――――― 1 ―――――

7 営利 **eiri** profit(-making)

13 営業 **eigyō** (running a) business

18 営繕 **eizen** building and repair, maintenance

――――― 2 ―――――

4 公営 **kōei** public, government-run

5 民営 **min'ei** private management, privately run

市営 **shiei** run by the city, municipal

7 私営 **shiei** privately run/managed

8 官営 **kan'ei** government-run

府営 **fuei** run by an urban prefecture

国営 **kokuei** government-run, state-managed

9 陣営 **jin'ei** camp

県営 **ken'ei** run by the prefecture

10 都営 **toei** city-run, metropolitan

11 運営 **un'ei** operation, management, administration

経営 **keiei** manage, operate, run

 ３

氵 土 扌 口 女 巾 犭 弓 彳 彡 艹 宀 ⺌ 山 吉 广 尸 口 ９

3n9.3 / 605

目 貝 小 冂
68 35 20

覺 | 覚 覚

KAKU, obo(eru) remember, bear in mind, learn; feel, experience
obo(ezu) involuntarily, unwittingly, in-spite of oneself **obo(shii)** looking like, apparently **sa(meru/masu)** (intr./tr.) awake, wake up **sato(ru)** realize
SATORU (m. given name)

─────── 1 ───────

10 覚書 **obo(e)ga(ki)** memorandum

覚悟 **kakugo** be prepared/resolved/resigned to

16 覚醒剤 **kakuseizai** stimulant drugs

─────── 2 ───────

3 才覚 **saikaku** ready wit; raise (money); a plan

4 不覚 **fukaku** imprudence, failure, mistake

幻覚 **genkaku** hallucination

5 目覚 **meza(meru)** wake up, come awake **meza(mashii)** striking, remarkable, spectacular

6 先覚者 **senkakusha** pioneer, leading spirit

自覚 **jikaku** consciousness, awareness, realization

7 見覚 **miobo(e)** recognition, familiarity

8 味覚 **mikaku** sense of taste

9 発覚 **hakkaku** be detected, come to light

11 視覚 **shikaku** sense of sight, vision

13 嗅覚 **kyūkaku** sense of smell

感覚 **kankaku** sense, the senses

触覚 **shokkaku** sense of touch

16 錯覚 **sakkaku** illusion

─────── 3 ───────

12 無感覚 **mukankaku** insensible, numb, callous

3n9.4 / 499

目 小 口 扌
35 24 23

掌 寧

SHŌ palm of the hand; administer
tsukasado(ru) administer, preside over **tanagokoro** palm of the hand

─────── 1 ───────

3 掌大 **shōdai** palm-size

4 掌中 **shōchū** in the hand; pocket (edition)

─────── 2 ───────

7 車掌 **shashō** (train) conductor

就→ **3d9.21**

─────── 10 ───────

嘗→嘗 **3n11.1**

3n10.1 / 802

目 言 小 儿
67 35 16

譽 | 誉 誉

YO, home(ru) praise **homa(re)** honor, glory

─────── 2 ───────

6 名誉 **meiyo** honor, glory, fame, prestige

名誉教授 **meiyo kyōju** professor emeritus

當→当 **3n3.3**

亂→乱 **3d4.21**

3n10.2 / 2208

田 小 夕 冂
35 30 20

舜 舜

SHUN type of morning glory; rose of Sharon, althea SHUN, KIYO, TOSHI, YOSHI, MITSU (part of given name)
HITOSHI, AKIRA (m. given name)

3n10.4 / 1332 | 田 小 寸 大
35 37 34

奬｜奬 奬

SHŌ, susu(meru) urge, encourage
SUSUMU (m. given name)

――――― 1 ―――――

7 奨励 **shōrei** encourage, promote,
give incentive

奨学生 **shōgakusei** student on a
scholarship

奨学金 **shōgakukin** a scholarship

3n10.5 | 川 厂 阝 子
18 7 6

孵孚 孵卵

FU, kae(su) hatch, incubate

――――― 1 ―――――

4 孵化 **fuka** incubation, hatching
7 孵卵器 **furanki** incubator

――――― 11 ―――――

3n11.1 | 目 日 小 口
43 35 24

嘗｜嘗 嘗

SHŌ lick; once; try **na(meru)** lick;
underrate **katsu(te)** once, formerly,
ever

3n11.2 | 目 衤 小 口
57 35 24

裳

裳 裳

SHŌ, mo (traditional type) skirt

――――― 12 ―――――

3n12.1 / 500 | 目 貝 小 口
68 35 24

賞 賞

SHŌ prize; praise

――――― 1 ―――――

3 賞与金 **shōyokin** bonus
7 賞状 **shōjō** certificate of merit
8 賞味 **shōmi** relish, appreciate
賞杯 **shōhai** trophy, prize cup
賞金 **shōkin** (cash) prize, monetary
reward
9 賞品 **shōhin** (nonmonetary) prize
15 賞賛 **shōsan** praise, admire

――――― 2 ―――――

2 入賞 **nyūshō** win a prize
8 受賞者 **jushōsha** prizewinner
10 恩賞 **onshō** a reward
11 授賞 **jushō** awarding a prize
13 嘆賞 **tanshō** praise, admire
15 褒賞 **hōshō** prize, reward
18 観賞 **kanshō** admiration, enjoyment
20 懸賞 **kenshō** offering prizes
23 鑑賞 **kanshō** appreciation, enjoyment

輝 → **7c8.8**

――――― 13 ―――――

鴬 → 鶯 **11b10.9**

靜 → 静 **4b10.9**

――――― 14 ―――――

3n14.1 / 822 | 目 耳 攵 小
65 49 35

嚴｜嚴 嚴

GEN, GON, kibi(shii) severe, strict,
rigorous, intense **ogoso(ka)** solemn,
grave, stately **ikame(shii)** solemn,
august IWAO (m. given name)

1

6 厳守 **genshu** strict observance/adherence

9 厳重 **genjū** strict, stringent, rigid

10 厳格 **genkaku** strict, stern, severe

11 厳粛 **genshuku** grave, serious, solemn

厳密 **genmitsu** strict, precise

13 厳禁 **genkin** strictly prohibited

14 厳罰 **genbatsu** severe punishment

2

7 戒厳令 **kaigenrei** martial law

9 荘厳 **sōgon** sublime, grand, majestic

威厳 **igen** dignity, majesty, stateliness

10 峻厳 **shungen** strict, stern, harsh

12 尊厳 **songen** dignity

3

3 土足厳禁 **dosoku genkin** Remove Shoes (sign)

4 火気厳禁 **kaki genkin** Danger: Flammable

17

黨 → 党 3n7.2

山 3o

山	出	岐	岩	岸	岳	峡	峠	炭	幽	峽	峻	峰
0.1	0a5.22	4.1	5.10	5.11	5.12	6.1	6.3	6.5	6.6	3o6.1	7.4	7.6

峯	島	崚	崎	崖	崩	崇	崖	嵌	崟	嵐	嵯	崟
3o7.6	7.9	8.1	8.3	3o8.11	8.7	8.9	8.11	9.2	3o8.3	9.4	10.2	3o10.2

嵩	嶋	嶺	嶽	豊	巌	巖
10.4	3o7.9	14.2	3o5.12	3d10.15	17.2	3o17.2

3o0.1 / 34

SAN, yama mountain

1

3 山川 **Yamakawa** (surname)

山下 **Yamashita** (surname)

山口 **Yamaguchi** (surname)

4 山内 **Yama(no)uchi, Yamauchi** (surname)

山中 **Yamanaka** (surname)

山中湖 **Yamanaka-ko** Lake Yamanaka (near Mt. Fuji)

山水画 **sansuiga** landscape painting; a landscape

山手 **yamate, yama(no)te** hilly residential section, bluff, uptown

5 山本 **Yamamoto** (surname)

山田 **Yamada** (surname)

6 山羊 **yagi** goat

山地 **sanchi, yamachi** mountainous area

7 山男 **yamaotoko** (back)woodsman, hillbilly; alpinist

8 山岳 **sangaku** mountains

山林学 **sanringaku** forestry

9 山彦 **yamabiko** echo

10 山根 **Yamane** (surname)

山脈 **sanmyaku** mountain range

11 山猫争議 **yamaneko sōgi** wildcat strike

山崎 **Yamazaki, Yamasaki** (surname)

山崩 **yamakuzu(re)** landslide

山梨県 **Yamanashi-ken** (prefecture)

山頂 **sanchō** summit

12 山登 **yamanobo(ri)** mountain climbing

山葵 **wasabi** Japanese horseradish

2

1 一山 **hitoyama** a pile (of bananas); the whole mountain

3 丸山 **Maruyama** (surname)

小山 **Koyama** (surname)

⁴ 内山 **Uchiyama** (surname)
中山 **Nakayama** (surname)
片山 **Katayama** (surname)
火山 **kazan** volcano
⁵ 本山 **honzan** head temple; this temple
本山 **Motoyama** (surname)
平山 **Hirayama** (surname)
氷山 **hyōzan** iceberg
立山 **Tateyama** (mountain, Toyama-ken)
⁶ 西山 **Nishiyama** (surname)
米山 **Yoneyama** (surname)
⁷ 沢山 **takusan** many, much, plenty
杉山 **Sugiyama** (surname)
村山 **Murayama** (surname)
⁸ 岡山県 **Okayama-ken** (prefecture)
松山 **Matsuyama** (city, Ehime-ken); (surname)
青山 **Aoyama** (surname)
⁹ 春山 **Haruyama** (surname)
神山 **Kamiyama** (surname)
¹⁰ 高山 **Takayama** (surname)
釜山 **Fuzan, Pusan** Pusan
柴山 **Shibayama** (surname)
¹¹ 黒山 **kuroyama** large crowd
¹² 遠山 **Tōyama, Toyama** (surname)
登山 **tozan** mountain climbing
富山 **Tomiyama, Toyama** (surname)
富山県 **Toyama-ken** (prefecture)
森山 **Moriyama** (surname)
奥山 **Okuyama** (surname)
¹³ 福山 **Fukuyama** (city, Hiroshima-ken)
鉱山 **kōzan** a mine
¹⁵ 影山 **Kageyama** (surname)
横山 **Yokoyama** (surname)
¹⁸ 藤山 **Fujiyama** (surname)

─────── 3 ───────

⁵ 比叡山 **Hieizan** (mountain, Kyōto-fu)
⁶ 死火山 **shikazan** extinct volcano
休火山 **kyūkazan** dormant volcano
⁸ 和歌山県 **Wakayama-ken** (prefecture)
和歌山 **Wakayama** (city, Wakayama-ken)
⁹ 活火山 **kakkazan** active volcano

¹⁰ 高野山 **Kōyasan** (mountain, Wakayama-ken)
¹² 富士山 **Fuji-san** Mt. Fuji
¹⁵ 磐梯山 **Bandai-san** (mountain, Fukushima-ken)

─────── 3 ───────

出 → **0a5.22**

─────── 4 ───────

3o4.1 / 872   ⊞ 山 十 又
                    36 12 9

岐   岐 岐

KI forked road

─────── 1 ───────

⁸ 岐阜県 **Gifu-ken** (prefecture)
¹³ 岐路 **kiro** fork in the road, crossroads

─────── 2 ───────

⁴ 分岐点 **bunkiten** branch/ramification/turning point, fork, junction
¹³ 隠岐諸島 **Oki shotō** (group of islands, Shimane-ken)

─────── 5 ───────

3o5.4 / 1363   ⊞ 日 山 丨
                    43 36 2

岬   岬 岬

misaki promontory, headland, cape, point (of land)

3o5.10 / 1345   ⊟ 石 山
                    53 36

岩   岩 岩

GAN, iwa rock

─────── 1 ───────

⁴ 岩手県 **Iwate-ken** (prefecture)
⁵ 岩本 **Iwamoto** (surname)

氵
扌
口
女
巾
犭
弓
彳
彡
艹
宀
⺌
山
耂
广
尸
口

5

岩石 **ganseki** rock
岩田 **Iwata** (surname)
[11] 岩崎 **Iwasaki** (surname)
[17] 岩礁 **ganshō** reef

——————— 2 ———————

[13] 溶岩 **yōgan** lava
[18] 鎔岩 **yōgan** lava

3o5.11 / 586

氏 山 厂 工
36 18 14

岸

岸 岸

GAN, kishi bank, shore, coast KISHI (surname)

——————— 1 ———————

[5] 岸本 **Kishimoto** (surname)
岸田 **Kishida** (surname)
[8] 岸和田 **Kishiwada** (city, Ōsaka-fu)

——————— 2 ———————

[3] 川岸 **kawagishi** riverbank
[6] 西岸 **seigan** west coast; west bank
[8] 東岸 **tōgan** eastern coast; east bank
沿岸 **engan** coast, shore
河岸 **kashi** riverside; (riverside) fish market; place, scene; one's field/trade **kagan** riverside, bank/shore of a river
彼岸 **higan** equinoctal week; Buddhist services during equinoctal week; the other shore; goal
[9] 海岸 **kaigan** seashore, coast

3o5.12 / 1358

目 斤 山 一
50 36 1

岳

嶽 ‖ 岳 岳

GAKU, take mountain, peak
TAKESHI (m. given name)

——————— 2 ———————

[3] 山岳 **sangaku** mountains
[14] 槍岳 **Yari(ga)take** (mountain, Nagano-ken)

——————— 3 ———————

[12] 雲仙岳 **Unzendake** (mountain, Nagasaki-ken)

——————— 6 ———————

3o6.1 / 1352

囗 山 大 儿
36 34 16

峡

峡 ‖ 峽 峡

KYŌ gorge, ravine

——————— 1 ———————

[7] 峡谷 **kyōkoku** gorge, ravine, canyon

——————— 2 ———————

[9] 海峡 **kaikyō** strait(s), channel, sound

——————— 4 ———————

[8] 宗谷海峡 **Sōya-kaikyō** (strait between Hokkaidō and Sakhalin)
[9] 津軽海峡 **Tsugaru-kaikyō** (strait between Honshū and Hokkaidō)
[14] 鳴門海峡 **Naruto-kaikyō** (strait between Shikoku and Awaji island)
関門海峡 **Kanmon-kaikyō** (strait between Shimonoseki and Moji)

3o6.3 / 1351

囗 山 卜 一
36 13 14

峠

峠 峠

tōge mountain pass

——————— 1 ———————

[11] 峠道 **tōgemichi** road through a mountain pass

3o6.5 / 1344

氏 火 山 厂
44 36 18

炭

炭 ‖ 炭 炭

TAN coal, charcoal, carbon
sumi charcoal

—————— 1 ——————

⁷ 炭坑 **tankō** coal mine
¹³ 炭鉱 **tankō** coal mine
¹⁴ 炭酸水 **tansansui** carbonated water

—————— 2 ——————

⁴ 木炭画 **mokutanga** charcoal drawing
⁵ 石炭 **sekitan** coal

3o6.6 / 1228　　　□… ⺍ 竹 丨
　　　　　　　　　36　17　2

YŪ quiet, deep **kasu(ka)** faint, dim, indistinct

—————— 1 ——————

⁵ 幽玄 **yūgen** the profound, occult
¹⁵ 幽霊 **yūrei** ghost

—————— 7 ——————

峡 → 峡 **3o6.1**

3o7.4 / 2053　　　田 夂 ⺍ 竹
　　　　　　　　　49　36　17

SHUN high, steep; severe, strict
SHUN, TAKA, TOSHI, MINE, CHIKA, MICHI (part of given name) TAKASHI (m. given name)

—————— 1 ——————

¹⁰ 峻烈 **shunretsu** severe, scathing, sharp
¹⁷ 峻厳 **shungen** strict, stern, harsh

3o7.6 / 1350　　　山 夂 ⺍ 十
　　　　　　　　　49　36　12

HŌ, mine peak, summit; back (of a sword)

峯 → 峰 **3o7.6**

3o7.9 / 286　　　日 尸 山 一
　　　　　　　　　40　36　1

島　　嶋 | 島 島

TŌ, shima island SHIMA (surname)

—————— 1 ——————

³ 島々 **shimajima** (many) islands
⁵ 島民 **tōmin** islanders
　島田 **Shimada** (surname)
⁷ 島村 **Shimamura** (surname)
⁸ 島国 **shimaguni** island country
¹⁰ 島根県 **Shimane-ken** (prefecture)
¹¹ 島崎 **Shimazaki** (surname)

—————— 2 ——————

³ 三島 **Mishima** (surname)
　川島 **Kawashima** (surname)
　大島 **Ōshima** (frequent name for an island); (surname)
　千島列島 **Chishima-rettō** the Kurile Islands
　小島 **Kojima** (surname)
⁴ 中島 **Nakajima** (surname)
　水島 **Mizushima** (surname)
　手島 **Teshima, Tejima** (surname)
⁵ 北島 **Kitajima** (surname)
　半島 **hantō** peninsula
　永島 **Nagashima** (surname)
　広島県 **Hiroshima-ken** (prefecture)
　田島 **Tajima** (surname)
⁶ 列島 **rettō** archipelago
⁷ 児島 **Kojima** (surname)
⁸ 長島 **Nagashima** (surname)
　松島 **Matsushima** (surname)
¹⁰ 高島 **Takashima** (surname)
¹³ 群島 **guntō** group of islands, archipelago
¹⁴ 徳島県 **Tokushima-ken** (prefecture)
¹⁵ 諸島 **shotō** islands
¹⁸ 藤島 **Fujishima** (surname)

3

⺡ 土 扌 口 女 巾 犭 弓 彳 彡 艹 宀 ⺍ 7 青 广 尸 口

3

氵
土
扌
日
女
巾
犭
弓
彳
彡
艹
宀
八 山
吉
广
尸
口

—————— 3 ——————

² 八丈島 **Hachijōjima** (island, Tōkyō-to)

⁷ 佐渡島 **Sado(ga)shima** (island, Niigata-ken)

択捉島 **Etorofu-tō** (island, Russian Hokkaidō)

⁸ 国後島 **Kunashiri-tō** (island, Russian Hokkaidō)

¹¹ 淡路島 **Awajishima** (island, Hyōgo-ken)

鹿児島県 **Kagoshima-ken** (prefecture)

¹⁴ 種子島 **Tanegashima** (island, Kagoshima-ken)

—————— 4 ——————

³ 千島列島 **Chishima-rettō** the Kurile Islands

⁶ 伊豆半島 **Izu-hantō** Izu Peninsula (Shizuoka-ken)

⁸ 奄美大島 **Amami Ōshima** (island, Kagoshima-ken)

¹⁰ 能登半島 **Noto-hantō** (peninsula, Ishikawa-ken)

¹³ 隠岐諸島 **Oki shotō** (group of islands, Shimane-ken)

—————— 8 ——————

3o8.1 / 2054 　　田 夂 凵 土
　　　　　　　 49 36 22

峻 峻

RYŌ towering in a row　RYŌ (part of given name)

3o8.3 / 1362 　　田 山 大 卩
　　　　　　　 36 34 24

崎 崎 崎

saki, misaki cape, promontory, headland, point (of land)

—————— 2 ——————

³ 川崎 **Kawasaki** (city, Kanagawaken); (surname)

山崎 **Yamazaki, Yamasaki** (surname)

⁵ 尼崎 **Amagasaki** (city, Hyōgo-ken)

⁶ 西崎 **Nishizaki** (surname)

⁷ 谷崎 **Tanizaki** (surname)

尾崎 **Ozaki** (surname)

⁸ 長崎県 **Nagasaki-ken** (prefecture)

岡崎 **Okazaki** (city, Aichi-ken); (surname)

岩崎 **Iwasaki** (surname)

松崎 **Matsuzaki** (surname)

¹⁰ 宮崎 **Miyazaki** (city, Miyazaki-ken); (surname)

宮崎県 **Miyazaki-ken** (prefecture)

島崎 **Shimazaki** (surname)

¹¹ 野崎 **Nozaki** (surname)

崕 → 崖 3o8.11

3o8.7 / 1122 　　日 月 山
　　　　　　　 42 36

崩 | 崩 崩

HŌ, kuzu(reru) crumble, fall to pieces, collapse **kuzu(su)** demolish; change, break (a large bill); simplify
kuzu(shi) simplified form (of a kanji)

—————— 1 ——————

¹⁶ 崩壊 **hōkai** collapse, disintegration

—————— 2 ——————

³ 山崩 **yamakuzu(re)** landslide

¹¹ 崖崩 **gakekuzu(re)** landslide

—————— 3 ——————

³ 土砂崩 **doshakuzu(re)** landslide, washout

3o8.9 / 1424 　　日 礻 山 宀
　　　　　　　 45 36 33

SŪ respect, revere; lofty, sublime
aga(meru) respect, revere　TAKASHI (m. given name)　TAKA (part of given name)

---1---

⁸ 崇拝 **sūhai** worship, adoration

3o8.11　　　　日 凵 土 厂
　　　　　　　　　　36　22　18

　屋｜崖崖

GAI, gake cliff

---1---

¹¹ 崖崩 **gakekuzu(re)** landslide

---9---

3o9.2　　　　田 夂 凵 卅
　　　　　　　　　49　36　32

筬｜嵌嵌

KAN, ha(meru) inlay, set in, fit into, put on (gloves/ring); throw into; take in, cheat **ha(maru)** fit/go/fall into; be deceived

---1---

⁴ 嵌込 **ha(me)ko(mu)** fit into, insert, inlay

嵜 → 崎　**3o8.3**

3o9.4 / 2055　　　日 虫 凵 冂
　　　　　　　　　64　36　20

　嵐嵐

RAN, arashi storm, tempest　ARASHI (surname)　RAN (part of given name)

---2---

³ 大嵐 **ōarashi** big storm
¹¹ 雪嵐 **yukiarashi** snowstorm

---3---

⁴ 五十嵐 **Igarashi** (surname)

---10---

3o10.2 / 2056　　　⋯ 王 凵 工
　　　　　　　　　46　36　38

崕｜嵯嵯

SA steep, rugged, craggy
SA, SHI (part of given name)

崕 → 嵯　**3o10.2**

3o10.4 / 2057　　　日 凵 口 宀
　　　　　　　　　36　24　11

嵩嵩

SŪ, kasa bulk, volume, size, quantity
kasa(mu) grow bulky, increase in volume; mount up　SŪ, SHŪ, TAKA, TAKE (part of given name)　TAKASHI, TAKABU (m. given name)

---1---

¹¹ 嵩張 **kasaba(ru)** be bulky/unwieldly

---11---

嶋 → 島　**3o7.9**

---14---

3o14.2 / 2058　　　田 頁 凵 亻
　　　　　　　　　77　36　3

　嶺嶺

REI, mine, ne peak, summit　REI, RYŌ, MINE, NE (part of given name)

嶽 → 岳　**3o5.12**

豐 → 豊　**3d10.15**

17

3o17.2 / 2059

日 耳 攵 山
65 49 36

巌

巌｜巌巌

GAN rock, crag **iwao** (massive) rock
GAN, GEN, IWA, YOSHI, O, MINE, MICHI,
TOSHI, ITSU (part of given name)
IWAO (m. given name)

20

巖 → 巌 3o17.2

3p

士 吉 壮 壯 志 壱 売 声 缶 表 壺 殻 喜
0.1 3.1 2b4.2 2b4.2 4.1 4.2 4.3 4.4 2k4.6 0a8.6 3p9.2 8.1 9.1

壷 壹 殻 聖 鼓 嘉 壽 皷 賣
9.2 3p4.2 3p8.1 4f9.9 10.2 11.1 0a7.15 3p10.2 3p4.3

0

3p0.1 / 572

口 士
22

士

士士

SHI samurai; man; scholar
TSUKASA (m. given name)

1

13 士農工商 **shinōkōshō** samurai-
farmers-artisans-merchants,
the military, agricultural, industrial, and mercantile classes

2

2 力士 **rikishi** sumo wrestler
6 同士 **dōshi** fellow, companion
7 兵士 **heishi** soldier
学士 **gakushi** Bachelor of Arts, university graduate
8 武士 **bushi, mononofu** samurai,
warrior
10 修士 **shūshi** master's degree, M.A.,
M.S.
准士官 **junshikan** warrant officer
11 紳士 **shinshi** gentleman
紳士用 **shinshiyō** men's, for men
紳士協定 **shinshi kyōtei** gentleman's agreement
紳士服 **shinshifuku** men's clothing
紳士録 **shinshiroku** a who's-who,
directory

12 博士 **hakase, hakushi** Ph.D.
富士山 **Fuji-san** Mt. Fuji
棋士 **kishi** (professional) go/shogi
player
13 戦士 **senshi** warrior, soldier
18 闘士 **tōshi** fighter for

3

3 工学士 **kōgakushi** Bachelor of Engineering
4 文学士 **bungakushi** Bachelor of
Arts
5 弁理士 **benrishi** patent attorney
弁護士 **bengoshi** lawyer, attorney
6 会計士 **kaikeishi** accountant
9 飛行士 **hikōshi** aviator
計理士 **keirishi** public accountant
11 経理士 **keirishi** public accountant
12 税理士 **zeirishi** tax accountant
16 操縦士 **sōjūshi** pilot
18 闘牛士 **tōgyūshi** matador, bull-
fighter

3

3p3.1 / 1141

口 士 口
22 24

吉

吉｜吉吉

KICHI, KITSU, yoshi good luck
YOSHI (part of given name)

---- 1 ----

3 吉川 **Yoshikawa, Kikkawa** (surname)

4 吉井 **Yoshii** (surname)

吉日 **kichinichi, kichijitsu** lucky day

5 吉本 **Yoshimoto** (surname)

吉田 **Yoshida** (surname)

6 吉兆 **kitchō** good/lucky omen

7 吉沢 **Yoshizawa** (surname)

吉村 **Yoshimura** (surname)

8 吉岡 **Yoshioka** (surname)

10 吉原 **Yoshiwara** (proper name); (a former red-light district in Tōkyō)

11 吉野 **Yoshino** (surname)

---- 2 ----

8 定吉 **Sadakichi, Sadayoshi, Teikichi** (m. given name)

壮 → **2b4.2**

---- 4 ----

壯 → 壮 **2b4.2**

3p4.1 / 573   日 心 士
                        51 22

志 志志

SHI will, intention; record; shilling
kokoroza(su) intend, aim at, have in mind **kokorozashi** will, intention, aim
YUKI (part of given name)

---- 1 ----

6 志向 **shikō** intention, inclination

11 志望 **shibō** desire, ambition, choice

18 志織 **Shiori** (f. given name)

19 志願者 **shigansha** applicant, candidate, volunteer, aspirant

---- 2 ----

3 大志 **taishi** ambition, aspiration

10 高志 **Takashi, Kōshi** (m. given name)

13 意志 **ishi** will, volition

16 篤志家 **tokushika** benefactor, volunteer

18 闘志 **tōshi** fighting spirit

3p4.2 / 1730   日 士 冂 卜
                         22 20 13

壱 壹|壱壱

ICHI, ITSU one (in documents)

3p4.3 / 239   日 士 冂 儿
                        22 20 16

売 賣|売売

BAI, u(ru) sell **u(reru)** sell, be in demand

---- 1 ----

2 売子 **u(rek)ko** popular person
u(ri)ko salesclerk

3 売上 **u(ri)a(ge)** sales

売上高 **uria(ge)daka** amount sold, sales

4 売切 **u(ri)ki(re)** sold out

売手 **u(ri)te** seller

8 売店 **baiten** (news)stand, kiosk

売国 **baikoku** betrayal of one's country

9 売春 **baishun** prostitution

売春婦 **baishunfu** prostitute

10 売値 **u(ri)ne** selling price

売家 **u(ri)ya, u(ri)ie** house for sale

12 売場 **u(ri)ba** sales counter, place where (tickets) are sold

売買 **baibai** buying and selling, trade, sale

---- 2 ----

3 大売出 **ōu(ri)da(shi)** big sale

小売 **kou(ri)** retail

6 安売 **yasuu(ri)** sell cheap

7 即売 **sokubai** sale on the spot

8 非売品 **hibaihin** article not for sale

直売 **chokubai** direct sales

押売 **o(shi)u(ri)** high-pressure/importunate selling

物売 **monou(ri)** peddler

9 発売 **hatsubai** sale

3

氵
土
扌
口
女
巾
犭
弓
彳
彡
艹
宀
屮
亠
广
尸
口

4

専売 **senbai** monopoly
卸売 **oroshiu(ri)** wholesale
前売券 **maeu(ri)ken** ticket sold in advance
10 特売 **tokubai** special sale
11 商売 **shōbai** business, trade, transaction; occupation
淫売 **inbai** prostitution
密売 **mitsubai** illicit sale, smuggling, bootlegging
販売 **hanbai** sales, selling
販売店 **hanbaiten** shop, store
12 量売 **haka(ri)u(ri)** sell by measure/weight
20 競売 **kyōbai, se(ri)u(ri)** auction

―――――― 3 ――――――

4 水商売 **mizu shōbai** trades dependent on public patronage (bars, restaurants, entertainment)
13 新発売 **shinhatsubai** new(ly marketed) product

―――――― 4 ――――――

6 自動販売機 **jidōhanbaiki** vending machine
8 委託販売 **itaku hanbai** selling on consignment/commission

3p4.4 / 746

| 曰 | 土 | 尸 | ｜ |
| 22 | 40 | 2 | |

声

聲｜声 声

SEI, SHŌ, koe, kowa- voice

―――――― 1 ――――――

8 声明 **seimei** declaration, (public) statement, proclamation
9 声音 **kowane** tone of voice, timbre
seion vocal sound
12 声援 **seien** (shouts of) encouragement, cheering
13 声楽 **seigaku** vocal music, (study) voice
17 声優 **seiyū** radio actor/actress, dubber

―――――― 2 ――――――

3 大声 **ōgoe** loud voice **taisei** loud voice; sonorous voice

6 叫声 **sake(bi)goe** a shout, cry, scream
名声 **meisei** fame, reputation
7 吠声 **ho(e)goe** bark, yelp, howl, roar
忍声 **shino(bi)goe** in a whisper
8 泣声 **na(ki)goe** crying, tearful voice, sob
拡声器 **kakuseiki** loudspeaker
呼声 **yo(bi)goe** a call, cry, shout
9 音声 **onsei, onjō** voice, audio
10 涙声 **namidagoe** tearful voice
12 喚声 **kansei, wame(ki)goe** shout, yell, scream, outcry
13 嗄声 **shaga(re)goe** hoarse voice
14 鳴声 **na(ki)goe** cry, call, chirping (of animals)
15 歓声 **kansei** shout of joy, cheer
罵声 **basei** jeers, boos, hisses
17 擬声語 **giseigo** onomatopoetic word
20 鐘声 **shōsei** sound/ringing of a bell

―――――― 3 ――――――

11 猫撫声 **nekona(de)goe** coaxing voice
21 鶴一声 **tsuru (no) hitokoe** the voice of authority

缶→ **2k4.6**

―――――― 6 ――――――

表→ **0a8.6**

―――――― 8 ――――――

壷→ 壺 **3p9.2**

3p8.1 / 1728

| 曰 | 土 | 冂 | 又 |
| 22 | 20 | 9 | |

殻

殻｜殻 殻

KAKU, kara husk, hull, shell

―――――― 2 ――――――

6 吸殻 **su(i)gara** cigar(ette) butt
7 卵殻 **rankaku** eggshell

貝殻 **kaigara** (sea) shell

───── **9** ─────

3p9.1 / 1143

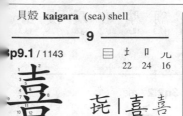

🔲 ⼟ 🔲 ⼉
22 24 16

毐 | 喜 喜

KI, yoroko(bu) be glad, rejoice
yoroko(bashii) joyful, glad YOSHI
(part of given name)

───── **1** ─────

7 喜寿 **kiju** one's 77th birthday
9 喜怒哀楽 **kidoairaku** joy-anger-sorrow-pleasure, emotions
12 喜雄 **Yoshio, Hisao** (m. given name)
14 喜歌劇 **kikageki** comic opera
15 喜劇 **kigeki** a comedy

───── **2** ─────

1 一喜一憂 **ikki ichiyū** alternation of joy and sorrow, hope and fear
3 大喜 **ōyoroko(bi)** great joy

3p9.2

🔲 ⼟ 🔲 ⼀
22 20 1

壷 | 壺 壺

KO, tsubo jar, pot; spot for applying moxa; one's aim

壹 → 壱 3p4.2

殼 → 殻 3p8.1

───── **10** ─────

聖 → 聖 4f9.9

3p10.2 / 1147

🔲 ⼟ 🔲 ⼉
22 24 16

皷 | 鼓 鼓

KO, tsuzumi hand drum

───── **1** ─────

11 鼓動 **kodō** (heart) beat
鼓笛隊 **kotekitai** drum-and-bugle corps, fife-and-drum band

───── **2** ─────

4 太鼓 **taiko** drum

───── **11** ─────

3p11.1 / 2041

🔲 ⼟ 🔲 ⼉
22 24 16

嘉 嘉

KA good, happy, auspicious
yomi(suru) praise, applaud YOSHI, YOMISHI, KONOMU (m. given name)
YOSHIMI (f. given name) KA, HIRO, TAKA, YOSHI (part of given name)

───── **1** ─────

5 嘉代 **Kayo, Yoshinori** (given name)
10 嘉納 **kanō** approve, appreciate; accept with pleasure

壽 → 寿 0a7.15

皷 → 鼓 3p10.2

───── **12** ─────

賣 → 売 3p4.3

3

氵
⼟
扌
⼥
⼱
犭
⼸
彳
彡
艹
宀
⺍
⼟ 11
广
⼫
⼝

───── 广 **3q** ─────

広 2.1	庁 2.2	庌 3q12.6	庀 3q13.3	庄 3.1	床 4.1	応 4.2	庇 4.3	序 4.4	府 5.2	底 5.3	店 5.4	庖 3q5.5
庖 5.5	度 6.1	庭 6.3	庫 7.1	座 7.2	唐 7.3	席 7.4	康 8.1	庸 8.2	麻 8.3	廊 8.4	鹿 8.5	庵 8.6

庶	廓	廊	廃	廉	腐	塵	廟	摩	廢	廣	慶	磨
8.7	9.1	3q8.4	9.3	10.1	11.3	11.4	12.3	12.6	3q9.3	3q2.1	12.8	13.3

應	麿	麒	麗	魔	鷹	廳
3q4.2	15.2	16.4	16.5	18.2	21.1	3q2.2

3

― 2 ―

3q2.1 / 694

□ 厂 竹
18 17

広 廣 | 広 広

KŌ, hiro(i), hiro(yaka) broad, wide, spacious, extensive **hiro(geru)** extend, enlarge **hiro(garu)** spread, expand **hiro(meru)** broaden, propagate **hiro(maru)** spread, be propagated HIROSHI (m. given name) HIRO (part of given name)

――― 1 ―――

- 3 広大 **kōdai** vast, extensive, huge
- 4 広太郎 **Hirotarō, Kōtarō** (m. given name)
- 5 広田 **Hirota** (surname)
- 7 広告 **kōkoku** advertisement
- 8 広治 **Hiroji, Kōji, Hiroharu** (m. given name)
- 10 広島県 **Hiroshima-ken** (prefecture)
- 12 広場 **hiroba** plaza, public square
  - 広報 **kōhō** publicity
  - 広間 **hiroma** hall; spacious room
- 13 広義 **kōgi** broad sense
  - 広辞苑 **Kōjien** (name of a dictionary)
- 19 広瀬 **Hirose** (surname)

――― 2 ―――

- 5 末広 **suehiro** folding fan
  - **suehiro(gari)** spreading/widening out toward the end; prospering as time goes on
- 9 背広 **sebiro** business suit
- 12 幅広 **habahiro(i)** broad, extensive
  - **habahiro** wide
- 16 燃広 **mo(e)hiro(garu)** (flames) spread

3q2.2 / 763

□ 厂
18 14

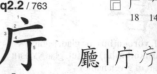

庁 廳 | 庁 庁

CHŌ government office, agency

――― 1 ―――

- 8 庁舎 **chōsha** government-office building

――― 2 ―――

- 8 官庁 **kanchō** government office/authorities

――― 3 ―――

- 6 気象庁 **Kishōchō** Meteorological Agency
  - 防衛庁 **Bōeichō** Defense Agency
- 8 法王庁 **Hōōchō** the Vatican
- 10 宮内庁 **Kunaichō** Imperial Household Agency
  - 特許庁 **Tokkyochō** Patent Office
  - 教皇庁 **Kyōkōchō** the Vatican
- 17 環境庁 **Kankyōchō** Environment Agency
- 19 警視庁 **Keishichō** Metropolitan Police Agency
  - 警察庁 **Keisatsuchō** National Police Agency

庁 → 摩 3q12.6

庁 → 磨 3q13.3

――― 3 ―――

3q3.1 / 2063

□ 土 厂
22 18

庄 庄 庄

SHŌ in the country; level SHŌ, SŌ, MASA (part of given name) TAIRA (m. given name)

4

3q4.1 / 826 　　　　□ 木 厂
　　　　　　　　　　　　41　18

床

牀 | 床 床

SHŌ, toko bed; floor **yuka** floor
yuka(shii) admirable; charming; tasteful

1

9 床屋 **tokoya** barber, barbershop
12 床間 **toko(no)ma** alcove (in a Japanese-style room)

2

9 臥床 **gashō** be confined to bed
10 起床 **kishō** wake up, rise
病床 **byōshō** sickbed
13 寝床 **nedoko** bed
17 臨床 **rinshō** clinical

3

3 万年床 **mannendoko** bedding/futon left spread out on the floor during the daytime

3q4.2 / 827 　　　　□ 心 厂
　　　　　　　　　　　　51　18

応

應 | 応 応

Ō reply, respond; comply with, fulfill, satisfy **kota(eru)** answer, respond; be felt keenly, be telling **ira(e)** reply
MASA (part of given name)

1

0 応じる **ō(jiru)** respond; consent to; satisfy, meet (a need)
5 応用 **ōyō** (practical) application
9 応急 **ōkyū** emergency, temporary, stopgap
応待 **ōtai** receive (visitors), wait on (customers)
11 応接 **ōsetsu** reception (of visitors)
応接間 **ōsetsuma** reception room, parlor
12 応援 **ōen** aid, support
応援団 **ōendan** rooting section, cheerleaders

応募 **ōbo** answer (an ad), apply for, enroll, enlist, subscribe for (shares)
応答 **ōtō** answer, reply, response

2

1 一応 **ichiō** once; tentatively; in outline
4 反応 **hannō** reaction, response
手応 **tegota(e)** response, effect, resistance
7 即応 **sokuō** conform/adapt to, meet
対応 **taiō** correspond to, be equivalent to; cope with
12 順応 **junnō** adapt/conform to
13 適応 **tekiō** adaptation, accommodation, adjustment
感応 **kannō** response; inspiration; sympathy; induce, influence
15 慶応 **Keiō** (a university); (era, 1865 – 1868)

3

15 質疑応答 **shitsugi-ōtō** question-and-answer (session)

4

9 連鎖反応 **rensa hannō** chain reaction

3q4.3 　　　　□ 厂 卜
　　　　　　　　　　18　13

庇

庇 庇

HI, kaba(u) protect, shield **hisashi** eaves; canopy; visor

1

20 庇護 **higo** protection, patronage

3q4.4 / 770 　　　　□ 厂 宀 一
　　　　　　　　　　18　14　1

序

序 序

JO beginning; preface; order, sequence
tsuide order; occasion, chance

3q5.2 (continued)

—————— 1 ——————

[4] 序文 **jobun** preface, foreword, introduction

[6] 序曲 **jokyoku** overture, prelude

[7] 序言 **jogen** preface, foreword, introduction

[14] 序説 **josetsu** introduction, preface

[15] 序論 **joron** introduction, preface

—————— 2 ——————

[6] 自序 **jijo** author's preface

[10] 秩序 **chitsujo** order, system, regularity

[12] 順序 **junjo** order, sequence; procedure

—————— 3 ——————

[12] 無秩序 **muchitsujo** disorder, chaos; anomie

—————— 4 ——————

[6] 安寧秩序 **annei-chitsujo** peace and order

—————— 5 ——————

3q5.2 / 504   □ 寸 厂 亻
                        37 18 3

府府

FU urban prefecture; government office; storehouse

—————— 1 ——————

[5] 府立 **furitsu** run by an urban prefecture

[9] 府県 **fuken** prefectures

[12] 府営 **fuei** run by an urban prefecture

—————— 2 ——————

[9] 政府 **seifu** the government

政府筋 **seifusuji** government sources

—————— 3 ——————

[10] 都道府県 **to-dō-fu-ken** prefectures

[11] 現政府 **genseifu** the present government

[12] 無政府 **museifu** anarchy

[14] 総理府 **sōrifu** Prime Minister's Office

3q5.3 / 562   □ 厂 十 一
                        18 12 1

底底

TEI, soko bottom

—————— 1 ——————

[2] 底力 **sokojikara** latent energy/strength

[7] 底抜 **sokonu(ke)** bottomless, unbounded

[10] 底値 **sokone** rock-bottom price

—————— 2 ——————

[4] 心底 **shinsoko, shintei** the bottom of one's heart

[7] 谷底 **tanizoko, tanisoko** bottom of a valley/ravine

[8] 到底 **tōtei** (cannot) possibly, (not) at all, utterly, absolutely

河底 **kawazoko, katei** river bed/bottom

[9] 海底 **kaitei** ocean floor, undersea

[12] 奥底 **okusoko, okuzoko** depths, bottom

[15] 徹底的 **tetteiteki** thorough, exhaustive

3q5.4 / 168   □ 口 厂 卜
                        24 18 13

店店

TEN, mise, tana- shop, store

—————— 1 ——————

[6] 店先 **misesaki** storefront

[8] 店長 **tenchō** store/shop manager

[10] 店員 **ten'in** store employee, clerk

—————— 2 ——————

[4] 支店 **shiten** a branch (store/office)

[5] 出店 **demise** branch store
    shutten open a new store

本店 **honten** head office; main store; this store

[7] 売店 **baiten** (news)stand, kiosk

[10] 酒店 **sakamise, saketen** liquor store

書店 **shoten** bookstore; publisher

¹¹ 商店 **shōten** store, shop
商店街 **shōtengai** shopping area
閉店 **heiten** store closing

¹² 開店 **kaiten** opening a new store; opening the store for the day

²¹ 露店 **roten** street stall, vending booth

───── 3 ─────

³ 工務店 **kōmuten** engineering firm

⁵ 代理店 **dairiten** agent, agency

⁶ 百貨店 **hyakkaten** department store

⁹ 食品店 **shokuhinten** grocery store

¹¹ 理髪店 **rihatsuten** barbershop
販売店 **hanbaiten** shop, store

¹² 喫茶店 **kissaten** teahouse, café

庖 → 庖 **3q5.5**

3q5.5
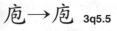

　庖｜庖庖

HŌ kitchen, cooking, cook

───── 1 ─────

² 庖丁 **hōchō** kitchen knife

───── 6 ─────

3q6.1 / 377

　度度

DO, TAKU, TO degree; extent, measure, limit; (how many) times **tabi** time, occasion **-ta(i)** (verb suffix) want to …

───── 1 ─────

³ 度々 **tabitabi** often, frequently

⁷ 度忘 **dowasu(re)** forget for the moment, slip one's mind

¹³ 度数 **dosū** number of times/degrees

───── 2 ─────

¹ 一度 **ichido, hitotabi** once, one time

² 丁度 **chōdo** exactly

⁴ 今度 **kondo** this time; next time
支度 **shitaku** preparation, arrangements
尺度 **shakudo** (linear) measure, scale, yardstick, standard

⁶ 年度 **nendo** fiscal/business year
毎度 **maido** each time; frequently; always
再度 **saido** twice, a second time, again
印度 **Indo** India

⁷ 何度 **nando** how many times; how many degrees
角度 **kakudo** angle

⁸ 限度 **gendo** limit
制度 **seido** system
歩度 **hodo** pace, cadence

⁹ 速度 **sokudo** speed, velocity
速度計 **sokudokei** speedometer

¹⁰ 高度 **kōdo** high(ly developed), advanced, sophisticated; altitude
純度 **jundo** purity

¹¹ 過度 **kado** excessive, too much
深度 **shindo** depth
密度 **mitsudo** density
経度 **keido** longitude

¹² 温度 **ondo** temperature
温度計 **ondokei** thermometer
湿度 **shitsudo** humidity
極度 **kyokudo** to the highest degree, extreme
程度 **teido** extent, degree, level

¹³ 適度 **tekido** proper degree/amount, moderation
零度 **reido** zero (degrees), the freezing point

¹⁴ 態度 **taido** attitude, stance, posture
精度 **seido** precision, accuracy

¹⁵ 震度 **shindo** earthquake intensity

¹⁶ 緯度 **ido** latitude

¹⁷ 頻度 **hindo** frequency, rate of occurrence
鮮度 **sendo** (degree of) freshness

───── 3 ─────

⁵ 加速度 **kasokudo** acceleration

3q6.3 / 1112 □ 王 厂 辶
46 18 19

庭

庭 庭

TEI, niwa garden, yard

— 1 —

13 庭園 **teien** garden

— 2 —

5 矢庭 **yaniwa (ni)** suddenly, immediately
10 家庭 **katei** home; family
家庭教師 **katei kyōshi** (priv.) tutor
校庭 **kōtei** schoolyard, campus

— 7 —

3q7.1 / 825 □ 車 厂
69 18

庫

庫 庫

KO, KU, kura storehouse
KURA (part of given name)

— 2 —

4 文庫 **bunko** stationery box; bookcase; library
文庫本 **bunkobon** small paperback book (page size 14.8 x 10.5 cm)
6 在庫 **zaiko** (in) stock, inventory
7 兵庫県 **Hyōgo-ken** (prefecture)
車庫 **shako** garage, carbarn
8 金庫 **kinko, kanegura** safe, vault; cashbox; depository, treasury; rich patron
10 倉庫 **sōko** warehouse

— 3 —

7 冷凍庫 **reitōko** freezer
冷蔵庫 **reizōko** refrigerator

3q7.2 / 786 □ 土 厂 亻
22 18 3

座

座 座

ZA seat; theater, troupe; constellation
suwa(ru) sit down

— 1 —

4 座込 **suwa(ri)ko(mu)** sit down, stage a sit-in
10 座席 **zaseki** seat
13 座蒲団 **zabuton** cushion
座禅 **zazen** (Zen) meditation
15 座敷 **zashiki** room, drawing room
座談会 **zadankai** round-table discussion, symposium

— 2 —

3 口座 **kōza** (bank) account
4 王座 **ōza** the throne, the crown
5 正座 **seiza** sit straight (on one's heels) **shōza** seat of honor
7 即座 **sokuza** prompt, on the spot
9 星座 **seiza** constellation
14 静座 **seiza** sit quietly
銀座 **ginza** silver mint; the Ginza
17 講座 **kōza** course (of lectures); professorship, chair

— 3 —

7 牡牛座 **Oushiza** (the constellation) Taurus

3q7.3 / 1697 □ ⧻ 口 厂
39 24 18

唐

唐 唐

TŌ Tang (dynasty); China; foreign
Kara China, Cathay; foreign

— 1 —

7 唐辛子 **tōgarashi** cayenne/red pepper
12 唐朝 **Tōchō** the Tang dynasty

3q7.4 / 379 □ 艹 巾 厂
32 26 18

席

席 席

SEKI seat, place

— 1 —

3 席上 **sekijō** at the meeting, on the occasion

¹² 席順 **sekijun** seating order, precedence

— 2 —

¹ 一席 **isseki** a speech/story/feast

⁴ 欠席 **kesseki** absence, nonattendance

⁵ 出席 **shusseki** attendance

主席 **shuseki** top place, first, head, chairman

⁶ 列席 **resseki** attend, be present

⁷ 即席 **sokuseki** extemporaneous, impromptu, instant (foods)

⁸ 空席 **kūseki** vacant seat, vacancy

⁹ 首席 **shuseki** head, chief, chairman

客席 **kyakuseki** seats for guests

¹⁰ 座席 **zaseki** seat

¹¹ 寄席 **yose** variety-show hall

¹² 着席 **chakuseki** take a seat

¹⁵ 隣席 **rinseki** the seat next to one

²⁰ 議席 **giseki** seat in parliament/congress

— 3 —

⁹ 指定席 **shiteiseki** reserved seats

——— 8 ———

3q8.1 / 894 　　□ 厂 氵 ヨ
　　　　　　　　　　18　21　39

康 康

KŌ peaceful YASUSHI (m. given name) YASU (part of given name)

— 1 —

² 康之 **Yasuyuki, Kōji** (m. given name)

康子 **Yasuko, Kōko, Sadako** (f. given name)

⁵ 康司 **Kōji, Yasushi, Kōshi** (m. given name)

¹² 康雄 **Yasuo, Michio** (m. given name)

— 2 —

¹⁰ 健康 **kenkō** health; healthy, sound

— 3 —

⁴ 不健康 **fukenkō** unhealthy, unhealthful

3q8.2 / 1696 　　□ 月 ヨ 厂
　　　　　　　　　　42　39　18

庸

 庸 庸

YŌ employ; ordinary; tax paid in cloth in lieu of in labor ISAO (m. given name) TSUNE (part of given name)

— 1 —

³ 庸才 **yōsai** mediocre talent

— 2 —

¹² 雇庸 **koyō** employment, hiring

3q8.3 / 1529 　　□ 木 厂
　　　　　　　　　　41　18

麻

 麻 麻

MA, asa flax, hemp

— 1 —

⁵ 麻生 **Asō** (surname)

麻布 **asanuno, mafu** hemp cloth, linen

⁶ 麻衣 **Mai** (f. given name)

⁹ 麻美 **Asami, Mami** (f. given name)

¹¹ 麻酔 **masui** anesthesia

麻雀 **mājan** mahjong

¹³ 麻痺 **mahi** paralysis

¹⁶ 麻薬 **mayaku** narcotics, drugs

— 2 —

³ 大麻 **taima** marijuana; Shinto paper amulet **ōasa** hemp

⁹ 胡麻 **goma** sesame (seeds)

— 3 —

³ 小児麻痺 **shōni mahi** infantile paralysis, polio

3q8.4 / 981 　　□ 食 厂 阝
　　　　　　　　　　73　18　7

廊

 廊 ｜ 廊 廊

RŌ corridor, hall

— 1 —

³ 廊下 **rōka** corridor, hall

8

— 2 —

⁸ 画廊 **garō** picture gallery

¹² 渡廊下 **wata(ri) rōka** covered passageway

3q8.5 / 2279 □ 厂 儿 冂
18 16 20

鹿

ROKU, shika deer ROKU, SHIKA, KA, SHISHI (part of given name)

— 1 —

⁷ 鹿児島県 **Kagoshima-ken** (prefecture)

— 2 —

¹⁰ 馬鹿 **baka** fool, idiot, stupid; to a ridiculous degree

— 3 —

¹⁶ 親馬鹿 **oyabaka** overfond parent

3q8.6 □ 日 大 厂
43 34 18

庵

AN, iori hermit's cottage, retreat

— 2 —

⁷ 沢庵 **takuan** pickled daikon

3q8.7 / 1766 □ 火 艹 厂
44 32 18

庶

SHO all; illegitimate child

— 1 —

⁵ 庶民 **shomin** the (common) people
¹¹ 庶務 **shomu** general affairs

— 9 —

3q9.1 □ 口 厂 宀
24 18 11

廓

KAKU enclosure; quarter; large; empty **kuruwa** enclosure; quarter; red-light district

廊 → 廊 **3q8.4**

3q9.3 / 961 □ 火 艹 厂
44 32 18

廃

HAI obsolete; discontinue, do away with; crippled **suta(reru), suta(ru)** become outmoded, go out of fashion

— 1 —

⁴ 廃止 **haishi** abolition, abrogation
⁵ 廃刊 **haikan** discontinue publication
⁸ 廃物 **haibutsu** waste, refuse, scrap
廃物利用 **haibutsu riyō** recycling
⁹ 廃品 **haihin** scrap, waste, discards, junk
¹² 廃絶 **haizetsu** become extinct
¹³ 廃業 **haigyō** going out of business
廃棄物 **haikibutsu** waste matter, wastes
¹⁴ 廃墟 **haikyo** ruins

— 2 —

¹⁵ 撤廃 **teppai** abolition, do away with, repeal
¹⁶ 興廃 **kōhai** rise and fall, destiny

— 10 —

3q10.1 / 1689 □ 厂 ヨ 儿
18 39 16

廉

REN purity; honest; low price
kado grounds, charge, suspicion; point

yasu(i) cheap, inexpensive
YASU (part of given name)

——————— 1 ———————

8 廉価 **renka** low price
10 廉恥心 **renchishin** sense of shame/
honor

——————— 2 ———————

10 破廉恥 **harenchi** shameless, disgraceful

——————— 11 ———————

3q11.3 / 1245   □ 厂 寸 亻
                         18 37 3

腐   腐 腐

FU, kusa(ru), kusa(reru) rot, decay
kusa(rasu) let rot/spoil, corrode
kusa(su) disparage

——————— 1 ———————

6 腐朽 **fukyū** decay, molder, rot, decompose
9 腐食 **fushoku** corrosion
11 腐敗 **fuhai** decomposition, decay;
corruption

——————— 2 ———————

6 防腐剤 **bōfuzai** a preservative, antiseptic
7 豆腐 **tōfu** tofu, bean curd

——————— 3 ———————

12 湯豆腐 **yudōfu** boiled tofu

3q11.4   □ 土 厂 儿
                      22 18 16

JIN dust; the mundane world
chiri dust; trash, rubbish
gomi garbage, trash

——————— 1 ———————

8 塵取 **chirito(ri)** dustpan
10 塵紙 **chirigami** coarse (toilet) paper

——————— 12 ———————

3q12.3   □ 日 月 厂
                      43 42 18

廟   廟 廟

BYŌ mausoleum; shrine; palace

3q12.6 / 1530   □ 木 厂 扌
                         41 18 23

摩   庁 ｜ 摩 摩

MA rub, scrape **sasu(ru)** pat, stroke,
rub

——————— 1 ———————

4 摩天楼 **matenrō** skyscraper
17 摩擦 **masatsu** friction

——————— 2 ———————

9 按摩 **anma** massage; masseur,
masseuse
16 薩摩 **Satsuma** (ancient kuni, Kagoshima-ken)
薩摩芋 **satsumaimo** sweet potato

廢 → 廃 **3q9.3**

廣 → 広 **3q2.1**

3q12.8 / 1632   □ 心 夂 厂
                         51 49 18

慶   慶 慶

KEI rejoice; congratulate
yoroko(bu) rejoice, be happy over
YOSHI (part of given name)

——————— 1 ———————

2 慶子 **Keiko, Yoshiko** (f. given
name)
4 慶弔 **keichō** congratulations and
condolences
7 慶応 **Keiō** (a university); (era, 1865
– 1868)

3

氵
土
口
女
巾
犭
弓
彳
彡
艹
宀
屮
聿
广 **12**
尸
口

— 3 —

⁴ 内弁慶 **uchi-Benkei** tough-acting at home (but meek before outsiders)

— 13 —

3q13.3 / 1531 　　　🀫 石 木 厂
　　　　　　　　　53 41 18

磨 庁丨磨磨

MA, miga(ku) polish, brush **su(ru)** rub, chafe, file; lose

— 1 —

¹⁰ 磨耗 **mamō** wear and tear, abrasion

— 2 —

¹¹ 達磨 **Daruma** Dharma (Indian priest who brought Zen Buddhism to China circa 520 A.D.); tumbler, legless figurine

球磨川 **Kumagawa** (river, Kumamoto-ken)

¹² 歯磨 **hamiga(ki)** toothpaste

— 3 —

¹¹ 雪達磨 **yuki daruma** snowman

— 14 —

應 → 応 3q4.2

— 15 —

3q15.2 / 2281 　　　🀫 木 口 厂
　　　　　　　　　41 24 18

麿 麿麿

maro I; (name suffix) MARO (part of given name)

— 16 —

3q16.4 　　　🀫 艹 厂 儿
　　　　　　　　　32 18 16

麒 麒鹿其

KI Chinese-mythical beast associated with wise rule; genius; giraffe

— 1 —

²⁴ 麒麟 **kirin** giraffe

3q16.5 / 1630 　　　日 厂 冂 儿
　　　　　　　　　18 20 16

麗 麗麗

REI, RAI, uruwa(shii) beautiful, pretty, lovely **urara(ka)** beautiful (weather), bright, serene URARA (f. given name)

— 1 —

² 麗人 **reijin** beautiful woman

³ 麗々 **reirei(shii)** ostentatious, pretentious

— 2 —

⁸ 佳麗 **karei** beautiful

奇麗 **kirei** pretty, beautiful; clean, neat

¹⁰ 華麗 **karei** splendid, magnificent

¹⁴ 綺麗 **kirei** pretty, beautiful; clean

— 3 —

⁹ 美辞麗句 **biji-reiku** flowery language

— 18 —

3q18.2 / 1528 　　　🀫 甲 木 厂
　　　　　　　　　58 41 18

魔 魔魔

MA demon, devil, evil spirit

— 1 —

³ 魔女 **majo** witch, sorceress

⁸ 魔法使 **mahōtsuka(i)** magician, wizard

魔法瓶 **mahōbin** thermos bottle

¹¹ 魔術 **majutsu** magic, sorcery, witchcraft

— 2 —

⁷ 邪魔 **jama** hinder, obstruct, get in the way, interfere, bother, disturb

¹⁴ 誤魔化 **gomaka(su)** cheat, deceive; gloss over; tamper with, doctor

21

3q21.1 / 2278

鳥 隹 厂
80 74 18

鷹

鷹 鷹

YŌ, Ō, taka hawk TAKA (m. given name) **YŌ, Ō** (part of given name)

1

9 鷹派 **takaha** the hawks, hardliners
鷹狩 **takaga(ri)** falconry

22

廳 → 庁 3q2.2

3

尸 **3r**

尺	尻	尼	尽	尿	尾	局	届	屈	屈	居	屎	眉
1.1	2.1	2.2	3.1	4.1	4.2	4.4	5.1	3r5.1	5.2	5.3	6.1	5c4.9

屍	屋	屏	昼	展	屑	屠	屏	属	屠	殿	層	履
6.2	6.3	6.5	4c5.15	7.2	7.4	3r9.2	3r6.5	9.1	9.2	10.1	11.2	12.1

層	屬
3r11.2	3r9.1

1

3r1.1 / 1895

尸 |
40 2

尺

尺 尺

SHAKU, SEKI (unit of length, about 30 cm); measure, length

1

2 尺八 **shakuhachi** bamboo flute/recorder
9 尺度 **shakudo** (linear) measure, scale, yardstick, standard

---

2

3r2.1 / 1960

尸 十
40 12

尻

尻 尻

KŌ, shiri buttocks, fanny, backside, rear end; tail end

1

7 尻尾 **shippo** tail; end
8 尻押 **shirio(shi)** push from behind, boost, back, abet; instigator, wirepuller

12 尻軽 **shirigaru** wanton, loose

3r2.2 / 1620

尸 ヒ
40 13

尼

尼 尼

NI, ama nun

1

6 尼寺 **amadera** convent
11 尼崎 **Amagasaki** (city, Hyōgo-ken)
13 尼僧 **nisō** nun

3

3r3.1 / 1726

尸 |
40 2

尽

盡 | 尽 尽

JIN, tsu(kusu) exhaust, use up; render (service), make efforts **tsu(kasu)** exhaust, use up, run out of **tsu(kiru)** become exhausted/depleted, run out, end **kotogoto(ku)** all, entirely, completely

1

2 尽力 **jinryoku** efforts, exertions; assistance

氵 土 扌 口 女 巾 犭 弓 彡 彳 艹 宀 丷 虫 士 广 尸 3 口

8 尽忠 **jinchū** loyalty

—— 2 ——

9 食尽 **ku(i)tsu(kusu), ta(be)tsu(kusu)** eat up, consume

12 焼尽 **ya(ki)tsuku(su)** burn up, consume, reduce to ashes
ya(ke)tsu(kiru) burn itself out

無尽 **mujin** inexhaustible, endless; mutual financing association

—————— 4 ——————

3r4.1 / 1869

口 尸 氵
40 21

尿

尿 尿

NYŌ, yubari urine

—— 1 ——

13 尿意 **nyōi** the urge to urinate

—— 2 ——

8 泌尿科 **hinyōka** urology

9 屎尿 **shinyō** excreta

11 排尿 **hainyō** urination

3r4.2 / 1868

口 尸 十 一
40 12 1

尾

尾 尾

BI, o tail

—— 1 ——

6 尾行 **bikō** shadow, tail (someone)

11 尾崎 **Ozaki** (surname)

17 尾翼 **biyoku** tail (of an airplane)

—— 2 ——

4 中尾 **Nakao** (surname)

5 末尾 **matsubi** end, last, final

尻尾 **shippo** tail; end

8 妹尾 **Senoo** (surname)

松尾 **Matsuo** (surname)

11 接尾辞 **setsubiji** suffix

接尾語 **setsubigo** suffix

14 語尾 **gobi** word ending

16 燕尾服 **enbifuku** swallow-tailed coat

23 鷲尾 **Washio** (surname)

3r4.4 / 170

口 尸 口 一
40 24 1

局

局 局

KYOKU bureau, office; (radio/TV) station; situation; local **tsubone** court lady('s apartment)

—— 1 ——

5 局外 **kyokugai** the outside

8 局長 **kyokuchō** bureau chief, director, postmaster

局限 **kyokugen** localize, limit

9 局面 **kyokumen** (chessboard) position; situation

10 局部 **kyokubu** part, section; local; the affected region; one's private parts

局留 **kyokudo(me)** general delivery

—— 2 ——

4 支局 **shikyoku** a branch (office)

分局 **bunkyoku** branch office

6 当局 **tōkyoku** the authorities

8 事局 **jikyoku** circumstances

9 政局 **seikyoku** political situation

10 時局 **jikyoku** the situation

破局 **hakyoku** catastrophe, ruin

11 終局 **shūkyoku** end, conclusion; endgame

12 結局 **kekkyoku** after all, in the end

16 薬局 **yakkyoku** pharmacy

—— 3 ——

8 放送局 **hōsōkyoku** broadcasting station

9 造幣局 **zōheikyoku** the mint

10 郵便局 **yūbinkyoku** post office

13 電話局 **denwakyoku** telephone office

5

3r5.1 / 992

□ 日 尸 丨
43 40 2

届

居丨届届

todo(ku) reach, arrive **todo(keru)** report, notify; send, deliver

— 1 —

5 届出 **todokeide, todokede** report, notification

6 届先 **todo(ke)saki** where to report, receiver's address

— 2 —

12 無届 **mutodo(ke)** without advance notice

居 → 届 **3r5.1**

3r5.2 / 1802

□ 尸 山 凵
40 36 20

屈

屈屈

KUTSU bend; yield **kaga(mu)** bend/lean over, stoop, crouch **kaga(meru)** bend (one's leg/body), incline

— 1 —

0 屈する **kus(suru)** bend, bend over; yield to, be daunted

6 屈曲 **kukkyoku** crookedness; refraction; curvature

7 屈折 **kussetsu** bending; refraction; inflection

10 屈辱 **kutsujoku** humiliation, indignity

— 2 —

8 退屈 **taikutsu** boring, dull

9 怠屈 **taikutsu** boredom, tedium

卑屈 **hikutsu** mean-spirited, servile

11 偏屈 **henkutsu** eccentric, bigoted, narrow-minded

理屈 **rikutsu** theory; reason, logic; argument; pretext

15 窮屈 **kyūkutsu** narrow, cramped; formal, stiff, straitlaced; ill at ease

3r5.3 / 171

□ 尸 口 土
40 24 12

居

居居

KYO, KO, i(ru) be (present), exist

— 1 —

7 居住者 **kyojūsha** resident, inhabitant

8 居直 **inao(ru)** sit up straight; change one's attitude, come on strong; turn violent, resort to threat

10 居候 **isōrō** hanger-on, dependent, sponger

居眠 **inemu(ri)** doze, drowse

居留守 **irusu** pretend not to be in (to avoid callers)

12 居間 **ima** living room

— 2 —

3 土居 **Doi** (surname)

5 芝居 **shibai** stage play, theater

6 同居 **dōkyo** live in the same house

7 住居 **jūkyo, sumai** residence, dwelling

別居 **bekkyo** (legal) separation, living apart

8 長居 **nagai** stay too long

11 転居 **tenkyo** moving, change of address

鳥居 **torii** Shinto shrine archway

13 隠居 **inkyo** retirement; retired person; old person

新居 **shinkyo** one's new residence/home

6

3r6.1

□ 米 尸
62 40

屎

屎屎

SHI, kuso shit

— 1 —

7 屎尿 **shinyō** excreta

眉 → **5c4.9**

3

氵
土
扌
口
女
巾
犭
弓
彳
彡
艹
宀
山
耂
广
尸 6
囗

3r6.2

□ 尸 夕 卜
40 30 13

屍 　　屍屍

SHI, shikabane corpse

— 1 —

7 屍体 **shitai** corpse

3r6.3 / 167

□ 尸 土 竹
40 22 17

屋 　　屋屋

OKU, ya roof, house; shop, dealer

— 1 —

3 屋上 **okujō** roof, rooftop
4 屋内 **okunai** indoor(s)
5 屋外 **okugai** outdoor(s)
10 屋根 **yane** roof
15 屋敷 **yashiki** mansion

— 2 —

5 瓦屋根 **kawara yane** tiled roof
　本屋 **hon'ya** bookstore
　平屋 **hiraya** one-story house
6 肉屋 **nikuya** butcher (shop)
7 花屋 **hanaya** flower shop, florist
　牢屋 **rōya** prison, jail
　床屋 **tokoya** barber, barbershop
9 茶屋 **chaya** teahouse; tea dealer
10 部屋 **heya** room, apartment
　酒屋 **sakaya** wine dealer, liquor store
　家屋 **kaoku** house; building
　殺屋 **koro(shi)ya** hired killer
　蚊屋 **kaya** mosquito net
11 宿屋 **yadoya** inn
　魚屋 **sakanaya** fish shop/seller
12 畳屋 **tatamiya** tatami maker/dealer/store
13 靴屋 **kutsuya** shoe store, shoemaker
15 質屋 **shichiya** pawnshop
16 薬屋 **kusuriya** drugstore
17 闇屋 **yamiya** black marketeer
　鮨屋 **sushiya** sushi shop

— 3 —

2 八百屋 **yaoya** vegetable store; jack-of-all-trades
4 犬小屋 **inugoya** doghouse, kennel
6 名古屋 **Nagoya** (city, Aichi-ken)
7 阿古屋貝 **akoyagai** pearl oyster
8 青物屋 **aomonoya** vegetable store, greengrocer
　玩具屋 **omochaya** toy shop
10 料理屋 **ryōriya** restaurant
11 菓子屋 **kashiya** candy store, confectionery shop
12 貸部屋 **ka(shi)beya** room for rent
13 電気屋 **denkiya** electrical appliance store/dealer

3r6.5

□ 尸 艹 儿
40 32 16

屏 　　屏I屏屏

BYŌ folding screen **HEI** wall, fence

— 1 —

9 屏風 **byōbu** folding screen

昼 → **4c5.15**

— 7 —

3r7.2 / 1129

□ 衤 尸 艹
57 40 32

展 　　展展

TEN expand **NOBU, NORI** (part of given name)

— 1 —

5 展示 **tenji** exhibition, display
　展示会 **tenjikai** show, exhibition
11 展望 **tenbō** view, outlook, prospects
12 展開 **tenkai** unfold, develop, evolve; deploy, fan out; expand (a math expression), develop (into a two-dimensional surface)
17 展覧会 **tenrankai** exhibition

─────── 2 ───────

9 発展 **hatten** expansion, growth, development

発展途上国 **hattentojōkoku** developing country

16 親展 **shinten** confidential, personal (letter)

3r7.4

□ 月 尸 小
42 40 35

屑 屑

SETSU, kuzu trash, waste, scrap; scum, dregs (of society)

─────── 1 ───────

2 屑入 **kuzui(re)** trash can/receptacle

22 屑籠 **kuzukago** wastebasket

─────── 2 ───────

16 鋸屑 **nokokuzu** sawdust

─────── 8 ───────

屠 → 屠   3r9.2

屏 → 屏   3r6.5

─────── 9 ───────

3r9.1 / 1637

□ 虫 尸 口
64 40 20

屬 | 属 属

ZOKU belong to, be attached to; genus; subordinate official   **SHOKU** belong to, be attached to

─────── 1 ───────

0 属する **zoku(suru)** belong to, fall under, be affiliated with

6 属名 **zokumei** generic name

8 属性 **zokusei** attribute

─────── 2 ───────

5 付属 **fuzoku** attached, associated, auxiliary

7 附属 **fuzoku** attached, affiliated, ancillary

8 所属 **shozoku** be attached/assigned to

金属 **kinzoku** metal

金属製 **kinzokusei** made of metal

10 帰属 **kizoku** revert to, belong to, be ascribed to

従属的 **jūzokuteki** subordinate, dependent

─────── 3 ───────

12 無所属 **mushozoku** unaffiliated, independent

3r9.2

□ 曰 尸 土
43 40 22

屠 | 屠 屠

TO, hofu(ru) slaughter, butcher

─────── 1 ───────

10 屠殺 **tosatsu** butchering, slaughter

─────── 10 ───────

3r10.1 / 1130

⊞ 尸 艹 儿
40 32 16

殿 殿

DEN, TEN hall, palace; mister
tono lord; mansion   **-dono** Mr.
shingari rear

─────── 1 ───────

3 殿下 **Denka** His/Your Highness

4 殿方 **tonogata** gentlemen, men's

14 殿様 **tonosama** lord, prince

─────── 2 ───────

6 妃殿下 **hidenka** Her Highness

9 神殿 **shinden** temple, shrine

10 宮殿 **kyūden** palace

─────── 11 ───────

3r11.2 / 1367

□ 曲 曰 尸
58 43 40

層 | 層 層

SŌ layer, level, stratum, (social) class

3

氵土扌口女巾犭弓彳彡艹宀丷辶丰广尸 11 口

──────── 1 ────────
12 層雲 **sōun** stratus clouds

──────── 2 ────────
1 一層 **issō** still more, all the more
6 地層 **chisō** stratum, layer
10 高層 **kōsō** high-altitude, high-rise (building)
11 階層 **kaisō** tier; social stratum, class

──────── 12 ────────

3r12.1 / 1635

□	日	夂	尸
	43	49	40

履 履履

ha(ku) put on, wear (shoes/pants)

──────── 1 ────────
6 履行 **rikō** perform, fulfill, implement
8 履物 **ha(ki)mono** footwear
14 履歴書 **rirekisho** personal history, vita

──────── 2 ────────
9 草履 **zōri** sandals, zori

層 → 層 **3r11.2**

──────── 18 ────────

屬 → 属 **3r9.1**

──────── □ 3s ────────

口	□	□	囚	四	回	因	団	困	囲	図	国	固
3d0.1	3s5.1	3s4.2	2.1	2.2	3.1	3.2	3.3	4.1	4.2	4.3	5.1	5.2

面	圃	恩	勉	國	圏	圈	園	圍	圓	團	圖	豫
6.1	7.1	4k6.23	2n8.1	3s5.1	3s9.1	9.1	10.1	3s4.2	2r2.1	3s3.3	3s4.3	0a4.12

齡	齡
3s21.1	21.1

──────── 0 ────────

口 → **3d0.1**

□ → 国 **3s5.1**

□ → 囲 **3s4.2**

──────── 2 ────────

3s2.1 / 1195

□	口	亻
	24	3

囚 囚囚

SHŪ arrest, imprison; prisoner
torawa(reru) be captured/apprehended; be in thrall to, be seized with

──────── 1 ────────
2 囚人 **shūjin** prisoner, convict

──────── 2 ────────
13 虜囚 **ryoshū** captive, prisoner (of war)
14 獄囚 **gokushū** prisoner

3s2.2 / 6

□	口	儿
	24	16

四 四四

SHI, yot(tsu), yo(tsu), yon, yo- four

──────── 1 ────────
2 四人 **yonin** four people
　四十 **yonjū, shijū** forty
4 四六時中 **shirokujichū** 24 hours a day, constantly
　四月 **shigatsu** April
　　yon(ka)getsu four months
　四日 **yokka** four days; the fourth (day of the month)
　四日市 **Yokkaichi** (city, Mie-ken)

四方 **shihō, yomo** all (four) directions/sides

四方八方 **shihō-happō** in every direction, far and wide

6 四百 **yonhyaku** four hundred

7 四角 **shikaku** square; quadrilateral **yo(tsu)kado** four corners; intersection

四角張 **shikakuba(ru)** be formal/stiff

四季 **shiki** the four seasons

8 四苦八苦 **shiku-hakku** agony, dire distress

四国 **Shikoku** (island)

9 四重奏 **shijūsō** (instrumental) quartet

四則 **shisoku** the four basic arithmetic operations (+, −, *, /)

10 四時 **yoji** four o'clock **shiji** the/all four seasons

11 四捨五入 **shisha-gonyū** rounding off

12 四割 **yonwari, shiwari** forty percent **yo(tsu)wa(ri)** divide into four, quarter

——————— 3 ———————

3s3.1 / 90

回

巴 | 回 | 回

KAI, E (how many) times, (which) round/inning; go around **mawa(ru)** go/turn around **mawa(ri)** turning around; circumference; surroundings, vicinity **mawa(su)** (tr.) turn; send around **mawa(shi)** loincloth **megu(ru)** make a cycle; make one's rounds; surround, concern **megu(rasu)** surround; ponder

——————— 1 ———————

7 回忌 **kaiki** anniversary of one's death

8 回送 **kaisō** forwarding, transportation; (bus) returning to the barn, Out of Service

10 回帰 **kaiki** recurrent; regression (coefficient)

回教徒 **kaikyōto** a Moslem

11 回道 **mawa(ri)michi** roundabout way

回転 **kaiten** revolve, rotate, swivel

12 回復 **kaifuku** recovery

回答 **kaitō** reply

13 回数券 **kaisūken** (train) coupon tickets

回想 **kaisō** retrospection, reminiscence

15 回避 **kaihi** avoid

21 回顧 **kaiko** recollect, look back on

回顧録 **kaikoroku** memoirs, reminiscences

——————— 2 ———————

1 一回 **ikkai** once, one time; a game; an inning **hitomawa(ri)** a turn/round

一回戦 **ikkaisen** first game/round (of tennis)

3 大回 **ōmawa(ri)** the long way around, circuitous route

上回 **uwamawa(ru)** be more than, exceed

下回 **shitamawa(ru)** be less than, fall short of

4 今回 **konkai** this time, lately

5 北回帰線 **Kita Kaikisen** the Tropic of Cancer

出回 **demawa(ru)** appear on the market

迂回 **ukai** detour

巡回 **junkai** tour, patrol, one's rounds

右回 **migimawa(ri)** clockwise

6 毎回 **maikai** every time

次回 **jikai** next time

先回 **sakimawa(ri)** anticipate, forestall; arrive ahead of

7 何回 **nankai** how many times

走回 **hashi(ri)mawa(ru)** run around

初回 **shokai** the first time

9 飛回 **to(bi)mawa(ru)** fly/jump/rush around

前回 **zenkai** last time

10 捜回 **saga(shi)mawa(ru)** search/hunt around

挽回 **bankai** retrieve, recover, restore

振回 **fu(ri)mawa(su)** wave about, brandish

根回 **nemawa(shi)** doing the groundwork, pre-selling (a proposal), consensus-building

胴回 **dōmawa(ri)** one's girth

11 旋回 **senkai** turning, revolving, circling

転回 **tenkai** rotate, revolve

12 遠回 **tōmawa(ri)** roundabout way, detour **tōmawa(shi)** roundabout expression

13 搔回 **ka(ki)mawa(su)** stir, churn; ransack, rummage around

腰回 **koshimawa(ri)** one's hip measurement

14 駆回 **ka(ke)mawa(ru), ka(kezuri)mawa(ru)** run around

15 暴回 **aba(re)mawa(ru)** run riot/ amuck, rampage

———————— 3 ————————

4 引搔回 **hi(k)ka(ki)mawa(su)** ransack, rummage through; carry on highhandedly

12 最終回 **saishūkai** the last time/inning

3s3.2 / 554

□ 冂 大
24 34

IN cause, factor **china(mu)** be associated with **china(mi ni)** in this connection, by the way **yo(ru)** be due to, be based on **yo(tte)** therefore, consequently

———————— 1 ————————

8 因果 **inga** cause and effect; fate; misfortune

15 因縁 **innen** fate; connection; origin; pretext

———————— 2 ————————

4 内因 **naiin** internal cause

5 主因 **shuin** main cause, primary factor

6 死因 **shiin** cause of death

10 原因 **gen'in** cause

11 悪因悪果 **akuin-akka** Evil breeds evil.

3s3.3 / 491

□ 冂 寸
24 37

DAN, TON, DON group

———————— 1 ————————

6 団地 **danchi** (public) housing development, apartment complex

7 団体 **dantai** group, organization

10 団扇 **uchiwa** round fan

12 団結 **danketsu** unity, solidarity

———————— 2 ————————

2 入団 **nyūdan** join, enlist

5 布団 **futon** bedding, sleeping mat, futon

7 社団法人 **shadan hōjin** corporate juridical person

8 師団 **shidan** (army) division

財団 **zaidan** foundation, financial group

財団法人 **zaidan hōjin** (incorporated) foundation

11 経団連 **Keidanren** Federation of Economic Organizations (Keidanren) (short for 経済団体連合)

12 集団 **shūdan** group, mass, crowd

13 蒲団 **futon** futon, mattress, bedding

楽団 **gakudan** orchestra, band

15 劇団 **gekidan** troupe, theatrical company

16 親団体 **oyadantai** parent organization

———————— 3 ————————

6 合唱団 **gasshōdan** chorus, choir

7 応援団 **ōendan** rooting section, cheerleaders

10 座蒲団 **zabuton** cushion

11 掛布団 **ka(ke)buton** quilt, coverlet

15 暴力団 **bōryokudan** gangster organization

敷布団 **shikibuton** floor mattress

———————— 4 ————————

14 管弦楽団 **kangen gakudan** orchestra

—————— **4** ——————

3s4.1 / 558   回 木 口
                    41 24

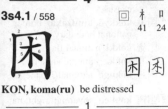

KON, koma(ru) be distressed

—————— 1 ——————

4 困切 **koma(ri)ki(ru)** be in a fix, be at a loss
8 困果 **koma(ri)ha(teru)** be greatly troubled/nonplussed
12 困惑 **konwaku** perplexity, dilemma
15 困窮 **konkyū** poverty, distress
18 困難 **konnan** difficulty, trouble

—————— 2 ——————

11 貧困 **hinkon** poverty; lack

3s4.2 / 1194   回 口 艹 一
                     24 32 1

I, kako(mu/u) surround, enclose, encircle

—————— 1 ——————

13 囲碁 **igo** go (the board game)

—————— 2 ——————

5 包囲 **hōi** surround, encircle, besiege
8 周囲 **shūi** circumference, perimeter; surroundings
    取囲 **to(ri)kako(mu)** surround, encircle
10 胸囲 **kyōi** girth/circumference of the chest
12 雰囲気 **fun'iki** atmosphere, ambience
15 範囲 **han'i** extent, scope, range
    範囲内 **han'inai** within the limits of

3s4.3 / 339   回 口 十 |
                     24 12 2

ZU drawing, diagram, plan

TO, haka(ru) plan, seek (to effect), strive/work for, (try to) bring about

—————— 1 ——————

8 図表 **zuhyō** chart, table, graph
9 図面 **zumen** drawing, sketch, plan, blueprints
10 図案 **zuan** (ornamental) design, device
    図書 **tosho** books
    図書館 **toshokan** library
13 図解 **zukai** explanatory diagram, illustration
14 図説 **zusetsu** explanatory diagram, illustration

—————— 2 ——————

4 不図 **futo** suddenly, unexpectedly, by chance
6 合図 **aizu** signal, sign
    地図 **chizu** map
7 系図 **keizu** genealogy, family tree
10 流図 **naga(re)zu** flowchart
    挿図 **sōzu** figure, illustration
11 略図 **ryakuzu** rough sketch, outline map
13 意図 **ito** intention, aim
14 製図 **seizu** drafting, drawing, cartography
17 縮図 **shukuzu** reduced/scaled-down drawing

—————— 3 ——————

10 家系図 **kakeizu** family tree
    案内図 **annaizu** information map
11 設計図 **sekkeizu** plan, blueprint

—————— **5** ——————

3s5.1 / 40   回 王 口 |
                     46 24 2

KOKU country **kuni** country; (ancient) province; one's native province/country

—————— 1 ——————

3 国々 **kuniguni** countries, nations
4 国内 **kokunai** domestic
    国文学 **kokubungaku** Japanese literature

5 国民 **kokumin** the/a people, a national; national

国民性 **kokuminsei** national character

国史 **kokushi** national/Japanese history

国字 **kokuji** native script; made-in-Japan kanji not found in Chinese

国立 **kokuritsu** national (park/library) **Kunitachi** (city, Tōkyō-to)

6 国会 **kokkai** national assembly, parliament, diet, congress

国防 **kokubō** national defense

国交 **kokkō** diplomatic relations

国有 **kokuyū** national ownership

7 国学者 **kokugakusha** Japanese-classics scholar

国利 **kokuri** national interests

8 国事 **kokuji** affairs of state

国宝 **kokuhō** national treasure

国定 **kokutei** quasi-national, state-prescribed

9 国連 **Kokuren** United Nations, UN (short for 国際連合)

国連総会 **Kokuren Sōkai** UN General Assembly

国後島 **Kunashiri-tō** (island, Russian Hokkaidō)

10 国益 **kokueki** national interests/benefit

国辱 **kokujoku** national disgrace

国家 **kokka** state, nation, country

国家主義 **kokka shugi** nationalism

11 国道 **kokudō** national highway

国務 **kokumu** affairs of state

国務長官 **kokumu chōkan** (U.S.) Secretary of State

国産 **kokusan** domestic-made

12 国葬 **kokusō** state funeral

国富 **kokufu** national wealth

国営 **kokuei** government-run, state-managed

13 国債 **kokusai** national debt/bonds

国際 **kokusai** international

国際化 **kokusaika** internationalization

国際連合 **Kokusai Rengō** United Nations

国勢調査 **kokusei chōsa** (national) census

14 国境 **kokkyō, kunizakai** border, national boundary

国旗 **kokki** national flag

国歌 **kokka** national anthem

国語 **kokugo** national/Japanese language

15 国権 **kokken** sovereign right; national prestige

20 国籍 **kokuseki** nationality, citizenship

———————— 2 ————————

1 一国 **ikkoku** stubborn, hotheaded; the whole country

2 入国 **nyūkoku** entering a country, immigration

3 万国 **bankoku** all nations

大国 **taikoku** large country; major nation

亡国 **bōkoku** ruined country, national ruin

4 天国 **tengoku** paradise, heaven

中国 **Chūgoku** China; Western tip of Honshū, comprising Hiroshima, Okayama, Shimane, Tottori, and Yamaguchi prefectures

中国地方 **Chūgoku chihō** the Chūgoku region (Hiroshima, Okayama, Shimane, Tottori, and Yamaguchi prefectures)

王国 **ōkoku** kingdom, monarchy

5 北国 **hokkoku, kitaguni** northern provinces, northern countries

出国 **shukkoku** departure from a country

本国 **hongoku** one's own country

母国 **bokoku** one's mother/native country

母国語 **bokokugo** one's mother/native tongue

他国 **takoku** foreign country; another province

外国 **gaikoku** foreign country; foreign

外国人 **gaikokujin** foreigner

外国語 **gaikokugo** foreign language

四国 **Shikoku** (island)

6 全国 **zenkoku, zengoku** the whole country, nationwide, national

全国民 **zenkokumin** the entire nation

列国 **rekkoku** the powers, all nations

各国 **kakkoku** all/various countries

自国 **jikoku** one's own country

米国 **Beikoku** the United States

7 我国 **wa(ga)kuni** our country

売国 **baikoku** betrayal of one's country

8 建国 **kenkoku** founding of a country

英国 **Eikoku** Britain, the U.K.

英国人 **Eikokujin** Briton, Englishman

9 軍国主義 **gunkoku shugi** militarism

帝国 **teikoku** empire

帝国主義 **teikoku shugi** imperialism

神国 **shinkoku** land of the gods

祖国 **sokoku** one's homeland/fatherland

10 帰国 **kikoku** return to one's country

島国 **shimaguni** island country

11 強国 **kyōkoku** strong country, great power

異国 **ikoku, kotokuni** foreign country

雪国 **yukiguni** snow country

13 戦国時代 **sengoku jidai** era of civil wars

靖国神社 **Yasukuni-jinja** (shrine in Tōkyō dedicated to fallen Japanese soldiers)

14 愛国心 **aikokushin** patriotism

15 隣国 **ringoku** neighboring country

諸国 **shokoku** all/various countries

18 韓国 **Kankoku** South Korea

鎖国 **sakoku** national isolation

---------- 3 ----------

5 出入国 **shutsunyūkoku** emigration and immigration

加盟国 **kameikoku** member nation, signatory

6 合衆国 **Gasshūkoku** United States

先進国 **senshinkoku** advanced/developed nation

共和国 **kyōwakoku** republic

7 君主国 **kunshukoku** a monarchy

8 法治国 **hōchikoku** constitutional state

11 密入国 **mitsunyūkoku** smuggle oneself into a country

12 満州国 **Manshūkoku** Manchukuo

13 戦敗国 **senpaikoku** defeated nation

戦勝国 **senshōkoku** victorious nation

---------- 4 ----------

4 中華民国 **Chūka Minkoku** Republic of China (Taiwan)

---------- 5 ----------

9 発展途上国 **hattentojōkoku** developing country

---------- 7 ----------

4 中華人民共和国 **Chūka Jinmin Kyōwakoku** People's Republic of China

3s5.2 / 972

□ 口 十
24 12

固 囗

KO, kata(i) hard, firm, solid   **kata(maru/meru)** (intr./tr.) harden, solidify   **moto(yori)** from the beginning; of course

---------- 1 ----------

6 固有 **koyū** its own, peculiar, characteristic

固有名詞 **koyū meishi** proper noun

8 固苦 **katakuru(shii)** stiff, formal, strict

固定 **kotei** fixed

11 固執 **koshitsu** hold fast to, persist in, insist on

---------- 2 ----------

7 牢固 **rōko** firm, solid, inflexible

11 断固 **danko** firm, resolute

13 頑固 **ganko** stubborn, obstinate

16 凝固 **gyōko** solidify, congeal, coagulate   **ko(ri)kata(maru)** coagulate; be fanatical

—————— 6 ——————

3s6.1 / 274

日 口 一 二
24 14 4

面

面 面

MEN face; mask; surface; aspect, facet; page **omote, omo, tsura** face

—————— 1 ——————

0 面する **men(suru)** face, border, front on

2 面子 **mentsu** face, honor
　menko cardboard game doll

5 面白 **omoshiro(i)** interesting; amusing

　面目 **menmoku, menboku** face, honor, dignity

6 面会 **menkai** interview, meeting

10 面倒 **mendō** trouble, difficulty; taking care of, tending to

　面倒臭 **mendōkusa(i)** troublesome, a big bother

11 面接 **mensetsu** interview

15 面影 **omokage** face, looks; trace, vestiges

16 面積 **menseki** area

—————— 2 ——————

1 一面 **ichimen** one side/phase; the whole surface; first page (of a newspaper)

3 三面記事 **sanmen kiji** page-3 news, police news, human-interest stories

　上面 **jōmen** surface, top, exterior
　uwatsura, uwa(t)tsura surface, appearances

4 内面 **naimen** inside, interior, inner

　反面 **hanmen** the other side, on the other hand

　方面 **hōmen** direction; district; standpoint; aspect, phase

5 凸面 **totsumen** convex (surface)

　凹面 **ōmen** concave (surface)

　半面 **hanmen** half the face; one side, half; the other side

　他面 **tamen** the other side, on the other hand

外面 **gaimen** exterior, outward appearance, surface

正面 **shōmen** front, head-on

白面 **hakumen** white/pale face; inexperience **shirafu** sober

6 両面刷 **ryōmenzu(ri)** printing on both sides

仮面 **kamen** mask, disguise

全面的 **zenmenteki** all-out, full, general

地面 **jimen** ground, surface, land

7 対面 **taimen** interview, meeting; facing each other

赤面 **sekimen** a blush **akatsura** red face; villain's role

局面 **kyokumen** (chessboard) position; situation

図面 **zumen** drawing, sketch, plan, blueprints

8 表面 **hyōmen** surface

画面 **gamen** scene, picture, (TV etc.) screen

直面 **chokumen** be faced with, confront

9 前面 **zenmen** front, front side

洗面所 **senmenjo** washroom, lavatory

背面 **haimen** rear, back, reverse

10 真面目 **majime** serious-minded, earnest, honest
　shinmenmoku one's true self/character; seriousness, earnestness

鬼面 **kimen** devil's face/mask; bluff

11 側面 **sokumen** side, flank

斜面 **shamen** slope, inclined plane

12 場面 **bamen** scene

腹面 **fuku(ret)tsura** sulky/sullen look, pout

13 路面 **romen** road surface

14 誌面 **shimen** page of a magazine

18 額面 **gakumen** face value, par

—————— 3 ——————

2 几帳面 **kichōmen** methodical, precise, punctilious

4 不真面目 **fumajime** not serious-minded, insincere

　仏頂面 **butchōzura** sour face, pout, scowl

3
氵
土
扌
口
女
巾
犭
弓
彳
彡
艹
宀
屮
耂
广
尸
6 口

⁶ 多方面 **tahōmen** various, different, many-sided, versatile

各方面 **kaku hōmen** every direction, all quarters

⁷ 社会面 **shakaimen** local-news page

初対面 **shotaimen** first meeting

¹⁰ 真正面 **ma(s)shōmen** directly opposite, right in front

¹⁷ 糞真面目 **kusomajime** humorless earnestness

7

3s7.1   ◻ 月 口 十
                             42 24 12

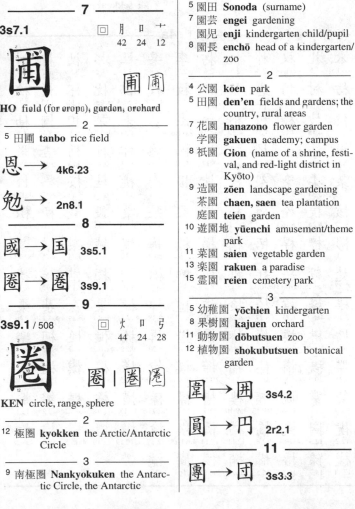

HO field (for crops), garden, orchard

--- 2 ---

⁵ 田圃 **tanbo** rice field

恩 → 4k6.23

勉 → 2n8.1

--- 8 ---

國 → 国 3s5.1

圈 → 圏 3s9.1

--- 9 ---

3s9.1 / 508   ◻ 火 口 弓
                            44 24 28

KEN circle, range, sphere

--- 2 ---

¹² 極圏 **kyokken** the Arctic/Antarctic Circle

--- 3 ---

⁹ 南極圏 **Nankyokuken** the Antarctic Circle, the Antarctic

10

3s10.1 / 447   ◻ 衤 口 土
                           57 24 22

EN, sono garden S**ONO** (surname)

--- 1 ---

⁵ 園田 **Sonoda** (surname)

⁷ 園芸 **engei** gardening

園児 **enji** kindergarten child/pupil

⁸ 園長 **enchō** head of a kindergarten/zoo

--- 2 ---

⁴ 公園 **kōen** park

⁵ 田園 **den'en** fields and gardens; the country, rural areas

⁷ 花園 **hanazono** flower garden

学園 **gakuen** academy; campus

⁸ 祇園 **Gion** (name of a shrine, festival, and red-light district in Kyōto)

⁹ 造園 **zōen** landscape gardening

茶園 **chaen, saen** tea plantation

庭園 **teien** garden

¹⁰ 遊園地 **yūenchi** amusement/theme park

¹¹ 菜園 **saien** vegetable garden

¹³ 楽園 **rakuen** a paradise

¹⁵ 霊園 **reien** cemetery park

--- 3 ---

⁵ 幼稚園 **yōchien** kindergarten

⁸ 果樹園 **kajuen** orchard

¹¹ 動物園 **dōbutsuen** zoo

¹² 植物園 **shokubutsuen** botanical garden

圍 → 囲 3s4.2

圓 → 円 2r2.1

--- 11 ---

團 → 団 3s3.3

圖 → 図　3s4.3

—————— 13 ——————

豫 → 予　0a4.12

—————— 16 ——————

鹹 → 鹼　3s21.1

3 ⚏

氵 土 扌 口 女 巾 犭 弓 彳 彡 艹 宀 丷 山 士 广 尸 口 **21**

—————— 21 ——————

3s21.1　　田 口 卜 十
　　　　　　24 13 12

鹼　鹸｜鹹鹸

KEN saltiness, brine; lye; soap

—————— 2 ——————

5 石鹸 **sekken** soap

————— 十 **4a** —————

木	札	权	朴	机	朽	李	朶	杜	杉	杖	杆	材
0.1	1.1	4a11.18	2.3	2.4	2.6	2.7	2.8	3.1	3.2	3.5	4a7.7	3.7
枴	村	杓	杏	条	林	枚	栈	梯	枕	杯	析	松
4a5.28	3.11	3.12	3.13	4i4.1	4.1	4.4	4a3.7	4a5.25	4.8	4.11	4.12	4.16
杭	枝	枠	板	枢	琳	杰	杰	采	枈	相	柵	柚
4.17	4.18	4.19	4.21	4.22	3q4.1	2a11.6	4a4.16	4.24	4a6.34	5.3	5.4	5.5
柑	柄	柱	柏	柾	柳	枷	柊	柿	枯	栃	査	果
5.6	5.9	5.12	5.14	5.15	5.17	5.19	5.24	5.25	5.26	5.28	5.32	0a8.8
某	柔	染	架	栈	株	根	桁	桃	桂	桜	格	桧
5.33	5.34	5.35	5.36	6.1	6.3	6.5	6.8	6.10	6.13	6.15	6.17	4a13.8
核	校	栓	梅	栢	桐	栗	栞	桑	殺	栽	梗	椒
6.22	6.24	6.26	6.27	4a5.14	6.30	6.32	6.34	2h8.1	6.35	4n6.1	7.1	4a8.7
彬	梓	桿	梧	梢	梯	桶	梅	梶	械	梨	梁	梦
7.3	7.5	7.7	7.9	7.13	7.17	7.18	4a6.27	7.19	7.22	7.24	7.25	3k10.14
梵	殺	耕	耗	椎	棟	椰	椒	棚	極	棋	椄	棲
7.27	4a6.35	0a10.13	0a10.12	8.1	8.3	8.6	8.7	8.10	8.11	8.14	8.15	8.16
棒	棧	棺	椅	検	椋	植	椁	槌	巣	森	椹	渠
8.20	4a6.1	8.25	8.27	8.28	8.31	8.32	8.38	4a9.27	3n8.1	8.39	4a8.14	8.40
楯	梻	楼	楕	椿	楊	楷	楫	楠	樋	槌	楓	楽
9.3	3k5.7	9.10	9.13	9.16	9.17	9.18	9.20	9.25	4a10.28	9.27	9.28	9.29
楪	概	構	榛	榴	樺	模	槍	様	槙	槇	樋	槃
9.31	10.2	10.10	10.11	10.12	10.15	10.16	10.20	10.25	4a10.27	10.27	10.28	10.30
榮	業	槻	橢	樓	槽	標	樣	横	権	樞	樂	機
3n6.1	0a13.3	11.4	4a9.13	4a9.10	11.7	11.8	4a10.25	11.13	11.18	4a4.22	4a9.29	12.1
樸	樹	槪	橋	橘	氈	横	橙	樽	橦	櫛	檜	檢
12.2	12.3	4a10.2	12.8	12.11	12.14	4a11.13	12.17	4a12.19	12.19	4a15.5	13.8	4a8.28
檀	鞣	櫓	櫛	欄	櫻	欄	欖	鬱				
13.11	14.7	15.2	15.5	16.4	4a6.15	4a16.4	22.1	25.1				

— 0 —

4a0.1 / 22   □ 木
                                        41

木

BOKU, MOKU, ki, ko- tree, wood

— 1 —

3 木下 **Kinoshita** (surname)
4 木内 **Kiuchi** (surname)
5 木本 **Kimoto** (surname)
木立 **kodachi** grove, thicket
木田 **Kida** (surname)
7 木材 **mokuzai** wood, lumber
木村 **Kimura** (surname)
8 木苺 **kiichigo** raspberry
木実 **ki(no)mi, ko(no)mi** fruit, nut, berry
9 木炭画 **mokutanga** charcoal drawing
木枯 **koga(rashi)** wintry wind
10 木陰 **kokage** tree shade
木原 **Kihara** (surname)
11 木彫 **kibo(ri), mokuchō** wood carving
12 木葉 **ki(no)ha, ko(no)ha** tree leaves, foliage
14 木製 **mokusei** wooden, made of wood
木綿 **momen** cotton (cloth)
kiwata cotton (plant)
18 木曜日 **mokuyōbi** Thursday

— 2 —

2 八木 **Yagi** (surname)
3 三木 **Miki** (surname)
大木 **Ōki** (surname)
土木 **doboku** civil engineering, public works
7 材木 **zaimoku** wood, lumber
8 並木 **namiki** row of trees; roadside tree
松木 **matsu(no)ki** pine tree
青木 **Aoki** (surname)
9 荒木 **Araki** (surname)
枯木 **ka(re)ki** dead tree
栃木県 **Tochigi-ken** (prefecture)
10 高木 **Takagi** (surname)

11 啄木鳥 **kitsutsuki** woodpecker
梶木 **kaji(no)ki** mulberry tree (used for paper)
黒木 **Kuroki** (surname)
12 喬木 **kyōboku** tall tree
植木 **ueki** garden/potted plant
植木鉢 **uekibachi** flowerpot
13 鈴木 **Suzuki** (surname)
14 雑木林 **zōkibayashi, zōbokurin** grove of trees of various species
16 樹木 **jumoku** trees

— 3 —

7 佐々木 **Sasaki** (surname)

— 1 —

4a1.1 / 1157   □ 木 |
                                        41 2

札

SATSU paper money, slip of paper; a bid, tender **fuda** label, tag, sign; chit, ticket; amulet

— 1 —

7 札束 **satsutaba** wad of money, bundle/roll of bills
13 札幌 **Sapporo** (city, Hokkaidō)

— 2 —

4 切札 **ki(ri)fuda** trump card
5 立札 **ta(te)fuda** bulletin/notice board
6 名札 **nafuda** name plate/tag
7 花札 **hanafuda** floral playing cards
改札口 **kaisatsuguchi** ticket gate, wicket
8 表札 **hyōsatsu** nameplate, doorplate
11 偽札 **nisesatsu** counterfeit paper money
15 標札 **hyōsatsu** nameplate, doorplate
19 贋札 **nisesatsu, gansatsu** counterfeit currency

4

木 1
月
日 火
禾
王 牛
方
攵
心
戸
戈

——— 2 ———

权 → 権 **4a11.18**

4a2.3 / 1466 ⯐ 木 卜
41 13

BOKU simple, plain **SUNAO** (m. given name)

——— 1 ———

8 朴直 **bokuchoku** simple and honest, ingenuous

——— 2 ———

10 淳朴 **junboku** simple and honest
素朴 **soboku** simple, artless, ingenuous
14 醇朴 **junboku** simple and honest

4a2.4 / 1305 ⯐ 木 几
41 20

KI, tsukue desk

——— 1 ———

3 机上 **kijō** desk-top, academic, theoretical, armchair

4a2.6 / 1628 ⯐ 木 丂
41 14

KYŪ, ku(chiru) rot, decay

——— 1 ———

8 朽果 **ku(chi)ha(teru)** rot away

——— 2 ———

4 不朽 **fukyū** immortal, everlasting
14 腐朽 **fukyū** decay, molder, rot, decompose

4a2.7 / 2104 ⯐ 木 子
41 6

RI, sumomo plum **Lee** (Chinese/Korean surname) **RI, MOMO** (part of given name)

4a2.8 ⯐ 木 力
41 8

DA branch; hang down

——— 3 ———

4a3.1 / 2103 ⯐ 木 土
41 22

TO, ZU crab apple, wild pear; stop, block, close **mori** woods, grove (with a shrine) **TO, ZU, MORI, AKANASHI** (part of given name)

——— 1 ———

12 杜絶 **tozetsu** be blocked/obstructed
15 杜撰 **zusan** slipshod, careless(ly done)

4a3.2 / 1872 ⯐ 木 彡
41 31

sugi Japan(ese) cedar, cryptomeria, sugi **SUGI** (surname)

——— 1 ———

3 杉山 **Sugiyama** (surname)
5 杉本 **Sugimoto** (surname)
杉田 **Sugita** (surname)
10 杉原 **Sugihara** (surname)

———————— 2 ————————

³ 上杉 **Uesugi** (surname)
⁸ 若杉 **Wakasugi** (surname)

4a3.5

木 十 |
41 12 2

杖 杖

JŌ, tsue staff, cane

———————— 3 ————————

⁸ 松葉杖 **matsubazue** crutches

杆 → 桿 **4a7.7**

4a3.7 / 552

木 十 |
41 12 2

材 材 材

ZAI wood, lumber; material; talent

———————— 1 ————————

⁴ 材木 **zaimoku** wood, lumber
¹⁰ 材料 **zairyō** materials, ingredients; data; factors

———————— 2 ————————

² 人材 **jinzai** man of talent, personnel
⁴ 木材 **mokuzai** wood, lumber
⁸ 取材 **shuzai** news gathering, coverage
¹⁰ 素材 **sozai** a material; subject matter
¹³ 適材 **tekizai** the right person

枥 → 栃 **4a5.28**

4a3.11 / 191

木 寸
41 37

村 村 村

SON, mura village

———————— 1 ————————

² 村人 **murabito** villager

³ 村上 **Murakami** (surname)
村山 **Murayama** (surname)
⁴ 村井 **Murai** (surname)
⁵ 村民 **sonmin** villagers
村田 **Murata** (surname)
⁸ 村長 **sonchō** village mayor
¹⁹ 村瀬 **Murase** (surname)

———————— 2 ————————

³ 川村 **Kawamura** (surname)
上村 **Uemura, Kamimura** (surname)
下村 **Shimomura** (surname)
⁴ 中村 **Nakamura** (surname)
今村 **Imamura** (surname)
木村 **Kimura** (surname)
⁵ 北村 **Kitamura** (surname)
田村 **Tamura** (surname)
⁶ 西村 **Nishimura** (surname)
吉村 **Yoshimura** (surname)
竹村 **Takemura** (surname)
⁷ 谷村 **Tanimura** (surname)
沢村 **Sawamura** (surname)
町村 **chōson** towns and villages, municipality
⁸ 岡村 **Okamura** (surname)
河村 **Kawamura** (surname)
松村 **Matsumura** (surname)
武村 **Takemura** (surname)
⁹ 津村 **Tsumura** (surname)
¹⁰ 島村 **Shimamura** (surname)
¹¹ 野村 **Nomura** (surname)
¹³ 農村 **nōson** farm village, rural community
¹⁸ 藤村 **Fujimura** (surname)

———————— 3 ————————

⁵ 市町村 **shichōson** cities, towns, and villages; municipalities

4a3.12

木 勹 |
41 15 2

杓 杓

SHAKU ladle, dipper; handle

———————— 1 ————————

² 杓子 **shakushi** dipper, ladle, scoop

4a3.13 / 2102

⊟ 木 口
41 24

杏 杏杏

KYŌ, anzu apricot
KYŌ, KŌ, AN (part of given name)
ANZU (f. given name)

――― 1 ―――

2 杏子 **Kyōko, Momoko, Yōko** (f. given name)

――― 2 ―――

14 銀杏 **ginnan** gingko nut **ichō** gingko tree

条 → 4i4.1

――― 4 ―――

4a4.1 / 127

⊞ 木
41

林 林林

RIN, hayashi woods, forest
HAYASHI (surname) SHIGE (part of given name)

――― 1 ―――

11 林道 **rindō** forest road/trail
13 林業 **ringyō** forestry
16 林檎 **ringo** apple

――― 2 ―――

3 小林 **Kobayashi** (surname)
山林学 **sanringaku** forestry
6 竹林 **takebayashi, chikurin** bamboo grove
9 造林 **zōrin** (re)forestation
11 密林 **mitsurin** jungle, dense forest
12 森林 **shinrin** woods, forest
13 農林水産省 **Nōrinsuisanshō** Ministry of Agriculture, Forestry and Fisheries

――― 3 ―――

14 雑木林 **zōkibayashi, zōbokurin** grove of trees of various species

4a4.4 / 1156

⊞ 木 攵
41 49

枚 枚枚

MAI (counter for thin, flat objects)

――― 1 ―――

13 枚数 **maisū** number of sheets

――― 2 ―――

1 一枚 **ichimai** one sheet
2 二枚目 **nimaime** (role of a) handsome man/beau
二枚舌 **nimaijita** forked tongue, duplicity

栈 → 材 4a3.7

梛 → 柿 4a5.25

4a4.8 / 1982

⊞ 木 冂 丨
41 20 2

枕 枕枕

CHIN, makura pillow

――― 1 ―――

12 枕詞 **makurakotoba** prefatory word, set epithet

――― 2 ―――

15 膝枕 **hizamakura** using someone's lap for a pillow

4a4.11 / 1155

⊞ 木 一 丨
41 14 2

杯 盃丨杯杯

HAI cup; (counter for cupfuls)
sakazuki winecup (for saké)

――― 2 ―――

1 一杯 **ippai** a cup of; a drink; full; to the upmost
9 祝杯 **shukuhai** a toast
11 乾杯 **kanpai** a toast; Cheers!

¹⁵ 賞杯 **shōhai** trophy, prize cup

松葉杖 **matsubazue** crutches

——— 3 ———

¹³ 腹一杯 **hara ippai** full stomach; to one's heart's content

——— 2 ———

³ 小松 **Komatsu** (surname)

⁸ 若松 **Wakamatsu** (surname)

門松 **kadomatsu** New Year's pine-and-bamboo decorations

¹⁴ 精一杯 **sei-ippai** with all one's might

¹⁰ 浜松 **Hamamatsu** (city, Shizuoka-ken)

4a4.12 / 1393

囗 木 斤
41 50

析析

SEKI divide, take apart, analyze

——— 2 ———

⁴ 分析 **bunseki** analysis

——— 4 ———

¹⁴ 精神分析 **seishin bunseki** psycho-analysis

4a4.16 / 696

囗 木 儿 竹
41 16 17

杰 | 松松

SHŌ, matsu pine

——— 1 ———

³ 松下 **Matsushita** (surname)

松山 **Matsuyama** (city, Ehime-ken); (surname)

⁴ 松井 **Matsui** (surname)

松木 **matsu(no)ki** pine tree

⁵ 松本 **Matsumoto** (surname)

松田 **Matsuda** (surname)

⁶ 松竹梅 **shō-chiku-bai** pine-bamboo-plum (as sign of congratulations or to designate three things of equal rank)

⁷ 松尾 **Matsuo** (surname)

松村 **Matsumura** (surname)

⁸ 松岡 **Matsuoka** (surname)

松茸 **matsutake, matsudake** (a kind of edible mushroom)

¹⁰ 松原 **Matsubara** (surname)

松島 **Matsushima** (surname)

¹¹ 松崎 **Matsuzaki** (surname)

¹² 松葉 **matsuba** pine needle

4a4.17

囗 木 宀 冂
41 11 20

杭杭

KŌ, kui stake, post, piling

——— 1 ———

⁵ 杭打 **kuiu(chi)** pile driving

4a4.18 / 870

囗 木 十 又
41 12 9

枝枝

SHI, eda branch ᴇ (part of given name)

——— 1 ———

⁷ 枝豆 **edamame** green soybeans

¹² 枝葉 **shiyō, edaha** branches and leaves; ramifications; unimportant details

——— 2 ———

³ 千枝 **Chie, Chieda** (f. given name)

⁹ 美枝 **Mie, Yoshie** (f. given name)

¹³ 楊枝 **yōji** toothpick; toothbrush

——— 3 ———

⁴ 爪楊枝 **tsumayōji** toothpick

4a4.19 / 1907

囗 木 十
41 12

枠枠

waku frame, framework; limit, confines

— 1 —

11 枠組 **wakugumi** frame, framework; framing

4a4.21 / 1047

□ 木 厂 又
41 18 9

HAN, BAN, ita board, plank

— 1 —

9 板前 **itamae** a cook
12 板塀 **itabei** board fence
　板間 **ita(no)ma** wooden floor

— 2 —

9 看板 **kanban** sign(board)
11 黒板 **kokuban** blackboard
13 溝板 **dobuita** boards covering a ditch
　鉄板 **teppan** steel plate; griddle
16 鋼板 **kōhan, kōban** steel plate

— 3 —

8 表看板 **omote-kanban** sign out in front; figurehead; mask
11 掲示板 **keijiban** bulletin board
16 鋼鉄板 **kōtetsuban** steel plate

4a4.22 / 1023

□ 木 冂 十
41 20 12

SŪ, toboso pivot

— 1 —

9 枢要 **sūyō** pivotal, important
12 枢軸 **sūjiku** pivot, axis, center

牀 → 床 3q4.1

杰 → 傑 2a11.6

枩 → 松 4a4.16

4a4.24 / 2153

□ 木 小 丨
41 35 2

SAI general's baton; dice; take; coloring; appearance; territory SAI, UNE, AYA, KOTO (part of given name)

— 2 —

11 喝采 **kassai** applause, cheers

 采 → 採 4a6.34

— 5 —

4a5.3 / 146

□ 目 木
55 41

SŌ each other, reciprocal; aspect, phase, physiognomy SHŌ (government) minister ai- together, fellow-, each other SUKE (part of given name)

— 1 —

3 相々傘 **aiaigasa (de)** under the same umbrella
4 相互 **sōgo** mutual, reciprocal
　相手 **aite** the other party, partner, opponent
6 相合傘 **aia(i)gasa (de)** under the same umbrella
　相次 **aitsu(gu)** follow in succession
　相当 **sōtō** suitable, appropriate; considerable; be equivalent to, correspond to
8 相性 **aishō** affinity, compatibility
9 相変 **aikawa(razu)** as usual
12 相違 **sōi** difference, discrepancy
　相場 **sōba** market price; speculation; estimation
　相棒 **aibō** pal, partner, accomplice
13 相槌 **aizuchi** (anvil) hammering in alternation; giving responses to make the conversation go smoothly

相続 **sōzoku** inheritance, succession

14 相模川 **Sagami-gawa** (river, Kanagawa-ken)

15 相撲 **sumō** sumo wrestling

相談 **sōdan** consult, confer; proposal; arrangements

———— 2 ————

2 人相 **ninsō** facial features, physiognomy

3 大相撲 **ōzumō** grand sumo tournament; exciting match

4 手相 **tesō** lines of the palm

5 世相 **sesō** phase of life, the times, world conditions

外相 **gaishō** the Foreign Minister

6 仮相 **kasō** appearance, phenomenon

血相 **kessō** a look, expression

7 位相 **isō** phase

8 厚相 **kōshō** Welfare Minister

法相 **hōshō** Minister of Justice

9 首相 **shushō** prime minister

10 真相 **shinsō** the truth/facts, the real situation

遊相手 **aso(bi)aite** playmate

宰相 **saishō** prime minister, premier

13 農相 **nōshō** Agriculture (, Forestry and Fisheries) Minister

話相手 **hanashi aite** someone to talk to; companion

14 様相 **yōsō** aspect, phase, condition

15 蔵相 **zōshō** Finance Minister

17 闇相場 **yamisōba** black-market price

———— 3 ————

5 可哀相 **kawaisō** poor, pitiable, pathetic

4a5.4

□ 朮 艹 冂
41 32 20

栅丨栅栅

SAKU fence, palisade, stockade
shigarami weir, small dam

4a5.5 / 2106

□ 朮 日 丨
41 43 2

柚柚

YŪ, YU, JIKU, yuzu citron
YŪ, YU, YUZU (part of given name)

———— 1 ————

2 柚子 **yuzu** citron

4a5.6

□ 朮 艹 二
41 32 4

柑柑

KAN citrus fruit

———— 1 ————

16 柑橘類 **kankitsurui** citrus fruits

———— 2 ————

14 蜜柑 **mikan** mandarin orange, tangerine

4a5.9 / 985

□ 朮 丆 冂
41 14 20

柄柄

HEI, e, tsuka handle, grip, hilt
gara pattern, design; build, physique; character

———— 2 ————

2 人柄 **hitogara** character, personality; personal appearance

3 大柄 **ōgara** large build; large pattern (on a kimono)

4 手柄 **tegara** meritorious deed(s), achievement

7 身柄 **migara** one's person

8 事柄 **kotogara** matters, affairs, circumstances

10 家柄 **iegara** lineage, parentage; (of) good family

12 間柄 **aidagara** relationship

14 銘柄 **meigara** name, brand, issue (of shares)

4

朮 5
月
日
火
礻
王
牛
方
攵
心
戸
戈

15 横柄 **ōhei** arrogant, haughty

4a5.12 / 598   田 朮 王 丨
            41 46 2

柱

柱柱

CHŪ, hashira pillar, column, pole

――――― 2 ―――――

6 帆柱 **hobashira** mast

7 貝柱 **kaibashira** (boiled scallop) adductor muscle

17 霜柱 **shimobashira** ice/frost columns

――――― 3 ―――――

3 大黒柱 **daikokubashira** central pillar; pillar, mainstay

4a5.14   田 朮 日 丨
            41 43 2

柏

栢丨柏柏

HAKU, BYAKU, kashiwa oak

――――― 1 ―――――

4 柏手 **kashiwade** clap one's hands (in worship at a shrine)

10 柏原 **Kashiwabara** (surname)

14 柏餅 **kashiwa mochi** rice cake wrapped in an oak leaf

4a5.15 / 2107   田 朮 Ｆ 一
            41 38 1

柾

masa straight grain **masaki** spindle tree **MASA** (part of given name) **MASAKI, MASASHI** (m. given name)

――――― 1 ―――――

5 柾目 **masame** straight grain

4a5.17 / 1871   田 朮 厂 阝
            41 18 7

柳

柳柳

RYŪ, yanagi willow tree
YANAGI (surname)

――――― 2 ―――――

7 花柳 **karyū** blossoms and willows; demimonde; red-light district

4a5.19   田 朮 口 力
            41 24 8

枷

枷枷

KA, kase shackles

――――― 2 ―――――

4 手枷 **tekase, tegase** handcuffs, manacles

4a5.24 / 2105   田 朮 攵 丨
            41 49 2

柊

柊柊

SHŪ, hiiragi holly tree
SHŪ, HIIRAGI (part of given name)

4a5.25   田 朮 巾 亠
            41 26 11

柿

SHI, kaki persimmon (tree/fruit)
kokera shingle

4a5.26 / 974   田 朮 口 十
            41 24 12

枯

枯枯

KO, ka(reru) wither, die (vegetation)
ka(rasu) cause to wither, kill (vegetation), let dry

---1---

⁴ 枯木 **ka(re)ki** dead tree
⁶ 枯死 **koshi** wither, die
¹¹ 枯野 **ka(re)no** desolate fields
¹² 枯葉 **ka(re)ha** dead leaf

---2---

⁴ 水枯 **mizuga(re)** drought
　木枯 **koga(rashi)** wintry wind

4a5.28

□ 木 厂 一
41 18 14

tochi horse chestnut tree

---1---

⁴ 栃木県 **Tochigi-ken** (prefecture)

4a5.32 / 624

目 木 月 一
41 42 1

SA investigate

---1---

⁸ 査定 **satei** assessment
¹² 査証 **sashō** visa; investigation and attestation

---2---

⁵ 巡査 **junsa** patrolman, cop
¹⁰ 捜査 **sōsa** investigation
¹² 検査 **kensa** inspection, examination
　検査官 **kensakan** inspector, examiner
¹⁵ 審査 **shinsa** examination, investigation
　監査 **kansa** inspection; auditing
　調査 **chōsa** investigation, inquiry, survey, research

---4---

⁸ 国勢調査 **kokusei chōsa** (national) census

果 → 0a8.8

4a5.33 / 1494

目 木 艹 二
41 32 4

BŌ a certain, one **nanigashi** a certain person/amount **soregashi** a certain person; I

---1---

⁴ 某氏 **bōshi** a certain person

4a5.34 / 774

目 木 一 一
41 14 1

JŪ, NYŪ, yawa(rakai/raka/i) soft **yawa(ra)** jujitsu

---1---

¹⁰ 柔弱 **nyūjaku** weakness, enervation
¹¹ 柔道 **jūdō** judo
　柔軟 **jūnan** soft, supple, flexible

---2---

⁸ 物柔 **monoyawa(raka)** mild, gentle, suave

4a5.35 / 779

田 木 氵 十
41 21 12

SEN, so(meru) dye, color **so(me)** dyeing **so(maru)** be dyed/imbued with **shi(miru)** soak in; be infected; smart, hurt **shi(mi)** stain, blot, smudge **SOME** (part of given name)

---1---

⁴ 染込 **shi(mi)ko(mu)** soak into, permeate; be instilled with **so(me)ko(mu)** dye in
⁶ 染色 **senshoku** dyeing, staining

¹⁰ 染料 **senryō** dye, dyestuffs

——————— 2 ———————

⁶ 伝染病 **densenbyō** contagious/communicable disease

色染 **irozo(me)** dyeing

汚染 **osen** pollution, contamination

¹³ 感染 **kansen** infection, contagion

馴染 **naji(mi)** familiar

——————— 3 ———————

⁵ 幼馴染 **osana najimi** childhood playmate

4a5.36 / 755   囗 木 口 力
                     41 24 8

KA hang up, mount, build; rack, shelf, stand **ka(keru)** build (a bridge)
ka(karu) hang, be built

——————— 1 ———————

⁸ 架空 **kakū** overhead, aerial; fanciful, fictitious

¹¹ 架設 **kasetsu** construction, laying

——————— 2 ———————

⁸ 担架 **tanka** stretcher

¹⁰ 高架 **kōka** elevated, overhead

——————— 3 ———————

² 十字架 **jūjika** cross, crucifix

——————— 6 ———————

4a6.1 / 1906   囗 木 戈 二
                     41 52 4

SAN suspension bridge; jetty; shelf; crosspiece, frame, bolt (of a door)

——————— 1 ———————

¹⁶ 桟橋 **sanbashi** wharf, jetty
    sankyō wharf; bridge

4a6.3 / 741   囗 木 牛 儿
                    41 47 16

kabu share (of stock); (tree) stump, (tulip) bulb

——————— 1 ———————

⁵ 株主 **kabunushi** shareholder, stockholder

⁶ 株式 **kabushiki** shares, stocks
    株式市場 **kabushiki shijō** stock market
    株式会社 **kabushiki-gaisha, kabushiki kaisha** corporation, Co., Ltd.

——————— 2 ———————

³ 大株主 **ōkabunushi** large shareholder

4a6.5 / 314   囗 食 木
                    73 41

KON root; perseverance **ne** root; base, origin

——————— 1 ———————

⁵ 根本主義 **konpon shugi** fundamentalism
    根本的 **konponteki** fundamental, radical
    根付 **netsu(ke)** ornamental button for suspending a pouch from a belt

⁶ 根気 **konki** patience, perseverance
    根回 **nemawa(shi)** doing the groundwork, pre-selling (a proposal), consensus-building

⁸ 根拠 **konkyo** basis, grounds, foundation
    根性 **konjō** disposition, spirit, nature

⁹ 根柢 **kontei** root, basis, foundation

¹¹ 根深 **nebuka(i)** deep-rooted, ingrained
    根基 **konki** root, origin

根強 **nezuyo(i)** firmly rooted/established

² 根絶 **konzetsu, nedaya(shi)** eradication

³ 根源 **kongen** root, origin, source, cause

─────── 2 ───────

³ 大根 **daikon** daikon, Japanese radish

山根 **Yamane** (surname)

⁷ 利根川 **Tone-gawa** (river, Chiba-ken)

⁸ 性根 **shōkon** perseverance
shōne one's disposition

⁹ 垣根 **kakine** fence, hedge

屋根 **yane** roof

¹⁰ 島根県 **Shimane-ken** (prefecture)

¹³ 禍根 **kakon** root of evil, source of calamity

¹⁵ 箱根 **Hakone** (resort area near Mt. Fuji)

─────── 3 ───────

⁵ 瓦屋根 **kawara yane** tiled roof

4a6.8   ▥ 木 彳 二
                          41 29 4

KŌ, keta beam, girder; digit, place (in numbers)

─────── 1 ───────

⁵ 桁外 **ketahazu(re)** extraordinary

─────── 2 ───────

¹ 一桁 **hitoketa** single digit

² 二桁 **futaketa** two digits, double-digit

³ 三桁 **miketa** three digits

¹⁶ 橋桁 **hashigeta** bridge girder

4a6.10 / 1567   ▥ 木 丿 儿
                          41 5 16

TŌ, momo peach

─────── 1 ───────

⁶ 桃色 **momo-iro** pink

⁷ 桃花 **Momoka** (f. given name)

¹³ 桃節句 **momo (no) sekku** Doll Festival (March 3)

─────── 2 ───────

⁹ 扁桃腺 **hentōsen** the tonsils

4a6.13 / 2109   ▥ 木 土
                          41 22

桂   桂桂

KEI cinnamon/cassia tree; bay-leaf tree; the moon **katsura** katsura tree **KATSURA** (surname) **KEI, YOSHI, KATSU** (part of given name)

─────── 1 ───────

⁹ 桂冠 **keikan** crown of laurel

4a6.15 / 928   ▥ 木 女 小
                          41 25 35

桜   櫻∣桜桜

Ō, sakura cherry tree

─────── 1 ───────

⁰ 桜んぼ **sakura(nbo)** cherry

⁴ 桜井 **Sakurai** (surname)

⁶ 桜肉 **sakuraniku** horsemeat

桜色 **sakura-iro** pink, cerise

4a6.17 / 643   ▥ 木 夂 口
                          41 49 24

格   格格

KAKU, KŌ status, rank; standard, rule; case (in grammar) **ITARU, TADASHI** (m. given name)

─────── 1 ───────

² 格子 **kōshi** lattice, bars, grating, grille

⁶ 格安 **kakuyasu** inexpensive

7 格別 **kakubetsu** particularly, exceptionally

10 格差 **kakusa** gap, differential

───── 2 ─────

2 人格 **jinkaku** character, personality

5 本格的 **honkakuteki** full-scale, genuine, in earnest

失格 **shikkaku** disqualification

6 合格 **gōkaku** pass (an exam/inspection)

7 別格 **bekkaku** special, exceptional

8 価格 **kakaku** price, cost, value

性格 **seikaku** character, personality

9 風格 **fūkaku** character, personality, style

10 骨格 **kokkaku** skeleton, frame, one's build

11 規格 **kikaku** standard, norm

13 適格 **tekikaku, tekkaku** competent, eligible

資格 **shikaku** qualifications, competence

17 厳格 **genkaku** strict, stern, severe

───── 3 ─────

4 不合格 **fugōkaku** failure (in an exam), rejection, disqualification

桧 → 檜 **4a13.8**

4a6.22 / 1212   田 木 宀 竹
41 11 17

核 | 核 核

KAKU core, nucleus; (as prefix) nuclear **sane** fruit stone, kernel, seed

───── 1 ─────

4 核分裂 **kakubunretsu** nuclear fission

7 核兵器 **kakuheiki** nuclear weapons

8 核実験 **kakujikken** nuclear testing

16 核燃料 **kakunenryō** nuclear fuel

───── 2 ─────

4 中核 **chūkaku** kernel, core, nucleus

───── 3 ─────

9 肺結核 **haikekkaku** pulmonary tuberculosis

4a6.24 / 115   田 木 宀 儿
41 11 16

校校

KŌ, KYŌ school; (printing) proof

───── 1 ─────

4 校友 **kōyū** schoolmate, alumnus

5 校正 **kōsei** proofreading

8 校長 **kōchō** principal, headmaster

校舎 **kōsha** school building

9 校庭 **kōtei** schoolyard, campus

校訂 **kōtei** revision

───── 2 ─────

5 母校 **bokō** one's alma mater

6 再校 **saikō** second proof

休校 **kyūkō** school closing

7 学校 **gakkō** school

初校 **shokō** first proofs

10 高校 **kōkō** senior high school (short for 高等学校)

高校生 **kōkōsei** senior-high-school student

───── 3 ─────

3 小学校 **shōgakkō** elementary school

4 予備校 **yobikō** preparatory school

中学校 **chūgakkō** junior high school

8 盲学校 **mōgakkō** school for the blind

4a6.26 / 1842   田 木 王 亻
41 46 3

栓栓

SEN stopper, cork, plug, spigot, tap, hydrant

───── 1 ─────

7 栓抜 **sennu(ki)** corkscrew; bottle opener

—————— 2 ——————

¹³ 塞栓 **sokusen** an embolism

—————— 3 ——————

¹⁰ 消火栓 **shōkasen** fire hydrant

4a6.27 / 1734   田 木 女 ヘ
41 25 15

梅 | 梅 梅

BAI, ume Japanese plum/apricot (tree)

—————— 1 ——————

⁰ 梅干 **umebo(shi)** pickled plums

⁸ 梅雨 **baiu, tsuyu** the rainy season

—————— 3 ——————

⁸ 松竹梅 **shō-chiku-bai** pine-bamboo-plum (as sign of congratulations or to designate three things of equal rank)

栢→柏   **4a5.14**

4a6.30 / 2110   田 木 口 冂
41 24 20

桐桐

TŌ, kiri paulownia tree   TŌ, DŌ, KIRI, HISA (part of given name)

—————— 2 ——————

⁴ 片桐 **Katagiri** (surname)

4a6.32 / 2111   田 木 口 一
41 24 14

栗 栗

RITSU, kuri chestnut   RITSU, KURI (part of given name)

—————— 1 ——————

⁵ 栗田 **Kurita** (surname)

¹³ 栗鼠 **risu** squirrel

4a6.34 / 2108   田 木 一 一
41 14 1

栞 | 栞 桒

KAN, shiori bent branch to mark a trail; bookmark; guidebook
KAN, KEN, KI (part of given name)
SHIORI (f. given name)

桑→   **2h8.1**

4a6.35 / 576   田 木 十 冂
41 12 20

殺 | 殺 殺

SATSU, SETSU kill   **SAI** lessen
koro(su) kill   **so(gu)** cut/slash off; diminish, dampen, spoil   **so(geru)** split, splinter; be sunken in

—————— 1 ——————

² 殺人 **satsujin** murder

⁶ 殺虫剤 **satchūzai** insecticide

⁸ 殺到 **sattō** rush, stampede

⁹ 殺屋 **koro(shi)ya** hired killer

¹⁰ 殺害 **satsugai** murder

¹¹ 殺菌 **sakkin** sterilize, disinfect, pasteurize

—————— 2 ——————

² 人殺 **hitogoro(shi)** murder; murderer

³ 女殺 **onnagoro(shi)** ladykiller

⁵ 生殺 **seisatsu** life and death
namagoro(shi) half-kill; keep in suspense

他殺 **tasatsu** murder

⁶ 忙殺 **bōsatsu** keep (someone) busily occupied

自殺 **jisatsu** suicide

自殺未遂 **jisatsu misui** attempted suicide

⁸ 毒殺 **dokusatsu** a poisoning

刺殺 **sa(shi)koro(su)** stab to death
shisatsu stab to death; put out (a runner)

殴殺 **nagu(ri)koro(su), ōsatsu** beat to death, strike dead

4

木 6
月
日
火
ネ
王
牛
方
攵
欠
心
戸
戈

9 虐殺 **gyakusatsu** massacre
10 射殺 **shasatsu, ikoro(su)** shoot to death
悩殺 **nōsatsu** enchant, captivate
11 惨殺 **zansatsu** murder, massacre, slaughter
12 屠殺 **tosatsu** butchering, slaughter
絞殺 **kōsatsu** strangle to death; hang
13 暗殺 **ansatsu** assassination
14 銃殺 **jūsatsu** shoot dead
15 撲殺 **bokusatsu** clubbing to death
黙殺 **mokusatsu** take no notice of, ignore
22 轢殺 **rekisatsu, hi(ki)koro(su)** run over and kill

————————— 4 —————————

9 飛込自殺 **tobiko(mi) jisatsu** suicide by jumping in front of an oncoming train

栽→ **4n6.1**

————————— 7 —————————

4a7.1   田 木 日 一   41 43 14

KŌ in general; block, close off

————————— 1 —————————

13 梗塞 **kōsoku** stoppage; (monetary) stringency; infarction

椒→ **4a8.7**

4a7.3 / 2069   田 木 彡   41 31

HIN splendid in both form and content **akiraka** clear AKIRA, SHIGESHI, HITOSHI (m. given name) HIN, AKI, YOSHI, MORI, AYA, HIDE (part of given name)

4a7.5 / 2113   田 立 木 十   54 41 12

SHI catalpa tree; (wood-block) printing; publishing **azusa** catalpa tree AZUSA (surname, f. given name) SHI (part of given name)

4a7.7   田 木 日 一   41 43 14

KAN rod, pole, stick

4a7.9 / 2112   田 木 口 一   41 24 14

GO, aogiri Chinese parasol tree, Phoenix tree GO (part of given name)

4a7.13 / 2114   田 木 月 小   41 42 35

SHI, kozue twig; treetop SHŌ, TAKA, SUE (part of given name) KOZUE (f. given name)

————————— 2 —————————

5 末梢 **masshō** tip of a twig; periphery; nonessentials, trifles

4a7.17   田 木 弓 儿   41 28 16

TEI, hashigo ladder; barhopping, pub-crawling

—— 1 ——

² 梯子 **hashigo** ladder; barhopping, pub-crawling

—— 2 ——

¹ 舷梯 **gentei** gangway (ladder)

⁵ 磐梯山 **Bandai-san** (mountain, Fukushima-ken)

4a7.18

田 木 月 一
41 42 1

桶桶

TŌ, oke tub, bucket

—— 2 ——

¹⁰ 秣桶 **magusaoke** manger

¹² 棺桶 **kan'oke** coffin

—— 3 ——

⁹ 風呂桶 **furooke** bathtub

梅→梅 4a6.27

4a7.19

田 木 尸 十
41 40 12

梶梶

BI, kaji mulberry tree; oar

—— 1 ——

⁴ 梶木 **kaji(no)ki** mulberry tree (used for paper)

4a7.22 / 529

田 木 戈 卄
41 52 32

械械

KAI fetters; machine

—— 2 ——

¹⁶ 機械 **kikai** machine

機械化 **kikaika** mechanization, mechanized

4a7.24 / 2115

田 禾 木 儿
56 41 16

梨梨

RI, nashi pear, pear tree   RI, NASHI (part of given name)

—— 1 ——

⁷ 梨沙 **Risa** (f. given name)

—— 2 ——

³ 山梨県 **Yamanashi-ken** (prefecture)

4a7.25

田 木 氵 力
41 21 8

梁梁

RYŌ bridge beams
hari, utsubari beam, girder
yana weir, fish trap

—— 2 ——

¹² 棟梁 **tōryō** pillar, mainstay; chief, leader, foreman

¹⁶ 橋梁 **kyōryō** bridge

梦→夢 3k10.14

4a7.27

田 木 门 丨
41 20 2

梵梵

BON Sanskrit; purity; Buddhist believer; Brahman

—— 1 ——

¹⁴ 梵語 **bongo** Sanskrit

殺→殺 4a6.35

耕→ 0a10.13

耗→ 0a10.12

4

木   7
月
日
火
礻
王
牛
方
攵
欠
心
戸
戈

— 8 —

4a8.1 / 2116

74 41

椎椎

TSUI hit; backbone **tsuchi** hammer
shii (a species of oak) TSUI, SUI,
TSUCHI, SHII (part of given name)

— 1 —

⁶ 椎名 **Shiina** (surname)

⁹ 椎茸 **shiitake** (a variety of edible
mushroom)

4a8.3 / 1406

□ 木 日

41 43

棟棟

TŌ, mune, muna- ridge of a roof;
ridgepole, ridge beam; (counter for
buildings)

— 1 —

³ 棟上式 **munea(ge)shiki** roof-raising ceremony

¹¹ 棟梁 **tōryō** pillar, mainstay; chief,
leader, foreman

— 2 —

¹⁰ 病棟 **byōtō** ward

4a8.6 / 2121

□ 耳 木 阝

65 41 7

椰椰

YA palm/coconut tree

YA, YASHI (part of given name)

— 1 —

² 椰子 **yashi** palm/coconut tree

4a8.7

□ 木 小 ト

41 35 13

椒

椒椒

SHŌ Japanese pepper tree

— 2 —

⁹ 胡椒 **koshō** pepper

4a8.10 / 1908

□ 木 月

41 42

棚

棚棚

tana shelf

— 1 —

⁴ 棚引 **tanabi(ku)** trail, hang over
(fog/smoke)

⁴ 戸棚 **todana** cupboard, cabinet,
closet

⁵ 本棚 **hondana** bookshelf

¹⁰ 書棚 **shodana** bookshelf

¹¹ 釣棚 **tsu(ri)dana** hanging shelf

4a8.11 / 336

□ 木 口 一

41 24 14

極

極極

KYOKU end, pole **GOKU** very,
extremely **kiwa(meru)** go to the end,
study thoroughly; carry to extremes
kiwa(mete) extremely
kiwa(maru) come to an end, reach an
extreme **kiwa(mi)** height, end
ki(me) arrangement, agreement
ki(mari) settlement, conclusion; rule,
convention

— 1 —

⁴ 極切 **kima(ri)ki(tta)** fixed, definite; stereotyped; self-evident

極手 **ki(me)te** winning move, decisive factor

⁸ 極東 **kyokutō** the Far East

極限 **kyokugen** limit, extremity

9 極度 **kyokudo** to the highest degree, extreme

10 極秘 **gokuhi** top-secret, confidential

12 極圏 **kyokken** the Arctic/Antarctic Circle

13 極楽 **gokuraku** paradise

14 極端 **kyokutan** extreme

——— 2 ———

5 北極 **hokkyoku** the North Pole

6 両極端 **ryōkyokutan** both extremes

7 究極 **kyūkyoku** final, ultimate

見極 **mikiwa(meru)** see through, discern, ascertain, grasp

9 南極 **Nankyoku** the South Pole

南極圏 **Nankyokuken** the Antarctic Circle, the Antarctic

10 消極的 **shōkyokuteki** passive, negative

16 積極的 **sekkyokuteki** positive, active

4a8.14 / 1835   田 木 艹 二
                                           41 32 4

KI go; shogi, Japanese chess

——— 1 ———

3 棋士 **kishi** (professional) go/shogi player

9 棋客 **kikyaku, kikaku** go/shogi player

——— 2 ———

10 将棋 **shōgi** shōgi, Japanese chess

4a8.15   田 立 木 女
                                           54 41 25

SETSU, tsu(gu) graft

4a8.16   田 木 彐 女
                                           41 39 25

SEI, su(mu) live, dwell

——— 1 ———

10 棲息 **seisoku** live in, inhabit

棲息地 **seisokuchi** habitat

——— 2 ———

6 同棲 **dōsei** live together, cohabit with

4a8.20 / 1543   田 木 大 二
                                           41 34 4

BŌ stick, pole

——— 1 ———

5 棒立 **bōda(chi)** standing bolt upright

13 棒暗記 **bōanki** indiscriminate memorization

——— 2 ———

4 心棒 **shinbō** axle, shaft, mandrel, stem

8 泥棒 **dorobō** thief, burglar

9 相棒 **aibō** pal, partner, accomplice

棧 → 桟   **4a6.1**

4a8.25 / 1825   田 木 宀 尸
                                           41 33 40

KAN, hitsugi coffin

——— 1 ———

11 棺桶 **kan'oke** coffin

4   8

木 月 日 火 礻 王 牛 方 欠 心 尸 戈

4a8.27 田 木 亠 口
41 34 24

椅椅

I chair

——— 1 ———

² 椅子 **isu** chair, seat, couch

——— 2 ———

⁷ 車椅子 **kurumaisu** wheelchair
⁸ 長椅子 **nagaisu** sofa, couch

4a8.28 / 531 田 木 口 亻
41 24 3

檢丨検檢

KEN investigation, inspection

——— 1 ———

⁶ 検死 **kenshi** coroner's inquest, autopsy
　検印 **ken'in** stamp of approval
⁸ 検事 **kenji** public procurator/prosecutor
　検定 **kentei** official approval, inspection
⁹ 検査 **kensa** inspection, examination
　検査官 **kensakan** inspector, examiner
　検疫 **ken'eki** quarantine
¹⁰ 検索 **kensaku** retrieval, lookup, reference
　検挙 **kenkyo** arrest, apprehend
　検討 **kentō** examine, study, look into
¹¹ 検問 **kenmon** inspect, examine, check
¹² 検証 **kenshō** verification, inspection
　検診 **kenshin** medical examination
¹⁴ 検察 **kensatsu** investigation and prosecution
¹⁵ 検閲 **ken'etsu** censorship; inspection (of troops)

——— 2 ———

⁷ 車検 **shaken** auto inspection (certificate)
⁹ 点検 **tenken** inspection
¹¹ 探検 **tanken** exploration, expedition

4a8.31 / 2117 田 木 口 小
41 24 35

椋椋

RYŌ, muku (type of deciduous tree); gray starling RYŌ, MUKU, KURA (part of given name)

4a8.32 / 424 田 日 木 十
55 41 12

植植

SHOKU, u(eru) plant **u(waru)** be planted TANE (part of given name)

——— 1 ———

⁴ 植木 **ueki** garden/potted plant
　植木鉢 **uekibachi** flowerpot
⁵ 植民地 **shokuminchi** colony
　植付 **u(e)tsu(keru)** plant, implant
　植字 **shokuji** typesetting
　植田 **Ueda** (surname)
⁸ 植物 **shokubutsu** plant
　植物園 **shokubutsuen** botanical garden
¹² 植替 **u(e)ka(eru)** transplant, replant
¹⁶ 植樹 **shokuju** tree planting

——— 2 ———

⁵ 田植 **tau(e)** rice-planting
¹³ 鉢植 **hachiu(e)** potted plant
¹⁴ 誤植 **goshoku** misprint

4a8.38 木 日 ⺊ 41 43 13

棹

棹 棹

TŌ, sao pole

槌→槌 4a9.27

巢→巣 3n8.1

4a8.39 / 128 木 41

森

森 森

SHIN, mori woods, forest
MORI (surname)

— 1 —

3 森下 **Morishita** (surname)
森山 **Moriyama** (surname)
5 森本 **Morimoto** (surname)
森田 **Morita** (surname)
8 森岡 **Morioka** (surname)
森林 **shinrin** woods, forest
12 森閑 **shinkan (to shita)** still, hushed, silent

— 2 —

3 大森 **Ōmori** (surname)
小森 **Komori** (surname)
8 青森県 **Aomori-ken** (prefecture)

棊→棋 4a8.14

4a8.40 木 氵 冂 41 21 20

渠

渠 渠

KYO ditch; ringleader; he

— 9 —

4a9.3 目 木 厂 55 41 18

楯

楯 楯

JUN, tate shield

— 1 —

8 楯突 **tatetsu(ku)** oppose, defy

— 2 —

9 後楯 **ushi(ro)date** backing, support

楙→茂 3k5.7

4a9.10 / 1841 米 木 女 62 41 25

楼

樓 | 楼 楼

RŌ tower, turret, lookout

— 3 —

15 摩天楼 **matenrō** skyscraper

4a9.13 木 月 工 41 42 38

楕

橢 | 楕 楕

DA ellipse

— 1 —

4 楕円形 **daenkei** ellipse, oval

4a9.16 / 2118 木 日 大 41 43 34

椿

椿 椿

CHIN, tsubaki camellia TSUBAKI (surname) CHIN, TSUBAKI (part of given name)

— 1 —

8 椿事 **chinji** accident; sudden occurrence

10 椿姫 **Tsubakihime** (Verdi's) La Traviata

4a9.17 / 2122

田 木 日 犭
41 43 27

楊 楊

YŌ purple willow   YŌ, YASU (part of given name)

— 1 —

2 楊子江 **Yōsukō** the Yangzi/Yangtze river

8 楊枝 **yōji** toothpick; toothbrush

— 2 —

4 爪楊枝 **tsumayōji** toothpick

4a9.18

田 木 日 匕
41 43 13

楷 楷

KAI block/noncursive style; rule, model

— 1 —

10 楷書 **kaisho** noncursive (kanji), printed style

4a9.20

田 耳 木 口
65 41 24

楫 楫

SHŪ, kaji rudder

4a9.25 / 2119

田 木 月 十
41 42 12

楠 楠

NAN, kusunoki camphor tree   NAN, DAN, NA, TOSHI, KUSU (part of given name)   KUSU, KUSUNOKI (surname)

— 1 —

5 楠田 **Kusuda** (surname)

 樋 → 樋 **4a10.28**

4a9.27

田 木 尸 辶
41 40 19

槌 | 槌 槌

TSUI, tsuchi hammer, mallet

— 2 —

9 相槌 **aizuchi** (anvil) hammering in alternation; giving responses to make the conversation go smoothly

4a9.28 / 2120

田 虫 木 冂
64 41 20

楓 楓

FŪ, kaede maple tree   KAEDE (f. given name)   FŪ (part of given name)

4a9.29 / 358

日 日 木 冫
43 41 5

樂 | 楽 楽

GAKU music   **RAKU** pleasure; comfort, ease, relief   **tanoshi(mu)** enjoy; look forward to   **tano(shii)** fun, enjoyable, pleasant

— 1 —

3 楽々 **rakuraku** comfortably, with great ease

4 楽天家 **rakutenka** optimist

6 楽曲 **gakkyoku** musical composition/piece

楽団 **gakudan** orchestra, band

11 楽隊 **gakutai** band, orchestra

楽章 **gakushō** a movement (of a symphony)

12 楽勝 **rakushō** easy victory

³ 楽園 **rakuen** a paradise
⁵ 楽器 **gakki** musical instrument
⁸ 楽観的 **rakkanteki** optimistic, hopeful
⁹ 楽譜 **gakufu** musical notation, sheet music, the score

─────── 2 ───────

⁴ 文楽 **bunraku** puppet theater
⁵ 打楽器 **dagakki** percussion instrument
⁶ 気楽 **kiraku** feeling at ease, easy-going, comfortable
行楽地 **kōrakuchi** pleasure resort
安楽 **anraku** ease, comfort
安楽死 **anrakushi** euthanasia
⁷ 享楽 **kyōraku** enjoyment
声楽 **seigaku** vocal music, (study) voice
快楽 **kairaku, keraku** pleasure
⁸ 弦楽器 **gengakki** string instrument, the strings
和楽 **wagaku** Japanese-style music
⁹ 奏楽 **sōgaku** instrumental music
音楽 **ongaku** music
音楽家 **ongakka, ongakuka** musician
¹⁰ 倶楽部 **kurabu** club
逸楽 **itsuraku** idle pursuit of pleasure
娯楽 **goraku** amusement, entertainment
能楽 **nōgaku** Noh drama
悦楽 **etsuraku** joy, pleasure, gaiety
¹¹ 道楽 **dōraku** hobby; dissipation, debauchery
絃楽 **gengaku** string music
絃楽器 **gengakki** stringed instrument
¹² 極楽 **gokuraku** paradise
¹³ 雅楽 **gagaku** ancient Japanese court music
¹⁵ 舞楽 **bugaku** old Japanese court-dance music
歓楽街 **kanrakugai** amusement center
¹⁸ 観楽街 **kanrakugai** amusement district

─────── 3 ───────

⁷ 吹奏楽 **suisōgaku** wind-instrument music, brass
¹⁴ 管弦楽団 **kangen gakudan** orchestra

─────── 4 ───────

¹² 喜怒哀楽 **kidoairaku** joy-anger-sorrow-pleasure, emotions

4a9.31   田 木 艹 宀   41 32 11

牒   牒牒

CHŌ label; a circular

─────── 2 ───────

¹¹ 符牒 **fuchō** mark, symbol, code

─────── 10 ───────

4a10.2 / 1459   冊 食 木 宀   73 41 14

概   概丨概概

GAI general, approximate
ōmu(ne) generally

─────── 1 ───────

⁷ 概見 **gaiken** overview, outline
⁸ 概念 **gainen** general idea, concept
概況 **gaikyō** general situation, outlook
⁹ 概括 **gaikatsu** summary, generalization
概要 **gaiyō** outline, synopsis
¹¹ 概略 **gairyaku** outline, summary
¹⁵ 概論 **gairon** general remarks, outline, introduction

─────── 2 ───────

¹ 一概 **ichigai** unconditionally, sweepingly
³ 大概 **taigai** in general; mostly; probably; moderate, reasonable

4

木 10
月
日
火
礻
王
牛
方
攵
心
戸
戈

4a10.10 / 1010   囲 木 王 艹
　　　　　　　　　　　41　46　32

構　　構|構構

KŌ, kama(eru) build, set up; assume a
stance/position **kama(e)** posture,
stance; structure, appearance; enclosure
radical **kama(u)** mind, care about;
meddle in; look after

───── 1 ─────

⁴ 構内 **kōnai** premises, grounds, pre-
　　　cincts
　　構文 **kōbun** sentence construction,
　　　syntax
⁶ 構成 **kōsei** composition, makeup
⁹ 構造 **kōzō** structure, construction

───── 2 ─────

⁴ 心構 **kokorogama(e)** mental atti-
　　　tude/readiness
⁶ 気構 **kigama(e)** readiness, antici-
　　　pation
¹¹ 虚構 **kyokō** fabricated, false, un-
　　　founded
¹² 結構 **kekkō** fine, good, alright;
　　　quite

4a10.11 / 2124   囲 禾 木 大
　　　　　　　　　　　56　41　34

榛　　榛榛

SHIN, hashibami hazel tree
han black alder   SHIN, HARU, HARI
(part of given name)

4a10.12   囲 甲 木 厂
　　　　　　　　58　41　18

榴　　榴榴

RYŪ pomegranate

───── 2 ─────

⁴ 手榴弾 **shuryūdan, teryūdan**
　　　hand grenade

4a10.15 / 2123   囲 木 艹 艹
　　　　　　　　　　　41　32　14

樺　　樺樺

KA, kaba, kanba birch
KANBA (surname)   KA, KABA (part
of given name)

───── 1 ─────

⁴ 樺太 **Karafuto** Sakhalin

───── 2 ─────

⁵ 白樺 **shirakaba, shirakanba** white
　　　birch

4a10.16 / 1425   囲 木 日 艹
　　　　　　　　　　　41　43　32

模　　模|模模

MO, BO copy, imitate

───── 1 ─────

⁵ 模写 **mosha** copy, replica
⁹ 模造 **mozō** imitation
　　模型 **mokei** (scale) model; a mold
¹⁰ 模倣 **mohō** copy, imitation
　　模索 **mosaku** groping, trial and er-
　　　ror
¹⁴ 模様 **moyō** pattern, design; appear-
　　　ance; situation
¹⁵ 模範 **mohan** model, exemplar
¹⁷ 模擬 **mogi** imitation, mock, dry-
　　　run, dummy, simulated

───── 2 ─────

⁷ 花模様 **hanamoyō** floral pattern/
　　　design
⁸ 空模様 **soramoyō** looks of the sky,
　　　weather
　　雨模様 **amamoyō, amemoyō** signs
　　　of rain
⁹ 相模川 **Sagami-gawa** (river, Kana-
　　　gawa-ken)
¹¹ 規模 **kibo** scale, scope
¹⁶ 縞模様 **shimamoyō** striped pattern

───── 3 ─────

³ 大規模 **daikibo** large-scale
　　小規模 **shōkibo** small-scale

4a10.20

☐ 木 尸 口
41 40 24

槍 槍

SŌ, yari spear, lance, javelin

— 1 —

7 槍投 **yarinage** javelin throwing

8 槍岳 **Yari(ga)take** (mountain, Nagano-ken)

4a10.25 / 403

☐ 王 木 儿
46 41 16

樣 | 様 樣

YŌ way, manner; similar, like; condition -**sama** Mr., Mrs., Miss **sama** condition **zama** state, predicament, spectacle

— 1 —

2 様子 **yōsu** situation, aspect, appearance

3 様々 **samazama** various, varied

6 様式 **yōshiki** style, form

9 様相 **yōsō** aspect, phase, condition

— 2 —

1 一様 **ichiyō** uniformity, evenness; equality, impartiality

4 仏様 **hotoke-sama** a Buddha; deceased person

  王様 **ōsama** king

5 母様 **(o)kāsama** mother, mama

  仕様 **shiyō** specifications; way, method

6 多様性 **tayōsei** diversity, variety

  同様 **dōyō** the same (kind/way), similar

  有様 **a(ri)sama, a(ri)yō** situation, circumstances, spectacle; the truth

8 逆様 **sakasama** upside-down, reverse, backwards

  姉様 **(o)nēsama, nēsama** elder sister

9 皆様 **minasama** all (of you), Ladies and Gentlemen!

  神様 **kamisama** God; god

10 宮様 **miyasama** prince, princess

  紋様 **mon'yō** (textile) pattern

12 奥様 **okusama** (your) wife, married lady, ma'am

13 殿様 **tonosama** lord, prince

14 模様 **moyō** pattern, design; appearance; situation

15 憚様 **habaka(ri)sama** Thanks for your trouble.

16 嬢様 **(o)jōsama** (your) daughter; young lady

— 3 —

7 花模様 **hanamoyō** floral pattern/design

8 空模様 **soramoyō** looks of the sky, weather

  雨模様 **amamoyō, amemoyō** signs of rain

13 愁傷様 **(go)shūshō-sama** My heartfelt sympathy.

16 縞模様 **shimamoyō** striped pattern

槙 → 槇   4a10.27

4a10.27 / 2125

☐ 目 木 卜
55 41 13

槇 | 槇 槇

TEN, SHIN twig **maki** Chinese black pine **KOZUE** (f. given name) **SHIGERU** (m. given name) **SHIN, MAKI** (part of given name)

4a10.28

☐ 木 月 辶
41 42 19

樋 | 樋 樋

TŌ, toi (wooden) pipe, gutter

— 1 —

3 樋口 **Higuchi** (surname)

木 10
月
日
火
礻
王
牛
方
欠
心
尸
戈

4

4a10.30

田 舟 木 冂
63 41 20

槃 槃

HAN tub

榮 → 栄 **3n6.1**

業 → **0a13.3**

――― 11 ―――

4a11.4 / 2126

⫴ 貝 木 大
68 41 34

槻 槻

KI, tsuki zelkova/keyaki tree
KI, TSUKI (part of given name)

楕 → 楕 **4a9.13**

樓 → 楼 **4a9.10**

4a11.7 / 1644

田 木 日 艹
41 43 32

槽 槽

SŌ tub, tank, vat

――― 2 ―――

4 水槽 **suisō** water tank/trough
10 浴槽 **yokusō** bathtub

4a11.8 / 923

田 礻 木 口
45 41 24

標 標

HYŌ sign, mark **shirube** guide,
handbook **shirushi** mark, sign, indication

――― 1 ―――

5 標札 **hyōsatsu** nameplate, doorplate
8 標的 **hyōteki** target, mark
13 標準 **hyōjun** standard, norm, criterion
標準語 **hyōjungo** the standard language
14 標語 **hyōgo** slogan, motto
18 標題 **hyōdai** title, heading, caption
19 標識 **hyōshiki** (land)mark, marking, sign, signal, tag

――― 2 ―――

5 目標 **mokuhyō** target, goal, objective
9 指標 **shihyō** index, indicator
11 商標 **shōhyō** trademark

様 → 様 **4a10.25**

4a11.13 / 781

田 木 日 艹
41 43 32

横 | 横 横

Ō horizontal **yoko** side; horizontal
direction

――― 1 ―――

0 横たわる **yoko(tawaru)** lie down;
be horizontal
3 横山 **Yokoyama** (surname)
4 横井 **Yokoi** (surname)
横切 **yokogi(ru)** cross, traverse, intersect
横文字 **yokomoji** European/hori-
zontal writing
5 横田 **Yokota** (surname)
7 横町 **yokochō** side street, lane, alley
8 横長 **yokonaga** oblong
9 横這 **yokoba(i)** sidle; level off
横柄 **ōhei** arrogant, haughty
10 横浜 **Yokohama** (city, Kanagawa-
ken)
横書 **yokoga(ki)** writing horizontally

11 横道 **yokomichi** side street, cross-road; wrong way; side issue, digression; path of evil

横断 **ōdan** cross, traverse

横断歩道 **ōdan hodō** pedestrian crossing

12 横着 **ōchaku** dishonest; cunning; impudent; lazy; selfish

横幅 **yokohaba** width, breadth

13 横溢 **ōitsu** be filled/overflowing with

14 横綱 **yokozuna** sumo champion

横領 **ōryō** misappropriate, embezzle, usurp

16 横縞 **yokojima** horizontal stripes

18 横顔 **yokogao** profile, side view, silhouette

——————— 2 ———————

16 縦横 **jūō, tate-yoko** length and breadth, vertical and horizontal

4a11.18 / 335   □ 隹 木 宀
                          74 41 15

権   权 | 権 権

KEN, GON authority, power; a right

——————— 1 ———————

0 スト権 **sutoken** right to strike

2 権力 **kenryoku** power, authority, influence

7 権利 **kenri** a right

8 権限 **kengen** authority, power, jurisdiction

9 権威 **ken'i** authority; an authority

——————— 2 ———————

2 人権 **jinken** human rights

人権蹂躙 **jinken jūrin** infringement of human rights

3 三権分立 **sanken bunritsu** separation of powers (legislative, executive, and judicial)

大権 **taiken** supreme power/authority

女権 **joken** women's rights

5 民権 **minken** civil rights

失権 **shikken** forfeiture of rights, disenfranchisement

主権 **shuken** sovereignty

主権者 **shukensha** sovereign, supreme ruler

6 全権大使 **zenken taishi** ambassador plenipotentiary

同権 **dōken** the same rights, equal rights

有権者 **yūkensha** qualified person, eligible voter

8 版権 **hanken** copyright

実権 **jikken** real power

国権 **kokken** sovereign right; national prestige

金権 **kinken** the power of money, plutocracy

9 政権 **seiken** political power, administration

10 特権 **tokken** privilege, prerogative; option (to buy)

12 越権 **ekken** overstepping one's authority

13 債権 **saiken** credit, claims

棄権 **kiken** abstain from voting; renounce one's rights, withdraw

19 覇権 **haken** hegemony, domination

——————— 3 ———————

5 市民権 **shiminken** citizenship, civil rights

主導権 **shudōken** leadership

9 専有権 **sen'yūken** exclusive right, monopoly

11 著作権 **chosakuken** copyright

12 統治権 **tōchiken** sovereignty

——————— 4 ———————

10 被選挙権 **hisenkyoken** eligibility for election

樞 → 枢 **4a4.22**

樂 → 楽 **4a9.29**

─────────── 12 ───────────

4a12.1 / 528   ☐ 木 戈 竹
                              41 52 17

機 機

KI machine; airplane; opportunity, occasion **hata** loom

─────────── 1 ───────────

⁴ 機内 **kinai** inside the airplane
⁶ 機会 **kikai** opportunity, occasion, chance
⁷ 機体 **kitai** fuselage
⁸ 機長 **kichō** (airplane) captain
¹⁰ 機能 **kinō** a function
   機敏 **kibin** astute, shrewd, quick
¹¹ 機動隊 **kidōtai** riot squad
   機密 **kimitsu** secret, secrecy
   機械 **kikai** machine
   機械化 **kikaika** mechanization, mechanized
   機転 **kiten** quick wit
¹³ 機業 **kigyō** the textile industry
   機嫌 **kigen** mood, humor, temper
¹⁴ 機種 **kishu** model, type of machine
   機関 **kikan** engine; machinery, organ(ization)
   機関車 **kikansha** locomotive
   機関誌 **kikanshi** organization's publication

─────────── 2 ───────────

⁶ 危機 **kiki** crisis
   危機一髪 **kiki-ippatsu** imminent/ hairbreadth danger
   有機的 **yūkiteki** organic
⁷ 投機 **tōki** speculation
⁹ 契機 **keiki** opportunity, chance
   軍機 **gunki** military secret
   待機 **taiki** wait for an opportunity, watch and wait, stand by
¹⁰ 時機 **jiki** opportunity, time, occasion
¹¹ 動機 **dōki** motive
   転機 **tenki** turning point

─────────── 3 ───────────

⁵ 芝刈機 **shibaka(ri)ki** lawn mower

⁷ 投影機 **tōeiki** projector
⁹ 飛行機 **hikōki** airplane
   洗濯機 **sentakki, sentakuki** washing machine
   計算機 **keisanki** computer
¹⁰ 旅客機 **ryokakki** passenger plane
   扇風機 **senpūki** (electric) fan
¹¹ 掃除機 **sōjiki** vacuum cleaner
¹³ 戦闘機 **sentōki** fighter (plane)
¹⁹ 警報機 **keihōki** warning device, alarm

─────────── 5 ───────────

⁶ 自動販売機 **jidōhanbaiki** vending machine

4a12.2   ☐ 木 王 儿
                        41 46 16

樸 樸

BOKU unprocessed (lumber), as is

─────────── 1 ───────────

⁸ 樸直 **bokuchoku** simple and honest

─────────── 3 ───────────

³ 大相樸 **ōzumō** grand sumo tournament; exciting match

4a12.3 / 1144   ▥ 木 土 口
                              41 22 24

樹 樹

JU, ki tree, bush **ta(teru)** set up, establish KI, JU, TATSU (part of given name) ŌKI (m. given name)

─────────── 1 ───────────

⁴ 樹木 **jumoku** trees
⁵ 樹氷 **juhyō** frost/ice on trees
¹⁰ 樹脂 **jushi** resin
¹³ 樹幹 **jukan** (tree) trunk

─────────── 2 ───────────

³ 大樹 **Daiki** (m. given name)
⁵ 弘樹 **Hiroki** (m. given name)
⁷ 秀樹 **Hideki, Hotsuki** (m. given name)
⁸ 果樹園 **kajuen** orchard

直樹 **Naoki** (m. given name)

和樹 **Kazuki** (m. given name)

9 美樹 **Miki, Yoshiki, Haruki** (given name)

祐樹 **Hiroki, Yūki** (m. given name)

12 植樹 **shokuju** tree planting

17 優樹 **Masaki, Yūki** (m. given name)

———————— 3 ————————

10 針葉樹 **shin'yōju** needle-leaf tree, conifer

11 菩提樹 **bodaiju** bo tree; linden tree; lime tree

12 落葉樹 **rakuyōju** deciduous tree

概 → 慨 **4a10.2**

4a12.8 / 597   ⊞ 木 大 口
                 41 34 24

橋橋

KYŌ, hashi bridge

———————— 1 ————————

5 橋本 **Hashimoto** (surname)

10 橋桁 **hashigeta** bridge girder

11 橋梁 **kyōryō** bridge

12 橋渡 **hashiwata(shi)** bridge building; mediation

———————— 2 ————————

5 石橋 **Ishibashi** (surname)

9 前橋 **Maebashi** (city, Gunma-ken)

10 高橋 **Takahashi** (surname)

桟橋 **sanbashi** wharf, jetty
sankyō wharf; bridge

11 釣橋 **tsu(ri)bashi** suspension bridge

13 鉄橋 **tekkyō** steel/railroad bridge

20 懸橋 **ka(ke)hashi** suspension bridge; viaduct

———————— 3 ————————

8 歩道橋 **hodōkyō** pedestrian overpass

4a12.11 / 2127   ⊞ 木 口 宀
                 41 24 14

橘

KITSU citrus fruits **tachibana** mandarin orange TACHIBANA (surname) KITSU (part of given name)

———————— 2 ————————

9 柑橘類 **kankitsurui** citrus fruits

4a12.14   ⊞ 木 艹 一
                  41 12 1

橇 橇橇

KYŌ, ZEI, sori sled, sleigh, sledge, skid

———————— 1 ————————

4 橇犬 **soriinu** sled dog

横 → 横 **4a11.13**

4a12.17   ⊞ 木 亻 广
                  41 3 11

檎 檎檎

KIN, GO apple

———————— 2 ————————

8 林檎 **ringo** apple

樽 → 樽 **4a12.19**

4a12.19   ⊞ 酉 木 寸
                  71 41 37

樽 樽|樽樽

SON, taru barrel, cask, keg, tub

———————— 1 ————————

13 樽詰 **taruzu(me)** barreled, in casks

─────────── 13 ───────────

櫛 → 櫛　**4a15.5**

4a13.8　　　⊞ 木 日 口
　　　　　　　　　41 43 24

桧 | 檜檜

KAI, hinoki, hi Japanese cypress, white cedar

─────── 1 ───────

15 檜舞台 **hinoki butai** cypress-floored stage; high-class stage, limelight

檢 → 検　**4a8.28**

4a13.11 / 2128　⊞ 木 日 口
　　　　　　　　　41 43 24

檀 | 檀檀

DAN, TAN sandalwood, rosewood, chinaberry tree **mayumi** spindle tree
DAN, SEN (part of given name)
MAYUMI (f. given name)

─────── 1 ───────

10 檀家 **danka** family supporting a temple

─────────── 14 ───────────

4a14.7　　　⊞ 木 艹 口
　　　　　　　　　41 32 24

鞣 鞣

JŪ, name(su) tan (hides)
nameshi, nameshigawa leather

─────── 1 ───────

5 鞣皮 **jūhi, name(shi)gawa** leather

─────────── 15 ───────────

4a15.2　　　⊞ 魚 木 日
　　　　　　　　　79 41 43

櫓

RO oar; tower **yagura** tower, turret; scaffolding

4a15.5　　　⊞ 食 竹 木
　　　　　　　　　73 66 41

櫛 | 櫛櫛

SHITSU, kushi comb

─────────── 16 ───────────

4a16.4 / 1202　⊞ 門 木 日
　　　　　　　　　76 41 43

欄 | 欄欄

RAN (newspaper) column, blank, space (on a form); railing
obashima handrail

─────── 1 ───────

5 欄外 **rangai** margin (of a page)

─────── 2 ───────

8 空欄 **kūran** blank column

─────── 3 ───────

11 経済欄 **keizairan** financial section/columns

─────────── 17 ───────────

櫻 → 桜　**4a6.15**

欄 → 欄　**4a16.4**

22

4a22.1

田 貝 目 木
68 55 41

欖

欖 欖

RAN Java almond tree

25

4a25.1

⺍ 木 山 彡
41 36 31

鬱

欝 | 鬱 鬱

UTSU melancholy, gloom, depression; accumulate, become congested,

be pent up; dense growth
fusa(gu) feel depressed, mope

――――― 1 ―――――
4 鬱込 **fusa(gi)ko(mu)** be depressed, feel low, mope
10 鬱陶 **uttō(shii)** gloomy, depressing

――――― 2 ―――――
6 気鬱 **kiutsu** gloom, melancholy, depression
15 憂鬱 **yūutsu** melancholy, dejection, gloom
20 躁鬱病 **sōutsubyō** manic-depressive psychosis

4

木
月
日
火
礻
王
牛
方
攵
欠
心
戸
戈

0

――――― 月 **4b** ―――――

月	肉	肋	肌	有	肝	肘	肛	朋	肪	肥	服	肢
0.1	2a4.20	2.1	2.2	2.3	3.2	3.3	3.4	4.1	4.2	4.5	4.6	4.7

股	青	肯	宥	冑	胞	胆	肺	胎	胡	背	胤	脅
4.8	4.10	4.11	3m6.1	4c5.6	5.5	5.6	5.9	5.10	5.12	5.15	5.16	6.3

脆	朕	脂	脈	胸	胴	朗	朔	脊	骨	能	豚	脚
6.4	6.6	6.7	6.8	6.9	6.10	6.11	6.12	6.13	6.14	6.15	7.2	7.3

脛	脳	脱	脉	朗	脣	脹	勝	腕	腔	臍	腋	腑
7.6	7.7	7.8	4b6.8	4b6.11	3d7.12	8.1	8.4	8.6	8.7	4b14.2	8.8	8.9

腱	腿	期	朝	腫	腰	腹	腺	腸	膣	腦	腿	腎
8.10	4b9.10	8.11	8.12	9.1	9.3	9.4	9.6	9.8	9.9	4b7.7	9.10	9.11

膜	膀	静	趙	膠	膝	腸	膣	膨	膳	骸	鞘	膽
10.6	10.7	10.9	10.11	11.3	11.4	4b9.8	4b9.9	12.1	12.2	12.7	12.8	13.1

膿	臆	膽	臍	髄	鵬	臓	覇	騰	臓	髄	體
13.2	13.3	4b5.6	14.2	14.3	15.1	15.2	15.4	16.3	4b15.2	4b14.3	2a5.6

0

4b0.1 / 17

囗 月
42

月

月 月

GETSU moon; month; Monday
GATSU month **tsuki** moon; month

――――― 1 ―――――
4 月日 **gappi** date **tsukihi** months and days, time
5 月末 **getsumatsu, tsukizue** end of the month
月刊 **gekkan** monthly publication
月払 **tsukibara(i)** monthly installments
6 月光 **gekkō** moonlight
7 月見 **tsukimi** viewing the moon

8 月夜 **tsukiyo** moonlit night
9 月食 **gesshoku** eclipse of the moon
10 月俸 **geppō** monthly salary
11 月産 **gessan** monthly production/ output
12 月給 **gekkyū** (monthly) salary
月給日 **gekkyūbi** payday
15 月賦 **geppu** monthly installments
17 月謝 **gessha** monthly tuition
18 月曜日 **getsuyōbi** Monday

─────── 2 ───────

1 一月 **ichigatsu** January **ik(ka)getsu, hitotsuki, ichigetsu** one month
2 二月 **nigatsu** February **futatsuki** two months
七月 **shichigatsu** July
九月 **kugatsu** September **kyū(ka)getsu, ku(ka)getsu** nine months
十月 **jūgatsu** October
八月 **hachigatsu** August
3 三月 **sangatsu** March **san(ka)getsu, mitsuki** three months
夕月 **yūzuki** evening moon
4 五月 **gogatsu** May **satsuki** fifth month of the lunar calendar
五月晴 **satsukiba(re)** fine weather during the rainy season
今月 **kongetsu** this month
六月 **rokugatsu** June
5 半月 **hantsuki** half a month **hangetsu** half moon, semicircle
本月 **hongetsu** this month
正月 **shōgatsu** the New Year; January
四月 **shigatsu** April **yon(ka)getsu** four months
6 年月日 **nengappi** date
毎月 **maigetsu, maitsuki** every month, monthly
先月 **sengetsu** last month
安月給 **yasugekkyū** meager salary
7 来月 **raigetsu** next month
何月 **nangatsu** what month **nan(ka)getsu** how many months
8 明月 **meigetsu** bright/full moon
10 祥月命日 **shōtsuki meinichi** anniversary of one's death

11 菜月 **Natsuki** (f. given name)
12 満月 **mangetsu** full moon
13 歳月 **saigetsu** time, years

─────── 3 ───────

2 十一月 **jūichigatsu** November
十二月 **jūnigatsu** December
3 三日月 **mikazuki** crescent moon
5 生年月日 **seinengappi** date of birth
6 先々月 **sensengetsu** the month before last

肉 → **2a4.20**

─────── 2 ───────

4b2.1   ⊞ 月 力
                           42   8

肋   肋 肋

ROKU, abara rib

─────── 1 ───────

10 肋骨 **rokkotsu, abarabone** ribs

4b2.2 / 1306   ⊞ 月 冂
                           42   20

肌   肌 肌

KI, hada skin; disposition

─────── 1 ───────

6 肌色 **hada-iro** flesh-colored
12 肌着 **hadagi** underwear
肌寒 **hadazamu(i), hadasamu(i)** chilly
13 肌触 **hadazawa(ri)** the touch/feel

4b2.3 / 265   ⊟ 月 十
                           42   12

有   有 有

YŪ, U, a(ru) be, exist; have
TAMOTSU (m. given name) **ARI** (part of given name)

——————— 1 ———————

0 有する **yū(suru)** have, possess, own

2 有力 **yūryoku** influential, powerful

5 有史 **yūshi** historical, in recorded history

有功 **yūkō** merit(orious)

有用 **yūyō** useful, serviceable, available

有田焼 **Arita-ya(ki)** Arita porcelainware

6 有合 **a(ri)a(u)** happen to be on hand **a(ri)a(wase)** what is on hand

有名 **yūmei** famous

7 有余 **a(ri)ama(ru)** be superfluous, be more than enough **yūyo** more than

有利 **yūri** advantageous, profitable, favorable

8 有毒 **yūdoku** poisonous

有価物 **yūkabutsu** valuables

有限会社 **yūgen-gaisha** limited liability company, Ltd.

9 有為 **yūi** capable, effective, promising **ui** vicissitudes of life

10 有益 **yūeki** beneficial, profitable

有害 **yūgai** harmful, noxious, injurious

有能 **yūnō** capable, competent

有料 **yūryō** fee-charging, toll (road), pay (toilet)

11 有得 **a(ri)u(ru)** could be, possible

12 有税 **yūzei** subject to tax, dutiable

有給 **yūkyū** salaried

13 有数 **yūsū** prominent, leading, top

有意 **yūi** intentional; (statistically) significant

有罪 **yūzai** guilty

14 有徳 **yūtoku** virtuous

有様 **a(ri)sama, a(ri)yō** situation, circumstances, spectacle; the truth

15 有権者 **yūkensha** qualified person, eligible voter

有線 **yūsen** by wire

16 有機的 **yūkiteki** organic

18 有職 **yūshoku** employed **yūsoku, yūshoku** person versed in court and military practices, scholar

有難 **a(ri)gata(i)** welcome, thankful **a(ri)ga(tō)** thank you

有難味 **a(ri)gatami** value, worth

——————— 2 ———————

4 公有 **kōyū** publicly owned

5 民有 **min'yū** privately owned

占有 **sen'yū** exclusive possession, occupancy

6 共有 **kyōyū** joint ownership

共有地 **kyōyūchi** public land, a common

7 含有量 **gan'yūryō** quantity of a constituent substance, content

享有 **kyōyu** enjoy, possess

私有 **shiyū** privately owned

私有物 **shiyūbutsu** private property

8 官有 **kan'yū** government-owned

国有 **kokuyū** national ownership

固有 **koyū** its own, peculiar, characteristic

固有名詞 **koyū meishi** proper noun

所有 **shoyū** ownership, possession

9 専有権 **sen'yūken** exclusive right, monopoly

保有 **hoyū** possess, hold, maintain

10 特有 **tokuyū** characteristic of, peculiar to

——————— 3 ———————

4b3.2 / 1272   冂 月 一一 一

             42 14 1

肝

肝肝

KAN liver **kimo** liver; pluck, courage

——————— 1 ———————

4 肝心 **kanjin** main, vital, essential

5 肝玉 **kimo(t)tama** pluck, courage, grit

9 肝要 **kan'yō** important, vital

肝胆 **kantan** liver and gall; one's inmost heart

13 肝腎 **kanjin** main, vital, essential

14 肝魂 **kimo(t)tama** pluck, courage, grit

19 肝臓 **kanzō** liver

木 月 日 火 ネ 王 牛 方 攵 欠 心 戸 戈

3

4b3.3

□ 月 寸
42 37

肘　肘肘

CHŪ, hiji elbow

────────── 1 ──────────

11 肘掛 **hijika(ke)** arm (of a chair)
13 肘鉄 **hijitetsu** rebuff, rejection

4b3.4

□ 月 工
42 38

肛　肛肛

KŌ the anus

────────── 1 ──────────

8 肛門 **kōmon** the anus

────────────── 4 ──────────────

4b4.1 / 2100

□ 月
42

朋　朋丨朋朋

HŌ (class)mate, comrade, companion
HŌ, TOMO, TOSHI (part of given name)

────────── 1 ──────────

4 朋友 **hōyū** friend, companion

4b4.2 / 1857

□ 月 方
42 48

肪　肪肪

BŌ (animal) fat

────────── 2 ──────────

10 脂肪 **shibō** fat, grease

4b4.5 / 1723

□ 月 尸 丨
42 40 2

肥　肥肥

HI, ko(eru) get fat; grow fertile
koe manure, night soil　**ko(yasu)** fertilize; fatten　**ko(yashi)** manure, night soil　**futo(ru)** get fat

────────── 1 ──────────

3 肥大 **hidai** fleshiness, corpulence
10 肥料 **hiryō** manure, fertilizer
12 肥満 **himan** corpulence, obesity

4b4.6 / 683

□ 月 阝 又
42 7 9

服　服服

FUKU clothes, dress; dose; obey, serve; admit to

────────── 1 ──────────

0 服する **fuku(suru)** yield/submit to, obey; admit; serve (in the army), discharge (duties)
6 服地 **fukuji** cloth, fabric, material
10 服部 **Hattori** (surname)
　　服従 **fukujū** obey, submit to
12 服装 **fukusō** dress, attire
　　服装随意 **fukusō zuii** informal attire
13 服飾 **fukushoku** clothing and accessories, attire

────────── 2 ──────────

1 一服 **ippuku** a dose; a smoke; a rest/break; a lull, calm market
4 不服 **fufuku** dissatisfaction, protest
5 礼服 **reifuku** formal dress
　　冬服 **fuyufuku** winter clothing
6 衣服 **ifuku** clothes, clothing
7 克服 **kokufuku** conquest, subjugation
　　呉服 **gofuku** cloth/dry goods, draperies
8 制服 **seifuku** uniform
　　征服 **seifuku** conquer, subjugate; master

（左欄外）

4

3

木 月 日 火 礻 王 牛 方 攵 欠 心 戸 戈

和服 **wafuku** Japanese clothes, kimono
9 軍服 **gunpuku** military uniform
洋服 **yōfuku** (Western-type) clothes
11 黒服 **kurofuku** black clothes
略服 **ryakufuku** everyday clothes,
informal dress
12 着服 **chakufuku** put on clothes;
embezzle
喪服 **mofuku** mourning clothes

―――――― 3 ――――――

11 紳士服 **shinshifuku** men's clothing
16 燕尾服 **enbifuku** swallow-tailed
coat

4b4.7 / 1146   田 月 十 又
                   42   12   9

肢

SHI limbs

―――――― 1 ――――――

7 肢体 **shitai** limbs; body and limbs

―――――― 2 ――――――

13 義肢 **gishi** artificial limb

4b4.8   田 月 冂 又
                   42   20   9

股

KO thigh; crotch **mata** crotch
momo upper leg, thigh, femur

―――――― 1 ――――――

14 股関節 **kokansetsu** hip joint

―――――― 2 ――――――

19 蟹股 **ganimata** bowlegged

4b4.10 / 208   日 月 土 一
                   42   22   1

青

青 | 青 青

SEI, SHŌ, ao(i), ao blue, green; unripe

―――――― 1 ――――――

3 青山 **Aoyama** (surname)
4 青天 **seiten** the blue sky
青少年 **seishōnen** young people,
the young
青木 **Aoki** (surname)
5 青写真 **aojashin, aoshashin** blueprints
青白 **aojiro(i)** pale, pallid, wan
6 青年 **seinen** young man/people, a
youth
青色 **seishoku** blue
8 青果物 **seikabutsu** vegetables and
fruits
青空 **aozora** the blue sky
青空市場 **aozora ichiba** open-air
market
青物 **aomono** green vegetables
青物屋 **aomonoya** vegetable store,
greengrocer
9 青信号 **aoshingō** green (traffic)
light
青春 **seishun** youth
青臭 **aokusa(i)** smelling grassy/un-
ripe; inexperienced
12 青葉 **aoba** green leaves/foliage,
greenery
青森県 **Aomori-ken** (prefecture)
13 青電話 **aodenwa** public telephone
14 青銅色 **seidōshoku** bronze-color
青銅器 **seidōki** bronze ware/tools

―――――― 2 ――――――

8 刺青 **shisei, irezumi** tattooing

4b4.11 / 1262   日 月 十 六
                   42   13   11

肯

肯 肯

KŌ, gae(njiru), gae(nzuru) agree to,
consent

―――――― 1 ――――――

8 肯定 **kōtei** affirm
肯定的 **kōteiteki** affirmative

 → **3m6.1**

冐 → 冒   **4c5.6**

— 5 —

4b5.5 / 1284   ⊞ 月 弓 宀   42 28 15

胞   胞｜胞胞

HŌ sac, sheath; placenta, afterbirth

— 1 —

2 胞子 **hōshi** spore

4b5.6 / 1273   ⊞ 月 日 一   42 43 1

胆   膽｜胆胆

TAN, kimo, i gallbladder; pluck, courage

— 1 —

2 胆力 **tanryoku** courage, mettle
9 胆勇 **tan'yū** courage, pluck, dauntlessness

— 2 —

3 大胆 **daitan** bold, daring
7 肝胆 **kantan** liver and gall; one's inmost heart
12 落胆 **rakutan** be discouraged/disheartened
14 魂胆 **kontan** soul; ulterior motive

4b5.9 / 1277   ⊞ 月 巾 亠   42 26 11

肺   肺肺

HAI lung

— 1 —

8 肺炎 **haien** pneumonia
10 肺病 **haibyō** lung/pulmonary disease
12 肺結核 **haikekkaku** pulmonary tuberculosis
17 肺癌 **haigan** lung cancer

4b5.10 / 1296   ⊞ 月 厶 竹   42 24 17

胎   胎胎

TAI womb, uterus

— 1 —

7 胎児 **taiji** fetus
15 胎盤 **taiban** placenta, afterbirth

— 2 —

5 母胎 **botai** womb, uterus
11 堕胎 **datai** abortion

4b5.12 / 2206   ⊞ 月 口 十   42 24 12

胡   胡胡

KO, GO, U barbarian, foreign
KO, GO, HISA (part of given name)

— 1 —

11 胡麻 **goma** sesame (seeds)
12 胡椒 **koshō** pepper

4b5.15 / 1265   ⊞ 月 ⼧ 一   42 13 1

背   背背

HAI, se back; one's height **sei** one's height **somu(ku)** turn one's back on, act contrary to, defy **somu(keru)** avert, turn away

— 1 —

3 背丈 **setake** one's height
4 背中 **senaka** one's back
5 背広 **sebiro** business suit
9 背負 **seo(u), sho(u)** carry on one's back, shoulder, be burdened with
   背後 **haigo** back, rear, behind
   背面 **haimen** rear, back, reverse
10 背部 **haibu** the back, posterior
   背骨 **sebone** backbone, spine
12 背景 **haikei** background

──── 4 ────

4 中肉中背 **chūniku-chūzei** medium height and build

4b5.16 / 2205　　　冂 月 儿 竹
　　　　　　　　　　　　42　16　17

IN, tane descendant, issue, offspring
TANE (f. given name)　TSUZUKI (m. given name)　IN, TSUGU, TSUGI, KAZU, MI, TANE (part of given name)

──── 6 ────

4b6.3　　　　　　冂 月 力
　　　　　　　　　　　42　8

脇　　　　　脇脇

KYŌ, waki side, armpit, flank; supporting role

──── 1 ────

5 脇目 **wakime** onlooker's eyes; looking aside
7 脇見 **wakimi** look aside/away
11 脇道 **wakimichi** byway, side road; digression

──── 2 ────

6 西脇 **Nishiwaki** (surname)

4b6.4　　　　　冂 月 宀 厂
　　　　　　　　　　42　15　18

脆　　　　　脆脆

ZEI, moro(i) fragile, brittle

──── 1 ────

10 脆弱 **zeijaku** fragile, frail, flimsy, brittle

4b6.6 / 1921　　　冂 月 大 儿
　　　　　　　　　　　42　34　16

朕 | 朕朕

CHIN (imperial) we

4b6.7 / 1042　　　冂 月 日 匕
　　　　　　　　　　　42　43　13

脂　　　　　脂脂

SHI, abura (animal) fat **yani** resin, gum, tar, nicotine; earwax, eye discharge

──── 1 ────

6 脂気 **aburake** oily, greasy
8 脂肪 **shibō** fat, grease
16 脂濃 **abura(k)ko(i)** greasy, rich (foods)

──── 2 ────

8 油脂 **yushi** fat, fats and oils
16 樹脂 **jushi** resin

4b6.8 / 913　　　冂 月 厂 乀
　　　　　　　　　　　42　18　10

脈　　　脈 | 脈脈

MYAKU pulse, vein, blood vessel

──── 1 ────

8 脈拍 **myakuhaku** pulse (rate)
12 脈絡 **myakuraku** logical connection, coherence

──── 2 ────

2 人脈 **jinmyaku** (network of) personal connections
3 山脈 **sanmyaku** mountain range
4 文脈 **bunmyaku** context
6 血脈 **ketsumyaku** blood vessel/relationship

──── 3 ────

3 大静脈 **daijōmyaku** the vena cava

4b6.9 / 1283

     月 ⼍ 勹
     42   15   20

胸

KYŌ, mune, muna- chest, breast; heart, feelings

—————— 1 ——————

4 胸中 **kyōchū** one's bosom, heart, feelings
6 胸先 **munasaki** the solar plexus; breast
7 胸囲 **kyōi** girth/circumference of the chest
8 胸苦 **munaguru(shii)** feeling oppressed in the chest
10 胸部 **kyōbu** the chest
12 胸焼 **muneya(ke)** heartburn
14 胸像 **kyōzō** (sculptured) bust
18 胸騒 **munasawa(gi)** uneasiness; apprehension

4b6.10 / 1300

     月 ⼝ 勹
     42   24   20

胴

DŌ torso, trunk

—————— 1 ——————

6 胴回 **dōmawa(ri)** one's girth
7 胴体 **dōtai** the body, torso; fuselage
胴忘 **dōwasu(re)** have a lapse of memory, forget for the moment

4b6.11 / 1754

     食 月
     73   42

朗

RŌ, hoga(raka) clear, bright, cheerful AKIRA (m. given name) AKI (part of given name)

—————— 1 ——————

3 朗々 **rōrō** clear, sonorous
12 朗詠 **rōei** recite

14 朗読 **rōdoku** read aloud

—————— 2 ——————

8 明朗 **meirō** clear, open, cheerful

4b6.12 / 2101

     日 月 ⼉ 一
     42   16   14

朔

SAKU beginning; north **tsuitachi** first day of the month HAJIME (m. given name) SAKU, KITA, MOTO (part of given name)

4b6.13

     ⼃ 月 ⼈ 二
     42   3   4

脊

SEKI back, spine **se** one's height

—————— 1 ——————

18 脊髄 **sekizui** spinal cord

4b6.14 / 1266

     ⼌ 月 ⼍ 一
     42   20   1

骨

KOTSU, hone bone

—————— 1 ——————

6 骨休 **honeyasu(me)** relaxation, recreation
骨肉 **kotsuniku** one's flesh and blood, kin
7 骨身 **honemi** flesh and bones; marrow
骨折 **kossetsu** broken bone, fracture **honeo(ru)** take pains, exert oneself
骨折損 **honeo(ri)zon** wasted effort
骨抜 **honenu(ki)** boned; emasculated, watered down
10 骨格 **kokkaku** skeleton, frame, one's build
11 骨惜 **honeo(shimi)** avoid effort, spare oneself

骨組 **honegu(mi)** skeleton; framework

12 骨董品 **kottōhin** curios, bric-a-brac

骨無 **honena(shi)** rickets; spineless/weak-willed person

───── 2 ─────

6 肋骨 **rokkotsu, abarabone** ribs

9 背骨 **sebone** backbone, spine

10 納骨 **nōkotsu** depositing the (deceased's) ashes

11 接骨 **sekkotsu** bonesetting

14 遺骨 **ikotsu** one's remains/ashes

16 骸骨 **gaikotsu** skeleton

21 露骨 **rokotsu** open, undisguised, frank; conspicuous; lewd

4b6.15 / 386

田 月 竹 ⺈
42 17 13

能 能

NŌ ability, function; Noh drama
yo(ku) skillfully **YOSHI** (part of given name)

───── 1 ─────

2 能力 **nōryoku** ability, capacity, talent

5 能弁 **nōben** eloquence, oratory

7 能狂言 **nōkyōgen** Noh farce; Noh drama and *kyōgen* farce

11 能率 **nōritsu** efficiency

12 能登半島 **Noto-hantō** (peninsula, Ishikawa-ken)

能筆 **nōhitsu** calligraphy, skilled penmanship

13 能楽 **nōgaku** Noh drama

───── 2 ─────

3 万能 **bannō** omnipotent, all-around, all-purpose **mannō** all-purpose

才能 **sainō** talent, ability

5 本能 **honnō** instinct

可能 **kanō** possible

可能性 **kanōsei** possibility

6 多能 **tanō** versatile

全能 **zennō** omnipotence

有能 **yūnō** capable, competent

7 低能 **teinō** low intelligence, mentally deficient

技能 **ginō** skill, technical ability

芸能 **geinō** (public) entertainment; accomplishments, attainments

8 非能率的 **hinōritsuteki** inefficient

効能 **kōnō** efficacy, effect

知能 **chinō** intelligence

官能 **kannō** bodily functions; sensual, carnal

12 堪能 **tannō** skill; be satisfied

無能 **munō** incompetent, ineffective

16 機能 **kinō** a function

───── 3 ─────

4 不可能 **fukanō** impossible

8 放射能 **hōshanō** radioactivity, radiation

━━━━━ 7 ━━━━━

4b7.2 / 796

⊞ 月 ⺨ ⺈
42 27 10

豚 豚

TON, buta pig

───── 1 ─────

6 豚肉 **butaniku** pork

15 豚箱 **butabako** police lockup, jail

───── 2 ─────

8 河豚 **fugu** globefish, blowfish, puffer

9 海豚 **iruka** porpoise, dolphin

15 養豚 **yōton** hog raising

4b7.3 / 1784

⊞ 月 土 竹
42 22 17

脚 脚

KYAKU, KYA, ashi leg

───── 1 ─────

5 脚本 **kyakuhon** script, play

6 脚色 **kyakushoku** dramatization, stage/film adaptation

8 脚注 **kyakuchū** footnote

12 脚註 **kyakuchū** footnote

4
━
━
━

7

木
月
日
火
⻂
王
牛
方
攵
欠
心
戸
戈

¹⁵ 脚線美 **kyakusenbi** leg beauty/ shapeliness

─────── 2 ───────

⁵ 失脚 **shikkyaku** lose one's standing, be overthrown, fall

4b7.6 田 月 エ 一
42 38 1

脛 脛脛

KEI, sune, hagi shin, (lower) leg

─────── 1 ───────

¹⁸ 脛囓 **sunekaji(ri)** hanger-on, sponger

4b7.7 / 1278 田 月 小 冂
42 35 20

脳 脳 | 脳脳

NŌ brain

─────── 1 ───────

⁶ 脳死 **nōshi** brain death
⁸ 脳卒中 **nōsotchū** cerebral apoplexy
脳味噌 **nōmiso** brains, gray matter

─────── 2 ───────

⁵ 主脳 **shunō** leader
主脳会談 **shunō kaidan** summit conference
主脳会議 **shunō kaigi** summit conference
⁹ 首脳 **shunō** leader
首脳会談 **shunō kaidan** summit conference
洗脳 **sennō** brainwashing
¹⁶ 頭脳 **zunō** brains, head

4b7.8 / 1370 田 月 口 儿
42 24 16

脱 脱 | 脱脱

DATSU omit; escape **nu(gu)** take off (clothes) **nu(gasu)** strip off clothes, undress (someone) **nu(geru)** come/ slip off

─────── 1 ───────

⁰ 脱する **das(suru)** escape from; be omitted; take off (clothes); omit
⁴ 脱毛 **datsumō, nu(ke)ge** falling-out/removal of hair
脱文 **datsubun** missing passage, lacuna
⁵ 脱出 **dasshutsu** escape from; prolapse **nu(ke)da(su)** slip away
脱字 **datsuji** omitted character/ word
⁶ 脱会 **dakkai** withdrawal (from an organization)
脱色 **dasshoku** decoloration, bleaching
脱衣所 **datsuisho, datsuijo** changing/dressing room
⁷ 脱走 **dassō** escape, flee
⁸ 脱退 **dattai** secede, withdraw
⁹ 脱臭剤 **dasshūzai** deodorant, deodorizer
¹⁰ 脱党 **dattō** leave/bolt the party
¹¹ 脱捨 **nu(gi)su(teru)** throw off (clothes), kick off (shoes)
¹² 脱帽 **datsubō** take off one's hat/cap
脱落 **datsuraku** fall off, molt; be omitted; defect, desert, drop out
脱税 **datsuzei** tax evasion
¹⁴ 脱獄 **datsugoku** escape from prison, jailbreak
¹⁵ 脱線 **dassen** derailment; digression

 脈 → 脈 4b6.8

朗 → 朗 4b6.11

脣 → 唇 3d7.12

─────── 8 ───────

4b8.1 / 1922 田 礻 月 卜
57 42 13

 脹脹

CHŌ, fuku(reru/ramu) swell, get big, expand **fuku(ramasu)** cause to swell, expand

───────── 1 ─────────

9 脹面 **fuku(ret)tsura** sulky/sullen look, pout

───────── 2 ─────────

16 膨脹 **bōchō** swelling, expansion

4b8.4 / 509

□ 月 火 二
42 44 4

勝 | 勝 勝

SHŌ, ka(tsu) win **ka(chi)** victory **-gachi** tend to **masa(ru)** excel, be superior to **sugu(reru)** excel, be excellent SHŌ, KATSU (part of given name)

───────── 1 ─────────

1 勝一 **Katsuichi, Shōichi** (m. given name)
2 勝人 **Katsuhito, Katsuto, Katsundo** (m. given name)
4 勝手 **katte** as one pleases, arbitrary; kitchen; the situation
6 勝気 **ka(chi)ki** determined to succeed
7 勝利 **shōri** victory
   Katsutoshi (m. given name)
8 勝者 **shōsha** winner, victor
9 勝負 **shōbu** victory or defeat; match, showdown
   勝負事 **shōbugoto** game of skill/ chance
   勝通 **ka(chi)tō(su)** win successive victories
10 勝残 **ka(chi)noko(ru)** make the finals
11 勝得 **ka(chi)e(ru)** win, achieve, earn, gain
   勝敗 **shōhai** victory or defeat
12 勝報 **shōhō** news of victory
   勝景 **shōkei** beautiful scenery, fine view
   勝越 **ka(chi)ko(shi)** ahead by (so many) wins
   勝訴 **shōso** winning a lawsuit
13 勝誇 **ka(chi)hoko(ru)** triumph, exult in victory

───────── 2 ─────────

3 大勝利 **daishōri** decisive victory

5 必勝 **hisshō** sure victory
6 先勝 **senshō** win the first game/ point
7 決勝 **kesshō** decision (in a contest)
10 健勝 **kenshō** healthy, robust, hale and hearty
13 楽勝 **rakushō** easy victory
   戦勝国 **senshōkoku** victorious nation
17 優勝 **yūshō** victory, championship

───────── 3 ─────────

13 準決勝 **junkesshō** semifinals

4b8.6 / 1299

□ 月 宀 夕
42 33 30

腕腕

WAN, ude arm; skill **kaina** arm

───────── 1 ─────────

2 腕力 **wanryoku** physical strength
6 腕次第 **ude-shidai** according to one's ability
   腕自慢 **udejiman** proud of one's skill
7 腕利 **udeki(ki)** skilled, able
9 腕前 **udemae** ability, skill
10 腕時計 **udedokei** wristwatch
11 腕組 **udegu(mi)** fold one's arms
13 腕節 **ude(p)pushi** muscular strength

───────── 2 ─────────

4 手腕 **shuwan** ability, skill
5 右腕 **uwan, migiude** right arm
10 敏腕 **binwan** able, capable
14 辣腕 **ratsuwan** astute, sharp

4b8.7

□ 月 宀 工
42 33 38

腔腔

KŌ, KŪ body cavity

臍 → 臍 **4b14.2**

木
月
日
火
礻
王
牛
方
攵
欠
心
戸
戈

4b8.8　　　　　田 月 夕 宀
　　　　　　　　　42　30　11

腋　　　　腋 腋

EKI, waki armpit, side

4b8.9　　　　　　田 月 寸 厂
　　　　　　　　　42　37　18

腑　　　　腑 腑

FU viscera, bowels; mind; reason, understanding

――――――― 1 ―――――――

¹² 腑落 **fu (ni) o(chinai)** cannot fathom/understand

4b8.10　　　　　　田 月 彐 辶
　　　　　　　　　42　39　19

腱　　　　腱 腱

KEN tendon

腿 → 腿　　**4b9.10**

4b8.11 / 449　　　田 月 卄 二
　　　　　　　　　42　32　4

期　　　　期 | 期 期

KI, GO time, period, term

――――――― 1 ―――――――

⁴ 期日 **kijitsu** (appointed) day/date, term, due date
⁵ 期末 **kimatsu** end of the term/period
⁸ 期限 **kigen** term, period, due date, deadline
⁹ 期待 **kitai** expect, anticipate, place one's hopes on

――――――― 2 ―――――――

¹ 一期 **ichigo** one's lifespan **ikki** a term, a half year, a quarter

⁴ 中期 **chūki** middle period
　今期 **konki** the present/current term
⁵ 半期 **hanki** half term, half year
　冬期 **tōki** winter season, wintertime
⁶ 死期 **shiki** time of death, one's last hour
　年期 **nenki** term of service, apprenticeship; experience
　任期 **ninki** term of office, tenure
　会期 **kaiki** term, session (of a legislature)
　刑期 **keiki** prison term
　同期 **dōki** the same period; the same class; synchronous
　早期 **sōki** early stage/phase
⁷ 延期 **enki** postpone, defer, prolong
　学期 **gakki** school term, semester
　初期 **shoki** early period/stage, beginning
⁸ 長期 **chōki** long-term, long-range
　画期的 **kakkiteki** epoch-making, revolutionary
　周期 **shūki** period, cycle
　定期 **teiki** fixed period/term/intervals, regular (meeting); (train) pass, commuting ticket (short for 定期券)
　雨期 **uki** the rainy season
⁹ 前期 **zenki** the first/preceding term
　後期 **kōki** latter period/term, late (Nara); latter half (of the year)
¹⁰ 残期 **zanki** remaining period, unexpired term
　時期 **jiki** time, season
　夏期 **kaki** the summer period
　納期 **nōki** payment date, delivery deadline
¹² 満期 **manki** expiration (date)
　短期 **tanki** short period, short-term
　最期 **saigo** one's last moments, death
　無期 **muki** indefinite
　無期限 **mukigen** indefinite, without time limit

――――――― 3 ―――――――

⁵ 半減期 **hangenki** halflife (in physics)
　氷河期 **hyōgaki** glacial period, ice age
⁶ 全盛期 **zenseiki** golden age, heyday

⁹ 思春期 **shishunki** puberty

¹¹ 過渡期 **katoki** transition period

¹² 最盛期 **saiseiki** golden age, heyday; the best season for

¹³ 農閑期 **nōkanki** farmers' slack season

4b8.12 / 469   田   月   日   十
               42   43   12

朝   朝 | 朝 朝

CHŌ morning; dynasty

asa, ashita morning   TOMO (part of given name)

--- 1 ---

⁴ 朝日 **asahi** morning/rising sun

⁵ 朝刊 **chōkan** morning paper/edition

   朝市 **asaichi** morning market/fair

⁹ 朝食 **chōshoku** breakfast

¹² 朝飯 **asahan, asameshi** breakfast

¹³ 朝寝坊 **asanebō** late riser

¹⁷ 朝鮮 **Chōsen** Korea

   朝鮮人 **Chōsenjin** a Korean

¹⁸ 朝顔 **asagao** morning glory

¹⁹ 朝霧 **asagiri** morning fog

²⁴ 朝靄 **asamoya** morning haze/mist

--- 2 ---

⁴ 今朝 **kesa, konchō** this morning

   王朝 **ōchō** dynasty

⁵ 北朝鮮 **Kita Chōsen** North Korea

⁶ 毎朝 **maiasa** every morning

   早朝 **sōchō** early morning

⁷ 宋朝 **Sōchō** Song dynasty

⁸ 明朝 **myōchō** tomorrow morning

   Minchō Ming dynasty; Ming style (of printed kanji)

¹⁰ 唐朝 **Tōchō** the Tang dynasty

¹¹ 清朝 **Shinchō** Manchu/Qing dynasty

   翌朝 **yokuchō, yokuasa** the next morning

--- 3 ---

⁵ 平安朝 **Heianchō** the Heian period (794 – 1185)

4b9.1   田   車   月   一
               69   42   1

腫   腫 腫

SHU tumor, swelling **ha(reru)** swell, become swollen **ha(rasu)** cause to swell, inflame

--- 1 ---

¹⁴ 腫瘍 **shuyō** tumor

--- 2 ---

¹⁷ 癌腫 **ganshu** cancer tumor, carcinoma

4b9.3 / 1298   田   月   口   女
               42   24   25

腰   腰 腰

YŌ, koshi the pelvic region, loins, hips, the small of the back

--- 1 ---

⁶ 腰回 **koshimawa(ri)** one's hip measurement

⁷ 腰抜 **koshinu(ke)** coward(ice), weak-kneed milksop

¹⁰ 腰部 **yōbu** the pelvic region, waist, hips, loins

¹¹ 腰掛 **koshika(keru)** sit down **koshika(ke)** seat; stepping-stone (to something else)

¹² 腰痛 **yōtsū** lumbago

4b9.4 / 1271   田   月   日   夂
               42   43   49

腹   腹 腹

FUKU, hara belly, stomach; heart, mind   **(o)naka** belly, stomach

--- 1 ---

¹ 腹一杯 **hara ippai** full stomach; to one's heart's content

4   木 月 日 火 礻 王 牛 方 欠 心 戸 戈   9

³ 腹下 **harakuda(shi)** diarrhea; laxative

⁴ 腹切 **haraki(ri)** suicide by disembowelment

腹心 **fukushin** confidant, trusted associate

⁵ 腹立 **harada(tsu)** get angry

⁹ 腹持 **haramo(chi)** slow digestion, feeling of fullness

¹⁰ 腹部 **fukubu** abdomen, belly

¹¹ 腹黒 **haraguro(i)** black-hearted, scheming

¹² 腹違 **harachiga(i)** born of a different mother but having the same father

腹痛 **fukutsū, haraita** stomachache, abdominal pain

¹⁵ 腹蔵 **fukuzō** being reserved, holding back

――――― 2 ―――――

⁴ 太腹 **futo(p)para** generous; bold

⁵ 立腹 **rippuku** get angry, lose one's temper

⁸ 空腹 **kūfuku, su(ki)hara** empty stomach, hunger

¹² 満腹 **manpuku** full stomach/belly

¹³ 裏腹 **urahara** the contrary, opposite

4b9.6　　　　　田　月　日　氵
　　　　　　　　　42　43　21

腺　　腺腺

SEN gland

――――― 2 ―――――

⁶ 汗腺 **kansen** sweat gland

――――― 3 ―――――

⁹ 扁桃腺 **hentōsen** the tonsils

¹¹ 淋巴腺 **rinpasen** lymph gland

4b9.8 / 1270　　田　月　日　犭
　　　　　　　　　42　43　27

腸　　腸丨腸腸

CHŌ, harawata, wata intestines, entrails

――――― 1 ―――――

¹³ 腸詰 **chōzu(me)** sausage

⁹ 胃腸 **ichō** stomach and intestines

胃腸薬 **ichōyaku** stomach and bowel medicine

4b9.9　　　　　田　月　宀　土
　　　　　　　　　42　33　22

膣　　膣丨膣膣

CHITSU vagina

脳 → 脳　**4b7.7**

4b9.10　　　　　田　食　月　辶
　　　　　　　　　73　42　19

腿　　腿丨腿腿

TAI, momo (upper) leg

4b9.11　　　　　田　月　冂　又
　　　　　　　　　42　20　9

腎　　腎腎

JIN kidney

――――― 1 ―――――

¹⁹ 腎臓 **jinzō** kidney

――――― 2 ―――――

⁷ 肝腎 **kanjin** main, vital, essential

――――――――― 10 ―――――――――

4b10.6 / 1426　　田　月　日　艹
　　　　　　　　　42　43　32

膜　　膜膜

MAKU membrane

4b10.7

⊞ 月 方 亠
42 48 11

膀 膀膀

BŌ bladder

4b10.9 / 663

⊞ 月 土 ヨ
42 22 39

静 静丨静静

SEI, JŌ, shizu, shizu(ka) quiet, peaceful, still **shizu(meru)** calm, soothe, quell **shizu(maru)** grow quiet/calm, subside SHIZU (part of given name)

──── 1 ────

3 静々 **shizushizu** quietly, calmly, gently
4 静止 **seishi** still, standstill, at rest, stationary, static state
6 静江 **Shizue** (f. given name)
8 静岡県 **Shizuoka-ken** (prefecture)
静的 **seiteki** static
10 静座 **seiza** sit quietly
11 静粛 **seishuku** silent, still, quiet
静寂 **seijaku** silent, still, quiet
14 静態 **seitai** static, stationary
15 静養 **seiyō** rest, recuperate

──── 2 ────

3 大静脈 **daijōmyaku** the vena cava
5 平静 **heisei** calm, serene, tranquil
7 冷静 **reisei** calm, cool, unruffled
12 閑静 **kansei** quiet, peaceful
18 鎮静剤 **chinseizai** tranquilizer, sedative

4b10.11

⸛ 月 土 小
42 22 35

趙 趙趙

CHŌ (proper name); stab; walk slowly

──── 11 ────

4b11.3

⊞ ヨ 月 彡
39 42 31

膠 膠膠

KŌ, nikawa glue

4b11.4

⊞ 月 木 氵
42 41 21

膝 膝膝

SHITSU, hiza knee; lap

──── 1 ────

8 膝枕 **hizamakura** using someone's lap for a pillow

腸 → 腸 **4b9.8**

膣 → 膣 **4b9.9**

──── 12 ────

4b12.1 / 1145

⊞ 月 士 口
42 22 24

膨 膨膨

BŌ swell, expand
fuku(reru/ramu) swell, expand; sulk

──── 1 ────

3 膨大 **bōdai** swelling; large, enormous
11 膨張 **bōchō** swelling, expansion
12 膨脹 **bōchō** swelling, expansion

4b12.2

⊞ 月 王 口
42 46 24

膳 膳膳

ZEN food offering; serving tray; (counter for pairs of chopsticks)

--- 2 ---

¹ 一膳 **ichizen** a bowl (of rice); a pair
(of chopsticks)

4b12.7   田 月 冂 一
                    42 20 11

骸骸

GAI bone, body **mukuro** body;
corpse

--- 1 ---

¹⁰ 骸骨 **gaikotsu** skeleton

4b12.8   田 朿 月 ⺾
                    41 42 32

鞘 | 鞘 鞘

SHŌ, saya scabbard, sheath, cap;
markup, margin, spread; (bean) shells

--- 13 ---

4b13.1 / 1779   田 言 月 火
                     67 42 44

謄 | 謄 謄

TŌ copy

--- 1 ---

⁵ 謄本 **tōhon** transcript, copy
  謄写 **tōsha** copy, duplication

4b13.2   田 衤 月 日
                    57 42 43

膿膿

NŌ pus **u(mu)** form pus, fester,
suppurate **umi** pus

4b13.3   田 立 月 日
                    54 42 43

臆

臆臆

OKU breast, heart, mind; timidity

--- 1 ---

¹⁰ 臆病 **okubyō** cowardly, timid

膽 → 胆 **4b5.6**

--- 14 ---

4b14.2   田 月 一 儿
                    42 11 16

臍

脐 | 臍 臍

SEI, SAI, heso, hozo navel, belly button

--- 1 ---

⁶ 臍曲 **hesoma(gari)** cranky person,
grouch

4b14.3 / 1740   田 月 冂 十
                     42 20 12

髄 | 髄 髄

ZUI marrow, pith

--- 2 ---

⁴ 心髄 **shinzui** the soul/essence of
⁹ 神髄 **shinzui** (quint)essence, soul
¹⁰ 脊髄 **sekizui** spinal cord

--- 15 ---

4b15.1 / 2276   川 鳥 月
                     80 42

鵬

鵬鵬 | 鵬鵬

HŌ, ōtori huge mythical bird
HŌ, TOMO, YUKI (part of given name)

4b15.2 / 1287   田 月 戈 艹
                42   52   32

臓   臓 | 臓 臓

ZŌ internal organs

— 1 —

15 臓器 **zōki** internal organs, viscera

— 2 —

4 内臓 **naizō** internal organs
   心臓 **shinzō** the heart; nerve, cheek
7 肝臓 **kanzō** liver
13 腎臓 **jinzō** kidney

4b15.4 / 1633   田 月 口 艹
                42   24   32

覇

HA supremacy, domination, hegemony

— 1 —

6 覇気 **haki** ambition, aspirations
15 覇権 **haken** hegemony, domination

— 2 —

6 那覇 **Naha** (city, Okinawa-ken)
8 制覇 **seiha** mastery, supremacy; championship

---

9 連覇 **renpa** successive championships

— 16 —

4b16.3 / 1780   田 馬 月 火
                78   42   44

騰   騰 | 騰 騰

TŌ rise (in prices)   **NOBORU** (m. given name)

— 1 —

12 騰貴 **tōki** rise (in prices)
13 騰勢 **tōsei** rising/upward trend

— 2 —

8 沸騰 **futtō** boiling; excitement, agitation
   昇騰 **shōtō** rise, go up, soar
10 高騰 **kōtō** steep rise (in prices)

— 18 —

臓 → 臓   4b15.2

髄 → 髄   4b14.3

— 19 —

體 → 体   2a5.6

— 日 **4c** —

日	旧	旦	白	早	旨	百	亘	旬	旭	早	兒	児
0.1	1.1	1.2	1.3	2.1	2.2	2.3	2.4	2.5	2.6	3.1	4c10.6	3.3
明	旺	昌	昇	易	昂	昆	昏	昔	冐	的	者	旺
4.1	4.2	4.4	4.5	4.9	4c5.11	4.10	4.11	3k5.28	4c5.6	4.12	4.13	4c14.1
映	昧	昨	昭	昵	冒	星	是	昂	昻	昆	春	皆
5.1	5.2	5.3	5.4	4c15.2	5.6	5.7	5.9	5.11	5.12	4c4.10	5.13	5.14
泉	昼	者	晒	時	晄	晦	晟	晏	晃	書	晋	皆
3a5.33	5.15	4c4.13	6.1	6.2	4c6.5	4c7.3	4c7.5	6.4	6.5	6.6	6.8	4c5.14
晋	殉	晩	晦	晟	晨	曼	曹	習	皐	匙	乾	兜
4c6.8	6.9	4c8.3	7.3	7.5	7.7	7.8	7.10	7.11	7.12	7.13	7.14	4c8.16
畫	暁	晴	暎	晩	暑	晶	景	量	最	曾	智	替
4c5.15	8.1	8.2	8.3	8.5	8.5	8.6	8.8	8.9	8.10	2o9.3	8.11	8.12

4

木 月 日 火 礻 王 牛 方 欠 心 戸 戈   16

皓	朝	兜	奢	暇	暗	暖	暉	暑	餀	幹	幹	暢
8.13	4b8.12	8.16	8.17	9.1	9.2	9.4	9.6	4c8.5	0a10.5	9.8	10.3	10.4

貌	暴	暫	瞭	曉	曇	翰	曙	曖	矇	曜	曙	韓
10.6	11.2	11.3	5c12.4	4c8.1	12.1	12.4	4c14.2	13.1	13.2	14.1	14.2	14.3

覆	曠	響	馨	響	曬
14.6	15.2	15.3	16.2	4c15.3	4c6.1

4

0

木 月 日 火 礻 王 牛 方 攵 欠 心 戸 戈

─────── **0** ───────

4c0.1 / 5

□ 日

43

日 ⎡2⎤

NICHI day; sun; Sunday; (as prefix or suffix) Japan **JITSU, hi** sun; day **-ka** day (of the month), (number of) days

─────── **1** ───────

² 日入 **hi(no)i(ri)** sunset

³ 日丸 **hi(no)maru** the Japanese/red-sun flag

日々 **hibi** daily; days
nichi-nichi daily, every day

⁴ 日中 **Nit-Chū** Japan and China
nitchū during the day
hinaka broad daylight, daytime

日仏 **Nichi-Futsu** Japan and France

⁵ 日出 **hi(no)de** sunrise

日本 **Nihon, Nippon** Japan

日本一 **Nihon-ichi, Nippon-ichi** Japan's best

日本人 **Nihonjin, Nipponjin** a Japanese

日本刀 **nihontō** Japanese sword

日本三景 **Nihon sankei** Japan's three noted scenic sights (Matsushima, Miyajima, Amanohashidate)

日本中 **Nihonjū, Nipponjū** all over Japan

日本史 **Nihonshi** Japanese history

日本学 **nihongaku** Japanology

日本画 **nihonga** Japanese-style painting/drawing

日本的 **nihonteki** (very) Japanese

日本風 **nihonfū** Japanese style

日本海 **Nihonkai** the Sea of Japan

日本酒 **nihonshu** saké

日本紙 **nihonshi** Japanese paper

日本晴 **nihonba(re)** clear cloudless sky, beautiful weather

日本間 **nihonma** Japanese-style room

日本製 **nihonsei** made in Japan

日本語 **nihongo** the Japanese language

日付 **hizuke** day, dating

日刊 **nikkan** a daily (newspaper)

日加 **Nik-Ka** Japan and Canada

日比 **Nip-Pi** Japan and the Philippines

日比野 **Hibino** (surname)

日用品 **nichiyōhin** daily necessities

日立 **hida(tsu)** grow up; recover (after childbirth)
Hitachi (city, Ibaraki-ken); (electronics company)

⁶ 日伊 **Nichi-I** Japan and Italy

日印 **Nichi-In** Japan and India

日向 **hinata(bokko)** bask in the sun **Hyūga** (ancient kuni, Miyazaki-ken)

日光 **nikkō** sunshine, sunlight
Nikkō (town in Tochigi-ken)

日光浴 **nikkōyoku** sunbath

日当 **hia(tari)** exposure to the sun; sunny place **nittō** per-diem allowance, daily wages

日米 **Nichi-Bei** Japan and America, Japan-U.S.

⁷ 日延 **hino(be)** postponement

日没 **nichibotsu** sunset

日赤 **Nisseki** Japan Red Cross (short for 日本赤十字社)

日系 **nikkei** of Japanese descent

⁸ 日夜 **nichiya** day and night, constantly

日英 **Nichi-Ei** Japan and Britain/England

日欧 **Nichi-Ō** Japan and Europe

日和 **hiyori** the weather; fair weather; the situation

日取 **hido(ri)** (set) the date, schedule

9 日除 **hiyo(ke)** sunshade, awning, blind

日独 **Nichi-Doku** Japan and Germany

10 日陰 **hikage** the shade

日帰 **higae(ri)** a one-day (trip)

日時 **nichiji** date and hour, time

日記 **nikki** diary, journal

11 日野 **Hino** (surname)

日常 **nichijō** everyday, routine

日産 **nissan** daily production/output **Nissan** (automobile company)

日貨 **nikka** Japanese goods/currency

日頃 **higoro** usually, always; for a long time

12 日傘 **higasa** parasol

日満 **Nichi-Man** Japan and Manchuria

日焼 **hiya(ke)** sunburn; suntan

日程 **nittei** the day's schedule/agenda

13 日蓮 **Nichiren** Buddhist priest (1222–1282) who founded the Nichiren sect

日照 **nisshō, hide(ri)** sunshine, drought, dry weather

日数 **nissū, hikazu** number of days

日電 **Nichiden** (short for 日本電気) NEC (Corporation)

14 日豪 **Nichi-Gō** Japan and Australia

日増 **hima(shi ni)** (getting …er) day by day

日銀 **Nichigin** Bank of Japan (short for 日本銀行)

15 日影 **hika(ge)** sunlight; shadow

17 日鮮 **Nis-Sen** Japan and Korea

18 日曜 **nichiyō** Sunday

日曜日 **nichiyōbi** Sunday

日韓 **Nik-Kan** Japan and South Korea

21 日露 **Nichi-Ro** Japan and Russia

2
---

1 一日 **tsuitachi** the 1st (day of the month)
ichinichi, ichijitsu one/a day

一日中 **ichinichi-jū** all day long

2 二日 **futsuka** the 2nd (day of the month); two days

二日酔 **futsukayo(i)** a hangover

入日 **i(ri)hi** the setting sun

七日 **nanoka, nanuka** the 7th (day of the month); seven days

九日 **kokonoka** the 9th (day of the month); nine days

十日 **tōka** the tenth (day of the month); ten days

八日 **yōka** eight days; the eighth (of the month)

3 三日 **mikka** the 3rd (day of the month); three days

三日月 **mikazuki** crescent moon

三日坊主 **mikka bōzu** one who can stick to nothing, "three-day monk"

夕日 **yūhi** the setting sun

大日本 **Dai-Nippon/-Nihon** (Great) Japan

4 五日 **itsuka** the 5th (day of the month); five days

中日 **Chū-Nichi** China and Japan
chūnichi day of the equinox
nakabi, chūnichi the middle day (of a sumo tournament)

今日 **kyō, konnichi** today

六日 **muika** the sixth (day of the month); six days

反日 **han-Nichi** anti-Japanese

厄日 **yakubi** unlucky/critical day

月日 **gappi** date **tsukihi** months and days, time

5 半日 **hannichi** half day

本日 **honjitsu** today

末日 **matsujitsu** last day (of a month)

平日 **heijitsu** weekday; everyday

四日 **yokka** four days; the fourth (day of the month)

四日市 **Yokkaichi** (city, Mie-ken)

白日 **hakujitsu** daytime, broad daylight

6 両日 **ryōjitsu** both days; two days

西日 **nishibi** the afternoon sun

西日本 **Nishi Nihon** western Japan

毎日 **mainichi** every day, daily

休日 **kyūjitsu** holiday, day off

全日本 **zen-Nihon, zen-Nippon** all Japan

全日空 **Zennikkū** ANA = All Nippon Airways (short for 全日本 空輸)

近日 **kinjitsu** soon, in a few days

同日 **dōjitsu** the same day

先日 **senjitsu** the other day

在日 **zai-Nichi** in Japan
a(rishi)hi bygone days; during one's lifetime

吉日 **kichinichi, kichijitsu** lucky day

旭日章 **Kyokujitsushō** the Order of the Rising Sun

7 来日 **rainichi** come to Japan

何日 **nannichi** how many days; what day of the month

即日 **sokujitsu** on the same day

対日 **tai-Nichi** toward/with Japan

8 表日本 **Omote Nihon** Pacific side of Japan

例日 **reijitsu** weekday

定日 **teijitsu** fixed/appointed date

明日 **myōnichi, asu** tomorrow
a(kuru) hi the next/following day

明日香 **Asuka** (f. given name)

或日 **a(ru) hi** one day

9 前日 **zenjitsu** the day before

連日 **renjitsu** day after day, every day

後日 **gojitsu, gonichi** the future, another day

昨日 **sakujitsu, kinō** yesterday

祝日 **shukujitsu, iwa(i)bi** festival day, holiday

10 週日 **shūjitsu** weekday

時日 **jijitsu** the date/time; time, days

純日本風 **jun-Nihon-fū** classical Japanese style

11 排日 **hai-Nichi** anti-Japanese

祭日 **saijitsu** holiday; festival day

翌日 **yokujitsu** the next/following day

訪日 **hō-Nichi** visiting Japan

12 隔日 **kakujitsu** every other day, alternate days

期日 **kijitsu** (appointed) day/date, term, due date

朝日 **asahi** morning/rising sun

幾日 **ikunichi** how many days; what day of the month

13 裏日本 **ura-Nihon, ura-Nippon** Sea-of-Japan side of Japan

滞日 **tai-Nichi** staying in Japan

聖日 **seijitsu** holy day; the Sabbath

数日 **sūjitsu** a few days, several days

15 駐日 **chū-Nichi** resident/stationed in Japan

16 親日 **shin-Nichi** pro-Japanese

親日家 **shin-Nichika** Nippophile

18 曜日 **yōbi** day of the week

───────── 3 ─────────

1 一昨日 **issakujitsu, ototoi, ototsui** the day before yesterday

2 二十日 **hatsuka** the 20th (day of the month); twenty days

3 三十日 **sanjūnichi** the 30th (day of the month); 30 days **misoka** the last day of the month

大晦日 **Ōmisoka** last day of the year; New Year's Eve

土曜日 **doyōbi** Saturday

4 予定日 **yoteibi** scheduled date, expected date (of birth)

文化日 **Bunka (no) Hi** Culture Day (November 3)

公休日 **kōkyūbi** legal holiday

水曜日 **suiyōbi** Wednesday

木曜日 **mokuyōbi** Thursday

月給日 **gekkyūbi** payday

月曜日 **getsuyōbi** Monday

日曜日 **nichiyōbi** Sunday

火曜日 **kayōbi** Tuesday

6 年月日 **nengappi** date

安息日 **ansokubi** sabbath
ansokunichi the (Jewish) sabbath **ansokujitsu** the (Christian) sabbath

7 何曜日 **nan'yōbi, naniyōbi** what day of the week

投票日 **tōhyōbi** voting day

8 定休日 **teikyūbi** regular holiday, Closed (Tuesday)s

明後日 **myōgonichi** the day after tomorrow

金曜日 **kin'yōbi** Friday

9 春分日 **shunbun (no) hi** the vernal equinox (a holiday, about March 21)

祝祭日 **shukusaijitsu** festival, holiday

10 記念日 **kinenbi** memorial day, anniversary

12 最終日 **saishūbi** the last day

給料日 **kyūryōbi** payday

14 誕生日 **tanjōbi** birthday

——————— 4 ———————

5 生年月日 **seinengappi** date of birth

10 振替休日 **furikae kyūjitsu** substitute holiday (for one falling on a Sunday)

祥月命日 **shōtsuki meinichi** anniversary of one's death

13 聖金曜日 **Seikin'yōbi** Good Friday

——————— 1 ———————

4c1.1 / 1216

KYŪ old, former

——————— 1 ———————

4 旧友 **kyūyū** an old friend

6 旧式 **kyūshiki** old-type, old-fashioned

8 旧姓 **kyūsei** former/maiden name

9 旧約 **kyūyaku** old promise/covenant; the Old Testament

14 旧暦 **kyūreki** the old (lunar) calendar

15 旧弊 **kyūhei** an old evil; old-fashioned, behind the times

——————— 2 ———————

12 復旧 **fukkyū, fukukyū** restoration, recovery

13 新旧 **shinkyū** new and old

16 懐旧 **kaikyū** yearning for the old days

4c1.2 / 2085   43 1

TAN morning, dawn   AKIRA, TADA-SHI (m. given name)   TAN, AKI, ASA, AKE, MASA (part of given name)

——————— 1 ———————

6 旦那 **danna** master; husband; gentleman

——————— 2 ———————

1 一旦 **ittan** once

4 元旦 **gantan** New Year's Day

13 歳旦 **saitan** New Year's Day; the New Year

4c1.3 / 205   43 2

HAKU white; Belgium   **BYAKU, shiro, shiro(i), shira-** white   **shira(mu)** grow light   **shira** feigned ignorance

——————— 1 ———————

2 白人 **hakujin** a white, Caucasian

3 白々 **shirojiro** pure white

shirajira dawning

shirajira(shii) feigning ignorance; barefaced (lie)

hakuhaku very clear

4 白井 **Shirai** (surname)

白日 **hakujitsu** daytime, broad daylight

5 白石 **Shiraishi** (surname)

6 白色 **hakushoku** white

白光 **hakkō** white light; corona

白衣 **hakui, byakue, byakui** white robe, lab coat

白米 **hakumai** polished rice

7 白身 **shiromi** whiteness; white meat; white of an egg

白状 **hakujō** confess, admit

9 白面 **hakumen** white/pale face; inexperience   **shirafu** sober

白昼 **hakuchū** daytime, broad daylight

10 白書 **hakusho** whitepaper, report

11 白黒 **shiro-kuro** black-and-white; right or wrong, guilty or innocent

白鳥 **hakuchō** swan

12 白雲 **shirakumo, hakuun** white/fleecy clouds

13 白痴 **hakuchi** idiot

14 白墨 **hakuboku** chalk

白髪 **hakuhatsu, shiraga** white/gray hair

白樺 **shirakaba, shirakanba** white birch

白旗 **shirahata, hakki** white flag (of truce/surrender)

15 白熱戦 **hakunetsusen** intense fighting, thrilling game

白線 **hakusen** white line

21 白露 **Hakuro** White Russia, Belarus

―――――― 2 ――――――

7 告白 **kokuhaku** confession

8 空白 **kūhaku** blank, empty space, vacuum

青白 **aojiro(i)** pale, pallid, wan

明白 **meihaku** clear, unmistakable

9 面白 **omoshiro(i)** interesting; amusing

紅白 **kōhaku** red and white

10 真白 **ma(s)shiro** pure white

純白 **junpaku** pure white

11 淡白 **tanpaku** light, plain, simple; candid; indifferent to

黒白 **kuro-shiro, kokuhaku, kokubyaku** black and white; right and wrong

蛋白 **tanpaku** protein; albumen

13 蒼白 **sōhaku** pale, pallid, wan

14 精白米 **seihakumai** polished rice

15 潔白 **keppaku** pure, upright, of integrity

―――――― 2 ――――――

4c2.1 / 248

43 12

早

SŌ, SA', SA, **haya(i)** early; fast
haya(meru) hasten, accelerate
haya(maru) be hasty

―――――― 1 ――――――

3 早川 **Hayakawa** (surname)

早々 **sōsō** early, immediately; Hurriedly yours, **hayabaya** early, immediately

早口 **hayakuchi, hayaguchi** fast talking

4 早分 **hayawa(kari)** quick understanding; guide, handbook

早引 **hayabi(ki)** leave early

5 早出 **hayade** early arrival (at the office)

早目 **hayame (ni)** a little early (leaving leeway)

6 早死 **hayaji(ni)** die young/prematurely

早合点 **hayagaten** hasty conclusion

早耳 **hayamimi** quick-eared, in the know

7 早技 **hayawaza** quick work; sleight of hand

早足 **hayaashi** quick pace, fast walking

8 早退 **sōtai** leave early

9 早急 **sōkyū, sakkyū** urgently, without delay

早速 **sassoku** at once, getting right to the point

早咲 **hayaza(ki)** early-blooming; precocious

早春 **sōshun** early spring

早紀 **Saki** (f. given name)

10 早起 **hayao(ki)** get up early

11 早婚 **sōkon** early marriage

早産 **sōzan** premature birth

12 早期 **sōki** early stage/phase

早朝 **sōchō** early morning

早晩 **sōban** sooner or later

早飯 **hayameshi** eating fast/early
13 早業 **hayawaza** quick work; sleight of hand
早寝 **hayane** retiring early
19 早瀬 **hayase** swift current, rapids
早瀬 **Hayase** (surname)

——— 2 ———

11 遅早 **oso(kare)haya(kare)** sooner or later
12 最早 **mohaya** already, by now; (not) any longer

4c2.2 / 1040

目 日 卜
43 13

旨 旨

SHI, mune purport, content, gist, (to the effect) that; instructions
uma(i) tasty, delicious; skillful, good at; successful; wise

——— 1 ———

8 旨味 **umami** tastiness, flavor

——— 2 ———

5 本旨 **honshi** the main purpose
主旨 **shushi** gist, purport, object
9 要旨 **yōshi** gist, purport, substance
15 趣旨 **shushi** purport, meaning, aim, object

4c2.3 / 14

百 日 一
43 14

百 百

HYAKU hundred **momo** hundred; many MOMO (part of given name)

——— 1 ———

2 百人一首 **hyakunin-isshu** 100 poems by 100 poets (a collection of 100 *tanka*; basis for the popular card game *uta karuta*)
3 百万 **hyakuman** million
6 百合 **yuri** lily
8 百姓 **hyakushō** farmer, peasant

9 百点 **hyakuten** 100 points, perfect score
百科事典 **hyakka jiten** encyclopedia
11 百貨店 **hyakkaten** department store

——— 2 ———

2 八百長 **yaochō** rigged affair, fixed game
八百屋 **yaoya** vegetable store; jack-of-all-trades
5 四百 **yonhyaku** four hundred

——— 3 ———

14 嘘八百 **usohappyaku** a pack of lies

4c2.4 / 2006

目 日 一
43 1

亘 亘

SEN, KŌ, wata(ru) range/extend over, span SEN, KŌ, KAN, NOBU, HIRO (part of given name) WATARU, TŌRU, HIROSHI, WATARI (m. given name)

4c2.5 / 338

日 日 勹
43 15

旬 旬

JUN ten-day period **shun** the season for (oysters/vegetables)

——— 2 ———

3 上旬 **jōjun** the first ten days of a month
下旬 **gejun** 21st through last day of a month
4 中旬 **chūjun** middle ten days of a month, mid-(May)

4 ≡

2

木 月 日 火 礻 王 牛 方 攵 欠 心 戸 戈

4c2.6 / 2086

□ 日 十
43 12

旭

旭 旭

KYOKU, asahi the morning/rising sun **AKIRA, ASAHI** (m. given name) **KYOKU, TERU, ASA** (part of given name)

───── 1 ─────

³ 旭川 **Asahikawa** (city, Hokkaidō)
⁴ 旭日章 **Kyokujitsushō** the Order of the Rising Sun

───── 3 ─────

4c3.1

曰 日 十 一
43 14 1

旱

旱 旱

KAN, hideri drought

───── 1 ─────

¹⁰ 旱害 **kangai** drought damage
¹⁵ 旱魃 **kanbatsu** drought

兒 → 貌 **4c10.6**

4c3.3 / 1217

臼 日 儿 丨
43 16 2

児

兒 丨 児 児

JI, NI, ko child

───── 1 ─────

¹⁰ 児島 **Kojima** (surname)
¹² 児童 **jidō** child, juvenile

───── 2 ─────

³ 小児科 **shōnika** pediatrics
  小児麻痺 **shōni mahi** infantile paralysis, polio
⁵ 幼児 **yōji** small child, tot, baby
⁷ 乳児 **nyūji** suckling baby, infant
⁸ 孤児 **koji, minashigo** orphan
  育児 **ikuji** care/raising of children

⁹ 胎児 **taiji** fetus
¹¹ 鹿児島県 **Kagoshima-ken** (prefecture)
¹³ 園児 **enji** kindergarten child/pupil
  稚児 **chigo** child; child in a Buddhist procession
¹⁴ 愛児 **aiji** one's dear child
²² 驕児 **kyōji** spoiled child

───── 3 ─────

⁴ 双生児 **sōseiji** twins
¹¹ 混血児 **konketsuji** person of mixed race, half-breed
¹³ 畸形児 **kikeiji** deformed child

───── 4 ─────

4c4.1 / 18

□ 日 月
43 42

明

明 明

MEI light **MYŌ** light; next, following **MIN** Ming (dynasty) **a(kari)** light, clearness **aka(rui)** bright **aki(raka)** clear **a(keru), aka(rumu/ramu)** become light **a(ku)** be open/visible **a(kasu)** pass (the night); divulge **a(kuru)** next, following **AKIRA** (m. given name) **MEI, AKI, AKE, HARU** (part of given name)

───── 1 ─────

² 明子 **Akiko, Haruko, Meiko, Akeko** (f. given name)
⁴ 明月 **meigetsu** bright/full moon
  明日 **myōnichi, asu** tomorrow **a(kuru) hi** the next/following day
  明日香 **Asuka** (f. given name)
⁵ 明白 **meihaku** clear, unmistakable
  明石 **Akashi** (city, Hyōgo-ken)
⁷ 明言 **meigen** declare, assert
⁸ 明盲 **a(ki)mekura** blind; illiterate
  明治 **Meiji** (emperor and era, 1868–1912)
  明治神宮 **Meiji Jingū** Meiji Shrine
  明治維新 **Meiji Ishin** the Meiji Restoration
⁹ 明美 **Akemi, Harumi** (f. given name)

明後日 **myōgonichi** the day after tomorrow

10 明朗 **meirō** clear, open, cheerful

明記 **meiki** clearly state, specify, stipulate

11 明細 **meisai** details, particulars

12 明朝 **myōchō** tomorrow morning **Minchō** Ming dynasty; Ming style (of printed kanji)

13 明暗 **meian** light and dark, shading

明解 **meikai** clear (explanation)

14 明察 **meisatsu** discernment, insight

15 明確 **meikaku** clear, distinct, well-defined

17 明瞭 **meiryō** clear, distinct, obvious

——— 2 ———

4 不明 **fumei** unclear, unknown, ignorance

文明 **bunmei** civilization, culture **Fumiaki, Bunmei, Fumiharu** (m. given name)

公明 **kōmei** just, fair

公明党 **Kōmeitō** (a political party)

5 未明 **mimei** (pre-)dawn

失明 **shitsumei** lose one's eyesight, go blind

弁明 **benmei** explanation, justification

打明 **u(chi)a(keru)** confide in, reveal

7 判明 **hanmei** become clear, be ascertained

究明 **kyūmei** study, investigation, inquiry

声明 **seimei** declaration, (public) statement, proclamation

利明 **Toshiaki, Rimei** (m. given name)

8 表明 **hyōmei** state, express, announce

夜明 **yoa(kashi)** stay up all night **yoa(ke)** dawn, daybreak

9 発明 **hatsumei** invention

透明 **tōmei** transparent

10 高明 **Takaaki, Kōmei, Takaharu** (m. given name)

11 釈明 **shakumei** explanation, vindication

12 証明 **shōmei** proof, corroboration

証明書 **shōmeisho** certificate

13 義明 **Yoshiaki, Noriaki, Nobuaki** (m. given name)

照明 **shōmei** illumination, lighting

14 徳明 **Noriaki, Tokuaki, Naruaki, Tokumei, Akira** (m. given name)

聡明 **sōmei** wise, sagacious

説明 **setsumei, to(ki)a(kashi)** explanation

説明書 **setsumeisho** (written) explanation, instructions, manual

15 黎明 **reimei** dawn, morning twilight

16 賢明 **kenmei** wise, intelligent

17 鮮明 **senmei** clear, distinct

——— 4 ———

6 行方不明 **yukue-fumei** missing

4c4.2 / 2087

Ō flourishing; beautiful AKIRA (m. given name) Ō, MORI (part of given name)

——— 1 ———

4 旺文社 **Ōbunsha** (name of publishing company)

11 旺盛 **ōsei** flourishing, in prime condition

4c4.4 / 2089

SHŌ prosperous; bright, clear SHŌ, MASA, AKI, YOSHI, SUKE (part of given name) AKIRA, MASASHI, MASARU (m. given name) SAKAE (given name)

——— 1 ———

2 昌子 **Masako, Shōko, Akiko** (f. given name)

3 昌三 **Shōzō, Masami, Masazō** (m. given name)

9 昌彦 **Masahiko, Akihiko** (m. given name)

4c4.5 / 1777   日 日 卝 丨
43 32 2

昇

昇 昇

SHŌ, nobo(ru) rise, be promoted
NORI (part of given name)

───── 1 ─────

9 昇降 **shōkō** rise and fall, ascend and descend
10 昇進 **shōshin** promotion, advancement
12 昇給 **shōkyū** pay raise
20 昇騰 **shōtō** rise, go up, soar

───── 2 ─────

3 上昇 **jōshō** rise, ascend, climb

4c4.9 / 759   日 日 犭
43 27

易

易 易

EKI divination **I, yasa(shii), -yasu(i)** easy **YASU** (part of given name)

───── 1 ─────

3 易々 **ii(taru), yasuyasu** easy, simple
8 易者 **ekisha** fortuneteller

───── 2 ─────

6 曲易 **ma(ge)yasu(i)** easy to bend, supple, pliant, flexible
安易 **an'i** easy, easygoing
10 容易 **yōi** easy, simple
12 貿易 **bōeki** trade, commerce
貿易会社 **bōeki-gaisha** trading firm
貿易商 **bōekishō** trader
14 読易 **yo(mi)yasu(i)** easy to read
16 燃易 **mo(e)yasu(i)** flammable
18 簡易 **kan'i** simple, easy

昂 → 昴   **4c5.11**

4c4.10 / 1874   日 日 ┝
43 13

昆

昆 昆

KON elder brother; later, descendants; insect

───── 1 ─────

5 昆布 **konbu, kobu** sea tangle, tang, kelp
6 昆虫 **konchū** insect

4c4.11   日 日 厂 十
43 18 12

昏

昏 昏

KON dark; evening, dusk
kura(i) dark

───── 1 ─────

8 昏迷 **konmei** be stupefied/bewildered

昔 →   **3k5.28**

冐 → 冒   **4c5.6**

4c4.12 / 210   日 日 勹 丨
43 15 2

的

的 丨 的 的

TEKI (attributive suffix), -istic; target, mark **mato** target, mark

───── 1 ─────

4 的中 **tekichū** hit the mark, come true, guess right
5 的外 **matohazu(re)** wide of the mark; out of focus
15 的確 **tekikaku, tekkaku** precise, accurate, unerring

───── 2 ─────

4 内的 **naiteki** inner, intrinsic
5 史的 **shiteki** historical

目的 **mokuteki** purpose, object, aim
目的語 **mokutekigo** object (in grammar)
8 法的 **hōteki** legal, legalistic
知的 **chiteki** intellectual, mental
物的 **butteki** material, physical
性的 **seiteki** sexual
9 美的 **biteki** esthetic
10 病的 **byōteki** morbid, diseased, abnormal
12 量的 **ryōteki** quantitative
13 詩的 **shiteki** poetic
14 静的 **seiteki** static
15 劇的 **gekiteki** dramatic
標的 **hyōteki** target, mark
質的 **shitsuteki** qualitative

—————— 3 ——————

1 一方的 **ippōteki** one-sided, unilateral
一時的 **ichijiteki** temporary
一義的 **ichigiteki** unambiguous
2 二義的 **nigiteki** secondary
人為的 **jin'iteki** artificial
力動的 **rikidōteki** dynamic
4 日本的 **nihonteki** (very) Japanese
5 本格的 **honkakuteki** full-scale, genuine, in earnest
本質的 **honshitsuteki** in substance, essential
写実的 **shajitsuteki** realistic, true to life, graphic
古典的 **kotenteki** classical
比喩的 **hiyuteki** figurative
比較的 **hikakuteki** relative(ly), comparative(ly)
圧倒的 **attōteki** overwhelming
打算的 **dasanteki** calculating, mercenary
示威的 **jiiteki** demonstrative, threatening
主観的 **shukanteki** subjective
立体的 **rittaiteki** three-dimensional
6 多角的 **takakuteki** many-sided, versatile, diversified, multilateral
両性的 **ryōseiteki** bisexual, androgynous
伝統的 **dentōteki** traditional

全面的 **zenmenteki** all-out, full, general
全般的 **zenpanteki** general, overall, across-the-board
合理的 **gōriteki** rational, reasonable, logical
肉体的 **nikutaiteki** sensual, corporal
肉感的 **nikkanteki** suggestive, sensual, voluptuous
近代的 **kindaiteki** modern
先天的 **sententeki** inborn, congenital, hereditary
有機的 **yūkiteki** organic
自発的 **jihatsuteki** spontaneous, voluntary
自動的 **jidōteki** automatic
7 良心的 **ryōshinteki** conscientious
抜打的 **nu(ki)u(chi)teki** without advance warning
8 画期的 **kakkiteki** epoch-making, revolutionary
典型的 **tenkeiteki** typical
抽象的 **chūshōteki** abstract
実質的 **jisshitsuteki** substantial, essential, material, real
官僚的 **kanryōteki** bureaucratic
肯定的 **kōteiteki** affirmative
物質的 **busshitsuteki** material, physical
具体的 **gutaiteki** concrete, specific, definite
具象的 **gushōteki** concrete, not abstract
9 飛躍的 **hiyakuteki** rapid, by leaps and bounds
保守的 **hoshuteki** conservative
逐語的 **chikugoteki** word for word, literal
活動的 **katsudōteki** active, dynamic
挑発的 **chōhatsuteki** provocative, suggestive
客観的 **kyakkanteki, kakkanteki** objective
神秘的 **shinpiteki** mystic(al), mysterious
恒常的 **kōjōteki** constant
科学的 **kagakuteki** scientific

10 個人的 **kojinteki** individual, personal, self-centered

部分的 **bubunteki** partial, here and there

原始的 **genshiteki** primitive, primeval, original

浪漫的 **rōmanteki** romantic (school)

消極的 **shōkyokuteki** passive, negative

従属的 **jūzokuteki** subordinate, dependent

根本的 **konponteki** fundamental, radical

致命的 **chimeiteki** fatal, lethal, deadly, mortal

耽美的 **tanbiteki** esthetic

11 野性的 **yaseiteki** wild, rough

偶発的 **gūhatsuteki** accidental, incidental, occasional

副次的 **fukujiteki** secondary

虚無的 **kyomuteki** nihilistic

基本的 **kihonteki** basic, fundamental

排他的 **haitateki** exclusive

常識的 **jōshikiteki** matter-of-fact, practical

理想的 **risōteki** ideal

経済的 **keizaiteki** economic, financial; economical

12 最終的 **saishūteki** final, ultimate

悲観的 **hikanteki** pessimistic

13 義務的 **gimuteki** obligatory, compulsory

楽観的 **rakkanteki** optimistic, hopeful

感情的 **kanjōteki** emotional, sentimental

意識的 **ishikiteki** consciously

15 徹底的 **tetteiteki** thorough, exhaustive

魅力的 **miryokuteki** attractive, charming, captivating

16 積極的 **sekkyokuteki** positive, active

19 爆発的 **bakuhatsuteki** explosive (popularity)

―――――― 4 ――――――

8 非人間的 **hiningenteki** inhuman, impersonal

非合理的 **higōriteki** unreasonable, irrational

非社交的 **hishakōteki** unsociable, retiring

非科学的 **hikagakuteki** unscientific

非能率的 **hinōritsuteki** inefficient

非現実的 **higenjitsuteki** unrealistic

非衛生的 **hieiseiteki** unsanitary, unhygienic

4c4.13 / 164   ⋯ 日 土 │

43 22 2

SHA, mono person

―――――― 2 ――――――

2 二者択一 **nisha-takuitsu** an alternative

6 死者 **shisha** dead person, the dead

両者 **ryōsha** both persons; both things

7 作者 **sakusha** author

医者 **isha** doctor, physician

役者 **yakusha** player, actor

芸者 **geisha** geisha

学者 **gakusha** scholar

忍者 **ninja** ninja, spy-assassin (historical)

8 使者 **shisha** messenger, envoy

侍者 **jisha** attendant, valet; altar boy

若者 **wakamono** young person/ people

易者 **ekisha** fortuneteller

武者振 **mushabu(ri)** valor, gallantry

9 信者 **shinja** believer, adherent, the faithful

前者 **zensha** the former

独者 **hito(ri)mono** single/unmarried person

後者 **kōsha** the latter

怠者 **nama(ke)mono** idler, lazybones

10 猛者 **mosa** man of courage, stalwart, veteran

晒者 **sara(shi)mono** (pilloried) criminal on public display

記者 **kisha** newspaper reporter, journalist

記者会見 **kisha kaiken** news/press conference

11 達者 **tassha** healthy, strong; proficient

著者 **chosha** author

悪者 **warumono** bad fellow, scoundrel

患者 **kanja** a patient

訳者 **yakusha** translator

敗者 **haisha** the defeated, loser

12 勝者 **shōsha** winner, victor

慌者 **awa(te)mono** absent-minded person, scatterbrain

筆者 **hissha** the writer/author

13 働者 **hatara(ki)mono** hard worker

傷者 **shōsha** injured person

適者生存 **tekisha seizon** survival of the fittest

愚者 **oro(ka)mono, gusha** fool, jackass

14 読者 **dokusha** reader

15 暴者 **aba(re)mono** rowdy, ruffian

編者 **hensha** editor, compiler

論者 **ronsha** disputant; advocate; this writer, I

16 賢者 **kenja** wise man, the wise

17 聴者 **chōsha** listener

────── 3 ──────

1 一人者 **hitorimono** someone alone; unmarried/single person

3 工学者 **kōgakusha** engineer

亡命者 **bōmeisha** exile, emigré

4 厄介者 **yakkaimono** a dependent; nuisance

5 失業者 **shitsugyōsha** unemployed person

生残者 **seizansha** survivor

代行者 **daikōsha** agent, proxy

代表者 **daihyōsha** a representative

加害者 **kagaisha** assailant, perpetrator

司会者 **shikaisha** emcee, chairman

主宰者 **shusaisha** president, chairman

主義者 **shugisha** -ist, advocate (of a theory/doctrine)

主権者 **shukensha** sovereign, supreme ruler

主謀者 **shubōsha** (ring)leader, mastermind

目医者 **meisha** ophthalmologist, optometrist

目撃者 **mokugekisha** (eye)witness

6 死傷者 **shishōsha** casualties, killed and wounded

年長者 **nenchōsha** a senior, older person

仲介者 **chūkaisha** mediator, intermediary, middleman

先任者 **senninsha** predecessor

先仕者 **senjusha** former occupant

先覚者 **senkakusha** pioneer, leading spirit

先駆者 **senkusha** forerunner, pioneer

共犯者 **kyōhansha** accomplice

有権者 **yūkensha** qualified person, eligible voter

7 労働者 **rōdōsha** worker, laborer

志願者 **shigansha** applicant, candidate, volunteer, aspirant

利用者 **riyōsha** user

初心者 **shoshinsha** beginner

8 使用者 **shiyōsha** user, consumer; employer

受益者 **juekisha** beneficiary

受賞者 **jushōsha** prizewinner

担当者 **tantōsha** the one in charge

妻帯者 **saitaisha** married man

参加者 **sankasha** participant

定住者 **teijūsha** permanent resident

歩行者 **hokōsha** pedestrian

居住者 **kyojūsha** resident, inhabitant

国学者 **kokugakusha** Japanese-classics scholar

9 保菌者 **hokinsha** carrier (of a disease)

前任者 **zenninsha** one's predecessor

浮浪者 **furōsha** street bum, tramp, hobo

指揮者 **shikisha** (orchestra) conductor, leader; commander, director

指導者 **shidōsha** leader

後継者 **kōkeisha** successor

為政者 **iseisha** statesman, administrator

科学者 **kagakusha** scientist

10 既婚者 **kikonsha** married person

残存者 **zansonsha** survivor, holdover

候補者 **kōhosha** candidate

高齢者 **kōreisha** elderly person

消費者 **shōhisha** consumer

荷担者 **katansha** participant, supporter, accomplice

容疑者 **yōgisha** a suspect

旅行者 **ryokōsha** traveler, tourist

扇動者 **sendōsha** instigator, agitator

被災者 **hisaisha** victim, sufferer

被害者 **higaisha** victim

被爆者 **hibakusha** bombing victims

配遇者 **haigūsha** spouse

11 偽善者 **gizensha** hypocrite

側近者 **sokkinsha** close associate

婚約者 **kon'yakusha** fiancé(e)

密航者 **mikkōsha** stowaway

常習者 **jōshūsha** habitual offender

移住者 **ijūsha** emigrant, immigrant

異端者 **itansha** heretic

第三者 **dai-sansha** third person/party

12 焼死者 **shōshisha** person burned to death

雇用者 **koyōsha** employer

歯医者 **haisha** dentist

13 戦没者 **senbotsusha** fallen soldier

戦歿者 **senbotsusha** fallen soldier

継承者 **keishōsha** successor

該当者 **gaitōsha** the said person

14 関係者 **kankeisha** interested party, those concerned

17 犠牲者 **giseisha** victim

聴視者 **chōshisha** (TV) viewer(s)

鍼医者 **hariisha** acupuncturist

18 藪医者 **yabuisha** a quack

翻訳者 **hon'yakusha** translator

— 4 —

11 第一人者 **dai-ichininsha** foremost/leading person

12 悲観論者 **hikanronsha** pessimist

15 億万長者 **okumanchōja** multimillionaire, billionaire

— 5 —

7 身体障害者 **shintai shōgaisha** physically handicapped person

— 5 —

旺 → 曜 4c14.1

4c5.1 / 352

☐ 日 六 冂
43 34 20

映 暎 | 映 映

EI, utsu(su) reflect; project; take (a photo) **utsu(ru)** be reflected/projected **ha(eru)** shine, be brilliant AKIRA (m. given name) AKI, TERU (part of given name)

— 1 —

8 映画 **eiga** movie, film

映画館 **eigakan** movie theater

14 映像 **eizō** image, reflection

— 2 —

3 上映 **jōei** screen, show, play (a movie)

4 反映 **han'ei** reflect, mirror

7 投映 **tōei** project (an image), cast

見映 **miba(e)** (attractive) appearance

4c5.2

☐ 日 木 一
43 41 1

昧 昧

MAI dark; foolish; dawn

— 2 —

17 曖昧 **aimai** vague, ambiguous, equivocal

4c5.3 / 361   □ 日 ⸜ 卜
                          43 15 13

昨   昨昨

SAKU past, yesterday, last (year)

――――― 1 ―――――

4 昨今 **sakkon** nowadays, recently
  昨日 **sakujitsu, kinō** yesterday
6 昨年 **sakunen** last year
8 昨夜 **sakuya, yūbe** last night/
    evening
12 昨晩 **sakuban** last evening/night

――――― 2 ―――――

1 一昨日 **issakujitsu, ototoi, ototsui**
    the day before yesterday
  一昨年 **issakunen, ototoshi** the
    year before last

4c5.4 / 997   ⊞ 日 口 力
                          43 24 8

昭   昭昭

SHŌ bright, clear AKIRA (m. given
name) AKI, TERU (part of given name)

――――― 1 ―――――

2 昭二 **Shōji, Akiji** (m. given name)
  昭子 **Akiko, Teruko** (f. given
    name)
8 昭和 **Shōwa** (emperor and era,
    1926 – 1989)

昿 → 曠 4c15.2

4c5.6 / 1104   ⊟ 日 日
                          55 43

冒   冐⎮冒冒

BŌ, oka(su) risk, brave, defy, dare

――――― 1 ―――――

10 冒険 **bōken** adventure
16 冒頭 **bōtō** beginning, opening
    (paragraph)

――――― 2 ―――――

13 感冒 **kanbō** a cold, the flu

4c5.7 / 730   目 日 牛 一
                          43 47 1

星   星星

SEI, hoshi star HOSHI (surname)

――――― 1 ―――――

5 星占 **hoshiurana(i)** astrology,
    horoscope
7 星条旗 **seijōki** the Stars and Stripes
    flag
8 星空 **hoshizora** starry sky
10 星座 **seiza** constellation

――――― 2 ―――――

5 占星術 **senseijutsu** astrology
10 流星 **ryūsei, naga(re)boshi** mete-
    or, shooting/falling star
11 彗星 **suisei, hōkiboshi** comet
  黒星 **kuroboshi** black spot/dot;
    bull's-eye; a defeat, failure
12 暁星 **gyōsei** morning star, Venus
  惑星 **wakusei** planet
16 衛星 **eisei** satellite

――――― 4 ―――――

5 北斗七星 **Hokuto Shichisei** the
    Big Dipper

4c5.9 / 1591   ⊟ 日 丁 亻
                          43 14 3

是   是是

ZE right, correct, just; policy
kore this KORE (part of given name)

――――― 1 ―――――

8 是非 **zehi** right and wrong; by all
    means

4

木
月
日 5
火
礻
王
牛
方
攵
欠
心
戸
戈

4c5.11 / 2088 　田 日 工 阝
43　38　7

KŌ rise　KŌ, TAKA, AKI (part of given name)　TAKASHI, NOBORU, AKIRA (m. given name)

─────── 1 ───────

16 昂奮 **kōfun** get excited

4c5.12 / 2090 　田 日 厂 阝
43　18　7

昴

昴 昴

BŌ, Subaru the Pleiades (constellation)　SUBARU (m. given name)　BŌ (part of given name)

 4c4.10

4c5.13 / 460 　⼩ 日 大 二
43　34　4

春

春 春

SHUN spring; beginning of the year; sex　**haru** spring

─────── 1 ───────

3 春山 **Haruyama** (surname)
4 春分日 **shunbun (no) hi** the vernal equinox (a holiday, about March 21)
6 春先 **harusaki** early spring
8 春雨 **harusame, shun'u** spring rain; bean-jelly sticks
9 春香 **Haruka** (f. given name)
10 春夏秋冬 **shun-ka-shū-tō** the four seasons, the year round
11 春菜 **Haruna** (f. given name)
18 春闘 **shuntō** spring labor offensive (short for 春季闘争)

─────── 2 ───────

6 迎春 **geishun** welcoming the new year
　早春 **sōshun** early spring
7 売春 **baishun** prostitution
　売春婦 **baishunfu** prostitute
　初春 **shoshun** early spring
8 青春 **seishun** youth
9 思春期 **shishunki** puberty

4c5.14 / 587 　田 日 比 丨
43　13　2

皆

皆 皆

KAI, mina, minna all

─────── 1 ───────

12 皆勤 **kaikin** perfect attendance
　皆無 **kaimu** nothing/none at all
14 皆様 **minasama** all (of you), Ladies and Gentlemen!

 3a5.33

4c5.15 / 470 　日 日 尸 一
43　40　1

昼

晝 丨昼昼

CHŪ, hiru daytime, noon

─────── 1 ───────

6 昼休 **hiruyasu(mi)** lunch/noon-time break
8 昼夜 **chūya** day and night
9 昼食 **chūshoku** lunch
12 昼飯 **hirumeshi, chūhan** lunch
　昼間 **hiruma, chūkan** daytime, during the day
13 昼寝 **hirune** nap, siesta

─────── 2 ───────

5 白昼 **hakuchū** daytime, broad daylight
10 真昼 **mahiru** broad daylight, midday

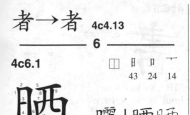

者 → 者 **4c4.13**

――――― **6** ―――――

4c6.1   □ | 日 口 一
                    43 24 14

曬 | 晒 晒

SAI, sara(su) bleach; expose to
sara(shi) bleaching; bleached cotton

――――― 1 ―――――

8 晒者 **sara(shi)mono** (pilloried)
criminal on public display

4c6.2 / 42   □ | 日 土 卄
                  43 22 37

時

時 時

JI, toki time; hour

――――― 1 ―――――

3 時下 **jika** now, at present
  時々 **tokidoki** sometimes
4 時日 **jijitsu** the date/time; time, days
5 時代 **jidai** era, period, age
  時代劇 **jidaigeki** period/costume
    drama
  時外 **tokihazu(re)** unseasonable,
    untimely, inopportune
7 時折 **tokio(ri)** at times, occasionally
  時局 **jikyoku** the situation
8 時事 **jiji** current events
  時限 **jigen** time limit; time (bomb)
  時刻表 **jikokuhyō** timetable,
    schedule
  時雨 **shigure** an off-and-on late-au-
    tumn/early-winter rain
9 時速 **jisoku** speed per hour
  時計 **tokei** clock, watch, timepiece
10 時候 **jikō** season, time of year;
    weather
  時候外 **jikōhazu(re)** unseasonable
  時差 **jisa** time difference, staggered
    jisa(boke) jet lag
  時流 **jiryū** trend of the times

11 時運 **jiun** tide of fortune
12 時報 **jihō** review; time signal
  時期 **jiki** time, season
  時給 **jikyū** payment by the hour
  時評 **jihyō** (editorial) commentary
  時間 **jikan** an hour; time
  時間表 **jikanhyō** timetable, sched-
    ule
13 時勢 **jisei** the times/Zeitgeist
  時節 **jisetsu** season; the times; op-
    portunity
16 時機 **jiki** opportunity, time, occa-
    sion

――――― 2 ―――――

1 一時 **ichiji** a time; at one time; for a
    time **ittoki** twelfth part of a
    day **hitotoki** a little while, a
    short period **ichidoki** at a/
    one time
  一時的 **ichijiteki** temporary
  一時預場 **ichiji azukarijō** baggage
    safekeeping area
4 今時 **imadoki** today, nowadays;
    this time of day
  日時 **nichiji** date and hour, time
5 四時 **yoji** four o'clock **shiji** the/
    all four seasons
6 同時 **dōji** at the same time, simulta-
    neous
7 何時 **nanji** what time, when
  何時間 **nanjikan** how many hours
  即時 **sokuji** immediately, on the
    spot
8 長時間 **chōjikan** a long time
  定時 **teiji** regular time/intervals,
    fixed period
10 随時 **zuiji** at any time, whenever re-
    quired
  夏時間 **natsujikan** daylight-sav-
    ing time
11 常時 **jōji** usually, habitually, ordi-
    narily
12 腕時計 **udedokei** wristwatch
13 戦時 **senji** wartime, war period
  戦時中 **senjichū** during the war,
    wartime
  歳時記 **saijiki** almanac
  新時代 **shinjidai** new era
  零時 **reiji** 12:00 (noon or midnight)

4

木
月
日 6
火
ネ
王
牛
方
攵
欠
心
戸
戈

15 潮時 **shiodoki** (waiting for) the tide, opportunity

暫時 **zanji** for a (short) time

17 臨時 **rinji** temporary, provisional, extraordinary

18 蟬時雨 **semishigure** outburst of cicada droning

— 3 —

5 幼年時代 **yōnen jidai** childhood

四六時中 **shirokujichū** 24 hours a day, constantly

石器時代 **sekki jidai** the Stone Age

9 食事時 **shokujidoki** mealtime

12 御飯時 **gohandoki** mealtime

13 戦国時代 **sengoku jidai** era of civil wars

晄→晃 4c6.5

晦→晦 4c7.3

晟→ 4c7.5

4c6.4 / 2091

⽇ 日 宀 女
43 33 25

晏

晏 晏

AN late; sunset; peaceful
YASUSHI (m. given name) AN, YASU, HARU, SADA, OSO (part of given name)

4c6.5 / 2092

⽇ 日 小 一
43 35 14

晃

晃 晃

KŌ clear, bright KŌ, AKI, TERU, MITSU, KIRA (part of given name) AKIRA, HIKARU, NOBORU (m. given name)

4c6.6 / 131

⽇ 日 土 ヨ
43 22 39

書

書 書

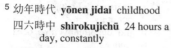

SHO, ka(ku) write; draw
fumi books; letter, note

— 1 —

2 書入 **ka(ki)i(reru)** write/fill in, enter

4 書込 **ka(ki)ko(mu)** write/fill in, enter

書手 **ka(ki)te** writer; calligrapher, painter

書方 **ka(ki)kata** how to write; penmanship

6 書名 **shomei** (book) title

書式 **shoshiki** (blank) form

7 書体 **shotai** style of calligraphy/type

書抜 **ka(ki)nu(ku)** copy out, excerpt, abstract

書改 **ka(ki)arata(meru)** rewrite

書言葉 **ka(ki)kotoba** written language

8 書表 **ka(ki)ara(wasu)** express/describe in writing

書直 **ka(ki)nao(su)** rewrite

書店 **shoten** bookstore; publisher

書物 **shomotsu** books

書房 **shobō** library; bookstore

10 書家 **shoka** good penman, calligrapher

書留 **kakitome** registered mail
ka(ki)to(meru) write down

11 書斎 **shosai** study, library, den

書道 **shodō** calligraphy

12 書棚 **shodana** bookshelf

書散 **ka(ki)chi(rasu)** scribble, scrawl

書評 **shohyō** book review

13 書置 **ka(ki)o(ki)** note left behind; will

14 書誌 **shoshi** bibliography

18 書簡 **shokan** letter, note

書類 **shorui** documents, papers

20 書籍 **shoseki** books

――――――― 2 ―――――――

3 下書 **shitaga(ki)** rough draft

4 分書 **wa(kachi)ga(ki)** writing with a space between words

手書 **shusho** write in one's own hand **tega(ki)** handwritten

5 史書 **shisho** history book, a history

白書 **hakusho** whitepaper, report

7 但書 **tada(shi)ga(ki)** proviso

別書 **waka(chi)ga(ki)** write leaving a space between words

走書 **hashi(ri)ga(ki)** flowing/hasty handwriting

抜書 **nu(ki)ga(ki)** excerpt, clipping

投書 **tōsho** letter to the editor, contribution

図書 **tosho** books

図書館 **toshokan** library

私書 **shisho** private document/letter

私書箱 **shishobako** post-office box

8 肩書 **kataga(ki)** one's title, degree

9 前書 **maega(ki)** preface, foreword

後書 **atoga(ki)** postscript

草書 **sōsho** cursive form of kanji, "grass hand"

珍書 **chinsho** rare book

10 秘書 **hisho** (private) secretary

11 清書 **seisho** fair/clean copy

添書 **tensho, so(e)ga(ki)** accompanying letter; letter of introduction; additional writing, postscript

12 落書 **rakuga(ki)** graffiti, scribblings

葉書 **hagaki** postcard

覚書 **obo(e)ga(ki)** memorandum

詔書 **shōsho** imperial edict/rescript

13 裏書 **uraga(ki)** endorsement; certificate of genuineness; proof

楷書 **kaisho** noncursive (kanji), printed style

聖書 **Seisho** the Bible

新書 **shinsho** new book; largish paperback size

辞書 **jisho** dictionary

14 読書 **dokusho** reading **yo(mi)ka(ki)** reading and writing

15 蔵書 **zōsho** book collection, one's library

横書 **yokoga(ki)** writing horizontally

篆書 **tensho** seal characters

調書 **chōsho** protocol, record

16 隷書 **reisho** (ancient squared style of kanji)

縦書 **tatega(ki)** vertical writing

18 叢書 **sōsho** series, library

19 願書 **gansho** written request, application

――――――― 3 ―――――――

4 公文書 **kōbunsho** official document

5 古文書 **komonjo, kobunsho** ancient documents

6 参考書 **sankōsho** reference book/work

9 計算書 **keisansho** statement (of account)

10 陳述書 **chinjutsusho** statement, declaration

陳情書 **chinjōsho** petition, representation

教科書 **kyōkasho** textbook

12 報告書 **hōkokusho** (written) report/statement

絵葉書 **ehagaki** picture postcard

証明書 **shōmeisho** certificate

14 遺言書 **yuigonsho** will, testament

説明書 **setsumeisho** (written) explanation, instructions, manual

領収書 **ryōshūsho** receipt

15 履歴書 **rirekisho** personal history, vita

請求書 **seikyūsho** application, claim, bill

20 議定書 **giteisho, gijōsho** a protocol

4c6.8 / 2093   日 日 工 儿
            43 38 16

SHIN advance **SUSUMU** (m. given name) SHIN, KUNI, YUKI, AKI, NOBU (part of given name)

4 ＝
木
月
日   6
火
礻
王
牛
方
攵
欠
心
戸
戈

皆 → **4c5.14**

晉 → 晋 **4c6.8**

4c6.9 / 1799 | 田 | 日 | 夕 | ケ
| | 43 | 30 | 15

殉

殉殉

JUN follow (someone) into death; lay down one's life

───── 1 ─────

0 殉じる/ずる **jun(jiru/zuru)** die a martyr; follow (someone) into death (by committing suicide)

18 殉職 **junshoku** dying in the line of duty

───── 7 ─────

晚 → 晚 **4c8.3**

4c7.3 | 田 | 日 | 女 | ケ
| | 43 | 25 | 15

晦

晦 | 晦 晦

KAI dark, night; last day of the month **kura(i)** dark **kura(masu)** hide, slip away **misoka, tsugomori** the last day of the month

───── 2 ─────

3 大晦日 **Ōmisoka** last day of the year; New Year's Eve

4c7.5 / 2094 | 日 | 日 | 戈 | ケ
| | 43 | 52 | 15

晟

晟 晟

SEI, JŌ clear **AKIRA, NOBORU, SHIGERU** (m. given name) **SEI, MASA, TERU** (part of given name)

4c7.7 / 2095 | 日 | 礻 | 日 | 厂
| | 57 | 43 | 18

晨

晨 晨

SHIN morning, dawn **SHIN, TOKI, AKI, ASA, MASA, TERU, TOYO** (part of given name) **AKIRA** (m. given name)

4c7.8 | 日 | 日 | 日 | 又
| | 55 | 43 | 9

曼

MAN wide; long; (used phonetically)

───── 1 ─────

7 曼陀羅 **mandara** mandala, picture of Buddha

4c7.10 / 1929 | 田 | 日 | 艹
| | 43 | 32

曹

曹 曹

SŌ, ZŌ friend, comrade; officer

───── 2 ─────

8 法曹 **hōsō** the legal profession

4c7.11 / 591 | 田 | 日 | ヨ | 丨
| | 43 | 39 | 2

習

SHŪ, nara(u) learn

───── 1 ─────

5 習字 **shūji** penmanship, calligraphy

9 習俗 **shūzoku** manners and customs, usages

11 習得 **shūtoku** learn, master

14 習慣 **shūkan** custom, habit

習練 **shūren** practice, training, drill

───── 2 ─────

4 予習 **yoshū** lesson preparation

8 実習 **jisshū** practice, drill

9 俗習 **zokushū** (popular) custom

風習 **fūshū** manners, customs, ways

11 常習 **jōshū** custom, common practice, habit

常習者 **jōshūsha** habitual offender

悪習慣 **akushūkan** bad habit, evil practice

12 復習 **fukushū** review

補習 **hoshū** supplementary/continuing (education)

14 演習 **enshū** practice, exercises; (military) maneuvers; seminar

慣習 **kanshū** custom, practice

練習 **renshū** practice, exercise

練習不足 **renshū-busoku** out/lack of training

17 講習 **kōshū** short course, training

4c7.12 / 2168

⊟ 日 十 二
43 12 4

皋 | 皋 皋

KŌ swamp; shore

SUSUMU, TAKASHI (m. given name)

KŌ, TAKA, SAWA (part of given name)

4c7.13

... 日 一 亻
43 14 3

匙 匙

SHI, saji spoon

4c7.14 / 1190

⊞ 日 十 乀
43 12 15

乾 乾

KAN dry **KEN** heaven; emperor
kawa(ku) become dry, dry up **kawa-(kasu)** dry (out), parch **ho(su)** dry; drink (a cup) dry INUI (surname)

— 1 —

7 乾季 **kanki** the dry season

8 乾杯 **kanpai** a toast; Cheers!

乾物 **kanbutsu** dry provisions, groceries

13 乾電池 **kandenchi** dry cell, battery

兜 → 4c8.16

晝 → 昼 4c5.15

— 8 —

4c8.1 / 1658

⊞ 日 艹 十
43 32 12

暁

曉 | 暁 暁

GYŌ, akatsuki dawn, daybreak; in the event of

— 1 —

9 暁星 **gyōsei** morning star, Venus

4c8.2 / 662

⊞ 日 月 土
43 42 22

晴

晴 | 晴 晴

SEI, ha(reru) clear up **ha(re)** fair/cloudless weather **ha(rete)** openly, publicly **ha(rasu)** dispel, clear away/up HARU (part of given name)

— 1 —

0 晴れやか **ha(reyaka)** clear, bright; beaming, cheerful

3 晴上 **ha(re)a(garu)** clear up

9 晴美 **Harumi, Haruyoshi** (given name)

12 晴間 **ha(re)ma** interval of clear weather

— 2 —

6 気晴 **kiba(rashi)** diversion, pastime, recreation

7 快晴 **kaisei** fine weather, clear skies

9 秋晴 **akiba(re)** clear autumn weather

¹⁰ 素晴 **suba(rashii)** splendid, magnificent

¹⁵ 憂晴 **u(sa)bara(shi)** diversion, distraction

――――― 3 ―――――

⁴ 五月晴 **satsukiba(re)** fine weather during the rainy season

日本晴 **nihonba(re)** clear cloudless sky, beautiful weather

暎 → 映　**4c5.1**

4c8.3 / 736

曰 日 口 宀
43 24 15

晩｜晩 晩

BAN evening, night

――――― 1 ―――――

⁶ 晩年 **bannen** latter part of one's life

¹⁰ 晩酌 **banshaku** an evening drink (of saké)

¹¹ 晩婚 **bankon** late marriage

¹⁶ 晩餐 **bansan** dinner, supper

――――― 2 ―――――

¹ 一晩 **hitoban** a night, one evening; all night

⁴ 今晩 **konban** this evening, tonight

⁶ 毎晩 **maiban** every evening, nightly

早晩 **sōban** sooner or later

⁹ 昨晩 **sakuban** last evening/night

4c8.5 / 638

曰 日 土 ｜
43 22 2

暑｜暑 暑

SHO, atsu(i) hot (weather)

――――― 1 ―――――

⁰ 暑がる **atsu(garu)** feel the heat, swelter

⁴ 暑中見舞 **shochū mima(i)** inquiry after (someone's) health in the hot season

⁸ 暑苦 **atsukuru(shii), atsuguru-(shii)** oppressively hot, sultry, sweltering

¹⁰ 暑凌 **atsu(sa)shino(gi)** relief from the heat

――――― 2 ―――――

⁸ 炎暑 **ensho** intense heat, hot weather

¹⁰ 残暑 **zansho** the lingering summer heat

猛暑 **mōsho** intense heat

¹² 蒸暑 **mu(shi)atsu(i)** hot and humid, sultry

¹⁴ 酷暑 **kokusho** intense/sweltering heat

¹⁵ 避暑地 **hishochi** summer resort

4c8.6 / 1645

曰 日
43

晶 晶

SHŌ clear; crystal　**AKIRA** (m. given name)　**SHŌ, AKI** (part of given name)

――――― 1 ―――――

² 晶子 **Akiko, Shōko** (f. given name)

――――― 2 ―――――

⁴ 水晶 **suishō** quartz, crystal

¹¹ 液晶 **ekishō** liquid crystal

4c8.8 / 853

曰 日 口 小
43 24 35

景

KEI view, scene　**KAGE** (part of given name)

――――― 1 ―――――

⁶ 景気 **keiki** business conditions

景色 **keshiki** scenery

⁸ 景況 **keikyō** the situation

⁹ 景品 **keihin** premium, present, giveaway

¹⁸ 景観 **keikan** spectacular view, a sight

—— 2 ——

4 不景気 **fukeiki** business slump, recession; cheerless, gloomy

6 全景 **zenkei** complete view, panorama

8 夜景 **yakei** night view

9 前景 **zenkei** foreground

風景 **fūkei** scene(ry), landscape, view

背景 **haikei** background

11 雪景色 **yukigeshiki** snowy landscape

12 勝景 **shōkei** beautiful scenery, fine view

—— 3 ——

12 跛行景気 **hakō keiki** spotty boom/prosperity

—— 4 ——

4 日本三景 **Nihon sankei** Japan's three noted scenic sights (Matsushima, Miyajima, Amanohashidate)

4c8.9 / 411

目 日 土 一
43 22 1

量 量

RYŌ quantity **haka(ru)** measure, weigh **KAZU** (part of given name)

—— 1 ——

7 量売 **haka(ri)u(ri)** sell by measure/weight

8 量的 **ryōteki** quantitative

11 量産 **ryōsan** mass production (short for 大量生産)

—— 2 ——

2 力量 **rikiryō** physical strength; ability, capacity

3 大量 **tairyō** large quantity

大量生産 **tairyō seisan** mass production

4 少量 **shōryō** small quantity/dose

5 用量 **yōryō** dosage, dose

6 多量 **taryō** large quantity, a great deal

8 定量 **teiryō** fixed quantity; to measure; dose

雨量 **uryō** (amount of) rainfall

9 重量 **jūryō** weight

計量 **keiryō** measure, weigh

10 容量 **yōryō** capacity, volume; capacitance

酌量 **shakuryō** consideration, extenuation

12 無量 **muryō** beyond measure, immense

13 数量 **sūryō** quantity

15 器量 **kiryō** looks; ability; dignity

—— 3 ——

7 含有量 **gan'yūryō** quantity of a constituent substance, content

—— 4 ——

13 感慨無量 **kangai-muryō** full of emotion

4c8.10 / 263

日 耳 日 又
65 43 9

最 最

SAI, motto(mo) the most **ito-** very, extremely **MASARU** (m. given name)

—— 1 ——

3 最大 **saidai** maximum, greatest, largest

最上 **saijō** best, highest

最上川 **Mogami-gawa** (river, Yamagata-ken)

最下 **saika** lowest; worst

最小 **saishō** smallest, minimum

4 最中 **saichū, sanaka** the midst/height of **monaka** middle; bean-jam-filled wafers

最少 **saishō** fewest; youngest

5 最古 **saiko** oldest

6 最近 **saikin** recently; latest, newest

最早 **mohaya** already, by now; (not) any longer

7 最良 **sairyō** best

最低 **saitei** lowest, minimum

最初 **saisho** the first/beginning

8 最長 **saichō** longest

9 最前線 **saizensen** forefront, front lines

最後 **saigo** the last; the end

¹⁰ 最高 **saikō** maximum, best; great

最高点 **saikōten** highest point/score

最高裁判所 **Saikō Saibansho** Supreme Court

最高潮 **saikōchō** highwater mark; climax, peak

¹¹ 最深 **saishin** deepest

最強 **saikyō** strongest

最悪 **saiaku** worst

最盛期 **saiseiki** golden age, heyday; the best season for

最終 **saishū** the last, the end; final

最終日 **saishūbi** the last day

最終回 **saishūkai** the last time/inning

最終的 **saishūteki** final, ultimate

¹² 最善 **saizen** (do one's) best

最短 **saitan** shortest

最期 **saigo** one's last moments, death

¹³ 最適 **saiteki** optimum, best suited

最新 **saishin** newest, latest

————— 2 —————

¹⁰ 真最中 **ma(s)saichū** right in the midst/middle of, at the height of

曾 → 曽 **2o9.3**

4c8.11 / 2099   田 日 大 日
             43 34 24

CHI knowledge, wisdom, intellect
CHI, TOMO, TOSHI, NORI, SATO (part of given name) SATOSHI, SATORU, MASARU, AKIRA (m. given name)

————— 1 —————

³ 智也 **Tomoya** (m. given name)

⁹ 智美 **Satomi, Tomomi** (f. given name)

智哉 **Tomoya** (m. given name)

¹⁵ 智慧 **chie** knowledge, wisdom

————— 2 —————

⁹ 美智子 **Michiko** (f. given name)

¹⁶ 叡智 **eichi** wisdom, intelligence; intellect

4c8.12 / 744   田 日 大 一
             43 34 1

TAI, ka(eru) replace **ka(e)-** spare, substitute, exchange **ka(waru)** be replaced

————— 1 —————

⁵ 替玉 **ka(e)dama** substitute, stand-in, ringer

————— 2 —————

² 入替 **i(re)ka(eru)** replace, substitute

⁴ 切替 **ki(ri)ka(eru)** change, exchange, convert; renew; replace; switch over

引替 **hikika(e)** exchange, conversion

⁵ 代替 **daitai, daiga(e)** substitute, alternative

立替 **ta(te)ka(eru)** pay in advance; pay for another

⁶ 両替 **ryōgae** money exchange

交替 **kōtai** take turns, alternate, relieve, work in shifts

衣替 **koromoga(e)** seasonal change of clothes

⁷ 吹替 **fu(ki)ka(e)** substitute actor, stand-in; dubbing; recasting, reminting

⁸ 建替 **ta(te)ka(e)** rebuilding, reconstruction

取替 **to(ri)ka(eru)** (ex)change, replace

⁹ 為替 **kawase** (foreign) exchange; money order

¹⁰ 振替 **fu(ri)ka(eru)** change to, transfer (funds)
furika(e) transfer

振替休日 **furikae kyūjitsu** substitute holiday (for one falling on a Sunday)

¹² 着替 **kiga(e)** changing clothes; change of clothes

植替 **u(e)ka(eru)** transplant, replant

畳替 **tatamiga(e)** replace old tatami with new ones

19 繰替 **ku(ri)ka(eru)** exchange, swap; divert (money)

4c8.13 / 2169
田 日 土 日
43 22 24

皓

皓 皓

KŌ white; clear, gleaming AKIRA, HIROSHI, HIKARU (m. given name)
KŌ, TERU, TSUGU, HIRO, AKI (part of given name)

—————— 1 ——————

12 皓歯 **kōshi** white/pearly teeth

朝→朝 **4b8.12**

4c8.16
目 日 厂 冂
43 18 20

兜

兜 兜

TŌ, TO, kabuto helmet, headpiece

—————— 1 ——————

7 兜町 **Kabuto-chō** (area of Tōkyō, site of Tōkyō Stock Exchange)

4c8.17
⋯ 日 土 大
43 22 34

奢

奢 奢

SHA, ogo(ru) be extravagant; treat (someone to)

—————— 9 ——————

4c9.1 / 1064
川 日 尸 二
43 40 4

暇

暇 暇

KA, hima free time, leisure
itoma leisure, spare time; leave-taking

—————— 1 ——————

15 暇潰 **himatsubu(shi)** wasting/killing time

—————— 2 ——————

6 休暇 **kyūka** holiday, vacation, leave of absence

7 余暇 **yoka** spare time, leisure

4c9.2 / 348
田 立 日
54 43

暗

暗 暗

AN, kura(i) dark **kura(gari)** darkness **kura(mu)** grow dark; be dazzled/blinded **kura(masu)** hide, slip away

—————— 1 ——————

5 暗号 **angō** code, cipher

暗示 **anji** suggestion, hint

8 暗夜 **an'ya** dark night

9 暗室 **anshitsu** darkroom

10 暗殺 **ansatsu** assassination

暗記 **anki** memorization

11 暗黒 **ankoku** darkness

15 暗黙 **anmoku** silence

—————— 2 ——————

3 丸暗記 **maruanki** learn by heart/rote

4 仄暗 **honogura(i)** dim(ly lit)

8 明暗 **meian** light and dark, shading

10 真暗 **makkura** pitch-dark

12 棒暗記 **bōanki** indiscriminate memorization

無暗 **muyami** thoughtless, rash; excessive; unnecessary

16 薄暗 **usugura(i), usukura(gari)** dimly lit, semi-dark, twilight

4c9.4 / 635
田 日 小 下
43 35 14

暖

暖 | 暖 暖

DAN, atata(kai/ka) warm **atata(maru/meru)** (intr./tr.) warm up

4
————
木
月
日 火
衤
王
牛 9
方
攵
欠
心
戸
戈

—— 1 ——

⁵ 暖冬 **dantō** warm/mild winter

⁸ 暖房 **danbō** heating

¹⁰ 暖流 **danryū** warm (ocean) current

—— 2 ——

⁵ 生暖 **namaatataka(i)** lukewarm

¹² 温暖 **ondan** warm, mild

4c9.6 / 2096   ⊞ 車 日 冂
      69 43 20

KI light; shine   KI, TERU, AKI (part of given name)   AKIRA, TERASU, HIKA-RU (m. given name)

暑 → 暑   **4c8.5**

既 → 既   **0a10.5**

4c9.8 / 1189   ⊞ 日 十 亻
      43 12 3

KAN main part   **miki** (tree) trunk TSUYOSHI (m. given name) MOTO (part of given name)

—————— 1 ——————

⁸ 幹事長 **kanjichō** executive secretary, secretary-general

¹⁰ 幹部 **kanbu** (top) executives, management

—————— 2 ——————

¹³ 新幹線 **Shinkansen** New Trunk Line, bullet train

¹⁴ 語幹 **gokan** stem, root of a word

¹⁶ 樹幹 **jukan** (tree) trunk

—— 10 ——

4c10.3   ⊞ 日 十 亻
      43 12 3

ATSU go around; ladle handle; rule, administer

—————— 1 ——————

¹¹ 斡旋 **assen** mediation, good offices, placement

4c10.4 / 2097   ⊞ 日 彡 丨
      43 27 2

CHŌ stretch, be relaxed   CHŌ, NOBU, MASA, MITSU, NAGA (part of given name) TŌRU, MITSURU, NOBORU, ITA-RU, NOBU (m. given name)

—————— 1 ——————

⁶ 暢気 **nonki** easygoing, happy-go-lucky

4c10.6   ⊞ 日 彡 儿
      43 27 16

BŌ form, appearance; countenance

—————— 2 ——————

⁹ 変貌 **henbō** transformation

¹⁰ 容貌 **yōbō** looks, personal appearance

—— 11 ——

4c11.2 / 1014   ⊟ 日 卅 氵
      43 32 21

暴暴

BŌ violence   **BAKU** expose, reveal **aba(reru)** act violently, rage, rampage,

run amuck **aba(ku)** disclose, expose, bring to light

――――― 1 ―――――

2 暴力 **bōryoku** violence, force
暴力団 **bōryokudan** gangster organization
6 暴行 **bōkō** act of violence, assault, outrage
暴回 **aba(re)mawa(ru)** run riot/amuck, rampage
7 暴走 **bōsō** run wild, run out of control
暴狂 **aba(re)kuru(u)** run amuck
8 暴者 **aba(re)mono** rowdy, ruffian
9 暴風 **bōfū** high winds, windstorm
暴風雨 **bōfūu** rainstorm
11 暴悪 **bōaku** violence, tyranny, savagery
12 暴飲 **bōin** heavy/excessive drinking
13 暴漢 **bōkan** ruffian, goon, thug
21 暴露 **bakuro** expose, bring to light

――――― 2 ―――――

4 凶暴 **kyōbō** ferocity, brutality, savagery
6 兇暴 **kyōbō** ferocity, brutality, savagery
7 乱暴 **ranbō** violence; rough, reckless
11 粗暴 **sobō** wild, rough, violent

4c11.3 / 1399 | 匚 車 斤 日
69 50 43

ZAN, shibara(ku) for a while

――――― 1 ―――――

8 暫定 **zantei** tentative, provisional
10 暫時 **zanji** for a (short) time

――――― 12 ―――――

瞭 → 瞭 **5c12.4**

曉 → 暁 **4c8.1**

4c12.1 / 637 | 目 雷 日 二
75 43 4

DON, kumo(ru) cloud up, get cloudy

――――― 1 ―――――

4 曇天 **donten** cloudy/overcast sky

――――― 2 ―――――

8 雨曇 **amagumo(ri)** overcast weather

4c12.4 | 田 日 ⼆ 十
43 39 12

KAN (a mountain bird); (feather) writing brush; letter

――――― 13 ―――――

曙 → 曙 **4c14.2**

4c13.1 | 田 日 心 夂
43 51 49

AI dark; not clear

――――― 1 ―――――

9 曖昧 **aimai** vague, ambiguous, equivocal

4c13.2 | 田 日 艹 犭
43 32 27

MŌ darkness

4

木
月
日 **13**
火
衤
王
牛
方
攵
欠
心
戸
戈

14

4c14.1 / 19

田 隹 日 三
74 43 39

曜

旺 | 曜 曜

YŌ day of the week; light; shine

─────── 1 ───────

4 曜日 **yōbi** day of the week

─────── 2 ───────

3 土曜日 **doyōbi** Saturday
4 水曜日 **suiyōbi** Wednesday
木曜日 **mokuyōbi** Thursday
月曜日 **getsuyōbi** Monday
日曜 **nichiyō** Sunday
日曜日 **nichiyōbi** Sunday
火曜日 **kayōbi** Tuesday
7 何曜日 **nan'yōbi, naniyōbi** what day of the week
8 金曜 **kin'yō** Friday
金曜日 **kin'yōbi** Friday

─────── 3 ───────

13 聖金曜日 **Seikin'yōbi** Good Friday

4c14.2 / 2098

田 日 日 土
55 43 22

曙

曙 | 曙 曙

SHO, akebono dawn, daybreak
SHO, AKE (part of given name)
AKIRA, AKEBONO (m. given name)

4c14.3 / 1977

田 日 口 十
43 24 12

韓

韓 韓

KAN, Kara Korea

─────── 1 ───────

8 韓国 **Kankoku** South Korea

─────── 2 ───────

4 日韓 **Nik-Kan** Japan and South Korea

4c14.6 / 1634

田 日 ㄆ 口
43 49 24

覆

覆 | 覆 覆

FUKU cover; overturn **ō(u)** cover; conceal **ō(i)** cover, covering
kutsugae(ru) be overturned
kutsugae(su) overturn, overthrow

─────── 1 ───────

4 覆水盆返 **fukusui bon (ni) kae(razu)** No use crying over spilt milk.
8 覆刻 **fukkoku** reproduce, republish
覆刻本 **fukkokubon** reissued book

─────── 2 ───────

11 転覆 **tenpuku** overturn, overthrow

15

4c15.2

田 日 艹 厂
43 32 18

曠

昿 | 曠 曠

KŌ clear; broad, large; empty

4c15.3 / 856

日 食 立 日
73 54 43

響

響 | 響 響

KYŌ, hibi(ku) sound, resound, be echoed; affect

─────── 1 ───────

12 響渡 **hibi(ki)wata(ru)** resound, reverberate

─────── 2 ───────

4 反響 **hankyō** echo, reverberation; repercussions, reaction
6 交響曲 **kōkyōkyoku** symphony
9 音響 **onkyō** sound
14 鳴響 **na(ri)hibi(ku)** resound, reverberate
15 影響 **eikyō** effect, influence

16

4c16.2 / 2267

田 禾 日 土
56 43 22

馨 馨

KEI, kao(ru) be fragrant **kanba(shii), kōba(shii)** fragrant; favorable **KEI, KYŌ, KA, KIYO, YOSHI** (part of given name) **KAORU, KAORI** (f. given name)

17

響 → 響 **4c15.3**

19

曬 → 晒 **4c6.1**

4

木 月 日 火 礻 王 牛 方 攵 欠 心 戸 戈

0

火 4d

火 0.1	灯 2.1	災 3.3	炊 4.1	炉 4.2	炬 4d5.5	炎 4.4	畑 5.1	炸 5.3	炬 5.5	為 5.8	烟 4d9.3	烈 6.3
烏 6.5	黒 7.2	煉 4d9.2	焙 8.1	焼 8.4	焚 8.7	無 8.8	黑 4d7.2	煮 8.9	然 8.10	爲 4d5.8	毯 8.11	煩 9.1
煉 9.2	煙 9.3	煌 9.7	煖 9.9	熙 9.11	照 9.12	煎 2o11.2	熔 8a10.1	煽 10.4	熏 4d14.1	熟 10.5	熈 4d9.11	熊 10.6
燵 4d12.6	勲 11.3	熱 11.4	黙 11.5	燃 12.2	燎 12.4	燈 4d2.1	燒 4d8.4	燵 12.6	燕 3k13.16	燦 13.3	燐 13.4	燭 13.5
燥 13.6	黛 13.7	點 2m7.2	燻 14.1	燿 14.3	爆 15.2	爐 4d4.2	爛 17.1				

0

4d0.1 / 20

□ 火
44

KA fire; Tuesday **hi, ho** fire

1

3 火口 **kakō** (volcano) crater
　　higuchi burner; muzzle (of a gun); origin of a fire
　火山 **kazan** volcano

4 火元 **himoto** origin of a fire
　火中 **kachū** in the fire, midst of the flames

5 火失 **kashitsu** accidental fire
　火付 **hitsu(ke)** arson; instigator, firebrand **hitsu(ki)** kindling

6 火気厳禁 **kaki genkin** Danger: Flammable

7 火災 **kasai** fire, conflagration

8 火事 **kaji** fire, conflagration
　火炎瓶 **kaenbin** firebomb, Molotov cocktail

10 火消 **hike(shi)** firefighter; fire extinguisher

12 火葬 **kasō** cremation

13 火傷 **kashō, yakedo** a burn
　火煙 **kaen** fire and smoke
　火鉢 **hibachi** charcoal brazier, hibachi

18 火曜日 **kayōbi** Tuesday

2

6 死火山 **shikazan** extinct volcano
　休火山 **kyūkazan** dormant volcano
　防火 **bōka** fire prevention, fire fighting, fireproof

7 劫火 **gōka** world-destroying conflagration
　花火 **hanabi** fireworks

8 放火 **hōka** arson

9 飛火 **to(bi)hi** flying sparks, leaping flames

発火 **hakka** ignition, combustion; discharge, firing

点火 **tenka** ignite

耐火 **taika** fireproof, fire-resistant

活火山 **kakkazan** active volcano

10 消火栓 **shōkasen** fire hydrant

消火器 **shōkaki** fire extinguisher

砲火 **hōka** gunfire, shellfire

12 焚火 **ta(ki)bi** open-air fire, bonfire

15 噴火 **funka** (volcanic) eruption

噴火口 **funkakō** crater

─────── 2 ───────

4d2.1 / 1333   囗 火 一
                          44 14

灯

燈丨灯灯

TŌ, hi, tomoshibi, akashi a light, lamp

─────── 1 ───────

5 灯台 **tōdai** lighthouse

6 灯光 **tōkō** light, lamplight, flashlight

15 灯影 **tōei** flicker of light

─────── 2 ───────

9 点灯 **tentō** light (a lamp) (cf. 消灯)

10 消灯 **shōtō** putting out the lights (cf. 点灯)

12 提灯 **chōchin** (paper) lantern

街灯 **gaitō** street lamp

13 電灯 **dentō** electric light

─────── 3 ───────

11 蛍光灯 **keikōtō** fluorescent lamp

─────── 4 ───────

16 懐中電灯 **kaichū dentō** flashlight

4d3.3 / 1335   日 火 丨
                          44 2

災

災災

SAI, wazawa(i) misfortune, disaster

─────── 1 ───────

10 災害 **saigai** disaster, accident

18 災難 **sainan** mishap, accident, calamity

─────── 2 ───────

4 天災 **tensai** natural disaster

火災 **kasai** fire, conflagration

10 被災者 **hisaisha** victim, sufferer

13 戦災 **sensai** war devastation

15 震災 **shinsai** earthquake disaster

─────── 4 ───────

4d4.1 / 1791   囗 火 攵
                          44 49

炊

炊炊

SUI, ta(ku) boil (rice), cook

─────── 1 ───────

8 炊事 **suiji** cooking

12 炊飯器 **suihanki** (electric) rice cooker

4d4.2 / 1790   囗 火 尸
                          44 40

炉

爐丨炉炉

RO furnace, hearth

炬→ **4d5.5**

4d4.4 / 1336   日 火
                          44

炎

炎炎

EN flame; (as suffix) inflammation of the ..., -itis **honō, homura** flame

─────── 1 ───────

3 炎上 **enjō** go up in flames, burst into flames

12 炎暑 **ensho** intense heat, hot weather

─────── 2 ───────

4 火炎瓶 **kaenbin** firebomb, Molotov cocktail

⁹ 肺炎 **haien** pneumonia

————— 5 —————

4d5.1 / 36　　　　　　囗　甲　火
　　　　　　　　　　　　　58　44

畑

畑・畑

hata, hatake cultivated field
HATA (surname)

————— 1 —————

¹¹ 畑野 **Hatano** (surname)
¹² 畑違 **hatakechiga(i)** out of one's
　　line

————— 2 —————

³ 川畑 **Kawabata** (surname)
　小畑 **Obata** (surname)
⁵ 田畑 **tahata** fields and rice
　　paddies **Tabata** (surname)
⁷ 花畑 **hanabatake** flower bed/garden
　麦畑 **mugibatake** wheat field
⁹ 茶畑 **chabatake** tea plantation
¹⁰ 高畑 **Takabatake, Takahata** (sur-
　　name)

————— 3 —————

⁹ 段々畑 **dandanbatake** terraced
　　fields

4d5.3　　　　　　囗　火　⼇　⼘
　　　　　　　　44　15　13

炸

炸・炸

SAKU explode; fry

————— 1 —————

¹² 炸裂 **sakuretsu** explode, burst

4d5.5　　　　　　囗　火　冂
　　　　　　　　44　20

炬

炬・炬

KO, KYO torch, signal fire

————— 1 —————

¹⁶ 炬燵 **kotatsu** heated floor well, foot
　　warmer

4d5.8 / 1484　　　　⼉　火　十　一
　　　　　　　　　44　12　1

為

爲 | 為 為

I, na(su), su(ru) do **na(ru)** be,
become **tame** for sake of, in order to;
because of TAME (part of given name)

————— 1 —————

⁹ 為政者 **iseisha** statesman, adminis-
　　trator
¹² 為替 **kawase** (foreign) exchange;
　　money order

————— 2 —————

² 人為的 **jin'iteki** artificial
⁶ 行為 **kōi** act, deed, conduct
　有為 **yūi** capable, effective,
　　promising **ui** vicissitudes of
　　life

————— 6 —————

烟 → 煙　4d9.3

4d6.3 / 1331　　　　囗　火　夕　⼉
　　　　　　　　44　30　16

烈

烈 烈

RETSU, hage(shii) violent, intense

————— 2 —————

¹⁰ 猛烈 **mōretsu** fierce, violent, in-
　　tense
　峻烈 **shunretsu** severe, scathing,
　　sharp
¹¹ 強烈 **kyōretsu** strong, intense,
　　powerful
¹² 痛烈 **tsūretsu** severe, bitter, scath-
　　ing
¹⁵ 熱烈 **netsuretsu** ardent, impas-
　　sioned

木
月
日
火
礻
王
牛
方
攵
欠
心
戸
戈

4

6

4d6.5

□… 火 尸 一
44 40 1

烏

烏 烏

U, O, karasu crow, raven

——————— 1 ———————

13 烏賊 **ika** squid, cuttlefish

——————— 7 ———————

4d7.2 / 206

曰 火 日 土
44 43 22

黒

黑 | 黒 黑

KOKU, kuro, kuro(i) black
kuro(bamu/zumu/maru) become
black/dark **kuro(meru)** make black,
blacken

——————— 1 ———————

2 黒人 **kokujin** a black, Negro
3 黒山 **kuroyama** large crowd
4 黒木 **Kuroki** (surname)
5 黒字 **kuroji** in the black
　黒白 **kuro-shiro, kokuhaku,
　kokubyaku** black and white;
　right and wrong
6 黒色 **kokushoku** black
　黒衣 **kokui** black clothes
8 黒板 **kokuban** blackboard
　黒服 **kurofuku** black clothes
9 黒点 **kokuten** black/dark spot; sun-
　spot
　黒海 **Kokkai** the Black Sea
　黒星 **kuroboshi** black spot/dot;
　bull's-eye; a defeat, failure
12 黒焦 **kuroko(ge)** charred, burned
　black
　黒雲 **kurokumo, kokuun** dark
　clouds
13 黒塗 **kuronu(ri)** black-lacquered,
　painted black
　黒幕 **kuromaku** black curtain; be-
　hind-the-scenes mastermind,
　wirepuller
　黒煙 **kokuen, kurokemuri** black
　smoke

黒褐色 **kokkasshoku** blackish
　brown
14 黒髪 **kurokami, kokuhatsu** black
　hair

——————— 2 ———————

3 大黒柱 **daikokubashira** central
　pillar; pillar, mainstay
5 白黒 **shiro-kuro** black-and-white;
　right or wrong, guilty or inno-
　cent
9 浅黒 **asaguro(i)** dark-colored,
　swarthy
13 腹黒 **haraguro(i)** black-hearted,
　scheming
　暗黒 **ankoku** darkness
14 漆黒 **shikkoku** jet-black, pitch-
　black
16 薄黒 **usuguro(i)** dark, dusky, umber

——————— 8 ———————

煉 → 煉 **4d9.2**

4d8.1

曰 立 火 口
54 44 24

焙

焙 焙

HŌ, abu(ru) roast, broil, toast, grill

——————— 1 ———————

9 焙茶 **hō(ji)cha** toasted/roasted tea

4d8.4 / 920

曰 火 艹 土
44 32 12

焼

燒 | 焼 焼

SHŌ, ya(ku) (tr.) burn; roast, broil,
bake **ya(keru)** (intr.) burn; be roasted/
broiled/baked

——————— 1 ———————

3 焼上 **ya(ki)a(geru)** burn up; bake
5 焼失 **shōshitsu** be destroyed by fire
　焼立 **ya(ki)ta(te)** fresh baked/
　roasted
6 焼死 **shōshi, ya(ke)ji(ni)** be burned
　to death

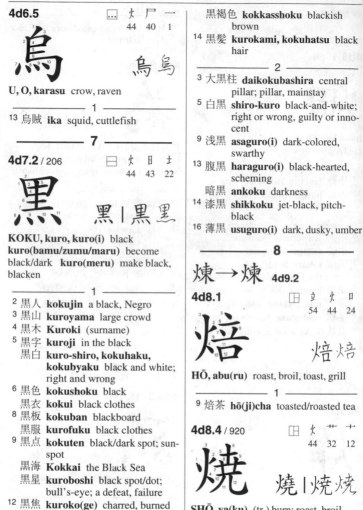

4

木 月 日 火 礻 王 牛 方 攵 欠 心 尸 戈

6

焼死者 **shōshisha** person burned to death

焼肉 **ya(ki)niku** roast/broiled meat

焼尽 **ya(ki)tsuku(su)** burn up, consume, reduce to ashes
ya(ke)tsu(kiru) burn itself out

7 焼却 **shōkyaku** destroy by fire, incinerate

10 焼残 **ya(ke)noko(ru)** remain unburned, escape the fire

11 焼過 **ya(ki)su(giru)** overcook

焼魚 **ya(ki)zakana** broiled fish

焼鳥 **ya(ki)tori** grilled chicken

14 焼餅 **ya(ki)mochi** toasted rice cake; jealousy

───── 2 ─────

3 夕焼 **yūya(ke)** red/glowing sunset

丸焼 **maruya(ki)** barbecue
maruya(ke) totally destroyed by fire

土焼 **tsuchiya(ki)** unglazed earthenware

4 日焼 **hiya(ke)** sunburn; suntan

5 好焼 **(o)kono(mi)ya(ki)** (unsweetened batter fried with vegetable bits into a thick griddlecake)

6 全焼 **zenshō** be totally destroyed by fire

10 胸焼 **muneya(ke)** heartburn

13 照焼 **te(ri)ya(ki)** fish broiled with soy sauce

15 鋤焼 **sukiya(ki)** sukiyaki

16 燃焼 **nenshō** combustion

17 鍋焼 **nabeya(ki)** boiled in a pot, baked in a casserole

───── 3 ─────

6 有田焼 **Arita-ya(ki)** Arita porcelainware

4d8.7

日 木 火
41 44

FUN, ta(ku) burn, light a fire; cook

───── 1 ─────

4 焚火 **ta(ki)bi** open-air fire, bonfire

4d8.8 / 93

目 火 艹 亠
44 32 15

無

無 無

MU, BU not; (as prefix) un-, without, -less, -free **na(shi)** not be; (as suffix) without **na(i)** not be **na(kusu)** lose; get rid of; run out of **na(ku naru)** be gone/lost/missing, run out of; die

───── 1 ─────

1 無一文 **muichimon** penniless

2 無二 **muni** peerless, unequaled

無人 **mujin, munin** uninhabited; unmanned **bunin** shortage of help

無力 **muryoku** powerless, ineffectual, feeble; incompetent

3 無口 **mukuchi** taciturn, reticent, laconic

4 無分別 **mufunbetsu** imprudent, thoughtless, rash

無辺 **muhen** limitless, boundless, infinite

無欠 **muketsu** flawless

無心 **mushin** absorbed in (play); request, cadge

5 無用 **muyō** useless; needless; without business; prohibited

無用心 **buyōjin** unsafe; incautious

無礼 **burei** discourtesy, rudeness

6 無気力 **mukiryoku** spiritless, flabby, gutless

無気味 **bukimi** ominous, eerie

無休 **mukyū** no holidays, always open (shop)

無防備 **mubōbi** defenseless, unfortified

無色 **mushoku** colorless, achromatic

無名 **mumei** anonymous; an unknown

無尽 **mujin** inexhaustible, endless; mutual financing association

無血 **muketsu** bloodless, without bloodshed

7 無我 **muga** selflessness, self-forgetfulness

無我夢中 **muga-muchū** total absorption, ecstasy

無作法 **busahō** bad manners, rudeness

無沙汰 **busata** silence, neglect to write/call

無形文化財 **mukei-bunkazai** intangible cultural asset

無学 **mugaku** unlettered, ignorant

無条件 **mujōken** unconditional

無私 **mushi** unselfish, disinterested

無言 **mugon** silent, mute

8 無表情 **muhyōjō** expressionless

無事 **buji** safe and sound

無念 **munen** regret, resentment, vexation

無念無想 **munen-musō** blank state of mind

無限 **mugen** infinite

無効 **mukō** null, void, invalid, ineffective

無免許 **mumenkyo** without a license

無法 **muhō** unjust, unlawful, outrageous

無味 **mumi** tasteless, flat, dry

無知 **muchi** ignorance

無届 **mutodo(ke)** without advance notice

無性 **musei** asexual
mushō thoughtless; inordinate **bushō** lazy

無所属 **mushozoku** unaffiliated, independent

9 無茶 **mucha** absurd; rash; excessive

無神経 **mushinkei** insensible to

無神論 **mushinron** atheism

無政府 **museifu** anarchy

10 無差別 **musabetsu** indiscriminate

無益 **mueki** useless, futile

無害 **mugai** harmless

無能 **munō** incompetent, ineffective

無秩序 **muchitsujo** disorder, chaos; anomie

無症状 **mushōjō** without symptoms

無料 **muryō** without charge, free

11 無偏 **muhen** unbiased, impartial

無視 **mushi** ignore, disregard

無理 **muri** unreasonable; impossible, beyond one's power, too difficult; by force, against one's will; strain oneself

無理矢理 **muriyari** forcibly, under compulsion

無欲 **muyoku** free from avarice

無情 **mujō** unfeeling, callous, cruel

無断 **mudan** unannounced; unauthorized

無責任 **musekinin** irresponsibility

12 無遠慮 **buenryo** unreserved, forward, impertinent

無報酬 **muhōshū** without pay, for free

無期 **muki** indefinite

無期限 **mukigen** indefinite, without time limit

無量 **muryō** beyond measure, immense

無税 **muzei** tax-free, duty-free

無給 **mukyū** unpaid, nonsalaried

13 無傷 **mukizu** uninjured, undamaged, unblemished

無慈悲 **mujihi** merciless, ruthless

無暗 **muyami** thoughtless, rash; excessive; unnecessary

無数 **musū** innumerable, countless

無感覚 **mukankaku** insensible, numb, callous

無意義 **muigi** meaningless, not significant

無意識 **muishiki** unconscious, involuntary

無罪 **muzai** innocent, not guilty

無罪判決 **muzai hanketsu** acquittal

14 無精 **bushō** lazy

無関心 **mukanshin** indifference, unconcern, apathy

無関係 **mukankei** unrelated, irrelevant

無駄 **muda** futile, useless, wasteful

無駄遣 **mudazuka(i)** waste, squander

15 無器用 **bukiyō** clumsy

無敵 **muteki** invincible, unrivaled

無線 **musen** wireless, radio

無縁 **muen** unrelated; with no surviving relatives

無論 **muron** of course, naturally

無調法 **buchōhō** impolite; clumsy, unaccustomed to
16 無糖 **mutō** sugar-free, unsweetened
18 無職 **mushoku** unemployed; no occupation
無難 **bunan** safe, acceptable

——— 2 ———
9 皆無 **kaimu** nothing/none at all
10 骨無 **honena(shi)** rickets; spineless/weak-willed person
11 虚無的 **kyomuteki** nihilistic
12 御無沙汰 **gobusata** neglect to visit/write

——— 3 ———
1 一文無 **ichimonna(shi)** penniless
4 勿体無 **mottaina(i)** more than one deserves, too good for; wasteful
7 何気無 **nanigena(ku)** unintentionally; nonchalantly
8 味気無 **ajikena(i)** irksome, wearisome, dreary
10 致方無 **ita(shi)kata (ga) na(i)** it can't be helped
12 無念無想 **munen-musō** blank state of mind
13 感慨無量 **kangai-muryō** full of emotion

黒 → 黑 **4d7.2**

4d8.9 / 1795
 日 火 土
43 44 22

SHA, ni(eru/ru) (intr./tr.) boil, cook **ni** cooking **ni(yasu)** (tr.) boil

——— 1 ———
3 煮上 **ni(e)a(garu), nia(garu)** boil up, be thoroughly cooked
8 煮沸 **shafutsu** boiling
12 煮湯 **ni(e)yu** boiling water

——— 2 ———
14 雑煮 **zōni** rice cakes boiled with vegetables

4d8.10 / 651
 火 夕 犭
44 30 27

然

ZEN, NEN as, like **sō, sa** such **sō(shite)** and **sa(ru)** a certain, such **sa(redo)** but, however **sa(ri to wa)** if so, well **shika** so, thus **shika(shi)** but, however **shika(ru ni)** but, nevertheless **shika(ru ni)** but, nevertheless **shika(ri)** yes, quite so **shika(rubeki)** as it should be, proper, right

——— 1 ———
12 然程 **sahodo** so much, very

——— 2 ———
4 天然 **tennen** natural
5 必然 **hitsuzen** inevitability, necessity
6 全然 **zenzen** entirely, utterly, (not) at all
当然 **tōzen** of course, naturally
自然 **shizen** nature; natural
自然主義 **shizen shugi** naturalism
自然科学 **shizen kagaku** the natural sciences
7 呆然 **bōzen (to)** in blank amazement
8 画然 **kakuzen (to)** distinctly, sharply
依然 **izen (to shite)** still, as ever
突然 **totsuzen** suddenly, unexpectedly
突然変異 **totsuzen hen'i** mutation
忽然 **kotsuzen** suddenly
9 茫然 **bōzen** vacantly, in a daze
10 泰然 **taizen** calm, composed; firm
浩然 **kōzen** expansive, free and easy, openly
11 偶然 **gūzen** by chance, happen to …
啞然 **azen (to)** dumbfounded, agape
寂然 **sekizen, jakunen** lonesome, desolate
断然 **danzen** resolutely, flatly, decidedly
12 愕然 **gakuzen** in surprise/terror, aghast, shocked

13 漠然 **bakuzen** vague, obscure
蓋然性 **gaizensei** probability
14 歴然 **rekizen** clear, unmistakable
15 憮然 **buzen** discouraged; surprised
憤然 **funzen** indignantly
16 整然 **seizen** orderly, regular, systematic, neat and trim
17 燦然 **sanzen** brilliant, radiant, resplendent

───── 3 ─────

3 大自然 **daishizen** Mother Nature
4 不自然 **fushizen** unnatural
12 超自然 **chōshizen** supernatural

───── 4 ─────

1 一目瞭然 **ichimoku ryōzen** clear at a glance, obvious

爲 → 為 **4d5.8**

4d8.11　　　　　`⟦⟧ 火 十 丨`
　　　　　　　　　44 12 2

毯 䄺

TAN wool rug

───── 2 ─────

12 絨毯 **jūtan** rug, carpet

───── 9 ─────

4d9.1 / 1849　　　`⟦⟧ 頁 火`
　　　　　　　　　　77 44

煩 煩

HAN, BON, wazura(u) worry about, be troubled by; be ill
wazura(wasu) trouble, bother, annoy
wazura(washii) troublesome, tangled
urusa(i) annoying, irksome, fastidious, noisy

───── 1 ─────

6 煩忙 **hanbō** busy, pressed with business
10 煩悩 **bonnō** evil passions, carnal desires

14 煩雑 **hanzatsu** complicated, troublesome

───── 2 ─────

10 恋煩 **koiwazura(i)** lovesickness

4d9.2　　　　`⟦⟧ 火 木 口`
　　　　　　　　44 41 24

煉 | 煉 煉

REN, ne(ru) refine (metals)
ne(ri) kneading over fire

───── 2 ─────

9 洗煉 **senren** refine, polish

4d9.3 / 919　　　`⟦⟧ 火 口 土`
　　　　　　　　　24 22

烟 | 煙 煙

EN, kemuri, kemu smoke
kemu(ru), kebu(ru) smoke, smolder
kemu(i), kebu(i) smoky

───── 1 ─────

8 煙突 **entotsu** chimney
19 煙霧 **enmu** mist, fog, smog

───── 2 ─────

4 火煙 **kaen** fire and smoke
11 黒煙 **kokuen, kurokemuri** black smoke
12 喫煙 **kitsuen** smoking
硝煙 **shōen** gunpowder smoke
紫煙 **shien** tobacco smoke
13 禁煙 **kin'en** No Smoking

4d9.7　　　　`⟦⟧ 火 日 王`
　　　　　　　　44 43 46

煌 煌

KŌ, kira(meku) sparkle, gleam, twinkle **kira(biyaka)** glittering, resplendent

4d9.9

田 火 厂 又
44 14 9

煖   煖 煖

DAN warm

───── 1 ─────

8 煖房 **danbō** heating

4d9.11 / 2148

田 火 口 尸
44 24 40

熙   熙 | 熙 熙

KI shine; wide; calm; enjoy   KI, I, HI-RO, TERU, SATO, OKI, YOSHI, NORI (part of given name) HIROSHI, HIROMU (m. given name)

4d9.12 / 998

田 日 火 口
43 44 24

照   照 照

SHŌ, te(ru) shine   **te(ri)** sunshine; dry weather; gloss, luster   **te(rasu)** shine on   **te(reru)** feel embarrassed

───── 1 ─────

2 照子 **Teruko, Shōko, Mitsuko** (f. given name)

4 照夫 **Teruo, Akio, Nobuo** (m. given name)

6 照合 **te(rashi)a(waseru)** check by comparison   **shōgō** check against, verify

8 照明 **shōmei** illumination, lighting

12 照焼 **te(ri)ya(ki)** fish broiled with soy sauce

───── 2 ─────

4 日照 **nisshō, hide(ri)** sunshine, drought, dry weather

7 対照 **taishō** contrast

8 参照 **sanshō** refer to, see, compare

───────────────

煎 → **2o11.2**

───── 10 ─────

熔 → 鎔 **8a10.1**

4d10.4

田 火 尸 彐
44 40 39

煽   煽 | 煽 煽

SEN, ao(ru) fan (flames), blow; incite   **ao(gu)** fan (a fire); instigate   **oda(teru)** incite; flatter

───── 1 ─────

5 煽立 **ao(gi)ta(teru)** instigate

熏 → 燻 **4d14.1**

4d10.5 / 687

田 火 口 亠
44 24 11

熟   熟 熟

JUKU, u(reru) ripen, come to maturity   **u(mu)** ripen; be overripe

───── 1 ─────

0 熟す **juku(su)** be ripe, reach maturity; (of words) come into common use; acquire skill

6 熟考 **jukkō** mature reflection, due deliberation

14 熟練 **jukuren** practiced skill, mastery

熟語 **jukugo** word of two or more kanji, compound; phrase

───── 2 ─────

6 老熟 **rōjuku** mature skill, maturity, mellowness

成熟 **seijuku** ripen; mature

熙 → 熙 **4d9.11**

4d10.6 / 2149   田 月 火 竹
     42 44 17

熊   熊 熊

YŪ, kuma bear
YŪ, KUMA, KAGE (part of given name)

——— 1 ———

4 熊手 **kumade** rake
5 熊本県 **Kumamoto-ken** (prefecture)

——— 11 ———

燻→ **4d12.6**

4d11.3 / 1773   田 車 火 力
     69 44 8

勲   勲 | 勲 勲

KUN merit **isao** meritorious deed
ISAO, KAORU (m. given name)

——— 1 ———

5 勲功 **kunkō** distinguished service, merits
11 勲章 **kunshō** order, decoration, medal

4d11.4 / 645   田 火 土 儿
     44 22 16

熱   熱 熱

NETSU heat; fever; mania, enthusiasm
atsu(i) hot

——— 1 ———

0 熱する **nes(suru)** heat, make hot; become hot/excited
4 熱中 **netchū** be enthusiastic/crazy about, be engrossed/absorbed in
    熱心 **nesshin** enthusiasm, zeal
7 熱狂 **nekkyō** wild enthusiasm, frenzy, mania
8 熱苦 **atsukuru(shii)** sultry, sweltering, stifling

10 熱帯 **nettai** torrid zone, the tropics
    熱烈 **netsuretsu** ardent, impassioned
11 熱情 **netsujō** fervor, ardor, passion
13 熱戦 **nessen** fierce fighting; close contest
    熱意 **netsui** enthusiasm, zeal, ardor
16 熱燗 **atsukan** hot saké
19 熱願 **netsugan** fervent plea, earnest entreaty

——— 2 ———

5 加熱 **kanetsu** heating
    白熱戦 **hakunetsusen** intense fighting, thrilling game
6 光熱費 **kōnetsuhi** heating and electricity expenses
7 亜熱帯 **anettai** subtropics
    余熱 **yonetsu** remaining heat
9 発熱 **hatsunetsu** generation of heat; have a fever
    耐熱 **tainetsu** heat-resistant
11 黄熱 **ōnetsu, kōnetsu** yellow fever
    情熱 **jōnetsu** passion, enthusiasm
13 微熱 **binetsu** a slight fever

4d11.5 / 1578   田 日 火 土
     43 44 22

黙   黙 | 黙 黙

MOKU, dama(ru) become/be silent, say nothing **danma(ri)** silence, reticence **moda(su)** be silent, not say; leave as is

——— 1 ———

4 黙込 **dama(ri)ko(mu)** fall silent, say no more
9 黙約 **mokuyaku** a tacit agreement
10 黙殺 **mokusatsu** take no notice of, ignore
    黙秘 **mokuhi** keep silent about, keep secret
11 黙許 **mokkyo** tacit permission, connivance
14 黙認 **mokunin** tacit approval/admission
15 黙諾 **mokudaku** tacit consent

4   木 月 日 火 礻 王 牛 方 攵 欠 心 尸 戈
10

— 2 —

7 沈黙 **chinmoku** silence
13 暗黙 **anmoku** silence
14 寡黙 **kamoku** taciturn, reticent

— 12 —

4d12.2 / 652   ⊞ 火 夕 犭
              44 30 27

燃 燃

NEN, mo(eru/yuru) burn, blaze
mo(yasu/su) (tr.) burn

— 1 —

3 燃上 **mo(e)a(garu)** blaze up, burst
    into flames
5 燃出 **mo(e)da(su)** begin to burn, ig-
    nite
   燃付 **mo(e)tsu(ku)** catch fire, ignite
   燃広 **mo(e)hiro(garu)** (flames)
    spread
   燃立 **mo(e)ta(tsu)** blaze up, be
    ablaze
8 燃易 **mo(e)yasu(i)** flammable
10 燃料 **nenryō** fuel
11 燃移 **mo(e)utsu(ru)** (flames)
    spread to
12 燃焼 **nenshō** combustion
   燃費 **nenpi** fuel cost; fuel economy
    (km/liter)

— 2 —

5 可燃性 **kanensei** combustible,
    flammable
10 核燃料 **kakunenryō** nuclear fuel

4d12.4 / 2150   ⊞ 火 日 小
              44 43 35

燎 燎

RYŌ bonfire; burn   RYŌ (part of giv-
en name)

燈 → 灯   **4d2.1**

燒 → 焼   **4d8.4**

4d12.6   ⊞ 立 火 土
                 54 44 22

燵 燵

TATSU heated floor well, foot-warmer

— 2 —

9 炬燵 **kotatsu** heated floor well, foot
    warmer

燕 →   **3k13.16**

— 13 —

4d13.3 / 2151   ⊞ 米 火 夕
              62 44 30

燦 燦

SAN bright, brilliant   SAN (part of
given name)

— 1 —

12 燦然 **sanzen** brilliant, radiant, re-
    splendent

4d13.4   ⊞ 米 火 夕
                62 44 30

燐 燐

RIN phosphorus

4d13.5   ⊞ 虫 日 火
                64 55 44

燭 燭

SHOKU (candle)light; a candlepower

— 1 —

5 燭台 **shokudai** candlestick, candle-
    stand

— 2 —
21 蠟燭 **rōsoku** candle

4d13.6 / 1656 　　田 火 木 口
44 41 24

燥　　燥燥

SŌ dry

4d13.7 / 2283 　　目 戈 日 火
52 43 44

黛　　黛黛

TAI, mayuzumi blue-black eyebrow coloring MAYUZUMI (surname) TAI (part of given name)

點 → 点 **2m7.2**

— 14 —

4d14.1 　　田 火 王 口
44 46 24

燻　　熏丨燻燻

KUN, ibu(ru) smoke, smolder, fume **ibu(su), kusu(beru), fusu(beru)** smoke, fumigate **kusu(buru), fusu(bu-ru/boru)** smoke, smolder, become sooty; stay indoors; remain in obscurity **kuyu(rasu)** smoke (a cigar)

— 1 —
14 燻製 **kunsei** smoked (fish)

4d14.3 / 2152 　　田 隹 火 三
74 44 39

燿　　燿燿

YŌ, kagaya(ku) shine, gleam **YŌ**, TERU (part of given name)

— 15 —

4d15.2 / 1015 　　田 火 日 艹
44 43 32

爆　　爆爆

BAKU explode **ha(zeru)** burst/pop open, split

— 1 —
6 爆死 **bakushi** death from bombing
9 爆発 **bakuhatsu** explosion
爆発的 **bakuhatsuteki** explosive (popularity)
爆音 **bakuon** (sound of an) explosion, roar (of an engine)
10 爆破 **bakuha** blast, blow up
爆笑 **bakushō** burst out laughing
12 爆弾 **bakudan** bomb
15 爆撃 **bakugeki** bombing
16 爆薬 **bakuyaku** explosives

— 2 —
4 水爆 **suibaku** hydrogen bomb (short for 水素爆弾)
10 原爆 **genbaku** atomic bomb (short for 原子爆弾)
被爆者 **hibakusha** bombing victims

— 16 —

爐 → 炉 **4d4.2**

— 17 —

4d17.1 　　田 門 火 木
76 44 41

爛　　爛爛

RAN inflamed; colorful **tada(reru)** be inflamed/sore

— 2 —
12 絢爛 **kenran(taru)** gorgeous, dazzling, gaudy

礻 4e

示	礼	社	祀	奈	祉	祇	祈	神	祓	秘	祐	祖
0.1	1.1	3.1	3.2	3.3	4.1	4.2	4.3	5.1	5.2	5d5.6	5.3	5.4

祝	祥	票	祭	尉	祷	視	禄	禁	福	禅	禎	禍
5.5	6.1	6.2	6.3	6.4	4e14.2	7.1	8.2	8.3	9.1	9.2	9.3	9.4

隷	禪	隸	禱	禮
11.1	4e9.2	4e11.1	14.2	4e1.1

0

4e0.1 / 615

□ 礻
45

示

示 示

JI, SHI, shime(su) show
shime(shi) deportment, discipline (by
example); revelation

— 1 —

9 示威的 **jiiteki** demonstrative,
threatening

10 示唆 **shisa** suggestion

示教 **shikyō** instruction, guidance

15 示談 **jidan** out-of-court settlement

— 2 —

4 公示 **kōji** public announcement

7 呈示 **teiji** present, bring up

告示 **kokuji** notification

8 表示 **hyōji** indicate, express, display

例示 **reiji** give an example of

9 指示 **shiji** indication, instructions,
directions **sa(shi)shime(su)**
indicate, point out

10 展示 **tenji** exhibition, display

展示会 **tenjikai** show, exhibition

教示 **kyōji** instruct, teach, enlighten

11 掲示 **keiji** notice, bulletin

掲示板 **keijiban** bulletin board

啓示 **keiji** revelation

13 暗示 **anji** suggestion, hint

18 顕示 **kenji** show, unveil, reveal

1

4e1.1 / 620

□ 礻 丨
45 2

礼

禮 丨礼礼

REI, RAI courtesy; salutation, salute,
bow; gratitude; return present
REI, NORI (part of given name)

— 1 —

2 礼子 **Reiko, Noriko** (f. given
name)

7 礼状 **reijō** letter of thanks

8 礼法 **reihō** courtesy, etiquette,
manners

礼拝 **reihai, raihai** worship, services

礼服 **reifuku** formal dress

礼金 **reikin** honorarium, fee

11 礼遇 **reigū** cordial reception; honors, privileges

15 礼儀 **reigi** courtesy, politeness, propriety

礼儀正 **reigitada(shii)** polite, courteous

礼儀作法 **reigisahō** etiquette,
courtesy, propriety

— 2 —

1 一礼 **ichirei** a bow/greeting

5 失礼 **shitsurei** rudeness, discourtesy

巡礼 **junrei** pilgrimage; pilgrim

6 返礼 **henrei** return gift, in return for

9 洗礼式 **senreishiki** baptism (ceremony)

11 祭礼 **sairei** festival, ritual

12 無礼 **burei** discourtesy, rudeness

17 謝礼 **sharei** remuneration, honorarium

木
月
日
火
礻
王
牛
方
欠
心
戸
戈

1

——— 3 ———

4e3.1 / 308 ☐ 礻 土
45 22

社

社╎社社

SHA company; Shinto shrine
yashiro Shinto shrine

——— 1 ———

4 社内 **shanai** in the company/shrine
5 社司 **shashi** Shinto priest
6 社会 **shakai** society, social
社会民主主義 **shakai minshu shugi** social democracy
社会主義 **shakai shugi** socialism
社会学 **shakaigaku** sociology
社会面 **shakaimen** local-news page
社会党 **shakaitō** socialist party
社会福祉 **shakai fukushi** social welfare
社交 **shakō** society, social life
社寺 **shaji** shrines and temples
社名 **shamei** company name
社団法人 **shadan hōjin** corporate juridical person
8 社長 **shachō** company president
10 社員 **shain** employee, staff
12 社費 **shahi** company expenses
13 社債 **shasai** (company) bonds, debentures
14 社説 **shasetsu** an editorial

——— 2 ———

2 入社 **nyūsha** joining a company
4 支社 **shisha** a branch (office)
公社 **kōsha** public corporation
5 出社 **shussha** go/come to the office
本社 **honsha** head office; main shrine; this shrine
正社員 **seishain** regular employee, full member of the staff
6 会社 **kaisha** company, corporation
会社員 **kaishain** company employee
寺社 **jisha** temples and shrines
当社 **tōsha** this/our company; this shrine
8 非社交的 **hishakōteki** unsociable, retiring

9 神社 **jinja** Shinto shrine
11 商社 **shōsha** trading company, business firm
12 結社 **kessha** association, society
貴社 **kisha** your company
15 弊社 **heisha** our company, we

——— 3 ———

2 子会社 **kogaisha** a subsidiary
8 旺文社 **Ōbunsha** (name of publishing company)
13 新聞社 **shinbunsha** newspaper (company)
16 親会社 **oyagaisha** parent company

——— 4 ———

6 合弁会社 **gōben-gaisha** joint venture (company)
有限会社 **yūgen-gaisha** limited liability company, Ltd.
10 株式会社 **kabushiki-gaisha, kabushiki kaisha** corporation, Co., Ltd.
11 運送会社 **unsō-gaisha** transport/express company
情報化社会 **jōhōka shakai** information-oriented society
12 貿易会社 **bōeki-gaisha** trading firm
13 靖国神社 **Yasukuni-jinja** (shrine in Tōkyō dedicated to fallen Japanese soldiers)
14 製薬会社 **seiyaku-gaisha** pharmaceutical company

4e3.2 ☐ 礻 尸
45 40

祀

SHI, matsu(ru) deify, worship; year

4e3.3 / 2044 ┉ 礻 大
45 34

奈

NA what?, how? NA, DAI, **NANI** (part of given name)

---- 1 ----

3 奈々 **Nana** (f. given name)
7 奈良県 **Nara-ken** (prefecture)
12 奈落 **naraku** hell, hades; theater basement

---- 2 ----

5 加奈 **Kana** (f: given name)
8 佳奈 **Kana** (f. given name)
9 神奈川県 **Kanagawa-ken** (prefecture)

---- 4 ----

4e4.1 / 1390   口 礻 十 亠
                   45 13 11

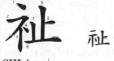

祉 | 祉 祉

SHI happiness

---- 2 ----

13 福祉 **fukushi** welfare, well-being

7 社会福祉 **shakai fukushi** social welfare

4e4.2   口 礻 厂 十
            45 18 12

祇 | 祇 祇

GI local god; the gods

---- 1 ----

13 祇園 **Gion** (name of a shrine, festival, and red-light district in Kyōto)

4e4.3 / 621   口 礻 斤
                  45 50

祈 | 祈 祈

KI, ino(ru) pray; wish **ino(ri)** prayer

---- 1 ----

8 祈念 **kinen** a prayer
19 祈願 **kigan** a prayer

---- 5 ----

4e5.1 / 310   口 礻 日 丨
                  45 43 2

神

神 | 神 神

SHIN, JIN, kami, kan-, kō- god, God
KA (part of given name)

---- 1 ----

3 神山 **Kamiyama** (surname)
4 神仏 **shinbutsu** gods and Buddha; Shinto and Buddhism
  神父 **shinpu** (Catholic) priest, Father
  神戸 **Kōbe** (city, Hyōgo-ken)
5 神主 **kannushi** Shinto priest
6 神気 **shinki** energy, spirits; mind
7 神谷 **Kamiya** (surname)
  神妙 **shinmyō** mysterious, marvelous; admirable; gentle
  神学 **shingaku** theology
  神社 **jinja** Shinto shrine
8 神官 **shinkan** Shinto priest
  神国 **shinkoku** land of the gods
  神奈川県 **Kanagawa-ken** (prefecture)
  神武 **Jinmu** (emperor, 660 – 585 B.C.)
9 神前結婚 **shinzen kekkon** Shinto wedding
  神政 **shinsei** theocracy
10 神宮 **jingū** Shinto shrine; the Ise Shrines
  神秘的 **shinpiteki** mystic(al), mysterious
11 神道 **shintō** Shintoism
  神経 **shinkei** nerve
  神経質 **shinkeishitsu** nervous, high-strung
13 神業 **kamiwaza** the work of God; superhuman feat
  神殿 **shinden** temple, shrine
  神聖 **shinsei** holy; sanctity, dignity
  神話 **shinwa** myth, mythology
14 神様 **kamisama** God; god
18 神髄 **shinzui** (quint)essence, soul

4

木 月 日 火 礻 王 牛 方 攵 欠 心 戸 戈
5

2

1 一神教 **isshinkyō** monotheism
3 大神宮 **Daijingū** the Grand Shrine (at Ise)
女神 **megami, joshin, nyoshin** goddess
4 氏神 **ujigami** patron deity
6 阪神 **Han-Shin** Ōsaka-Kōbe area
守神 **mamo(ri)gami** guardian deity
12 無神経 **mushinkei** insensible to
無神論 **mushinron** atheism
14 精神 **seishin** mind, spirit
精神力 **seishinryoku** force of will
精神分析 **seishin bunseki** psycho-analysis
精神病 **seishinbyō** mental illness/disorder

3

8 京阪神 **Kei-Han-Shin** Kyōto-Ōsaka-Kōbe
明治神宮 **Meiji Jingū** Meiji Shrine
13 靖国神社 **Yasukuni-jinja** (shrine in Tōkyō dedicated to fallen Japanese soldiers)

4

6 伊勢大神宮 **Ise Daijingū** the Grand Shrines of Ise

4e5.2　　　　　□　ネ　犭　丨
　　　　　　　　　　45　27　2

FUTSU, hara(u) exorcise
harai purification, exorcism

1

11 祓清 **hara(i)kiyo(meru)** purify, exorcise

祕 → 秘　**5d5.6**

4e5.3 / 2178　　　□　ネ　口　十
　　　　　　　　　　　45　24　12

YŪ help　YŪ, YU, SUKE, HIRO, SACHI, MASA, YOSHI, MASU (part of given name) TASUKU (m. given name)

1

1 祐一 **Yūichi, Sukekazu, Sukeichi** (m. given name)
2 祐子 **Yūko, Sachiko** (f. given name)
4 祐太 **Yūta** (m. given name)
14 祐輔 **Yūsuke** (m. given name)
16 祐樹 **Hiroki, Yūki** (m. given name)

2

6 圭祐 **Keisuke** (m. given name)

4e5.4 / 622　　　□　ネ　月　一
　　　　　　　　　　45　42　1

SO ancestor

1

4 祖父 **sofu** grandfather
祖父母 **sofubo** grandparents
5 祖母 **sobo** grandmother
6 祖先 **sosen** ancestor, forefathers
8 祖国 **sokoku** one's homeland/fatherland

2

4 父祖 **fuso** forefathers, ancestors
6 先祖 **senzo** ancestor
8 宗祖 **shūso** founder of a sect
10 教祖 **kyōso** founder of a sect
11 曽祖父 **sōsofu, hiijiji** great-grandfather
曽祖母 **sōsobo, hiibaba** great-grandmother

4e5.5 / 851 ⊞ ネ 日 儿
45 24 16

祝 | 祝祝

SHUKU, SHŪ, iwa(u) celebrate,
congratulate **HAJIME** (m. given
name) **NORI** (part of given name)

───────── 1 ─────────

4 祝日 **shukujitsu, iwa(i)bi** festival
day, holiday
6 祝返 **iwa(i)gae(shi)** return gift
7 祝言 **shūgen** congratulations; celebration; wedding
8 祝事 **iwa(i)goto** auspicious/festive
occasion
祝杯 **shukuhai** a toast
10 祝宴 **shukuen** congratulatory banquet, feast
11 祝祭日 **shukusaijitsu** festival, holiday
12 祝賀 **shukuga** celebration; congratulations
13 祝福 **shukufuku** blessing, benediction
祝辞 **shukuji** (speech of) congratulations
祝電 **shukuden** telegram of congratulations

───────── 3 ─────────

14 誕生祝 **tanjō iwa(i)** birthday celebration

───────── 6 ─────────

4e6.1 / 1576 ⊞ ネ 王 儿
45 46 16

祥 | 祥祥

SHŌ, JŌ happiness; good omen
SACHI, YOSHI (part of given name)

───────── 1 ─────────

1 祥一 **Shōichi, Yoshikazu** (m. given
name)
2 祥子 **Shōko, Sachiko, Yoshiko, Yōko, Toshiko** (f. given name)
4 祥月命日 **shōtsuki meinichi** anniversary of one's death

───────── 2 ─────────

9 発祥地 **hasshōchi** cradle, birthplace

4e6.2 / 922 ⊞ ネ 日 ⼀
45 24 14

票 票

HYŌ slip of paper, ballot, vote

───────── 1 ─────────

7 票決 **hyōketsu** vote, voting
13 票数 **hyōsū** number of votes

───────── 2 ─────────

1 一票 **ippyō** a vote
6 伝票 **denpyō** slip of paper
7 投票 **tōhyō** vote
投票日 **tōhyōbi** voting day
12 開票 **kaihyō** ballot counting

4e6.3 / 617 ⊞ ネ 夕 又
45 30 9

祭 祭

SAI, matsu(ru) deify; worship
matsu(ri) festival

───────── 1 ─────────

4 祭日 **saijitsu** holiday; festival day
5 祭礼 **sairei** festival, ritual
8 祭典 **saiten** festival, ritual
16 祭壇 **saidan** altar

───────── 2 ─────────

9 盆祭 **Bon-matsu(ri)** Bon Festival
後祭 **ato (no) matsu(ri)** too late
(for the fair)
祝祭日 **shukusaijitsu** festival, holiday
10 宵祭 **yoimatsu(ri)** eve (of a festival), vigil
18 雛祭 **hinamatsu(ri)** Girls' Doll
Festival (March 3)

───────── 3 ─────────

9 前夜祭 **zen'yasai** (Christmas) Eve
12 復活祭 **Fukkatsusai** Easter
13 聖誕祭 **Seitansai** Christmas

4

6

木 月 日 火 ネ 王 牛 方 攵 欠 心 戸 戈

15 慰霊祭 **ireisai** memorial service

——— 4 ———

9 冠婚葬祭 **kankonsōsai** ceremonial occasions

4e6.4 / 1617 　　□ 礻 尸 寸
45 40 37

尉 尉

I officer

——— 1 ———

8 尉官 **ikan** officer below the rank of major

——— 2 ———

3 大尉 **taii** captain; lieutenant

——— 7 ———

祷 → 禱 **4e14.2**

4e7.1 / 606 　　□ 貝 礻
68 45

視 | 視 視

SHI see, look at; (as suffix) regard as

——— 1 ———

2 視力 **shiryoku** visual acuity, eyesight
7 視角 **shikaku** angle of vision; viewpoint
9 視点 **shiten** center of one's field of view; viewpoint
11 視野 **shiya** field of vision/view
12 視覚 **shikaku** sense of sight, vision
14 視察 **shisatsu** inspection, observance
15 視線 **shisen** line of vision, one's eyes/gaze
17 視聴率 **shichōritsu** (TV show popularity) rating

——— 2 ———

5 巡視 **junshi** inspection tour, patrol
6 近視 **kinshi** nearsightedness
9 重視 **jūshi** attach great importance to

透視 **tōshi** see through; fluoroscopy; clairvoyance
12 遠視 **enshi** farsightedness
無視 **mushi** ignore, disregard
軽視 **keishi** belittle, neglect, scorn
14 蔑視 **besshi** look down on, regard with contempt
15 敵視 **tekishi** regard with hostility
監視 **kanshi** monitor, keep watch over
16 凝視 **gyōshi** stare, steady gaze, fixation
17 聴視者 **chōshisha** (TV) viewer(s)
19 警視庁 **Keishichō** Metropolitan Police Agency

——— 8 ———

4e8.2 / 2179 　　□ 礻 彐 氵
45 39 21

禄 | 禄 禄

ROKU fief, stipend, allowance; happiness ROKU, YOSHI, TOSHI, SACHI, TOMI (part of given name)

4e8.3 / 482 　　□ 礻 木
45 41

禁 禁

KIN prohibition

——— 1 ———

0 禁じる/ずる **kin(jiru/zuru)** prohibit, ban, forbid; abstain from
4 禁止 **kinshi** prohibition
5 禁句 **kinku** tabooed word/phrase
7 禁忌 **kinki** taboo; contraindication
8 禁制品 **kinseihin** contraband
禁物 **kinmotsu** forbidden things, taboo
10 禁酒 **kinshu** abstinence from alcohol, Prohibition
11 禁欲 **kin'yoku** control of passions, self-denial, abstinence
13 禁煙 **kin'en** No Smoking
16 禁輸品 **kin'yuhin** contraband

————— 2 —————

9 独禁法 **dokkinhō** antitrust laws, the Anti-Monopoly Law (short for 独占禁止法)

13 解禁 **kaikin** lifting a ban, open season

17 厳禁 **genkin** strictly prohibited

————— 3 —————

5 立入禁止 **tachiiri kinshi** Keep Out

11 張紙禁止 **ha(ri)gami kinshi** Post No Bills

————— 4 —————

3 土足厳禁 **dosoku genkin** Remove Shoes (sign)

4 火気厳禁 **kaki genkin** Danger: Flammable

————— 9 —————

4e9.1 / 1379

田 田 ネ 口
58 45 24

 福 | 福福

FUKU fortune, blessing, happiness; wealth, welfare   YOSHI   (part of given name)

————— 1 —————

3 福山 **Fukuyama** (city, Hiroshima-ken)

4 福井 **Fukui** (city, Fukui-ken); (surname)

福井県 **Fukui-ken** (prefecture)

5 福田 **Fukuda** (surname)

7 福寿 **fukuju** happiness and longevity

福利 **fukuri** welfare, well-being

8 福祉 **fukushi** welfare, well-being

9 福音 **fukuin** the Gospel; good news

8 幸福 **kōfuku** happiness

9 祝福 **shukufuku** blessing, benediction

12 裕福 **yūfuku** wealth, affluence

13 禍福 **kafuku** fortune and misfortune, weal or woe

————— 3 —————

7 社会福祉 **shakai fukushi** social welfare

4e9.2 / 1540

田 ネ 日 小
45 43 35

 禪 | 禅禅

ZEN Zen Buddhism

————— 1 —————

6 禅寺 **zendera** Zen temple

8 禅宗 **zenshū** the Zen sect

禅定 **zenjō** meditative concentration

11 禅問答 **zen mondō** Zen/incomprehensible dialog

13 禅僧 **zensō** Zen priest

————— 2 —————

10 座禅 **zazen** (Zen) meditation

4e9.3 / 2180

田 貝 ネ ⊥
68 45 13

 禎 | 禎禎

TEI happy; correct   TEI, SADA, YOSHI, TADA, SACHI, TSUGU, TOMO   (part of given name)   TADASHI, SADAMU (m. given name)

4e9.4 / 1809

田 ネ 口 冂
45 24 20

 禍 | 禍禍

KA, maga, wazawai calamity, misfortune

————— 1 —————

10 禍根 **kakon** root of evil, source of calamity

13 禍福 **kafuku** fortune and misfortune, weal or woe

————— 2 —————

3 大禍 **taika** great disaster

11 黄禍 **kōka** the Yellow Peril

13 戦禍 **senka** war damage, ravages of war

4

木
月
日
火
ネ
王
牛
方
攵
欠
心
戸
戈

9

11

4e11.1 / 1934

田 示 土 三
45 22 39

隷

隷 | 隷 隷

REI servant; criminal; follow; (a style of kanji)

— 1 —

10 隷従 **reijū** slavery

隷書 **reisho** (ancient squared style of kanji)

— 2 —

5 奴隷 **dorei** slave

12

禪 → 禅 4e9.2

隸 → 隷 4e11.1

14

4e14.2

田 示 土 王
57 22 38

禱

祷 | 禱 祷

TŌ, ino(ru) pray

16

禮 → 礼 4e1.1

王 **4f**

王 0.1	玉 0.2	主 1.1	玉 4f0.2	全 2a4.16	玖 3.1	弄 3.2	玩 4.1	珊 5.1	珪 4f6.4	珍 5.6	珎 4f5.6	玲 5.7
皇 5.9	珠 6.2	班 6.3	珪 6.4	理 7.1	球 7.2	琅 4f9.1	琢 4f8.1	現 7.3	琉 7.5	望 7.6	琢 8.1	琳 8.2
斑 8.3	瑛 8.6	琶 8.9	琵 8.10	琴 8.11	瑚 9.3	瑤 9.5	瑞 9.6	聖 9.9	瑠 10.3	瑤 4f9.5	璃 10.5	瑳 10.6
對 2j5.5	業 0a13.3	瑠 4f10.3	璠 4f10.3	躬 12.2	環 13.1	璧 13.2	璽 14.2					

0

4f0.1 / 294

口 王
46

王

王 王

Ō king **Wang** (Chinese surname)

— 1 —

2 王子 **ōji** prince

3 王女 **ōjo** princess

7 王位 **ōi** the throne, the crown

8 王国 **ōkoku** kingdom, monarchy

9 王政 **ōsei** imperial rule, monarchy

10 王座 **ōza** the throne, the crown

12 王朝 **ōchō** dynasty

14 王様 **ōsama** king

— 2 —

3 女王 **joō** queen

8 法王 **hōō** the pope

法王庁 **Hōōchō** the Vatican

9 帝王 **teiō** monarch, emperor

帝王切開 **teiō sekkai** Caesarean section

4f0.2 / 295

⊡ 王 丨
46 2

玉

玉 玉

GYOKU gem, jewel **tama** ball

— 1 —

2 玉子 **tamago** egg

9 玉砕 **gyokusai** death for honor

─────────── 2 ───────────

4 水玉 **mizutama** drop of water/dew; polka dots

7 肝玉 **kimo(t)tama** pluck, courage, grit

11 埼玉県 **Saitama-ken** (prefecture)

12 替玉 **ka(e)dama** substitute, stand-in, ringer

─────────── 1 ───────────

4f1.1 / 155

□ 王 丨
46 2

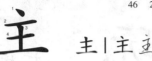

SHU, SU, SHŪ master, Lord, the main thing **nushi** owner; master **omo** main, principal **aruji** master KAZU (part of given name)

─────────── 1 ───────────

0 主として **shu (to shite)** mainly, chiefly

2 主人 **shujin** master; one's husband
主人公 **shujinkō** main character, hero (of a story)

6 主任 **shunin** person in charge
主因 **shuin** main cause, primary factor
主旨 **shushi** gist, purport, object

7 主位 **shui** leading position, first place
主体 **shutai** the subject; main part
主役 **shuyaku** major role; star

9 主要 **shuyō** main, principal, essential, key

10 主将 **shushō** commander-in-chief; captain (of a team)
主部 **shubu** main part; subject (in grammar)
主流 **shuryū** mainstream
主宰者 **shusaisha** president, chairman
主席 **shuseki** top place, first, head, chairman

11 主唱 **shushō** advocate, promote, suggest
主婦 **shufu** housewife

主張 **shuchō** assertion, contention
主脳 **shunō** leader
主脳会談 **shunō kaidan** summit conference
主脳会議 **shunō kaigi** summit conference

13 主催 **shusai** sponsor, promote
主義 **shugi** -ism, principle
主義者 **shugisha** -ist, advocate (of a theory/doctrine)

14 主演 **shuen** starring
主導 **shudō** leadership
主導権 **shudōken** leadership
主語 **shugo** subject (in grammar)

15 主潮 **shuchō** the main current
主賓 **shuhin** guest of honor
主権 **shuken** sovereignty
主権者 **shukensha** sovereign, supreme ruler

16 主謀者 **shubōsha** (ring)leader, mastermind

18 主観 **shukan** subjectivity; subject, ego
主観的 **shukanteki** subjective
主題 **shudai** theme, subject matter

─────────── 2 ───────────

5 民主主義 **minshu shugi** democracy

6 地主 **jinushi** landlord
自主 **jishu** independent, autonomous

7 坊主 **bōzu** Buddhist priest, bonze; shaven head; boy, rascal
坊主頭 **bōzuatama** shaven/close-cropped head
君主国 **kunshukoku** a monarchy

9 亭主 **teishu** husband; master, host
持主 **mo(chi)nushi** owner, possessor
神主 **kannushi** Shinto priest

10 借主 **ka(ri)nushi** borrower, renter
家主 **yanushi, ienushi** house-owner, landlord
株主 **kabunushi** shareholder, stockholder

12 落主 **o(toshi)nushi** owner of a lost/found article
雇主 **yato(i)nushi** employer
貸主 **ka(shi)nushi** lender; landlord

13 飼主 **ka(i)nushi** (pet) owner, master
18 藩主 **hanshu** lord of a feudal clan

――――――― 3 ―――――――

3 大株主 **ōkabunushi** large shareholder
丸坊主 **marubōzu** close-cropped,
shaven (head)
5 民本主義 **minpon shugi** democracy
民主主義 **minshu shugi** democracy
世帯主 **setainushi** head of a household
6 共産主義 **kyōsan shugi** communism
自然主義 **shizen shugi** naturalism
7 社会主義 **shakai shugi** socialism
8 国家主義 **kokka shugi** nationalism
9 軍国主義 **gunkoku shugi** militarism
帝国主義 **teikoku shugi** imperialism
10 根本主義 **konpon shugi** fundamentalism
11 理想主義 **risō shugi** idealism
13 資本主義 **shihon shugi** capitalism

――――――― 4 ―――――――

3 三日坊主 **mikka bōzu** one who can
stick to nothing, "three-day
monk"
7 社会民主主義 **shakai minshu
shugi** social democracy

――――――― 5 ―――――――

7 社会民主主義 **shakai minshu
shugi** social democracy

玉 → 4f0.2

――――――― 2 ―――――――

全 → 全 2a4.16

――――――― 3 ―――――――

4f3.1 / 2156　　　田 王 宀 丨
　　　　　　　　　46 15 2

玖

玖玖

KYŪ beautiful black jewel; nine
KYŪ, KU, KI, HISA, TAMA (part of giv-
en name)

4f3.2　　　田 王 艹
　　　　　　46 32

弄

弄弄

RŌ, iji(ru), iji(kuru), moteaso(bu)
play/trifle/tamper with

――――――― 2 ―――――――

15 嘲弄 **chōrō** ridicule

――――――― 4 ―――――――

4f4.1　　　田 王 二 几
　　　　　　46 4 16

玩

玩玩

GAN, moteaso(bu) play/toy/trifle with

――――――― 1 ―――――――

8 玩具 **gangu, omocha** toy
玩具屋 **omochaya** toy shop

――――――― 5 ―――――――

4f5.1　　　田 王 艹 冂
　　　　　　46 32 20

珊

珊珊

SAN coral; jingling, rustling

――――――― 1 ―――――――

13 珊瑚礁 **sangoshō** coral reef

珪 → 4f6.4

4f5.6 / 1215　　　田 王 彡 亻
　　　　　　　　46 31 3

珍

珎丨珍珍

CHIN rare, strange, curious
mezura(shii) new, novel; rare, unusual

――――――― 1 ―――――――

9 珍重 **chinchō** value highly, prize
珍品 **chinpin** rare article, curio

¹⁰ 珍書 **chinsho** rare book

珍 → 珍 **4f5.6**

4f5.7 / 2157   ⊞ 王 亻 一
                           46 3 1

玲 玲

REI sound of jewels, tinkling; clear, brilliant REI, RE, RYŌ, RŌ, TAMA, AKI (part of given name) AKIRA (m. given name)

4f5.9 / 297   目 日 王 丨
                          43 46 2

皇 皇

KŌ, Ō emperor

――――― 1 ―――――

⁴ 皇太子 **kōtaishi** crown prince
  皇太后 **kōtaikō, kōtaigō** empress dowager, queen mother
⁶ 皇后 **kōgō** empress, queen
  皇后陛下 **Kōgō Heika** Her Majesty the Empress
⁹ 皇帝 **kōtei** emperor
  皇室 **Kōshitsu** the Imperial Household, the reigning line
¹¹ 皇族 **kōzoku** (member of) the imperial family

――――― 2 ―――――

⁴ 天皇 **tennō** Emperor of Japan
  天皇陛下 **Tennō Heika** His Majesty the Emperor
¹⁰ 教皇庁 **Kyōkōchō** the Vatican

――――― 6 ―――――

4f6.2 / 1504   ⊞ 王 牛 儿
                          46 47 16

珠 珠

SHU, JU, tama gem, jewel
TAMA (part of given name)

¹⁴ 珠算 **shuzan** calculation on the abacus

4f6.3 / 1381   ⊞ 王 儿
                           46 16

班 班

HAN squad, corps, group

――――― 1 ―――――

⁸ 班長 **hanchō** group leader
⁹ 班点 **hanten** spot, dot, fleck, speck

――――― 2 ―――――

⁹ 首班 **shuhan** head, leader

――――― 3 ―――――

¹¹ 救護班 **kyūgohan** relief squad, rescue party

4f6.4   ⊞ 王 土
                   46 22

珪 硅丨珪 珪

KEI silicon

――――― 7 ―――――

4f7.1 / 143   ⊞ 王 日 土
                          46 43 22

理 理

RI reason, justice, truth, principle
kotowari reason OSAMU (m. given name) RI, MASA, MICHI (part of given name)

――――― 1 ―――――

⁵ 理由 **riyū** reason, cause
  理外 **rigai** transcendental, supernatural
⁷ 理沙 **Risa** (f. given name)
  理学 **rigaku** physical sciences, science
⁸ 理事 **riji** director, trustee

4

木 月 日 火 礻 王 牛 方 攵 欠 心 戸 戈

7

理事会 **rijikai** board of directors/ trustees

理事長 **rijichō** chairman, president

理念 **rinen** idea, doctrine, ideology

理屈 **rikutsu** theory; reason, logic; argument; pretext

理性 **risei** reason, reasoning power

10 理恵 **Rie** (f. given name)

13 理解 **rikai** understand, comprehend

理想 **risō** ideal

理想主義 **risō shugi** idealism

理想的 **risōteki** ideal

理想家 **risōka** idealist

14 理髪店 **rihatsuten** barbershop

理髪師 **rihatsushi** barber, hairdresser

15 理論 **riron** theory

──────── 2 ────────

1 一理 **ichiri** a principle, a reason

4 心理 **shinri** mental state, psychology

心理学 **shinrigaku** psychology

5 生理 **seiri** physiology; menstruation

弁理士 **benrishi** patent attorney

代理人 **dairinin** agent, proxy, substitute, representative

代理店 **dairiten** agent, agency

処理 **shori** treat, manage, deal with

6 合理化 **gōrika** rationalization, streamlining

合理的 **gōriteki** rational, reasonable, logical

地理 **chiri** geography

8 受理 **juri** accept

法理学 **hōrigaku** jurisprudence

物理学 **butsurigaku** physics

9 計理士 **keirishi** public accountant

10 修理 **shūri** repair

倫理 **rinri** ethics, morals

真理 **shinri** truth

真理 **Mari, Makoto, Masayoshi** (given name)

病理学 **byōrigaku** pathology

料理 **ryōri** cooking, cuisine; dish, food

料理人 **ryōrinin** a cook

料理屋 **ryōriya** restaurant

11 道理 **dōri, kotowari** reason, right, truth

推理 **suiri** reasoning, inference

推理小説 **suiri shōsetsu** detective story, whodunit

経理士 **keirishi** public accountant

12 無理 **muri** unreasonable; impossible, beyond one's power, too difficult; by force, against one's will; strain oneself

無理矢理 **muriyari** forcibly, under compulsion

税理士 **zeirishi** tax accountant

13 義理 **giri** sense of duty/honor, decency, courtesy, debt of gratitude

義理人情 **giri-ninjō** duty versus/ and human feelings

14 総理大臣 **sōri daijin** prime minister

総理府 **sōrifu** Prime Minister's Office

管理 **kanri** administration, supervision, control, management

管理人 **kanrinin** manager, superintendent

15 論理 **ronri** logic

論理上 **ronrijō** logically (speaking)

調理 **chōri** cooking

16 整理 **seiri** arrangement, adjustment; liquidation, reorganization; retrenchment, curtailment

──────── 3 ────────

4 不合理 **fugōri** unreasonable, irrational

手料理 **teryōri** home cooking

8 非合理的 **higōriteki** unreasonable, irrational

13 節料理 **(o)sechi ryōri** New Year's foods

──────── 4 ────────

4 中華料理 **chūka ryōri** Chinese cooking/food

12 無理矢理 **muriyari** forcibly, under compulsion

4f7.2 / 726 　　　口 王 氵 一
　　　　　　　　　46 21 1

KYŪ, tama ball, sphere, globe, bulb

――――――― 1 ―――――――

7 球技 **kyūgi** game in which a ball is used

球形 **kyūkei** spherical, globular

12 球場 **kyūjō** baseball grounds/stadium

16 球磨川 **Kuma-gawa** (river, Kumamoto-ken)

――――――― 2 ―――――――

0 地球 **chikyū** earth, globe

地球儀 **chikyūgi** a globe of the world

8 卓球 **takkyū** table tennis, pingpong

11 野球 **yakyū** baseball

琉球 **Ryūkyū** the Ryukyu islands; (ancient kuni, Okinawa-ken)

13 電球 **denkyū** light bulb

――――――― 3 ―――――――

5 北半球 **kita hankyū** Northern Hemisphere

6 西半球 **nishi hankyū** Western Hemisphere

9 南半球 **minami hankyū** Southern Hemisphere

琢 → 琢 **4f8.1**

4f7.3 / 298 　　　口 貝 王
　　　　　　　　　68 46

GEN present, existing, actual
ara(wasu) show, indicate, express
ara(wareru) appear, emerge, be expressed **utsutsu** reality; consciousness; reverie, absent-mindedness

――――――― 1 ―――――――

5 現出 **genshutsu, ara(ware)de(ru)** appear, emerge

現世紀 **genseiki** this century

現代 **gendai** the present age, today, modern times

現代人 **gendaijin** people today

現代化 **gendaika** modernization

現代語 **gendaigo** modern language

現存 **genson, genzon** living, existing, extant

6 現地 **genchi** the actual place; on the scene, in the field, local

現在 **genzai** now, present, current; present tense; actually

現行犯 **genkōhan** crime/criminal witnessed in the act, flagrante delicto

7 現状 **genjō** present situation, current state of affairs

8 現実 **genjitsu** actuality, reality

現金 **genkin** cash

現金払 **genkinbara(i)** cash payment

9 現政府 **genseifu** the present government

12 現象 **genshō** phenomenon

現場 **genba, genjō** the actual spot; on the scene, at the site, in the field

14 現像 **genzō** developing (film)

18 現職 **genshoku** present post, incumbent

――――――― 2 ―――――――

5 出現 **shutsugen** appear, show up

6 再現 **saigen** reappearance, return; revival

8 非現実的 **higenjitsuteki** unrealistic

表現 **hyōgen** expression

実現 **jitsugen** come true, realize, materialize

9 発現 **hatsugen** revelation, manifestation

13 夢現 **yumeutsutsu** dream and reality; half-dreaming

4f7.5

田 王 宀 竹
46 11 17

琉琉

RYŪ, RU lapis lazuli

— 1 —

11 琉球 **Ryūkyū** the Ryukyu islands; (ancient kuni, Okinawa-ken)

4f7.6 / 673

田 王 夕 宀
46 30 11

望望

BŌ, MŌ hope, desire; look into the distance; full moon **nozo(mu)** desire, hope for; see, command a view of **nozo(mashii)** desirable, advisable **mochi** full NOZOMI (f. given name)

— 1 —

9 望通 **nozo(mi)dō(ri)** as desired
10 望郷 **bōkyō** homesickness, nostalgia
12 望遠鏡 **bōenkyō** telescope

— 2 —

3 大望 **taimō, taibō** ambition, aspirations
5 本望 **honmō** long-cherished desire; satisfaction
失望 **shitsubō** disappointment, despair
6 多望 **tabō** promising, with bright prospects
7 希望 **kibō** wish, hope, desire
志望 **shibō** desire, ambition, choice
9 要望 **yōbō** demand, cry for
待望 **taibō** wait for expectantly, hope for, look forward to
10 展望 **tenbō** view, outlook, prospects
11 宿望 **shukubō** long-cherished desire
欲望 **yokubō** desire, craving
眺望 **chōbō** a view (from a window)
12 絶望 **zetsubō** despair

13 羨望 **senbō** envy
19 願望 **ganbō, ganmō** wish, desire

— 8 —

4f8.1 / 2158

田 王 犭 匕
46 27 10

琢 | 琢琢

TAKU polish TAKU, TAKA, AYA, SHIGE (part of given name) MIGAKU, MIGAKI (m. given name)

4f8.2 / 2160

川 王 木
46 41

琳琳

RIN jewel; tinkling of jewelry
RIN (part of given name)

4f8.3

川 王 宀 十
46 11 12

斑斑

HAN spot **buchi, madara, hadara, fu** spots, patches, streaks, spotted, speckled, mottled, dappled **mura** unevenness, lack of uniformity; blotches, blemishes; capriciousness

— 1 —

9 斑点 **hanten** spot, speck

4f8.6 / 2159

田 王 艹 大
46 32 34

瑛瑛

EI sparkle of jewelry, crystal AKIRA (m. given name) EI, YŌ, TERU, AKI (part of given name)

4f8.9

田 王 尸 |
46 40 2

琵

琵 琶

HA lute

― 2 ―

12 琵琶 **biwa** lute
琵琶湖 **Biwa-ko** Lake Biwa

4f8.10

田 王 ヒ
46 13

琵

琵 琵

BI, HI lute

― 1 ―

12 琵琶 **biwa** lute
琵琶湖 **Biwa-ko** Lake Biwa

4f8.11 / 1251

田 王 イ 一
46 3 1

琴

琴 琴

KIN harp **koto** koto (the musical instrument)

― 1 ―

15 琴線 **kinsen** heartstrings

― 2 ―

14 竪琴 **tategoto** harp, lyre

― 9 ―

4f9.3 / 2161

⽥ 王 月 口
46 42 24

瑚

瑚 瑚

KO, GO coral; ancestral-offering receptacle　KO, GO (part of given name)

― 2 ―

9 珊瑚礁 **sangoshō** coral reef

4f9.5 / 2163

田 王 爫 山
46 35 36

瑤

瑤 | 瑤 瑤

YŌ (beautiful as a) jewel
YŌ, TAMA (part of given name)

4f9.6 / 2162

田 王 山 一
46 36 14

瑞

瑞 瑞

ZUI good omen; Switzerland; Sweden **mizu** good omen; young and fresh　ZUI, SUI, MIZU, TAMA, MITSU (part of given name)　MAKOTO, YUTAKA (m. given name)

4f9.9 / 674

田 耳 王 口
65 46 24

聖

聖 | 聖 聖

SEI, SHŌ holy, sacred; saint, sage
hijiri emperor; sage; saint; master
KIYOSHI (m. given name)　SEI, SHŌ, KIYO, MASA (part of given name)

― 1 ―

2 聖人 **seijin** sage, saint, holy man
　聖子 **Seiko, Kiyoko, Satoko, Shōko** (f. given name)
4 聖日 **seijitsu** holy day; the Sabbath
5 聖母 **Seibo** the Holy Mother
6 聖地 **seichi** the Holy Land; sacred ground
8 聖夜 **seiya** Christmas Eve
　聖典 **seiten** sage's writings; holy book, scriptures
　聖金曜日 **Seikin'yōbi** Good Friday
10 聖哲 **seitetsu** sage, wise man
　聖書 **Seisho** the Bible
11 聖域 **seiiki** holy ground, sacred precincts
　聖堂 **seidō** Confucian temple; sanctuary, church

― 右欄外 ―

4

木 月 日 火 礻 王 牛 方 攵 欠 心 戸 戈

9

¹³ 聖戦 **seisen** holy war, crusade

¹⁴ 聖像 **seizō** sacred image, icon

聖誕祭 **Seitansai** Christmas

¹⁵ 聖霊 **Seirei** Holy Spirit

¹⁶ 聖賢 **seiken** sages, saints

¹⁸ 聖職 **seishoku** ministry, clergy, holy orders

— 2 —

⁹ 神聖 **shinsei** holy; sanctity, dignity

— 10 —

4f10.3 / 2165   田 甲 王 厂
                 58 46 18

瑠   瑠 | 瑠瑠

RU lapis lazuli RU, RYŪ (part of given name)

— 1 —

¹⁴ 瑠璃色 **ruri-iro** sky blue, azure

— 9 —

⁹ 浄瑠璃 **jōruri** (type of ballad-drama)

瑤 → 瑶 4f9.5

4f10.5 / 2166   田 王 宀 冂
                 46 11 20

璃   璃璃

RI lapis lazuli RI, AKI (part of given name)

— 2 —

¹⁴ 瑠璃色 **ruri-iro** sky blue, azure

— 3 —

⁹ 浄瑠璃 **jōruri** (type of ballad-drama)

4f10.6 / 2164   ⼞ 王 工 儿
                 46 38 16

瑳   瑳瑳

SA polish SA (part of given name)

對 → 対 2j5.5

業 → 0a13.3

— 11 —

瑠 → 4f10.3

— 12 —

璢 → 瑠 4f10.3

4f12.2   田 月 王 大
                 42 46 34

躾   躾躾

shitsuke teaching manners, upbringing, discipline **shitsu(keru)** teach manners, rear, train

— 2 —

⁴ 不躾 **bushitsuke** ill-breeding, bad manners

— 13 —

4f13.1 / 865   田 目 衣 王
                55 57 46

環   環 | 環環

KAN, wa, tamaki ring, circle, loop TAMAKI (f. given name) TAMA (part of given name)

— 1 —

⁷ 環状線 **kanjōsen** loop/belt line

¹⁴ 環境 **kankyō** environment

環境庁 **Kankyōchō** Environment Agency

¹² 循環 **junkan** circulation, cycle

¹¹ 悪循環 **akujunkan** vicious cycle/ spiral

4f13.2 　　　田 立 王 尸
　　　　　　54 46 40

璧

璧 璧

HEKI, tama pierced jewel-disk, jewel; splendid

⁷ 完璧 **kanpeki** perfect, flawless

4f14.2 / 1887 　　　日 雫 王 儿
　　　　　　　75 46 16

璽

璽 璽

JI imperial seal

牛 4g

牛 生 牝 牟 告 牧 物 牲 特 解 犠 犠
0.1 0a5.29 2.1 2.2 3d4.18 4.1 4.2 5.1 6.1 9.1 13.1 4g13.1

4g0.1 / 281 　　　口 牛
　　　　　　　47

牛

牛 牛

GYŪ, GO, ushi cow, bull, ox, cattle

⁶ 牛肉 **gyūniku** beef
⁷ 牛乳 **gyūnyū** (cow's) milk

⁷ 牡牛座 **Oushiza** (the constellation) Taurus
¹⁸ 闘牛士 **tōgyūshi** matador, bull- fighter

生 → 　**0a5.29**

4g2.1 　　　口 牛 ┝
　　　　　　47 13

牝

牝 牝

HIN, mesu, men, me- female

⁴ 牝犬 **mesu inu, meinu** female dog, bitch
⁷ 牝牡 **mesu-osu** male and female

4g2.2 　　　日 牛 竹
　　　　　　47 17

牟

牟 牟

MU, BŌ mooing of a cow; greedy, gluttonous; barley

⁴ 牡牛座 **Oushiza** (the constellation) Taurus
²⁰ 牡蠣 **kaki** oyster

⁶ 牝牡 **mesu-osu** male and female

告 → 　**3d4.18**

4g4.1 / 731 　　　口 牛 攵
　　　　　　　47 49

牧

牧 牧

— 1 —

6 牧地 **bokuchi** grazing land, pasture
9 牧草 **bokusō** grass, pasturage, meadow
10 牧畜 **bokuchiku** livestock/cattle raising
牧師 **bokushi** pastor, minister
11 牧野 **Makino** (surname)
12 牧場 **bokujō, makiba** pasture, meadow, ranch

4g4.2 / 79

□ 牛 犭
47 27

物物

BUTSU, MOTSU, mono thing, object

— 1 —

5 物好 **monozu(ki)** curious, whimsical, eccentric
6 物件 **bukken** thing, article, physical object, a property
7 物体 **buttai** body, object, substance
物忘 **monowasu(re)** forgetfulness
物売 **monou(ri)** peddler
8 物事 **monogoto** things, matters
物価 **bukka** (commodity) prices
物知 **monoshi(ri)** knowledgeable, erudite
物知顔 **monoshi(ri)gao** knowing look
物的 **butteki** material, physical
9 物指 **monosa(shi)** ruler, measure, yardstick
物品 **buppin** goods, article, commodity
物柔 **monoyawa(raka)** mild, gentle, suave
10 物陰 **monokage** cover, hiding; a form, shape
物差 **monosa(shi)** ruler, measure, yardstick
11 物理学 **butsurigaku** physics
物産 **bussan** products, produce, commodities
13 物置 **monoo(ki)** storeroom, shed
物資 **busshi** goods, resources
14 物語 **monogatari** tale, story

15 物影 **monokage** a form, shape
物憂 **monou(i)** languid, weary, dull
物質的 **busshitsuteki** material, physical

— 2 —

1 一物 **ichimotsu** an article, a thing; ulterior motive, designs
2 入物 **i(re)mono** receptacle, container
人物 **jinbutsu** person; one's character; character (in a story); man of ability
3 万物 **banbutsu, banmotsu** all things, all creation
大物 **ōmono** big thing; great man, big shot; big game
刃物 **hamono** edged tool, cutlery
干物 **himono** dried fish
ho(shi)mono laundry (hung up) to be dried
4 化物 **ba(ke)mono** ghost, spook
反物 **tanmono** dry/piece goods, textiles
5 出物 **demono** rash, boil; secondhand article **da(shi)mono** performance, program
本物 **honmono** genuine article, the real thing
生物 **seibutsu, i(ki)mono** living creature, life **namamono** uncooked food, unbaked cake
古物 **furumono, kobutsu** old things, secondhand goods, curios, antiques
比物 **kura(be)mono** comparison, match
汁物 **shirumono** soups
好物 **kōbutsu** a favorite food
冬物 **fuyumono** winter clothing
6 汚物 **obutsu** dirt, filth; sewage **yogo(re)mono** soiled things, the wash/laundry
吸物 **su(i)mono** soup
名物 **meibutsu** noted product (of a locality)
安物 **yasumono** cheap goods
7 忘物 **wasu(re)mono** something forgotten

見物 **kenbutsu** sightseeing
mimono a sight, spectacle, attraction

8 果物 **kudamono** fruit

事物 **jibutsu** things, affairs

供物 **kumotsu, sona(e)mono** votive offering

建物 **tatemono** a building

拵物 **koshira(e)mono** imitation, fake

呼物 **yo(bi)mono** attraction, feature, main event

宝物 **takaramono, hōmotsu** treasure

実物 **jitsubutsu** the real thing, the original

実物大 **jitsubutsudai** actual size

青物 **aomono** green vegetables

青物屋 **aomonoya** vegetable store, greengrocer

9 巻物 **ma(ki)mono** scroll

乗物 **no(ri)mono** vehicle

俗物 **zokubutsu** worldly-minded person, person of vulgar tastes

拾物 **hiro(i)mono** something picked up, a find; a bargain

品物 **shinamono** goods, merchandise

施物 **hodoko(shi)mono** alms, charity

食物 **ta(be)mono, shokumotsu, ku(i)mono** food
ku(wase)mono a fake; imposter

10 残物 **zanbutsu, noko(ri)mono** remnants, scraps, leftovers

進物 **shinmotsu** present, gift

荷物 **nimotsu** baggage; load

書物 **shomotsu** books

夏物 **natsumono** summer clothing

11 偽物 **gibutsu, nisemono** a counterfeit/fake

動物 **dōbutsu** animal

動物園 **dōbutsuen** zoo

唯物論 **yuibutsuron** materialism

乾物 **kanbutsu** dry provisions, groceries

産物 **sanbutsu** product

疵物 **kizumono** defective article; deflowered girl

貨物 **kamotsu** freight, cargo

貨物船 **kamotsusen** freighter

12 割物 **wa(re)mono** broken article; fragile article

博物館 **hakubutsukan** museum

着物 **kimono** clothes, kimono

揚物 **a(ge)mono** fried food

尋物 **tazu(ne)mono** thing being searched for, lost article

落物 **o(toshi)mono** lost article

廃物 **haibutsu** waste, refuse, scrap

廃物利用 **haibutsu riyō** recycling

植物 **shokubutsu** plant

植物園 **shokubutsuen** botanical garden

買物 **ka(i)mono** shopping, purchase

貰物 **mora(i)mono** present, gift

酢物 **su(no)mono** vinegared dish

飲物 **no(mi)mono** (something to) drink, beverage

13 催物 **moyō(shi)mono** public event, show

塗物 **nu(ri)mono** lacquerware

禁物 **kinmotsu** forbidden things, taboo

置物 **o(ki)mono** ornament; figurehead

鉱物 **kōbutsu** mineral

14 漬物 **tsukemono** pickled vegetables

穀物 **kokumotsu** grain

読物 **yo(mi)mono** reading matter

15 履物 **ha(ki)mono** footwear

敷物 **shikimono** carpet, rug, cushion

編物 **a(mi)mono** knitting; knitted goods

縫物 **nu(i)mono** sewing, needlework

調物 **shira(be)mono** matter for inquiry

賜物 **tamamono** gift

鋳物 **imono** article of cast metal, a casting

16 獲物 **emono** game, a catch, spoils

薬物 **yakubutsu** medicines, drugs

憑物 **tsu(ki)mono** possessing spirit, curse, obsession

4

木
月
日
火
ネ
王
牛
方
攵
欠
心
戸
戈

4

17 鍋物 **nabemono** food served in the pot

18 儲物 **mō(ke)mono** good bargain, windfall

織物 **orimono** cloth, fabric, textiles

織物業 **orimonogyō** the textile business

贈物 **oku(ri)mono** gift, present

19 贋物 **ganbutsu, nisemono** imitation, counterfeit, forgery

————— 3 —————

1 一人物 **ichijinbutsu** a person of consequence

3 大人物 **daijinbutsu** great man

4 水産物 **suisanbutsu** marine products

手荷物 **tenimotsu** luggage, (hand) baggage

5 生産物 **seisanbutsu** product, produce

古生物学 **koseibutsugaku** paleontology

6 危険物 **kikenbutsu** hazardous articles, explosives and combustibles

有価物 **yūkabutsu** valuables

7 夾雑物 **kyōzatsubutsu** admixture, impurities

抗生物質 **kōsei busshitsu** an antibiotic

投射物 **tōshabutsu** projectile

見世物 **misemono** show, exhibition

私有物 **shiyūbutsu** private property

8 建造物 **kenzōbutsu** a building, structure

抵当物 **teitōbutsu** security, pawn, collateral

青果物 **seikabutsu** vegetables and fruits

9 海産物 **kaisanbutsu** marine products

拾得物 **shūtokubutsu** found article

10 耕作物 **kōsakubutsu** farm products

特産物 **tokusanbutsu** special product (of a locality), indigenous to

11 副産物 **fukusanbutsu** by-product

添加物 **tenkabutsu** additives

掘出物 **ho(ri)da(shi)mono** treasure trove; lucky find, bargain

12 廃棄物 **haikibutsu** waste matter, wastes

絵巻物 **emakimono** picture scroll

飲食物 **inshokubutsu** food and drink

13 障害物 **shōgaibutsu** obstacle, obstruction

農産物 **nōsanbutsu** agricultural products

源氏物語 **Genji Monogatari** The Tale of Genji

微生物 **biseibutsu** microorganism, microbe

絹織物 **kinuorimono** silk fabrics

14 綿織物 **men'orimono** cotton goods

19 瀬戸物 **setomono** porcelain, china, earthenware

————— 4 —————

10 哺乳動物 **honyū dōbutsu** mammal

————— 5 —————

4g5.1 / 729 　　　田 牜 一
　　　　　　　　　47　1

牲 牲牲

SEI, nie sacrifice, offering

————— 2 —————

17 犠牲 **gisei** sacrifice

犠牲者 **giseisha** victim

————— 6 —————

4g6.1 / 282 　　　田 牜 土 寸
　　　　　　　　47 22 37

特 特特

TOKU special

————— 1 —————

3 特大 **tokudai** extra large

6 特色 **tokushoku** characteristic, distinguishing feature, peculiarity

特有 **tokuyū** characteristic of, peculiar to

7 特別 **tokubetsu** special, extraordinary

特売 **tokubai** special sale

8 特長 **tokuchō** distinctive feature, characteristic; strong point, forte, merit

特価 **tokka** special/reduced price

特例 **tokurei** special case, exception

特定 **tokutei** specify

特性 **tokusei** distinctive quality, characteristic, trait

9 特点 **tokuten** special favor, privilege

特急 **tokkyū** limited express (train)

特派員 **tokuhain** (news) correspondent; delegate

10 特殊 **tokushu** special

11 特産物 **tokusanbutsu** special product (of a locality), indigenous to

特異 **tokui** singular, peculiar, unique

特許 **tokkyo** patent; special permission

特許庁 **Tokkyochō** Patent Office

特許品 **tokkyohin** patented article

12 特集 **tokushū** special edition/collection

14 特選 **tokusen** specially selected

特徴 **tokuchō** distinctive feature, characteristic

特種 **tokudane** exclusive news, scoop **tokushu** special kind/type

特製 **tokusei** special make, deluxe

15 特権 **tokken** privilege, prerogative; option (to buy)

特質 **tokushitsu** characteristic, trait

———— 2 ————

9 独特 **dokutoku** unique, peculiar to

———— 9 ————

4g9.1 / 474   田 月 牛 宀
               42 47 15

解   解 解 解

KAI, GE explanation, solution

to(ku) untie, loosen, unravel; cancel,

release **to(kasu)** comb **to(keru)** come loose; be solved **hodo(ku)** untie **hodo(keru)** come untied **waka(ru)** understand

———— 1 ————

6 解任 **kainin** dismissal, release

7 解体 **kaitai** dismantle

解決 **kaiketsu** solution, settlement

8 解放 **kaihō, to(ki)hana(tsu)** liberate, release, set free

9 解除 **kaijo** cancel, rescind; release from

解約 **kaiyaku** cancellation of a contract

10 解剖 **kaibō** dissection, autopsy; analysis

解消 **kaishō** dissolution, liquidation; annulment; be settled/solved

11 解釈 **kaishaku** interpretation, elucidation

12 解散 **kaisan** disperse, break up, disband, dissolve

解雇 **kaiko** discharge, dismissal

解答 **kaitō** answer, solution

13 解禁 **kaikin** lifting a ban, open season

14 解読 **kaidoku** decipher, decrypt

解説 **kaisetsu** explanation, commentary

———— 2 ————

1 了解 **ryōkai** understand, comprehend; Roger!

4 分解 **bunkai** analysis, breakdown, decomposition, disassembly, disintegration

5 未解決 **mikaiketsu** unsolved, unsettled

弁解 **benkai** explanation, vindication, justification, defense, excuse, apology

氷解 **hyōkai** thaw, melt away, be dispelled

打解 **u(chi)to(keru)** open one's heart, be frank

6 曲解 **kyokkai** strained interpretation, distortion

7 図解 **zukai** explanatory diagram, illustration

見解 **kenkai** opinion, view

8 例解 **reikai** example, illustration

明解 **meikai** clear (explanation)

和解 **wakai** amicable settlement, compromise

11 理解 **rikai** understand, comprehend

12 註解 **chūkai** notes, commentary

13 溶解 **yōkai** (intr.) melt, dissolve

14 誤解 **gokai** misunderstanding

16 融解 **yūkai** fuse, melt, dissolve

18 鎔解 **yōkai** melt, fuse

— 3 —

4 不可解 **fukakai** mysterious, baffling

— 13 —

4g13.1 / 728

田 牜 王 戈
47 46 52

犧 犧|犧犧

GI sacrifice

— 1 —

9 犧牲 **gisei** sacrifice

犧牲者 **giseisha** victim

— 16 —

犧 → 犠 **4g13.1**

方 **4h**

方	放	於	施	旅	旋	族	旗
0.1	4.1	4.2	5.1	6.4	7.2	7.3	10.1

— 0 —

4h0.1 / 70

□ 方
48

方 方

HŌ direction, side; square **kata** person (polite); direction; (as verb suffix) way/method of …ing, how to …
masa (ni) precisely, indeed MASA, MICHI (part of given name)

— 1 —

3 方々 **katagata** people, ladies and gentlemen **hōbō** every direction

6 方向 **hōkō** direction

方式 **hōshiki** formula; form; method, system; formalities, usage

7 方言 **hōgen** dialect

8 方法 **hōhō** method, way, means

9 方面 **hōmen** direction; district; standpoint; aspect, phase

10 方案 **hōan** plan

方針 **hōshin** compass needle; course, policy

— 2 —

1 一方 **ippō** one side; on one hand, on the other hand; one party, the other party; nothing but, only **hitokata(narazu)** greatly, immensely

一方的 **ippōteki** one-sided, unilateral

一方通行 **ippō tsūkō** one-way traffic

2 二方 **futakata** both people

八方 **happō** all sides/directions

八方美人 **happō bijin** one who is affable to everybody

3 夕方 **yūgata** evening

大方 **ōkata** probably; almost, mostly; people in general

下方 **kahō** lower part, downward, below

4 双方 **sōhō** both parties/sides

片方 **katahō, katappō, katakata** one side/party, the other side/party

父方 **chichikata** on the father's side, paternal

5 北方 **hoppō** north, northward, northern

左方 **sahō** the left

母方 **hahakata** the mother's side (of the family)

仕方 **shikata** way, method, means, how to

他方 **tahō** another side/direction; on the other hand

平方 **heihō** square (of a number); square (meter)

正方形 **seihōkei** square

右方 **uhō** right side, the right

四方 **shihō, yomo** all (four) directions/sides

四方八方 **shihō-happō** in every direction, far and wide

立方 **rippō** cube (of a number), cubic (meter)

6 多方面 **tahōmen** various, different, many-sided, versatile

両方 **ryōhō** both

西方 **seihō** west, western, westward

考方 **kanga(e)kata** way of thinking, viewpoint

地方 **chihō** region, area **jikata** rural locality

行方不明 **yukue-fumei** missing

当方 **tōhō** I, we, on our part/side

各方面 **kaku hōmen** every direction, all quarters

7 作方 **tsuku(ri)kata** how to make; style of building, construction, workmanship

快方 **kaihō** recovery, convalescence

見方 **mikata** viewpoint, way of looking at

言方 **i(i)kata** way of saying

8 東方 **tōhō** east, eastward, eastern

使方 **tsuka(i)kata** how to use, management

味方 **mikata** friend, ally, supporter

9 南方 **nanpō** south, southern, southward

前方 **zenpō** front **maekata** before; immature

途方暮 **tohō (ni) ku(reru)** be at a loss, not know what to do

10 書方 **ka(ki)kata** how to write; penmanship

教方 **oshi(e)kata** teaching method

致方無 **ita(shi)kata (ga) na(i)** it can't be helped

12 遣方 **ya(ri)kata** way of doing, method

遠方 **enpō** great distance, long way, far-off

貴方 **kihō, anata** you

13 漢方 **kanpō** Chinese herbal medicine

漢方薬 **kanpōyaku** a herbal medicine

殿方 **tonogata** gentlemen, men's

話方 **hana(shi)kata** way of speaking

14 暮方 **ku(re)gata** dusk, evening **ku(rashi)kata** manner of living

綴方 **tsuzu(ri)kata** spelling; composition, theme **to(ji)kata** binding

読方 **yo(mi)kata** reading, pronunciation (of a character)

16 薬方 **yakuhō** prescription

——————— 4 ———————

4 中国地方 **Chūgoku chihō** the Chūgoku region (Hiroshima, Okayama, Shimane, Tottori, and Yamaguchi prefectures)

5 北陸地方 **Hokuriku chihō** the Hokuriku region (Fukui, Ishikawa, Toyama, Niigata prefectures)

四方八方 **shihō-happō** in every direction, far and wide

——————— 4 ———————

4h4.1 / 512   方 攵
                   48 49

HŌ, hana(tsu) set free, release; fire (a gun); emit **hana(su)** set free, release, let go **hana(reru)** get free of **hō(ru)** throw; leave as is **ho(ttarakasu)** neglect, lay aside, leave undone

——————— 1 ———————

4 放水 **hōsui** drainage, discharge

放火 **hōka** arson

5 放出 **hōshutsu** release, discharge, emit **hō(ri)da(su)** throw out; expel; abandon

8 放送 **hōsō** broadcast

放送局 **hōsōkyoku** broadcasting station

10 放射 **hōsha** radiation, emission, discharge

放射能 **hōshanō** radioactivity, radiation

放射線 **hōshasen** radiation

放浪 **hōrō** wander, rove

放流 **hōryū** set adrift, discharge, stock (with fish)

13 放棄 **hōki** abandon, renounce, waive, forfeit

放置 **hōchi** let alone, leave as is, leave to chance

14 放漫 **hōman** lax, loose, reckless

15 放談 **hōdan** random/unreserved talk

18 放題 **-hōdai** (as verb suffix) as much as one pleases, all you can (eat)

——— 2 ———

4 手放 **tebana(su)** let go of, part with; leave unattended
tebana(shi) without holding on to, left unattended; unreservedly

5 生放送 **namahōsō** live broadcast

仕放題 **shihōdai** have one's own way

6 再放送 **saihōsō** rebroadcast

8 追放 **tsuihō** banishment; purge

9 食放題 **ta(be)hōdai, ku(i)hōdai** eating as much as one pleases, all-you-can-eat

11 野放 **nobana(shi)** putting to pasture; leaving things to themselves

釈放 **shakuhō** release, discharge

12 開放 **kaihō, a(ke)hana(su)** (fling/leave) open
a(kep)pana(shi) left open; open, frank

13 解放 **kaihō, to(ki)hana(tsu)** liberate, release, set free

——— 3 ———

6 仮釈放 **karishakuhō** release on parole

4h4.2 / 2084

O, (ni) oi(te) at, in, on, as for, as to **(ni) o(keru)** at, in **O** (part of given name)

——— 5 ———

4h5.1 / 1004

 施施

SHI, SE, hodoko(su) give, bestow; carry out, perform, conduct

——— 1 ———

6 施行 **shikō** enforce; put into operation

8 施物 **hodoko(shi)mono** alms, charity

9 施政 **shisei** administration, governing

11 施設 **shisetsu** facilities, institution

12 施策 **shisaku** a measure/policy

——— 2 ———

5 布施 **fuse** alms, charity
Fuse (city, Ōsaka-fu)

——— 6 ———

4h6.4 / 222

 旅旅

RYO, tabi trip, travel, journey

——— 1 ———

5 旅立 **tabida(tsu)** start on a journey

6 旅先 **tabisaki** destination

旅行 **ryokō** trip, travel

旅行者 **ryokōsha** traveler, tourist
8 旅券 **ryoken** passport
9 旅客機 **ryokakki** passenger plane
12 旅程 **ryotei** distance to be covered; itinerary
旅費 **ryohi** traveling expenses
16 旅館 **ryokan** inn, hotel

——————— 2 ———————

11 船旅 **funatabi** voyage

——————— 3 ———————

10 修学旅行 **shūgaku ryokō** school excursion, field trip
13 新婚旅行 **shinkon ryokō** honeymoon

═══════ **7** ═══════

4h7.2 / 1005   ⊞ 方 ⺉ ⼇
                         48 15 14

旋   旋 旋

SEN go around, revolve, rotate

——————— 1 ———————

6 旋回 **senkai** turning, revolving, circling
9 旋律 **senritsu** melody

——————— 2 ———————

8 周旋 **shūsen** good offices, recommendation, mediation
12 凱旋門 **gaisenmon** arch of triumph
14 斡旋 **assen** mediation, good offices, placement
17 螺旋 **rasen** spiral, helix
   neji screw; stopcock; (wind-up) spring

4h7.3 / 221   ⊞ 方 ⼤ ⼃
                         48 34 15

族   族 族

ZOKU family, tribe **yakara** family, relatives; fellows, gang

——————— 1 ———————

0 ながら族 **nagarazoku** those who do two things at once (eat/study while watching TV)
15 族縁 **zokuen** family ties

——————— 2 ———————

1 一族 **ichizoku** a family/household
4 水族館 **suizokukan** (public) aquarium
5 民族 **minzoku** race, a people
6 血族 **ketsuzoku** blood relative, kin
9 皇族 **kōzoku** (member of) the imperial family
10 部族 **buzoku** tribe
家族 **kazoku** family
家族連 **kazokuzu(re)** taking the family along
12 貴族 **kizoku** the nobility
14 遺族 **izoku** surviving family
閥族 **batsuzoku** clan, clique
16 親族 **shinzoku** relatives

——————— 3 ———————

13 漢民族 **Kan minzoku** the Han/Chinese people

——————— 4 ———————

6 先住民族 **senjū minzoku** aborigines

═══════ **10** ═══════

4h10.1 / 1006   ⊞ 方 ⾋ ⼇
                          48 32 15

旗   旗 旗

KI, hata flag, banner

——————— 1 ———————

4 旗手 **kishu** standardbearer

——————— 2 ———————

5 白旗 **shirahata, hakki** white flag (of truce/surrender)
8 国旗 **kokki** national flag

——————— 3 ———————

9 星条旗 **seijōki** the Stars and Stripes flag

4

木
月
日
火
⻂
王
牛
方 10
攵
欠
心
戸
戈

攵 **4i**

攷	冬	処	改	収	攻	各	条	麦	政	故	教	致
2k4.4	2.1	2.2	3.1	2h2.2	3.2	3.3	4.1	4.2	5.1	5.2	6.1	6.2

效	敏	敕	救	赦	敦	夏	敏	務	散	敬	敢	麥
2g6.2	6.3	2g7.1	7.1	7.3	7.4	7.5	4i6.3	7.6	8.1	8.4	8.5	4i4.2

数	愛	數	敷	敵	髪	弊	憂	整	麺	麵	變
9.1	10.1	4i9.1	11.1	11.2	3j11.3	11.3	12.1	12.3	4i17.1	17.1	2j7.3

4

木 月 日 火 礻 王 牛 方 攵 欠 心 戸 戈

2

——— 2 ———

攷 → 考 **2k4.4**

4i2.1 / 459

曰 攵 ｜
49   2

冬

冬 冬

TŌ, fuyu winter

——— 1 ———

6 冬休 **fuyuyasu(mi)** winter vacation

　冬至 **tōji** winter solstice

　冬向 **fuyumu(ki)** for winter

7 冬季 **tōki** winter(time), the winter season

8 冬空 **fuyuzora** winter sky

　冬服 **fuyufuku** winter clothing

　冬物 **fuyumono** winter clothing

10 冬眠 **tōmin** hibernation

12 冬期 **tōki** winter season, wintertime

——— 2 ———

10 真冬 **mafuyu** dead of winter, midwinter

13 暖冬 **dantō** warm/mild winter

——— 4 ———

9 春夏秋冬 **shun-ka-shū-tō** the four seasons, the year round

4i2.2 / 1137

口 攵 冂
49   20

処

處 ｜ 処 処

SHO manage, deal with; punish
tokoro place

——— 1 ———

3 処女作 **shojosaku** one's first (published) work

4 処分 **shobun** disposal, disposition; punishment

6 処刑 **shokei** punish, execute

11 処理 **shori** treat, manage, deal with

13 処置 **shochi** disposition, measures, steps

14 処罰 **shobatsu** punishment, penalty

——— 2 ———

5 出処 **shussho, dedokoro** source, origin

6 此処 **koko** here, this place

7 何処 **izuko, izuku, doko** where

　対処 **taisho** deal/cope with

——— 3 ———

4i3.1 / 514

口 攵 弓
49   28

改

改 改

KAI, arata(meru) alter, renew, reform **arata(mete)** anew; again, on another occasion **arata(maru)** be altered/renewed/corrected

——— 1 ———

4 改心 **kaishin** reform (oneself)

5 改正 **kaisei** revision, amendment; improvement

　改札口 **kaisatsuguchi** ticket gate, wicket

6 改名 **kaimei** changing one's/the name

7 改良 **kairyō** improvement, reform

8 改宗 **kaishū** conversion (to another religion)

9 改革 **kaikaku** reform, reorganization

改訂 **kaitei** revision

改訂版 **kaiteiban** revised edition

改訂増補 **kaitei-zōho** revised and enlarged

10 改修 **kaishū** repair, improvement

改進 **kaishin** reform, progress

改悟 **kaigo** repentance, remorse, contrition

改称 **kaishō** rename, retitle

11 改悪 **kaiaku** change for the worse, deterioration

12 改善 **kaizen** improvement

改装 **kaisō** remodel, refurbish

13 改新 **kaishin** renovation, reformation

14 改選 **kaisen** reelection

16 改築 **kaichiku** rebuild, remodel, alter

18 改題 **kaidai** retitle, rename

———— 2 ————

10 書改 **ka(ki)arata(meru)** rewrite

 収→収 **2h2.2**

4i3.2 / 819   ⊞ 攵 工   49 38

攻   攻攻

KŌ, se(meru) attack OSAMU (m. given name)

———— 1 ————

6 攻防 **kōbō** offense and defense

13 攻勢 **kōsei** the offensive

15 攻撃 **kōgeki** attack

———— 2 ————

4 反攻 **hankō** counteroffensive, counterattack

9 専攻 **senkō** academic specialty, one's major

4i3.3 / 642   ⊟ 攵 口   49 24

各   各各

KAKU, onoono each, every; various

———— 1 ————

3 各々 **onoono** each, every, respectively

4 各方面 **kaku hōmen** every direction, all quarters

6 各地 **kakuchi** every area; various places

各自 **kakuji** each person, everyone

8 各国 **kakkoku** all/various countries

各所 **kakusho** each place, various places

14 各種 **kakushu** every kind, various types

各駅停車 **kakuekiteisha** local train

15 各論 **kakuron** detailed discussion

———— 4 ————

4i4.1 / 564   ⊟ 攵 木   49 41

条   條|条糸

JŌ article, clause; line, stripe

———— 1 ————

4 条文 **jōbun** the text, provisions

5 条令 **jōrei** law, ordinance, rule, regulation

6 条件 **jōken** condition, stipulation

条件付 **jōkentsu(ki)** conditional

8 条例 **jōrei** regulation, law, ordinance, rule

9 条約 **jōyaku** treaty

12 条項 **jōkō** articles and paragraphs, stipulations

———— 2 ————

1 一条 **ichijō** a line/streak; a matter; a passage (from a book)

4

木 月 日 火 ネ 王 牛 方 攵 4 欠 心 戸 戈

9 星条旗 **seijōki** the Stars and Stripes flag
10 索条 **sakujō** cable, rope
12 無条件 **mujōken** unconditional
13 鉄条網 **tetsujōmō** barbed-wire entanglements
14 箇条 **kajō** article, provision, item

4i4.2 / 270 日 攵 土 一 49 22 1

BAKU, mugi wheat, barley, rye, oats

——————— 1 ———————
9 麦畑 **mugibatake** wheat field
10 麦粉 **mugiko** (wheat) flour
12 麦飯 **mugimeshi** boiled barley and rice

——————— 2 ———————
3 小麦 **komugi** wheat
15 蕎麦 **soba** buckwheat; buckwheat noodles

——————————— 5 ———————————

4i5.1 / 483 攵 工 一 49 38 1

SEI, SHŌ, matsurigoto government, rule MASA (part of given name)

——————— 1 ———————
5 政令 **seirei** government ordinance, cabinet order
政司 **Masashi, Masaji** (m. given name)
7 政体 **seitai** form/system of government
政局 **seikyoku** political situation
8 政況 **seikyō** political situation
政治 **seiji** politics
政治学 **seijigaku** political science
政治家 **seijika** politician
政府 **seifu** the government

政府筋 **seifusuji** government sources
10 政党 **seitō** political party
11 政務 **seimu** political/government affairs
政務次官 **seimu jikan** parliamentary vice-minister
政務官 **seimukan** parliamentary official
政略 **seiryaku** political strategy; expedient
政経学 **seikeigaku** politics and economics
12 政策 **seisaku** policy
15 政権 **seiken** political power, administration

——————— 2 ———————
4 内政 **naisei** domestic/internal affairs
王政 **ōsei** imperial rule, monarchy
5 民政 **minsei** civil/civilian government
失政 **shissei** misgovernment, misrule
6 地政学 **chiseigaku** geopolitics
行政 **gyōsei** administration
9 軍政 **gunsei** military government/administration
為政者 **iseisha** statesman, administrator
神政 **shinsei** theocracy
施政 **shisei** administration, governing
10 郵政省 **Yūseishō** Ministry of Posts and Telecommunications
家政婦 **kaseifu** housekeeper
財政 **zaisei** (public) finances
11 現政府 **genseifu** the present government
12 無政府 **museifu** anarchy
13 新政 **shinsei** new government/regime
16 憲政 **kensei** constitutional government

4i5.2 / 173   田 夂 口 十
                          49 24 12

故   故 故

KO old, former; deceased, (as prefix)
the late …; intentional; matter
yue reason, cause; circumstances
furu(i) old

— 1 —

0 それ故 **soreyue** therefore, hence,
that is why

8 故事 **koji** historical event

10 故郷 **kokyō, furusato** birthplace,
home town

13 故障 **koshō** out of order, breakdown, trouble, accident, hindrance, obstacle; objection

故意 **koi** intention, purpose

— 2 —

7 何故 **naze, naniyue** why

8 事故 **jiko** accident; unavoidable
circumstances

— 6 —

4i6.1 / 245   田 夂 土 子
                          49 22 6

教   敎 | 教 教

KYŌ teaching; religion
oshi(eru) teach **oshi(e)** a teaching,
precept **oso(waru)** be taught
NORI (part of given name)

— 1 —

4 教方 **oshi(e)kata** teaching method

5 教示 **kyōji** instruct, teach, enlighten

6 教会 **kyōkai** church

8 教育 **kyōiku** education

教育費 **kyōikuhi** school/education
expenses

9 教室 **kyōshitsu** classroom

教祖 **kyōso** founder of a sect

教皇庁 **Kyōkōchō** the Vatican

教科書 **kyōkasho** textbook

10 教唆 **kyōsa** instigate, abet

教員 **kyōin** teacher, instructor;
teaching staff

教師 **kyōshi** instructor, teacher

教徒 **kyōto** believer, adherent

教案 **kyōan** teaching/lesson plan

教訓 **kyōkun** lesson, precept,
moral

11 教授 **kyōju** professor; teaching

教務 **kyōmu** school/educational affairs

15 教養 **kyōyō** culture, education, refinement

16 教諭 **kyōyu** instructor, teacher

教頭 **kyōtō** head teacher

— 2 —

3 女教師 **jokyōshi** female teacher

4 仏教 **bukkyō** Buddhism

5 正教 **seikyō** orthodoxy; Greek Orthodox Church

示教 **shikyō** instruction, guidance

6 回教徒 **kaikyōto** a Moslem

7 邪教 **jakyō** heretical religion, heathenism

助教授 **jokyōju** assistant professor

8 宗教 **shūkyō** religion

9 信教 **shinkyō** religion, religious belief

宣教師 **senkyōshi** missionary

11 道教 **dōkyō** Taoism

密教 **mikkyō** esoteric Buddhism;
religious mysteries

異教 **ikyō** heathenism, paganism,
heresy

13 新教 **shinkyō** Protestantism

14 説教 **sekkyō** sermon

— 3 —

1 一神教 **isshinkyō** monotheism

6 名誉教授 **meiyo kyōju** professor
emeritus

10 家庭教師 **katei kyōshi** (private) tutor

— 4 —

3 大乗仏教 **Daijō Bukkyō** Mahayana Buddhism, Great-Vehicle
Buddhism

4

木
月
日
火
礻
王
牛
方
夂 6
欠
心
戸
戈

4i6.2 / 903

攵 土 竹
49 22 17

致致

CHI, ita(su) do (deferential); bring about, cause

——————— 1 ———————

⁴ 致方無 **ita(shi)kata (ga) na(i)** it can't be helped

⁶ 致死 **chishi** fatal, lethal, deadly, mortal

⁸ 致命的 **chimeiteki** fatal, lethal, deadly, mortal

致命傷 **chimeishō** fatal wound/injury

——————— 2 ———————

¹ 一致 **itchi** agree

⁶ 合致 **gatchi** agreement, concurrence, conforming to

⁹ 風致 **fūchi** taste, elegance; scenic beauty

——————— 3 ———————

⁴ 不一致 **fuitchi** disagreement, incompatibility

效 → 効 2g6.2

4i6.3 / 1735

攵 女 宀
49 25 15

敏|敏敏

BIN agile, alert SATOSHI (m. given name) TOSHI (part of given name)

——————— 1 ———————

⁸ 敏郎 **Toshirō, Toshio** (m. given name)

⁹ 敏速 **binsoku** promptness, alacrity

敏活 **binkatsu** quick, alert, active, agile

¹² 敏腕 **binwan** able, capable

¹³ 敏感 **binkan** sensitive

——————— 2 ———————

¹¹ 過敏 **kabin** oversensitive, nervous

¹⁵ 鋭敏 **eibin** sharp, keen, acute

¹⁶ 機敏 **kibin** astute, shrewd, quick

——————— 7 ———————

敕 → 勅 2g7.1

4i7.1 / 725

攵 氵 一
49 21 1

救救

KYŪ, suku(u) rescue, save, aid

——————— 1 ———————

⁵ 救出 **kyūshutsu** rescue **suku(i)da(su)** rescue from, help out of

⁷ 救助 **kyūjo** rescue, relief, aid

⁸ 救命 **kyūmei** lifesaving

⁹ 救急 **kyūkyū** emergency (relief)

救急車 **kyūkyūsha** ambulance

¹¹ 救済 **kyūsai** relief, aid; emancipation

救済策 **kyūsaisaku** relief measure

¹² 救援 **kyūen** relief, rescue

²⁰ 救護 **kyūgo** relief, aid, rescue

救護所 **kyūgosho** first-aid station

救護班 **kyūgohan** relief squad, rescue party

4i7.3 / 1570

攵 土 儿
49 22 16

赦赦

SHA, yuru(su) forgive, pardon

——————— 1 ———————

⁸ 赦免 **shamen** pardon, clemency

¹³ 赦罪 **shazai** pardon, absolution

——————— 2 ———————

³ 大赦 **taisha** amnesty; plenary indulgence

¹⁰ 容赦 **yōsha** mercy, pardon, forgiveness

恩赦 **onsha** amnesty, general pardon

4i7.4 / 2081 田 攵 口 亠
                  49 24 11

敦 敦

TON warm, kindly; work hard; big
TON, TAI, ATSU, TOSHI, TSURU, YOI
(part of given name) ATSUSHI, TSUTO-
MU, OSAMU (m. given name)

4i7.5 / 461 目 目 攵 亠
                55 49 14

夏 夏

KA, GE, natsu summer

───── 1 ─────

0 夏ばて **natsu(bate)** listlessness
    during hot summer weather

6 夏休 **natsuyasu(mi)** summer vaca-
    tion

夏至 **geshi** summer solstice

夏向 **natsumu(ki)** for summer

7 夏季 **kaki** summer(time), the sum-
    mer season

8 夏服 **natsufuku** summer clothes/
    wear

夏物 **natsumono** summer clothing

9 夏美 **Natsumi** (f. given name)

10 夏時間 **natsujikan** daylight-sav-
    ing time

12 夏場 **natsuba** summertime, the
    summer season

夏期 **kaki** the summer period

14 夏痩 **natsuya(se)** loss of weight in
    summer

───── 2 ─────

7 初夏 **shoka** early summer

9 春夏秋冬 **shun-ka-shū-tō** the four
    seasons, the year round

10 真夏 **manatsu** midsummer

敏 → 敏 4i6.3

4i7.6 / 235 田 攵 宀 力
                49 14 8

務 務

MU, tsuto(meru) work, serve
TSUTOMU (m. given name)

───── 2 ─────

3 工務店 **kōmuten** engineering firm

4 内務省 **Naimushō** (prewar) Minis-
    try of Home Affairs

公務員 **kōmuin** government em-
    ployee

5 外務 **gaimu** foreign affairs

外務大臣 **gaimu daijin** Minister of
    Foreign Affairs

外務省 **Gaimushō** Ministry of For-
    eign Affairs

6 任務 **ninmu** duty, task, function

刑務所 **keimusho** prison

8 事務 **jimu** business, clerical work

事務長官 **jimuchōkan** chief secre-
    tary

事務官 **jimukan** administrative of-
    ficial, secretary, commissioner

事務所 **jimusho** office

法務 **hōmu** legal/judicial affairs

法務省 **Hōmushō** Ministry of Jus-
    tice

国務 **kokumu** affairs of state

国務長官 **kokumu chōkan** (U.S.)
    Secretary of State

9 専務 **senmu** special duty; principal
    business; managing/executive
    (director)

乗務員 **jōmuin** train/plane crew

急務 **kyūmu** urgent business,
    pressing need

政務 **seimu** political/government
    affairs

政務次官 **seimu jikan** parliamen-
    tary vice-minister

政務官 **seimukan** parliamentary
    official

10 教務 **kyōmu** school/educational af-
    fairs

財務 **zaimu** financial affairs

11 商務 **shōmu** commercial affairs

4

木
月
日
火
礻
王
牛
方
攵 7
欠
心
戸
戈

常務 **jōmu** regular business, routine duties, executive (director)

庶務 **shomu** general affairs

責務 **sekimu** duty, obligation

12 勤務 **kinmu** service, work, duty

勤務先 **kinmusaki** place of employment, employer

税務署 **zeimusho** tax office

13 業務 **gyōmu** business, work, operations, duties

債務 **saimu** debt, liabilities

義務 **gimu** obligation, duty

義務的 **gimuteki** obligatory, compulsory

14 総務 **sōmu** general affairs; manager

総務長官 **sōmu chōkan** director-general

総務課 **sōmuka** general affairs section

——— 8 ———

4i8.1 / 767

田 夂 月 艹
49 42 32

SAN, chi(ru) scatter, (leaves) fall, disperse **chi(rasu)** scatter, strew **chi(rashi)** handbill **chi(rakasu)** scatter, disarrange **chi(rakaru)** lie scattered, be in disorder **chi(rabaru)** be scattered about

——— 1 ———

4 散文 **sanbun** prose

7 散乱 **sanran** dispersion, scattering **chi(ri)mida(reru)** be scattered about; be routed

8 散歩 **sanpo** walk, stroll

14 散髪 **sanpatsu** get/give a haircut; disheveled hair

——— 2 ———

4 分散 **bunsan** breakup, dispersion, variance

9 飛散 **hisan, to(bi)chi(ru)** scatter, disperse

発散 **hassan** give forth, emit, exhale, radiate, evaporate; divergent

10 書散 **ka(ki)chi(rasu)** scribble, scrawl

12 閑散 **kansan** leisure; (market) inactivity

13 解散 **kaisan** disperse, break up, disband, dissolve

15 撒散 **ma(ki)chi(rasu)** scatter about; squander

18 離散 **risan** scatter, disperse

19 蹴散 **kechi(rasu)** kick around, put to rout

4i8.4 / 705

田 夂 艹 口
49 32 24

KEI, KYŌ, uyama(u) respect, revere TAKASHI (m. given name) KEI, TAKA, NORI, HIRO, YUKI, YOSHI (part of given name)

——— 1 ———

2 敬子 **Keiko, Takako** (f. given name)

6 敬老 **keirō** respect for the aged

8 敬具 **keigu** Sincerely yours,

10 敬称 **keishō** honorific title

12 敬遠 **keien** keep (someone) at a respectful distance

13 敬愛 **keiai** love and respect, veneration

敬意 **keii** respect, homage

14 敬語 **keigo** an honorific, term of respect

——— 2 ———

12 尊敬 **sonkei** respect, esteem, honor

4i8.5 / 1691

田 耳 夂 一
65 49 14

KAN daring, bold **ae(te)** daringly, positively, venture to … **ae(nai)** sad, tragic, pitiful; frail, feeble; transitory ISAMU (m. given name)

— 2 —

9 勇敢 **yūkan** courageous, brave, heroic

麥 → 麦 **4i4.2**

— 9 —

4i9.1 / 225

田 半 夂 女
62 49 25

数

數 | 数 数

SŪ number; (as prefix) several, a number of **SU, kazu** number
kazo(eru) count

— 1 —

2 数人 **sūnin** several persons
数十 **sūjū** dozens/scores of
3 数万 **sūman** tens of thousands
数上 **kazo(e)a(geru)** count up, enumerate
数々 **kazukazu** many
4 数切 **kazo(e)kire(nai)** countless
数日 **sūjitsu** a few days, several days
5 数字 **sūji** digit, numeral, figures
6 数多 **kazuō(ku), amata** many, great numbers of
数年 **sūnen** several years
kazo(e)doshi one's calendar-year age (reckoned racehorse-style)
7 数学 **sūgaku** mathematics
9 数秒 **sūbyō** for several seconds
10 数倍 **sūbai** several times as (large), several-fold
12 数量 **sūryō** quantity
数詞 **sūshi** numeral, number word
13 数損 **kazo(e)soko(nau)** miscount

— 2 —

2 人数 **ninzū, ninzu, hitokazu** number of people
十数 **jūsū** ten-odd, a dozen or so
3 小数点 **shōsūten** decimal point
4 手数 **tesū** trouble, pains, care
tekazu trouble; number of moves (in a game)

手数料 **tesūryō** handling charge, fee
少数 **shōsū** few; minority
日数 **nissū, hikazu** number of days
戸数 **kosū** number of houses/households
6 多数 **tasū** a large number; majority
多数決 **tasūketsu** decision by the majority
全数 **zensū** the whole number, all
回数券 **kaisūken** (train) coupon tickets
有数 **yūsū** prominent, leading, top
8 画数 **kakusū** number of strokes (of a kanji)
坪数 **tsubosū** number of tsubo, area
奇数 **kisū** odd number
枚数 **maisū** number of sheets
9 点数 **tensū** points, marks, score
指数 **shisū** index (number); exponent
単数 **tansū** singular (not plural)
度数 **dosū** number of times/degrees
10 部数 **busū** number of copies, circulation
軒数 **kensū** number of houses
11 偶数 **gūsū** even number
票数 **hyōsū** number of votes
12 無数 **musū** innumerable, countless
14 複数 **fukusū** plural
総数 **sōsū** total (number)
算数 **sansū** arithmetic, math, calculation

— 3 —

3 大多数 **daitasū** the great majority
8 周波数 **shūhasū** frequency
11 過半数 **kahansū** majority, more than half

— 10 —

4i10.1 / 259

目 心 夂 小
51 49 35

AI love; (as prefix) beloved, favorite
me(deru) love; admire, appreciate
ito(shii) dear, beloved **mana-** beloved,

favorite MEGUMU (m. given name)
YOSHI (part of given name) AI (f. given name)

——————— 1 ———————
2 愛人 **aijin** lover
4 愛犬 **aiken** pet dog
5 愛好 **aikō** love, have a liking/taste for
7 愛児 **aiji** one's dear child
8 愛妻 **aisai** one's beloved wife
　愛国心 **aikokushin** patriotism
10 愛称 **aishō** term of endearment, pet name
11 愛情 **aijō** love, affection
12 愛着 **aichaku, aijaku** attachment, affection
　愛媛県 **Ehime-ken** (prefecture)
13 愛想 **aiso, aisō** amiability, sociability
14 愛慕 **aibo** love, attachment, yearning
　愛憎 **aizō** love and/or hate
　愛読 **aidoku** like to read
15 愛嬌 **aikyō** charm, winsomeness, attractiveness, courtesy

——————— 2 ———————
4 仁愛 **jin'ai** benevolence, charity, love
5 他愛 **taai** altruism
　可愛 **kawai(i)** cute, dear, sweet
6 自愛 **jiai** self-love, self-regard; selfishness
8 性愛 **seiai** sexual love
10 恋愛 **ren'ai** love
12 博愛 **hakuai** philanthropy
　敬愛 **keiai** love and respect, veneration
16 親愛 **shin'ai** affection, love; dear

——————— 3 ———————
6 同性愛 **dōseiai** homosexuality

——————— 11 ———————

數 → 数 4i9.1

4i11.1 / 1451　　　田 日 方 攵
　　　　　　　　　　43 48 49

敷　　　敷 敷

FU, shi(ku) spread, lay, put down

——————— 1 ———————
5 敷布 **shikifu** (bed) sheet
　敷布団 **shikibuton** floor mattress
8 敷物 **shikimono** carpet, rug, cushion
　敷金 **shikikin** (security) deposit
11 敷設 **fusetsu** lay (cable/mines), build (a railway/road) (also spelled 布設)

——————— 2 ———————
3 下敷 **shitaji(ki)** mat, desk pad; pinned under, crushed beneath; model, pattern
9 屋敷 **yashiki** mansion
10 座敷 **zashiki** room, drawing room

——————— 3 ———————
9 風呂敷 **furoshiki** (square of cloth used to wrap goods and presents in)

4i11.2 / 416　　　田 攵 口 亠
　　　　　　　　　　49 24 11

敵　　　敵 敵

TEKI enemy, competitor, opponent
kataki enemy, rival; revenge

——————— 1 ———————
0 敵する **teki(suru)** fight against, face, be a match for
7 敵対心 **tekitaishin** enmity, animosity
9 敵軍 **tekigun** enemy army, hostile forces
11 敵視 **tekishi** regard with hostility
13 敵意 **tekii** enmity, hostility, animosity

——————— 2 ———————
3 大敵 **taiteki** archenemy; formidable opponent

4 不敵 **futeki** bold, daring, fearless
天敵 **tenteki** natural enemy
仇敵 **kyūteki** bitter enemy
匹敵 **hitteki** rival, compare with, be a match for

10 恋敵 **koigataki** one's rival in love
素敵 **suteki** splendid, marvelous, great

12 無敵 **muteki** invincible, unrivaled

髪 → **3j11.3**

4i11.3 / 1782

田 夂 小 艹
49 35 32

弊

HEI evil, abuse, vice; (as prefix) our (humble)

――――――― 1 ―――――――

7 弊社 **heisha** our company, we
10 弊害 **heigai** an evil, ill effects

――――――― 2 ―――――――

5 旧弊 **kyūhei** an old evil; old-fashioned, behind the times
7 余弊 **yohei** a lingering evil

―――――――――― 12 ――――――――――

4i12.1 / 1032

目 月 心 夂
42 51 49

憂

YŪ, ure(eru), ure(u) grieve, be distressed/anxious **ure(e), ure(i)** grief, distress, anxiety **u(i)** sad, unhappy, gloomy

――――――― 1 ―――――――

5 憂目 **u(ki)me** grief, misery, hardship
11 憂患 **yūkan** sorrow, distress, cares
12 憂晴 **u(sa)bara(shi)** diversion, distraction
13 憂愁 **yūshū** melancholy, grief, gloom

18 憂顔 **ure(i)gao** sorrowful face, troubled look
29 憂鬱 **yūutsu** melancholy, dejection, gloom

――――――― 2 ―――――――

8 物憂 **monou(i)** languid, weary, dull

――――――― 4 ―――――――

1 一喜一憂 **ikki ichiyū** alternation of joy and sorrow, hope and fear

---

4i12.3 / 503

田 木 夂 口
41 49 24

整

SEI, totono(eru) put in order, arrange, prepare **totono(u)** be put in order, be arranged/prepared **HITOSHI** (m. given name)

――――――― 1 ―――――――

7 整形 **seikei** orthopedics
11 整理 **seiri** arrangement, adjustment; liquidation, reorganization; retrenchment, curtailment
12 整備 **seibi** make/keep ready for use, maintain, equip
整然 **seizen** orderly, regular, systematic, neat and trim

――――――― 2 ―――――――

7 均整 **kinsei** symmetry, balance
15 調整 **chōsei** adjust, regulate, coordinate

―――――――――― 13 ――――――――――

麺 → 麺 **4i17.1**

―――――――――― 17 ――――――――――

4i17.1

⋯ 木 夂 口
41 49 24

麺

MEN noodles; wheat flour

19

變 → 変 **2j7.3**

欠 4j

欠	欣	欧	欲	欺	款	歌	歎	歓	歐	歡
0.1	4.1	4.2	7.1	8.1	8.2	10.2	10.3	11.1	4j4.2	4j11.1

4

木 月 日 火 禾 王 牛 方 攵 欠 心 戸 戈

0

0

4j0.1 / 383

□ 攵
49

欠

缺 | 欠 欠

KETSU, ka(ku) lack **ka(kasu)** miss (a meeting) **ka(keru)** be lacking **ka(ke/kera)** broken piece, fragment **akubi** yawn

---

1

3 欠乏 **ketsubō** lack, scarcity, shortage, deficiency
7 欠伸 **akubi** yawn
9 欠陥 **kekkan** defect, deficiency, shortcoming
　欠点 **ketten** defect, flaw, faults
10 欠員 **ketsuin** vacant position, opening
　欠席 **kesseki** absence, nonattendance
12 欠勤 **kekkin** absence (from work)
13 欠損 **kesson** deficit, loss

2

5 出欠 **shukketsu** attendance or absence
8 金欠 **kinketsu** shortage of money
12 無欠 **muketsu** flawless

3

4 不可欠 **fukaketsu** indispensable, essential

4

4j4.1 / 2129

□ 斤 攵
50 49

欣

欣 欣

KIN rejoice **KIN, GON,** YOSHI (part of given name) YASUSHI, MOTOMU (m. given name)

4j4.2 / 1022

□ 攵 冂 十
49 20 12

欧

歐 | 欧 欧

Ō Europe

1

4 欧文 **ōbun** European language, roman script
6 欧州 **Ōshū** Europe
　欧州同盟 **Ōshū Dōmei** the European Union
　欧米 **Ō-Bei** Europe and America, the West
7 欧亜 **Ō-A** Europe and Asia

2

4 中欧 **Chūō** central Europe
　日欧 **Nichi-Ō** Japan and Europe
5 北欧 **Hokuō** Northern Europe
6 西欧 **Seiō** Western Europe, the West
7 対欧 **tai-Ō** toward/with Europe
8 東欧 **Tōō** Eastern Europe
13 滞欧 **tai-Ō** staying in Europe

7

4j7.1 / 1127

□ 火 攵 口
44 49 24

欲

慾 | 欲 欲

YOKU covetousness; desire
ho(shii) want **hos(suru)** desire, want

1

7 欲求 **yokkyū** wants, desires

欲求不満 **yokkyū fuman** frustration

11 欲張(り) **yokuba(ri)** greed, covetousness

欲望 **yokubō** desire, craving

欲情 **yokujō** passions, desires

2

3 大欲 **taiyoku** greed, avarice, covetousness

6 肉欲 **nikuyoku** carnal desires

7 我欲 **gayoku** selfishness

8 性欲 **seiyoku** sexual desire

9 食欲 **shokuyoku** appetite

11 強欲 **gōyoku** greedy, avaricious

12 無欲 **muyoku** free from avarice

13 禁欲 **kin'yoku** control of passions, self-denial, abstinence

意欲 **iyoku** will, desire, zest

8

4j8.1 / 1499   田 夂 艹 二
                49 32 4

GI, azamu(ku) deceive, cheat, dupe

1

16 欺瞞 **giman** deception, fraud, trickery

2

12 詐欺 **sagi** fraud

詐欺師 **sagishi** swindler, con man

4j8.2 / 1727   田 ネ 夂 士
                45 49 22

KAN article, section; goodwill, friendship

1

9 款待 **kantai** warm welcome, hospitality

2

8 定款 **teikan** articles of incorporation, charter

10 借款 **shakkan** loan

10

4j10.2 / 392   田 夂 口 丅
                49 24 14

KA, uta song; poem **uta(u)** sing; recite

1

2 歌人 **kajin** poet

4 歌手 **kashu** singer

11 歌唱 **kashō** singing; song

12 歌詞 **kashi** the lyrics/words (of a song)

歌集 **kashū** poetry anthology

15 歌舞伎 **kabuki** kabuki

歌劇 **kageki** opera

16 歌謡曲 **kayōkyoku** popular song

2

6 舟歌 **funauta** sailor's song, chantey

8 国歌 **kokka** national anthem

和歌山県 **Wakayama-ken** (prefecture)

和歌山 **Wakayama** (city, Wakayama-ken)

11 唱歌 **shōka** singing

12 短歌 **tanka** 31-syllable poem, tanka

喜歌劇 **kikageki** comic opera

童歌 **warabeuta** traditional children's song

13 詩歌 **shiika, shika** poetry

14 演歌 **enka** (a style of singing)

鼻歌 **hanauta** humming, crooning

15 賛歌 **sanka** paean, praise

3

10 流行歌 **ryūkōka, haya(ri)uta** popular song

4

5 古今和歌集 **Kokinwakashū** (poetry anthology, early tenth century)

4 木 月 日 火 ネ 王 牛 方 夂 欠 心 戸 戈 10

4j10.3

田 夊 艹 刂
49 32 24

歎

歎 歎

TAN, nage(ku) sigh, grieve over, lament, bemoan, deplore

— 1 —

10 歎息 **tansoku** sigh, lament
19 歎願 **tangan** petition, appeal

— 2 —

12 詠歎 **eitan** exclamation; admiration

— 11 —

4j11.1 / 1052

田 隹 夊 宀
74 49 15

歡

歡 | 歡 歡

KAN joy, pleasure

— 1 —

4 歡心買 **kanshin (o) ka(u)** curry favor
6 歡迎 **kangei** welcome
7 歡声 **kansei** shout of joy, cheer
8 歡送会 **kansōkai** farewell party, send-off
9 歡待 **kantai** hospitality
13 歡楽街 **kanrakugai** amusement center
15 歡談 **kandan** pleasant chat

— 2 —

9 哀歡 **aikan** joys and sorrows

歐 → 欧 **4j4.2**

— 17 —

歡 → 歡 **4j11.1**

— 忄 **4k** —

心	必	忙	忍	忌	忘	快	忠	忽	性	怖	怯	怜
0.1	0a5.16	3.2	3.3	3.4	2j5.4	4.2	4.6	4.7	5.4	5.6	5.9	5.10

怪	怒	怨	急	怠	恨	悖	恒	恰	悔	恵	息	恕
5.11	5.19	5.20	2n7.2	5.21	6.2	6.4	6.5	6.10	6.12	6.16	6.17	6.18

恐	恣	恩	恭	悧	悸	悍	悟	悩	惇	悌	悦	悔
6.19	6.22	6.23	3k7.16	7.2	7.3	7.4	7.5	7.11	7.12	7.14	7.15	4k6.12

悪	患	悠	惟	惨	情	惚	惜	悼	恵	惑	悪	惣
7.17	7.18	7.20	8.1	8.5	8.9	8.10	8.11	8.13	4k6.16	8.16	4k7.17	8.17

悲	愕	惰	慌	悩	愉	愚	愁	想	慈	感	悪	慨
8.18	9.4	9.6	9.10	4k7.11	9.13	9.15	9.16	9.18	2o11.1	9.21	4k7.17	10.3

博	慎	態	悪	慈	惨	憎	慢	慣	慰	憖	慾	慧
2k10.1	10.4	10.14	4k7.17	2o11.1	4k8.5	11.7	11.8	11.9	11.13	4k12.10	4j7.1	11.16

慨	憮	憚	憧	憤	憎	憩	憑	憾	憐	憶	懐	懇
4k10.3	12.3	12.4	12.5	12.6	4k11.7	12.10	12.12	13.3	13.4	13.5	13.9	13.12

懦	懲	應	懲	懐	懸	戀
14.1	14.3	3q4.2	4k14.3	4k13.9	16.2	2j8.2

—————— 0 ——————

4k0.1 / 97　　　　　　□ 心
　　　　　　　　　　　　　　51

心

心 心

SHIN, kokoro heart, mind; core

—————— 1 ——————

4 心中 **shinjū** lovers' double suicide; murder-suicide **shinchū** in one's heart

6 心地 **kokochi(yoi)** pleasant, comfortable

7 心身 **shinshin** mind and body, psychosomatic

8 心底 **shinsoko, shintei** the bottom of one's heart

9 心変 **kokoroga(wari)** change of mind, inconstancy

10 心配 **shinpai** worry, anxiety, concern

心配事 **shinpaigoto** cares, worries, troubles

11 心掛 **kokoroga(ke)** intention; attention, care

心強 **kokorozuyo(i)** reassuring, heartening

心得 **kokoroe** knowledge, understanding **kokoroe(ru)** know, understand

心得違 **kokoroechiga(i)** mistaken idea; indiscretion

心寂 **kokorosabi(shii)** lonely, lonesome

心理 **shinri** mental state, psychology

心理学 **shinrigaku** psychology

心情 **shinjō** one's heart/feelings

心細 **kokoroboso(i)** forlorn, disheartened

心酔 **shinsui** be fascinated by, ardently admire

12 心遣 **kokorozuka(i)** solicitude, consideration **kokoroya(ri)** diversion, recreation; thoughtfulness

心棒 **shinbō** axle, shaft, mandrel, stem

14 心境 **shinkyō** state of mind

心構 **kokorogama(e)** mental attitude/readiness

17 心優 **kokoroyasa(shii)** kind, considerate

18 心髄 **shinzui** the soul/essence of

19 心臓 **shinzō** the heart; nerve, cheek

心願 **shingan** heartfelt desire; prayer

—————— 2 ——————

1 一心 **isshin, hito(tsu)kokoro** one mind; the whole heart, whole-hearted

3 女心 **onnagokoro** a woman's heart

4 内心 **naishin** one's heart/mind, inward thoughts

中心 **chūshin** center

仏心 **busshin, hotokegokoro** Buddha's heart

5 本心 **honshin** one's right mind, one's senses; real intention/motive, true sentiment; conscience

失心 **shisshin** faint, lose consciousness

幼心 **osanagokoro** child's mind/heart

用心 **yōjin** care, caution

用心深 **yōjinbuka(i)** careful, cautious, wary

6 安心 **anshin** feel relieved/reassured

7 良心 **ryōshin** conscience

良心的 **ryōshinteki** conscientious

身心 **shinshin** body and mind

里心 **satogokoro** homesickness, nostalgia

住心地 **su(mi)gokochi** livability, comfort

決心 **kesshin** determination, resolution

肝心 **kanjin** main, vital, essential

改心 **kaishin** reform (oneself)

初心者 **shoshinsha** beginner

8 苦心 **kushin** pains, efforts

9 衷心 **chūshin** one's inmost heart/feelings

乗心地 **no(ri)gokochi** riding comfort

信心 **shinjin** faith, belief, piety

4

木
月
日
火
礻
王
牛
方
攵
欠
心　0
戸
戈

狭心症 **kyōshinshō** stricture of the heart, angina pectoris

10 都心 **toshin** heart of the city, mid-town

恋心 **koigokoro** (awakening of) love

11 野心 **yashin** ambition

唯心論 **yuishinron** idealism, spiritualism

情心 **nasa(ke)gokoro** sympathy, compassion

12 着心地 **kigokochi** fit and feel (of clothes)

遠心力 **enshinryoku** centrifugal force

無心 **mushin** absorbed in (play); request, cadge

焦心 **shōshin** impatience, anxiousness

13 傷心 **shōshin** heartbreak, sorrow

腹心 **fukushin** confidant, trusted associate

感心 **kanshin** be impressed by, admire

14 関心 **kanshin** interest, concern

15 熱心 **nesshin** enthusiasm, zeal

歓心買 **kanshin (o) ka(u)** curry favor

————— 3 —————

1 一安心 **hitoanshin** feeling relieved for a while

4 不用心 **buyōjin, fuyōjin** unsafe, insecure; careless

5 好奇心 **kōkishin** curiosity, inquisitiveness

6 自尊心 **jisonshin** self-esteem; conceit

9 勇猛心 **yūmōshin** intrepid spirit

11 虚栄心 **kyoeishin** vanity, vainglory

12 無用心 **buyōjin** unsafe; incautious

無関心 **mukanshin** indifference, unconcern, apathy

13 廉恥心 **renchishin** sense of shame/honor

14 愛国心 **aikokushin** patriotism

15 敵対心 **tekitaishin** enmity, animosity

必 → **0a5.16**

————— 3 —————

4k3.2 / 1373   日 心 亠 丨
                     51 11 2

忙忙

BŌ, isoga(shii), sewa(shii) busy

————— 1 —————

10 忙殺 **bōsatsu** keep (someone) busily occupied

————— 2 —————

6 多忙 **tabō** busy

13 煩忙 **hanbō** busy, pressed with business

16 繁忙 **hanbō** busy, pressed

————— 3 —————

12 御多忙中 **gotabōchū** while you are so busy

4k3.3 / 1414   日 心 力 丨
                     51 8 2

忍丨忍忍

NIN, shino(bu) bear, endure; hide, lie hidden **shino(baseru)** hide, conceal **shino(bi)** stealing into; incognito/surreptitious visit; spy, scout; sneak thief

————— 1 —————

0 忍びやか **shino(biyaka)** stealthy, secret

7 忍声 **shino(bi)goe** in a whisper

忍足 **shino(bi)ashi** stealthy steps

8 忍者 **ninja** ninja, spy-assassin (historical)

9 忍耐 **nintai** perseverance, patience, endurance

忍耐強 **nintaizuyo(i)** patient, persevering

18 忍難 **shino(bi)gata(i)** unbearable

————— 2 —————

12 堪忍 **kannin** patience, forbearance; forgiveness

4k3.4 / 1797

日 忌 弓
51 28

忌忌

KI mourning; death anniversary; avoid, shun **i(mu)** hate, loathe; avoid, shun **i(mi)** mourning; abstinence, taboo **ima(washii)** abominable, disgusting, scandalous; ominous

―――――― 1 ――――――

4 忌中 **kichū** in mourning
7 忌言葉 **i(mi)kotoba** tabooed word
15 忌避 **kihi** evasion, shirking; (legal) challenge

―――――― 2 ――――――

6 年忌 **nenki** anniversary of a death
　回忌 **kaiki** anniversary of one's death
8 周忌 **shūki** anniversary of a death
13 禁忌 **kinki** taboo; contraindication

忘→ **2j5.4**

―――――― 4 ――――――

4k4.2 / 1409

川 忌 大 一
51 34 1

快快

KAI, kokoroyo(i) pleasant, delightful **kokoroyo(shi)** be willing/pleased to **kokoroyo(ge)** pleasant **YOSHI** (part of given name)

―――――― 1 ――――――

4 快方 **kaihō** recovery, convalescence
9 快速 **kaisoku** high-speed; express (train)
　快活 **kaikatsu** cheerful, lively, merry
10 快記録 **kaikiroku** a fine record
12 快晴 **kaisei** fine weather, clear skies
13 快適 **kaiteki** comfortable, pleasant, agreeable
　快楽 **kairaku, keraku** pleasure

快感 **kaikan** pleasant/agreeable feeling
15 快調 **kaichō** harmony; excellent condition

―――――― 2 ――――――

4 不快 **fukai** unpleasant, uncomfortable; displeased
6 全快 **zenkai** complete recovery, full cure
11 爽快 **sōkai** thrilling, exhilarating
12 愉快 **yukai** pleasant, merry, cheerful
　痛快 **tsūkai** keen pleasure, thrill, delight
　軽快 **keikai** light, nimble, jaunty, lilting

―――――― 3 ――――――

4 不愉快 **fuyukai** unpleasant, disagreeable

4k4.6 / 1348

日 忌 口 丨
51 24 2

忠忠

CHŪ loyalty, faithfulness TADASHI (m. given name) CHŪ, TADA (part of given name)

―――――― 1 ――――――

6 忠孝 **Tadataka, Tadanori, Chūkō** (m. given name)
7 忠告 **chūkoku** advice, admonition
8 忠実 **chūjitsu** faithful, devoted, loyal
13 忠誠 **chūsei** loyalty, allegiance

―――――― 2 ――――――

6 尽忠 **jinchū** loyalty

4k4.7

日 忌 犭
51 27

忽忽

KOTSU, tachima(chi) immediately, all of a sudden **yuruga(se)** neglect, slight

木
月
日
火
礻
王
牛
方
攵
欠
心　4
戸
戈

4

——————— 1 ———————

12 忽然 **kotsuzen** suddenly

——————— 5 ———————

4k5.4 / 98   □ 忄 牛 一
                        51 47 1

性   性性

4 ⬚

木
相
月
日
火
礻
王
牛
方
攵
欠
5 心
戸
戈

SEI sex; nature, character; (as suffix)
-ness, -ity **SHŌ** temperament,
propensity **saga** one's nature; custom

——————— 1 ———————

4 性分 **shōbun** nature, disposition
5 性生活 **sei seikatsu** sex life
  性犯罪 **sei hanzai** sex crime
6 性交 **seikō** sexual intercourse
7 性別 **seibetsu** sex, whether male or
  female
8 性的 **seiteki** sexual
10 性根 **shōkon** perseverance
  shōne one's disposition
  性格 **seikaku** character, personality
  性病 **seibyō** sexually-transmitted/
  venereal disease
11 性欲 **seiyoku** sexual desire
13 性愛 **seiai** sexual love
18 性癖 **seiheki** disposition, proclivity

——————— 2 ———————

2 人性 **jinsei** human nature; humanity
3 女性 **josei** woman; feminine gender
4 中性 **chūsei** neuter; (chemically)
  neutral; sterile
  水性 **suisei** aqueous, water
  mizushō flirtatious, wanton
5 本性 **honshō, honsei** true nature/
  character
6 気性 **kishō** disposition, temper-
  ment, spirit
  両性の **ryōseiteki** bisexual, androgynous
  仮性 **kasei** false (symptoms)
  同性愛 **dōseiai** homosexuality
7 良性 **ryōsei** benign (tumor)
  男性 **dansei** man, male; masculinity
8 毒性 **dokusei** virulence, toxicity

9 急性 **kyūsei** acute (not chronic)
  相性 **aishō** affinity, compatibility
10 個性 **kosei** individuality, idiosyncrasy
  陰性 **insei** negative; dormant
  根性 **konjō** disposition, spirit, nature
  特性 **tokusei** distinctive quality,
  characteristic, trait
11 野性的 **yaseiteki** wild, rough
  陽性 **yōsei** positive
  理性 **risei** reason, reasoning power
  悪性 **akusei** malignant, vicious,
  pernicious **akushō** evil nature; licentiousness
  異性 **isei** the opposite sex
12 堪性 **kora(e)shō** patience
  属性 **zokusei** attribute
  無性 **musei** asexual
  mushō thoughtless;
  inordinate **bushō** lazy
  惰性 **dasei** inertia
13 適性 **tekisei** aptitude, suitability
  感性 **kansei** sensitivity; the senses
14 慢性 **mansei** chronic
  酸性 **sansei** acidity
16 凝性 **ko(ri)shō** single-minded enthusiasm, fastidiousness
17 優性 **yūsei** dominant (gene)
  癇性 **kanshō** irritability, irascibility

——————— 3 ———————

1 一過性 **ikkasei** transient, temporary
2 人間性 **ningensei** human nature,
  humanity
4 内向性 **naikōsei** introverted
  水溶性 **suiyōsei** water-soluble
5 甲斐性 **kaishō** resourcefulness,
  competence
  外向性 **gaikōsei** extroverted, outgoing
  可能性 **kanōsei** possibility
  可燃性 **kanensei** combustible,
  flammable
6 多発性 **tahatsusei** multiple (sclerosis)
  多様性 **tayōsei** diversity, variety
  合憲性 **gōkensei** constitutionality

8 国民性 **kokuminsei** national character

9 信憑性 **shinpyōsei** credibility, authenticity

12 弾力性 **danryokusei** elasticity, resilience, flexibility

13 蓋然性 **gaizensei** probability

感受性 **kanjusei** sensibility, sensitivity

4k5.6 / 1814   囗 心 巾 十
                    51 26 12

怖怖

FU, kowa(i) frightening, scary
kowa(garu) fear, be afraid
kowa(gari) timidity, cowardice
o(jiru/jikeru) fear, be afraid
oso(reru) fear, be apprehensive

—————— 1 ——————

6 怖気 **o(ji)ke, ozoke** fear, timidity, nervousness

—————— 2 ——————

10 恐怖 **kyōfu** fear, terror
恐怖感 **kyōfukan** sense of fear

4k5.9   囗 心 土 竹
                51 22 17

怯怯

KYŌ fear, cowardice **obi(eru)** become frightened, be scared
hiru(mu) flinch, wince, be daunted

4k5.10 / 2070   囗 心 亻 一
                    51 3 1

怜怜

REI wise REI, RYŌ, REN, SATO, TOKI (part of given name) SATOSHI, SATORU (m. given name)

4k5.11 / 1476   囗 心 土 又
                    51 22 9

怪

性丨怪怪

KAI, KE mystery; apparition
aya(shimu) doubt, be skeptical; marvel at, be surprised **aya(shii/shige)** dubious, suspicious-looking; strange, mysterious **ke(shikaran/shikaranu)** disgraceful, outrageous, shameful, rude

—————— 1 ——————

6 怪気 **aya(shi)ge** suspicious, questionable, shady; faltering

7 怪我 **kega** injury, wound; accident, chance

8 怪事件 **kaijiken** strange/mystery case

怪奇 **kaiki** mysterious, grotesque, eerie

15 怪談 **kaidan** ghost story

4k5.19 / 1596   囗 心 女 又
                    51 25 9

怒

怒怒

DO, oko(ru), ika(ru) become angry
ika(ri) anger, wrath

—————— 1 ——————

0 怒りっぽい **oko(rippoi)** touchy, snappish, irascible

6 怒気 **doki** (fit of) anger

14 怒鳴 **dona(ru)** shout at

—————— 2 ——————

12 喜怒哀楽 **kidoairaku** joy-anger-sorrow-pleasure, emotions

4k5.20   囗 心 夕 阝
                51 30 7

怨

怨怨

EN, ON, ura(mu) bear a grudge, resent, reproach **ura(meshii)** reproachful, resentful, rueful

4

木
月
日
火
礻
王
牛
方
攵
欠
心
戸
戈

5

───────── 1 ─────────

⁹ 怨恨 **enkon** grudge, enmity

急 → **2n7.2**

4k5.21 / 1297

目 心 口 竹
51 24 17

怠 怠

TAI laziness, neglect **okota(ru)** neglect, be remiss in, default on **nama(keru)** be idle/lazy, neglect

───────── 1 ─────────

⁸ 怠屈 **taikutsu** boredom, tedium

怠者 **nama(ke)mono** idler, lazy-bones

¹² 怠惰 **taida** idleness, laziness, sloth

¹⁴ 怠慢 **taiman** negligence, dereliction, inattention

───────── 2 ─────────

¹⁰ 倦怠感 **kentaikan** fatigue

───────── 6 ─────────

4k6.2 / 1755

回 食 心
73 51

恨 恨

KON, ura(mu) bear a grudge, resent, reproach **ura(meshii)** reproachful, resentful, rueful

───────── 1 ─────────

⁷ 恨言 **ura(mi)goto** grudge, grievance, reproach

───────── 2 ─────────

⁹ 怨恨 **enkon** grudge, enmity

悔恨 **kaikon** remorse, regret, contrition

4k6.4

口 心 宀 子
51 33 6

悖 悖

HAI, moto(ru) go against, be contrary to

4k6.5 / 1275

口 心 日 二
51 43 4

恆 | 恒 恒

KŌ always, constant, fixed **tsune (ni)** always HISASHI, WATARU (m. given name) TSUNE (part of given name)

───────── 1 ─────────

³ 恒久 **kōkyū** permanence, perpetuity

⁴ 恒夫 **Tsuneo, Hisao** (m. given name)

⁸ 恒例 **kōrei** established practice, custom

¹¹ 恒常的 **kōjōteki** constant

4k6.10

田 心 口 亻
51 24 3

恰 恰

KŌ, KA', ataka(mo) as if, just like

───────── 1 ─────────

⁵ 恰好 **kakkō** shape, form, figure, appearance; reasonable; approximately

4k6.12 / 1733

田 心 女 厶
51 25 15

悔 | 悔 悔

KAI, KE, ku(iru) regret **ku(yamu)** regret; mourn for, offer condolences **kuya(shii)** vexatious, vexing

─────── 1 ───────

7 悔状 **ku(yami)jō** letter of condolence

悔言 **ku(yami)goto** words of condolence

9 悔恨 **kaikon** remorse, regret, contrition

─────── 2 ───────

9 後悔 **kōkai** regret

4k6.16 / 1219   日 日 心 十
                      43 51 12

KEI, E, megu(mu) bless, bestow a
favor MEGUMI, KEI (f. given name)
SATOSHI (m. given name) E, KEI,
SHIGE, YOSHI (part of given name)

─────── 1 ───────

2 恵子 **Keiko, Shigeko** (f. given name)
9 恵美 **Emi** (f. given name)
恵美子 **Emiko** (f. given name)

─────── 2 ───────

4 仁恵 **jinkei** graciousness, benevolence, mercy

7 寿恵 **Toshie, Hisae, Sue, Kazue** (f.
given name)

8 幸恵 **Yukie, Sachie** (f. given name)
知恵 **chie** knowledge, intelligence,
wisdom

9 美恵 **Mie, Yoshie** (f. given name)
11 理恵 **Rie** (f. given name)

─────── 3 ───────

9 浅知恵 **asajie** shallow-witted
11 悪知恵 **warujie** cunning, guile
13 猿知恵 **sarujie** shallow cleverness

4k6.17 / 1242   目 日 心 丨
                      55 51 2

SOKU son; breath **iki** breath
iki(mu) strain, bear down (in defecat-
ing or giving birth)

─────── 1 ───────

2 息子 **musuko** son
4 息切 **ikigi(re)** shortness of breath
6 息休 **kyūsoku** a rest, breather

─────── 2 ───────

1 一息 **hitoiki** a breath; a pause/
break; (a little more) effort
2 子息 **shisoku** son
6 休息 **kyūsoku** rest
安息 **ansoku** rest, repose
安息日 **ansokubi** sabbath
ansokunichi the (Jewish)
sabbath **ansokujitsu** the
(Christian) sabbath
7 利息 **risoku** interest (on a loan)
10 消息 **shōsoku** news, hearing from
(someone)
11 窒息 **chissoku** suffocation, asphyxiation
12 棲息 **seisoku** live in, inhabit
棲息地 **seisokuchi** habitat
13 溜息 **ta(me)iki** sigh
嘆息 **tansoku** sigh; lament
14 歎息 **tansoku** sigh, lament

─────── 3 ───────

1 一人息子 **hitori musuko** an only
son

4k6.18 / 2071   田 心 女 口
                      51 25 24

JO magnanimity, tolerance; consider-
ateness, sympathy JO, SHO, HIRO,
YOSHI, MICHI, NORI, YUKI (part of given
name) HIROSHI, HAKARU (m. given
name) YUKI (f. given name)

4k6.19 / 1602   田 心 工 冂
                      51 38 20

KYŌ, oso(reru) fear, be afraid
oso(re) fear, danger, risk of
oso(roshii) terrible, frightful, awful

oso(raku) perhaps kowa(i) frightening, scary

<hr>1

⁰ 恐れながら **oso(renagara)** most humbly/respectfully

² 恐入 **oso(re)i(ru)** be overwhelmed (with gratitude/shame), be astonished, be sorry to trouble, beg pardon; be defeated, yield; plead guilty

⁵ 恐乍 **oso(re)naga(ra)** most humbly/respectfully

⁸ 恐妻家 **kyōsaika** henpecked husband

　恐怖 **kyōfu** fear, terror

　恐怖感 **kyōfukan** sense of fear

¹¹ 恐喝 **kyōkatsu** threat, intimidation, blackmail

¹² 恐慌 **kyōkō** panic

¹⁷ 恐縮 **kyōshuku** be very grateful/sorry

4k6.22　　　　田 夂 心 冫
　　　　　　　　49 51 5

恣 恣

SHI, hoshiimama as one pleases, self-indulgent, arbitrary

<hr>1

¹³ 恣意 **shii** arbitrariness, selfishness

4k6.23 / 555　　　日 心 口 大
　　　　　　　　51 24 34

恩 恩

ON kindness, goodness, favor

<hr>1

² 恩人 **onjin** benefactor, patron

⁶ 恩返 **ongae(shi)** repayment of a favor

⁸ 恩知 **onshi(razu)** ingratitude; ingrate

¹⁰ 恩師 **onshi** one's honored teacher

¹¹ 恩赦 **onsha** amnesty, general pardon

¹² 恩給 **onkyū** pension

¹⁵ 恩賞 **onshō** a reward

<hr>2

¹⁷ 鴻恩 **kōon** great benevolence/blessings

恭 → **3k7.16**

<hr>7

4k7.2　　　　田 禾 心 儿
　　　　　　　　56 51 16

俐 俐 俐 俐

RI clever

4k7.3　　　　田 禾 心 子
　　　　　　　　56 51 6

悸 悸 悸

KI pulsate; tremble

4k7.4　　　　田 心 日 一
　　　　　　　　51 43 14

悍 悍 悍

KAN strong, violent, rough, spirited

4k7.5 / 1438　　田 心 口 一
　　　　　　　　51 24 14

悟 悟 悟

GO, sato(ru) perceive, understand, realize, be enlightened **sato(ri)** comprehension, understanding; satori, spiritual awakening

---

<hr>2

⁷ 改悟 **kaigo** repentance, remorse, contrition

¹² 覚悟 **kakugo** be prepared/resolved/resigned to

4k7.11 / 1279   田 心 小 冂
            51   35   20

悩 ｜ 悩 悩

NŌ, naya(mu) be troubled/distressed, suffer **naya(masu)** afflict, beset, worry

———— 1 ————

10 悩殺 **nōsatsu** enchant, captivate

———— 2 ————

7 伸悩 **no(bi)naya(mu)** be sluggish, stagnate, level off, mark time

8 苦悩 **kunō** suffering, agony, distress

13 煩悩 **bonnō** evil passions, carnal desires

4k7.12 / 2075   田 心 口 亠
            51   24   11

悙 悙

SHUN, TON, atsu(i) kind, considerate TON, JUN, ATSU, TOSHI (part of given name) JUN, ATSUSHI, MAKOTO, TSU-TOMU, SUNAO (m. given name)

———— 1 ————

2 悙子 **Junko, Atsuko** (f. given name)

4k7.14 / 2072   田 心 弓 儿
            51   28   16

悌 悌

TEI deferring to one's elders YASU-SHI, SUNAO (m. given name) TEI, YA-SU, YOSHI, TOMO (part of given name)

4k7.15 / 1368   田 心 口 儿
            51   24   16

悦 ｜ 悦 悦

ETSU joy **yoroko(bu)** rejoice, be glad YOSHI (part of given name)

———— 1 ————

13 悦楽 **etsuraku** joy, pleasure, gaiety

悔 → 悔 4k6.12

4k7.17 / 304   日 心 工 口
            51   38   24

惡 ｜ 悪 悪

AKU evil, vice **waru(i)** bad **a(shikarazu)** without taking offense **-niku(i)** difficult, hard to …

———— 1 ————

2 悪人 **akunin** evildoer, scoundrel, the wicked

3 悪口 **warukuchi, aku(tare)guchi, akkō** verbal abuse, speaking ill/evil of

悪女 **akujo** wicked/ugly woman

4 悪天候 **akutenkō** bad weather

悪化 **akka** worsening, deterioration

6 悪気 **warugi** evil intent, malice, ill will

悪行 **akugyō, akkō** evildoing, wickedness

悪因悪果 **akuin-akka** Evil breeds evil.

7 悪役 **akuyaku** the villain('s role)

8 悪事 **akuji** evil deed

悪例 **akurei** bad example/precedent

悪知恵 **warujie** cunning, guile

悪者 **warumono** bad fellow, scoundrel

悪性 **akusei** malignant, vicious, pernicious **akushō** evil nature; licentiousness

9 悪臭 **akushū** offensive odor, stench

11 悪運 **aku'un** evildoer's good luck; bad luck

悪習慣 **akushūkan** bad habit, evil practice

悪酔 **waruyo(i)** drink oneself sick; become unpleasant when drunk

12 悪循環 **akujunkan** vicious cycle/ spiral

悪評 **akuhyō** bad reputation; unfavorable criticism

13 悪漢 **akkan** scoundrel, crook, ruffian, knave

悪夢 **akumu** nightmare, disturbing dream

悪感情 **akukanjō, akkanjō** ill will, animosity, unfavorable impression

悪意 **akui** evil intent, malice, ill will

14 悪銭 **akusen** ill-gotten money

15 悪戯 **akugi, itazura** prank, mischief

悪質 **akushitsu** evil, vicious, unscrupulous; of poor quality

16 悪賢 **warugashiko(i)** cunning, sly, crafty, wily

18 悪癖 **akuheki, waruguse** bad habit, vice

——————— 2 ———————

4 凶悪 **kyōaku** heinous, brutal, fiendish

7 改悪 **kaiaku** change for the worse, deterioration

9 俗悪 **zokuaku** vulgar, coarse

10 険悪 **ken'aku** dangerous, threatening, serious

害悪 **gaiaku** an evil (influence), harm

11 粗悪 **soaku** coarse, crude, inferior

12 善悪 **zen'aku** good and evil
yo(shi)waru(shi),
yo(shi)a(shi) good and bad, good or bad
yo(kare)a(shikare) right or wrong, for better or worse

最悪 **saiaku** worst

13 嫌悪 **ken'o** hatred, dislike, loathing

罪悪感 **zaiakukan** guilty conscience

14 憎悪 **zōo** hatred, abhorrence

15 暴悪 **bōaku** violence, tyranny, savagery

17 醜悪 **shūaku** ugly, abominable, scandalous

——————— 3 ———————

11 悪因悪果 **akuin-akka** Evil breeds evil.

13 意地悪 **ijiwaru(i)** ill-tempered, crabby

4k7.18 / 1315

日 心 口 丨
51 24 2

患患

KAN, wazura(u) be ill, suffer from

——————— 1 ———————

8 患者 **kanja** a patient

10 患部 **kanbu** diseased part, the affected area

——————— 2 ———————

9 急患 **kyūkan** emergency patient/ case

10 疾患 **shikkan** disease, ailment

15 憂患 **yūkan** sorrow, distress, cares

4k7.20 / 1597

巴 心 夂 イ
51 49 3

悠悠

YŪ distant; leisure

——————— 1 ———————

3 悠々 **yūyū** calm, composed, leisurely

4 悠介 **Yūsuke** (m. given name)

——————— 8 ———————

4k8.1 / 2073

口 隹 心
74 51

惟惟

I, omonmi(ru) ponder, reflect on
omo(u) think over **YUI** (f. given

name) I, KORE, TADA, NOBU, YOSHI, ARI (part of given name) TAMOTSU (m. given name)

4k8.5 / 1725   田 心 大 彡
51 34 31

惨 | 惨 惨

SAN, ZAN, miji(me) piteous, wretched, miserable **mugo(i)** cruel, harsh

—————— 1 ——————

⁶ 惨死 **zanshi** tragic/violent death
⁸ 惨事 **sanji** disaster, tragic accident
¹⁰ 惨殺 **zansatsu** murder, massacre, slaughter
¹¹ 惨敗 **zanpai** crushing defeat
¹⁵ 惨劇 **sangeki** tragedy, tragic event

—————— 2 ——————

¹⁰ 凄惨 **seisan** ghastly, gruesome, lurid
¹² 悲惨 **hisan** tragic, wretched, pitiable

4k8.9 / 209   田 心 月 士
51 42 22

情 | 情 情

JŌ, SEI feelings, emotion; circumstances **nasa(ke)** sympathy, compassion

—————— 1 ——————

⁴ 情心 **nasa(ke)gokoro** sympathy, compassion
⁷ 情状 **jōjō** circumstances, conditions
⁸ 情況 **jōkyō** circumstances, state of affairs
¹¹ 情深 **nasa(ke)buka(i)** compassionate, kindhearted
¹² 情報 **jōhō** information
情報化社会 **jōhōka shakai** information-oriented society
¹³ 情勢 **jōsei** situation, condition, circumstances
¹⁵ 情熱 **jōnetsu** passion, enthusiasm

—————— 2 ——————

² 人情 **ninjō** human feelings, humanity, kindness
⁴ 友情 **yūjō** friendship, fellowship
心情 **shinjō** one's heart/feelings
⁶ 色情 **shikijō** sexual desire, lust
同情 **dōjō** sympathy
⁸ 表情 **hyōjō** (facial) expression
事情 **jijō** circumstances, reasons
苦情 **kujō** complaint, grievance
実情 **jitsujō** actual state of affairs
⁹ 発情 **hatsujō** sexual arousal, (in) heat
衷情 **chūjō** one's inmost feelings
叙情詩 **jojōshi** lyric poem/poetry
¹⁰ 陳情書 **chinjōsho** petition, representation
純情 **junjō** pure-minded emotion, naïveté, devotion
¹¹ 強情 **gōjō** stubbornness, obstinacy
欲情 **yokujō** passions, desires
¹² 温情 **onjō** warm, cordial, kindly
無情 **mujō** unfeeling, callous, cruel
¹³ 感情 **kanjō** feelings, emotion
感情的 **kanjōteki** emotional, sentimental
痴情 **chijō** blind love, passion, infatuation
¹⁴ 慕情 **bojō** longing, love, affection
愛情 **aijō** love, affection
¹⁵ 熱情 **netsujō** fervor, ardor, passion
¹⁶ 薄情 **hakujō** unfeeling, heartless, coldhearted

—————— 3 ——————

¹¹ 悪感情 **akukanjō, akkanjō** ill will, animosity, unfavorable impression
¹² 無表情 **muhyōjō** expressionless

—————— 4 ——————

¹³ 義理人情 **giri-ninjō** duty versus/ and human feelings

4

木
月
日
火
礻
王
牛
方
攵
欠
心
戸
戈

8

4k8.10

田 忄 犭
51 27

KOTSU, ho(reru) fall in love with
bo(keru) become dull-witted/senile;
be out of focus, fade

─────── 2 ───────
13 寝惚 **nebo(keru)** be half asleep

─────── 3 ───────
1 一目惚 **hitomebo(re)** love at first
sight

4k8.11 / 765

田 忄 日 艹
51 43 32

SEKI, o(shii) regrettable; precious;
wasteful **o(shimu)** regret; value; be-
grudge, be sparing of, be reluctant to
part with

─────── 1 ───────
11 惜敗 **sekihai** narrow defeat

─────── 2 ───────
9 哀惜 **aiseki** grief, sorrow
負惜 **ma(ke)o(shimi)** unwilling-
ness to admit defeat
10 骨惜 **honeo(shimi)** avoid effort,
spare oneself

4k8.13 / 1680

田 忄 日 卜
51 43 13

TŌ, ita(mu) grieve over, mourn

─────── 2 ───────
8 追悼 **tsuitō** mourning; memorial
(address)

惠 → 恵 4k6.16

4k8.16 / 969

日 戈 心 口
52 51 24

WAKU, mado(u) go astray, be mis-
guided/tempted

─────── 1 ───────
9 惑星 **wakusei** planet

─────── 2 ───────
4 戸惑 **tomado(i)** become disorient-
ed/confused
6 当惑 **tōwaku** be perplexed/non-
plussed, be at a loss
7 困惑 **konwaku** perplexity, dilemma
8 迷惑 **meiwaku** trouble, annoyance,
inconvenience
10 眩惑 **genwaku** blind, dazzle, daze
14 疑惑 **giwaku** suspicion, distrust,
misgivings
誘惑 **yūwaku** temptation, seduction

惡 → 悪 4k7.17

4k8.17 / 2074

日 牛 心 犭
47 51 27

SŌ all **SŌ, SU, NOBU, FUSA, MICHI**
(part of given name) **OSAMU** (m. giv-
en name)

4k8.18 / 1034

日 心 儿 二
51 16 4

HI, kana(shii) sad **kana(shimu)** be
sad, mourn for, regret

─────── 1 ───────
9 悲哀 **hiai** sorrow, grief, sadness

11 悲惨 **hisan** tragic, wretched, pitiable

12 悲痛 **hitsū** bitter, grief, sorrow

13 悲嘆 **hitan** grief, sorrow

14 悲鳴 **himei** shriek, scream

15 悲劇 **higeki** tragedy

18 悲観 **hikan** pessimism

悲観的 **hikanteki** pessimistic

悲観論者 **hikanronsha** pessimist

─────── 2 ───────

13 慈悲 **jihi** compassion, mercy, charity

─────── 3 ───────

19 無慈悲 **mujihi** merciless, ruthless

─────── 9 ───────

4k9.4

田　忄　月　二
51　24　4

愕愕

GAKU, odoro(ku) be surprised/frightened

─────── 1 ───────

12 愕然 **gakuzen** in surprise/terror, aghast, shocked

─────── 2 ───────

22 驚愕 **kyōgaku** astonishment; alarm, consternation

4k9.6 / 1743

田　忄　月　工
51　42　38

惰惰

DA lazy, inactive **okota(ru)** neglect

─────── 1 ───────

8 惰性 **dasei** inertia

─────── 2 ───────

9 怠惰 **taida** idleness, laziness, sloth

4k9.10 / 1378

田　忄　艹　亠
51　32　11

慌慌

KŌ, awa(teru) get flustered, be in a flurry, panic **awa(tadashii)** bustling, flurried, confused

─────── 1 ───────

8 慌者 **awa(te)mono** absent-minded person, scatterbrain

─────── 2 ───────

10 恐慌 **kyōkō** panic

惱 → 悩 **4k7.11**

4k9.13 / 1598

田　忄　月　亻
51　42　3

愉｜愉愉

YU joy, pleasure **tano(shii)** pleasant, delightful, fun

─────── 1 ───────

7 愉快 **yukai** pleasant, merry, cheerful

─────── 2 ───────

4 不愉快 **fuyukai** unpleasant, disagreeable

4k9.15 / 1642

日　心　竹
43　51　17

愚愚

GU foolish; (self-deprecatory prefix) **oro(ka), oro(kashii)** foolish, stupid

─────── 1 ───────

6 愚劣 **guretsu** stupid, foolish

8 愚者 **oro(ka)mono, gusha** fool, jackass

9 愚連隊 **gurentai** hooligans, street gang

13 愚痴 **guchi** idle complaint, grumbling

15 愚論 **guron** foolish argument/opinion

4k9.16 / 1601   田 禾 火 心
                  56 44 51

SHŪ, ure(i) grief, sorrow, distress; anxiety, cares **ure(eru)** grieve, be distressed; fear, be apprehensive

—————— 1 ——————

13 愁傷様 **(go)shūshō-sama** My heartfelt sympathy.

—————— 2 ——————

9 哀愁 **aishū** sadness, sorrow, grief

10 郷愁 **kyōshū** homesickness, nostalgia

15 憂愁 **yūshū** melancholy, grief, gloom

4k9.18 / 147   田 目 木 心
                  55 41 51

SŌ, SO idea, thought **omo(u)** think of, call to mind

—————— 1 ——————

14 想像 **sōzō** imagine

想像力 **sōzōryoku** (powers of) imagination

—————— 2 ——————

4 幻想 **gensō** fantasy, illusion

予想 **yosō** expect, anticipate, conjecture, imagine; estimate

6 仮想 **kasō** imaginary, supposed, virtual (mass), hypothetical

妄想 **mōsō, bōsō** wild fantasy, delusion

回想 **kaisō** retrospection, reminiscence

7 狂想曲 **kyōsōkyoku** rhapsody

8 迷想 **meisō** illusion, fallacy

追想 **tsuisō** recollection, reminiscences

空想 **kūsō** idle fancy, fiction, daydream

9 発想 **hassō** conception; expression (in music)

連想 **rensō** association (of ideas)

思想 **shisō** thought, idea

思想家 **shisōka** thinker

10 随想録 **zuisōroku** occasional thoughts, essays

11 理想 **risō** ideal

理想主義 **risō shugi** idealism

理想的 **risōteki** ideal

理想家 **risōka** idealist

12 着想 **chakusō** idea, conception

13 夢想 **musō** dream, vision, fancy

夢想家 **musōka** dreamer, visionary

感想 **kansō** one's thoughts, impressions

14 愛想 **aiso, aisō** amiability, sociability

15 瞑想 **meisō** meditation, contemplation

—————— 4 ——————

12 無念無想 **munen-musō** blank state of mind

慈 → 2o11.1

4k9.21 / 262   日 戈 心 口
                  52 51 24

KAN feeling, sensation

—————— 1 ——————

0 感じる/ずる **kan(jiru/zuru)** feel

感じ **kan(ji)** feeling, sensation

4 感心 **kanshin** be impressed by, admire

7 感応 **kannō** response; inspiration; sympathy; induce, influence

8 感受性 **kanjusei** sensibility, sensitivity

感性 **kansei** sensitivity; the senses

9 感染 **kansen** infection, contagion

感冒 **kanbō** a cold, the flu

11 感動 **kandō** impression, inspiration, emotion, excitement

感情 **kanjō** feelings, emotion

感情的 **kanjōteki** emotional, sentimental

12 感覚 **kankaku** sense, the senses

13 感傷 **kanshō** sentimentality

感嘆 **kantan** admiration, wonder, exclamation

感嘆符 **kantanfu** exclamation point (!)

感想 **kansō** one's thoughts, impressions

感慨無量 **kangai-muryō** full of emotion

感触 **kanshoku** the touch/feel, texture

16 感激 **kangeki** be deeply impressed/grateful

17 感謝 **kansha** gratitude, appreciation

——————— 2 ———————

4 予感 **yokan** premonition, hunch

五感 **gokan** the five senses

反感 **hankan** antipathy, animosity

6 多感 **takan** sensitive, sentimental, emotional

肉感的 **nikkanteki** suggestive, sensual, voluptuous

同感 **dōkan** the same sentiment, sympathy, concurrence

7 快感 **kaikan** pleasant/agreeable feeling

8 直感 **chokkan** intuition

実感 **jikkan** actual sensation, realization

10 流感 **ryūkan** flu, influenza (short for 流行性感網)

敏感 **binkan** sensitive

11 悪感情 **akukanjō, akkanjō** ill will, animosity, unfavorable impression

12 無感覚 **mukankaku** insensible, numb, callous

鈍感 **donkan** obtuse, thick, insensitive

15 霊感 **reikan** inspiration

——————— 3 ———————

6 劣等感 **rettōkan** inferiority complex

10 倦怠感 **kentaikan** fatigue

恐怖感 **kyōfukan** sense of fear

11 第六感 **dai-rokkan** sixth sense

責任感 **sekininkan** sense of responsibility

12 違和感 **iwakan** feeling ill at ease, discomfort, malaise

13 罪悪感 **zaiakukan** guilty conscience

17 優越感 **yūetsukan** superiority complex

惡 → 悪   **4k7.17**

——————— 10 ———————

4k10.3 / 1460   冂 食 心 一
                           73 51 14

慨   慨丨慨慨

GAI, nage(ku) regret, lament, bemoan

——————— 1 ———————

13 慨嘆 **gaitan** regret, lament, deplore

——————— 2 ———————

13 感慨無量 **kangai-muryō** full of emotion

15 憤慨 **fungai** indignation, resentment

博 → 博   **2k10.1**

4k10.4 / 1785   囗 目 心 十
                           55 51 12

慎   愼丨慎慎

SHIN, tsutsushi(mu) be discreet/careful; restrain oneself, refrain from **tsutsu(mashii)** modest, reserved MAKOTO (m. given name)

—— 1 ——

³ 慎也 **Shin'ya** (m. given name)

⁹ 慎重 **shinchō** cautious

¹¹ 慎深 **tsutsushi(mi)buka(i)** discreet, cautious

4k10.14 / 387

田 月 心 竹
42 51 17

態

態態

TAI condition, appearance
waza (to) intentionally

—— 1 ——

³ 態々 **wazawaza** on purpose, deliberately

⁹ 態度 **taido** attitude, stance, posture

—— 2 ——

⁵ 失態 **shittai** blunder, mismanagement; disgrace

生態学 **seitaigaku** ecology

⁷ 状態 **jōtai** state of affairs, situation

形態 **keitai** form, shape, configuration

⁸ 事態 **jitai** situation, state of affairs

実態 **jittai** actual conditions

⁹ 重態 **jūtai** in serious/critical condition

変態 **hentai** metamorphosis; abnormal, perverted

¹⁰ 容態 **yōdai** (patient's) condition

¹² 媚態 **bitai** coquetry

¹⁴ 静態 **seitai** static, stationary

惡 → 悪 4k7.17

慈 → 慈 2o11.1

—— 11 ——

惨 → 惨 4k8.5

4k11.7 / 1365

田 心 田 日
51 58 43

憎

憎 憎 憎

ZŌ, niku(mu/garu) hate **niku(i/rashii)** hateful, horrible, repulsive
niku(shimi) hatred, animosity

—— 1 ——

³ 憎々 **nikuniku(shii)** hateful, loathsome, malicious

憎口 **niku(mare)guchi** offensive/malicious remarks

⁶ 憎合 **niku(mi)a(u)** hate one another

¹¹ 憎悪 **zōo** hatred, abhorrence

—— 2 ——

⁵ 生憎 **ainiku** unfortunately

¹⁴ 愛憎 **aizō** love and/or hate

4k11.8 / 1410

田 日 心 日
55 51 43

慢

慢 慢

MAN lazy; scorn, deride; prolonged, chronic; boasting

—— 1 ——

⁸ 慢性 **mansei** chronic

—— 2 ——

⁶ 自慢 **jiman** be proud of

⁷ 我慢 **gaman** put up with, bear, endure, be patient

⁹ 怠慢 **taiman** negligence, dereliction, inattention

¹⁰ 高慢 **kōman** proud, haughty, supercilious

¹³ 傲慢 **gōman** proud, arrogant, haughty

¹⁵ 緩慢 **kanman** sluggish, slack

—— 3 ——

¹² 腕自慢 **udejiman** proud of one's skill

¹⁴ 痩我慢 **ya(se)gaman** endure for sake of pride

4k11.9 / 915   田 貝 心 女
                    68 51 25

慣慣

KAN, na(reru) get used to
na(rasu) accustom to; tame

—————— 1 ——————

5 慣用句 **kan'yōku** idiom, common
   expression
   慣用語 **kan'yōgo** idiom, colloquial
   word/phrase
8 慣例 **kanrei** custom, precedent
11 慣習 **kanshū** custom, practice

—————— 2 ——————

4 手慣 **tena(reru)** get used to, become practiced in
7 見慣 **mina(reru)** get used to seeing,
   be familiar to
11 習慣 **shūkan** custom, habit

—————— 3 ——————

11 悪習慣 **akushūkan** bad habit, evil
   practice

4k11.13 / 1618   田 礻 心 尸
                      45 51 40

慰慰

I, nagusa(meru) comfort, console;
amuse, cheer up **nagusa(mu)** be di-
verted/amused; banter; make a play-
thing of YASU (part of given name)

—————— 1 ——————

6 慰安 **ian** comfort, recreation,
   amusement
   慰安婦 **ianfu** comfort girl/woman,
   army prostitute
11 慰問 **imon** consolation, sympathy
15 慰霊祭 **ireisai** memorial service
17 慰謝料 **isharyō** consolation money, solatium

—————— 2 ——————

4 弔慰 **chōi** condolences, sympathy

慭 → 憩 **4k12.10**

慾 → 欲 **4j7.1**

4k11.16 / 2076   目 心 ヨ 十
                      51 39 12

慧慧

KEI wise, clever, astute KEI, E, SATO,
TOSHI (part of given name) SATOSHI,
SATORU, AKIRA, TOSHI (m. given
name)

—————— 2 ——————

12 智慧 **chie** knowledge, wisdom

—————— 12 ——————

慨 → 慨 **4k10.3**

4k12.3   田 心 火 艹
             51 44 32

憮憮

BU be disappointed/surprised

—————— 1 ——————

12 憮然 **buzen** discouraged; surprised

4k12.4   田 心 日 口
             51 43 24

憚憚

TAN, habaka(ru) be afraid of, shrink
from; (clouds) spread

—————— 1 ——————

14 憚様 **habaka(ri)sama** Thanks for
   your trouble.

木
月
日
火
礻
王
牛
方
攵
欠 **12**
心
尸
戈

4k12.5 / 2077

田 立 忄 日
54 51 43

憧 憧

DŌ, SHŌ, akoga(reru) yearn for, aspire to, admire　**DŌ, SHŌ, TŌ** (part of given name)

4k12.6 / 1661

田 貝 忄 艹
68 51 32

憤 憤

FUN, ikidō(ru) resent, be indignant/enraged

——————— 1 ———————
12 憤然 **funzen** indignantly
13 憤慨 **fungai** indignation, resentment

——————— 2 ———————
9 発憤 **happun** be roused to action
13 義憤 **gifun** righteous indignation

憎 → 憎　4k11.7

4k12.10 / 1243

田 目 忄 口
55 51 24

憩｜憩 憩

KEI, iko(u) rest, relax　**iko(i)** rest, relaxation

——————— 2 ———————
6 休憩 **kyūkei** recess, break, intermission

4k12.12

田 馬 忄 阝
78 51 7

憑 憑

HYŌ be based on, rely on; be demon-possessed　**tsu(ku)** possess, haunt,

obsess　**tsu(kareru)** be spirit-possessed, be haunted by

——————— 1 ———————
8 憑物 **tsu(ki)mono** possessing spirit, curse, obsession

——————— 2 ———————
9 信憑性 **shinpyōsei** credibility, authenticity

——————————— 13 ———————————

4k13.3 / 1815

田 忄 戈 口
51 52 24

憾 憾

KAN, ura(mu) regret, be sorry for

——————— 1 ———————
7 憾言 **ura(mi)goto** words of regret

——————— 2 ———————
14 遺憾 **ikan** regrettable

4k13.4

田 米 忄 夕
62 51 30

憐 憐

REN, awa(remu) pity, feel compassion, sympathize with　**awa(remi)** pity, compassion

——————— 1 ———————
11 憐深 **awa(remi)buka(i)** compassionate

4k13.5 / 381

田 立 忄 日
54 51 43

憶｜憶 憶

OKU remember, think　**omo(u)** think of, remember

——————— 1 ———————
10 憶病 **okubyō** cowardice, timidity
12 憶測 **okusoku** speculation, conjecture

10 記憶 **kioku** memory

4k13.9 / 1408   田 日 衤 心
                          55 57 51

懐｜懐懐

KAI pocket; nostalgia **natsu(kashii)**
dear, fond, longed-for **natsu(kashimu)**
yearn for **natsu(ku)** take kindly to
natsu(keru) win over; tame **futokoro**
breast (pocket)

───────── 1 ─────────

4 懐中 **kaichū** one's pocket
   懐中電灯 **kaichū dentō** flashlight
5 懐古 **kaiko** nostalgia
   懐旧 **kaikyū** yearning for the old
      days
7 懐妊 **kainin** pregnancy
10 懐郷 **kaikyō** nostalgic reminis-
      cence
14 懐疑論 **kaigiron** skepticism

4k13.12 / 1135   田 食 心 犭
                          73 51 27

懇懇

KON, nengo(ro) friendly, cordial, intimate, kind

───────── 1 ─────────

13 懇意 **kon'i** intimacy, friendship,
      kindness
15 懇談会 **kondankai** get-together,
      friendly discussion
16 懇親会 **konshinkai** social gather-
      ing

───────── 14 ─────────

4k14.1   田 雨 心 而
                   75 51 14

懦懦

DA timidity, cowardice

───────── 1 ─────────

10 懦弱 **dajaku** effete, soft

4k14.3 / 1421   日 王 攵 心
                          46 49 51

懲｜懲懲

CHŌ, ko(riru) learn from experience,
be taught a lesson, be sick of
ko(rasu) chastise, punish, discipline

───────── 1 ─────────

0 懲らしめる **ko(rashimeru)** chas-
      tise, punish, discipline, teach a
      lesson
7 懲役 **chōeki** penal servitude, im-
      prisonment
14 懲罰 **chōbatsu** disciplinary mea-
      sure, punishment

應 → 応 3q4.2

───────── 15 ─────────

懲 → 懲 4k14.3

───────── 16 ─────────

懐 → 懐 4k13.9

4k16.2 / 911   田 糸 日 心
                          61 55 51

懸懸

KEN, KE, ka(karu) hang
ka(keru) hang; offer, give

───────── 1 ─────────

8 懸念 **kenen** fear, apprehension
  懸命 **kenmei** eager, going all-out;
      risking one's life
15 懸賞 **kenshō** offering prizes
16 懸橋 **ka(ke)hashi** suspension
      bridge; viaduct

───────── 2 ─────────

8 命懸 **inochiga(ke)** life-or-death,
      risky, desperate

4
木
月
日
火
衤
王
牛
方
攵
欠
心 16
戸
戈

14 踊懸 **odo(ri)ka(karu)** spring upon, jump at
21 躍懸 **odo(ri)ka(karu)** spring upon, jump at

一所懸命 **isshokenmei** with all one's might

——— 3 ———

1 一生懸命 **isshōkenmei** with all one's might

——— 19 ———

戀 → 恋 **2j8.2**

——— 戸 4m ———

戸	戻	戻	肩	房	所	扁	扇	雇	扉	肇
0.1	3.1	4m3.1	4.1	4.2	4.3	5.1	6.1	8.1	8.2	10.1

——— 0 ———

4m0.1 / 152

□ 尸
40

戸

戸｜尸 尸

KO door; house(hold) **to** door

——— 1 ———

5 戸外 **kogai** outdoor, open-air
戸田 **Toda** (surname)
12 戸棚 **todana** cupboard, cabinet, closet
戸惑 **tomado(i)** become disoriented-ed/confused
13 戸数 **kosū** number of houses/households
20 戸籍 **koseki** family register

——— 2 ———

1 一戸 **ikko** a house; a household
3 下戸 **geko** nondrinker, teetotaler
4 井戸 **ido** (water) well
水戸 **Mito** (city, Ibaraki-ken)
6 江戸 **Edo** (old name for Tōkyō, 1603 – 1867)
8 雨戸 **amado** storm door, shutter
9 神戸 **Kōbe** (city, Hyōgo-ken)
18 鎧戸 **yoroido** Venetian blinds
19 瀬戸 **seto** strait(s), channel; porcelain
瀬戸内海 **Setonaikai** the Inland Sea
瀬戸物 **setomono** porcelain, china, earthenware
瀬戸際 **setogiwa** crucial moment, crisis, brink

——— 3 ———

4m3.1 / 1238

□ 尸 大
40 34

戻

戻｜戻 戻

REI, modo(ru) go/come back, return **modo(su)** give/send back, return, restore; throw up, vomit

——— 1 ———

11 戻道 **modo(ri)michi** the way back

——— 2 ———

5 払戻 **hara(i)modo(su)** refund, reimburse
立戻 **ta(chi)modo(ru)** return to
8 取戻 **to(ri)modo(su)** take back, regain, recoup, catch up on
9 巻戻 **ma(ki)modo(shi)** rewind (a tape)
15 舞戻 **ma(i)modo(ru)** find one's way back, return

——— 4 ———

戻 → 戻 **4m3.1**

4m4.1 / 1264

□ 月 尸
42 40

肩

肩｜肩 肩

KEN, kata shoulder

⁵ 肩代 **kataga(wari)** change of palanquin bearers; takeover, transfer (of a business)

¹⁰ 肩書 **kataga(ki)** one's title, degree

4m4.2 / 1237

□ 方 尸
48 40

房 | 房 房

BŌ a room; tassel **fusa** tassel, tuft, cluster

----------- 1 -----------

³ 房々 **fusafusa** tufty, bushy, profuse (hair)

----------- 2 -----------

³ 女房 **nyōbō** wife; court lady

⁷ 冷房 **reibō** air conditioning
乳房 **chibusa** breast

⁸ 官房長官 **kanbō chōkan** Chief Cabinet Secretary

¹⁰ 書房 **shobō** library; bookstore

¹³ 暖房 **danbō** heating
煖房 **danbō** heating

¹⁵ 監房 **kanbō** (prison) cell

4m4.3 / 153

□ 尸 斤
40 50

所 | 所 所

SHO, tokoro, toko place

----------- 1 -----------

⁶ 所在 **shozai** whereabouts, location, site
所有 **shoyū** ownership, possession

⁸ 所長 **shochō** director, head, manager
所定 **shotei** fixed, prescribed, stated

⁹ 所信 **shoshin** one's belief, conviction, opinion
所持 **shoji** possess, have on one's person, carry

¹⁰ 所員 **shoin** (member of the) staff, personnel
所帯 **shotai** household, home
所帯持 **shotaimo(chi)** housekeeping; married (wo)man

¹¹ 所得 **shotoku** income, earnings
所得税 **shotokuzei** income tax
所産 **shosan** product, result

¹² 所属 **shozoku** be attached/assigned to

¹³ 所詮 **shosen** after all
所載 **shosai** printed, published

¹⁵ 所蔵 **shozō** in one's possession

----------- 2 -----------

¹ 一所 **ik(ka)sho, issho, hitotokoro** one place; the same place
一所懸命 **isshokenmei** with all one's might

² 入所 **nyūsho** entrance, admission; imprisonment

³ 3ヶ所 **sankasho** three places

⁵ 出所 **shussho** source, origin; be released from prison
dedokoro source, origin
他所 **tasho** another place
台所 **daidokoro** kitchen

⁶ 近所 **kinjo** neighborhood, vicinity
至所 **ita(ru) tokoro** everywhere
名所 **meisho** noted places/sights
各所 **kakusho** each place, various places

⁷ 住所 **jūsho, su(mi)dokoro** address; residence, domicile
余所 **yoso** another place; other, strange
役所 **yakusho** government office
見所 **midokoro** the part most worth seeing; promise, merit **mi(ta) tokoro** judging from the appearance

⁸ 長所 **chōsho** one's strong point, advantages
狙所 **nera(i)dokoro** aim, objective

⁹ 便所 **benjo** toilet, lavatory
急所 **kyūsho** vital point, vulnerable spot; crux, key (to)

¹⁰ 高所 **kōsho** elevation, height; altitude; broad view

¹¹ 勘所 **kandokoro** vital point, crux

¹² 場所 **basho** place, location

4

木
月
日
火
礻
王
牛
方
攵
欠
心
尸 4
戈

短所 **tansho** shortcoming, defect, fault

御所 **gosho** imperial palace

無所属 **mushozoku** unaffiliated, independent

13 預所 **azu(kari)sho** depository, warehouse

14 箇所 **kasho** place, part, passage (in a book)

--- 3 ---

4 収容所 **shūyōjo** home, asylum, camp

区役所 **kuyakusho** ward office

5 市役所 **shiyakusho** city hall

6 刑務所 **keimusho** prison

7 初場所 **hatsubasho** New Year's grand sumo tournament

8 事務所 **jimusho** office

9 発電所 **hatsudensho** power plant, generating station

洗面所 **senmenjo** washroom, lavatory

派出所 **hashutsujo** police box; branch office

研究所 **kenkyūjo** (research) institute, laboratory

秋場所 **akibasho** autumn sumo tournament

10 案内所 **annaijo** information office/ booth

11 停留所 **teiryūjo** stopping place, (bus) stop

脱衣所 **datsuisho, datsuijo** changing/dressing room

救護所 **kyūgosho** first-aid station

12 裁判所 **saibansho** (law) court

給油所 **kyūyusho** filling/gas station

13 碁会所 **gokaisho, gokaijo** go club

14 製鉄所 **seitetsujo** ironworks

16 興信所 **kōshinjo** detective/investigative agency

17 療養所 **ryōyōjo** sanitarium

20 醸造所 **jōzōsho** brewery, distillery

--- 5 ---

11 商工会議所 **Shōkō Kaigisho** Chamber of Commerce and Industry

12 最高裁判所 **Saikō Saibansho** Supreme Court

--- 5 ---

4m5.1　　□ 尸 艹 冂
　　　　　　40 32 20

扁｜扁扁

HEN doorplate, nameplate; flat; small

--- 1 ---

5 扁平足 **henpeisoku** flat feet

10 扁桃腺 **hentōsen** the tonsils

--- 6 ---

4m6.1 / 1555　　□ 尸 ⦿
　　　　　　　40 39

扇扇

SEN, ōgi folding fan　**ao(gu)** fan

--- 1 ---

2 扇子 **sensu** folding fan

7 扇形 **ōgigata, senkei** fan shape, sector, segment

9 扇風機 **senpūki** (electric) fan

11 扇動者 **sendōsha** instigator, agitator

--- 2 ---

6 団扇 **uchiwa** round fan

--- 8 ---

4m8.1 / 1553　　□ 隹 尸
　　　　　　　74 40

雇｜雇雇

KO, yato(u) employ, hire; charter
yato(i) employee

--- 1 ---

2 雇入 **yato(i)i(reru)** employ, hire; charter

雇人 **yato(i)nin** employee; servant

5 雇用 **koyō** employment

雇用者 **koyōsha** employer

雇主 **yato(i)nushi** employer

¹¹ 雇傭 **koyō** employment, hiring

━━━ 2 ━━━

¹³ 解雇 **kaiko** discharge, dismissal

4m8.2 / 1556   口 尸 儿 二
           40 16 4

 扉 | 扉 扉

HI, tobira door (hinged, not sliding)

━━━ 10 ━━━

4m10.1 / 2204   田 夂 尸 彐
           49 40 39

 肇 肇

CHŌ begin, found; rectify CHŌ, TŌ, HATSU, TADA, TOSHI, KOTO (part of given name) HAJIME, TADASHI (m. given name)

━━━ 弋 **4n** ━━━

成	戒	式	弍	我	或	威	武	哉	戚	栽	戚	越
2.1	3.1	3.2	3.3	0a7.10	4.2	5.2	5.3	5.4	4n7.2	6.1	7.2	8.2

殘	幾	裁	戰	感	歲	越	鳶	戲	戰	戯	戴	鹹
0a10.11	8.4	5e6.9	9.2	4k9.21	9.5	4n8.2	11b3.1	11.1	4n9.2	4n11.1	5f12.2	16.1

━━━ 2 ━━━

4n2.1 / 261   口 戈 ノ
           52 15

 成 成

SEI, JŌ, na(ru) become, consist of **na(su)** do; form SEI, SHIGE, NARI (part of given name)

━━━ 1 ━━━

² 成人 **seijin** adult

成人式 **seijinshiki** Coming-of-Age-Day (Jan. 15) ceremony

⁴ 成文 **seibun** composition, writing

成分 **seibun** composition, content, ingredient, component

⁵ 成功 **seikō** success

成句 **seiku** set phrase, idiomatic expression

成立 **seiritsu** come into being, be formed/effected **na(ri)ta(tsu)** consist of; be effected, come into being **na(ri)ta(chi)** origin, history, makeup

⁶ 成年 **seinen** (age of) majority, adulthood

成行 **na(ri)yu(ki)** course (of events), developments

⁸ 成長 **seichō** growth

成果 **seika** result, fruit **na(ri)-ha(teru)** become, be reduced to **na(re) (no) ha(te)** the wreck of one's former self

成育 **seiiku** growth, development

成金 **narikin** new rich, parvenu

⁹ 成美 **Shigemi, Shigeyoshi, Narumi, Seibi** (given name)

¹¹ 成章 **Nariaki, Shigeaki, Seishō, Narikira, Shigeaya** (m. given name)

¹⁴ 成熟 **seijuku** ripen; mature

成語 **seigo** set phrase, idiomatic expression

¹⁷ 成績 **seiseki** results, (business) performance

成績表 **seisekihyō** report/score card

━━━ 2 ━━━

³ 大成 **taisei** complete, accomplish; compile; attain greatness

⁴ 化成 **kasei** transformation, chemical synthesis

⁵ 未成年 **miseinen** minority, not of age

生成 **seisei** creation, formation, generation

平成 **Heisei** (era, 1989 –)

6 合成 **gōsei** synthetic, composite, combined

7 作成 **sakusei** draw up, prepare

助成金 **joseikin** subsidy, grant

形成 **keisei** formation, makeup

完成 **kansei** completion, accomplishment

8 育成 **ikusei** rearing, training

10 既成事実 **kisei jijitsu** fait accompli

11 達成 **tassei** achieve, attain

組成 **sosei** composition, makeup

12 結成 **kessei** formation, organization

集成 **shūsei** collect, compile

14 構成 **kōsei** composition, makeup

15 養成 **yōsei** train, educate, cultivate

編成 **hensei** organize, put together

賛成 **sansei** agreement, approbation

16 錬成 **rensei** training

——————— 3 ———————

5 未完成 **mikansei** incomplete, unfinished

6 光合成 **kōgōsei** photosynthesis

——————— 3 ———————

4n3.1 / 876

□ 戈 艹
52 32

戒 戒

KAI, imashi(meru) admonish, warn
imashi(me) instructions

——————— 1 ———————

7 戒告 **kaikoku** warning, admonition

17 戒厳令 **kaigenrei** martial law

——————— 2 ———————

11 斎戒 **saikai** purification

19 警戒 **keikai** warning, (pre)caution; vigilance

4n3.2 / 525

□ 戈 工
52 38

式
式 式

SHIKI ceremony, rite; formula, expression (in math); (as suffix) type, style, system NORI (part of given name)

——————— 1 ———————

8 式典 **shikiten** ceremonies

12 式場 **shikijō** ceremonial hall

13 式辞 **shikiji** address, message, oration

——————— 2 ———————

1 一式 **isshiki** a complete set; all, the whole

4 公式 **kōshiki** formula, formality

方式 **hōshiki** formula; form; method, system; formalities, usage

5 正式 **seishiki** formal, official

旧式 **kyūshiki** old-type, old-fashioned

7 形式 **keishiki** form; formality

8 定式 **jōshiki, teishiki** prescribed/established form, formula, formality

9 洋式 **yōshiki** Western-style

10 挙式 **kyoshiki** (wedding) ceremony

株式 **kabushiki** shares, stocks

株式市場 **kabushiki shijō** stock market

株式会社 **kabushiki-gaisha, kabushiki kaisha** corporation, Co., Ltd.

書式 **shoshiki** (blank) form

12 葬式 **sōshiki** funeral

13 新式 **shinshiki** new-type, new-style, modern

14 様式 **yōshiki** style, form

15 儀式 **gishiki** ceremony

——————— 3 ———————

6 成人式 **seijinshiki** Coming-of-Age-Day (Jan. 15) ceremony

8 定礎式 **teisoshiki** cornerstone-laying ceremony

金婚式 **kinkonshiki** golden wedding anniversary

9 除幕式 **jomakushiki** unveiling (ceremony)

洗礼式 **senreishiki** baptism (ceremony)

10 訓令式 **kunreishiki** (a system of romanization which differs from Hepburn romanization in such syllables as *shi/si, tsu/tu, cha/tya*)

11 組立式 **kumita(te)shiki** prefab, collapsible

12 棟上式 **munea(ge)shiki** roof-raising ceremony

結婚式 **kekkonshiki** wedding

開会式 **kaikaishiki** opening ceremony

14 銀婚式 **ginkonshiki** silver wedding anniversary

17 戴冠式 **taikanshiki** coronation

4n3.3 / 1030

     □ 弋 二 丨
     52 4 2

弍   貳丨弍式

NI two (in documents)

我 → 0a7.10

───── 4 ─────

4n4.2 / 1994

     冂 弋 口 丨
     52 24 2

或   或 或

WAKU, a(ru) a certain, a, some, one **arui(wa)** or; perhaps

───── 1 ─────

4 或日 **a(ru) hi** one day

───── 5 ─────

4n5.2 / 1339

     冂 弋 女 一
     52 25 1

威   威 威

I authority, dignity, majesty; threat **odo(su)** threaten TAKESHI (m. given name)

───── 1 ─────

2 威力 **iryoku** power, might, authority, influence

11 威張 **iba(ru)** be proud, swagger

13 威勢 **isei** power, influence; high spirits

17 威嚇 **ikaku** menace, threat

威厳 **igen** dignity, majesty, stateliness

───── 2 ─────

5 示威的 **jiiteki** demonstrative, threatening

10 脅威 **kyōi** threat, menace

15 権威 **ken'i** authority; an authority

4n5.3 / 1001

     □ 弋 卜 一
     52 13 1

武   武 武

BU, MU military TAKESHI (m. given name) TAKE (part of given name)

───── 1 ─────

3 武士 **bushi, mononofu** samurai, warrior

4 武内 **Takeuchi, Takenouchi** (surname)

武中 **Takenaka** (surname)

武井 **Takei** (surname)

5 武本 **Takemoto** (surname)

武田 **Takeda** (surname)

7 武村 **Takemura** (surname)

8 武者振 **mushabu(ri)** valor, gallantry

9 武彦 **Takehiko, Takeyoshi** (m. given name)

10 武家 **buke** samurai

11 武道 **budō** military/martial arts, bushido

武術 **bujutsu** military/martial arts

12 武装 **busō** arms; armed (neutrality)

15 武器 **buki** weapon, arms

武蔵 **Musashi** (ancient kuni, Saitama-ken and Tōkyō-to)

18 武藤 **Mutō** (surname)

───── 2 ─────

8 非武装 **hibusō** demilitarized (zone), unarmed (neutrality)

4

木
月
日
火
礻
王
牛
方
欠
心
戸
戈 5

⁹ 神武 **Jinmu** (emperor, 660 – 585 B.C.)

4n5.4 / 2037 　　　🔲 戈 口 十
　　　　　　　　　　　52　24　12

哉 　　　哉 哉

SAI how, what, alas, (question particle) SAI, YA, CHIKA, KA, KANA, KI, TOSHI, SUKE, EI (part of given name)　HAJIME (m. given name)

――――――― 2 ―――――――

⁴ 友哉 **Tomoya** (m. given name)
⁸ 直哉 **Naoya** (m. given name)
　拓哉 **Takuya** (m. given name)
¹² 智哉 **Tomoya** (m. given name)

――――――― 6 ―――――――

戚 → **4n7.2**

4n6.1 / 1125 　　　🔲 戈 木 十
　　　　　　　　　　　52　41　12

栽 　　　栽 栽

SAI planting

――――――― 1 ―――――――

¹¹ 栽培 **saibai** cultivate, grow

――――――― 2 ―――――――

⁹ 盆栽 **bonsai** bonsai, potted dwarf tree

――――――― 7 ―――――――

4n7.2 　　　　🔲 戈 小 卜
　　　　　　　　　52　35　13

戚 　　　戚 戚

SEKI battleax; relatives, kin; sadness

――――――― 2 ―――――――

¹⁶ 親戚 **shinseki** a relative

――――――― 8 ―――――――

4n8.2 / 1001 　　　🔲 戈 土 卜
　　　　　　　　　　52　22　13

越 　　　越 越

ETSU cross, go beyond, exceed; Vietnam　**ko(su), ko(eru)** cross, go beyond, exceed　**-go(shi)** across, over, through

――――――― 1 ―――――――

¹⁴ 越境 **ekkyō** (illegally) crossing the border
¹⁵ 越権 **ekken** overstepping one's authority

――――――― 2 ―――――――

⁴ 引越 **hi(k)ko(su)** move (to a new residence)
⁷ 呉越同舟 **Go-Etsu dōshū** enemies in the same boat
⁸ 追越 **o(i)ko(su)** overtake
¹⁰ 借越 **ka(ri)ko(su)** overdraw
¹² 超越 **chōetsu** transcend, rise above
　勝越 **ka(chi)ko(shi)** ahead by (so many) wins
¹⁷ 優越感 **yūetsukan** superiority complex
¹⁹ 繰越 **ku(ri)ko(su)** transfer, carry forward

残 → 残 **0a10.11**

4n8.4 / 877 　　　🔲 戈 竹 亻
　　　　　　　　　52　17　3

幾 　　　幾 幾

KI, iku- how much/many; some, several

――――――― 1 ―――――――

⁰ 幾つ **iku(tsu)** how many/old
　幾ら **iku(ra)** how much
² 幾人 **ikunin** how many people
³ 幾千 **ikusen** thousands
⁴ 幾分 **ikubun** some, a portion

幾日 **ikunichi** how many days;
what day of the month

6 幾年 **ikunen, ikutose** how many
years

7 幾何学 **kikagaku** geometry

8 幾夜 **ikuyo** how many nights; many
a night

裁→ 5e6.9

───────── 9 ─────────

4n9.2 / 301

田 日 戈 小
43 52 35

SEN, ikusa war, battle **tataka(u)**
wage war; fight **onono(ku)** shudder,
tremble **wanana(ku)** tremble
soyo(gu) rustle, stir, sway, tremble,
quiver

───────── 1 ─────────

3 戦士 **senshi** warrior, soldier

5 戦史 **senshi** military/war history

戦犯 **senpan** war crime/criminal

6 戦死 **senshi** death in battle, killed in
action

戦争 **sensō** war

戦争中 **sensōchū** during the war

戦地 **senchi** battlefield, the front

7 戦没者 **senbotsusha** fallen soldier

戦乱 **senran** the upheavals of war,
war-torn (region)

戦災 **sensai** war devastation

戦車 **sensha** tank

8 戦果 **senka** war results

戦殁者 **senbotsusha** fallen soldier

戦国時代 **sengoku jidai** era of civil
wars

9 戦前 **senzen** before the war, prewar

戦後 **sengo** after the war, postwar

10 戦時 **senji** wartime, war period

戦時中 **senjichū** during the war,
wartime

戦記 **senki** account of a war

11 戦術 **senjutsu** tactics

戦略 **senryaku** strategy

戦敗国 **senpaikoku** defeated nation

12 戦備 **senbi** military preparedness

戦渦 **senka** the turmoil of war

戦場 **senjō** battlefield, the front

戦勝国 **senshōkoku** victorious nation

戦費 **senpi** war expenditures

13 戦禍 **senka** war damage, ravages of
war

15 戦線 **sensen** battle line, front

18 戦闘 **sentō** combat, battle, fighting

戦闘機 **sentōki** fighter (plane)

21 戦艦 **senkan** battleship

───────── 2 ─────────

3 大戦 **taisen** great/world war

4 内戦 **naisen** civil war

反戦 **hansen** antiwar

6 死戦 **shisen** death struggle

休戦 **kyūsen** truce, cease-fire

合戦 **kassen** battle

7 作戦 **sakusen** (military) operation,
tactics

冷戦 **reisen** cold war

決戦 **kessen** decisive battle; play-
offs

抗戦 **kōsen** resistance

乱戦 **ransen** melee, free-for-all
fight

9 海戦 **kaisen** naval battle

挑戦 **chōsen** challenge

宣戦布告 **sensen fukoku** declaration of war

11 接戦 **sessen** close combat/contest

終戦 **shūsen** end of the war

敗戦 **haisen** lost battle, defeat

13 聖戦 **seisen** holy war, crusade

15 熱戦 **nessen** fierce fighting; close
contest

16 激戦 **gekisen** fierce fighting, hard-
fought contest

───────── 3 ─────────

1 一回戦 **ikkaisen** first game/round
(of tennis)

5 白熱戦 **hakunetsusen** intense
fighting, thrilling game

6 争奪戦 **sōdatsusen** contest/scram-
ble/struggle for

10 遊撃戦 **yūgekisen** guerrilla warfare

4

木
月
日
火
礻
王
牛
方
攵
欠
心
戸
戈 9

¹¹ 終盤戦 **shūbansen** endgame, final
battle

¹⁴ 選挙戦 **senkyosen** election campaign

感 → 感 **4k9.21**

歳

歳 歳

□ 弋 小 卜
52 35 13

SAI year; harvest; (as suffix) … years
old **SEI** year **toshi** year, one's age
TOSHI (part of given name)

― 1 ―

² 歳入 **sainyū** annual revenue
⁴ 歳月 **saigetsu** time, years
⁵ 歳出 **saishutsu** annual expenditures
  歳市 **toshi (no) ichi** year-end market (cf. 節季市)
  歳旦 **saitan** New Year's Day; the New Year
¹⁰ 歳時記 **saijiki** almanac
¹⁴ 歳暮 **seibo** year's end; year-end present

― 2 ―

³ 万歳 **banzai** hurrah
  千歳 **chitose** a thousand years

― 3 ―

² 二十歳 **hatachi** 20 years old, age 20

越 → **4n8.2**

― 11 ―

鳶 → **11b3.1**

戯

戯 I 戯 戯

□ 弋 厂 十
52 18 12

GI, GE, tawamu(reru) play, sport;
jest; flirt **tawa(keru)** act foolish
ja(reru), za(reru) be playful, gambol

― 1 ―

⁶ 戯曲 **gikyoku** drama, play
⁸ 戯画 **giga** a caricature

― 2 ―

¹⁰ 遊戯 **yūgi** games, amusement, entertainment **aso(bi)-tawamu(reru)** play, frolic
¹¹ 悪戯 **akugi, itazura** prank, mischief

――― 12 ―――

戦 → 戦 **4n9.2**

――― 13 ―――

戯 → 戯 **4n11.1**

戴 → **5f12.2**

――― 16 ―――

□ 弋 口 卜
52 24 13

鹹

鹹 鹹

KAN, kara(i) salty

― 1 ―

⁴ 鹹水魚 **kansuigyo** saltwater fish

――――――― 石 **5a** ―――――――

石	研	砂	砒	砕	破	砲	砥	研	硅	硬	硯	硫
0.1	4.1	4.3	4.5	4.6	5.1	5.3	5.4	5a4.1	4f6.4	7.1	7.2	7.3

硝	碑	碍	碇	碗	砕	碁	碩	碑	碵	磁	碧	碼
7.6	5a9.2	8.4	8.6	8.7	5a4.6	8.9	9.1	9.2	5a9.1	9.6	9.7	10.1

確 磐 礫 磯 礁 礎 礙 礫
10.3 10.9 11.2 12.1 12.2 13.2 5a8.4 15.1

─── 0 ───

5a0.1 / 78 · □ 石 53

石

石 石

SEKI, SHAKU, ishi stone
KOKU (unit of volume, about 180
liters) **IWA** (part of given name)

─── 1 ───

3 石川 **Ishikawa** (surname)
  石川県 **Ishikawa-ken** (prefecture)
4 石井 **Ishii** (surname)
  石仏 **ishibotoke, sekibutsu** stone
    image of Buddha
  石文 **ishibumi** (inscribed) stone
    monument
5 石田 **Ishida** (surname)
8 石油 **sekiyu** petroleum, oil, kero-
    sene
  石門 **sekimon** stone gate
9 石段 **ishidan** stone steps
  石垣 **ishigaki** stone wall
  石狩川 **Ishikari-gawa** (river, Hok-
    kaidō)
  石炭 **sekitan** coal
10 石原 **Ishihara** (surname)
12 石塔 **sekitō** tombstone, stone mon-
    ument
  石塀 **ishibei** stone wall
13 石塊 **sekkai, ishikoro, ishikure**
    pebble, stones
14 石像 **sekizō** stone image/statue
  石碑 **sekihi** tombstone, (stone)
    monument
15 石器時代 **sekki jidai** the Stone Age
16 石橋 **Ishibashi** (surname)
24 石鹸 **sekken** soap

─── 2 ───

1 一石二鳥 **isseki nichō** killing two
    birds with one stone
3 大石 **Ōishi** (surname)
5 白石 **Shiraishi** (surname)
  立石 **Tateishi** (surname)

8 宝石 **hōseki** precious stone, gem,
    jewel
  岩石 **ganseki** rock
  明石 **Akashi** (city, Hyōgo-ken)
9 砕石 **saiseki** rubble, broken stone
10 高石 **Takaishi** (surname)
  流石 **sasuga** as might be expected
  砥石 **toishi** whetstone
13 墓石 **hakaishi, boseki** gravestone
  碁石 **goishi** go stone
  鉱石 **kōseki** ore, mineral, (radio)
    crystal
14 磁石 **jishaku, jiseki** magnet
  磁石盤 **jishakuban** (mariner's)
    compass
18 礎石 **soseki** foundation (stone)

─── 4 ───

5a4.1 / 896 · □ 石 艹 一 53 32 1

研

研｜研 研

KEN, to(gu) whet, hone, sharpen; polish; wash (rice)

─── 1 ───

7 研究 **kenkyū** research
  研究所 **kenkyūjo** (research) insti-
    tute, laboratory
  研究室 **kenkyūshitsu** laboratory,
    study room
  研学 **kengaku** study
10 研修 **kenshū** study and training

5a4.3 / 1151 · □ 石 小 ｜ 53 35 2

砂

砂 石少

SA, SHA, suna, isago sand

─── 1 ───

5 砂丘 **sakyū** dune
7 砂利 **jari** gravel

10 砂浜 **sunahama, sahin** sand beach

13 砂漠 **sabaku** desert

16 砂糖 **satō** sugar

—————— 2 ——————

3 土砂降 **doshabu(ri)** downpour

土砂崩 **doshakuzu(re)** landslide, washout

5 氷砂糖 **kōrizatō** rock candy, crystal sugar

5a4.5

石 卜
53 13

HI arsenic

5a4.6 / 1710

石 十
53 12

碎丨砕砕

SAI, kuda(ku) break, smash, pulverize **kuda(keru)** break, be crushed; become familiar **kuda(keta)** broken; plain, familiar, friendly

—————— 1 ——————

4 砕片 **saihen** fragment, splinter

5 砕石 **saiseki** rubble, broken stone

—————— 2 ——————

5 玉砕 **gyokusai** death for honor

16 擂砕 **su(ri)kuda(ku)** grind down/fine, pulverize

—————— 5 ——————

5a5.1 / 665

石 厂 又
53 18 9

破破

HA, yabu(ru), yabu(ku) tear, rip, break **yabu(reru), yabu(keru)** get torn/broken

—————— 1 ——————

4 破片 **hahen** broken piece, fragment, splinter

7 破局 **hakyoku** catastrophe, ruin

9 破約 **hayaku** breach of contract/promise

11 破産 **hasan** bankruptcy

破船 **hasen** shipwreck

12 破裂 **haretsu** bursting, rupture, explosion

13 破棄 **haki** annulment, repudiation, abrogation, reversal

破滅 **hametsu** ruin, destruction, downfall

破損 **hason** damage, breakage, breach

破廉恥 **harenchi** shameless, disgraceful

16 破壊 **hakai** destroy, demolish, collapse

—————— 2 ——————

7 牢破 **rōyabu(ri)** jailbreak

8 突破 **toppa** break through, overcome **tsu(ki)yabu(ru)** break/crash through

19 爆破 **bakuha** blast, blow up

5a5.3 / 1764

石 弓 宀
53 28 15

砲丨砲砲

HŌ gun, cannon **tsutsu** gun

—————— 1 ——————

4 砲火 **hōka** gunfire, shellfire

12 砲弾 **hōdan** shell, cannonball

15 砲撃 **hōgeki** shelling, bombardment

—————— 2 ——————

9 発砲 **happō** firing, discharge, shooting

13 鉄砲 **teppō** gun

14 銃砲 **jūhō** guns, firearms

5a5.4

口 石 厂 广
53 18 12

砥

砥 石氐

SHI, to, toishi whetstone **to(gu)** whet, hone, polish

———————— 1 ————————

5 砥石 **toishi** whetstone

———————— 6 ————————

研 → 研 **5a4.1**

硅 → 珪 **4f6.4**

———————— 7 ————————

5a7.1 / 1009

口 石 日 一
53 43 14

硬

硬硬

KŌ, kata(i) hard, firm

———————— 1 ————————

4 硬化 **kōka** hardening
硬水 **kōsui** hard water
9 硬派 **kōha** tough elements, hardliners, hardcore
11 硬貨 **kōka** coin; hard currency
12 硬筆 **kōhitsu** pen or pencil (rather than brush)

———————— 2 ————————

11 強硬 **kyōkō** firm, resolute, vigorous

5a7.2

口 貝 石
68 53

硯硯

KEN, suzuri inkstone

———————— 1 ————————

15 硯箱 **suzuribako** inkstone case

5a7.3 / 1856

口 石 宀 竹
53 11 17

硫

硫 石流

RYŪ sulfur

———————— 1 ————————

11 硫黄 **iō** sulfur
硫黄泉 **iōsen** sulfur springs

5a7.6 / 1855

口 石 月 小
53 42 35

硝

硝石肖

SHŌ saltpeter

———————— 1 ————————

2 硝子 **garasu** glass
13 硝煙 **shōen** gunpowder smoke

———————— 8 ————————

碑 → 碑 **5a9.2**

5a8.4

口 石 日 寸
53 43 37

碍

礙 | 碍碍

GAI obstacle

———————— 1 ————————

2 碍子 **gaishi** insulator

5a8.6

口 石 宀 疋
53 33 14

碇

碇碇

TEI, ikari anchor

———————— 1 ————————

8 碇泊 **teihaku** lie at anchor, be berthed/moored

5

石 8
立
目
禾
ネ
罒
皿
广

5a8.7

田 石 宀 夕
53 33 30

碗

碗 碗

WAN porcelain bowl, teacup

――― 2 ―――

9 茶碗 **chawan** teacup; (rice) bowl

茶碗蒸 **chawanmu(shi)** steamed non-sweet custard of vegetables, egg, and meat

碎 → 砕 5a4.6

5a8.9 / 1834

田 石 艹 二
53 32 4

碁

碁 碁

GO (the board game) go

――― 1 ―――

5 碁石 **goishi** go stone

6 碁会所 **gokaisho, gokaijo** go club

15 碁盤 **goban** go board

――― 2 ―――

7 囲碁 **igo** go (the board game)

――― 9 ―――

5a9.1 / 2265

田 頁 石
77 53

碩 | 碩 碩

SEKI great SEKI, HIRO, MICHI, Ō (part of given name) HIROSHI, MITSURU, YUTAKA (m. given name)

――― 1 ―――

7 碩学 **sekigaku** erudition; great scholar

5a9.2 / 1522

田 石 田 十
53 58 12

碑

碑 | 碑 碑

HI tombstone, monument
ishibumi (inscribed) stone monument

――― 1 ―――

4 碑文 **hibun** epitaph, inscription

14 碑銘 **himei** inscription, epitaph

――― 2 ―――

5 石碑 **sekihi** tombstone, (stone) monument

13 墓碑 **bohi** tombstone

――― 3 ―――

10 記念碑 **kinenhi** monument

碩 → 碩 5a9.1

5a9.6 / 1548

田 石 几 竹
53 16 17

磁 磁

JI magnetism; porcelain

――― 1 ―――

5 磁石 **jishaku, jiseki** magnet

磁石盤 **jishakuban** (mariner's) compass

6 磁気 **jiki** magnetism, magnetic

12 磁場 **jiba, jijō** magnetic field

15 磁器 **jiki** porcelain

――― 2 ―――

10 陶磁器 **tōjiki** ceramics, china and porcelain

5a9.7 / 2176

田 石 王 日
53 46 43

碧

碧 碧

HEKI blue, green MIDORI (f. given name) KIYOSHI (m. given name) HEKI, AO, TAMA (part of given name)

─────── 10 ───────

5a10.1　　　　　□ 馬 石
　　　　　　　　　78 53

碼

碼碼馬

BA, ME number; wharf; agate
yādo, yāru yard (91.44 cm)

5a10.3 / 603　　　□ 隹 石 冂
　　　　　　　　　74 53 20

確

確確

KAKU, tashi(ka) certain, sure
tashi(kameru) make sure of, verify
shika(to) certainly, definitely, exactly, clearly, fully, firmly

─────── 1 ───────

5 確立 **kakuritsu** establishment, settlement
8 確実 **kakujitsu** certain, reliable
　確定 **kakutei** decision, definite
9 確信 **kakushin** firm belief, conviction
　確保 **kakuho** secure, ensure
11 確率 **kakuritsu** probability
14 確認 **kakunin** confirm, verify

─────── 2 ───────

5 正確 **seikaku** exact, precise, accurate
6 再確認 **saikakunin** reaffirmation
8 明確 **meikaku** clear, distinct, well-defined
　的確 **tekikaku, tekkaku** precise, accurate, unerring

─────── 3 ───────

4 不正確 **fuseikaku** inaccurate

5a10.9　　　　　□ 舟 石 冂
　　　　　　　　　63 53 20

磐

磐磐

BAN, HAN, iwa rock, crag

─────── 1 ───────

11 磐梯山 **Bandai-san** (mountain, Fukushima-ken)

─────── 11 ───────

5a11.2　　　　　□ 石 木 夕
　　　　　　　　　53 41 30

磔

磔磔

TAKU crucifixion; pulling limb from limb; exposing a (criminal's) corpse
haritsuke crucifixion

─────── 1 ───────

6 磔刑 **haritsuke, takkei** crucifixion

─────── 12 ───────

5a12.1 / 2177　　　□ 石 戈 竹
　　　　　　　　　53 52 17

磯

磯磯

KI, iso (rocky) beach, seashore
KI, ISO, SHI (part of given name)

─────── 1 ───────

4 磯辺 **isobe** (rocky) beach, seashore
5 磯田 **Isoda** (surname)

5a12.2 / 1768　　　□ 隹 石 火
　　　　　　　　　74 53 44

礁

礁礁

SHŌ sunken rock

─────── 2 ───────

8 岩礁 **ganshō** reef

─────── 3 ───────

9 珊瑚礁 **sangoshō** coral reef

5

石 12
立
目
禾
衤
罒
皿
疒

————— 13 —————

5a13.2 / 1515

田 石 木 一
53 41 14

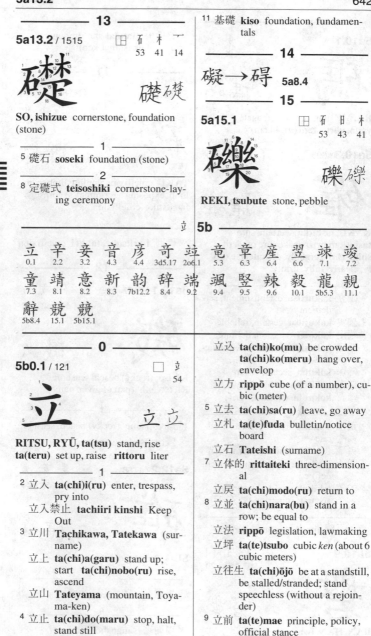

礎 礎

SO, ishizue cornerstone, foundation (stone)

————— 1 —————

5 礎石 **soseki** foundation (stone)

————— 2 —————

8 定礎式 **teisoshiki** cornerstone-laying ceremony

11 基礎 **kiso** foundation, fundamentals

————— 14 —————

礙 → 碍 5a8.4

————— 15 —————

5a15.1

田 石 日 木
53 43 41

礫 礫

REKI, tsubute stone, pebble

————— 立 5b —————

立	辛	妾	音	彦	奇	竝	竜	章	産	翌	竦	竣
0.1	2.2	3.2	4.3	4.4	3d5.17	2o6.1	5.3	6.3	6.4	6.6	7.1	7.2
童	靖	意	新	韵	辞	端	颯	竪	辣	毅	龍	親
7.3	8.1	8.2	8.3	7b12.2	8.4	9.2	9.4	9.5	9.6	10.1	5b5.3	11.1
辭	競	競										
5b8.4	15.1	5b15.1										

————— 0 —————

5b0.1 / 121

口 立
54

立 立

RITSU, RYŪ, ta(tsu) stand, rise
ta(teru) set up, raise **rittoru** liter

————— 1 —————

2 立入 **ta(chi)i(ru)** enter, trespass, pry into
立入禁止 **tachiiri kinshi** Keep Out

3 立川 **Tachikawa, Tatekawa** (surname)
立上 **ta(chi)a(garu)** stand up; start **ta(chi)nobo(ru)** rise, ascend
立山 **Tateyama** (mountain, Toyama-ken)

4 立止 **ta(chi)do(maru)** stop, halt, stand still

立込 **ta(chi)ko(mu)** be crowded **ta(chi)ko(meru)** hang over, envelop
立方 **rippō** cube (of a number), cubic (meter)

5 立去 **ta(chi)sa(ru)** leave, go away
立札 **ta(te)fuda** bulletin/notice board
立石 **Tateishi** (surname)

7 立体的 **rittaiteki** three-dimensional
立戻 **ta(chi)modo(ru)** return to

8 立並 **ta(chi)nara(bu)** stand in a row; be equal to
立法 **rippō** legislation, lawmaking
立坪 **ta(te)tsubo** cubic *ken* (about 6 cubic meters)
立往生 **ta(chi)ōjō** be at a standstill, be stalled/stranded; stand speechless (without a rejoinder)

9 立前 **ta(te)mae** principle, policy, official stance

立派 **rippa** splendid, fine, magnificent

立食 **ta(chi)gu(i), risshoku** eating while standing

11 立寄 **ta(chi)yo(ru)** drop in on, stop at

12 立場 **tachiba** standpoint, position, viewpoint

立替 **ta(te)ka(eru)** pay in advance; pay for another

立飲 **ta(chi)no(mi)** drinking while standing

13 立腹 **rippuku** get angry, lose one's temper

立話 **ta(chi)banashi** standing and chatting

14 立読 **ta(chi)yo(mi)** read while standing (at a magazine rack)

——————— 2 ———————

3 夕立 **yūdachi** sudden afternoon shower

4 中立 **chūritsu** neutrality

分立 **bunritsu** separation (of powers), independence

公立 **kōritsu** public (institution)

木立 **kodachi** grove, thicket

日立 **hida(tsu)** grow up; recover (after childbirth) **Hitachi** (city, Ibaraki-ken); (electronics company)

5 生立 **u(mi)ta(te)** fresh-laid (eggs) **u(mare)ta(te)** newborn **o(i)ta(chi)** one's childhood, growing up

申立 **mō(shi)ta(teru)** state, declare

仕立 **shita(te)** sewing, tailoring; outfitting

市立 **shiritsu** municipal, city(-run)

目立 **meda(tsu)** be conspicuous, stand out

6 両立 **ryōritsu** coexist, be compatible

仲立 **nakada(chi)** intermediation; agent, broker; go-between

先立 **sakida(tsu)** go before, precede; die before; take precedence

帆立貝 **hotategai** scallop (shell)

成立 **seiritsu** come into being, be formed/effected

na(ri)ta(tsu) consist of; be effected, come into being

na(ri)ta(chi) origin, history, makeup

自立 **jiritsu** stand on one's own, be independent

7 対立 **tairitsu** confrontation, opposing

角立 **kadoda(tsu)** be pointed/ sharp, be rough; sound harsh

役立 **yakuda(tsu), yaku (ni) ta(tsu)** be useful, serve the purpose

私立 **shiritsu** private (sometimes pronounced *watakushiritsu* to avoid confusion with 市立, municipal)

足立 **Adachi** (surname)

8 孤立 **koritsu** be isolated

建立 **konryū** erection, building

逆立 **sakada(chi)** handstand, standing on one's head **sakada(tsu)** stand on end **sakada(teru)** set on end, bristle/ruffle up

沸立 **wa(ki)ta(tsu)** boil up, seethe

泡立 **awada(teru)** beat into a froth, whip

苛立 **irada(tsu)** get irritated/ exasperated **irada(teru)** irritate, exasperate

府立 **furitsu** run by an urban prefecture

国立 **kokuritsu** national (park/ library) **Kunitachi** (city, Tōkyō-to)

9 重立 **omoda(tta)** principal, leading, prominent

独立 **dokuritsu** independence **hito(ri)da(chi)** stand alone, be on one's own

荒立 **arada(tsu)** be agitated/ aggravated **arada(teru)** exacerbate, exasperate

県立 **kenritsu** prefectural

思立 **omo(i)ta(tsu)** set one's mind on, plan

10 都立 **toritsu** metropolitan, municipal

埋立地 **u(me)ta(te)chi** reclaimed land

起立 **kiritsu** stand up

旅立 **tabida(tsu)** start on a journey

11 巣立 **suda(chi)** leave the nest, become independent

組立 **ku(mi)ta(teru)** construct, assemble

組立式 **kumita(te)shiki** prefab, collapsible

設立 **setsuritsu** establishment, founding

12 傘立 **kasata(te)** umbrella stand

創立 **sōritsu** establishment, founding

湧立 **wa(ki)ta(tsu)** well up, seethe

棒立 **bōda(chi)** standing bolt upright

焼立 **ya(ki)ta(te)** fresh baked/roasted

粟立 **awada(tsu)** have gooseflesh

13 際立 **kiwada(tsu)** be conspicuous/prominent

隠立 **kaku(shi)da(te)** keep secret

塗立 **nu(ri)ta(teru)** put on thick makeup **nu(ri)ta(te)** freshly painted/plastered, Wet Paint

搗立 **tsu(ki)ta(te)** freshly pounded (*mochi*)

献立 **kondate** menu; arrangements, plan, program

献立表 **kondatehyō** menu

腹立 **harada(tsu)** get angry

14 煽立 **ao(gi)ta(teru)** instigate

15 褒立 **ho(me)ta(teru)** praise, applaud

確立 **kakuritsu** establishment, settlement

16 燃立 **mo(e)ta(tsu)** blaze up, be ablaze

積立 **tsu(mi)ta(teru)** save up, amass

積立金 **tsumitatekin** a reserve (fund)

18 騒立 **sawa(gi)ta(teru)** raise a big fuss/furor **sawa(gi)ta(tsu)** be agitated

——— 3 ———

1 一本立 **ipponda(chi)** independence

——— 4 ———

3 三権分立 **sanken bunritsu** separation of powers (legislative, executive, and judicial)

——— 2 ———

5b2.2 / 1487   日 立 十
                          54   12

SHIN bitter, trying; eighth in a series, "H" **kanoto** eighth calendar sign **kara(i)** hot, spicy, salty; hard, trying **karo(ujite), kara(kumo)** barely **tsura(i)** painful, trying, tough

——— 1 ———

3 辛口 **karakuchi** salty, spicy, dry (saké); preference for sharp taste

6 辛気臭 **shinkikusa(i)** fretful

8 辛抱 **shinbō** perseverance, patience

辛苦 **shinku** hardship, privation, trouble

——— 2 ———

9 香辛料 **kōshinryō** spices, seasoning

10 唐辛子 **tōgarashi** cayenne/red pepper

——— 3 ———

5b3.2   日 立 女
                          54   25

SHŌ, mekake concubine, mistress **warawa** I, me (in feminine speech)

——— 4 ———

5b4.3 / 347   日 立 日
                          54   43

ON, IN, oto, ne sound

――――― 1 ―――――

⁷ 音声 **onsei, onjō** voice, audio

⁹ 音便 **onbin** (for sake of) euphony

¹⁰ 音訓 **on-kun** Chinese and Japanese pronunciations of a kanji

¹¹ 音階 **onkai** (musical) scale

音符 **onpu** (musical) note; the part of a kanji indicating its pronunciation

音訳 **on'yaku** transliteration

¹³ 音楽 **ongaku** music

音楽家 **ongakka, ongakuka** musician

音痴 **onchi** tone deaf

¹⁴ 音読 **ondoku** reading aloud
on'yo(mi) the Chinese reading of a kanji

¹⁹ 音響 **onkyō** sound

音譜 **onpu** (written) notes, the score

音韻 **on'in** phoneme

――――― 2 ―――――

² 子音 **shiin** consonant

⁵ 本音 **honne** real intention, underlying motive

母音 **boin** vowel

⁶ 防音 **bōon** sound-deadening, soundproof(ing)

同音異義 **dōon-igi** the same pronunciation but different meanings

同音語 **dōongo** homophone, homonym

⁷ 低音 **teion** bass (in music); low voice, sotto voce

余音 **yoin** lingering tone, reverberation; aftertaste, suggestiveness

声音 **kowane** tone of voice, timbre
seion vocal sound

足音 **ashioto** sound of footsteps

⁸ 長音 **chōon** a long sound/vowel, long tone, dash

表音文字 **hyōon moji** phonetic symbol/script

拗音 **yōon** diphthong (written with a small や, ゆ, or よ, as in きゅ)

⁹ 発音 **hatsuon** pronunciation

促音 **sokuon** assimilated sound (represented by a small っ or, in romanization, a doubled letter)

¹² 超音波 **chōonpa** ultrasonic waves

超音速 **chōonsoku** supersonic speed

¹³ 福音 **fukuin** the Gospel; good news

¹⁴ 雑音 **zatsuon** noise, static

¹⁵ 撥音 **hatsuon** the sound of the kana "ん"

¹⁶ 濁音 **dakuon** voiced sound

録音 **rokuon** (sound) recording

¹⁸ 観音 **Kannon** the Goddess of Mercy

騒音 **sōon** noise

¹⁹ 爆音 **bakuon** (sound of an) explosion, roar (of an engine)

²¹ 轟音 **gōon** deafening roar/boom

――――― 3 ―――――

⁴ 五十音順 **gojūon-jun** in "*aiueo*" order of the kana alphabet

⁵ 半濁音 **handakuon** semivoiced sound, *p*-sound

5b4.4 / 2067　　　日 立 彡 丨
　　　　　　　　　　　54 31 2

 彦 丨 彦 彦

GEN, hiko fine young man　GEN, HI-KO, YOSHI, YASU, O, SATO, HIRO, TSUNE (part of given name)

――――― 2 ―――――

³ 山彦 **yamabiko** echo

⁸ 昌彦 **Masahiko, Akihiko** (m. given name)

武彦 **Takehiko, Takeyoshi** (m. given name)

和彦 **Kazuhiko** (m. given name)

¹⁰ 真彦 **Masahiko, Nobuhiko, Mahiko** (m. given name)

竒 → 奇　3d5.17

――――― 5 ―――――

竝 → 並　2o6.1

5
石
立
目
禾
罒
皿
扩
4

5b5.3 / 1758

日 立 日 │
54 43 2

竜

龍│竜竜

RYŪ, RYŌ, tatsu dragon
RYŌ (part of given name)

——————— 1 ———————

8 竜巻 **tatsuma(ki)** tornado

——————— 6 ———————

5b6.3 / 857

日 立 日 十
54 43 12

章

章章

SHŌ chapter; badge, mark
AKIRA (m. given name) SHŌ, AKI
(part of given name)

——————— 1 ———————

4 章夫 **Akio, Fumio, Yukio** (m. giv-
en name)
11 章魚 **tako** octopus

——————— 2 ———————

4 文章 **bunshō** composition, writing;
article, essay
6 成章 **Nariaki, Shigeaki, Seishō,
Nariakira, Shigeaya** (m. giv-
en name)
10 紋章 **monshō** crest, coat of arms
13 楽章 **gakushō** a movement (of a
symphony)
15 褒章 **hōshō** medal
勲章 **kunshō** order, decoration,
medal

——————— 3 ———————

6 旭日章 **Kyokujitsushō** the Order
of the Rising Sun

5b6.4 / 278

日 立 牛 一
54 47 1

産

産│産産

SAN give birth to; produce, (as suffix)
product of; property **u(mu)** give birth/

rise to **u(mareru)** be born **ubu** birth;
infant

——————— 1 ———————

5 産出 **sanshutsu** production, yield,
output
6 産地 **sanchi** producing area
8 産物 **sanbutsu** product
9 産前 **sanzen** before childbirth/de-
livery
産後 **sango** after childbirth
産科 **sanka** obstetrics
産科医 **sankai** obstetrician
11 産婦 **sanpu** woman in/nearing
childbirth
産婦人科 **sanfujinka** obstetrics
and gynecology
産婆 **sanba** midwife
13 産業 **sangyō** industry
産業界 **sangyōkai** (the) industry
16 産親 **u(mi no) oya** one's biological
parent; originator, the father of
18 産額 **sangaku** output, yield, production

——————— 2 ———————

3 土産 **miyage** souvenir, present
4 水産物 **suisanbutsu** marine products
水産業 **suisangyō** fisheries, marine
products industry
月産 **gessan** monthly production/
output
日産 **nissan** daily production/
output **Nissan** (automobile
company)
5 出産 **shussan** childbirth
生産 **seisan** production
生産物 **seisanbutsu** product, produce
生産高 **seisandaka** output, production, yield
6 多産 **tasan** multiparous; fecund,
prolific
死産 **shizan** stillbirth
年産 **nensan** annual production
共産 **kyōsan** communist
共産主義 **kyōsan shugi** communism
共産党 **kyōsantō** communist party

安産 **anzan** easy delivery/child-birth

早産 **sōzan** premature birth

米産 **beisan** rice production

7 助産婦 **josanpu** midwife

8 国産 **kokusan** domestic-made

物産 **bussan** products, produce, commodities

所産 **shosan** product, result

9 通産省 **Tsūsanshō** MITI, Ministry of International Trade and Industry (short for 通商産業省)

海産物 **kaisanbutsu** marine products

10 倒産 **tōsan** bankruptcy

畜産 **chikusan** livestock raising

流産 **ryūzan** miscarriage

特産物 **tokusanbutsu** special product (of a locality), indigenous to

破産 **hasan** bankruptcy

財産 **zaisan** estate, assets, property

財産税 **zaisanzei** property tax

11 副産物 **fukusanbutsu** by-product

12 減産 **gensan** lower production

量産 **ryōsan** mass production (short for 大量生産)

殖産 **shokusan** increase in production/assets

13 農産物 **nōsanbutsu** agricultural products

資産 **shisan** assets, property

14 遺産 **isan** inheritance, estate

増産 **zōsan** increase in production

――――――― 3 ―――――――

4 不動産 **fudōsan** immovable property, real estate

――――――― 4 ―――――――

3 大量生産 **tairyō seisan** mass production

13 農林水産省 **Nōrinsuisanshō** Ministry of Agriculture, Forestry and Fisheries

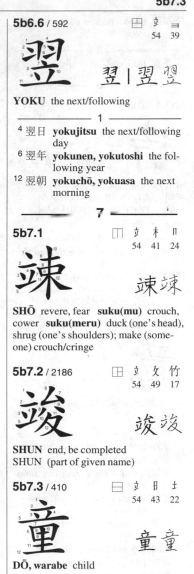

5b6.6 / 592   田 立 彐
            54 39

翌 | 翌 翌

YOKU the next/following

――――――― 1 ―――――――

4 翌日 **yokujitsu** the next/following day

6 翌年 **yokunen, yokutoshi** the following year

12 翌朝 **yokuchō, yokuasa** the next morning

――――――― 7 ―――――――

5b7.1   田 立 木 刂
          54 41 24

竦 竦

SHŌ revere, fear **suku(mu)** crouch, cower **suku(meru)** duck (one's head), shrug (one's shoulders); make (someone) crouch/cringe

5b7.2 / 2186   田 立 夂 竹
          54 49 17

竣 竣

SHUN end, be completed
SHUN (part of given name)

5b7.3 / 410   田 立 日 土
          54 43 22

童 童

DŌ, warabe child

――――――― 1 ―――――――

13 童話 **dōwa** children's story, fairy tale

14 童歌 **warabeuta** traditional children's song

¹⁶ 童謡 **dōyō** children's song, nursery rhyme

——————— 2 ———————

⁷ 児童 **jidō** child, juvenile

——————— 8 ———————

5b8.1 / 2187

| 立 | 月 | 士 |
| 54 | 42 | 22 |

靖

靖 | 靖 靖

SEI, yasu(i) peaceful   SEI, JŌ, YASU, NOBU, SHIZU, HARU (part of given name)   YASUSHI, KIYOSHI, OSAMU (m. given name)

——————— 1 ———————

² 靖子 **Yasuko, Seiko, Shizuko** (f. given name)

⁸ 靖国神社 **Yasukuni-jinja** (shrine in Tōkyō dedicated to fallen Japanese soldiers)

5b8.2 / 132

| 立 | 日 | 心 |
| 54 | 43 | 51 |

意

意 意

I will, heart, mind, thought; meaning, sense

——————— 1 ———————

⁵ 意外 **igai** unexpected, surprising
⁶ 意気 **iki** spirits, morale
意気揚々 **iki-yōyō** exultant, triumphant
意地 **iji** temperament; will power; obstinacy
意地悪 **ijiwaru(i)** ill-tempered, crabby
意向 **ikō** intention, inclination
⁷ 意志 **ishi** will, volition
意図 **ito** intention, aim
意見 **iken** opinion
⁸ 意味 **imi** meaning, significance
¹¹ 意欲 **iyoku** will, desire, zest
¹³ 意義 **igi** meaning, significance

¹⁹ 意識 **ishiki** consciousness, awareness
意識的 **ishikiteki** consciously

——————— 2 ———————

³ 大意 **taii** gist, outline, summary
⁴ 不意 **fui** sudden, unexpected
介意 **kaii** care about, concern oneself with
反意語 **han'igo** antonym
⁵ 失意 **shitsui** despair, disappointment; adversity
生意気 **namaiki** conceited, impertinent, smart-alecky
用意 **yōi** preparations, arrangements
好意 **kōi** good will, kindness, favor, friendliness
⁶ 任意 **nin'i** optional, voluntary, discretionary, arbitrary
合意 **gōi** mutual consent, agreement
同意 **dōi** the same meaning; the same opinion; consent, agreement
同意見 **dōiken** the same opinion, like views
同意語 **dōigo** synonym
有意 **yūi** intentional; (statistically) significant
⁷ 含意 **gan'i** implication
決意 **ketsui** determination, resolution
尿意 **nyōi** the urge to urinate
⁸ 表意文字 **hyōi moji** ideograph
厚意 **kōi** kindness, favor, courtesy
注意 **chūi** attention, caution, warning
注意報 **chūihō** (storm) warning
⁹ 発意 **hatsui** initiative, suggestion, original idea
便意 **ben'i** urge to go to the toilet, call of nature
故意 **koi** intention, purpose
¹⁰ 恣意 **shii** arbitrariness, selfishness
¹¹ 得意 **tokui** pride, triumph; one's strong point; customer; prosperity
悪意 **akui** evil intent, malice, ill will
¹² 隔意 **kakui** reserve, estrangement

善意 **zen'i** good faith; well-intentioned; favorable sense

寓意 **gūi** allegory, moral

無意義 **muigi** meaningless, not significant

無意識 **muishiki** unconscious, involuntary

敬意 **keii** respect, homage

13 誠意 **seii** sincerity, good faith

14 語意 **goi** meaning of a word

15 熱意 **netsui** enthusiasm, zeal, ardor

敵意 **tekii** enmity, hostility, animosity

17 懇意 **kon'i** intimacy, friendship, kindness

謝意 **shai** gratitude; apology

18 翻意 **hon'i** change one's mind

——————— 3 ———————

4 不本意 **fuhon'i** reluctant, unwilling, to one's regret

不用意 **fuyōi** unprepared, unguarded, careless

不注意 **fuchūi** carelessness

不得意 **futokui** one's weak point

15 潜在意識 **senzai ishiki** subconscious

——————— 4 ———————

8 服装随意 **fukusō zuii** informal attire

5b8.3 / 174

田 立 木 斤
54 41 50

新 新 新

SHIN, atara(shii), ara(ta), nii- new
HAJIME (m. given name)

——————— 1 ———————

2 新人 **shinjin** newcomer, new face

4 新井 **Arai** (surname)

5 新生活 **shinseikatsu** a new life

新刊 **shinkan** new publication

新旧 **shinkyū** new and old

6 新年 **shinnen** the New Year

新式 **shinshiki** new-type, new-style, modern

7 新作 **shinsaku** a new work/composition

新車 **shinsha** new car

8 新郎新婦 **shinrō-shinpu** the bride and groom

新版 **shinpan** new publication/edition

新居 **shinkyo** one's new residence/home

9 新発売 **shinhatsubai** new(ly marketed) product

新派 **shinpa** new school (of thought/art)

新型 **shingata** new model/style

新品 **shinpin** new article, brand new

新政 **shinsei** new government/regime

新約 **shin'yaku** the New Testament

新訂版 **shinteiban** newly revised edition

10 新修 **shinshū** new compilation

新時代 **shinjidai** new era

新書 **shinsho** new book; largish paperback size

新教 **shinkyō** Protestantism

11 新婚旅行 **shinkon ryokō** honeymoon

新設 **shinsetsu** newly established

12 新装 **shinsō** new equipment, refurbishing, redecorated

13 新幹線 **Shinkansen** New Trunk Line, bullet train

14 新製品 **shinseihin** new product

新緑 **shinryoku** fresh verdure

新語 **shingo** new word, neologism

新聞 **shinbun** newspaper

新聞社 **shinbunsha** newspaper (company)

新聞紙 **shinbunshi** newspaper (paper)

15 新潟県 **Niigata-ken** (prefecture)

16 新興 **shinkō** new, rising

新築 **shinchiku** newly built

17 新鮮 **shinsen** fresh

18 新顔 **shingao** new face, newcomer

——————— 2 ———————

1 一新 **isshin** complete change, reform, renovation

7 更新 **kōshin** renew, renovate, update

改新 **kaishin** renovation, reformation

8 刷新 **sasshin** reform, renovation

9 革新 **kakushin** reform, innovation

11 清新 **seishin** fresh, new

12 最新 **saishin** newest, latest

14 維新 **ishin** (the Meiji) restoration

―――――――― 3 ――――――――

5 外字新聞 **gaiji shinbun** foreign-language newspaper

8 英字新聞 **eiji shinbun** English-language newspaper

10 恭賀新年 **kyōga shinnen** Happy New Year

13 新郎新婦 **shinrō-shinpu** the bride and groom

17 謹賀新年 **kinga shinnen** Happy New Year

―――――――― 4 ――――――――

8 明治維新 **Meiji Ishin** the Meiji Restoration

韵 → 韻 **7b12.2**

5b8.4 / 688

54 24 12

辭 | 辞 辞

JI word; resign, quit **ya(meru)** quit, resign

―――――――― 1 ――――――――

6 辞任 **jinin** resign

8 辞典 **jiten** dictionary

10 辞書 **jisho** dictionary

15 辞儀 **jigi** bow, greeting; decline, refuse

18 辞職 **jishoku** resignation, quitting

―――――――― 2 ――――――――

4 弔辞 **chōji** message of condolence, memorial address

5 世辞 **seji** flattery, compliment

広辞苑 **Kōjien** (name of a dictionary)

6 式辞 **shikiji** address, message, oration

9 美辞麗句 **biji-reiku** flowery language

祝辞 **shukuji** (speech of) congratulations

10 修辞学 **shūjigaku** rhetoric

11 接辞 **setsuji** an affix, prefixes and suffixes

12 御辞儀 **ojigi** bow, greeting

―――――――― 3 ――――――――

11 接尾辞 **setsubiji** suffix

接頭辞 **settōji** prefix

13 漢和辞典 **Kan-Wa jiten** kanji dictionary

―――――――― 9 ――――――――

5b9.2 / 1418

54 36 14

端 端

TAN end, tip; origin; correct **hashi** end, edge **hata** side, edge, nearby **ha** edge **hana** beginning, inception; end, tip TADASHI (m. given name) TADA (part of given name)

―――――――― 1 ――――――――

4 端午 **tango** Boys' Day (May 5)

7 端折 **hasho(ru)** tuck up; cut short, abridge

14 端緒 **tansho, tancho** beginning, first step, clue

―――――――― 2 ――――――――

1 一端 **ittan** a part; a general idea

5 半端 **hanpa** fragment; incomplete set; fraction; remnant; incomplete

末端 **mattan** end, tip, terminal

6 先端 **sentan** tip, point, end; the latest, advanced (technology)

尖端 **sentan** pointed tip; spearhead, leading edge, latest (technology)

9 発端 **hottan** origin, beginning

途端 **totan** the (very) moment/minute, just when

11 道端 **michibata** roadside, wayside

異端者 **itansha** heretic

12 極端 **kyokutan** extreme

— 3 —
6 両極端 **ryōkyokutan** both extremes

— 4 —
4 中途半端 **chūto-hanpa** half finished, incomplete

5b9.4 / 2266

巴　虫　立　冂
　　64　54　20

颯　颯颯

SATSU, sat(to) sudden, quick SATSU, SŌ, HAYA (part of given name)

— 1 —
11 颯爽 **sassō** dashing, smart, gallant

5b9.5

曰　立　冂　又
　54　20　9

豎｜豎豎

JU, tate vertical, upright

— 1 —
12 豎琴 **tategoto** harp, lyre

5b9.6

田　立　木　口
　54　41　24

辣辣

RATSU bitter, severe

— 1 —
12 辣腕 **ratsuwan** astute, sharp

— 10 —

5b10.1 / 2131

田　立　犭　乀
　54　27　10

毅毅

KI strong KI, GI, TAKE (part of given name) TAKESHI, TSUYOSHI, KO-

WASHI, TSUYOKI, HATASU (m. given name)

— 2 —
10 剛毅 **gōki** hardy, stout-hearted

— 11 —

龍 → 竜 5b5.3

5b11.1 / 175

田　貝　立　木
　68　54　41

親親

SHIN intimacy; parent; (as prefix) pro-(American) **oya** parent
shita(shii) intimate, close (friend)
shita(shimu) get to know better, become friendly with CHIKASHI (m. given name) CHIKA (part of given name)

— 1 —
2 親子 **oyako, shinshi** parent and child
　親子丼 **oyako donburi** bowl of rice topped with chicken and egg
4 親不孝 **oyafukō** lack of filial piety
　親切 **shinsetsu** kind, friendly
　親友 **shin'yū** close friend
　親分 **oyabun** boss, chief
　親父 **oyaji** one's father; the old man, the boss
　親日 **shin-Nichi** pro-Japanese
　親日家 **shin-Nichika** Nippophile
5 親字 **oyaji** first character (of a dictionary entry)
6 親会社 **oyagaisha** parent company
　親交 **shinkō** friendship, intimacy
　親孝行 **oyakōkō** filial piety
　親団体 **oyadantai** parent organization
　親米 **shin-Bei** pro-American
7 親身 **shinmi** blood relation; kind, cordial
9 親指 **oyayubi** thumb
10 親展 **shinten** confidential, personal (letter)
　親馬鹿 **oyabaka** overfond parent
11 親族 **shinzoku** relatives

5

石
立 11
目
禾
礻
田
皿
疒

親戚 **shinseki** a relative

12 親善 **shinzen** friendship, amity, goodwill

13 親愛 **shin'ai** affection, love; dear

18 親類 **shinrui** relatives

———— 2 ————

2 二親 **futaoya** (both) parents

4 父親 **chichioya, teteoya** father

5 生親 **u(mi no) oya** one's biological father; originator, creator

母親 **hahaoya** mother

6 両親 **ryōshin** (both) parents

肉親 **nikushin** blood relationship/relative

7 里親 **sato oya** foster parent

8 育親 **soda(te no) oya** foster parent

11 産親 **u(mi no) oya** one's biological parent; originator, the father of

17 懇親会 **konshinkai** social gathering

———— 14 ————

辭 → 辞 **5b8.4**

———— 15 ————

5b15.1 / 852

田 立 日 儿
54 24 16

競 | 競 競

KYŌ, KEI, kiso(u), kio(u) compete, vie for **se(ru)** compete, vie; bid for **se(ri)** auction **-kura** race, contest

———— 1 ————

6 競合 **kyōgō** competition, rivalry **se(ri)a(u)** compete with, vie for

競争 **kyōsō** competition

7 競走 **kyōsō** race

競技 **kyōgi** competition, match

競売 **kyōbai, se(ri)u(ri)** auction

8 競泳 **kyōei** swimming race

10 競馬 **keiba** horse race/racing

12 競艇 **kyōtei** boat race/racing

15 競輪 **keirin** bicycle race/racing

———— 17 ————

競 → 競 **5b15.1**

目 5c

目	自	見	具	直	盾	眄	眇	臭	看	眈	省	盾
0.1	1.1	2.1	3.1	2k6.2	5c4.8	4.1	4.2	4.3	4.4	4.5	4.7	4.8

眉	眠	眄	眩	臭	眼	眺	眸	眷	規	覗	殖	睡
4.9	5.2	5c4.1	5.3	5c4.3	6.1	6.2	6.3	6.6	6.9	7.3	7.4	8.2

睫	睨	睦	督	鼎	鼻	導	瞑	瞞	瞠	瞳	瞭	瞰
8.4	8.5	8.6	8.9	8.10	5f9.3	9.3	10.3	11.2	11.3	12.2	12.4	12.6

鼾	覧	覯	瞬	瞼	観	覚	覧
5f12.3	12.7	12.8	13.1	13.4	13.7	3n9.3	5c12.7

———— 0 ————

5c0.1 / 55

口 目
55

目 目

MOKU, BOKU eye; classification, order (in taxonomy) **me** eye; (suffix for ordinals), -th **ma** eye

———— 1 ————

3 目上 **meue** one's superior/senior

目下 **meshita** one's subordinate/junior **mokka** at present, now

5 目付 **metsu(ki)** a look, expression of the eyes

目立 **meda(tsu)** be conspicuous, stand out

6 目次 **mokuji** table of contents

目印 **mejirushi** mark, sign

目安 **meyasu** standard, yardstick

7 目医者 **meisha** ophthalmologist, optometrist

8 目的 **mokuteki** purpose, object, aim

目的語 **mokutekigo** object (in grammar)

9 目前 **me (no) mae, mokuzen** before one's eyes; immediate (gain)

目指 **meza(su)** aim at

12 目測 **mokusoku** measure by eye

目覚 **meza(meru)** wake up, come awake **meza(mashii)** striking, remarkable, spectacular

14 目算 **mokusan** expectation, estimate

15 目撃者 **mokugekisha** (eye)witness

目標 **mokuhyō** target, goal, objective

————— 2 —————

1 一目 **hitome, ichimoku** a glance/look **hito(tsu)me** one-eyed (goblin)

一目惚 **hitomebo(re)** love at first sight

一目瞭然 **ichimoku ryōzen** clear at a glance, obvious

2 丁目 **chōme** city block-size area (used in addresses)

3 大目見 **ōme (ni) mi(ru)** overlook (faults), let go, view with tolerance

4 分目 **wa(kare)me** turning point, junction, parting of the ways

5 付目 **tsu(ke)me** purpose; weak point to take advantage of

6 羽目 **hame** situation, predicament; panel, wainscoting

名目 **meimoku** name, pretext; nominal, ostensible

早目 **hayame (ni)** a little early (leaving leeway)

7 折目 **o(ri)me** fold, crease

役目 **yakume** one's duty, role

利目 **ki(ki)me** effect, efficacy

8 効目 **ki(ki)me** effect, efficacy

注目 **chūmoku** attention, notice

9 変目 **ka(wari)me** change, turning point, transition

面目 **menmoku, menboku** face, honor, dignity

柾目 **masame** straight grain

科目 **kamoku** subject, course (of study); item, classification

10 脇目 **wakime** onlooker's eyes; looking aside

11 控目 **hika(e)me** moderate, reserved

細目 **saimoku** details, particulars
hosome narrow eyes/opening

12 遠目 **tōme** distant view; farsightedness

落目 **o(chi)me** declining fortunes, on the wane

裂目 **sa(ke)me** rip, split, crack, fissure

衆目 **shūmoku** public attention

痛目 **ita(i) me** a painful experience

項目 **kōmoku** heading, item

13 裏目 **urame** the reverse (of the intended outcome)

継目 **tsu(gi)me** joint, seam

節目 **fushime** knot (in wood); turning point

14 境目 **sakaime** borderline; crisis

総目録 **sōmokuroku** complete catalog

綱目 **kōmoku** gist, main points

酷目 **hido(i)me** a bitter experience, a hard time

駄目 **dame** no good

15 憂目 **u(ki)me** grief, misery, hardship

課目 **kamoku** subject (in school), item

16 瞳目 **dōmoku** stare in wonder

17 霞目 **kasumime** purblind/blurred eyes

19 繋目 **tsuna(gi)me** joint

————— 3 —————

2 二枚目 **nimaime** (role of a) handsome man/beau

二番目 **nibanme** No. 2, second

10 真面目 **majime** serious-minded, earnest, honest **shinmenmoku** one's true self/character; seriousness, earnestness

—————— 4 ——————

4 不真面目 **fumajime** not serious-minded, insincere

17 糞真面目 **kusomajime** humorless earnestness

—————— 1 ——————

5c1.1 / 62   日 丨 丨

55   2

自 自

JI self; (as prefix) from (date/place)
SHI self **mizuka(ra)** oneself, personally, on one's own **ono(zukara/zuto)** of itself, spontaneously, naturally
YORI (part of given name)

—————— 1 ——————

0 自…至… **ji…shi…** from (place/date) to (place/date)

2 自力 **jiryoku** one's own strength/efforts **jiriki** one's own strength/efforts; (Buddhist) salvation by works

3 自己 **jiko** self-, oneself, one's own
自己紹介 **jiko shōkai** introduce oneself

4 自分 **jibun** oneself, one's own
自分自身 **jibun-jishin** oneself

5 自民党 **Jimintō** LDP, Liberal Democratic Party (short for 自由民主党)
自由 **jiyū** freedom, liberty; free
自由自在 **jiyū-jizai** free, unrestricted
自由党 **jiyūtō** liberal party
自由業 **jiyūgyō** freelance occupation, self-employed
自他 **jita** self and others; transitive and intransitive
自主 **jishu** independent, autonomous
自立 **jiritsu** stand on one's own, be independent

6 自伝 **jiden** autobiography
自宅 **jitaku** at one's home

7 自我 **jiga** self, ego
自体 **jitai** itself; one's own body

自決 **jiketsu** self-determination; resignation (from a post); suicide
自序 **jijo** author's preface
自利 **jiri** self-interest, personal gain

8 自制 **jisei** self-control, self-restraint
自治 **jichi** self-government
自治体 **jichitai** self-governing body, municipality
自治省 **Jichishō** Ministry of Home Affairs
自国 **jikoku** one's own country

9 自発的 **jihatsuteki** spontaneous, voluntary
自乗 **jijō** square (of a number)
自信 **jishin** confidence (in oneself)
自叙伝 **jijoden** autobiography
自律 **jiritsu** autonomy, self-control
自省 **jisei** self-examination, reflection

10 自家製 **jikasei** homemade, home-brewed
自殺 **jisatsu** suicide
自殺未遂 **jisatsu misui** attempted suicide
自称 **jishō** self-styled; first person (in grammar)

11 自動 **jidō** automatic
自動車 **jidōsha** motor vehicle, automobile
自動的 **jidōteki** automatic
自動販売機 **jidōhanbaiki** vending machine
自動詞 **jidōshi** intransitive verb
自転車 **jitensha** bicycle

12 自尊心 **jisonshin** self-esteem; conceit
自覚 **jikaku** consciousness, awareness, realization
自然 **shizen** nature; natural
自然主義 **shizen shugi** naturalism
自然科学 **shizen kagaku** the natural sciences
自給自足 **jikyū-jisoku** self-sufficiency
自筆 **jihitsu** one's own handwriting
自評 **jihyō** self-criticism
自費 **jihi** at one's own expense

自費出版 **jihi shuppan** publishing at one's own expense, vanity press

13 自愛 **jiai** self-love, self-regard; selfishness

14 自慢 **jiman** be proud of

自認 **jinin** acknowledge, admit

15 自縄自縛 **jijō-jibaku** tied up with one's own rope, caught in one's own trap

自賛 **jisan** self-praise

16 自衛隊 **Jieitai** Self Defense Forces

— 2 —

3 大自然 **daishizen** Mother Nature

4 不自由 **fujiyū** inconvenience, discomfort; privation; disability, handicap

不自然 **fushizen** unnatural

6 各自 **kakuji** each person, everyone

7 私自身 **watakushi jishin** personally, as for me

9 独自 **dokuji** original, characteristic, indivudual, personal

12 超自然 **chōshizen** supernatural

腕自慢 **udejiman** proud of one's skill

軽自動車 **keijidōsha** light car

— 3 —

6 自分自身 **jibun-jishin** oneself

自由自在 **jiyū-jizai** free, unrestricted

自給自足 **jikyū-jisoku** self-sufficiency

自縄自縛 **jijō-jibaku** tied up with one's own rope, caught in one's own trap

9 飛込自殺 **tobiko(mi) jisatsu** suicide by jumping in front of an oncoming train

— 2 —

5c2.1 / 63 □ 貝 68

見 見

KEN, mi(ru) see **mi(eru)** be visible, can see **mi(seru)** show **mami(eru)** have an audience with, see

— 1 —

0 見せしめ **mi(seshime)** object lesson, warning, example

3 見下 **mio(rosu)** command a view of **mikuda(su)** look down on, despise **misa(geru)** look down on, despise

4 見分 **miwa(keru)** tell apart, distinguish between, recognize; judge, identify

見込 **miko(mi)** prospects, promise, hope, possibility

見方 **mikata** viewpoint, way of looking at

5 見出 **miida(su)** find, discover, pick out **mida(shi)** heading, caption, headline

見出語 **mida(shi)go** headword, entry word

見本 **mihon** sample, specimen

見世物 **misemono** show, exhibition

見付 **mitsu(keru)** find **mitsu(karu)** be found

見比 **mikura(beru)** compare (by eying)

6 見合 **mia(u)** look at each other; offset **mia(i)** arranged-marriage interview **mia(waseru)** exchange glances; set off against; postpone, abandon

見返 **mikae(ru)** look back at **mikae(shi)** inside the cover

見守 **mimamo(ru)** watch over

見当 **miata(ru)** be found, turn up **kentō** aim, mark, guess, estimate, hunch; direction; approximately

見当違 **kentōchiga(i)** wrong guess

7 見学 **kengaku** study by observation, tour (a factory)

8 見事 **migoto** beautiful, splendid

見直 **minao(su)** take another look at, reevaluate; think better of; get better

見逃 **minoga(su)** overlook

見送 **mioku(ru)** see (someone) off, watch till out of sight

見物 **kenbutsu** sightseeing **mimono** a sight, spectacle, attraction

5
石
立
目 2
ネ
田
皿
扩

見所 **midokoro** the part most worth seeing; promise, merit **mi(ta) tokoro** judging from the appearance

9 見通 **mitō(shi)** prospects, outlook, forecast; unobstructed view

見栄 **mie** (for sake of) appearance, show

見映 **miba(e)** (attractive) appearance

11 見捨 **misu(teru)** desert, abandon, forsake

見張 **miha(ru)** watch, be on the lookout for, stake out; open (one's eyes) wide

12 見違 **michiga(eru)** mistake for, not recognize **michiga(i)** misperception, mistake

見渡 **miwata(su)** look out over

見覚 **miobo(e)** recognition, familiarity

見極 **mikiwa(meru)** see through, discern, ascertain, grasp

13 見解 **kenkai** opinion, view

見詰 **mitsu(meru)** gaze/stare at

14 見慣 **mina(reru)** get used to seeing, be familiar to

見聞 **kenbun, kenmon, miki(ki)** information, knowledge, experience

15 見舞 **mima(u)** inquire after (someone's health), visit (someone in hospital)

───── 2 ─────

1 一見 **ikken** take a look at, glance at

了見 **ryōken** idea; intention; decision, discretion; forgive

2 人見知 **hitomishi(ri)** be bashful before strangers

4 月見 **tsukimi** viewing the moon

6 会見 **kaiken** interview

先見 **senken** foresight

7 形見 **katami** keepsake, memento

花見 **hanami** viewing cherry blossoms

8 拝見 **haiken** see, have a look at

9 発見 **hakken** discover

10 脇見 **wakimi** look aside/away

11 偏見 **henken** biased view, prejudice

13 夢見 **yumemi** dreaming, dream

意見 **iken** opinion

14 概見 **gaiken** overview, outline

15 謁見 **ekken** have an audience with

18 顔見知 **kaomishi(ri)** knowing someone by sight, a nodding acquaintance

19 識見 **shikiken, shikken** knowledge, discernment

21 露見 **roken** be found out, come to light

───── 3 ─────

3 大目見 **ōme (ni) mi(ru)** overlook (faults), let go, view with tolerance

6 同意見 **dōiken** the same opinion, like views

9 垣間見 **kaimami(ru)** peek in, get a glimpse

12 暑中見舞 **shochū mima(i)** inquiry after (someone's) health in the hot season

───── 4 ─────

10 記者会見 **kisha kaiken** news/press conference

───── 3 ─────

5c3.1 / 420

目 目 儿 一
55 16 1

具 | 具 具

GU tool, equipment, gear; (soup) ingredients, (pizza) topping **sona(eru)** equip, furnish, provide **sona(waru)** be furnished/provided with **tsubusa (ni)** minutely, in detail TOMO (part of given name)

───── 1 ─────

7 具体化 **gutaika** embodiment, materialization

具体的 **gutaiteki** concrete, specific, definite

12 具象的 **gushōteki** concrete, not abstract

───── 2 ─────

4 仏具 **butsugu** Buddhist altar articles

8 拝具 **haigu** Sincerely yours
　玩具 **gangu, omocha** toy
　玩具屋 **omochaya** toy shop
　金具 **kanagu** metal fittings, bracket
　雨具 **amagu** rain gear, rainwear
10 家具 **kagu** furniture, furnishings
11 道具 **dōgu** tool, implement
12 敬具 **keigu** Sincerely yours,
13 寝具 **shingu** bedding
15 器具 **kigu** utensil, appliance, tool, apparatus

直 → **2k6.2**

盾 → **5c4.8**

—————— 4 ——————

5c4.1　　　　　
　　　　　　　55　14　1

眄

眄眄

BEN look at askance, glare at

5c4.2　　　　　囗 日 小 ｜
　　　　　　　55　35　2

眇

眇眇

BYŌ small; distant **sugame** one eye smaller/injured/blind; squinting, cross-eyed, wall-eyed

5c4.3 / 1244　　　目 日 大 ｜
　　　　　　　55　34　2

臭｜臭臭

SHŪ odor **kusa(i)** foul-smelling; (as suffix) smelling of **nio(i)** odor, smell

—————— 1 ——————

6 臭気 **shūki** offensive odor, stink, stench

—————— 2 ——————

5 生臭 **namagusa(i)** smelling of fish/blood
　古臭 **furukusa(i)** old, musty, outdated, trite, stale
6 汚臭 **oshū** foul odor
7 体臭 **taishū** body odor; a characteristic
8 青臭 **aokusa(i)** smelling grassy/unripe; inexperienced
9 俗臭 **zokushū** vulgarity, worldly-mindedness
11 脱臭剤 **dasshūzai** deodorant, deodorizer
　悪臭 **akushū** offensive odor, stench
12 焦臭 **ko(ge)kusa(i), kinakusa(i)** smelling burnt
23 黴臭 **kabikusa(i)** moldy, musty

—————— 3 ——————

7 辛気臭 **shinkikusa(i)** fretful
9 面倒臭 **mendōkusa(i)** troublesome, a big bother

5c4.4 / 1316　　　囗 日 扌
　　　　　　　55　23

看

看看

KAN, mi(ru) see, watch

—————— 1 ——————

8 看板 **kanban** sign(board)
10 看病 **kanbyō** tending the sick, nursing
20 看護婦 **kangofu** (female) nurse

—————— 2 ——————

8 表看板 **omote-kanban** sign out in front; figurehead, mask

5c4.5　　　　　囗 日 冂 ｜
　　　　　　　55　20　2

眈眈

TAN watch intently

5

石
立
目
禾
衤
罒
皿
疒

4

5c4.7 / 145　　　　　□˙˙　日　小　|
　　　　　　　　　　　55　35　2

省　　　　　　　省省

SEI, kaeri(miru) reflect upon, give heed to　**SHŌ** (government) ministry; province (in China); be sparing of, save (space)　**habu(ku)** omit, eliminate; curtail, cut down on

――――― 1 ―――――

0　省エネ **shōene** energy saving
7　省吾 **Shōgo, Seigo** (m. given name)
11　省略 **shōryaku** abbreviate, omit

――――― 2 ―――――

4　反省 **hansei** reflection, introspection; reconsideration
6　自省 **jisei** self-examination, reflection
10　帰省 **kisei** returning to one's home town (for the holidays)

――――― 3 ―――――

3　大蔵省 **Ōkurashō** Ministry of Finance
4　内務省 **Naimushō** (prewar) Ministry of Home Affairs
　　文部省 **Monbushō** Ministry of Education
5　外務省 **Gaimushō** Ministry of Foreign Affairs
6　自治省 **Jichishō** Ministry of Home Affairs
7　労働省 **Rōdōshō** Ministry of Labor
8　厚生省 **Kōseishō** Ministry of Health and Welfare
　　建設省 **Kensetsushō** Ministry of Construction
　　法務省 **Hōmushō** Ministry of Justice
9　通産省 **Tsūsanshō** MITI, Ministry of International Trade and Industry (short for 通商産業省)
10　郵政省 **Yūseishō** Ministry of Posts and Telecommunications
11　運輸省 **Un'yushō** Ministry of Transport

――――― 5 ―――――

13　農林水産省 **Nōrinsuisanshō** Ministry of Agriculture, Forestry and Fisheries

5c4.8 / 772　　　　　□□　日　厂　十
　　　　　　　　　　　55　18　12

盾　　　　　　　盾盾

JUN, tate shield

――――― 2 ―――――

5　矛盾 **mujun** contradiction

5c4.9 / 2170　　　　　□□　日　尸　|
　　　　　　　　　　　55　40　2

眉　　　　　　　眉眉

BI, MI, mayu eyebrow　BI, MI, MA-YU (part of given name)

――――― 1 ―――――

4　眉毛 **mayuge** eyebrows

――――― 5 ―――――

5c5.2 / 849　　　　　□□　日　尸　十
　　　　　　　　　　　55　40　12

眠　　　　　　　眠眠

MIN, nemu(ru) sleep　**nemu(i), nemu(tai)** sleepy, drowsy, tired

――――― 1 ―――――

6　眠気 **nemuke** sleepiness, drowsiness
16　眠薬 **nemu(ri)gusuri** sleeping drug/pills

――――― 2 ―――――

1　一眠 **hitonemu(ri)** a short sleep, a nap
4　不眠症 **fuminshō** insomnia
5　冬眠 **tōmin** hibernation
6　仮眠 **kamin** nap
8　居眠 **inemu(ri)** doze, drowse
13　催眠術 **saiminjutsu** hypnotism

5

石
立
目
禾
皿
罒
广

睡眠 **suimin** sleep

睡眠薬 **suimin'yaku** sleeping drug/pills

眂→ **5c4.1**

5c5.3　　　　　田 目 宀 竹
　　　　　　　　55 11 17

GEN, kurume(ku) get dizzy **mabu(shii), mabayu(i)** glaring, blinding, dazzling

———————— 1 ————————

¹² 眩惑 **genwaku** blind, dazzle, daze

臭→ 臭 **5c4.3**

———————— 6 ————————

5c6.1 / 848　　　　　田 食 目
　　　　　　　　73 55

GAN, GEN, me, manako eye

———————— 1 ————————

⁹ 眼科 **ganka** ophthalmology
¹⁹ 眼鏡 **megane, gankyō** (eye)glasses

———————— 2 ————————

¹ 一眼 **ichigan** one eye; single lens
⁴ 双眼鏡 **sōgankyō** binoculars
⁶ 肉眼 **nikugan** the naked/unaided eye

　　老眼 **rōgan** farsightedness

　　色眼鏡 **iromegane** colored glasses; prejudiced view

　　近眼 **kingan, chikame** nearsighted; shortsighted

¹⁰ 隻眼 **sekigan** one-eyed
¹² 着眼 **chakugan** notice, observe

———————— 3 ————————

³ 千里眼 **senrigan** clairvoyant

5c6.2 / 1565　　　　田 目 冫 儿
　　　　　　　　55 5 16

CHŌ, naga(meru) look/gaze at, watch

———————— 1 ————————

¹¹ 眺望 **chōbō** a view (from a window)

5c6.3 / 2171　　　　田 目 牛 竹
　　　　　　　　55 47 17

BŌ pupil (of the eye)　**HITOMI** (f. given name)　**BŌ** (part of given name)

5c6.6　　　　　… 目 火 二
　　　　　　　　55 44 4

眷 眷

KEN look around; regard with affection

———————— 1 ————————

²¹ 眷顧 **kenko** favor, patronage

5c6.9 / 607　　　　　田 貝 大 一
　　　　　　　　68 34 1

規 規

KI standard, measure　**TADASHI, TADASU** (m. given name)　**NORI** (part of given name)

———————— 1 ————————

⁸ 規制 **kisei** regulation, control
　　規定 **kitei** stipulations, provisions, regulations
⁹ 規則 **kisoku** regulation, rule
¹⁰ 規格 **kikaku** standard, norm
¹⁴ 規模 **kibo** scale, scope

———————— 2 ————————

³ 大規模 **daikibo** large-scale

小規模 **shōkibo** small-scale
4 不規則 **fukisoku** irregular, unsystematic
5 正規 **seiki** regular, normal, formal, legal
8 法規 **hōki** laws and regulations
定規 **teiki** prescribed **jōgi** ruler, (T-)square; standard

————— 7 —————

5c7.3

□ 貝 口 一
68 24 1

覘 覘

SHI, nozo(ku) peek, peep, peer

————— 1 —————

4 覘込 **nozo(ki)ko(mu)** look/peek/peer into
5 覘穴 **nozo(ki)ana** peephole

5c7.4 / 1506

田 歹 夕 十
55 30 12

殖 殖

SHOKU, fu(eru) increase, grow in number **fu(yasu)** increase, add to SHIGERU (m. given name)

————— 1 —————

11 殖産 **shokusan** increase in production/assets

————— 2 —————

5 生殖 **seishoku** reproduction, procreation
8 拓殖 **takushoku** colonization, exploitation
15 養殖 **yōshoku** raising, culture, cultivation

————— 8 —————

5c8.2 / 1071

□ 目 王 艹
55 46 32

睡 睡

SUI sleep

————— 1 —————

10 睡眠 **suimin** sleep
睡眠薬 **suimin'yaku** sleeping drug/pills

5c8.4

□ 目 ヨ 十
55 39 12

睫 睫

SHŌ, matsuge eyelashes

————— 1 —————

4 睫毛 **matsuge** eyelashes

5c8.5

□ 目 ヨ 厂
55 39 18

睨 睨

GEI, nira(mu) glare/scowl at; watch with suspicion; estimate

————— 1 —————

6 睨合 **nira(mi)a(u)** glare at each other **nira(mi)a(waseru)** take (something) for comparison

5c8.6 / 2172

□ 目 土 儿
55 22 16

睦 睦

BOKU, mutsu(majii) getting along well together, harmonious, friendly, intimate BOKU, MUTSU, CHIKA, NOBU (part of given name) MUTSUMI (f. given name) ATSUSHI, CHIKASHI (m. given name)

————— 1 —————

9 睦美 **Mutsumi, Mutsuyoshi** (given name)

5c8.9 / 1670

田 日 小 ⊢
55 35 13

督 督督

TOKU lead, command; superintend, supervise

――――― 1 ―――――
7 督励 **tokurei** encourage, urge
9 督促 **tokusoku** urge, press, dun

――――― 2 ―――――
15 監督 **kantoku** supervision, direction; (movie) director, (team) manager

5c8.10

⺌ 日 ⼀ |
55 14 2

鼎 鼎鼎

TEI, kanae three-legged kettle

――――― 9 ―――――
鼻 → **5f9.3**

5c9.3 / 703

田 日 寸 儿
55 37 16

導 導導

DŌ, michibi(ku) lead, guide
shirube guide(post)

――――― 1 ―――――
2 導入 **dōnyū** bring in, introduce
7 導体 **dōtai** conductor (of electricity/heat)

――――― 2 ―――――
5 主導 **shudō** leadership
   主導権 **shudōken** leadership
6 先導 **sendō** guidance, leadership
8 盲導犬 **mōdōken** seeing-eye dog
9 指導 **shidō** guidance, leadership
   指導者 **shidōsha** leader
14 誘導 **yūdō** induction; incitement; guidance

――――― 3 ―――――
12 超伝導 **chōdendō** superconductivity

――――― 10 ―――――

5c10.3

田 日 日 冂
55 43 20

瞑 瞑

MEI, tsubu(ru) close (one's eyes)

――――― 1 ―――――
13 瞑想 **meisō** meditation, contemplation

――――― 11 ―――――

5c11.2

田 日 ⺾ 巾
55 32 26

瞞 瞞瞞

MAN deception; dim, obscure

――――― 1 ―――――
12 瞞着 **manchaku** deceive, trick, dupe

――――― 2 ―――――
12 欺瞞 **giman** deception, fraud, trickery

5c11.3

田 日 小 口
55 35 24

瞠 瞠瞠

DŌ stare at

――――― 1 ―――――
5 瞠目 **dōmoku** stare in wonder

――――― 12 ―――――

5c12.2 / 2173

田 日 立 日
55 54 43

瞳 瞳|瞳瞳

DŌ, hitomi pupil (of the eye) **DŌ, TŌ** (part of given name) **HITOMI** (f. given name) **AKIRA** (m. given name)

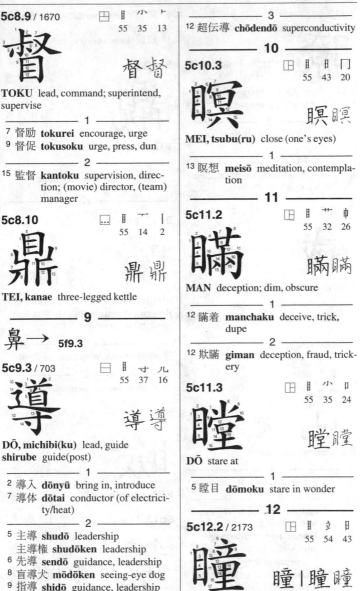

石
立
日 12
禾
衤
田
皿
疒

5

5c12.4 / 2174

田 日 火 日
55 44 43

瞭

瞭 | 瞭 瞭

RYŌ clear AKIRA (m. given name)
RYŌ, AKI (part of given name)

——— 2 ———

8 明瞭 **meiryō** clear, distinct, obvious

——— 3 ———

1 一目瞭然 **ichimoku ryōzen** clear at a glance, obvious

5c12.6

田 日 戈 口
55 52 24

馘

馘 馘

KAKU sever an ear; behead

——— 1 ———

9 馘首 **kakushu** decapitate; dismissal

鼾→ **5f12.3**

5c12.7 / 1291

田 貝 门 ハ
68 20 15

覧

覧 | 覧 覧

RAN, mi(ru) see, look at

——— 1 ———

0 ご覧 **goran** see, look at (honorific)

——— 2 ———

1 一覧 **ichiran** a look/glance; a summary; catalog
5 巡覧 **junran** tour, sightseeing
10 遊覧 **yūran** excursion, sightseeing
展覧会 **tenrankai** exhibition
12 博覧会 **hakurankai** exhibition, exposition, fair
御覧 **goran** see, look at; give it a try
15 閲覧 **etsuran** perusal, inspection, reading

閲覧室 **etsuranshitsu** reading room
18 観覧 **kanran** view, see, inspect

5c12.8

田 貝 艹 土
68 32 22

覯

覯 覯

KŌ (happen to) meet

——— 2 ———

12 稀覯本 **kikōbon** rare book

——— 13 ———

5c13.1 / 1732

田 日 小 夕
55 35 30

瞬

瞬 | 瞬 瞬

SHUN, matata(ku), mabata(ku), majiro(gu), shibatata(ku), shibata(ku) wink, blink, twinkle

——— 1 ———

12 瞬間 **shunkan** instant, moment

——— 2 ———

1 一瞬 **isshun** a moment, an instant

5c13.4

田 日 口 イ
55 24 3

瞼

瞼 瞼

KEN, mabuta eyelid

5c13.7 / 604

田 隹 貝 ハ
74 68 15

観

觀 | 観 観

KAN appearance; view, outlook
mi(ru) see, view MI (part of given name)

─────────── 1 ───────────
6 観光 **kankō** sightseeing

観光客 **kankōkyaku** tourist, sightseer

8 観念 **kannen** idea; sense (of duty)

9 観点 **kanten** viewpoint

観客 **kankyaku** audience, spectators

観音 **Kannon** the Goddess of Mercy

12 観測 **kansoku** observation, survey; thinking, opinion

観衆 **kanshū** audience, spectators

13 観楽街 **kanrakugai** amusement district

14 観察 **kansatsu** observe, view

15 観賞 **kanshō** admiration, enjoyment

17 観覧 **kanran** view, see, inspect

─────────── 2 ───────────
3 大観 **taikan** comprehensive view, general survey; philosophical outlook

5 史観 **shikan** view of history

外観 **gaikan** external appearance

主観 **shukan** subjectivity; subject, ego

主観的 **shukanteki** subjective

8 直観 **chokkan** intuition

拝観料 **haikanryō** (museum) admission fee

参観 **sankan** visit, inspect

9 美観 **bikan** fine view, beautiful sight

客観的 **kyakkanteki, kakkanteki** objective

12 傍観 **bōkan** look on, remain a spectator

景観 **keikan** spectacular view, a sight

悲観 **hikan** pessimism

悲観的 **hikanteki** pessimistic

悲観論者 **hikanronsha** pessimist

13 楽観的 **rakkanteki** optimistic, hopeful

─────────── 3 ───────────
6 先入観 **sennyūkan** preconception, preoccupation, prejudice

─────────── 15 ───────────
覺 → 覚 **3n9.3**

─────────── 17 ───────────
覽 → 覧 **5c12.7**

禾 **5d**

利 2.1	私 2.2	季 2.3	秀 2.4	禿 2.5	和 3.1	委 3.2	秋 4.1	秒 4.2	科 4.3	香 4.5	秣 5.1	秩 5.2
秤 5.4	秘 5.6	租 5.7	称 5.8	秦 5.10	移 6.1	程 7.2	税 7.4	稀 7.5	黍 7.6	稚 8.1	稜 8.4	稔 8.5
種 9.1	稱 5d5.8	稲 9.2	穀 9.4	穂 10.2	稻 5d9.2	稼 10.3	稿 10.5	黎 3a10.29	穀 5d9.4	稽 11.3	穏 11.4	積 11.5
穐 5d4.1	穗 5d10.2	穉 5d8.1	黏 6b5.4	穣 13.2	穫 13.4	穩 5d11.4	馨 4c16.2	穰 5d13.2				

─────────── 2 ───────────

5d2.1 / 329

□ 禾 儿
56 16

RI advantage; interest (on a loan)
ki(ku) take effect, work **ki(kasu)**

make effective, use, exercise RI, TOSHI (part of given name)

─────────── 1 ───────────
2 利子 **rishi** interest (on a loan)

3 利己 **riko** self-interest

利口 **rikō** smart, clever, bright

5 利用 **riyō** use, make use of

利用者 **riyōsha** user

利目 **ki(ki)me** effect, efficacy

8 利明 **Toshiaki, Rimei** (m. given name)

10 利益 **rieki** profit, gain; benefit, advantage **(go)riyaku** divine favor

利害 **rigai** advantages and disadvantages, interests

利害関係 **rigai kankei** interests

利根川 **Tone-gawa** (river, Chiba-ken)

利息 **risoku** interest (on a loan)

11 利率 **riritsu** rate of interest

15 利潤 **rijun** profit

————— 2 —————

1 一利 **ichiri** one advantage

4 元利 **ganri** principal and interest

毛利 **Mōri** (surname)

5 左利 **hidariki(ki)** left-handed; left-hander; a drinker

功利 **kōri** utility; utilitarian

右利 **migiki(ki)** righthanded; right-hander

6 気利 **ki (ga) ki(ku)** be clever, be considerate; be stylish

年利 **nenri** annual interest

有利 **yūri** advantageous, profitable, favorable

自利 **jiri** self-interest, personal gain

7 低利 **teiri** low interest

8 国利 **kokuri** national interests

9 便利 **benri** convenient, handy

砂利 **jari** gravel

10 射利 **shari** love of money

冥利 **myōri** divine favor, providence, luck

純利 **junri** net profit

12 営利 **eiri** profit(-making)

勝利 **shōri** victory

勝利 **Katsutoshi** (m. given name)

腕利 **udeki(ki)** skilled, able

13 福利 **fukuri** welfare, well-being

14 徳利 **tokuri, tokkuri** (pinch-necked) saké bottle

15 権利 **kenri** a right

鋭利 **eiri** sharp, keen

————— 3 —————

3 大勝利 **daishōri** decisive victory

12 廃物利用 **haibutsu riyō** recycling

SHI private **watakushi, watashi** I, me, my **hiso(ka)** secret, private

————— 1 —————

3 私大 **shidai** private college (short for 私立大学)

私小説 **watakushi shōsetsu** novel narrated in the first person; autobiographical novel **shishōsetsu** autobiographical novel

5 私生活 **shiseikatsu** one's private life

私用 **shiyō** private use

私立 **shiritsu** private (sometimes pronounced *watakushiritsu* to avoid confusion with 市立, municipal)

6 私有 **shiyū** privately owned

私有物 **shiyūbutsu** private property

私自身 **watakushi jishin** personally, as for me

7 私学 **shigaku** private school

8 私事 **shiji, watakushigoto** personal affairs

10 私案 **shian** one's own plan

私書 **shisho** private document/letter

私書箱 **shishobako** post-office box

私財 **shizai** private funds

11 私達 **watakushitachi** we, us, our

私設 **shisetsu** private, nongovernmental

12 私営 **shiei** privately run/managed

13 私鉄 **shitetsu** private railway line

————— 2 —————

12 無私 **mushi** unselfish, disinterested

5d2.3 / 465

目 禾 子
56 6

季

季 季

KI season SUE, TOSHI (part of given name)

─────── 1 ───────

5 季刊誌 **kikanshi** a quarterly (magazine)

10 季候 **kikō** climate

13 季節 **kisetsu** season, time of year
季節風 **kisetsufū** seasonal wind, monsoon

14 季語 **kigo** word indicating the season (in haiku)

─────── 2 ───────

5 四季 **shiki** the four seasons
冬季 **tōki** winter(time), the winter season

10 夏季 **kaki** summer(time), the summer season

11 乾季 **kanki** the dry season

5d2.4 / 1683

目 禾 力
56 8

秀

秀 秀

SHŪ, hii(deru) excel, surpass
SHIGERU (m. given name) SHŪ, HIDE (part of given name)

─────── 1 ───────

3 秀才 **shūsai** talented man, bright boy/girl

10 秀逸 **shūitsu** superb, masterly

12 秀雄 **Hideo, Shūyū** (m. given name)

16 秀樹 **Hideki, Hotsuki** (m. given name)

─────── 2 ───────

14 閨秀作家 **keishū sakka** woman writer

17 優秀 **yūshū** superior, excellent

5d2.5

目 禾 儿
56 16

禿

禿 禿

TOKU, ha(geru) become bald
hage baldness **chibi(ru)** wear away

─────── 1 ───────

16 禿頭 **hageatama, tokutō** bald head

─────── 3 ───────

5d3.1 / 124

田 禾 口
56 24

和

和 和

WA, O peace, harmony; Japan(ese)
yawa(rageru) soften, make calm
yawa(ragu) soften, become calm
nago(mu) soften, become mild
nago(yaka) mild, gentle, congenial
a(eru) dress (food with vinegar/miso, sesame seeds, etc.) HITOSHI, YAWARA (m. given name) KAZU (part of given name)

─────── 1 ───────

2 和人 **Kazuto, Kazuhito, Nagito** (m. given name)

3 和也 **Kazuya** (m. given name)

4 和文 **wabun** Japanese (writing)

5 和田 **Wada** (surname)

6 和名 **wamyō** Japanese name (of a Chinese) **wamei** Japanese name (of a plant/animal)

7 和男 **Kazuo, Yasuo, Yoshio** (m. given name)

8 和英 **Wa-Ei** Japanese-English (dictionary), Japan and England
和服 **wafuku** Japanese clothes, kimono

9 和美 **Kazumi, Kazuyoshi** (given name)
和風 **wafū** Japanese style
和洋折衷 **wayō setchū** blending of Japanese and Western styles

和独 **Wa-Doku** Japanese-German (dictionary), Japan and Germany

和室 **washitsu** Japanese-style room

和彦 **Kazuhiko** (m. given name)

和食 **washoku** Japanese food

10 和紙 **washi** Japanese paper

11 和菓子 **wagashi** Japanese-style confections

和訳 **wayaku** translation into Japanese

12 和雄 **Kazuo, Toshio** (m. given name)

13 和漢 **Wa-Kan** Japanese and Chinese

和楽 **wagaku** Japanese-style music

和解 **wakai** amicable settlement, compromise

14 和歌山県 **Wakayama-ken** (prefecture)

和歌山 **Wakayama** (city, Wakayama-ken)

和語 **wago** (native) Japanese word

16 和樹 **Kazuki** (m. given name)

——————— 2 ———————

3 大和 **Yamato** ancient Japan

大和撫子 **Yamato nadeshiko** daughter/woman of Japan

4 不和 **fuwa** discord, trouble, strife

中和 **chūwa** neutralize

日和 **hiyori** the weather; fair weather; the situation

5 付和 **fuwa** blindly follow others

平和 **heiwa** peace

6 共和国 **kyōwakoku** republic

共和党 **kyōwatō** republican party

8 英和 **Ei-Wa** English-Japanese (dictionary)

岸和田 **Kishiwada** (city, Ōsaka-fu)

9 独和 **Doku-Wa** German-Japanese (dictionary)

宥和 **yūwa** appease, placate

昭和 **Shōwa** (emperor and era, 1926 – 1989)

10 浦和 **Urawa** (city, Saitama-ken)

12 違和感 **iwakan** feeling ill at ease, discomfort, malaise

温和 **onwa** mild, gentle

13 漢和 **Kan-Wa** China and Japan, Chinese and Japanese (languages)

漢和辞典 **Kan-Wa jiten** kanji dictionary

15 緩和 **kanwa** relieve, ease, alleviate, relax

調和 **chōwa** harmony

16 穏和 **onwa** mild, gentle, genial

17 講和 **kōwa** make peace with

——————— 3 ———————

5 古今和歌集 **Kokinwakashū** (poetry anthology, early tenth century)

——————— 6 ———————

4 中華人民共和国 **Chūka Jinmin Kyōwakoku** People's Republic of China

---

5d3.2 / 466   日 禾 女   56 25

I, yuda(neru) entrust to **maka(seru/su)** entrust/leave to **kuwa(shii)** detailed, full

——————— 1 ———————

6 委任 **inin** trust, mandate, authorization

10 委員 **iin** committee member

委員会 **iinkai** committee

委託 **itaku** entrust to, put in (someone's) charge

委託販売 **itaku hanbai** selling on consignment/commission

11 委細 **isai** details, particular

——————— 3 ———————

11 常任委員会 **jōnin iinkai** standing committee

——————— 4 ———————

5d4.1 / 462   囗 禾 火   56 44

SHŪ, aki autumn, fall

――――― 1 ―――――

5 秋田 **Akita** (city, Akita-ken); (surname)

秋田県 **Akita-ken** (prefecture)
8 秋空 **akizora** autumn sky
9 秋風 **akikaze, shūfū** autumn breeze
12 秋場所 **akibasho** autumn sumo tournament

秋晴 **akiba(re)** clear autumn weather

――――― 3 ―――――

9 春夏秋冬 **shun-ka-shū-tō** the four seasons, the year round

5d4.2 / 1152   禾 小 丨   30 35 2

秒秒

BYŌ second (of time/arc)

――――― 1 ―――――

10 秒針 **byōshin** second hand (of a clock)
14 秒読 **byōyo(mi)** countdown

――――― 2 ―――――

13 数秒 **sūbyō** for several seconds

5d4.3 / 320   禾 十 丨   56 12 2

科科

KA course (of study), branch, department, faculty, family (in taxonomy)
toga fault, blame **shina** actions, deportment; coquetry

――――― 1 ―――――

5 科目 **kamoku** subject, course (of study); item, classification
7 科学 **kagaku** science
科学的 **kagakuteki** scientific
科学者 **kagakusha** scientist

――――― 2 ―――――

3 工科 **kōka** engineering course
4 内科 **naika** internal medicine

分科 **bunka** department, section, branch, course
5 外科 **geka** surgery
外科医 **gekai** surgeon
6 百科事典 **hyakka jiten** encyclopedia
8 非科学的 **hikagakuteki** unscientific
9 前科…犯 **zenka …-han/-pan** (a criminal record of three) previous convictions
10 教科書 **kyōkasho** textbook
11 産科 **sanka** obstetrics
産科医 **sankai** obstetrician
眼科 **ganka** ophthalmology
12 歯科医 **shikai** dentist

――――― 3 ―――――

3 小児科 **shōnika** pediatrics
6 自然科学 **shizen kagaku** the natural sciences
耳鼻科 **jibika** otorhinology
8 泌尿科 **hinyōka** urology
11 婦人科医 **fujinkai** gynecologist

――――― 4 ―――――

11 産婦人科 **sanfujinka** obstetrics and gynecology

――――― 5 ―――――

6 耳鼻咽喉科 **jibiinkōka** ear, nose, and throat specialty

5d4.5 / 1682   日 禾 日   56 43

香香

KŌ, KYŌ, kao(ri), ka fragrance, aroma **kao(ru)** smell good/sweet

――――― 1 ―――――

3 香川県 **Kagawa-ken** (prefecture)
4 香水 **kōsui** perfume
6 香気 **kōki** fragrance, aroma
7 香辛料 **kōshinryō** spices, seasoning
10 香料 **kōryō** spice; perfume; condolence gift
12 香港 **Honkon** Hong Kong
15 香澄 **Kasumi** (f. given name)

5

石
立
目
禾 4
衤
田
皿
疒

¹⁸ 香織 **Kaori** (f. given name)

───────── 2 ─────────

⁶ 色香 **iroka** color and scent; beauty, loveliness

⁷ 芳香 **hōkō** fragrance, perfume, aroma(tic)

⁸ 抹香 **makkō** incense powder; incense

⁹ 春香 **Haruka** (f. given name)

¹¹ 彩香 **Ayaka** (f. given name)

¹³ 遥香 **Haruka** (f. given name)

¹⁴ 綾香 **Ayaka** (f. given name)

¹⁵ 線香 **senkō** incense/joss stick

¹⁷ 優香 **Yūka** (f. given name)

───────── 3 ─────────

⁸ 明日香 **Asuka** (f. given name)

───────── 4 ─────────

¹⁰ 蚊取線香 **katori senkō** mosquito-repellent incense

───────── 5 ─────────

5d5.1 ⬚ 禾 木 一
56 41 1

秣 秣秣

MATSU, magusa fodder, forage, hay, feed

───────── 1 ─────────

¹¹ 秣桶 **magusaoke** manger

5d5.2 / 1508 ⬚ 禾 失 ⺈
56 34 15

秩 秩秩

CHITSU order, sequence; salary

───────── 1 ─────────

⁷ 秩序 **chitsujo** order, system, regularity

───────── 2 ─────────

¹² 無秩序 **muchitsujo** disorder, chaos; anomie

───────── 3 ─────────

⁶ 安寧秩序 **annei-chitsujo** peace and order

5d5.4 ⬚ 禾 一 儿
56 14 16

秤 秤秤

SHŌ, BIN, hakari (weighing) scales, balance

5d5.6 / 807 ⬚ 禾 心 丨
56 51 2

秘 祕丨秘秘

HI secret **hi(meru)** conceal, keep secret **hiso(ka)** secret

───────── 1 ─────────

¹⁰ 秘書 **hisho** (private) secretary

¹¹ 秘密 **himitsu** a secret, confidential

¹⁵ 秘蔵 **hizō** treasure, prize, cherish

───────── 2 ─────────

⁹ 便秘 **benpi** constipation

神秘的 **shinpiteki** mystic(al), mysterious

¹² 極秘 **gokuhi** top-secret, confidential

¹⁵ 黙秘 **mokuhi** keep silent about, keep secret

5d5.7 / 1083 ⬚ 禾 月 一
56 42 1

租 租租

SO crop tax, tribute

───────── 1 ─────────

¹² 租税 **sozei** taxes

5d5.8 / 978 ⬚ 禾 小 ⺈
56 35 15

称 稱丨称称

SHŌ name, title **tona(eru)** name, call, entitle **tata(eru)** praise, admire

——————— 1 ———————

0 称する **shō(suru)** name, call, entitle; claim, purport

5 称号 **shōgō** title, degree

——————— 2 ———————

6 仮称 **kashō** tentative/provisional/
working name

自称 **jishō** self-styled; first person
(in grammar)

7 対称 **taishō** symmetry; second person (in grammar)

改称 **kaishō** rename, retitle

9 俗称 **zokushō** popular/vernacular
name

11 略称 **ryakushō** abbreviation

12 敬称 **keishō** honorific title

14 愛称 **aishō** term of endearment, pet
name

——————— 3 ———————

1 一人称 **ichininshō** first person (in
grammar)

2 二人称 **nininshō** second person (in
grammar)

3 三人称 **sanninshō** third person (in
grammar)

5d5.10 / 2181 ⬚ 禾 大 二
56 34 4

秦 秦

SHIN Manchu dynasty HATA (surname) SHIN, KUNI, HATA (part of giv-
en name)

——————— 6 ———————

5d6.1 / 1121 ⬚ 禾 夕
56 30

移 移

I, utsu(ru) move (to a new residence),
change, pass to, (of a disease) be
catching **utsu(su)** move (one's
residence/office), transfer, pass on (one's

cold to someone) **utsu(rou)** change,
shift, fade

——————— 1 ———————

5 移民 **imin** immigration, emigration; immigrant, emigrant, settler

6 移行 **ikō** move, shift to

7 移住 **ijū** migration, moving

移住者 **ijūsha** emigrant, immigrant

11 移動 **idō** moving, migration

移転 **iten** move, change of address

——————— 2 ———————

6 気移 **kiutsu(ri)** fickleness

11 転移 **ten'i** change, spread, metastasis

16 燃移 **mo(e)utsu(ru)** (flames)
spread to

——————— 7 ———————

5d7.2 / 417 ⬚ 禾 王 口
56 46 24

程 程

TEI, hodo extent, degree

——————— 1 ———————

9 程度 **teido** extent, degree, level

——————— 2 ———————

3 工程 **kōtei** process; progress of the
work

4 日程 **nittei** the day's schedule/
agenda

6 先程 **sakihodo** a while ago

行程 **kōtei** distance; journey;
march; itinerary; stroke (of a
piston)

7 余程 **yohodo, yo(p)podo** very,
much, to a great degree

走程 **sōtei** distance covered

9 後程 **nochihodo** later on

10 射程 **shatei** range (of a gun/mis-
sile)

旅程 **ryotei** distance to be covered;
itinerary

11 過程 **katei** process

12 然程 **sahodo** so much, very

5

石
立
目
禾 7
衤
毋
皿
广

¹⁵ 課程 **katei** course, curriculum

5d7.4 / 399
禾 口 儿
56 24 16

税

税税

ZEI tax

─────── 1 ───────

⁴ 税収 **zeishū** tax revenues
税込 **zeiko(mi)** including tax
⁸ 税制 **zeisei** tax system
税金 **zeikin** tax
¹¹ 税理士 **zeirishi** tax accountant
税務署 **zeimusho** tax office
¹⁴ 税関 **zeikan** customs; customs-house

─────── 2 ───────

⁶ 印税 **inzei** royalties
有税 **yūzei** subject to tax, dutiable
⁸ 免税 **menzei** tax exemption
免税品 **menzeihin** duty-free goods
¹⁰ 酒税 **shuzei** liquor tax
租税 **sozei** taxes
納税 **nōzei** payment of taxes
¹¹ 脱税 **datsuzei** tax evasion
¹² 減税 **genzei** tax cut/reduction
無税 **muzei** tax-free, duty-free
¹⁴ 増税 **zōzei** tax increase
徴税 **chōzei** tax collection, taxation
関税 **kanzei** customs, tariff, duty
¹⁵ 課税 **kazei** taxation

─────── 3 ───────

⁸ 非課税 **hikazei** tax exemption
所得税 **shotokuzei** income tax
¹⁰ 財産税 **zaisanzei** property tax
¹¹ 累進税 **ruishinzei** progressive/graduated tax
¹² 間接税 **kansetsuzei** indirect tax
¹⁶ 輸入税 **yunyūzei** import duties/tariff

─────── 5 ───────

⁵ 付加価値税 **fuka-kachi zei** value-added tax

5d7.5 / 2182
禾 巾 十
56 26 12

稀

稀稀

KI, KE, mare rare
KI, KE, MARE (part of given name)

─────── 1 ───────

¹⁷ 稀覯本 **kikōbon** rare book

5d7.6
禾 氵 亻
56 21 3

黍

黍黍

SHO, kibi millet

─────── 8 ───────

5d8.1 / 1230
隹 禾
74 56

稚

稺|稚稚

CHI, itokena(i) young (child)
WAKA (part of given name)

─────── 1 ───────

⁷ 稚児 **chigo** child; child in a Buddhist procession

─────── 2 ───────

⁵ 幼稚園 **yōchien** kindergarten

5d8.4 / 2184
禾 夂 土
56 49 22

稜

稜稜

RYŌ corner; majesty **RYŌ, TAKA, TARU, IZU, KADO, SUMI** (part of given name)

5

石
立
目
禾
衤
囲
皿
疒

7

5d8.5 / 2183   田 禾 心 亻
     56   51   3

JIN, NEN ripen, harvest; year
MINORU, YUTAKA (m. given name)
JIN, NEN, TOSHI, NARU, NARI, NORI,
MINE (part of given name)

---9---

5d9.1 / 228   田 車 禾 一
     69   56   1

SHU kind, type, species; seed
tane seed; kind, species; cause, source
kusa, -gusa cause, source (of ridicule/
conversation)

---1---

² 種子島 **Tanegashima** (island, Ka-
     goshima-ken)
³ 種々 **shuju, kusagusa** various
¹⁸ 種類 **shurui** kind, type, sort

---2---

² 人種 **jinshu** race (of people)
⁶ 各種 **kakushu** every kind, various
     types
¹⁰ 特種 **tokudane** exclusive news,
     scoop **tokushu** special kind/
     type
¹¹ 接種 **sesshu** inoculation, vaccination
¹³ 業種 **gyōshu** type of industry, cate-
     gory of business
¹⁴ 雑種 **zasshu** of various kinds;
     mixed breed
¹⁶ 機種 **kishu** model, type of machine

稱 → 称 **5d5.8**

5d9.2 / 1220   田 禾 日 小
     56   43   35

TŌ, ine, ina- rice plant

---1---

⁴ 稲刈 **ineka(ri)** rice mowing/reap-
     ing
⁵ 稲田 **Inada** (surname)
⁶ 稲光 **inabikari** lightning
⁸ 稲妻 **inazuma** lightning
¹⁰ 稲荷 **Inari** god of harvests, fox de-
     ity

5d9.4 / 1729   田 禾 土 冂
     56   22   20

KOKU grain, cereals

---1---

⁸ 穀物 **kokumotsu** grain
¹⁸ 穀類 **kokurui** grains

---2---

⁶ 米穀 **beikoku** rice

---10---

5d10.2 / 1221   田 禾 日 心
     56   43   51

SUI, ho ear/head of grain

---1---

⁶ 穂先 **hosaki** tip of an ear/spear/
     knife/brush
⁸ 穂波 **honami** waves of grain

---2---

⁹ 美穂 **Miho, Yoshiho** (given name)

稻 → 稲 **5d9.2**

5d10.3 / 1750   田 禾 宀 犭
     56   33   27

KA, kase(gu) work, earn (a living)

5
石
立
日
禾
衤
田
皿 10
疒

5d10.5

—————— 1 ——————

4 稼手 **kase(gi)te** breadwinner; hard worker

13 稼業 **kagyō** one's trade/occupation

—————— 2 ——————

5 出稼 **dekase(gi)** working away from home

6 共稼 **tomokase(gi)** (husband and wife) both working, dual income

5d10.5 / 1120   56 24 11

稿   稾|稿稿

KŌ manuscript, draft; straw

—————— 1 ——————

10 稿料 **kōryō** payment for a manuscript

—————— 2 ——————

7 投稿 **tōkō** contribution (to a magazine)

9 草稿 **sōkō** (rough) draft, notes, manuscript

10 原稿 **genkō** manuscript

原稿用紙 **genkō yōshi** manuscript paper

14 遺稿 **ikō** (deceased's) unpublished works

黎→ 3a10.29

穀→穀 5d9.4

—————— 11 ——————

5d11.3   56 43 27

稽   稽|稽稽

KEI think, consider; stop; reach; bow low

—————— 1 ——————

5 稽古 **keiko** practice, training, drill, rehearsal

—————— 2 ——————

13 滑稽 **kokkei** comic, funny; joke

5d11.4 / 869   56 51 35

穏   穏|穏穏

ON, oda(yaka) calm, quiet, peaceful, mild, moderate

—————— 1 ——————

6 穏当 **ontō** proper, reasonable, moderate

8 穏和 **onwa** mild, gentle, genial

10 穏健 **onken** moderate

5d11.5 / 656   68 56 22

積   積積

SEKI accumulate; product (in math); size, area, volume **tsu(mu)** heap up, load **tsu(mi)** loading, shipment; capacity **tsu(moru)** be piled up, accumulate; estimate **tsu(mori)** intention; estimate

—————— 1 ——————

3 積上 **tsu(mi)a(geru)** heap up

4 積込 **tsu(mi)ko(mu)** load, take on (board)

5 積立 **tsu(mi)ta(teru)** save up, amass

積立金 **tsumitatekin** a reserve (fund)

9 積重 **tsu(mi)kasa(naru)** be piled/stacked up

10 積荷 **tsu(mi)ni** load, freight, cargo, shipment

11 積過 **tsu(mi)su(giru)** overload

12 積極的 **sekkyokuteki** positive, active

—————— 2 ——————

7 体積 **taiseki** volume

9 面積 **menseki** area

11 累積 **ruiseki** cumulative

船積 **funazu(mi)** shipment, lading

13 蓄積 **chikuseki** accumulation, amassing

稝→秋 **5d4.1**

───── 12 ─────

穂→穂 **5d10.2**

稺→稚 **5d8.1**

黏→粘 **6b5.4**

───── 13 ─────

5d13.2 / 2185   ⊞ 禾 衤
                        56 57 32

穰   穣⎮穰穰

JŌ harvest, abundance MINORU, YU-
TAKA, YUZURA, MINORI, OSAMU (m.
given name) JŌ, SHIGE (part of given
name)

5d13.4 / 1314   ⊞ 隹 禾 艹
                        74 56 32

穫   穫穫

KAKU harvest

───── 2 ─────

⁴ 収穫 **shūkaku** harvest

───── 14 ─────

穏→穏 **5d11.4**

───── 15 ─────

馨→ **4c16.2**

───── 17 ─────

穰→穣 **5d13.2**

───────── 衤 **5e** ─────────

| 衣 | 初 | 表 | 衿 | 袖 | 袢 | 被 | 袈 | 袋 | 袴 | 裂 | 装 | 裁 |
|0.1|2.1|0a8.6|4.5|5.1|5.2|5.3|5.10|5.11|6.4|6.7|6.8|6.9|

| 補 | 裡 | 裕 | 裔 | 装 | 裟 | 裸 | 褐 | 裾 | 製 | 褐 | 褌 | 複 |
|7.1|2j11.2|7.3|7.4|5e6.8|7.6|8.1|8.7|8.8|8.9|5e8.7|9.2|9.3|

| 褪 | 襖 | 襖 | 襟 | 襦 | 襲 |
|9.5|5e13.1|13.1|13.2|14.1|16.2|

───────── 0 ─────────

5e0.1 / 677   □ 衤
                      57

衣   衣衣

I, E, koromo garment, clothes **kinu**
clothing, kimono **I** (part of given name)

───── 1 ─────

⁸ 衣服 **ifuku** clothes, clothing
⁹ 衣食住 **ishokujū** food, clothing,
and shelter
¹¹ 衣笠 **Kinugasa** (surname)
¹² 衣替 **koromoga(e)** seasonal change
of clothes

¹⁸ 衣類 **irui** clothing

───── 2 ─────

³ 上衣 **uwagi** coat, jacket
⁵ 白衣 **hakui, byakue, byakui** white
robe, lab coat
⁷ 更衣室 **kōishitsu** clothes-changing
room
¹⁰ 真衣 **Mai** (f. given name)
浴衣 **yukata, yokui** light cotton kimono, bathrobe
¹¹ 麻衣 **Mai** (f. given name)
脱衣所 **datsuisho, datsuijo** chang-
ing/dressing room
黒衣 **kokui** black clothes
¹⁷ 濡衣 **nu(re)ginu** wet clothes; false
charge

─────── 2 ───────

5e2.1 / 679 ⊞ 礻 力
57 8

初 初初

SHO, haji(me) beginning
haji(mete) for the first time
hatsu-, ui- first **-someru** begin to

─────── 1 ───────

4 初心者 **shoshinsha** beginner
5 初代 **shodai** the first generation; the founder
6 初任給 **shoninkyū** starting salary
初老 **shorō** early old age (formerly 40, now about 60)
初回 **shokai** the first time
7 初対面 **shotaimen** first meeting
8 初版 **shohan** first edition
初歩 **shoho** rudiments, ABCs
9 初春 **shoshun** early spring
初級 **shokyū** beginners' class
10 初恋 **hatsukoi** one's first love
初校 **shokō** first proofs
初夏 **shoka** early summer
11 初雪 **hatsuyuki** first snow of the season
12 初場所 **hatsubasho** New Year's grand sumo tournament
初期 **shoki** early period/stage, beginning
13 初詣 **hatsumōde** first shrine/temple visit in the new year
14 初演 **shoen** first performance, premiere

─────── 2 ───────

12 最初 **saisho** the first/beginning
13 馴初 **na(re)so(me)** beginning of a romance

─────── 3 ───────

表→ **0a8.6**

─────── 4 ───────

5e4.5 / 2237 ⊞ 礻 亻 一
57 3 1

衿 衿衿

KIN, eri neck, collar, lapel
KIN, ERI (part of given name)

─────── 5 ───────

5e5.1 ⊞ 礻 曰 丨
57 43 2

袖 袖袖

SHŪ, sode sleeve

─────── 1 ───────

3 袖丈 **sodetake** sleeve length

─────── 2 ───────

5 半袖 **hansode** short sleeves
8 長袖 **nagasode** long sleeves

5e5.2 ⊞ 礻 十 儿
57 12 16

袢 袢袢

HAN short summer kimono

─────── 2 ───────

19 襦袢 **juban** underwear (worn under kimono)

5e5.3 / 976 ⊞ 礻 厂 又
57 18 9

被 被被

HI receive; (prefix indicating being acted upon), -ed, -ee **kōmu(ru)** incur, suffer, receive **kabu(ru)** wear, put on (one's head); take (the blame)
kabu(seru) place/pour on top of,

cover **kabu(saru)** get covered, hang
over **ō(u)** cover **ō(i)** a cover(ing)

───────── 1 ─────────

7 被告 **hikoku** defendant
　被災者 **hisaisha** victim, sufferer
10 被害 **higai** damage, harm, injury
　被害者 **higaisha** victim
14 被選挙権 **hisenkyoken** eligibility
　for election
19 被爆者 **hibakusha** bombing vic-
　tims

5e5.10 / 2238
　　　　　　　　田 礻 口 力
　　　　　　　　57 24 8

KE (used phonetically)
KE, KA, KESA (part of given name)

───────── 1 ─────────

13 袈裟掛 **kesaga(ke)** hanging/
　slashed diagonally from the
　shoulder

───────── 2 ─────────

3 大袈裟 **ōgesa** exaggerated

5e5.11 / 1329
　　　　　　　　田 礻 戈 亻
　　　　　　　　57 52 3

TAI, fukuro sack, bag, pouch

───────── 1 ─────────

0 ビニール袋 **binīru-bukuro** plas-
　tic (vinyl) bag
2 袋入 **fukuroi(ri)** in bags, sacked,
　pouched
3 袋小路 **fukurokōji** blind alley,
　cul-de-sac

───────── 2 ─────────

4 匂袋 **nioibukuro** sachet
　手袋 **tebukuro** gloves, mittens
5 布袋 **Hotei** (a potbellied god of for-
　tune)
7 足袋 **tabi** Japanese socks, tabi
9 胃袋 **ibukuro** stomach

10 紙袋 **kamibukuro** paper sack/bag
13 寝袋 **nebukuro** sleeping bag

───────── 6 ─────────

5e6.4
　　　　　　　　田 礻 大 一
　　　　　　　　57 34 14

KO, hakama (divided skirt for men's
formal wear)

5e6.7 / 1330
　　　　　　　　田 礻 夕 儿
　　　　　　　　57 30 16

RETSU, sa(keru/ku) (intr./tr.) split,
tear, rip, burst

───────── 1 ─────────

5 裂目 **sa(ke)me** rip, split, crack, fis-
　sure
13 裂傷 **resshō** laceration

───────── 2 ─────────

4 分裂 **bunretsu** dissolution, break-
　up, division
9 炸裂 **sakuretsu** explode, burst
10 破裂 **haretsu** bursting, rupture, ex-
　plosion
11 亀裂 **kiretsu** crack, fissure

───────── 3 ─────────

10 核分裂 **kakubunretsu** nuclear fis-
　sion

5e6.8 / 1328
　　　　　　　　田 礻 土 冫
　　　　　　　　57 22 5

SŌ, SHŌ, yosō(u) wear; feign, pretend, disguise oneself as **yosō(i)** dress,
garb, equipment

───────── 1 ─────────

12 装備 **sōbi** equipment
　装着 **sōchaku** equip, fit, put, place

5
石
立
目
禾
礻 6
罒
疒

13 装置 **sōchi** device, apparatus, equipment

装飾 **sōshoku** ornament, decoration

装飾品 **sōshokuhin** ornaments, decorations, accessories

———— 2 ————

5 包装 **hōsō** packaging, packing, wrapping

6 仮装 **kasō** disguise, fancy dress; converted (cruiser)

7 改装 **kaisō** remodel, refurbish

8 服装 **fukusō** dress, attire

服装随意 **fukusō zuii** informal attire

武装 **busō** arms; armed (neutrality)

9 変装 **hensō** disguise

11 偽装 **gisō** camouflage

12 軽装 **keisō** light dress/equipment

13 塗装 **tosō** painting, coating

新装 **shinsō** new equipment, refurbishing, redecorated

15 舗装 **hosō** pavement, paving

———— 3 ————

8 非武装 **hibusō** demilitarized (zone), unarmed (neutrality)

5e6.9 / 1123

□□ 衤 戈 十
57   52   12

裁裁

SAI, saba(ku) pass judgment
ta(tsu) cut out (cloth/leather)

———— 1 ————

7 裁判 **saiban** trial, hearing

裁判官 **saibankan** the judge

裁判所 **saibansho** (law) court

裁決 **saiketsu** decision, ruling

8 裁定 **saitei** decision, ruling, arbitration

15 裁縫 **saihō** sewing, tailoring, dressmaking **ta(chi)nu(i)** cutting and sewing

———— 2 ————

6 仲裁 **chūsai** arbitration, mediation

7 体裁 **teisai** decency, form, appearance, effect

8 制裁 **seisai** sanctions, punishment

9 洋裁 **yōsai** (Western) dressmaking

独裁 **dokusai** autocracy, dictatorship

10 高裁 **kōsai** High Court (short for 高等裁判所)

14 総裁 **sōsai** president, governor

———— 3 ————

12 最高裁判所 **Saikō Saibansho** Supreme Court

———— 7 ————

5e7.1 / 889

□□ 衤 月 十
57   42   12

補補

HO assist, supplement **ogina(u)** supply, make up for, compensate for, offset

———— 1 ————

6 補充 **hojū** supplement, replacement

7 補助 **hojo** assistance, supplement, subsidy

補助金 **hojokin** subsidy, grant

補足 **hosoku** supply, replenish, supplement

11 補習 **hoshū** supplementary/continuing (education)

12 補給 **hokyū** supply, replenish

14 補遺 **hoi** supplement, addendum, appendix

17 補償 **hoshō** compensation, indemnification

補償金 **hoshōkin** indemnity, compensation (money)

———— 2 ————

10 候補者 **kōhosha** candidate

13 填補 **tenpo** fill up; compensate for, make good; replenish, complete

———— 4 ————

7 改訂増補 **kaitei-zōho** revised and enlarged

裡→裏 **2j11.2**

5e7.3 / 1391   田 衤 火 口
                57   44   24

裕裕

YŪ surplus   HIROSHI, YUTAKA (m. given name)   YŪ, HIRO, YASU (part of given name)

─────── 1 ───────

¹ 裕一 **Yūichi, Hirokazu, Hiroichi** (m. given name)
² 裕之 **Hiroyuki, Yūji, Yasuyuki** (m. given name)
   裕子 **Yūko, Hiroko** (f. given name)
⁴ 裕太 **Yūta** (m. given name)
   裕介 **Yūsuke** (m. given name)
⁹ 裕美 **Hiromi, Yumi** (f. given name)
¹² 裕貴 **Yūki, Hiroki** (m. given name)
¹³ 裕福 **yūfuku** wealth, affluence

─────── 2 ───────

⁷ 余裕 **yoyū** surplus, leeway, room, margin
¹² 富裕 **fuyū** wealthy, affluent
   貴裕 **Takahiro** (m. given name)

5e7.4   日 衤 口 冂
                57   24   20

裔裔

EI descendant; border

─────── 2 ───────

⁹ 後裔 **kōei** descendant

裝→装 **5e6.8**

5e7.6 / 2239   田 衤 氵 小
                57   21   35

裟裟

SA (used phonetically)
SA, SHA (part of given name)

─────── 2 ───────

¹¹ 袈裟掛 **kesaga(ke)** hanging/ slashed diagonally from the shoulder

─────── 3 ───────

³ 大袈裟 **ōgesa** exaggerated

─────── 8 ───────

5e8.1 / 1536   田 衤 日 木
                57   43   41

裸裸

RA, hadaka naked

─────── 1 ───────

⁷ 裸体 **ratai** naked body, nudity
   裸足 **hadashi** bare feet, barefooted
¹¹ 裸婦 **rafu** nude woman

─────── 2 ───────

⁷ 赤裸々 **sekirara** stark naked; frank, outspoken
⁴ 辻褄 **tsujitsuma** coherence, consistency

5e8.7 / 1623   田 衤 日 宀
                57   43   15

褐 | 褐褐

KATSU rough woolen clothing; brown

─────── 1 ───────

⁶ 褐色 **kasshoku** brown

─────── 2 ───────

¹¹ 黒褐色 **kokkasshoku** blackish brown

5

石
立
目
禾
衤
田
皿
疒

8

5e8.8

□ 礻 尸 ㅁ
57 40 24

裾

裾 裾

KYO, suso hem, skirt, cuff; foot of a mountain

―――――――― 1 ――――――――

11 裾野 **susono** foot of a mountain

5e8.9 / 428

田 礻 牛 ㄇ
57 47 20

製

製 製

SEI make, manufacture; (as suffix) made in/of/by …

―――――――― 1 ――――――――

5 製本 **seihon** bookbinding
7 製作 **seisaku** manufacturing, production
　製図 **seizu** drafting, drawing, cartography
9 製造 **seizō** manufacture
　製品 **seihin** product, manufactured goods
13 製鉄所 **seitetsujo** ironworks
16 製薬会社 **seiyaku-gaisha** pharmaceutical company

―――――――― 2 ――――――――

3 土製 **dosei** earthen, terra cotta
4 手製 **tesei** handmade, homemade
　木製 **mokusei** wooden, made of wood
7 作製 **sakusei** manufacture
　即製 **sokusei** manufacture on the spot
8 金製 **kinsei** made of gold
10 既製 **kisei** ready-made
　特製 **tokusei** special make, deluxe
11 粗製 **sosei** crudely made
13 新製品 **shinseihin** new product
14 複製 **fukusei** reproduction, duplication
　精製 **seisei** refining; careful manufacture

　銀製 **ginsei** made of silver
18 燻製 **kunsei** smoked (fish)

―――――――― 3 ――――――――

4 日本製 **nihonsei** made in Japan
6 自家製 **jikasei** homemade, home-brewed
8 金属製 **kinzokusei** made of metal

―――――――― 9 ――――――――

褐 → 褐 **5e8.7**

5e9.2

田 車 礻 ㄇ
69 57 20

褌

褌 褌

KON, fundoshi loincloth

5e9.3 / 916

田 礻 日 夂
57 43 49

複

複 複

FUKU double, multiple, composite, compound, again

―――――――― 1 ――――――――

5 複写 **fukusha** copying, duplication; a copy, facsimile
6 複合 **fukugō** composite, compound, complex
　複合語 **fukugōgo** compound word
13 複数 **fukusū** plural
14 複製 **fukusei** reproduction, duplication
　複雑 **fukuzatsu** complicated, complex

―――――――― 2 ――――――――

9 重複 **chōfuku, jūfuku** duplication, repetition, overlapping, redundancy

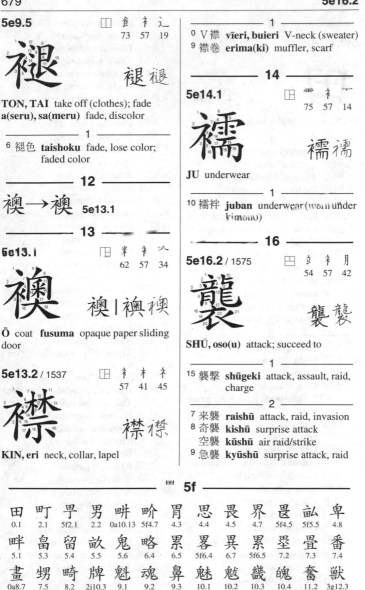

5e9.5

☐ 衤 衤 辶
73 57 19

褪 褪褪

TON, TAI take off (clothes); fade
a(seru), sa(meru) fade, discolor

— 1 —

6 褪色 **taishoku** fade, lose color;
  faded color

— 12 —

襖→襖 5e13.1

— 13 —

5e13.1

☐ 半 衤 八
62 57 34

襖 襖|襖襖

Ō coat **fusuma** opaque paper sliding
door

5e13.2 / 1537

☐ 衤 衤 衤
57 41 45

襟 襟襟

KIN, eri neck, collar, lapel

— 1 —

0 V襟 **vīeri, buieri** V-neck (sweater)
9 襟巻 **erima(ki)** muffler, scarf

— 14 —

5e14.1

☐ 需 衤 宀
75 57 14

襦 襦襦

JU underwear

— 1 —

10 襦袢 **juban** underwear (worn under
   kimono)

— 16 —

5e16.2 / 1575

☐ 立 衤 月
54 57 42

襲 襲襲

SHŪ, oso(u) attack; succeed to

— 1 —

15 襲撃 **shūgeki** attack, assault, raid,
   charge

— 2 —

7 来襲 **raishū** attack, raid, invasion
8 奇襲 **kishū** surprise attack
  空襲 **kūshū** air raid/strike
9 急襲 **kyūshū** surprise attack, raid

⊞ **5f**

田	町	甼	男	畉	昤	胃	思	畏	界	畐	甿	卑
0.1	2.1	5f2.1	2.2	0a10.13	5f4.7	4.3	4.4	4.5	4.7	5f4.5	5f5.5	4.8

畔	畠	留	畝	鬼	略	累	暑	異	累	塁	畳	番
5.1	5.3	5.4	5.5	5.6	6.4	6.5	5f6.4	6.7	5f6.5	7.2	7.3	7.4

畫	甥	畸	牌	魁	魂	鼻	魅	魃	畿	魄	奮	獸
0a8.7	7.5	8.2	2j10.3	9.1	9.2	9.3	10.1	10.2	10.3	10.4	11.2	3g12.3

戴	鼾	壘	翻	疊								
12.2	12.3	5f7.2	6b12.3	5f7.3								

5

石
立
目
禾
衤
田
皿
疒

16

——— 0 ———

5f0.1 / 35

□ 田
58

田

田 田

DEN, ta rice field, paddy

——— 1 ———

³ 田口 **Taguchi** (surname)
⁴ 田中 **Tanaka** (surname)
  田辺 **Tanabe** (surname)
⁵ 田代 **Tashiro** (surname)
⁷ 田村 **Tamura** (surname)
⁸ 田舎 **inaka** the country, rural areas
⁹ 田畑 **tahata** fields and rice paddies
  田畑 **Tabata** (surname)
¹⁰ 田原 **Tahara** (surname)
  田島 **Tajima** (surname)
  田圃 **tanbo** rice field
¹² 田植 **tau(e)** rice-planting
¹³ 田園 **den'en** fields and gardens;
    the country, rural areas

——— 2 ———

³ 三田 **Mita** (surname)
  上田 **Ueda** (surname)
  下田 **Shimoda** (surname)
  小田 **Oda** (surname)
  小田原 **Odawara** (city, Kanagawa-
    ken)
  山田 **Yamada** (surname)
⁴ 太田 **Ōta** (surname)
  内田 **Uchida** (surname)
  中田 **Nakada, Nakata** (surname)
  今田 **Imada** (surname)
  水田 **suiden** paddy
  木田 **Kida** (surname)
  戸田 **Toda** (surname)
⁵ 半田 **Handa** (surname)
  本田 **Honda, Motoda** (surname)
  古田 **Furuta** (surname)
  平田 **Hirata** (surname)
  広田 **Hirota** (surname)
  石田 **Ishida** (surname)
⁶ 多田 **Tada, Ōta** (surname)
  西田 **Nishida** (surname)
  仲田 **Nakada, Nakata** (surname)

羽田 **Haneda** (airport in Tōkyō)
池田 **Ikeda** (surname)
寺田 **Terada** (surname)
安田 **Yasuda** (surname)
守田 **Morita** (surname)
吉田 **Yoshida** (surname)
有田焼 **Arita-ya(ki)** Arita porce-
    lainware
米田 **Yoneda** (surname)
竹田 **Takeda** (surname)
⁷ 角田 **Tsunoda, Kadota** (surname)
  沢田 **Sawada** (surname)
  坂田 **Sakata** (surname)
  杉田 **Sugita** (surname)
  村田 **Murata** (surname)
⁸ 長田 **Osada, Nagata** (surname)
  岡田 **Okada** (surname)
  油田 **yuden** oil field
  岩田 **Iwata** (surname)
  岸田 **Kishida** (surname)
  松田 **Matsuda** (surname)
  武田 **Takeda** (surname)
  和田 **Wada** (surname)
  金田 **Kaneda** (surname)
⁹ 前田 **Maeda** (surname)
  浅田 **Asada** (surname)
  秋田 **Akita** (city, Akita-ken); (sur-
    name)
  秋田県 **Akita-ken** (prefecture)
¹⁰ 桑田 **Kuwata, Kuwada** (surname)
  高田 **Takada** (surname)
  原田 **Harada** (surname)
  浜田 **Hamada** (surname)
  宮田 **Miyata** (surname)
  島田 **Shimada** (surname)
  栗田 **Kurita** (surname)
  柴田 **Shibata** (surname)
¹¹ 野田 **Noda** (surname)
  隅田川 **Sumida-gawa** (river,
    Tōkyō-to)
  亀田 **Kameda** (surname)
  堀田 **Hotta, Horita** (surname)
  菊田 **Kikuta** (surname)
¹² 富田 **Tomita** (surname)
  植田 **Ueda** (surname)
  森田 **Morita** (surname)
  飯田 **Iida** (surname)
¹³ 豊田 **Toyoda, Toyota** (surname)
  園田 **Sonoda** (surname)

楠田 **Kusuda** (surname)
福田 **Fukuda** (surname)
14 増田 **Masuda** (surname)
窪田 **Kubota** (surname)
稲田 **Inada** (surname)
15 横田 **Yokota** (surname)
17 磯田 **Isoda** (surname)
篠田 **Shinoda** (surname)
18 藤田 **Fujita** (surname)
21 鶴田 **Tsuruta** (surname)

———————— 3 ————————

3 久保田 **Kubota** (surname)
8 岸和田 **Kishiwada** (city, Ōsaka-fu)

———————— 2 ————————

5f2.1 / 182

田丁   58 14

町   甲丨町町

CHŌ street, town; (unit of length, about l09 m); (unit of area, 3000 *tsubo*, or about 0.992 hectares) **machi** street, town, quarter

———————— 1 ————————

2 町人 **chōnin** merchant
5 町民 **chōmin** townspeople
7 町村 **chōson** towns and villages, municipality
8 町長 **chōchō** town mayor

———————— 2 ————————

3 下町 **shitamachi** part of the city near the sea or river, downtown
5 市町村 **shichōson** cities, towns, and villages; municipalities
9 室町 **Muromachi** (era, 1338 – 1573)
12 港町 **minatomachi** port town/city
兜町 **Kabuto-chō** (area of Tōkyō, site of Tōkyō Stock Exchange)
13 裏町 **uramachi** back street, alley
15 横町 **yokochō** side street, lane, alley

———————— 3 ————————

9 城下町 **jōkamachi** castle town

甲→町 **5f2.1**

5f2.2 / 101

日 甲 力
58   8

男   男 男

DAN, NAN, otoko man, male
O (part of given name)

———————— 1 ————————

2 男子 **danshi** man, male, boy, son
otoko(no)ko boy

男子用 **danshiyō** for men, men's
3 男女 **danjo, nannyo** men and women
8 男性 **dansei** man, male; masculinity
12 男尊女卑 **danson-johi** predominance of men over women
13 男嫌 **otokogira(i)** man-hater
17 男優 **dan'yū** actor
男爵 **danshaku** baron

———————— 2 ————————

1 一男 **Kazuo, Ichio, Ichidan** (m. given name)
3 大男 **ōotoko** tall/large man
山男 **yamaotoko** (back)woodsman, hillbilly; alpinist
5 正男 **Masao** (m. given name)
6 次男 **jinan** second son
行男 **Yukio, Ikuo** (m. given name)
8 長男 **chōnan** eldest son
幸男 **Yukio, Sachio, Yoshio** (m. given name)
征男 **Masao, Yukio, Ikuo** (m. given name)
和男 **Kazuo, Yasuo, Yoshio** (m. given name)
9 美男子 **bidanshi, binanshi** handsome man
14 彰男 **Akio, Teruo** (m. given name)

———————— 3 ————————

3 女尊男卑 **joson-danpi** putting women above men

5

石
立
目
禾
ネ
田 2
皿
疒

─────── **4** ───────

畊 → 耕 **0a10.13**

畍 → 界 **5f4.7**

5f4.3 / 1268 　　日 甲 月
58　42

胃
胃 胃

I stomach

─────── 1 ───────

11 胃袋 **ibukuro** stomach
12 胃痛 **itsū** stomachache
13 胃腸 **ichō** stomach and intestines
　　胃腸薬 **ichōyaku** stomach and bowel medicine
17 胃癌 **igan** stomach cancer

5f4.4 / 99 　　日 甲 心
58　51

思
思 思

SHI, omo(u) think

─────── 1 ───────

3 思上 **omo(i)a(garu)** be conceited
4 思切 **omo(i)ki(ru)** resolve, make up one's mind; resign oneself, give up **omo(i)ki(tta)** radical, drastic
　　思込 **omo(i)ko(mu)** have the idea that, be convinced that; set one's heart on
5 思出 **omo(i)de** memory, remembrance **omo(i)da(su)** remember
　　思付 **omo(i)tsu(ki)** idea, thought that comes to mind
　　思外 **omo(ino)hoka** unexpectedly, more than expected
　　思立 **omo(i)ta(tsu)** set one's mind on, plan
6 思考力 **shikōryoku** mental faculties

9 思通 **omo(i)dō(ri)** as one likes, to one's satisfaction
　　思春期 **shishunki** puberty
10 思索 **shisaku** thinking, speculation, meditation
　　思案 **shian** thought, consideration, mulling over; plan
11 思掛 **omo(i)ga(kenai)** unexpected
12 思遣 **omo(i)ya(ri)** consideration, sympathy, compassion
13 思想 **shisō** thought, idea
　　思想家 **shisōka** thinker
　　思詰 **omo(i)tsu(meru)** think hard, brood over
14 思慕 **shibo** yearning, deep affection

─────── 2 ───────

1 一思 **hitoomo(i)** with one effort, once and for all, resolutely
4 不思議 **fushigi** wonder, mystery, marvel
　　片思 **kataomo(i)** unrequited love

5f4.5 　　日 甲 衤
58　57

畏
畏 畏 畏

I, oso(reru) fear, be overawed
kashiko(maru) obey respectfully; sit respectfully **kashiko(kumo)** graciously, condescendingly

─────── 1 ───────

17 畏縮 **ishuku** cower, quail, be awe-struck, shrink from

5f4.7 / 454 　　日 甲 亻 几
58　3　16

界
畍 界 界

KAI boundary, limits, circle, world

─────── 2 ───────

4 分界線 **bunkaisen** line of demarcation
5 世界 **sekai** the world
　　他界 **takai** the next world; die

7 学界 **gakkai** academic/scientific world

8 限界 **genkai** limit, boundary; marginal; critical

9 俗界 **zokkai** the workaday/secular world

10 財界 **zaikai** financial world

13 業界 **gyōkai** the business world, industry, the trade

14 境界 **kyōkai** boundary, border

15 霊界 **reikai** the spiritual world

17 臨界 **rinkai** critical (temperature)

─────── 3 ───────

6 全世界 **zensekai** the whole world

11 産業界 **sangyōkai** (the) industry

14 銀世界 **ginsekai** vast silvery/snowy scene

畠 → 畏 5f4.5

畝 → 畝 5f5.5

5f4.8 / 1521

	罒	十		
	58	12	2	

卑 | 卑 卑

HI, iya(shimeru), iya(shimu) despise, look down on **iya(shii)** humble, lowly; base, ignoble, vulgar

─────── 1 ───────

6 卑劣 **hiretsu** mean, contemptible, sneaking

8 卑屈 **hikutsu** mean-spirited, servile

9 卑俗 **hizoku** vulgar, coarse

14 卑語 **higo** vulgar word/expression

─────── 4 ───────

3 女尊男卑 **joson-danpi** putting women above men

7 男尊女卑 **danson-johi** predominance of men over women

─────── 5 ───────

5f5.1 / 1945

	罒	小	二	
	58	35	4	

畔 | 畔 畔

HAN, aze, kuro ridge between rice paddies

─────── 2 ───────

12 湖畔 **kohan** lakeshore, lakeside

5f5.3

	罒	日		
	58	43	2	

畠 畠

hatake, hata (cultivated) field

5f5.4 / 761

	罒	厂	力	
	58	18	8	

畄 | 留 留

RYŪ, RU stop; hold fast; detain; keep **to(maru/meru), todo(maru/meru)** (intr./tr.) stop TOME (part of given name)

─────── 1 ───────

6 留守 **rusu** absence, being away from home; looking after the house (while someone is away); neglecting

留守番 **rusuban** looking after the house (while someone is away); caretaker

留守番電話 **rusuban denwa** answering machine

7 留学 **ryūgaku** studying abroad

留学生 **ryūgakusei** student studying abroad

13 留置 **ryūchi** detention, custody, lockup **to(me)o(ku)** detain, keep (after school); leave until called for

— 2 —

4 勾留 **kōryū** detention, custody
6 在留 **zairyū** reside, stay
7 抑留 **yokuryū** detention, intern-
ment
　　局留 **kyokudo(me)** general delivery
8 拘留 **kōryū** detention, custody
　　居留守 **irusu** pretend not to be in
(to avoid callers)
9 係留 **keiryū** moor, anchor
　　保留 **horyū** reserve, defer
　　逗留 **tōryū** stay, sojourn
　　逗留客 **tōryūkyaku** guest, visitor,
sojourner
10 残留 **zanryū** remain behind
　　書留 **kakitome** registered mail
ka(ki)to(meru) write down
11 停留所 **teiryūjo** stopping place,
(bus) stop
15 駐留軍 **chūryūgun** stationed/occu-
pying troops

5f5.5 / 1901

58　11　15

畝 | 畝畝

se (unit of area, about 1 are) **une** ridge
between furrows; rib (in fabric)

— 1 —

18 畝織 **uneori** rep, ribbed fabric

5f5.6 / 1523

目　田　几　竹
58　16　17

鬼鬼

KI, oni demon (with horns and fangs),
ogre, devil; "it" in a game of tag; spirits
of the dead; (as prefix) a fiend (for work),
fanatic; strict, fearsome (boss); abnor-
mally large

— 1 —

3 鬼才 **kisai** genius, man of remarkable talent

9 鬼面 **kimen** devil's face/mask;
bluff
10 鬼畜 **kichiku** devil, brutal man

— 6 —

5f6.4 / 841

田　夂　卩
58　49　24

署 | 略略

RYAKU abbreviation, abridgment;
omission; outline; capture, seize
hobo roughly, approximately

— 1 —

0 略す **ryaku(su)** abbreviate; omit
5 略字 **ryakuji** simplified character;
abbreviation
7 略図 **ryakuzu** rough sketch, outline
map
8 略服 **ryakufuku** everyday clothes,
informal dress
10 略称 **ryakushō** abbreviation
　　略記 **ryakki** brief account, outline
14 略歴 **ryakureki** brief personal history, résumé
　　略語 **ryakugo** abbreviation
　　略奪 **ryakudatsu** pillage, plunder,
looting

— 2 —

3 大略 **tairyaku** summary, outline;
great plan; roughly, approximately
9 侵略 **shinryaku** aggression, invasion
　　前略 **zenryaku** first part omitted;
(salutation in a letter)
　　政略 **seiryaku** political strategy;
expedient
　　省略 **shōryaku** abbreviate, omit
　　計略 **keiryaku** stratagem, plan,
ruse
12 策略 **sakuryaku** strategem,
scheme, tactic
13 戦略 **senryaku** strategy
14 概略 **gairyaku** outline, summary
16 謀略 **bōryaku** strategem, scheme

5f6.5 / 1060   日 糸 田
           61   58

累

累 累

RUI accumulate, pile up; incessantly; encumber

———————— 1 ————————

3 累々 **ruirui(taru)** piled up, in heaps
5 累加 **ruika** acceleration, progressive increase
   累犯 **ruihan** repeated offense
9 累計 **ruikei** total
10 累進 **ruishin** successive promotions; progressive, graduated
   累進税 **ruishinzei** progressive/graduated tax
16 累積 **ruiseki** cumulative

———————— 2 ————————

19 繋累 **keirui** encumbrances, dependents

 署 → 略 **5f6.4**

5f6.7 / 1061   日 田 卅 儿
           58   32   16

異

異 異

I uncommon, strange; difference
koto(naru), koto (ni suru) be different, vary; be unusual

———————— 1 ————————

3 異才 **isai** genius, prodigy
6 異色 **ishoku** different color; unique, novel
7 異体 **itai** different form, variant
   異状 **ijō** something wrong, abnormality
8 異国 **ikoku, kotokuni** foreign country
   異性 **isei** the opposite sex
9 異変 **ihen** accident, disaster, unforeseen occurrence
10 異教 **ikyō** heathenism, paganism, heresy

11 異動 **idō** change, reshuffling
13 異義 **igi** different meaning
14 異端者 **itansha** heretic

———————— 2 ————————

10 特異 **tokui** singular, peculiar, unique
22 驚異 **kyōi** wonder, miracle, marvel

———————— 3 ————————

6 同名異人 **dōmei-ijin** different person of the same name
   同音異義 **dōon-igi** the same pronunciation but different meanings

———————— 4 ————————

8 突然変異 **totsuzen hen'i** mutation

———————— 7 ————————

 累 → **5f6.5**

5f7.2 / 1694   日 田 土 冫
           58   22   5

塁

塁 塁 塁

RUI fort; base (in baseball)

———————— 1 ————————

5 塁打 **ruida** base hit, single

5f7.3 / 1087   日 田 月 冂
           58   42   20

畳

 畳 畳 畳

JŌ repetition; (counter for mats)
tatami straw mat; (as prefix) folding, collapsible **tata(mu)** fold, fold up; shut; bear in mind; finish off

———————— 1 ————————

9 畳屋 **tatamiya** tatami maker/dealer/store
12 畳替 **tatamiga(e)** replace old tatami with new ones

———————— 2 ————————

1 一畳 **ichijō** one mat
7 折畳 **o(ri)tata(mu)** fold up

石
立
目
禾
衣
田
皿
疒

7

日 米 甲 丨
62 58 2

番 番

BAN keeping watch; one's turn; number, order **tsuga(u)** pair, mate, copulate **tsuga(i)** pair, couple **tsuga(eru)** (tr.) to mate; pair; fit (an arrow) to (the string)

___ 1 ___

2 番人 **bannin** watchman, guard

4 番犬 **banken** watchdog

5 番付 **banzu(ke)** graded list, ranking

番号 **bangō** number

6 番地 **banchi** lot/house number

9 番茶 **bancha** coarse tea

11 番組 **bangumi** program

___ 2 ___

1 一番 **ichiban** number one, the first; most, best; a game/bout

2 二番目 **nibanme** No. 2, second

6 交番 **kōban** police box/stand; alternation **kawa(ri)ban(koni)** taking turns

当番 **tōban** being on duty

9 通番号 **tō(shi)bangō** serial number

12 順番 **junban** order, one's turn

___ 3 ___

10 留守番 **rusuban** looking after the house (while someone is away); caretaker

留守番電話 **rusuban denwa** answering machine

畫 → 画 0a8.7

5f7.5

田 甲 牛 力
58 47 8

甥 甥

SEI, oi nephew

___

8

5f8.2

田 甲 大 口
58 34 24

畸 畸

KI different, strange, crippled

___ 1 ___

7 畸形 **kikei** deformity, abnormality

畸形児 **kikeiji** deformed child

牌 → 牌 2j10.3

___ 9 ___

5f9.1 / 2083

… 甲 儿 竹
58 16 17

魁 魁

KAI, sakigake in the forefront; harbinger ISAO, ISAMU, TSUTOMU, HAJIME, YASUSHI (m. given name) KAI, O (part of given name)

5f9.2 / 1525

田 甲 二 竹
58 4 17

魂 魂

KON, tamashii, tama soul, spirit

___ 1 ___

9 魂胆 **kontan** soul; ulterior motive

___ 2 ___

7 肝魂 **kimo(t)tama** pluck, courage, grit

9 負魂 **ma(keji)damashii** unyielding spirit, striving to keep ahead of others

15 霊魂 **reikon** soul, spirit

18 闘魂 **tōkon** fighting spirit

5f9.3 / 813   目 目 甲 艹
                          55 58 32

鼻鼻

BI, hana nose

——— 1 ———

6 鼻先 **hanasaki** tip of the nose
  鼻血 **hanaji** nosebleed, bloody
       nose
14 鼻歌 **hanauta** humming, crooning
16 鼻髭 **hanahige** mustache

——— 2 ———

6 耳鼻咽喉科 **jibiinkōka** ear, nose,
       and throat specialty
  耳鼻科 **jibika** otorhinology

——— 10 ———

5f10.1 / 1526   ... 甲 木 儿
                          58 41 16

魅魅

MI charm, enchant, fascinate

——— 1 ———

1 魅了 **miryō** charm, captivate, hold
       spellbound
2 魅力 **miryoku** charm, appeal, fasci-
       nation
  魅力的 **miryokuteki** attractive,
       charming, captivating

5f10.2   ... 甲 犭 儿
                          58 27 16

魃魃

HATSU drought; god of drought

——— 2 ———

7 旱魃 **kanbatsu** drought

5f10.3   ... 甲 戈 竹
                          58 52 17

畿畿

KI capital; capital region

——— 2 ———

6 近畿 **Kinki** the Ōsaka-Kyōto area

5f10.4   甲 甲 日 儿
                          58 43 16

魄

魄魄

TAKU, HAKU soul, spirit

——— 2 ———

12 落魄 **rakuhaku** straitened
        circumstances
        o(chi)bu(reru) be ruined, be
        reduced to poverty

——— 11 ———

5f11.2 / 1309   目 隹 甲 大
                          74 58 34

奮奮

FUN, furu(u) be enlivened/invigorat-
ed, rouse forth (one's courage); wield;
thrive

——— 1 ———

0 奮って **furu(tte)** energetically,
       heartily
9 奮発 **funpatsu** exertion, strenuous
       effort; splurge
18 奮闘 **funtō** struggle, strive, fight
       hard

——— 2 ———

9 昂奮 **kōfun** get excited
16 興奮 **kōfun** get excited

獣 → **3g12.3**

石
立
目
禾
甲 11
皿
疒

5

— 12 —

5f12.2 ⣀ 畐 戈 艹
58 52 32

戴 　戴 戴

TAI, itada(ku) be crowned with; receive, accept

— 1 —
9 戴冠式 **taikanshiki** coronation

— 2 —
11 頂戴 **chōdai** accept, receive; please (give me)

5f12.3 田 耳 畐 一
55 58 14

鼾 　鼾 鼾

KAN, ibiki snoring

— 13 —

疊 → 塁 **5f7.2**

翻 → **6b12.3**

— 17 —

疊 → 畳 **5f7.3**

⣿ 5g

| 詈 | 買 | 署 | 罰 | 罪 | 罨 | 置 | 署 | 罰 | 罵 | 詈 | 罷 | 爵 |
|7.1|7.2|8.1|8.2|8.4|8.5|8.8|5g8.1|9.1|10.1|5g9.1|10.2|12.1|

| 羅 | 爨 |
|14.1|4a25.1|

— 7 —

5g7.1 目 言 畐
67 55

詈 　詈 詈

RI vilification, vituperation

5g7.2 / 241 目 貝 畐
68 55

買 　買 買

BAI, ka(u) buy

— 1 —
2 買入 **ka(i)i(reru)** purchase, stock up on
3 買上 **ka(i)a(geru)** buy (up/out)
4 買込 **ka(i)ko(mu)** buy, stock up on
　買手 **ka(i)te** buyer
5 買占 **ka(i)shi(meru)** buy up, corner (the market)

8 買物 **ka(i)mono** shopping, purchase
11 買過 **ka(i)su(giru)** buy too much/many
13 買置 **ka(i)o(ki)** stocking up on, hoarding

— 2 —
6 仲買 **nakaga(i)** broking, brokerage
7 売買 **baibai** buying and selling, trade, sale
11 掛買 **ka(ke)ga(i)** credit purchase
17 購買 **kōbai** purchasing

— 3 —
15 歓心買 **kanshin (o) ka(u)** curry favor

— 8 —

5g8.1 / 860 目 耳 日 土
55 43 22

署 　署 | 署 署

SHO government office, (police) station; sign one's name

1

⁶ 署名 **shomei** signature
署名捺印 **shomei-natsuin** signature and seal

3

¹⁰ 消防署 **shōbōsho** fire station
¹² 税務署 **zeimusho** tax office

5g8.2

55 22 13

KEI, KE ruled line

1

¹⁵ 罫線 **keisen** ruled line

5g8.4 / 885

55 16 4

ZAI, tsumi crime, sin, guilt

1

² 罪人 **zainin** criminal
tsumibito sinner
¹¹ 罪悪感 **zaiakukan** guilty conscience
¹³ 罪滅 **tsumihorobo(shi)** atonement, amends, expiation, penance, conscience money

---

2

⁵ 犯罪 **hanzai** crime
⁶ 死罪 **shizai** capital punishment
有罪 **yūzai** guilty
⁹ 重罪 **jūzai** serious crime, felony
¹¹ 赦罪 **shazai** pardon, absolution
¹² 無罪 **muzai** innocent, not guilty
無罪判決 **muzai hanketsu** acquittal
¹⁷ 謝罪 **shazai** apology

3

⁸ 性犯罪 **sei hanzai** sex crime
⁹ 窃盗罪 **settōzai** theft, larceny

5g8.5

55 43 34

AN cover

5g8.8 / 426

55 12 2

CHI, o(ku) put, place, set; leave behind, leave as is -o(ki) skipping ..., at intervals of ..., every (other/third day), (five meters) apart

---

1

⁵ 置去 **o(ki)za(ri)** desert, leave in the lurch
⁸ 置物 **o(ki)mono** ornament; figurehead
¹² 置違 **o(ki)chiga(eru)** put in the wrong place
置場 **o(ki)ba** place to put something
置換 **o(ki)kae(ru)** replace, transpose, rearrange **chikan** substitute, replace

---

2

¹ 一置 **hito(tsu)o(ki)** every other one
⁵ 処置 **shochi** disposition, measures, steps
⁷ 位置 **ichi** position, location
⁸ 併置 **heichi** juxtapose, place side by side
拘置 **kōchi** keep in detention, confine, hold
物置 **monoo(ki)** storeroom, shed
放置 **hōchi** let alone, leave as is, leave to chance
⁹ 前置 **maeo(ki)** preface, introduction
¹⁰ 差置 **sa(shi)o(ku)** leave, let alone; ignore
書置 **ka(ki)o(ki)** note left behind, will
留置 **ryūchi** detention, custody, lockup **to(me)o(ku)** detain,

keep (after school); leave until called for

配置 **haichi** arrangement, placement, layout

11 措置 **sochi** measure, steps

据置 **su(e)o(ku)** leave as is, let stand

12 装置 **sōchi** device, apparatus, equipment

買置 **ka(i)o(ki)** stocking up on, hoarding

15 箸置 **hashio(ki)** chopstick rest

─────── 9 ───────

署 → 署 5g8.1

5g9.1 / 886

石 言 目 儿
67 55 16

罰 罰罰

BATSU punishment, penalty
BACHI (divine) punishment, retribution

─────── 1 ───────

0 罰する **bas(suru)** punish, penalize
6 罰当 **bachia(tari)** damned, cursed
8 罰金 **bakkin** a fine
9 罰点 **batten** demerit marks

─────── 2 ───────

4 天罰 **tenbatsu** divine punishment
5 処罰 **shobatsu** punishment, penalty
6 刑罰 **keibatsu** punishment, penalty
7 体罰 **taibatsu** corporal punishment
17 厳罰 **genbatsu** severe punishment
18 懲罰 **chōbatsu** disciplinary measure, punishment

─────── 10 ───────

5g10.1

馬 目
78 55

罵 罵罵

BA, nonoshi(ru) speak ill of, revile, inveigh against

7 罵声 **basei** jeers, boos, hisses

詈 → 罰 **5g9.1**

5g10.2 / 1861

目 月 竹
55 42 17

罷 罷罷

HI, ya(meru/mu) (tr./intr.) end, discontinue, stop **maka(ru)** leave, withdraw

─────── 1 ───────

8 罷免 **himen** dismissal (from one's post)
13 罷業 **higyō** strike, walkout

─────── 2 ───────

14 総罷業 **sōhigyō** general strike

─────── 12 ───────

5g12.1 / 1923

爪 目 小
73 55 35

爵 爵爵

SHAKU peerage, court rank

─────── 1 ───────

7 爵位 **shakui** peerage, court rank

─────── 2 ───────

4 公爵 **kōshaku** prince, duke
7 伯爵 **hakushaku** count, earl
男爵 **danshaku** baron
9 侯爵 **kōshaku** marquis, marquess

─────── 14 ───────

5g14.1 / 1860

隹 糸 目
74 61 55

羅 羅羅

RA silk gauze, thin silk; (used phonetically)

———— 1 ————

10 羅針盤 **rashinban** compass

———— 2 ————

14 網羅 **mōra** include, be comprehensive

———— 3 ————

4 天麩羅 **tenpura** tempura, Japanese-style fried foods

11 曼陀羅 **mandara** mandala, picture of Buddha

———— 21 ————

爵 → 鬱 4a25.1

5h

皿	血	盂	盃	盆	盛	盗	盜	衆	盟	盡	監	盤
0.1	1.1	3.1	4a4.11	2o7.6	6.1	6.2	5h6.2	7.1	8.1	3r3.1	10.1	10.2

鹽	爵
3b10.4	4a25.1

———— 0 ————

5h0.1 / 1107   59

皿   皿 四

sara plate, dish, saucer

———— 1 ————

9 皿洗 **saraara(i)** dishwashing; dishwasher

———— 2 ————

1 一皿 **hitosara** a plate/dish (of food)
6 灰皿 **haizara** ashtray

5h1.1 / 789   59   2

血   血 血

KETSU, chi blood

———— 1 ————

0 血だらけ **chi(darake)** bloodstained
5 血圧 **ketsuatsu** blood pressure
9 血相 **kessō** a look, expression
10 血脈 **ketsumyaku** blood vessel/relationship
11 血液 **ketsueki** blood
   血族 **ketsuzoku** blood relative, kin

12 血統 **kettō** lineage, pedigree, family line
   血筋 **chisuji** blood relationship, lineage
13 血塗 **chimami(re)** bloodstained
   chinu(ru) smear with blood
14 血管 **kekkan** blood vessel
15 血縁 **ketsuen** blood relationship/relative

———— 2 ————

5 出血 **shukketsu** bleeding, hemorrhage
10 高血圧 **kōketsuatsu** high blood pressure
   流血 **ryūketsu** bloodshed
11 貧血 **hinketsu** anemia
   混血児 **konketsuji** person of mixed race, half-breed
12 無血 **muketsu** bloodless, without bloodshed
13 献血 **kenketsu** blood donation
14 鼻血 **hanaji** nosebleed, bloody nose
16 輸血 **yuketsu** blood transfusion

———— 3 ————

5h3.1   59   14   1

盂   盂 盂

U bowl

5

石
立
目
禾
示
田
皿 3
疒

─── 1 ───

19 盂蘭盆 **Urabon** o-Bon festival

─── 4 ───

盃 → 杯 **4a4.11**

盆 → 盆 **2o7.6**

─── 6 ───

5h6.1 / 719

日 皿 戊 ノ
59 52 15

盛 盛

SEI, JŌ, SHŌ, saka(n) prosperous, energetic **saka(ru)** flourish, prosper **mo(ru)** heap up; serve (food)
SAKARI (m. given name) MORI (part of given name)

─── 1 ───

3 盛大 **seidai** thriving, grand, magnificent

盛上 **mo(ri)a(geru)** heap/pile up

8 盛岡 **Morioka** (city, Iwate-ken)

12 盛場 **saka(ri)ba** bustling place, popular resort, amusement center

─── 2 ───

1 一盛 **hitomo(ri)** a pile **hito-saka(ri)** temporary prosperity

3 女盛 **onnazaka(ri)** the prime of womanhood

6 全盛期 **zenseiki** golden age, heyday

7 花盛 **hanazaka(ri)** in full bloom

8 旺盛 **ōsei** flourishing, in prime condition

10 隆盛 **ryūsei** prosperous, flourishing, thriving

12 最盛期 **saiseiki** golden age, heyday; the best season for

16 繁盛 **hanjō** prosperity; success

5h6.2 / 1100

日 皿 夂 冫
59 49 5

盗 | 盜盗

TŌ, nusu(mu) steal

─── 1 ───

7 盗作 **tōsaku** plagiarism

9 盗品 **tōhin** stolen goods, loot

17 盗聴 **tōchō** surreptitious listening, bugging, wiretapping

18 盗癖 **tōheki** kleptomania, larcenousness

盗難 **tōnan** (loss from) theft

─── 2 ───

9 窃盗 **settō** theft, larceny; thief

窃盗犯 **settōhan** thief

窃盗罪 **settōzai** theft, larceny

11 強盗 **gōtō** burglar(y), robber(y)

─── 7 ───

盜 → 盗 **5h6.2**

5h7.1 / 792

日 皿 衤 |
59 57 2

衆 衆

SHŪ, SHU multitude, populace

─── 1 ───

5 衆目 **shūmoku** public attention

8 衆参両院 **shū-san ryōin** both Houses of the Diet

20 衆議院 **Shūgiin** the House of Representatives

─── 2 ───

3 大衆 **taishū** a crowd; the masses, the general public

大衆向 **taishūmu(ki)** for the general public, popular

4 公衆 **kōshū** public (telephone, toilet, etc.)

5 民衆 **minshū** people, populace, masses

6 合衆国 **Gasshūkoku** United States

¹³ 群衆 **gunshū** crowd, multitude

¹⁷ 聴衆 **chōshū** audience

¹⁸ 観衆 **kanshū** audience, spectators

───────── 8 ─────────

5h8.1 / 717   田 皿 日 月
                   59 43 42

盟   盟 盟

MEI oath; alliance

───────── 1 ─────────

⁹ 盟約 **meiyaku** pledge, pact; alliance

───────── 2 ─────────

⁵ 加盟国 **kameikoku** member nation, signatory

⁶ 同盟 **dōmei** alliance, league, union

⁹ 連盟 **renmei** league, federation, union

───────── 4 ─────────

⁸ 欧州同盟 **Ōshū Dōmei** the European Union

───────── 9 ─────────

盡 → 尽 3r3.1

───────── 10 ─────────

5h10.1 / 1663   田 皿 冂 𠆢
                   59 20 15

監   監 監

KAN keep watch over

───────── 1 ─────────

⁶ 監守 **kanshu** keeping watch over, custody

⁸ 監房 **kanbō** (prison) cell

⁹ 監査 **kansa** inspection; auditing

¹⁰ 監修 **kanshū** (editorial) supervision

¹¹ 監視 **kanshi** monitor, keep watch over

¹³ 監督 **kantoku** supervision, direction; (movie) director, (team) manager

¹⁴ 監察 **kansatsu** inspection; inspector, supervisor

5h10.2 / 1098   田 舟 皿 冂
                   63 59 20

盤   盤 盤

BAN (chess/go) board, tray, platter, basin

───────── 2 ─────────

⁶ 地盤 **jiban** the ground; footing, base, constituency

⁹ 胎盤 **taiban** placenta, afterbirth

¹¹ 基盤 **kiban** base, basis, foundation

    終盤戦 **shūbansen** endgame, final battle

¹³ 碁盤 **goban** go board

¹⁴ 算盤 **soroban** abacus

───────── 3 ─────────

¹⁴ 磁石盤 **jishakuban** (mariner's) compass

¹⁹ 羅針盤 **rashinban** compass

───────── 20 ─────────

鹽 → 塩 3b10.4

───────── 21 ─────────

欝 → 鬱 4a25.1

───────── 广 **5i** ─────────

疫	疲	病	症	疹	疾	痕	疵	痔	痢	痩	痙	痣
4.2	5.2	5.3	5.4	5.10	5.12	6.2	6.3	6.4	7.2	5i9.1	7.5	7.6

痛	痘	痴	痺	瘤	痹	瘦	瘍	瘤	瘡	療	癌	痼
7.7	7.8	8.1	8.4	8.8	5i8.4	9.1	9.3	10.3	10.5	12.3	12.4	5i12.6

5   石 立 目 禾 衤 田 皿 10 广

癇 癖 癒 癡 癩 癪 癲
12.6　13.2　13.3　5i8.1　16.1　16.2　19.1

—————— 4 ——————

5i4.2 / 1319　　□　疒　冂　又
　　　　　　　　　60　20　9

疫　疫疫

EKI, YAKU epidemic

——————— 1 ———————

10 疫病 **ekibyō, yakubyō** epidemic,
　　plague

——————— 2 ———————

8 免疫 **men'eki** immunity (from a
　　disease)

12 検疫 **ken'eki** quarantine

—————— 5 ——————

5i5.2 / 1321　　□　疒　厂　又
　　　　　　　　　60　18　9

疲　疲疲

HI, tsuka(reru) get tired
tsuka(rasu) tire, exhaust

——————— 1 ———————

7 疲労 **hirō** fatigue

8 疲果 **tsuka(re)ha(teru)** get tired
　　out, be exhausted

——————— 2 ———————

6 気疲 **kizuka(re)** mental fatigue,
　　nervous strain

5i5.3 / 380　　□　疒　丙　冂
　　　　　　　　　60　14　20

病　病病

BYŌ, HEI, ya(mu), ya(meru) get
sick, be ill, suffer from **yamai** illness,
disease; bad habit; weakness for

——————— 1 ———————

2 病人 **byōnin** sick person, patient,
　　invalid

4 病中 **byōchū** during an illness

6 病死 **byōshi** death from illness, nat-
　　ural death

病気 **byōki** sickness, illness; sick,
　　ill

7 病状 **byōjō** patient's condition

病床 **byōshō** sickbed

8 病苦 **byōku** suffering from illness

病的 **byōteki** morbid, diseased, ab-
　　normal

9 病院 **byōin** hospital

病後 **byōgo** after an illness, convales-
　　cence

病室 **byōshitsu** sickroom, ward, in-
　　firmary

10 病弱 **byōjaku** delicate constitution

病症 **byōshō** nature of a disease

11 病理学 **byōrigaku** pathology

12 病棟 **byōtō** ward

——————— 2 ———————

6 死病 **shibyō** fatal disease

仮病 **kebyō** feigned illness

7 余病 **yobyō** secondary disease,
　　complications

8 性病 **seibyō** sexually-transmitted/
　　venereal disease

9 発病 **hatsubyō** be taken ill

重病 **jūbyō** serious illness

急病 **kyūbyō** sudden illness

肺病 **haibyō** lung/pulmonary dis-
　　ease

看病 **kanbyō** tending the sick, nurs-
　　ing

疫病 **ekibyō, yakubyō** epidemic,
　　plague

11 淋病 **rinbyō** gonorrhea

16 憶病 **okubyō** cowardice, timidity

17 臆病 **okubyō** cowardly, timid

20 躁病 **sōbyō** mania

21 癩病 **raibyō** leprosy, Hansen's dis-
　　ease

——————— 3 ———————

6 伝染病 **densenbyō** contagious/
　　communicable disease

7 狂犬病 **kyōkenbyō** rabies

14 精神病 **seishinbyō** mental illness/ disorder
18 職業病 **shokugyōbyō** occupational disease
20 躁鬱病 **sōutsubyō** manic-depressive psychosis

5i5.4 / 1318   口 疒 工 一
                                       60 38 1

症 症

SHŌ illness, patient's condition, symptoms

――――― 1 ―――――
7 症状 **shōjō** symptoms
10 症候 **shōkō** symptom
――――― 2 ―――――
10 病症 **byōshō** nature of a disease
12 無症状 **mushōjō** without symptoms
――――― 3 ―――――
4 不眠症 **fuminshō** insomnia
9 狭心症 **kyōshinshō** stricture of the heart, angina pectoris
10 健忘症 **kenbōshō** forgetfulness, amnesia
18 鞭打症 **muchiu(chi)shō** whiplash

5i5.10   口 疒 彡 亻
                                    60 31 3

疹 疹

SHIN measles, rash **CHIN** febrile disease

――――― 2 ―――――
12 湿疹 **shisshin** eczema, rash

5i5.12 / 1812   口 疒 矢 宀
                                    60 34 15

疾 疾

SHITSU illness, disease; fast, swift **to(ku)** fast, swiftly **to(kku ni)** already,

quite a while ago **yama(shii)** feel ashamed, have qualms of conscience

――――― 1 ―――――
11 疾患 **shikkan** disease, ailment
――――― 2 ―――――
6 耳疾 **jishitsu** ear ailments
11 痔疾 **jishitsu** hemorrhoids
13 痼疾 **koshitsu** chronic illness

――――― 6 ―――――

5i6.2   口 食 疒
                                     73 60

痕 痕

KON, ato scar, mark; footprint

――――― 1 ―――――
13 痕跡 **konseki** traces, vestiges, evidence

5i6.3   口 疒 卜 丨
                                     60 13 2

疵 疵

SHI, kizu flaw, blemish, defect

――――― 1 ―――――
5 疵付 **kizutsu(keru)** wound, injure; mar; besmirch
8 疵物 **kizumono** defective article; deflowered girl

5i6.4   口 疒 土 寸
                                     60 22 37

痔 痔

JI hemorrhoids

――――― 1 ―――――
10 痔疾 **jishitsu** hemorrhoids

5

石
立
目
禾
礻
罒

疒 6

—————— 7 ——————

5i7.2 / 1811 　　□ 疒 禾 儿
　　　　　　　　　60　56　16

RI diarrhea

—————— 2 ——————

³ 下痢 **geri** diarrhea

瘦 → 痩 5i9.1

5i7.5 　　□ 疒 工 一
　　　　　　60　38　1

KEI, tsu(ru) have a cramp

—————— 1 ——————

²³ 痙攣 **keiren** cramp, spasm, convulsions

5i7.6 　　□ 疒 心 士
　　　　　　60　51　22

SHI, aza birthmark

5i7.7 / 1320 　　□ 疒 月 一
　　　　　　　　60　42　1

TSŪ pain **ita(i)** painful **ita(mu)** be painful, hurt; be damaged, spoil **ita(meru)** hurt, pain, afflict **ita(mi)** pain, ache

—————— 1 ——————

⁰ 痛がる **ita(garu)** complan of pain
⁴ 痛止 **ita(mi)do(me)** painkiller
　痛手 **itade** serious wound; hard blow

⁵ 痛目 **ita(i)me** a painful experience
⁷ 痛快 **tsūkai** keen pleasure, thrill, delight
¹⁰ 痛烈 **tsūretsu** severe, bitter, scathing

—————— 2 ——————

⁸ 苦痛 **kutsū** pain
⁹ 陣痛 **jintsū** labor (pains)
　胃痛 **itsū** stomachache
¹² 悲痛 **hitsū** bitter, grief, sorrow
　歯痛 **shitsū, haita** toothache
¹³ 腰痛 **yōtsū** lumbago
　腹痛 **fukutsū, haraita** stomachache, abdominal pain
¹⁶ 頭痛 **zutsū** headache
¹⁸ 鎮痛剤 **chintsūzai** painkiller

—————— 3 ——————

¹¹ 偏頭痛 **henzutsū, hentōtsu** migraine headache

5i7.8 / 1942 　　□ 疒 口 儿
　　　　　　　　60　24　16

TŌ smallpox

—————— 1 ——————

⁸ 痘苗 **tōbyō** vaccine

—————— 8 ——————

5i8.1 / 1813 　　□ 疒 矢 口
　　　　　　　　60　34　24

CHI foolish

—————— 1 ——————

² 痴人 **chijin** fool, idiot
¹¹ 痴情 **chijō** blind love, passion, infatuation
¹³ 痴漢 **chikan** molester of women, masher

—————— 2 ——————

⁵ 白痴 **hakuchi** idiot
⁹ 音痴 **onchi** tone deaf

13 愚痴 **guchi** idle complaint, grumbling

5i8.4 □ 疒 日 十
60 43 12

痺 痺｜痺痺

HI palsy **shibi(reru)** go numb, tingle, be paralyzed

— 1 —
16 痺薬 **shibi(re)gusuri** anesthetic

— 2 —
11 麻痺 **mahi** paralysis

— 4 —
3 小児麻痺 **shōni mahi** infantile paralysis, polio

5i8.8 □ 疒 冂 十
60 24 12

痼 痼痼

KO chronic illness

— 1 —
10 痼疾 **koshitsu** chronic illness

痹 → 痺 **5i8.4**

— 9 —

5i9.1 □ 疒 ヨ 厂
60 39 18

瘦 瘦｜瘦瘦

SŌ, SHŪ, ya(seru) become thin

7 瘦我慢 **ya(se)gaman** endure for sake of pride
10 瘦衰 **ya(se)otoro(eru)** become emaciated, waste away

— 2 —
10 夏瘦 **natsuya(se)** loss of weight in summer

5i9.3 □ 疒 日 犭
60 43 27

瘍 瘍瘍

YŌ ulcer, boil, carbuncle

— 2 —
13 腫瘍 **shuyō** tumor
15 潰瘍 **kaiyō** ulcer

— 10 —

5i10.3 □ 疒 罒 厂
60 58 18

瘤 瘤瘤

RYŪ, kobu wen, lump, bump, swelling, nodule

— 1 —
5 瘤付 **kobutsu(ki)** wen; nuisance; with a child along

— 2 —
2 力瘤 **chikarakobu** flexed biceps

5i10.5 □ 食 疒 口
73 60 24

瘡 瘡瘡

SŌ wound; boil **kasa** syphilis

— 12 —

5i12.3 / 1322 □ 疒 火 日
60 44 43

療 療療

RYŌ heal, cure

— 1 —
8 療法 **ryōhō** treatment, therapy, remedy
  療治 **ryōji** medical treatment, remedy

5

石
立
目
禾
衤
罒
皿

疒 **12**

15 療養 **ryōyō** medical treatment/care

療養所 **ryōyōjo** sanitarium

—————— 2 ——————

7 医療 **iryō** medical treatment, health care; medical

8 治療 **chiryō** medical treatment

5i12.4 　□ 疒 口 凵
　　　　　　60 24 36

癌 癌癌

GAN cancer

—————— 1 ——————

13 癌腫 **ganshu** cancer tumor, carcinoma

—————— 2 ——————

7 乳癌 **nyūgan** breast cancer

9 発癌 **hatsugan** cancer-causing, carcinogenic

肺癌 **haigan** lung cancer

胃癌 **igan** stomach cancer

瘤 → 瘤 5i12.6

5i12.6 　□ 門 疒 月
　　　　　　76 60 42

癇 癇|癇癇

KAN quick temper, irritability, peevishness; nervousness, sensitivity

—————— 1 ——————

8 癇性 **kanshō** irritability, irascibility

21 癇癪 **kanshaku** passion, temper, irritability

—————— 2 ——————

24 癲癇 **tenkan** epilepsy, epileptic fit

—————— 13 ——————

5i13.2 / 1490 　□ 疒 立 尸
　　　　　　　60 54 40

癖 癖癖

HEKI, kuse habit, peculiarity

—————— 1 ——————

4 癖毛 **kusege** curly/kinky hair

—————— 2 ——————

1 一癖 **hitokuse** trait, peculiarity; slyness

3 口癖 **kuchiguse** habit of saying, favorite saying

8 性癖 **seiheki** disposition, proclivity

10 酒癖 **sakekuse, sakeguse, shuheki** drinking habits

11 悪癖 **akuheki, waruguse** bad habit, vice

盗癖 **tōheki** kleptomania, larcenousness

15 潔癖 **keppeki** love of cleanliness, fastidiousness

5i13.3 / 1600 　□ 疒 月 心
　　　　　　　60 42 51

癒 癒|癒癒

YU, i(yasu) heal, cure; satisfy, quench; soothe **i(eru)** be healed, recover

—————— 1 ——————

12 癒着 **yuchaku** adhere, knit together, heal up; too close a relationship (with an organization)

—————— 2 ——————

8 治癒 **chiyu** heal, cure, recover

—————— 14 ——————

癡 → 痴 5i8.1

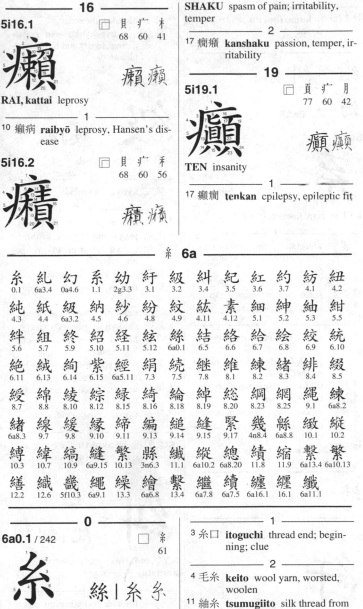

16

5i16.1   □ 貝 疒 木
           68   60   41

癩   癩癩

RAI, kattai leprosy

1

10 癩病 **raibyō** leprosy, Hansen's disease

5i16.2   □ 貝 疒 耒
           68   60   56

癪   癪癪

SHAKU spasm of pain; irritability, temper

2

17 癇癪 **kanshaku** passion, temper, irritability

19

5i19.1   □ 頁 疒 月
           77   60   42

癲   癲癲

TEN insanity

1

17 癲癇 **tenkan** epilepsy, epileptic fit

糸 6a

糸	糺	幻	系	幼	紆	級	糾	紀	紅	約	紡	紐
0.1	6a3.4	0a4.6	1.1	2g3.3	3.1	3.2	3.4	3.5	3.6	3.7	4.1	4.2
純	紙	級	納	紗	紛	紋	紘	素	細	紳	紬	紺
4.3	4.4	6a3.2	4.5	4.6	4.8	4.9	4.11	4.12	5.1	5.2	5.3	5.5
絆	組	終	紹	経	絃	絲	結	絡	給	絵	絞	統
5.6	5.7	5.9	5.10	5.11	5.12	6a0.1	6.5	6.6	6.7	6.8	6.9	6.10
絶	絨	絢	紫	經	絹	続	継	維	練	緒	緋	綴
6.11	6.13	6.14	6.15	6a5.11	7.3	7.5	7.8	8.1	8.2	8.3	8.4	8.5
綬	綿	綾	綜	緑	綺	綸	綽	総	綱	網	縄	練
8.7	8.8	8.10	8.12	8.15	8.16	8.18	8.19	8.20	8.23	8.25	9.1	6a8.2
緒	線	緩	縁	締	編	縋	縫	緊	幾	縣	緻	縦
6a8.3	9.7	9.8	9.10	9.11	9.13	9.14	9.15	9.17	4n8.4	6a8.8	10.1	10.2
縛	緯	縞	縫	繁	縣	纖	縦	總	績	縮	繋	繁
10.3	10.7	10.9	6a9.15	10.13	3n6.3	11.1	6a10.2	6a8.20	11.8	11.9	6a13.4	6a10.13
繕	織	畿	縄	繰	繪	繋	繼	續	纏	繮	纎	
12.2	12.6	5f10.3	6a9.1	13.3	6a6.8	13.4	6a7.8	6a7.5	6a16.1	16.1	6a11.1	

0

6a0.1 / 242   □ 糸
               61

糸   絲｜糸 糸

SHI, ito thread

1

3 糸口 **itoguchi** thread end; beginning; clue

2

4 毛糸 **keito** wool yarn, worsted, woolen

11 紬糸 **tsumugiito** silk thread from waste cocoons

—————— 3 ——————
¹⁴ 蜘蛛糸 **kumo (no) ito** spider's thread

—————— 1 ——————

糺→糾 **6a3.4**

幻→ **0a4.6**

6a1.1 / 908   日 糸 ｜
                                       61 2

系

KEI system; lineage, group

系系

—————— 1 ——————
⁶ 系列 **keiretsu** system, series; ownership affiliation, corporate group
⁷ 系図 **keizu** genealogy, family tree
¹² 系統 **keitō** system; lineage, descent
¹⁹ 系譜 **keifu** genealogy, family tree
—————— 2 ——————
³ 大系 **taikei** outline, overview, survey
　 女系 **jokei** female line(age), on the mother's side
⁴ 日系 **nikkei** of Japanese descent
⁵ 母系 **bokei** maternal line
⁷ 体系 **taikei** system, organization
⁸ 直系 **chokkei** lineal descendant, direct line
¹⁰ 家系図 **kakeizu** family tree

—————— 2 ——————

幼→ **2g3.3**

—————— 3 ——————

6a3.1   日 糸 一 一
                                 61 14 1

紆

紆紆

U bend; crouch

—————— 3 ——————
⁶ 紆曲 **ukyoku** meander
⁷ 紆余曲折 **uyo-kyokusetsu** meandering, twists and turns, complications

6a3.2 / 568   日 糸 力 ｜
                                       61 8 2

級

級｜級級

KYŪ rank, class, grade

—————— 1 ——————
⁴ 級友 **kyūyū** classmate
—————— 2 ——————
¹ 一級 **ikkyū** one grade; first class
³ 上級 **jōkyū** upper grade, senior
　 下級 **kakyū** lower grade/class, junior, subordinate
⁶ 同級生 **dōkyūsei** classmate
⁷ 低級 **teikyū** low-grade, lowbrow, vulgar
　 学級 **gakkyū** school class, grade
　 初級 **shokyū** beginners' class
¹⁰ 高級 **kōkyū** high-grade, high-class; high rank
　 進級 **shinkyū** promotion (to a higher grade)
¹¹ 階級 **kaikyū** (social) class; (military) rank
¹² 等級 **tōkyū** class, grade, rank
—————— 3 ——————
⁵ 比較級 **hikakukyū** the comparative degree (in grammar)

6a3.4 / 1703   日 糸 十 ｜
                                        61 12 2

糾

糺｜糾糾

KYŪ, tada(su) rectify, clear up
azana(u) twist (rope)

—————— 2 ——————
¹⁰ 紛糾 **funkyū** complication, entanglement

粉糾 **funkyū** complications, entanglement

6a3.5 / 372　　囗 糹 弓
　　　　　　　　61　28

紀紀

KI account, narrative, history; (geological) period OSAMU (m. given name)
KI, TOSHI, NORI, MICHI (part of given name)

―――――― 1 ――――――

⁴ 紀元 **kigen** era (of year reckoning)
紀元前 **kigenzen** B.C.
紀元後 **kigengo** A.D.
紀元節 **kigensetsu** Empire Day
紀夫 **Norio, Toshio** (m. given name)
⁶ 紀行 **kikō** account of a journey
⁹ 紀要 **kiyō** bulletin, record, proceedings

―――――― 2 ――――――

⁵ 世紀 **seiki** century
⁶ 早紀 **Saki** (f. given name)
⁹ 美紀 **Miki** (f. given name)
風紀 **fūki** discipline, public morals

―――――― 3 ――――――

¹ 一世紀 **isseiki** a century; first century
⁵ 半世紀 **hanseiki** half century
¹¹ 現世紀 **genseiki** this century

6a3.6 / 820　　囗 糹 エ
　　　　　　　　61　38

紅紅

KŌ, KU, GU, kurenai red, crimson
beni rouge, lipstick; red **momi** red silk cloth

―――――― 1 ――――――

⁵ 紅白 **kōhaku** red and white
⁹ 紅海 **Kōkai** the Red Sea
紅茶 **kōcha** black tea

¹² 紅葉 **kōyō** red (autumn) leaves
momiji maple tree; red (autumn) leaves
¹⁵ 紅潮 **kōchō** redden, flush, blush; menstruate

6a3.7 / 211　　囗 糹 冖 丨
　　　　　　　　61　15　2

約約

YAKU promise; approximately; curtail; factor (in math) **tsuzu(maru)** shrink; be summarized **tsuzu(meru)** condense, shorten, curtail

―――――― 1 ――――――

⁰ 約する **yaku(suru)** promise, reduce, abbreviate
⁵ 約半分 **yaku hanbun** about half
⁷ 約束 **yakusoku** promise; appointment

―――――― 2 ――――――

⁴ 予約 **yoyaku** reservations, booking, advance order, subscription, contract
⁵ 旧約 **kyūyaku** old promise/covenant; the Old Testament
⁶ 先約 **sen'yaku** previous engagement; prior contract
⁷ 条約 **jōyaku** treaty
⁸ 制約 **seiyaku** restriction, limitation, condition
協約 **kyōyaku** agreement, convention, pact
⁹ 契約 **keiyaku** contract, agreement
要約 **yōyaku** summary
¹⁰ 倹約 **ken'yaku** thrift, frugality
倹約家 **ken'yakuka** thrifty person, economizer
破約 **hayaku** breach of contract/promise
¹¹ 婚約 **kon'yaku** engagement, betrothal
婚約者 **kon'yakusha** fiancé(e)
¹² 違約 **iyaku** breach of contract, default
¹³ 解約 **kaiyaku** cancellation of a contract

糹 3
米
舟
虫
耳
艹

新約 **shin'yaku** the New Testament
盟約 **meiyaku** pledge, pact; alliance
節約 **setsuyaku** economizing, saving on
14 誓約 **seiyaku** oath, vow, pledge
15 黙約 **mokuyaku** a tacit agreement

———— 4 ————

6a4.1 / 1859
□ 糸 方
61 48

紡 紡紡

BŌ, tsumu(gu) spin, make yarn

———— 1 ————
17 紡績 **bōseki** spinning

———— 2 ————
20 鐘紡 **Kanebō** (company name)

6a4.2
□ 糸 十 一
61 12 1

紐 紐紐

CHŪ, JŪ, himo string(s), cord, (shoe)lace, strap

———— 1 ————
5 紐付 **himotsu(ki)** with strings attached

———— 2 ————
13 靴紐 **kutsuhimo** shoelaces

6a4.3 / 965
□ 糸 十 冂
61 12 20

純 純純

JUN pure　JUN, ATSUSHI (m. given name)　JUN, SUMI (part of given name)

———— 1 ————
1 純一 **Jun'ichi, Yoshikazu, Jun'itsu** (m. given name)

2 純子 **Junko, Sumiko** (f. given name)
4 純毛 **junmō** all-wool
　純文学 **junbungaku** pure literature, belles lettres
　純日本風 **jun-Nihon-fū** classical Japanese style
5 純正 **junsei** pure, genuine
　純白 **junpaku** pure white
7 純利 **junri** net profit
8 純金 **junkin** pure/solid gold
9 純度 **jundo** purity
10 純益 **jun'eki** net profit
　純粋 **junsui** pure, genuine
11 純情 **junjō** pure-minded emotion, naïveté, devotion
15 純潔 **junketsu** pure, unsullied, chaste

———— 2 ————
4 不純 **fujun** impure
9 単純 **tanjun** simple
11 清純 **seijun** pure (and innocent)

6a4.4 / 180
□ 糸 厂 十
61 18 12

紙 帋|紙紙

SHI, kami paper

———— 1 ————
3 紙上 **shijō** on paper; by letter; in the newspapers
4 紙切 **kamiki(re)** scrap of paper
　紙片 **shihen** scrap of paper
11 紙袋 **kamibukuro** paper sack/bag
15 紙幣 **shihei** paper money

———— 2 ————
4 手紙 **tegami** letter
5 包紙 **tsutsu(mi)gami** wrapping paper
　用紙 **yōshi** form (to be filled out); stationery
6 色紙 **irogami** colored paper
　　 shikishi (a type of calligraphy paper)
7 別紙 **besshi** attached sheet, enclosure

6

4 糸
米
舟
虫
耳
⺮

折紙 **o(ri)gami** the art of paper folding; colored origami paper; authentication, testimonial

8 表紙 **hyōshi** cover, binding

和紙 **washi** Japanese paper

11 張紙禁止 **ha(ri)gami kinshi** Post No Bills

12 貼紙 **ha(ri)gami** sticker, poster

14 塵紙 **chirigami** coarse (toilet) paper

16 壁紙 **kabegami** wallpaper

18 濾紙 **roshi, ko(shi)gami** filter paper

─────── 3 ───────

3 上表紙 **uwabyōshi** outer cover, (book) jacket

4 日本紙 **nihonshi** Japanese paper

8 画用紙 **gayōshi** drawing paper

12 絵草紙 **ezōshi** picture book

13 新聞紙 **shinbunshi** newspaper (paper)

17 藁半紙 **warabanshi** (a low-grade paper)

─────── 4 ───────

10 原稿用紙 **genkō yōshi** manuscript paper

級 → 級 **6a3.2**

6a4.5 / 758   囗 糸 亻 冂
             61   3   20

納 納

NŌ, TŌ, NA, NA', NAN, osa(meru) pay; supply; accept; store **osa(maru)** be paid (in), be supplied; stay (in the stomach); be contented **OSAMU** (m. given name)

─────── 1 ───────

2 納入 **nōnyū** pay, deliver, supply

5 納本 **nōhon** book delivery; presentation copy

納付 **nōfu** payment, delivery

7 納豆 **nattō** fermented soybeans

9 納品 **nōhin** delivery

10 納骨 **nōkotsu** depositing the (deceased's) ashes

11 納得 **nattoku** assent to, be convinced of

12 納期 **nōki** payment date, delivery deadline

納税 **nōzei** payment of taxes

─────── 2 ───────

4 不納 **funō** nonpayment, default

収納 **shūnō** receipts; harvest; put in, store

分納 **bunnō** payment/delivery in installments

5 加納 **Kanō** (surname)

8 奉納 **hōnō** dedication, offering

13 滞納 **tainō** delinquency (in payment)

14 嘉納 **kanō** approve, appreciate, accept with pleasure

6a4.6 / 2191   囗 糸 小 丨
             61   35   2

紗 紗

SA, SHA gauze, cloth **SA, SHA, TAE, SUZU** (part of given name) **SUZU** (f. given name)

─────── 1 ───────

7 紗希 **Saki** (f. given name)

6a4.8 / 1702   囗 糸 儿 力
             61   16   8

紛 紛

FUN, magi(reru) be mistaken for, be hardly distinguishable; get mixed, disappear among; be diverted **magi(rawasu), magi(rasu)** divert, distract; conceal; evade **magi(rawashii)** ambiguous, misleading **maga(u)** be mistaken for; be confused with

─────── 1 ───────

5 紛失 **funshitsu** loss, be missing

6 紛争 **funsō** dispute, strife

9 紛糾 **funkyū** complication, entanglement

6

—————— 2 ——————

⁶ 気紛 **kimagu(re)** whimsical, capricious

6a4.9 / 1454　　　　　□ 糸 亠 十
　　　　　　　　　　　　61　11　12

紋　　　　　紋紋

MON (family) crest; (textile) pattern
AYA (part of given name)

—————— 1 ——————

⁴ 紋切型 **monki(ri)gata** conventional

¹¹ 紋章 **monshō** crest, coat of arms

¹⁴ 紋様 **mon'yō** (textile) pattern

—————— 2 ——————

⁸ 波紋 **hamon** ripples; repercussions

⁹ 指紋 **shimon** fingerprints, thumbprint

¹⁰ 家紋 **kamon** family crest

6a4.11 / 2190　　　□ 糸 十 竹
　　　　　　　　　　　61　12　17

紘　　　　　紘紘

KŌ reins; boundary; large　KŌ, HIRO, AYA, TSUNA (part of given name)　HIROSHI, HIROMU, OSAMU (m. given name)

6a4.12 / 271　　　　□ 糸 土 一
　　　　　　　　　　　61　22　1

素　　　　　素素

SO element; beginning　**SU** naked, uncovered, simple　**moto** beginning, base

—————— 1 ——————

² 素人 **shirōto** amateur, layman

⁶ 素朴 **soboku** simple, artless, ingenuous

⁷ 素材 **sozai** a material; subject matter

素足 **suashi** bare feet, barefooted

⁸ 素直 **sunao** gentle, meek, docile; frank, honest

¹⁰ 素振 **sobu(ri)** manner, bearing, behavior

¹¹ 素描 **sobyō** rough sketch

¹² 素晴 **suba(rashii)** splendid, magnificent

¹⁵ 素敵 **suteki** splendid, marvelous, great

¹⁸ 素顔 **sugao** face without makeup; sober face

—————— 2 ——————

⁸ 画素 **gaso** picture element, pixel, dot

⁹ 要素 **yōso** element, factor

¹⁴ 酸素 **sanso** oxygen

¹⁵ 質素 **shisso** simple, plain, frugal

¹⁸ 簡素 **kanso** plain and simple

—————— 5 ——————

6a5.1 / 695　　　　□ 糸 田
　　　　　　　　　　　61　58

細　　　　　細細

SAI narrow, small, fine　**hoso(i)** thin, narrow, slender　**hoso(ru)** get thin　**hoso(meru)** make narrow　**koma(kai/ka)** small, detailed　**sasa(yaka)** small

—————— 1 ——————

³ 細川 **Hosokawa** (surname)

細工 **saiku** work(manship); artifice, trick

細々 **komagoma** in pieces, in detail　**hosoboso** slender; scanty (livelihood)

⁴ 細井 **Hosoi** (surname)

⁵ 細目 **saimoku** details, particulars　**hosome** narrow eyes/opening

⁷ 細谷 **Hosoya, Hosotani** (surname)

⁸ 細長 **hosonaga(i)** long and thin

細雨 **saiu** fine/misty rain, drizzle

¹¹ 細道 **hosomichi** narrow lane, path

細密 **saimitsu** minute, close, miniature

6 ◀ 糸 米 舟 虫 耳 ⺮

14 細説 **saisetsu** detailed explanation

――― 2 ―――

4 仔細 **shisai** reasons, circumstances; significance; details

心細 **kokoroboso(i)** forlorn, disheartened

6 竹細工 **takezaiku** bamboo handicrafts

8 明細 **meisai** details, particulars

委細 **isai** details, particular

金細工 **kinzaiku** goldwork, gold ware

13 微細 **bisai** minute, fine, detailed

詳細 **shōsai** details, particulars

14 精細 **seisai** detailed, precise

17 繊細 **sensai** delicate, fine, subtle

6a5.2 / 1109

61 43 2

紳紳

SHIN gentleman

――― 1 ―――

3 紳士 **shinshi** gentleman

紳士用 **shinshiyō** men's, for men

紳士協定 **shinshi kyōtei** gentleman's agreement

紳士服 **shinshifuku** men's clothing

紳士録 **shinshiroku** a who's-who, directory

6a5.3 / 2193

61 43 2

紬紬

CHŪ, tsumugi pongee CHŪ, SHŪ, TSUMUGI (part of given name)

――― 1 ―――

6 紬糸 **tsumugiito** silk thread from waste cocoons

6a5.5 / 1493

糸 艹 二
61 32 4

紺紺

KON dark/navy blue

――― 1 ―――

6 紺色 **kon'iro** dark/navy blue

6a5.6

糸 十 九
61 12 16

絆絆

HAN, BAN, hoda(su) tie, bind **kizuna** ties, bonds

――― 1 ―――

12 絆創膏 **bansōkō** adhesive plaster

6a5.7 / 418

糸 月 一
61 42 1

組組

SO, kumi group, set, crew, class, company **ku(mu)** put together

――― 1 ―――

4 組分 **kumiwa(ke)** sorting, grouping

5 組立 **ku(mi)ta(teru)** construct, assemble

組立式 **kumita(te)shiki** prefab, collapsible

6 組合 **ku(mi)a(u)** form a partnership; grapple with **kumiai** association, union **ku(mi)a(waseru)** combine; fit together **ku(mi)a(wase)** combination

組成 **sosei** composition, makeup

14 組閣 **sokaku** formation of a cabinet

18 組織 **soshiki** organization; tissue

――― 2 ―――

1 一組 **hitokumi, ichikumi** one set, one class

6

糸 5

米
角
虫
耳
艹

5 仕組 **shiku(mi)** construction; contrivance, mechanism; plan

7 労組 **rōso, rōkumi** labor union (short for 労働組合)

8 枠組 **wakugumi** frame, framework; framing

取組 **to(ri)ku(mu)** grapple with **to(ri)kumi** (sumo) match

9 乗組員 **norikumiin** crew

10 骨組 **honegu(mi)** skeleton; framework

12 腕組 **udegu(mi)** fold one's arms

番組 **bangumi** program

—————— 3 ——————

2 二人組 **niningumi** twosome, duo

6a5.9 / 458   田 糸 夂 丨
                   61 49 2

  終終

SHŪ, o(waru), o(eru) come/bring to an end   **o(wari)** end, conclusion
tsui (ni) finally, in the end

—————— 1 ——————

1 終了 **shūryō** end, conclusion, completion, expiration

4 終止 **shūshi** come to an end

5 終末 **shūmatsu** end, conclusion

7 終身刑 **shūshinkei** life sentence

終決 **shūketsu** settlement, conclusion

終局 **shūkyoku** end, conclusion; endgame

9 終点 **shūten** end of the line, last stop, terminus

12 終着駅 **shūchakueki** terminal station

終結 **shūketsu** conclusion, termination

13 終業 **shūgyō** close of work/school

終幕 **shūmaku** curtainfall, end, close

終戦 **shūsen** end of the war

終電車 **shūdensha** the last train/streetcar for the day

14 終演 **shūen** end of a performance

15 終審 **shūshin** final trial, last instance

終盤戦 **shūbansen** endgame, final battle

—————— 2 ——————

8 始終 **shijū** from first to last, all the while

12 最終 **saishū** the last, the end; final

最終日 **saishūbi** the last day

最終回 **saishūkai** the last time/inning

最終的 **saishūteki** final, ultimate

17 臨終 **rinjū** one's last moments, deathbed

—————— 4 ——————

1 一部始終 **ichibu shijū** full particulars

6a5.10 / 456   田 糸 口 力
                   61 24 8

  紹紹

SHŌ introduce; help; inherit
TSUGU (part of given name)

—————— 1 ——————

4 紹介 **shōkai** introduction, presentation

紹介状 **shōkaijō** letter of introduction

—————— 3 ——————

6 自己紹介 **jiko shōkai** introduce oneself

6a5.11 / 548   田 糸 土 又
                   61 22 9

 經丨経経

KEI, KYŌ longitude; sutra; passage of time; pass through, via   **he(ru)** pass, elapse; pass through   **ta(tsu)** pass, elapse, expire   **TSUNE** (part of given name)

—————— 1 ——————

5 経由 **keiyu** via, by way of

⁶ 経団連 **Keidanren** Federation of Economic Organizations (Keidanren) (short for 経済団体連合)

⁹ 経度 **keido** longitude

¹¹ 経過 **keika** lapse, passage of time; progress, course, developments

経済 **keizai** economy, economics, economical use

経済学 **keizaigaku** economics

経済的 **keizaiteki** economic, financial; economical

経済欄 **keizairan** financial section/columns

経理士 **keirishi** public accountant

¹² 経営 **keiei** manage, operate, run

経費 **keihi** expenses, cost

¹³ 経路 **keiro** course, route

¹⁴ 経歴 **keireki** personal history, career

¹⁸ 経験 **keiken** experience

————— 2 —————

⁴ 不経済 **fukeizai** poor economy, waste

⁹ 神経 **shinkei** nerve

神経質 **shinkeishitsu** nervous, high-strung

政経学 **seikeigaku** politics and economics

————— 3 —————

¹² 無神経 **mushinkei** insensible to

6a5.12 / 2192   田 糸 宀 竹
                 61 11 17

GEN, ito strings (on musical instruments) GEN, KEN, TSURU, ITO, O, FUSA (part of given name)

————— 1 —————

¹³ 絃楽 **gengaku** string music

絃楽器 **gengakki** stringed instrument

————— 6 —————

絲 → 糸 **6a0.1**

6a6.5 / 485   田 糸 土 口
                 61 22 24

結結

KETSU, KECHI, musu(bu) tie, bind; conclude (a contract); bear (fruit)
yu(waeru) bind, tie **yu(u), i(u)** do up (one's hair)

————— 1 —————

⁵ 結末 **ketsumatsu** end, conclusion, upshot

結付 **musu(bi)tsu(keru)** tie together, link

⁶ 結合 **ketsugō** union, combination
musu(bi)a(waseru) tie together, combine

結成 **kessei** formation, organization

⁷ 結束 **kessoku** band together, be united

結局 **kekkyoku** after all, in the end

結社 **kessha** association, society

⁸ 結果 **kekka** result, consequence, effect

¹¹ 結婚 **kekkon** marriage

結婚式 **kekkonshiki** wedding

¹² 結着 **ketchaku** conclusion, settlement

結集 **kesshū** concentrate, marshal together

¹⁴ 結構 **kekkō** fine, good, alright; quite

¹⁵ 結論 **ketsuron** conclusion

————— 2 —————

⁶ 団結 **danketsu** unity, solidarity

⁸ 直結 **chokketsu** direct connection

⁹ 連結 **renketsu** coupling, connection; consolidated

肺結核 **haikekkaku** pulmonary tuberculosis

¹⁰ 凍結 **tōketsu** freeze

¹¹ 終結 **shūketsu** conclusion, termination

6

糸 6
米
舟
虫
耳
⺍

¹⁵ 締結 **teiketsu** conclude, contract

————— 3 —————

⁹ 神前結婚 **shinzen kekkon** Shinto wedding

6a6.6 / 840 　　□ 糸 攵 口
　　　　　　　　　61 49 24

絡絡

RAKU, kara(mu), kara(maru) get entangled

————— 1 —————

⁶ 絡合 **kara(mi)a(u)** intertwine

————— 2 —————

⁹ 連絡 **renraku** contact, liaison, communication; get/be in touch

連絡船 **renrakusen** ferryboat

¹⁰ 脈絡 **myakuraku** logical connection, coherence

¹² 短絡 **tanraku** short circuit

6a6.7 / 346 　　□ 糸 口 亻
　　　　　　　　　61 24 3

給給

KYŪ supply **tama(u)** give, grant, deign to **-tama(e)** (imperative verb suffix)

————— 1 —————

³ 給与 **kyūyo** allowance, grant, wages

⁴ 給水 **kyūsui** water supply

⁵ 給仕 **kyūji** wait on; waiter, waitress, bellhop

⁸ 給油 **kyūyu** supplying oil, fueling, oiling

給油所 **kyūyusho** filling/gas station

¹⁰ 給料 **kyūryō** pay, wages, salary

給料日 **kyūryōbi** payday

————— 2 —————

⁴ 支給 **shikyū** provide, furnish, issue, grant

月給 **gekkyū** (monthly) salary

月給日 **gekkyūbi** payday

⁶ 有給 **yūkyū** salaried

自給自足 **jikyū-jisoku** self-sufficiency

⁸ 供給 **kyōkyū** supply

昇給 **shōkyū** pay raise

¹⁰ 俸給 **hōkyū** salary

時給 **jikyū** payment by the hour

恩給 **onkyū** pension

配給 **haikyū** distribution, rationing

¹² 減給 **genkyū** salary reduction, pay cut

無給 **mukyū** unpaid, nonsalaried

補給 **hokyū** supply, replenish

¹⁴ 需給 **jukyū** supply and demand

————— 3 —————

⁶ 安月給 **yasugekkyū** meager salary

⁷ 初任給 **shoninkyū** starting salary

6a6.8 / 345 　　□ 糸 亻 二
　　　　　　　　　61 3 4

繪|絵絵

KAI, E picture

————— 1 —————

⁵ 絵本 **ehon** picture book

⁸ 絵画 **kaiga** pictures, paintings, drawings

⁹ 絵巻物 **emakimono** picture scroll

絵美 **Emi** (f. given name)

絵草紙 **ezōshi** picture book

¹¹ 絵描 **eka(ki)** painter, artist

¹² 絵葉書 **ehagaki** picture postcard

————— 2 —————

³ 口絵 **kuchie** frontispiece

⁸ 油絵 **aburae** oil painting

¹⁰ 挿絵 **sa(shi)e** illustration (in a book)

¹³ 蒔絵 **makie** (gold) lacquerwork

¹⁴ 墨絵 **sumie** India-ink drawing

¹⁵ 影絵 **kagee** shadow picture, silhouette

¹⁶ 錦絵 **nishikie** colored woodblock print

—— 3 ——

7 似顔絵 **nigaoe** portrait, likeness

9 浮世絵 **ukiyoe** (type of Japanese woodblock print)

6a6.9 / 1452   田 糸 亠 几
              61   11   16

KŌ, shi(meru) strangle, wring
shi(maru) be wrung out, be pressed together **shibo(ru)** wring, squeeze, press, milk **shibo(ri)** (camera's) iris diaphragm; throttling; dapple, white-spotted cloth

—— 1 ——

0 お絞り **(o)shibo(ri)** hot wet towel (in restaurants)

5 絞出 **shibo(ri)da(su)** press/ squeeze out

9 絞首刑 **kōshukei** (execution by) hanging

10 絞殺 **kōsatsu** strangle to death; hang

6a6.10 / 830   田 糸 亠 竹
              61   11   17

TŌ, su(beru) govern, control
OSAMU (m. given name)

—— 1 ——

1 統一 **tōitsu** unity, unification, uniformity

6 統合 **tōgō** unify, integrate, combine

8 統制 **tōsei** control, regulation

統治 **tōchi, tōji** reign, rule

統治権 **tōchiken** sovereignty

9 統計 **tōkei** statistics

—— 2 ——

1 一統 **ittō** a lineage; bringing under one rule; all (of you)

3 大統領 **daitōryō** president

5 正統派 **seitōha** orthodox school, fundamentalists

6 伝統 **dentō** tradition

伝統的 **dentōteki** traditional

血統 **kettō** lineage, pedigree, family line

7 系統 **keitō** system; lineage, descent

—— 3 ——

11 副大統領 **fukudaitōryō** vice president

6a6.11 / 742   田 糸 尸 ク
              61   40   15

ZETSU, ta(eru) die out, end, fail
ta(yasu) kill off, let die out
ta(tsu) cut off, interrupt; eradicate

—— 1 ——

0 絶えず **ta(ezu)** constantly, unceasingly; all the time

5 絶句 **zekku** stop short, forget one's lines; (Chinese poetry form)

絶好 **zekkō** splendid, first-rate

7 絶対 **zettai** absolute

9 絶食 **zesshoku** fasting

11 絶望 **zetsubō** despair

絶頂 **zetchō** summit, peak, climax

12 絶間 **ta(e)ma** interval, pause, gap
ta(e)ma(naku) continually, without letup

13 絶滅 **zetsumetsu** eradicate; become extinct

15 絶縁 **zetsuen** insulation; breaking off a relationship

—— 2 ——

4 中絶 **chūzetsu** interruption, discontinuation, termination; abortion

6 死絶 **shizetsu** extinction
shi(ni)ta(eru) die out, become extinct

気絶 **kizetsu** faint, pass out

壮絶 **sōzetsu** sublime, magnificent

7 杜絶 **tozetsu** be blocked/obstructed

8 拒絶 **kyozetsu** refusal, rejection, repudiation

6

糸 6

米

舟

虫

耳

⺮

⁹ 途絶 **toda(eru)** come to a stop
tozetsu suspension, interruption

¹⁰ 根絶 **konzetsu, nedaya(shi)** eradication

¹¹ 断絶 **danzetsu** become extinct; sever

¹² 隔絶 **kakuzetsu** be isolated/separated

廃絶 **haizetsu** become extinct

¹⁷ 謝絶 **shazetsu** refuse, decline

——————— 4 ———————

⁷ 妊娠中絶 **ninshin chūzetsu** abortion

6a6.13　　　　□ 糸 戈 十
　　　　　　　　　61 52 12

JŪ wool cloth

——————— 1 ———————

¹² 絨毯 **jūtan** rug, carpet

6a6.14 / 2194　　□ 糸 日 ⌐
　　　　　　　　　61 43 15

絢

KEN (colorful/beautiful) design
KEN, JUN, AYA (part of given name)
AYA (f. given name)

——————— 1 ———————

²¹ 絢爛 **kenran(taru)** gorgeous, dazzling, gaudy

6a6.15 / 1389　　□ 糸 ⊢ 丨
　　　　　　　　　61 13 2

SHI, murasaki purple, violet

——————— 1 ———————

⁶ 紫色 **murasaki-iro** purple
¹³ 紫煙 **shien** tobacco smoke

———— 7 ————

 經 → 経 6a5.11

6a7.3 / 1261　　□ 糸 月 口
　　　　　　　　　61 42 24

絹

KEN, kinu silk

——————— 1 ———————

¹⁸ 絹織物 **kinuorimono** silk fabrics

6a7.5 / 243　　□ 糸 土 冂
　　　　　　　　　61 22 20

 續丨続 続

ZOKU, tsuzu(ku/keru) (intr./tr.) continue **TSUGI** (part of given name)

——————— 1 ———————

³ 続々 **zokuzoku** successively, one after another

⁵ 続出 **zokushutsu** appear one after another

⁹ 続発 **zokuhatsu** occur one after another

¹⁵ 続編 **zokuhen** sequel

——————— 2 ———————

⁴ 手続 **tetsuzu(ki)** procedure, formalities

引続 **hi(ki)tsuzu(ki)** continuing

⁵ 存続 **sonzoku** continued existence, duration

永続 **eizoku, nagatsuzu(ki)** perpetuity

⁹ 連続 **renzoku** continuous, consecutive, in a row

持続 **jizoku** continuation, maintenance

相続 **sōzoku** inheritance, succession

¹¹ 接続詞 **setsuzokushi** a conjunction

¹² 勤続 **kinzoku** long service

¹³ 継続 **keizoku** continuance

6a7.8 / 1025

⬚ 糸 米 |
61 62 2

継 | 継 継 継

KEI, tsu(gu) succeed to, inherit; follow; patch, join together TSUGI (part of given name)

———— 1 ————

⁴ 継父 **keifu** stepfather
⁵ 継目 **tsu(gi)me** joint, seam
⁷ 継承 **keishō** succession, inheritance
　継承者 **keishōsha** successor
¹⁰ 継続 **keizoku** continuance

———— 2 ————

⁴ 中継 **chūkei** (remote broadcast) relay
⁸ 受継 **u(ke)tsu(gu)** inherit, succeed to
⁹ 後継者 **kōkeisha** successor
¹³ 跡継 **atotsu(gi)** successor, heir

———— 3 ————

⁵ 生中継 **namachūkei** live (remote) broadcast

———— 8 ————

6a8.1 / 1231

⬚ 隹 糸
74 61

維 | 維 維

I tie up; rope KORE, TSUNA (part of given name)

———— 1 ————

⁹ 維持 **iji** maintenance, support
¹³ 維新 **ishin** (the Meiji) restoration

———— 2 ————

¹⁷ 繊維 **sen'i** fiber, textiles

———— 3 ————

⁸ 明治維新 **Meiji Ishin** the Meiji Restoration

6a8.2 / 743

⬚ 糸 木 日
61 41 43

練 | 練 練

REN, ne(ru) knead; train; polish up **ne(reru)** be mellowed/mature

———— 1 ————

¹¹ 練習 **renshū** practice, exercise
　練習不足 **renshū-busoku** out/lack of training

———— 2 ————

⁵ 未練 **miren** lingering affection
⁹ 洗練 **senren** refine, polish
¹⁰ 修練 **shūren** training, discipline, drill
　訓練 **kunren** training
¹¹ 習練 **shūren** practice, training, drill
¹³ 試練 **shiren** trial, test, ordeal
¹⁴ 熟練 **jukuren** practiced skill, mastery

6a8.3 / 862

⬚ 糸 日 土
61 43 22

緒 | 緒 緒

SHO, CHO beginning **o** cord, strap, thong **itoguchi** thread end; beginning; clue

———— 1 ————

⁷ 緒言 **chogen, shogen** preface, foreword

———— 2 ————

¹ 一緒 **issho** together
⁴ 内緒 **naisho** secret
　内緒話 **naishobanashi** confidential talk, whispering
⁵ 由緒 **yuisho** history, lineage
¹⁴ 端緒 **tansho, tancho** beginning, first step, clue

6 = 8
糸
米
舟
虫
耳
⺮

6a8.4 / 2197 ⊞ 糸 二 卜
        61 4 13

緋緋

HI scarlet **HI, AKA** (part of given name)

―――――――― 1 ――――――――

18 緋鯉 **higoi** red/gold carp

6a8.5 ⊞ 糸 又
        61 9

綴 綴

TEI, tsuzu(ru) spell; bind; patch; write, compose **tsuzu(re)** rags, tatters **to(jiru)** stitch together, bind, file

―――――――― 1 ――――――――

4 綴方 **tsuzu(ri)kata** spelling; composition, theme **to(ji)kata** binding

---

6a8.7 ⊞ 糸 小 冂
        61 35 20

綬 綬

JU cordon, ribbon (on a medal)

6a8.8 / 1191 ⊞ 糸 日 巾
        61 43 26

緜 | 綿 綿

MEN, wata cotton

―――――――― 1 ――――――――

11 綿密 **menmitsu** minute, close, meticulous
18 綿織物 **men'orimono** cotton goods

―――――――― 2 ――――――――

4 木綿 **momen** cotton (cloth)
      kiwata cotton (plant)

---

9 海綿 **kaimen** sponge

6a8.10 / 2198 ⊞ 糸 夂 土
        61 49 22

綾綾

RYŌ, aya figured cloth, twill
AYA (f. given name) **RYŌ, AYA** (part of given name)

―――――――― 1 ――――――――

9 綾香 **Ayaka** (f. given name)
16 綾錦 **ayanishiki** twill damask and brocade

6a8.12 / 2196 ⊞ 糸 礻 宀
        61 45 33

綜綜

SŌ rule over **SŌ, OSA** (part of given name)

―――――――― 1 ――――――――

6 綜合 **sōgō** comprehensive, composite, synthetic

6a8.15 / 537 ⊞ 糸 彐 氵
        61 39 21

緑 | 緑 緑

RYOKU, ROKU, midori green

―――――――― 1 ――――――――

6 緑色 **midori-iro, ryokushoku** green
  緑地 **ryokuchi** green tract of land

―――――――― 2 ――――――――

11 深緑 **shinryoku, fukamidori** dark green
13 新緑 **shinryoku** fresh verdure

6
8 糸
米 舟
虫 耳
⺮

6a8.16 / 2195　　　田　糸　大　口
　　　　　　　　　　　　　61　34　24

綺綺

KI figured cloth; beautiful
KI, AYA (part of given name)

——— 1 ———

19 綺麗 **kirei** pretty, beautiful; clean

6a8.18 / 2199　　　田　糸　艹　亻
　　　　　　　　　　　　　61　32　3

綸

綸綸

RIN thread, string, line; reign, rule
RIN, O, KUMI (part of given name)

6a8.19　　　　　　田　糸　日　卜
　　　　　　　　　　　　　61　43　13

綽

綽綽

SHAKU gentle, graceful

——— 1 ———

6 綽名 **adana** nickname

6a8.20 / 697　　　田　糸　忩　儿
　　　　　　　　　　　　　61　51　16

總 | 総総

SŌ general, overall　su(beru) control, supervise　**fusa** tuft, cluster

——— 1 ———

4 総支出 **sōshishutsu** gross expenditures
5 総代 **sōdai** representative, delegate
　総司令 **sōshirei** general headquarters, supreme command
　総目録 **sōmokuroku** complete catalog
6 総合 **sōgō** synthesis, comprehensive

総合大学 **sōgō daigaku** university
総会 **sōkai** general meeting, plenary session
8 総長 **sōchō** (university) president
9 総括 **sōkatsu** summarize, generalize
　総計 **sōkei** (sum) total
10 総索引 **sōsakuin** general index
　総益 **sōeki** gross profit
　総員 **sōin** all hands, in full force
11 総動員 **sōdōin** general mobilization
　総理大臣 **sōri daijin** prime minister
　総理庁 **sōrifu** Prime Minister's Office
　総務 **sōmu** general affairs; manager
　総務長官 **sōmu chōkan** director-general
　総務課 **sōmuka** general affairs section
12 総裁 **sōsai** president, governor
　総評 **Sōhyō** General Council of Trade Unions of Japan (short for 日本労働組合総評議会)
13 総数 **sōsū** total (number)
14 総選挙 **sōsenkyo** general election
　総領事 **sōryōji** consul-general
　総領事館 **sōryōjikan** consulate-general
15 総罷業 **sōhigyō** general strike
18 総額 **sōgaku** total amount

——— 3 ———

8 国連総会 **Kokuren Sōkai** UN General Assembly

6a8.23 / 1609　　　田　糸　屮　冂
　　　　　　　　　　　　　61　36　20

綱綱

KŌ rope; rule; classification
tsuna rope, cord

——— 1 ———

5 綱目 **kōmoku** gist, main points

6

糸　8
米
舟
虫
耳
竹

— 2 —

3 大綱 **ōzuna** hawser, cable
taikō general principles; outline, general features
4 手綱 **tazuna** reins, bridle
8 命綱 **inochizuna** lifeline
15 横綱 **yokozuna** sumo champion

6a8.25 / 1612 ◫ 糸 冂 儿 61 42 16

網

網 網

MŌ, ami net

— 1 —

0 デジタル網 **dejitaru ami** digital net
19 網羅 **mōra** include, be comprehensive

— 3 —

13 鉄条網 **tetsujōmō** barbed-wire entanglements
鉄道網 **tetsudōmō** railway network

— 9 —

6a9.1 / 1760 ◫ 糸 日 | 61 43 2

縄

縄 | 繩 繩

JŌ, nawa rope TSUNA (part of given name)

— 1 —

4 縄文 **jōmon** (ancient Japanese) straw-rope pattern
11 縄張 **nawaba(ri)** rope off; one's domain, bailiwick

— 2 —

6 自縄自縛 **jijō-jibaku** tied up with one's own rope, caught in one's own trap
7 沖縄県 **Okinawa-ken** (prefecture)

練→練 **6a8.2**

緒→緒 **6a8.3**

6a9.7 / 299 ◫ 糸 日 氵 61 43 21

線

線 線

SEN line

— 1 —

9 線香 **senkō** incense/joss stick
13 線路 **senro** (railroad) track

— 2 —

4 内線 **naisen** (telephone) extension; indoor wiring; inner line
5 外線 **gaisen** outside (telephone) line; outside wiring
白線 **hakusen** white line
6 曲線 **kyokusen** a curve
有線 **yūsen** by wire
8 直線 **chokusen** straight line
沿線 **ensen** along the (train) line
弦線 **gensen** (violin) string, catgut
9 点線 **tensen** dotted/perforated line
前線 **zensen** front lines, the front; a (cold) front
11 斜線 **shasen** oblique line
脚線美 **kyakusenbi** leg beauty/shapeliness
脱線 **dassen** derailment; digression
視線 **shisen** line of vision, one's eyes/gaze
断線 **dansen** disconnection, broken wire
12 無線 **musen** wireless, radio
琴線 **kinsen** heartstrings
13 戦線 **sensen** battle line, front
罫線 **keisen** ruled line
路線 **rosen** route, line
電線 **densen** electric wire/line/cable
16 縦線 **jūsen** vertical line

— 3 —

3 三味線 **shamisen, samisen** samisen (three-stringed instrument)
4 分界線 **bunkaisen** line of demarcation

6
8 糸 米 舟 虫 耳 竹

水平線 **suiheisen** the horizon; horizontal line

6 地平線 **chiheisen** the horizon

7 赤外線 **sekigaisen** infrared rays

8 放射線 **hōshasen** radiation

10 蚊取線香 **katori senkō** mosquito-repellent incense

12 最前線 **saizensen** forefront, front lines

13 新幹線 **Shinkansen** New Trunk Line, bullet train

17 環状線 **kanjōsen** loop/belt line

——————— 4 ———————

5 北回帰線 **Kita Kaikisen** the Tropic of Cancer

12 寒冷前線 **kanrei zensen** cold front

6a9.8 / 1089   田 糸 小 一
                              61 35 14

緩 緩

KAN, yuru(mu) become loose, abate, slacken **yuru(meru)** loosen, relieve, relax, slacken **yuru(i)** loose; generous; lax; gentle (slope); slow
yuru(yaka) loose, slack; magnanimous; gentle, easy, slow

——————— 8 ———————

8 緩和 **kanwa** relieve, ease, alleviate, relax

14 緩慢 **kanman** sluggish, slack

6a9.10 / 1131   田 糸 ヨ 丬
                              61 39 27

縁 | 縁 縁

EN relation, connection; marriage; fate; veranda **enishi** relation, connection; marriage; fate **fuchi, heri** edge, brink, rim, border **yukari** relation, affinity **yosuga** means, way

——————— 1 ———————

4 縁切 **enki(ri)** severing of a relationship

---

10 縁起 **engi** history, origin; omen, luck

11 縁側 **engawa** veranda, porch, balcony

15 縁談 **endan** marriage proposal

——————— 2 ———————

4 内縁 **naien** common-law marriage

5 由縁 **yuen** relationship, reason, way

6 因縁 **innen** fate; connection; origin; pretext

血縁 **ketsuen** blood relationship/relative

7 良縁 **ryōen** good (marital) match

11 族縁 **zokuen** family ties

12 無縁 **muen** unrelated, with no surviving relatives

絶縁 **zetsuen** insulation; breaking off a relationship

18 離縁 **rien** divorce, disowning

6a9.11 / 1180   田 糸 巾 亠
                              61 26 11

締 締

TEI, shi(meru) tie, tighten; control strictly; shut **shi(maru)** become taut/tight/firm; be thrifty

——————— 1 ———————

4 締切 **shi(me)ki(ru)** close
shi(me)ki(ri) closing (date), deadline

5 締出 **shi(me)da(su)** shut/lock out

12 締結 **teiketsu** conclude, contract

——————— 2 ———————

4 引締 **hi(ki)shi(meru)** tighten, stiffen, brace

8 取締役 **torishimariyaku** (company) director

6a9.13 / 682   田 糸 尸 艹
                              61 40 32

編 編

HEN, a(mu) knit; compile, edit

───────── 1 ─────────

⁶ 編年史 **hennenshi** chronicle, annals

編曲 **henkyoku** (musical) arrangement

編成 **hensei** organize, put together

⁸ 編者 **hensha** editor, compiler

編物 **a(mi)mono** knitting; knitted goods

¹² 編集 **henshū** editing, compilation

───────── 2 ─────────

⁶ 全編 **zenpen** the whole book

共編 **kyōhen** joint editorship

⁸ 長編 **chōhen** long (article), full-length (novel), feature-length (movie)

⁹ 後編 **kōhen** concluding part/volume

¹² 短編 **tanpen** short piece/story/film

¹³ 続編 **zokuhen** sequel

6a9.14　　　▯　糸　尸　辶
　　　　　　　　　61　40　19

TSUI, suga(ru) hang/hold on to; depend on, appeal to

───────── 1 ─────────

⁵ 縋付 **suga(ri)tsu(ku)** cling to, depend on

6a9.15 / 1349　　　▯　糸　夂　辶
　　　　　　　　　61　49　19

HŌ, nu(u) sew

───────── 1 ─────────

⁸ 縫物 **nu(i)mono** sewing, needlework

¹⁰ 縫針 **nu(i)bari** sewing needle

───────── 2 ─────────

¹² 裁縫 **saihō** sewing, tailoring, dressmaking **ta(chi)nu(i)** cutting and sewing

---

6a9.17 / 1290　　　田　糸　冂　又
　　　　　　　　61　20　9

KIN tense, tight

───────── 1 ─────────

⁷ 緊迫 **kinpaku** tension

⁹ 緊急 **kinkyū** emergency

¹¹ 緊張 **kinchō** tension

緊密 **kinmitsu** close, tight

¹⁷ 緊縮 **kinshuku** contraction; austerity

幾 → **4n8.4**

緜 → 綿 **6a8.8**

───────── 10 ─────────

6a10.1　　　▯　糸　夂　土
　　　　　　　61　49　22

CHI fine, close, minute

───────── 1 ─────────

¹¹ 緻密 **chimitsu** fine, close, minute, exact

6a10.2 / 1483　　　▯　糸　彳　儿
　　　　　　　61　29　16

JŪ, tate height, length; vertical
hoshiimama self-indulgent
yo(shi) even if

───────── 1 ─────────

¹⁰ 縦書 **tatega(ki)** vertical writing

¹⁵ 縦横 **jūō, tate-yoko** length and breadth, vertical and horizontal

縦線 **jūsen** vertical line

16 操縦 **sōjū** control, operate, manipulate

操縦士 **sōjūshi** pilot

6a10.3 / 1448
田 糸 日 寸
61 43 37

縛 | 縛 縛

BAKU, shiba(ru) tie up, bind
imashi(me) bonds, bondage

——————— 1 ———————
5 縛付 **shiba(ri)tsu(keru)** tie/fasten to

——————— 2 ———————
7 束縛 **sokubaku** restraint, constraint, shackles
10 捕縛 **hobaku** arrest, capture

——————— 4 ———————
6 自縄自縛 **jijō-jibaku** tied up with one's own rope, caught in one's own trap

6a10.7 / 1054
田 糸 口 十
61 24 12

緯 緯

I woof (horizontal thread in weaving); latitude **nuki** woof

——————— 1 ———————
9 緯度 **ido** latitude

——————— 2 ———————
5 北緯 **hokui** north latitude
9 南緯 **nan'i** south latitude

6a10.9
田 糸 口 亠
61 24 11

縞 縞

KŌ, shima stripe

——————— 1 ———————
10 縞馬 **shimauma** zebra

14 縞模様 **shimamoyō** striped pattern

——————— 2 ———————
15 横縞 **yokojima** horizontal stripes

縫 → 縫 6a9.15

6a10.13 / 1292
田 糸 夂 女
61 49 25

繁 | 繁 繁

HAN fullness, luxury; frequency
shige(ru) grow thick/luxuriantly
shige(mi) thicket **shige(ku)** densely, frequently **Shigeru** (m. given name) **SHIGE** (part of given name)

——————— 1 ———————
6 繁忙 **hanbō** busy, pressed
8 繁茂 **hanmo** luxuriant/dense growth
9 繁栄 **han'ei** prosperity
10 繁華街 **hankagai** busy (shopping/entertainment) area
11 繁盛 **hanjō** prosperity; success

——————— 2 ———————
17 頻繁 **hinpan** frequent, incessant

縣 → 県 3n6.3

——————— 11 ———————

6a11.1 / 1571
田 糸 戈 十
61 52 12

纖 | 繊 繊

SEN fine, slender

——————— 1 ———————
10 繊弱 **senjaku** frail, delicate
11 繊細 **sensai** delicate, fine, subtle
14 繊維 **sen'i** fiber, textiles

——————— 2 ———————
4 化繊 **kasen** synthetic fiber

縦 → 縦 6a10.2

6

糸 11
米
舟
虫
耳
艹

總 → 総   **6a8.20**

6a11.8 / 1117   ⊞ 貝 糸 土
                   68 61 22

績   績 績

SEKI achievements; (silk) spinning
Isao (m. given name)

——— 2 ———

5 功績 **kōseki** meritorious service
6 成績 **seiseki** results, (business) performance
    成績表 **seisekihyō** report/score card
7 学績 **gakuseki** student's record
8 事績 **jiseki** achievements, exploits
    実績 **jisseki** actual results, record of performance
10 紡績 **bōseki** spinning
13 業績 **gyōseki** (business) performance, results, achievement

6a11.9 / 1110   ⊞ 糸 日 宀
                   61 43 33

       縮 縮

SHUKU, chiji(maru/mu) shrink, contract **chiji(mi)** shrinkage; crepe **chiji(meru)** shorten, condense **chiji(rasu/reru)** make/become curly

——— 1 ———

3 縮小 **shukushō** reduction, cut
5 縮写 **shukusha** reduced copy, miniature reproduction
7 縮図 **shukuzu** reduced/scaled-down drawing
8 縮刷版 **shukusatsuban** small-size edition

——— 2 ———

4 収縮 **shūshuku** contraction, constriction
7 伸縮 **shinshuku, no(bi)chiji(mi)** expansion and contraction; elastic, flexible

9 軍縮 **gunshuku** arms reduction, disarmament
    畏縮 **ishuku** cower, quail, be awestruck, shrink from
10 恐縮 **kyōshuku** be very grateful/sorry
11 萎縮 **ishuku** wither, atrophy; be dispirited
12 短縮 **tanshuku** shorten, curtail, abridge
15 緊縮 **kinshuku** contraction; austerity
16 凝縮 **gyōshuku** condensation
    濃縮 **nōshuku** concentrate, enrich

繋 → 繋   **6a13.4**

繁 → 繁   **6a10.13**

——— 12 ———

6a12.2 / 1140   ⊞ 糸 王 ⼌
                   61 46 24

       繕 繕

ZEN, tsukuro(u) repair, mend

——— 2 ———

8 取繕 **to(ri)tsukuro(u)** repair, patch up, gloss over
10 修繕 **shūzen** repair
12 営繕 **eizen** building and repair, maintenance

6a12.6 / 680   ⊞ 糸 戈 日
                   61 52 43

織   織 織

SHOKU, SHIKI, o(ru) weave **o(ri)** fabric, weave ORI (part of given name)

——— 1 ———

4 織込 **o(ri)ko(mu)** weave into
8 織物 **orimono** cloth, fabric, textiles
    織物業 **orimonogyō** the textile business

—— 2 ——

6 羽織 **haori** Japanese half-coat
    hao(ru) put on

7 沙織 **Saori** (f. given name)
   志織 **Shiori** (f. given name)

9 香織 **Kaori** (f. given name)

10 畝織 **uneori** rep, ribbed fabric

11 組織 **soshiki** organization; tissue

13 絹織物 **kinuorimono** silk fabrics

14 綿織物 **men'orimono** cotton goods

畿 → **5f10.3**

—— 13 ——

縄 → 縄 **6a9.1**

6a13.3 / 1654   ⊞ 糸 木 口
                              61 41 24

繰 繰 繰

SŌ, ku(ru) reel, wind; spin (thread);
turn (pages); look up (a word); count

—— 1 ——

4 繰込 **ku(ri)ko(mu)** stream into;
    count in, round up

6 繰返 **ku(ri)kae(su)** repeat

7 繰延 **ku(ri)no(be)** postponement,
    deferment

   繰言 **ku(ri)goto** same old story,
    complaint

12 繰替 **ku(ri)ka(eru)** exchange,
    swap; divert (money)

   繰越 **ku(ri)ko(su)** transfer, carry
    forward

—— 2 ——

4 引繰返 **hi(k)ku(ri)kae(ru)** be
    overturned, capsize, collapse;
    be reversed **hi(k)ku(ri)-
    kae(su)** overturn, turn upside
    down, turn inside out

繪 → 絵 **6a6.8**

6a13.4   ⊞ 車 糸 冂
                      69 61 20

繋 | 繋 繋

KEI, tsuna(gu) connect, tie, tether
tsuna(garu) be connected
kaka(ru) be tied together; lie at anchor

—— 1 ——

5 繋目 **tsuna(gi)me** joint

6 繋合 **tsuna(gi)a(waseru)** join/tie
    together

   繋争 **keisō** dispute, contention

11 繋累 **keirui** encumbrances, depen-
    dents

—— 14 ——

繼 → 継 **6a7.8**

—— 15 ——

續 → 続 **6a7.5**

纏 → 纏 **6a16.1**

—— 16 ——

6a16.1   ⊞ 糸 日 火
                      61 43 44

纏 纏 | 纏 纏

TEN, mato(meru) gather/put together; settle, arrange **mato(maru)** be col-
lected/brought together; take shape; be
settled/arranged **matsu(waru)** coil
around; surround, hang about
mato(u) put on, wear **mato(i)** (firemen's) standard

—— 1 ——

7 纏役 **mato(me)yaku** mediator

—— 17 ——

纖 → 繊 **6a11.1**

6   糸 **16**
              米
              舟
              虫
              耳
              ⺮

米 **6b**

米	料	粋	粉	氣	粒	粗	粘	釈	断	粧	粟	奥
0.1	4.4	4.5	4.6	0a6.8	5.1	5.2	5.4	5.5	5.6	6.1	6.6	6.9

番	歯	粛	粮	精	粋	糊	模	糖	糟	糠	糞	齢
5f7.4	6.11	0a11.8	6b12.1	8.1	6b4.5	9.2	4a10.16	10.3	11.1	11.2	11.3	11.5

鞠	糧	翻	釋	飜	麟
11.6	12.1	12.3	6b5.5	6b12.3	18.1

— **0** —

6b0.1 / 224 ☐ 米
62

米米

BEI rice; America, U.S.; meter **kome, yone** rice **mētoru** meter

— 1 —

3 米山 **Yoneyama** (surname)
4 米中 **Bei-Chū** America and China
5 米田 **Yoneda** (surname)
7 米兵 **beihei** U.S. soldier/sailor
8 米価 **beika** (government-set) rice price
米国 **Beikoku** the United States
9 米軍 **beigun** U.S. armed forces
米食 **beishoku** rice diet
11 米産 **beisan** rice production
米粒 **kometsubu** grain of rice
米貨 **beika** U.S. currency, the dollar
14 米穀 **beikoku** rice
米語 **beigo** American English
21 米艦 **beikan** U.S. warship

— 2 —

4 中米 **Chūbei** Central America
反米 **han-Bei** anti-American
日米 **Nichi-Bei** Japan and America, Japan-U.S.
5 北米 **Hokubei** North America
玄米 **genmai** unpolished/unmilled rice
白米 **hakumai** polished rice
6 全米 **zen-Bei** all-America(n), pan-American
在米 **zai-Bei** in America

7 対米 **tai-Bei** toward/with America
8 英米 **Ei-Bei** Britain and the U.S.
欧米 **Ō-Bei** Europe and America, the West
9 南米 **Nanbei** South America
11 排米 **hai-Bei** anti-American
12 渡米 **to-Bei** going to America
13 滞米 **tai-Bei** staying in America
15 駐米 **chū-Bei** resident/stationed in America
16 親米 **shin-Bei** pro-American

— 3 —

4 中南米 **Chūnanbei** Central and South America
14 精白米 **seihakumai** polished rice

— 4 —

6b4.4 / 319 ☐ 米 十 ｜
62 12 2

料料

RYŌ materials; fee, charge

— 1 —

8 料金 **ryōkin** fee, charge, fare
9 料亭 **ryōtei** restaurant
11 料理 **ryōri** cooking, cuisine; dish, food
料理人 **ryōrinin** a cook
料理屋 **ryōriya** restaurant

— 2 —

4 手料理 **teryōri** home cooking
6 有料 **yūryō** fee-charging, toll (road), pay (toilet)
7 材料 **zairyō** materials, ingredients; data; factors

8 送料 **sōryō** shipping charges, postage

肥料 **hiryō** manure, fertilizer

9 染料 **senryō** dye, dyestuffs

香料 **kōryō** spice; perfume; condolence gift

食料 **shokuryō** food

食料品 **shokuryōhin** food(stuffs)

10 原料 **genryō** raw materials

12 無料 **muryō** without charge, free

給料 **kyūryō** pay, wages, salary

給料日 **kyūryōbi** payday

貸料 **ka(shi)ryō** rent; loan charges

飲料水 **inryōsui** drinking water

13 塗料 **toryō** paint, paint and varnish

節料理 **(o)sechi ryori** New Year's foods

資料 **shiryō** material, data

15 稿料 **kōryō** payment for a manuscript

16 燃料 **nenryō** fuel

———————— 3 ————————

2 入場料 **nyūjōryō** admission fee

3 口止料 **kuchido(me)ryō** hush money

4 中華料理 **chūka ryōri** Chinese cooking/food

手数料 **tesūryō** handling charge, fee

5 甘味料 **kanmiryō** sweetener

8 拝観料 **haikanryō** (museum) admission fee

9 香辛料 **kōshinryō** spices, seasoning

10 郵送料 **yūsōryō** postage

核燃料 **kakunenryō** nuclear fuel

13 賃借料 **chinshakuryō** rent

電話料 **denwaryō** telephone charges

15 慰謝料 **isharyō** consolation money, solatium

調味料 **chōmiryō** condiments, seasonings

17 購読料 **kōdokuryō** subscription price/fee

———————— 4 ————————

11 清涼飲料 **seiryō inryō** carbonated beverage

6b4.5 / 1708

田 米 十
62 12

粹丨粋粋

SUI purity, essence; elite, choice; refined, elegant, fashionable, urbane

iki chic, stylish

———————— 1 ————————

2 粋人 **suijin** man of refined tastes

———————— 2 ————————

7 抜粋 **bassui** excerpt, extract, selection

10 純粋 **junsui** pure, genuine

6b4.6 / 1701

田 米 儿 力
62 16 8

粉粉

FUN, kona, ko flour, powder

deshimētoru decimeter, tenth of a meter

———————— 1 ————————

3 粉々 **konagona** into tiny pieces

5 粉末 **funmatsu** powder

7 粉状 **funjō** powder(ed)

9 粉糾 **funkyū** complications, entanglement

———————— 2 ————————

5 汁粉 **shiruko** sweet adzuki-bean soup with rice cake

7 麦粉 **mugiko** (wheat) flour

氣 → 気 **0a6.8**

———————— 5 ————————

6b5.1 / 1700

田 米 立
62 54

粒粒

RYŪ, tsubu a grain; drop(let)

糸
米   5
舟
虫
耳
⺮

─────────── 1 ───────────

² 粒子 **ryūshi** (atomic) particle; grain (in film)

─────────── 2 ───────────

¹ 一粒 **hitotsubu** a grain

⁶ 米粒 **kometsubu** grain of rice

6b5.2 / 1084   田 米 月 一
                 62 42 1

粗   粗粗

SO, ara(i) coarse, rough   **ara** flaw, defect

─────────── 1 ───────────

³ 粗大 **sodai** coarse, rough, bulky
  粗大ゴミ **sodai gomi** large-item trash (discarded washing machines, TV sets, etc.)

⁵ 粗末 **somatsu** coarse, plain, crude, rough, rude

⁹ 粗食 **soshoku** coarse food, plain diet

¹¹ 粗野 **soya** rustic, loutish, vulgar
  粗悪 **soaku** coarse, crude, inferior

¹² 粗筋 **arasuji** outline, summary, synopsis

¹⁴ 粗製 **sosei** crudely made

¹⁵ 粗暴 **sobō** wild, rough, violent

6b5.4 / 1707   田 米 口 ⻌
                 62 24 13

粘   黏丨粘粘

NEN, neba(ru) be sticky; stick to it, persist

─────────── 1 ───────────

¹¹ 粘液 **nen'eki** mucus
  粘強 **neba(ri)zuyo(i)** tenacious, persistent

¹² 粘着 **nenchaku** adhesion
  粘着 **neba(ri)tsu(ku)** be sticky
  粘着力 **nenchakuryoku** adhesion, viscosity

¹⁵ 粘質 **nenshitsu** viscosity, stickiness

6b5.5 / 595   田 米 尸 丨
                 62 40 2

釈   

SHAKU explanation

─────────── 1 ───────────

⁷ 釈迦 **Shaka** Gautama, Buddha

⁸ 釈明 **shakumei** explanation, vindication
  釈放 **shakuhō** release, discharge

─────────── 2 ───────────

⁶ 仮釈放 **karishakuhō** release on parole
  会釈 **eshaku** salutation, greeting, bow

⁷ 希釈 **kishaku** dilute

⁹ 保釈 **hoshaku** bail

¹² 註釈 **chūshaku** annotation, commentary

¹³ 解釈 **kaishaku** interpretation, elucidation

6b5.6 / 1024   田 米 斤 丨
                 62 50 2

断

DAN decision, judgment; cut off; abstain from   **ta(tsu)** cut off; abstain from   **kotowa(ru)** decline, refuse; give notice/warning; prohibit

─────────── 1 ───────────

⁰ 断じて **dan(jite)** decidedly, absolutely

⁴ 断切 **ta(chi)ki(ru)** cut off, sever
  断片 **danpen** fragment, snippet
  断水 **dansui** water supply cutoff

⁶ 断交 **dankō** break off relations with

⁸ 断固 **danko** firm, resolute

¹² 断然 **danzen** resolutely, flatly, decidedly
  断絶 **danzetsu** become extinct; sever

¹⁵ 断線 **dansen** disconnection, broken wire

— 2 —

3 寸断 **sundan** cut/tear to pieces

4 不断 **fudan** constant, ceaseless; usually

中断 **chūdan** break off, interrupt, suspend

切断 **setsudan** cutting, section; cut, sever, amputate

7 判断 **handan** judgment

決断 **ketsudan** decision, resolve

8 油断 **yudan** inattentiveness, lack of vigilance

10 酒断 **sakada(chi), sakeda(chi)** swearing off from drinking

12 無断 **mudan** unannounced; unauthorized

診断 **shindan** diagnosis

16 遮断 **shadan** interception, isolation, cutoff

15 横断 **ōdan** cross, traverse

横断歩道 **ōdan hodō** pedestrian crossing

— 6 —

6b6.1 / 1699

粧 粧

SHŌ adorn (one's person)

— 2 —

4 化粧品 **keshōhin** cosmetics, makeup

— 3 —

8 厚化粧 **atsugeshō** heavy makeup

16 薄化粧 **usugeshō** light makeup

6b6.6

粟 粟

ZOKU, awa millet

— 1 —

5 粟立 **awada(tsu)** have gooseflesh

6b6.9 / 476

| 目 | 米 | 大 | 冂 |
| 62 | 34 | 20 | |

奥

Ō, oku interior **oku(maru)** extend far back, lie deep in OKU (surname)

— 1 —

0 奥さん **oku(san)** (your) wife, married lady, ma'am

3 奥山 **Okuyama** (surname)

5 奥付 **okuzu(ke)** colophon

6 奥行 **okuyu(ki)** depth (vs. height and width)

8 奥底 **okusoko, okuzoko** depths, bottom

11 奥野 **Okuno** (surname)

13 奥義 **okugi, ōgi** secrets, esoteric mysteries

14 奥様 **okusama** (your) wife, married lady, ma'am

番 → **5f7.4**

6b6.11 / 478

| 目 | 米 | 卜 | 亠 |
| 62 | 13 | 11 | |

歯

SHI, ha tooth

— 1 —

7 歯医者 **haisha** dentist

歯車 **haguruma** gear, cogwheel

9 歯科医 **shikai** dentist

12 歯痛 **shitsū, haita** toothache

16 歯磨 **hamiga(ki)** toothpaste

— 2 —

6 臼歯 **kyūshi, usuba** molar

虫歯 **mushiba** decayed tooth, cavity

12 皓歯 **kōshi** white/pearly teeth

13 義歯 **gishi** artificial/false tooth, dentures

粛 → **0a11.8**

6

糸
米   6
舟
虫
耳
⺮

---7---

粮 → 糧 6b12.1

---8---

6b8.1 / 659   田 米 月 土
        62 42 22

精

精 | 精 精

SEI, SHŌ spirit; energy, vitality; semen; precise; refine, polish (rice)
kuwa(shii) in detail, full   KIYOSHI (m. given name)   KIYO (part of given name)

---1---

1 精一杯 **sei-ippai** with all one's might
2 精力 **seiryoku** energy, vigor, vitality
3 精々 **seizei** to the utmost; at most
5 精白米 **seihakumai** polished rice
9 精度 **seido** precision, accuracy
   精神 **seishin** mind, spirit
   精神力 **seishinryoku** force of will
   精神分析 **seishin bunseki** psychoanalysis
   精神病 **seishinbyō** mental illness/disorder
10 精進 **shōjin** diligence, devotion; purification
   精華 **seika** (quint)essence
11 精密 **seimitsu** precision
   精細 **seisai** detailed, precise
12 精勤 **seikin** diligence, good attendance
14 精選 **seisen** careful/choice selection
   精製 **seisei** refining; careful manufacture
   精算 **seisan** exact calculation, (fare) adjustment, settling of accounts

---2---

4 不精 **bushō** lazy, indolent
   不精髭 **bushōhige** stubbly beard
   丹精 **tansei** diligence
12 無精 **bushō** lazy

粋 → 粋 6b4.5

---9---

6b9.2   田 米 月 口
        62 42 24

糊

KO, nori paste, glue; starch, sizing

---1---

5 糊付 **noritsu(ke)** starching; pasting
13 糊塗 **koto** patch up, temporize

---10---

模 → 模 4a10.16

6b10.3 / 1698   田 米 彐 口
        62 39 24

糖

糖 糖

TŌ sugar

---1---

4 糖分 **tōbun** sugar content
11 糖菓 **tōka** candy, sweets

---2---

8 果糖 **katō** fruit sugar, fructose
9 砂糖 **satō** sugar
12 無糖 **mutō** sugar-free, unsweetened

---3---

5 氷砂糖 **kōrizatō** rock candy, crystal sugar

---11---

6b11.1   田 米 日 艹
        62 43 32

糟

SŌ, kasu saké lees, dregs, dross

6b11.2

	米	ヨ	シ
62	39	21	

KŌ, nuka rice bran

6b11.3

	米	田	业
62	58	32	

糞糞

FUN excrement, droppings **kuso** shit

—————— 1 ——————

8 糞垂 **kusota(re), kuso(t)ta(re)** (shit-dripping) son-of-a-bitch

10 糞真面目 **kusomajime** humorless earnestness

6b11.5 / 833

	米	上	一
62	13	11	

齢 | 齢齢

REI, yowai age TOSHI (part of given name)

—————— 2 ——————

6 年齢 **nenrei** age

老齢 **rōrei** old age

10 高齢者 **kōreisha** elderly person

6b11.6 / 2262

	米	业	目
62	32	24	

鞠鞠

KIKU nurture, raise; to bend, bow **mari** ball KIKU, KYŪ, MITSU, TSUGU (part of given name) MARI (f. given name)

—————— 12 ——————

6b12.1 / 1704

	米	日	土
62	43	22	

粮 | 糧糧

RYŌ, RŌ, kate food, provisions

—————— 1 ——————

9 糧食 **ryōshoku** provisions, food

—————— 2 ——————

9 食糧 **shokuryō** food

6b12.3 / 596

	米	田	羽
62	58	49	

飜 | 番羽翻羽

HON, hirugae(su) (tr.) turn over; change (one's opinion); wave (a flag) **hirugae(ru)** (intr.) turn over; wave, flutter **kobo(su)** overturn, spill

—————— 1 ——————

8 翻刻 **honkoku** reprint

11 翻訳 **hon'yaku** translation

翻訳者 **hon'yakusha** translator

13 翻意 **hon'i** change one's mind

—————— 14 ——————

釋 → 釈 6b5.5

—————— 15 ——————

飜 → 翻 6b12.3

—————— 18 ——————

6b18.1 / 2280

	米	厂	几
62	18	16	

麟 | 麐

RIN Chinese-mythological beast associated with wise rule; genius; giraffe; bright, shining RIN (part of given name)

糸
米 18
舟
虫
耳
竹

6

────────── 2 ──────────

19 麒麟 **kirin** giraffe

────────── 舟 **6c** ──────────

舟	航	舩	般	舶	舵	船	舷	艇	艦
0.1	4.2	6c5.4	4.3	5.2	5.3	5.4	5.5	6.2	15.2

────────── 0 ──────────

6c0.1 / 1094 　　　□ 舟
　　　　　　　　　63

舟 | 舟 舟

SHŪ, fune, funa- boat

────────── 1 ──────────

12 舟艇 **shūtei** boat, craft
14 舟歌 **funauta** sailor's song, chantey

────────── 2 ──────────

12 渡舟 **wata(shi)bune** ferryboat

────────── 4 ──────────

7 呉越同舟 **Go-Etsu dōshū** enemies in the same boat

────────── 4 ──────────

6c4.2 / 823 　　　□ 舟 亠 冂
　　　　　　　　63 11 20

航 航

KŌ navigation　Kō (m. given name)

────────── 1 ──────────

6 航行 **kōkō** navigation, sailing
8 航空 **kōkū** aviation, flight, aero-
　航空母艦 **kōkū bokan** aircraft carrier
　航空券 **kōkūken** flight/airplane ticket
　航空便 **kōkūbin** airmail
　航空路 **kōkūro** air route
9 航海 **kōkai** voyage, ocean navigation
13 航路 **kōro** (sea) route, course

────────── 2 ──────────

5 出航 **shukkō** departure, sailing
6 休航 **kyūkō** suspension of ship or airline service
8 直航 **chokkō** nonstop flight, direct voyage
9 発航 **hakkō** departure, sailing
11 密航者 **mikkōsha** stowaway
12 渡航 **tokō** voyage, passage, sailing, flight

舩 → 船 **6c5.4**

6c4.3 / 1096 　　　□ 舟 冂 又
　　　　　　　　63 20 9

般 般

HAN carry; all, general

────────── 2 ──────────

1 一般 **ippan** general
　一般化 **ippanka** generalization, popularization
6 全般的 **zenpanteki** general, overall, across-the-board

────────── 5 ──────────

6c5.2 / 1095 　　　□ 舟 日 丨
　　　　　　　　63 43 2

舶 舶

HAKU ship

────────── 1 ──────────

7 舶来 **hakurai** imported
　舶来品 **hakuraihin** imported goods

2

11 船舶 **senpaku** ship, vessel; shipping

6c5.3　　　　　⊞ 舟 宀 卜
　　　　　　　　63 33 13

舵　　舵舵

DA, kaji rudder, helm

6c5.4 / 376　　　⊞ 舟 口 几
　　　　　　　　63 24 16

船　　船丨船船

SEN, fune, funa- ship

1

4 船中 **senchū** in/aboard the ship
5 船号 **sengō** ship's name
8 船長 **senchō** (ship's) captain
9 船乗 **funano(ri)** seaman, sailor
　 船便 **funabin** sea mail; ship transportation
　 船客 **senkyaku** (ship) passenger
　 船室 **senshitsu** cabin, stateroom
10 船員 **sen'in** crewman, seaman
　 船荷 **funani** (ship's) cargo
　 船旅 **funatabi** voyage
11 船隊 **sentai** fleet
　 船舶 **senpaku** ship, vessel; shipping
　 船酔 **funayo(i)** seasickness
16 船積 **funazu(mi)** shipment, lading

2

6 帆船 **hansen, hobune** sailing ship, sailboat
7 助船 **tasu(ke)bune** lifeboat
　 汽船 **kisen** steamship, steamer
9 造船 **zōsen** shipbuilding
　 風船 **fūsen** balloon
　 客船 **kyakusen** passenger ship/boat
10 破船 **hasen** shipwreck
12 湯船 **yubune** bathtub
　 渡船 **wata(shi)bune, tosen** ferry

14 漁船 **gyosen, ryōsen** fishing boat/vessel
　 漕船 **ko(gi)bune** rowboat
21 艦船 **kansen** warships and other vessels

3

6 宇宙船 **uchūsen** spaceship
8 油送船 **yusōsen** oil tanker
9 連絡船 **renrakusen** ferryboat
11 貨物船 **kamotsusen** freighter

6c5.5　　　　　⊞ 舟 亠 竹
　　　　　　　　63 11 17

舷　　舷舷

GEN ship's side, gunwale

1

8 舷門 **genmon** gangway
11 舷梯 **gentei** gangway (ladder)

6

6c6.2 / 1666　　　⊡ 舟 王 辶
　　　　　　　　63 46 19

艇　　艇艇

TEI small boat

1

7 艇身 **teishin** boat length
10 艇員 **teiin** (boat's) crew
11 艇隊 **teitai** flotilla

2

6 舟艇 **shūtei** boat, craft
20 競艇 **kyōtei** boat race/racing
21 艦艇 **kantei** naval vessels

15

6c15.2 / 1665　　　⊞ 舟 皿 囗
　　　　　　　　63 59 20

艦　　艦艦

KAN warship

糸
米
舟 **15**
虫
耳
⺮

6

1	9 軍艦 **gunkan** warship, battleship
8 艦長 **kanchō** the captain (of a warship)	13 戦艦 **senkan** battleship
11 艦隊 **kantai** fleet, squadron	**3**
艦船 **kansen** warships and other vessels	15 潜水艦 **sensuikan** a submarine
12 艦艇 **kantei** naval vessels	**4**
2	10 航空母艦 **kōkū bokan** aircraft carrier
6 米艦 **beikan** U.S. warship	

虫 6d

虫	虱	虹	蛇	蚊	蚤	蚕	蛇	蛉	蛋	蛍	蛛	蛙
0.1	2.1	3.1	3.2	4.5	4.7	4.8	5.7	5.8	5.11	3n8.2	6.1	6.4

蛮	蛸	蜂	触	蝿	蜘	蜻	蝋	蝦	蝶	蝗	蝎	蝠
2j10.1	7.5	7.6	7.10	6d13.1	8.2	8.7	6d15.1	9.4	9.7	9.8	9.10	9.12

蝉	蝙	蟲	融	螢	螺	蟬	蟲	蠅	蟹	蠍	蟻	蟹
6d12.3	9.14	6d2.1	10.5	3n8.2	11.3	12.3	6d0.1	13.1	6d13.7	6d9.10	13.6	13.7

觸	蠟	蠻	蠶
6d7.10	15.1	2j10.1	6d4.8

0

6d0.1 / 873

虫

□ 虫
64

蟲 | 虫 虫

CHŪ, mushi bug, insect

1

9 虫除 **mushiyo(ke)** insect repellent, charm against insects
10 虫害 **chūgai** damage from insects
12 虫歯 **mushiba** decayed tooth, cavity

2

4 毛虫 **kemushi** caterpillar
5 甲虫 **kabutomushi, kōchū** beetle
8 毒虫 **dokumushi** poisonous insect
泣虫 **na(ki)mushi** crybaby
油虫 **aburamushi** aphid; cockroach
昆虫 **konchū** insect
10 弱虫 **yowamushi** weakling, coward, sissy
害虫 **gaichū** harmful insect, pest
殺虫剤 **satchūzai** insecticide

15 蝗虫 **batta** grasshopper, locust

2

6d2.1

虱

□ 虫 一 |
64 I 2

蝨 | 虱 虱

SHITSU, shirami louse, lice

1

15 虱潰 **shiramitsubu(shi ni)** one by one, thoroughly, with a fine-tooth comb

3

6d3.1 / 2235

虹

□ 虫 工
64 38

虹 虹

KŌ, niji rainbow **KŌ, NIJI** (part of given name)

1

23 虹鱒 **nijimasu** rainbow trout

6d3.2

口	虫	宀	丨
	64	11	2

蛇

蚹蛇

BŌ, abu horsefly

— 1 —

13 虻蜂取 **abu-hachi to(razu)** trying to catch both a fly and a bee in one swoop of the hand and failing to catch either

— 4 —

0d4.5 / 1876

口	虫	宀	十
	64	11	12

蚊

蚊蚊

ka mosquito

— 1 —

8 蚊取線香 **katori senkō** mosquito-repellent incense
9 蚊屋 **kaya** mosquito net
11 蚊帳 **kaya, kachō** mosquito net

6d4.7

口	虫	又	丨
	64	9	2

蚤

蚤蚤

SŌ early; flea **nomi** flea

— 1 —

5 蚤市 **nomi (no) ichi** flea market

6d4.8 / 1877

口	虫	大	一
	64	34	1

蚕

蠶 | 蚕 蚕

SAN, kaiko silkworm

— 1 —

9 蚕食 **sanshoku** encroachment, inroads

13 蚕業 **sangyō** sericulture

— 5 —

6d5.7 / 1875

口	虫	宀	匕
	64	33	13

蛇

蛇蛇

JA, DA, hebi, kuchinawa snake

— 1 —

3 蛇口 **jaguchi** faucet, tap
6 蛇行 **dakō** meander, zigzag
7 蛇足 **dasoku** superfluous (no legs on a snake)

— 2 —

8 長蛇 **chōda** long snake; long line of people, long queue
毒蛇 **dokuhebi, dokuja** poisonous snake

6d5.8

口	虫	亻	一
	64	3	1

蛉

蛉蛉

REI dragonfly; caterpillar

— 2 —

14 蜻蛉 **tonbo** dragonfly

— 3 —

7 赤蜻蛉 **akatonbo** red dragonfly

6d5.11

口	虫	宀	亻
	64	14	3

蛋

蛋蛋

TAN egg

— 1 —

5 蛋白 **tanpaku** protein; albumen

蛍 → 3n8.2

糸
米
舟
虫   5
耳
竹

---------------------- 6 ----------------------

6d6.1 | 虫 牛 几
64 47 16

蛛

蛛蛛

CHU spider

---------------------- 2 ----------------------

14 蜘蛛 **kumo** spider
蜘蛛糸 **kumo (no) ito** spider's thread
蜘蛛巣 **kumo(no)su** spiderweb

6d6.4 | 虫 土
64 22

蛙

蛙蛙

A, kaeru, kawazu frog

蛮 → **2j10.1**

---------------------- 7 ----------------------

6d7.5 | 虫 月 小
64 42 35

蛸

蛸 | 蛸蛸

SHŌ, tako octopus

---------------------- 1 ----------------------

10 蛸配当 **takohaitō** bogus dividends

6d7.6 | 虫 夂 十
64 49 12

蜂

蜂蜂

HŌ, hachi bee, wasp

---------------------- 1 ----------------------

11 蜂巣 **hachi (no) su** beehive, honeycomb
14 蜂蜜 **hachimitsu** honey

---------------------- 2 ----------------------

9 虻蜂取 **abu-hachi to(razu)** trying to catch both a fly and a bee in one swoop of the hand and failing to catch either
14 蜜蜂 **mitsubachi** honeybee

6d7.10 / 874 | 虫 月 宀
64 42 15

触

觸 | 触触

SHOKU, sawa(ru) touch, feel
fu(reru) touch (upon); announce

---------------------- 1 ----------------------

6 触合 **fu(re)a(u)** touch, come in contact with
12 触覚 **shokkaku** sense of touch

---------------------- 2 ----------------------

6 先触 **sakibu(re)** preliminary/previous announcement
肌触 **hadazawa(ri)** the touch/feel
9 前触 **maebu(re)** advance notice/warning
11 接触 **sesshoku** touch, contact; catalytic
接触点 **sesshokuten** point of contact/tangency
13 感触 **kanshoku** the touch/feel, texture
15 膚触 **hadazawa(ri)** the touch, the feel
18 顔触 **kaobu(re)** personnel, lineup, cast

---------------------- 8 ----------------------

6d8.2 | 虫 大 口
64 34 24

蜘

蜘蜘

CHI spider

---------------------- 1 ----------------------

12 蜘蛛 **kumo** spider
蜘蛛糸 **kumo (no) ito** spider's thread

蜘蛛巣 **kumo(no)su** spiderweb

6d8.7

田 虫 土 冂
64 22 20

蜻蜻

SEI dragonfly; mayfly; cicada; cricket

———————— 1 ————————

11 蜻蛉 **tonbo** dragonfly

———————— 2 ————————

7 赤蜻蛉 **akatonbo** red dragonfly

蝋 → 蠟 6d15.1

———————— 9 ————————

6d9.4

田 虫 尸 二
64 40 4

蝦蝦

KA, ebi shrimp, prawn, lobster

———————— 1 ————————

6 蝦夷 **Ezo** Ainu; Hokkaidō

———————— 3 ————————

6 伊勢蝦 **ise-ebi** spiny lobster

6d9.7 / 2236

田 虫 朮 艹
64 41 32

蝶蝶

CHŌ butterfly   CHŌ (part of given name)

———————— 1 ————————

0 蝶ネクタイ **chōnekutai** bow tie

3 蝶々 **chōchō** butterfly

6d9.8

田 虫 日 王
64 43 46

蝗蝗

KŌ, inago, batta locust, grasshopper

———————— 1 ————————

6 蝗虫 **batta** grasshopper, locust

6d9.10

田 虫 日 勹
64 43 15

蠍 | 蝎蝎

KATSU, sasori scorpion

6d9.12

田 虫 罒 口
64 58 24

蝙蝠

FUKU bat

———————— 2 ————————

15 蝙蝠 **kōmori** bat
蝙蝠傘 **kōmorigasa** umbrella

蝉 → 蟬 6d12.3

6d9.14

田 虫 尸 艹
64 40 32

蝙 | 蝙蝙

HEN bat

———————— 1 ————————

15 蝙蝠 **kōmori** bat
蝙蝠傘 **kōmorigasa** umbrella

蠢 → 虫 6d2.1

10

6d10.5 / 1588 | 🁢 虫 口 冂
64 24 20

融

融 融

YŪ, to(keru) melt, dissolve
TŌRU (m. given name)

--- 1 ---

6 融合 **yūgō** fusion
9 融通 **yūzū** accommodation, loan; versatility
13 融解 **yūkai** fuse, melt, dissolve
融資 **yūshi** financing, loan

--- 2 ---

8 金融 **kin'yū** money, credit, financing

螢 → 蛍 **3n8.2**

11

6d11.3 | 🁢 虫 糸 田
64 61 58

螺

螺 螺

RA, nishi spiral shellfish

--- 1 ---

2 螺子 **neji** screw; stopcock; (wind-up) spring
11 螺旋 **rasen** spiral, helix

12

6d12.3 | 🁢 虫 日 口
64 43 24

蟬

蝉 | 蝉 蟬

SEN, ZEN, semi cicada

--- 1 ---

10 蟬時雨 **semishigure** outburst of cicada droning

蟲 → 虫 **6d0.1**

13

6d13.1 | 🁢 虫 彐 卜
64 39 13

蠅

蝿 | 蠅 蠅

YŌ, hae, hai a fly

--- 1 ---

5 蠅叩 **haetata(ki)** fly swatter

蟹 → 蟹 **6d13.7**

蠍 → 蝎 **6d9.10**

6d13.6 | 🁢 虫 王 戈
64 46 52

蟻

蟻 蟻

GI, ari ant

--- 1 ---

6 蟻地獄 **arijigoku** antlion, doodle-bug
12 蟻塚 **arizuka** anthill

6d13.7 | 🁢 虫 月 牛
64 42 47

蟹

蠏 | 蟹 蟹

KAI, kani crab

--- 1 ---

8 蟹股 **ganimata** bowlegged

--- 3 ---

22 鱈場蟹 **tarabagani** king crab

觸 → 触 **6d7.10**

15

6d15.1

□ 虫 口 十
64 24 12

蠟

蝋 | 蝋 蜡

RŌ wax

— 1 —

17 蠟燭 **rōsoku** candle

18

蠅 → 蠅 6d13.1

19

蠻 → 蛮 2j10.1

20

蠶 → 蚕 6d4.8

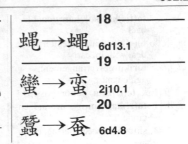

耳 6e

耳	耶	取	恥	耻	耽	耘	聊	聖	聡	聯	趣	聰
0.1	2.1	2.2	4.2	6e4.2	4.3	6e12.1	5.1	4f9.9	8.2	6e11.2	9.1	6e8.2

聯	聴	聲	聳	職	叢	聽	聾
11.2	11.3	3p4.4	11.4	12.1	12.3	6e11.3	16.1

糸
米
舟
虫
耳 2
⺮

0

6e0.1 / 56

□ 耳
65

耳

耳 耳

JI, mimi ear

— 1 —

5 耳打 **mimiu(chi)** whisper in (some-one's) ear

10 耳疾 **jishitsu** ear ailments

14 耳鳴 **mimina(ri)** ringing in the ears

耳鼻咽喉科 **jibiinkōka** ear, nose, and throat specialty

耳鼻科 **jibika** otorhinology

— 2 —

6 早耳 **hayamimi** quick-eared, in the know

10 馬耳東風 **bajitōfū** utter indifference, turn a deaf ear

2

6e2.1 / 2253

□ 耳 阝
65 7

耶

耶 耶

YA (question mark); (used phonetically) YA, JA, SHA (part of given name)

6e2.2 / 65

□ 耳 又
65 9

取

取 取

SHU, to(ru) take **to(reru)** can be taken; come off **(ni) to(tte)** to, for, as far as … is concerned

— 1 —

2 取入 **to(ri)i(reru)** take in, accept, adopt; harvest **to(ri)i(ru)** win (someone's) favor

3 取上 **to(ri)a(geru)** take up, adopt; take away

4 取分 **to(ri)wa(ke)** especially **to(ri)wa(keru)** divide, portion out **to(ri)bun** share, portion

取引 **torihiki** transaction, deal, business

5 取出 **to(ri)da(su)** take/pick out

取外 **to(ri)hazu(su)** remove, dismantle

6 取次 **to(ri)tsu(gu)** act as agent; transmit, convey

取返 **to(ri)kae(su)** get back, regain, recover, recoup, catch up on

to(tte)kae(su) hurry/double back

取扱 to(ri)atsuka(u) treat, handle, deal with/in, carry

7 取決 toriki(me) arrangement, agreement

取沙汰 to(ri)zata rumor, gossip

取囲 to(ri)kako(mu) surround, encircle

取材 shuzai news gathering, coverage

取戻 to(ri)modo(su) take back, regain, recoup, catch up on

8 取逃 to(ri)ni(gasu) fail to catch, miss

10 取消 to(ri)ke(su) cancel, revoke, rescind

11 取組 to(ri)ku(mu) grapple with to(ri)kumi (sumo) match

12 取替 to(ri)ka(eru) (ex)change, replace

15 取締役 torishimariyaku (company) director

取調 to(ri)shira(beru) investigate, look into

16 取壊 to(ri)kowa(su) tear down, demolish

18 取繕 to(ri)tsukuro(u) repair, patch up, gloss over

─────── 2 ───────

4 刈取 ka(ri)to(ru) mow, cut down, reap

切取 ki(ri)to(ru) cut off/out

日取 hido(ri) (set) the date, schedule

6 汲取 ku(mi)to(ru) draw (water), dip up (night soil); take into consideration, make allowances for

先取 senshu take/score first, preoccupy sakido(ri) receive in advance; anticipate

7 位取 kuraido(ri) positioning of the ones digit within a number

8 受取 u(ke)to(ru) receive, accept, take uketo(ri) receipt, acknowledgment

9 乗取 no(t)to(ru) hijack, commandeer, capture, occupy

窃取 sesshu steal

10 剥取 ha(gi)to(ru) strip/tear off; rob of

蚊取線香 katori senkō mosquito-repellent incense

11 隈取 kumado(ru) tint, shade; make up (one's face) kumado(ri) shading; makeup

採取 saishu gather, pick, harvest, extract

鳥取県 Tottori-ken (prefecture)

13 鼠取 nezumito(ri) rat poison; mousetrap, rattrap

摂取 sesshu ingest, take in

搾取 sakushu exploitation

14 摘取 tsu(mi)to(ru) pick, pluck

攫取 tsuka(mi)to(ru) snatch off, grasp

塵取 chirito(ri) dustpan

奪取 uba(i)to(ru) plunder dasshu capture, seize, wrest

聞取 ki(ki)to(ru) hear and understand, catch, follow

関取 sekitori ranking sumo wrestler

17 聴取 chōshu listening

闇取引 yamitorihiki black-market dealings, illegal transaction

─────── 3 ───────

9 虻蜂取 abu-hachi to(razu) trying to catch both a fly and a bee in one swoop of the hand and failing to catch either

─────── 4 ───────

6e4.2 / 1690

口 耳 心
65 51

恥 | 恥 恥

CHI, haji shame, disgrace **ha(jiru/ zuru)** feel shame **ha(jirau)** be shy/ bashful **ha(zukashii)** shy, bashful, ashamed **ha(zubeki)** disgraceful, unbecoming

─────── 1 ───────

0 恥ずかしがる ha(zukashigaru) be shy/bashful

8 恥知 hajishi(razu) shameless person

10 耻部 **chibu** the private parts
耻辱 **chijoku** disgrace, humiliation

———— 2 ————

6 気恥 **kiha(zukashii)** embarrassed, ashamed, bashful
13 廉恥心 **renchishin** sense of shame/honor

———— 3 ————

10 破廉恥 **harenchi** shameless, disgraceful

耻 → 恥 **6e4.2**

6e4.3   田 耳 冂 丨
                    65 20 2

耽 耽

TAN, fuke(ru) be addicted to, be engrossed in

———— 1 ————

9 耽美的 **tanbiteki** esthetic
13 耽溺 **tandeki** addiction, dissipation

耺 → 職 **6e12.1**

———— 5 ————

6e5.1   田 耳 厂 阝
                    65 18 7

聊 聊

RYŌ ringing in the ears; enjoyment
isasa(ka) a little

———— 7 ————

聖 → 聖 **4f9.9**

———— 8 ————

6e8.2 / 2203   田 耳 心 儿
                      65 51 16

聡 聰 ｜ 聡 聡

SŌ, sato(i) wise, quick-witted, keen (of hearing) SATOSHI, AKIRA, SATORU, TOSHI (m. given name) SŌ, SATO, FUSA, AKI, TOMI, TOKI, TOSHI (part of given name)

———— 1 ————

8 聡明 **sōmei** wise, sagacious

———— 9 ————

聯 → 聯 **6e11.2**

6e9.1 / 1002   … 耳 土 卜
                      65 22 13

趣 趣

SHU, omomuki purport, gist; taste, elegance; appearance

———— 1 ————

6 趣向 **shukō** plan, idea
趣旨 **shushi** purport, meaning, aim, object
8 趣味 **shumi** interest, liking, tastes; hobby

———— 2 ————

6 多趣味 **tashumi** many-sided interests
11 野趣 **yashu** rural beauty, rustic air

———— 11 ————

聰 → 聡 **6e8.2**

6e11.2   田 耳 竹 丨
                      65 17 2

聯 聯 ｜ 聯 聯

REN group, accompaniment (now usually written with 連)

———— 1 ————

6 聯合 **rengō** combination, league, coalition

6

糸
米
舟
虫
耳 11
⺮

6e11.3 / 1039 　田 耳 目 心　65 55 51

聴　　聴 | 聴 聴

CHŌ, ki(ku) hear, listen to

――――――― 1 ―――――――

2 聴力 **chōryoku** hearing ability
8 聴者 **chōsha** listener
　聴取 **chōshu** listening
11 聴視者 **chōshisha** (TV) viewer(s)
12 聴衆 **chōshū** audience
14 聴聞会 **chōmonkai** public hearing
17 聴講 **chōkō** attendance at a lecture

――――――― 2 ―――――――

4 公聴会 **kōchōkai** public hearing
11 視聴率 **shichōritsu** (TV show popularity) rating
　盗聴 **tōchō** surreptitious listening, bugging, wiretapping
12 傍聴 **bōchō** hearing, attendance, auditing
13 傾聴 **keichō** listen (attentively) to
　試聴 **shichō** audition

聲 → 声　3p4.4

6e11.4　田 耳 彳 亻　65 29 3

聳　　聳 聳

SHŌ, sobi(eru) rise, tower above
sobi(yakasu) raise, throw back (one's shoulders)

――――――― 1 ―――――――

11 聳動 **shōdō** electrify, startle, shock

――――――― 12 ―――――――

6e12.1 / 385　田 耳 日 戈　65 43 52

職　　耺 | 職 職

SHOKU employment, job, occupation, office

――――――― 1 ―――――――

2 職人 **shokunin** craftsman, workman
3 職工 **shokkō** (factory) worker
6 職安 **shokuan** (public) employment security office (short for 公共職業安定所)
10 職員 **shokuin** personnel, staff (member)
12 職場 **shokuba** workplace, job site
13 職業 **shokugyō** occupation, profession
　職業病 **shokugyōbyō** occupational disease

――――――― 2 ―――――――

4 内職 **naishoku** at-home work, side job, cottage industry
5 本職 **honshoku** one's regular occupation; an expert; I
6 休職 **kyūshoku** temporary retirement from office, layoff
　汚職 **oshoku** corruption, graft
　在職 **zaishoku** hold office, remain in office
　有職 **yūshoku** employed **yūsoku, yūshoku** person versed in court and military practices, scholar
7 求職 **kyūshoku** job hunting, Situation Wanted
8 免職 **menshoku** dismissal, discharge
　退職 **taishoku** retirement
　定職 **teishoku** regular occupation, steady job
10 兼職 **kenshoku** concurrent post
　殉職 **junshoku** dying in the line of duty
11 現職 **genshoku** present post, incumbent
　転職 **tenshoku** change of post/occupation
12 就職 **shūshoku** find employment
　就職口 **shūshokuguchi** job opening, employment
　無職 **mushoku** unemployed; no occupation

13 聖職 **seishoku** ministry, clergy, holy orders

辞職 **jishoku** resignation, quitting

6e12.3 / 1998

目 耳 儿 丆
65 16 14

叢叢

SŌ congregate, cluster **kusamura** thicket, the bush **mura-** massing together

— 1 —

10 叢書 **sōsho** series, library

— 16 —

聽 → 聴 6e11.3

6e16.1

田 耳 立 月
65 54 42

聾聾

RŌ, tsunbo deaf

— 1 —

11 聾啞 **rōa** deaf and mute

—— ⺮ 6f ——

竹	竿	笑	笠	笹	笙	第	笛	符	笥	筆	策	筋
0.1	3.3	4.1	5.1	5.3	5.4	5.5	5.6	5.12	5.15	6.1	6.2	6.4

筑	等	筈	答	筒	節	泛	筱	貿	箸	箔	算	箋
6.6	6.9	6.10	6.12	6.15	7.3	6f13.4	6f11.3	7b8.7	6f9.1	8.5	8.7	8.9

管	箇	箸	範	節	箱	單	篆	篇	篤	篭	築	篠
8.12	8.15	9.1	9.3	6f7.3	9.4	6f12.2	9.8	9.9	10.1	6f16.1	10.5	11.3

簞	簡	簿	簾	籍	纂	籃	籤	籠	籤
12.2	12.5	13.4	13.8	14.1	14.4	15.2	6f17.2	16.1	17.2

糸 米 舟 虫 耳 ⺮ 3

— 0 —

6f0.1 / 129

口 ⺮
66

竹竹

CHIKU, take bamboo

— 1 —

2 竹子 **take(no)ko** bamboo shoots

竹刀 **shinai** bamboo sword (for kendo)

3 竹下 **Takeshita** (surname)

4 竹内 **Takeuchi** (surname)

竹中 **Takenaka** (surname)

5 竹本 **Takemoto** (surname)

竹田 **Takeda** (surname)

7 竹村 **Takemura** (surname)

8 竹林 **takebayashi, chikurin** bamboo grove

9 竹竿 **takezao** bamboo pole

11 竹細工 **takezaiku** bamboo handicrafts

18 竹藪 **takeyabu** bamboo grove/thicket

— 2 —

3 大竹 **Ōtake** (surname)

7 佐竹 **Satake** (surname)

8 松竹梅 **shō-chiku-bai** pine-bamboo-plum (as sign of congratulations or to designate three things of equal rank)

— 3 —

6f3.3

日 ⺮ 丆 一
66 14 1

竿竿

KAN, sao pole

6f4.1

— 2 —

⁶ 竹竿 **takezao** bamboo pole

¹¹ 釣竿 **tsu(ri)zao** fishing rod

— 4 —

6f4.1 / 1235

笑   笑笑

□ ⺮ 大 |
66 34 2

SHŌ, wara(u) laugh, smile
e(mu) smile   EMI (part of given name)

— 1 —

⁵ 笑出 **wara(i)da(su)** burst out
laughing

⁷ 笑声 **wara(i)goe, shōsei** laughter

⁹ 笑草 **wara(i)gusa** topic of amuse-
ment

¹³ 笑話 **wara(i)banashi, shōwa** fun-
ny story

¹⁸ 笑顔 **egao, wara(i)gao** smiling face

— 2 —

³ 大笑 **ōwara(i), taishō** a big laugh

⁷ 冷笑 **reishō** derisive smile, scornful
laugh, sneer

⁸ 苦笑 **kushō, nigawara(i)** bitter/
wry smile

¹³ 微笑 **bishō, hohoe(mi)** smile

¹⁵ 談笑 **danshō** chat, friendly talk

¹⁶ 頬笑 **hohoe(mi)** smile

¹⁹ 爆笑 **bakushō** burst out laughing

— 5 —

6f5.1

笠   笠笠

□ ⺮ 立
66 54

RYŪ, kasa bamboo hat; (lamp)shade,
hood

— 1 —

⁴ 笠井 **Kasai** (surname)

— 2 —

⁶ 衣笠 **Kinugasa** (surname)

6f5.3 / 2189

笹   笹笹

□ ⺮ 廿 一
66 32 1

sasa bamboo grass   SASA (part of giv-
en name)

— 1 —

¹⁸ 笹薮 **sasayabu** bamboo-grass
thicket

6f5.4 / 2188

笙   笙笙

□ ⺮ 牛 一
66 47 1

SHŌ (a type of reed flute)
SHŌ, SEI (part of given name)

6f5.5 / 404

第   才|第第

□ ⺮ 弓 |
66 28 2

DAI (prefix for ordinals), No. (1, 2,
etc.); a residence; (passing an) examination

— 1 —

¹ 第一 **dai-ichi** No. 1, first, best, main

第一人者 **dai-ichininsha** fore-
most/leading person

第一次 **dai-ichiji** first

³ 第三者 **dai-sansha** third person/
party

⁴ 第六感 **dai-rokkan** sixth sense

— 2 —

³ 及第 **kyūdai** passing (an exam),
make the grade

⁶ 次第 **shidai** order, precedence; cir-
cumstances; as soon as; accord-
ing to; gradually

¹² 落第 **rakudai** failure in an exam

— 3 —

⁶ 安全第一 **anzen dai-ichi** Safety
First

6

糸
米
舟
虫
耳

4 ⺮

12 腕次第 **ude-shidai** according to one's ability

6f5.6 / 1471　　日 ∧∧ 日 丨　66 43 2

TEKI, fue flute, whistle

---- 2 ----

3 口笛 **kuchibue** whistling
7 汽笛 **kiteki** (steam) whistle, siren
13 鼓笛隊 **kotekitai** drum-and-bugle corps, fife-and-drum band
10 警笛 **keiteki** alarm whistle, horn

6f5.12 / 505　　日 ∧∧ 寸 亻　66 37 3

FU sign, mark; amulet

---- 1 ----

5 符号 **fugō** mark, symbol, code
13 符牒 **fuchō** mark, symbol, code

---- 2 ----

4 切符 **kippu** ticket
9 音符 **onpu** (musical) note; the part of a kanji indicating its pronunciation
20 護符 **gofu** amulet, talisman

---- 3 ----

4 引用符 **in'yōfu** quotation marks
13 感嘆符 **kantanfu** exclamation point (!)
14 疑問符 **gimonfu** question mark

6f5.15　　日 ∧∧ 口 一　66 24 1

SHI, SU box; clothes chest

---- 2 ----

18 箪笥 **tansu** chest of drawers, dresser

---- 6 ----

6f6.1 / 130　　日 ∧∧ 彐 十　66 39 12

HITSU, fude writing brush

---- 1 ----

5 筆写 **hissha** copy, transcribe
6 筆先 **fudesaki** brush tip; writings
　筆名 **hitsumei** pen name, pseudonym
8 筆者 **hissha** the writer/author
12 筆答 **hittō** written reply
　筆順 **hitsujun** stroke order

---- 2 ----

1 一筆 **ippitsu, hitofude** a stroke of the pen, a few lines
4 毛筆 **mōhitsu** writing/painting brush
6 自筆 **jihitsu** one's own handwriting
7 乱筆 **ranpitsu** hasty writing, scrawl
8 画筆 **gahitsu** artist's brush
　毒筆 **dokuhitsu** spiteful/poison pen
10 随筆 **zuihitsu** essay, miscellaneous writings
　能筆 **nōhitsu** calligraphy, skilled penmanship
11 執筆 **shippitsu** write (for a magazine)
12 硬筆 **kōhitsu** pen or pencil (rather than brush)
13 鉛筆 **enpitsu** pencil

---- 3 ----

3 万年筆 **mannenhitsu** fountain pen

6f6.2 / 880　　日 ∧∧ 木 冂　66 41 20

SAKU plan, means, measure, policy

___ 1 ___

11 策略 **sakuryaku** stratagem, scheme, tactic

16 策謀 **sakubō** stratagem, machinations

___ 2 ___

5 失策 **shissaku** blunder, slip, error

7 良策 **ryōsaku** good plan/policy
対策 **taisaku** (counter)measures

8 拙策 **sessaku** poor policy, imprudent measure

9 施策 **shisaku** a measure/policy
政策 **seisaku** policy

11 術策 **jussaku** stratagem, artifice, tricks

15 窮策 **kyūsaku** desperate measure, last resort

___ 3 ___

11 救済策 **kyūsaisaku** relief measure

6f6.4 / 1090

□ ⺮ 月 力
66 42 8

KIN muscle, sinews **suji** muscle, tendon; blood vessel; line; stripe, steak; reason, logic, coherence; plot (of a story); source (of information)

___ 1 ___

6 筋肉 **kinniku** muscle

11 筋道 **sujimichi** reason, logic, coherence

12 筋違 **sujichiga(e)** a cramp **sujichiga(i)** illogical; diagonal **sujika(i)** diagonal; brace

___ 2 ___

1 一筋 **hitosuji** a line; earnestly, wholeheartedly

5 本筋 **honsuji** plot, main thread (of a story)

6 血筋 **chisuji** blood relationship, lineage

11 粗筋 **arasuji** outline, summary, synopsis

___ 3 ___

9 政府筋 **seifusuji** government sources

6f6.6

□ ⺮ 工 口
66 38 20

筑 筑

CHIKU (ancient koto-like instrument)

___ 1 ___

8 筑波 **Tsukuba** (city and university, Ibaraki-ken)

6f6.9 / 569

目 ⺮ 土 寸
66 22 37

等 等

TŌ class, grade; equal; etc.
hito(shii) equal **-nado** and so forth, etc. **-ra** and others, and the like; (plural suffix) **HITOSHI** (m. given name)

___ 1 ___

4 等分 **tōbun** (division into) equal parts

5 等号 **tōgō** equal sign (=)

9 等級 **tōkyū** class, grade, rank

15 等質 **tōshitsu** homogeneous

___ 2 ___

1 一等 **ittō** first class/rank, the most/best

3 上等 **jōtō** first-rate, superior
下等 **katō** low, lower (animals/plants), inferior, base, vulgar

4 不等 **futō** inequality
中等 **chūtō** medium/secondary grade, average quality

5 平等 **byōdō** equality, impartiality

6 同等 **dōtō** equal, on a par with
劣等 **rettō** inferiority
劣等感 **rettōkan** inferiority complex

7 我等 **warera** we
何等 **nanra** what, whatever

均等 **kintō** equality, uniformity, parity

10 高等 **kōtō** high-grade, high-class

17 優等生 **yūtōsei** honors student

———— 3 ————

4 不平等 **fubyōdō** unequal

6f6.10

	^^	口	十
	66	24	12

KATSU, hazu arrow/bow notch; to be expected, surely

6f6.12 / 160

	^^	口	亻
	66	24	3

TŌ, kota(eru) answer **kota(e)** an answer

———— 1 ————

5 答弁 **tōben** reply, explanation, defense

答申 **tōshin** report

———— 2 ————

3 口答 **kuchigota(e)** backtalk, retort

口答 **kōtō** oral reply

4 手答 **tegota(e)** response, effect, resistance

6 返答 **hentō** reply

回答 **kaitō** reply

7 即答 **sokutō** prompt reply

応答 **ōtō** answer, reply, response

11 問答 **mondō** questions and answers

12 筆答 **hittō** written reply

13 解答 **kaitō** answer, solution

———— 3 ————

13 禅問答 **zen mondō** Zen/incomprehensible dialog

———— 4 ————

15 質疑応答 **shitsugi-ōtō** question-and-answer (session)

6f6.15 / 1472

	^^	口	冂
	66	24	20

TŌ, tsutsu pipe, tube

———— 1 ————

4 筒井 **Tsutsui** (surname)

7 筒抜 **tsutsunu(ke)** directly, clearly

———— 2 ————

4 水筒 **suitō** water flask, canteen

9 封筒 **fūtō** envelope

———— 7 ————

6f7.3 / 464

	^^	食	阝
	66	73	7

SETSU, SECHI season; occasion; section, paragraph, verse; joint; be moderate in, use sparingly; knot (nautical miles per hour) **fushi** joint, knuckle; knot (in wood); melody; point, item TAKASHI (m. given name) MISAO (given name) SETSU, TOKI (part of given name)

———— 1 ————

2 節子 **Setsuko, Sadako** (f. given name)

5 節句 **sekku** seasonal festival

節目 **fushime** knot (in wood); turning point

8 節制 **sessei** moderation, temperance

9 節約 **setsuyaku** economizing, saving on

10 節料理 **(o)sechi ryōri** New Year's foods

13 節電 **setsuden** saving on electricity

16 節操 **sessō** fidelity, integrity; chastity

———— 2 ————

7 季節 **kisetsu** season, time of year

季節風 **kisetsufū** seasonal wind, monsoon

8 使節 **shisetsu** envoy; mission, delegation

6

糸
米
舟
虫
耳
^^ **7**

9 貞節 **teisetsu** fidelity, chastity
10 桃節句 **Momo (no) Sekku** Doll Festival (March 3)

時節 **jisetsu** season; the times; opportunity
11 菊節句 **Kiku (no) Sekku** Chrysanthemum Festival
12 腕節 **ude(p)pushi** muscular strength
15 調節 **chōsetsu** adjust, control, regulate
23 鰹節 **katsuobushi** dried bonito shavings

——————— 3 ———————

8 股関節 **kokansetsu** hip joint
9 紀元節 **kigensetsu** Empire Day

�""→薄 **6f13.4**

筱→篠 **6f11.3**

質→ **7b8.7**

——————— 8 ———————

箸→箸 **6f9.1**

6f8.5 〼 ⺮ 日 氵
66 43 21

箔

箔箔

HAKU foil, leaf, gilt

6f8.7 / 747 〼 ⺮ 目 卝
66 55 32

算

算算

SAN calculate KAZU (part of given name)

——————— 1 ———————

8 算定 **santei** calculate, estimate
13 算数 **sansū** arithmetic, math, calculation
15 算盤 **soroban** abacus

——————— 2 ———————

4 予算 **yosan** budget, estimate
引算 **hi(ki)zan** subtraction (in math)
5 打算的 **dasanteki** calculating, mercenary
目算 **mokusan** expectation, estimate
7 決算 **kessan** settlement (of accounts); liquidation
足算 **ta(shi)zan** addition (in math)
9 計算 **keisan** computation, calculation
計算書 **keisansho** statement (of account)
計算機 **keisanki** computer
10 珠算 **shuzan** calculation on the abacus
11 清算 **seisan** liquidation, settlement
推算 **suisan** calculate, reckon, estimate
掛算 **ka(ke)zan** multiplication (in math)
採算 **saisan** profit
12 割算 **wa(ri)zan** division (in math)
換算 **kansan** conversion, exchange
14 精算 **seisan** exact calculation, (fare) adjustment, settling of accounts
誤算 **gosan** miscalculation

6f8.9 目 ⺮ 戈
66 52

箋

箋箋

SEN paper; label; letter, writing

——————— 2 ———————

9 便箋 **binsen** stationery, notepaper

6f8.12 / 328 目 ⺮ 宀 尸
66 33 40

管

管管

KAN control, jurisdiction; pipe, tube; wind instrument **kuda** pipe, tube

—— 1 ——

4 管区 **kanku** district, precinct

8 管制塔 **kanseitō** control tower
管弦楽団 **kangen gakudan** orchestra

11 管理 **kanri** administration, supervision, control, management
管理人 **kanrinin** manager, superintendent

17 管轄 **kankatsu** jurisdiction

—— 2 ——

6 気管 **kikan** windpipe, trachea
血管 **kekkan** blood vessel

8 弦管 **genkan** wind and string instruments

9 保管 **hokan** custody, deposit, storage

13 鉛管 **enkan** lead pipe, plumbing

6f8.15 / 1473 ▢ ⺮ 口 十 66 24 12

KA, KO (counter for inanimate objects)

—— 1 ——

0 りんご1ケ **ringo ikko** one apple

6 1ケ年 **ikkanen** one year

7 箇条 **kajō** article, provision, item

8 3ケ所 **sankasho** three places
箇所 **kasho** place, part, passage (in a book)

—— 2 ——

1 一箇 **ikko** one; a piece
一ケ年 **ikkanen** one year

—— 9 ——

6f9.1 ▢ ⺮ 日 土 66 43 22

CHO, CHAKU, hashi chopsticks

—— 1 ——

13 箸置 **hashio(ki)** chopstick rest

—— 2 ——

12 割箸 **wa(ri)bashi** half-split chopsticks

13 塗箸 **nu(ri)bashi** lacquered chopsticks

6f9.3 / 1092 ▢ 車 ⺮ 阝 69 66 7

HAN example, model, pattern; limit
NORI (part of given name)

—— 1 ——

7 範囲 **han'i** extent, scope, range
範囲内 **han'inai** within the limits of

8 範例 **hanrei** example

—— 2 ——

9 軌範 **kihan** model, example

10 師範 **shihan** teacher, instructor

14 模範 **mohan** model, exemplar

節 → 節 6f7.3

箴 → 嵌 3o9.2

6f9.4 / 1091 ▢ ⺮ 目 木 66 55 41

箱

hako box

—— 1 ——

2 箱入 **hakoi(ri)** boxed, in cases
箱入娘 **hakoi(ri)musume** girl who has led a sheltered life

10 箱根 **Hakone** (resort area near Mt. Fuji)

13 箱詰 **hakozume** packed in cases, boxed

—— 2 ——

7 芥箱 **gomibako** garbage box/bin, waste basket

11 豚箱 **butabako** police lockup, jail

6

糸
米
角
虫
耳
⺮ 9

¹² 硯箱 **suzuribako** inkstone case

――――― 3 ―――――

⁷ 私書箱 **shishobako** post-office box
¹⁰ 郵便箱 **yūbinbako** mailbox
¹² 貯金箱 **chokinbako** savings box, (piggy) bank

箪 → 箪 **6f12.2**

6f9.8   目 ⺮ 犭 丶
          66 27 10

篆   篆 篆

TEN (a style of kanji used on seals and inscriptions)

――――― 1 ―――――

⁵ 篆字 **tenji** seal characters
¹⁰ 篆書 **tensho** seal characters

6f9.9   目 ⺮ 尸 卄
          66 40 32

篇   篇 篇

HEN book, volume, edition; chapter, part; (counter for literary works)

――――― 2 ―――――

⁹ 前篇 **zenpen** the first volume/part
¹² 短篇小説 **tanpen shōsetsu** short story/novel

――――― 10 ―――――

6f10.1 / 1883   目 馬 ⺮
               78 66

篤   篤 篤

TOKU, atsu(i) kind, cordial; fervent; serious (illness) **ATSUSHI** (m. given name) **ATSU** (part of given name)

――――― 1 ―――――

⁷ 篤学 **tokugaku** love of learning

篤志家 **tokushika** benefactor, volunteer

――――― 2 ―――――

⁶ 危篤 **kitoku** critically ill, near death
⁹ 重篤 **jūtoku** serious (illness)

竜 → 籠 **6f16.1**

6f10.5 / 1603   目 ⺮ 木 工
                  66 41 38

築   築 築

CHIKU, kizu(ku), tsu(ku) build

――――― 1 ―――――

³ 築上 **kizu(ki)a(geru)** build up

――――― 2 ―――――

⁷ 改築 **kaichiku** rebuild, remodel, alter
⁸ 建築 **kenchiku** building, construction, architecture
    建築家 **kenchikuka** architect, building contractor
¹³ 新築 **shinchiku** newly built
¹⁴ 増築 **zōchiku** build on, extend, enlarge

――――― 11 ―――――

6f11.3   目 ⺮ 攵 木
               66 49 41

篠   篠 篠

SHŌ, shino (a variety of small bamboo)

――――― 1 ―――――

⁵ 篠田 **Shinoda** (surname)

――――― 12 ―――――

6f12.2   目 ⺮ 日 口
               66 43 24

箪   箪 箪 箪

TAN (a variety of bamboo); round woven-bamboo lunch box

——————— 1 ———————

11 簞笥 **tansu** chest of drawers, dresser

6f12.5 / 1533 　　日 門 ㅅㅅ 日
　　　　　　　76 66 43

簡

簡 简

KAN, KEN simple, brief

——————— 1 ———————

8 簡易 **kan'i** simple, easy
9 簡単 **kantan** simple, brief
10 簡素 **kanso** plain and simple

——————— 2 ———————

10 書簡 **shokan** letter, note

——————— 13 ———————

6f13.4 / 1450 　　日 ㅅㅅ 日 氵
　　　　　　　66 43 21

簿

泍 | 簿 簿

BO record book, ledger, register, list

——————— 1 ———————

10 簿記 **boki** bookkeeping

——————— 2 ———————

6 名簿 **meibo** name list, roster, roll
11 帳簿 **chōbo** (account) books, book (value)

6f13.8 　　日 ㅅㅅ 彐 厂
　　　　　　　66 39 18

簾

簾 簾

REN, sudare, su bamboo/rattan (venetian-type) blind

——————— 14 ———————

6f14.1 / 1198 　　日 ㅅㅅ 耒 日
　　　　　　　66 41 43

籍

籍 籍

SEKI (family) register

——————— 2 ———————

2 入籍 **nyūseki** have one's name entered on the family register
4 戸籍 **koseki** family register
5 本籍 **honseki** one's legal domicile
8 国籍 **kokuseki** nationality, citizenship
10 書籍 **shoseki** books

6f14.4 　　日 ㅅㅅ 糸 日
　　　　　　　66 61 55

纂

纂 纂

SAN edit, compile

——————— 15 ———————

6f15.2 　　日 ㅅㅅ 皿 冂
　　　　　　　66 59 20

籃

籃 籃

RAN basket

籤 → 籤 **6f17.2**

——————— 16 ———————

6f16.1 　　日 ㅅㅅ 立 月
　　　　　　　66 54 42

籠

篭 | 籠 籠

RŌ, komo(ru) seclude oneself, hole up; be full of **ko(meru)** put into **kago** (palanquin/carrying) basket, (bird) cage **ko** basket

6

糸
米
角
虫
耳
ㅅㅅ 16

2

10 屑籠 **kuzukago** wastebasket
11 鳥籠 **torikago** bird cage

1

4 籤引 **kujibi(ki)** drawing lots

2

6 当籤 **tōsen** win (a lottery)
8 抽籤 **chūsen** drawing, lottery
宝籤 **takarakuji** lottery, raffle

17

6f17.2

日 ⺮ 戈 亻
66 52 3

籤

籤|籤籤

SEN, kuji written oracle; lottery, raffle

言 **7a**

言	計	訂	託	討	記	訓	訪	訣	許	訟	設	訳
0.1	2.1	2.3	3.1	3.3	3.5	3.6	4.1	4.2	4.3	4.6	4.7	4.8
訴	評	註	詛	証	詐	診	詔	註	詠	詞	誠	詩
5.2	5.3	7a5.11	5.4	5.5	5.6	5.9	5.10	5.11	5.14	5.15	6.3	6.5
詫	詰	話	誇	詮	該	詭	詳	詣	詮	詢	試	誤
6.6	6.7	6.8	6.9	7a6.14	6.10	6.11	6.12	6.13	6.14	6.17	6.18	7.2
誘	語	誌	読	認	諄	説	誦	誕	誓	誰	諫	課
7.4	7.6	7.8	7.9	7.10	7.11	7.12	7.14	7.15	7.17	8.1	7a9.1	8.2
諸	諏	誹	謁	談	請	諾	誼	論	諒	謎	調	諫
8.3	8.4	8.5	8.6	8.7	8.8	8.10	8.11	8.13	8.14	7a9.20	8.16	9.1
諸	諮	諺	諜	謀	謁	謡	諧	諭	諺	謎	諷	謝
7a8.3	9.4	7a9.15	9.7	9.8	7a8.6	9.9	9.11	9.13	9.15	9.20	9.21	10.1
講	詞	謠	譁	謹	謙	謹	譜	證	識	警	譯	讓
10.3	4j10.2	7a9.9	3d10.7	10.6	10.10	7a10.6	12.2	7a5.5	12.6	12.7	7a4.8	13.1
護	議	譜	譽	辯	讃	讀	讓	讚				
13.3	13.4	7a12.2	3n10.1	0a5.30	15.1	7a7.9	7a13.1	7a15.1				

0

7a0.1 / 66

口 言
67

言

言言

GEN, GON, koto word **i(u)** say
i(waba) so to speak, as it were
NOBU (part of given name)

1

4 言分 **i(i)bun** one's say; objection
言方 **i(i)kata** way of saying

6 言伝 **i(i)tsuta(eru)** hand down (a
  legend), spread (a rumor)
  kotozu(te) hearsay; message
言争 **i(i)araso(i)** quarrel, altercation
8 言直 **i(i)nao(su)** rephrase, correct
11 言過 **i(i)su(giru)** overstate, go too
  far
言張 **i(i)ha(ru)** insist on, maintain
言訳 **i(i)wake** excuse, explanation,
  apology
12 言葉 **kotoba** words, expression,
  language **koto(no)ha** words;
  tanka poem

13 言損 **i(i)soko(nau)** misspeak; fail to mention

14 言語 **gengo** language, speech
i(wazu)kata(razu) tacitly

言語学 **gengogaku** linguistics, philology

15 言論 **genron** speech, discussion

18 言難 **i(i)gata(i)** difficult to say, inexpressible

─────── 2 ───────

1 一言 **hitokoto, ichigen, ichigon** a word

一言二言 **hitokoto futakoto** a word or two

2 二言 **futakoto** two words
nigon double-dealing

4 予言 **yogen** prediction
kanegoto prediction; promise

片言 **katakoto** baby talk, broken (English) **hengen** few words

方言 **hōgen** dialect

5 失言 **shitsugen** verbal slip/impropriety

甘言 **kangen** honeyed words, flattery, blarney

用言 **yōgen** declinable word

7 体言 **taigen** uninflected word

助言 **jogen** advice

狂言 **kyōgen** play, drama; program; Noh farce; trick, sham

序言 **jogen** preface, foreword, introduction

忌言葉 **i(mi)kotoba** tabooed word

8 毒言 **dokugen** abusive language

明言 **meigen** declare, assert

金言 **kingen** wise saying, maxim

9 発言 **hatsugen** utterance, speaking; proposal

独言 **hito(ri)goto** talking to oneself; soliloquy; monolog

宣言 **sengen** declaration, statement

祝言 **shūgen** congratulations; celebration; wedding

恨言 **ura(mi)goto** grudge, grievance, reproach

悔言 **ku(yami)goto** words of condolence

10 書言葉 **ka(ki)kotoba** written language

11 過言 **kagon, kagen** exaggeration

12 換言 **kangen (sureba)** in other words

無言 **mugon** silent, mute

証言 **shōgen** testimony

13 話言葉 **hana(shi)kotoba** spoken language

14 遺言 **yuigon** will, last wishes

遺言書 **yuigonsho** will, testament

緒言 **chogen, shogen** preface, foreword

16 憾言 **ura(mi)goto** words of regret

諫言 **kangen** remonstrate with, admonish

19 繰言 **ku(ri)goto** same old story, complaint

─────── 3 ───────

10 能狂言 **nōkyōgen** Noh farce; Noh drama and *kyōgen* farce

─────── 4 ───────

1 一言二言 **hitokoto futakoto** a word or two

─────── 2 ───────

7a2.1 / 340   □ 言 十
                                    67 12

KEI measure, (as suffix) meter, gauge; plan; total **haka(ru)** measure, compute **haka(rau)** arrange, dispose of, see about KAZU (part of given name)

─────── 1 ───────

8 計画 **keikaku** plan, project

11 計理士 **keirishi** public accountant

計略 **keiryaku** stratagem, plan, ruse

12 計量 **keiryō** measure, weigh

14 計算 **keisan** computation, calculation

計算書 **keisansho** statement (of account)

計算機 **keisanki** computer

─────── 2 ───────

3 小計 **shōkei** subtotal

5 生計費 **seikeihi** living expenses

6 合計 **gōkei** total

会計 **kaikei** accounting; the bill
会計士 **kaikeishi** accountant

7 余計 **yokei** more than enough, extra; unneeded, uncalled-for

10 家計 **kakei** family finances; livelihood
時計 **tokei** clock, watch, timepiece

11 累計 **ruikei** total
設計 **sekkei** design, planning
設計図 **sekkeizu** plan, blueprint

12 統計 **tōkei** statistics

14 総計 **sōkei** (sum) total

———— 3 ————

7 体温計 **taionkei** (clinical) thermometer

9 速度計 **sokudokei** speedometer

12 温度計 **ondokei** thermometer
腕時計 **udedokei** wristwatch

7a2.3 / 1019　　□ 言 一
67 14

訂　　訂訂

TEI correcting

———— 1 ————

5 訂正 **teisei** correction, revision

———— 2 ————

7 改訂 **kaitei** revision
改訂版 **kaiteiban** revised edition
改訂増補 **kaitei-zōho** revised and enlarged

10 校訂 **kōtei** revision

13 新訂版 **shinteiban** newly revised edition

———— 3 ————

7a3.1 / 1636　　□ 言 十 丨
67 12 2

託　　託託

TAKU entrust **kako(tsu)** complain of, bemoan **kakotsu(keru)** make a pretext of **kotozu(keru)** send word, have (someone) deliver

———— 1 ————

0 託する **taku(suru)** entrust to, leave in the care of

———— 2 ————

8 依託 **itaku** request, entrust
受託 **jutaku** be entrusted with
委託 **itaku** entrust to, put in (someone's) charge
委託販売 **itaku hanbai** selling on consignment/commission

9 信託 **shintaku** trust, entrusting

15 嘱託 **shokutaku** put in charge of, commission; part-time employee

7a3.3 / 1018　　□ 言 寸
67 37

討　　討討

TŌ, u(tsu) attack

———— 1 ————

15 討論 **tōron** debate, discussion
討論会 **tōronkai** forum, debate, discussion

20 討議 **tōgi** discussion, deliberation, debate

———— 2 ————

4 仇討 **adau(chi)** vendetta, revenge

12 検討 **kentō** examine, study, look into

7a3.5 / 371　　□ 言 弓
67 28

記　　記記

KI write down, note **shiru(su)** write/note down NORI (part of given name)

———— 1 ————

2 記入 **kinyū** entry (in a form/ledger)

5 記号 **kigō** mark, symbol

6 記名 **kimei** register/sign one's name

7 記述 **kijutsu** description, account

8 記事 **kiji** article, report

記念 **kinen** commemoration, remembrance

記念日 **kinenbi** memorial day, anniversary

記念碑 **kinenhi** monument

記者 **kisha** newspaper reporter, journalist

記者会見 **kisha kaiken** news/press conference

¹³ 記載 **kisai** record, report, note

¹⁶ 記憶 **kioku** memory

記録 **kiroku** record, document(ary)

——— 2 ———

³ 上記 **jōki** the above-mentioned/aforesaid

下記 **kaki** the following

⁴ 日記 **nikki** diary, journal

⁵ 左記 **saki** the following

⁶ 伝記 **denki** biography

⁷ 快記録 **kaikiroku** a fine record

⁸ 表記 **hyōki** inscription, indication, declaration; orthography

追記 **tsuiki** postscript, P.S.

明記 **meiki** clearly state, specify, stipulate

⁹ 前記 **zenki** the above-mentioned

速記 **sokki** shorthand

後記 **kōki** postscript

¹¹ 略記 **ryakki** brief account, outline

¹² 登記 **tōki** registration, recording

¹³ 暗記 **anki** memorization

戦記 **senki** account of a war

¹⁹ 簿記 **boki** bookkeeping

——— 3 ———

³ 三面記事 **sanmen kiji** page-3 news, police news, human-interest stories

丸暗記 **maruanki** learn by heart/rote

⁵ 古事記 **Kojiki** (Japan's) Ancient Chronicles

⁹ 風土記 **fudoki** description of the natural features of a region, a topography

¹² 棒暗記 **bōanki** indiscriminate memorization

¹³ 歳時記 **saijiki** almanac -

7a3.6 / 771   言 儿 丨
                 67 16 2

訓   訓 訓

KUN Japanese reading of a kanji; teachings, precept SATOSHI (m. given name) KUNI, NORI (part of given name)

——— 1 ———

⁵ 訓令 **kunrei** instructions, directive

訓令式 **kunreishiki** (a system of romanization which differs from Hepburn romanization in such syllables as *shi/si, tsu/tu, cha/tya*)

¹⁴ 訓練 **kunren** training

訓読 **kundoku, kun'yo(mi)** native-Japanese reading of a kanji

——— 2 ———

⁹ 音訓 **onkun** Chinese and Japanese pronunciations of a kanji

¹⁰ 教訓 **kyōkun** lesson, precept, moral

——— 4 ———

7a4.1 / 1181   言 方
                 67 48

訪   訪 訪

HŌ, tazu(neru), otozu(reru), to(u) visit

——— 1 ———

⁴ 訪日 **hō-Nichi** visiting Japan

⁹ 訪客 **hōkyaku, hōkaku** visitor, guest

¹¹ 訪問 **hōmon** visit

——— 2 ———

⁷ 来訪 **raihō** visit, call

7a4.2   言 𠂉 一
                67 34 1

訣   訣 訣

KETSU separation, parting; secret

—————— 1 ——————

7 訣別 **ketsubetsu** parting, farewell

7a4.3 / 737

□ 言 ⺅ 十
67　15　12

許

許 許

KYO, yuru(su) permit, allow
moto with, at (someone's house)
-baka(ri) approximately; only; almost;
nothing but

—————— 1 ——————

5 許可 **kyoka** permission, approval,
　　authorization
7 許否 **kyohi** approval or disapproval
10 許容 **kyoyō** permission, tolerance

—————— 2 ——————

4 允許 **inkyo** permission, license
　　手許 **temoto** at hand; in one's care;
　　　ready cash
8 免許 **menkyo** license, permission
　　免許証 **menkyoshō** license, certifi-
　　　cate, permit
10 特許 **tokkyo** patent; special permis-
　　　sion
　　特許庁 **Tokkyochō** Patent Office
　　特許品 **tokkyohin** patented article
15 黙許 **mokkyo** tacit permission,
　　　connivance

—————— 3 ——————

12 無免許 **mumenkyo** without a li-
　　　cense

7a4.6 / 1403

□ 言 ⼏ 竹
67　16　17

訟

訟 訟

SHŌ accuse

—————— 2 ——————

12 訴訟 **soshō** lawsuit, litigation

7a4.7 / 577

田 言 冂 又
67　20　9

設

設 設

SETSU, mō(keru) provide, prepare,
establish, set up

—————— 1 ——————

5 設立 **setsuritsu** establishment,
　　founding
8 設定 **settei** establishment, creation
9 設計 **sekkei** design, planning
　　設計図 **sekkeizu** plan, blueprint
12 設備 **setsubi** equipment, facilities,
　　accommodations

—————— 2 ——————

4 公設 **kōsetsu** public
5 布設 **fusetsu** lay (cable/mines),
　　build (a railway/road) (also
　　spelled 敷設)
7 私設 **shisetsu** private, nongovern-
　　mental
8 建設 **kensetsu** construction
　　建設省 **Kensetsushō** Ministry of
　　Construction
9 架設 **kasetsu** construction, laying
　　施設 **shisetsu** facilities, institution
13 新設 **shinsetsu** newly established
14 増設 **zōsetsu** build on, extend, es-
　　tablish/install more
15 敷設 **fusetsu** lay (cable/mines),
　　build (a railway/road) (also
　　spelled 布設)

7a4.8 / 594

田 言 尸 丨
67　40　2

訳

譯 | 訳 訳

YAKU translation **wake** reason,
cause; meaning; circumstances, the case

—————— 1 ——————

0 訳す **yaku(su)** translate
8 訳注 **yakuchū** translation and an-
　　notation
　　訳者 **yakusha** translator

14 訳語 **yakugo** translated term, an equivalent

───── 2 ─────

4 内訳 **uchiwake** itemization, breakdown

5 申訳 **mō(shi)wake** excuse, apology

6 全訳 **zen'yaku** complete translation

邦訳 **hōyaku** translation into Japanese

7 対訳 **taiyaku** bilingual text (with Japanese and English side by side)

言訳 **i(i)wake** excuse, explanation, apology

8 直訳 **chokuyaku** literal translation

英訳 **eiyaku** English translation

和訳 **wayaku** translation into Japanese

9 通訳 **tsūyaku** interpreting; interpreter

音訳 **on'yaku** transliteration

14 誤訳 **goyaku** mistranslation

18 翻訳 **hon'yaku** translation

翻訳者 **hon'yakusha** translator

───── 3 ─────

9 逐語訳 **chikugoyaku** word-for-word/literal translation

───── 5 ─────

7a5.2 / 1402

□	言	斤	l
67	50	2	

訴訴

SO, utta(eru) sue; complain of; appeal to

───── 1 ─────

11 訴訟 **soshō** lawsuit, litigation

19 訴願 **sogan** petition, appeal

───── 2 ─────

7 告訴 **kokuso** accuse, charge, bring suit

8 免訴 **menso** dismissal (of a case), acquittal

10 起訴 **kiso** prosecute, indict; sue, bring action against

11 控訴院 **kōsoin** court of appeal

12 勝訴 **shōso** winning a lawsuit

7a5.3 / 1028

□	言	小	二
67	35	4	

評評

HYŌ criticism, comment

───── 1 ─────

7 評判 **hyōban** fame, popularity; rumor, gossip

8 評価 **hyōka** appraisal

15 評論 **hyōron** criticism, critique, commentary

評論家 **hyōronka** critic, commentator

───── 2 ─────

3 寸評 **sunpyō** brief review/commentary

大評判 **daihyōban** sensation, smash

5 好評 **kōhyō** favorable reception, popularity

6 再評価 **saihyōka** reassessment, reevaluation

自評 **jihyō** self-criticism

7 批評 **hihyō** criticism, critique, review

10 時評 **jihyō** (editorial) commentary

書評 **shohyō** book review

11 悪評 **akuhyō** bad reputation; unfavorable criticism

14 総評 **Sōhyō** General Council of Trade Unions of Japan (short for 日本労働組合総評議会)

酷評 **kokuhyō** sharp/harsh criticism

15 論評 **ronpyō** comment, criticism, review

───── 3 ─────

3 下馬評 **gebahyō** outsiders' irresponsible talk, rumor

註 → 註 7a5.11

7

言 5
貝
車
足
酉

7a5.4 　　　田 言 月 一
67 42 1

詛詛

SO, noro(u) curse

7a5.5 / 484 　　　田 言 エ 一
67 38 1

證 | 証証

SHŌ proof, evidence; certificate
akashi proof, evidence

------ 1 ------

2 証人 **shōnin** witness
6 証印 **shōin** seal on a document
7 証言 **shōgen** testimony
8 証券 **shōken** securities
　証拠 **shōko** evidence, proof
　証明 **shōmei** proof, corroboration
　証明書 **shōmeisho** certificate
13 証跡 **shōseki** evidence, traces

------ 2 ------

4 内証 **naishō** secret; internal evidence; one's circumstances
8 実証 **jisshō** actual proof
9 保証 **hoshō** guarantee
　保証人 **hoshōnin** guarantor
　査証 **sashō** visa; investigation and attestation
11 偽証 **gishō** false testimony, perjury
12 検証 **kenshō** verification, inspection
14 認証 **ninshō** certify, attest, authenticate
15 論証 **ronshō** demonstration, proof

------ 3 ------

8 免許証 **menkyoshō** license, certificate, permit
14 領収証 **ryōshūshō** receipt

7a5.6 / 1498 　　　田 言 𠂉 𠃊
67 15 13

詐詐

SA, itsuwa(ru) lie, deceive

------ 1 ------

12 詐欺 **sagi** fraud
　詐欺師 **sagishi** swindler, con man

7a5.9 / 1214 　　　田 言 彡 亻
67 31 3

診診

SHIN, mi(ru) see (a patient), examine, diagnose

------ 1 ------

11 診断 **shindan** diagnosis
14 診察 **shinsatsu** medical examination

------ 2 ------

5 打診 **dashin** percussion, tapping (in medicine); sound/feel out
6 休診 **kyūshin** see no patients, Clinic Closed
8 受診 **jushin** receive a medical examination
12 検診 **kenshin** medical examination
14 誤診 **goshin** misdiagnosis

7a5.10 / 1885 　　　田 言 口 力
67 24 8

詔詔

SHŌ, mikotonori imperial edict

------ 1 ------

9 詔勅 **shōchoku** imperial proclamation
10 詔書 **shōsho** imperial edict/rescript

7a5.11 / 1978   田 言 王 丨
67 46 2

註 丨 註 詿

CHŪ note, comment, annotation

———— 1 ————
¹¹ 註釈 **chūshaku** annotation, commentary
¹³ 註解 **chūkai** notes, commentary

———— 2 ————
¹¹ 脚註 **kyakuchū** footnote

7a5.14 / 1209   田 言 氵 丨
67 21 2

詠 丨 詠 詠

EI poem, song; singing; composing
yo(mu) compose, write (a poem)

———— 1 ————
¹³ 詠嘆 **eitan** exclamation; admiration
¹⁴ 詠歎 **eitan** exclamation; admiration

———— 2 ————
⁷ 吟詠 **gin'ei** sing, recite; (compose a) poem
¹⁰ 朗詠 **rōei** recite

7a5.15 / 843   田 言 口 一
67 24 1

詞 詞

SHI, kotoba words

———— 2 ————
⁵ 台詞 **serifu** (actor's) lines, what one says
⁶ 名詞 **meishi** noun
⁷ 助詞 **joshi** a particle (in grammar)
⁸ 枕詞 **makurakotoba** prefatory word, set epithet
⁹ 冠詞 **kanshi** article (in grammar)
¹¹ 副詞 **fukushi** adverb
動詞 **dōshi** verb

¹³ 数詞 **sūshi** numeral, number word
¹⁴ 歌詞 **kashi** the lyrics/words (of a song)

———— 3 ————
⁵ 代名詞 **daimeishi** pronoun
他動詞 **tadōshi** transitive verb
⁶ 自動詞 **jidōshi** intransitive verb
⁷ 助動詞 **jodōshi** auxiliary verb
形容詞 **keiyōshi** adjective
¹¹ 接続詞 **setsuzokushi** a conjunction
¹² 間投詞 **kantōshi** an interjection

———— 4 ————
⁷ 形容動詞 **keiyōdōshi** quasi-adjective used with -na (e.g., shi-zuka, kirei)
⁸ 固有名詞 **koyū meishi** proper noun

———— 6 ————

7a6.3 / 718   田 言 戈 宀
67 52 15

誠 誠

SEI, makoto sincerity, fidelity; truth, reality **MAKOTO** (m. given name)
SEI, MASA (part of given name)

———— 1 ————
¹ 誠一 **Seiichi, Makoto** (m. given name)
⁸ 誠実 **seijitsu** sincere, faithful, truthful
¹³ 誠意 **seii** sincerity, good faith

———— 2 ————
⁴ 丹誠 **tansei** sincerity; diligence
⁸ 忠誠 **chūsei** loyalty, allegiance

7a6.5 / 570   田 言 土 寸
67 22 37

詩 詩

SHI poem, poetry **UTA** (part of given name)

———— 1 ————
² 詩人 **shijin** poet
⁸ 詩的 **shiteki** poetic

7 言 6
貝
車
足
酉

12 詩集 **shishū** a collection of poems
14 詩選 **shisen** poetry anthology
   詩歌 **shiika, shika** poetry

――――――― 3 ―――――――

9 叙情詩 **jojōshi** lyric poem/poetry

7a6.6

田 言 宀 十
67 33 12

詫 詫

TA apologize; boast; bewail
wa(biru) apologize, make an excuse
wa(bi) apology, excuse

――――――― 1 ―――――――

7 詫状 **wa(bi)jō** written apology

7a6.7 / 1142

田 言 土 口
67 22 24

詰 詰

KITSU, tsu(meru) cram, stuff; shorten
-zu(me) packed in (cans/bottles)
tsu(maru) be stopped up, be jammed;
shrink; be cornered **tsu(mu)** be
pressed/packed in **naji(ru)** reprove, re-
buke

――――――― 1 ―――――――

4 詰込 **tsu(me)ko(mu)** cram, stuff,
   pack in
11 詰掛 **tsu(me)ka(keru)** throng to,
   besiege, crowd
   詰問 **kitsumon** cross-examination,
   grilling

――――――― 2 ―――――――

3 大詰 **ōzu(me)** finale, final scene
4 切詰 **ki(ri)tsu(meru)** shorten; reduce, economize, curtail, retrench
6 気詰 **kizu(mari)** feeling of awkwardness, ill at ease
   缶詰 **kanzume** canned goods
   行詰 **yu(ki)zu(mari), i(ki)-
   zu(mari)** dead end, deadlock,
   standstill

7 折詰 **o(ri)zu(me)** (food/lunch)
   packed in a cardboard/thin-
   wood box
   見詰 **mitsu(meru)** gaze/stare at
8 追詰 **o(i)tsu(meru)** corner, drive to
   the wall, hunt down
9 思詰 **omo(i)tsu(meru)** think hard,
   brood over
11 瓶詰 **binzu(me)** bottling; bottled
13 腸詰 **chōzu(me)** sausage
15 箱詰 **hakozume** packed in cases,
   boxed
16 樽詰 **taruzu(me)** barreled, in casks

7a6.8 / 238

田 言 口 十
67 24 12

話 話

WA, hanashi talk, conversation,
story **hana(su)** speak

――――――― 1 ―――――――

4 話中 **hana(shi)chū** in the midst of
   speaking; (phone is) busy
   話手 **hana(shi)te** speaker
   話方 **hana(shi)kata** way of speaking
6 話合 **hana(shi)a(u)** talk over, discuss
7 話言葉 **hana(shi)kotoba** spoken
   language
9 話相手 **hanashi aite** someone to
   talk to; companion
11 話掛 **hana(shi)ka(keru)** speak to,
   accost
18 話題 **wadai** topic, subject

――――――― 2 ―――――――

4 手話 **shuwa** sign language
5 民話 **minwa** folk tale, folklore
   世話 **sewa** help, assistance; good
   offices, recommendation; take
   care of; everyday life
   立話 **ta(chi)banashi** standing and
   chatting
6 会話 **kaiwa** conversation
7 作話 **tsuku(ri)banashi** made-up
   story, fabrication, fable
   伽話 **(o)togibanashi** fairy tale

8 長話 **nagabanashi** a long/tedious talk

受話器 **juwaki** (telephone) receiver

昔話 **mukashibanashi** old tale, legend

9 通話 **tsūwa** telephone call/conversation

指話 **shiwa** finger language, dactylology

茶話会 **sawakai, chawakai** tea party

神話 **shinwa** myth, mythology

10 逸話 **itsuwa** anecdote

笑話 **wara(i)banashi, shōwa** funny story

12 寓話 **gūwa** fable, parable, allegory

童話 **dōwa** children's story, fairy tale

13 裏話 **urabanashi** inside story, story behind the story

電話 **denwa** telephone

電話局 **denwakyoku** telephone office

電話料 **denwaryō** telephone charges

電話帳 **denwachō** telephone directory

14 説話 **setsuwa** tale, narrative

15 噂話 **uwasabanashi** rumor, gossip, hearsay

談話 **danwa** conversation

――――――― 3 ―――――――
7 身上話 **mi(no)uebanashi** one's life story

8 英会話 **eikaiwa** English conversation

青電話 **aodenwa** public telephone

――――――― 5 ―――――――
10 留守番電話 **rusuban denwa** answering machine

7a6.9 / 1629   言 大 二
                    67 34 4

KO, hoko(ru) boast of, be proud of

――――――― 1 ―――――――
3 誇大 **kodai** exaggeration
11 誇張 **kochō** exaggeration

――――――― 2 ―――――――
12 勝誇 **ka(chi)hoko(ru)** triumph, exult in victory

詮 → 詮 **7a6.14**

7a6.10 / 1213   言 亠 竹
                     67 11 17

GAI the said

――――――― 1 ―――――――
6 該当 **gaitō** pertain to, come/fall under

該当者 **gaitōsha** the said person
12 該博 **gaihaku** profound, vast (learning)

7a6.11   言 勹 厂
             67 15 18

KI lie, deceive

――――――― 1 ―――――――
5 詭弁 **kiben** sophistry, logic-chopping

詭弁家 **kibenka** sophist, quibbler

7a6.12 / 1577   言 王 儿
                     67 46 16

SHŌ, kuwa(shii), tsumabi(raka) detailed, full; familiar with (something)

――――――― 1 ―――――――
7 詳述 **shōjutsu** detailed explanation, full account

11 詳細 **shōsai** details, particulars

2

⁴ 不詳 **fushō** unknown, unidentified

⁵ 未詳 **mishō** unknown, unidentified

7a6.13 / 1974

67 43 13

詣　詣詣

KEI, mō(de), mai(ri) visit to a temple/shrine

2

⁷ 初詣 **hatsumōde** first shrine/temple visit in the new year

7a6.14

67 46 3

詮｜詮詮

SEN clarity, reason, truth; investigation; efficacy

1

¹⁰ 詮索 **sensaku** search, inquiry

2

⁸ 所詮 **shosen** after all

7a6.17 / 2240

67 43 15

詢詢

JUN consult with　JUN, SHUN (part of given name)　MAKOTO (m. given name)

7a6.18 / 526

67 52 38

試試

SHI, kokoro(miru), tame(su) give it a try, try out, attempt

1

⁶ 試合 **shiai** game, match

試行錯誤 **shikō-sakugo** trial and error

⁹ 試食 **shishoku** sample, taste

¹⁰ 試案 **shian** draft, tentative plan

¹¹ 試運転 **shiunten** trial run

¹⁴ 試演 **shien** rehearsal, preview

試練 **shiren** trial, test, ordeal

¹⁷ 試聴 **shichō** audition

¹⁸ 試験 **shiken** examination, test; experiment, test

試験地獄 **shiken jigoku** the hell of (entrance) exams

2

⁶ 再試合 **saishiai** rematch, resumption of a game

3

² 入学試験 **nyūgaku shiken** entrance exams

7

7a7.2 / 906

67 24 16

誤｜誤誤

GO, ayama(ru) err, make a mistake

1

⁵ 誤用 **goyō** misuse

誤字 **goji** incorrect character, misprint

¹⁰ 誤差 **gosa** error, aberration

¹¹ 誤訳 **goyaku** mistranslation

¹² 誤報 **gohō** erroneous report/information

誤植 **goshoku** misprint

誤診 **goshin** misdiagnosis

¹³ 誤解 **gokai** misunderstanding

¹⁴ 誤算 **gosan** miscalculation

誤読 **godoku** misreading

誤聞 **gobun** mishearing; misinformation

¹⁵ 誤審 **goshin** error in refereeing

²¹ 誤魔化 **gomaka(su)** cheat, deceive; gloss over; tamper with, doctor

——— 2 ———

5 正誤表 **seigohyō** errata

14 読誤 **yo(mi)ayama(ru)** misread

16 錯誤 **sakugo** error

——— 4 ———

13 試行錯誤 **shikō-sakugo** trial and error

7a7.4 / 1684

田 言 禾 力
67 56 8

誘 誘

YŪ, saso(u) invite; induce; entice, lure **izana(u)** invite; lead; entice **obi(ku)** lure, entice

——— 1 ———

8 誘拐 **yūkai** kidnapping, abduction

12 誘惑 **yūwaku** temptation, seduction

14 誘導 **yūdō** induction; incitement; guidance

——— 2 ———

13 勧誘 **kan'yū** solicitation, invitation, canvassing

7a7.6 / 67

田 言 口 丁
67 24 14

語 語

GO word **kata(ru)** talk, relate **kata(rau)** converse, chat

——— 1 ———

4 語手 **kata(ri)te** narrator, storyteller

5 語末 **gomatsu** word ending
語句 **goku** words and phrases

6 語合 **kata(ri)a(u)** talk together, chat

7 語学 **gogaku** language learning; linguistics
語尾 **gobi** word ending

8 語法 **gohō** phraseology, usage, diction

13 語彙 **goi** vocabulary
語源 **gogen** derivation, etymology

語幹 **gokan** stem, root of a word
語意 **goi** meaning of a word

——— 2 ———

1 一語 **ichigo** one word

3 口語 **kōgo** colloquial language

4 文語 **bungo** literary language
文語体 **bungotai** literary style

5 古語 **kogo** archaic/obsolete word; old saying
用語 **yōgo** term, terminology, vocabulary
主語 **shugo** subject (in grammar)

6 死語 **shigo** dead language; obsolete word
成語 **seigo** set phrase, idiomatic expression
米語 **belgo** American English

7 述語 **jutsugo** predicate
季語 **kigo** word indicating the season (in haiku)
言語 **gengo** language, speech **i(wazu)kata(razu)** tacitly
言語学 **gengogaku** linguistics, philology

8 英語 **eigo** the English language
国語 **kokugo** national/Japanese language
物語 **monogatari** tale, story
和語 **wago** (native) Japanese word

9 俗語 **zokugo** colloquial language, slang
勅語 **chokugo** imperial rescript
逐語的 **chikugoteki** word for word, literal
逐語訳 **chikugoyaku** word-for-word/literal translation
造語 **zōgo** coined word
単語 **tango** word
卑語 **higo** vulgar word/expression

11 剰語 **jōgo** redundancy
梵語 **bongo** Sanskrit
略語 **ryakugo** abbreviation
訳語 **yakugo** translated term, an equivalent

12 落語 **rakugo** comic storytelling
落語家 **rakugoka** comic storyteller
敬語 **keigo** an honorific, term of respect

13 隠語 **ingo** secret language; argot, jargon

鄙語 **higo** vulgar word/expression

新語 **shingo** new word, neologism

14 熟語 **jukugo** word of two or more kanji, compound; phrase

15 標語 **hyōgo** slogan, motto

—————— 3 ——————

4 反対語 **hantaigo** antonym

反意語 **han'igo** antonym

日本語 **nihongo** the Japanese language

5 母国語 **bokokugo** one's mother/native tongue

外来語 **gairaigo** word of foreign origin, loanword

外国語 **gaikokugo** foreign language

目的語 **mokutekigo** object (in grammar)

6 同音語 **dōongo** homophone, homonym

同義語 **dōgigo** synonym

同意語 **dōigo** synonym

7 見出語 **mida(shi)go** headword, entry word

10 流行語 **ryūkōgo** popular phrase, catchword

11 接尾語 **setsubigo** suffix

現代語 **gendaigo** modern language

14 慣用語 **kan'yōgo** idiom, colloquial word/phrase

複合語 **fukugōgo** compound word

15 標準語 **hyōjungo** the standard language

17 擬声語 **giseigo** onomatopoetic word

18 類義語 **ruigigo** words of similar meaning

—————— 4 ——————

7 学術用語 **gakujutsu yōgo** technical term

13 源氏物語 **Genji Monogatari** The Tale of Genji

7a7.8 / 574

SHI write down, chronicle; magazine

—————— 1 ——————

3 誌上 **shijō** in a magazine

9 誌面 **shimen** page of a magazine

—————— 2 ——————

10 書誌 **shoshi** bibliography

14 雑誌 **zasshi** magazine

—————— 3 ——————

7 季刊誌 **kikanshi** a quarterly (magazine)

10 週刊誌 **shūkanshi** a weekly (magazine)

16 機関誌 **kikanshi** organization's publication

7a7.9 / 244

DOKU, TOKU, TŌ, yo(mu) read

—————— 1 ——————

3 読上 **yo(mi)a(geru)** read aloud/out; finish reading

4 読方 **yo(mi)kata** reading, pronunciation (of a character)

5 読本 **tokuhon** reader, book of readings

6 読返 **yo(mi)kae(su)** reread

8 読易 **yo(mi)yasu(i)** easy to read

読者 **dokusha** reader

読物 **yo(mi)mono** reading matter

9 読点 **tōten** comma

読通 **yo(mi)tō(su)** read it through

10 読書 **dokusho** reading

yo(mi)ka(ki) reading and writing

12 読違 **yo(mi)chiga(i)** misreading

読落 **yo(mi)o(tosu)** overlook in reading

14 読誤 **yo(mi)ayama(ru)** misread

18 読難 **yo(mi)niku(i)** hard to read

確認 **kakunin** confirm, verify

―――― 2 ――――

1 一読 **ichidoku** a perusal/reading

5 必読 **hitsudoku** required reading, a must read

句読点 **kutōten** punctuation mark

立読 **ta(chi)yo(mi)** read while standing (at a magazine rack)

9 音読 **ondoku** reading aloud
on'yo(mi) the Chinese reading of a kanji

秒読 **byōyo(mi)** countdown

10 朗読 **rōdoku** read aloud

訓読 **kundoku, kun'yo(mi)** native-Japanese reading of a kanji

13 解読 **kaidoku** decipher, decrypt

14 愛読 **aidoku** like to read

誤読 **godoku** misreading

17 購読 **kōdoku** subscription

購読料 **kōdokuryō** subscription price/fee

18 難読 **nandoku** a difficult reading

7a7.10 / 738   田 言 忌 力
                                     67 51 8

NIN, mito(meru) perceive; recognize; approve **shitata(meru)** write, draw up; eat

―――― 1 ――――

5 認可 **ninka** approval

8 認定 **nintei** approval, acknowledgment

10 認容 **nin'yō** admit, accept

12 認証 **ninshō** certify, attest, authenticate

19 認識 **ninshiki** (re)cognition, perception, knowledge

―――― 2 ――――

4 公認 **kōnin** officially authorized, certified

6 自認 **jinin** acknowledge, admit

7 承認 **shōnin** approval

否認 **hinin** deny, repudiate

15 黙認 **mokunin** tacit approval/admission

―――― 3 ――――

6 再確認 **saikakunin** reaffirmation

7a7.11 / 2242   田 言 口 亠
                                      67 24 11

JUN carefully, earnestly, repeatedly
JUN, SHUN, ATSU, SHIGE, TOMO, NOBU, SANE (part of given name) ATSUSHI, MAKOTO, ITARU, SHUN (m. given name)

7a7.12 / 400   田 言 口 儿
                                    67 24 16

SETSU opinion, theory
ZEI, to(ku) explain; persuade

―――― 1 ――――

8 説明 **setsumei, to(ki)a(kashi)** explanation

説明書 **setsumeisho** (written) explanation, instructions, manual

10 説教 **sekkyō** sermon

11 説得 **settoku** persuasion

12 説落 **to(ki)o(tosu)** win over, talk into

13 説話 **setsuwa** tale, narrative

―――― 2 ――――

1 一説 **issetsu** one/another view

3 口説 **kudo(ku)** persuade, entreat, woo, court **kuzetsu** quarrel; curtain lecture

小説 **shōsetsu** novel, story, fiction

小説家 **shōsetsuka** novelist, (fiction) writer

6 伝説 **densetsu** legend

仮説 **kasetsu** hypothesis, tentative theory

7 序説 **josetsu** introduction, preface

図説 **zusetsu** explanatory diagram, illustration

社説 **shasetsu** an editorial

7

言
貝
車
足
酉

8 逆説 **gyakusetsu** paradox
定説 **teisetsu** established/accepted opinion
9 俗説 **zokusetsu** common saying; folklore
11 細説 **saisetsu** detailed explanation
13 解説 **kaisetsu** explanation, commentary
14 演説 **enzetsu** speech, address
15 諸説 **shosetsu** various views/accounts
論説 **ronsetsu** dissertation; editorial

— 3 —

7 私小説 **watakushi shōsetsu** novel narrated in the first person; autobiographical novel
shishōsetsu autobiographical novel

— 4 —

11 推理小説 **suiri shōsetsu** detective story, whodunit
12 短篇小説 **tanpen shōsetsu** short story/novel

7a7.14

| ⊞ | 言 | 月 | 一 |
| 67 | 42 | 1 |

誦誦

SHŌ, JU recite, chant

7a7.15 / 1116

| ⊞ | 言 | 辶 | 卜 |
| 67 | 19 | 13 |

誕誕

TAN birth

— 1 —

5 誕生 **tanjō** birth
誕生日 **tanjōbi** birthday
誕生祝 **tanjō iwa(i)** birthday celebration

— 2 —

13 聖誕祭 **Seitansai** Christmas

7a7.17 / 1395

| ⊞ | 言 | 斤 | 扌 |
| 67 | 50 | 23 |

誓誓

SEI, chika(u) swear, pledge, vow

— 1 —

9 誓約 **seiyaku** oath, vow, pledge

— 2 —

9 宣誓 **sensei** oath, vow, pledge

— 8 —

7a8.1 / 1979

| □ | 隹 | 言 |
| 74 | 67 |

誰誰

SUI, dare, tare who

— 1 —

1 誰一人 **dare hitori (mo)** (with negative) no one

諌 → 諫 **7a9.1**

7a8.2 / 488

| □ | 言 | 日 | 木 |
| 67 | 43 | 41 |

課課

KA lesson; section; levy, impose

— 1 —

5 課目 **kamoku** subject (in school), item
8 課長 **kachō** section chief
12 課程 **katei** course, curriculum
課税 **kazei** taxation
18 課題 **kadai** subject, theme, topic, problem; (school) assignment

— 2 —

5 正課 **seika** regular curriculum/course
7 学課 **gakka** lessons, schoolwork
8 非課税 **hikazei** tax exemption

——————— 3 ———————

¹⁴ 総務課 **sōmuka** general affairs section

7a8.3 / 861　　　　□ 言 日 土
　　　　　　　　　　67 43 22

諸 | 諸 諸

SHO- all, various, many, (prefix indicating plural) **moro-** various, all, both, every sort of

——————— 1 ———————

³ 諸々 **moromoro** various, all, every sort of

⁸ 諸国 **shokoku** all/various countries

¹⁰ 諸島 **shotō** islands

¹⁴ 諸説 **shosetsu** various views/accounts

——————— 3 ———————

¹³ 隠岐諸島 **Oki shotō** (group of islands, Shimane-ken)

7a8.4　　　　　　□ 言 耳 又
　　　　　　　　　　67 65 9

諏 諏

SHU, SU consult with

7a8.5　　　　　　□ 言 二 ト
　　　　　　　　　　67 4 13

誹 誹

HI speak ill of, slander

——————— 1 ———————

¹⁶ 誹諧 **haikai** humorous poem; 17-syllable poem

7a8.6 / 1920　　　□ 言 日 亠
　　　　　　　　　　67 43 15

謁 | 謁 謁

ETSU audience (with someone)

——————— 1 ———————

⁷ 謁見 **ekken** have an audience with

7a8.7 / 593　　　　□ 言 火
　　　　　　　　　　67 44

談 談

DAN conversation

——————— 1 ———————

¹⁰ 談笑 **danshō** chat, friendly talk

¹³ 談話 **danwa** conversation

——————— 2 ———————

⁴ 冗談 **jōdan** a joke

⁵ 示談 **jidan** out-of-court settlement

⁶ 会談 **kaidan** conversation, conference

⁷ 対談 **taidan** face-to-face talk, conversation, interview

⁸ 放談 **hōdan** random/unreserved talk

　 怪談 **kaidan** ghost story

⁹ 相談 **sōdan** consult, confer; proposal; arrangements

¹⁰ 座談会 **zadankai** round-table discussion, symposium

¹¹ 商談 **shōdan** business talks/negotiations

¹² 猥談 **waidan** indecent talk, dirty story

¹⁴ 雑談 **zatsudan** chitchat, idle conversation

¹⁵ 歓談 **kandan** pleasant chat

　 縁談 **endan** marriage proposal

¹⁷ 懇談会 **kondankai** get-together, friendly discussion

——————— 4 ———————

⁵ 主脳会談 **shunō kaidan** summit conference

7

言 **8**
貝
車
足
酉

9 首脳会談 **shunō kaidan** summit conference

7a8.8 / 661

67 42 22

SEI, SHIN, SHŌ request; invite **ko(u)** ask for **u(keru)** receive, undertake

——— 1 ———

6 請合 **u(ke)a(u)** undertake; guarantee, vouch for **u(ke)a(i)** sure, certain, guaranteed
7 請求 **seikyū** demand, request
請求書 **seikyūsho** application, claim, bill
9 請負 **u(ke)o(u)** contract for, undertake **ukeoi** contracting
19 請願 **seigan** petition, application

——— 2 ———

3 下請 **shitauke** subcontract
5 申請 **shinsei** application, petition
9 要請 **yōsei** demand, call for, require

7a8.10 / 1770

 67 32 24

DAKU consent, agree to **ubena(u)** agree to

——— 1 ———

7 諾否 **dakuhi** acceptance or refusal, definite reply

——— 2 ———

7 承諾 **shōdaku** consent
15 黙諾 **mokudaku** tacit consent

7a8.11 / 2241

 67 42 33

GI friendship, fellowship; good **yoshi(mi)** friendship, fellowship, good will GI, YOSHI, KOTO (part of given name) YOSHIMI (f. given name)

7a8.13 / 293

 67 32 3

RON discussion, argument; thesis, dissertation **agetsura(u)** discuss, comment on

——— 1 ———

0 論じる/ずる **ron(jiru/zuru)** discuss, argue, comment on, deal with, consider
4 論文 **ronbun** thesis, essay
6 論考 **ronkō** a study
論争 **ronsō** dispute, controversy
8 論拠 **ronkyo** grounds, basis
論者 **ronsha** disputant; advocate; this writer, I
11 論理 **ronri** logic
論理上 **ronrijō** logically (speaking)
12 論評 **ronpyō** comment, criticism, review
論証 **ronshō** demonstration, proof
14 論説 **ronsetsu** dissertation; editorial
20 論議 **rongi** discussion, argument

——— 2 ———

4 勿論 **mochiron** of course, naturally
反論 **hanron** counterargument, refutation
5 弁論 **benron** argument, debate; oral proceedings, pleading
世論 **seron, yoron** public opinion
6 争論 **sōron** dispute, argument, controversy
各論 **kakuron** detailed discussion

7 序論 **joron** introduction, preface

言論 **genron** speech, discussion

10 討論 **tōron** debate, discussion

討論会 **tōronkai** forum, debate, discussion

11 理論 **riron** theory

12 無論 **muron** of course, naturally

結論 **ketsuron** conclusion

評論 **hyōron** criticism, critique, commentary

評論家 **hyōronka** critic, commentator

13 愚論 **guron** foolish argument/opinion

14 概論 **gairon** general remarks, outline, introduction

駁論 **bakuron** refutation, rebuttal

16 激論 **gekiron** heated argument

20 議論 **giron** argument, discussion, controversy

——————— 3 ———————

2 二元論 **nigenron** dualism

6 多元論 **tagenron** pluralism

11 唯心論 **yuishinron** idealism, spiritualism

唯物論 **yuibutsuron** materialism

12 無神論 **mushinron** atheism

悲観論者 **hikanronsha** pessimist

16 懐疑論 **kaigiron** skepticism

7a8.14 / 2243   口 言 口 小
                  67 24 35

諒   諒 諒

RYŌ understanding, sympathy; true, sincere **MAKOTO** (m. given name) RYŌ, MASA, AKI, ASA (part of given name)

——————— 1 ———————

7 諒承 **ryōshō** acknowledge, understand, note

 謎 → 謎   **7a9.20**

7a8.16 / 342   口 言 月 口
                      67 42 24

調   調 | 調 調

CHŌ investigate; order, harmony; tune, tone **shira(beru)** investigate, check **shira(be)** investigation; melody, tune **totono(eru)** prepare, arrange, put in order **totono(u)** be prepared/arranged, be in order

——————— 1 ———————

2 調子 **chōshi** tone; mood; condition

5 調号 **chōgō** key signature (in music)

6 調合 **chōgō** compounding, mixing

調印 **chōin** signing (of a treaty)

8 調味料 **chōmiryō** condiments, seasonings

調物 **shira(be)mono** matter for inquiry

調和 **chōwa** harmony

9 調査 **chōsa** investigation, inquiry, survey, research

10 調書 **chōsho** protocol, record

11 調停 **chōtei** arbitration, mediation, conciliation

調理 **chōri** cooking

13 調節 **chōsetsu** adjust, control, regulate

16 調整 **chōsei** adjust, regulate, coordinate

——————— 2 ———————

3 下調 **shitashira(be)** preliminary investigation; prepare (lessons)

4 不調 **fuchō** failure to agree; out of sorts

不調法 **buchōhō** impoliteness; carelessness; misconduct; awkward, inexperienced

5 失調 **shitchō** malfunction, lack of coordination

好調 **kōchō** good, favorable, satisfactory

6 同調 **dōchō** alignment; tuning

7 低調 **teichō** low-pitched; dull, inactive, sluggish (market)

快調 **kaichō** harmony; excellent condition

8 協調 **kyōchō** cooperation, conciliation

步調 **hochō** pace, step

取調 **to(ri)shira(beru)** investigate, look into

9 変調 **henchō** change of tone/key; irregular, abnormal; modulation (in radio)

単調 **tanchō** monotonous

11 強調 **kyōchō** emphasis, stress

12 短調 **tanchō** minor key

無調法 **buchōhō** impolite; clumsy, unaccustomed to

順調 **junchō** favorable, smooth, without a hitch

16 諧調 **kaichō** harmony, euphony

——— 3 ———

1 一本調子 **ipponchōshi, ipponjōshi** monotony

8 国勢調査 **kokusei chōsa** (national) census

——— 9 ———

7a9.1 ⊞ 言 木 口
67 41 24

諫 | 諫 諫

KAN, isa(meru) remonstrate with, admonish

——— 1 ———

4 諫止 **kanshi** dissuade from

7 諫言 **kangen** remonstrate with, admonish

諸 → 諸 7a8.3

7a9.4 / 1769 ⊞ 言 夂 口
67 49 24

諮 諮

SHI, haka(ru) consult, confer, solicit advice

——— 1 ———

11 諮問 **shimon** question, inquiry; question, inquiry; consultive, advisory (body)

諺 → 諺 7a9.15

7a9.7 ⊞ 言 木 艹
67 41 32

謀 謀 謀

CHŌ spy out, reconnoiter

——— 1 ———

12 諜報 **chōhō** intelligence, espionage

7a9.8 / 1495 ⊞ 言 木 艹
67 41 32

謀 謀

BŌ, MU, haka(ru) plan, devise; deceive **tabaka(ru)** cheat, take in **hakarigoto** plan, scheme, plot

——— 1 ———

11 謀略 **bōryaku** stratagem, scheme

——— 2 ———

5 主謀者 **shubōsha** (ring)leader, mastermind

6 共謀 **kyōbō** conspiracy

8 参謀 **sanbō** staff officer; adviser

10 陰謀 **inbō** conspiracy, plot, intrigue

12 策謀 **sakubō** stratagem, machinations

謁 → 謁 7a8.6

7a9.9 / 1647 ⊞ 言 小 山
67 35 36

謡 | 謡 謡

YŌ song; (Noh) chanting **uta(u)** sing (without accompaniment), chant **utai** Noh chanting

—— 2 ——

⁵ 民謡 **min'yō** folk song

¹² 童謡 **dōyō** children's song, nursery rhyme

¹⁴ 歌謡曲 **kayōkyoku** popular song

7a9.11

口　言　月　闩
67　43　13

諧　諧

KAI order, harmony

—— 1 ——

¹⁵ 諧調 **kaichō** harmony, euphony

—— 2 ——

¹⁵ 誹諧 **haikai** humorous poem; 17-syllable poem

7a9.13 / 1599

口　言　月　亻
67　42　3

諭 | 諭 諭

YU, sato(su) admonish, remonstrate, warn, counsel　SATOSHI (m. given name)

—— 2 ——

¹⁰ 教諭 **kyōyu** instructor, teacher

7a9.15

口　言　立　彡
67　54　31

諺 | 諺 諺

GEN, kotowaza proverb

7a9.20

口　言　米　辶
67　62　19

謎 | 謎 謎

MEI, nazo riddle, puzzle, enigma

7a9.21

口　言　虫　冂
67　64　20

諷

諷 諷

FŪ hint at, allude to

—— 1 ——

⁸ 諷刺 **fūshi** satire, sarcasm, lampoon
諷刺画 **fūshiga** caricature, cartoon

—— 10 ——

7a10.1 / 901

口　言　月　寸
67　42　37

謝

謝 謝

SHA gratitude; apology
ayama(ru) apologize

—— 1 ——

⁵ 謝礼 **sharei** remuneration, honorarium

¹² 謝絶 **shazetsu** refuse, decline

¹³ 謝意 **shai** gratitude; apology
謝罪 **shazai** apology

—— 2 ——

⁴ 月謝 **gessha** monthly tuition

⁵ 代謝 **taisha** metabolism

¹³ 感謝 **kansha** gratitude, appreciation

¹⁵ 慰謝料 **isharyō** consolation money, solatium

7a10.3 / 783

口　言　王　艹
67　46　32

講

講 | 講 講

KŌ lecture, study; club, association

—— 1 ——

⁸ 講和 **kōwa** make peace with

¹⁰ 講師 **kōshi** lecturer, instructor
講座 **kōza** course (of lectures); professorship, chair

¹¹ 講習 **kōshū** short course, training

7

言 10
貝
車
足
酉

13 講義 **kōgi** lecture

14 講演 **kōen** lecture, address

講演会 **kōenkai** lecture meeting

— 2 —

8 受講 **jukō** take lectures

17 聴講 **chōkō** attendance at a lecture

詞 → 歌 **4j10.2**

謡 → 謡 **7a9.9**

譁 → 嘩 **3d10.7**

7a10.6 / 1247 ⊞ 言 艹 口   67 32 24

謹 | 謹 謹

KIN, tsutsushi(mu) be respectful

— 1 —

7 謹呈 **kintei** Respectfully presented, With the compliments of the author

12 謹賀新年 **kinga shinnen** Happy New Year

7a10.10 / 1687 ⊞ 言 彐 几   67 39 16

謙 | 謙 謙

KEN modesty, humility

— 1 —

11 謙遜 **kenson** modesty, humility

20 謙譲 **kenjō** modesty, humility

— 11 —

謹 → 謹 **7a10.6**

— 12 —

7a12.2 / 1167 ⊞ 言 日   67 43 38

譜 | 譜 譜

FU (sheet) music, notes, staff, score; a genealogy; record

— 2 —

7 系譜 **keifu** genealogy, family tree

9 音譜 **onpu** (written) notes, the score

10 家譜 **kafu** a genealogy, family tree

13 楽譜 **gakufu** musical notation, sheet music, the score

證 → 証 **7a5.5**

7a12.6 / 681 ⊞ 言 戈 日   67 52 43

識 識

SHIKI know, discriminate

— 1 —

7 識別 **shikibetsu** discrimination, recognition

識見 **shikiken, shikken** knowledge, discernment

— 2 —

8 知識 **chishiki** knowledge

知識人 **chishikijin** an intellectual

11 常識 **jōshiki** common sense/knowledge

常識的 **jōshikiteki** matter-of-fact, practical

13 意識 **ishiki** consciousness, awareness

意識的 **ishikiteki** consciously

14 認識 **ninshiki** (re)cognition, perception, knowledge

15 標識 **hyōshiki** (land)mark, marking, sign, signal, tag

— 3 —

12 無意識 **muishiki** unconscious, involuntary

—— 4 ——

¹⁵ 潜在意識 **senzai ishiki** subconscious

7a12.7 / 706   田 言 攵 ⁺⁺
67 49 32

警

KEI, imashi(meru) warn, admonish

—— 1 ——

⁷ 警告 **keikoku** warning, admonition
警戒 **keikai** warning, (pre)caution; vigilance
⁸ 警官 **keikan** policeman
¹¹ 警視庁 **Keishichō** Metropolitan Police Agency
警笛 **keiteki** alarm whistle, horn
¹² 警備 **keibi** security, guard, defense
警報 **keihō** warning, alarm
警報機 **keihōki** warning device, alarm
¹⁴ 警察 **keisatsu** police
警察庁 **Keisatsuchō** National Police Agency
警察官 **keisatsukan** police officer

—— 2 ——

¹¹ 婦警 **fukei** policewoman

—— 13 ——

譯 → 訳 7a4.8

7a13.1 / 1013   田 言 礻 ⁺⁺
67 57 32

讓 |

JŌ, yuzu(ru) turn over to, transfer, assign; yield to, concede

—— 1 ——

⁶ 譲合 **yuzu(ri)a(u)** defer/yield to each other, compromise
¹² 譲渡 **jōto** assign, transfer, convey
yuzu(ri)wata(su) turn over to, transfer

—— 2 ——

⁴ 互譲 **gojō** mutual concession, compromise, conciliation
¹⁷ 謙譲 **kenjō** modesty, humility

7a13.3 / 1312   田 隹 言 ⁺⁺
74 67 32

護 護

GO, mamo(ru) defend, protect
MAMORU (m. given name)
MORI (part of given name)

—— 1 ——

¹¹ 護符 **gofu** amulet, talisman
¹⁹ 護衛 **goei** guard, escort

—— 2 ——

⁵ 弁護士 **bengoshi** lawyer, attorney
⁷ 庇護 **higo** protection, patronage
⁹ 保護 **hogo** protect, shelter, take care of
看護婦 **kangofu** (female) nurse
¹¹ 救護 **kyūgo** relief, aid, rescue
救護所 **kyūgosho** first-aid station
救護班 **kyūgohan** relief squad, rescue party
¹² 援護 **engo** protection, support, relief
¹⁵ 養護 **yōgo** protection, care
¹⁶ 擁護 **yōgo** protect, defend

7a13.4 / 292   田 言 王 弋
67 46 52

議 議

GI deliberation; proposal

—— 1 ——

⁶ 議会 **gikai** parliament, diet, congress
⁷ 議決 **giketsu** decision, resolution
⁸ 議長 **gichō** chairman, president
議事 **giji** proceedings
議事堂 **gijidō** assembly hall, parliament/diet building
議定書 **giteisho, gijōsho** a protocol

9 議院 **giin** house of a legislature, diet
10 議員 **giin** M.P., dietman, congressman
   議席 **giseki** seat in parliament/congress
15 議論 **giron** argument, discussion, controversy
18 議題 **gidai** topic for discussion, agenda

━━━━━━━ 2 ━━━━━━━

1 一議 **ichigi** a word, an opinion, an objection
5 代議員 **daigiin** representative, delegate
6 両議院 **ryōgiin** both houses (of parliament/congress)
   再議 **saigi** reconsideration, redeliberation
   合議制 **gōgisei** parliamentary system
   会議 **kaigi** conference, meeting
   会議録 **kaigiroku** minutes, proceedings
7 決議 **ketsugi** resolution, decision, vote
   批議 **higi** criticize, censure, blame
   抗議 **kōgi** protest, objection
8 協議 **kyōgi** consultation, conference
   建議 **kengi** proposal
   参議院 **Sangiin** House of Councilors
10 討議 **tōgi** discussion, deliberation, debate
11 動議 **dōgi** a (parliamentary) motion
12 衆議院 **Shūgiin** the House of Representatives
13 稟議 **ringi** decision-making by circular letter (instead of holding a meeting)
14 閣議 **kakugi** cabinet meeting
15 審議会 **shingikai** deliberative assembly, commission, council
   論議 **rongi** discussion, argument

━━━━━━━ 3 ━━━━━━━

4 不思議 **fushigi** wonder, mystery, marvel

━━━━━━━ 4 ━━━━━━━

3 山猫争議 **yamaneko sōgi** wildcat strike
5 主脳会議 **shunō kaigi** summit conference
11 商工会議所 **Shōkō Kaigisho** Chamber of Commerce and Industry

譜 → 譜　7a12.2

誉 → 誉　3n10.1

━━━━━━━ 14 ━━━━━━━

辯 → 弁　0a5.30

━━━━━━━ 15 ━━━━━━━

7a15.1　　　　　　田 言 貝 大
　　　　　　　　　　 67 68 34

讃 ｜ 讃 讃

SAN praise; inscription on a picture

━━━━━━━ 1 ━━━━━━━

9 讃美 **sanbi** praise, glorification

讀 → 読　7a7.9

━━━━━━━ 17 ━━━━━━━

讓 → 譲　7a13.1

━━━━━━━ 19 ━━━━━━━

讚 → 讃　7a15.1

━━━━━━━ 貝 **7b** ━━━━━━━

貝	則	財	貢	敗	賊	販	貫	責	貨	貧	质	貯
0.1	2.1	3.1	3.3	4.1	7b3.1	4.2	4.3	4.4	4.5	2o9.5	7b8.7	5.1

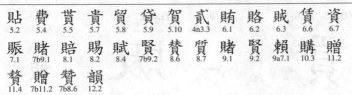

貼 5.2 費 5.4 貰 5.5 貴 5.7 貿 5.8 貸 5.9 賀 5.10 貳 4n3.3 賄 6.1 賂 6.2 賊 6.3 賃 6.6 資 6.7

賑 7.1 賭 7b9.1 賠 8.1 賜 8.2 賦 8.4 賢 7b9.2 贅 8.6 質 8.7 賭 9.1 賢 9.2 賴 9a7.1 購 10.3 贈 11.2

贅 11.4 贈 7b11.2 賛 7b8.6 韻 12.2

0

7b0.1 / 240 □ 貝 68

貝 貝

kai shellfish, (sea) shell

--- 1 ---

9 貝柱 **kaibashira** (boiled scallop) adductor muscle

11 貝殻 **kaigara** (sea) shell

18 貝類 **kairui** shellfish (plural)

--- 3 ---

6 帆立貝 **hotategai** scallop (shell)

--- 4 ---

7 阿古屋貝 **akoyagai** pearl oyster

2

7b2.1 / 608 □ 貝 儿 68 16

則 則

SOKU, nori rule, law **notto(ru)** follow, conform to **sunawa(chi)** in that case, whereupon NORI (part of given name)

--- 2 ---

5 付則 **fusoku** supplementary provisions, bylaws

四則 **shisoku** the four basic arithmetic operations (+, −, *, /)

8 法則 **hōsoku** law, rule

10 原則 **gensoku** principle, general rule

11 規則 **kisoku** regulation, rule

13 鉄則 **tessoku** hard-and-fast rule

---

3 不規則 **fukisoku** irregular, unsystematic

3

7b3.1 / 553 □ 貝 十 丨 68 12 2

財 賊 丨 財 財

ZAI, SAI money, wealth, property

--- 1 ---

5 財布 **saifu** purse, pocketbook, wallet

6 財団 **zaidan** foundation, financial group

財団法人 **zaidan hōjin** (incorporated) foundation

9 財政 **zaisei** (public) finances

財界 **zaikai** financial world

11 財務 **zaimu** financial affairs

財産 **zaisan** estate, assets, property

財産税 **zaisanzei** property tax

13 財源 **zaigen** revenue source; resourcefulness

14 財閥 **zaibatsu** financial clique

--- 2 ---

7 私財 **shizai** private funds

10 借財 **shakuzai** debt

--- 3 ---

4 文化財 **bunkazai** cultural asset

--- 5 ---

12 無形文化財 **mukei-bunkazai** intangible cultural asset

7

言 貝 車 跙 酉 3

7b3.3 / 1719

□ 貝 工
68 38

貢

貢 貢

KŌ, KU, mitsu(gu) pay tribute; support (financially)

---- 1 ----

13 貢献 **kōken** contribution, services

---- 4 ----

7b4.1 / 511

□ 貝 攵
68 49

敗

敗 敗

HAI, yabu(ru) defeat
yabu(reru) be defeated

---- 1 ----

5 敗北 **haiboku** defeat
8 敗者 **haisha** the defeated, loser
13 敗戦 **haisen** lost battle, defeat

---- 2 ----

3 大敗 **taihai** a crushing defeat
4 不敗 **fuhai** invincible, undefeated
5 失敗 **shippai** failure, blunder, mistake
7 完敗 **kanpai** complete defeat
9 連敗 **renpai** successive defeats, losing streak
11 惨敗 **zanpai** crushing defeat
惜敗 **sekihai** narrow defeat
12 勝敗 **shōhai** victory or defeat
13 戦敗国 **senpaikoku** defeated nation
14 腐敗 **fuhai** decomposition, decay; corruption

賎 → 財 **7b3.1**

7b4.2 / 1048

□ 貝 厂 又
68 18 9

販

販 販

HAN sell

---- 1 ----

7 販売 **hanbai** sales, selling
販売店 **hanbaiten** shop, store

---- 2 ----

9 通販 **tsūhan** mail order (short for 通信販売)

---- 3 ----

6 自動販売機 **jidōhanbaiki** vending machine
8 委託販売 **itaku hanbai** selling on consignment/commission

7b4.3 / 914

□ 貝 母 丨
68 25 2

貫

貫 貫

KAN pierce, go through; place of domicile; (unit of weight, about 3.75 kg)
tsuranu(ku) pierce; carry through/out, attain **nuki** brace, crosspiece **TŌRU** (m. given name) **TSURA** (part of given name)

---- 1 ----

9 貫通 **kantsū** pass through, pierce
tsuranu(ki)tō(su) carry out (one's will)
15 貫徹 **kantetsu** carry through, attain, realize

7b4.4 / 655

□ 貝 士 一
68 22 1

責

責 責

SEKI responsibility; censure
se(meru) condemn, censure; torture

——————— 1 ———————

6 責任 **sekinin** responsibility, liability

責任感 **sekininkan** sense of responsibility

11 責務 **sekimu** duty, obligation

——————— 2 ———————

5 叱責 **shisseki** reproach, reprimand

9 重責 **jūseki** heavy responsibility

12 無責任 **musekinin** irresponsibility

7b4.5 / 752

⊔ 貝 亻 ┝
68 3 13

 貨 貨

KA freight; goods, property

——————— 1 ———————

8 貨物 **kamotsu** freight, cargo

貨物船 **kamotsusen** freighter

15 貨幣 **kahei** money, currency, coin

——————— 2 ———————

4 日貨 **nikka** Japanese goods/currency

5 外貨 **gaika** foreign currency; imported goods

6 邦貨 **hōka** Japanese currency; yen

百貨店 **hyakkaten** department store

米貨 **beika** U.S. currency, the dollar

9 通貨 **tsūka** currency

12 硬貨 **kōka** coin; hard currency

14 銅貨 **dōka** copper coin

貧 → 貧 **2o9.5**

質 → 質 **7b8.7**

——————— 5 ———————

7b5.1 / 762

⊞ 貝 宀 丆
68 33 14

 貯貯

CHO, takuwa(eru) store, lay in stock, save

——————— 1 ———————

8 貯金 **chokin** savings, deposit

貯金通帳 **chokin tsūchō** bankbook

貯金箱 **chokinbako** savings box, (piggy) bank

13 貯蓄 **chochiku** savings

15 貯蔵 **chozō** storage, preservation

7b5.2

⊞ 貝 口 ┝
68 24 13

 貼貼

CHŌ, TEN stick on, affix; (counter for medicine packages) **ha(ru)** stick on, paste, affix

——————— 1 ———————

5 貼付 **chōfu, tenpu, ha(ri)tsu(keru)** stick, paste, affix

10 貼紙 **ha(ri)gami** sticker, poster

7b5.4 / 749

⊟ 貝 弓 儿
68 28 16

 費費

HI expenses, cost **tsui(yasu)** spend **tsui(eru)** be wasted

——————— 1 ———————

5 費用 **hiyō** expenses, cost

——————— 2 ———————

4 冗費 **jōhi** unnecessary expenses

巨費 **kyohi** great cost

5 出費 **shuppi** expenses, disbursements

7

言 貝 車 足 酉

5

失費 **shippi** expenses, expenditures

6 自費 **jihi** at one's own expense

自費出版 **jihi shuppan** publishing at one's own expense, vanity press

7 社費 **shahi** company expenses

8 実費 **jippi** actual expense; cost price

官費 **kanpi** government expense

9 食費 **shokuhi** food expenses, board

10 浪費 **rōhi** waste, squander

消費 **shōhi** consumption

消費者 **shōhisha** consumer

旅費 **ryohi** traveling expenses

11 経費 **keihi** expenses, cost

13 戦費 **senpi** war expenditures

14 雑費 **zappi** miscellaneous expenses

16 燃費 **nenpi** fuel cost; fuel economy (km/liter)

18 濫費 **ranpi** waste, extravagance

——————— 3 ———————

2 人件費 **jinkenhi** personnel expenses

5 生計費 **seikeihi** living expenses

6 光熱費 **kōnetsuhi** heating and electricity expenses

10 教育費 **kyōikuhi** school/education expenses

16 輸送費 **yusōhi** shipping costs

7b5.5 / 1986   曰 貝 艹 一
               68   32   1

SEI, mora(u) get, obtain, receive; (with verb) have (someone do something), get (someone to do something)

——————— 1 ———————

8 貰泣 **mora(i)na(ki)** weeping in sympathy

貰物 **mora(i)mono** present, gift

7b5.7 / 1171   曰 貝 口 亠
               68   24   11

KI valuable; noble; esteemed, your **tatto(i), tōto(i)** valuable; noble, exalted **tatto(bu), tōto(bu)** value, esteem, respect   TAKASHI (m. given name)   KI, TAKA (part of given name)

——————— 1 ———————

4 貴方 **kihō, anata** you

7 貴社 **kisha** your company

9 貴重 **kichō** valuable, precious

貴重品 **kichōhin** valuables

11 貴族 **kizoku** the nobility

12 貴裕 **Takahiro** (m. given name)

15 貴賓 **kihin** distinguished guest

——————— 2 ———————

5 兄貴 **aniki** elder brother; one's senior

12 裕貴 **Yūki, Hiroki** (m. given name)

20 騰貴 **tōki** rise (in prices)

7b5.8 / 760   凹 貝 厂 力
               68   18   8

BŌ exchange

——————— 1 ———————

8 貿易 **bōeki** trade, commerce

貿易会社 **bōeki-gaisha** trading firm

貿易商 **bōekishō** trader

7b5.9 / 748   凹 貝 戈 亻
               68   52   3

TAI, ka(su) rent out, lend

——————— 1 ———————

4 貸切 **ka(shi)ki(ri)** reservations, booking

⁵ 貸出 **ka(shi)da(su)** lend/hire out
貸付 **ka(shi)tsu(keru)** lend
貸主 **ka(shi)nushi** lender; landlord
¹⁰ 貸部屋 **ka(shi)beya** room for rent
貸家 **ka(shi)ie, kashiya** house for rent
貸料 **ka(shi)ryō** rent; loan charges
¹³ 貸賃 **ka(shi)chin** rent, charge

—————— 2 ——————

² 又貸 **mataga(shi)** lend what one has borrowed, sublet, sublease
¹³ 賃貸 **chintai, chinga(shi)** leasing, renting

7b5.10 / 756　　▦ 貝 口 力
　　　　　　　　　68 24 8

賀

GA congratulations, felicitations
KA, YOSHI (part of given name)

—————— 1 ——————

⁷ 賀状 **gajō** greeting card

—————— 2 ——————

⁶ 年賀状 **nengajō** New Year's card
⁷ 佐賀県 **Saga-ken** (prefecture)
⁹ 祝賀 **shukuga** celebration; congratulations
¹⁰ 恭賀新年 **kyōga shinnen** Happy New Year
¹² 滋賀県 **Shiga-ken** (prefecture)
¹⁷ 謹賀新年 **kinga shinnen** Happy New Year

貳 → 弐 **4n3.3**

—————— 6 ——————

7b6.1 / 1739　　▦ 貝 月 十
　　　　　　　　　68 42 12

賄

WAI, makana(u) pay, cover, meet (expenses); provide (meals)

—————— 1 ——————

¹³ 賄賂 **wairo** bribe, bribery

—————— 2 ——————

⁴ 収賄 **shūwai** accepting bribes, graft
¹⁸ 贈賄 **zōwai** bribery

—————— 3 ——————

¹⁸ 贈収賄 **zōshūwai** bribery

7b6.2　　　　　　▦ 貝 夂 口
　　　　　　　　　68 49 24

賂

RO, mainai bribe

—————— 2 ——————

¹³ 賄賂 **wairo** bribe, brlbery

7b6.3 / 1807　　▦ 貝 戈 十
　　　　　　　　　68 52 12

賊

ZOKU rebel; robber

—————— 1 ——————

⁹ 賊軍 **zokugun** rebel army, rebels
¹⁰ 賊徒 **zokuto** rebels, traitors

—————— 2 ——————

⁹ 海賊 **kaizoku** pirate
海賊版 **kaizokuban** pirate edition
¹⁰ 烏賊 **ika** squid, cuttlefish

7b6.6 / 751　　▦ 貝 王 亻
　　　　　　　　　68 46 3

賃

CHIN rent, wages, fare, fee

—————— 1 ——————

³ 賃上 **chin'a(ge)** raise in wages
⁸ 賃金 **chingin** wages, pay
¹⁰ 賃借 **chinshaku, chinga(ri)** lease, rent, hire
賃借料 **chinshakuryō** rent
¹² 賃貸 **chintai, chinga(shi)** leasing, renting

---- 2 ----

10 借賃 **ka(ri)chin** the rent
家賃 **yachin** (house) rent
11 運賃 **unchin** fare; shipping/freight charges
宿賃 **yadochin** hotel charges
12 貸賃 **ka(shi)chin** rent, charge

---- 3 ----

13 電車賃 **denshachin** tramfare, trainfare

7b6.7 / 750 | 田 貝 女 冫
68 49 5

資 資資

SHI resources, capital, funds
TASUKU (m. given name)
SUKE (part of given name)

---- 1 ----

5 資本 **shihon** capital
資本主義 **shihon shugi** capitalism
8 資金 **shikin** funds
10 資格 **shikaku** qualifications, competence
資料 **shiryō** material, data
11 資産 **shisan** assets, property
13 資源 **shigen** resources

---- 2 ----

5 出資 **shusshi** investment, financing, contribution
7 投資 **tōshi** investment
労資 **rōshi** labor(ers) and capital(ists)
8 物資 **busshi** goods, resources
9 軍資 **gunshi** war funds/materiel; campaign funds
16 融資 **yūshi** financing, loan

---- 7 ----

7b7.1 | 田 貝 衤 厂
68 57 18

賑 賑賑

SHIN, nigi(wau) flourish, thrive, be bustling/lively **nigi(yaka)** lively, bustling

---- 1 ----

3 賑々 **niginigi(shii)** thriving; merry, gay

---- 8 ----

賭 → 賭 **7b9.1**

7b8.1 / 1829 | 田 貝 立 口
68 54 24

賠 賠賠

BAI indemnify

---- 1 ----

17 賠償 **baishō** reparation, indemnification
賠償金 **baishōkin** indemnities, reparations, damages

7b8.2 / 1831 | 田 貝 日 勿
68 43 27

賜 賜賜

SHI, tamawa(ru), tama(u) grant, bestow, confer

---- 1 ----

8 賜物 **tamamono** gift

7b8.4 / 1808 | 田 貝 戈 ⼂
68 52 13

賦 賦賦

FU tribute; payment, installment; give, confer; prose poem

---- 1 ----

3 賦与 **fuyo** grant, give

---- 2 ----

4 月賦 **geppu** monthly installments
6 年賦 **nenpu** annual installment

賢 → **7b9.2**

7b8.6 / 745 　　田 貝 大 一
　　　　　　　68 34 1

賛 | 賛 賛

SAN praise; agreement; assistance

— 1 —

6 賛成 **sansei** agreement, approbation

7 賛助 **sanjo** support, backing

9 賛美 **sanbi** praise, glorification

14 賛歌 **sanka** paean, praise

— 2 —

6 自賛 **jisan** self-praise

15 賞賛 **shōsan** praise, admire

7b8.7 / 176 　　田 貝 斤
　　　　　　　68 50

质 | 質 質

SHITSU quality, nature; inquire
SHICHI, CHI hostage; pawn
tada(su) ask, inquire, verify
tachi nature, temperament
TADASHI (m. given name)

— 1 —

8 質的 **shitsuteki** qualitative

9 質屋 **shichiya** pawnshop

10 質素 **shisso** simple, plain, frugal

11 質問 **shitsumon** question

14 質疑応答 **shitsugi-ōtō** question-and-answer (session)

— 2 —

2 人質 **hitojichi** hostage

5 本質的 **honshitsuteki** in substance, essential

6 気質 **katagi, kishitsu** disposition, temperament, spirit

　地質 **chishitsu** geology, geological features; nature of the soil

　　jishitsu quality/texture (of cloth)

7 良質 **ryōshitsu** good quality

8 実質的 **jisshitsuteki** substantial, essential, material, real

　物質的 **busshitsuteki** material, physical

9 変質 **henshitsu** deterioration, degeneration

　品質 **hinshitsu** quality

10 特質 **tokushitsu** characteristic, trait

11 悪質 **akushitsu** evil, vicious, unscrupulous; of poor quality

　粘質 **nenshitsu** viscosity, stickiness

12 等質 **tōshitsu** homogeneous

— 3 —

8 侍気質 **samurai katagi** samurai spirit

9 神経質 **shinkeishitsu** nervous, high-strung

— 4 —

7 抗生物質 **kōsei busshitsu** an antibiotic

— 9 —

7b9.1 　　田 貝 日 土
　　　　　　　68 43 22

賭 | 賭 賭

TO, ka(keru) bet, wager, stake, gamble **kake** a bet, wager, gamble

— 1 —

8 賭事 **kakegoto** betting, gambling

12 賭博 **tobaku** gambling

7b9.2 / 1288 　　田 貝 门 又
　　　　　　　68 20 9

賢 賢

KEN, kashiko(i) wise, intelligent **saka(shii)** bright, clever, wise **saka(shira)** pert, impertinent **MASARU** (m. given name) **KEN** (part of given name)

───────────── 1 ─────────────

1 賢一 **Ken'ichi, Yoshikazu, Toshikazu** (m. given name)
2 賢人 **kenjin** wise man, sage, the wise
8 賢明 **kenmei** wise, intelligent
　賢者 **kenja** wise man, the wise

───────────── 2 ─────────────

11 悪賢 **warugashiko(i)** cunning, sly, crafty, wily
13 聖賢 **seiken** sages, saints

頼 → 頼 **9a7.1**

───────────── 10 ─────────────

7b10.3 / 1011　　田 貝 王 艹
　　　　　　　　　68 46 32

購

購購

KŌ, agana(u) buy, purchase

───────────── 1 ─────────────

2 購入 **kōnyū** purchase
12 購買 **kōbai** purchasing
14 購読 **kōdoku** subscription
　購読料 **kōdokuryō** subscription price/fee

───────────── 11 ─────────────

7b11.2 / 1364　　田 貝 田 日
　　　　　　　　　68 58 43

贈

贈|贈贈

ZŌ, SŌ, oku(ru) give (as a gift), present, bestow

───────────── 1 ─────────────

3 贈与 **zōyo** gift, donation

4 贈収賄 **zōshūwai** bribery
5 贈本 **zōhon** gift book, complimentary copy
7 贈呈 **zōtei** presentation, gift
8 贈物 **oku(ri)mono** gift, present
13 贈賄 **zōwai** bribery

───────────── 2 ─────────────

11 寄贈 **kizō** donate, present
14 遺贈 **izō** bequest, legacy

7b11.4　　田 貝 方 攵
　　　　　　　68 48 49

贅

贅贅

ZEI luxury, extravagance, redundance, waste; wen, wart; son-in-law

───────────── 1 ─────────────

7 贅沢 **zeitaku** luxury, extravagance

───────────── 12 ─────────────

贈 → 贈 **7b11.2**

賛 → 賛 **7b8.6**

7b12.2 / 349　　田 貝 立 日
　　　　　　　　68 54 43

韻

韵|韻韻

IN rhyme; elegant

───────────── 1 ─────────────

4 韻文 **inbun** verse, poetry

───────────── 2 ─────────────

8 押韻 **ōin** rhyme
9 音韻 **on'in** phoneme

───────────── 車 **7c** ─────────────

車	軌	重	軒	軟	転	輿	軸	軽	輌	較	載	輔
0.1	2.1	0a9.18	3.1	4.1	4.3	7c14.2	5.1	5.3	7c8.1	6.3	6.5	7.1

輕	軻	輪	輩	輝	輻	輯	輸	轄	轉	轟	轢
7c5.3	8.1	8.4	8.7	8.8	9.3	9.4	9.5	10.1	7c4.3	14.2	15.1

— 0 —

7c0.1 / 133   □ 車
69

車 車

SHA, kuruma vehicle, car, cart; wheel

— 1 —

3 車上 **shajō** aboard (the train/vehicle)
4 車内 **shanai** inside the car
車中 **shachū** in the car/vehicle
6 車両 **sharyō** vehicles, cars, rolling stock
10 車庫 **shako** garage, carbarn
11 車道 **shadō** roadway
車窓 **shasō** car/train window
12 車掌 **shashō** (train) conductor
車椅子 **kurumaisu** wheelchair
車検 **shaken** auto inspection (certificate)
15 車輛 **sharyō** vehicles, cars, rolling stock
車輪 **sharin** wheel

— 2 —

3 下車 **gesha** get off (a train/bus)
4 水車 **suisha** water wheel, turbine
5 外車 **gaisha** foreign car
6 列車 **ressha** train
7 汽車 **kisha** train (drawn by a steam locomotive)
8 空車 **kūsha, karaguruma** empty car, (taxi) For Hire
9 発車 **hassha** start, departure (of a train)
乗車 **jōsha** get on (a train)
降車 **kōsha** get off (a train)
風車 **fūsha** windmill
kazaguruma pinwheel; windmill
洗車 **sensha** car wash
11 停車 **teisha** stopping a vehicle
12 歯車 **haguruma** gear, cogwheel
13 滑車 **kassha** pulley

戦車 **sensha** tank
新車 **shinsha** new car
電車 **densha** electric car, streetcar, train
電車賃 **denshachin** tramfare, trainfare
15 駐車場 **chūshajō** parking lot

— 3 —

6 自動車 **jidōsha** motor vehicle, automobile
自転車 **jitensha** bicycle
7 乳母車 **ubaguruma** baby carriage/buggy
9 乗用車 **jōyōsha** passenger car
11 救急車 **kyūkyūsha** ambulance
終電車 **shūdensha** the last train/streetcar for the day
16 機関車 **kikansha** locomotive

— 4 —

6 各駅停車 **kakuekiteisha** local train
9 途中下車 **tochū gesha** stopover, layover
12 軽自動車 **keijidōsha** light car

— 2 —

7c2.1 / 1787   □ 車 十
69   12

軌 軌

KI wheel track, rut; railway, track; orbit NORI (part of given name)

— 1 —

11 軌道 **kidō** (railroad) track; orbit
15 軌範 **kihan** model, example

重 → 0a9.18

——————— 3 ———————

7c3.1 / 1187 　　　□ 車 　一 一
　　　　　　　　　　　69　14　1

軒 軒

KEN (counter for buildings)
noki eaves

——————— 1 ———————

6 軒先 **nokisaki** edge of the eaves; front of the house
8 軒並 **nokina(mi), nokinara(bi)** row of houses
13 軒数 **kensū** number of houses

——————— 2 ———————

1 一軒 **ikken** a house

——————— 4 ———————

7c4.1 / 1788 　　　□ 車 攵
　　　　　　　　　　　69　49

軟 軟

NAN, yawa(rakai/raka) soft

——————— 1 ———————

4 軟化 **nanka** softening
10 軟弱 **nanjaku** weak(-kneed)
12 軟着陸 **nanchakuriku** soft landing

——————— 2 ———————

9 柔軟 **jūnan** soft, supple, flexible

7c4.3 / 433 　　　田 車 二 竹
　　　　　　　　　　　69　4　17

轉 | 転 転

TEN turn; change **koro(bu)** tumble, fall down; roll over **koro(garu/geru)** roll, tumble, fall, lie down/about **koro(gasu/basu)** roll (a ball), knock down, trip (someone) **utata** more and more, all the more; somehow; indeed

——————— 1 ———————

0 転じる **ten(jiru)** revolve; turn, shift, change; move, be transferred
5 転出 **tenshutsu** move out, be transferred
6 転任 **tennin** change of assignments/personnel
　転地 **tenchi** change of air/scene
　転回 **tenkai** rotate, revolve
8 転送 **tensō** transmit, forward (mail)
　転居 **tenkyo** moving, change of address
10 転倒 **tentō** fall down violently, turn upside down, reverse
11 転移 **ten'i** change, spread, metastasis
12 転勤 **tenkin** be transferred (to another office)
　転換 **tenkan** conversion, changeover; diversion
　転落 **tenraku, koro(ge)o(chiru)** fall, slip down
16 転機 **tenki** turning point
18 転覆 **tenpuku** overturn, overthrow
　転職 **tenshoku** change of post/occupation

——————— 2 ———————

1 一転 **itten** a turn, complete change
4 反転 **hanten** turn/roll over, reverse directions, invert
6 回転 **kaiten** revolve, rotate, swivel
　自転車 **jitensha** bicycle
9 急転 **kyūten** sudden change
11 運転 **unten** operate, run (a machine), drive (a car)
　運転手 **untenshu** driver, chauffeur
　移転 **iten** move, change of address
16 機転 **kiten** quick wit

——————— 3 ———————

6 気分転換 **kibun tenkan** a (refreshing) change, diversion
13 試運転 **shiunten** trial run

 7c14.2

─────────────── 5 ───────────────

7c5.1 / 988   ⊞ 車 日 丨
                          69 43 2

軸   軸軸

JIKU axis; axle, shaft; (picture) scroll

─────── 2 ───────

8 枢軸 **sūjiku** pivot, axis, center
11 掛軸 **ka(ke)jiku** hanging scroll

7c5.3 / 547   ⊞ 車 土 又
                          69 22 ㇉

軽   輕丨軽軽

KEI, karu(i), karo(yaka) light
karo(njiru) make light of, slight

─────── 1 ───────

3 軽工業 **keikōgyō** light industry
6 軽自動車 **keijidōsha** light car
7 軽快 **keikai** light, nimble, jaunty, lilting
9 軽食 **keishoku** light meal
11 軽率 **keisotsu** rash, hasty
   軽視 **keishi** belittle, neglect, scorn
12 軽装 **keisō** light dress/equipment
13 軽業 **karuwaza** acrobatics
   軽傷 **keishō** minor injury
14 軽蔑 **keibetsu** contempt, scorn, disdain
16 軽薄 **keihaku** insincere, frivolous, fickle

─────── 2 ───────

4 手軽 **tegaru** easy, readily, simple, informal, without ado
5 尻軽 **shirigaru** wanton, loose
6 気軽 **kigaru** lightheartedly, readily, feel free to
7 身軽 **migaru** light, agile, nimble
9 津軽海峡 **Tsugaru-kaikyō** (strait between Honshū and Hokkaidō)

─────────────── 6 ───────────────

輌 → 輌 **7c8.1**

7c6.3 / 1453   ⊞ 車 亠 儿
                          69 11 16

較   較較

KAKU, KŌ, kura(beru) compare

─────── 2 ───────

5 比較 **hikaku** compare; comparative (literature)
   比較的 **hikakuteki** relative(ly), comparative(ly)
   比較級 **hikakukyū** the comparative degree (in grammar)

7c6.5 / 1124   ⋯ 車 戈 十
                          69 52 12

載   載載

SAI, no(ru) be recorded, appear (in print) **no(seru)** place on top of; load (luggage); publish, run (an ad)

─────── 2 ───────

8 所載 **shosai** printed, published
9 連載 **rensai** serialization
10 記載 **kisai** record, report, note
11 掲載 **keisai** publish, print, carry/run (an ad)
12 搭載 **tōsai** load; embark; mounting (of electronic components)
   登載 **tōsai** register, record, enter

─────────────── 7 ───────────────

7c7.1 / 2245   ⊞ 車 月 亠
                          69 42 12

輔   輔輔

HO help HO, FU, BU, SUKE (part of given name) TASUKU, TASUKE (m. given name)

言
貝
車 7
足
酉

───────── 1 ─────────

7 輔佐 **hosa** assistance; assistant, adviser

───────── 2 ─────────

3 大輔 **Daisuke, Taisuke** (m. given name)

9 祐輔 **Yūsuke** (m. given name)

輕 → 軽 **7c5.3**

───────── 8 ─────────

7c8.1　　　田 車 巾 イ
　　　　　　　69 26 3

輌

輌 | 輌 車 輌

RYŌ (counter for railroad cars, etc.)

───────── 2 ─────────

7 車輌 **sharyō** vehicles, cars, rolling stock

7c8.4 / 1164　　田 車 艹 イ
　　　　　　　　69 32 3

輪

輪 輪

RIN wheel, circle, revolve; (counter for flowers) **wa** circle, ring, hoop, loop, wheel

───────── 1 ─────────

0 輪ゴム **wagomu** rubber band

9 輪郭 **rinkaku** outline, contours

───────── 2 ─────────

7 車輪 **sharin** wheel

9 前輪 **zenrin, maewa** front wheel

指輪 **yubiwa** (finger) ring

20 競輪 **keirin** bicycle race/racing

7c8.7 / 1037　　日 車 儿 二
　　　　　　　　69 16 4

輩

輩 輩

HAI fellow, colleague, companion
yakara fellows, gang; family, kin

───────── 1 ─────────

5 輩出 **haishutsu** appear one after another

───────── 2 ─────────

6 年輩 **nenpai** age; elderly age

先輩 **senpai** senior, superior, elder, older graduate

9 後輩 **kōhai** one's junior, younger generation

10 党輩 **tōhai** companions, associates

───────── 3 ─────────

6 同年輩 **dōnenpai** persons of the same age

7c8.8 / 1653　　田 車 ⺌ 儿
　　　　　　　　69 35 16

輝

輝 輝

KI, kagaya(ku) shine, gleam, sparkle, be brilliant **AKIRA** (m. given name)
TERU (part of given name)

───────── 1 ─────────

9 輝美 **Terumi, Teruyoshi** (given name)

───────── 2 ─────────

1 一輝 **Kazuki** (m. given name)

───────── 9 ─────────

7c9.3　　　　田 車 田 口
　　　　　　　　69 58 24

輻

輻 輻

FUKU, ya spoke

7c9.4　　　　田 車 耳 口
　　　　　　　　69 65 24

輯

輯 輯

SHŪ collect, gather; soften, relent

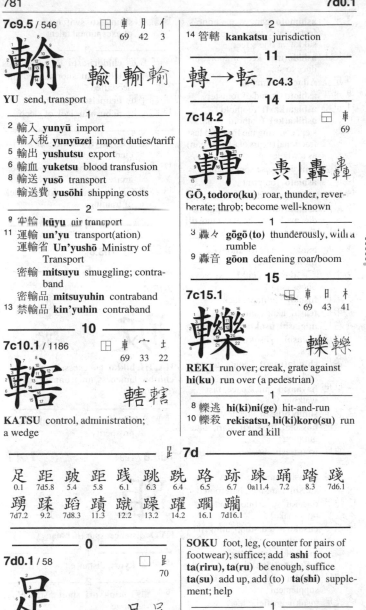

7c9.5 / 546 ⊞ 車 月 亻 69 42 3

輸

輸|輸輸

YU send, transport

— 1 —

2 輸入 **yunyū** import
輸入税 **yunyūzei** import duties/tariff
5 輸出 **yushutsu** export
6 輸血 **yuketsu** blood transfusion
8 輸送 **yusō** transport
輸送費 **yusōhi** shipping costs

— 2 —

8 空輸 **kūyu** air transport
11 運輸 **un'yu** transport(ation)
運輸省 **Un'yushō** Ministry of Transport
密輸 **mitsuyu** smuggling; contraband
密輸品 **mitsuyuhin** contraband
13 禁輸品 **kin'yuhin** contraband

— 10 —

7c10.1 / 1186 ⊞ 車 宀 土 69 33 22

轄

轄轄

KATSU control, administration; a wedge

— 2 —

14 管轄 **kankatsu** jurisdiction

— 11 —

轉→転 **7c4.3**

— 14 —

7c14.2 ⊟ 車 69

轟

軣|轟轟

GŌ, todoro(ku) roar, thunder, reverberate; throb; become well-known

— 1 —

3 轟々 **gōgō (to)** thunderously, with a rumble
9 轟音 **gōon** deafening roar/boom

— 15 —

7c15.1 ⊞ 車 日 木 69 43 41

轢

轢轢

REKI run over; creak, grate against
hi(ku) run over (a pedestrian)

— 1 —

8 轢逃 **hi(ki)ni(ge)** hit-and-run
10 轢殺 **rekisatsu, hi(ki)koro(su)** run over and kill

— 足 **7d** —

足 0.1	距 7d5.8	跛 5.4	距 5.8	践 6.1	跳 6.3	跣 6.4	路 6.5	跡 6.7	踈 0a11.4	踊 7.2	踏 8.3	踐 7d6.1
踴 7d7.2	蹂 9.2	蹈 7d8.3	蹟 11.3	蹴 12.2	躁 13.2	躍 14.2	躙 16.1	躪 7d16.1				

— 0 —

7d0.1 / 58 □ 足 70

足

足𧾷

SOKU foot, leg, (counter for pairs of footwear); suffice; add **ashi** foot
ta(riru), ta(ru) be enough, suffice
ta(su) add up, add (to) **ta(shi)** supplement; help

— 1 —

0 1足 **issoku** one pair (of shoes/socks) **hitoashi** a step

³ 足下 **ashimoto** gait, pace; at one's feet; (watch your) step
sokka at one's feet

⁴ 足止 **ashido(me)** keep indoors; induce to stay

⁵ 足立 **Adachi** (surname)

⁹ 足音 **ashioto** sound of footsteps

¹¹ 足掛 **ashiga(kari)** foothold
ashika(ke) foothold, pedal, step; counting the first and last fractional (years of a time span) as a whole

足袋 **tabi** Japanese socks, tabi

¹³ 足跡 **ashiato** footprint

¹⁴ 足算 **ta(shi)zan** addition (in math)

¹⁵ 足踏 **ashibu(mi)** step, stamp; treadle; mark time, be at a standstill

───── 2 ─────

¹ 一足 **issoku** a pair (of shoes)
hitoashi a step

³ 土足厳禁 **dosoku genkin** Remove Shoes (sign)

⁴ 不足 **fusoku** shortage, lack
手足 **teashi** hands and feet

⁵ 右足 **migiashi, usoku** right foot/leg

⁶ 両足 **ryōashi, ryōsoku** both feet/legs
舌足 **shitata(razu)** lisping, tongue-tied
早足 **hayaashi** quick pace, fast walking

⁷ 忍足 **shino(bi)ashi** stealthy steps

⁹ 発足 **hossoku, hassoku** start, inauguration
急足 **iso(gi)ashi** brisk pace, hurried steps
後足 **atoashi** hind leg/foot

¹⁰ 素足 **suashi** bare feet, barefooted

¹¹ 蛇足 **dasoku** superfluous (as legs on a snake)

¹² 遠足 **ensoku** excursion, outing, picnic, hike
満足 **manzoku** satisfaction
mi(chi)ta(riru) be contented
補足 **hosoku** supply, replenish, supplement

¹³ 義足 **gisoku** artificial leg
裸足 **hadashi** bare feet, barefooted

¹⁴ 駆足 **ka(ke)ashi** running, galloping

¹⁷ 駿足 **shunsoku** swift horse; person of exceptional talent

───── 3 ─────

³ 千鳥足 **chidori-ashi** tottering steps

⁴ 手不足 **tebusoku** shorthanded, understaffed

⁹ 扁平足 **henpeisoku** flat feet

¹³ 寝不足 **nebusoku** lack of sleep

───── 4 ─────

⁶ 自給自足 **jikyū-jisoku** self-sufficiency

¹¹ 運動不足 **undō-busoku** lack of exercise

¹⁴ 練習不足 **renshū-busoku** out/lack of training

───── 4 ─────

距 → **7d5.8**

───── 5 ─────

7d5.4 □ 𧾷 厂 又
70 18 9

HA, HI, bikko lameness, limp
chinba lameness, limp; unmatched pair (of shoes)

───── 1 ─────

⁶ 跛行景気 **hakō keiki** spotty boom/prosperity

7d5.8 / 1294 □ 𧾷 冂
70 20

KYO distance; spur (in botany)

───── 1 ─────

¹⁸ 距離 **kyori** distance

───── 2 ─────

⁶ 近距離 **kinkyori** short distance/range

⁸ 長距離 **chōkyori** long-distance, long-range

12 遠距離 **enkyori** long distance, long-range

短距離 **tankyori** short distance, short-range

——————— 6 ———————

7d6.1 / 1568 □ ⻊ 戈 二
70 52 4

践 │ 践 践

SEN step (up to); realize, put into practice

——————— 2 ———————

8 実践 **jissen** in practice

7d6.3 / 1563 □ ⻊ ⼃ 儿
70 5 16

跳 跳

CHŌ, ha(neru), to(bu) leap, spring up, jump, bounce

——————— 1 ———————

3 跳上 **ha(ne)a(garu), to(bi)a(garu)** jump up

跳下 **to(bi)o(ri)** jumping off
6 跳返 **ha(ne)kae(su)** bounce back, repel
21 跳躍 **ha(ne)odo(ru)** prance/frisk about **chōyaku** spring, jump, leap

——————— 2 ———————

9 飛跳 **to(bi)hane(ru)** jump up and down, hop
12 幅跳 **habato(bi)** longjump

7d6.4 □ ⻊ 土 儿
70 22 16

跣 跣

SEN, hadashi barefoot

7d6.5 / 151 □ ⻊ 夂 口
70 49 24

路 路

RO, -ji, michi road, path, way, street
MICHI (part of given name)

——————— 1 ———————

3 路上 **rojō** on the road
6 路地 **roji** alley, lane, path
9 路面 **romen** road surface
15 路線 **rosen** route, line

——————— 2 ———————

6 曲路 **ma(gari)michi** roundabout road; winding road
7 岐路 **kiro** fork in the road, crossroads
8 迷路 **meiro** maze, labyrinth
径路 **keiro** course, route, process
空路 **kūro** air route; by air/plane
9 通路 **tsūro** aisle, passageway, path **kayo(i)ji** path, route
10 進路 **shinro** course, way, route
姫路 **Himeji** (city, Hyōgo-ken)
航路 **kōro** (sea) route, course
11 道路 **dōro** road, street, highway
淡路島 **Awajishima** (island, Hyōgo-ken)
経路 **keiro** course, route
釧路 **Kushiro** (city, Hokkaidō)
12 街路 **gairo** street
15 線路 **senro** (railroad) track

——————— 3 ———————

2 丁字路 **teijiro** T-junction of roads/streets
十字路 **jūjiro** crossroads, intersection
3 三叉路 **sansaro** Y-junction of roads
10 航空路 **kōkūro** air route
11 袋小路 **fukurokōji** blind alley, cul-de-sac
13 滑走路 **kassōro** runway

7d6.7 / 1569   田 足 亠 儿
                70   11   16

跡

SEKI, ato mark, traces, vestiges, remains, ruins

———— 1 ————

8 跡始末 **atoshimatsu** winding-up,
settlement, straightening up
(afterwards)
13 跡継 **atotsu(gi)** successor, heir

———— 2 ————

5 古跡 **koseki, furuato** historic spot,
ruins
7 形跡 **keiseki** traces, signs, evidence
  足跡 **ashiato** footprint
8 追跡 **tsuiseki** pursue, track, stalk
  奇跡 **kiseki** miracle
11 痕跡 **konseki** traces, vestiges, evidence
12 証跡 **shōseki** evidence, traces
14 遺跡 **iseki** remains, ruins, relics

———— 7 ————

疎 → 疎 **0a11.4**

7d7.2 / 1558   田 足 月 一
                70   42   1

踊

YŌ, odo(ru) dance **odo(ri)** a dance,
dancing

———— 1 ————

2 踊子 **odo(ri)ko** dancer, dancing girl
20 踊懸 **odo(ri)ka(karu)** spring upon,
jump at

———— 2 ————

15 舞踊 **buyō** dancing; dance
  ma(i)odo(ru) dance

———— 8 ————

7d8.3 / 1559   田 足 日 氵
                70   43   21

踏

TŌ, fu(mu) step on **fu(maeru)** stand
on, be based on

———— 1 ————

4 踏切 **fu(mi)ki(ru)** cross; take the
plunge, take action, make bold
to **fumikiri** railroad (grade)
crossing
  踏込 **fu(mi)ko(mu)** step/rush into
5 踏付 **fu(mi)tsu(keru)** trample; oppress; despise
  踏外 **fu(mi)hazu(su)** miss one's
footing
11 踏張 **fu(n)ba(ru)** brace one's legs,
stand firm, hold out, persist in

———— 2 ————

5 未踏 **mitō** untrodden, unexplored
7 足踏 **ashibu(mi)** step, stamp; treadle; mark time, be at a standstill
14 雑踏 **zattō** hustle and bustle, congestion
15 舞踏 **butō** dancing
  舞踏会 **butōkai** ball, dance

践 → 践 **7d6.1**

———— 9 ————

踴 → 踊 **7d7.2**

7d9.2   田 足 木 丆
                70   41   14

躁

JŪ step on

———— 1 ————

23 躁躪 **jūrin** trampling upon; infringement, violation

―――――――――― 3 ――――――――――

² 人権蹂躙 **jinken jūrin** infringement of human rights

―――――――――― 10 ――――――――――

蹈 → 踏 **7d8.3**

―――――――――― 11 ――――――――――

7d11.3   ⊞ ⻊ 貝 士
                        70 68 22

蹟   蹟 蹟

SEKI, SHAKU remains, vestiges

―――――――――― 12 ――――――――――

7d12.2   ⊞ ⻊ 口 小
                        70 24 35

蹴   蹴 蹴

SHŪ, SHUKU, ke(ru) kick

⁹ 蹴飛 **keto(basu)** kick away/out, reject
¹² 蹴散 **kechi(rasu)** kick around, put
  to rout

―――――――――― 2 ――――――――――

¹ 一蹴 **isshū** kick; reject

―――――――――― 13 ――――――――――

7d13.2   ⊞ ⻊ 口 木
                        70 24 41

躁   躁 躁

SŌ be clamorous

―――――――――― 1 ――――――――――

¹⁰ 躁病 **sōbyō** mania
²⁹ 躁鬱病 **sōutsubyō** manic-depressive psychosis

―――――――――― 14 ――――――――――

7d14.2 / 1560   田 隹 ⻊ ⺲
                          74 70 39

躍   躍 躍

YAKU, odo(ru) jump, leap, hop

―――――――――― 1 ――――――――――

¹⁰ 躍進 **yakushin** advance by leaps
  and bounds
²⁰ 躍懸 **odo(ri)ka(karu)** spring upon,
  jump at

―――――――――― 2 ――――――――――

¹ 一躍 **ichiyaku** one bound; in one
  leap
⁰ 飛躍 **hiyaku** leap; activity; rapid
  progress
  飛躍的 **hiyakuteki** rapid, by leaps
  and bounds
  活躍 **katsuyaku** be active
¹³ 跳躍 **ha(ne)odo(ru)** prance/frisk
  about **chōyaku** spring, jump,
  leap

―――――――――― 16 ――――――――――

7d16.1   ⊟ 門 隹 ⻊
                        76 74 70

躪   躙 | 躪 躪

RIN, niji(ru) edge forward; trample
down

―――――――――― 1 ――――――――――

¹¹ 躙寄 **niji(ri)yo(ru)** edge/crawl/si-
  dle up to

―――――――――― 2 ――――――――――

¹⁶ 蹂躪 **jūrin** trampling upon; infringement, violation

―――――――――― 4 ――――――――――

² 人権蹂躙 **jinken jūrin** infringement of human rights

―――――――――― 19 ――――――――――

躙 → 躪 **7d16.1**

酉 7e

酉	西	配	酌	酔	酢	尊	酵	酬	酪	酷	酸	醇
0.1	0a6.20	3.2	3.3	4.3	5.3	2o10.3	6.1	6.2	6.4	7.1	7.2	7.5

醉	醜	醤	醫	醬	醸	釀
7e4.3	10.1	7e11.2	2t5.2	11.2	13.1	7e13.1

——————— 0 ———————

7e0.1 / 2254   □ 酉
                                            71

YŪ, tori tenth horary sign (bird)
YŪ, YU, TORI, NAGA (part of given
name) MINORU (m. given name)

——————— 1 ———————

⁵ 酉市 **tori (no) ichi** year-end fair

  0a6.20

——————— 3 ———————

7e3.2 / 515   □ 酉 弓
                                        71 28

HAI distribute, allot; arrange, place;
be together; exile **kuba(ru)** distribute, pass out, allocate

——————— 1 ———————

⁴ 配分 **haibun** distribution, alloca-
  tion
  配水 **haisui** water supply/distribu-
  tion
⁵ 配布 **haifu** distribution, apportionment
⁶ 配列 **hairetsu** arrangement, grouping
  配当 **haitō** allotment, share, dividend
¹¹ 配遇者 **haigūsha** spouse
  配達 **haitatsu** deliver
¹² 配給 **haikyū** distribution, rationing

¹³ 配置 **haichi** arrangement, placement, layout
¹⁵ 配慮 **hairyo** consideration, care

——————— 2 ———————

⁴ 勾配 **kōbai** slope, incline, gradient
  支配 **shihai** management, control,
  rule
  分配 **bunpai** division, sharing, allotment
  心配 **shinpai** worry, anxiety, concern
  心配事 **shinpaigoto** cares, worries,
  troubles
⁶ 気配 **kehai** sign, indication **kihai**
  market trend **kikuba(ri)** vigilance, attentiveness
  宅配便 **takuhaibin** parcel delivery
  business
¹³ 蛸配当 **takohaitō** bogus dividends

——————— 3 ———————

⁹ 急勾配 **kyūkōbai** steep slope

7e3.3 / 1863   □ 酉 宀 丨
                                71 15 2

SHAKU, ku(mu) pour (saké); take
into consideration

——————— 1 ———————

¹² 酌量 **shakuryō** consideration, extenuation

——————— 2 ———————

¹² 媒酌人 **baishakunin** matchmaker,
  go-between
  晩酌 **banshaku** an evening drink
  (of saké)

— 4 —

7e4.3 / 1709 田 酉 十
71 12

酔

酔 | 酔 醉

SUI, yo(u) get drunk, be intoxicated;
feel (sea)sick

— 1 —

5 酔払 **yo(p)para(i)** a drunk
15 酔潰 **yo(i)tsubu(reru)** be dead
drunk

— 2 —

4 心酔 **shinsui** be fascinated by, ardently admire
8 泥酔 **deisui** dead drunk
10 陶酔 **tōsui** intoxication; fascination, rapture
11 麻酔 **masui** anesthesia
悪酔 **waruyo(i)** drink oneself sick;
become unpleasant when drunk
船酔 **funayo(i)** seasickness

— 3 —

2 二日酔 **futsukayo(i)** a hangover

— 5 —

7e5.3 / 1867 田 酉 ⺈ 卜
71 15 13

酢

醋 | 酢 酢

SAKU, su vinegar

— 1 —

8 酢物 **su(no)mono** vinegared dish

 尊→尊 2o10.3

— 6 —

7e6.1 / 1866 田 酉 土 子
71 22 6

酵

酵 酵

KŌ fermentation; yeast

---

5 酵母 **kōbo** yeast

7e6.2 / 1864 田 酉 ⼉
71 16

酬

酬 酬

SHŪ, mukui reward, compensation;
retribution

— 2 —

12 報酬 **hōshū** remuneration

— 3 —

12 無報酬 **muhōshū** without pay, for
free

7e6.4 / 1865 田 酉 夂 口
71 49 24

酪

酪 酪

RAKU whey

— 1 —

13 酪農 **rakunō** dairy farming

— 7 —

7e7.1 / 1711 田 酉 士 口
71 22 24

酷

酷 酷

KOKU, hido(i), mugo(i) severe,
harsh, cruel, intense

— 1 —

5 酷目 **hido(i)me** a bitter experience,
a hard time
8 酷使 **kokushi** work (someone) hard
12 酷暑 **kokusho** intense/sweltering
heat
酷評 **kokuhyō** sharp/harsh criticism

— 2 —

7 冷酷 **reikoku** cruel, callous
8 苛酷 **kakoku** harsh, rigorous, cruel

10 残酷 **zankoku** cruel, brutal
11 過酷 **kakoku** severe, harsh

7e7.2 / 516 　酉 夂 竹 　71 49 17

酸

酸 酸

SAN acid **su(i), su(ppai)** sour, tart

— 1 —

4 酸化 **sanka** oxidation
8 酸味 **sanmi, su(i)mi** acidity, sourness
酸性 **sansei** acidity
10 酸素 **sanso** oxygen

— 2 —

9 炭酸水 **tansansui** carbonated water

7e7.5 / 2255 　酉 口 亠 　71 24 11

醇

醇 醇

JUN pure; kind; sweet saké
JUN, SHUN, ATSU (part of given name) ATSUSHI (m. given name)

— 1 —

6 醇朴 **junboku** simple and honest

— 8 —

醉 → 酔 **7e4.3**

— 10 —

7e10.1 / 1527 　酉 田 儿 　71 58 16

醜

醜 醜

SHŪ, miniku(i) ugly; indecent

— 1 —

11 醜悪 **shūaku** ugly, abominable, scandalous
14 醜聞 **shūbun** scandal

醬 → 醤 **7e11.2**

— 11 —

醫 → 医 **2t5.2**

7e11.2 　酉 夕 寸 　71 30 37

醤

醤 | 醤 醤

SHŌ salted or fermented food

— 1 —

8 醤油 **shōyu** soy sauce

— 13 —

7e13.1 / 1837 　酉 衤 艹 　71 57 32

醸

醸 | 醸 醸

JŌ, kamo(su) brew; bring about, give rise to

— 1 —

9 醸造 **jōzō** brewing, distilling
醸造所 **jōzōsho** brewery, distillery

— 17 —

釀 → 醸 **7e13.1**

— 金 **8a** —

金	釖	針	釘	釧	釣	欽	鈍	鈎	鉢	鉄	鈴	鉛
0.1	2f0.1	2.3	2.4	3.4	3.5	4.1	4.2	8a5.17	5.4	5.6	5.11	5.14

鉱	鉤	銭	銀	銘	銃	銃	銅	鋳	鋏	鋤	鋭	錐
5.15	5.17	6.1	6.3	6.4	6.6	6.9	6.12	7.2	7.4	7.5	7.12	8.1

錘	錬	錦	錢	錆	錯	錠	錨	録	鎚	鍵	鋸	鋼
8.2	8.3	8.6	8a6.1	8.8	8.10	8.12	8.14	8.16	8a9.10	8.18	8.19	8.20

錬	鍛	鎚	鍼	鍋	鎔	鎖	鎧	鎮	鎌	鏡	鐘	鐵
8a8.3	9.5	9.10	9.12	9.13	10.1	10.2	10.3	10.6	10.8	11.6	12.6	8a5.6

鑄	鑑	鑛	鑒
8a7.2	15.2	8a5.15	8a15.2

—————— 0 ——————

8a0.1 / 23   □ 金
                           72

金   金 金

KIN gold; metal; money; Friday
Kim (Korean surname) **KON** gold
kane money; metal **kana-** metal

—————— 1 ——————

0 サラ金 **sarakin** consumer/no-col-
   lateral loan business (short for
   サラリーマン金融)

金メダル **kinmedaru** gold medal

2 金入 **kanei(re)** purse, wallet; till
  金子 **Kaneko** (surname)
  金力 **kinryoku** the power of money

4 金井 **Kanai, Kanei** (surname)
  金欠 **kinketsu** shortage of money

5 金本 **Kanemoto, Kanamoto** (surname)
  金田 **Kaneda** (surname)

6 金色 **kinshoku, kin-iro, konjiki**
  golden color

7 金沢 **Kanazawa** (city, Ishikawa-
  ken)
  金言 **kingen** wise saying, maxim

8 金具 **kanagu** metal fittings, bracket

9 金持 **kanemo(chi)** rich person

10 金高 **kindaka** amount of money
  金庫 **kinko, kanegura** safe, vault;
  cashbox; depository, treasury;
  rich patron

11 金婚式 **kinkonshiki** golden wedding anniversary
  金細工 **kinzaiku** goldwork, gold
  ware

金魚 **kingyo** goldfish

12 金属 **kinzoku** metal
  金属製 **kinzokusei** made of metal

14 金髪 **kinpatsu** blond hair
  金製 **kinsei** made of gold
  金銭 **kinsen** money
  金閣寺 **Kinkakuji** Temple of the
  Golden Pavilion

15 金権 **kinken** the power of money,
  plutocracy

16 金融 **kin'yū** money, credit, financing

18 金儲 **kanemō(ke)** moneymaking
  金曜 **kin'yō** Friday
  金曜日 **kin'yōbi** Friday
  金額 **kingaku** amount of money

—————— 2 ——————

2 入金 **nyūkin** payment, money received

3 大金 **taikin** large amount of money

4 元金 **gankin, motokin** the principal, capital
  内金 **uchikin** partial payment, earnest money

5 代金 **daikin** price, charge, the mon-
  ey/bill
  礼金 **reikin** honorarium, fee

6 年金 **nenkin** annuity, pension
  合金 **gōkin** alloy
  成金 **narikin** new rich, parvenu

7 冶金 **yakin** metallurgy
  即金 **sokkin** (payment in) cash

8 送金 **sōkin** remittance
  拝金 **haikin** worship of money
  官金 **kankin** government funds

9 前金 **maekin, zenkin** advance payment

10 残金 **zankin** balance, surplus
  借金 **shakkin** debt

8 金 0

金
食
隹
雨
門

純金 **junkin** pure/solid gold
料金 **ryōkin** fee, charge, fare
針金 **harigane** wire
11 基金 **kikin** fund, endowment
掛金 **ka(ke)kin** installment (payment) **ka(ke)gane** latch, hasp
黄金 **ōgon, kogane** gold
現金 **genkin** cash
現金払 **genkinbara(i)** cash payment
12 換金 **kankin** realize, convert into money
募金 **bokin** fund raising
税金 **zeikin** tax
貯金 **chokin** savings, deposit
貯金通帳 **chokin tsūchō** bankbook
貯金箱 **chokinbako** savings box, (piggy) bank
集金 **shūkin** collecting money
13 献金 **kenkin** gift of money, contribution
聖金曜日 **Seikin'yōbi** Good Friday
賃金 **chingin** wages, pay
資金 **shikin** funds
預金 **yokin** deposit, bank account **azu(ke)kin** money on deposit
14 罰金 **bakkin** a fine
15 賞金 **shōkin** (cash) prize, monetary reward
敷金 **shikikin** (security) deposit

— 3 —

5 加入金 **kanyūkin** entrance/initiation fee
7 身代金 **mi(no)shirokin** ransom money
助成金 **joseikin** subsidy, grant
12 補助金 **hojokin** subsidy, grant
補償金 **hoshōkin** indemnity, compensation (money)
13 奨学金 **shōgakukin** a scholarship
15 賞与金 **shōyokin** bonus
賠償金 **baishōkin** indemnities, reparations, damages
16 積立金 **tsumitatekin** a reserve (fund)

— 4 —

1 一刻千金 **ikkoku senkin** Every minute counts.

2

釖 → 刀 2f0.1

8a2.3 / 341

⿰ 金 十
72 12

針　針針

SHIN, hari needle

— 1 —

5 針仕事 **hari shigoto** needlework, sewing
7 針医 **harii** acupuncturist
針灸 **shinkyū** acupuncture and moxibustion
8 針金 **harigane** wire
12 針葉樹 **shin'yōju** needle-leaf tree, conifer

— 2 —

4 方針 **hōshin** compass needle; course, policy
9 秒針 **byōshin** second hand (of a clock)
15 縫針 **nu(i)bari** sewing needle
19 羅針盤 **rashinban** compass

8a2.4

⿰ 金 丁
72 14

釘　釘釘

TEI, kugi nail, spike

— 1 —

5 釘付 **kugizu(ke)** nailing (down); pegging (a price)

8
2 金 食 隹 雨 門

8a3.4

□ 釒 儿 丨
72 16 2

釧 釧釧

SEN bracelet

1
---

13 釧路 **Kushiro** (city, Hokkaidō)

8a3.5 / 1862

□ 釒 ⺈ 丨
72 15 2

釣 釣釣

CHŌ, tsu(ru) fish, angle; lure, entice, take in; (see 吊) hang, suspend **tsu(ri)** (rod-and-reel) fishing; change (money returned when the amount paid is greater than the price)

1
---

0 お釣り **(o)tsu(ri)** change (money returned when the amount paid is greater than the price)
6 釣合 **tsu(ri)a(u)** be in balance, match **tsu(ri)a(i)** balance, equilibrium, proportion
9 釣竿 **tsu(ri)zao** fishing rod
11 釣堀 **tsu(ri)bori** fishpond
12 釣棚 **tsu(ri)dana** hanging shelf
14 釣銭 **tsu(ri)sen** change (money returned when the amount paid is greater than the price)
16 釣橋 **tsu(ri)bashi** suspension bridge

2
---

11 魚釣 **uotsu(ri), sakanatsu(ri)** fishing, angling

4

8a4.1 / 2130

□ 釒 攵
72 49

欽 欽欽

KIN respect, revere **KIN, YOSHI, TA-DA, KOKU, UYA** (part of given name)

HITOSHI, MAKOTO, SHITAU (m. given name)

8a4.2 / 966

□ 釒 十 凵
72 12 20

鈍 鈍鈍

DON, nibu(i) dull, thick, slow-witted, sluggish, blunt, dim **nibu(ru)** become dull/blunt, weaken **noro(i)** slow, dull; doting, flirtatious **nama(ru)** become dull/blunted **nama(su)** anneal

---
1
---

13 鈍感 **donkan** obtuse, thick, insensitive
15 鈍器 **donki** blunt object (used as a weapon)

鈎 → 鉤 8a5.17

5

8a5.4 / 1820

□ 釒 木 一
72 41 1

鉢 鉢鉢

HACHI, HATSU bowl, pot; brainpan, crown

1
---

6 鉢合 **hachia(wase)** bump heads; run into
12 鉢植 **hachiu(e)** potted plant

2
---

4 火鉢 **hibachi** charcoal brazier, hibachi

3
---

12 植木鉢 **uekibachi** flowerpot

8a5.6 / 312

□ 釒 𠂤 乚
72 34 15

鐵 | 鉄鉄

TETSU, kurogane iron

—————— 1 ——————

³ 鉄工場 **tekkōjō** ironworks

⁷ 鉄条網 **tetsujōmō** barbed-wire entanglements

⁸ 鉄板 **teppan** steel plate; griddle

⁹ 鉄則 **tessoku** hard-and-fast rule

¹⁰ 鉄砲 **teppō** gun

¹¹ 鉄道 **tetsudō** railroad

鉄道網 **tetsudōmō** railway network

¹³ 鉄鉱 **tekkō** iron ore

¹⁶ 鉄橋 **tekkyō** steel/railroad bridge

鉄鋼業 **tekkōgyō** the steel industry

—————— 2 ——————

⁷ 肘鉄 **hijitetsu** rebuff, rejection

私鉄 **shitetsu** private railway line

¹³ 電鉄 **dentetsu** electric railway

¹⁴ 製鉄所 **seitetsujo** ironworks

銑鉄 **sentetsu** pig iron

¹⁶ 鋼鉄 **kōtetsu** steel

鋼鉄板 **kōtetsuban** steel plate

—————— 3 ——————

⁶ 地下鉄 **chikatetsu** subway

8a5.11 / 1822 　　　田 金 亻 一
　　　　　　　　　　　72 　3 　1

 鈴鈴

REI, RIN, suzu bell

—————— 1 ——————

⁴ 鈴木 **Suzuki** (surname)

¹⁹ 鈴蘭 **suzuran** lily-of-the-valley

—————— 2 ——————

⁹ 風鈴 **fūrin** wind chime

8a5.14 / 1606 　　　田 金 口 儿
　　　　　　　　　　　72 24 16

 鉛鉛

EN, namari lead (the metal)

—————— 1 ——————

⁶ 鉛色 **namari-iro** lead color, gray

⁸ 鉛毒 **endoku** lead poisoning

¹² 鉛筆 **enpitsu** pencil

¹⁴ 鉛管 **enkan** lead pipe, plumbing

8a5.15 / 1604 　　　田 金 厂 竹
　　　　　　　　　　　72 18 17

 鑛 | 鉱鉱

KŌ ore

—————— 1 ——————

³ 鉱山 **kōzan** a mine

⁵ 鉱石 **kōseki** ore, mineral, (radio) crystal

⁸ 鉱物 **kōbutsu** mineral

⁹ 鉱泉 **kōsen** mineral springs

¹³ 鉱業 **kōgyō** mining

—————— 2 ——————

⁹ 炭鉱 **tankō** coal mine

¹¹ 採鉱 **saikō** mining

¹³ 鉄鉱 **tekkō** iron ore

8a5.17 　　　　　田 金 口 ㇇
　　　　　　　　　　　72 24 15

 鉤 | 鉤鉤

KŌ, kagi hook

—————— 1 ——————

⁴ 鉤手 **kagi(no)te** right-angle bend

—————— 6 ——————

8a6.1 / 648 　　　田 金 戈 二
　　　　　　　　　　　72 52 4

 錢 | 銭銭

SEN money; 1/100 yen **zeni** money

—————— 1 ——————

¹² 銭湯 **sentō** public bath

¹⁸ 銭儲 **zenimō(ke)** money-making

—————— 2 ——————

⁶ 守銭奴 **shusendo** miser, niggard

⁸ 金銭 **kinsen** money

¹¹ 悪銭 **akusen** ill-gotten money

8

5 金
食
隹
雷
門

釣銭 **tsu(ri)sen** change (money returned when the amount paid is greater than the price)

8a6.3 / 313

銀 銀

GIN, shirogane silver KANE (part of given name)

———————— 1 ————————

0 銀メダル **ginmedaru** silver medal
5 銀世界 **ginsekai** vast silvery/snowy scene
6 銀色 **gin-iro, ginshoku** silver color
  銀行 **ginkō** bank
7 銀杏 **ginnan** gingko nut
  ichō gingko tree
10 銀座 **ginza** silver mint; the Ginza
11 銀婚式 **ginkonshiki** silver wedding anniversary
14 銀製 **ginsei** made of silver
  銀閣寺 **Ginkakuji** (temple in Kyōto)

———————— 2 ————————

4 水銀 **suigin** mercury
  日銀 **Nichigin** Bank of Japan (short for 日本銀行)

8a6.4 / 1552

銘 銘

MEI inscription, signature, name; precept, motto

———————— 1 ————————

9 銘茶 **meicha** quality-brand tea
  銘柄 **meigara** name, brand, issue (of shares)

———————— 2 ————————

13 墓銘 **bomei** epitaph
14 碑銘 **himei** inscription, epitaph

8a6.6 / 1905

銑 銑

SEN pig iron

———————— 1 ————————

13 銑鉄 **sentetsu** pig iron

8a6.9 / 829

銃 銃

JŪ, tsutsu gun

———————— 1 ————————

10 銃殺 **jūsatsu** shoot dead
  銃砲 **jūhō** guns, firearms
12 銃弾 **jūdan** bullet
13 銃傷 **jūshō** gunshot wound
15 銃撃 **jūgeki** shooting

———————— 2 ————————

10 拳銃 **kenjū** pistol, handgun
11 猟銃 **ryōjū** hunting gun, shotgun

8a6.12 / 1605

銅 銅

DŌ, aka, akagane copper

———————— 1 ————————

0 銅メダル **dōmedaru** bronze medal
6 銅色 **dōshoku** copper-colored
11 銅貨 **dōka** copper coin
14 銅像 **dōzō** bronze statue

———————— 2 ————————

8 青銅色 **seidōshoku** bronze-color
  青銅器 **seidōki** bronze ware/tools

───────────────── 7 ─────────────────

8a7.2 / 1551   金 寸 十
                  72 37 12

鑄

鑄 | 鑄鋳

CHŪ, i(ru) cast (metal)

───────────────── 1 ─────────────────

⁸ 鋳物 **imono** article of cast metal, a casting
⁹ 鋳造 **chūzō** casting; minting, coinage
  鋳型 **igata** a mold, cast

8a7.4   金 大 亻
                  72 34 3

鋏

鋏鋏

KYŌ, hasami scissors; (ticket) punch
yattoko pliers, pincers

8a7.5   金 月 力
                  72 42 8

鋤

鋤鋤

JO, su(ku) till, plow **suki** spade, plow

───────────────── 1 ─────────────────

¹² 鋤焼 **sukiya(ki)** sukiyaki

8a7.12 / 1371   金 口 儿
                  72 24 16

鋭

 鋭 | 鋭鋭

EI, surudo(i) sharp, keen
TOSHI (part of given name)

───────────────── 1 ─────────────────

⁷ 鋭利 **eiri** sharp, keen
¹⁰ 鋭敏 **eibin** sharp, keen, acute

───────────────── 2 ─────────────────

⁶ 先鋭 **sen'ei** radical
  尖鋭 **sen'ei** acute; radical

───────────────── 8 ─────────────────

8a8.1   金 隹
                  72 74

錐

 錐錐

SUI gimlet; pyramid, cone **kiri** gimlet, auger, awl, drill

8a8.2 / 1904   金 王 艹
                  72 46 32

錘

 錘錘

SUI, tsumu spindle **omori** weight, plumb bob, sinker

8a8.3 / 1816   金 木 日
                  72 41 43

錬

錬 | 錬錬

REN, ne(ru) forge, temper, refine; polish up; train, drill

───────────────── 1 ─────────────────

⁶ 錬成 **rensei** training

───────────────── 2 ─────────────────

¹⁷ 鍛錬 **tanren** temper, anneal; train, harden

8a8.6 / 2256   金 日 巾
                  72 43 26

錦

 錦錦

KIN, nishiki brocade **KIN, NISHIKI, KANE** (part of given name)

───────────────── 1 ─────────────────

¹² 錦絵 **nishikie** colored woodblock print

—————— 2 ——————
14 綾錦 **ayanishiki** twill damask and brocade

錢 → 銭 8a6.1

8a8.8 ⊞ 金 月 土
72 42 22

錆 | 錆 錆

SHŌ, sabi rust **sa(biru)** rust, get rusty

—————— 1 ——————
5 錆付 **sabitsu(ku)** rust (together/fast)

8a8.10 / 1199 ⊞ 金 日 艹
72 43 32

錯 錯 錯

SAKU mix, be in disorder

—————— 1 ——————
7 錯乱 **sakuran** distraction, derangement
12 錯覚 **sakkaku** illusion
14 錯誤 **sakugo** error

—————— 2 ——————
10 倒錯 **tōsaku** perversion

—————— 3 ——————
13 試行錯誤 **shikō-sakugo** trial and error

8a8.12 / 1818 ⊞ 金 宀 疋
72 33 14

錠 錠 錠

JŌ lock, padlock; pill, tablet, (counter for pills)

—————— 1 ——————
9 錠前 **jōmae** a lock
10 錠剤 **jōzai** tablet, pill

—————— 2 ——————
4 手錠 **tejō** handcuffs

8a8.14 ⊞ 金 田 艹
72 58 32

錨 錨 錨

BYŌ, ikari anchor

—————— 1 ——————
8 錨泊 **byōhaku** anchorage

8a8.16 / 538 ⊞ 金 ヨ 氵
72 39 21

録 | 録 録

ROKU, to(ru) record

—————— 1 ——————
8 録画 **rokuga** (videotape) recording
9 録音 **rokuon** (sound) recording

—————— 2 ——————
4 収録 **shūroku** collect, record
5 付録 **furoku** supplement, appendix
7 抄録 **shōroku** excerpt, abstract, summary
10 記録 **kiroku** record, document(ary)
12 登録 **tōroku** registration

—————— 3 ——————
6 会議録 **kaigiroku** minutes, proceedings
　回顧録 **kaikoroku** memoirs, reminiscences
7 芳名録 **hōmeiroku** visitor's book, name list
　快記録 **kaikiroku** a fine record
10 随想録 **zuisōroku** occasional thoughts, essays
11 紳士録 **shinshiroku** a who's-who, directory
14 総目録 **sōmokuroku** complete catalog

鎚 → 鎚 8a9.10

8

金
食
隹
雨
門

8a8.18

□ 釒 ⺕ 廴
72 39 19

鍵 鍵

KEN, kagi key

——————— 1 ———————

² 鍵子 **kagi(k)ko** latchkey child (who carries a key to school because no one will be home when he returns)

⁵ 鍵穴 **kagiana** keyhole

8a8.19

□ 釒 尸 口
72 40 24

鋸 鋸

KYO, nokogiri, noko saw

——————— 1 ———————

¹⁰ 鋸屑 **nokokuzu** sawdust

8a8.20 / 1608

□ 釒 ⺵ 冂
72 36 20

鋼 鋼

KŌ, hagane steel

——————— 1 ———————

⁸ 鋼板 **kōhan, kōban** steel plate

¹³ 鋼鉄 **kōtetsu** steel

鋼鉄板 **kōtetsuban** steel plate

——————— 2 ———————

¹³ 鉄鋼業 **tekkōgyō** the steel industry

——————— 9 ———————

錬 → 錬 8a8.3

8a9.5 / 1817

□ 釒 厂 二
72 18 4

鍛 鍛

TAN, kita(eru) forge, temper; train, drill, discipline

——————— 1 ———————

³ 鍛工 **tankō** metalworker, smith

¹⁶ 鍛錬 **tanren** temper, anneal; train, harden

8a9.10

□ 釒 尸 辶
72 40 19

鎚 鎚 鎚

TSUI, tsuchi hammer

8a9.12

□ 釒 戈 口
72 52 24

鍼 鍼

SHIN, hari (acupuncture) needle

——————— 1 ———————

⁷ 鍼医者 **hariisha** acupuncturist

¹¹ 鍼術 **shinjutsu** acupuncture

8a9.13

□ 釒 口 冂
72 24 20

鍋 鍋

KA, nabe pot, saucepan

——————— 1 ———————

⁸ 鍋物 **nabemono** food served in the pot

¹² 鍋焼 **nabeya(ki)** boiled in a pot, baked in a casserole

—————— 10 ——————

8a10.1   田 金 火 宀
                                 72 44 33

熔｜鎔鎔

YŌ, to(keru) melt, become molten

—————— 1 ——————
8 鎔岩 **yōgan** lava
13 鎔解 **yōkai** melt, fuse

8a10.2 / 1819   田 金 貝 小
                                 72 68 35

鎖鎖

SA close, shut **kusari** chain
to(zasu) close, shut

—————— 1 ——————
8 鎖国 **sakoku** national isolation

—————— 2 ——————
9 連鎖反応 **rensa hannō** chain reaction
    封鎖 **fūsa** blockade; freeze (assets)
11 閉鎖 **heisa** closing, closure, lockout

8a10.3   田 金 山 凵
                                 72 36 24

鎧鎧

GAI, yoro(u) put on armor
yoroi (suit of) armor

—————— 1 ——————
4 鎧戸 **yoroido** Venetian blinds

8a10.6 / 1786   田 金 目 十
                                 72 55 12

鎮｜鎮鎮

CHIN, shizu(meru) calm, quell
shizu(maru) calm down **SHIZU** (part
of given name)

—————— 1 ——————
12 鎮痛剤 **chintsūzai** painkiller
14 鎮静剤 **chinseizai** tranquilizer,
    sedative

8a10.8 / 2257   田 金 彐 儿
                                 72 39 16

鎌｜鎌鎌

REN, kama sickle **REN, KEN, KA-
MA, KANE, KATA** (part of given name)

—————— 1 ——————
10 鎌倉 **Kamakura** (city, Kanagawa-
    ken); (era, 1185 – 1333)

—————— 11 ——————

8a11.6 / 863   田 金 立 日
                                 72 54 43

鏡鏡

KYŌ, kagami mirror

—————— 2 ——————
11 眼鏡 **megane, gankyō** (eye)glasses

—————— 3 ——————
4 双眼鏡 **sōgankyō** binoculars
6 色眼鏡 **iromegane** colored glasses;
    prejudiced view
8 拡大鏡 **kakudaikyō** magnifying
    glass
11 望遠鏡 **bōenkyō** telescope

—————— 12 ——————

8a12.6 / 1821   田 金 立 日
                                 72 54 43

鐘鐘

SHŌ, kane bell

8
釒 12
食
隹
雨
門

8a15.2

7 鐘声 **shōsei** sound/ringing of a bell
10 鐘紡 **Kanebō** (company name)

——— 13 ———

鐵 → 鉄 **8a5.6**

——— 14 ———

鑄 → 鋳 **8a7.2**

——— 15 ———

8a15.2 / 1664

田 金 m. 冂
72 59 20

鑑

鑑鑑

KAN, kagami model, paragon, example; mirror **kanga(miru)** take into
consideration, in view of; follow (an
example) AKIRA (m. given name)

——— 1 ———
8 鑑定 **kantei** appraisal, expert opinion
15 鑑賞 **kanshō** appreciation, enjoyment

——— 2 ———
6 年鑑 **nenkan** yearbook
印鑑 **inkan** one's seal; seal impression

鑛 → 鉱 **8a5.15**

鑒 → 鑑 **8a15.2**

食 8b

食 飢 飲 飩 飯 飽 飴 飾 飼 蝕 餌 餅 餓
0.1 2.1 4.1 4.2 4.5 5.1 5.2 5.3 5.4 6.1 6.2 6.4 7.1

餝 餘 餐 館 餡 饂 饅
8b5.3 2a5.24 7.4 8.3 8.4 10.2 11.1

——— 0 ———

8b0.1 / 322

食 73

食

食 食

SHOKU food, eating; (counter for
meals); eclipse **JIKI** food; eating
ta(beru) eat **ku(u/rau)** eat, drink; receive (a blow) **ku(eru)** can eat
ku(enai) cannot eat; shrewd, cunning
ku(rawasu/wasu) feed; make (someone) eat, give (someone a punch), play
(someone a trick) **ha(mu)** eat, feed
on; receive (an allowance)

——— 1 ———
0 食ってかかる **ku(ttekakaru)** lash
out at, defy
食パン **shokupan** (sliced white)
bread

4 食切 **ku(i)ki(ru)** bite off/through;
eat (it) all up
5 食生活 **shokuseikatsu** eating/di-
etary habits
食用 **shokuyō** edible, used for food
6 食尽 **ku(i)tsu(kusu), ta(be)-
tsu(kusu)** eat up, consume
7 食坊 **ku(ishin)bō** glutton, gourmand
8 食事 **shokuji** meal, dining
食事時 **shokujidoki** mealtime
食券 **shokken** meal ticket
食卓 **shokutaku** dining table
食物 **ta(be)mono, shokumotsu,
ku(i)mono** food **ku(wase)-
mono** a fake; imposter
食放題 **ta(be)hōdai, ku(i)hōdai**
eating as much as one pleases,
all-you-can-eat
9 食前 **shokuzen** before a meal
食通 **shokutsū** gourmet
食品 **shokuhin** food(stuffs)
食品店 **shokuhinten** grocery store

食後 **shokugo** after a meal
10 食料 **shokuryō** food
食料品 **shokuryōhin** food(stuffs)
11 食過 **ta(be)su(gi), ku(i)su(gi)** overeating
食堂 **shokudō** dining hall, cafeteria
食欲 **shokuyoku** appetite
12 食費 **shokuhi** food expenses, board
食間 **shokkan** between meals
13 食塩 **shokuen** table salt
15 食器 **shokki** eating utensils
18 食糧 **shokuryō** food

――――― 2 ―――――

1 一食 **isshoku** a meal
3 三食 **sanshoku** three meals (a day)
乞食 **kojiki** beggar
夕食 **yūshoku** supper, evening meal
4 水食 **suishoku** erosion
月食 **gesshoku** eclipse of the moon
5 外食 **gaishoku** eating out
立食 **ta(chi)gu(i), risshoku** eating while standing
6 肉食 **nikushoku** meat eating
衣食住 **ishokujū** food, clothing, and shelter
米食 **beishoku** rice diet
8 定食 **teishoku** regular meal, table d'hôte
和食 **washoku** Japanese food
9 美食家 **bishokuka** epicure, gourmet
洋食 **yōshoku** Western food
昼食 **chūshoku** lunch
10 浸食 **shinshoku** erosion, corrosion
蚕食 **sanshoku** encroachment, inroads
11 偏食 **henshoku** unbalanced diet
副食 **fukushoku** side dish; supplementary food
菜食 **saishoku** vegetarian/herbivorous diet
粗食 **soshoku** coarse food, plain diet
12 朝食 **chōshoku** breakfast
絶食 **zesshoku** fasting
軽食 **keishoku** light meal
飲食 **inshoku, no(mi)ku(i)** food and drink, eating and drinking
飲食物 **inshokubutsu** food and drink

13 試食 **shishoku** sample, taste
14 腐食 **fushoku** corrosion
餌食 **ejiki** food, bait, prey
18 糧食 **ryōshoku** provisions, food

――――― 4 ―――――

10 弱肉強食 **jakuniku-kyōshoku** survival of the fittest

――――― 2 ―――――

8b2.1 / 1304　　　□□ 食 冂
　　　　　　　　　　73　20

飢　　　　飢 飢

KI, u(eru) starve

――――― 1 ―――――

6 飢死 **u(e)ji(ni)** starve to death
15 飢餓 **kiga** hunger, starvation

――――― 4 ―――――

8b4.1 / 323　　　□□ 食 夊
　　　　　　　　　　73　49

飲　　　　飲丨飲 飲

IN, no(mu) drink

――――― 1 ―――――

4 飲水 **no(mi)mizu** drinking water
5 飲用水 **in'yōsui** drinking water
8 飲物 **no(mi)mono** (something to) drink, beverage
9 飲食 **inshoku, no(mi)ku(i)** food and drink, eating and drinking
飲食物 **inshokubutsu** food and drink
10 飲料水 **inryōsui** drinking water
11 飲過 **no(mi)su(giru)** drink too much

――――― 2 ―――――

1 一飲 **hitono(mi)** a mouthful; a swallow/sip; an easy prey
3 口飲 **kuchino(mi)** drink from the bottle
5 立飲 **ta(chi)no(mi)** drinking while standing

8
金
食 4
隹
雨
門

7 乳飲子 **chino(mi)go** suckling infant, babe in arms

10 酒飲 **sakeno(mi)** drinker

15 暴飲 **bōin** heavy/excessive drinking

— 3 —

11 清涼飲料 **seiryō inryō** carbonated beverage

8b4.2 　　□ 食 十 冂
　　　　　　73 12 20

飩飩

TON, DON noodles

— 2 —

19 饂飩 **udon** noodles, udon

8b4.5 / 325 　　□ 食 厂 又
　　　　　　73 18 9

飯飯

HAN, meshi, mama cooked rice; meal, food　**ii** cooked rice

— 1 —

0 ご飯 **(go)han** cooked rice; meal, food

5 飯田 **Iida** (surname)

12 飯塚 **Iizuka** (surname)

— 2 —

3 夕飯 **yūhan, yūmeshi** evening meal

6 早飯 **hayameshi** eating fast/early

7 赤飯 **sekihan, akameshi** (festive) rice with red beans

麦飯 **mugimeshi** boiled barley and rice

8 炊飯器 **suihanki** (electric) rice cooker

9 茶飯事 **sahanji** everyday occurrence

昼飯 **hirumeshi, chūhan** lunch

12 御飯 **gohan** boiled rice; a meal

御飯時 **gohandoki** mealtime

朝飯 **asahan, asameshi** breakfast

— 5 —

8b5.1 / 1763 　　□ 食 弓 宀
　　　　　　73 28 15

飽飽

HŌ, a(kiru/ku) get (sick and) tired of, have had enough of　**a(kasu)** cloy, satiate, surfeit; tire, bore, make (someone) fed up　**a(kanu)** unwearied of, untiring　**a(kippoi)** fickle, be soon tired of

— 1 —

0 飽くまで/くまでも **a(kumade/kumade mo)** to the last, throughout, strictly

12 飽満 **hōman** satiety, satiation

8b5.2 　　□ 食 口 竹
　　　　　　73 24 17

飴 | 飴飴

I, ame starch-jelly candy, hard candy

— 1 —

6 飴色 **ame-iro** amber, light brown

8b5.3 / 979 　　□ 食 巾 宀
　　　　　　73 26 15

餝 | 飾飾

SHOKU, kaza(ru) decorate, adorn

— 1 —

5 飾付 **kaza(ri)tsu(ke)** decoration

6 飾気 **kaza(ri)ke** affectation, love of display

— 2 —

8 服飾 **fukushoku** clothing and accessories, attire

9 首飾 **kubikaza(ri)** necklace

10 修飾 **shūshoku** decorate, adorn; modify (in grammar)

12 着飾 **kikaza(ru)** dress up

装飾 **sōshoku** ornament, decoration

装飾品 **sōshokuhin** ornaments, decorations, accessories

13 電飾 **denshoku** decorative lighting
15 潤飾 **junshoku** embellishment
16 頸飾 **kubikaza(ri)** necklace

8b5.4 / 1762   ⬚ 食 口 一
73 24 1

飼   飼飼

SHI, ka(u) raise, keep (animals)

——————— 1 ———————

4 飼犬 **ka(i)inu** pet dog
5 飼主 **ka(i)nushi** (pet) owner, master
8 飼育 **shiiku** raising, breeding
13 飼馴 **ka(i)na(rasu)** domesticate, tame

——————— 2 ———————

18 鵜飼 **uka(i)** fishing with cormorants

——————— 6 ———————

8b6.1   ⬚ 食 虫
73 64

蝕   蝕｜蝕蝕

SHOKU eclipse, occultation; be worm-eaten; be eroded **mushiba(mu)** be worm-eaten; gnaw at

8b6.2   ⬚ 食 耳
73 65

餌   餌｜餌餌

JI, e, esa feed, food; bait

——————— 1 ———————

9 餌食 **ejiki** food, bait, prey

8b6.4   ⊞ 食 艹 儿
73 32 16

餅   餅｜餅餅

HEI, mochi rice cake

——————— 2 ———————

9 柏餅 **kashiwa mochi** rice cake wrapped in an oak leaf
12 焼餅 **ya(ki)mochi** toasted rice cake; jealousy
13 煎餅 **senbei** (rice) cracker

——————— 7 ———————

8b7.1 / 1303   ⬚ 食 戈 十
73 52 12

餓   餓餓

GA, u(eru) starve, be hungry
katsu(eru) be starving for, hunger for

——————— 1 ———————

6 餓死 **gashi** starve to death

——————— 2 ———————

10 飢餓 **kiga** hunger, starvation

餝→飾 **8b5.3**

餘→余 **2a5.24**

8b7.4   … 食 夕 ⺊
73 30 13

餐   餐餐

SAN eat, drink

——————— 2 ———————

12 晩餐 **bansan** dinner, supper

——————— 8 ———————

8b8.3 / 327   ⬚ 食 宀 尸
73 33 40

館   舘｜館館

KAN (large) building, hall **yakata** mansion, manor **tate, tachi** fort; mansion TACHI (surname)

——————— 1 ———————

8 館長 **kanchō** director, curator

8
金食催雫門 8

2

5 本館 **honkan** main building; this building
6 会館 **kaikan** (assembly) hall
7 別館 **bekkan** annex
8 函館 **Hakodate** (city, Hokkaidō)
10 旅館 **ryokan** inn, hotel

3

3 大使館 **taishikan** embassy
4 公民館 **kōminkan** public hall, community center
　水族館 **suizokukan** (public) aquarium
6 迎賓館 **geihinkan** reception hall, residence for guests
7 体育館 **taiikukan** gymnasium
　図書館 **toshokan** library
9 美術館 **bijutsukan** art gallery
　映画館 **eigakan** movie theater
12 博物館 **hakubutsukan** museum
14 領事館 **ryōjikan** consulate

4

14 総領事館 **sōryōjikan** consulate-general

8b8.4　　　　　囗 食 彐 宀
　　　　　　　　73 39 15

館

館館

AN bean jam

1

0 餡パン **anpan** bean-jam-filled roll

10

8b10.2　　　　　囗 食 罒 口
　　　　　　　　73 59 24

饂

饂饂

UN noodles

1

13 饂飩 **udon** noodles, udon

11

8b11.1　　　　　囗 食 日 日
　　　　　　　　73 55 43

饅

饅饅

MAN dumpling

1

16 饅頭 **manjū** steamed dumpling (with bean-jam/meat filling)

隹 8c

隻 隼 雀 雄 集 焦 雅 雅 雌 雑 奪 雛 難
2.1 2.2 3.2 4.1 4.2 4.3 8c5.1 5.1 6.1 6.2 6.4 10.1 10.2

離 雑 難 耀 罐 観
10.3 8c6.2 8c10.2 12.1 2k4.6 5c13.7

2

8c2.1 / 1311　　　　　日 隹 又
　　　　　　　　74 9

隻

隻隻

SEKI (counter for ships); one (of a pair)

1

11 隻眼 **sekigan** one-eyed

8c2.2 / 2259 　　　　　　　日　隹　亠
　　　　　　　　　　　　74　12

隼隼

JUN, SHUN, hayabusa falcon JUN, SHUN, HAYA, TAKA, TOSHI (part of given name) HAYASHI, HAYATO, HAYABUSA (m. given name)

――――― 1 ―――――

² 隼人 **Hayato** (m. given name)

――――― 3 ―――――

8c3.2 　　　　　　　亠…　隹　小　｜
　　　　　　　　　　　74　35　2

雀雀

JAKU, suzume sparrow

――――― 2 ―――――

³ 孔雀 **kujaku** peacock
¹¹ 麻雀 **mājan** mahjong

――――― 4 ―――――

8c4.1 / 1387 　　　　　　口　隹　十　竹
　　　　　　　　　　　74　12　17

雄

雄雄

YŪ male; brave; great **osu, o-, on-** male TAKESHI (m. given name) YŪ, O, TAKA, TAKE (part of given name)

――――― 1 ―――――

³ 雄三 **Yūzō, Takemi** (m. given name)
　雄大 **yūdai** grand, magnificent **Yūdai** (m. given name)
⁴ 雄太 **Yūta** (m. given name)
　雄犬 **osuinu** male dog
⁹ 雄姿 **yūshi** gallant figure

――――― 2 ―――――

¹ 一雄 **Kazuo, Ichio, Kunio** (m. given name)
⁵ 正雄 **Masao** (m. given name)

⁷ 辰雄 **Tatsuo** (m. given name)
　秀雄 **Hideo, Shūyū** (m. given name)
⁸ 英雄 **eiyū** hero **Hideo, Fusao** (m. given name)
　和雄 **Kazuo, Toshio** (m. given name)
¹¹ 達雄 **Tatsuo, Michio** (m. given name)
　康雄 **Yasuo, Michio** (m. given name)
¹² 喜雄 **Yoshio, Hisao** (m. given name)
¹⁴ 雌雄 **shiyū** male and female; (decide) winner and loser, (vie for) supremacy **mesuosu** male and female

8c4.2 / 436 　　　　　　日　隹　木
　　　　　　　　　　　74　41

集集

SHŪ, atsu(meru) gather, collect **atsu(maru)** gather, come together **tsudo(u)** gather, assemble, meet

――――― 1 ―――――

⁴ 集中 **shūchū** concentration
⁶ 集合 **shūgō** gathering, meeting; set (in math)
　集会 **shūkai** meeting, assembly
　集団 **shūdan** group, mass, crowd
　集成 **shūsei** collect, compile
⁸ 集金 **shūkin** collecting money

――――― 2 ―――――

⁴ 文集 **bunshū** anthology
⁵ 召集 **shōshū** call together, convene
⁶ 全集 **zenshū** complete works
¹⁰ 特集 **tokushū** special edition/collection
¹¹ 採集 **saishū** collecting (butterflies)
¹² 募集 **boshū** recruiting; solicitation
　結集 **kesshū** concentrate, marshal together
¹³ 群集 **gunshū** crowd, multitude, mob (psychology)
　蒐集 **shūshū** collect, gather, accumulate

8

金
食
隹
雨
門

4

詩集 **shishū** a collection of poems
14 選集 **senshū** selection, anthology
歌集 **kashū** poetry anthology
駆集 **ka(ri)atsu(meru)** muster, round up
15 撰集 **senshū** anthology
編集 **henshū** editing, compilation

───── 3 ─────

3 万葉集 **Man'yōshū** (Japan's oldest anthology of poems)
5 古今集 **Kokinshū** (short for 古今和歌集, see next entry)

───── 5 ─────

5 古今和歌集 **Kokinwakashū** (poetry anthology, early tenth century)

8c4.3 / 999

焦

日 隹 火
74 44

焦 焦

SHŌ fire; impatience; yearning **ko(geru)** get scorched **ko(gasu)** scorch, singe; pine for **ko(gareru)** pine/yearn for **ase(ru)** be in a hurry, be hasty/impatient **ji(reru)** fret, be irritated **ji(rasu)** irritate, nettle, tease

───── 1 ─────

4 焦心 **shōshin** impatience, anxiousness
9 焦臭 **ko(ge)kusa(i), kinakusa(i)** smelling burnt

───── 2 ─────

10 恋焦 **ko(i)ko(gareru)** pine for, be desperately in love
11 黒焦 **kuroko(ge)** charred, burned black

雅 → 雅 8c5.1

───── 5 ─────

8c5.1 / 1456

雅

田 隹 一 亠
74 14 11

雅 | 雅 雅

GA elegance, gracefulness **miya(bita), miya(biyaka)** elegant, refined MIYABI (f. given name) TADASHI (m. given name) GA, MASA (part of given name)

───── 1 ─────

2 雅人 **Masato, Gajin** (m. given name)
雅子 **Masako, Motoko, Utako, Tsuneko** (f. given name)
3 雅也 **Masaya** (m. given name)
9 雅美 **Masami, Masayoshi, Motomi, Tsuneyoshi** (given name)
13 雅楽 **gagaku** ancient Japanese court music

───── 2 ─────

17 優雅 **yūga** elegant, graceful, refined

───── 6 ─────

8c6.1 / 1388

雌

止 隹 匕 |
74 13 2

雌 雌

SHI, mesu, me- female

───── 1 ─────

4 雌犬 **mesuinu** female dog, bitch
12 雌雄 **shiyū** male and female; (decide) winner and loser, (vie for) supremacy **mesuosu** male and female

8c6.2 / 575

雑

日 隹 木 十
74 41 12

雜 | 雑 雑

ZATSU, ZŌ miscellaneous, a mix **ma(zeru), maji(eru)** (tr.) mix **ma(zaru/jiru)** (intr.) mix, mingle

───── 1 ─────

4 雑木林 **zōkibayashi, zōbokurin** grove of trees of various species
7 雑学 **zatsugaku** knowledge of various subjects

9 雑音 **zatsuon** noise, static

12 雑煮 **zōni** rice cakes boiled with vegetables

雑費 **zappi** miscellaneous expenses

14 雑種 **zasshu** of various kinds; mixed breed

雑誌 **zasshi** magazine

15 雑談 **zatsudan** chitchat, idle conversation

雑踏 **zattō** hustle and bustle, congestion

───── 2 ─────

3 大雑把 **ōzappa** rough (guess); generous

7 夾雑物 **kyōzatsubutsu** admixture, impurities

乱雑 **ranzatsu** disorder, confusion

11 混雑 **konzatsu** confusion, disorder, congestion

13 煩雑 **hanzatsu** complicated, troublesome

14 複雑 **fukuzatsu** complicated, complex

8c6.4 / 1310   ⊟ 隹 寸 大
74 37 34

奪 奪

DATSU, uba(u) snatch away, take by force; captivate

───── 1 ─────

8 奪取 **uba(i)to(ru)** plunder
dasshu capture, seize, wrest

───── 2 ─────

6 争奪 **sōdatsu** contend/scramble for
争奪戦 **sōdatsusen** contest/scramble/struggle for

11 掠奪 **ryakudatsu** plunder, loot, despoil

強奪 **gōdatsu** rob, plunder, hijack, hold up

略奪 **ryakudatsu** pillage, plunder, looting

───── **10** ─────

8c10.1 / 2260   ⊟ 隹 勹 冂
74 15 20

雛 **雛 雛**

SŪ, hina chick; (Girls' Festival) doll
hiyoko chick   SŪ, SU, JU, HINA (part of given name)

───── 1 ─────

2 雛人形 **hina ningyō** (Girls' Festival) doll

11 雛祭 **hinamatsu(ri)** Girls' Doll Festival (March 3)

8c10.2 / 557   ⊟ 隹 艹 口
74 32 24

難 難 | 難 難

NAN difficulty; distress **muzuka(shii), kata(i)** difficult **-nlku(i), -gata(i)** difficult/hard to …, un…able

───── 1 ─────

5 難民 **nanmin** refugees

8 難波 **Nanba** (surname)

9 難点 **nanten** difficult point

14 難読 **nandoku** a difficult reading
難関 **nankan** barrier, obstacle, difficulty

18 難題 **nandai** difficult topic/problem

───── 2 ─────

1 一難 **ichinan** one difficulty, one danger

3 大難 **tainan** great misfortune, calamity

4 水難 **suinan** sea disaster, flood, drowning

6 気難 **kimuzuka(shii)** hard to please, grouchy

至難 **shinan** extreme difficulty

有難 **a(ri)gata(i)** welcome, thankful   **a(ri)ga(tō)** thank you

有難味 **a(ri)gatami** value, worth

7 困難 **konnan** difficulty, trouble

8
金
食
隹 **10**
雨
門

災難 **sainan** mishap, accident, calamity

忍難 **shino(bi)gata(i)** unbearable

言難 **i(i)gata(i)** difficult to say, inexpressible

8 非難 **hinan** criticize, denounce

受難 **junan** ordeal, sufferings; (Jesus's) Passion

9 海難 **kainan** sea disaster, shipwreck

11 盗難 **tōnan** (loss from) theft

12 無難 **bunan** safe, acceptable

13 遭難 **sōnan** disaster, accident, mishap, distress

14 読難 **yo(mi)niku(i)** hard to read

15 避難 **hinan** refuge, evacuation

避難民 **hinanmin** refugees, evacuees

---

9 飛離 **to(bi)hana(reru)** fly apart; tower above; out of the ordinary

10 遊離 **yūri** isolate, separate

12 隔離 **kakuri** isolate, segregate

距離 **kyori** distance

——— 3 ———

6 近距離 **kinkyori** short distance/range

8 長距離 **chōkyori** long-distance, long-range

12 遠距離 **enkyori** long distance, long-range

短距離 **tankyori** short distance, short-range

15 膚身離 **hadami-hana(sazu)** always kept on one's person, highly treasured

---

雜 → 雑 8c6.2

難 → 難 8c10.2

——— 12 ———

8c10.3 / 1281   田 隹 亠 冂
                     74 11 20

    离 | 離 離

RI, hana(reru) separate, leave
hana(su) separate, keep apart

——— 1 ———

10 離陸 **ririku** (airplane) takeoff

離宮 **rikyū** detached palace

11 離婚 **rikon** divorce

12 離散 **risan** scatter, disperse

15 離縁 **rien** divorce, disowning

——— 2 ———

4 切離 **ki(ri)hana(su)** cut off/apart, sever, separate

分離 **bunri** separation, division

引離 **hi(ki)hana(su)** pull apart; outdistance

7 別離 **betsuri** parting, separation

8c12.1 / 2202   田 隹 小 彐
                     74 35 39

耀   耀 | 耀 耀

YŌ, kagaya(ku) shine, sparkle, gleam
AKIRA (m. given name) YŌ, AKI, TERU (part of given name)

——— 15 ———

罐 → 缶 2k4.6

——— 16 ———

觀 → 観 5c13.7

——— 8d ———

雨 雪 雲 霧 雷 電 雹 零 需 霊 震 霞 霜
0.1 3.2 4.1 4.2 5.1 5.2 5.3 5.4 6.1 7.2 7.3 9.1 9.2

8
金 食 隹
10 隹 霝
門

霧　霸　露　靁　霊
11.1　4b15.4　13.1　16.1　8d7.2

0

8d0.1 / 30

75

雨　　雨雨

U, ame, ama- rain

1

4　雨天　**uten** rainy weather
　雨水　**amamizu, usui** rainwater
　雨戸　**amado** storm door, shutter
8　雨垂　**amada(re)** raindrops, eaves-
　　　drops
　雨具　**amagu** rain gear, rainwear
12　雨傘　**amagasa** umbrella
　雨期　**uki** the rainy season
　雨量　**uryō** (amount of) rainfall
　雨雲　**amagumo** rain cloud
13　雨靴　**amagutsu** rubbers, overshoes
14　雨滴　**uteki** raindrop
　雨模様　**amamoyō, amemoyō** signs
　　　of rain
16　雨曇　**amagumo(ri)** overcast
　　　weather

2

1　一雨　**hitoame** a shower/rainfall
3　大雨　**ōame, taiu** heavy rainfall,
　　　downpour
　小雨　**kosame** light rain, drizzle
9　俄雨　**niwakaame** (sudden) shower
　降雨　**kōu** rain(fall)
　風雨　**fūu** wind and rain, rainstorm
　春雨　**harusame, shun'u** spring
　　　rain; bean-jelly sticks
10　梅雨　**baiu, tsuyu** the rainy season
　時雨　**shigure** an off-and-on late-au-
　　　tumn/early-winter rain
11　細雨　**saiu** fine/misty rain, drizzle
13　雷雨　**raiu** thunderstorm
14　豪雨　**gōu** heavy rain, downpour
19　霧雨　**kirisame** misty rain, drizzle

3

15　暴風雨　**bōfūu** rainstorm

18　蟬時雨　**semishigure** outburst of ci-
　　　cada droning

3

8d3.2 / 949

75　39

雪　　雪｜雪雪

SETSU, yuki snow **susu(gu),
soso(gu)** rinse, wash, clear (one's
name)

1

7　雪花　**sekka** snowflakes
8　雪空　**yukizora** snowy sky
　雪国　**yukiguni** snow country
11　雪達磨　**yuki daruma** snowman
12　雪嵐　**yukiarashi** snowstorm
　雪景色　**yukigeshiki** snowy land-
　　　scape
13　雪搔　**yukika(ki)** snow shovel(ing)/
　　　plow(ing)

2

3　大雪　**ōyuki, taisetsu** heavy snow
7　吹雪　**fubuki** snowstorm, blizzard
　初雪　**hatsuyuki** first snow of the
　　　season
10　残雪　**zansetsu** lingering snow

4

8d4.1 / 636

目　　二　竹
75　4　17

雲　　雲雲

UN, kumo cloud

1

5　雲仙岳　**Unzendake** (mountain, Na-
　　　gasaki-ken)
8　雲泥差　**undei (no) sa** a great differ-
　　　ence
13　雲隠　**kumogaku(re)** be hidden be-
　　　hind clouds; disappear

— 2 —

⁵ 出雲 **Izumo** (ancient kuni, Shimane-ken)

白雲 **shirakumo, hakuun** white/fleecy clouds

⁸ 雨雲 **amagumo** rain cloud

¹¹ 黒雲 **kurokumo, kokuun** dark clouds

¹⁴ 層雲 **sōun** stratus clouds

²⁴ 鱗雲 **urokogumo** cirrocumulus clouds

8d4.2 / 1824   日 雨 儿 力   75 16 8

雰 雰

FUN fog

— 1 —

⁷ 雰囲気 **fun'iki** atmosphere, ambience

— 5 —

8d5.1 / 952   日 雨 田   75 58

雷 雷

RAI, kaminari, ikazuchi thunder

— 1 —

⁸ 雷雨 **raiu** thunderstorm

¹³ 雷電 **raiden** thunder and lightning, thunderbolt

¹⁴ 雷鳴 **raimei** thunder

— 2 —

⁴ 水雷 **suirai** torpedo; mine

⁶ 地雷 **jirai** land mine

¹² 落雷 **rakurai** be struck by lightning

8d5.2 / 108   日 雨 日 | 75 43 2

電 電

DEN electricity

— 1 —

² 電子レンジ **denshi renji** microwave oven

電子 **denshi** electron
電子- **denshi-** electronic

電力 **denryoku** electric power

⁵ 電圧 **den'atsu** voltage

⁶ 電気 **denki** electricity; electric light

電気屋 **denkiya** electrical appliance store/dealer

電池 **denchi** battery, dry cell

電灯 **dentō** electric light

⁷ 電車 **densha** electric car, streetcar, train

電車賃 **denshachin** tramfare, trainfare

⁸ 電卓 **dentaku** (desktop) calculator (short for 電子式卓上計算機)

電送 **densō** electrical transmission

電波 **denpa** electromagnetic waves, radio

⁹ 電信 **denshin** telegraph, telegram, cable

¹⁰ 電流 **denryū** electric current

¹¹ 電球 **denkyū** light bulb

¹² 電報 **denpō** telegram

¹³ 電源 **dengen** power source

電話 **denwa** telephone

電話局 **denwakyoku** telephone office

電話料 **denwaryō** telephone charges

電話帳 **denwachō** telephone directory

電鉄 **dentetsu** electric railway

電飾 **denshoku** decorative lighting

¹⁵ 電線 **densen** electric wire/line/cable

— 2 —

⁴ 日電 **Nichiden** (short for 日本電気) NEC (Corporation)

⁵ 市電 **shiden** municipal railway, trolley

⁶ 充電 **jūden** recharge (a battery)

⁸ 青電話 **aodenwa** public telephone

⁹ 発電 **hatsuden** generation of electricity; sending a telegram

発電所 **hatsudensho** power plant, generating station

祝電 **shukuden** telegram of congratulations

10 起電力 **kidenryoku** electromotive force

家電 **kaden** household electrical products/appliances, consumer electronics (short for 家庭用電気製品)

11 停電 **teiden** cutoff of electricity, power outage

乾電池 **kandenchi** dry cell, battery

終電車 **shūdensha** the last train/streetcar for the day

13 蓄電池 **chikudenchi** storage battery

節電 **setsuden** saving on electricity

雷電 **raiden** thunder and lightning, thunderbolt

14 漏電 **rōden** leakage of electricity, short circuit

——————— 3 ———————

16 懐中電灯 **kaichū dentō** flashlight

——————— 4 ———————

10 留守番電話 **rusuban denwa** answering machine

8d5.3

電　日　⻗　尸　ヘ
　　　75　40　15

 電電

HAKU, hyō hail

——————— 1 ———————

10 雹害 **hyōgai** hail damage

8d5.4 / 1823

零　日　⻗　亻　一
　　　75　3　1

 零零

REI zero **kobo(reru)** (intr.) spill **kobo(su)** (tr.) spill

——————— 1 ———————

3 零下 **reika** below zero, subzero

9 零点 **reiten** (a score/temperature of) zero

零度 **reido** zero (degrees), the freezing point

10 零時 **reiji** 12:00 (noon or midnight)

——————— 6 ———————

8d6.1 / 1416

需　日　⻗　丆　冂
　　　75　14　20

 需需

JU request, need, demand

——————— 1 ———————

9 需要 **juyō** demand

12 需給 **jukyū** supply and demand

——————— 2 ———————

4 内需 **naiju** domestic demand

5 必需品 **hitsujuhin** necessities, essentials

9 軍需 **gunju** military demand/supplies

——————— 7 ———————

8d7.2 / 1168

霊　日　⻗　工　儿
　　　75　38　16

 霊｜霊霊

REI, RYŌ, tama soul, spirit

——————— 1 ———————

9 霊界 **reikai** the spiritual world

13 霊園 **reien** cemetery park

霊感 **reikan** inspiration

14 霊魂 **reikon** soul, spirit

——————— 2 ———————

3 亡霊 **bōrei** departed soul, ghost

9 幽霊 **yūrei** ghost

13 聖霊 **Seirei** Holy Spirit

15 慰霊祭 **ireisai** memorial service

8d7.3 / 953

75 57 18

震

震 震

SHIN, furu(eru), furu(u) shake, tremble

--- 1 ---

5 震央 **shin'ō** epicenter
7 震災 **shinsai** earthquake disaster
9 震度 **shindo** earthquake intensity
10 震害 **shingai** earthquake damage
11 震動 **shindō** tremor, vibration
13 震源地 **shingenchi** epicenter

--- 2 ---

6 地震 **jishin** earthquake
7 身震 **miburu(i)** shiver, tremble, shudder
余震 **yoshin** aftershock
11 強震 **kyōshin** violent earthquake
13 微震 **bishin** slight earthquake/tremor
16 激震 **gekishin** severe earthquake

--- 3 ---

3 大地震 **ōjishin, daijishin** major earthquake

--- 9 ---

8d9.1 / 2261

75 40 4

霞

霞 霞

KA, kasumi haze, mist; dimness of sight **kasu(mu)** be hazy; (eyes) grow dim **KA, KO** (part of given name) KASUMI (f. given name)

--- 1 ---

5 霞目 **kasumime** purblind/blurred eyes
14 霞関 **Kasumi(ga)seki** (area of Tōkyō, where government ministries are located)

8d9.2 / 948

75 55 41

霜

霜 霜

SŌ, shimo frost

--- 1 ---

9 霜降 **shimofu(ri)** marbled (meat), salt-and-pepper pattern
霜柱 **shimobashira** ice/frost columns
10 霜害 **sōgai** frost damage

--- 11 ---

8d11.1 / 950

75 49 14

霧

霧 霧

MU, kiri fog

--- 1 ---

4 霧中 **muchū** in the fog
8 霧雨 **kirisame** misty rain, drizzle

--- 2 ---

3 夕霧 **yūgiri** evening mist
12 朝霧 **asagiri** morning fog
13 煙霧 **enmu** mist, fog, smog
16 濃霧 **nōmu** dense fog

--- 13 ---

霸 → 覇 4b15.4

8d13.1 / 951

75 70 49

露

露 露

RO in the open, exposed; dew; Russia **RŌ** open, public **tsuyu** dew **ara(wa)** open, public, frank

--- 1 ---

5 露出 **roshutsu** (indecent/film) exposure

8
金
食
隹
7
雨
門

7 露見 **roken** be found out, come to light

8 露店 **roten** street stall, vending booth

10 露骨 **rokotsu** open, undisguised, frank; conspicuous; lewd

18 露顕 **roken** be found out, come to light

— 2 —

4 日露 **Nichi-Ro** Japan and Russia

5 白露 **Hakuro** White Russia, Belarus

7 対露 **tai-Ro** toward/with Russia

8 披露 **hirō** announcement

披露宴 **hirōen** (wedding) reception

15 暴露 **bakuro** expose, bring to light

— **16** —

8d16.1 ⊞ 雨 言 日 75 67 43

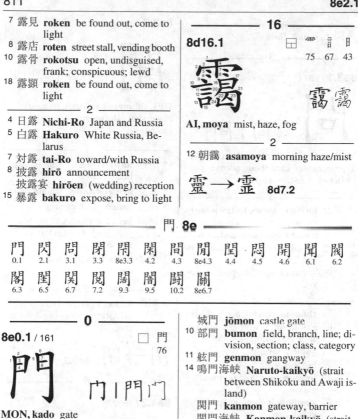

AI, moya mist, haze, fog

— 2 —

12 朝靄 **asamoya** morning haze/mist

靈 → 霊 **8d7.2**

門 **8e**

門 閃 問 閉 閂 閑 間 閖 閨 悶 開 聞 閾
0.1 2.1 3.1 3.3 8e3.3 4.2 4.3 8e4.3 4.4 4.5 4.6 6.1 6.2

閣 閏 関 閲 闊 闇 闘 關
6.3 6.5 6.7 7.2 9.3 9.5 10.2 8e6.7

8

金
食
隹
雨
門 2

— **0** —

8e0.1 / 161   ⊟ 門 76

門

門 丨 門 门

MON, kado gate

— 1 —

5 門外 **mongai** outside the gate; outside one's specialty

門外漢 **mongaikan** outsider; layman

8 門限 **mongen** closing time

門松 **kadomatsu** New Year's pine-and-bamboo decorations

9 門前払 **monzenbara(i)** turning (someone) away at the gate, refusing to see (someone)

— 2 —

2 入門 **nyūmon** admission, entrance; introduction, handbook, primer

5 石門 **sekimon** stone gate

7 肛門 **kōmon** the anus

9 専門 **senmon** specialty

城門 **jōmon** castle gate

10 部門 **bumon** field, branch, line; division, section; class, category

11 舷門 **genmon** gangway

14 鳴門海峡 **Naruto-kaikyō** (strait between Shikoku and Awaji island)

関門 **kanmon** gateway, barrier

関門海峡 **Kanmon-kaikyō** (strait between Shimonoseki and Moji)

— 3 —

4 天安門 **Ten'anmon** Tiananmon, Gate of Heavenly Peace (in Beijing)

12 凱旋門 **gaisenmon** arch of triumph

— 2 —

8e2.1   ▣ 門 亻 76 3

閃

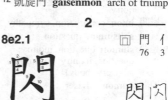

SEN, hirame(ku) (intr.) flash
hirame(kasu) (tr.) flash, brandish

—————— 1 ——————

⁶ 閃光 **senkō** flash

—————— 3 ——————

8e3.1 / 162 　　　□ 門 ㅁ
　　　　　　　　　76　24

問

問 | 問 問

MON question, problem　**to(u)** ask, inquire; matter, care about; accuse **to(i), ton** question, inquiry

—————— 1 ——————

⁶ 問合 **to(i)a(waseru), to(i)a(wasu)** inquire
¹² 問答 **mondō** questions and answers
¹⁸ 問題 **mondai** problem, question, issue
　　問題点 **mondaiten** the point at issue

—————— 2 ——————

⁴ 弔問 **chōmon** condolence call/visit
⁷ 学問 **gakumon** learning, scholarship, education, science
⁹ 拷問 **gōmon** torture
¹¹ 訪問 **hōmon** visit
¹² 尋問 **jinmon** questioning, interrogation
　　検問 **kenmon** inspect, examine, check
¹³ 禅問答 **zen mondō** Zen/incomprehensible dialog
　　詰問 **kitsumon** cross-examination, grilling
¹⁴ 疑問 **gimon** question, doubt
　　疑問符 **gimonfu** question mark
¹⁵ 審問 **shinmon** trial, hearing, inquiry
　　慰問 **imon** consolation, sympathy
　　質問 **shitsumon** question
¹⁶ 諮問 **shimon** question, inquiry; question, inquiry; consultive, advisory (body)
²¹ 顧問 **komon** adviser

—————— 3 ——————

⁶ 先決問題 **senketsu mondai** question to be settled first

8

金
食
隹
雷

3 門

8e3.3 / 397 　　□ 門 十 丨
　　　　　　　　76　12　2

閉

閉 | 閉 閉

HEI, shi(meru), to(jiru), to(zasu) close, shut　**shi(maru)** be(come) closed

—————— 1 ——————

⁴ 閉込 **to(ji)ko(meru)** shut in, confine
⁶ 閉会 **heikai** closing, adjournment
⁸ 閉店 **heiten** store closing
¹³ 閉塞 **heisoku** blockade; obstruction **to(ji)fusa(geru)** close up, cover over
¹⁸ 閉鎖 **heisa** closing, closure, lockout

—————— 2 ——————

¹² 開閉 **kaihei** opening and closing **a(ke)ta(te)** opening and shutting

閑 → 閉　8e3.3

—————— 4 ——————

8e4.2 / 1532 　　□ 門 木
　　　　　　　　　76　41

閑

閑 閑

KAN leisure　SHIZU (part of given name)

—————— 1 ——————

¹² 閑散 **kansan** leisure; (market) inactivity
¹⁴ 閑静 **kansei** quiet, peaceful

—————— 2 ——————

¹² 森閑 **shinkan (to shita)** still, hushed, silent
¹³ 農閑期 **nōkanki** farmers' slack season

8e4.3 / 43

囗 門 日
76 43

間

閒｜間间

KAN interval, space between; (as suffix) between, among **KEN** between, among; (counter for spaces on a go board); (unit of length, about 1.8 m) **aida** interval (of space or time), between, among **ai** interval, between, cross(breed) **ma** space, room; pause, a rest (in music); a room; time, leisure; luck, the situation

───────────── 1 ─────────────

⁰ 間もなく **ma(monaku)** presently, in a little while, soon

¹ 間一髪 **kan ippatsu** a hair's breadth

⁶ 間合 **ma (ni) a(u)** be in time for; serve the purpose, suffice

間近 **majika** nearby, close, affecting one personally

⁷ 間投詞 **kantōshi** an interjection

⁹ 間柄 **aidagara** relationship

¹¹ 間接 **kansetsu** indirect

間接税 **kansetsuzei** indirect tax

¹² 間隔 **kankaku** space, spacing; interval

間違 **machiga(u)** be mistaken/ wrong **machiga(eru)** mistake

¹³ 間際 **magiwa** on the verge of, just before

───────────── 2 ─────────────

² 人間 **ningen** human being, man

人間性 **ningensei** human nature, humanity

³ 大間違 **ōmachiga(i)** big mistake

⁴ 中間 **chūkan** middle, midway, intermediate; midterm, interim

区間 **kukan** section, interval

手間 **tema** time, labor, trouble; wages

⁵ 民間 **minkan** private (not public)

本間 **Honma** (surname)

世間 **seken** the world, people, the public, society, life; rumor, gossip

広間 **hiroma** hall; spacious room

⁶ 年間 **nenkan** period of a year; during the year

仲間 **nakama** member of a group, mate, fellow **chūgen** samurai's attendant

仲間外 **nakamahazu(re)** being left out

合間 **a(i)ma** interval

⁷ 束間 **tsuka(no)ma** brief time, moment

谷間 **tanima, taniai** valley, ravine

床間 **toko(no)ma** alcove (in a Japanese-style room)

⁸ 空間 **kūkan** space **a(ki)ma** vacant room

居間 **ima** living room

板間 **ita(no)ma** wooden floor

⁹ 透間 **su(ki)ma** crevice, gap, opening, space

垣間見 **kaimami(ru)** peek in, get a glimpse

茶間 **cha(no)ma** living room

客間 **kyakuma** guest room, parlor

昼間 **hiruma, chūkan** daytime, during the day

食間 **shokkan** between meals

¹⁰ 週間 **shūkan** week

時間 **jikan** an hour; time

時間表 **jikanhyō** timetable, schedule

¹² 隙間 **sukima** crevice, opening, gap, space

晴間 **ha(re)ma** interval of clear weather

絶間 **ta(e)ma** interval, pause, gap **ta(e)ma(naku)** continually, without letup

¹⁸ 瞬間 **shunkan** instant, moment

───────────── 3 ─────────────

¹ 一週間 **isshūkan** a week

⁴ 日本間 **nihonma** Japanese-style room

⁷ 何時間 **nanjikan** how many hours

応接間 **ōsetsuma** reception room, parlor

8

金
食
隹
雷
門 4

8 非人間的 **hiningenteki** inhuman, impersonal

長時間 **chōjikan** a long time

10 夏時間 **natsujikan** daylight-saving time

閒 → 間 8e4.3

8e4.4

 門 王
76 46

閏 閏

JUN leap (year); extra; pretending to the throne **urū** leap (year)

――――― 1 ―――――

6 閏年 **urūdoshi** leap year

8e4.5

 門 忄
76 51

悶 悶

MON, moda(eru) be in agony

――――― 1 ―――――

6 悶死 **monshi, moda(e)ji(ni)** die in agony

12 悶着 **monchaku** trouble; dispute

8e4.6 / 396

 門 艹 一
76 32 1

開 闱

KAI opening; development **a(ku/ keru)** (intr./tr.) open **hira(keru)** be opened, become developed **hira(ku)** (intr. or tr.) open, develop **hira(ki)** opening; difference, margin; (hinged) door

――――― 1 ―――――

6 開会 **kaikai** opening a meeting

開会式 **kaikaishiki** opening ceremony

7 開花 **kaika** bloom, flower, blossom

8 開拓 **kaitaku** opening up land, development

開始 **kaishi** begin, commence, start

開店 **kaiten** opening a new store; opening the store for the day

開放 **kaihō, a(ke)hana(su)** (fling/ leave) open **a(kep)pana(shi)** left open; open, frank

9 開発 **kaihatsu** development

11 開票 **kaihyō** ballot counting

開閉 **kaihei** opening and closing **a(ke)ta(te)** opening and shutting

12 開場 **kaijō** opening

13 開業 **kaigyō** opening/starting a business

開業医 **kaigyōi** doctor in private practice

開催 **kaisai** hold (a meeting)

開幕 **kaimaku** opening/raising the curtain

16 開墾 **kaikon** clear (land), bring under cultivation

――――― 2 ―――――

4 公開 **kōkai** open to the public

5 打開 **dakai** a break, development, new turn

6 再開 **saikai** reopen, resume, reconvene

全開 **zenkai** open fully

10 展開 **tenkai** unfold, develop, evolve; deploy, fan out; expand (a math expression), develop (into a two-dimensional surface)

11 疎開 **sokai** dispersal, removal, evacuation

12 満開 **mankai** in full bloom

13 幕開 **makua(ki), makua(ke)** opening of a play; beginning

――――― 4 ―――――

9 帝王切開 **teiō sekkai** Caesarean section

8
金
食
催
雷
4 門

—— 6 ——

8e6.1 / 64 囗 門 耳
76 65

聞

BUN, MON, ki(ku) hear, listen to; heed; ask **ki(koeru)** be heard/audible **ki(koe)** reputation, publicity

—— 1 ——

2 聞入 **ki(ki)i(reru)** accede to, comply with **ki(ki)i(ru)** listen attentively

4 聞手 **ki(ki)te** listener

6 聞返 **ki(ki)kae(su)** ask back

8 聞直 **ki(ki)nao(su)** ask/inquire again

聞取 **ki(ki)to(ru)** hear and understand, catch, follow

9 聞洩 **ki(ki)mo(rasu)** miss hearing, not catch

13 聞損 **ki(ki)sokona(u)** mishear, not catch

14 聞漏 **ki(ki)mo(rasu)** miss hearing, not catch

—— 2 ——

2 又聞 **matagi(ki)** hearsay, secondhand information

4 仄聞 **sokubun** hear (by chance)

6 伝聞 **denbun** hearsay, report, rumor

7 見聞 **kenbun, kenmon, miki(ki)** information, knowledge, experience

13 新聞 **shinbun** newspaper

新聞社 **shinbunsha** newspaper (company)

新聞紙 **shinbunshi** newspaper (paper)

14 誤聞 **gobun** mishearing; misinformation

17 聴聞会 **chōmonkai** public hearing

醜聞 **shūbun** scandal

—— 4 ——

5 外字新聞 **gaiji shinbun** foreign-language newspaper

8 英字新聞 **eiji shinbun** English-language newspaper

9 前代未聞 **zendai-mimon** unprecedented

8e6.2 / 1510 囗 門 戈 亻
76 52 3

閥

BATSU clique, clan, faction

—— 1 ——

11 閥族 **batsuzoku** clan, clique

—— 2 ——

7 学閥 **gakubatsu** clique of graduates from the same school, old boy network

9 軍閥 **gunbatsu** military clique, militarist party

派閥 **habatsu** clique, faction

10 党閥 **tōbatsu** faction, clique

財閥 **zaibatsu** financial clique

18 藩閥 **hanbatsu** clanship, clannishness

8e6.3 / 837 囗 門 夂 口
76 49 24

閣

KAKU tower, palace; the cabinet

—— 1 ——

14 閣僚 **kakuryō** cabinet members

20 閣議 **kakugi** cabinet meeting

—— 2 ——

4 内閣 **naikaku** the cabinet

仏閣 **bukkaku** Buddhist temple

8 金閣寺 **Kinkakuji** Temple of the Golden Pavilion

10 倒閣 **tōkaku** overthrowing the cabinet

11 組閣 **sokaku** formation of a cabinet

14 銀閣寺 **Ginkakuji** (temple in Kyōto)

8

金
食
隹
雨
門 6

8e6.5 □ 門 土
76 22

閨 閨

KEI, neya bedroom

———————— 1 ————————

7 閨秀作家 **keishū sakka** woman writer

8e6.7 / 398 □ 門 大 儿
76 34 16

關 | 関 関

KAN barrier, (border) checkpoint; relating to, concerning **seki** barrier, (border) checkpoint **kaka(waru)** be related to, have to do with **kaka(wari)** relation, connection **SEKI** (surname)

———————— 1 ————————

0 関する **kan(suru)** be related to, concern, involve

3 関口 **Sekiguchi** (surname)

4 関心 **kanshin** interest, concern

6 関西 **Kansai** (region including Ōsaka and Kyōto)

8 関東 **Kantō** (region including Tōkyō)

関取 **sekitori** ranking sumo wrestler

関門 **kanmon** gateway, barrier

関門海峡 **Kanmon-kaikyō** (strait between Shimonoseki and Moji)

9 関係 **kankei** relation(ship), connection

関係者 **kankeisha** interested party, those concerned

関連 **kanren** connection, relation, association

12 関税 **kanzei** customs, tariff, duty

———————— 2 ————————

3 大関 **ōzeki** sumo wrestler of second-highest rank

下関 **Shimonoseki** (city, Yamaguchi-ken)

5 玄関 **genkan** entranceway, vestibule, front door

8 股関節 **kokansetsu** hip joint

12 無関心 **mukanshin** indifference, unconcern, apathy

無関係 **mukankei** unrelated, irrelevant

税関 **zeikan** customs; customshouse

16 機関 **kikan** engine; machinery, organ(ization)

機関車 **kikansha** locomotive

機関誌 **kikanshi** organization's publication

17 霞関 **Kasumi(ga)seki** (area of Tōkyō, where government ministries are located)

18 難関 **nankan** barrier, obstacle, difficulty

———————— 3 ————————

7 利害関係 **rigai kankei** interests

8 表玄関 **omote genkan** front entrance/door

———————— 7 ————————

8e7.2 / 1369 □ 門 口 儿
76 24 16

閲 閲

ETSU inspection, review, revision

———————— 1 ————————

17 閲覧 **etsuran** perusal, inspection, reading

閲覧室 **etsuranshitsu** reading room

———————— 2 ————————

12 検閲 **ken'etsu** censorship; inspection (of troops)

———————— 9 ————————

8e9.3 □ 門 氵 口
76 21 24

濶 | 闊 濶

KATSU wide; broad-minded

———————— 1 ————————

11 闊達 **kattatsu** magnanimous, generous

8

金
食
隹

雷

6 門

⁵ 迂闊 **ukatsu** careless, stupid

8e9.5 / 1972   門 立 日
               76 54 43

闇　　闇 闇

AN, yami darkness; gloom; black market

---- 1 ----

⁸ 闇夜 **yamiyo, an'ya** dark night
闇取引 **yamitorihiki** black-market dealings, illegal transaction
⁹ 闇屋 **yamiya** black marketeer
闇相場 **yamisōba** black-market price
¹⁰ 闇値 **yamine** black-market price

---- 2 ----

³ 夕闇 **yūyami** dusk, twilight

---- 10 ----

8e10.2 / 1511   門 口 寸
               76 24 37

鬪　　鬭 鬪

TŌ, tataka(u) fight, struggle

---

³ 闘士 **tōshi** fighter for
⁴ 闘犬 **tōken** dogfight(ing); fighting dog
闘牛士 **tōgyūshi** matador, bull-fighter
⁶ 闘争 **tōsō** struggle, conflict; strike
⁷ 闘志 **tōshi** fighting spirit
¹⁴ 闘魂 **tōkon** fighting spirit

---- 2 ----

⁷ 決闘 **kettō** duel
⁹ 春闘 **shuntō** spring labor offensive (short for 春季闘争)
¹⁰ 健闘 **kentō** put up a good fight, make strenuous efforts
拳闘 **kentō** boxing
¹³ 戦闘 **sentō** combat, battle, fighting
戦闘機 **sentōki** fighter (plane)
¹⁶ 奮闘 **funtō** struggle, strive, fight hard

---- 11 ----

鬪 → 関 8e6.7

頁 **2**

頁 9a

頁	頂	頃	項	順	須	頓	頒	頌	預	頑	頸	領
0.1	2.1	2.2	3.1	3.2	3j9.1	4.1	4.3	4.4	4.5	4.6	9a7.4	5.2

頬	頼	頰	頻	頸	頭	頻	類	顎	顔	顕	額	顏
9a7.2	7.1	7.2	9a8.2	7.4	7.6	8.2	9.1	9.2	9.3	9.5	9.6	9a9.3

題	類	願	顧	鬚	顯
9.7	9a9.1	10.2	12.2	13.2	9a9.5

---- 0 ----

9a0.1   頁
               77

頁　　頁 頁

KETSU, pēji page

---- 2 ----

9a2.1 / 1440   頁 一
               77 14

頂　　頂 頂

CHŌ, itadaki summit, top
itada(ku) be capped with; receive

——————— 1 ———————

3 頂上 **chōjō** summit, peak, top, climax

9 頂点 **chōten** zenith, peak, climax

17 頂戴 **chōdai** accept, receive; please (give me)

——————— 2 ———————

3 山頂 **sanchō** summit

4 仏頂面 **butchōzura** sour face, pout, scowl

12 絶頂 **zetchō** summit, peak, climax

9a2.2 / 1985 　　□　頁　卜
　　　　　　　　77　13

頃頃

KEI, koro, -goro time; about, toward
koro(shimo) at that time

——————— 1 ———————

6 頃合 **koroa(i)** suitable time; propriety; moderation

——————— 2 ———————

4 中頃 **nakagoro** about the middle

今頃 **imagoro** at about this time

日頃 **higoro** usually, always; for a long time

6 年頃 **toshigoro** age; marriageable age

近頃 **chikagoro** recently, nowadays

先頃 **sakigoro** recently, the other day

——————— 3 ———————

9a3.1 / 1439 　　□　頁　工
　　　　　　　　77　38

項項

KŌ item, clause, paragraph; term (in math) **unaji** nape of the neck

——————— 1 ———————

5 項目 **kōmoku** heading, item

——————— 2 ———————

7 条項 **jōkō** articles and paragraphs, stipulations

8 事項 **jikō** matters, facts, items

9 要項 **yōkō** the essential point(s)

9a3.2 / 769 　　□　頁　儿　丨
　　　　　　　　77　16　2

順順

JUN order, sequence; obey, follow
NOBU, MASA, YORI (part of given name)

——————— 1 ———————

0 ＡＢＣ順 **ē-bī-shī-jun** alphabetic order

1 順一 **Jun'ichi, Masakazu** (m. given name)

2 順子 **Junko, Yoriko, Noriko, Nobuko** (f. given name)

7 順位 **jun'i** ranking, standing

順応 **junnō** adapt/conform to

順序 **junjo** order, sequence; procedure

12 順番 **junban** order, one's turn

15 順調 **junchō** favorable, smooth, without a hitch

——————— 2 ———————

3 大順 **ō(kii) jun** decreasing order, largest first

小順 **chii(sai) jun** increasing order, smallest first

4 手順 **tejun** procedure, routine, process

10 席順 **sekijun** seating order, precedence

11 道順 **michijun** route, itinerary

12 筆順 **hitsujun** stroke order

——————— 3 ———————

6 年代順 **nendaijun** chronological order

先着順 **senchakujun** by order of arrival, in the order of receipt, (on a) first-come-first-served basis

——————— 4 ———————

4 五十音順 **gojūon-jun** in *"aiueo"* order of the kana alphabet

9

2 頁

須 → **3j9.1**

──────── **4** ────────

9a4.1   臼 頁 十 冂
               77 12 20

頓 頓

TON sudden; bow low; stumble; be in order **tomi** sudden

──────── 1 ────────

⁶ 頓死 **tonshi** sudden death

9a4.3 / 1850   臼 頁 儿 力
               77 16 8

頒 頒

HAN, waka(tsu) divide, distribute

──────── 1 ────────

⁵ 頒布 **hanpu** distribute, circulate

9a4.4 / 2264   臼 頁 儿 竹
               77 16 17

頌 頌

SHŌ praise, eulogy **SHŌ, JU, NOBU, TSUGU, TADA, UTA, OTO, YOMU** (part of given name)

──────── 1 ────────

¹⁴ 頌徳 **shōtoku** eulogizing someone's virtues

9a4.5 / 394   臼 頁 亠 一
               77 14 1

預 預

YO, azu(keru) entrust/receive for safekeeping **YO, azu(karu)** entrust/ receive for safekeeping

──────── 1 ────────

⁸ 預所 **azu(kari)sho** depository, warehouse

預金 **yokin** deposit, bank account **azu(ke)kin** money on deposit

──────── 3 ────────

¹ 一時預場 **ichiji azukarijō** baggage safekeeping area

9a4.6 / 1848   臼 頁 二 儿
               77 4 16

頑 頑

GAN, kataku(na) stubborn, obstinate

──────── 1 ────────

³ 頑丈 **ganjō** solid, firm, robust
⁸ 頑固 **ganko** stubborn, obstinate
¹¹ 頑張 **ganba(ru)** persist in, stick to it, hang in there

──────── **5** ────────

頚 → 頸 **9a7.4**

9a5.2 / 834   臼 頁 亻 一
               77 3 1

領 領

RYŌ govern, rule; territory; neck, collar; (counter for suits of armor)

──────── 1 ────────

³ 領土 **ryōdo** territory
⁴ 領収書 **ryōshūsho** receipt
    領収証 **ryōshūshō** receipt
⁷ 領承 **ryōshō** understand, acknowledge, estimate
⁸ 領事 **ryōji** consul
    領事館 **ryōjikan** consulate
¹¹ 領域 **ryōiki** territory; domain, field

──────── 2 ────────

⁵ 占領 **senryō** occupation, capture; have all to oneself

9

頁 **5**

8 受領 **juryō** receive, accept
9 要領 **yōryō** gist, substance, synopsis
14 総領事 **sōryōji** consul-general
　　総領事館 **sōryōjikan** consulate-general
15 横領 **ōryō** misappropriate, embezzle, usurp

―――――― 3 ――――――
3 大統領 **daitōryō** president

―――――― 4 ――――――
11 副大統領 **fukudaitōryō** vice president

―――――― 6 ――――――
頬→頰 **9a7.2**

―――――― 7 ――――――

9a7.1 / 1512　　　□ 頁 木 口
　　　　　　　　　　　77 41 24

頼 | 頼頼

RAI, tano(mu) ask for, request; entrust to **tano(moshii)** reliable, dependable; promising **tayo(ru)** rely/depend on YORI (part of given name)

―――――― 1 ――――――
4 頼込 **tano(mi)ko(mu)** earnestly request

―――――― 2 ――――――
8 依頼 **irai** request; entrust; rely on
9 信頼 **shinrai** reliance, trust, confidence

9a7.2　　　□ 頁 大 亻
　　　　　　　77 34 3

頬 | 頬頬

KYŌ, hō, hoho cheek

―――――― 1 ――――――
0 頬っぺた **ho(ppeta)** cheek
10 頬笑 **hohoe(mi)** smile

頻→頻 **9a8.2**

9a7.4　　　□ 頁 エ 一
　　　　　　　77 38 1

頸 | 頸頸

KEI, kubi neck

―――――― 1 ――――――
13 頸飾 **kubikaza(ri)** necklace

9a7.6 / 276　　　□ 頁 口 儿
　　　　　　　77 24 16

頭頭

TŌ, ZU, TO, atama, kōbe, kaburi head **kashira** head, leader, top

―――――― 1 ――――――
3 頭上 **zujō** overhead
4 頭文字 **kashiramoji** initials; capital letter
11 頭脳 **zunō** brains, head
12 頭痛 **zutsū** headache
14 頭髪 **tōhatsu** hair (on the head)

―――――― 2 ――――――
5 出頭 **shuttō** appear, attend, be present
　　叩頭 **kōtō** kowtow, bow deeply
6 年頭 **nentō** beginning of the year
　　　　toshigashira the oldest person
　　先頭 **sentō** (in the) lead, (at the) head
7 没頭 **bottō** be engrossed/absorbed in
　　禿頭 **hageatama, tokutō** bald head
8 阜頭 **futō** wharf
9 冒頭 **bōtō** beginning, opening (paragraph)
10 教頭 **kyōtō** head teacher
11 偏頭痛 **henzutsū, hentōtsu** migraine headache
　　接頭辞 **settōji** prefix

¹² 街頭 **gaitō** street
²⁰ 饅頭 **manjū** steamed dumpling (with bean-jam/meat filling)

———— 3 ————

⁷ 坊主頭 **bōzuatama** shaven/close-cropped head

———— 8 ————

9a8.2 / 1847   　田 頁 小 ├
　　　　　　　　77 35 13

頻│頻頻

HIN occur repeatedly **shiki(ri)** frequently, repeatedly, incessantly, intently

———— 1 ————

⁹ 頻度 **hindo** frequency, rate of occurrence
¹⁶ 頻繁 **hinpan** frequent, incessant

———— 9 ————

9a9.1 / 226   　田 頁 半 大
　　　　　　　　77 62 34

類│類類

RUI kind, type, genus; similarity
tagui kind, sort; match, equal

———— 1 ————

⁷ 類似 **ruiji** similarity, resemblance
¹³ 類義語 **ruigigo** words of similar meaning

———— 2 ————

² 人類 **jinrui** mankind, man
　人類学 **jinruigaku** anthropology
⁴ 分類 **bunrui** classification
⁵ 比類 **hirui** a parallel, an equal
⁶ 衣類 **irui** clothing
⁷ 貝類 **kairui** shellfish (plural)
¹⁰ 酒類 **shurui** alcoholic beverages, liquor
　書類 **shorui** documents, papers
¹¹ 魚類 **gyorui** fishes

　鳥類 **chōrui** birds, fowl
¹⁴ 種類 **shurui** kind, type, sort
　穀類 **kokurui** grains
¹⁶ 獣類 **jūrui** beasts, animals, brutes
　親類 **shinrui** relatives
¹⁹ 藻類 **sōrui** water plants, seaweeds

———— 3 ————

⁹ 柑橘類 **kankitsurui** citrus fruits

9a9.2   　田 頁 口 二
　　　　　　　77 24 4

顎│顎顎

GAKU, ago jaw, chin **agito** gills

———— 1 ————

²² 顎鬚 **agohige** beard

9a9.3 / 277   　田 頁 立 彡
　　　　　　　　77 54 31

顔

顔│顔顔

GAN, kao face

———— 1 ————

⁵ 顔付 **kaotsu(ki)** face, look(s), expression
⁶ 顔色 **kaoiro, ganshoku** complexion; expression
⁷ 顔見知 **kaomishi(ri)** knowing someone by sight, a nodding acquaintance
¹³ 顔触 **kaobu(re)** personnel, lineup, cast

———— 2 ————

⁷ 似顔絵 **nigaoe** portrait, likeness
⁸ 泣顔 **na(ki)gao** crying/tearful face
　知顔 **shi(ran) kao, shi(ranu) kao** pretending not to know, nonchalant **shi(ri)gao** knowing look
¹⁰ 涙顔 **namidagao** tearful face
　素顔 **sugao** face without makeup; sober face

9
頁 9

笑顔 **egao, wara(i)gao** smiling face
12 朝顔 **asagao** morning glory
13 新顔 **shingao** new face, newcomer
15 横顔 **yokogao** profile, side view, silhouette
憂顔 **ure(i)gao** sorrowful face, troubled look

--- 3 ---

8 物知顔 **monoshi(ri)gao** knowing look

9a9.5 / 1170

田 頁 日 儿
77 43 16

顯 | 顕 顕

KEN clear, plain, obvious
ara(wareru) appear, become evident
ara(wasu) show, exhibit, manifest
AKIRA (m. given name) AKI (part of given name)

--- 1 ---

5 顕示 **kenji** show, unveil, reveal
11 顕著 **kencho** notable, striking, marked

--- 2 ---

21 露顕 **roken** be found out, come to light

9a9.6 / 838

田 頁 夂 宀
77 49 33

額 額

GAKU amount; framed picture
hitai forehead

--- 1 ---

9 額面 **gakumen** face value, par

--- 2 ---

3 小額 **shōgaku** small amount
4 巨額 **kyogaku** enormous amount, vast sum
5 半額 **hangaku** half the amount/price

6 多額 **tagaku** large sum/amount
年額 **nengaku** annual amount
全額 **zengaku** the full amount
8 定額 **teigaku** fixed amount, flat sum
金額 **kingaku** amount of money
10 残額 **zangaku** remaining amount, balance
倍額 **baigaku** double the amount
11 産額 **sangaku** output, yield, production
14 増額 **zōgaku** increase (the amount)
総額 **sōgaku** total amount

顔 → 顔 9a9.3

9a9.7 / 354

… 頁 日 丷
77 43 14

題 題

DAI subject, topic, theme; title

--- 1 ---

6 題名 **daimei** title

--- 2 ---

5 主題 **shudai** theme, subject matter
7 改題 **kaidai** retitle, rename
8 表題 **hyōdai** title, heading, caption
例題 **reidai** example, exercise (in a textbook)
放題 **-hōdai** (as verb suffix) as much as one pleases, all you can (eat)
11 副題 **fukudai** subtitle, subheading
宿題 **shukudai** homework
問題 **mondai** problem, question, issue
問題点 **mondaiten** the point at issue
13 話題 **wadai** topic, subject
15 標題 **hyōdai** title, heading, caption
課題 **kadai** subject, theme, topic, problem; (school) assignment
18 難題 **nandai** difficult topic/problem
20 議題 **gidai** topic for discussion, agenda

9 頁

9

─────── 3 ───────

5 仕放題 **shihōdai** have one's own way

9 食放題 **ta(be)hōdai, ku(i)hōdai** eating as much as one pleases, all-you-can-eat

─────── 4 ───────

6 先決問題 **senketsu mondai** question to be settled first

─────── 10 ───────

類 → 類 9a9.1

9a10.2 / 581   田 頁 日 小
77 43 35

願顧

GAN, nega(u) petition, request, desire

─────── 1 ───────

8 願事 **nega(i)goto** one's wish/prayer

10 願書 **gansho** written request, application

11 願望 **ganbō, ganmō** wish, desire

─────── 2 ───────

3 大願 **taigan** ambition, aspiration; earnest wish

4 心願 **shingan** heartfelt desire; prayer

5 出願 **shutsugan** application

7 志願者 **shigansha** applicant, candidate, volunteer, aspirant

8 念願 **nengan** one's heart's desire, earnest wish

祈願 **kigan** a prayer

9 哀願 **aigan** entreat, implore, petition

12 訴願 **sogan** petition, appeal

13 嘆願 **tangan** entreaty, petition

14 歎願 **tangan** petition, appeal

15 熱願 **netsugan** fervent plea, earnest entreaty

請願 **seigan** petition, application

─────── 12 ───────

9a12.2 / 1554   田 頁 隹 尸
77 74 40

顧 ┃ 顧 顧

KO, kaeri(miru) look back; take into consideration

─────── 1 ───────

11 顧問 **komon** adviser

─────── 2 ───────

6 回顧 **kaiko** recollect, look back on
回顧録 **kaikoroku** memoirs, reminiscences

11 眷顧 **kenko** favor, patronage

─────── 13 ───────

9a13.2   田 頁 彡 卜
77 31 13

鬚 鬚

SHU, hige beard (on the chin)

─────── 2 ───────

18 顎鬚 **agohige** beard

─────── 14 ───────

顯 → 顕 9a9.5

9

頁 **13**

─────── 馬 **10a** ───────

馬	馴	駄	駁	駅	駆	駐	駝	駒	馴	駱	駿	騎
0.1	3.2	4.1	4.3	4.4	4.5	5.2	5.3	5.5	2f4.1	6.2	7.1	8.3

験	騒	騙	騰	騒	駆	驕	驚	駅	験
8.4	8.5	9.1	4b16.3	10a8.5	10a4.5	12.2	12.4	10a4.4	10a8.4

0

10a0.1 / 283   □ 馬
                78

馬

馬 馬

BA, uma, ma horse

1

2 馬力 **bariki** horsepower
6 馬耳東風 **bajitōfū** utter indifference, turn a deaf ear
11 馬術 **bajutsu** horseback riding, dressage
   馬鹿 **baka** fool, idiot, stupid; to a ridiculous degree
12 馬場 **Baba** (surname)

2

3 下馬評 **gebahyō** outsiders' irresponsible talk, rumor
9 乗馬 **jōba, no(ri)uma** horseback riding; riding horse
13 群馬県 **Gunma-ken** (prefecture)
16 親馬鹿 **oyabaka** overfond parent
   縞馬 **shimauma** zebra
18 騎馬 **kiba** on horseback, mounted
20 競馬 **keiba** horse race/racing

3

8 弥次馬 **yajiuma** bystanders, spectators, crowd of onlookers

10a3.2   Ⅲ 馬 九 │
             78 16 2

馴

馴 馴

JUN, na(reru) get used to
na(rasu) tame, train

1

7 馴初 **na(re)so(me)** beginning of a romance
9 馴染 **naji(mi)** familiar

2

5 幼馴染 **osana najimi** childhood playmate

13 飼馴 **ka(i)na(rasu)** domesticate, tame

4

10a4.1 / 1880   Ⅲ 馬 大 │
             78 34 2

駄

駄 駄

DA, TA pack horse; of poor quality

1

5 駄弁 **daben** foolish talk, bunk
   駄目 **dame** no good
7 駄作 **dasaku** poor work, worthless stuff

2

3 下駄 **geta** clogs
12 無駄 **muda** futile, useless, wasteful
   無駄遣 **mudazuka(i)** waste, squander

10a4.3   Ⅲ 馬 十
             78 12

駁

駁 駁

BAKU speckled, piebald; refutation

1

15 駁撃 **bakugeki** argue against, attack, refute
   駁論 **bakuron** refutation, rebuttal

10a4.4 / 284   Ⅲ 馬 尸 │
             78 40 2

駅

驛 │ 駅 駅

EKI (train) station

1

5 駅弁 **ekiben** box lunch sold at a train station
8 駅長 **ekichō** stationmaster
9 駅前 **ekimae** in front of the station
10 駅員 **ekiin** station employee/staff

— 2 —

6 各駅停車 **kakuekiteisha** local train

— 3 —

11 終着駅 **shūchakueki** terminal station

10a4.5 / 1882

⊞ 馬 冂 十
78 20 12

驅 | 駆駆

KU, ka(keru) gallop; run, rush
ka(ru) drive, spur on

— 1 —

4 駆込 **ka(ke)ko(mu)** rush into, seek refuge in
駆引 **ka(ke)hi(ki)** bargaining, haggling, maneuvering

5 駆出 **ka(ke)da(su)** rush out, start running **ka(ke)da(shi)** beginner **ka(ri)da(su)** round up, muster

6 駆回 **ka(ke)mawa(ru), ka(kezuri)-mawa(ru)** run around

7 駆足 **ka(ke)ashi** running, galloping

9 駆逐 **kuchiku** drive away, expel, get rid of

11 駆寄 **ka(ke)yo(ru)** rush up to

12 駆集 **ka(ri)atsu(meru)** muster, round up

— 2 —

6 先駆 **sakiga(ke)** the lead/initiative
先駆者 **senkusha** forerunner, pioneer

— 5 —

10a5.2 / 599

⊞ 馬 王 |
78 46 2

駐駐

CHŪ be resident/stationed in; stop

— 1 —

4 駐屯地 **chūtonchi** (army) post

駐日 **chū-Nichi** resident/stationed in Japan

6 駐在 **chūzai** stay, residence
駐米 **chū-Bei** resident/stationed in America

7 駐車場 **chūshajō** parking lot

10 駐留軍 **chūryūgun** stationed/occupying troops

— 2 —

11 常駐 **jōchū** permanently stationed

10a5.3

⊞ 馬 宀 匕
78 33 13

駝駝

DA camel; ostrich

— 1 —

11 駝鳥 **dachō** ostrich

— 2 —

16 駱駝 **rakuda** camel

10a5.5 / 2268

⊞ 馬 口 勹
78 24 15

駒駒

KU, koma colt, pony; (shōgi) chessman; (samisen) fret, bridge; frame (of a film) KU, KOMA (part of given name)

— 6 —

馴 → 州 **2f4.1**

10a6.2

⊞ 馬 夂 口
78 49 24

駱駱

RAKU black-maned white horse; camel

— 1 —

15 駱駝 **rakuda** camel

10
馬 6

────────── 7 ──────────

10a7.1 / 2269   ⊞ 馬 夊 竹
                 78 49 17

駿駿

SHUN a fine horse; swiftness;
excellence TOSHI, HAYASHI, HAYAO,
TAKASHI, SUSUMU (m. given name)
SHUN (part of given name)

────────── 1 ──────────

⁴ 駿介 **Shunsuke** (m. given name)
⁷ 駿足 **shunsoku** swift horse; person
    of exceptional talent

────────── 8 ──────────

10a8.3 / 1881   ⊞ 馬 大 口
                 78 34 24

騎騎

KI horse riding; (counter for horse-
men)

────────── 1 ──────────

⁴ 騎手 **kishu** rider, jockey
¹⁰ 騎馬 **kiba** on horseback, mounted

10a8.4 / 532   ⊞ 馬 口 亻
                 78 24 3

驗 | 驗驗

KEN effect; testing **GEN** beneficial
effect **shirushi** sign, indication; effect, benefit

────────── 2 ──────────

⁷ 体験 **taiken** experience
⁸ 受験 **juken** take an examination
    実験 **jikken** experiment
    実験室 **jikkenshitsu** laboratory
¹¹ 経験 **keiken** experience
¹³ 試験 **shiken** examination, test; ex-
    periment, test
    試験地獄 **shiken jigoku** the hell of
    (entrance) exams

────────── 3 ──────────

¹⁰ 核実験 **kakujikken** nuclear testing

────────── 4 ──────────

² 入学試験 **nyūgaku shiken** en-
    trance exams

10a8.5 / 875   ⊞ 馬 虫 又
                 78 64 9

騒 | 騷騒

SŌ, sawa(gu) make a noise/fuss
zawame(ku), zawatsu(ku) be noisy

────────── 1 ──────────

⁵ 騒立 **sawa(gi)ta(teru)** raise a big
    fuss/furor **sawa(gi)ta(tsu)** be
    agitated
⁹ 騒音 **sōon** noise
¹¹ 騒動 **sōdō** disturbance, riot

────────── 2 ──────────

³ 大騒 **ōsawa(gi)** clamor, uproar
¹⁰ 胸騒 **munasawa(gi)** uneasiness;
    apprehension
¹⁵ 潮騒 **shiosai** roar of the sea

────────── 9 ──────────

10a9.1   ⊞ 馬 尸 艹
                 78 40 32

騙 | 騙騙

HEN, dama(su/kasu) deceive, trick,
fool, cheat, swindle; humor, soothe,
coax **kata(ru)** swindle, cheat; misrepresent

────────── 1 ──────────

⁶ 騙合 **dama(shi)a(i)** cheating each
    other

────────── 10 ──────────

騰 → 騰 4b16.3

騒 → 騒 10a8.5

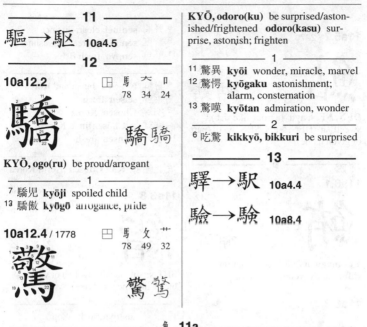

11

驅 → 駆 10a4.5

12

10a12.2 | 田 馬 大 刂
| 78 34 24

驕 驕驕

KYŌ, ogo(ru) be proud/arrogant

― 1 ―

7 驕児 **kyōji** spoiled child
13 驕傲 **kyōgō** arrogance, pride

10a12.4 / 1778 | 田 馬 夂 艹
| 78 49 32

驚 驚驚

KYŌ, odoro(ku) be surprised/astonished/frightened **odoro(kasu)** surprise, astonish; frighten

― 1 ―

11 驚異 **kyōi** wonder, miracle, marvel
12 驚愕 **kyōgaku** astonishment; alarm, consternation
13 驚嘆 **kyōtan** admiration, wonder

― 2 ―

6 吃驚 **kikkyō, bikkuri** be surprised

13

驛 → 駅 10a4.4

驗 → 験 10a8.4

― **11a** ―

| 魚 | 鮎 | 鮪 | 鮭 | 鮫 | 鮮 | 鮨 | 鯉 | 鮹 | 鯡 | 鯨 | 鯛 | 鰊 |
| 0.1 | 5.7 | 6.1 | 6.3 | 6.5 | 6.7 | 6.8 | 7.2 | 7.6 | 8.2 | 8.9 | 8.11 | 9.1 |

| 鰕 | 鰐 | 鰯 | 鱈 | 鰻 | 鰹 | 鱒 | 鱗 |
| 9.4 | 9.5 | 10.3 | 11.1 | 11.5 | 12.1 | 12.6 | 13.2 |

魚 0
鳥

― **0** ―

11a0.1 / 290 | □ 魚
| 79

魚 魚魚

GYO, sakana, uo fish NA (part of given name)

― 1 ―

5 魚市場 **uoichiba** fish market
9 魚屋 **sakanaya** fish shop/seller
11 魚釣 **uotsu(ri), sakanatsu(ri)** fishing, angling
18 魚類 **gyorui** fishes

― 2 ―

3 干魚 **ho(shi)uo, ho(shi)zakana** dried fish
5 生魚 **namazakana, seigyo** raw/fresh fish
8 金魚 **kingyo** goldfish
9 海魚 **kaigyo** ocean/saltwater fish
11 章魚 **tako** octopus
12 焼魚 **ya(ki)zakana** broiled fish
17 鮮魚 **sengyo** fresh fish

― 3 ―

11 淡水魚 **tansuigyo** freshwater fish
20 鹹水魚 **kansuigyo** saltwater fish

5

11a5.7 / 2270 ⊞ 魚 口 宀
79 24 13

鮎

鮎鮎

DEN, NEN, ayu (a trout-like fish),
sweetfish   DEN, NEN, SEN, AYU (part
of given name)

6

11a6.1 ⊞ 魚 月 十
79 42 12

鮪

鮪鮪

YŪ, maguro (bluefin) tuna, tunny
shibi tunny, yellowfin tuna

11a6.3 ⊞ 魚 土
79 22

鮭

鮭鮭

KAI, KEI, sake, shake salmon

11a6.5 ⊞ 魚 亠 儿
79 11 16

鮫

鮫鮫

KŌ, same shark

11a6.7 / 701 ⊞ 魚 王 儿
79 46 16

鮮

鮮鮮

SEN fresh, vivid, clear; Korea
aza(yaka) vivid, clear, brilliant,
bright, colorful

1
8 鮮明 **senmei** clear, distinct
9 鮮度 **sendo** (degree of) freshness
11 鮮魚 **sengyo** fresh fish

2
4 日鮮 **Nis-Sen** Japan and Korea
5 生鮮 **seisen** fresh
12 朝鮮 **Chōsen** Korea
朝鮮人 **Chōsenjin** a Korean
13 新鮮 **shinsen** fresh

3
5 北朝鮮 **Kita Chōsen** North Korea

11a6.8 ⊞ 魚 日 宀
79 43 13

鮨

鮨鮨

SHI, sushi sushi (raw fish or vegetables with vinegared rice)

1
9 鮨屋 **sushiya** sushi shop

7

11a7.2 / 2271 ⊞ 魚 日 土
79 43 22

鯉

鯉鯉

RI, koi carp   RI, KOI (part of given
name)

1
15 鯉幟 **koinobori** carp streamer
(Boys' Festival decoration)

2
14 緋鯉 **higoi** red/gold carp

11a7.6 ⊞ 魚 月 小
79 42 35

鮹

鮹鮹

SHŌ, tako octopus

─────────── 8 ───────────

11a8.2   ⊞ 魚 十 二
                 79 12 4

鯡

鯡鯡

HI, nishin herring

11a8.9 / 700   ⊞ 魚 口 小
                    79 24 35

鯨

鯨鯨

GEI, kujira whale

─────────── 1 ───────────
6 鯨肉 **geiniku** whale meat

─────────── 2 ───────────
10 捕鯨 **hogei** whaling

11a8.11 / 2272   ⊞ 魚 月 口
                      79 42 24

鯛

鯛鯛

CHŌ, tai sea bream, porgy
CHŌ, TAI (part of given name)

─────────── 9 ───────────

11a9.1   ⊞ 魚 木 口
                 79 41 24

鰊

鰊鰊

REN, nishin herring

11a9.4   ⊞ 魚 尸 二
                 79 40 4

鰕

鰕鰕

KA, ebi shrimp, prawn

11a9.5   ⊞ 魚 口 二
                 79 24 4

鰐

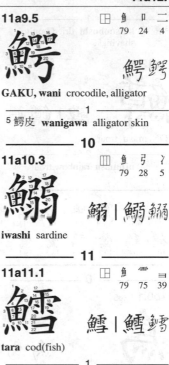

鰐鰐

GAKU, wani crocodile, alligator

─────────── 1 ───────────
5 鰐皮 **wanigawa** alligator skin

─────────── 10 ───────────

11a10.3   ⊞ 魚 弓 冫
                  79 28 5

鰯

鰯 | 鰯鰯

iwashi sardine

─────────── 11 ───────────

11a11.1   ⊞ 魚 雨 彐
                  79 75 39

鱈

鱈 | 鱈鱈

tara cod(fish)

─────────── 1 ───────────
12 鱈場蟹 **tarabagani** king crab

11a11.5   ⊞ 魚 日 日
                  79 55 43

鰻

鰻鰻

MAN, unagi eel

─────────── 1 ───────────
5 鰻丼 **unagi donburi, unadon** bowl
of eel and rice

─────────── 12 ───────────

11a12.1   ⊞ 魚 土 冂
                  79 22 20

鰹

鰹鰹

KEN, katsuo bonito, skipjack

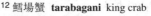

≡11
≡
魚 12
鳥

1

13 鰹節 **katsuobushi** dried bonito shavings

11a12.6

⊞ 魚 酉 寸
79 71 37

鱒

鱒｜鱒鱒

SON, masu trout

2

9 虹鱒 **nijimasu** rainbow trout

13

11a13.2

⊞ 魚 米 夕
79 62 30

鱗

鱗鱗

RIN, uroko, kokera scales (on a fish)

1

12 鱗雲 **urokogumo** cirrocumulus clouds

鳥 11b

鳥 烏 島 鳩 鳶 鴎 鴨 鴉 鴬 鵞 鵜 鷲 鶏
0.1 4d6.5 3o7.9 2.1 3.1 11b11.3 5.2 5.3 11b10.9 11b7.7 7.6 7.7 8.4

鶴 鷄 鶯 鴎 鷲 鸞
10.1 11b8.4 10.9 11.3 12.5 19.1

0

11b0.1 / 285

▢ 鳥
80

鳥

鳥 鳥

CHŌ, tori bird

1

6 鳥肉 **toriniku** chicken (meat)
8 鳥居 **torii** Shinto shrine archway
鳥取県 **Tottori-ken** (prefecture)
16 鳥獣 **chōjū** birds and animals, wildlife
18 鳥類 **chōrui** birds, fowl
22 鳥籠 **torikago** bird cage

2

3 千鳥足 **chidori-ashi** tottering steps
5 白鳥 **hakuchō** swan
11 野鳥 **yachō** wild birds
12 渡鳥 **wata(ri)dori** migratory bird
焼鳥 **ya(ki)tori** grilled chicken
15 駝鳥 **dachō** ostrich
18 鵞鳥 **gachō** goose

3

11 啄木鳥 **kitsutsuki** woodpecker

4

1 一石二鳥 **isseki nichō** killing two birds with one stone

烏 → **4d6.5**

島 → **3o7.9**

2

11b2.1 / 2273

▢ 鳥 十
80 12

鳩

鳩鳩

KYŪ, hato dove, pigeon KYŪ, KU, KATO, YASU (part of given name)

1

9 鳩派 **hatoha** the doves, soft-liners

3

11b3.1

… 鳥 戈
80 52

鳶

鳶鳶

左側欄外:

11

12 魚
鳥

EN, tobi, tonbi kite (the bird); fireman; scaffolding worker

— 4 —

鴎 → 鷗 **11b11.3**

— 5 —

11b5.2　　　　　　□ 鳥 日 |
　　　　　　　　　80 43 2

鴨

鴨鴨

O, kamo duck, mallard; easily deceived person

11b5.3　　　　　　□ 鳥 ' ―
　　　　　　　　　80 14 11

鴉

鴉鴉

A, karasu crow; raven

鴬 → 鶯 **11b10.9**

— 7 —

鵝 → 鵞 **11b7.7**

11b7.6　　　　　　□ 鳥 弓 儿
　　　　　　　　　80 28 16

鵜

鵜鵜

TEI, u cormorant

— 1 —

13 鵜飼 **uka(i)** fishing with cormorants

11b7.7　　　　　　□ 鳥 戈 艹
　　　　　　　　　80 52 12

鵞

鵝 | 鵞鵞

GA goose

— 1 —

11 鵞鳥 **gachō** goose

— 8 —

11b8.4 / 926　　　　□ 鳥 小 大
　　　　　　　　　80 35 34

鶏

鶏 | 鶏鶏

KEI, niwatori chicken, hen, rooster

— 1 —

6 鶏肉 **keiniku** chicken (meat)
7 鶏卵 **keiran** chicken egg
14 鶏鳴 **keimei** cockcrow, rooster's crowing

— 2 —

8 若鶏 **wakadori** (spring) chicken, pullet

— 10 —

11b10.1 / 2277　　　□ 鳥 隹 冂
　　　　　　　　　80 74 20

鶴

鶴鶴

KAKU, tsuru crane, stork TSURU (f. given name) KAKU, ZU, TAZU, TSU, KAZU, TSURU (part of given name)

— 1 —

1 鶴一声 **tsuru (no) hitokoe** the voice of authority
5 鶴田 **Tsuruta** (surname)

— 2 —

3 千鶴 **Chizu, Chizuru** (f. given name)

鷄 → 鶏 **11b8.4**

11b10.9　　　　　　□ 鳥 火 冂
　　　　　　　　　80 44 20

鶯

鴬 | 鶯鶯

Ō, uguisu bush warbler

11
魚
鳥 10

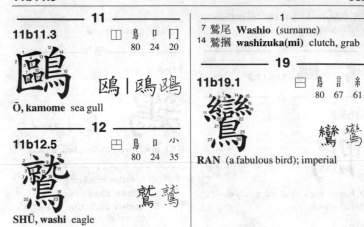

	11	

11b11.3

□|　鳥　口　冂
　　　80　24　20

鷗

鴎 | 鴎 鸥

Ō, kamome sea gull

	12	

11b12.5

□|　鳥　口　小
　　　80　24　35

鷲

鷲 鷲

SHŪ, washi eagle

	1	

7 鷲尾 **Washio** (surname)
14 鷲摑 **washizuka(mi)** clutch, grab

	19	

11b19.1

□|　鳥　言　糸
　　　80　67　61

鸞

鸞 鸞

RAN (a fabulous bird); imperial

11

魚

11 鳥

APPENDICES

付録

The 100 Most Frequent Surnames (1 – 50)

1	佐藤	Satō	26	石川	Ishikawa
2	鈴木	Suzuki	27	橋本	Hashimoto
3	高橋	Takahashi	28	小川	Ogawa
4	田中	Tanaka	29	石井	Ishii
5	伊藤	Itō	30	長谷川	Hasegawa
6	渡辺	Watanabe	31	後藤	Gotō
7	小林	Kobayashi	32	斉藤	Saitō
8	中村	Nakamura	33	山下	Yamashita
9	山本	Yamamoto	34	藤田	Fujita
10	加藤	Katō	35	遠藤	Endō
11	吉田	Yoshida	36	前田	Maeda
12	山田	Yamada	37	岡田	Okada
13	斎藤	Saitō	38	近藤	Kondō
14	佐佐木	Sasaki	39	青木	Aoki
15	山口	Yamaguchi	40	村上	Murakami
16	松本	Matsumoto	41	金子	Kaneko
17	木村	Kimura	42	三浦	Miura
18	井上	Inoue	43	坂本	Sakamoto
19	清水	Shimizu	44	福田	Fukuda
20	林	Hayashi	45	太田	Ōta
21	阿部	Abe	46	田村	Tamura
22	山崎	Yamasaki	47	小野	Ono
23	池田	Ikeda	48	藤井	Fujii
24	中島	Nakajima	49	竹内	Takeuchi
25	森	Mori	50	中川	Nakagawa

The 100 Most Frequent Surnames (51 – 100)

51	西村	Nishimura	76	大野	Ōno
52	松田	Matsuda	77	丸山	Maruyama
53	中野	Nakano	78	今井	Imai
54	原田	Harada	79	大塚	Ōtsuka
55	和田	Wada	80	千葉	Chiba
56	中山	Nakayama	81	菅原	Sugawara
57	岡本	Okamoto	82	村田	Murata
58	石田	Ishida	83	武田	Takeda
59	小島	Kojima	84	新井	Arai
60	内田	Uchida	85	野口	Noguchi
61	森田	Morita	86	小山	Koyama
62	工藤	Kudō	87	増田	Masuda
63	横山	Yokoyama	88	高田	Takada
64	酒井	Sakai	89	平野	Hirano
65	柴田	Shibata	90	岩崎	Iwasaki
66	原	Hara	91	上野	Ueno
67	藤原	Fujiwara	92	佐野	Sano
68	高木	Takagi	93	杉山	Sugiyama
69	島田	Shimada	94	谷口	Taniguchi
70	宮崎	Miyazaki	95	高野	Takano
71	菊地	Kikuchi	96	松井	Matsui
72	上田	Ueda	97	野村	Nomura
73	桜井	Sakurai	98	渡部	Watanabe
74	安藤	Andō	99	河野	Kawano
75	宮本	Miyamoto	100	古川	Furukawa

The 10 Most Frequent Kanji
Used in Surnames

1	田	ta, -da	6	木 ki
2	藤	TŌ, -DŌ	7	井 i
3	山	yama	8	村 mura
4	野	no, YA	9	本 moto
5	川	kawa, gawa	10	中 naka

The 10 Most Frequent Female Given Names
(for children born in 1912)

1	千代 Chiyo	6	ヨシ Yoshi
2	ハル Haru	7	千代子 Chiyoko
3	ハナ Hana	8	キヨ Kiyo
4	正子 Masako, Seiko, Shōko	9	静子 Shizuko
5	文子 Fumiko, Ayako	10	はる Haru

The 10 Most Frequent Male Given Names
(for children born in 1912)

1	正一 Shōichi, Masakazu, Masaichi, Seiichi, Tadakazu	6	武雄 Takeo
2	清 Kiyoshi, Shin, Shō	7	正治 Masaharu, Shōji, Masaji, Seiji, Tadaharu
3	正雄 Masao, Tadao	8	三郎 Saburō, Mitsuo, Kazuo
4	正 Tadashi, Masa	9	正夫 Masao, Tadao
5	茂 Shigeru	10	一郎 Ichirō, Kazu

The 50 Most Frequent Female Given Names

(for children born in 1994)

1	美咲	Misaki		26	未来	Mirai
2	愛	Ai			楓	Kaede
3	萌	Moe		28	彩夏	Ayaka
4	愛美	Aimi			菜摘	Natsumi
5	遥	Haruka			綾香	Ayaka
6	千夏	Chinatsu		31	唯	Yui
	彩香	Ayaka		32	七海	Nanami
	葵	Aoi		33	恵	Kei
9	舞	Mai			晴香	Haruka
	麻衣	Mai			春菜	Haruna
	桃子	Momoko			奈々	Nana
12	理奈	Rina			玲奈	Reina
13	千尋	Chihiro			綾乃	Ayano
	彩	Aya		39	菜月	Natsuki
15	杏奈	Anna		40	智美	Tomomi
16	成美	Narumi			瞳	Hitomi
	栞	Shiori			莉奈	Rina
	茜	Akane		43	春香	Haruka
19	彩乃	Ayano		44	真美	Mami
20	美里	Misato			春奈	Haruna
	早紀	Saki		46	真衣	Mai
22	美穂	Miho			理沙	Risa
	明日香	Asuka			彩加	Ayaka
	佳奈	Kana			彩花	Ayaka
	詩織	Shiori			由佳	Yuka

The 50 Most Frequent Male Given Names

(for children born in 1994)

1	健太	Kenta	26	涼	Ryō
2	翔太	Shōta		一樹	Kazuki
3	拓也	Takuya		光	Hikaru
4	翼	Tsubasa		諒	Ryō
5	翔	Shō	30	匠	Takumi
6	大樹	Daiki		雄太	Yūta
7	大輔	Daisuke	32	裕也	Yūya, Hiroya
8	亮太	Ryōta		駿	Shun
9	大輝	Daiki	34	啓太	Keita
10	大貴	Daiki	35	和樹	Kazuki
11	雄大	Yūdai		拓海	Takumi
12	達也	Tatsuya	37	翔平	Shōhei
13	大地	Daichi	38	直也	Naoya
14	健太郎	Kentarō	39	涼太	Ryōta
15	拓哉	Takuya		航	Kō
16	直人	Naoto		亮	Ryō
17	康平	Kōhei	42	健	Ken
	一輝	Kazuki		良太	Ryōta
19	修平	Shūhei	44	恭平	Kyōhei
	凌	Ryō		祐介	Yūzuke
21	優太	Yūta		貴大	Kidai
22	和也	Kazuya	47	竜也	Tatsuya
	健人	Taketo		優	Yū, Masaru
	直樹	Naoki		優樹	Masaki, Yūki
25	裕太	Yūta		裕貴	Yūki, Hiroki

The 284 Kanji for Use in Given Names

丑	丞	乃	之	也	亙	亦	亥	亨	亮	伊	伎	伍	伽	佑
1	2	3	4	5	6	7	8	9	10	11	12	13	14	15
伶	侃	侑	倭	倖	偲	允	冴	冶	凌	凜	凪	凱	勁	匡
16	17	18	19	20	21	22	23	24	25	26	27	28	29	30
卯	叡	叶	只	吾	呂	哉	啄	唄	喬	嘉	圭	尭	奈	奎
31	32	33	35	36	37	38	39	40	41	42	43	44	45	
爽	媛	嬉	孟	宏	宥	寅	峻	崚	嵐	嵯	嵩	嶺	巌	巳
46	47	48	49	50	51	52	53	54	55	56	57	58	59	60
巴	巽	庄	弘	弥	彗	彦	彪	彬	怜	恕	悌	惟	惣	惇
61	62	63	64	65	66	67	68	69	70	71	72	73	74	75
慧	憧	拳	捷	捲	敦	斐	魁	於	旦	旭	旺	昂	昌	昴
76	77	78	79	80	81	82	83	84	85	86	87	88	89	90
晏	晃	晋	晟	晨	暉	暢	曙	智	朋	朔	杏	杜	李	柊
91	92	93	94	95	96	97	98	99	100	101	102	103	104	105
柚	柾	栞	桂	桐	栗	梧	梓	梢	梨	椎	椋	椿	楠	楓
106	107	108	109	110	111	112	113	114	115	116	117	118	119	120
椰	楊	樺	榛	槙	槻	橘	檀	欣	欽	毅	毬	汀	汐	沙
121	122	123	124	125	126	127	128	129	130	131	132	133	134	135
汰	洸	洲	洵	浩	淳	渚	渥	湧	滉	漱	澪	熙	熊	燎
136	137	138	140	141	142	143	144	145	146	147	148	149	150	
燦	耀	采	爾	猪	玖	玲	琢	瑛	琳	瑚	瑞	瑶	瑳	瑠
151	152	153	154	155	156	157	158	159	160	161	162	163	164	165
璃	甫	皐	皓	眉	眸	睦	瞳	瞭	矩	碧	磯	祐	禄	禎
166	167	168	169	170	171	172	173	174	175	176	177	178	179	180
秦	稀	稔	稜	穣	竣	靖	笙	笹	紘	紗	絃	紬	絢	綺
181	182	183	184	185	186	187	188	189	190	191	192	193	194	195
綜	緋	綾	綸	翔	翠	耀	聡	肇	胤	胡	脩	舜	艶	芹
196	197	198	199	200	201	202	203	204	205	206	207	208	209	210
芙	苑	茄	茅	茉	茜	莞	莉	菫	菖	萌	葵	萩	蒔	蒼
211	212	213	214	215	216	217	218	219	220	221	222	223	224	225
蓉	蓮	蔦	蕉	蕗	藤	藍	蘭	虎	虹	蝶	衿	袈	裟	詢
226	227	228	229	230	231	232	233	234	235	236	237	238	239	240
誼	諄	諒	赳	輔	辰	迪	遥	遼	邑	那	郁	耶	酉	醇
241	242	243	244	245	246	247	248	249	250	251	252	253	254	255
錦	鎌	阿	隼	雛	霞	鞠	須	頌	碩	颯	馨	駒	駿	鮎
256	257	258	259	260	261	262	263	264	265	266	267	268	269	270
鯉	鯛	鳩	鳳	鴻	鵬	鶴	鷹	鹿	麟	麿	黎	黛	亀	
271	272	273	274	275	276	277	278	279	280	281	282	283	284	

The 214 Historical Radicals in Comparison
with the 79 Radicals

	- 1 -			23	匸	--
1	一	--		24	十	= 2k 十
2	丨	--		25	卜	= 2m 丨
3	丶	--		26	卩	= 2e 卩
4	丿	--		27	厂	= 2p 厂
5	乙	--		28	厶	--
6	亅	--		29	又	= 2h 又
	- 2 -				**- 3 -**	
7	二	--		30	口	= 3d 口
8	亠	= 2j 亠		31	囗	= 3s 囗
9	人, 亻	= 2a 亻		32	土	= 3b 土
10	儿	--		33	士	= 3p 士
11	入	--		34	夂	= 4i 夂
12	八	= 2o ˇ		35	夊	--
13	冂	= 2r 冂		36	夕	--
14	冖	= 2i 冖		37	大	--
15	冫	= 2b 冫		38	女	= 3e 女
16	几	= 2s 几		39	子	= 2c 子
17	凵	--		40	宀	= 3m 宀
18	刀, 刂	= 2f 刂		41	寸	--
19	力	= 2g 力		42	小	= 3n ˇ
20	勹	--		43	尢	--
21	匕	--		44	尸, 尸	= 3r 尸
22	匚	= 2t 匚		45	屮	--

46	山	= 3o ㄩ	71	无	--
47	川	--	72	日	= 4c 日
48	工	--	73	曰	→ 3s 口
49	己	--	74	月	= 4b 月
50	巾	= 3f 巾	75	木	= 4a 木
51	干	--	76	欠	= 4j 欠
52	幺	--	77	止	→ 2m 止
53	广	= 3q 广	78	歹	--
54	廴	= 2q 廴	79	殳	→ 2s 几
55	廾, 卅	--	80	世	--
56	弋	= 4n 弋	81	比	--
57	弓	= 3h 弓	82	毛	--
58	彐, ⺕, ⺕	--	83	氏	--
59	彡	= 3j 彡	84	气	--
60	彳	= 3i 彳	85	水, 氵	= 3a 氵

- 4 -

61	心, 忄, ⺗	= 4k 忄

86	火, 灬	= 4d 火
87	爪	--

62	戈	= 4n 戈	88	父	→ 2o ⺀
63	戶, 户	= 4m 戶	89	爻	--
64	手, 扌	= 3c 扌	90	爿, 丬	--, 2b 丬
65	支	→ 2k 十	91	片	→ 2j 亠
66	攴	→ 2m 止	92	牙	--
67	文	→ 2j 亠	93	牛	= 4g 牛
68	斗	--	94	犬, 犭	= 3g 犭
69	斤	--			**- 5 -**
70	方	= 4h 方	95	玄	→ 2j 亠

96	玉, 王	= 4f	王
97	瓜	--	
98	瓦	--	
99	甘	--	
100	生	--	
101	用	→ 2r	冂
102	田	= 5f	田
103	疋, 疋	→ 2m	⺊
104	疒	= 5i	疒
105	癶	--	
106	白	→ 4c	日
107	皮	→ 2h	又
108	皿	= 5h	皿
109	目	= 5c	目
110	矛	--	
111	矢	--	
112	石	= 5a	石
113	示, 礻	= 4e	礻
114	内	--	
115	禾	= 5d	禾
116	穴	→ 3m	宀
117	立	= 5b	立

- 6 -

118	竹	= 6f	竹
119	米	= 6b	米
120	糸, 糹	= 6a	糸

121	缶	→ 2k	艹
122	网, 罒	= 5g	罒
123	羊	→ 2o	ⸯ
124	羽, 羽	→ 2b	冫
125	老	→ 2k	艹
126	而	→ 2r	冂
127	耒	--	
128	耳	= 6e	耳
129	聿	--	
130	肉, 月	→ 2a	亻,
		= 4b	月
131	臣	→ 2t	匚
132	自	→ 5c	目
133	至	→ 3b	士
134	臼	--	
135	舌	→ 3d	口
136	舛	--	
137	舟	= 6c	舟
138	艮, 艮	--	
139	色	→ 2n	勹
140	艸, 艹	= 3k	艹
141	虍	→ 2m	⺊
142	虫	= 6d	虫
143	血	→ 5h	皿
144	行	→ 3i	彳
145	衣, 礻	= 5e	礻

146	西		--	169	門	= 8e	門

170	阜, 阝	→ 2k	十,

147	見	→ 5c	目			= 2d	阝
148	角	→ 2n	⺈	171	隶	→ 2b	冫
149	言	= 7a	訁	172	隹	= 8c	隹
150	谷	→ 2o	⸜	173	雨	= 8d	雨
151	豆	→ 3d	口	174	靑, 青	→ 4b	月
152	豕		--	175	非		--
153	豸		--				

154	貝	= 7b	貝	176	面	→ 3s	囗
155	赤	→ 3b	土	177	革	→ 3k	艹
156	走	→ 3b	土	178	韋	→ 3d	口
157	足	= 7d	𧾷	179	韭		--
158	身		--	180	音	→ 5b	立
159	車	= 7c	車	181	頁	= 9a	頁
160	辛	→ 5b	立	182	風	→ 2s	几
161	辰	→ 2p	厂	183	飛		--
162	辵, 辶	= 2q	辶	184	食	= 8b	飠
163	邑, 阝	= 2d	阝	185	首	→ 2o	⸜
164	酉	= 7e	酉	186	香	→ 5d	禾
165	釆	→ 6b	米				

166	里		--	187	馬	= 10a	馬

188	骨	→ 4b	月

167	金	= 8a	釒	189	高	→ 2j	亠
168	長		--	190	髟	→ 3j	彡

191	鬥	→ 8e 門			**- 13 -**	
192	鬯	--	205	黽	--
193	鬲	→ 2r 冂	206	鼎	→ 5c 目
194	鬼	→ 5f 田	207	鼓	→ 3p 壴
			208	鼠	--

- 11 -

195	魚	= 11a 魚			**- 14 -**	
196	鳥	= 11b 鳥	209	鼻	→ 5f 田
197	鹵	→ 2m 卜	210	齊, 斉	→ 2j 亠
198	鹿	→ 3q 广			**- 15 -**	
199	麥, 麦	→ 4i 夂	211	齒, 歯	→ 2a 亻,
200	麻	→ 3q 广			→ 6b 米

- 12 -

201	黃, 黄	→ 3k 艹	212	龍, 竜	→ 5b 立
202	黍	→ 5d 禾			**- 17 -**	
203	黑, 黒	→ 4d 火	213	龜, 亀	→ 2n 宀
204	黹	--	214	龠	→ 2a 亻

The above table shows the similarities and differences between the historical 214-radical system and our modern 79-radical system. The 214 historical radicals are numbered and listed in order. Correspondence between a historical radical and a modern radical is indicated with an equal sign (=) followed by the name of the modern radical and its standard form. An arrow (→) instead of an equal sign indicates a limited correspondence, and those historical radicals for which there is no corresponding modern radical are marked with a hyphen (--).

SOURCES

The page numbers below refer to the sources that have been essential for preparing the respective tables.

834–835   日本語百科大事典. 金田一春彦編. Tokyo 1988

836   1912年生まれの子供の名前. Compiled by Meiji Seimei. Tokyo 1996

837   『1994年生まれ』の名前ベスト100（女の子）Compiled by Meiji Seimei. Tokyo 1996

838   『1994年生まれ』の名前ベスト100（男の子）Compiled by Meiji Seimei. Tokyo 1996

839–844   The Kanji Dictionary. By M. Spahn and W. Hadamitzky. Tokyo 1996

ALPHABETICAL INDEX
OF READINGS

音訓索引

—— A ——

Reading	Kanji (code)
A	亜 0a7.14, 啞 3d8.3, (悪) AKU, 蛙 6d6.4, 窪 3m11.9, 阿 2d5.6, 鴉 11b5.3
a	吾 3d4.17
aba(ku)	発 0a9.5, 暴 4c11.2
abara	肋 4b2.1
aba(reru)	暴 4c11.2
a(biru)	浴 3a7.18
a(biseru)	浴 3a7.18
abu	虻 6d3.2
abuku	泡 3a5.18
abu(nai)	危 2n4.3
abura	脂 4b6.7, 膏 2j12.1, 油 3a5.6
abu(ru)	焙 4d8.1
ada	仇 2a2.4, 徒 3i7.1
ade(yaka)	艶 3d16.3
ae(nai)	敢 4i8.5
a(eru)	和 5d3.1
ae(te)	敢 4i8.5
afu(reru)	溢 3a10.19
aga(meru)	崇 3o8.9
agana(u)	購 7b10.3
a(gari)	上 2m1.1
a(garu)	挙 3n7.1, 揚 3c9.5, 上 2m1.1
Agata	県 3n6.3
agata	県 3n6.3
a(gattari)	上 2m1.1
a(ge)	揚 3c9.5
a(geru)	挙 3n7.1, 揚 3c9.5, 上 2m1.1
a(gete)	挙 3n7.1
agetsura(u)	論 7a8.13
-a(gezu)	上 2m1.1
agito	顎 9a9.2
ago	顎 9a9.2
agu(mu)	倦 2a8.13
AI	愛 4i10.1, 曖 4c13.1, 哀 2j7.4, (衰) SUI, 挨 3c7.12, 靄 8d16.1
Ai	愛 4i10.1
ai	間 8e4.3, 藍 3k15.5
ai-	相 4a5.3
aida	間 8e4.3
aji	味 3d5.3
aji(na)	味 3d5.3
aji(wau)	味 3d5.3
aka	赤 3b4.10, 垢 3b6.3, 緋 6a8.4, 銅 8a6.12
akagane	銅 8a6.12
aka(i)	赤 3b4.10
aka(meru)	赤 3b4.10
akanashi	杜 4a3.1
Akane	茜 3k6.3
akane	茜 3k6.3
a(kanu)	飽 8b5.1
aka(rameru)	赤 3b4.10
aka(ramu)	赤 3b4.10, 明 4c4.1
a(kari)	明 4c4.1
aka(rui)	明 4c4.1
aka(rumu)	明 4c4.1
akashi	灯 4d2.1, 証 7a5.5
a(kasu)	明 4c4.1, 飽 8b5.1
akatsuki	暁 4c8.1
ake	旦 4c1.2, 明 4c4.1, 曙 4c14.2, 朱 0a6.13
Akebono	曙 4c14.2
akebono	曙 4c14.2
a(keru)	空 3m5.12, 明 4c4.1, 開 8e4.6
aki	旦 4c1.2, 明 4c4.1, 昌 4c4.4, 映 4c5.1, 昭 4c5.4, 昂 4c5.11, 晃 4c6.5, 晋 4c6.8, 者 3k8.4, 晨 4c7.7, 章 5b6.3, 晶 4c8.6, 皓 4c8.13, 暉 4c9.6, 彰 3j11.1, 瞭 5c12.4, 顕 9a9.5, 玲 4f5.7, 瑛 4f8.6, 璃 4f10.5, 亨 2j4.2, 亮 2j7.6, 諒 7a8.14, 圭 3b3.2, 堯 3b9.3, 秋 5d4.1, 朗 4b6.11, 爽 0a11.7, 彬 4a7.3, 聡 6e8.2, 耀 8c12.1
akina(u)	商 2j9.7
a(kippoi)	飽 8b5.1
Akira	旦 4c1.2, 旭 4c2.6, 明 4c4.1, 旺 4c4.2, 昌 4c4.4, 映 4c5.1, 昭 4c5.4, 昂 4c5.11, 晃 4c6.5, 陽 2d9.5, 晟 4c7.5, 晨 4c7.7, 章 5b6.3, 晶 4c8.6, 智 4c8.11, 皓 4c8.13, 滉 3a10.12, 暉 4c9.6, 彰 3j11.1, 瞳 5c12.2, 曦 5c12.4, 曙 4c14.2, 顕 9a9.5, 光 3n3.2, 洸 3a6.15, 輝 7c8.8, 耀 8c12.1, 侃 2a6.12, 信 2a7.1, 爽 0a11.7, 爾 0a14.3, 玲 4f5.7, 瑛 4f8.6, 徴 3i11.2, 聡 6e8.2, 慧 4k11.16, 憲 3m13.2, 卯 2e3.1, 丞 2c4.3, 亨 2j4.2, 亮 2j7.6, 朗 4b6.11, 啓 3d8.17, 彪 3j8.3, 彬 4a7.3, 斐 2j10.4, 堯 3b9.3, 舜 3n10.2, 翠 2k12.2

	痕	5i6.2		合	2a4.18
	跡	7d6.7		会	2a4.19
ATSU	圧	2p3.1	awa	泡	3a5.18
(庄)		SHŌ		粟	6b6.6
atsu	幹	4c10.3	awa(i)	淡	3a8.15
	淳	3a7.19	awa(re)	哀	2j7.4
	惇	4k7.12	awa(remi)	憐	4k13.4
	敦	4i7.4	awa(remu)		
	諄	7a7.11		哀	2j7.4
	醇	7e7.5		憐	4k13.4
	厚	2p6.1	awa(seru)	併	2a6.17
	温	3a9.21	a(waseru)	合	2a4.18
	渥	3a9.33	a(wasu)	合	2a4.18
(屋)		OKU	awa(tadashii)		
	宏	3m4.3		慌	4k9.10
	農	2p11.1	awa(teru)	慌	4k9.10
	篤	6f10.1	Aya	文	2j2.4
atsu(i)	厚	2p6.1		斐	2j10.4
	暑	4c8.5		彩	3j8.1
	惇	4k7.12		絢	6a6.14
	熱	4d11.4	aya	紘	6a4.11
	篤	6f10.1		絢	6a6.14
atsuka(u)	扱	3c3.5		綾	6a8.10
atsu(maru)				綺	6a8.16
	集	8c4.2		文	2j2.4
atsu(meru)				紋	6a4.9
	集	8c4.2		斐	2j10.4
Atsumu	伍	2a4.8		彩	3j8.1
	侑	2a6.5		彪	3j8.3
Atsushi	淳	3a7.19		彬	4a7.3
	惇	4k7.12		郁	2d6.6
	敦	4i7.4		采	4a4.24
	諄	7a7.11		亀	2n9.1
	醇	7e7.5		琢	4f8.1
	厚	2p6.1	aya(bumu)	危	2n4.3
	温	3a9.21	ayaka(ru)	肖	3n4.1
	純	6a4.3	ayama(chi)		
	渥	3a9.33		過	2q9.18
	睦	5c8.6	ayama(ru)	誤	7a7.2
	濃	3a13.7		謝	7a10.1
	篤	6f10.1	ayama(tsu)		
a(u)	逢	2q7.15		過	2q9.18
	遇	2q9.1	Ayame	菖	3k8.22
	遭	2q11.2	Ayaru	斐	2j10.4
			aya(shige)	怪	4k5.11

aya(shii)	怪	4k5.11		(海)	KAI
aya(shimu)				(敏)	BIN
	怪	4k5.11		(毎)	MAI
ayatsu(ru)	操	3c13.3		唄	3d7.1
ayau(i)	危	2n4.3		買	5g7.2
ayu	鮎	11a5.7		(貝)	kai
Ayumi	歩	3n5.3		媒	3e9.2
Ayumu	歩	3n5.3		(某)	BŌ
ayu(mu)	歩	3n5.3		(謀)	BŌ
aza	字	3m2.1		売	3p4.3
	痣	5i7.6		黴	3i20.1
azake(ru)	嘲	3d12.2		許	7a4.3
azamu(ku)	欺	4j8.1	-baka(ri)		
azana	字	3m2.1	ba(kasu)	化	2a2.6
azana(u)	糾	6a3.4	ba(keru)	化	2a2.6
aza(yaka)	鮮	11a6.7	BAKU	莫	3k7.13
aze	畦	5f5.1		漠	3a10.18
azu(karu)	預	9a4.5		幕	3k10.19
azu(keru)	預	9a4.5		(漢)	KAN
Azuma	東	0a8.9		(募)	BO
azuma	東	0a8.9		(墓)	BO
Azusa	梓	4a7.5		(暮)	BO
azusa	梓	4a7.5		(膜)	MAKU
				(模)	MO
	— B —			博	2k10.1
				縛	6a10.3
BA	馬	10a0.1		(専)	SEN
	碼	5a10.1		暴	4c11.2
	罵	5g10.1		爆	4d15.2
	(篤)	TOKU		麦	4i4.2
	婆	3e8.9		駁	10a4.3
	(波)	HA	BAN	伴	2a5.4
ba	芭	3k4.6		判	2f5.2
	場	3b9.6		絆	6a5.6
-ba	羽	2b4.5		(半)	HAN
babā	婆	3e8.9		磐	5a10.9
BACHI	罰	5g9.1		盤	5h10.2
bachi	撥	3c12.11		(般)	HAN
BAI	倍	2a8.14		挽	3c7.13
	陪	2d8.3		晩	4c8.3
	培	3b8.6		(免)	MEN
	賠	7b8.1		番	5f7.4
	(部)	BU		(審)	SHIN
	(剖)	BŌ		(藩)	HAN
	苺	3k5.4		板	4a4.21
	梅	4a6.27			

(反) HAN	-biki 引 3h1.1	(昂) KŌ	煩 4d9.1
蛮 2j10.1	bikko 跛 7d5.4	(卵) RAN	BOTSU 没 3a4.15
(変) HEN	BIN 便 2a7.5	尨 3j4.2	殁 2h6.3
万 0a3.8	(更) KŌ	彪 2p7.2	BU 無 4d8.8
卍 2k4.7	敏 4i6.3	某 4a5.33	撫 3c12.7
-ban 判 2f5.2	(毎) MAI	謀 7a9.8	蕪 3k12.7
bā(san) 婆 3e8.9	貧 2o9.5	冒 4c5.6	憮 4k12.3
BATSU 伐 2a4.5	(分) BUN	帽 3f9.1	舞 0a15.1
閥 8e6.2	秤 5d5.4	牟 4g2.2	葡 3k9.30
抜 3c4.10	瓶 2o9.6	眸 5c6.3	蒲 3k10.8
(髪) HATSU	BO 莫 3k7.13	剖 2f8.1	輔 7c7.1
(友) YŪ	募 3k9.23	(倍) BAI	(甫) HO
末 0a5.26	墓 3k10.18	(部) BU	奉 0a8.13
罰 5g9.1	慕 3k11.12	棒 4a8.20	(俸) HŌ
batta 蝗 6d9.8	暮 3k11.14	(俸) HŌ	(棒) BŌ
bā(ya) 婆 3e8.9	模 4a10.16	(奉) BU	部 2d8.15
be 部 2d8.15	(漢) KAN	乏 0a3.11	(倍) BAI
-be 辺 2q2.1	(漠) BAKU	(之) SHI	(剖) BŌ
BEI 米 6b0.1	簿 6f13.4	呆 3d4.13	侮 2a6.20
吠 3d4.1	(専) SEN	(保) HO	(毎) MAI
BEN 便 2a7.5	(薄) HAKU	茅 3k5.26	不 0a4.2
鞭 3k15.8	母 0a5.36	萌 3k8.11	分 2o2.1
(更) KŌ	菩 3k8.21	貌 4c10.6	歩 3n5.3
弁 0a5.30	BO' 坊 3b4.1	暴 4c11.2	武 4n5.3
眄 5c4.1	BŌ 防 2d4.1	膨 4b12.1	斑 4f8.3
勉 2n8.1	坊 3b4.1	bo(keru) 惚 4k8.10	BUN 聞 8e6.1
beni 紅 6a3.6	妨 3e4.1	BOKU 僕 2a12.1	(門) MON
BETSU 別 2f5.3	肪 4b4.2	撲 3c12.1	文 2j2.4
捌 3c7.4	房 4m4.2	模 4a12.2	分 2o2.1
蔑 3k11.11	紡 6a4.1	(業) GYŌ	-bu(ri) 振 3c7.14
BI 尾 3r4.2	傍 2a10.6	木 4a0.1	buta 豚 4b7.2
梶 4a7.19	膀 4b10.7	朴 4a2.3	BUTSU 勿 0a4.11
(毛) MŌ	(方) HŌ	目 5c0.1	物 4g4.2
微 3i10.1	亡 2j1.1	睦 5c8.6	仏 2a2.5
薇 3k13.13	妄 2j4.6	墨 3b11.4	(払) FUTSU
(徴) CHŌ	忙 4k3.2	(黒) KOKU	bu(tsu) 打 3c2.3
眉 5c4.9	忘 2j5.4	(里) RI	BYAKU 白 4c1.3
媚 3e9.5	盲 2j6.6	牧 4g4.1	柏 4a5.14
琵 4f8.10	茫 3k6.6	BON 凡 2s1.1	BYŌ 苗 3k5.2
(比) HI	蛇 6d3.2	梵 4a7.27	描 3c8.21
弥 3h5.2	望 4f7.6	(帆) HAN	猫 3g8.5
美 2o7.4	卯 2e3.1	盆 2o7.6	錨 8a8.14
備 2a10.4	昂 4c5.12	(分) BUN	眇 5c4.2
鼻 5f9.3	貿 7b5.8		秒 5d4.2

(少) SHŌ	乳 3n4.4	(咲) saku	長 0a8.2
(砂) SA	chiga(eru) 違 2q10.5	鎮 8a10.6	帳 3f8.2
病 5i5.3	chiga(u) 違 2q10.5	(真) SHIN	張 3h8.1
(丙) HEI	chigi(ru) 契 2f7.6	椿 4a9.16	脹 4b8.1
廟 3q12.3	chii(sai) 小 3n0.1	(春) SHUN	彫 3j8.2
(朝) CHŌ	chiji(maru)	china(mi ni)	調 7a8.16
平 2k3.4	縮 6a11.9	因 3s3.2	鯛 11a8.11
屏 3r6.5	chiji(meru)	china(mu) 因 3s3.2	(周) SHŪ
	縮 6a11.9	chinba 跛 7d5.4	牒 4a9.31
— C —	chiji(mi) 縮 6a11.9	chi(rabaru)	蝶 6d9.7
	chiji(mu) 縮 6a11.9	散 4i8.1	諜 7a9.7
CHA 茶 3k6.19	chiji(rasu) 縮 6a11.9	chi(rakaru)	(葉) YŌ
CHAKU 著 3k8.4	chiji(reru) 縮 6a11.9	散 4i8.1	朝 4b8.12
箸 6f9.1	chika 允 0a4.13	chi(rakasu)	潮 3a12.1
着 2o10.1	近 2q4.3	散 4i8.1	嘲 3d12.2
(差) SA	周 2r6.1	chi(rashi) 散 4i8.1	腸 4b9.8
嫡 3e11.5	哉 4n5.4	chi(rasu) 散 4i8.1	暢 4c10.4
CHI 知 3d5.14	峻 3o7.4	chiri 塵 3q11.4	(場) JŌ
智 4c8.11	睦 5c8.6	chi(ru) 散 4i8.1	(湯) TŌ
痴 5i8.1	親 5b11.1	CHITSU 窒 3m8.9	鳥 11b0.1
蜘 6d8.2	chika(i) 近 2q4.3	腟 4b9.9	蔦 3k11.1
値 2a8.30	chikara 力 2g0.1	(室) SHITSU	(島) TŌ
置 5g8.8	Chikashi 即 2e5.1	秩 5d5.2	徴 3i11.2
(直) CHOKU	睦 5c8.6	(失) SHITSU	懲 4k14.3
致 4i6.2	爾 0a14.3	CHO 猪 3g8.1	(微) BI
緻 6a10.1	親 5b11.1	著 3k8.4	澄 3a12.11
(至) SHI	chika(u) 誓 7a7.17	緒 6a8.3	(豆) TŌ
池 3a3.4	CHIKU 竹 6f0.1	箸 6f9.1	(登) TŌ
地 3b3.1	筑 6f6.6	儲 2a16.1	超 3b9.18
治 3a5.28	築 6f10.5	(署) SHO	(召) SHŌ
(始) SHI	畜 2j8.7	(諸) SHO	趙 4b10.11
(台) DAI	蓄 3k10.16	(者) SHA	(肖) SHŌ
(冶) YA	逐 2q7.6	貯 7b5.1	弔 0a4.41
恥 6e4.2	CHIN 珍 4f5.6	(丁) CHŌ	(弓) KYŪ
遅 2q9.17	疹 5i5.10	CHŌ 丁 0a2.4	聴 6e11.3
稚 5d8.1	(診) SHIN	打 3c2.3	(徳) TOKU
質 7b8.7	沈 3a4.9	庁 3q2.2	提 3c9.4
chi 血 5h1.1	枕 4a4.8	町 5f2.1	(堤) TEI
(皿) sara	陳 2d8.2	頂 9a2.1	吊 3d3.8
千 2k1.2	(陣) JIN	兆 2b4.4	重 0a9.18
乳 3n4.4	(東) TŌ	挑 3c6.5	釣 8a3.5
茅 3k5.26	賃 7b6.6	眺 5c6.2	塚 3b9.10
chibi(ru) 禿 5d2.5	(任) NIN	跳 7d6.3	貼 7b5.2
chichi 父 2o2.3	朕 4b6.6	(桃) TŌ	
		(逃) TŌ	

	肇 4m10.1	(訂) TEI	(炎) EN	桐 4a6.30
Chō	長 0a8.2	(灯) TŌ	楠 4a9.25	胴 4b6.10
chō	長 0a8.2	妥 3e4.9	(南) NAN	銅 8a6.12
CHOKU	直 2k6.2	(桜) Ō	団 3s3.3	(筒) TŌ
	(値) CHI	駄 10a4.1	段 2s7.2	童 5b7.3
	勅 2g7.1	(太) TAI	断 6b5.6	憧 4k12.5
	(束) SOKU	那 2d4.6	danma(ri) 黙 4d11.5	瞳 5c12.2
CHU	蛛 6d6.1	朵 4a2.8	dare 誰 7a8.1	動 2g9.1
CHŪ	中 0a4.40	唾 3d8.2	da(shi) 出 0a5.22	働 2a11.1
	仲 2a4.7	懦 4k14.1	da(su) 出 0a5.22	(重) CHŌ
	虫 6d0.1	DAI 台 3d2.11	dāsu 打 3c2.3	道 2q9.14
	沖 3a4.5	殆 3d6.21	-da(te) 建 2q6.2	導 5c9.3
	忠 4k4.6	(胎) TAI	DATSU 脱 4b7.8	(首) SHU
	注 3a5.16	大 0a3.18	(説) SETSU	堂 3n8.4
	柱 4a5.12	奈 4e3.3	(悦) ETSU	瞳 5c11.3
	註 7a5.11	(太) TAI	奪 8c6.4	(党) TŌ
	駐 10a5.2	弟 2o5.1	(奮) FUN	萄 3k8.31
	(主) SHU	第 6f5.5	DE 弟 2o5.1	(陶) TŌ
	宙 3m5.5	代 2a3.3	(第) DAI	(缶) KAN
	抽 3c5.7	(袋) TAI	de 出 0a5.22	藤 3k15.3
	紬 6a5.3	(貸) TAI	DEI 泥 3a5.29	dobu 溝 3a10.9
	(由) YŪ	乃 0a2.10	(尼) NI	do(keru) 退 2q6.3
	丑 0a4.39	内 0a4.23	溺 3a10.1	DOKU 読 7a7.9
	紐 6a4.2	題 9a9.7	DEKI 溺 3a10.1	(続) ZOKU
	衷 0a9.9	DAKU 諾 7a8.10	DEN 淀 3a8.23	(売) BAI
	(哀) AI	(若) JAKU	(定) TEI	毒 0a8.14
	鋳 8a7.2	濁 3a13.8	殿 3r10.1	(母) BO
	(寿) JU	da(ku) 抱 3c5.15	(展) TEN	独 3g6.1
	肘 4b3.3	dama(kasu)	田 5f0.1	do(ku) 退 2q6.3
	昼 4c5.15	騙 10a9.1	伝 2a4.14	domo(ru) 吃 3d3.7
-chū	中 0a4.40	dama(ru) 黙 4d11.5	電 8d5.2	DON 鈍 8a4.2
		dama(su) 騙 10a9.1	鮎 11a5.7	飩 8b4.2
—— D ——		DAN 暖 4c9.4	de(ru) 出 0a5.22	(屯) TON
DA	陀 2d5.5	煖 4d9.9	deshimētoru	(純) JUN
	舵 6c5.3	(援) EN	粉 6b4.6	曇 4c12.1
	蛇 6d5.7	(緩) KAN	DO 奴 3e2.2	(雲) UN
	駝 10a5.3	壇 3b13.5	努 2g5.6	団 3s3.3
	堕 3b8.14	檀 4a13.11	怒 4k5.19	呑 3d4.19
	惰 4k9.6	弾 3h9.3	度 3q6.1	donburi 丼 0a5.40
	楕 4a9.13	(単) TAN	(渡) TO	-dono 殿 3r10.1
	(随) ZUI	男 5f2.2	(席) SEKI	何 2a5.21
	(髄) ZUI	(田) DEN	土 3b0.1	do(re) 何 2a5.21
	打 3c2.3	談 7a8.7	(吐) TO	-dō(ri) 通 2q7.18
	(丁) TEI		do(re) 何 2a5.21	doro 泥 3a5.29
			DŌ 同 2r4.2	
			洞 3a6.25	

—E—

E	衣	5e0.1
	依	2a6.1
	壊	3b13.3
	会	2a4.19
	絵	6a6.8
	回	3s3.1
	歪	2m7.4
	恵	4k6.16
	慧	4k11.16
e	枝	4a4.18
	柄	4a5.9
	江	3a3.8
	餌	8b6.2
-e	重	0a9.18
ebi	蝦	6d9.4
	鰕	11a9.4
ebisu	夷	0a6.24
eda	枝	4a4.18
ega(ku)	画	0a8.7
	描	3c8.21
EI	永	3a1.1
	泳	3a5.14
	詠	7a5.14
	(水)	SUI
	(氷)	HYŌ
	英	3k5.5
	映	4c5.1
	瑛	4f8.6
	(央)	Ō
	栄	3n6.1
	営	3n9.2
	(宮)	KYŪ
	鋭	8a7.12
	(悦)	ETSU
	(税)	ZEI
	(説)	SETSU
	影	3j12.1
	(京)	KEI
	(景)	KEI
	衛	3i13.3
	(偉)	I
	曳	0a6.23

	彗	0a11.9
	裔	5e7.4
	叡	2h14.1
ei	哉	4n5.4
EKI	液	3a8.29
	腋	4b8.8
	(夜)	YA
	役	3i4.2
	疫	5i4.2
	亦	2j4.4
	易	4c4.9
	益	2o8.5
	駅	10a4.4
emi	笑	6f4.1
e(mu)	笑	6f4.1
EN	兎	3k5.17
	宛	3m5.9
	怨	4k5.20
	遠	2q10.4
	猿	3g10.3
	園	3s10.1
	援	3c9.7
	媛	3e9.4
	(緩)	KAN
	(暖)	DAN
	奄	0a8.10
	俺	2a8.25
	沿	3a5.23
	鉛	8a5.14
	延	2q5.4
	(廷)	TEI
	(正)	SEI
	炎	4d4.4
	(火)	KA
	縁	6a9.10
	(緑)	RYOKU
	垣	3b6.5
	(亘)	KAN
	咽	3d6.14
	(因)	IN
	允	0a4.13
	円	2r2.1
	宴	3m7.3

	淵	3a9.3
	塩	3b10.4
	煙	4d9.3
	厭	2p12.1
	演	3a11.13
	鳶	11b3.1
	燕	3k13.16
	艶	3d16.3
enishi	縁	6a9.10
era(bu)	選	2q12.3
	撰	3c12.9
	択	3c4.21
era(garu)	偉	2a10.5
era(i)	偉	2a10.5
eri	衿	5e4.5
	襟	5e13.2
e(ru)	得	3i8.4
	選	2q12.3
	獲	3g13.1
esa	餌	8b6.2
e(tari)	得	3i8.4
e(te)	得	3i8.4
ETSU	悦	4k7.15
	閲	8e7.2
	(脱)	DATSU
	(説)	SETSU
	謁	7a8.6
	(渇)	KATSU
	(掲)	KEI
	(喝)	KATSU
	(褐)	KATSU
	咽	3d6.14
	越	4n8.2

—F—

FU	付	2a3.6
	附	2d5.4
	府	3q5.2
	俯	2a8.35
	符	6f5.12
	腑	4b8.9
	腐	3q11.3
	布	3f2.1
	怖	4k5.6
	婦	3e8.6

fu
FŪ

	(帰)	KI
	(掃)	SŌ
	夫	0a4.31
	扶	3c4.4
	芙	3k4.4
	父	2o2.3
	斧	2o6.4
	釜	2o8.7
	甫	0a7.11
	蒲	3k10.8
	輔	7c7.1
	浮	3a6.11
	孵	3n10.5
	(乳)	NYŪ
	歩	3n5.3
	賦	7b8.4
	(武)	BU
	普	2o10.5
	譜	7a12.2
	富	3m9.5
	(副)	FUKU
	(幅)	FUKU
	(福)	FUKU
	膚	2m13.1
	(胃)	I
	敷	4i11.1
	(激)	GEKI
	不	0a4.2
	缶	2k4.6
	巫	2a5.26
	阜	2k6.3
	負	2n7.1
	風	2s7.1
	赴	3b6.14
	斑	4f8.3
	風	2s7.1
	楓	4a9.28
	諷	7a9.21
	(虫)	CHŪ
	封	3b6.13
	(圭)	KEI
	(卦)	KE
	夫	0a4.31

	(扶) FU	fuku(meru)		furu(bokeru)		FUTSU	仏 2a2.5
	富 3m9.5	含 2a5.25		古 2k3.1			払 3c2.2
	鳳 2s12.1	fuku(mu) 含 2a5.25		furu(eru) 震 8d7.3			沸 3a5.3
fuchi	淵 3a9.3	fuku(ramasu)		furu(i) 古 2k3.1			祓 4e5.2
	縁 6a9.10	脹 4b8.1		故 4i5.2		fu(yasu)	殖 5c7.4
fuda	札 4a1.1	fuku(ramu)		furu(mekashii)			増 3b11.3
fude	筆 6f6.1	脹 4b8.1		古 2k3.1		fuyu	冬 4i2.1
fue	呂 3d4.16	膨 4b12.1		-furu(su) 古 2k3.1			那 2d4.6
	笛 6f5.6	fuku(reru) 脹 4b8.1		furu(u) 震 8d7.3			
fu(eru)	殖 5c7.4	膨 4b12.1		奮 5f11.2		—— G ——	
	増 3b11.3	fukuro 袋 5e5.11		fu(ruu) 振 3c7.14		GA	我 0a7.10
Fuji	藤 3k15.3	fu(maeru) 踏 7d8.3		fusa 総 6a8.20			俄 2a7.4
fuji	藤 3k15.3	Fumi 史 0a5.38		聡 6e8.2			餓 8b7.1
fuka(i)	深 3a8.21	fumi 文 2j2.4		房 4m4.2			鵞 11b7.7
fuka(maru)		史 0a5.38		寅 3m8.4			(義) GI
	深 3a8.21	迪 2q5.1		絃 6a5.12			
fuka(meru)		郁 2d6.6		惣 4k8.17			牙 0a4.28
	深 3a8.21	奎 3b6.12		fusa(garu) 塞 3m10.2			芽 3k5.9
Fukashi	宏 3m4.3	書 4c6.6		fusa(gu) 塞 3m10.2			雅 8c5.1
	洸 3a6.15	fu(mu) 踏 7d8.3		鬱 4a25.1			(邪) JA
fu(kasu)	更 0a7.12	FUN 分 2o2.1		fuse(gu) 防 2d4.1			(冴) GO
	蒸 3k9.19	紛 6a4.8		fu(seru) 伏 2a4.1			
fuke(ru)	耽 6e4.3	粉 6b4.6		臥 2a7.22			伽 2a5.12
fu(keru)	老 2k4.5	雰 8d4.2		俯 2a8.35			賀 7b5.10
	更 0a7.12			fushi 節 6f7.3			(加) KA
	蒸 3k9.19	墳 3b12.1		fu(shite) 伏 2a4.1			
fuki	蕗 3k13.4	噴 3d12.8		伏 2a4.1			瓦 0a5.11
FUKU	副 2f9.2	憤 4k12.6		fu(su) 臥 2a7.22			画 0a8.7
	幅 3f9.2	奮 5f11.2		俯 2a8.35			臥 2a7.22
	福 4e9.1	(奪) DATSU		fusu(beru)		GA'	合 2a4.18
	蝠 6d9.12	焚 4d8.7		燻 4d14.1		-gachi 勝 4b8.4
	輻 7c9.3	糞 6b11.3		fusu(boru)		gae(njiru) 肯 4b4.11
	(富) FU	funa- 舟 6c0.1		燻 4d14.1		gae(nzuru)	
		船 6c5.4		fusu(buru)			肯 4b4.11
	復 3i9.4	fundoshi 褌 5e9.2		燻 4d14.1		GAI	亥 2j4.1
	腹 4b9.4	fune 舟 6c0.1		fusuma 襖 5e13.1			刻 2g6.1
	複 5e9.3	船 6c5.4		futa 双 2h2.1			咳 3d6.10
	覆 4c14.6	fu(rareru) 振 3c7.14		蓋 3k10.15			該 7a6.10
	(履) RI	fu(reru) 狂 3g4.2		futa- 二 0a2.1			骸 4b12.7
	伏 2a4.1	振 3c7.14		futata(bi) 再 0a6.26			(核) KAKU
	(犬) KEN	触 6d7.10		futa(tsu) 二 0a2.1			(刻) KOKU
	服 4b4.6	furi 風 2s7.1		futo(i) 太 0a4.18			
	(報) HŌ	fu(ri) 振 3c7.14		futokoro 懐 4k13.9			涯 3a8.33
		fu(ru) 降 2d7.7		futo(ru) 太 0a4.18			崖 3o8.11
fu(ku)	吹 3d4.3	振 3c7.14		肥 4b4.5			街 3i9.2
	噴 3d12.8	furu(biru) 古 2k3.1		Futoshi 太 0a4.18			(術) JUTSU
	葺 3k9.25						慨 4k10.3
							概 4a10.2

	(既) KI		
	凱 2s10.1		
	鎧 8a10.3		
	刈 2f2.1		
	外 2m3.1		
	害 3m7.4		
	蓋 3k10.15		
	碍 5a8.4		
-ga(kari)	掛 3c8.6		
-ga(karu)	掛 3c8.6		
gake	崖 3o8.11		
-ga(ke)	掛 3c8.6		
GAKU	愕 4k9.4		
	顎 0a9.2		
	鰐 11a9.5		
	齶 3d21.1		
	額 9a9.6		
	(各) KAKU		
	(客) KAKU		
	岳 3o5.12		
	(丘) KYŪ		
	(兵) HEI		
	学 3n4.2		
	(字) JI		
	楽 4a9.29		
	(薬) YAKU		
gama	蒲 3k10.8		
GAN	元 0a4.5		
	玩 4f4.1		
	頑 9a4.6		
	顔 9a9.3		
	願 9a10.2		
	(原) GEN		
	岩 3o5.10		
	岸 3o5.11		
	巌 3o17.2		
	癌 5i12.4		
	雁 2p10.3		
	贋 2p17.2		
	含 2a5.25		
	(吟) GIN		
	(今) KON		
	丸 0a3.28		

	(九) KYŪ		
	眼 5c6.1		
	(眠) MIN		
gara	柄 4a5.9		
-ga(ri)	狩 3g6.5		
-gata	形 3j4.1		
	型 3b6.11		
-gata(i)	難 8c10.2		
GATSU	月 4b0.1		
-gawa	側 2a9.4		
GE	下 2m1.2		
	牙 0a4.28		
	外 2m3.1		
	夏 4i7.5		
	解 4g9.1		
	戯 4n11.1		
GEI	鯨 11a8.9		
	(京) KEI		
	迎 2q4.4		
	芸 3k4.12		
	睨 5c8.5		
GEKI	逆 2q6.8		
	隙 2d10.4		
	劇 2f13.2		
	撃 3c11.7		
	激 3a13.1		
GEN	幻 0a4.6		
	玄 2j3.2		
	弦 3h5.1		
	眩 5c5.3		
	絃 6a5.12		
	舷 6c5.5		
	(幼) YŌ		
	言 7a0.1		
	諺 7a9.15		
	彦 5b4.4		
	限 2d6.1		
	眼 5c6.1		
	(銀) GIN		
	(根) KON		
	(恨) KON		
	原 2p8.1		
	源 3a10.25		
GIN	(願) GAN		
	厳 3n14.1		

	巌 3o17.2		
	(敢) KAN		
GO	験 10a8.4		
	(倹) KEN		
	(検) KEN		
	(険) KEN		
	現 4f7.3		
	(見) KEN		
	嫌 3e10.7		
	(謙) KEN		
	元 0a4.5		
	拳 3c6.18		
	減 3a9.37		
	還 2q13.4		
GETSU	月 1b0.1		
GI	義 2o11.3		
	儀 2a13.4		
	犠 4g13.1		
	蟻 6d13.6		
	議 7a13.4		
	(我) GA		
	伎 2a4.13		
	技 3c4.16		
	妓 3e4.7		
	(岐) KI		
	(支) SHI		
	宜 3m5.7		
	誼 7a8.11		
	(且) SHO		
	疑 2m12.1		
GO-	擬 3c14.2		
GŌ	(凝) GYŌ		
	偽 2a9.2		
	(為) I		
	欺 4j8.1		
	(期) KI		
	祇 4e4.2		
	葵 3k9.17		
	戯 4n11.1		
	毅 5b10.1		
GIN	吟 3d4.8		
	(含) GAN		
	(今) KIN		

	銀 8a6.3		
	(金) KIN		
GO	五 0a4.27		
	伍 2a4.8		
	吾 3d4.17		
	悟 4k7.5		
	梧 4a7.9		
	語 7a7.6		
	呉 2o5.7		
	娯 3e7.3		
	誤 7a7.2		
	胡 4b5.12		
	瑚 4f9.3		
	(古) KO		
	(湖) KO		
	期 4b8.11		
	碁 5a8.9		
	午 2k2.2		
	牛 4g0.1		
	護 7a13.3		
	(獲) KAKU		
	(穫) KAKU		
	冴 2b5.2		
	(牙) GA		
	檎 4a12.17		
	(禽) KIN		
	互 0a4.15		
	后 3d3.11		
	後 3i6.5		
	御 3i9.1		
GO-	号 3d2.10		
GŌ	合 2a4.18		
	噛 3d15.2		
	豪 2j12.3		
	濠 3a14.9		
	(口) KŌ		
	拷 3c6.2		
	(考) KŌ		
	郷 2d8.14		
	剛 2f8.7		
	強 3h8.3		
	業 0a13.3		
	傲 2a11.2		

	轟 7c14.2	GYO	魚 11a0.1	habu(ku)	省 5c4.7		肺 4b5.9
Gō	郷 2d8.14		漁 3a11.1	HACHI	八 2o0.1		背 4b5.15
GOKU	極 4a8.11		御 3i9.1		捌 3c7.4		悖 4k6.4
	獄 3g11.1	GYŌ	凝 2b14.1		鉢 8a5.4		唄 3d7.1
gomi	芥 3k4.10		(疑) GI	hachi	八 2o0.1		配 7e3.2
	塵 3q11.4		(擬) GI		蜂 6d7.6		敗 7b4.1
GON	厳 3n14.1		仰 2a4.10	hada	肌 4b2.2		廃 3q9.3
	(敢) KAN		(抑) YOKU		膚 2m13.1	hai	灰 2p4.1
	言 7a0.1		倖 2a8.23	hadaka	裸 5e8.1		蠅 6d13.1
	欣 4j4.1		(幸) KŌ	hadara	斑 4f8.3	hai(ru)	入 0a2.3
	勤 2g10.1		業 0a13.3	hadashi	跣 7d6.4	haji	恥 6e4.2
	権 4a11.18		(叢) SŌ	hae	蠅 6d13.1	haji(keru)	弾 3h9.3
-goro	頃 9a2.2		行 3i3.1	ha(e)	栄 3n6.1	haji(ki)	弾 3h9.3
Gorō	吾 3d4.17		形 3j4.1	ha(eru)	生 0a5.29	haji(ku)	弾 3h9.3
-go(shi)	越 4n8.2		堯 3b9.3		栄 3n6.1	haji(maru)	始 3e5.9
-goto	毎 0a6.25		暁 4c8.1		映 4c5.1	Hajime	一 0a1.1
goto(ki)	如 3e5.1	GYOKU	玉 4f0.2	hagane	鋼 8a8.20		元 0a4.5
goto(ku)	如 3e5.1		(王) Ō	ha(gasu)	剥 2f8.4		甫 0a7.11
goto(shi)	如 3e5.1	GYŪ	牛 4g0.1	hage	禿 5d2.5		孟 2c5.1
GU	具 5c3.1			hage(masu)			始 3e5.9
	俱 2a8.15	**—— H ——**			励 2g5.4		祝 4e5.5
	遇 2q9.1	HA	巴 0a4.16	hage(mu)	励 2g5.4		哉 4n5.4
	(隅) GŪ		把 3c4.5	ha(geru)	禿 5d2.5		朔 4b6.12
	供 2a6.13		琶 4f8.9		剥 2f8.4		基 3b8.12
	紅 6a3.6		(肥) HI	hage(shii)	烈 4d6.3		巽 2o10.7
	虞 2m11.1		波 3a5.9		激 3a13.1		源 3a10.25
	愚 4k9.15		破 5a5.1	hagi	脛 4b7.6		新 5b8.3
GŪ	偶 2a9.1		跛 7d5.4		萩 3k9.5		肇 4m10.1
	隅 2d9.1		(皮) HI	ha(gu)	剥 2f8.4		魁 5f9.1
	遇 2q9.1		派 3a6.21		接 3c8.10	haji(me)	初 5e2.1
	寓 3m9.1		(脈) MYAKU	haguki	齦 3d21.1	haji(meru)	始 3e5.9
	(愚) GU		覇 4b15.4	haguku(mu)		haji(mete)	初 5e2.1
	宮 3m7.5	HA'	法 3a5.20		育 2j6.4	ha(jirau)	恥 6e4.2
	(営) EI	ha	刃 0a3.22	haha	母 0a5.36	ha(jiru)	恥 6e4.2
GUN	郡 2d7.12		羽 2b4.5	HAI	俳 2a8.8	haka	墓 3k10.18
	群 3d10.14		葉 3k9.21		排 3c8.8	hakama	袴 5e6.4
	(君) KUN		歯 6b6.11		輩 7c8.7	haka(rau)	計 7a2.1
	軍 2i7.1		端 5b9.2		(非) HI	hakari	秤 5d5.4
	(運) UN	haba	巾 3f0.1		(悲) HI	hakarigoto	
	(車) SHA		幅 3f9.2		牌 2j10.3		謀 7a9.8
-gurai	位 2a5.1	habaka(ru)			(卑) HI	Hakaru	恕 4k6.18
guramu	瓦 0a5.11		憚 4k12.4		(碑) HI	haka(ru)	計 7a2.1
-gusa	種 5d9.1	haba(mu)	阻 2d5.1		吠 3d4.1		諮 7a9.4
GYAKU	逆 2q6.8	habe(ru)	侍 2a6.11		拝 3c5.3		謀 7a9.8
	虐 2m7.3				杯 4a4.11		図 3s4.3
							測 3a9.4

	量	4c8.9	槃	4a10.30	Hara	原	2p8.1
ha(ke)	捌	3c7.4	磐	5a10.9	hara	原	2p8.1
hako	函	2b6.3	凡	2s1.1		腹	4b9.4
	箱	6f9.4	汎	3a3.11	harai	祓	4e5.2
hako(bu)	運	2q9.10	帆	3f3.1	hara(mu)	妊	3e4.3
HAKU	白	4c1.3	幡	3f12.2	ha(rasu)	晴	4c8.2
	伯	2a5.7	藩	3k15.4		腫	4b9.1
	迫	2q5.5	(番)	BAN	hara(u)	払	3c2.2
	泊	3a5.15	(審)	SHIN		祓	4e5.2
	拍	3c5.14	班	4f6.3	harawata	腸	4b9.8
	柏	4a5.14	斑	4f8.3	ha(re)	晴	4c8.2
	舶	6c5.2	犯	3g2.1	ha(reru)	晴	4c8.2
	箔	6f8.5	煩	4d9.1		腫	4b9.1
	魄	5f10.4	頒	0a1.3	ha(rete)	晴	4c8.2
	博	2k10.1	範	8i4.3	hari	針	8a2.3
	薄	3k13.11	繁	6a10.13		鍼	8a9.17
	(簿)	BO	han 榛	4a10.11		梁	4a7.25
	(専)	SEN	hana 花	3k4.7		榛	4a10.11
	剥	2f8.4	華	3k7.1	haritsuke	磔	5a11.2
	電	8d5.3	端	5b9.2	haru	東	0a8.9
ha(ku)	吐	3d3.1	鼻	5f9.3		明	4c4.1
	穿	3m7.10	Hanabusa 英	3k5.5		春	4c5.13
	掃	3c8.22	hanaha(da)			晏	4c6.4
	履	3r12.1	甚	0a9.10		陽	2d9.5
hama	浜	3a7.7	hanaha(dashii)			晴	4c8.2
ha(maru)	嵌	3o9.2	甚	0a9.10		玄	2j3.2
ha(meru)	嵌	3o9.2	hana(reru) 放	4h4.1		治	3a5.28
ha(mu)	食	8b0.1	離	8c10.3		美	2o7.4
HAN	反	2p2.2	hanashi 話	7a6.8		浩	3a7.9
	阪	2d4.4	hana(su) 放	4h4.1		脩	2a9.6
	坂	3b4.7	話	7a6.8		遙	2q10.3
	版	2j6.8	離	8c10.3		靖	5b8.1
	板	4a4.21	hana(tsu) 放	4h4.1		榛	4a10.11
	叛	2p7.3	hana(yagu)		ha(ru)	張	3h8.1
	販	7b4.2	花	3k4.7		貼	7b5.2
	飯	8b4.5	華	3k7.1	Haruka	遙	2q10.3
	(仮)	KA	hana(yaka)			遼	2q12.5
	半	0a5.24	花	3k4.7	haru(ka)	遙	2q10.3
	伴	2a5.4	華	3k7.1	hasa(maru)		
	判	2f5.2	hane	羽	2b4.5		挟	3c6.1
	袢	5e5.2	ha(nekasu)		hasami	鋏	8a7.4
	畔	5f5.1	撥	3c12.11	hasa(mu)	挟	3c6.1
	絆	6a5.6	跳	7d6.3		挿	3c7.2
	般	6c4.3	ha(neru) 撥	3c12.11	hashi	端	5b9.2
	搬	3c10.2	ha(ppa) 葉	3k9.21		箸	6f9.1

	嘴	3d13.7
	橋	4a12.8
hashibami	榛	4a10.11
hashigo	梯	4a7.17
hashira	柱	4a5.12
hashi(ri)	走	3b4.9
hashi(ru)	走	3b4.9
	奔	2k6.5
hasu	芙	3k4.4
	蓉	3k10.20
	蓮	3k10.31
	斜	2a9.21
Hata	畑	4d5.1
	秦	5d5.10
hata	畑	4d5.1
	畠	5f5.3
	幡	3f12.2
	傍	2a10.6
	旗	4h10.1
	秦	5d5.10
	側	2a9.4
	端	5b9.2
	機	4a12.1
hatake	畑	4d5.1
	畠	5f5.3
hatara(ki)	働	2a11.1
hatara(ku)	働	2a11.1
ha(tashite)		
	果	0a8.8
Hatsu	毅	5b10.1
ha(tasu)	果	0a8.8
ha(te)	果	0a8.8
ha(teru)	果	0a8.8
ha(teshi)	果	0a8.8
hato	鳩	11b2.1
HATSU	発	0a9.5
	撥	3c12.11
	捌	3c7.4
	(別)	BETSU
	鉢	8a5.4
	髪	3j11.3
	魃	5f10.2
hatsu	八	2o0.1
	肇	4m10.1
hatsu-	初	5e2.1

Reading	Kanji	Code
ha(u)	這	2q7.1
haya	速	2q7.4
	逸	2q8.6
	隼	8c2.2
	捷	3c8.4
	颯	5b9.4
Hayabusa	隼	8c2.2
hayabusa	隼	8c2.2
haya(i)	早	4c2.1
	速	2q7.4
haya(maru)	早	4c2.1
haya(meru)	早	4c2.1
	速	2q7.4
Hayao	駿	10a7.1
haya(ru)	逸	2q8.6
Hayashi	林	4a4.1
	隼	8c2.2
	駿	10a7.1
hayashi	林	4a4.1
	囃	3d18.1
haya(su)	囃	3d18.1
ha(yasu)	生	0a5.29
Hayato	隼	8c2.2
ha(zeru)	爆	4d15.2
hazu	筈	6f6.10
ha(zubeki)	恥	6e4.2
ha(zukashii)		
	恥	6e4.2
hazukashi(meru)		
	辱	2p8.2
hazu(mu)	弾	3h9.3
hazu(reru)		
	外	2m3.1
ha(zuru)	恥	6e4.2
hazu(su)	外	2m3.1
hebi	蛇	6d5.7
heda(taru)		
	隔	2d10.2
heda(teru)		
	隔	2d10.2
HEI	併	2a6.17
	屏	3r6.5
	瓶	2o9.6
	塀	3b9.11

Reading	Kanji	Code
	餅	8b6.4
	丙	0a5.21
	柄	4a5.9
	病	5i5.3
	幣	3f12.4
	蔽	3k12.1
	弊	4i11.3
	平	2k3.4
	坪	3b5.4
	兵	2o5.6
	並	2o6.1
	陛	2d7.6
	閉	8e3.3
HEKI	壁	3b13.7
	璧	4f13.2
	癖	5i13.2
	碧	5a9.7
heko(masu)		
	凹	0a5.14
heko(mu)	凹	0a5.14
HEN	扁	4m5.1
	偏	2a9.16
	遍	2q9.16
	編	6a9.13
	蝙	6d9.14
	篇	6f9.9
	騙	10a9.1
	片	2j2.5
	辺	2q2.1
	返	2q4.5
	変	2j7.3
	減	3a9.37
heri	縁	6a9.10
herikuda(ru)		
	遜	2q9.4
he(ru)	経	6a5.11
	減	3a9.37
	歴	2p12.4
heso	臍	4b14.2
he(su)	減	3a9.37
hezu(ru)	剥	2f8.4
HI	非	0a8.1
	斐	2j10.4
	悲	4k8.18
	扉	4m8.2

Reading	Kanji	Code
	緋	6a8.4
	誹	7a8.5
	鯡	11a8.2
	(俳)	HAI
	(排)	HAI
	(輩)	HAI
	皮	2h3.1
	披	3c5.13
	彼	3i5.2
	被	5e5.3
	疲	5i5.2
	跛	7d5.4
	(波)	HA
	(破)	HA
	比	2m3.5
	批	3c4.13
	庇	3q4.3
	砒	5a4.5
	琵	4f8.10
	卑	5f4.8
	痺	5i8.4
	碑	5a9.2
	泌	3a5.10
	秘	5d5.6
	(必)	HITSU
	罷	5g10.2
	(能)	NŌ
	妃	3e3.2
	否	3d4.20
	肥	4b4.5
	飛	0a9.4
	費	7b5.4
	鄙	2d11.4
	避	2q13.3
hi	日	4c0.1
	陽	2d9.5
	檜	4a13.8
	火	4d0.1
	灯	4d2.1
	一	0a1.1
	氷	3a1.2
hibi(ku)	響	4c15.3
hidari	左	0a5.20
hide	之	0a2.9

Reading	Kanji	Code
	秀	5d2.4
	英	3k5.5
	栄	3n6.1
	彬	4a7.3
	豪	2j12.3
hideri	旱	4c3.1
	酷	7e7.1
hido(i)	酷	7e7.1
hi(eru)	冷	2b5.3
Higashi	東	0a8.9
higashi	東	0a8.9
hige	髭	3j13.2
	鬚	9a13.2
hii(deru)	秀	5d2.4
hiiragi	柊	4a5.24
hiji	肘	4b3.3
hijiri	聖	4f9.9
hika(e)	控	3c8.11
hika(eru)	控	3c8.11
hikari	光	3n3.2
Hikaru	光	3n3.2
	晃	4c6.5
	皓	4c8.13
	暉	4c9.6
hika(ru)	光	3n3.2
hi(keru)	引	3h1.1
hiki	匹	2t2.3
	率	2j9.1
hiki(iru)	率	2j9.1
hiko	彦	5b4.4
hiku	渥	3a9.33
hi(ku)	引	3h1.1
	弾	3h9.3
	抽	3c5.7
	挽	3c7.13
	曳	0a6.23
	退	2q6.3
	轢	7c15.1
hiku(i)	低	2a5.15
hiku(maru)		
	低	2a5.15
hiku(meru)		
	低	2a5.15
hima	隙	2d10.4
	暇	4c9.1
hime	姫	3e7.11
	媛	3e9.4

hi(meru)	秘	5d5.6		大	0a3.18		伍	2a4.8		私	5d2.2
himo	紐	6a4.2		丑	0a4.39		亘	4c2.4		窃	3m6.5
HIN	賓	3m12.3		巨	2t2.2		宙	3m5.5	hiso(maru)		
	頻	9a8.2		亘	4c2.4		洋	3a6.19		潜	3a12.6
	品	3d6.15		弥	3h5.2		宥	3m6.1	hiso(meru)		
	稟	2j11.3		洋	3a6.19		恕	4k6.18		潜	3a12.6
	彬	4a7.3		宥	3m6.1		博	2k10.1	hiso(mu)	潜	3a12.6
	(林)	RIN		祐	4e5.3		裕	5e7.3	hitai	額	9a9.6
	(杉)	sugi		彦	5b4.4		寛	3m10.3	hita(ru)	浸	3a7.17
	浜	3a7.7		恕	4k6.18		熙	4d9.11	hita(su)	浸	3a7.17
	(兵)	HEI		啓	3d8.17		碩	5a9.1	hito	人	2a0.1
	牝	4g2.1		博	2k10.1		鴻	3a14.2		仁	2a2.8
	貧	2o9.5		普	2o10.5	hiro(u)	拾	3c6.14	hito-	一	0a1.1
hina	鄙	2d11.4		尋	3d9.29	hiro(yaka)	広	3q2.1	hitoe (ni)	偏	2a9.16
	雛	8c10.1		敬	4i8.4	hiru	昼	4c5.15	Hitomi	眸	5c6.3
hina(biru)	鄙	2d11.4		粕	5b7.3	hi(ru)	干	2k1.1		瞳	5c12.2
hine(kuru)	捻	3c8.25		寛	3m10.3	hirugae(ru)			hitomi	瞳	5c12.2
hine(ri)	捻	3c8.25		熙	4d9.11		翻	6b12.3	hito(ri)	独	3g6.1
hine(ru)	捻	3c8.25		嘉	3p11.1	hirugae(su)			hito(rideni)		
hinoe	丙	0a5.21		碩	5a9.1		翻	6b12.3		独	3g6.1
hinoki	檜	4a13.8		鴻	3a14.2	hiru(mu)	怯	4k5.9	Hitoshi	一	0a1.1
hinoto	丁	0a2.4	hiro(garu)	広	3q2.1	hisa	久	0a3.7		仁	2a2.8
hira	片	2j2.5		拡	3c5.25		玖	4f3.1		均	3b4.8
	迪	2q5.1	hiro(geru)	広	3q2.1		之	0a2.9		斉	2j6.5
	衡	3i13.1		拡	3c5.25		央	0a5.33		和	5d3.1
hira-	平	2k3.4	hiro(i)	弘	3h2.1		寿	0a7.15		洵	3a6.23
hira(keru)	開	8e4.6		広	3q2.1		弥	3h5.2		倫	2a8.28
hira(ki)	開	8e4.6	hiro(maru)				尚	3n5.2		斎	2j9.6
Hiraku	啓	3d8.17		広	3q2.1		胡	4b5.12		彬	4a7.3
hira(ku)	拓	3c5.1	hiro(meru)				桐	4a6.30		等	6f6.9
	開	8e4.6		広	3q2.1		亀	2n9.1		欽	8a4.1
hirame(kasu)				弘	3h2.1		藤	3k15.3		準	2k11.1
	閃	8e2.1	Hiromu	紘	6a4.11	Hisashi	久	0a3.7		舜	3n10.2
hirame(ku)				熙	4d9.11		央	0a5.33		整	4i12.3
	閃	8e2.1	Hiroshi	弘	3h2.1		永	3a1.1		鴻	3a14.2
hira(tai)	平	2k3.4		広	3q2.1		寿	0a7.15	hito(shii)	均	3b4.8
hiro	弘	3h2.1		宏	3m4.3		長	0a8.2		斉	2j6.5
	広	3q2.1		拡	3c5.25		弥	3h5.2		等	6f6.9
	宏	3m4.3		紘	6a4.11		尚	3n5.2	hito(tsu)	一	0a1.1
	紘	6a4.11		洸	3a6.15		恒	4k6.5	HITSU	必	0a5.16
	洸	3a6.15		滉	3a10.12		亀	2n9.1		泌	3a5.10
	滉	3a10.12		浩	3a7.9		庇	3q4.3		(秘)	HI
	浩	3a7.9		皓	4c8.13	hisa(shii)	久	0a3.7		匹	2t2.3
	皓	4c8.13		公	2o2.2	hishi	菱	3k8.20		筆	6f6.1
				央	0a5.33	hiso(ka)	秘	5d5.6	hitsugi	棺	4a8.25
							密	3m8.5	hitsuji	未	0a5.27

	羊 2o4.1		縫 6a9.15	hōmu(ru)	葬 3k9.15	hoto(ri)	辺 2q2.1
hi(ya)	冷 2b5.3		朋 4b4.1	HON	反 2p2.2	HOTSU	発 0a9.5
hi(yakasu)			萌 3k8.11		叛 2p7.3	ho(ttarakasu)	
	冷 2b5.3		崩 3o8.7		翻 6b12.3		放 4h4.1
hi(yasu)	冷 2b5.3		鵬 4b15.1	(番)	BAN	hozo	臍 4b14.2
hiyoko	雛 8c10.1		奉 0a8.13		本 0a5.25	HYAKU	百 4c2.3
hiza	膝 4b11.4		俸 2a8.18		奔 2k6.5	(白)	HAKU
hizu(mi)	歪 2m7.4		捧 3c8.12	hone	骨 4b6.14	HYŌ	票 4e6.2
hizu(mu)	歪 2m7.4		呆 3d4.13	honō	炎 4d4.4		剽 2f11.1
HO	甫 0a7.11		保 2a7.11	honoka	仄 2p2.1		漂 3a11.9
	浦 3a7.2		褒 2j13.1	hono(mekasu)			標 4a11.8
	捕 3c7.3		邦 2d4.7		仄 2p2.1		表 0a8.6
	哺 3d7.4		亨 2j4.2	hono(meku)			俵 2a8.21
	圃 3s7.1		法 3a5.20		仄 2p2.1		氷 3a1.2
	葡 3k9.30		宝 3m5.2	hora	洞 3a6.25	(永)	EI
	補 5e7.1		封 3b6.13	ho(reru)	惚 4k8.10		兵 2o5.6
	蒲 3k10.8		報 3b9.16	Hori	堀 3b8.11		拍 3c5.14
	輔 7c7.1		焙 4d8.1	hori	堀 3b8.11		彪 3j8.3
	舗 3b12.4		豊 3d10.15		濠 3a14.9		評 7a5.3
	保 2a7.11		鳳 2s12.1	horo	幌 3f10.1		憑 4k12.12
(呆)	HŌ	hō	頬 9a7.2	horo(biru)	亡 2j1.1		雹 8d5.3
	布 3f2.1	hobo	略 5f6.4		滅 3a10.26	hyō	彪 3j8.3
	歩 3n5.3	hoda(su)	絆 6a5.6	horo(bosu)		HYŪ	彪 3j8.3
HO'	法 3a5.20	hodo	程 5d7.2		亡 2j1.1		
ho	火 4d0.1	hodo(keru)			滅 3a10.26		— I —
	帆 3f3.1		解 4g9.1	ho(ru)	掘 3c8.32	I	偉 2a10.5
	穂 5d10.2	hodoko(su)			彫 3j8.2		違 2q10.5
HŌ	包 0a5.9		施 4h5.1	hō(ru)	放 4h4.1		葦 3k10.21
	泡 3a5.18	hodo(ku)	解 4g9.1	Hoshi	星 4c5.7		緯 6a10.7
	抱 3c5.15	ho(eru)	吠 3d4.1	hoshi	星 4c5.7	(衛)	EI
	疱 3q5.5	hofu(ru)	屠 3r9.2	ho(shii)	欲 4j7.1		唯 3d8.1
	胞 4b5.5	hoga(raka)		hoshiimama			惟 4k8.1
	砲 5a5.3		朗 4b6.11		恣 4k6.22		維 6a8.1
	飽 8b5.1	hoho	頬 9a7.2		縦 6a10.2	(准)	JUN
	鞄 3k11.25	hojiku(ru)	穿 3m7.10	hoso(i)	細 6a5.1	(推)	SUI
	方 4h0.1	hoji(ru)	穿 3m7.10	hoso(meru)		(稚)	CHI
	芳 3k4.1	hoka	他 2a3.4		細 6a5.1		委 5d3.2
	放 4h4.1		外 2m3.1	hoso(ru)	細 6a5.1		倭 2a8.16
	倣 2a8.7	hoko	矛 0a5.6	hos(suru)	欲 4j7.1		萎 3k8.18
	訪 7a4.1	hoko(ru)	誇 7a6.9	ho(su)	干 2k1.1		胃 5f4.3
	傍 2a10.6	HOKU	北 0a5.5		乾 4c7.14		畏 5f4.5
(防)	BŌ	homa(re)	誉 3n10.1	hotaru	蛍 3n8.2		異 5f6.7
	逢 2q7.15	home(ru)	誉 3n10.1	hotohoto	殆 3d6.21		衣 5e0.1
	峰 3o7.6	ho(meru)	褒 2j13.1	hotoke	仏 2a2.5		依 2a6.1
	蜂 6d7.6	homura	炎 4d4.4	hoton(do)	殆 3d6.21		尉 4e6.4

iso(gu) 急 2n7.2
ita 板 4a4.21
itadaki 頂 9a2.1
itada(ku) 頂 9a2.1
戴 5f12.2
ita(i) 痛 5i7.7
ita(ku) 甚 0a9.10
ita(meru) 痛 5i7.7
傷 2a11.10
ita(mi) 痛 5i7.7
ita(mu) 悼 4k8.13
痛 5i7.7
傷 2a11.10
ita(ranai) 至 3b3.6
Itaru 之 0a2.9
到 2f6.4
格 4a6.17
達 2q9.8
暢 4c10.4
諄 7a7.11
ita(ru) 至 3b3.6
到 2f6.4
迪 2q5.1
ita(su) 致 4i6.2
ita(tte) 至 3b3.6
itawa(ru) 労 3n4.3
itazu(ra) 徒 3i7.1
i(teru) 凍 2b8.2
ito 糸 6a0.1
絃 6a5.12
ito- 幼 2g3.3
最 4c8.10
itoguchi 緒 6a8.3
itokena(i) 幼 2g3.3
稚 5d8.1
itoma 暇 4c9.1
itona(mu) 営 3n9.2
ito(shii) 愛 4i10.1
ito(u) 厭 2p12.1
ITSU 一 0a1.1
壱 3p4.2
逸 2q8.6
溢 3a10.19
itsu 伍 2a4.8
巌 3o17.2
itsu- 五 0a4.27
Itsuki 斎 2j9.6
itsuku(shimu)
慈 2o11.1
itsu(tsu) 五 0a4.27
itsuwa(ru) 偽 2a9.2
詐 7a5.6
i(u) 云 0a4.4
言 7a0.1
結 6a6.5
iwa 石 5a0.1
岩 3o5.10
磐 5a10.9
巌 3o17.2
i(waba) 言 7a0.1
iwa(n'ya) 況 3a5.21
Iwao 厳 3n14.1
巌 3o17.2
iwao 巌 3o17.2
iwashi 鰯 11a10.3
iwa(u) 祝 4e5.5
iwaya 窟 3m10.6
iya 否 3d4.20
弥 3h5.2
嫌 3e10.7
i(ya) 厭 2p12.1
iya(garu) 嫌 3e10.7
iya(shii) 卑 5f4.8
iya(shimeru)
卑 5f4.8
iya(shimu)
卑 5f4.8
i(yasu) 癒 5i13.3
izana(u) 誘 7a7.4
izu 稜 5d8.4
Izumi 泉 3a5.33
izumi 泉 3a5.33
izu(re) 何 2a5.21
Izuru 出 0a5.22

— J —

JA 邪 2d5.8
耶 6e2.1
蛇 6d5.7
JAKU 若 3k5.12
弱 3h7.2
寂 3m8.2
雀 8c3.2
着 2o10.1
ja(reru) 戯 4n11.1
JI 寺 3b3.5
侍 2a6.11
持 3c6.8
時 4c6.2
痔 5i6.4
蒔 3k10.7
(待) TAI
(詩) SHI
(等) TŌ
滋 3a9.27
慈 2o11.1
磁 5a9.6
耳 6e0.1
餌 8b6.2
爾 0a14.3
璽 4f14.2
地 3b3.1
(池) CHI
仕 2a3.2
(士) SHI
字 3m2.1
(子) SHI
治 3a5.28
(冶) YA
除 2d7.10
(余) YO
似 2a5.11
(以) I
示 4e0.1
次 2b4.1
自 5c1.1
児 4c3.3
事 0a8.15
辞 5b8.4
JI' 十 2k0.1
ji 二 0a2.1
-ji 路 7d6.5
jika (ni) 直 2k6.2
JIKI 直 2k6.2
食 8b0.1
JIKU 柚 4a5.5
軸 7c5.1
JIN 人 2a0.1
仁 2a2.8
刃 0a3.22
(刀) TŌ
臣 2t4.3
(巨) KYO
尽 3r3.1
(尺) SHAKU
沈 3a4.9
(枕) CHIN
陣 2d7.1
(陳) CHIN
神 4e5.1
(申) SHIN
稔 5d8.5
(念) NEN
迅 2q3.5
甚 0a9.10
尋 3d9.29
腎 4b9.11
塵 3q11.4
儘 2a14.2
ji(rasu) 焦 8c4.3
ji(reru) 焦 8c4.3
JITSU 日 4c0.1
実 3m5.4
JO 女 3e0.1
如 3e3.1
茹 3k6.7
恕 4k6.18
除 2d7.10
叙 2h7.1
徐 3i7.2
(余) YO
助 2g5.1
鋤 8a7.5
序 3q4.4
JŌ 壌 3b13.4
嬢 3e13.1
穣 5d13.2
譲 7a13.1
醸 7e13.1

情	4k8.9
靖	5b8.1
静	4b10.9
浄	3a6.18
(青)	SEI
(争)	SŌ
成	4n2.1
城	3b6.1
晟	4c7.5
盛	5h6.1
丞	2c4.3
承	0a7.7
蒸	3k9.19
上	2m1.1
貞	2m7.1
又	0a2.26
杖	4a3.5
定	3m5.8
錠	8a8.12
乗	0a9.19
剰	2f9.1
祥	4e6.1
(羊)	YŌ
(洋)	YŌ
常	3n8.3
(党)	TŌ
(堂)	DŌ
場	3b9.6
(湯)	TŌ
(腸)	CHŌ
娘	3e7.2
(女)	JO
(良)	RYŌ
茸	3k6.1
(耳)	JI
縄	6a9.1
(亀)	KI
冗	2i2.1
状	2b5.1
条	4i4.1
畳	5f7.3
JOKU 辱	2p8.2
(唇)	SHIN

JU

需	8d6.1
儒	2a14.1
濡	3a14.4
糯	5e14.1
受	2h6.2
授	3c8.15
綬	6a8.7
珠	4f6.2
(朱)	SHU
(殊)	SHU
(株)	kabu
呪	3d5.11
(兄)	KEI
就	3d9.21
(京)	KYŌ
従	3i7.3
(縦)	JŪ
入	0a2.3
寿	0a7.15
頌	9a4.4
竪	5b9.5
誦	7a7.14
樹	4a12.3
雛	8c10.1
樹	4a12.3
柔	4a5.34
揉	3c9.2
蹂	7d9.2
鞣	4a14.7
十	2k0.1
汁	3a2.1
充	2j4.5
銃	8a6.9
従	3i7.3
縦	6a10.2

Ju / JŪ

住	2a5.19
(主)	SHU
(注)	CHŪ
(駐)	CHŪ
拾	3c6.14
(合)	GŌ
重	0a9.18
紐	6a4.2

渋	3a8.19
絨	6a6.13
獣	3g12.3
-jū 中	0a4.40
JUKU 塾	3b10.7
熟	4d10.5
JUN 旬	4c2.5
洵	3a6.23
殉	4c6.9
絢	6a6.14
詢	7a6.17
(句)	KU
淳	3a7.19
惇	4k7.12
諄	7a7.11
醇	7e7.5
(享)	KYŌ
(亨)	KYŌ
准	2b8.1
隼	8c2.2
準	2k11.1
(集)	SHŪ
順	9a3.2
馴	10a3.2
巡	2q3.3
(訓)	KUN
盾	5c4.8
循	3i9.6
楯	4a9.3
閏	8e4.4
潤	3a12.20
純	6a4.3
(鈍)	DON
(屯)	TON
遵	2q12.8
(尊)	SON
Jun 惇	4k7.12
純	6a4.3
jun 絢	6a6.14
JUTSU 述	2q5.3
術	3i8.2

—— K ——

KA 加	2g3.1
伽	2a5.12
迦	2q5.6
茄	3k5.19
枷	4a5.19
架	4a5.36
袈	5e5.10
嘉	3p11.1
可	3d2.12
何	2a5.21
河	3a5.30
苛	3k5.30
荷	3k7.10
歌	4j10.2
化	2a2.6
花	3k4.7
貨	7b4.5
靴	3k10.34
過	2q9.18
渦	3a9.36
禍	4e9.4
鍋	8a9.13
暇	4c9.1
蝦	6d9.4
鰕	11a9.4
霞	8d9.1
果	0a8.8
菓	3k8.2
課	7a8.2
家	3m7.1
嫁	3e10.6
稼	5d10.3
華	3k7.1
嘩	3d10.7
樺	4a10.15
佳	2a6.10
卦	2m6.1
(圭)	KEI
個	2a8.36
箇	6f8.15
仮	2a4.15
(反)	HAN
下	2m1.2
火	4d0.1

	瓜	0a6.3
	価	2a6.3
	科	5d4.3
	夏	4i7.5
	寡	3m11.2
KA'	合	2a4.18
	恰	4k6.10
ka	香	5d4.5
	馨	4c16.2
	甲	0a5.34
	圭	3b3.2
	郁	2d6.6
	神	4e5.1
	哉	4n5.4
	蚊	6d4.5
	鹿	3q8.5
	賀	7b5.10
	蘭	3k16.9
-ka	日	4c0.1
kaba	樺	4a10.15
kaban	鞄	3k11.25
kabane	姓	3e5.3
kaba(u)	庇	3q4.3
kabe	壁	3b13.7
kabi	黴	3i20.1
kabi(ru)	黴	3i20.1
ka(biru)	黴	3i20.1
kabu	株	4a6.3
	蕪	3k12.7
kabura	蕪	3k12.7
kaburi	頭	9a7.6
kabu(ru)	被	5e5.3
kabu(saru)	被	5e5.3
kabu(seru)	被	5e5.3
kabuto	兜	4c8.16
kachi	徒	3i7.1
	捷	3c8.4
ka(chi)	勝	4b8.4
kado	圭	3b3.2
	角	2n5.1
	門	8e0.1
	矩	2t7.1
	廉	3q10.1
	稜	5d8.4

ka(e)-	替	4c8.12
Kaede	楓	4a9.28
kaede	楓	4a9.28
kaeri(miru)	省	5c4.7
	顧	9a12.2
kaeru	蛙	6d6.4
kae(ru)	返	2q4.5
	帰	2f8.8
	還	2q13.4
ka(eru)	代	2a3.3
	変	2j7.3
	換	3c9.15
	替	4c8.12
kae(su)	返	2q4.5
	帰	2f8.8
	孵	3n10.5
kae(tte)	却	2e5.3
kaga(meru)	屈	3r5.2
kagami	鏡	8a11.6
	鑑	8a15.2
kaga(mu)	屈	3r5.2
kagaya(ku)	輝	7c8.8
	耀	8c12.1
	燿	4d14.3
kage	陰	2d8.7
	蔭	3k10.10
	景	4c8.8
	影	3j12.1
	熊	4d10.6
kage(ru)	陰	2d8.7
kagi	鈎	8a5.17
	鍵	8a8.18
kagi(ri)	限	2d6.1
kagi(ru)	限	2d6.1
kago	籠	6f16.1
ka(gu)	嗅	3d10.3
KAI	皆	4c5.14
	階	2d9.6
	楷	4a9.18
	諧	7a9.11
	海	3a6.20
	悔	4k6.12

	晦	4c7.3
(毎)	MAI	
	介	2a2.9
	芥	3k4.10
	界	5f4.7
	会	2a4.19
	絵	6a6.8
	檜	4a13.8
	街	3i9.2
	鮭	11a6.3
(圭)	KEI	
	塊	3b10.2
	魁	5f9.1
(鬼)	KI	
	解	4g9.1
	蟹	6d13.7
(角)	KAKU	
	戒	4n3.1
	械	4a7.22
	壊	3b13.3
	懐	4k13.9
	潰	3a12.14
(貴)	KI	
(遺)	I	
	快	4k4.2
(決)	KETSU	
	刈	2f2.1
	亥	2j4.1
	灰	2p4.1
	回	3s3.1
	改	4i3.1
	拐	3c5.21
	怪	4k5.11
	凱	2s10.1
	喙	3d9.14
	開	8e4.6
kai	貝	7b0.1
kaiko	蚕	6d4.8
kaina	腕	4b8.6
kaji	梶	4a7.19
	舵	6c5.3
	楫	4a9.20
kaka(e)	抱	3c5.15
kaka(eru)	抱	3c5.15

kaka(geru)	揭	3c8.13
kakari	係	2a7.8
	掛	3c8.6
ka(kari)	掛	3c8.6-
kaka(ru)	係	2a7.8
	繋	6a13.4
ka(karu)	架	4a5.36
	掛	3c8.6
	懸	4k16.2
ka(kasu)	欠	4j0.1
kakawa(razu)	拘	3c5.28
kakawa(ri)	関	8e6.7
kakawa(ru)	拘	3c5.28
kaka(waru)	係	2a7.8
	関	8e6.7
kake	賭	7b9.1
ka(ke)	欠	4j0.1
	掛	3c8.6
ka(kera)	欠	4j0.1
ka(keru)	欠	4j0.1
	架	4a5.36
	掛	3c8.6
	翔	2o10.8
	駆	10a4.5
	賭	7b9.1
	懸	4k16.2
(ni) ka(kete wa)	掛	3c8.6
kaki	垣	3b6.5
	柿	4a5.25
ka(ki)-	搔	3c10.11
kako(mu)	囲	3s4.2
kako(tsu)	託	7a3.1
kakotsu(keru)	託	7a3.1
kako(u)	囲	3s4.2
KAKU	各	4i3.3
	客	3m6.3
	格	4a6.17
	閣	8e6.3
(略)	RYAKU	
(絡)	RAKU	

(額)	GAKU	
礭	5a10.3	
鶴	11b10.1	
獲	3g13.1	
穫	5d13.4	
(隹)	SEKI	
(護)	GO	
郭	2d7.14	
廓	3q9.1	
(享)	KYŌ	
摑	3c11.6	
馘	5c12.6	
核	4a6.22	
(亥)	GAI	
(劾)	GAI	
(該)	GAI	
(刻)	KOKU	
拡	3c5.25	
(広)	KŌ	
殻	3p8.1	
(穀)	KOKU	
隔	2d10.2	
(融)	YŪ	
覚	3n9.3	
(見)	KEN	
嚇	3d14.1	
(赤)	SEKI	
角	2n5.1	
画	0a8.7	
革	3k6.2	
較	7c6.3	
ka(ku) 欠	4j0.1	
書	4c6.6	
描	3c8.21	
搔	3c10.11	
kakuma(u)		
匿	2t8.2	
kaku(reru)		
隠	2d11.3	
kaku(su) 隠	2d11.3	
kama 缶	2k4.6	
釜	2o8.7	
窯	3m12.5	
鎌	8a10.8	

kamabisu(shii)		
喧	3d9.12	
kama(e) 構	4a10.10	
kama(eru) 構	4a10.10	
kama(u) 構	4a10.10	
kame 亀	2n9.1	
瓶	2o9.6	
kami 上	2m1.1	
守	3m3.2	
神	4e5.1	
紙	6a4.4	
髪	3j11.3	
kaminari 雷	8d5.1	
kamo 鴨	11b5.2	
kamome 鷗	11b11.3	
kamo(su) 醸	7e13.1	
ka(mu) 嚙	3d15.2	
KAN 干	2k1.1	
刊	2f3.1	
汗	3a3.6	
奸	3e3.3	
肝	4b3.2	
旱	4c3.1	
竿	6f3.3	
栞	4a6.34	
悍	4k7.4	
桿	4a7.7	
幹	4c9.8	
靬	5f12.3	
閑	8e4.2	
間	8e4.3	
関	8e6.7	
癇	5i12.6	
簡	6f12.5	
(門)	MON	
(問)	MON	
(聞)	BUN	
官	3m5.6	
菅	3k8.27	
棺	4a8.25	
管	6f8.12	
館	8b8.3	
完	3m4.6	
冠	2i7.2	
莞	3k7.14	

(元)	GEN	
(宗)	SHŪ	
監	5h10.1	
艦	6c15.2	
鑑	8a15.2	
(濫)	RAN	
(覧)	RAN	
勧	2g11.1	
歓	4j11.1	
観	5c13.7	
(権)	KEN	
感	4k9.21	
憾	4k13.3	
鹹	4n16.1	
(減)	GEN	
乾	4c7.14	
翰	4c12.4	
韓	4c14.3	
甘	0a5.32	
柑	4a5.6	
嵌	3o9.2	
勘	2g9.3	
堪	3b9.1	
(甚)	JIN	
貫	7b4.3	
慣	4k11.9	
換	3c9.15	
喚	3d9.19	
還	2q13.4	
環	4f13.1	
串	0a7.13	
患	4k7.18	
緩	6a9.8	
(暖)	DAN	
(援)	EN	
漢	3a10.17	
(難)	NAN	
(漠)	BAKU	
巻	0a9.11	
(券)	KEN	
款	4j8.2	
(隷)	REI	

寛	3m10.3	
(見)	KEN	
甲	0a5.34	
缶	2k4.6	
亘	4c2.4	
侃	2a6.12	
函	2b6.3	
陥	2d7.11	
姦	3e6.9	
看	5c4.4	
寒	3m9.3	
敢	4i8.5	
諫	7a9.1	
Kan 菅	3k8.27	
kan- 神	4e5.1	
kana 哉	4n5.4	
kana- 金	8a0.1	
kana(deru)		
奏	0a9.17	
kanae 鼎	5c8.10	
kana(eru) 叶	3d2.1	
Kanai 叶	3d2.1	
Kaname 要	3e6.11	
kaname 要	3e6.11	
kanara(zu)		
必	0a5.16	
悲	4k8.18	
kana(shii) 悲	4k8.18	
kana(shimu)		
悲	4k8.18	
kana(u) 叶	3d2.1	
適	2q11.3	
Kanba 樺	4a10.15	
kanba 樺	4a10.15	
kanba(shii)		
芳	3k4.1	
馨	4c16.2	
kane 金	8a0.1	
銀	8a6.3	
錦	8a8.6	
鎌	8a10.8	
鐘	8a12.6	
包	0a5.9	
矩	2t7.1	
兼	2o8.1	
ka(neru) 兼	2o8.1	

kawa(ku)	渇	3a8.13	(反)	HAN	傾	2a11.3	剣	2f8.5

kawa(ku)	渇 3a8.13	(反) HAN	傾 2a11.3	剣 2f8.5
	乾 4c7.14	袈 5e5.10	(項) KŌ	検 4a8.28
kawara	瓦 0a5.11	(加) KA	(頂) CHŌ	瞼 5c13.4
ka(waru)	代 2a3.3	懸 4k16.2	敬 4i8.4	験 10a8.4
	変 2j7.3	(県) KEN	警 7a12.7	鹸 3s21.1
	換 3c9.15	気 0a6.8	(驚) KYŌ	券 2f6.10
	替 4c8.12	怪 4k5.11	兄 3d2.9	巻 0a9.11
ka(wasu)	交 2j4.3	華 3k7.1	競 5b15.1	倦 2a8.13
kawazu	蛙 6d6.4	家 3m7.1	系 6a1.1	拳 3c6.18
kaya	茅 3k5.26	ke 毛 0a4.33	係 2a7.8	捲 3c8.9
	萱 3k9.26	kebu(i) 煙 4d9.3	京 2j6.3	眷 5c6.6
kayo(u)	通 2q7.18	kebu(ru) 煙 4d9.3	景 4c8.8	圏 3s9.1
kaza-	風 2s7.1	KECHI 結 6a6.5	渓 3a8.16	兼 2o8.1
kaza(ru)	飾 8b5.3	kedamono 獣 3g12.3	鶏 11b8.4	嫌 3e10.7
kaze	風 2s7.1	蓋 3k10.15	繋 6a13.4	謙 7a10.10
kazo(eru)	数 4i9.1	keda(shi)	繋 4c16.2	鎌 8a10.9
kazu	一 0a1.1	keda(rawashii)	契 2f7.6	建 2q6.2
	三 0a3.1	汚 3a3.5	(喫) KITSU	健 2a8.34
	万 0a3.8	kega(reru)	継 6a7.8	腱 4b8.10
	五 0a4.27	汚 3a3.5	(米) BEI	鍵 8a8.18
	主 4f1.1	kega(su) 汚 3a3.5	慧 4k11.16	堅 3b9.13
	和 5d3.1	KEI 圭 3b3.2	(彗) EI	賢 7b9.2
	胤 4b5.16	奎 3b6.12	計 7a2.1	鰹 11a12.1
	計 7a2.1	桂 4a6.13	恵 4k6.16	(緊) KIN
	倭 2a8.16	珪 4f6.4	掲 3c8.13	間 8e4.3
	員 3d7.10	罫 5g8.2	啓 3d8.17	簡 6f12.5
	運 2q9.10	閨 8e6.5	蛍 3n8.2	犬 3g0.1
	量 4c8.9	鮭 11a6.3	卿 2e10.1	献 3g9.6
	数 4i9.1	(佳) KA	携 3c10.4	見 5c2.1
	算 6f8.7	(封) FŪ	詣 7a6.13	硯 5a7.2
	鶴 11b10.1	径 3i5.5	境 3b11.1	県 3n6.3
KE	圭 3b3.2	茎 3k5.23	慶 3q12.8	懸 4k16.2
	卦 2m6.1	経 6a5.11	憩 4k12.10	栞 4a6.34
	奎 3b6.12	軽 7c5.3	稽 5d11.3	軒 7c3.1
	罫 5g8.2	(怪) KAI	Kei 佳 2a6.10	喧 3d9.12
	(佳) KA	勁 2g7.2	恵 4k6.16	萱 3k9.26
	(封) FŪ	脛 4b7.6	kei 佳 2a6.10	件 2a4.4
	化 2a2.6	痙 5i7.5	kemono 獣 3g12.3	(牛) GYŪ
	花 3k4.7	頸 9a7.4	kemu 煙 4d9.3	絃 6a5.12
	希 3f4.1	刑 2f4.2	kemu(i) 煙 4d9.3	(玄) GEN
	稀 5d7.5	形 3j4.1	kemuri 煙 4d9.3	遣 2q10.2
	悔 4k6.12	型 3b6.11	kemu(ru) 煙 4d9.3	(遺) I
	(毎) MAI	(研) KEN	KEN 倹 2a8.27	絢 6a6.14
	(海) KAI	頃 9a2.2	険 2d8.8	
	仮 2a4.15			

(旬)	JUN
肩	4m4.1
研	5a4.1
乾	4c7.14
絹	6a7.3
権	4a11.18
憲	3m13.2
繭	3k15.7
顕	9a5.5
ke(ru) 蹴	7d12.2
kesa 袈	5e5.10
ke(shikaran)	
怪	4k5.11
ke(shikaranu)	
怪	4k5.11
ke(su) 消	3a7.16
keta 桁	4a6.8
KETSU 決	3a4.6
訣	7a4.2
欠	4j0.1
穴	3m2.2
血	5h1.1
頁	9a0.1
結	6a6.5
傑	2a11.6
潔	3a12.10
kewa(shii) 険	2d8.8
kezu(ru) 削	2f7.4
KI 奇	3d5.17
埼	3b8.8
寄	3m8.8
畸	5f8.2
綺	6a8.16
騎	10a8.3
己	0a3.12
忌	4k3.4
紀	6a3.5
起	3b7.11
記	7a3.5
基	3b8.12
棋	4a8.14
期	4b8.11
旗	4h10.1
麒	3q16.4
幾	4n8.4

畿	5f10.3
機	4a12.1
磯	5a12.1
伎	2a4.13
妓	3e4.7
岐	3o4.1
(支)	SHI
揮	3c9.14
暉	4c9.6
輝	7c8.8
(軍)	GUN
机	4a2.4
肌	4b2.2
飢	8b2.1
芹	3k4.5
祈	4e4.3
(斤)	KIN
(近)	KIN
揆	3c9.3
葵	3k9.17
(発)	HATSU
(廃)	HAI
季	5d2.3
悸	4k7.3
(委)	I
気	0a6.8
汽	3a4.16
危	2n4.3
詭	7a6.11
希	3f4.1
稀	5d7.5
規	5c6.9
槻	4a11.4
喜	3p9.1
嬉	3e12.3
毀	3b10.14
毅	5b10.1
帰	2f8.8
(婦)	FU
(掃)	SŌ
企	2a4.17
(止)	SHI

奎	3b6.12
(圭)	KEI
軌	7c2.1
既	0a10.5
姫	3e7.11
鬼	5f5.6
亀	2n9.1
貴	7b5.7
棄	2j11.5
熙	4d9.11
器	3d12.13
ki 木	4a0.1
栞	4a6.34
樹	4a12.3
城	3b6.1
哉	4n5.4
甲	0a5.34
玖	4f3.1
黄	3k8.16
牙	0a4.28
kiba 黄	3k8.16
ki(bamu) 黍	5d7.6
kibi 厳	3n14.1
kibi(shii)	
KICHI 吉	3p3.1
ki(eru) 消	3a7.16
ki(kasu) 利	5d2.1
ki(koe) 聞	8e6.1
ki(koeru) 聞	8e6.1
KIKU 菊	3k8.30
鞠	6b11.6
ki(ku) 聞	8e6.1
聴	6e11.3
利	5d2.1
効	2g6.2
Kim 金	8a0.1
ki(mari) 極	4a8.11
ki(maru) 決	3a4.6
ki(me) 極	4a8.11
ki(meru) 決	3a4.6
kimi 公	2o2.2
君	3d4.23
侯	2a7.21
kimo 肝	4b3.2
胆	4b5.6
KIN 斤	0a4.3

近	2q4.3
芹	3k4.5
欣	4j4.1
(祈)	KI
金	8a0.1
欽	8a4.1
錦	8a8.6
(銀)	GIN
今	2a2.10
衿	5e4.5
琴	4f8.11
菫	3k8.1
勤	2g10.1
謹	7a10.6
禽	2a10.8
檎	4a12.17
禁	4e8.3
襟	5e13.2
巾	3f0.1
均	3b4.8
菌	3k8.32
筋	6f6.4
緊	6a9.17
kin 公	2o2.2
kinoe 甲	0a5.34
kinoko 茸	3k6.1
kinoto 乙	0a1.5
kinu 衣	5e0.1
絹	6a7.3
kio(u) 競	5b15.1
kira 晃	4c6.5
kira(biyaka)	
煌	4d9.7
kira(i) 嫌	3e10.7
kira(meku)	
煌	4d9.7
kira(rasu) 切	2f2.2
kira(u) 嫌	3e10.7
ki(re) 切	2f2.2
ki(reru) 切	2f2.2
kiri 桐	4a6.30
錐	8a8.1
霧	8d11.1
ki(ri) 切	2f2.2
ki(ru) 切	2f2.2

	著	3k8.4	潔	3a12.10	戸	4m0.1	浩	3a7.9

著 3k8.4
着 2o10.1
kisaki 后 3d3.11
ki(seru) 着 2o10.1
Kishi 岸 3o5.11
kishi 岸 3o5.11
kiso(u) 競 5b15.1
Kita 北 0a5.5
kita 北 0a5.5
朔 4b6.12
kita(eru) 鍛 8a9.5
kitana(i) 汚 3a3.5
ki(taru) 来 0a7.6
ki(tasu) 来 0a7.6
KITSU 乞 0a3.4
迄 2q3.4
吃 3d3.7
吉 3p3.1
詰 7a6.7
喫 3d9.7
(契) KEI
橘 4a12.11
kitsune 狐 3g6.4
-ki(tte no) 切 2f2.2
kiwa 際 2d11.1
kiwa(doi) 際 2d11.1
kiwa(maru) 極 4a8.11
窮 3m12.4
kiwa(meru) 究 3m4.5
極 4a8.11
窮 3m12.4
kiwa(mete) 極 4a8.11
kiwa(mi) 極 4a8.11
Kiwamu 究 3m4.5
kiyo 清 3a8.18
精 6b8.1
汐 3a3.9
圭 3b3.2
浄 3a6.18
淳 3a7.19
舜 3n10.2
聖 4f9.9

潔 3a12.10
馨 4c16.2
kiyo(i) 清 3a8.18
kiyo(maru)
清 3a8.18
kiyo(meru)
浄 3a6.18
清 3a8.18
kiyo(raka) 清 3a8.18
Kiyoshi 清 3a8.18
靖 5b8.1
精 6b8.1
圭 3b3.2
浄 3a6.18
浩 3a7.9
淳 3a7.19
犂 4f9.9
碧 5a9.7
潔 3a12.10
澄 3a12.11
kizahashi 陛 2d7.6
階 2d9.6
kiza(mi) 刻 2f6.7
kiza(mu) 刻 2f6.7
Kizashi 萌 3k8.11
kiza(shi) 兆 2b4.4
萌 3k8.11
kiza(su) 兆 2b4.4
萌 3k8.11
kizu 疵 5i6.3
傷 2a11.10
kizu(ku) 築 6f10.5
kizuna 絆 6a5.6
KO 古 2k3.1
居 3r5.3
固 3s5.2
枯 4a5.26
胡 4b5.12
故 4i5.2
個 2a8.36
湖 3a9.8
葫 3k9.7
瑚 4f9.3
痼 5i8.8
箇 6f8.15
糊 6b9.2

戸 4m0.1
雇 4m8.1
顧 9a12.2
孤 2c6.2
狐 3g6.4
弧 3h6.2
虎 2m6.3
虚 2m9.1
袴 5e6.4
誇 7a6.9
拠 3c5.26
(処) SHO
炬 4d5.5
(巨) KYO
霞 8d9.1
(暇) KA
冴 2b5.2
(牙) GA
己 0a3.12
去 3b2.2
呼 3d5.4
股 4b4.8
庫 3q7.1
壺 3p9.2
鼓 3p10.2
子 2c0.1
仔 2a2.1
巨 2t2.2
児 4c3.3
粉 6b4.6
黄 3k8.16
籠 6f16.1
小 3n0.1
木 4a0.1
口 3d0.1
叩 3d2.3
亨 2j4.2
向 3d3.10
后 3d3.11
杏 4a3.13
拘 3c5.28
垢 3b6.3
恰 4k6.10
高 2j8.6

ko

ko-

KŌ

浩 3a7.9
格 4a6.17
皓 4c8.13
鈎 8a5.17
膏 2j12.1
稿 5d10.5
興 2o14.2
縞 6a10.9
藁 3k14.6
嚙 3d15.2
工 0a3.6
巧 0a5.7
功 2g3.2
江 3a3.8
肛 4b3.4
攻 4l3.2
昂 4c6.11
紅 6a3.6
虹 6d3.1
貢 7b3.3
控 3c8.11
腔 4b8.7
項 9a3.1
鴻 3a14.2
勾 0a4.8
公 2o2.2
弘 3h2.1
広 3q2.1
宏 3m4.3
紘 6a4.11
鉱 8a5.15
交 2j4.3
郊 2d6.8
効 2g6.2
校 4a6.24
絞 6a6.9
較 7c6.3
鮫 11a6.5
光 3n3.2
洸 3a6.15
晃 4c6.5
滉 3a10.12
幌 3f10.1
溝 3a10.9
構 4a10.10

Reading	Kanji	Code
	覯	5c12.8
	講	7a10.3
	購	7b10.3
	坑	3b4.6
	抗	3c4.15
	杭	4a4.17
	航	6c4.2
	行	3i3.1
	後	3i6.5
	桁	4a6.8
	衡	3i13.1
	皇	4f5.9
	皐	4c7.12
	煌	4d9.7
	蝗	6d9.8
	更	0a7.12
	梗	4a7.1
	硬	5a7.1
	孔	2c1.1
	好	3e2.1
	厚	2p6.1
	孝	2k4.3
	酵	7e6.1
	考	2k4.4
	侯	2a7.21
	候	2a8.10
	喉	3d9.6
	仰	2a4.10
	昂	4c5.11
(昂)		BŌ
(迎)		GEI
	幸	3b5.9
	倖	2a8.23
(辛)		SHIN
	亘	4c2.4
	恒	4k6.5
	耗	0a10.12
	耕	0a10.13
	黄	3k8.16
	曠	4c15.2
	康	3q8.1
	糠	6b11.2
	洪	3a6.14
	港	3a9.13
	荒	3k6.18
	慌	4k9.10
	綱	6a8.23
	鋼	8a8.20
	甲	0a5.34
	尻	3r2.1
	肯	4b4.11
	降	2d7.7
	香	5d4.5
	膠	4b11.3
Kō	航	6c4.2
kō-	神	4e5.1
koba(mu)	拒	3c5.29
kōba(shii)	馨	4c16.2
kō(bashii)	芳	3k4.1
kōbe	首	2o7.2
	頭	9a7.6
ko(biru)	媚	3e9.5
kobo(reru)	溢	3a10.19
	毀	3b10.14
	零	8d5.4
kobo(su)	溢	3a10.19
	零	8d5.4
	翻	6b12.3
kobo(tsu)	毀	3b10.14
kobu	瘤	5i10.3
kobushi	拳	3c6.18
koe	声	3p4.4
	肥	4b4.5
ko(eru)	超	3b9.18
	越	4n8.2
	肥	4b4.5
ko(gareru)	焦	8c4.3
ko(gasu)	焦	8c4.3
ko(geru)	焦	8c4.3
kogo(eru)	凍	2b8.2
kogo(ru)	凝	2b14.1
ko(gu)	漕	3a11.7
koi	恋	2j8.2
	鯉	11a7.2
ko(i)	濃	3a13.7
koinega(u)	希	3f4.1
koi(shii)	恋	2j8.2
koji(rasu)	拗	3c5.16
koji(reru)	拗	3c5.16
koke	苔	3k5.27
kokera	柿	4a5.25
	鱗	11a13.2
ko(keru)	倒	2a8.5
kokono-	九	0a2.15
kokono(tsu)	九	0a2.15
kokoro	心	4k0.1
kokoro(miru)	試	7a6.18
kokoroyo(ge)	快	4k4.2
kokoroyo(i)	快	4k4.2
kokoroyo(shi)	快	4k4.2
kokorozashi	志	3p4.1
kokoroza(su)	志	3p4.1
KOKU	告	3d4.18
	酷	7e7.1
	刻	2f6.7
(亥)		GAI
(劾)		GAI
	国	3s5.1
(玉)		GYOKU
	黒	4d7.2
(里)		RI
	穀	5d9.4
(殻)		KAKU
	石	5a0.1
	克	2k5.1
	谷	2o5.3
koku	欽	8a4.1
ko(ku)	扱	3c3.5
koma	駒	10a5.5
koma(ka)	細	6a5.1
koma(kai)	細	6a5.1
koma(ru)	困	3s4.1
koma(yaka)	濃	3a13.7
kome	米	6b0.1
ko(meru)	込	2q2.3
	籠	6f16.1
-ko(mi)	込	2q2.3
komo	薦	3k13.25
komo(ru)	籠	6f16.1
ko(mu)	込	2q2.3
kōmu(ru)	被	5e5.3
	蒙	3k10.23
KON	恨	4k6.2
	根	4a6.5
	痕	5i6.2
	墾	3b13.6
	懇	4k13.12
	昆	4c4.10
	混	3a8.14
	昏	4c4.11
	婚	3e8.4
	献	3g9.6
(南)		NAN
	褌	5e9.2
(軍)		GUN
	魂	5f9.2
(鬼)		KI
	今	2a2.10
	困	3s4.1
	建	2q6.2
	金	8a0.1
	紺	6a5.5
Kon	今	2a2.10
kona	粉	6b4.6
ko(no)	此	2m4.2
Konomu	嘉	3p11.1
kono(mu)	好	3e2.1
kora(eru)	堪	3b9.1
ko(rasu)	凝	2b14.1
	懲	4k14.3
kō(rasu)	凍	2b8.2
kore	惟	4k8.1
	維	6a8.1
	之	0a2.9
	也	0a3.29
	只	3d2.8
	伊	2a4.6

是 4c5.9
ko(re) 此 2m4.2
kōri 氷 3a1.2
ko(riru) 懲 4k14.3
koro 頃 9a2.2
koro(basu)
　転 7c4.3
koro(bu) 転 7c4.3
koro(garu)
　転 7c4.3
koro(gasu)
　転 7c4.3
koro(geru) 転 7c4.3
koromo 衣 5e0.1
koro(shimo)
　頃 9a2.2
koro(su) 殺 4a6.35
ko(ru) 凝 2b14.1
kō(ru) 氷 3a1.2
　凍 2b8.2
koshi 腰 4b9.3
　輿 2o15.1
koshira(eru)
　拵 3c5.24
ko(su) 超 3b9.18
　越 4n8.2
　濾 3a15.8
kosu(ru) 擦 3c14.5
kota(e) 答 6f6.12
kota(eru) 応 3q4.2
　堪 3b9.1
　答 6f6.12
koto 事 0a8.15
　肇 4m10.1
　言 7a0.1
　諠 7a8.11
　采 4a4.24
　琴 4f8.11
koto (ni) 殊 0a10.7
koto (ni suru)
　異 5f6.7
kotoba 詞 7a5.15
kotobuki 寿 0a7.15
kotogoto(ku)
　尽 3r3.1

kotoho(gu)
　寿 0a7.15
koto(naru)
　異 5f6.7
kotowari 理 4f7.1
kotowa(ru)
　断 6b5.6
kotowaza 諺 7a9.15
kotozu(keru)
　託 7a3.1
KOTSU 骨 4b6.14
　滑 3a10.6
　忽 4k4.7
　惚 4k8.10
　乞 0a3.4
ko(tta) 凝 2b14.1
ko(u) 乞 0a3.4
　恋 2j8.2
　請 7a8.8
　声 3p4.4
kowa-
kowa(gari)
　怖 4k5.6
kowa(garu)
　怖 4k5.6
kowa(i) 怖 4k5.6
　恐 4k6.19
　強 3h8.3
kowa(reru)
　毀 3b10.14
　壊 3b13.3
Kowashi 毅 5b10.1
kowa(su) 毀 3b10.14
　壊 3b13.3
ko(yashi) 肥 4b4.5
ko(yasu) 肥 4b4.5
koyomi 暦 2p12.3
kozo(tte) 挙 3n7.1
Kozue 梢 4a7.13
　槙 4a10.27
kozue 梢 4a7.13
KU 口 3d0.1
　句 3d2.13
　狗 3g5.5
　苦 3k5.24
　垢 3b6.3

宮 3m7.5
駒 10a5.5
軀 3d15.5
工 0a3.6
功 2g3.2
紅 6a3.6
貢 7b3.3
九 0a2.15
鳩 11b2.1
久 0a3.7
玖 4f3.1
区 2t2.1
駆 10a4.5
供 2a6.13
(共) KYŌ
矩 2t7.1
(巨) KYO
俱 2a8.15
(具) GU
孔 2c1.1
公 2o2.2
庫 3q7.1
KŪ 空 3m5.12
　腔 4b8.7
　弘 3h2.1
kuba(ru) 配 7e3.2
kubi 首 2o7.2
　頸 9a7.4
kubi(reru) 括 3c6.12
kubo 凹 0a5.14
　窪 3m11.9
kubo(mi) 窪 3m11.9
kubo(mu) 窪 3m11.9
kuchi 口 3d0.1
kuchibashi
　喙 3d9.14
　嘴 3d13.7
kuchibiru 唇 3d7.12
kuchinawa
　蛇 6d5.7
　朽 4a2.6
kuda 管 6f8.12
kuda(keru)
　砕 5a4.6

kuda(keta)
　砕 5a4.6
kuda(ku) 砕 5a4.6
kudan 件 2a4.4
kuda(ranai)
　下 2m1.2
kudari 件 2a4.4
　行 3i3.1
kuda(ru) 下 2m1.2
　降 2d7.7
kuda(sai) 下 2m1.2
kuda(saru)
　下 2m1.2
kuda(su) 下 2m1.2
　降 2d7.7
kuda(tte) 降 2d7.7
ku(enai) 食 8b0.1
ku(eru) 食 8b0.1
kugi 釘 8a2.4
kugu(ri) 潜 3a12.6
kugu(ru) 潜 3a12.6
kui 杭 4a4.17
ku(iru) 悔 4k6.12
kuji 籤 6f17.2
kuji(keru) 挫 3c7.15
kuji(ku) 挫 3c7.15
kujira 鯨 11a8.9
kuki 茎 3k5.23
kuku(ru) 括 3c6.12
kuma 阿 2d5.6
　熊 4d10.6
kumi 組 6a5.7
　綸 6a8.18
　伍 2a4.8
kumi(suru)
　与 0a3.23
kumo 雲 8d4.1
kumo(ru) 曇 4c12.1
ku(mu) 汲 3a3.7
　酌 7e3.9
　組 6a5.7
KUN 勲 4d11.3
　薫 3k13.17
　燻 4d14.1
　訓 7a3.6
(馴) JUN

Reading	Kanji	Code
	君	3d4.23
kuni	邦	2d4.7
	郁	2d6.6
	郡	2d7.12
	州	2f4.1
	洲	3a6.10
	之	0a2.9
	邑	3d4.15
	国	3s5.1
	晋	4c6.8
	秦	5d5.10
	訓	7a3.6
kura	倉	2a8.37
	庫	3q7.1
	椋	4a8.31
	蔵	3k12.17
-kura	競	5b15.1
kura(beru)		
	比	2m3.5
	較	7c6.3
kura(gari)	暗	4c9.2
kurai	位	2a5.1
kura(i)	晦	4c7.3
	暗	4c9.2
	昏	4c4.11
kura(masu)		
	晦	4c7.3
	暗	4c9.2
kura(mu)	暗	4c9.2
ku(rashi)	暮	3k11.14
ku(rasu)	暮	3k11.14
kura(u)	喰	3d9.1
ku(rau)	食	8b0.1
ku(rawasu)		
	食	8b0.1
Kure	呉	2o5.7
ku(re)	暮	3k11.14
kurenai	紅	6a3.6
ku(reru)	呉	2o5.7
	暮	3k11.14
kuri	栗	4a6.32
kurikaeshi kigō		
	々	2n1.1
kuro	畔	5f5.1
	黒	4d7.2
kuro(bamu)		
	黒	4d7.2
kurogane	鉄	8a5.6
kuro(i)	黒	4d7.2
kuro(maru)		
	黒	4d7.2
kuro(meru)		
	黒	4d7.2
kuro(zumu)		
	黒	4d7.2
ku(ru)	来	0a7.6
	繰	6a13.3
kuru(i)	狂	3g4.2
kuruma	車	7c0.1
kurume(ku)		
	眩	5c5.3
kuru(meru)		
	包	0a5.9
	括	3c6.12
kuru(mu)	包	0a5.9
	括	3c6.12
kuru(oshii)		
	狂	3g4.2
kuru(shigaru)		
	苦	3k5.24
kuru(shii)	苦	3k5.24
kuru(shimeru)		
	苦	3k5.24
kuru(shimu)		
	苦	3k5.24
kuru(u)	狂	3g4.2
kuruwa	郭	2d7.14
	廓	3q9.1
kuru(waseru)		
	狂	3g4.2
kuru(washii)		
	狂	3g4.2
kuru(wasu)		
	狂	3g4.2
kusa	草	3k6.13
	種	5d9.1
kusa(i)	臭	5c4.3
kusamura	叢	6e12.3
kusa(rasu)		
	腐	3q11.3
kusa(reru)	腐	3q11.3
kusari	鎖	8a10.2
kusa(ru)	腐	3q11.3
kusa(su)	腐	3q11.3
kuse	癖	5i13.2
kushi	串	0a7.13
	櫛	4a15.5
ku(shiki)	奇	3d5.17
ku(shikumo)		
	奇	3d5.17
kuso	屎	3r6.1
	糞	6b11.3
Kusu	楠	4a9.25
kusu	楠	4a9.25
kusu(beru)		
	燻	4d14.1
kusu(buru)		
	燻	4d14.1
Kusunoki	楠	4a9.25
kusunoki	楠	4a9.25
kusuri	薬	3k13.15
KUTSU	屈	3r5.2
	掘	3c8.32
	窟	3m10.6
	(出)	SHUTSU
kutsu	靴	3k10.34
kutsugae(ru)		
	覆	4c14.6
kutsugae(su)		
	覆	4c14.6
kutsuro(geru)		
	寛	3m10.3
kutsuro(gu)		
	寛	3m10.3
ku(u)	食	8b0.1
	喰	3d9.1
kuwa	桑	2h8.1
kuwada(teru)		
	企	2a4.17
kuwa(eru)	加	2g3.1
kuwa(shii)	委	5d3.2
	詳	7a6.12
	精	6b8.1
ku(wasu)	食	8b0.1
kuwa(waru)	加	2g3.1
ku(yamu)	悔	4k6.12
kuya(shii)	悔	4k6.12
kuyu(rasu)		
	燻	4d14.1
kuzu	屑	3r7.4
	葛	3k9.22
kuzu(reru)	崩	3o8.7
kuzu(shi)	崩	3o8.7
kuzu(su)	崩	3o8.7
KYA	伽	2a5.12
	脚	4b7.3
KYAKU	却	2e5.3
	脚	4b7.3
	(去)	KYO
KYO	客	3m6.3
	巨	2t2.2
	拒	3c5.29
	炬	4d5.5
	渠	4a8.40
	距	7d5.8
	居	3r5.3
	据	3c8.33
	裾	5e8.8
	鋸	8a8.19
	(古)	KO
	虚	2m9.1
	嘘	3d11.7
	拠	3c5.26
	(処)	SHO
	去	3b2.2
	挙	3n7.1
	許	7a4.3
KYŌ	喬	3d9.25
	嬌	3e12.1
	蕎	3k12.8
	橋	4a12.8
	矯	3d14.5
	驕	10a12.2
	兄	3d2.9
	況	3a5.21
	競	5b15.1
	共	3k3.3
	供	2a6.13
	恭	3k7.16
	亨	2j4.2

享 2j5.1	旭 4c2.6	(末) MATSU	妹 3e5.4
京 2j6.3	局 3r4.4　ma	万 0a3.8	昧 4c5.2
挟 3c6.1	極 4a8.11	目 5c0.1	枚 4a4.4
狭 3g6.2　KYŪ	及 0a3.24	馬 10a0.1	埋 3b7.2
峡 3o6.1	汲 3a3.7	満 3a9.25　Mai	舞 0a15.1
凶 0a4.19	扱 3c3.5	間 8e4.3　mai	舞 0a15.1
兇 0a6.12	吸 3d3.5　ma-	真 2k8.1　mainai	賂 7b6.2
胸 4b6.9	級 6a3.2　maba(ra)	疎 0a11.4　mai(ri)	詣 7a6.13
協 2k6.1	求 2b5.5　mabata(ku)		(o)mai(ri) 参 3j5.1
脅 2g8.2	毬 2b9.1	瞬 5c13.1　mai(ru)	参 3j5.1
脇 4b6.3	球 4f7.2　mabayu(i)		maji(eru) 交 2j4.3
匡 2t4.1	救 4i7.1	眩 5c5.3	雑 8c6.2
狂 3g4.2	九 0a2.15　maboroshi		majina(i) 呪 3d5.11
(王) Ō	仇 2a2.4	幻 0a4.6　majiro(gu)	瞬 5c13.1
郷 2d8.14	究 3m4.5　mabu(shii)		ma(jiru) 交 2j4.3
響 4c15.3	鳩 11b2.1	眩 5c5.3	混 3a8.14
香 5d4.5	久 0a3.7　mabu(su)	塗 3b10.10	雑 8c6.2
馨 4c16.2	玖 4f3.1　mabuta	瞼 5c13.4　maji(waru)	
敬 4i8.4	弓 3h0.1　machi	町 5f2.1	交 2j4.3
驚 10a12.4	窮 3m12.4	街 3i9.2　makana(u)	
境 3b11.1	糾 6a3.4　mada	未 0a5.27	賄 7b6.1
鏡 8a11.6	赳 3b7.10　madara	斑 4f8.3　maka(ru)	罷 5g10.2
鋏 8a7.4	宮 3m7.5　made	迄 2q3.4　ma(karu)	負 2n7.1
頬 9a7.2	(営) EI　mado	窓 3m8.7　maka(seru)	
経 6a5.11	丘 0a5.12　Madoka	円 2r2.1	任 2a4.9
(怪) KAI	旧 4c1.1　mado(ka)	円 2r2.1	委 5d3.2
(径) KEI	臼 0a6.4　mado(u)	惑 4k8.16　maka(su)	任 2a4.9
怯 4k5.9	休 2a4.2　mae	前 2o7.3	委 5d3.2
(去) KYO	朽 4a2.6　maga	禍 4e9.4　ma(kasu)	負 2n7.1
校 4a6.24	泣 3a5.1　maga(i)	擬 3c14.2　(o)ma(ke)	負 2n7.1
(交) KŌ	急 2n7.2　ma(garu)	曲 0a6.27　ma(keru)	負 2n7.1
教 4i6.1	給 6a6.7　maga(u)	紛 6a4.8　Maki	牧 4g4.1
(孝) KŌ	嗅 3d10.3　ma(geru)	曲 0a6.27　maki	牧 4g4.1
叶 3d2.1	鞠 6b11.6　magi(rasu)		巻 0a9.11
叫 3d3.4		紛 6a4.8	蒔 3k10.7
杏 4a3.13	**— L —**	magi(rawashii)	槙 4a10.27
恐 4k6.19	Lee 李 4a2.7	紛 6a4.8	薪 3k13.3
強 3h8.3		magi(rawasu)	Makoto 淳 3a7.19
卿 2e10.1	**— M —**	紛 6a4.8	惇 4k7.12
興 2o14.2	MA 麻 3q8.3　magi(reru)		諄 7a7.11
橇 4a12.14	摩 3q12.6	紛 6a4.8	真 2k8.1
	磨 3q13.3　mago	孫 2c7.1	慎 4k10.4
KYOKU	魔 3q18.2　maguro	鮪 11a6.1	洵 3a6.23
曲 0a6.27	茉 3k5.6　magusa	秣 5d5.1	詢 7a6.17
(典) TEN		MAI 毎 0a6.25	一 0a1.1
		苺 3k5.4	

	允	0a4.13	mana(bu)	学	3n4.2		順	9a3.2	mata(wa)	又	2h0.1

Reading	Kanji	Code	Reading	Kanji	Code	Reading	Kanji	Code	Reading	Kanji	Code
	允	0a4.13	mana(bu)	学	3n4.2		順	9a3.2	mata(wa)	又	2h0.1
	周	2r6.1	manako	眼	5c6.1		雅	8c5.1	mato	的	4c4.12
	実	3m5.4	mane(ku)	招	3c5.22		暢	4c10.4	mato(i)	纏	6a16.1
	信	2a7.1	manimani	随	2d8.10		諒	7a8.14	mato(maru)		
	亮	2j7.6	manji	卍	2k4.7		叡	2h14.1		纏	6a16.1
	欽	8a4.1	manuka(reru)				優	2a15.1	mato(meru)		
	瑞	4f9.6		免	2n6.1	masa (ni)	方	4h0.1		纏	6a16.1
	誠	7a6.3	mare	希	3f4.1		正	2m3.3	mato(u)	纏	6a16.1
	諒	7a8.14		稀	5d7.5		当	3n3.3	MATSU	末	0a5.26
makoto	信	2a7.1	Mari	鞠	6b11.6		将	2b8.3		抹	3c5.9
	誠	7a6.3	mari	毬	2b9.1	Masaki	柾	4a5.15		茉	3k5.6
	実	3m5.4		鞠	6b11.6	masaki	柾	4a5.15		秣	5d5.1
	真	2k8.1	maro	麿	3q15.2	Masaru	大	0a3.18		(未)	MI
MAKU	幕	3k10.19	maro(yaka)				多	0a6.5	matsu	松	4a4.16
	膜	4b10.6		円	2r2.1		克	2k5.1		須	3j9.1
ma(ku)	巻	0a9.11	maru	丸	0a3.28		昌	4c4.4	ma(tsu)	待	3i6.4
	捲	3c8.9	maru (de)	丸	0a3.28		捷	3c8.4	matsuge	睫	5c8.4
	蒔	3k10.7	maru(i)	丸	0a3.28		最	4c8.10	matsu(ri)	祭	4e6.3
	撒	3c12.2		円	2r2.1		智	4c8.11	matsurigoto		
makura	枕	4a4.8	maru(kkoi)				賢	7b9.2		政	4i5.1
maku(reru)				丸	0a3.28		優	2a15.1	matsu(ru)	祀	4e3.2
	捲	3c8.9	maru(meru)			masa(ru)	勝	4b8.4		祭	4e6.3
maku(ru)	捲	3c8.9		丸	0a3.28		優	2a15.1	matsu(waru)		
mama	飯	8b4.5	masa	正	2m3.3	ma(saru)	増	3b11.3		纏	6a16.1
	儘	2a14.2		征	3i5.3	Masashi	匡	2t4.1	matta(ku)	全	2a4.16
mame	豆	3d4.22		柾	4a5.15		昌	4c4.4	matto(u suru)		
mami(eru)				政	4i5.1		柾	4a5.15		全	2a4.16
	見	5c2.1		全	2a4.16	masa(shiku)			ma(u)	舞	0a15.1
mami(reru)				匡	2t4.1		正	2m3.3	mawa(ri)	回	3s3.1
	塗	3b10.10		聖	4f9.9	ma(shi)	増	3b11.3	mawa(ru)	回	3s3.1
Mamoru	葵	3k9.17		晨	4c7.7	mashira	猿	3g10.3	mawa(shi)	回	3s3.1
	衛	3i13.3		晟	4c7.5	ma(shite)	況	3a5.21	mawa(su)	回	3s3.1
	護	7a13.3		誠	7a6.3	masu	升	0a4.32	mayo(i)	迷	2q6.1
mamo(ru)	守	3m3.2		允	0a4.13		祐	4e5.3	mayo(u)	迷	2q6.1
	護	7a13.3		方	4h0.1		益	2o8.5	mayo(wasu)		
MAN	曼	4c7.8		旦	4c1.2		鱒	11a12.6		迷	2q6.1
	漫	3a11.11		庄	3q3.1	ma(su)	益	2o8.5	mayu	眉	5c4.9
	慢	4k11.8		甫	0a7.11		増	3b11.3		繭	3k15.7
	饅	8b11.1		応	3q4.2	mata	又	2h0.1	Mayumi	檀	4a13.11
	鰻	11a11.5		昌	4c4.4		叉	2h1.1	mayumi	檀	4a13.11
	満	3a9.25		祐	4e5.3		也	0a3.29	Mayuzumi	黛	4d13.7
	瞞	5c11.2		倭	2a8.16		亦	2j4.4	mayuzumi	黛	4d13.7
	万	0a3.8		将	2b8.3		股	4b4.8	ma(zaru)	交	2j4.3
	卍	2k4.7		真	2k8.1		復	3i9.4		混	3a8.14
mana-	愛	4i10.1		理	4f7.1	matata(ku)				雑	8c6.2
							瞬	5c13.1	ma(zeru)	交	2j4.3

Reading	Kanji	Code
	混	3a8.14
	雑	8c6.2
ma(zu)	先	3b3.7
mazu(i)	拙	3c5.11
mazu(shii)	貧	2o9.5
ME	碼	5a10.1
me	目	5c0.1
	眼	5c6.1
me-	芽	3k5.9
	萌	3k8.11
me-	女	3e0.1
	牝	4g2.1
	雌	8c6.1
me(deru)	愛	4i10.1
Megumi	恵	4k6.16
	萌	3k8.11
Megumu	愛	4i10.1
megu(mu)	恵	4k6.16
me(gumu)	芽	3k5.9
megu(rasu)	巡	2q3.3
	回	3s3.1
megu(ru)	巡	2q3.3
	回	3s3.1
MEI	迷	2q6.1
	謎	7a9.20
	名	3d3.12
	銘	8a6.4
	明	4c4.1
	盟	5h8.1
	冥	2i8.2
	瞑	5c10.3
	命	2a6.26
	鳴	3d11.1
mekake	妾	5b3.2
mekura	盲	2j6.6
meku(ru)	捲	3c8.9
memi	萌	3k8.11
MEN	面	3s6.1
	麺	4i17.1
	免	2n6.1
	綿	6a8.8
men	牝	4g2.1
me(ru)	減	3a9.37
meshi	飯	8b4.5
meshii	盲	2j6.6
mesu	牝	4g2.1
	雌	8c6.1
me(su)	召	2f3.3
mētoru	米	6b0.1
METSU	滅	3a10.26
mezura(shii)	珍	4f5.6
MI	未	0a5.27
	味	3d5.3
	魅	5f10.1
	(妹)	MAI
	(末)	MATSU
	弥	3h5.2
	眉	5c4.9
	微	3i10.1
mi	已	0a3.16
	水	3a0.1
	身	0a7.5
	弥	3h5.2
	実	3m5.4
	美	2o7.4
	海	3a6.20
	胤	4b5.16
	深	3a8.21
	御	3i9.1
mi-	爾	0a14.3
	観	5c13.7
	三	0a3.1
	御	3i9.1
michi	迪	2q5.1
	通	2q7.18
	達	2q9.8
	道	2q9.14
	遙	2q10.3
	方	4h0.1
	亨	2j4.2
	吾	3d4.17
	紀	6a3.5
	倫	2a8.28
	峻	3o7.4
	恕	4k6.18
	理	4f7.1
	惣	4k8.17
	路	7d6.5
	碩	5a9.1
	巌	3o17.2
michibi(ku)	迪	2q5.1
	導	5c9.3
mi(chiru)	満	3a9.25
mida(ra)	淫	3a8.17
	猥	3g9.2
mida(reru)	乱	3d4.21
mida(ri ni)	妄	2j4.6
	濫	3a15.3
mida(rigamashii)		
	猥	3g9.2
mida(ou)	乱	3d4.21
Midori	翠	2k12.2
	碧	5a9.7
midori	翠	2k12.2
	緑	6a8.15
mi(eru)	見	5c2.1
Migaki	琢	4f8.1
Migaku	琢	4f8.1
miga(ku)	磨	3q13.3
migi	右	3d2.15
Migiwa	汀	3a2.2
migiwa	汀	3a2.2
mijika(i)	短	3d9.27
miji(me)	惨	4k8.5
mikado	帝	2j7.1
miki	幹	4c9.8
mikoto	命	2a6.26
	尊	2o10.3
mikotonori		
	勅	2g7.1
	詔	7a5.10
mimi	耳	6e0.1
MIN	民	0a5.23
	眠	5c5.2
	明	4c4.1
mina	南	2k7.1
	皆	4c5.14
Minami	南	2k7.1
minami	南	2k7.1
Minamoto	源	3a10.25
minamoto	源	3a10.25
minato	港	3a9.13
mine	峻	3o7.4
	峰	3o7.6
	嶺	3o14.2
	巌	3o17.2
	稔	5d8.5
miniku(i)	醜	7e10.1
minna	皆	4c5.14
Minori	穣	5d13.2
Minoru	酉	7e0.1
	実	3m5.4
	稔	5d8.5
	穣	5d13.2
mino(ru)	実	3m6.1
Mio	澪	3a13.6
mio	澪	3a13.6
mi(ru)	見	5c2.1
	覧	5c12.7
	観	5c13.7
	看	5c4.4
	診	7a5.9
misa	操	3c13.3
misaki	岬	3o5.4
	崎	3o8.3
Misao	節	6f7.3
misao	操	3c13.3
misasagi	陵	2d8.5
mise	店	3q5.4
mi(seru)	見	5c2.1
misoka	晦	4c7.3
mi(tasu)	充	2j4.5
	満	3a9.25
mito(meru)		
	認	7a7.10
MITSU	密	3m8.5
	蜜	3m11.7
	(必)	HITSU
mitsu	光	3n3.2
	晃	4c6.5
	允	0a4.13
	充	2j4.5
	弘	3h2.1
	弥	3h5.2

	満	3a9.25	MOCHI	勿	0a4.11	mono	者	4c4.13

mu(keru)	向	3d3.10
	剥	2f8.4
muko	婿	3e9.3
mu(kō)	向	3d3.10
muku	尨	3j4.2
	椋	4a8.31
mu(ku)	向	3d3.10
	剥	2f8.4
mukui	酬	7e6.2
muku(iru)	報	3b9.16
mukuro	骸	4b12.7
	軀	3d15.5
muna-	胸	4b6.9
	棟	4a8.3
muna(shii)		
	空	3m5.12
	虚	2m9.1
mune	旨	4c2.2
	宗	3m5.1
	胸	4b6.9
	棟	4a8.3
mura	邑	3d4.15
	村	4a3.11
	斑	4f8.3
	群	3d10.14
mura-	叢	6e12.3
mura(garu)		
	群	3d10.14
Muraji	連	2q7.2
murasaki	紫	6a6.15
mu(rasu)	蒸	3k9.19
mu(re)	群	3d10.14
mu(reru)	蒸	3k9.19
	群	3d10.14
muro	室	3m6.4
muse(bu)	咽	3d6.14
mushi	虫	6d0.1
mushiba(mu)		
	蝕	8b6.1
mushi(ro)	寧	3m11.8
mu(su)	蒸	3k9.19
musu(bu)	結	6a6.5
musume	娘	3e7.2
mutsu	陸	2d8.4
	睦	5c8.6
mu(tsu)	六	2j2.2

mutsu(majii)		
	睦	5c8.6
Mutsumi	睦	5c8.6
mut(tsu)	六	2j2.2
muzuka(shii)		
	難	8c10.2
MYAKU	脈	4b6.8
	(派)	HA
MYŌ	名	3d3.12
	妙	3e4.5
	命	2a6.26
	苗	3k5.2
	明	4c4.1
	冥	2i8.2

— N —

NA	納	6a4.5
	(内)	NAI
	那	2d4.6
	奈	4e3.3
	南	2k7.1
NA'	納	6a4.5
na	名	3d3.12
	菜	3k8.25
	魚	11a0.1
	楠	4a9.25
nabe	鍋	8a9.13
nada(meru)		
na(deru)	撫	3c12.7
-nado	等	6f6.9
nae	苗	3k5.2
na(eru)	萎	3k8.18
naga	永	3a1.1
	亨	2j4.2
	孟	2c5.1
	呂	3d4.16
	酉	7e0.1
	長	0a8.2
	脩	2a9.6
	斐	2j10.4
	暢	4c10.4
naga(i)	永	3a1.1
	長	0a8.2
naga(meru)		
	眺	5c6.2

-naga(ra)	乍	0a5.10
naga(raeru)		
	長	0a8.2
naga(reru)		
	流	3a7.10
Nagashi	亀	2n9.1
naga(su)	流	3a7.10
naga(tarashii)		
	長	0a8.2
nage(kawashii)		
	嘆	3d10.8
nage(ku)	嘆	3d10.8
	歓	4j10.3
	慨	4k10.3
na(geru)	投	3c4.18
nagi	凪	2s4.3
Nagisa	汀	3a2.2
	渚	3a9.1
nagisa	渚	3a9.1
nago(mu)	和	5d3.1
nago(yaka)		
	和	5d3.1
nagu	凪	2s4.3
na(gu)	凪	2s4.3
nagu(ru)	殴	2t6.1
nagusa(meru)		
	慰	4k11.13
nagusa(mu)		
	慰	4k11.13
NAI	乃	0a2.10
	内	0a4.23
na(i)	無	4d8.8
naji(ru)	詰	7a6.7
naka	中	0a4.40
	仲	2a4.7
	斐	2j10.4
(o)naka	腹	4b9.4
Nakaba	央	0a5.33
naka(ba)	半	0a5.24
nakadachi	媒	3e9.2
naka(re)	勿	0a4.11
	莫	3k7.13
na(kaseru)		
	泣	3a5.1
na(kasu)	泣	3a5.1

na(keru)	泣	3a5.1
na(ki)	亡	2j1.1
na(ku)	泣	3a5.1
	鳴	3d11.1
na(ku naru)		
	無	4d8.8
na(kunaru)		
	亡	2j1.1
na(kusu)	無	4d8.8
nama	生	0a5.29
nama(keru)		
	怠	4k5.21
namame(kashii)		
	艶	3d16.3
namame(ku)		
	艶	3d16.3
namari	鉛	8a5.14
nama(ru)	鈍	8a4.2
nama(su)	鈍	8a4.2
name(raka)		
	滑	3a10.6
na(meru)	嘗	3n11.1
nameshi	鞣	4a14.7
nameshigawa		
	鞣	4a14.7
name(su)	鞣	4a14.7
nami	波	3a5.9
	浪	3a7.5
	甫	0a7.11
na(mi)	並	2o6.1
namida	涙	3a7.21
NAN	南	2k7.1
	楠	4a9.25
	納	6a4.5
	(内)	NAI
	難	8c10.2
	(漢)	KAN
	男	5f2.2
	軟	7c4.1
nan	何	2a5.21
nana	七	0a2.13
nana(me)	斜	2a9.21
nana(tsu)	七	0a2.13
nani	何	2a5.21
	奈	4e3.3

nanigashi	某 4a5.33	natsu(kashimu)		年 0a6.16	nigi(wau)	賑 7b7.1
nano-	七 0a2.13		懐 4k13.9	nengo(ro)	懇 4k13.12	nigi(yaka)	賑 7b7.1
nao	侃 2a6.12	natsu(keru)		nera(u)	狙 3g5.3	nigo(ri)	濁 3a13.8
	直 2k6.2		懐 4k13.9	ne(reru)	練 6a8.2	nigo(ru)	濁 3a13.8
	尚 3n5.2	natsu(ku)	懐 4k13.9	ne(ri)	煉 4d9.2	nigo(su)	濁 3a13.8
	脩 2a9.6	nawa	苗 3k5.2	ne(ru)	煉 4d9.2	nii-	新 5b8.3
	猶 3g9.5		縄 6a9.1		練 6a8.2	(o)nii(san)	兄 3d2.9
nao(ru)	直 2k6.2	naya(masu)			錬 8a8.3	niji	虹 6d3.1
	治 3a5.28		悩 4k7.11		寝 3m10.1	niji(ru)	躙 7d16.1
nao(su)	直 2k6.2	naya(mu)	悩 4k7.11	nē(san)	姉 3e5.8	nikawa	膠 4b11.3
	治 3a5.28	nazo	謎 7a9.20	neta(mu)	妬 3e5.1	NIKU	肉 2a4.20
nara(beru)		nazora(eru)		NETSU	熱 4d11.4	niku(garu)	憎 4k11.7
	並 2o6.1		準 2k11.1	neya	閨 8e6.5	niku(i)	憎 4k11.7
nara(bi ni)	並 2o6.1	ne	子 2c0.1	nē(ya)	姉 3e5.8	-niku(i)	悪 4k7.17
nara(bu)	並 2o6.1		音 5b4.3	nezumi	鼠 0a13.1		難 8c10.2
nara(su)	均 3b4.8		値 2a8.30	NI	二 0a2.1	niku(mu)	憎 4k11.7
na(rasu)	馴 10a3.2		根 4a6.5		仁 2a2.8		
	鳴 3d11.1		寝 3m10.1		弐 4n3.3		憎 4k11.7
	慣 4k11.9		嶺 3o14.2		尼 3r2.2	niku(rashii)	
nara(u)	倣 2a8.7	neba(ru)	粘 6b5.4		児 4c3.3		
	習 4c7.11	nega(u)	願 9a10.2		爾 0a14.3	niku(shimi)	
na(reru)	馴 10a3.2	negi	葱 3k9.20	ni	丹 0a4.34		憎 4k11.7
	慣 4k11.9	negira(u)	労 3n4.3		荷 3k7.10	NIN	刃 0a3.22
nari	也 0a3.29	NEI	寧 3m11.8		煮 4d8.9		忍 4k3.3
	成 4n2.1	neji(keru)	拗 3c5.16	(ni) ka(kete wa)			認 7a7.10
	形 3j4.1	neji(kureru)			掛 3c8.6		人 2a0.1
	斉 2j6.5		拗 3c5.16	(ni) oi(te)	於 4h4.2		仁 2a2.8
	得 3i8.4	neji(reru)	捻 3c8.25	(ni) o(keru)			任 2a4.9
	就 3d9.21		捩 3c8.31		於 4h4.2		妊 3e4.3
	業 0a13.3	neji(ru)	拗 3c5.16	(ni) to(tte)	取 6e2.2	nina(u)	担 3c5.20
	稔 5d8.5		捻 3c8.25	(ni) tsu(ite)		ninniku	葫 3k9.7
naru	稔 5d8.5		捩 3c8.31		就 3d9.21	nio(i)	匂 0a4.7
na(ru)	成 4n2.1	ne(kasu)	寝 3m10.1	(ni) tsu(rete)			臭 5c4.3
	為 4d5.8	neko	猫 3g8.5		連 2q7.2	nio(u)	匂 0a4.7
	鳴 3d11.1	nemu(i)	眠 5c5.2	nibu(i)	鈍 8a4.2	nira(mu)	睨 5c8.5
nasa(ke)	情 4k8.9	nemu(ru)	眠 5c5.2	nibu(ru)	鈍 8a4.2	ni(ru)	似 2a5.11
nashi	梨 4a7.24	nemu(tai)	眠 5c5.2	NICHI	日 4c0.1		煮 4d8.9
na(shi)	無 4d8.8	NEN	念 2a6.24	nie	牲 4g5.1	nise	偽 2a9.2
na(su)	成 4n2.1		捻 3c8.25	ni(eru)	煮 4d8.9		贋 2p17.2
	為 4d5.8		稔 5d8.5	niga(i)	苦 3k5.24	ni(seru)	似 2a5.11
	済 3a8.30		粘 6b5.4	niga(ru)	苦 3k5.24	Nishi	西 0a6.20
nasu(ru)	擦 3c14.5		鮎 11a5.7	ni(gasu)	逃 2q6.5	nishi	西 0a6.20
NATSU	捺 3c8.17		(占) SEN	ni(geru)	逃 2q6.5		螺 6d11.3
natsu	夏 4i7.5		然 4d8.10	nigi(ri)	握 3c9.17	nishiki	錦 8a8.6
natsu(kashii)			燃 4d12.2	nigi(ru)	握 3c9.17	nishin	鯡 11a8.2
	懐 4k13.9						鰊 11a9.1
						niwa	庭 3q6.3

柔 4a5.34

— O —

o 汚 3a3.5
阿 2d5.6
於 4h4.2
和 5d3.1
烏 4d6.5

o 絃 6a5.12
緒 6a8.3
緖 6a8.18
夫 0a4.31
弘 3h2.1
阿 2d5.6
尾 3r4.2
男 5f2.2
彦 5b4.4
魁 5f9.1

o- 巌 3o17.2
小 3n0.1
御 3i9.1
雄 8c4.1

Ō 鴨 11b5.2
鷺 11b10.9
鷗 11b11.3
鷹 3q21.1
(鳥) CHŌ
王 4f0.1
旺 4c4.2
皇 4f5.9
殴 2t6.1
欧 4j4.2
黄 3k8.16
横 4a11.13
奥 6b6.9
襖 5e13.1
押 3c5.5
(甲) KŌ
拗 3c5.16
(幼) YŌ
翁 2o8.6
(公) KŌ
桜 4a6.15
(楼) RŌ

凹 0a5.14
央 0a5.33
応 3q4.2
往 3i5.6

ō 碩 5a9.1
艶 3d16.3
大 0a3.18

ō- 欄 4a16.4
obashima
obi 帯 3f7.1
obi(eru) 怯 4k5.9
obi(ku) 誘 7a7.4
o(biru) 帯 3f7.1
obiya(kasu)
脅 2g8.2
obo(eru) 覚 3n9.3
obo(ezu) 覚 3n9.3
obo(rasu) 溺 3a10.1
obo(reru) 溺 3a10.1
obo(shii) 覚 3n9.3
o(busaru) 負 2n7.1
o(buu) 負 2n7.1
o(chi) 落 3k9.13
ochii(ru) 陥 2d7.11
o(chiru) 落 3k9.13
oda(teru) 煽 4d10.4
oda(yaka) 穏 5d11.4
odo(kasu) 脅 2g8.2
嚇 3d14.1
odo(ri) 踊 7d7.2
odoriji 々 2n1.1
odoro(kasu)
驚 10a12.4
odoro(ku) 愕 4k9.4
驚 10a12.4
odo(ru) 踊 7d7.2
躍 7d14.2
odo(su) 威 4n5.2
脅 2g8.2
嚇 3d14.1
o(eru) 終 6a5.9
oga(mu) 拝 3c5.3
ogi 荻 3k7.8
ōgi 扇 4m6.1
ogina(u) 補 5e7.1
ogo(ru) 奢 4c8.17
驕 10a12.2

ogoso(ka) 厳 3n14.1
oi 甥 5f7.5
o(i) 老 2k4.5
Ōi 浩 3a7.9
ō(i) 多 0a6.5
被 5e5.3
覆 4c14.6
ō(i ni) 大 0a3.18
ō(inaru) 大 0a3.18
oi(raku) 老 2k4.5
o(iru) 老 2k4.5
(ni) oi(te) 於 4h4.2
o(jikeru) 怖 4k5.6
o(jiru) 怖 4k5.6
Oka 岡 2r6.2
oka 丘 0a5.12
岡 2r6.2
陸 2d8.4
(o)kage 陰 2d8.7
ōkami 狼 3g7.3
(o)kā(san) 母 0a5.36
oka(su) 犯 3g2.1
侵 2a7.15
冒 4c5.6
oke 桶 4a7.18
(ni) o(keru)
於 4h4.2
oki 沖 3a4.5
起 3b7.11
熙 4d9.11
興 2o14.2
-o(ki) 置 5g8.8
Ōki 樹 4a12.3
ō(kii) 大 0a3.18
okina 翁 2o8.6
o(kiru) 起 3b7.11
okona(u) 行 3i3.1
oko(ru) 怒 4k5.19
興 2o14.2
起 3b7.11
o(koru) 起 3b7.11
oko(su) 興 2o14.2
起 3b7.11
okota(ru) 怠 4k5.21
惰 4k9.6
OKU 億 2a13.6
憶 4k13.5

臆 4b13.3
屋 3r6.3
Oku 奥 6b6.9
oku 奥 6b6.9
o(ku) 措 3c8.20
置 5g8.8
奥 6b6.9
oku(maru)
oku(rasu) 遅 2q9.17
oku(reru) 後 3i6.5
遅 2q9.17
oku(ru) 送 2q6.9
贈 7b11.2
(o)mai(ri) 参 3j5.1
(o)ma(ke) 負 2n7.1
omi 臣 2t4.3
omo 主 4f1.1
面 3s6.1
omo(i) 重 0a9.18
omo(mi) 重 0a9.18
omomuki 趣 6e9.1
omomu(ku)
赴 3b6.14
omomu(ro)
徐 3i7.2
omone(ru)
阿 2d5.6
omo(njiru)
重 0a9.18
omonmi(ru)
惟 4k8.1
omonpaka(ri)
慮 2m13.2
omo(nzuru)
重 0a9.18
omori 錘 8a8.2
omo(sa) 重 0a9.18
omo(tai) 重 0a9.18
omote 表 0a8.6
面 3s6.1
omo(u) 思 5f4.4
惟 4k8.1
想 4k9.18
憶 4k13.5
概 4a10.2
ōmu(ne) 苑 3k5.17
ON

Reading	Kanji	Code
	怨	4k5.20
	隠	2d11.3
	穏	5d11.4
	音	5b4.3
	陰	2d8.7
	恩	4k6.23
	遠	2q10.4
	温	3a9.21
on-	御	3i9.1
	雄	8c4.1
ona(ji)	同	2r4.2
(o)naka	腹	4b9.4
o(nbu)	負	2n7.1
(o)nē(san)	姉	3e5.8
oni	鬼	5f5.6
(o)nii(san)	兄	3d2.9
onna	女	3e0.1
ono	斧	2o6.4
onono(ku)	戦	4n9.2
onoono	各	4i3.3
onore	己	0a3.12
ono(zukara)		
	自	5c1.1
ono(zuto)	自	5c1.1
ore	俺	2a8.25
o(reru)	折	3c4.7
ori	折	3c4.7
	織	6a12.6
o(ri)	織	6a12.6
o(riru)	下	2m1.2
	降	2d7.7
oro(ka)	愚	4k9.15
oro(kashii)		
	愚	4k9.15
oroshi	卸	2e7.1
oroso(ka)	疎	0a11.4
oro(su)	卸	2e7.1
o(rosu)	降	2d7.7
o(ru)	折	3c4.7
	織	6a12.6
osa	孟	2c5.1
	長	0a8.2
	脩	2a9.6
	綜	6a8.12
o(sae)	押	3c5.5
osa(eru)	抑	3c4.12
o(saeru)	押	3c5.5
osa(maru)	収	2h2.2
	治	3a5.28
	修	2a8.11
	納	6a4.5
osa(meru)		
	収	2h2.2
	治	3a5.28
	修	2a8.11
	納	6a4.5
	紀	6a3.5
Osamu	納	6a4.5
	紘	6a4.11
	統	6a6.10
	修	2a8.11
	脩	2a9.6
	乃	0a2.10
	収	2h2.2
	伊	2a4.6
	攻	4i3.2
	治	3a5.28
	宰	3m7.2
	理	4f7.1
	敦	4i7.4
	惣	4k8.17
	摂	3c10.6
	靖	5b8.1
	蔵	3k12.17
	穣	5d13.2
osana(i)	幼	2g3.3
ōse	仰	2a4.10
ō(seru)	果	0a8.8
oshi	唖	3d8.3
o(shi)	押	3c5.5
oshi(e)	教	4i6.1
oshi(eru)	教	4i6.1
o(shii)	惜	4k8.11
o(shimu)	惜	4k8.11
o(shite)	押	3c5.5
oso	晏	4c6.4
oso(i)	遅	2q9.17
oso(raku)	恐	4k6.19
osore	虞	2m11.1
oso(re)	恐	4k6.19
oso(reru)	怖	4k5.6
	恐	4k6.19
	畏	5f4.5
oso(roshii)		
	恐	4k6.19
oso(u)	襲	5e16.2
oso(waru)	教	4i6.1
os(sharu)	仰	2a4.10
osu	雄	8c4.1
o(su)	押	3c5.5
	推	3c8.1
	捺	3c8.17
	圧	2p3.1
(o)taka(ku)		
	高	2j8.6
oto	乙	3d4.16
	音	5b4.3
	頌	9a4.4
otoko	男	5f2.2
Ōtori	鳳	2s12.1
ōtori	鵬	4b15.1
otoro(eru)	衰	2j8.1
oto(ru)	劣	3n3.4
(o)tō(san)	父	2o2.3
o(toshi)	落	3k9.13
otoshii(reru)		
	陥	2d11.11
o(tosu)	落	3k9.13
otōto	弟	2o5.1
otozu(reru)		
	訪	7a4.1
OTSU	乙	0a1.5
o(tte)	追	2q6.4
otto	夫	0a4.31
o(u)	追	2q6.4
	逐	2q7.6
	生	0a5.29
	負	2n7.1
ō(u)	被	5e3.3
	蔽	3k12.1
	覆	4c14.6
o(wari)	終	6a5.9
o(waru)	終	6a5.9
	負	2n7.1
o(waseru)	負	2n7.1
oya	親	5b11.1
ōyake	公	2o2.2
oyo(bi)	及	0a3.24
oyo(bosu)	及	0a3.24
oyo(bu)	及	0a3.24
oyo(gu)	泳	3a5.14
oyo(so)	凡	2s1.1

— P —

Reading	Kanji	Code
pai	牌	2j10.3
pēji	頁	9a0.1

— R —

Reading	Kanji	Code
RA	裸	5e8.1
	(果)	KA
	(課)	KA
	羅	5g14.1
	(維)	I
	螺	6d11.3
	(累)	RUI
-ra	等	6f6.9
RAI	頼	9a7.1
	癩	5i16.1
	礼	4e1.1
	来	0a7.6
	雷	8d5.1
	麗	3q16.5
RAKU	落	3k9.13
	絡	6a6.6
	酪	7e6.4
	駱	10a6.2
	(各)	KAKU
	(略)	RYAKU
RAN	楽	4a9.29
	覧	5c12.7
	濫	3a15.3
	藍	3k15.5
	籃	6f15.2
	欖	4a22.1
	(監)	KAN
	(艦)	KAN
	(鑑)	KAN
	蘭	3k16.9
	欄	4a16.4
	爛	4d17.1

卵 2e5.2
(卵) U
乱 3d4.21
(舌) ZETSU
嵐 3o9.4
(風) FŪ
鷲 11b19.1

RATSU 辣 5b9.6
RE 玲 4f5.7
(令) REI

REI 令 2a3.9
伶 2a5.17
冷 2b5.3
怜 4k5.10
玲 4f5.7
蛉 6d5.8
鈴 8a5.11
零 8d5.4
澪 3a13.6
嶺 3o14.2
齢 6b11.5
(領) RYŌ
(今) KON
戻 4m3.1
捩 3c8.31
(涙) RUI
隷 4e11.1
(逮) TAI
(款) KAN
例 2a6.7
(列) RETSU
莉 3k7.5
(利) RI
礼 4e1.1
励 2g5.4
黎 3a10.29
霊 8d7.2
麗 3q16.5

REKI 暦 2p12.3
歴 2p12.4
礫 5a15.1
櫟 7c15.1

REN 煉 4d9.2
練 6a8.2
錬 8a8.3
鰊 11a9.1
(東) TŌ
廉 3q10.1
鎌 8a10.8
簾 6f13.8
(兼) KEN
連 2q7.2
蓮 3k10.31
怜 4k5.10
(令) REI
憐 4k13.4
(隣) RIN
恋 2j8.2
聯 6e11.2
攣 3c19.3

RETSU 列 2f4.4
烈 4d6.3
裂 5e6.7
劣 3n3.4
(少) SHŌ
捩 3c8.31
(戻) REI

RI 利 5d2.1
莉 3k7.5
悧 4k7.2
梨 4a7.24
痢 5i7.2
里 0a7.9
狸 3g7.2
理 4f7.1
裏 2j11.2
鯉 11a7.2
璃 4f10.5
離 8c10.3
吏 0a6.22
(史) SHI
李 4a2.7
(季) KI
履 3r12.1
(復) FUKU
罟 5g7.1
黎 3a10.29

ri 亥 2j4.1
RICHI 律 3i6.1
RIKI 力 2g0.1
riki(mu) 力 2g0.1
RIKU 陸 2d8.4
(睦) BOKU
六 2j2.2
Riku 陸 2d8.4
RIN 隣 2d13.1
燐 4d13.4
麟 6b18.1
鱗 11a13.2
倫 2a8.28
綸 6a8.18
輪 7c8.4
(論) RON
林 4a4.1
淋 3a8.6
琳 4f8.2
稟 2j11.3
凛 2b13.1
厘 2p7.1
(里) RI
鈴 8a5.11
臨 2t15.1
躙 7d16.1

RITSU 立 5b0.1
律 3i6.1
栗 4a6.32
率 2j9.1
rittoru 立 5b0.1
RO 略 7b6.2
路 7d6.5
蕗 3k13.4
露 8d13.1
(各) KAKU
(足) SOKU
芦 3k4.3
炉 4d4.2
(戸) KO
呂 3d4.16
濾 3a15.8
櫓 4a15.2
RŌ 郎 2d6.5
浪 3a7.5
狼 3g7.3
朗 4b6.11
廊 3q8.4
(良) RYŌ
弄 4f3.2
玲 4f5.7
(王) Ō
(令) REI
漏 3a11.19
露 8d13.1
(雨) U
(路) RO
聾 6e16.1
籠 6f16.1
老 2k4.5
(考) KŌ
牢 3m4.2
(牛) GYŪ
楼 4a9.10
(桜) Ō
糧 6b12.1
(量) RYŌ
労 3n4.3
蠟 6d15.1

ROKU 禄 4e8.2
緑 6a8.15
録 8a8.16
(縁) EN
六 2j2.2
肋 4b2.1
陸 2d8.4
鹿 3q8.5
論 7a8.13
RON 流 3a7.10
RU 琉 4f7.5
留 5f5.4
瑠 4f10.3
累 5f6.5
塁 5f7.2
RUI 涙 3a7.21
(戻) REI
類 9a9.1

RYAKU	掠 3c8.28		良 0a7.3		唆 3d7.8	Sadamu	禎 4e9.3	
	(京) KYŌ		亮 2j7.6		(酸) SAN	sae	冴 2b5.2	
	略 5f6.4		竜 5b5.3		(俊) SHUN	saegi(ru)	遮 2q11.4	
	(各) KAKU		猟 3g8.6		叉 2h1.1	sa(eru)	冴 2b5.2	
	暦 2p12.3		梁 4a7.25		(又) mata	saga	性 4k5.4	
	(歴) REKI		聊 6e5.1		再 0a6.26	sa(garu)	下 2m1.2	
RYO	虜 2m11.2		霊 8d7.2		早 4c2.1	saga(su)	捜 3c7.5	
	慮 2m13.2	RYOKU	緑 6a8.15		茶 3k6.19		探 3c8.16	
	旅 4h6.4		(録) ROKU		査 4a5.32	sa(geru)	下 2m1.2	
	(族) ZOKU		力 2g0.1		嗄 3d10.5		提 3c9.4	
	呂 3d4.16	RYŪ	留 5f5.4		鎖 8a10.2	sagesu(mu)		
RYO	凌 2b8.5		溜 3a10.11	SA'	早 4c2.1		蔑 3k11.11	
	陵 2d8.5		榴 4a10.12	sa	三 0a3.1	sagu(ru)	探 3c8.16	
	菱 3k8.20		瑠 4f10.3		小 3n0.1	SAI	斎 2j9.6	
	峻 3o8.1		瘤 5i10.3		狭 3g6.2		祭 4e6.3	
	稜 5d8.4		(貿) BŌ		齊 0a11.7		際 2d11.1	
	綾 6a8.10		立 5b0.1		然 4d8.10		歳 4n6.0	
	(陸) RIKU		竜 5b5.3	sa-	狭 3g6.2		(察) SATSU	
	令 2a3.9		粒 6b5.1	saba(keru)			采 4a4.24	
	怜 4k5.10		笠 6f5.1		捌 3c7.4		採 3c8.14	
	玲 4f5.7		流 3a7.10	saba(ku)	捌 3c7.4		彩 3j8.1	
	領 9a5.2		琉 4f7.5		裁 5e6.9		菜 3k8.25	
	澪 3a13.6		硫 5a7.3	sabi	寂 3m8.2		哉 4n5.4	
	嶺 3o14.2		隆 2d8.6		錆 8a8.8		栽 4n6.1	
	僚 2a12.4		(降) KŌ	sabi(reru)	寂 3m8.2		裁 5e6.9	
	遼 2q12.5		柳 4a5.17	sa(biru)	錆 8a8.8		載 7c6.5	
	寮 3m12.2			sabi(shii)	淋 3a8.6		才 0a3.27	
	燎 4d12.4		—— S ——		寂 3m8.2		財 7b3.1	
	瞭 5c12.4	SA	左 0a5.20	sabu	三 0a3.1		(材) ZAI	
	療 5i12.3		佐 2a5.9	sachi	祐 4e5.3		西 0a6.20	
	涼 3a8.31		差 2o8.4		祥 4e6.1		晒 4c6.1	
	椋 4a8.31		嵯 3o10.2		禄 4e8.2		債 2a11.11	
	諒 7a8.14		瑳 4f10.6		禎 4e9.3		(責) SEKI	
	(京) KYŌ		(着) CHAKU		幸 3b5.9		(積) SEKI	
	量 4c8.9		沙 3a4.13		倖 2a8.23		(績) SEKI	
	糧 6b12.1		砂 5a4.3	sada	貞 2m7.1		砕 5a4.6	
	両 0a6.11		紗 6a4.6		禎 4e9.3		(粋) SUI	
	輔 7c8.1		裟 5e7.6		定 3m5.8		(酔) SUI	
	漁 3a11.1		(少) SHŌ		晏 4c6.4		(粋) waku	
	(魚) GYO		乍 0a5.10	sada(ka)	定 3m5.8		済 3a8.30	
	料 6b4.4		作 2a5.10	sada(maru)			(剤) ZAI	
	(科) KA		詐 7a5.6		定 3m5.8		(斉) SEI	
	了 2c0.3		(昨) SAKU	sada(me)	定 3m5.8		塞 3m10.2	
			(酢) SAKU	sada(meru)			(寒) KAN	
					定 3m5.8			

	(基) KI	前 2o7.3	(昔) SEKI
	偲 2a9.7	咲 3d6.12	参 3j5.1
	(思) SHI	sakigake 魁 5f9.1	惨 4k8.5
	宰 3m7.2	SAKU 作 2a5.10	賛 7b8.6
	(辛) SHIN	昨 4c5.3	讃 7a15.1
	最 4c8.10	炸 4d5.3	餐 8b7.4
	(取) SHU	窄 3m7.11	燦 4d13.3
	切 2f2.2	酢 7e5.3	算 6f8.7
	再 0a6.26	搾 3c10.9	纂 6f14.4
	災 4d3.3	(詐) SA	桟 4a6.1
	妻 3e5.10	冊 0a5.42	(残) ZAN
	殺 4a6.35	柵 4a5.4	(浅) SEN
	細 6a5.1	錯 8a8.10	(銭) SEN
	催 2a11.12	(昔) SEKI	酸 7e7.2
	臍 4b14.2	(惜) SEKI	(唆) SA
saina(mu)	苛 3k5.30	(借) SHAKU	(俊) SHUN
saiwa(i)	幸 3b5.9	(措) SO	産 5b6.4
saji	匙 4c7.13	朔 4b6.12	(生) SEI
Saka	坂 3b4.7	(逆) GYAKU	(彦) GEN
saka	阪 2d4.4	(塑) SO	珊 4f5.1
	坂 3b4.7	策 6f6.2	(冊) SATSU
saka-	逆 2q6.8	(刺) SHI	三 0a3.1
	酒 3a7.1	削 2f7.4	山 3o0.1
Sakae	昌 4c4.4	(肖) SHŌ	蚕 6d4.8
	栄 3n6.1	索 2k8.2	傘 2a10.7
saka(eru)	栄 3n6.1	(糸) SHI	蒜 3k10.5
sakai	境 3b11.1	sa(ku) 割 2f10.1	sanaga(ra)
saka(n)	壮 2b4.2	裂 5e6.7	宛 3m5.9
	盛 5h6.1	咲 3d6.12	sane 実 3m5.4
sakana	魚 11a0.1	sakura 桜 4a6.15	真 2k8.1
saka(rau)	逆 2q6.8	sama 様 4a10.25	核 4a6.22
Sakari	盛 5h6.1	-sama 様 4a10.25	脩 2a9.6
saka(ru)	盛 5h6.1	sa(masu) 冷 2b5.3	翔 2o10.8
saka(shii)	賢 7b9.2	覚 3n9.3	諄 7a7.11
saka(shira)		samata(geru)	sao 竿 6f3.3
	賢 7b9.2	妨 3e4.1	棹 4a8.38
sakazuki	杯 4a4.11	same 鮫 11a6.5	sara 皿 5h0.1
sake	酒 3a7.1	sa(meru) 冷 2b5.3	更 0a7.12
	鮭 11a6.3	覚 3n9.3	sara (ni) 更 0a7.12
sake(bu)	叫 3d3.4	褪 5e9.5	sara(naru)
sa(keru)	裂 5e6.7	samu(i) 寒 3m9.3	更 0a7.12
	避 2q13.3	samurai 侍 2a6.11	sara(shi) 晒 4c6.1
saki	埼 3b8.8	SAN 散 4i8.1	sara(su) 晒 4c6.1
	崎 3o8.3	撒 3c12.2	sa(redo) 然 4d8.10
	先 3b3.7		

sa(ri to wa)	
	然 4d8.10
saru	申 0a5.39
	猿 3g10.3
sa(ru)	去 3b2.2
	然 4d8.10
sasa	笹 6f5.3
sasa(eru)	支 2k2.1
sasa(geru)	
	捧 3c8.12
	献 3g9.6
sa(saru)	刺 2f6.2
sasa(yaka)	
	細 6a5.1
sasaya(ku)	
	囁 3d18.5
sa(shi)-	差 2o8.4
sa(shi de)	差 2o8.4
sashigane	矩 2t7.1
sashihasa(mu)	
	挟 3c6.1
sasori	蝎 6d9.10
saso(u)	誘 7a7.4
sa(su)	指 3c6.15
	挿 3c7.2
	刺 2f6.2
	注 3a5.16
	射 0a10.8
	差 2o8.4
sasu(ru)	摩 3g12.6
sato	里 0a7.9
	邑 3d4.15
	怜 4k5.10
	彦 5b4.4
	郷 2d8.14
	智 4c8.11
	熙 4d9.11
	聡 6e8.2
	慧 4k11.16
	叡 2h14.1
sato(i)	聡 6e8.2
sato(ri)	悟 4k7.5
Satoru	学 3n4.2
	怜 4k5.10
	堯 3b9.3
	覚 3n9.3

	智 4c8.11	Sayako 爽 0a11.7	斉 2j6.5	(淑) SHUKU

智 4c8.11
聡 6e8.2
慧 4k11.16

sato(ru)
悟 4k7.5
覚 3n9.3

Satoshi
邑 3d4.15
怜 4k5.10
哲 3d7.13
敏 4i6.3
恵 4k6.16
訓 7a3.6
捷 3c8.4
智 4c8.11
聡 6e8.2
慧 4k11.16
叡 2h14.1
諭 7a9.13

sato(su)
論 7a9.13

SATSU
察 3m11.6
擦 3c14.5
(祭) SAI
(際) SAI
刹 2f6.8
殺 4a6.35
撮 3c12.13
(最) SAI
冊 0a5.42
札 4a1.1
刷 2f6.9
拶 3c6.13
颯 5b9.4
撒 3c12.2
薩 3k13.14

sat(to)
颯 5b9.4

Sawa
爽 0a11.7

sawa
沢 3a4.18
爽 0a11.7
皐 4c7.12

sawa(gu)
騒 10a8.5

sawa(ru)
障 2d11.2
触 6d7.10

sawa(yaka)
爽 0a11.7

saya
爽 0a11.7
鞘 4b12.8

sazu(karu)
授 3c8.15

sazu(keru)
授 3c8.15

SE
施 4h5.1
(旋) SEN
世 0a5.37
勢 2g11.6

se
背 4b5.15
脊 4b6.13
畝 5f5.5
瀬 3a16.3

seba(maru)
狭 3g6.2

seba(meru)
狭 3g6.2

SECHI
節 6f7.3

SEI
青 4b4.10
清 3a8.18
情 4k8.9
晴 4c8.2
靖 5b8.1
静 4b10.9
精 6b8.1
蜻 6d8.7
請 7a8.8
生 0a5.29
姓 3e5.3
性 4k5.4
星 4c5.7
牲 4g5.1
笙 6f5.4
甥 5f7.5
正 2m3.3
征 3i5.3
政 4i5.1
婿 3e9.3
整 4i12.3
(症) SHŌ
(証) SHŌ
成 4n2.1
晟 4c7.5
盛 5h6.1
誠 7a6.3

斉 2j6.5
済 3a8.30
臍 4b14.2
逝 2q7.8
誓 7a7.17
(折) SETSU
井 0a4.46
穽 3m6.6
世 0a5.37
貰 7b5.5
制 2f6.1
製 5e8.9
凄 2b8.4
棲 4a8.16
勢 2g11.6
(熱) NETSU
西 0a6.20
声 3p4.4
省 5c4.7
聖 4f9.9
歳 4n9.5

sei / SEKI
背 4b5.15
昔 3k5.28
惜 4k8.11
藉 3k14.2
籍 6f14.1
(錯) SAKU
(借) SHAKU
(措) SO
責 7b4.4
積 5d11.5
績 6a11.8
蹟 7d11.3
(債) SAI
斥 0a5.18
析 4a4.12
(斤) KIN
(折) SETSU
赤 3b4.10
跡 7d6.7
(亦) YAKU
寂 3m8.2
戚 4n7.2

(淑) SHUKU
夕 0a3.14
汐 3a3.9
石 5a0.1
碩 5a9.1
席 3q7.4
(度) DO
尺 3r1.1
脊 4b6.13
隻 8c2.1
潟 3a12.9

Seki
関 8e6.7

seki
咳 3d6.10
関 8e6.7

se(ku)
急 2n7.2
咳 3d6.10
塞 3m10.2

sema(i)
狭 3g6.2

sema(ru)
迫 2q5.5

se(meru)
攻 4i3.2
責 7b4.4

semi
蝉 6d12.3

SEN
浅 3a6.4
践 7d6.1
銭 8a6.1
箋 6f8.9
(桟) SAN
(残) ZAN
先 3b3.7
洗 3a6.12
跣 7d6.4
銑 8a6.6
泉 3a5.33
腺 4b9.6
線 6a9.7
亘 4c2.4
宣 3m6.2
(恒) KŌ
栓 4a6.26
詮 7a6.14
(全) ZEN
選 2q12.3
撰 3c12.9
(巽) SON

揃 3c9.16	設 7a4.7	叉 2h1.1	髭 3j13.2
煎 2o11.2	切 2f2.2	(又) mata	司 3d2.14
(前) ZEN	窃 3m6.5	写 2i3.1	伺 2a5.23
占 2m3.2	(刀) TŌ	(与) YO	笥 6f5.15
鮎 11a5.7	接 3c8.10	遮 2q11.4	覗 5c7.3
扇 4m6.1	椄 4a8.15	(庶) SHO	詞 7a5.15
煽 4d10.4	説 7a7.12	赦 4i7.3	嗣 3d10.13
羨 2o11.4	(鋭) EI	(赤) SEKI	飼 8b5.4
鮮 11a6.7	(悦) ETSU	社 4e3.1	次 2b4.1
川 0a3.2	(税) ZEI	車 7c0.1	姿 3e6.10
釧 8a3.4	折 3c4.7	耶 6e2.1	茨 3k6.11
船 6c5.4	(析) SEKI	這 2q7.1	恣 4k6.22
(沿) EN	(斤) KIN	斜 2a9.21	資 7b6.7
(鉛) EN	拙 3c5.11	shaga(reru)	諮 7a9.4
(舟) SHŪ	(出) SHUTSU	嗄 3d10.5	(欠) KETSU
潜 3a12.6	屑 3r7.4	鮭 11a6.3	市 2j3.1
(賛) SAN	(肖) SHŌ	shake	姉 3e5.8
(替) TAI	節 6f7.3	SHAKU 勺 0a3.5	柿 4a5.25
仙 2a3.1	(即) SOKU	杓 4a3.12	師 3f7.2
(山) SAN	雪 8d3.2	酌 7e3.3	獅 3g10.1
茜 3k6.3	摂 3c10.6	(釣) tsu(ru)	(帥) SUI
(西) SEI	setsu (na) 切 2f2.2	昔 3k5.28	士 3p0.1
閃 8e2.1	setsu(nai) 切 2f2.2	借 2a8.22	仕 2a3.2
(門) MON	sewa(shii)	(錯) SAKU	志 3p4.1
旋 4h7.2	忙 4k3.2	(惜) SEKI	痣 5i7.6
(施) SE	SHA	(措) SO	誌 7a7.8
千 2k1.2	沙 3a4.13	尺 3r1.1	旨 4c2.2
尖 3n3.1	砂 5a4.3	釈 6b5.5	指 3c6.15
専 0a9.16	紗 6a4.6	(沢) TAKU	脂 4b6.7
染 4a5.35	裟 5e7.6	(訳) YAKU	匙 4c7.13
穿 3m7.10	(少) SHŌ	(駅) EKI	鮨 11a6.8
戦 4n9.2	者 4c4.13	蹟 7d11.3	支 2k2.1
遷 2q12.1	奢 4c8.17	癪 5i16.2	伎 2a4.13
薦 3k13.25	煮 4d8.9	石 5a0.1	枝 4a4.18
檀 4a13.11	(著) CHO	赤 3b4.10	肢 4b4.7
繊 6a11.1	(暑) SHO	綽 6a8.19	氏 0a4.25
蟬 6d12.3	(署) SHO	爵 5g12.1	砥 5a5.4
籤 6f17.2	借 2a8.22	SHI 止 2m2.2	紙 6a4.4
seri 芹 3k4.5	藉 3k14.2	此 2m4.2	蒔 3k10.7
se(ri) 競 5b15.1	(昔) SEKI	祉 4e4.1	詩 7a6.5
se(ru) 競 5b15.1	舍 2a6.23	疵 5i6.3	(寺) JI
SETSU 刹 2f6.8	捨 3c8.26	紫 6a6.15	(侍) JI
殺 4a6.35	射 0a10.8	歯 6b6.11	(持) JI
	謝 7a10.1	雌 8c6.1	(時) JI
		嘴 3d13.7	

寝 3m10.1	shino(bu) 忍 4k3.3	shitaga(eru)	shizu(ka) 静 4b10.9	倭 2a8.16
新 5b8.3	偲 2a9.7	従 3i7.3	shizuku 滴 3a11.14	閑 8e4.2
薪 3k13.3	Shinogu 凌 2b8.5	shitaga(tte)	shizu(maru)	鎮 8a10.6
親 5b11.1	shino(gu) 凌 2b8.5	従 3i7.3	静 4b10.9	
清 3a8.18	shi(nu) 死 0a6.6	shitaga(u)	鎮 8a10.6	
請 7a8.8	殁 2h6.3	随 2d8.10	shizu(meru)	
(青) SEI	shio 汐 3a3.9	従 3i7.3	沈 3a4.9	
(晴) SEI	潮 3a12.1	shita(shii) 親 5b11.1	静 4b10.9	
(精) SEI	塩 3b10.4	shita(shimu)	鎮 8a10.6	
疹 5i5.10	shio(reru) 萎 3k8.18	親 5b11.1	shizu(mu) 沈 3a4.9	
診 7a5.9	Shiori 栞 4a6.34	shitata(meru)	SHO 渚 3a9.1	
(珍) CHIN	shiori 栞 4a6.34	認 7a7.10	暑 4c8.5	
秦 5d5.10	shira- 白 4c1.3	shitata(ru)	署 5g8.1	
榛 4a10.11	shira(be) 調 7a8.16	滴 3a11.14	緒 6a8.3	
臣 2t4.3	shira(beru)	Shitau 欽 8a4.1	曙 4c14.2	
(巨) KYO	調 7a8.16	shita(u) 慕 3k11.12	(者) SHA	
辛 5b2.2	shirami 虱 6d2.1	shita(washii)	(著) CHO	
(幸) KŌ	shira(mu) 白 4c1.3	慕 3k11.12	(都) TO	
津 3a6.1	shi(rase) 知 3d5.14	shito(yaka)	庶 3q8.7	
(律) RITSU	shiri 尻 3r2.1	淑 3a8.5	(遮) SHA	
深 3a8.21	shirizo(keru)	SHITSU 失 0a5.28	恕 4k6.18	
(探) TAN	斥 0a5.18	疾 5i5.12	(如) JO	
審 3m12.1	退 2q6.3	嫉 3e10.8	且 0a5.15	
(番) BAN	shirizo(ku) 退 2q6.3	(矢) SHI	処 4i2.2	
晋 4c6.8	shiro 代 2a3.3	漆 3a11.10	初 5e2.1	
(普) FU	白 4c1.3	膝 4b11.4	所 4m4.3	
心 4k0.1	城 3b6.1	室 3m6.4	書 4c6.6	
身 0a7.5	shirogane 銀 8a6.3	(屋) OKU	黍 5d7.6	
信 2a7.1	shiro(i) 白 4c1.3	(至) SHI	諸 7a8.3	
進 2q8.1	shiru 汁 3a2.1	虱 6d2.1	SHO-	
針 8a2.3	shi(ru) 知 3d5.14	(風) FŪ	SHŌ 肖 3n4.1	
森 4a8.39	shirube 導 5c9.3	執 3b8.15	消 3a7.16	
鍼 8a9.12	標 4a11.8	(幸) KŌ	宵 3m7.7	
shina	shirushi 印 2e4.1	叱 3d2.2	梢 4a7.13	
品 3d6.15	徴 3i11.2	湿 3a9.22	硝 5a7.6	
科 5d4.3	標 4a11.8	質 7b8.7	蛸 6d7.5	
shina(biru)	験 10a8.4	櫛 4a15.5	鞘 4b12.8	
萎 3k8.18	shiru(su) 記 7a3.5	躾 4f12.2	鮹 11a7.6	
shingari 殿 3r10.1	shishi 猪 3g8.1	shitsuke 躾 4f12.2	(削) SAKU	
shino 篠 6f11.3	獅 3g10.1	shitsu(keru)	小 3n0.1	
shino(baseru)	鹿 3q8.5	躾 4f12.2	少 3n1.1	
忍 4k3.3	shis(suru) 失 0a5.28	shiwabuki 咳 3d6.10	抄 3c4.11	
shino(bi) 忍 4k3.3	shita 下 2m1.2	shiwaga(reru)	尚 3n5.2	
Shinobu 偲 2a9.7	舌 3d3.9	嗄 3d10.5		
		shizu 靖 5b8.1		
		静 4b10.9		

省	5c4.7	
称	5d5.8	
渉	3a8.20	
(砂)	SA	
(秒)	BYŌ	
(妙)	MYŌ	
召	2f3.3	
沼	3a5.24	
招	3c5.22	
昭	4c5.4	
紹	6a5.10	
詔	7a5.10	
照	4d9.12	
青	4b4.10	
清	3a8.18	
精	6b8.1	
請	7a8.8	
錆	8a8.8	
(情)	JŌ	
(静)	JŌ	
(晴)	SEI	
昌	4c4.4	
唱	3d8.9	
娼	3e8.3	
菖	3k0.22	
晶	4c8.6	
掌	3n9.4	
嘗	3n11.1	
裳	3n11.2	
賞	3n12.1	
償	2a15.4	
正	2m3.3	
政	4i5.1	
症	5i5.4	
証	7a5.5	
将	2b8.3	
奨	3n10.4	
漿	3a11.21	
醤	7e11.2	
生	0a5.29	
姓	3e5.3	
性	4k5.4	
笙	6f5.4	
松	4a4.16	

訟	7a4.6	
頌	9a4.4	
(公)	KŌ	
(総)	SŌ	
聖	4f9.9	
聳	6e11.4	
囁	3d18.5	
(耳)	JI	
章	5b6.3	
障	2d11.2	
彰	3j11.1	
焦	8c4.3	
蕉	3k12.6	
礁	5a12.2	
祥	4e6.1	
詳	7a6.12	
(羊)	YŌ	
(洋)	YŌ	
庄	3q3.1	
粧	6b6.1	SHOKU
(圧)	ATSU	
荘	3k6.12	
装	5e6.8	
(壮)	SŌ	
憧	4k12.5	
鐘	8a12.6	
(童)	DŌ	
升	0a4.32	
昇	4c4.5	
丞	2c4.3	
承	0a7.7	
捷	3c8.4	
睫	5c8.4	
象	2n10.1	
像	2a12.8	
翔	2o10.8	SHU
摺	3c11.3	
焼	4d8.4	
(暁)	GYŌ	
匠	2t4.2	
(斤)	KIN	
衝	3i12.1	

(重)	CHŌ	
上	2m1.1	
井	0a4.46	
声	3p4.4	
床	3q4.1	
妾	5b3.2	
咲	3d6.12	
相	4a5.3	
従	3i7.3	
秤	5d5.4	
笑	6f4.1	
商	2j9.7	
盛	5h6.1	
椒	4a8.7	
勝	4b8.4	
竦	5b7.1	
傷	2a11.10	SHŪ
誦	7a7.14	
薔	3k13.20	
篠	6f11.3	
食	8b0.1	
飾	8b5.3	
蝕	8b6.1	
(飼)	SHI	
(餌)	JI	
植	4a8.32	
殖	5c7.4	
(直)	CHOKU	
(値)	CHI	
織	6a12.6	
職	6e12.1	
(識)	SHIKI	
属	3r9.1	
嘱	3d12.11	
触	6d7.10	
燭	4d13.5	
色	2n4.1	
朱	0a6.13	
殊	0a10.7	
珠	4f6.2	
(株)	kabu	
取	6e2.2	
趣	6e9.1	
諏	7a8.4	

腫	4b9.1	
種	5d9.1	
(重)	JŪ	
守	3m3.2	
狩	3g6.5	
須	3j9.1	
鬚	9a13.2	
修	2a8.11	
(候)	KŌ	
手	3c0.1	
主	4f1.1	
首	2o7.2	
酒	3a7.1	
衆	5h7.1	
鼠	0a13.1	
就	3d9.21	
蹴	7d12.2	
鷲	11b12.5	
(京)	KYŌ	
州	2f4.1	
洲	3a6.10	
酬	7e6.2	
茸	3k9.25	
楫	4a9.20	
輯	7c9.4	
秋	5d4.1	
萩	3k9.5	
愁	4k9.16	
蒐	3k10.12	
醜	7e10.1	
(鬼)	KI	
(塊)	KAI	
柊	4a5.24	
終	6a5.9	
(冬)	TŌ	
修	2a8.11	
脩	2a9.6	
周	2r6.1	
週	2q8.7	
袖	5e5.1	
紬	6a5.3	
習	4c7.11	
摺	3c11.3	

側 2a9.4	園 3s10.1	子 2c0.1	suge 菅 3k8.27	
測 3a9.4	so(no) 其 2o6.6	主 4f1.1	Sugi 杉 4a3.2	
束 0a7.8	sora 空 3m5.12	洲 3a6.10	sugi 杉 4a3.2	
速 2q7.4	so(rasu) 反 2p2.2	須 3j9.1	su(giru) 過 2q9.18	
足 7d0.1	逸 2q8.6	雛 8c10.1	sugo(i) 凄 2b8.4	
促 2a7.3	sore 其 2o6.6	蘇 3k16.1	sugo(mu) 凄 2b8.4	
仄 2p2.1	so(re) 夫 0a4.31	su 州 2f4.1	su(gosu) 過 2q9.18	
即 2e5.1	soregashi 某 4a5.33	洲 3a6.10	su(gu) 直 2k6.2	
息 4k6.17	so(reru) 逸 2q8.6	沙 3a4.13	sugu(reru)	
塞 3m10.2	sori 橇 4a12.14	巣 3n8.1	勝 4b8.4	
so(maru) 染 4a5.35	-sōrō 候 2a8.10	酢 7e5.3	傑 2a11.6	
some 染 4a5.35	soro(eru) 揃 3c9.16	簾 6f13.8	優 2a15.1	
so(me) 染 4a5.35	soro(i) 揃 3c9.16	SŪ 崇 3o8.9	Suguru 英 3k5.5	
-someru 初 5e2.1	soro(u) 揃 3c9.16	(宗) SHŪ	捷 3c8.4	
so(meru) 染 4a5.35	so(ru) 反 2p2.2	嵩 3o10.4	sugu(ru) 選 2q12.3	
somosomo	剃 2f7.5	(高) KŌ	SUI 推 3c8.1	
抑 3c4.12	sō(shite) 然 4d8.10	枢 4a4.22	椎 4a8.1	
somu(keru)	soso(gu) 注 3a5.16	(区) KU	誰 7a8.1	
背 4b5.15	濯 3a14.5	数 4i9.1	錐 8a8.1	
somu(ku) 叛 2p7.3	雪 8d3.2	(楼) RŌ	(維) I	
背 4b5.15	sosonoka(su)	雛 8c10.1	(准) JUN	
SON 尊 2o10.3	唆 3d7.8	Subaru 昴 4c5.12	(唯) YUI	
噂 3d12.10	soto 外 2m3.1	sube 術 3i8.2	垂 0a8.12	
樽 4a12.19	SOTSU 卒 2j6.2	subeka(raku)	睡 5c0.2	
鱒 11a12.6	率 2j9.1	須 3j9.1	錘 8a8.2	
存 2c3.1	so(u) 沿 3a5.23	sube(kkoi) 滑 3a10.6	(郵) YŪ	
拵 3c5.24	添 3a8.22	sube(ru) 滑 3a10.6	粋 6b4.5	
孫 2c7.1	副 2f9.2	su(beru) 統 6a6.10	酔 7e4.3	
遜 2q9.4	soyo(gu) 戦 4n9.2	総 6a8.20	(砕) SAI	
損 3c10.12	sozo(ro) 漫 3a11.11	sube(te) 凡 2s1.1	吹 3d4.3	
(員) IN	SU 守 3m3.2	subo(maru)	炊 4d4.1	
村 4a3.11	寿 0a7.15	窄 3m7.11	(欠) KETSU	
(寸) SUN	(寸) SUN	subo(meru)	出 0a5.22	
巽 2o10.7	素 6a4.12	窄 3m7.11	瑞 4f9.6	
(選) SEN	(麦) BAKU	subo(mu) 窄 3m7.11	帥 3f6.1	
sona(eru) 供 2a6.13	(表) HYŌ	sudare 簾 6f13.8	(師) SHI	
備 2a10.4	筍 6f5.15	sude (ni) 既 0a10.5	(追) TSUI	
具 5c3.1	(司) SHI	sue 末 0a5.26	衰 2j8.1	
sona(waru)	惣 4k8.17	季 5d2.3	(哀) AI	
具 5c3.1	(物) BUTSU	梢 4a7.13	遂 2q9.13	
備 2a10.4	数 4i9.1	su(eru) 据 3c8.33	(逐) CHIKU	
sone(mu) 嫉 3e10.8	(楼) RŌ	Suga 菅 3k8.27	翠 2k12.2	
Sono 園 3s10.1	諏 7a8.4	sugame 眇 5c4.2	(卒) SOTSU	
sono 苑 3k5.17	(取) SHU	suga(ru) 縋 6a9.14	穂 5d10.2	
		sugata 姿 3e6.10		

(惠) KEI	su(manai) 済 3a8.30	剃 2f7.5	su(teru) 捨 3c8.26	
水 3a0.1	su(masu) 清 3a8.18	為 4d5.8	棄 2j11.5	
彗 0a11.9	済 3a8.30	摺 3c11.3	su(u) 吸 3d3.5	
su(i) 酸 7e7.2	澄 3a12.11	擂 3c13.2	suwa(ru) 坐 3b4.11	
suji 筋 6f6.4	su(mau) 住 2a5.19	磨 3g13.3	座 3q7.2	
su(kasazu)	sumi 住 2a5.19	擦 3c14.5	su(waru) 据 3c8.33	
透 2q7.10	角 2n5.1	surudo(i) 鋭 8a7.12	Suzu 紗 6a4.6	
su(kashi) 透 2q7.10	邑 3d4.15	susa(bi) 遊 2q8.3	suzu 紗 6a4.6	
su(kasu) 透 2q7.10	炭 3o6.5	susa(bu) 荒 3k6.18	鈴 8a5.11	
suke 右 3d2.15	純 6a4.3	susa(majii)	suzume 雀 8c3.2	
佑 2a5.8	隅 2d9.1	凄 2b8.4	suzu(mu) 涼 3a8.31	
祐 4e5.3	遙 2q10.3	susa(mu) 荒 3k6.18	suzuri 硯 5a7.2	
甫 0a7.11	稜 5d8.4	sushi 鮨 11a6.8	Suzushi 涼 3a8.31	
輔 7c7.1	墨 3b11.4	suso 裾 5e8.8	suzu(shii) 涼 3a8.31	
允 0a4.13	澄 3a12.11	Susugu 漱 3a11.4		
介 2a2.9	su(mi) 済 3a8.30	susu(gu) 雪 8d3.2	**— T —**	
丞 2c4.3	sumi(kko) 隅 2d9.1	漱 3a11.4	TA 太 0a4.18	
佐 2a5.9	su(mimasen)	濯 3a14.5	汰 3a4.8	
助 2g5.1	済 3a8.30	susuki 薄 3k13.11	駄 10a4.1	
昌 4c4.4	Sumire 菫 3k8.1	susu(meru)	(大) TAI	
亮 2j7.6	sumire 菫 3k8.1	進 2q8.1	侘 2a6.14	
宥 3m6.1	sumi(yaka)	勧 2g11.1	詫 7a6.6	
相 4a5.3	速 2q7.4	奨 3n10.4	(宅) TAKU	
哉 4n5.4	sumomo 李 4a2.7	薦 3k13.25	他 2a3.4	
脩 2a9.6	su(mu) 住 2a5.19	Susumu 亨 2j4.2	(也) YA	
喬 3d9.25	済 3a8.30	享 2j5.1	多 0a6.5	
資 7b6.7	棲 4a8.16	将 2b8.3	ta 田 5f0.1	
su(keru) 透 2q7.10	澄 3a12.11	奨 3n10.4	ta- 手 3c0.1	
suki 隙 2d10.4	SUN 寸 0a3.17	迪 2q5.1	taba 束 0a7.8	
鋤 8a7.5	suna 沙 3a4.13	達 2q9.8	tabaka(ru) 謀 7a9.8	
su(ki) 好 3e2.1	砂 5a4.3	勤 2g10.1	taba(neru)	
suko(shi) 少 3n1.1	Sunao 淳 3a7.19	勧 2g11.1	束 0a7.8	
suko(yaka)	惇 4k7.12	丞 2c4.3	ta(beru) 食 8b0.1	
健 2a8.34	朴 4a2.3	侑 2a6.5	tabi 度 3q6.1	
su(ku) 好 3e2.1	侃 2a6.12	益 2o8.5	旅 4h6.4	
空 3m5.12	直 2k6.2	晋 4c6.8	Tachi 館 8b8.3	
透 2q7.10	悌 4k7.14	肅 0a11.8	tachi 質 7b8.7	
鋤 8a7.5	sunawa(chi)	亀 2n9.1	館 8b8.3	
suku(meru)	乃 0a2.10	皐 4c7.12	-tachi 達 2q9.8	
竦 5b7.1	即 2e5.1	駿 10a7.1	Tachibana 橘 4a12.11	
suku(mu) 竦 5b7.1	則 7b2.1	susu(mu) 迪 2q5.1	tachibana 橘 4a12.11	
suku(nai) 少 3n1.1	sune 脛 4b7.6	進 2q8.1	tachima(chi)	
suku(u) 救 4i7.1	su(neru) 拗 3c5.16	suta(reru) 廃 3q9.3	忽 4k4.7	
su(kuu) 巣 3n8.1	su(ppai) 酸 7e7.2	suta(ru) 廃 3q9.3	tada 唯 3d8.1	
su(mai) 住 2a5.19	su(reru) 擦 3c14.5	sute 捨 3c8.26	惟 4k8.1	
	su(ru) 刷 2f6.9			

只 3d2.8
侃 2a6.12

也 0a3.29
允 0a4.13
伊 2a4.6
匡 2t4.1
但 2a5.14
迪 2q5.1
直 2k6.2
忠 4k4.6
徒 3i7.1
董 3k8.1
喬 3d9.25
欽 8a4.1
禎 4e9.3
頌 9a4.4
肇 4m10.1
端 5b9.2
叡 2h14.1
tada(chi ni) 直 2k6.2
tada(reru) 爛 4d17.1
Tadashi 正 2m3.3
旦 4c1.2
匡 2t4.1
迪 2q5.1
侃 2a6.12
直 2k6.2
忠 4k4.6
衷 0a9.9
矩 2t7.1
淳 3a7.19
格 4a6.17
規 5c6.9
喬 3d9.25
義 2o11.3
禎 4e9.3
雅 8c5.1
肇 4m10.1
端 5b9.2
質 7b8.7
tada(shi) 但 2a5.14
tada(shii) 正 2m3.3
Tadasu 匡 2t4.1
迪 2q5.1
矩 2t7.1
規 5c6.9
tada(su) 正 2m3.3
糾 6a3.4
質 7b8.7
tadayo(u) 漂 3a11.9
tado(ru) 辿 2q3.1
tae 妙 3e4.5
紗 6a4.6
tae(naru) 妙 3e4.5
tae(ru) 堪 3b9.1
ta(eru) 耐 2r7.1
絶 6a6.11
taga(eru) 違 2q10.5
taga(i) 互 0a4.15
taga(u) 違 2q10.5
tagaya(su)
耕 0a10.13
tagui 比 2m3.5
倫 2a8.28
類 9a9.1
TAI 台 3d2.11
苔 3k5.27
殆 3d6.21
胎 4b5.10
怠 4k5.21
(始) SHI
(治) JI

代 2a3.3
袋 5e5.11
貸 7b5.9
黛 4d13.7

大 0a3.18
太 0a4.18
汰 3a4.8

退 2q6.3
腿 4b9.10
褪 5e9.5

対 2j5.5
耐 2r7.1
(寸) SUN

帯 3f7.1
滞 3a10.14

待 3i6.4
(寺) JI
(侍) JI
(持) JI
(時) JI

体 2a5.6
(休) KYŪ
(本) HON

替 4c8.12
(賛) SAN
(潜) SEN

態 4k10.14
(熊) YŪ
(能) NŌ

逮 2q8.2
(康) KŌ

隊 2d9.7
(遂) SUI

戴 5f12.2
(異) I

泰 3a5.34
敦 4i7.4
tai 鯛 11a8.11
-ta(i) 度 3q6.1
Taira 平 2k3.4
庄 3q3.1
tai(ra) 平 2k3.4
Taka 鷹 3q21.1
taka 高 2j8.6
嵩 3o10.4
喬 3d9.25

鳳 2s12.1
鴻 3a14.2
鷹 3q21.1

堯 3b9.3
琢 4f8.1

孝 2k4.3
圭 3b3.2
卓 2m6.2
昂 4c5.11
隆 2d8.6
挙 3n7.1
峻 3o7.4
隼 8c2.2
寅 3m8.4
崇 3o8.9
梢 4a7.13
皐 4c7.12
尊 2o10.3
敬 4i8.4
貴 7b5.7
雄 8c4.1
稜 5d8.4
嘉 3p11.1
Takabu 嵩 3o10.4
taka(buru)
高 2j8.6
taka(ga) 高 2j8.6
taka(i) 高 2j8.6
(o)taka(ku)
高 2j8.6
taka(maru)
高 2j0.0
taka(meru)
高 2j8.6
takara 宝 3m5.2
taka(raka) 高 2j8.6
Takashi 喬 3d9.25
嵩 3o10.4

峻 3o7.4
駿 10a7.1

充 2j4.5
孝 2k4.3
郁 2d6.6
京 2j6.3
卓 2m6.2
洸 3a6.15
昂 4c5.11
隆 2d8.6
崇 3o8.9
皐 4c7.12
堯 3b9.3
敬 4i8.4
貴 7b5.7
節 6f7.3
take 孟 2c5.1
猛 3g7.4

虎 2m6.3
彪 3j8.3

建 2q6.2
健 2a8.34

丈 0a3.26

	竹	6f0.1
	長	0a8.2
	岳	3o5.12
	武	4n5.3
	茸	3k6.1
	剛	2f8.7
	赳	3b7.10
	偉	2a10.5
	雄	8c4.1
	嵩	3o10.4
	毅	5b10.1
ta(keru)	長	0a8.2
	猛	3g7.4
Takeshi	孟	2c5.1
	猛	3g7.4
	豪	2j12.3
	毅	5b10.1
	岳	3o5.12
	武	4n5.3
	洸	3a6.15
	威	4n5.2
	健	2a8.34
	剛	2f8.7
	赳	3b7.10
	彪	3j8.3
	雄	8c4.1
Taki	滝	3a10.8
taki	滝	3a10.8
takigi	薪	3k13.3
tako	蛸	6d7.5
	鮹	11a7.6
	凧	2s3.1
TAKU	沢	3a4.18
	択	3c4.21
	(尺)	SHAKU
	(訳)	YAKU
	(駅)	EKI
	宅	3m3.4
	託	7a3.1
	啄	3d8.4
	琢	4f8.1
	拓	3c5.1
	磔	5a11.2
	濯	3a14.5

	(躍)	YAKU
	(曜)	YŌ
	魄	5f10.4
	(鬼)	KI
	度	3q6.1
	(席)	SEKI
	卓	2m6.2
ta(ku)	炊	4d4.1
	焚	4d8.7
Takumi	工	0a3.6
	匠	2t4.2
takumi	工	0a3.6
	匠	2t4.2
taku(mi)	巧	0a5.7
taku(ramu)		
	企	2a4.17
takuwa(eru)		
	貯	7b5.1
	蓄	3k10.16
tama	玉	4f0.2
	玖	4f3.1
	玲	4f5.7
	珠	4f6.2
	球	4f7.2
	瑶	4f9.5
	瑞	4f9.6
	環	4f13.1
	璧	4f13.2
	圭	3b3.2
	弾	3h9.3
	適	2q11.3
	碧	5a9.7
	魂	5f9.2
	霊	8d7.2
tama (ni)	偶	2a9.1
-tama(e)	給	6a6.7
tamago	卵	2e5.2
Tamaki	環	4f13.1
tamaki	環	4f13.1
tama(ranai)		
	堪	3b9.1
tama(ri)	溜	3a10.11
tama(ru)	堪	3b9.1
	溜	3a10.11
tamashii	魂	5f9.2

tamatama	偶	2a9.1
tama(u)	給	6a6.7
	賜	7b8.2
tamawa(ru)		
	賜	7b8.2
tame	為	4d5.8
ta(me)	溜	3a10.11
ta(meru)	溜	3a10.11
	矯	3d14.5
tameshi	例	2a6.7
tame(su)	試	7a6.18
tami	民	0a5.23
	蒼	3k10.22
	黎	3a10.29
Tamotsu	存	2c3.1
	全	2a4.16
	有	4b2.3
	惟	4k8.1
tamo(tsu)	保	2a7.11
tamuro	屯	0a4.35
TAN	旦	4c1.2
	担	3c5.20
	胆	4b5.6
	檀	4a13.11
	(但)	tada(shi)
	炭	3o6.5
	淡	3a8.15
	毯	4d8.11
	(炎)	EN
	(灰)	KAI
	(談)	DAN
	単	3n6.2
	憚	4k12.4
	簞	6f12.2
	(巣)	SŌ
	嘆	3d10.8
	歎	4j10.3
	(漢)	KAN
	段	2s7.2
	鍛	8a9.5
	眈	5c4.5
	耽	6e4.3
	探	3c8.16
	(深)	SHIN

	湯	3a9.23
	(場)	JŌ
	短	3d9.27
	(豆)	TŌ
	誕	7a7.15
	(延)	EN
	丼	0a5.40
	(井)	SEI
	丹	0a4.34
	反	2p2.2
	蛋	6d5.11
	堪	3b9.1
	端	5b9.2
tana	棚	4a8.10
tana-	店	3q5.4
tanagokoro	掌	3n9.4
Tane	胤	4b5.16
tane	胤	4b5.16
	植	4a8.32
	種	5d9.1
Tani	谷	2o5.3
tani	谷	2o5.3
tano(moshii)		
	頼	9a7.1
tano(mu)	頼	9a7.1
Tanoshi	凱	2s10.1
tano(shii)	愉	4k9.13
	楽	4a9.29
tanoshi(mu)		
	楽	4a9.29
tanuki	狸	3g7.2
tao(reru)	倒	2a8.5
tao(su)	倒	2a8.5
tara	鱈	11a11.1
ta(rasu)	垂	0a8.12
tare	垂	0a8.12
	誰	7a8.1
ta(reru)	垂	0a8.12
ta(riru)	足	7d0.1
taru	垂	0a8.12
	稜	5d8.4
	樽	4a12.19
ta(ru)	足	7d0.1
ta(shi)	足	7d0.1

Reading	Kanji	Code
tashi(ka)	確	5a10.3
tashi(kameru)		
	確	5a10.3
ta(su)	足	7d0.1
tasu(karu)	助	2g5.1
Tasuke	輔	7c7.1
tasu(keru)	助	2g5.1
	扶	3c4.4
	援	3c9.7
Tasuku	佑	2a5.8
	祐	4e5.3
	丞	2c4.3
	匡	2t4.1
	助	2g5.1
	侑	2a6.5
	資	7b6.7
	輔	7c7.1
tata(eru)	称	5d5.8
tataka(u)	戦	4n9.2
	闘	8e10.2
tata(ku)	叩	3d2.3
tatami	畳	5f7.3
tata(mu)	畳	5f7.3
tate	盾	5c4.8
	楯	4a9.3
	干	2k1.1
	建	2q6.2
	竪	5b9.5
	縦	6a10.2
	館	8b8.3
tatematsu(ru)		
	奉	0a8.13
ta(teru)	立	5b0.1
	建	2q6.2
	樹	4a12.3
tato(eba)	例	2a6.7
tato(eru)	例	2a6.7
	喩	3d9.15
TATSU	達	2q9.8
	燵	4d12.6
tatsu	辰	2p5.1
	竜	5b5.3
	樹	4a12.3
ta(tsu)	立	5b0.1
	建	2q6.2
	起	3b7.11
	経	6a5.11
	断	6b5.6
	裁	5e6.9
	絶	6a6.11
Tatsumi	巽	2o10.7
tatsumi	巽	2o10.7
tatta	唯	3d8.1
tat(te)	達	2q9.8
tatto(bu)	尊	2o10.3
	貴	7b5.7
tatto(i)	尊	2o10.3
	貴	7b5.7
tawa(keru)		
	戯	4n11.1
tawamu(reru)		
	戯	4n11.1
Tawara	俵	2a8.21
tawara	俵	2a8.21
ta(yasu)	絶	6a6.11
tayo(ri)	便	2a7.5
tayo(ru)	頼	9a7.1
tazu	鶴	11b10.1
tazu(neru)	訪	7a4.1
	尋	3d9.29
tazusa(eru)		
	携	3c10.4
tazusa(waru)		
	携	3c10.4
te	手	3c0.1
TEI	丁	0a2.4
	汀	3a2.2
	亭	2j7.5
	訂	7a2.3
	釘	8a2.4
	停	2a9.14
	(打)	DA
	(灯)	TŌ
	弟	2o5.1
	剃	2f7.5
	悌	4k7.14
	梯	4a7.17
	鵜	11b7.6
	(第)	DAI
	低	2a5.15
	邸	2d5.10
	抵	3c5.18
	底	3q5.3
	(氏)	SHI
	廷	2q4.2
	庭	3q6.3
	艇	6c6.2
	(延)	EN
	貞	2m7.1
	偵	2a9.15
	禎	4e9.3
	堤	3b9.7
	提	3c9.4
	(是)	ZE
	定	3m5.8
	碇	5a8.6
	帝	2j7.1
	締	6a9.11
	呈	3d4.14
	程	5d7.2
	体	2a5.6
	(本)	HON
	(休)	KYŪ
	逓	2q7.5
	鼎	5c8.10
	綴	6a8.5
TEKI	適	2q11.3
	滴	3a11.14
	摘	3c11.5
	敵	4i11.2
	迪	2q5.1
	笛	6f5.6
	的	4c4.12
	(約)	YAKU
TEN	荻	3k7.8
	店	3q5.4
	点	2m7.2
	貼	7b5.2
	(占)	SEN
	填	3b10.5
	槙	4a10.27
	巓	5i19.1
	(県)	KEN
	伝	2a4.14
	転	7c4.3
	天	0a4.21
	添	3a8.22
	展	3r7.2
	殿	3r10.1
	典	2o6.5
	(曲)	KYOKU
	迪	2q3.1
	淀	3a8.23
	篆	6f9.8
	纏	6a16.1
tera	寺	3b3.5
Terasu	暉	4c9.6
te(rasu)	照	4d9.12
te(reru)	照	4d9.12
te(ri)	照	4d9.12
teru	光	3n3.2
	晃	4c6.5
	暉	4c9.6
	輝	7c8.8
	耀	8c12.1
	燿	4d14.3
	映	4c5.1
	瑛	4f8.6
	晟	4c7.5
	晨	4c7.7
	旭	4c2.6
	昭	4c5.4
	皓	4c8.13
	熙	4d9.11
te(ru)	照	4d9.12
TETSU	撤	3c12.3
	徹	3i12.2
	(徴)	CHŌ
	(微)	BI
	迭	2q5.2
	鉄	8a5.6
	(失)	SHITSU
	哲	3d7.13
	(誓)	SEI
	(逝)	SEI
	(折)	SETSU

TO
土 3b0.1
吐 3d3.1
杜 4a3.1
徒 3i7.1
(走) SŌ
都 2d8.13
屠 3r9.2
賭 7b9.1
(者) SHA
登 3d9.26
頭 9a7.6
(豆) TŌ
塗 3b10.10
途 2q7.16
度 3q6.1
渡 3a9.35
斗 0a4.17
図 3s4.3
兎 0a8.5
妬 3e5.1
兜 4c8.16

to
人 2a0.1
戸 4m0.1
外 2m3.1
砥 5a5.4
富 3m9.5

to-
十 2k0.1

TŌ
豆 3d4.22
逗 2q7.19
登 3d9.26
痘 5i7.8
頭 9a7.6
闘 8e10.2
(豊) HŌ
東 0a8.9
凍 2b8.2
棟 4a8.3
(陳) CHIN
(練) REN
(錬) REN
刀 2f0.1
到 2f6.4
倒 2a8.5
(至) SHI

逃 2q6.5
桃 4a6.10
(兆) CHŌ
(挑) CHŌ
(眺) CHŌ
(跳) CHŌ
湯 3a9.23
蕩 3k12.4
(場) JŌ
(揚) YŌ
(陽) YŌ
塔 3b9.9
搭 3c9.10
(合) GŌ
桐 4a6.30
筒 6f6.15
(同) DŌ
悼 4k8.13
棹 4a8.38
(卓) TAKU
憧 4k12.5
瞳 5c12.2
(童) DŌ
陶 2d8.11
萄 3k8.31
(缶) KAN
島 3o7.9
搗 3c10.1
唐 3q7.3
糖 6b10.3
桶 4a7.18
樋 4a10.28
膽 4b13.1
騰 4b16.3
党 3n7.2
(堂) DŌ
(常) JŌ
統 6a6.10
(充) JŪ
(銃) JŪ
読 7a7.9
(売) BAI
(続) ZOKU

透 2q7.10
(秀) SHŪ
套 0a10.3
(長) CHŌ
董 3k9.1
(重) JŪ
等 6f6.9
(寺) JI
道 2q9.14
(首) SHU
冬 4i2.1
当 3n3.3
灯 4d2.1
投 3c4.18
納 6a4.5
討 7a3.3
盗 5h6.2
兜 4c8.16
答 6f6.12
肇 4m10.1
稲 5d9.2
踏 7d8.3
藤 3k15.3
檮 4e14.2

tō
十 2k0.1
遙 2q10.3
遼 2q12.5
tobari
帳 3f8.2
to(basu)
飛 0a9.4
tobi
鳶 11b3.1
tobira
扉 4m8.2
tobo(shii)
乏 0a3.11
toboso
枢 4a4.22
to(bu)
飛 0a9.4
跳 7d6.3
tochi
栃 4a5.28
todo(keru)
届 3r5.1
todokō(ru)
滞 3a10.14
todo(ku)
届 3r5.1
todo(maru)
止 2m2.2
留 5f5.4
停 2a9.14
todo(me)
止 2m2.2

todo(meru)
止 2m2.2
留 5f5.4
停 2a9.14
todoro(ku)
轟 7c14.2
toga 科 5d4.3
toga(rasu) 尖 3n3.1
toga(ru) 尖 3n3.1
toge 刺 2f6.2
tōge 峠 3o6.3
to(geru) 遂 2q9.13
togi 伽 2a5.12
to(gu)
研 5a4.1
砥 5a5.4
toi 樋 4a10.28
to(i) 問 8e3.1
tō(i) 遠 2q10.4
toishi 砥 5a5.4
to(jiru)
閉 8e3.3
綴 6a8.5
to(kasu)
溶 3a10.15
解 4g9.1
to(keru)
溶 3a10.15
鎔 8a10.1
解 4g9.1
融 6d10.5
toki
辰 2p5.1
晨 4c7.7
怜 4k5.10
時 4c6.2
凱 2s10.1
節 6f7.3
聡 6e8.2
鴻 3a14.2
to(kku ni) 疾 5i5.12
toko
床 3q4.1
所 4m4.3
toko- 常 3n8.3
tokoro
処 4i2.2
所 4m4.3
tokoshi(e) 長 0a8.2
TOKU 特 4g6.1
(寺) JI
(持) JI

	啄	3d8.4
	(琢)	TAKU
	(豚)	TON
	督	5c8.9
	(叔)	SHUKU
	(目)	MOKU
	読	7a7.9
	(売)	BAI
	(続)	ZOKU
	匿	2t8.2
	(若)	JAKU
	徳	3i11.3
	(聴)	CHŌ
	篤	6f10.1
	(馬)	BA
	禿	5d2.5
	得	3i8.4
to(ku)	疾	5i5.12
	溶	3a10.15
	解	4g9.1
	説	7a7.12
to(maru)	止	2m2.2
	泊	3a5.15
	留	5f5.4
	停	2a9.14
tome	留	5f5.4
to(meru)	止	2m2.2
	泊	3a5.15
	留	5f5.4
tomi	臣	2t4.3
	宝	3m5.2
	堯	3b9.3
	富	3m9.5
	禄	4e8.2
	頓	9a4.1
	聡	6e8.2
tomo	共	3k3.3
	供	2a6.13
	朋	4b4.1
	鵬	4b15.1
	具	5c3.1
	倶	2a8.15
	知	3d5.14
	智	4c8.11

	与	0a3.23
	巴	0a4.16
	友	2h2.3
	伍	2a4.8
	那	2d4.6
	伴	2a5.4
	孟	2c5.1
	呂	3d4.16
	奉	0a8.13
	悌	4k7.14
	寅	3m8.4
	朝	4b8.12
	禎	4e9.3
	諄	7a7.11
Tomoe	巴	0a4.16
tomoe	巴	0a4.16
tomona(u)		
	伴	2a5.4
tomo(ru)	点	2m7.2
tomoshibi	灯	4d2.1
tomo(su)	点	2m7.2
to(mu)	富	3m9.5
tomura(i)	弔	0a4.41
tomura(u)	弔	0a4.41
TON	屯	0a4.35
	鈍	8b4.2
	頓	9a4.1
	(鈍)	DON
	(純)	JUN
	惇	4k7.12
	敦	4i7.4
	(亨)	KYŌ
	丼	0a5.40
	(井)	SEI
	豚	4b7.2
	(啄)	TOKU
	褪	5e9.5
	(退)	TAI
	団	3s3.3
ton	問	8e3.1
tona(eru)	称	5d5.8
	唱	3d8.9
tonari	隣	2d13.1
tona(ru)	隣	2d13.1
tonbi	鳶	11b3.1

tonga(ru)	尖	3n3.1
tono	殿	3r10.1
Tora	虎	2m6.3
tora	虎	2m6.3
	彪	3j8.3
	寅	3m8.4
to(raeru)	捕	3c7.3
torawa(reru)		
	囚	3s2.1
to(rawareru)		
	捕	3c7.3
to(reru)	取	6e2.2
tori	酉	7e0.1
	鳥	11b0.1
	禽	2a10.8
tō(ri)	通	2q7.18
toriko	虜	2m11.2
toro(kasu)		
	蕩	3k12.4
toro(keru)	蕩	3k12.4
to(ru)	取	6e2.2
	撮	3c12.13
	捕	3c7.3
	執	3b8.15
	採	3c8.14
	録	8a8.16
Tōru	亨	2j4.2
	亮	2j7.6
	公	2o2.2
	亘	4c2.4
	透	2q7.10
	達	2q9.8
	貫	7b4.3
	暢	4c10.4
	徹	3i12.2
	叡	2h14.1
	融	6d10.5
tō(ru)	透	2q7.10
	通	2q7.18
(o)tō(san)	父	2o2.3
Toshi	遼	2q12.5
	聡	6e8.2
	慧	4k11.16
	駿	10a7.1
toshi	俊	2a7.10

	峻	3o7.4
	惇	4k7.12
	敦	4i7.4
	年	0a6.16
	甫	0a7.11
	寿	0a7.15
	利	5d2.1
	季	5d2.3
	朋	4b4.1
	哉	4n5.4
	紀	6a3.5
	敏	4i6.3
	隼	8c2.2
	淑	3a8.5
	捷	3c8.4
	捵	3c8.17
	智	4c8.11
	禄	4e8.2
	舜	3n10.2
	楠	4a9.25
	歳	4n9.5
	稔	5d8.5
	遼	2q12.5
	肇	4m10.1
	聡	6e8.2
	慧	4k11.16
	鋭	8a7.12
	叡	2h14.1
	齢	6b11.5
	厳	3o17.2
tō(su)	透	2q7.10
	通	2q7.18
tōto(bu)	尊	2o10.3
	貴	7b5.7
tōto(i)	尊	2o10.3
	貴	7b5.7
tōto(mu)	尊	2o10.3
totono(eru)		
	調	7a8.16
	整	4i12.3
totono(u)		
	調	7a8.16
	整	4i12.3
TOTSU	凸	0a5.13
	突	3m5.11
totsu(gu)	嫁	3e10.6

(ni) to(tte)	取 6e2.2	tsue	杖 4a3.5	tsui(yasu)	費 7b5.4		漬 3a11.12
to(u)	訪 7a4.1	tsuga(eru)	番 5f7.4	Tsuji	辻 2q2.2	tsuki	月 4b0.1
	問 8e3.1	tsuga(i)	番 5f7.4	tsuji	辻 2q2.2		槻 4a11.4
toyo	晨 4c7.7	tsuga(u)	番 5f7.4	tsuka	束 0a7.8	tsu(kiru)	尽 3r3.1
	豊 3d10.15	tsu(geru)	告 3d4.18		柄 4a5.9	tsu(ku)	付 2a3.6
to(zasu)	閉 8e3.3	tsugi	次 2b4.1		塚 3b9.10		附 2d5.4
	鎖 8a10.2		胤 4b5.16	tsuka(eru)	支 2k2.1		吐 3d3.1
TSU	通 2q7.18		嗣 3d10.13		仕 2a3.2		即 2e5.1
	都 2d8.13		続 6a7.5	tsuka(i)	使 2a6.2		突 3m5.11
Tsu	津 3a6.1		継 6a7.8	tsuka(maeru)			点 2m7.2
tsu	津 3a6.1	tsugomori	晦 4c7.3		捕 3c7.3		着 2o10.1
	藤 3k15.3	tsugu	丞 2c4.3		摑 3c11.6		就 3d9.21
	鶴 11b10.1		承 0a7.7	tsuka(maru)	捕 3c7.3		搗 3c10.1
TSŪ	通 2q7.18		胤 4b5.16		摑 3c11.6		憑 4k12.12
	痛 5i7.7		紹 6a5.10	tsuka(maseru)			築 6f10.5
tsuba	唾 3d8.2		皓 4c8.13		摑 3c11.6	tsukue	机 4a2.4
Tsubaki	椿 4a9.16		嗣 3d10.13	tsuka(mi)	摑 3c11.6	tsukuro(u)	
tsubaki	唾 3d8.2		禎 4e9.3	tsuka(mu)	摑 3c11.6		繕 6a12.2
	椿 4a9.16		頌 9a4.4	Tsukane	束 0a7.8	tsuku(ru)	作 2a5.10
tsubame	燕 3k13.16		鞠 6b11.6	tsuka(neru)			造 2q7.11
Tsubasa	翼 2o15.2	tsu(gu)	接 3c8.10		束 0a7.8	tsu(kusu)	尽 3r3.1
tsubasa	翼 2o15.2		楱 4a8.15	tsuka(rasu)		tsuma	妻 3e5.10
tsubo	坪 3b5.4		次 2b4.1		疲 5i5.2	tsuma-	爪 0a4.9
	壺 3p9.2		注 3a5.16	tsuka(reru)		tsumabi(raka)	
tsubo(maru)			継 6a7.8		疲 5i5.2		詳 7a6.12
	窄 3m7.11	tsuguna(u)		tsu(kareru)			審 3m12.1
tsubo(meru)			償 2a15.4		憑 4k12.12	tsuma(mi)	撮 3c12.13
	窄 3m7.11	TSUI	追 2q6.4	tsu(karu)	浸 3a7.17	tsuma(mu)	
tsubo(ne)	局 3r4.4		槌 4a9.27		漬 3a11.12		摘 3c11.5
tsubu	粒 6b5.1		縋 6a9.14	Tsukasa	士 3p0.1		撮 3c12.13
tsubu(reru)			鎚 8a9.10		司 3d2.14	tsu(maru)	詰 7a6.7
	潰 3a12.14		墜 3b11.7		宰 3m7.2	tsuma(shii)	
tsubu(ru)	瞑 5c10.3		(隊) TAI	tsukasa	司 3d2.14		倹 2a8.27
tsubusa (ni)			対 2j5.5	tsukasado(ru)		tsume	爪 0a4.9
	具 5c3.1		椎 4a8.1		司 3d2.14	tsu(meru)	詰 7a6.7
tsubu(su)	潰 3a12.14	tsui (ni)	遂 2q9.13		掌 3n9.4	tsume(tai)	
tsubute	礫 5a15.1		終 6a5.9	tsu(kasu)	尽 3r3.1		冷 2b5.3
tsuchi	槌 4a9.27	tsuiba(mu)		tsuka(u)	使 2a6.2	tsumi	罪 5g8.4
	鎚 8a9.10		啄 3d8.4		遣 2q10.2	tsu(mi)	積 5d11.5
	土 3b0.1	tsuide	序 3q4.4	tsuka(wasu)		tsu(mori)	積 5d11.5
	椎 4a8.1	tsui(eru)	費 7b5.4		遣 2q10.2	tsu(moru)	積 5d11.5
tsuchika(u)			潰 3a12.14	tsu(keru)	付 2a3.6	tsumu	錘 8a8.2
	培 3b8.6	tsuitachi	朔 4b6.12		附 2d5.4	tsu(mu)	詰 7a6.7
tsuchinoto		(ni) tsu(ite)			着 2o10.1		摘 3c11.5
	己 0a3.12		就 3d9.21		就 3d9.21		積 5d11.5
tsudo(u)	集 8c4.2					tsumugi	紬 6a5.3

tsumu(gu)		
紡	6a4.1	
tsuna		
綱	6a8.23	
(網)	ami	
紘	6a4.11	
維	6a8.1	
縄	6a9.1	
tsuna(garu)		
繋	6a13.4	
tsuna(gu) 繋	6a13.4	
tsunbo 聾	6e16.1	
tsune 凡	2s1.1	
毎	0a6.25	
矩	2t7.1	
恒	4k6.5	
彦	5b4.4	
常	3n8.3	
庸	3q8.2	
経	6a5.11	
tsune (ni) 恒	4k6.5	
tsuno 角	2n5.1	
tsuno(ru) 募	3k9.23	
tsura 面	3s6.1	
寅	3m8.4	
貫	7b4.3	
tsura(i) 辛	5b2.2	
tsura(naru)		
列	2f4.4	
連	2q7.2	
tsura(neru)		
列	2f4.4	
連	2q7.2	
tsuranu(ku)		
貫	7b4.3	
tsu(re) 連	2q7.2	
tsu(reru) 連	2q7.2	
(ni) tsu(rete)		
連	2q7.2	
tsu(ri) 釣	8a3.5	
Tsuru 鶴	11b10.1	
tsuru 弦	3h5.1	
絃	6a5.12	
敦	4i7.4	
鶴	11b10.1	
tsu(ru) 吊	3d3.8	

釣	8a3.5	
痙	5i7.5	
tsurugi 剣	2f8.5	
tsuru(shi) 吊	3d3.8	
tsuru(su) 吊	3d3.8	
tsuta 蔦	3k11.1	
Tsutae 伝	2a4.14	
tsuta(eru) 伝	2a4.14	
tsuta(u) 伝	2a4.14	
tsuta(waru)		
伝	2a4.14	
tsuto(maru)		
勤	2g10.1	
tsuto(meru)		
努	2g5.6	
勉	2n8.1	
務	4i7.6	
勤	2g10.1	
Tsutomu 力	2g0.1	
功	2g3.2	
励	2g5.4	
努	2g5.6	
勉	2n8.1	
務	4i7.6	
勤	2g10.1	
惇	4k7.12	
敦	4i7.4	
孟	2c5.1	
拳	3c6.18	
強	3h8.3	
魁	5f9.1	
tsutsu 砲	5a5.3	
筒	6f6.15	
銃	8a6.9	
tsutsu(ku)		
突	3m5.11	
tsutsu(mashii)		
慎	4k10.4	
Tsutsumi 堤	3b9.7	
tsutsumi 堤	3b9.7	
tsutsu(mi) 包	0a5.9	
tsutsu(mu)		
包	0a5.9	
tsutsushi(mu)		
慎	4k10.4	

謹	7a10.6	
tsuwamono		
兵	2o5.6	
Tsuya 艶	3d16.3	
tsuya 艶	3d16.3	
艶	3d16.3	
tsuya(meku)		
艶	3d16.3	
tsuya(ppoi)		
艶	3d16.3	
tsuyo(i) 強	3h8.3	
Tsuyoki 毅	5b10.1	
tsuyo(maru)		
強	3h8.3	
tsuyo(meru)		
強	3h8.3	
Tsuyoshi 侃	2a6.12	
勁	2g7.2	
剛	2f8.7	
強	3h8.3	
彪	3j8.3	
幹	4c9.8	
毅	5b10.1	
tsuyu 汁	3a2.1	
液	3a8.29	
露	8d13.1	
tsuzu(keru)		
続	6a7.5	
Tsuzuki 胤	4b5.16	
tsuzu(ku) 続	6a7.5	
tsuzu(maru)		
約	6a3.7	
tsuzuma(yaka)		
倹	2a8.27	
tsuzu(meru)		
約	6a3.7	
tsuzumi 鼓	3p10.2	
tsuzura 葛	3k9.22	
tsuzu(re) 綴	6a8.5	
tsuzu(ru) 綴	6a8.5	

—— U ——

U 迂	2q3.2	
芋	3k3.1	
宇	3m3.3	
盂	5h3.1	
紆	6a3.1	

右	3d2.15	
佑	2a5.8	
(石)	SEKI	
羽	2b4.5	
有	4b2.3	
雨	8d0.1	
胡	4b5.12	
烏	4d6.5	
u 卯	2e3.1	
(卵)	RAN	
鵜	11b7.6	
uba(u) 奪	8c6.4	
ubena(u) 諾	7a8.10	
ubu 産	5b6.4	
uchi 内	0a4.23	
中	0a4.40	
u(daru) 茹	3k6.7	
ude 腕	4b8.6	
u(deru) 茹	3k6.7	
ue 上	2m1.1	
u(eru) 飢	8b2.1	
餓	8b7.1	
植	4a8.32	
uga(tsu) 穿	3m7.10	
ugo(kasu) 動	2g9.1	
ugo(ku) 動	2g9.1	
uguisu 鶯	11b10.9	
ui- 初	5e2.1	
u(i) 憂	4i12.1	
u(ita) 浮	3a6.11	
uji 氏	0a4.25	
u(kaberu) 浮	3a6.11	
u(kabu) 浮	3a6.11	
ukaga(i) 伺	2a5.23	
ukaga(u) 伺	2a5.23	
u(kanu) 浮	3a6.11	
u(kareru) 浮	3a6.11	
u(karu) 受	2h6.2	
u(kasareru)		
浮	3a6.11	
u(kasu) 浮	3a6.11	
u(ke) 受	2h6.2	
u(keru) 享	2j5.1	
受	2h6.2	
請	7a8.8	

uketamawa(ru)			uraya(mashigaru)		usu(ragu)	薄 3k13.11	utsuwa	器 3d12.13
	承 0a7.7		羨 2o11.4	usu(reru)	薄 3k13.11	utta(eru)	訴 7a5.2
u(ki)	浮 3a6.11	uraya(mashii)		uta	唄 3d7.1	uwa-	上 2m1.1
u(ku)	浮 3a6.11		羨 2o11.4		詩 7a6.5	u(waru)	植 4a8.32
uma	午 2k2.2	uraya(mu)			頌 9a4.4	uwasa	噂 3d12.10
	馬 10a0.1		羨 2o11.4		歌 4j10.2	uya	欽 8a4.1
uma(i)	甘 0a5.32	ure(e)	憂 4i12.1	utaga(u)	疑 2m12.1	uyama(u)	敬 4i8.4
	旨 4c2.2	ure(eru)	愁 4k9.16	utaga(washii)		uyauya(shii)	
u(mareru)	生 0a5.29		憂 4i12.1		疑 2m12.1		恭 3k7.16
	産 5b6.4	ure(i)	愁 4k9.16	utage	宴 3m7.3	uzu	渦 3a9.36
u(maru)	埋 3b7.2		憂 4i12.1	utagu(ru)	疑 2m12.1	uzu(maru)	
ume	梅 4a6.27	u(reru)	売 3p4.3	utai	謡 7a9.9		埋 3b7.2
u(meru)	埋 3b7.2		熟 4d10.5	utata	転 7c4.3	uzu(meru)	埋 3b7.2
umi	海 3a6.20	ure(shii)	嬉 3e12.3	uta(u)	歌 4j10.2	uzu(moreru)	
	膿 4b13.2	ure(u)	憂 4i12.1		謡 7a9.9		埋 3b7.2
u(moreru)		uri	瓜 0a6.3	utena	台 3d2.11		
	埋 3b7.2	uro	虚 2m9.1	uto(i)	疎 0a11.4		**—— W ——**
u(mu)	生 0a5.29	uroko	鱗 11a13.2	uto(mashii)			
	産 5b6.4	u(ru)	売 3p4.3		疎 0a11.4	WA	和 5d3.1
	倦 2a8.13		得 3i8.4	uto(mu)	疎 0a11.4		倭 2a8.16
	熟 4d10.5	urū	閏 8e4.4	uto(njiru)	疎 0a11.4		(委) I
	膿 4b13.2	uru(mu)	潤 3a12.20	UTSU	鬱 4a25.1		話 7a6.8
UN	云 0a4.4	uruo(i)	潤 3a12.20	u(tsu)	打 3c2.3		(舌) ZETSU
	雲 8d4.1	uruo(su)	潤 3a12.20		拍 3c5.14		(活) KATSU
	(曇) DON	uruo(u)	潤 3a12.20		撲 3c12.1		窪 3m11.9
	運 2q9.10	urusa(i)	煩 4d9.1		撃 3c11.7	wa	我 0a7.10
	(軍) GUN	urushi	漆 3a11.10		伐 2a4.5		輪 7c8.4
	饂 8b10.2	uruwa(shii)			討 7a3.3		環 4f13.1
unaga(su)	促 2a7.3		麗 3q16.5	utsubari	梁 4a7.25	-wa	羽 2b4.5
unagi	鰻 11a11.5	usagi	兎 0a8.5	utsuke	空 3m5.12	wa(bi)	侘 2a6.14
unaji	項 9a3.1	u(seru)	失 0a5.28	utsuku(shii)			詫 7a6.6
une	采 4a4.24	ushi	丑 0a4.39		美 2o7.4	wa(biru)	侘 2a6.14
	畝 5f5.5		牛 4g0.1	utsumu(keru)			詫 7a6.6
uo	魚 11a0.1	ushina(u)	失 0a5.28		俯 2a8.35	wa(bishii)	侘 2a6.14
ura	浦 3a7.2	Ushio	潮 3a12.1	utsumu(ku)		waga	吾 3d4.17
	裏 2j11.2	ushio	潮 3a12.1		俯 2a8.35	wa(ga)	我 0a7.10
ura(meshii)		ushi(ro)	後 3i6.5	utsu(ro)	空 3m5.12	WAI	賄 7b6.1
	怨 4k5.20	uso	嘘 3d11.7	utsu(rou)	移 5d6.1		(有) YŪ
	恨 4k6.2	usu	臼 0a6.4	utsu(ru)	写 2i3.1		(侑) YŪ
ura(mu)	怨 4k5.20	usu(i)	薄 3k13.11		映 4c5.1		歪 2m7.4
	恨 4k6.2	usu(maru)			移 5d6.1		猥 3g9.2
	憾 4k13.3		薄 3k13.11		遷 2q12.1	waka	若 3k5.12
urana(u)	占 2m3.2	usu(meru)		utsu(su)	写 2i3.1		湧 3a9.31
Urara	麗 3q16.5		薄 3k13.11		映 4c5.1		稚 5d8.1
urara(ka)	麗 3q16.5	usu(ppera)			移 5d6.1	waka(chi)	別 2f5.3
			薄 3k13.11	utsutsu	現 4f7.3	waka(i)	若 3k5.12

Reading	Kanji	Code
waka(reru)		
	別	2f5.3
wa(kareru)		
	分	2o2.1
waka(ru)	判	2f5.2
	解	4g9.1
wa(karu)	分	2o2.1
wa(kasu)	沸	3a5.3
waka(tsu)	別	2f5.3
	頒	9a4.3
wa(katsu)	分	2o2.1
wake	訳	7a4.8
wa(keru)	分	2o2.1
	別	2f5.3
wa(kete)	別	2f5.3
waki	腋	4b6.3
	脇	4b8.8
	湧	3a9.31
wakima(eru)		
	弁	0a5.30
WAKU	或	4n4.2
	惑	4k8.16
	(域)	IKI
waku	枠	4a4.19
	湧	3a9.31
wa(ku)	沸	3a5.3
	湧	3a9.31
wame(ku)	喚	3d9.19
WAN	腕	4b8.6
	碗	5a8.7
	(苑)	EN
	湾	3a9.15
wanana(ku)		
	戦	4n9.2
Wang	王	4f0.1
wani	鰐	11a9.5
wara	藁	3k14.6
warabe	童	5b7.3
wara(u)	笑	6f4.1
warawa	妾	5b3.2
ware	我	0a7.10
	吾	3d4.17
wa(reru)	割	2f10.1
wari	割	2f10.1
wa(ru)	割	2f10.1
waru(i)	悪	4k7.17
washi	鷲	11b12.5
wasu(reru)		
	忘	2j5.4
wata	腸	4b9.8
	綿	6a8.8
watakushi	私	5d2.2
Watari	亘	4c2.4
Wataru	亘	4c2.4
	恒	4k6.5
	弥	3h5.2
	凌	2b8.5
	渉	3a8.20
	済	3a8.30
wata(ru)	亘	4c2.4
	渡	3a9.35
watashi	私	5d2.2
wata(su)	渡	3a9.35
waza	技	3c4.16
	業	0a13.3
waza (to)	態	4k10.14
wazawai	禍	4e9.4
	災	4d3.3
wazawa(i)	災	4d3.3
wazura(u)	患	4k7.18
	煩	4d9.1
wazura(washii)		
	煩	4d9.1
wazura(wasu)		
	煩	4d9.1

— Y —

Reading	Kanji	Code
YA	耶	6e2.1
	椰	4a8.6
	也	0a3.29
	(他)	TA
	冶	2b5.4
	(治)	JI
	夜	2j6.1
	野	0a11.5
ya	八	2o0.1
	谷	2o5.3
	矢	0a5.19
	弥	3h5.2
	屋	3r6.3
	哉	4n5.4
	輻	7c9.3
-ya	谷	2o5.3
	家	3m7.1
yabu	藪	3k15.1
yabu(keru)		
	破	5a5.1
yabu(ku)	破	5a5.1
yabu(reru)		
	破	5a5.1
	敗	7b4.1
yabu(ru)	破	5a5.1
	敗	7b4.1
yado	宿	3m8.3
yādo	碼	5a10.1
yado(ri)	宿	3m8.3
yado(su)	宿	3m8.3
yagura	櫓	4a15.2
yaiba	刃	0a3.22
yakama(shii)		
	喧	3d9.12
yakara	族	4h7.3
	輩	7c8.7
yakata	館	8b8.3
ya(keru)	焼	4d8.4
yakko	奴	3e2.2
YAKU	役	3i4.2
	疫	5i4.2
	訳	7a4.8
	(尺)	SHAKU
	(沢)	TAKU
	(駅)	EKI
	躍	7d14.2
	(濯)	TAKU
	(曜)	YŌ
	亦	2j4.4
	(赤)	SEKI
	薬	3k13.15
	(楽)	GAKU
	厄	2p2.3
	約	6a3.7
	益	2o8.5
ya(ku)	焼	4d8.4
yama	山	3o0.1
yamai	病	5i5.3
yama(shii)		
	疾	5i5.12
Yamato	倭	2a8.16
ya(meru)	止	2m2.2
	病	5i5.3
	辞	5b8.4
	罷	5g10.2
yami	闇	8e9.5
ya(mu)	止	2m2.2
	病	5i5.3
	罷	5g10.2
yana	梁	4a7.25
Yanagi	柳	4a5.17
yanagi	柳	4a5.17
yani	脂	4b6.7
yari	槍	4a10.20
yāru	碼	5a10.1
ya(ru)	遣	2q10.2
yasa-	優	2a15.1
yasa(shige)		
	優	2a15.1
yasa(shii)	易	4c4.9
	優	2a15.1
ya(seru)	痩	5i9.1
yashi	椰	4a8.6
yashiki	邸	2d5.10
yashina(u)		
	養	2o13.1
yashiro	社	4e3.1
yasu	安	3m3.1
	晏	4c6.4
	休	2a4.2
	那	2d4.6
	侃	2a6.12
	育	2j6.4
	易	4c4.9
	保	2a7.11
	彦	5b4.4
	倭	2a8.16
	泰	3a5.34
	恭	3k7.16
	容	3m7.8
	悌	4k7.14
	康	3q8.1
	喬	3d9.25
	裕	5e7.3

	廉 3q10.1		軟 7c4.1		拗 3c5.16		翼 2o15.2	
	楊 4a9.17	yawa(rakai)		(幻) GEN		(羽) U	
	靖 5b8.1		柔 4a5.34		夭 0a4.22		抑 3c4.12	
	鳩 11b2.1		軟 7c4.1		妖 3e4.4		(卯) U	
	養 2o13.1	YO	予 0a4.12		要 3e6.11		(仰) GYŌ	
	慰 4k11.13		預 9a4.5		腰 4b9.3	yo(ku)	克 2k5.1	
yasu(i)	安 3m3.1		(序) JO		湧 3a9.31		能 4b6.15	
	廉 3q10.1		(矛) MU		(勇) YŪ	yome	嫁 3c10.6	
	靖 5b8.1		与 0a3.23		葉 3k9.21	yomigae(ru)		
-yasu(i)	易 4c4.9		余 2a5.24		(蝶) CHŌ		蘇 3k16.1	
yasu(maru)			誉 3n10.1		瑛 4f8.6	Yomishi	嘉 3p11.1	
	休 2a4.2		輿 2o15.1		(英) EI	yomi(suru)		
yasu(meru)		yo	世 0a5.37		遙 2q10.3		嘉 3p11.1	
	休 2a4.2		代 2a3.3		厭 2p12.1	yomu	頌 9a4.4	
yasu(mi)	休 2a4.2		夜 2j6.1		擁 3c13.5	yo(mu)	詠 7a5.14	
yasu(mu)	休 2a4.2		四 3s2.2		蠅 6d13.1		読 7a7.9	
yasu(raka)		yo-	羊 2o4.1		鷹 3q21.1	yon	四 3s2.2	
	安 3m3.1	YŌ	洋 3a6.19		浩 3a7.9	yone	米 6b0.1	
Yasushi	安 3m3.1		様 4a10.25	yō	瑛 4f8.6	yori	之 0a2.9	
	晏 4c6.4		養 2o13.1	yō-	八 2o0.1		自 5c1.1	
	欣 4j4.1		窯 3m12.5	yo(bu)	呼 3d5.4		依 2a6.1	
	泰 3a5.34		陽 2d9.5	yodo	淀 3a8.23		亮 2j7.6	
	恭 3k7.16		揚 3c9.5	yodo(mu)	淀 3a8.23		寄 3m8.8	
	悌 4k7.14		楊 4a9.17	yo(giru)	過 2q9.18		順 9a3.2	
	康 3q8.1		瘍 5i9.3	yogo(reru)			頼 9a7.1	
	靖 5b8.1		(場) JŌ		汚 3a3.5	yoroi	鎧 8a10.3	
	寧 3m11.8		(湯) TŌ	yogo(su)	汚 3a3.5	yoroko(bashii)		
	魁 5f9.1		容 3m7.8	yoi	宵 3m7.7		喜 3p9.1	
yato(i)	雇 4m8.1		溶 3a10.15		敦 4i7.4	yoroko(bu)		
yato(u)	雇 4m8.1		蓉 3k10.20	yo(i)	好 3e2.1		悦 4k7.15	
yatsu	奴 3e2.2		鎔 8a10.1		良 0a7.3		喜 3p9.1	
ya(tsu)	八 2o0.1		(谷) KOKU		佳 2a6.10		慶 3q12.8	
yatsu(reru)			曜 4c14.1		善 2o10.2	yoro(shii)	宜 3m5.7	
	窶 3m13.5		燿 4d14.3	yoji(ru)	捩 3c8.31	yoro(shiku)		
yatsu(su)	窶 3m13.5		耀 8c12.1	-yo(ke)	除 2d7.10		宜 3m5.7	
yattoko	鋏 8a7.4		(濯) TAKU	yo(keru)	避 2q13.3	yoro(u)	鎧 8a10.3	
yat(tsu)	八 2o0.1		(躍) YAKU	yoko	横 4a11.13	yorozu	万 0a3.8	
yawa(i)	柔 4a5.34		揺 3c9.8	yokoshima		yoru	夜 2j6.1	
Yawara	和 5d3.1		瑶 4f9.5		邪 2d5.8	yo(ru)	由 0a5.35	
yawa(ra)	柔 4a5.34		謡 7a9.9	YOKU	浴 3a7.18		因 3s3.2	
yawa(rageru)			用 2r3.1		欲 4j7.1		依 2a6.1	
	和 5d3.1		庸 3q8.2		(谷) KOKU		拠 3c5.26	
yawa(ragu)			踊 7d7.2		(俗) ZOKU		寄 3m8.8	
	和 5d3.1		幼 2g3.3		翌 5b6.6		選 2q12.3	
yawa(raka)						yo(seru)	寄 3m8.8	
	柔 4a5.34					Yoshi	佳 2a6.10	

yoshi	嘉 3p11.1		悌 4k7.14		癒 5i13.3
	美 2o7.4		悦 4k7.15		由 0a5.35
	祥 4e6.1		淑 3a8.5		油 3a5.6
	善 2o10.2		啓 3d8.17		柚 4a5.5
	義 2o11.3		彬 4a7.3		(抽) CHŪ
	儀 2a13.4		惟 4k8.1		祐 4e5.3
	吉 3p3.1		斐 2j10.4		(右) YŪ
	喜 3p9.1		巽 2o10.7		酉 7e0.1
	嬉 3e12.3		凱 2s10.1		遊 2q8.3
	嘉 3p11.1		禄 4e8.2		弓 3h0.1
	圭 3b3.2		敬 4i8.4		友 2h2.3
	佳 2a6.10		賀 7b5.10	yu	湯 3a9.23
	桂 4a6.13		葦 3k10.21		有 4b2.3
	舜 3n10.2		熙 4d9.11	YŪ	侑 2a6.5
	愛 4i10.1		福 4e9.1		宥 3m0.1
	慶 3q12.8		禎 4e9.3		鮪 11a6.1
	宜 3m5.7		叡 2h14.1		右 3d2.15
	誼 7a8.11		艶 3d16.3		佑 2a5.8
	欣 4j4.1		巌 3o17.2		祐 4e5.3
	欽 8a4.1		馨 4c16.2		由 0a5.35
	之 0a2.9	yo(shi)	好 3e2.1		油 3a5.6
	允 0a4.13		縦 6a10.2		柚 4a5.5
	由 0a5.35	Yoshimi	嘉 3p11.1		勇 2g7.3
	令 2a3.9	yoshi(mi)	誼 7a8.11		湧 3a9.31
	功 2g3.2		誼 7a8.11		(男) DAN
	好 3e2.1	yosō(i)	装 5e6.8		酉 7e0.1
	休 2a4.2	yosō(u)	装 5e6.8		猶 3g9.5
	伊 2a4.6	yo(su)	止 2m2.2		憂 4i12.1
	至 3b3.6	yosuga	便 2a7.5		優 2a15.1
	良 0a7.3		縁 6a9.10		裕 5e7.3
	甫 0a7.11	yo(tsu)	四 3s2.2		(谷) KOKU
	克 2k5.1	yo(tte)	因 3s3.2		(俗) ZOKU
	辰 2p5.1	yot(tsu)	四 3s2.2		(浴) YOKU
	芳 3k4.1	yo(u)	酔 7e4.3		郵 2d8.12
	芦 3k4.3		齢 6b11.5		(垂) SUI
	快 4k4.2	yowai	弱 3h7.2		悠 4k7.20
	弥 3h5.2	yowa(i)			(修) SHŪ
	昌 4c4.4	yowa(maru)			熊 4d10.6
	亮 2j7.6		弱 3h7.2		(態) TAI
	栄 3n6.1	yowa(meru)			誘 7a7.4
	祐 4e5.3		弱 3h7.2		(秀) SHŪ
	彦 5b4.4	yowa(ru)	弱 3h7.2		融 6d10.5
	能 4b6.15	yōya(ku)	漸 3a11.2		(隔) KAKU
	恵 4k6.16	YU	喩 3d9.15		
	恕 4k6.18		愉 4k9.13		
			諭 7a9.13		
			輸 7c9.5		

	友 2h2.3
	邑 3d4.15
	幽 3o6.6
	遊 2q8.3
	雄 8c4.1
yū	夕 0a3.14
yubari	尿 3r4.1
yū(be)	夕 0a3.14
yubi	指 3c6.15
yuda(neru)	
	委 5d3.2
yu(daru)	茹 3k6.7
yu(deru)	茹 3k6.7
yue	故 4i5.2
yuga(meru)	
	歪 2m7.4
	歪 2m7.4
yuga(mi)	歪 2m7.4
yuga(mu)	歪 2m7.4
YUI	唯 3d8.1
	(推) SUI
	(惟) I
	(維) I
	遺 2q12.4
	(貴) KI
	由 0a5.35
Yui	惟 4k8.1
yuka	床 3q4.1
yukari	縁 6a9.10
yuka(shii)	床 3q4.1
Yuki	恕 4k6.18
yuki	之 0a2.9
	乃 0a2.10
	亨 2j4.2
	至 3b3.6
	行 3i3.1
	志 3p4.1
	侑 2a6.5
	幸 3b5.9
	征 3i5.3
	晋 4c6.8
	恕 4k6.18
	雪 8d3.2
	敬 4i8.4
	鵬 4b15.1
yuku	巽 2o10.7

yu(ku)	行	3i3.1		稔	5d8.5	zawatsu(ku)			
	往	3i5.6		碩	5a9.1		騒	10a8.5	
	之	0a2.9		穣	5d13.2	ZE	是	4c5.9	
	逝	2q7.8	yuta(ka)	豊	3d10.15	ZEI	税	5d7.4	
yume	夢	3k10.14	yu(u)	結	6a6.5		説	7a7.12	
yumi	弓	3h0.1	yu(waeru)	結	6a6.5	(脱)	DATSU	
yu(ragu)	揺	3c9.8	yuzu	柚	4a5.5		脆	4b6.4	
yu||(rameku)			Yuzura	穣	5d13.2		橇	4a12.14	
	揺	3c9.8	Yuzuru	弦	3h5.1		贅	7b11.4	
yu(rasu)	揺	3c9.8	yuzu(ru)	譲	7a13.1	ZEN	善	2o10.2	
yu(reru)	揺	3c9.8					膳	4b12.2	
yu(ru)	揺	3c9.8	**— Z —**				繕	6a12.2	
yuruga(se)			ZA	坐	3b4.11		禅	4e9.2	
	忽	4k4.7		座	3q7.2		蟬	6d12.3	
yu(rugasu)				挫	3c7.15	(単)	TAN	
	揺	3c9.8	ZAI	材	4a3.7	(戦)	SEN	
yu(rugu)	揺	3c9.8		財	7b3.1	(弾)	DAN	
yuru(i)	緩	6a9.8	(才)	SAI			然	4d8.10	
yuru(meru)				剤	2f8.6	(燃)	NEN	
	緩	6a9.8	(斉)	SEI		(黙)	MOKU	zoku(ppoi)
yuru(mu)	緩	6a9.8	(済)	SAI			漸	3a11.2	
yuru(su)	赦	4i7.3		在	3b3.8	(暫)	ZAN	ZON
	許	7a4.3	(存)	SON			全	2a4.16	
yuru(yaka)				罪	5g8.4		前	2o7.3	ZU
	緩	6a9.8	(非)	HI		zeni	銭	8a6.1	
yu(saburu)			zama	様	4a10.25	zenmai	薇	3k13.13	
	揺	3c9.8	ZAN	残	0a10.11	ZETSU	絶	6a6.11	
yu(suburu)			(桟)	SAN		(色)	SHOKU	
	揺	3c9.8	(浅)	SEN			舌	3d3.9	zu
yusu(gu)	濯	3a14.5	(銭)	SEN		ZŌ	増	3b11.3	
yu(suru)	揺	3c9.8		惨	4k8.5		憎	4k11.7	ZUI
Yutaka	宥	3m6.1	(参)	SAN			贈	7b11.2	
	泰	3a5.34		暫	4c11.3	(僧)	SŌ	
	浩	3a7.9	(漸)	ZEN			象	2n10.1	-zu(ki)
	温	3a9.21	za(reru)	戯	4n11.1		像	2a12.8	-zu(me)
	堯	3b9.3	ZATSU	雑	8c6.2		蔵	3k12.17	-zu(mi)
	裕	5e7.3	zawame(ku)				臓	4b15.2	-zutsu
	寛	3m10.3		騒	10a8.5				
	瑞	4f9.6							

	造	2q7.11
(告)	KOKU	
	三	0a3.1
	曹	4c7.10
	雑	8c6.2
ZOKU	俗	2a7.17
(谷)	KOKU	
(浴)	YOKU	
(裕)	YŪ	
	続	6a7.5
(売)	BAI	
(読)	DOKU	
	属	3r9.1
(嘱)	SHOKU	
	賊	7b6.3
(賦)	FU	
	族	4h7.3
	粟	6b6.6
	俗	2a7.17
ZON	存	2c3.1
(在)	ZAI	
ZU	豆	3d4.22
	頭	9a7.6
	図	3s4.3
	杜	4a3.1
	事	0a8.15
zu	津	3a6.1
	鶴	11b10.1
ZUI	随	2d8.10
	髄	4b14.3
	瑞	4f9.6
-zu(ki)	好	3e2.1
-zu(me)	詰	7a6.7
-zu(mi)	済	3a8.30
-zutsu	宛	3m5.9

OTHER TITLES BY THE SAME AUTHORS

W. Hadamitzky, M. Spahn
Kanji and Kana. A Handbook of the Japanese Writing System
Rutland (Vermont) and Tokyo: Tuttle 1981. Rev.ed. 1997

W. Hadamitzky, M. Spahn
A Guide to Writing Kanji & Kana. Book 1.2
Rutland (Vermont) and Tokyo: Tuttle 1991

M. Spahn, W. Hadamitzky
Japanese Character Dictionary. With Compound Look-up via Any Kanji.
Tokyo: Nichigai Associates 1989

M. Spahn, W. Hadamitzky
The Kanji Dictionary. Find Any Compound Using Any of Its Component
Characters.
Rutland (Vermont) and Tokyo: Tuttle 1996

W. Hadamitzky
Japanese, Chinese, and Korean Surnames And How to Read Them
München, New Providence, London, Paris: K.G. Saur 1997

W. Hadamitzky, M. Spahn, K. Fujie-Winter
Japanese. Step 1.2 (With audio cassette tapes)
Berlin: Ostasien-Verlag (Vol. 1, 1985), JAPAN Media (Vol. 2, 1987)

W. Hadamitzky, M. Kocks
Japan-Bibliography. German-language Publications on Japan.
Series A: Monographs, Periodicals and Maps. 1477–1985. Vol. 1–3/2.
1990–1997
Series B: Articles. ?–1985. Vol. 1– . 1997–
München, New Providence, London, Paris: K.G. Saur 1990–

W. Hadamitzky, M. Spahn, and others
SUNRISE Script. Electronic Reference and Learning System for Kanji.
1 CD-ROM + 2 floppy disks + Manual
Berlin: JAPAN Media 1989 (In English, German, French, Spanish,
Portuguese, Italian, Hungarian)

W. Hadamitzky, M. Spahn, and others
SUNRISE Kanji Dictionary. With Kanji and Compound Look-up via Any
Grapheme. 1 CD-ROM + 2 floppy disks + Manual
Berlin: JAPAN Media 1993 (In English and German)

W. Hadamitzky, J. Ruminski, and others
SUNRISE Japan Tour. Travel, Culture, and Language.
1 CD-ROM
Berlin: JAPAN Media 1997 (In English and German)

Mark Spahn has a background in mathematics, engineering, and computer science. He has worked in Japan as a teacher, computer magazine writer, programmer, and translator. He presently resides in the United States, where he is active as a technical translator and consultant.

Wolfgang Hadamitzky is a librarian of the East Asia section of the Berlin State Library. He has worked in Oslo and Tokyo on the staff of the German Cultural Institute (Goethe Institute).